THE INDEX LIBRARY

General Editor
Peter Spufford, M.A., Ph.D., Litt.D., F.S.A., F.R.Hist.S.

SURREY PROBATE RECORDS TO 1649

ISSUED BY

THE BRITISH RECORD SOCIETY

[99]

THE INDEX LIBRARY

UNION INDEX OF SURREY PROBATE RECORDS WHICH SURVIVE FROM BEFORE THE YEAR 1650

Edited by

Cliff Webb, M.A.

Issued to Subscribers by

THE BRITISH RECORD SOCIETY, LONDON

1990

Published by the British Record Society,
c/o Patric Dickinson,
The College of Arms,
Queen Victoria Street,
London EC4V 4BT.

I.S.B.N. 0 901505 27 7

Printed by Parchment (Oxford) Ltd., Oxford

CONTENTS

FOREWORD

It gives me great pleasure to be able to present to the subscribers to the British Record Society's *Index Library* and to the general public, these two volumes of index to all those Surrey probate records which survive from before the Civil War. It is not, as many of our volumes have been, an index to the probate records of a single jurisdiction, but to all the records, from whatever jurisdiction they may have come, which concern the county of Surrey. This is in the tradition of our Essex volumes, except that in that case the records were all in one place, the Essex Record Office at Chelmsford. In this case the records are still scattered, with, ironically, virtually none in the Surrey Record Office itself. The present volumes go further than the Essex volumes in that they include cross references to the Surrey material in the Prerogative Court of Canterbury, an innovation much to be welcomed. The Introduction, by the editor, is also innovative. The courts that generated the documents are considered in much more detail than is usual, and the substance of the records are analysed in ways that will be most useful to social and economic historians. Details are given of the number of wills surviving year by year, which, with the accompanying histogram, bring out something of the tradition of record keeping in the Archdeaconry Court of Surrey. This indicates the periods for which these Surrey records are safely susceptible to statistical analysis. He also brings out the social distribution of the testators, and makes clear what sections of the community have left probate records in this county. These innovations will surely stand the test of time and are surely precedents for all future editors of probate volumes who have access to modern technology. Of more instant use to larger numbers of people are the references to the microfilm copies and to abstracts of these records. We realise that this information will become out-dated in due course, but it is of such value in the short term that we thought its immense practical value today outweighed its anachronistic appearance to users in fifty or a hundred years time who we trust will still be consulting this index. I therefore have the greatest pleasure in thanking Mr Webb on behalf of the Society and congratulating him on such an exemplary and innovative index. I look foreward with pleasurable anticipation to being able to publish the index to the Surrey probate records surviving from after the Civil War on which he has now embarked.

The Society would also like to thank Mr Jeremy Gibson for permission to use his outline map of Surrey probate jurisdictions on p.xii, whilst the detailed map of Surrey parishes, appearing on p.l, is adapted from that in the series covering parochial and probate boundaries for every county, and is reproduced by kind permission of the Trustees of The Institute of Heraldic and Genalogical Studies.

Peter Spufford
General Editor
Cambridge, July 1990

Acknowledgements

Any work of this kind tends to be the product of many hands. Mr Bernard Campbell Cooke started work on the will registers in 1934; he completed slips for registers 'Spage', 'Mathewe', 'Michell', 'Heats', 'Pykman', 'Tully', 'Herringman', 'Berry' and 'Stoughton'. He also made slips for all unregistered wills prior to 1595, and a rough list of unregistered wills 1595-1620. He examined every will, registered and unregistered to approximately 1558, and noted not merely the parish of the testator, but any other parish in which he owned land or to which he made a charitable bequest; these details have been preserved in this index, but it has not been possible to continue on that basis, and for later wills only the main named parish, and occupation (where given) of the testator has been noted. Mr Campbell Cooke saw active service in both World Wars, and this terminated his work on the index. After the war he was appointed archivist to both East and West Sussex, being the first Sussex County Archivist, and, no doubt, though a Putney man by birth, his interests moved away from Surrey. He died in 1953.

In the interim, in 1947, a Miss Willis made a list of, and slips to register Peter. Both Mr Campbell Cooke and Miss Willis made a note of the exact date of both the making of the will, and of probate. The exact dates have been omitted in this index. Without the work done by these two previous slip writers this work would undoubtedly never have appeared.

In the period 1983-1989, the present editor made slips for registers 'Yeast', 'Farmer' and 'Harding', and for unregistered wills 1595-1649. I also added the references to each original will, which had been added to the documents since Mr Campbell Cooke and Miss Willis had done their work. The slip index as left by him, was in several sequences, and there had been very little attempt at surname grouping, and all christian names, place names and occupations had been left in their manuscript forms. I have put all of these in modern form, supplied cross-references and compiled the supplementary indexes of places and occupations. I also prepared this introduction, and produced the text on a word processor.

I should like to thank Elizabeth Stazicker of the Surrey Record Office who unearthed the slips, and suggested that I might complete the index and bring it to publication. Thanks are also due to the Surrey Record Society, under whose auspices the work began. It was at one time intended to be the subject of a joint publication with them, but it was felt in the event to be better the responsibility of a single society which specialised in will indexes.

The bulk of the wills here indexed are in the custody of the Greater London Record Office, and my thanks are due to Miss J. Coburn and her staff, and in particular Mrs J. Kenealy, without whom this index would most certainly have never appeared. I am particularly indebted to Mrs Kenealy for arranging for the numbering of previously unnumbered items, and for her most useful and helpful comments on the introduction. Many other archivists have helped with exhaustive lists of Surrey wills in their custody, in particular Miss F. Younson of the Hampshire Record Office, Mrs S. Corke of the Guildford Muniment Room and Mr Stephen Humphreys of the Southwark Local Studies Library. Thanks are due also to the British Library, for access to Add. Ms 24,925 and the Lambeth Palace Library, for allowing references to wills in their custody to be made in this volume.

I am most grateful to Peter Spufford for all his help and advice during the production stages of the volume, to Jeremy Gibson for the map, and for proof-reading the first draft of the introduction with Peter Spufford. Jeanne Bunting and Tim Wilcock helped unstintingly with advice regarding the word-processing program on which the index was compiled. I should also like to thank Elizabeth Munn for introducing me (and at times herself) to the higher arcana of computer graphics, which enabled me to add the graphs.

I need hardly add that the remaining defects in this index and introduction are my sole responsibility.

Last but very far from least, I should like to acknowledge the patience and forbearance over many years of my wife, Dianne, with 'slips, slips, slips', and to her I should like to dedicate this work.

Cliff Webb May 1990

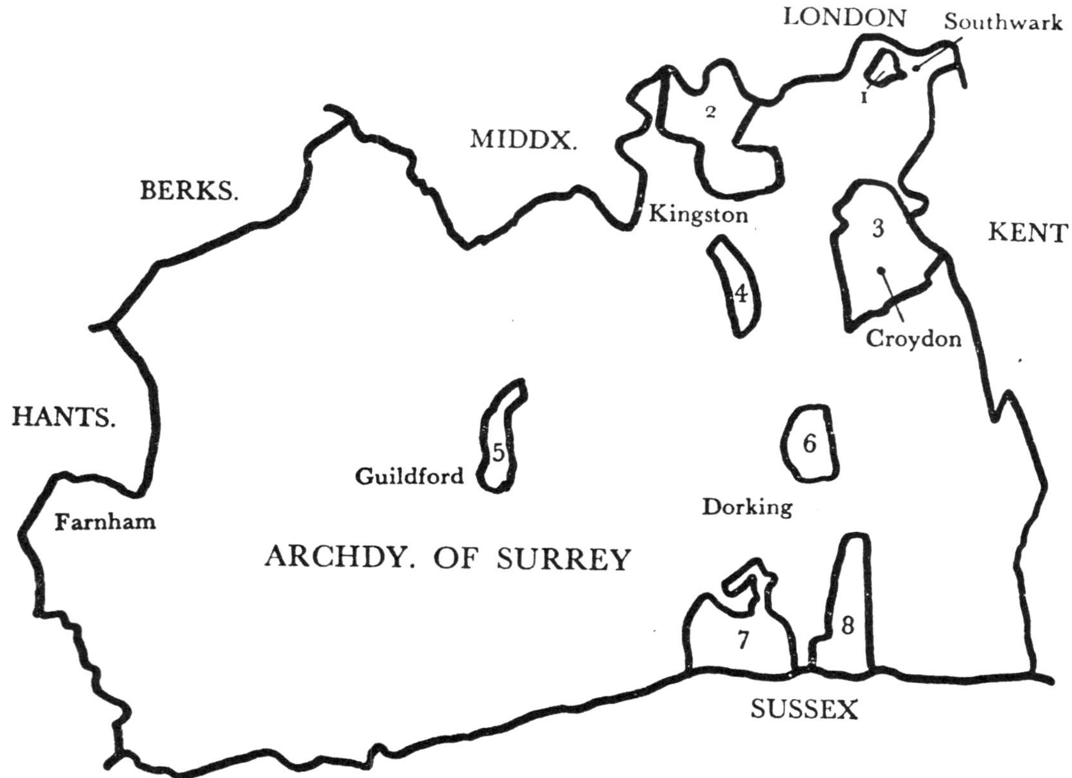

SURREY

Peculiar Deanery of Croydon

Barnes, 2
Burstow, 8
Charlwood, 7
Cheam, 4
Croydon, 3
East Horsley, 5
Merstham, 6
Mortlake, 2
Church Newington, 1
Putney, 2
Roehampton, 2
Walworth, St. Peter, 1
Wimbledon, 2

SURREY PROBATE JURISIDTIONS

The ancient county of Surrey extended into what is now south London, as far east as Rotherhithe. Large areas were detached from the ancient county and incorporated into London in 1889 and 1965, and in the latter year an area around Staines was transferred from Middlesex to the new administrative county of Surrey. There have been some other, more minor changes in the county boundary.

All these changes postdated the abolition of ecclesiastical jurisdiction over probate matters in 1858. The ancient county of Surrey is, therefore, what is meant whenever Surrey is mentioned here.

Surrey was in the province of Canterbury, and, mainly, in the diocese of Winchester. The Archdeaconry of Surrey consisted of that part of Surrey within the diocese of Winchester and the parish of Bentley in Hampshire, which was originally a chapelry of Farnham. Thirteen parishes in the county formed part of the exemnpt Deanery of Croydon, a peculiar of the Archbishop of Canterbury. For these parishes see the map opposite, on page xii.

The probate records of the county of Surrey survive, therefore, among the records of a number of courts. The senior court for all England was the Archbishop's Prerogative Court, the superior court for all England (see Public Record Office, p.xliv), many early wills however are only preserved in the Archbishop's registers (see Lambeth Palace Library, page xliii). When the see of Canterbury was vacant, the archbishop's jurisdiction could be exercised by the Prior (later Dean) and Chapter of Canterbury (see Canterbury Cathedral Archives and Library, page xlv). Similarly, on a diocesan level, some Surrey wills appear in the medieval registers of the bishops of Winchester and many more in his Consistory Court (see Hampshire Record Office, page xlii). After the Restoration, the bishop appointed a Commissary to act for the Archdeaconry of Surrey, and no further wills of Surrey testators are to be found in the Consistory Court. Most Surrey wills, however, are to be found in records of the Archdeaconry Court of Surrey (see Greater London Record Office, page xv) with a few strays in the British Library (see page xli). Wills proved in the Deanery of Croydon are also in Lambeth Palace Library (see page xliii). Part of the deanery together with most of south London was transferred to the diocese of London in 1845, and some Surrey wills very late in the period of ecclesiastical jurisdiction over probate matters are to be found in the records of the Consistory Court of London at the Greater London Record Office.

There is a map of Surrey probate jurisdiction on page xii and diagrammatic representation on page xiv.

Hierarchy of Courts

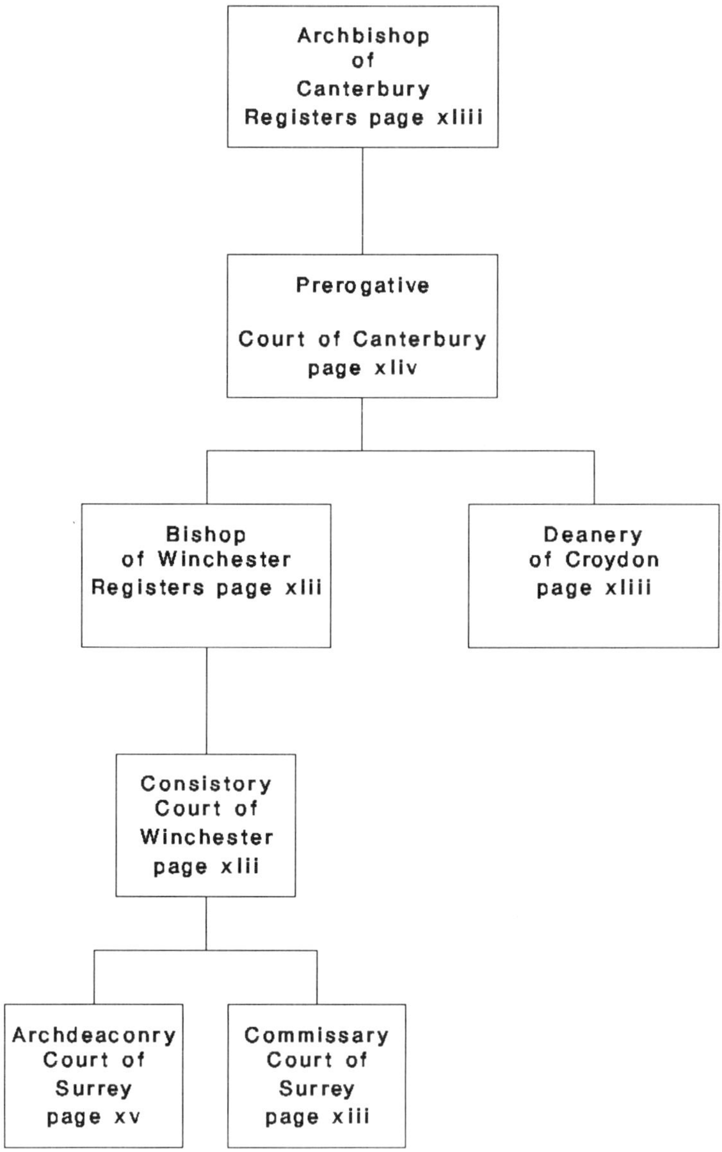

Probate Archives Covered by this Index

A. Greater London Record Office (GLRO)

I. Introduction

For this section of the introduction I have been especially reliant on the kindness of the GLRO for supplying me with their internally compiled interim lists of the records of the Archdeaconry Court of Surrey. These records were transferred from the Principal Probate Registry, Somerset House, Strand, London WC2 to the GLRO, The County Hall, London SE1 7PB on the 25th of March 1970. They were, of course, removed with the GLRO itself, on its relocation in 1982 to 40 Northampton Road, Clerkenwell. I have here listed the records of this court for the period covered by this index, and I have added to the listing of the registers of wills, the notes made Mr Campbell Cooke on Registers 'Spage', 'Mathewe', 'Mychell', 'Heats', 'Pykman', 'Tully', 'Herringman', 'Berry' and 'Stoughton' [DW/PA/7/1-9] as to the physical composition etc. of the registers. However, I have updated, and in some cases substantially corrected these notes. I have added similar notes for Registers 'Peter', 'Yeast', 'Farmer' and 'Harding' [DW/PA/7/10-13], including a full listing of the years represented. In many of the registers, strict chronological order is by no means maintained.

These records have not always been stored in the conditions which they enjoy today, and they have suffered considerably from the ravages of time. While it has been possible to assign an original GLRO reference number to every document, this should not be taken to indicate that the original is currently fit for production or available for consultation. While many of the documents have been repaired, guarded and filed, much remains to be done in this way (for example, currently, all of the original wills for 1623 are in too fragile a condition to be handled), and in any case, the documents are too precious to allow frequent consultation. Registers are large, bulky items, very prone to damage at the edges and of the binding; the original wills are, for the most part, still filed in their original bundles, and once again, frequent handling of them is most undesirable. Fortunately, there are substitutes readily available at the GLRO (and in some cases elsewhere) which make such consultation only very rarely necessary, even where it is possible.

Firstly, most (though unfortunately not all) of the documents in the collection were microfilmed by the Latter-Day Saints in the early 1950's. Copies of these films are available at Salt Lake City (and through Mormon Branch Libraries) and, of course, at the GLRO. Copies of all the films have recently been purchased by the Local Studies Library, North Street, Guildford.

Consultation of these documents even at the GLRO must in all normal circumstances be by microfilm. Accordingly, the lists which follow give the microfilm references where films are available, and searchers should convert the original document references given to the microfilm reference to examine either the original will or the register copy, or both, if both indeed survive. The first microfilm reference (beginning X/32) is the GLRO microfilm reference. After this, in brackets (and beginning 0097) is the Mormon microfilm reference, and this should be used to locate the desired film in Mormon libraries or the Local Studies Library, Guildford.

Searchers should note that there is no surviving will register in the 1560-1594 period, and recourse has to be to the films of the original wills, but these, as described, may not be complete. In addition, inevitably, as with any filming operation, there are a few occasions when a will, or a page of a register has been missed, and it must be confessed that the film is not ideal. However, as documents were filmed regardless of their condition (deplorable as this may be by present archival standards) many appear on the film which are not currently, and are unlikely for some while to be, available in their original form in any circumstances. Wherever it has been noted in the indexing operation that the filming has missed a single will, or a folio or more of a register, a full transcript has been made of the missing material and a copy deposited at the GLRO, so that again, unnecessary consultation of the originals can be avoided. Furthermore a programme of abstracting wills has been started; these abstracts will contain all names, places, relationships and far as possible, subjects mentioned in the originals, so once again consultation of the originals should only rarely be necessary, even where possible.

Where the searcher comes across a reference which includes a register (i.e. a DW/PA/7/ reference), it will usually be easier to search for that, rather than for an original will, as the folio number, also given in this index, will be readily found in the top left hand corner on the film. Where only an original will reference (beginning DW/PA/5/) is found, or where it is necessary to consult an original as opposed to a register entry, then searchers will find it easiest to locate a will, after finding the desired year, by turning the film for each will to the frame showing the folded will, on which has been annotated in a modern hand the name of the testator, until they locate the will they want.

Two of the will registers ('Spage' and 'Herringman') have been printed in abstract form by the Surrey Record Society (Vol.4 [Herringman] and Vol.5 [Spage]) (1915-1922). Much of Register 'Pykman' has also been abstracted, and copies of the abstracts are to be found at the GLRO and the SRO. An abstract has also been made of all the wills appearing in the will register now in the British Museum. An indexed abstract of all unfilmed wills in the period 1595-1649 is available at the GLRO and the Local Studies Library, Guildford. Wills in this abstract are denoted in this index by having a 'U' preceding their abstract number, so that a will reference followed by <Abs U1> means that this will is unfilmed, and is the first abstract in the volume.

Furthermore, many will abstracts appear in the pages of *Surrey Archaeological Society Collections*. In all cases where an abstract has been noticed a note has been put in angle brackets <>. <Abs 1>, for example means that the will concerned is the first will abstracted in the printed calendar of the register concerned. Other abstract references give the volume and page number of the Surrey Archaeological Society Collections where the abstract appears. Searchers finding references to these abstracted wills should be able to obtain all their information from the abstracts. A systematic search has been made of the S.A.C. volumes for will abstracts, of which many appear especially in the first few volumes.

II. Document and Microfilm References

(a) Original wills [DW/PA/5/]

As stated above, the original wills are filed in annual bundles. Each bundle 1595-1649 is kept in alphabetical order by initial letter, but there has been some missorting of the bundles, so this is not always to be relied upon totally. For 1593 and before this help is generally not there, and wills are usually filed in strict chronological order within the year's bundle (except for 1558 and 1579 which have been rearranged in alphabetical order), though inevitably there has been some disturbance to this chronological order. In addition it is obvious from the current arrangement and the notes made by Campbell Cooke, together with a note on DW/PA/5/1558/302, that originally there were two sequences of unregistered wills, at least prior to 1593. It is apparent that there has been some substantial rearrangement between the filming in the fifties, and the arrival of the records at the GLRO in 1970. In any case, for the sake of the record, an asterisk appears in this list after the square bracket containing the reference of those wills listed by Campbell Cooke as being 'Unregistered Wills I'. This is a much smaller sequence than 'Unregistered Wills II' which contains most wills before 1593. The asterisk is not, of course, in the GLRO reference, and should not be used in official references to the wills. Happily, one can report that only very few of the wills recorded by Campbell Cooke cannot now be traced.

Many individual wills are unfit for production within the bundles, though some years have been repaired, guarded and filed. The bundles are kept in boxes, and the wills are listed below by these boxes. Wills are occasionally found out of their correct year of probate, but the year used is fairly consistently the Old Style year, i.e. from 25 March to 24 March. The reference is in three parts, firstly DW/PA/5/ which is the overall reference for original wills of this court, secondly the year, and finally the number of the will within the bundle. Searchers are warned that they has undoubtedly been some (though hopefully limited) disturbance within the bundles, between the time of filming and the time of numbering each document. All the registers have been filmed, but not (as described above) all the original wills, and since the filming predated the numbering, the reference numbers which are now on original wills do not appear on the films.

For the early part of this period, both the terms original wills, and unregistered wills, though freely used herein, are misnomers. Documents in the 'Original Wills' series prior to 1595 are very rarely original wills, but in fact registered copies of original wills, even though they are not kept in registers (but often on sheets containing more than one will). Quite apart from the fact of the illiteracy of most people even of the will-making class, therefore, wills from this period do not make available the signatures of either testators or witnesses.

DW/PA/5/ 1534-1554 Original wills

Microfilm Ref, X/32/24; this film only covers wills from 1547, The Mormon microfilm reference is 0097180, and they list the film as covering all these wills,

DW/PA/5/ 1555-1557 Original wills

Microfilm Ref, X/32/24 (0097180) (to Oct 1557); X/32/25 (0097181) (Oct 1557-March 1557/58)

DW/PA/5/ 1558 Original wills

Microfilm Ref, X/32/25 (A-M) (0097181); X/32/26 (0097182) (M-Z)

DW/PA/5/ 1559-1560 Original wills

No microfilm available for original wills, use film of register; microfilm ref, X/32/5-6 (0097153)

DW/PA/5/ 1561-1563 Original wills

Microfilm Ref, X/32/26 (0097183) (March 1561-March 1562/63); X/32/27 (0097184) (March 1562/63-March 1563/64)

DW/PA/5/ 1564-1571 Original wills

Microfilm Ref, X/32/27 (0097184) (June 1564-April 1569); X/32/28 (0097185) (1569-March 1571/72)

DW/PA/5/ 1572-1576 Original wills

Microfilm Ref, X/32/29 (0097186-7)

DW/PA/5/ 1577-1581 Original wills

Microfilm Ref, X/32/29 (0097187-9)(March 1578-March 1578/79); X/32/31 (0097187-9) (July 1581-March 1581/82); these films cover 1578 and 1581 only; there are no wills for 1577

DW/PA/5/ 1582-1587 Original wills

Microfilm Ref, X/32/31 (0097191) (April 1582-Jan/March 1586/87); X/32/32 (0097192) (August 1586-March 1587/88)

DW/PA/5/ 1588-1591 Original wills

Microfilm Ref, X/32/32 (0097192) (April-Oct 1588, March 1588/89, various 1589-1590); X/32/33 (0097193) (Oct 1588-March 1588/89, April 1591-March 1591/92)

DW/PA/5/ 1592-1594 Original wills

Microfilm Ref, X/32/33 (0097193) (March-Oct 1592); X/32/34 (0097194) (Oct 1592-Oct 1593, Jan-March 1593/94); X/32/35 (0097195) (Oct-Dec 1593, May 1594)

DW/PA/5/ 1595-1597 Original wills

No microfilm available for original wills, use film of register; microfilm ref, X/32/6 (0097154), or printed abstracts of will register

DW/PA/5/ 1598-1599 Original wills

No microfilm available for original wills, use film of register; microfilm ref, X/32/6 (0097154), or printed abstracts of will register

DW/PA/5/ 1600-1602 Original wills
No microfilm available for original wills, use film of register; microfilm ref. X/32/6 (0097154), or printed abstracts of will register

DW/PA/5/ 1603-1604 Original wills
No microfilm available for original wills, use film of register; microfilm ref. X/32/6 (0097154), or printed abstracts of will register

DW/PA/5/ 1605-1606 Original wills
No microfilm available for original wills, use film of register; microfilm ref. X/32/6 (0097154), or printed abstracts of will register

DW/PA/5/ 1607-1608 Original wills
No microfilm available for original wills, use film of register; microfilm ref. X/32/6 (0097154), or printed abstracts of will register

DW/PA/5/ 1609-1611 Original wills
No microfilm available for original wills, use film of register; microfilm ref. X/32/7 (0097155)

DW/PA/5/ 1612 Original wills
No microfilm available for original wills, use film of register; microfilm ref. X/32/7 (0097155)

DW/PA/5/ 1613-1614 Original wills
No microfilm available for original wills, use film of registers; microfilm ref. X/32/7-8 (0097155-6)

DW/PA/5/ 1615-1616 Original wills
No microfilm available for original wills, use film of register; microfilm ref. X/32/7-8 (0097155-6)

DW/PA/5/ 1617, 1619 (A-H) Original wills
No microfilm available for original wills, use film of register; microfilm ref. X/32/8-9 (0097156-7); no original wills survive for 1618

DW/PA/5/ 1619 (I-Z), 1620-1621 Original wills
No microfilm available for original wills, use film of register; microfilm ref. X/32/7-8 (0097155-6)

DW/PA/5/ 1622-1624 Original wills
Microfilm Ref. X/32/35 (0097197) (1622, 1623 A-H); X/32/36 (0097198)

DW/PA/5/ 1625 Original wills
Microfilm Ref. X/32/37 (0097199); X/32/38 (0097200)

DW/PA/5/ 1626-1627 Original wills
Microfilm Ref. X/32/38 (0097201); X/32/39 (0097202)

DW/PA/5/ 1628-1630 Original wills
Microfilm Ref. X/32/39 (0097202); X/32/40 (0097203); X/32/41 (0097204)

DW/PA/5/ 1631-1633 Original wills
No microfilm available for original wills, use film of register; microfilm ref. X/32/9 (0097158)

DW/PA/5/ 1634-1636 Original wills
No microfilm available for original wills, use film of register; microfilm ref. X/32/9 (0097158)

DW/PA/5/ 1637-1638 Original wills
No microfilm available for original wills, use film of register; microfilm ref. X/32/9 (0097158)

DW/PA/5/ 1639-1640 Original wills
No microfilm available for original wills, use film of register; microfilm ref. X/32/10 (0097159)

DW/PA/5/ 1641-1642 Original wills
No microfilm available for original wills, use film of register; microfilm ref. X/32/10 (0097159)

DW/PA/5/ 1643-1649 Original wills
No microfilm available for original wills, use film of register; microfilm ref. X/32/10 (0097159)

There follows a list of the numbers of original wills filed in each year, with a note as to the numbering used, and of errors in numbering discovered during the compilation of this work. From 1534 to 1593 the documents are sorted chronologically within each year, except 1558 and 1579, which are sorted alphabetically.

1534/1 (1) (William Upfold of Cranleigh - was originally misfiled in 1596)
1535 no original wills survive for this year
1536 no original wills survive for this year
1537 no original wills survive for this year
1538/1 (1) (Robert Richardson of St Margaret Southwark)
1539 no original wills survive for this year
1534-1539 (2)
1540 no original wills survive for this year
1541 no original wills survive for this year
1542 no original wills survive for this year
1543/1-16 (16)
1544/1-13 (no.4 is a sheet containing four wills; no.5 is a sheet containing four wills; no.6 is a sheet containing four wills; no.8 is a sheet containing three wills; no.9 has seven wills on four pages) (30)
1545/1-21 (nos.19 and 20 are labels only) (19)
1546/1-94 (nos.2,4,6,7,8,9,13,21,22,26,51,52,53,61,62,63,72,73,74,76,78, 79,81 and 92 are labels only; no.10 is a sheet containing three wills; no.11 is a sheet containing two wills; no.23 is a sheet containing two wills; no.24 is a sheet containing two wills; no.75 is a sheet containing four wills) (78)
1547/1-29 (29)
1548/1-3 (3)
1549/1-3 (3)
1540-1549 (178)

1550/1-114 (nos,72,74 and 75 are labels only; no,76 is a sheet containing two wills) (112)

1551 no original wills survive for this year

1552/1-31 (nos,29 and 30 are two copies of the same will) (30)

1553 no original wills survive for this year

1554 no original wills survive for this year

1555/1-85 (nos,17,18,20,21,23,32,41,60,61,62,63 and 64 are labels only; no,1 is a quasi-register with four wills on four pages; no,14 is a quasi-register with five wills on four pages; no,67 is a quasi-register with three wills on four pages; no,68 is a quasi-register with three wills on four pages; no,6 is a proxy for no,33) (83)

1556/1-16 (nos,1 and 2 are labels only) (14)

1557/1-145 (nos,9,33,57,76,77,80-86 incl.,107 and 109 are labels only; there are two x no,60; no,72 is a sheet with two wills on it; no,75 is a quasi-register containing eight pages and ten wills; no,88 is a sheet with two wills on it; no,120 is a sheet with two wills on it; no,97 is the first will not examined by Campbell Cooke) (144)

1558/1-302 (this year is arranged in alphabetical order; nos, 61,62,71,93, 96,97,99,123,130,156,164,171,176,183,199,203,235,248,251,264,265 and 302 are labels only; no,301 consists of three lists of names, but contains no will; no,76 is a quasi-register containing seven wills on four pages; no,166 is a quasi-register containing eight wills on four pages; no,186 is a quasi-register containing four wills on four pages; no,302 is a piece of cardboard on which are listed the names of testator's in the 'Supplementary' series of wills, and from which it is clear that when there was such a series, it was not kept in alphabetical order - this is in any case clear from Campbell Cooke's notes) (295)

1559/1-244 (nos, 23,24,44,103,147,169,172,184,190,191,205 and 218 are labels only; no,29 is a quasi-register having two wills on four pages (one of which is registered in 'Tully' and one is not); no, 30 is a quasi-register also having two wills on four pages; no,174 is a quasi-register having six wills on four pages; no,195 is a proxy for no,193; a few wills from 1560 are filed with, and numbered as, 1559) (238)

1550-1559 (916)

1560 the few original wills for this year are filed with 1559

1561/1-90 (2 x no,18) (91)

1562/1-88 (this year has been repaired, guarded and filed) (88)

1563/1-124 (nos,54-59 incl, are labels only; no,64 is a quasi-register of twelve pages (11¾" x 8") containing six wills, but three have originals filed also; no,65 is a quasi-register of sixteen pages (11½" x 8") containing ten wills; no,120 is a sheet containing two wills) (130)

1564 the few original wills for this year are filed in 1565

1565/1-12 (12)

1566 no original wills survive for this year

1567 no original wills survive for this year

1568/1-89 (nos,4,15,16,54 and 67 are labels only) (84)

1569/1-86 (86)

1560-1569 (491)

1570/1-104 (nos,1,3,30,31 and 36 are labels only; there are two x no,27) (100)

1571/1-96 (nos,12,42,43 and 72 are labels only; no,22 is the note of a grant of administration in respect of four people) (95)

1572/1-27 (nos,1 and 24 are labels only) (25)

1573 no original wills survive for this year

1574/1-45 (nos,2,10,28-33 incl, and 40 are labels only; but 1574/14 is a quasi-register (11½" x 7½") of twenty-six pages (six of them blank) containing nine wills) (44)

1575/1-90 (nos,1,24,67 and 88 are labels only) (86)

1576/1-156 (nos,1,31,84,87,88,104,105 and 139 are labels or wrappers only, while no,142 is a proxy for no,141) (147)

1577 no original wills survive for this year

1578/1-112 (nos,30,57 and 86 are labels or wrappers only, and nos,68 and 70, and nos,69 and 72, are the same wills) (107)

1579/1-107 (nos,48,57,61 and 62 are labels only) (103)

1570-1579 (707)

1580/1-72 (no,9 is only a label) (71)

1581/1-67 (no,1 is not a will, but a note of "the names of such testaments as were delivered to William Philipps to registred [*sic*] for the year 1581 hereafter followeth"; nos,3 and 39 are labels or wrappers only and nos,34 and 45 are identical wills) (64)

1582/1-108 (nos,1,20,54,55,87 and 103 are labels or wrappers only) (102)

1583/1-4 (on no,2 a pencil note "is this the will, one of a list of seven given on the back of Averie, 1592") (4)

1584/1-3 (3)

1585/1-4 (4)

1586/1-45 (45) (this year's wills have been repaired, guarded and filed)

1587/1-126 (nos,1,2,4 and 121 are only labels or wrappers, and no,89 is a proxy for no,88) (121)

1588/1-92 (92)

1589/1-2 (2)

1580-1589 (504)

1590/1 (1)

1591/1-115 (115)

1592/1-124 (2 x no,102) (125)

1593/1-208 (nos,104,111,112,140,143,145,177,192 and 205 are only labels or covers, but two x no,180) (200) (this year's wills have been repaired, guarded and filed)

1594 no original wills survive for this year

[From 1595-1649 the original wills have been, sorted within each year, into bundles for each letter of the alphabet, though there has been some limited missorting,]

1595/1-97 (97) (this year's wills have been repaired, guarded and filed)

1596/1-67 (67) (this year's wills have been repaired, guarded and filed)

1597/1-122 (122) (this year's wills have been repaired, guarded and filed)

1598/1-94 (94) (this year's wills have been repaired, guarded and filed)

1599/1-101 (101) (this year's wills have been repaired, guarded and filed)

1590-1599 (922)

1600/1-56 (56) (this year's wills have been repaired, guarded and filed)

1601/1-92 (92) (this year's wills have been repaired, guarded and filed)

1602/1-94 (no nos,51,57,71 or 88) (90) (this year's wills have been repaired, guarded and filed)

1603/1-191 (3 x no,16) (188)

1604/1-75 (2 x no,39, two x no,40 and two x no,53) (72)

1605/1-105 (nos,95 and 96 refer to the same man) (104) (this year's wills have been repaired, guarded and filed)

1606/1-107 (107) (this year's wills have been repaired, guarded and filed)

1607/1-110 (nos,20 and 21,25 and 26, 67 and 68 and 95 and 96 are of the same man in each case) (106) (this year's wills have been repaired, guarded and filed)
1608/1-119 (119)
1609/1-131 (two x no,55) (132)
1600-1609 (1066)
1610/1-150 (150)
1611/1-126 (126)
1612/1-178 (178)
1613/1-144 (144)
1614/1-142 (142)
1615/1-146 (146)
1616/1-153 (153)
1617/1-142 (142)
1618 no original wills survive for this year
1619/1-136 (136)
1610-1619 (1317)
1620/1-142 (142)
1621/1-136 (two x no,34) (137)
1622/1-112 (two x no,52) (113)
1623/1-137 (137) (all wills from this year are unfit for production)
1624/1-147 (two x no,28 & two x no,29) (149)
1625/1-282 (two x no,243) (283)
1626/1-137 (two x no,37 & two x no,38) (139)
1627/1-111 (two x no,59) (112)
1628/1-115 (115)
1629/1-112 (112)
1620-1629 (1439)
1630/1-126 (126)
1631/1-122 (no,68 and 69 same item + wrapper; two x no,92) (122)
1632/1-112 (two x no,7) (113)
1633/1-115 (two x no,41) (116)
1634/1-115 (115)
1635/1-135 (135)
1636/1-114 (114)
1637/1-105 (two x no,41, two x no,67) (107)
1638/1-160 (no nos,43-47, but two x no,138) (156)
1639/1-156 (+ one due to misnumbering) (157)
1630-1639 (1261)
1640/1-173 (173)
1641/1-148 (- one due to label; + two due to misnumbering) (149)
1642/1-94 (+ one due to misnumbering) (95)
1643/1-98 (+ two because of misnumbering) (100)
1644/1-20 (+ cover) (20)
1645/1-65 (65)
1646/1-60 (60)
1647/1-20 (20)
1648/1-46 (46)
1649/1-19 (19)
1640-1649 (747)
1534-1649 (8,554)

(b) Registers of wills [DW/PA/7/1-13]

These are the registers into which most but not all wills were copied. However, not only were not all wills registered during periods covered by registers, but registers either were not kept, or do not survive for several periods. There is one known early register which has strayed from archdiaconal custody, and is in the Department of Western Manuscripts, The British Library (Add.MS.24,925) which fills a small part of the gap between Register 'Pykman' ending in 1541 and Register 'Tully' beginning in 1559, having 65 wills registered dating mainly from 1543-1544. This register contains 23 leaves and there are two leaves of an index of a later date. An abstract of the entries in it has been made and copies deposited with the British Library itself, the Greater London Record Office, the Surrey Record Office, the Guildhall Library, the Guildford Muniment Room, the Society of Genealogists and West and East Surrey Family History Society libraries.

It was the custom in some courts for will registers to be named after the first testator recorded in them, and this was the pre-Commonwealth practice in the Archdeaconry Court of Surrey. For details of probate procedure reference should be made to Surrey Record Society number 17 (Dec 1922). At this time (1989), registers 'Spage', 'Michell', 'Pykman', 'Tully' and 'Herringman' are unfit for production; the other registers are not available for consultation, as they are fully covered by microfilms. Careful note should be taken of the folio numbers given in this index; none of the volumes are in perfect chronological order, and the later ones, from 1608 onwards, are in some considerable chronological disarray, with register 'Yeast' having some entries repeated. It would appear that these registers were compiled by a clerk working at dictation; this is the strong impression gained by the archivist who has done most work on them, though in the absence of procedural records of the court, this must remain conjectural.

For the first two registers, especially, but for all registers to some extent, the years' numbers are approximate, as the date of probate is frequently omitted, when the date of *making* the will is all that can be used. The years used in these calculations are Old Style, i.e. 25 March to 25 March. In the notes on earliest and latest entries however, as in the body of the index, wherever a year appears in isolation (i.e. *not* where it forms part of the reference) it has been rendered in New Style. The registers are foliated in roman numerals up to and including 'Tully' and in arabic numerals thereafter.

DW/PA/7/1 Oct 1480, July 1482, July 1484-Jan 1490 Will register 'Spage' Microfilm Ref. X/32/4 (0097152); printed calendar (Surrey Record Society No.17, alternatively known as Vol.5 of the Society's publications).

The register is 11" x 8", paper, bound in vellum but some sections now loose; the whole is boxed, with folios numbered from 1 to 101. The lower half of f.44 is torn off and missing, mutilating two wills; possibly others are missing. A folio is missing which Rodman states to be f.93. The register has suffered from damp damage.

Year	Folios	No.of wills in yr	Year	Folios	No.of wills in yr
1469	77	1	1485	7,12-32	67
1480	4	1	1486	31-52,68	64
1481	none		1487	35,47,51-80 38	
1482	48	1	1488	58,77-90	43
1483	none		1489	90-101	25
1484	1-11	36			

Total number of wills 276

Earliest entry: *made* 12 Sep 1469 (William Hooke)
Latest entry: *made* 26 Feb 1490 (William Woodstock)

DW/PA/7/2 Oct 1490-Oct 1524 Will register 'Mathewe' Microfilm Ref. X/32/4 (0097152)

The register is 12" x 8¼", paper, rebound in whole linen and boxed. Folios run from 1-209, with folio 11 missing. A manuscript index has been inserted in front of folio 1. The register contains nine administration acts on folios 7, 8, 21, 23, 35, 42, 46, 47; 2 sequestrations on folios 16, 25; one com. ad colligend. on folio 29; wills and administrations are, according to the date of probate or administration, out of place on folios 29, 34, 35 and 79.

Year	Folios	No.of wills in yr	Year	Folios	No.of wills in yr
1488	13,34	1	1496	47-50	9
1489	13	1	1497	35,51-55	11
1490	1-12,16	31	1498	29,55,59	14
1491	4-5,12-25,27	24	1499	29,34,56-61	14
1492	25-35	23	1500	61-75,83	35
1493	36-41	19	1501	76-81,83	6
1494	32,41-46	20	1502	82-86	7
1495	46-47	3	1503	87-89	6

Year	Folios	No.of wills in yr	Year	Folios	No.of wills in yr
1504	89	1	1517	79,111-120, 191,198	24
1505	90-91	4			
1506-1508		none	1518	121-133	21
1509	92-93	3	1519	134-138,140	10
1510-1511		none	1520	139,141-150	19
1512	93	1	1521	151-172	27
1513	94-96	6	1522	172-187	21
1514	97-102	14	1523	187-191, 193-196, 199,204	17
1515	102-106	10			
1516	106-110,133	12			
			1524	195,197-209	14

Total number of wills 438

Earliest entry: 13 Sep 1488 (Alice Bissett)
Latest entry: 25 Jan 1525 (John Millest)

Testators who merit brief individual mention are two gentlemen (Newdigate f.110; Brampton f.149); a knight of St George (De Norbon (f.119); a yeoman porter to Henry VIII (Scharpe f.144); three yeomen of the Guard (Brown f.148; Gough f.148; Stokes f.151); a squire (Gainsford f.163); a yeoman purveyor for the king's fish and a yeoman taker for the king's ale (witnesses to Cowper f.194).

DW/PA/7/3 June 1529-June 1532 Will register 'Michell'
Microfilm Ref. X/32/4 (0097152)

The register is 11" x 8", paper, and was repaired, guarded and filed in 1975. The folios do not commence until number 97 (and then run to folio 208), which presumably accounts for the gap between it and register 'Mathewe' of the years 1525-1529. Mention is made on the last page that the book belonged to Ralph White, notary public in Bath and Wells and official in the Court of Arches, and after his death to Robert Johnson, notary public, his successor as Registrar to the Archdeacon of Surrey.

Year	Folios	No.of wills in yr	Year	Folios	No.of wills in yr
1525-1528		none	1531	173,175-203	78
1529	97-130	74	1532	200,203-207	8
1530	131-174	99			

Total number of wills 259

Earliest entry: 11 Jun 1529 (William Mitchell alias Burley)
Latest entry: 28 Jun 1532 (Robert Wells)

Testators who merit mention are a yeoman to the crown (Stondon f.128); an esquire (Skerne f.134); two gentleman (Stoughton f.143; Sutton f.155); a notary and one of the proctors of the arches (Butterye f.147)

DW/PA/7/4 June 1532-February 1538 Will register 'Heats'
Microfilm Ref. X/32/4 (0097152) (fols.1-67); X/32/5 (0097153) (fols.65-237)

The register is 12" x 8¾", paper, rebound in whole cloth and boxed. Folios run from 1 to 237, part of folios 13 and 31 have been torn off. There are two folios 168, one of which has been lettered 'a' in pencil, but 'bis' in a contemporary hand in ink. An abstract is in the course of preparation.

Year	Folios	No.of wills in yr	Year	Folios	No.of wills in yr
1527	236	1	1534	64,74-112	97
1528-1530		none	1535	113-144	76
1531	3,73	2	1536	145-206	120
1532	1-2,4-32	65	1537	207-235	69
1533	32-74	83			

Total number of wills 513

Earliest entry: 3 Apr 1527 (John Thowcard)
Latest entry: 28 Feb 1538 (Nicholas Banbridge)

Individual entries worth mentioning are a gentleman (Perkyn f.12); a groom of the privy larder to the king (Dalton f.131); a groom almoner with our sovereign lord the king (Smith f.136); a squire (Scott f.15); a gift of 20s. towards the building of a kitchen at the sign of St George in Guildford (Norbrige f.19); a mention of the glasshouse at Chiddingfold (Peto f.150); yeoman of the chamber to the right honourable marquis of Exeter (who witnesses) (Thesther f.210); and a yeoman of the guard (Alcock f.220).

DW/PA/7/5 February 1538-May 1541 Will register 'Pykman'
Microfilm Ref, X/32/5 (0097153) (on the film the folios appear in the following order; 1-63; 89-137; 186-221; 224-231; 63-88; 138-185; 223)

The register is 10½" x 7¾", paper, rebound in whole cloth and boxed, The register, as far as can be told, was originally of 231 folios, At the time this register was rebound, paginated and an index compiled, certain folios (63-88, 137-160 and 164-184 were missing, Most of these were later recovered and are kept separately from the bound register, Folios 149, 152, 155, 158-160 and 222 remain missing, Rodman corrected the index, added foliation to the pagination in the index, and had bound in the list of entries, He then provided a contents list for ff,63-88, 137-184 (excluding the gaps) and 223, When the register was rebound (apparently late in the 18th or early in the 19th century), the binder cropped the folios, which were originally 11¼" x 8", Folios 63,150-151, 153-154,156-157 and 223, though loose were cropped in like manner, the remainder of the loose folios remain their original size, Folio 3 is inserted reversed (so that f,3r appears after f,3v), as are folios 5 and 6,

Year	Folios	No,of wills in yr	Year	Folios	No,of wills in yr
1537	1-10	11	1540	124,150-225	137
1538	11-70	117	1541	225-230	10
1539	70-148	121			

Total number of wills 396

Earliest entry; 20 Feb 1538 (several entries, including Richard Pikeman or Pykman)
Latest entry; 30 May 1541 (Thomas Norris)

Entries of interest include a gentleman (Hull f,42); Charles, duke of Suffolk (Chandler f,69); a servant at confectionaries of the king as a witness (Ford f,21); yeoman of the king's household (Jenner f,12) and a servant of the elder duchess of Norfolk (Shanke f,227),

DW/PA/7/6 November 1559-November 1560 Will register 'Tully'
Microfilm Ref, X/32/5 (0097153) (fols,1-165); X/32/6 (0097154) (fols,163-299)

The register is 11¾" x 8¼", paper and there are 299 folios, The binding case is missing and several leaves are loose; the whole is kept in a box case, Due to misfoliation there are no folios 31-39 and there are two folios numbered 214, At least one folio at the end is missing,

Year	Folios	No. of wills in yr	Year	Folios	No. of wills in yr
1542-1558		none	1561	91,116,241, 261-262	4
1559	1-54,56-192, 229	228			
1560	4,9,55,58,193-260,263-299	153			

Total number of wills 385

Earliest entry: 1 Apr 1559 (Thomas Goring)
Latest entry: 3 Jul 1561 (Thomas Page)

Entries of interest include two yeomen of the queen's chamber (Weale f.30; Norman f.147); keeper of the queen's park of Woking (Pullman f.107); one of the queen's most honourable guard (Spencer f.112); a minstrel (May f.230); one of the queen's watermen (Tibbold f.261) and a gentleman (Bray f.293).

DW/PA/7/7 March 1595-August 1608 Will register 'Herringman' Microfilm Ref. X/32/6 (0097154) (fols.1-470); X/32/7 (0097155) (fols.469-645); printed calendar (Surrey Record Society Vol.4, also known as parts 3, 7, 15).

The register is 16¼" x 11", paper, rebound in whole cloth with additional leather back. There are 645 folios. Folios 184, 408, 464, 490v-494 and 556 are blank.

Year	Folios	No. of wills in yr	Year	Folios	No. of wills in yr
1562-1574		none	1604	456,465, 467-490	50
1575	505 (admon)	1	1605	422,490-516, 607	44
1576-1594		none	1606	519-525, 527-529,531-574, 576-577,579-582, 591,597,612	101
1595	1-50,77,105	96	1607	524-527, 530,532,534, 539,554,578, 583-625	94
1596	51-76,78-104, 106-114,117	117	1608	626-645	45
1597	115-182	121	1609	575	1
1598	183-188, 191-243	93	1610-1612		none
1599	189-190, 243-290	92	1613	517	1
1600	291-321,390	58			
1601	322-354, 363,389	77			
1602	354-362, 364-389	71			
1603	389,391-455, 457-463,466	152			

Total number of wills 1214

Earliest entry: 27 Sep 1575 (John Bartholomew)
Latest entry: 7 Sep 1613 (Katherine English) apart from this exceptional entry, the latest is 4 Nov 1609 (John Terrell)

Entries of especial interest include a yeoman of the queen's privy backhouse (f.46); a prisoner in the king's bench prison in Southwark (f.142); a servant of the queen (f.139); one of the queen's yeomen in ordinary of the chamber (f.201); and a master of the queen's barges (f.202).

DW/PA/7/8 August 1608-March 1615 Will register 'Berry'
Microfilm Ref. X/32/7 (0097155)

The register is 16¾" x 10¾", paper, bound in whole cloth with an additional leather back. There are 410 folios. There are two folios marked f.28. ff.365-368 are bound in after f.265*. f. 386 is blank and ff.387-388 are missing. In addition at f.254 the hand changes and the probates are for 1611, whereas between f.236 and f.253, the year is 1613. The register from internal evidence was not made before 1619 (see will of Henry Chitty f.196).

Year	Folios	No.of wills in yr	Year	Folios	No.of wills in yr
1607	40-42	4	1612	207-235, 365-368*,273-276, 325,330,336-384*, 390-402	205
1608	1-31	74			
1609	31-99	134			
1610	99-140, 166-199	150	1613	236-253, 268-272,277-315, 325-330,389	142
1611	140-165, 200-206,254-265, 316-324,380	128			
			1614	331-335, 403-410	24

Total number of wills 861

Earliest entry: 13 Apr 1607 (Thomas Wright)
Latest entry: 22 Mar 1615 (Jasper Creamer)

Mention is made of the Catherine Wheel in Egham (Petty f.40, f.93); one of the gentlemen of his majesty's chapel (Plumley f.145); one of his majesty's woodyards (Hunt f.272) and keeper and servant to the right honourable Sir George Moore, knight (Harman f.274).

DW/PA/7/9 April 1614-March 1621 Will register 'Stoughton'
Microfilm Ref. X/32/8 (0097156)

The register is 16¼" x 10½", paper, bound in whole cloth with an additional leather back. The folios are numbered 1-344. There are two ff.25, marked 'a' and 'b' and ff. 62-66 are missing, while f.174 follows f.175, and is in turn followed by a second f.175; the first is marked '175a', the second '175b'; there is no f.254 and f.38 and ff.343-348 at the end of the volume are blank. In the filming ff.170v-171r have been missed, so an abstract has been made.

Year	Folios	No.of wills in yr	Year	Folios	No.of wills in yr
1614	21-80,		1617	213-263	102
	83,96-105	122	1618	264-299	63
1615	1-12,80-82,		1619	299-328	56
	84-90,104-156	126	1620	329-342	36
1616	13-20,90-95,157-213				123

Total number of wills 628

Earliest entry: 28 Mar 1614 (Joan Hall)
Latest entry: 10 Mar 1621 (Robert Best)

DW/PA/7/10 April 1615-September 1623 Will register 'Peter'
Microfilm Ref. X/32/8 (0097156) (fols.1-269); X/32/9 (0097157) (fols.265-299)

The register is 15½" x 10½". There are 299 folios. Folio 111 is marked '111 and 112' and there is no f.112, the entry at the end of f.111 continuing without interruption at the beginning of f.113; there are 2 x f.257; one is marked f.257A. Some early entries are of wills proved during a Metropolitan visitation. In the filming ff.44v-45r have been missed, so an abstract has been prepared.

Year	Folios	No.of wills in yr	Year	Folios	No.of wills in yr
1615	18-20,24,		1618	42-74	69
	27-29,32,83-93	25	1619	4-12,74-82, 80	
1616	1-4,13-18,			94-99,101,107-115,	
	21-23,26-27,			151-153,172-176,	
	30-32,93-94	35		184-185	
1617	33-41,299	20			

1620	20,115-145, 153,177-183, 185-189,201-213, 237,277-278	104	1622	244-274, 280-283,291-299	78
			1623	283-290	20
1621	99-106,146-150,154-171,189-201, 214-236,238-243,275-276,278				135

Total number of wills 566

Earliest entry; 6 Apr 1615 (Margaret Smither)
Latest entry; 18 Sep 1623 (Bartholomew Woodger)

DW/PA/7/11 April 1622-March 1631 Will register 'Yeast'
Microfilm Ref.X/32/11 (0097156) (fols.1-230); X/32/12 (0097157) (fols.227-615)

The register is 15½" x 10½". The folios run from 1 to 615. The top right hand corner of f.615 is missing; there are two ff.1, not differentiated. Wills appearing on the first f.1 are marked f.1A in this index, on the second f.1B, but this is not reflected in the original; there is no ff.43, 85, 236, 305 or 542 - all would appear to be errors in foliation rather than missing leaves; ff.237, 303 and 304 are blank; there are two ff.267, 327 and 437, in all cases marked A & B in the originals; there are also two ff.286, but the will of Andrew Baxter runs right through both of them. In the filming ff.42v-43r have been missed so an abstract has been made.

Year	Folios	No.of wills in yr	Year	Folios	No.of wills in yr
1620	221-223	7	1626	33,201, 292-321,361-395, 417-421,477	143
1621		none			
1622	1-11,34,39	24			
1623	11-54, 58-86,88-89,123	121	1627	396-416, 421-434	71
1624	1,55-57,87, 90-122,124-145, 156-163,187, 189-190,192, 195,197,327A	124	1628	435-494	117
			1629	495-523, 526,530-555,614	111
			1630	524-529, 555-613	130
1625	145-156,164-291,322-360,389				294

Total number of wills 1,142

DW/PA/7/12 April 1627-February 1628, April 1631-February 1639
Will register 'Farmer' Microfilm Ref. X/32/9 (0097157)

The register is 15½" x 10½". The folios run from 1-529. There are no ff.86-89; there are two ff.114, 127, 159 and 182, none of which are differentiated in the original, but which are in this indexed separately references with 'A' and 'B' numbers; there are also two f.468, but these are differentiated in the original too. In the filming f.235v-236r have been missed, so an abstract has been made.

Year	Folios	No.of wills	Year	Folios	No.of wills
1627	367-372	23	1635	247-254,	142
1628,1630		none		267-310,522-528	
1629	42-44	1	1636	311-353,	115
1631	1-42,45-70, 134			357-362,438	
1631	105	134	1637	354-356,	141
1632	71-140,217 130			363-367,372-437,	
1633	141-202,	106		439-441,528	
	209-219	106	1638	442-521,529	168
1634	203-208,219-246,255-267,269,295-296	125			

Total number of wills 1,085

DW/PA/7/13 April 1639-May 1649 Will register 'Harding'
Microfilm Ref. X/32/9 (0097158) (fols.1-55); X/32/10 (0097159)(fols.53-504)

The register is 15½" x 10½". The folios run from 1-504. There is no f.495-498v, while ff.312 and 504 are blank; there are two ff.149 in the original, not differentiated therein. In the filming ff.490v-491r have been missed so an abstract has been made.

Year	Folios	No.of wills	Year	Folios	No.of wills
1638	37,45	2	1644	261,272,	103
1639	1-52,66-71, 149			287,295,306,	
	112-118,140			320,325-380,400	
1640	53-64,	170	1645	243,311,	79
	72-111,119-141,			320,381-426,435	
	199,244-252		1646	311,319,427-52	44
1641	142-198	143	1647	351,453-472	32
1642	64,199-242,	88	1648	473-495	37
	303-305,307,402		1649	499-503	12
1643	253-260,	102			
	262-302,306-310,				
	313-318,321-324				

Total number of wills in register 961

III. Number of Wills Surviving

Listed first are the number of wills to appear in the annual bundle of original wills, with a note of how many wills are unregistered. Then is listed the number of wills in each register for that year, and then a total figure for all material available for all years. There are some discrepancies between years, probably caused by wills being filed in the wrong years. However, this list provides a guide to the size of the archive.

Headings; O = Original Wills;
U = Unregistered wills
R = Registered Wills
T = Total

Year	O	U	R	T	Year	O	U	R	T
1469	0	0	1	1	1490	0	0	31	31
1480	0	0	1	1	1491	0	0	24	24
1481	0	0	0	0	1492	0	0	23	23
1482	0	0	1	1	1493	0	0	19	19
1483	0	0	0	0	1494	0	0	20	20
1484	0	0	36	36	1495	0	0	3	3
1485	0	0	67	67	1496	0	0	9	9
1486	0	0	64	64	1497	0	0	11	11
1487	0	0	38	38	1498	0	0	14	14
1488	0	0	44	44	1499	0	0	14	14
1489	0	0	26	26					
Pre-1500						0	0	444	444
1500	0	0	35	35	1513	0	0	6	6
1501	0	0	6	6	1514	0	0	14	14
1502	0	0	7	7	1515	0	0	10	10
1503	0	0	6	6	1516	0	0	12	12
1504	0	0	1	1	1517	0	0	24	24
1505	0	0	4	4	1518	0	0	21	21
1506	0	0	0	0	1519	0	0	10	10
1507	0	0	0	0	1520	0	0	19	19
1508	0	0	0	0	1521	0	0	27	27
1509	0	0	3	3	1522	0	0	21	21
1510	0	0	0	0	1523	0	0	17	17
1511	0	0	0	0	1524	0	0	14	14
1512	0	0	1	1					
1500-1524						0	0	258	258

1525	0	0	0	0	1535	0	0	76	76
1526	0	0	0	0	1536	0	0	120	120
1527	0	0	1	1	1537	0	0	80	80
1528	0	0	0	0	1538	1	1	117	118
1529	0	0	74	74	1539	0	0	121	121
1530	0	0	93	93	1540	0	0	137	137
1531	0	0	80	80	1541	0	0	10	10
1532	0	0	73	73	1542	0	0	0	0
1533	0	0	83	83	1543	16	16	0	16
1534	1	0	97	97	1544	30	30	0	30
1545	19	19	0	19	1548	3	3	0	3
1546	78	78	0	78	1549	3	3	0	3
1547	29	29	0	29					

1525-1549 180 179 994 1173

1550	112	112	0	112	1563	130	130	0	130
1551	0	0	0	0	1564	0	0	0	0
1552	30	30	0	30	1565	12	12	0	12
1553	0	0	0	0	1566	0	0	0	0
1554	0	0	0	0	1567	0	0	0	0
1555	83	83	0	83	1568	84	84	0	84
1556	14	14	0	14	1569	86	86	0	86
1557	144	144	0	144	1570	100	100	0	100
1558	295	295	0	295	1571	95	95	0	95
1559	238	9	228	237	1572	25	25	0	25
1560	0	0	153	153	1573	0	0	0	0
1561	91	91	4	95	1574	44	44	0	44
1562	88	88	0	88					

1550-1574 1671 1442 385 1827

1575	86	85	1	86	1588	92	92	0	92
1576	147	147	0	147	1589	2	2	0	2
1577	0	0	0	0	1590	1	1	0	1
1578	107	107	0	107	1591	115	115	0	115
1579	103	103	0	103	1592	125	125	0	125
1580	71	71	0	71	1593	200	200	0	200
1581	64	64	0	64	1594	0	0	0	0
1582	102	102	0	102	1595	97	1	96	97
1583	4	4	0	4	1596	67	10	117	127
1584	3	3	0	3	1597	122	2	121	123
1585	4	4	0	4	1598	94	8	93	101
1586	45	45	0	45	1599	101	6	92	98
1587	121	121	0	121					

1575-1599 1873 1418 519 1938

1600	56	2	58	60	1613	144	1	143	144
1601	92	12	77	89	1614	142	2	146	144
1602	90	18	71	89	1615	146	3	141	144
1603	188	38	152	190	1616	153	5	158	163
1604	72	28	50	78	1617	142	20	122	142
1605	104	59	44	103	1618	0	0	132	132
1606	107	5	101	106	1619	136	4	136	140
1607	106	8	98	106	1620	142	5	147	152
1608	119	0	119	119	1621	137	7	135	142
1609	132	0	135	135	1622	113	11	102	113
1610	150	0	150	150	1623	137	4	141	145
1611	126	1	128	129	1624	149	29	124	153
1612	178	1	205	206					

1600-1624 3061 263 3015 3278

1625	283	16	294	310	1638	156	0	170	170
1626	139	4	143	147	1639	157	1	149	150
1627	112	26	94	120	1640	173	1	170	171
1628	115	2	117	119	1641	149	0	143	143
1629	112	7	112	119	1642	95	1	88	89
1630	126	6	130	136	1643	100	1	102	103
1631	122	0	134	134	1644	20	0	103	103
1632	113	0	130	130	1545	65	0	79	79
1633	116	0	106	106	1646	60	0	44	44
1634	115	0	125	125	1647	20	1	32	33
1635	135	2	142	144	1648	46	0	37	37
1636	114	1	115	116	1649	19	0	12	12
1637	107	1	141	142					

1625-1649 2769 70 2912 2982

1469-1649; Original wills 9,554; Unregistered wills 3,372; Registered wills 8,527; Total 11,900.

A bar chart is appended showing the number of wills in this court. A comparison with other provincial courts brings out some similarities in the patterns of survival of records. As elsewhere, a significant run of surviving wills only begins in the Archdeaconry of Surrey in Henry VIII's reign. They start to survive in significant numbers in 1529, which is similar to the Archdeaconry of Leicester (regular from 1515), the Diocese of Worcester (regular from 1527) and the Diocese of Ely (regular from 1537).[1] However, sporadic losses mean that the totals surviving in Surrey are somewhat erratic as late as the 1590s, which is rather later than in other provincial courts which have been counted so far. The number of wills surviving in the Archdeaconry of Surrey went on increasing, like the population, decade by decade, from the mid-sixteenth century to the second decade of the seventeenth century, and then dropped slightly, until the numbers collapsed totally in the disturbed circumstances of the 1640s. By the early seventeenth century we can believe that the numbers surviving are a very high proportion of those proved. The slight decline in the decades before the Civil War is similar to that in other provincial courts, for, from this point onwards, the numbers proved in the Prerogative Court, already growing faster than the provincial courts in Elizabeth's reign, incrased yet further at their expense. As in other courts some of the epidemics of Tudor and Stuart England show up in Surrey wills; plague in the years after its return from Germany in 1535, and again in 1563, 1591-1593 and 1603, the great influenza pandemic in the years after 1557, and diseases related to harvest failure in 1587, 1597 and 1625.

It is hardly surprising that a few christian names dominate the records. John alone was the name of over 30% of testators, and just seven male names predominate. Similarly, only a few names cover most female testators.

Most testators are identified by at least one place. Some of the early PCC calendars are defective in that they only list the county, especially where the testator left property in more than one county. On the other hand for many testators it has been possible to list more than one place. Approximately 20,000 place references are given in the index, apart from the Southwark entries, which despite the omission of the Southwark PCC entries still amount to some 3,000 further entries. No other place dominates the index, though as might be expected there are a very large number of testators from the area which was already virtually part of London, such as Bermondsey and Rotherhithe, and from the principal centres of population in the rural county, such as Guildford, Kingston and Farnham. The number of entries in the index presumably provides a rough guide to the size of any place. It should be remembered, however, that probate records for the peculiar do not exist prior to 1614, and so parishes in that area are underrepresented in this index.

By no means every testator identifies his trade in his will; it seems likely as a subjective impression, that more of the rural population of yeomen and husbandmen omitted this information than their urban contemporaries. In particular, citizens of London seem usually to have regarded their citizenship as almost part of their name, and it will usually be recorded. Despite this, Surrey was basically still an agricultural county, and the agricultural occupations predominate. No doubt, the omission of Southwark PCC wills from the index artificially increases this domination. There are approximately 9,000 listed descriptions of trade, occupation or status listed. 3,810 (42.3%) of these are of either husbandmen or yeoman. 1,218 (13.5%) were either gentlemen or esquires, while just over 5% (458 testators) described themselves as citizens of London and 412 (4.6%) were clergymen. There were a very few peers, but nearly 200 knights, while at the other end of the social scale there were 133 (1.4%) labourers. The docks and shipyards of Bermondsey and Rotherhithe produced 111 mariner testators, while 182 watermen demonstrate the importance to the Surrey economy of the Thames. Surrey's proximity to London has always resulted in Royal palaces being located in it or near it, and 88 testators were Royal servants. A few other occupations represent more than 1% of the total; tailors (248), weavers (193), carpenters and joiners (186), victuallers, innkeepers, etc. (149), blacksmiths and smiths (114), clothiers and clothworkers (100) and brewers (89).

Charts also follow showing the frequency of christian names and occupations in the probate records covered by this index.

[1]For other courts see M.Takahashi *The Number of Wills proved in the Sixteenth and Seventeenth Centuries. Graphs, with tables and commentary* in G.H. Martin and P. Spufford (eds.) Records of the Nation, pp.179-205 (Woodbridge, 1990)

Surrey wills
Archdeaconry Court

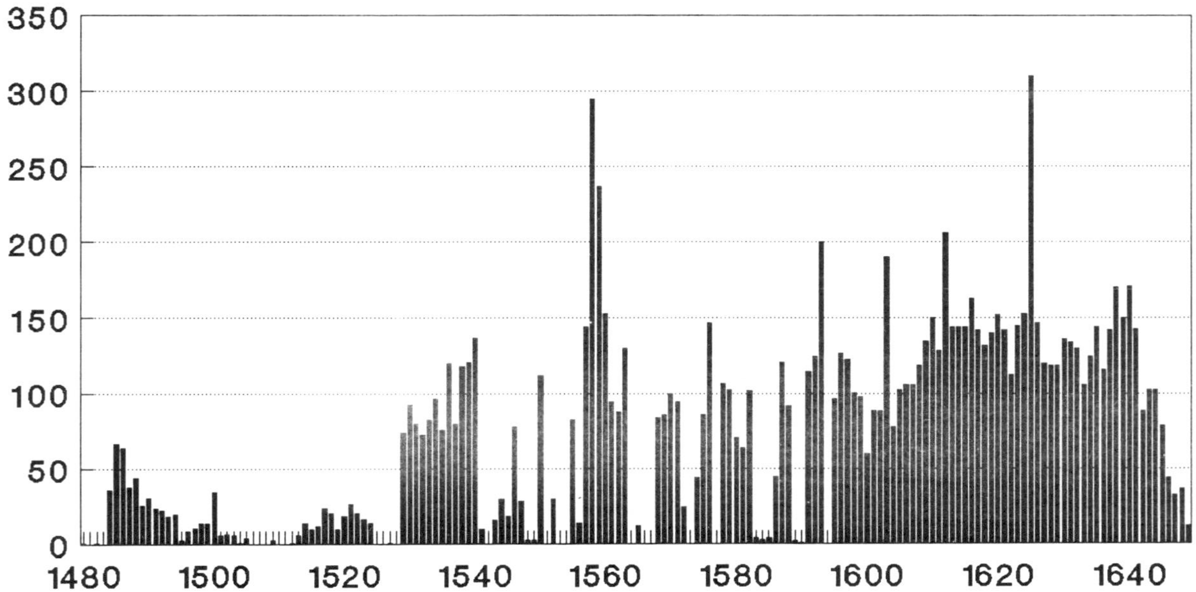

A. Women

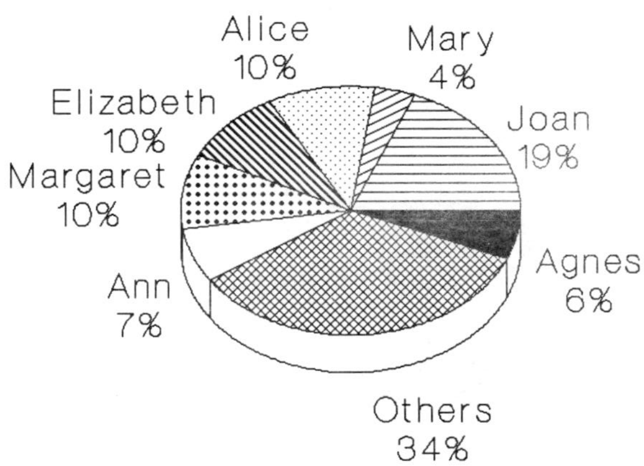

Alice 10%
Mary 4%
Joan 19%
Elizabeth 10%
Margaret 10%
Ann 7%
Agnes 6%
Others 34%

B. Men

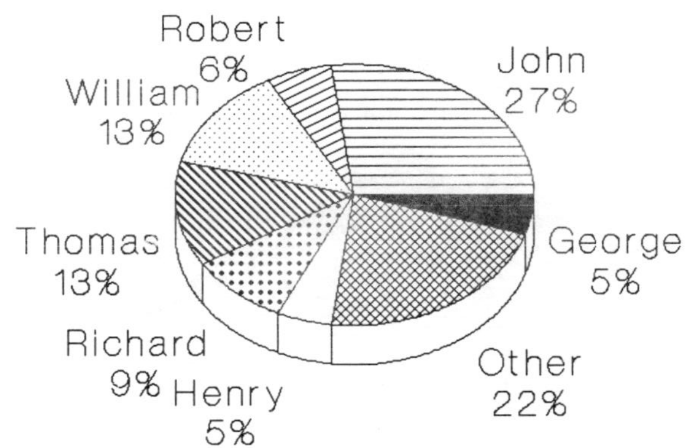

Robert 6%
John 27%
William 13%
Thomas 13%
George 5%
Richard 9%
Henry 5%
Other 22%

Occupations

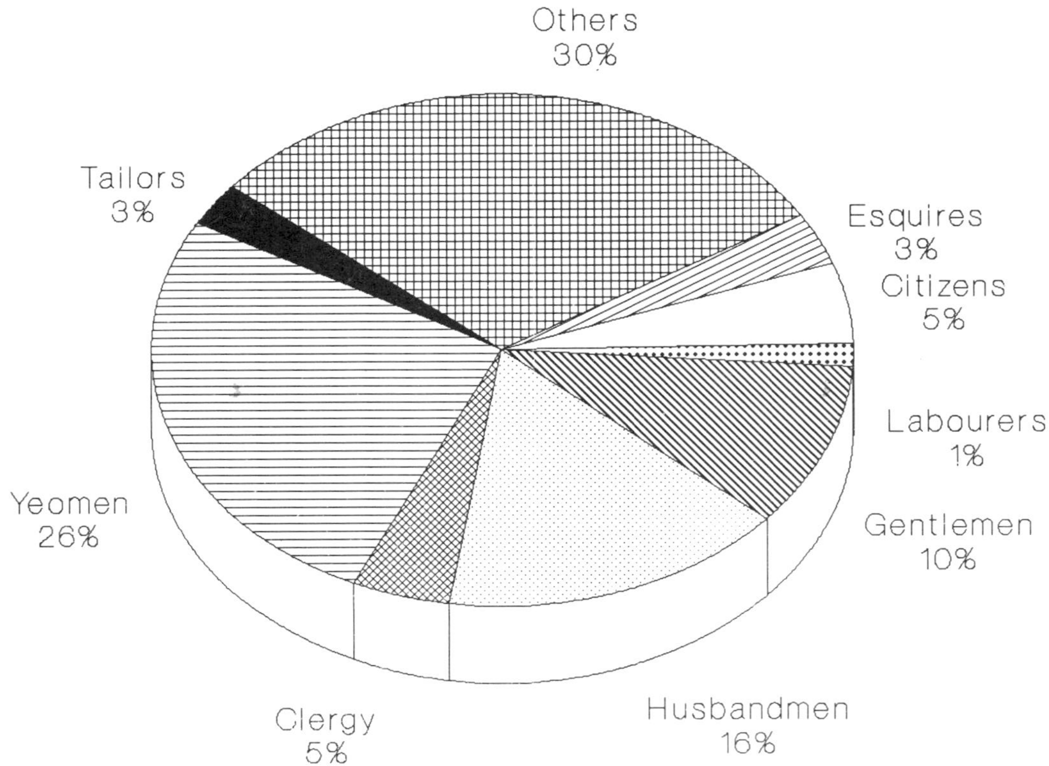

B. British Library

This Library's main holding of Surrey probate material is what appears to be a stray will register from the Archdeaconry Court of Surrey from the early 1540's. This document (Additional Ms. 24,925) came into the library from the sale room in the early nineteenth century, and its earlier provenance is unknown.

Abstracts have been made (and indexed) of all the wills appearing in this register, and copies supplied to various libraries, including the British Library itself, the Surrey Record Office and the Greater London Record Office.

Entries are here referenced in the form:

[BM: Add.Ms 24,925 f.17v; 1542] <Abs 38>

As can be seen, an indication of the year has been given, as well as the number of the abstract.

This volume fills a small part of the gap between registers Pykman and Tully (Greater London Record Office refs. DW/PA/7/5-6) (1541-1559), which is only very partially filled by the surviving original wills, none of which is duplicated in Add. Ms 24,925.

The register is of paper and 8½" x 12¼", and has a late eighteenth or early nineteenth century binding of morocco leather, with ornate marbled end-papers. At the front there is a note that the register was 'purchased at Messrs Boon 12 July 1862'. Its prior provenance is unknown.

The first two folios of the register consist of a nineteenth century list of the wills it contains. This has not been copied. The main portion of the text consists of folios 3-25, and contain the details of some 60-odd wills. This modern foliation in pencil and arabic numerals supercedes the original, contemporary foliation in ink and roman numerals. At an intermediate, probably nineteenth century, date, the volume has been paginated in ink; this pagination, which follows the current order of the folios has been ignored in this work. When the register was re-bound, the folios were not kept in the same order as the original foliation. There follows a concordance of the new and original folio numbers:

New	Original	New	Original	New	Original	New	Original
3	25	9	24	15	11	21	18
4	4	10	8	16	13	22	19
5	5	11	7	17	14	23	20
6	22	12	8	18	15	24	21
7	23	13	9	19	16	25	2
8	3	14	10	20	17		

This rearrangement causes less disruption to the text than one might suppose, since the clerks did not frequently allow a will to run on from one folio to the next, but that there was originally more to this register than now survives is shown by the fact that folios 1 and 12 are missing and that the will of John Alynson (which is the last will on original f.25) ends in mid-sentence, and clearly continued on now-lost f.26. Most of the text is in a single hand, though there are some wills in other hands.

C. Hampshire Record Office, Winchester

The office has two holdings of Surrey testamentary material, Firstly, it holds the registers of the bishop of Winchester in which many wills and probates were entered, presumably for security, While such registrations continued until near the end of our period, the main bulk are from the medieval registers,

Secondly, the bishop proved wills of Surrey testators in the Consistory Court of Winchester at this time, This court was superior to the Archdeaconry Court of Surrey, so tends to have the wills of testators of a standing between those proved in the Archdeaconry Court, and those proved in the Prerorogative Court of Canterbury, At the Restoration, the bishop appointed a Commissary for the Archdeaconry of Surrey, and ceased to prove the wills of Surrey testators in the Consistory Court, The records of the Commissary Court, dating from 1662, are in the Greater London Record Office, Both the Consistory Court, and its Surrey successor, the Commissary Court, were able to grant administrations, The Archdeaconry Court was only able to grant administrations with will annexed, Most wills and administrations proved in the Consistory Court have an inventory attached, These inventories, and the wills to which they refer are being abstracted for the Elizabethan period by Miss Marion Herridge and the Domestic Buildings Research Group, with a view to publication by the Surrey Record Society, *Surrey Probate Inventories* (ed, J,Holman & M,Herridge, 1986) lists all known Surrey probate inventories,

The first series are referenced by the abbreviated name of the bishop (followed by the number of the register, if the bishop concerned had more than one) and then a page reference and year, in the form;

[HRO; Reg, Edn 2 p,10; 1347]

The second series are very simply referenced at the Hampshire Record Office and this reference has been adopted here, A few wills are in class 'U' (unidentified court series), but most in class 'B', while the administrations form class 'Ad', The reference consists of the year the class number, and the number of the document within the year, in the form;

[HRO; 1584 B37]

A few Surrey wills also appear in various registers and act books of the bishop; again the HRO reference has been used here,

Two problems should be noted with regard to the Hampshire Record Office holdings, Firstly, previous lists of Surrey wills proved in the bishop's courts (especially that made by Willis which went to the Surrey Record Office) have often listed testators from Hampshire parishes which have the same or similar names as Surrey parishes, The main problems lie with;

Banstead, Surrey and Binstead, Hampshire
Bramley, Surrey and Hampshire
Chilworth [St Martha's], Surrey and Chilworth, Hampshire
Ewhurst, Surrey and Hampshire
Farleigh, Surrey and Hampshire
Headley, Surrey and Hampshire
Kingston, Surrey and Hampshire
Sutton, Surrey and Bishops Sutton, Hampshire
Wotton, Surrey and Wootton, Hampshire,

Most of these have been eliminated, but an element of doubt remains in a few cases. In any case, in Appendix I will be found a list of all wills noted by Willis as of Surrey testators not included in the main index.

Typescript calendars were made of the Consistory Court wills many years ago, directly from early manuscript ones. These calendars list a number of wills which never appear to have come into the HRO, especially for the first thirty years of the sixteenth century, though there are one or two later ones which appear to be missing, too. The reference used here for such wills is:

[? HRO; 1529]

D. Lambeth Palace Library

There are two series of records of Surrey testamentary material in the Lambeth Palace Library.

Firstly, many wills, probates and administrations were entered, presumably for safe-keeping, in the registers of the archbishops of Canterbury. While this continued for most of our period, the bulk of such entries date from the medieval period, and are not duplicated in the surviving records of any other court. Printed indexes have appeared to these records in *The Genealogist*, later consolidated as far as wills are concerned in *Index to Wills recorded in the Archiepiscopal Registers at Lambeth Palace* (edited by J. Challoner Smith, 1919). Entries appear here in the form:

[LPL; Reg. Abp Arundel ii f.103; Will 1408]

There are 481 early wills in a larger series, as a result of the archbishop of Canterbury's direct peculiar jurisdiction over, *inter alia*, the Deanery of Croydon. This peculiar comprised the following parishes:

Barnes; Burstow; Charlwood; Cheam; Croydon; East Horsley; Merstham; Mortlake; Newington; Putney; Wimbledon

Testators in these parishes could either prove in the court of the Deanery of Croydon, or in the Prerogative Court of Canterbury. Neither the Archdeaconry Court nor the Consistory Court of Winchester had jurisdiction over testators from these parishes. The records only survive from 1614, however. Originally they were transferred from Somerset House (where they had been deposited since the end of ecclesiastical testamentary authority in 1858) to the Kent Archives Office, Maidstone. While they were there they, and the records of two other archiepiscopal peculiars (the Deanery of the Arches and the Deanery of Shoreham) were filmed by the Mormons (film nos. 189094-189130). They are, therefore, available at Mormon Centres. Later, however, the records of all three peculiars were transferred to the Lambeth Palace Library, which already held the bishop's transcripts and allegations for marriage licences of these peculiars. All will references are preceded by the reference VH 96/; the documents being numbered in alphabetical order. There is also an Act Book, reference VH 98/1. Finally, there are testamentary case papers c.1629-1832 (class VH 82), however there is only one pre-Commonwealth case, and this does not concern a Surrey testator. Act book entries are in Latin and give record the act of probate or grant of administration or renunciation only. Where there is no VH 96 reference, therefore, there is no original will. For ease of reference VH has been omitted in this index, entries being in the form:

[LPL; 96/1160; Will 1627].

E. The Public Record Office

The vast majority of the Surrey wills in the Public Record Office are those proved in the Prerogative Court of Canterbury, which exercised superior jurisdiction over the whole country. Indexes to these wills have been printed already from their beginning in 1383 to after the end of our period, by the British Record Society and others. However, it was felt useful to have a union listing of early wills, and therefore each of the printed indexes has been searched for Surrey testators, and references inserted herein. The only exception is that Southwark testators have been omitted as they would have unreasonably swelled this index.

It is noteworthy that a number of wills proved in local courts were also proved in the Prerogative Court, no doubt for the additional security entailed. This is not just a case of wills being referred to a superior jurisdiction, though this happens; a number of wills are proved, successively in two separate courts.

Indexes have also been printed to all the administrations granted in the Prerogative Court for our period, from their beginning in 1558. Again all Surrey references, with the exception of Southwark, have been noted, and entries made in this index.

Many of these wills and administrations have surviving inventories; only this court and the Consistory Court of Winchester have surviving inventories of Surrey testators in any numbers.

Many abstracts of Prerogative Court Surrey wills have appeared in *Surrey Archaeological Collections* including a fairly systematic series for the first decade of the seventeenth century. Registers "Soame" (1620) and "Scroope" (1630) have been abstracted and printed. All the abstracts in this journal and these two published works have been noted here, but no attempt has been made to search for abstracts in the many other possible sources for them.

In addition to the Prerogative Court of Canterbury, there are stray Surrey wills in various of the collections at the Public Record Office. Many have been listed, and those falling within our period have been given references here, but many others, no doubt, remain to be discovered.

F. Surrey Record Office; G. Guildford Muniment Room; H. London Borough of Lambeth Archives Department; I. Southwark Local Studies Library

There are no archives of wills as such in these record offices. There are, however, a number of stray wills in collections of deeds and other muniments. Many may remain in unlisted collections. The list of those at Guildford was kindly provided by Mrs S. Cork, the archivist in charge, the others were abstracted from the lists and calendars in the two offices concerned by the editor. While most of the wills in these offices will also be found in the regular series, a number are not. For example, in the London Borough of Lambeth Archives Department (formerly called the Minet Library) there is an inventory to a will preserved elsewhere without a copy of the inventory.

These wills may be copies kept by executors or they may never have gone to probate. Alternatively, they may have been lost from the regular series, which all have gaps and missing items.

J. Cathedral Archives and Library, Canterbury

This library holds those wills proved in the Court of the Prior (later Dean) and Chapter of Christ Church, Canterbury. This court had jurisdiction during archiepiscopal vacancies in place of the Prerogative Court of Canterbury. Known therefore as *Sede Vacante* wills, an index to its records was printed in Kent Archaeological Society, Records Branch Vol.3 (1914).

Most of the wills date from the periods 1500-1501 and 1503, and are mainly duplicated in the records of the Prerogative Court. They are referenced here in the form:

[CCAL: 1500 f.201]

Editorial method

1, Surnames

Surnames have been standardised as far as possible and grouped, with full cross-referencing from aberrant forms, Minor differences, such as 'i' for 'y' and 'ei' for 'ie' have been noted in the surname heading, and fully cross-referenced, but it has not been noted for which specific entries within each surname such varieties occur, In these latter cases, the manuscript form will be found in single inverted commas after the christian name, More major differences have been noted in the specific entry, Some 100 (approximately two-thirds) of Surrey parishes have surviving burial records prior to 1649, and for the sixty-odd parishes for which transcripts were easily available to the editor, then doubtful entries have been cross-checked with the burial register and notes made,

For some surnames, it is impossible to avoid some confusion in early records between what are now distinct names, To give just one example, 'Blak' may be Black or Blake, Every attempt has been made to cross-reference these confusabilia, but undoubtedly some remain unnoticed,

Surnames of foreigners, mainly French and Dutch people in Southwark, have not been modernised or grouped, as this would generally be most dangerous, unless the manuscript form of the surname also occurs for natives, and has been grouped there, Wherever a foreigner was noted during the indexing, this has been mentioned in the index entry,

Entries of testators using aliases have been been fully entered under both (or in a few cases, all) surnames, except where the alias has been used by the original clerk merely to indicate a variant of the same surname, Similarly, entries beginning with de, le, van etc, are given full entries under both elements of the surname, In the few cases of Welshmen etc, where the name consists of a patronymic, again full entries have been made under all elements of the name,

2, Christian names

All Christian names have been modernised to their standard modern form, apart from foreigners, Particularly aberrant forms (and doubtful ones) have been signalled by the manuscript forms appearing in single inverted commas after the modernised forms, Few standardised forms will give rise to any problem, but it may be noted that Catherine has been consistently rendered Katherine and Jeffrey, Geoffrey, When Denis, Julian and Phillip clearly refer to women, these names have been given as Denise, Juliana and Phillipa, 'Jhon' a quite frequent name, may be either John or Joan, It has therefore been left in its manuscript form, within single inverted commas, when the will itself gives no indication of the sex of the testator, Happily, the name almost always comes between Joan and John in the alphabetical sequence of christian names for any given surname, 'Jhone', 'Jone' have been rendered Joan in all cases, 'Johis' etc, as John, Wherever the name Frances, Francis or other variant occurs, Frances has been used for female testators, Francis for male, and the manuscript form in single inverted commas for entries where the sex is not clear, 'Betteres' etc, has been rendered into its modern form of Beatrice, but the occasional foreigner of this name has been given the more correct foreign form of Beatrix, In Appendix II will be found a list of unusual Christian names keyed to the appropriate surname or surnames,

3. Places

All indentifiable places have been spelled in their modern forms as used in the English Place Name Society's work on Surrey placenames, or for places outside of Surrey, in their modern gazetteer spelling. Any placenames which are unidentifiable have been left in their manuscript forms and enclosed in single inverted commas.

Every attempt has been made to assign minor placenames to their correct ancient parish. Where the ancient parish is not given in the will it has been given in square brackets after the minor placename. A few places give rise to minor difficulties in Surrey. For the purposes of this index, I have used ancient parish to mean any place which habitually kept its own parish registers prior to 1800. This includes several places which were not technically parishes, such as Ripley [in Send] and Bramley [in Shalford]. Wanborough ceased keeping registers in the seventeenth century, but is clearly a parish for our purposes; Cuddington kept no registers as far as is known, but again is clearly a parish. Waverley, a liberty totally surrounded by Farnham, has been treated as a place within the latter parish. Wallington and Walworth kept no registers, though they were separate from their mother parishes of Beddington and Newington for most purposes, and are thus indexed under the latter. Chilworth has always been entered as St Martha's.

For some reason, many indexers in the past have given the dedication of certain churches in south London in index entries; in particular St Mary Magdalen Bermondsey; St Mary Newington Butts; St Mary Rotherhithe and, more occasionally, and inconsistently, St Giles Camberwell and St Mary Lambeth. Since prior to 1800 these parishes only had one parish church, this is wasteful of space, and the parishes concerned have been consistently rendered Bermondsey, Newington, Rotherhithe, Camberwell and Lambeth herein. It is, of course, necessary to give the parochial dedication in the case of the Southwark churches; and as there is often some confusion as to these, a short note of explanation is appended.

For some wills, it has been possible to include every place name mentioned in the will, for most, only the testator's parish has been listed.

There were five parishes in Southwark in late medieval times; St George, St Margaret, St Mary Overy, St Olave and St Thomas. The situation was complicated, because St Mary Overy was a 'double church'. St Mary Overy itself was appropriated to the services of the priory, while the church building was also dedicated to St Mary *Magdalene* Overy which was the appropriated to the parish and served the people. There has additionally been some confusion between St Mary Magdalene Overy, Southwark, and St Mary Magdalen Bermondsey, a completely separate parish church. This confusion is increased by Bermondsey Monastery being dedicated to St Saviour and this dedication being given to the new parish church which was founded when the monasteries were dissolved, the priory suppressed, and the two entities of St Mary Overy and the parish of St Margaret united. The name St Mary Overy was still used in records well into the nineteenth century. St Thomas was basically a charitable foundation, then as now, a hospital, but the hospital was moved to a new site in Lambeth, and in 1898 the parish of St Thomas Southwark was merged with St Saviour. There were also a number of gaols in Southwark, the Clink, the Compter, the King's Bench, the Marshalsea, and the White Lion, and occasionally testators are found who were unfortunate enough to be incarcerated there at the time of making their wills.

With the growth of Southwark's population, new parishes were created; Christ Church in 1670 from the old Paris Garden liberty of St Saviour, and St John Horsleydown in 1733 from St Olave. St Olave is situated in Tooley Street (itself a corruption of Olave's) and is often to be found as 'St Toolies' or similar in records. In this index, there are a few early testators who give their parish as St Margaret Southwark, and this has naturally been retained, and any rendering of St Olave modernised. St Mary Overy has also been retained where found, and St Mary Magdalene Southwark, though it is to be feared that there has been some misconflation with Bermondsey testators.

4. Trades and Occupations

All identifiable trades and occupations have been rendered in their modern form. Those few not identifiable have been placed in single inverted commas. As far as possible cognate occupations have been grouped and cross-referred in the Index of Trades and Occupations.

5. References

Apart from wills and administrations in the Prerogative Court of Canterbury, which have been referenced simply by 'PCC' followed by either 'Will' or 'Admon' and the year of probate, the call numbers of the various repositaries have been used in referencing the documents indexed herein. All references have been enclosed in square brackets. The Greater London Record Office and the Hampshire Record Office include the year of probate within the reference of original wills; in all cases where the reference does not give the year of probate, this has been noted in the index entry. In the few cases at the Greater London Record Office where the reference as given does not reflect the actual year of probate, this has been noted in the index, and estimates of the date have been made in the few cases where this is in doubt.

6. Abstracts

Where an abstract of a will is available, this has been noted in angle brackets. S.A.C. refers to the Surrey Archæological Society's Collections; for the printed calendars to registers Spage and Herringman [DW/PA/7/1 and DW/PA/7/7] merely the abstract number within the printed volume has been given, and this practice has been followed with the abstracts now being made to other will sequences. A similar practice has been followed with regard to the printed abstracts to the PCC will registers Soame (1620) and Scroope (1630).

Comprehensive notes have been made of will abstracts in the Surrey Archaeological Collections but no other journals or other secondary works have been searched for them.

Quick Guide to Finding Documents from Index Entries

1. All references begin with an abbreviation denoting the repository where the item is to be found, except those beginning DW/ which are at the Greater London Record Office.

The few other places of deposit are spelled out in full.

2. All entries which do not include a year within the body of the reference have had one assigned to aid identification.

3. Most of the wills at the Greater London Record Office have been filmed by the Mormons and will be available at Mormon Family History Centres (films 97150-97213). There is also a copy of these films at the Local Studies Library, North Street, Guildford. Almost all of those in this period not filmed have had abstracts made and indexed and copies deposited with various libraries, including the Greater London Record Office and the Local Studies Library, Guildford. The Mormons have also filmed the wills at Lambeth Palace Library in the Deanery of Croydon series (films 189094-189130).

4. It will generally be found easier to find registered copies of wills (references beginning DW/PA/7/) on the films than original wills (references beginning DW/PA/5/), as the latter were not numbered when the wills were filmed, whereas the registers are foliated, and the folio numbers included in this index.

5. A note has been made in angle brackets <> wherever an abstract is known to exist, usually in print. Where such a note is found, the searcher should refer to the note on abstracts on page xlvii. Abstracts are continually being made, and in this respect the index is bound to be out of date before it is published. For example, register 'Heats' is currently being abstracted, so all wills with references beginning DW/PA/7/4 should have abstracts available shortly.

A TOOTING GRAVENEY
B GUILDFORD ST MARY
C GUILDFORD HOLY TRINITY
D WEST CLANDON
E LITTLE BOOKHAM
F WOODMANSTERNE
G HASCOMBE
H CHILWORTH or ST MARTHA ON-THE-HILL

BERMONDSEY
St James
St Mary Magdalene

CAMBERWELL
St George
St Giles

CLAPHAM
Holy Trinity
St James, Clapham Park

LAMBETH
Renfrew Road, Workhouse
St John, Waterloo
St Luke, W. Norwood
St Mark, Kennington
St Mary
St Matthew, Brixton

NEWINGTON
Holy Trinity
St Mary
St Peter, Walworth

SOUTHWARK
Christ Church
St George the Martyr
St John Horsleydown
St Olave
St Saviour
St Thomas

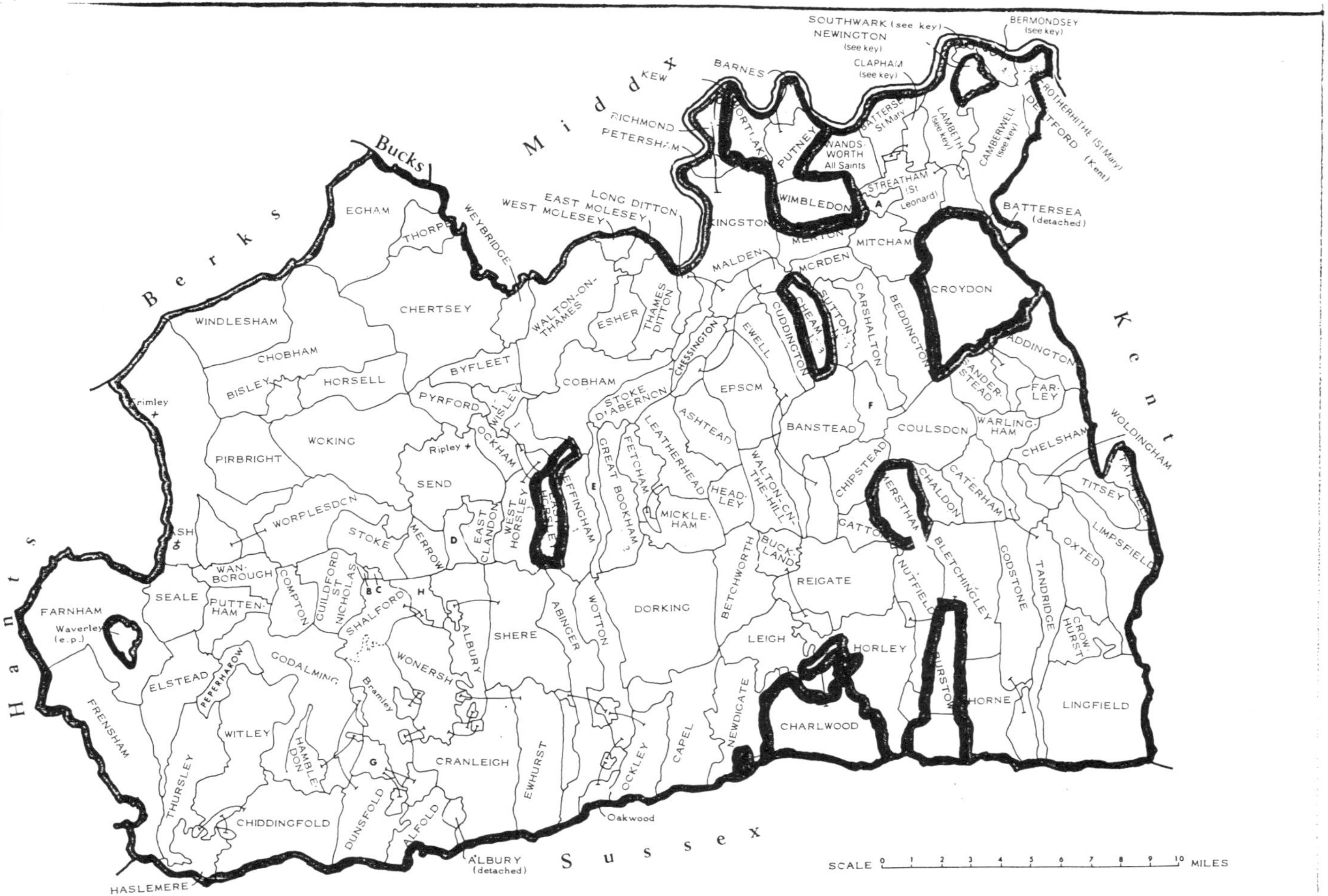

MAP OF SURREY PARISHES

The map opposite indicates the boundaries of parishes as they were in 1832. The broader lines indicate probate jurisdictions. The lighter line, enclosing most of the county, indicates the jurisdiction of the Archdeaconry Court of Surrey, whilst the darker line indicates that of the Deanery of Croydon. For details of these jurisdictions see above p.xiii.

Abbreviations

Abs = Abstract
Admon = Administration
BM = British Library Manuscripts Department
CCAL = Cathedral Archives and Library, Canterbury
esq. = esquire
gent. = gentleman
GL = Guildhall Library
GMR = Guildford Muniment Room
HRO = Hampshire Record Office
LBLAD = London Borough of Lambeth Archives Department
LPL = Lambeth Palace Library
PRO = Public Record Office
SAC = Surrey Archaeological Collections
SRO = Surrey Record Office
Swk = Southwark

[] enclose document references, and any editorial notes, the latter being in italics
<> enclose references to abstracts

AN INDEX

TO

PRE-1650 SURREY PROBATE RECORDS

ABARTON
  Richard of Wotton; Ockley; Oakwood [DW/PA/7/5 f,214; 1541]
    see also BARTON
ABBOTT (ABBOT,ABOT)
  Bridget of ..., widow of Robert, bishop of Salisbury [PRO; PCC Will 1646]
    <Abs, SAC v,3 pp,261-262>
  Elizabeth of Camberwell, widow [PRO; PCC 1645]
  Elizabeth of Guildford St Mary, widow [DW/PA/7/6 f,167; DW/PA/5/1559/163]
  John of Cobham, yeoman [DW/PA/7/7 f,271; DW/PA/5/1599/1] <Abs 477>
  Mary of Croydon, widow [PRO; PCC Will 1614]
  Maurice of Hackney, Middlesex; Guildford, knight and alderman [PRO; PCC
    Will 1644] <Abs, SAC v,3 pp,260-261>
  Richard of Guildford, gent, [DW/PA/7/11 f,576; DW/PA/5/1630/1]
  Robert of ..., bishop of Salisbury [PRO; PCC Will 1617] <Abs, SAC v,3
    p,260>
ABDYE
  Humphrey of Streatham, gent, [PRO; PCC Will 1626]
ABEFELD *see* ATFIELD
a BEKE *see* BECK
ABERCROMBY
  Eufhonsa of Cuddington - Nonsuch, widow [PRO; PCC Admon 1607]
ABLEWHITE
  Edward of Newington, yeoman [LPL; 96/1; 98/1 f,65v; Will 1635]
a BOROWGH,ABOROWGHT *see* ABURROW
ABOT *see* ABBOTT
ABOURNE (ABURNE)
  Edward of Albury, husbandman [HRO; 1599 B1]
  Francis of West Clandon [PRO; PCC Admon 1637]
  Thomas of Shere, husbandman [DW/PA/7/7 f,177; DW/PA/5/1597/2] <Abs 328>
    see also BOURNE,BYRNE
ABRAHAM
  Thomas of Lambeth - Brixton, husbandman [DW/PA/5/1586/17]
  Walter of Swk St Thomas [DW/PA/5/1570/75]
ABRE
  Thomas of Swk St Olave [DW/PA/7/3 f,206; 1532]

ABROOKE (ABROKE,ABROOCKE)
Robert of Swk St Olave, victualler [DW/PA/7/13 f.232; DW/PA/5/1642/4]
Thomas of Esher, husbandman [DW/PA/7/10 f.13; DW/PA/5/1616/2]
William of Kingston , cooper [DW/PA/7/12 f.214; DW/PA/5/1633/2]
see also BROOK
ABURNE *see* ABOURNE
ABURROW (a BOROWGH,ABOROUGHE,ABOROWGHT,ABORROWE,ABURROWE)
Alice of Chiddingfold, widow [DW/PA/7/2 f.93; 1512]
Ralph of Stoke next Guildford, shearman [DW/PA/5/1591/40]
Richard of Chiddingfold, yeoman [DW/PA/7/8 f.311; 1613]
Thomas of Chiddingfold [PRO; PCC Will 1504]
Thomas of Chiddingfold [DW/PA/5/1561/84]
see also BORROW,BURROWE
ACARMAN *see* ACREMAN
ACE
Richard of Reigate, senior, yeoman [DW/PA/7/9 f.49; DW/PA/5/1614/1]
Richard of Reigate [DW/PA/7/11 f.283; DW/PA/5/1625/1]
Richard of Reigate [PRO; PCC 1636]
William of Reigate, senior, yeoman [DW/PA/7/2 f.111; 1517]
ACHARTE
John of Burstow [PRO; PCC Will 1535]
see also CHART
ACHE
William of Carshalton [DW/PA/5/1569/37]
ACLAND
Thomas of Swk St Saviour [DW/PA/7/12 f.243; DW/PA/5/1634/2]
a COLLIS (a COLLYS) *see* COLLIS
a COWLES *see* COLES
ACRAKYLL
John of Kingston; Richmond [DW/PA/5/1545/6]
ACREMAN (ACARMAN)
Martin of Horley [DW/PA/5/1571/47]
ACRES
Helen of Poplar, Stepney, Middlesex; Swk St George, widow
[GL; Commissary Court of London Will 1607]
see also ATTACRE
ACTON
John of Swk St Saviour, tailor [DW/PA/7/8 f.45; DW/PA/5/1609/1]
ADAMS (ADAM,ADAMES,ADARNS,ADDAM,ADDAMS)
Alexander of East Clandon, clerk [DW/PA/7/10 f.299; DW/PA/5/1622/1]
Edward of ... [DW/PA/7/9 f.192; DW/PA/5/1616/1]
Edward of Reigate [PRO; PCC Admon 1610]
Elizabeth of Swk St Olave, widow [DW/PA/5/1576/89]
Francis of Kingston, blacksmith [DW/PA/7/13 f.140; DW/PA/5/1640/5]
James of Clapham, yeoman [DW/PA/5/1580/31]
John of Clapham, husbandman [DW/PA/5/1557/60B]
John of Horley [DW/PA/7/1 f.3; 1484] <Abs 9>
John of Horley [DW/PA/5/1576/77]
John of Merrow [DW/PA/7/3 f.145; 1530]
John of Merrow [DW/PA/5/1546/71]
John of Merrow, yeoman [DW/PA/5/1591/96]
John of Swk St Olave [DW/PA/7/4 f.95; 1534]
John of Swk St Olave, carman [DW/PA/7/8 f.390; DW/PA/5/1612/2]
John of Swk St Olave, waterman [DW/PA/7/13 f.331; 1644]

ADAMS (ADAM,ADAMES,ADARNS,ADDAM,ADDAMS) [*continued*]
  Margaret of Lambeth [PRO; PCC Admon 1594]
  Millicent of Merrow, widow [DW/PA/5/1550/23]
  Richard of Lambeth, gent. [PRO; PCC Will 1590]
  Thomas of Horley [DW/PA/5/1558/4]*
  Thomas of Mortlake [LPL; 98/1 f.121v; Will 1641]
  Thomas of Wimbledon [LPL; 96/2; 98/1 f.27v; Will 1631]
  William of Bermondsey, tailor [DW/PA/5/1586/34]
  William of Dorking - Betchworth Castle [PRO; PCC Will 1608] <Abs. SAC v.13 p.185>
  William of Byfleet [PRO; PCC Will 1603] <Abs. SAC v.11 p.107>
ADDERTON
  Thomas of 'Cheane' (? Sheen or Cheam) [PRO; PCC Admon 1593]
ADDEY (ADDYE)
  John of Rotherhithe, shipwright [PRO; PCC Will 1606]
  Thomas of Rotherhithe, parson [DW/PA/5/1592/26]
ADDEYSON *see* ADDISON
ADDINGTON (ADINGTON)
  Joan of Putney [PRO; PCC Will 1603] <Abs. SAC v.11 p.106>
  Margaret of Putney [LPL; 98/1 f.105r; Will 1639]
ADDIS (ADDYS,ADIS)
  John of Egham [DW/PA/7/8 f.146; DW/PA/5/1611/1]
  John of Swk St Saviour, cutler [DW/PA/5/1593/169]
ADDISON (ADDEYSON)
  Christian of Swk St Saviour, widow [DW/PA/7/11 f.63; DW/PA/5/1623/1]
  Edward of Swk St Saviour [DW/PA/7/7 f.505; DW/PA/5/1605/1] <Abs 944>
  William of Swk St Saviour, haberdasher [DW/PA/7/9 f.237; DW/PA/5/1617/1]
ADDYE *see* ADDEY
ADE
  William, alias William Ede, of Farnham [PRO; PCC Will 1529]
ADEANE (a DEANE,ADEEN)
  Philomusis of Fetcham; Leatherhead; Stoke, beer brewer [PRO; PCC Will 1612]
  Thomas of Fetcham [DW/PA/5/1579/7]*
  William of Capel [DW/PA/5/1545/6]
  William of Capel [DW/PA/5/1591/69]
  see also DEANE
ADENELL
  Thomas of Swk St Olave, citizen and leatherseller [DW/PA/7/5 f.203; 1540]
ADENSONNE *see* ATKINSON
ADERLE
  (Dame) Joan (formerly Brocas) of Peper Harow [PRO; PCC Will 1487]
ADHELARD *see* ADLER
ADINGTON *see* ADDINGTON
ADIS *see* ADDIS
ADKIN, ADKINS, ADKINSON *see* ATKINS, ATKINSON
ADLAND
  John of Guildford [HRO; 1623 AD1]
  Thomas of Guildford St Nicolas - Artington, yeoman [PRO; PCC Will 1610] <Abs. SAC v.24 p.65>
ADLER (ADHELARD,ADLAR,ADLARE)
  Elizabeth of Godalming [DW/PA/7/4 f.231; 1537]
  Joan of Elstead, widow [DW/PA/5/1593/9]
  John of Guildford St Mary [DW/PA/7/2 f.27; 1492]

ADLER (ADHELARD,ADLAR,ADLARE) [*continued*]
John, or John Alder, of Godalming, yeoman, senior [DW/PA/7/8 f.252; DW/PA/5/1613/2]
Richard of Godalming, bachelor [DW/PA/5/1556/9]
Thomas of Godalming, senior [DW/PA/7/4 f.199; 1537]
ADLINGTON (ADLYNGTON)
Michael of 'Farnisham' (?Frensham) [PRO; PCC Will 1558]
William of 'Chercherleys Aley in Towr strete', Swk St Saviour, innholder [DW/PA/5/1557/55]
ADLYE *see* ATLEE
ADMON
John of Kingston; Twickenham - Whitton, Middlesex, bachelor [DW/PA/7/6 f.228; 1561]
ADNOT
William of Swk St Olave, woodmonger [DW/PA/5/1557/61]
ADOWNE (a DOWNE)
Robert of Leatherhead [PRO; PCC 1632]
Thomas of Cobham; Thames Ditton; Walton on Thames - Pains Hill; Weybridge, gent. [PRO; PCC Will 1607] <Abs. SAC v.12 pp.99-100>
Thomas of Cobham; Thames Ditton; Walton on Thames - Pains Hill, gent. [DW/PA/7/8 f.6; DW/PA/5/1608/1]
William of Cobham; Walton on Thames, yeoman [*in* DW/PA/5/1557/72]
see also DOWN
ADRIANSON
Adrian of Swk St Olave, baptist minister and citizen of London [DW/PA/7/13 f.212; DW/PA/5/1643/1]
ADWICKE *see* ATWICK
ADYNSONNE *see* ATKINSON
AEGAR *see* EAGER
Ælfred, duke of Surrey [BM; Stowe Ms 20; 9th century]
AFFELL (a FELL,AFELL)
John of Bermondsey, citizen and leatherseller [PRO; PCC Will 1563]
Thomas of Swk St George, bachelor, servant to Stephen England [DW/PA/5/1579/9]*
AGAS
Amy of Shere, widow [PRO; PCC Will 1559]
AGALLIAWAY
Geanes, alias Geanes Gallawaie, of Morden [DW/PA/5/1575/63]
AGATE (AGAYTTE)
John of West Molesey [DW/PA/5/1546/5]
see also ATGATE,GATES
AGLAND (AGLANDE,AGLOND)
John of Ewell [HRO; Reg. WAY1 p.55; 1458]
John of Ewell, sawyer [DW/PA/7/4 f.156; 1536]
John of Ewell, husbandman [DW/PA/5/1562/56]
Margaret of Ewell, widow [DW/PA/7/4 f.147; 1536]
William of Ewell [DW/PA/5/1568/17]
AGMONDESHAM (AGMONDESAM,AGMONDISHAM,AGMUNDYSHAM)
John of Surrey, gent. [PRO; PCC Will 1509]
John of East Horsley, gent. [PRO; PCC Will 1506]
John of East Horsley - Rowbarns, esq. [PRO; PCC Will 1572]
John of East Horsley - Rowbarns, esq. [PRO; PCC Will 1597 *and* 1599] <Abs. SAC v.28 p.52>
John of Kingston [DW/PA/5/1546/68]

AGMONDESHAM (AGMONDESAM,AGMONDISHAM,AGMUNDYSHAM) [*continued*]
John of Kingston, gent. [PRO; PCC Will 1615]
John of Stoke Dabernon [DW/PA/7/2 f.174; 1523]
Margaret of Walton on Thames - Apps [PRO; PCC Will 1493]
Philip of Surrey [PRO; PCC Will 1490]
Ralph of East Horsley [PRO; PCC Will 1458]
Ralph of Walton on Thames [PRO; PCC Will 1506]
Thomas of East Horsley [PRO; PCC Will 1508]
a HOWELL *see* ap POWELL,POWELL
AIREY (AYRYE)
William of Thames Ditton, yeoman [DW/PA/7/12 f.448; DW/PA/5/1639/2]
ALAM *see* ALLAM
ALARD (ALLERDE)
Alice of Swk St Olave, widow [DW/PA/5/1570/99]
Francis of Swk St Olave, citizen and dyer [DW/PA/7/11 ff.253,281; DW/PA/5/1625/2]
ALBANY
(Sir) Robert of Farnham - Badshot, knight [PRO; PCC Admon 1639]
William of Oxted [PRO; PCC Admon 1621]
ALBERTON
William of Camberwell [LPL; Reg. Abp Kemp f.292b; Admon 1453]
ALBERY *see* ALBURY
ALBROOK (ALBROCKE,ALBROKE,ALBROOKE,ALLBROKE,ALROCKE)
Henry, alias Henry Pretty, of Walton on Thames, weaver [DW/PA/7/7 f.26; DW/PA/5/1595/1] <Abs 55>
James of Walton on Thames [DW/PA/7/6 f.186; DW/PA/5/1559/188]
John of Thames Ditton, husbandman [DW/PA/5/1558/5]
Richard of Walton on Thames [DW/PA/7/4 f.170; 1536]
Robert of Walton, fisher [DW/PA/5/1575/86]
Thomas of ... [DW/PA/5/1571/6]
Thomas of Esher [DW/PA/7/6 f.137; DW/PA/5/1559/140]
Thomas of Kingston; Thames Ditton [DW/PA/5/1547/28]
Thomas of Kingston, labourer [DW/PA/7/7 f.230; DW/PA/5/1598/1] <Abs 406>
ALBURY (ALBERY)
William, alias William Sayers, of Ockham [DW/PA/5/1557/22]
ALBY
William of Woking [DW/PA/7/12 f.324; DW/PA/5/1636/2]
ALCEY
Nathaniel of Swk St Olave, joiner [DW/PA/7/12 f.5; DW/PA/5/1631/1]
ALCOCK (ALKOCKE)
John of Swk St Margaret, yeoman of the guard [DW/PA/7/4 f.220; 1537]
ALDEN (ALDIN)
Andrew of Newington [LPL; f.94v; ren. 1638]
Nicholas of Mortlake; Barnes; Malden, servant to Mr Milles [PRO; PCC Will 1609] <Abs. SAC v.24 pp.58-59>
Richard of Malden, yeoman [HRO; 1591 B2]
ALDER
Ralph of Bermondsey, fellmonger [PRO; PCC Will 1614]
Robert of Bermondsey, citizen and draper [PRO; PCC Will 1622]
see also ADLER
ALDERICHE *see* ALDRIDGE
ALDERMAN
Henry of Swk St Saviour, waterman [DW/PA/7/9 f.257;DW/PA/5/1617/3]

ALDERMASTON
John of Croydon [LPL; Reg. Abp Arundel i f.212; Will 1403]
ALDERSEY
Ann of Morden, widow [PRO; PCC Will 1641]
ALDERTON
Alice of Cheam, widow [LPL; 96/23 Will 1623]
Richard of Send [DW/PA/7/6 f.253; 1560]
Robert of Send, husbandman [DW/PA/5/1571/51]
ALDRIDGE (ALDERICHE,ALDRED,ALLDRIDGE)
Elizabeth of Tooting [DW/PA/7/13 f.82; DW/PA/5/1641/2]
George of Albury, yeoman [DW/PA/7/11 f.35; DW/PA/5/1623/2]
Gregory of ...., citizen and joiner of London [DW/PA/5/1582/98]
John of Swk St George, gent. [DW/PA/5/1572/9]
Ralph of Swk St Olave, turner [DW/PA/5/1572/14]
Richard of Tooting Graveney, weaver [DW/PA/7/13 f.80; DW/PA/5/1640/2]
ALDWYN
John of Puttenham [CCAL; 1500; Reg.R f.152b]
ALEE (a LEE,ALEIGH)
Robert of Bermondsey [PRO; PCC Will 1587]
Robert of Lingfield, yeoman, senior [PRO; PCC Will 1618]
Thomas of Streatham [PRO; PCC Will 1504] <Abs SAC v.52 pp.34-35>
see also ATLEE,LEE
ALEN *see* ALLEN
ALEVYN *see* ALWYN
ALEWORD (ALWARD,AYLEWARD,AYLEWARDE)
John of Wandsworth, fisherman [DW/PA/7/12 f.384; DW/PA/5/1637/1]
Lyon of Newington, broom-man [LPL; 96/44 Will 1618]
Richard of Woking, carpenter [DW/PA/7/4 f.103; 1535]
Thomas of Ewell, senior [GL; Commissary Court of London Will 1477]
ALEXANDER
Michael of ...., citizen and merchant tailor of London [DW/PA/7/13 f.317; DW/PA/5/1644/3]
(Sir) Robert, alias Sir Robert Zinzan, of Walton on Thames, knight [PRO; PCC Will 1608] <Abs. SAC v.12 p.105>
ALEYN *see* ALLEN
ALEYNSON *see* ALLINSON
ALFORD (ALFORDE,ALFURTHE)
John of Swk St George, wheeler [DW/PA/7/2 f.51 c1496]
John of Bermondsey, citizen and white baker [DW/PA/7/8 f.50; DW/PA/5/1609/2]
William of Chertsey, yeoman [DW/PA/7/4 f.198; 1537]
William of Swk St George [DW/PA/7/4 f.99; 1534]
ALFRAY
Thomas of Surrey, esq. [PRO; PCC Will 1507]
ALFURTHE *see* ALFORD
ALIF *see* AYLIFFE
ALINGHAM *see* ALLINGHAM
ALISON *see* ALLISON
ALKOCKE *see* ALCOCK
ALLAM (ALAM)
Elizabeth of Bermondsey, widow [DW/PA/7/13 f.401; DW/PA/5/1645/1]
Eugenius of Bermondsey (widow Ursula) [PRO; PCC Will 1634]
James of Rotherhithe; *the Ship*, Tower Hill, London [DW/PA/5/1550/14]

ALLAM (ALAM) [*continued*]

Stephen of Swk St Olave [DW/PA/7/8 f.70; DW/PA/5/1609/3]

Stephen of Swk St Olave [DW/PA/7/8 f.174; DW/PA/5/1610/2]

ALLARD *see* ALARD

ALLBROKE *see* ALBROOK

ALLCHIN

Thomas of Betchworth, senior [HRO; 1626 B1]

ALLCOTT

William of Lambeth [DW/PA/7/12 f.257; DW/PA/5/1634/3]

ALLDRIDGE *see* ALDRIDGE

ALLEN (ALEN,ALEYN,ALLEYN,ALLEYNE,ALLIN,ALLYN,ALYN)

Alice of Farnham, widow [DW/PA/7/7 f.280; DW/PA/5/1599/2] <Abs 499>

Ann of Lambeth - Lambeth Marsh, widow [DW/PA/7/12 f.125; DW/PA/5/1632/3]

Edward of Camberwell - Dulwich, esq. [PRO; PCC Will 1626]

Edward of Swk St Olave, leatherdresser [DW/PA/7/7 f.441; DW/PA/5/1603/1] <Abs 833>

Edward of Swk St Saviour, clothworker [DW/PA/5/1591/48]

Eleanor of Oxted, widow [DW/PA/5/1591/8]

Elias of Rotherhithe, sailor [DW/PA/7/8 f.49; DW/PA/5/1609/4]

Elizabeth of Merstham, widow of John [LPL; 96/31; 98/1 f.63v; Will 1634]

George of Guildford St Mary - Losely; Wotton, servant to (Sir) George More, knight [PRO; PCC Will 1610] <Abs. SAC v.24 p.64>

Henry, alias Henry Laiforthe, of Kingston, clerk [DW/PA/5/1579/6]*

Henry of Swk St Mary Overy [DW/PA/5/1569/25]

Henry of Swk St Olave, citizen and fishmonger [DW/PA/7/13 f.393; DW/PA/5/1646/1]

Humphrey, alias Humphrey Sallows, of Rotherhithe, mariner [PRO; PCC Will 1626]

James of Godstone, clerk [DW/PA/7/13 f.363; 1644]

James of Lambeth, gent. [PRO; PCC Will 1618]

Joan, alias Joan Knight, of West Clandon [DW/PA/7/1 f.12; 1485] <Abs 41>

Joan of Swk St Saviour, sp. [DW/PA/7/7 f.343; DW/PA/5/1601/1] <Abs 624>

Joan of Thorpe, widow [DW/PA/5/1592/116]

John of the ship *Charles* [DW/PA/7/11 f.392; DW/PA/5/1626/2]

John of Bermondsey [DW/PA/5/1591/131]

John, alias John Marshall,of Blechingley, yeoman, senior [DW/PA/5/1581/8]

John of Chertsey; Thorpe, husbandman [DW/PA/5/1557/93]

John of Esher [*in* DW/PA/5/1546/10]

John of Ewhurst, yeoman [PRO; PCC Will 1625]

John of Lambeth [PRO; PCC Will 1579]

John, alias John Staplese, of Leigh, husbandman [DW/PA/5/1592/10]

John of Merstham, husbandman [LPL; 96/30; 98/1 f.63v; Will 1634]

John, alias John Sallowes of Rotherhithe [DW/PA/7/7 f.631; DW/PA/5/1608/2] <Abs 1180>

John, alias John Sallowes, of Rotherhithe, mariner, on the ship *Darling* [PRO; PCC Will 1609]

John, *or* John Alley, of Swk St Olave, vintner [DW/PA/7/11 f.206; DW/PA/5/1625/3]

John of Thorpe [DW/PA/7/3 f.152; 1530]

John of Woking, servant to George Simmons [DW/PA/7/6 f.203; 1560]

John of Thorpe [DW/PA/5/1579/2]*

John of Thorpe [DW/PA/5/1588/30]

Juliana of Ewhurst; Rudgwick [*Sussex*], widow [DW/PA/7/7 f.213; DW/PA/5/1598/2] <Abs 381>

ALLEN (ALEN,ALEYN,ALLEYN,ALLEYNE,ALLIN,ALLYN,ALYN) [*continued*]

Mary of Betchworth, widow [HRO; 1630 B1]
Matthias of Camberwell - Dulwich, gent, (son John) [PRO; PCC 1642]
Richard of Betchworth, husbandman [DW/PA/7/11 f.496; DW/PA/5/1629/1]
Richard of Burstow [PRO; PCC Admon 1592]
Richard of Ockley, clerk [PRO; PCC Will 1622]
Richard of Thorpe; Egham; Chertsey [HRO; 1582 B2]
Robert of Wandsworth, vicar [DW/PA/7/12 f.21; DW/PA/5/1631/2]
Sybil of Thorpe, widow [DW/PA/7/4 f.30; 1533]
Thomas of Bermondsey (died overseas) [PRO; PCC Admon 1641]
Thomas of Frensham - Pitfold [HRO; 1575 AD1]
Thomas of Godalming, weaver [DW/PA/7/7 f.180; DW/PA/5/1597/3] <Abs 332>
Thomas of Horley, weaver [DW/PA/7/12 f.371; 1627]
Thomas of East Molesey, yeoman [PRO; PCC Will 1608]
Thomas of Thorpe, yeoman [DW/PA/7/5 f.170; 1540]
William of Bermondsey [DW/PA/7/2 f.122; 1518]
William of Bramley, blacksmith [DW/PA/7/12 f.492; DW/PA/5/1638/2]
William of Camberwell - Peckham, gent. [PRO; PCC 1632]
William of Lambeth - Water Lambeth [DW/PA/7/4 f.71; 1534]
William of Richmond [DW/PA/5/1546/89]
William, alias William Sallowe, of Rotherhithe, mariner [PRO; PCC Will 1600]
William of Swk St Olave [DW/PA/7/4 f.70; 1534]
William of Streatham, miller [DW/PA/5/1569/70]

ALLERDE *see* ALARD

a LLEWELLYN *see* LLEWELLYN

ALLEY

John, *or* John Allen, of Swk St Olave, vintner [DW/PA/7/11 f.206; DW/PA/5/1625/3]

ALLIN *see* ALLEN

ALLINGHAM (ALINGHAM,ALLYNGHAM,ALLYNGHAME,ALYNGGAM,ALYNGHAM)

Bridget of Camberwell - Peckham [DW/PA/7/11 f.397; DW/PA/5/1627/1]
Charles of Burstow, husbandman [LPL; 96/38; 98/1 f.44r; Will 1633]
Ellen of Burstow, widow [LPL; 96/39 f.75v; Will 1636]
John of Burstow [LPL; 98/1 f.53v; Will 1633]
John of Horley [DW/PA/5/1561/80]
John of Horley [DW/PA/7/7 f.506; DW/PA/5/1605/2] <Abs 946>
John of Leatherhead [DW/PA/5/1557/74]
John of Leatherhead [DW/PA/5/1582/26]
John of Nutfield [BM; Add.Ms 24925 f.21v; 1544] <Abs 50>
John of Nutfield - South Hale [DW/PA/5/1547/17]
Nicholas of Camberwell [DW/PA/7/12 f.371; DW/PA/5/1627/2]
Nicholas of Coulsdon; Nutfield; Merstham, husbandman [DW/PA/7/6 f.187; DW/PA/5/1559/196]
Nicholas of Horley, husbandman [HRO; 1565 B1]
Nicholas of Horley, husbandman [DW/PA/5/1565/5]
Richard of Nutfield [DW/PA/7/4 f.136; 1536]
Richard of Nutfield - South Hale, husbandman [DW/PA/5/1578/4]
Richard of Nutfield [HRO; 1586 B2]
Robert of Nutfield [DW/PA/7/2 f.3; 1490]
Thomas of Reigate, husbandman [DW/PA/7/9 f.304; DW/PA/5/1619/1]

ALLINGTON

Edward of Newington [PRO; PCC 1646]
George of Richmond, junior [PRO; PCC Admon 1633]

ALLINSON (ALEYNSON,ALYNSON)
  Joan of Swk St Olave, widow [DW/PA/5/1555/3]
  John of Swk St Olave, citizen and barber surgeon [BM; Add,Ms 24925 f,3b; 1543] <Abs 4> [*and*] <Abs SAC v,1 p,199>
  William, alias William Allison of Newington [LPL; 96/41; 98/1 ff,56r-v; Will 1634]
ALLISON (ALISON,ALLISONN,ALYSON)
  George of Rotherhithe [PRO; PCC Will 1612]
  George of Streatham [DW/PA/7/12 f,320; DW/PA/5/1636/1]
  Henry of Swk St Olave, scrivener [DW/PA/7/7 f,473; 1604/1] <Abs 892>
  James of Rotherhithe [DW/PA/5/1546/86]
  William, alias William Allinson, of Newington [LPL; 96/41; 98/1 f,56r-v; Will 1634]
a LLOELLEN *see* ap LLOELLEN
ALLOTT
  (Dame) Ann of Sanderstead; Croydon - Church Street, widow [PRO; PCC Will 1617]
ALLWYNE *see* ALWYN
ALLYN *see* ALLEN
ALLYNGGAM,ALLYNGHAM,ALLYNGHAME *see* ALLINGHAM
ALMAN
  John of Farnham [DW/PA/7/2 f,132; 1519]
ALROCKE *see* ALBROOKE
ALSOP
  John of Lambeth - Water Lambeth, esq, [PRO; PCC Will 1611] <Abs, SAC v,35 p,41>
  Titus of Limpsfield, servant to (Sir) Thomas Gresham, knight [PRO; PCC Will 1628]
ALTHAM (ALTAM)
  John of Swk St George, innholder [DW/PA/5/1570/23]
  Richard of Mickleham [PRO; PCC Admon 1624]
  Robert of Tooting Graveney, yeoman [HRO; 1570 AD2]
ALTON
  William of Swk St Olave, shipwright [DW/PA/7/11 f,35; DW/PA/5/1623/3]
ALVIN,ALVYN *see* ALWYN and ELVIN
ALWARD *see* ALEWORD
ALWYN (ALEVYN,ALVIN,ALVYN,AYLEWIN,AYLEWYN,AYLWYN)
  Bridges ('Breges') of Richmond [DW/PA/7/5 f,115; 1539]
  Edmund of Lambeth [PRO; PCC Will 1504]
  Elizabeth of Haslemere, widow [PRO; PCC Will 1624]
  Nicholas of Blechingley [PRO; PCC Will 1505]
  Richard of Haslemere, yeoman [DW/PA/7/10 f,286; DW/PA/5/1623/5]
  Thomas of Haslemere [HRO; 1567 B9]
  Thomas of Horley [DW/PA/7/2 f,1; 1490]
  William of St Nicholas [? Guildford] [DW/PA/7/1 f,5; 1484] <Abs 16>
ALYEFE *see* AYLIFFE
ALYN *see* ALLEN
ALYNGGAM,ALYNGHAM *see* ALLINGHAM
ALYNSON *see* ALLINSON
ALYSON *see* ALLISON
AMAMAN
  John of Tandridge [DW/PA/7/12 f,309; DW/PA/5/1635/2]

AMBER
Christopher, alias Christopher Brownebrede, of Farnham [LPL; Reg. Abp Morton f.252v; Admon 1488]
AMBLER
John of Camberwell - Dulwich [DW/PA/7/7 f.605; DW/PA/5/1607/1]<Abs 1130>
AMBLIN (AMBLYN)
John of Swk St Olave, yeoman [DW/PA/7/9 f.176; DW/PA/5/1616/3]
AMBRE *see* AMBER
AMBROSE (AMBROS)
Henry of Weybridge - 'Coke' [DW/PA/5/1550/16]
John of Swk St Olave, citizen and chandler [DW/PA/7/5 f.100; 1539]
AMCOTTES
(Sir) Henry of Surrey, knight [PRO; PCC Will 1554]
AMELL
John of Newington, senior [PRO; PCC Will 1473]
AMERY (AMERIE)
John of Ham; Swk - Paris Garden, gent. [PRO; PCC Will 1612]
Juliana of Swk St Saviour, widow [DW/PA/7/8 f.211; DW/PA/5/1612/1]
Robert of Bermondsey [PRO; PCC Will 1597]
William of Swk St Saviour; Brentford, Middlesex [DW/PA/7/8 f.124; DW/PA/5/1610/3]
AMES (AYMES)
Charles of Swk St Saviour, citizen and clothworker [DW/PA/7/11 f.229; DW/PA/5/1625/4]
Joan of Swk St Olave, widow [DW/PA/7/8 f.235; DW/PA/5/1612/7]
Peter of Wonersh, husbandman [HRO; 1609 AD2] [*This entry appears thus in the list but is actually of Peter Amy.*]
AMEY *see* AMY
AMIAS *see* AMYAS
a MOORE, a MORE *see* ATMORE, MOORE
AMOR John of Swk St Saviour [DW/PA/5/1642/3] [*The will is so labelled on the outside, but appears to be that of a John Oliver.*]
AMY (AMYE, AMYES)
George of Wanborough, esq. [PRO; PCC 1635]
Jane of Worplesdon, widow [PRO; PCC Will 1624]
John of Shere, husbandman [DW/PA/7/13 f.15; DW/PA/5/1639/3]
Margaret of Cranleigh, widow [HRO; 1565 B3-6]
Margaret of Cranleigh, widow [DW/PA/5/1565/8]
Peter of Wonersh, husbandman [HRO; 1609 AD02]
Richard of Cranleigh [DW/PA/5/1558/11]*
Richard of Wanborough, yeoman [PRO; PCC Will 1617]
Robert[?] of Cranleigh [DW/PA/5/1565/12] [*It is very uncertain to which year this will belongs.*]
Thomas of Dorking [DW/PA/7/8 f.295; DW/PA/5/1613/3]
William of Shere, husbandman [DW/PA/7/11 f.498; DW/PA/5/1629/2]
AMYAS (AMIAS, AMYES)
John, alias John Elvyn, of Horley, yeoman [DW/PA/5/1591/59]
John, alias John Elvyn, of Horley [PRO; PCC Will 1591 *and* 1592]
John, alias John Elvyn, of Reigate, junior [DW/PA/7/11 f.473; DW/PA/5/1628/33]
Philip of Farnham, gent. [PRO; PCC Will 1626]
Roger of ... [DW/PA/7/7 f.432; DW/PA/5/1603/2] <Abs 818>
William of Reigate, husbandman [HRO; 1566 B3]
AMYE *see* AMY

AMYES *see* AMYAS
AMYOT
  Thomas of Kingston [DW/PA/7/1 f.3; 1484] <Abs 10>
ANACE
  John of Dorking [*in* DW/PA/5/1557/75]
ANCELL *see* ANSELL
ANDERSON
  Ann of Swk St Olave; 'St Legerhow'; Swk St George, widow [DW/PA/7/10 f.8; DW/PA/5/1619/2]
  John of Swk St Olave, baker, widower [DW/PA/7/12 f.377; DW/PA/5/1637/2]
  (Sir) John of Walton on Thames - Apps Court, knight [PRO; PCC Admon 1630]
  Rowland of Swk - St Thomas's Hospital [DW/PA/7/6 f.218; 1561]
ANDREWS (ANDREW,ANDREWES,ANDROES,ANDROW,ANDROWE,ANDROWES,ANDRUS)
  Cicely of Blechingley, widow [DW/PA/7/11 f.116; DW/PA/5/1624/1]
  Edward of Swk St Olave, citizen and weaver [DW/PA/7/13 f.307; DW/PA/5/1643/2]
  Henry of Chessington, yeoman [DW/PA/7/11 f.108; DW/PA/5/1624/2]
  John of Rotherhithe, husbandman, senior [DW/PA/7/8 f.134;DW/PA/5/1610/4]
  John, alias John Mayer, of Walton on Thames - Hersham; Byfleet; Hampton, Middlesex, labouringman [DW/PA/5/1604/38]
  Margaret of Swk St Olave, widow [DW/PA/7/9 f.251; DW/PA/5/1617/2]
  Mary of Kingston; Chessington, widow of Henry [DW/PA/7/12 f.39; DW/PA/5/1631/6]
  Peter of Swk St Olave [DW/PA/5/1587/106]
  Robert of Kingston [HRO; 1568 B3-4]
  Robert of Rotherhithe [PRO; PCC Will 1592]
  Thomas of Addington [DW/PA/7/1 ff.4,5; 1484] <Abs 12>
  Thomas of Chessington [DW/PA/7/12 f.216; DW/PA/5/1633/3]
  Thomas of Rotherhithe [PRO; PCC Will 1593]
  William of Reigate [DW/PA/7/5 f.165; 1540]
ANEVE
  Thomas of Stoke next Guildford; Guildford Holy Trinity, yeoman [HRO; 1592 B2]
ANFIELD (ANFEILD)
  Sybil of Blechingley, widow of William [DW/PA/7/8 f.153; DW/PA/5/1611/2]
  William of Blechingley, gent. [PRO; PCC Will 1610] <Abs. SAC v.24 p.61>
ANGELL (UNGILL)
  John of Swk St George [DW/PA/7/4 f.168; 1536]
  Susan of Camberwell - Peckham, spinster [PRO; PCC 1635]
  Thomas of Kingston [PRO; PCC Will 1490]
ANNESLEY (ANNSLEY,ANSLEY)
  James of Chobham [PRO; PCC Will 1546]
  James of Richmond, esq., junior [PRO; PCC Will 1606]
  Thomas of Surrey [PRO; PCC Will 1514]
ANSCOMBE (AYNESCOMBE,AYNSCOMBE,ENSCOMBE)
  Ann of Merstham - Alderstead, widow [PRO; PCC Will 1598]
  Dorothy of Godstone, widow [DW/PA/7/10 f.46; 1618]
  Gabriel of Chaldon (widow, Katherine) [PRO; PCC 1632]
  Joan of Merstham, widow [LPL; 96/882; Will 1629]
  Katherine of Merstham; Chaldon, widow of William yeoman [DW/PA/7/7 f.94; 1596] <Abs 173>
  Michael of Merstham [PRO; PCC Admon 1649]
  Richard of Merstham, yeoman [LPL; 96/108; 98/1 f.103r; Will 1639]

ANSCOMBE (AYNESCOMBE,AYNSCOMBE,ENSCOMBE) [*continued*]
Robert of Camberwell [HRO; Reg.CCB 20 p.10; 1563]
Robert of Camberwell, carpenter [DW/PA/5/1563/73; *in* DW/PA/5/1563/65]
William of Chaldon [PRO; PCC Admon 1593]
ANSELL (ANCELL,AUNCELL,AUNSELL,ENSALL,ENSOLL)
Christian of St Mary Woolchurch, London, and 'Thethers', Woodmansterne widow of George Ockley & ... Ansell [GL; Commissary Court of London Will 1595]
Edward of Windlesham, husbandman [DW/PA/7/12 f.124; DW/PA/5/1632/2]
George of Swk St Olave [DW/PA/7/11 f.426; DW/PA/5/1627/34]
Henry of Swk St George; Feltham, Middlesex [DW/PA/5/1557/95]
John of Dorking [DW/PA/7/5 f.204; 1540]
John of Dorking - Logmore, yeoman [DW/PA/7/11 f.108; DW/PA/5/1624/3]
John of Swk St Olave, whitster [DW/PA/5/1557/124]
Richard of Cobham, innholder [DW/PA/7/9 f.100; DW/PA/5/1614/3]
Robert of Dorking, yeoman [DW/PA/5/1558/6]*
Robert of Elstead, yeoman [DW/PA/7/8 f.302; DW/PA/5/1613/4]
Thomas of Dorking [DW/PA/7/3 f.173; 1531]
Thomas of Swk St Olave [DW/PA/7/3 f.190; 1531]
Walter of Swk St Olave, brewer [DW/PA/5/1603/48] <Abs U68>
William of Mitcham, vicar [DW/PA/7/7 f.301; DW/PA/5/1600/1] <Abs 538>
see also HOUNSELL
ANSLEY *see* ANNESLEY
ANSLOW (ANSLOE)
William of St Peter Paul's Wharf, London; Thames Ditton, citizen and dyer [GL; Commissary Court of London Will 1615]
ANSON
Thomas of Swk [DW/PA/5/1562/6]
ANSTED
John of Bermondsey [PRO; PCC Admon 1625]
ANSTY (ANSTYE,ENSTY)
Ninian of Lambeth [PRO; PCC 1648]
Richard, alias Richard Feild, of Charlwood, servant to Edmund Jordan, esq. [LPL; 96/66; Will 1629]
Thomas, alias Thomas Feilds, of Limpsfield, bachelor [PRO; PCC Admon 1646]
ANTEKEP *see* ENTICKNAP
ANTELL
Thomas of Chessington, yeoman [DW/PA/7/13 f.49; DW/PA/5/1639/4]
ANTHONY (ANTONIE)
Barbara of Chertsey [DW/PA/7/12 f.398; DW/PA/5/1637/3]
Edward of Chertsey [PRO; PCC Admon 1618]
John of Malden [PRO; PCC Will 1628]
John of Newington [PRO; PCC Admon 1627]
ANTON
James of Bermondsey [PRO; PCC Admon 1609]
ANTONIE *see* ANTHONY
ANVYK
Velze' of Swk St Olave [DW/PA/5/1558/10]*
ANWICKE
Thomas of St Martin Vintry, London; Swk St Olave - Battle Bridge [GL; Commissary Court of London Will 1591]
ANYMY
Thomas of Guildford St Mary [DW/PA/7/1 f.62; 1487] <Abs 209>

ap DAVID ap EIGN
Griff of Richmond [PRO; PCC Will 1501]
APFIELD *see* ARFIELD
ap DAVID
Ewan of Swk St George; Melverly, Shropshire), baker [DW/PA/5/1558/12]*
ap EIGN
Griff ap David of Richmond [PRO; PCC Will 1501]
ap HOWELL (a POWELL)
Phillip of Swk St George [DW/PA/7/4 f.86; 1534]
see also HOWELL, POWELL
ap JOHN
Edward, alias Edward King, of Bermondsey [PRO; PCC Will 1587]
Hugh, alias Hugh ap John ap Hugh, of Swk St Olave ; 'Clandils' [?Llandeilo], Radnorshire [DW/PA/7/7 f.489; 1604]
a PEW, APEW *see* HUGHES
APLE,APLETON *see* APPLE,APPLETON
ap LLOELLEN *see* LLEWELLYN
a POWELL
Phillip, or Phillip ap Howell, of Swk St George [DW/PA/7/4 f.86; 1534]
APPLE (APLE)
Angel of Alfold, widow [PRO; PCC Will 1592]
Angel of Alfold, widow [DW/PA/5/1592/5]
James of Alfold, merchant [DW/PA/5/1592/4]
James of Alfold [PRO; PCC Will 1592]
James of Alfold [PRO; PCC Will 1595]
APPLETON (APLETON,APYLTON)
Audrey of Walton on Thames, widow of Thomas [DW/PA/7/8 f.276; DW/PA/5/1612/3]
Thomas of Bermondsey, yeoman [DW/PA/7/2 f.74; 1501]
APPRICHARD (ap RICHERD)
Ann of Bermondsey, widow [PRO; PCC Will 1621]
John of Swk St Olave [DW/PA/7/5 f.58; 1539] <Abs 100>
see also RICHARDS
ap PUE *see* HUGHES
ap RICHARD (ap RICHERD) *see* RICHARDS
APSLEY
John of Surrey, esq. [PRO; PCC Will 1507]
Michael of Abinger, esq. [PRO; PCC Will 1618]
ap TELLER *see* ELLIS
APYLTON *see* APPLETON
ARBERRY
Eusebius of Bermondsey, citizen and leatherdresser [DW/PA/7/12 f.189; DW/PA/5/1633/1]
Margaret of Bermondsey, widow [DW/PA/7/12 f.204; DW/PA/5/1634/1]
ARCHARD *see* ORCHARD
ARCHER
Edward of Swk St Olave, yeoman [DW/PA/7/10 f.222; DW/PA/5/1621/1]
Joan of Wandsworth, widow [DW/PA/7/11 f.366; DW/PA/5/1626/3]
Lemuel of Swk, fishmonger [DW/PA/7/12 f.92; DW/PA/5/1632/1]
Richard of Swk St George,, prisoner in the King's Bench Prison [DW/PA/5/1604/3] <Abs U97>
Robert of Rotherhithe [PRO; PCC Admon 1638]
Thomas of Swk St George [DW/PA/5/1603/3] <Abs U59>

ARCHER [*continued*]

William of Wandsworth, yeoman [DW/PA/7/7 f.334; DW/PA/5/1601/2]<Abs 603>

ARDEN (ARDERN, ARDERNE, ARDYN)

John of Whitefriars, London and Leigh, high sheriff of Surrey and Sussex [LPL; Reg. Abp Stafford f.172; Will 1449] <Abs SAC v.11 pp.144-145 *and* v.29 p.136>

John of Lambeth [PRO; PCC Admon 1619]

John of Lambeth [PRO; PCC Admon 1621]

Richard of Bosham, Chichester, Sussex; Addington; Leigh [PRO; PCC Will 1499] <Abs SAC v.11 pp.147-148 *and* v.29 p.138>

Walter of Cheam, clerk [PRO; PCC Will 1492]

ARFEILD *see* ATTFIELD

ARGAR

Richard of Bermondsey (son Nicholas) [PRO; PCC 1632]

ARGENTYNE

Agnes of East Horsley [PRO; PCC Will 1544]

ARMESTRONGE *see* ARMSTRONG

ARMISBY *see* ARMYSBYE

ARMITSTEAD

Thomas of Swk St Thomas, draper [DW/PA/7/12 f.303; DW/PA/5/1635/1]

ARMSTRONG (ARMESTRONGE)

Arthur of Farnham [PRO; PCC Admon 1612]

Clement of Richmond; Kew, coachman to the Queen [PRO; PCC Will 1610]

ARMYSBYE

John of London, leatherseller [DW/PA/5/1558/7]*

ARNOLD (ARNOLDE, ARNOLL, ARNOLT, ARNOOLDE)

Alice of Ashtead, widow [DW/PA/7/4 f.17; 1532]

Alice of Swk St Olave, widow [DW/PA/7/11 f.308; DW/PA/5/1626/4]

Ann, alias Ann Fiett, of Croydon [PRO; PCC Admon 1597]

Ann of Lambeth - Water Lambeth, widow [PRO; PCC 1635]

Francis of Lambeth [PRO; PCC Admon 1632]

Henry of Guildford [PRO; PCC Admon 1593]

Henry of Swk St George, cordwainer [DW/PA/7/8 f.182; DW/PA/5/1610/5]

Henry of Stoke next Guildford [PRO; PCC Will 1594]

Joan of Mickleham [DW/PA/7/4 f.116; 1535]

John of Chaldon, husbandman [DW/PA/7/11 f.130; DW/PA/5/1624/4]

John of Chertsey, tilemaker [DW/PA/7/9 f.121; DW/PA/5/1615/2]

John of Ewell [PRO; PCC Will 1482]

John of Mickleham, yeoman [DW/PA/5/1587/46]

John of Reigate [DW/PA/7/11 f.471; DW/PA/5/1628/1]

Katherine of Swk St Olave; St Andrew Hubbard, London [DW/PA/5/1555/24]

Nathaniel of Hambledon, husbandman [DW/PA/7/13 f.189; DW/PA/5/1641/3]

Ralph of Dorking, senior, husbandman [DW/PA/5/1605/3] <Abs U125>

Ralph of Mickleham, senior, husbandman [DW/PA/5/1576/114]

Ralph of Mickleham; Wotton, yeo. [DW/PA/7/7 f.296; DW/PA/5/1600/2] <Abs 530>

Richard of Great Bookham [DW/PA/5/1557/100]

Richard of Mickleham, husbandman [DW/PA/5/1558/8]

Robert of Mickleham, husbandman [DW/PA/7/2 f.122; 1518]

Simon of Lambeth [PRO; PCC Will 1498]

Stephen of Woking, husbandman [DW/PA/5/1586/9]

Thomas of Swk St Olave [DW/PA/7/3 f.151; 1530]

Thomas, alias Thomas Stint, alias Thomas Stidall, of Stoke Dabernon [PRO; PCC Admon 1572]

ARNOLD (ARNOLDE,ARNOLL,ARNOLT,ARNOOLDE) [*continued*]
Thomas, senior, of Stoke Dabernon, yeoman [DW/PA/7/7 f.128; DW/PA/5/1597/4] <Abs 235>
William of Ashtead [DW/PA/7/2 f.199; 1524]
William of Great Bookham; Effingham; Little Bookham; Cobham, weaver [DW/PA/5/1593/97]
William of Croydon [LPL; 98/1 f.25r; Will 1631]
William of Lambeth, bachelor [PRO; PCC Admon 1632]
William of Mickleham [DW/PA/7/4 f.130; 1535]
William of Mickleham; Wotton, yeoman [HRO; 1589 B1]
William of Mickleham; Dorking, yeoman [DW/PA/7/9 f.85; DW/PA/5/1615/1]
William of Reigate, yeoman [HRO; 1599 B2]
William of Weybridge; Chertsey, yeoman [DW/PA/7/7 f.291; DW/PA/5/1600/3] <Abs 520>

ARNOLDSON
Gilbert of Swk St Olave [DW/PA/5/1563/97]

ARRETT
William of Swk St Saviour, pewterer [DW/PA/5/1570/78]

ARSLATT
Richard of Farnham [PRO; PCC Will 1518]

ARTEM (de ARTEM)
John of Swk St Olave [DW/PA/7/4 f.121; 1535]

ARTHOIS
Gerard of Swk [DW/PA/5/1587/107]

ARTHUR
John of Charlwood, weaver [LPL; 96/76; Will 1624]
Robert of Walton on Thames, esq. [PRO; PCC Will 1608] <Abs. SAC v.13 p.180>

ARUNDELL (ARUNDEL, de ARUNDEL)
Eleanor of Lytchett Maltravers, Dorset; Lingfield [PRO; PCC Will 1404] <Abs SAC v.2 pp.186-190>
John of Newington [LPL; 98/1 f.21r Will 1631]
Nathaniel (widow, Ellen) of Ockham, clerk [PRO; PCC 1639]
Thomas of Ewell, esq. [PRO; PCC Will 1571]
William of Mickleham, rector [PRO; E327 771; 1295]
(Sir) William of Rochester Priory [Kent]; Swk, knight [LPL; Reg. Abp Arundel i f.172; Will 1400]

ASCH in BRABANCIA
'Ludocus de' of Swk St Olave [DW/PA/7/2 f.66; 1500]

ASCHTON *see* ASHTON

ASCHYNE
John of Swk St Olave [DW/PA/7/6 f.65; DW/PA/5/1559/43]

ASCLOYT *see* ASTLOYT

ASCOMBE (OSCOMBE,OSCUMBE)
John of Walton on Thames; Thames Ditton, yeoman [DW/PA/7/9 f.321; DW/PA/5/1619/3]
John of Walton [on Thames] [PRO; PCC Admon 1643]
Thomas of Carshalton, smith [DW/PA/7/4 f.74; 1534]
William of Thames Ditton [DW/PA/5/1556/8]

ASH (ASHE,ASSHE)
Nicholas of Swk St Thomas's Hospital, goldfiner [DW/PA/7/6 f.199; 1560]
Thomas of Lambeth [PRO; PCC Admon 1587]

ASH (ASHE,ASSHE) [*continued*]
William of Swk St Saviour [DW/PA/7/7 f,414; DW/PA/5/1603/4] <Abs 771>
ASHBORNE (ASHBOURNE)
Fulk of Bermondsey, tanner [DW/PA/7/9 f,340; 1620]
Richard of Nutfield, husbandman [DW/PA/7/6 f,76; DW/PA/5/1559/114]
William of Horne, husbandman [DW/PA/5/1619/4] <Abs U235>
William of Horne, husbandman [DW/PA/7/10 f,78; DW/PA/5/1620/2]
ASHBURNHAM
Isabel of Lambeth [PRO; PCC Will 1584]
ASHBY (ASHBYE,ASSHEBY)
Emma of Newington, widow [PRO; PCC Will 1619]
Thomas of Beddington [PRO; PCC Admon 1630]
Thomas of Bermondsey - Bermondsey Abbey, gent, [PRO; PCC Will 1497]
ASHE *see* ASH
ASHELEY *see* ASHLEY
ASHELL *see* ASHWELL
ASHEMORE *see* ASHMORE
ASHEN
William of Charlwood [LPL; 98/1 f,121r; Will 1641]
ASHENDEN
William of Merton - Merton Abbey, citizen and scrivener [PRO; PCC Will 1613]
ASHEWELL *see* ASHWELL
ASHLEY (ASHELEY)
Alice (widow of Rees) of Battersea [DW/PA/7/8 f,280; DW/PA/5/1613/5]
Margaret of Battersea, widow [DW/PA/5/1558/14]*
Rees of Battersea [DW/PA/7/8 f,153; DW/PA/5/1611/3]
ASHLIN (ASHLYN)
John of Swk St Olave, citizen and pewterer [DW/PA/7/2 f,104; 1515]
ASHMORE
John of Swk St Saviour [DW/PA/5/1587/43]*
Richard of Lambeth, victualler [DW/PA/7/9 f,195; DW/PA/5/1616/4]
ASHPOOLE
Samuel of ...., joiner [DW/PA/7/7 f,429; DW/PA/5/1603/5] <Abs 808>
ASHTED
Thomas, alias Thomas Easted, of Nutfield, yeoman [HRO; 1571 B62]
ASHTON (ASCHTON,ASSHETON)
Anthony of Bermondsey [PRO; PCC Admon 1648]
Edmund of Swk St Saviour, citizen and brewer [DW/PA/7/11 f,246; DW/PA/5/1625/5]
Edward of Godstone [PRO; PCC Will 1537]
Nicholas of Godstone [PRO; PCC Will 1511]
ASHURST (ASSHURST)
John of Betchworth, gent, [PRO; PCC Will 1507]
Thomas of Surrey [PRO; PCC Will 1420]
ASHWELL (ASHELL,ASHEWELL,ASSHELL)
Alice (widow of Harry) of Swk St Saviour [DW/PA/7/5 f,225; 1541]
Henry of Swk St Saviour [DW/PA/7/5 f,184; 1540]
Katherine of Swk St Olave, widow [DW/PA/7/7 f,380; DW/PA/5/1602/2] <Abs 704>
Thomas of Thames Ditton, fisherman [DW/PA/7/9 f,334; DW/PA/5/1620/1]
William of Swk St Olave, porter [DW/PA/7/7 f,61; DW/PA/5/1596/1]<Abs 115>

ASHWORTH (AYSHWORTH)
Henry of Farnham [PRO; PCC 1641]
Henry of Farnham [PRO; PCC Admon 1641]
a SKAFE
John of Swk St George, victualler [DW/PA/5/1568/14]
ASKEW (ASKEWE,AYSCUE)
Francis of Egham, yeoman [DW/PA/7/7 f,382; DW/PA/5/1602/3] <Abs 708>
Grisell (wife of William) of Lambeth, esq, [PRO; PCC Will 1619]
John of Bermondsey [DW/PA/5/1555/43]
William of Gatton; Swk, gent, [PRO; PCC Will 1611]
ASKHAM
William of Newington - Walworth [PRO; PCC Will 1414]
ASKOLL
Henry of Godalming - Farncombe, weaver [DW/PA/5/1576/25]
ASLETT
John of Farnham - Runfold, husbandman [HRO; 1576 B2]
John of Swk St Saviour, waterman [DW/PA/7/11 f,362; DW/PA/5/1626/5]
see also Haslett
ASPIN
John of Swk St Olave [DW/PA/7/11 f,315; DW/PA/5/1626/6]
ASPULL
Thomas of West Horsley, parson [HRO; 1558 B12]
ASSER
Henry of Pirbright, preacher of God's word [DW/PA/7/8 f,409; 1615]
ASSHE *see* ASH
ASSHEBY *see* ASHBY
ASSHELL *see* ASHWELL
ASSHETON *see* ASHTON
ASSHURST *see* ASHURST
ASSITER
Thomas of Mitcham [PRO; PCC Admon 1617]
a STABLE *see* STABLE
ASTILL (ASTALL,ASTELL)
Joan of Morden, widow [PRO; PCC Will 1599]
Margaret of Kingston, widow [DW/PA/5/1558/17]*
Richard of Esher, widower [PRO; PCC Admon 1639]
William of Swk St Saviour, weaver [DW/PA/5/1568/85]
ASTLET (ASCLOYT,ASTLOYT)
Nicholas Astloyt *or* Ascloyt of Farnham, husbandman [DW/PA/7/3 f,117; 1529]
ASTON (ASTOANE,a STONE,ASTONE,AYSTON)
Eleanor of Cranleigh, widow [DW/PA/7/8 f,355; DW/PA/5/1612/4]
Henry, senior, of Capel; Ockley, yeoman [DW/PA/7/7 f,482; DW/PA/5/1604/4] <Abs 908>
John of Abinger, yeoman [DW/PA/7/8 f,121; DW/PA/5/1610/6]
John of Albury, senior [DW/PA/7/5 f,215; 1541]
John of Albury [DW/PA/7/6 f,77; DW/PA/5/1559/48]
John of Capel, yeoman [DW/PA/5/1582/67]
John of Farnham - Dogflood [DW/PA/7/7 f,541; DW/PA/5/1606/1] <Abs 1015>
John of Shere [DW/PA/7/5 f,38; 1538] <Abs 81>
John of Swk St Margaret [DW/PA/7/4 f,191; 1536]
John of Swk St Olave [DW/PA/7/4 f,24; 1532]
John of Wotton, yeoman [DW/PA/5/1591/76]
Mary of Shere [HRO; 1627 B3]

ASTON (ASTOANE,a STONE,ASTONE,AYSTON) [*continued*]
Matthew of Wotton, yeoman [DW/PA/5/1570/48]
Ralph of Capel, yeoman [PRO: PCC Will 1606] <Abs, SAC v.12 p.201>
Richard of Shere - Dilton, yeoman [DW/PA/5/1576/106]
Robert of Farnham, gent. [PRO: PCC Will 1588]
Robert of Farnham, esq. [PRO: PCC Will 1626]
Robert of Shere - Dilton, yeoman [DW/PA/7/8 f.63; DW/PA/5/1609/5]
Thomas of Farleigh; Albury, husbandman [DW/PA/7/7 f.524; DW/PA/5/1607/3] <Abs 987>
Thomas of Rotherhithe [PRO: PCC Admon 1638]
Thomas of Wotton; Carshalton; Dorking [PRO: PCC Will 1587]
see also STONE

ASTREET (a STREAT,ASTREATE,ASTREETE,ASTRET,a STRETE,ASTRETE,ATSTRETE)
Edward, alias Edward Barber, of Shalford; Wonersh [DW/PA/7/4 f.82; 1534]
Elizabeth of Guildford [DW/PA/7/11 f.477; DW/PA/5/1626/7]
Harry of Wonersh [DW/PA/5/1550/73]
Henry of Bramley; Wonersh, carpenter [DW/PA/7/7 f.247; DW/PA/5/1599/73] <Abs 437>
John of Albury [DW/PA/7/3 f.160; 1530]
John of Shalford; Guildford St Mary, yeoman [DW/PA/7/7 f.595; DW/PA/5/1607/4] <Abs 1116>
John of Wonersh, husbandman [DW/PA/5/1571/24]
John, alias John Street, of Wonersh [DW/PA/7/7 f.328; DW/PA/5/1601/76] <Abs 587>
John of Wonersh - Tangley; Guildford; Stoke; Newdigate; Godalming; Bramley, yeoman [PRO: PCC Will 1607] <Abs, SAC v.12 pp.203-204>
Richard of Wonersh [DW/PA/7/1 f.9; 1484] <Abs 29>
Richard of Wonersh [DW/PA/5/1591/21]
Robert of Alfold, husbandman [DW/PA/7/8 f.384; DW/PA/5/1612/5]
Robert of Wonersh, weaver [DW/PA/5/1570/46]
Thomas of Shalford - Chinthurst, husbandman [HRO: 1614 B1]
Thomas of Wonersh - Farnehill, weaver [DW/PA/5/1579/5]*
Thomas of Wonersh, husbandman [HRO: 1584 AD2]
Thomas of Wonersh, husbandman [HRO: 1612 AD4]
Walter of Wonersh - Smarkham, husbandman [DW/PA/7/9 f.20; DW/PA/5/1616/5]
William of Wonersh [DW/PA/5/1547/19]
William of Wonersh, tailor [DW/PA/7/7 f.356; DW/PA/5/1602/4] <Abs 651>
see also STREET

ASTRY
Barbara, alias Barbara Cooper, of Titsey [PRO: PCC Admon 1648]
(Sir) Ralph, alias (Sir) Ralph Ostriche of Surrey, knight and Lord Mayor of London [PRO: PCC Will 1494]

ATFEELD,ATFEELDE,ATFEILD,ATFELD,ATFELDE,ATFEYLD,ATFIELD *see* ATTFIELD,FIELD

ATGATE (at GAYTE)
John of Walton on Thames - Apps [DW/PA/7/5 f.177; 1540]
see also GATES

ATHEATH (ATHETH)
Michael of Battersea - Penge [DW/PA/7/2 f.42; 1494]
Walter of Caterham [DW/PA/7/1 f.79; 1488] <Abs 258>
see also HEATH

ATHERTON
Peter (widow Elizabeth) of Woking [PRO: PCC 1649]

ATHILL (ATHILD,at HOLE,ATHULL,ATHYLL,ATTEHILLE,atte HYLD)
John of Chiddingfold [PRO; PCC Will 1455]
John of Hambledon [PRO; PCC Will 1489] <Abs SAC v,29 p,81>
Robert of Elstead [DW/PA/7/1 f,76; 1488] <Abs 248>
Walter of Ewhurst [DW/PA/7/2 f,206; 1524]
William of Egham - Egham Wick [DW/PA/7/1 ff,55,90; 1486] <Abs 182,305>
see also HILL,HULL

ATHOW
John of Cranleigh [DW/PA/7/4 f,86; 1534]
Walter of Cranleigh - Boucheries - Vachery - Wyphurst; Ewhurst; Wonersh - Tylie; Guildford; Shere - Gomshall [DW/PA/5/1593/10]
see also HOW

ATHULL,ATHYLL *see* ATHILL

ATKINS (ADKIN,ADKINS)
Edward of Burstow [LPL; 96/15; 98/1 f,28r; Will 1631]
(Sir) Henry of Clapham, knight [PRO; PCC 1638]
Richard of Shoreditch, Middlesex); Swk St Saviour, basketmaker [DW/PA/7/11 f,390; DW/PA/5/1626/1]
Sidney of Lambeth - Lambeth Marsh, gent, [PRO; PCC Will 1629]
William of Godalming, gent, [PRO; PCC Will 1612]

ATKINSON (ADENSONNE,ADKINSON,ADYNSONNE,ATKINSONNE,ATKYNSON,ATKYNSTON, ATTKINSON,HATKYNSON)
Agnes of Swk St Saviour, widow [DW/PA/5/1579/1]*
Albert of ..., citizen and carpenter [DW/PA/7/8 f,152; DW/PA/5/1611/4]
Edmund of Swk St Margaret [HRO Reg, Fox 3 p,64; 1513]
Edward of Swk St Olave, citizen and innholder [DW/PA/7/7 f,410; DW/PA/5/1603/6] <Abs 760>
Elizabeth of Rotherhithe, widow [DW/PA/5/1562/48]
Elizabeth of Swk St Saviour, widow of Rowland [DW/PA/5/1593/115]
Geoffrey of Lambeth [LPL; Reg, Abp Abbot i f,280; Admon 1616]
George of Newington, yeoman [LPL; 96/90; Will 1624]
Henry of Lambeth [DW/PA/7/2 f,107; 1516]
James of Streatham [DW/PA/5/1579/3]*
Joan of Swk St Saviour, widow [DW/PA/7/9 f,303; DW/PA/5/1619/5]
John of West Horsley, butcher [HRO; 1567 B3]
John of Swk [DW/PA/5/1602/6] <Abs U41>
John of Swk St George, armourer [DW/PA/5/1568/11]
John of Swk St Olave; Essex, cooper [HRO; 1587 B2]
John of Swk St Olave, cooper [DW/PA/5/1587/31]
Nicholas of Swk - Paris Garden Liberty, waterman [DW/PA/7/8 f,72; DW/PA/5/1609/6]
Peter of Walton on Thames, husbandman [DW/PA/5/1575/44]
Robert of Bermondsey [DW/PA/5/1587/98]
Robert of Kingston [DW/PA/7/11 f,282; DW/PA/5/1625/6]
Robert of Swk, feltmaker [DW/PA/7/7 f,460; DW/PA/5/1603/7] <Abs 869>
Roger of Tooting Bec, husbandman [DW/PA/7/10 f,97; DW/PA/5/1619/6]
Thomas of Guildford [? HRO; 1505]
Thomas of Guildford [HRO; 1524 B4]
Thomas of Swk St Saviour [DW/PA/5/1578/91]
Thomas of Swk St Saviour, brewer [DW/PA/5/1598/3] <Abs U13>
William of Swk, saddler [DW/PA/5/1558/15]*
William of Swk St Saviour, leatherdresser [DW/PA/7/8 f,384; DW/PA/5/1612/6]

ATLAKE (ATTLAKE)
Thomas of Nutfield [DW/PA/7/3 f.133; 1530]

ATLEE (a LEE,ATLE,at LEE,ATLEIGH,ATTELEY,ATTLEE)
Alan of Chobham; Windlesham; Pirbright, yeoman [DW/PA/7/6 f.61; DW/PA/5/1559/52]
Alice of Woking [DW/PA/7/6 f.113; DW/PA/5/1559/51]
Edward of Effingham, yeoman [DW/PA/5/1582/28]
Edward of Effingham; Dorking; Worplesdon; Cobham; Horsley; Ockham, yeoman [DW/PA/5/1598/4] <Abs U14>
Elizabeth, alias Elizabeth Lyghe, of Ockham, widow [DW/PA/5/1571/73]
George of Tandridge [PRO; PCC Admon 1642]
Harry of West Horsley [DW/PA/5/1580/59]
Henry of East Clandon; West Horsley [DW/PA/7/4 f.12; 1532]
Joan of Addington [HRO; Reg. Fox 3 p.61; 1511] <Abs SAC v.7 pp.118-119>
Joan of Effingham, widow [DW/PA/7/2 f.146; 1520]
John of West Clandon, weaver [DW/PA/7/10 f.91; DW/PA/5/1615/82]
John of Effingham [HRO; 1605 B3]
John of Mitcham [DW/PA/7/2 f.5; 1490]
John of Woking, carpenter [DW/PA/5/1556/13]
Lawrence of Cobham, husbandman [DW/PA/7/8 f.60; DW/PA/5/1609/7]
Lawrence of West Horsley, husbandman [DW/PA/7/8 f.116; DW/PA/5/1610/1]
Maud *or* Matilda of East Clandon, widow of William, yeoman [DW/PA/7/7 f.25; DW/PA/5/1595/2] <Abs 54>
Peter of Godalming [DW/PA/7/1 ff.47,57; 1487] <Abs 157,189>
Phillip of Ockham, yeoman [DW/PA/5/1570/47]
Richard of Little Bookham; Shere; Abinger; Effingham, yeoman [DW/PA/7/8 f.135; DW/PA/5/1610/7]
Richard of Effingham [DW/PA/7/2 f.201; 1524]
Richard of Effingham, yeoman [DW/PA/7/6 f.68; DW/PA/5/1559/53]
Robert of East Clandon [DW/PA/7/3 f.169; 1531]
Robert of Wotton, yeoman [DW/PA/7/12 f.70; DW/PA/5/1631/7]
Thomas of East Clandon, yeoman [DW/PA/7/7 f.541; DW/PA/5/1606/2] <Abs 1016>
Thomas of Ockham [DW/PA/5/1579/4]*
William of East Clandon [DW/PA/7/3 f.180; 1531]
William of East Clandon [DW/PA/5/1591/109]
William of East Clandon, yeoman [DW/PA/7/8 f.16; DW/PA/5/1608/3]
William of Dorking [DW/PA/5/1579/8]*
William of West Horsley [HRO; 1592 B4]
William of West Molesey, yeoman [DW/PA/7/7 f.377; DW/PA/5/1602/1] <Abs 698>
William, *or* William Atwood, of Woking [DW/PA/5/1558/16]*
see also ALEE,LEE

ATMORE (a MOORE, a MORE)
John of Esher [DW/PA/7/4 f.216; 1537]
John of Esher [DW/PA/7/5 f.139; 1540]
see also MOORE

ATRIDE (at RIDE, at RYDE, att RIDD, ATTRIDE)
Elizabeth of Ewhurst, widow [DW/PA/7/13 f.315; DW/PA/5/1643/3]
Henry, alias Henry Ryde, of Send; West Clandon; Merrow, yeoman [DW/PA/7/7 f.299; DW/PA/5/1600/44] <Abs 535>
Henry of West Clandon, yeoman [HRO; 1638 B2]
John of [*? Surrey*] [LPL; Reg. Abp Grindal f.508a; Admon 1583]
John of Ewhurst, yeoman [DW/PA/7/6 f.153; DW/PA/5/1559/162]

ATRIDE (at RIDE, at RYDE, att RIDD, ATTRIDE) [*continued*]
John of Ewhurst, yeoman [DW/PA/5/1569/40]
John of Ewhurst, yeoman [DW/PA/7/12 f.521; DW/PA/5/1638/3]
Margaret, alias Margaret Harman, of Ewhurst [PRO; PCC Admon 1649]
Robert of East Clandon; Worplesdon; Stoke [DW/PA/7/4 f.143; 1536]
Thomas, alias Thomas Ride of Ewhurst, senior [DW/PA/7/8 f.250; DW/PA/5/1613/108]
Thomas of Ewhurst, yeoman [DW/PA/7/12 f.24; DW/PA/5/1631/3]
Thomas of Horsell [DW/PA/7/5 f.191; 1540]
Thomas, alias Thomas Ride, of Send - Dedswell [PRO; PCC Admon 1613]
Thomas of Wonersh, husbandman [DW/PA/5/1576/35]
see also RIDE

at ROKE
Robert of Steep, Hampshire; East Molesey [DW/PA/5/1565/1]
see also ROAKE

at RYDE *see* ATRIDE

at SMITH (at SMITHE)
John, alias John Smither, of Wonersh [DW/PA/5/1576/83]
see also SMITH

at STRETE, ATSTRETE *see* ASTREET,STREET

ATTACRE
Alan of Dorking, husbandman [DW/PA/7/13 f.78; DW/PA/5/1640/1]
Ursula of Dorking, widow [DW/PA/7/13 f.106; DW/PA/5/1640/4]

atte DENNE *see* DEAN

atte GRENE *see* GREEN

atte HILLE, atte HYLD *see* ATHILL,HILL

ATTELEY *see* ATLEE,LEE

atte WEDE, atte WODE *see* ATWOOD,WOOD

ATTFIELD (ARFEILD,ATFEELD,ATFEELDE,ATFEILD,ATFEILDE,ATFELD,ATFELDE,ATFEYLD, ATFIELD,ATFYLD,ATFYLDE,ATTFEILD,ATTFEILDE,ATTFELD)
Agnes of Bisley, spinster [DW/PA/7/11 f.144; DW/PA/5/1624/5]
Agnes, alias Agnes Ripley, of Worplesdon - Burpham, widow [DW/PA/5/1574/3]
Alan of Chobham [DW/PA/5/1562/20]
Alan of Chobham, husbandman [DW/PA/7/7 f.110; 1597] <Abs 201>
Edward of Egham [DW/PA/7/6 f.58; DW/PA/5/1559/50]
Gilbert of Windlesham, husbandman [DW/PA/7/12 f.27; DW/PA/5/1631/4]
Harry of Chobham, carpenter [DW/PA/5/1555/40]
Harry of Cobham [PRO; PCC Will 1592]
Henry of Chobham, husbandman [DW/PA/7/7 f.67; DW/PA/5/1596/2] <Abs 127>
Henry of 'at Heathside', Chobham, husbandman [DW/PA/7/13 f.86; DW/PA/5/1640/3]
Henry, alias Henry Field, of Chobham [PRO; PCC Admon 1648]
Henry of Egham - Stroud, gent. [PRO; PCC Will 1616]
Henry, alias Henry Ripley, of Stoke [DW/PA/7/13 f.364; 1644]
Henry, alias Henry Ripley, of Worplesdon - Burpham, yeo. [DW/PA/5/1578/87]
Henry, alias Henry Ripley, of Worplesdon, husbandman, senior [HRO; 1588 B1]
Henry, alias Henry Ripley, of Worplesdon - Burpham; Stoke; Merrow, yeoman [DW/PA/7/9 f.67; DW/PA/5/1614/100]
Henry, alias Henry Ripley, of Worplesdon - Burpham [DW/PA/7/11 f.535; DW/PA/5/1629/3]

ATTFIELD (ARFEILD,ATFEELD,ATFEELDE,ATFEILD,ATFEILDE,ATFELD,ATFELDE,ATFEYLD, ATFIELD,ATFYLD,ATFYLDE,ATTFEILD,ATTFEILDE,ATTFELD) [*continued*]
Henry, alias Henry Ripley, of Worplesdon - Burpham, yeoman [DW/PA/7/13 f.351; 1644]
Joan of Chobham, widow [DW/PA/5/1550/67]
John of Chobham, labourer [DW/PA/7/4 f.7; 1532]
John of Chobham, yeoman [DW/PA/5/1580/60]
John of Cobham [? HRO; 1534]
John of Egham [DW/PA/5/1546/47]
John of Pirbright [PRO; PCC Admon 1648]
John of Windlesham - Bagshot [DW/PA/5/1592/81]
John of Windlesham, carpenter [DW/PA/7/8 f.236; DW/PA/5/1613/6]
John, alias John Field, of Windlesham, yeoman, senior [PRO; PCC Will 1627]
John, alias John Ripley, of Worplesdon, yeoman [DW/PA/7/9 f.140; DW/PA/5/1615/3]
Juliana, alias Juliana Ripley, of Woking - Sutton, widow [DW/PA/5/1587/3]
Nicholas of Windlesham [DW/PA/5/1587/101]
Ralph of Egham - Stroud, gardener [PRO; PCC Will 1615]
Robert of Chobham [DW/PA/7/6 f.110; DW/PA/5/1559/49]
Thomas of Chertsey, yeoman [HRO; 1642 B2]
Thomas, alias Thomas Ripley, of Worplesdon - Burpham, senior [DW/PA/7/11 f.380; DW/PA/5/1626/8]
Thomas, alias Thomas Ripley of Worplesdon, yeoman [DW/PA/7/12 f.33; DW/PA/5/1631/5]
Walter of Chobham [DW/PA/5/1574/25]
Walter of Guildford [DW/PA/7/11 f.476; DW/PA/5/1628/2]
William of Chobham, husbandman [DW/PA/7/5 f.171; 1540]
William of Chobham, husbandman [DW/PA/5/1593/194]
William of Windlesham, yeoman [DW/PA/7/10 f.239; DW/PA/5/1621/2]

ATTKINSON *see* ATKINSON

ATTLAKE *see* ATLAKE,LAKE

ATTLEE *see* ATLEE,LEE

ATTRIDE,ATTRYDE *see* ATRIDE,RIDE

ATTYE
Richard of Chipstead [DW/PA/7/2 f.31; 1492]

at VODDE *see* ATWOOD,WOOD

at WALL *see* ATWELL,WELLS

ATWATER (ATTWATER,at WATTUR)
Richard, alias Richard Hill, of Kingston, shoemaker [DW/PA/5/1605/4] <Abs U128>
Robert of Shalford [DW/PA/7/1 f.29; 1486] <Abs 95,97>
William of Woking, husbandman [*in* DW/PA/5/1555/14]

ATWATERER
Richard of Woking, yeoman [DW/PA/5/1557/130]
see also WATERER

ATWEECKE,ATWEEKE,ATWEKE,ATWEKES *see* ATWICK

ATWELL (ATTWELL,at WALL,ATWELS,ATWILL,AWELLES)
Agnes of Headley, widow [DW/PA/7/6 f.140; DW/PA/5/1559/54]
Harry, alias Harry Wells, of Headley [DW/PA/5/1562/4]
Joan, alias Joan Cooper, of Bentley, Hampshire, widow [DW/PA/7/11 f.318; DW/PA/5/1626/9]
Joan of Headley, widow [DW/PA/5/1562/72]
John of West Clandon [DW/PA/5/1582/21]

ATWELL (ATTWELL,at WALL,ATWELS,ATWILL,AWELLES) [*continued*]
John of Fetcham, husbandman [HRO; 1587 B3] [*and*] [DW/PA/5/1587/33]
John of Headley [DW/PA/7/3 f,195; 1531]
John of Headley [? HRO; 1545]
John, alias John Weller of Headley, husbandman [DW/PA/5/1574/44]
John, of Leatherhead, senior [DW/PA/7/2 f,111; 1517]
Lawrence of Godalming [PRO; PCC Will 1588]
Richard of Headley [DW/PA/7/6 f,72; DW/PA/5/1559/55]
William of Kingston [HRO; Reg, Way 1 p,54; 1458]
William of Kingston [DW/PA/7/1 f,71; ?1487] <Abs 233>
see also WELLS
ATWICK (ADWICKE,ATWEECKE,ATWEEKE,ATWEKE,ATWEKES,ATWICKE,ATWYKE)
Agnes of Chertsey, widow [DW/PA/7/11 f,261; DW/PA/5/1625/7]
Alice of Thorpe, widow [DW/PA/5/1558/9]*
Henry of Chertsey, yeoman [DW/PA/7/13 f,214; DW/PA/5/1642/2]
Henry of Thorpe, yeoman [DW/PA/5/1574/20]
James of Egham - Stroud, yeoman [DW/PA/7/11 f,581; DW/PA/5/1630/2]
John of Egham [PRO; PCC 1635]
John of Egham [PRO; PCC 1639]
John of Thorpe [DW/PA/7/4 f,19; 1532]
Richard of Egham [PRO; PCC Will 1516]
Richard of Thorpe; Staines [Middlesex]; Egham; Chertsey; Laleham, Middlesex [DW/PA/5/1550/4]
Richard, alias Richard Weecke, of Thorpe; Egham - Stroud [PRO; PCC Will 1592]
Robert of Chertsey; Egham [DW/PA/7/4 f,89; 1534]
Robert of Chertsey [PRO; PCC Admon 1647]
William of Chertsey, yeoman [DW/PA/5/1558/13]*
William of Chertsey, innholder, senior [DW/PA/7/12 f,420; DW/PA/5/1637/4]
William of Egham - Stroud, yeoman [DW/PA/5/1557/97]
William of Egham, tanner [DW/PA/7/7 f,542; DW/PA/5/1606/3] <Abs 1017>
William of Rotherhithe, mariner [DW/PA/5/1575/23]
see also WICKS
ATWILL *see* ATWELL
ATWOOD (atte WEDE,atte WODE,ATTWOD,ATTWOOD,ATTWOODE,at VODDE,ATWODE, ATWOODE,AWOD,a WOODD,AWOODE)
Agnes of Coulsdon [DW/PA/7/2 f,9; 1491]
Charles of Effingham, yeoman [DW/PA/7/7 f,394; DW/PA/5/1603/8] <Abs 732>
Denise of Sanderstead, widow of John [DW/PA/7/3 f,174; 1531] <Abs SAC v,7 p,20>
Gillian of Woking, widow [DW/PA/5/1562/9]
Henry of Shere, husbandman [DW/PA/7/7 f,326; DW/PA/5/1601/3] <Abs 584>
Joan of Mickleham [HRO; 1527 B2]
John of Little Bookham, husbandman [DW/PA/7/8 f,37; DW/PA/5/1609/8]
John of Chobham [HRO; 1555 U5]
John of Headley [DW/PA/5/1556/6]
John of Malden [PRO; PCC Will 1563]
John of Woking; Chobham [DW/PA/7/7 f,317; DW/PA/5/1600/4] <Abs 564>
John of Woodmansterne [PRO; PCC Will 1529]
Mathew of Rotherhithe [PRO; PCC Admon 1598]
Richard of Coulsdon [DW/PA/7/2 f,143; 1520]
Richard of Horley [DW/PA/5/1562/51]
Richard of Reigate [DW/PA/7/4 f,11; 1532]
Richard of Tooting [GL; Commissary Court of London Will 1455]

ATWOOD (atte WEDE,atte WODE,ATTWOD,ATTWOOD,ATTWOODE,at VODDE,ATWODE, ATWOODE,AWOD,a WOODD,AWOODE) [*continued*]

Thomas, of Great Bookham - Bagden, yeoman, senior [DW/PA/7/7 f.30; DW/PA/5/1595/3] <Abs 63>

Thomas of Coulsdon, senior [DW/PA/5/1562/27]

William, of Charlwood, husbandman, senior [DW/PA/7/2 f.24; 1491]

William, *or* William Atlee of Woking [DW/PA/5/1558/16]*

William of Wonersh [DW/PA/7/1 f.84; 1488] <Abs 283>

see also BITHEWOOD,WOOD

ATWYKE *see* ATWICK

AUBREY (AWBERYE,AWBREY,AWBRYE)

Harry of Camberwell [PRO; PCC Will 1472]

John of Lambeth, gent. [PRO; PCC Will 1590]

Richard of Surrey [PRO; PCC Will 1474]

Thomas of Long Ditton - Tolworth, victualler [DW/PA/7/9 f.309; DW/PA/5/1619/7]

AUDITOR (AWDYTOR)

Roger of Swk St Mary Magdalen, wiredrawer [DW/PA/7/3 f.176; 1531]

AUDLEY (AUDSLEY,AWDELEYE,AWDLAY)

(Lady) Ann (formerly Rogers) of Bermondsey - Bermondsey Abbey [PRO; PCC Will 1498]

Ann of Swk St Margaret, widow [DW/PA/7/4 f.192; 1537]

Joan of Richmond, widow [DW/PA/5/1574/38]

Richard of Surrey [PRO; PCC 1643, at Oxford]

Thomas of Richmond [PRO; PCC Will 1572]

Thomas, alias Thomas Luke, of Swk St Saviour; Rotherhithe - Rotherhithe Marsh, butcher [PRO; PCC Will 1610]

AUGHTON

Richard of Puttenham [PRO; PCC Will 1440]

AUSTEN (AUSTYN,AWSTEN)

Daniel of Shalford; London, merchant [PRO; PCC Will 1615]

George of Shalford, esq. [PRO; PCC Will 1621]

George of Shalford, gent. [DW/PA/7/11 f.86; DW/PA/5/1623/4]

Jane of Camberwell, spinster [PRO; PCC Will 1610]

Joan of Guildford, widow [DW/PA/5/1582/35]

John of Guildford [PRO; PCC Will 1572]

John of Shalford; Guildford, gent., senior [PRO; PCC Will 1611]

Richard of Swk St Olave, brewer [DW/PA/7/5 f.219; 1541]

Robert of Bermondsey [PRO; PCC Admon 1565]

Robert of Carshalton [DW/PA/5/1568/56]

William of Beddington [PRO; PCC 1646 *and* PCC Admon 1646]

William of Swk St Saviour, waterman [DW/PA/7/12 f.394; DW/PA/5/1638/1]

AVENELL

George of Farnham [DW/PA/7/9 f.273; 1618]

John of Godalming, butcher, senior [DW/PA/7/12 f.446; DW/PA/5/1639/1]

John of Godalming - Enton, husbandman [DW/PA/7/13 f.274; DW/PA/5/1644/4]

Richard of Farnham, butcher [HRO; 1563 B12]

Thomas of Puttenham, yeoman, senior [DW/PA/7/11 f.120; DW/PA/5/1624/6]

William of Farnham, sherman [DW/PA/7/7 f.356; DW/PA/5/1602/5] <Abs 652>

AVERED *see* EVERED

AVERY (OVERY,OVERYE)

Anthony of Carshalton [PRO; PCC Admon 1648]

Edward of Croydon; Blechingley [DW/PA/7/10 f.126; DW/PA/5/1620/87]

George of Blechingley, tanner [DW/PA/7/8 f.213; DW/PA/5/1612/115]

AVERY (OVERY,OVERYE) [*continued*]
Peter of Cranleigh, husbandman [DW/PA/7/13 f.213; DW/PA/5/1642/1]
Reynold of Swk St Saviour, tailor [DW/PA/5/1570/85]
Rosse of Swk St George, widower [DW/PA/5/1591/64 *and* DW/PA/5/1592/19*]
William of Kingston, cooper [HRO; 1637 B1]
a VICARS,a VYCARS *see* VICKERS
AWBERYE,AWBREY,AWBRYE *see* AUBREY
AWBORNE
Robert of Swk Christ Church [DW/PA/5/1593/173]
AWBREY,AWBRYE *see* AUBREY
AWCHER
John of Kingston, town clerk [DW/PA/5/1568/89]
AWCOCKE
Gertrude of Bermondsey, spinster [PRO; PCC Will 1597]
AWDELEYE,AWDLAY,AWDLEY *see* AUDLEY
AWDYTOR *see* AUDITOR
AWELLES *see* ATWELL
AWOOD,AWOODD *see* ATWOOD
AWSIBROOKE
Richard of Newington - Walworth, yeoman [LPL; 96/99; Will 1614]
AWSTEN *see* AUSTEN
AWYKELDER *see* ENTICKNAP
AYLE
Dorothy of Swk St Saviour, widow [DW/PA/7/13 f.343; 1644]
AYLEWARD *see* ALEWORD
AYLEWYN *see* ALWYN
AYLIFFE (ALIF,ALYEFE,AYLIFF,AYLOFFE)
Joan of Reigate, widow [DW/PA/5/1570/17]
John of Ockley [? HRO; 1523]
John, of Reigate, husbandman, senior [DW/PA/7/6 f.145; DW/PA/5/1559/223]
John of Reigate, weaver [DW/PA/5/1587/50]
Margaret of Runwell, Essex; Crowhurst, widow of William, esq. [PRO; PCC Will 1579] <Abs Emmison pp.52-54>
AYLING
John of Wonersh [DW/PA/7/13 f.400; 1645]
AYLMER (EYMERS)
Anthony of Kingston [DW/PA/7/5 f.153; 1540]
Thomas of Kingston - Surbiton; Harmondsworth - Longford, Middlesex, husbandman [DW/PA/7/7 f.165; DW/PA/5/1597/5] <Abs 304>
AYLEWARDE *see* ALEWORD
AYLEWYN,AYLWYN *see* ALWYN
AYLOFFE *see* AYLIFFE
AYMES *see* AMES
AYNESCOMBE,AYNSCOMBE *see* ANSCOMBE
AYRE,AYRES *see* EYRES
AYRYE *see* AIREY
AYSCUE *see* ASKEW
AYSHWORTH *see* ASHWORTH
AYSTON *see* ASTON

BABB (BABBE,BABES)
Edmund of Frensham - Pitfold, miller (yeoman in inv.) [HRO; 1633 AD6]
Edward of Bramley, clothier [DW/PA/7/6 f.92; DW/PA/5/1559/58]
George of Guildford, sherman [DW/PA/5/1558/18] (2 copies)
George of Guildford, sherman [DW/PA/5/1558/18]* [*there is a Ms note in the calendar 'compare with George B. ent^d in MS Calendar no.4 - transferred 1867'*]
John of Shalford - Snowdenham; Bramley, yeoman [DW/PA/7/7 f.39; DW/PA/5/1595/4] <Abs 78>
Mary of Bramley, widow [HRO; 1628 B3]
Richard of Wonersh, weaver [HRO; 1584 B4]
Robert of Bramley; Shalford; Dunsfold; Godalming, yeoman [DW/PA/7/9 f.115; DW/PA/5/1615/4]
William of Bramley, yeoman [PRO; PCC Will 1626]
BABINGTON (BABBINGTON)
Ellen, alias Ellen Vyne of Chertsey [PRO; PCC Admon 1630]
Ellen of Chertsey, widow [PRO; PCC Admon 1631]
Ralph of Swk St Saviour, citizen and haberdasher [DW/PA/7/11 f.465; DW/PA/5/1628/3]
BACHELER (BACHILER,BATCHELER,BATCHELLOR,BATCHELOR,BAYCHELER)
Agnes of Capel, widow [PRO; PCC Will 1598]
Eleanor of Putney [PRO; PCC Admon 1584]
Joan of Wotton; Ockley, widow of John [DW/PA/7/6 f.184; DW/PA/5/1559/206]
John of Guildford [PRO; PCC Will 1593]
John of Guildford [PRO; PCC Will 1595]
John of Horley, yeoman [PRO; PCC Will 1596]
Richard of Pirbright [DW/PA/7/8 f.22; DW/PA/5/1608/8]
Richard of Stoke next Guildford, yeoman [DW/PA/7/4 f.102; 1535]
Richard of Wotton, husbandman [DW/PA/5/1561/57]
BACK
Mary of ... [DW/PA/5/1611/5] <Abs U199>
BACKBORNE
John of Croydon [PRO; PCC Admon 1630]
BACKES *see* BAX
BACKETT *see* BECKETT
BACKHOUSE
Frances of Swk St Olave, widow [DW/PA/7/7 f.270; DW/PA/5/1599/3] <Abs 474>
Hans Williamson of Steen, Belgium [DW/PA/5/1570/12]
BACON
James of Rotherhithe (died overseas) [PRO; PCC Admon 1643]
John of Swk St Saviour - Clink Liberty [DW/PA/7/8 f.141; DW/PA/5/1611/6]
Richard, or Richard Baron of Farnham - Wrecclesham [DW/PA/7/1 f.1; 1485] <Abs 56>
BADCOCK (BADCOCKE,BADCOKE)
Daniel of Kingston, cutler [DW/PA/7/12 f.493; DW/PA/5/1638/17]
Richard of Swk St Saviour [DW/PA/5/1588/55]
Samuel of Kingston, cutler [DW/PA/7/9 f.219; DW/PA/5/1617/5]
... of Kingston [DW/PA/5/1570/4]
BADGER
Denise of Chertsey, widow [PRO; PCC Will 1626]
Isaac of Long Ditton, husbandman [DW/PA/7/9 f.109; DW/PA/5/1615/5]
John of Camberwell - Dulwich [PRO; PCC 1648]

BADGER [*continued*]
  Ralph of Chertsey - Steven's Bridge, yeoman [PRO; PCC Will 1615]
  Thomas of Battersea [PRO; PCC 1648]
  Thomas of Shalford; Wonersh; Wisborough Green, Sussex, yeoman
    [DW/PA/7/8 f.376; DW/PA/5/1612/8]
  William of Swk St George, citizen and cook [DW/PA/5/1593/38]
  William of Swk St Saviour, cordwainer [DW/PA/7/9 f.75; DW/PA/5/1614/33]
BADSEYE
  John of Newington - Walworth, yeoman [LPL; 96/111; Will 1617]
BAGENAWLE *see* BAGNALL
BAGENT (BAGINT)
  Thomas of Seale [DW/PA/7/10 f.240; DW/PA/5/1621/3]
    see also BEYGEN
BAGFORD (BAGFORDE)
  Clement of Chobham, yeoman [DW/PA/5/1591/50]
  John of Chobham, yeoman [DW/PA/7/12 f.422; DW/PA/5/1637/12]
  Lewis of Merton, yeoman [DW/PA/7/13 f.177; DW/PA/5/1641/15]
BAGINT *see* BAGENT
BAGNALL (BAGENAWLE,BAGNOWLL)
  Humphrey of ...., tailor [DW/PA/5/1582/106]
  Ralph of Tooting, clerk and parson [PRO; PCC Will 1578]
  William of Swk St Olave [DW/PA/5/1547/1]
    see also BIGNELL
BAGSETT
  Benjamin of Swk St George [DW/PA/7/11 f.259; DW/PA/5/1625/8]
BAILDON *see* BAYLDON
BAILEY, BAILY *see* BAYLEY
BAINBRIDGE (BAINBRIGG,BANBRYGE,BAYNBRYCKE)
  Barbaby of East Horsley - New Marsh, mercer [PRO; PCC Will 1613]
  Nicholas of Mortlake - Sheen, servant to the prior of Charterhouse of
    Sheen and to the convent [DW/PA/7/4 f.235; 1538]
  Ralph of Farnham, yeoman [DW/PA/5/1557/116]
    see also BENBRICKE
BAINES (BAION,BANE,BANES)
  John of Swk St Olave, yeoman [DW/PA/7/7 f.243; DW/PA/5/1598/5] <Abs 427>
  Robert of Farnham - Wrecclesham [DW/PA/7/4 f.85; 1534]
  William of Swk St Olave, citizen and butcher [DW/PA/7/13 f.145;
    DW/PA/5/1641/8]
BAINHAM (BAYNAM)
  Robert of Swk St George [DW/PA/5/1592/77]
  Thomas of Newington, citizen and merchant tailor [PRO; PCC Will 1582]
BAION *see* BAINES
BAISMORE *see* BASSMORE
BAKER (BAKAR,le BAKERES)
  Abraham of Shalford; Dunsfold; Bramley [DW/PA/7/7 f.389;
    DW/PA/5/1601/4] <Abs 723>
  Agnes of Camberwell [PRO; PCC Will 1503; CCAL; 1503 f.259v]
  Agnes of Guildford St Nicolas [DW/PA/7/11 f.164; DW/PA/5/1625/9]
  Christiana of Shalford, widow [HRO; 1619 B3]
  Eleanor of Newington [PRO; PCC Admon 1593]
  Elizabeth of Crowhurst [DW/PA/7/2 f.13; 1489]
  Elizabeth of Windlesham - Bagshot, widow [PRO; PCC Will 1615]
  George of Thursley; Haslemere, husbandman [DW/PA/7/7 f.561;
    DW/PA/5/1606/4] <Abs 1049>

BAKER (BAKAR, le BAKERES) [*continued*]
Gillian of Mitcham, widow [DW/PA/7/7 f.161; DW/PA/5/1597/6] <Abs 298>
Henry of Camberwell - Peckham; Camberwell - Dulwich; Newington - Walworth, gent. [DW/PA/5/1557/52]
Henry of Dorking [DW/PA/7/2 f.7; 1491]
Humphrey of Swk St Saviour, innholder [DW/PA/7/10 f.286; DW/PA/5/1623/6]
James of Reigate, weaver [DW/PA/7/7 f.643; DW/PA/5/1608/4] <Abs 1209>
Joan of Burstow, widow [DW/PA/5/1561/46]
Joan of Charlwood, widow [LPL; 96/116; Will 1648]
Joan of Kingston [HRO; Reg. Edn 2 p.18; 1348]
Joan of Kingston, widow [DW/PA/5/1546/20]
John of Camberwell - Peckham Rye [PRO; PCC Will 1492]
John of Camberwell, senior [PRO; PCC Will 1500; CCAL; 1500 f.11a]
John of Compton [DW/PA/5/1568/37]
John of Guildford Holy Trinity [DW/PA/7/5 f.65; 1539] <Abs 53>
John, alias John Leadford of Ockley [PRO; PCC 1637]
John of Pirbright [PRO; PCC Will 1586]
John of Pirbright, yeoman [PRO; PCC Will 1626]
John of Reigate [DW/PA/7/2 f.209; ?1490-1524]
John of East Greenwich, Kent - H.M.Armoury; Reigate; Croydon [LPL; Reg. Abp Whitgift i f.250; Will 1589]
John of Richmond [PRO; PCC Admon 1613]
John of Rotherhithe; ship *Expedition* [PRO; PCC Will 1614]
John of Shalford - East Shalford [DW/PA/5/1550/91]
John of Shalford - East Shalford, husbandman [DW/PA/7/7 f.588; DW/PA/5/1607/5] <Abs 1096>
John of Swk St Olave; Horsham, Sussex [LPL; Reg. Abp Arundel i f.232; Will 1406]
John of Swk St Olave, cordwainer [DW/PA/7/8 f.86; DW/PA/5/1609/16]
Leonard of Molesey [PRO; PCC Will 1591]
Margaret of Selborne, Hampshire, widow [DW/PA/7/11 f.434; DW/PA/5/1627/3]
Margery of Mortlake [PRO; PCC Will 1471]
Nicholas of 'the highway between Sow Street and Wood Lane' [DW/PA/5/1557/58]
Nicholas of Charlwood, husbandman [LPL; Reg. Abp Abbot i f.279; Will 1615]
Phillis of Pirbright, widow [DW/PA/7/6 f.102; DW/PA/5/1559/56]
Richard of Camberwell - Peckham [PRO; PCC Will 1517]
Richard of Dorking, gent. [PRO; PCC Will 1560]
Richard, alias Richard Chapman of Kingston - Ham, yeoman [DW/PA/5/1568/3]
Richard of Reigate; Horley; West Hoathly, Sussex; Horsted Keynes, Sussex, senior [DW/PA/7/7 f.341; DW/PA/5/1601/5] <Abs 619>
Richard of Reigate, yeoman [DW/PA/7/11 f.78; DW/PA/5/1623/7]
Richard of Reigate, yeoman [DW/PA/7/11 f.441; DW/PA/5/1628/4]
Richard of Reigate [PRO; PCC Admon 1648]
Richard of Send [DW/PA/7/1 f.59; 1487] <Abs 195>
Richard of Shalford; Albury, husbandman [DW/PA/7/5 f.210; 1541]
Richard of Shalford - East Shalford, brickmaker [DW/PA/7/7 f.146; DW/PA/5/1597/7] <Abs 269>
Robert of Guildford St Nicolas [HRO; 1614 B2]
Robert of Swk St Saviour, waterman [DW/PA/7/11 f.9; DW/PA/5/1622/2]
Robert of Wonersh [DW/PA/5/1558/21]*
Sarah of Bentley, Hampshire [DW/PA/7/10 f.12; DW/PA/5/1619/8]
Thomas of Albury [*in* DW/PA/5/1544/6]

BAKER (BAKAR, le BAKERES) [*continued*]
  Thomas of Chessington [DW/PA/7/11 f.484; DW/PA/5/1628/5]
  Thomas of East Horsley, blacksmith [PRO; PCC Will 1605] <Abs SAC v.12 p.97>
  Thomas of Guildford, clothier [PRO; PCC Will 1585]
  Thomas, alias Thomas Chapman of Kingston - Ham Hatch, yeoman [PRO; PCC Will 1600]
  Thomas of Pirbright [DW/PA/7/8 f.41; DW/PA/5/1607/6]
  Thomas of Reigate [DW/PA/7/12 f.180; DW/PA/5/1633/11]
  Thomas of Windlesham - Bagshot, innholder [DW/PA/7/8 f.212; DW/PA/5/1612/9]
  William of ... [DW/PA/7/2 f.30; 1492]
  William of ...., citizen and leatherdresser [DW/PA/5/1601/6] <Abs U29>
  William of Blechingley [HRO; 1518 B1]
  William of Dunsfold [HRO; 1570 AD6]
  William of Mitcham, yeoman [DW/PA/5/1596/2] <Abs U1>
  William of Newington [LPL; 98/1 f.9v; Will 1630]
  William of Putney [LPL; 98/1 f.119v ren.; 1640]
  William of Reigate [DW/PA/7/5 f.193; 1540]
  William of Reigate, cordwainer [DW/PA/5/1571/59]
  William of Shalford - West Shalford [DW/PA/7/11 f.363; DW/PA/5/1626/10]
BALCH *see* BALCHIN
BALCHILD (BALDCHILDE, BALCHYLD, BALCHYLDE, BULCHILL)
  Henry of Bramley; Shalford; Godalming, husbandman [DW/PA/7/8 f.232; DW/PA/5/1612/10]
  Joan, alias Joan Balchen of Cranleigh [DW/PA/5/1584/1]*
  John of Bramley, carpenter [DW/PA/7/7 f.640; DW/PA/5/1608/5] <Abs 1199>
  John of Cranleigh, husbandman [DW/PA/7/7 f.583; DW/PA/5/1607/7] <Abs 1085>
  Richard of Cranleigh, husbandman [DW/PA/5/1571/25]
  Thomas of Cranleigh [DW/PA/7/4 f.117; 1535]
  William of Shalford [DW/PA/7/6 f.173; DW/PA/5/1559/155]
BALCHIN (BALCH, BALCHEN, BALCHINNE)
  Henry of Bramley, yeoman [DW/PA/7/13 f.412; DW/PA/5/1645/5]
  Joan, alias Joan Baldchilde of Cranleigh [DW/PA/5/1584/1]*
  John of Bramley, yeoman [DW/PA/7/13 f.43; DW/PA/5/1639/22]
  John of Cranleigh, husbandman [DW/PA/7/7 f.173; DW/PA/5/1597/8] <Abs 319>
  Richard of Farnham [PRO; PCC Will 1495]
  William of Witley - Brook, senior [PRO; PCC 1648]
BALDCHILDE *see* BALCHILD
BALDEN *see* BALDWIN
BALDING, BALDINGE *see* BALDWIN
BALDOCKE
  George of Kingston, yeoman of the king's chamber [DW/PA/7/7 f.225; DW/PA/5/1598/6] <Abs 398>
BALDWIN (BALDEN, BALDINGE, BALDWINE, BALDWYN, BALDYNG, BALLDING, BAULDIN, BAULDING)
  Agnes of Farnham - Tilford [DW/PA/7/4 ff.72,73; 1534]
  Edmund of Battersea - Penge [PRO; PCC Will 1618]
  John of Albury, tanner [DW/PA/7/12 f.270; DW/PA/5/1635/4]
  John of Charlwood, husbandman [LPL; 96/121; 98/1 f.63v; Will 1634]
  John of Compton, husbandman [DW/PA/7/12 f.295; DW/PA/5/1635/8]
  John of Elstead, carpenter [DW/PA/7/12 f.429; DW/PA/5/1637/14]
  John of Farnham - Tilford [DW/PA/7/3 f.138; 1530]
  John of Farnham - Wrecclesham, yeoman [DW/PA/7/12 f.108; DW/PA/5/1632/6]

BALDWIN(BALDEN,BALDINGE,BALDWINE,BALDWYN,BALDYNG,BALLDING,BAULDIN,BAULDING)
[*continued*]

John of Frensham; Haslemere; Linchmere, Sussex, tanner [DW/PA/7/7 f.17; DW/PA/5/1595/5] <Abs 38>

John of Godalming - Shackleford, husbandman, senior [DW/PA/5/1605/5] <Abs U126>

Marlyan of Shalford; Godalming, yeoman [DW/PA/7/11 f.436; DW/PA/5/1628/12]

Nicholas of Croydon [LPL; 98/1 f.108r; Will 1639]

Peter of Croydon [PRO; PCC Admon 1569]

Richard of Battersea - Penge, yeoman [PRO; PCC Will 1616]

Robert of Cranleigh [DW/PA/7/11 f.538; DW/PA/5/1629/4]

Thomas of Swk St George, feltmaker [DW/PA/7/8 f.184; DW/PA/5/1610/13]

William of Charlwood, husbandman [LPL; 96/122; 98/1 f.116r; Will 1640]

William of Godalming - Catteshall, husbandman [DW/PA/7/8 f.19; DW/PA/5/1608/6]

William of Lingfield, yeoman [DW/PA/7/12 f.304; DW/PA/5/1636/3]

BALE, BALEY *see* BAYLEY

BALINFORD

Joan of Swk St Olave, widow [DW/PA/7/12 f.331; DW/PA/5/1636/13]

BALL (BALLE,BAULE)

Dorothy of Swk St Saviour [DW/PA/7/11 f.371; DW/PA/5/1626/11]

Edward of Lambeth - Stockwell, esq. [PRO; PCC *and* PCC Admon 1649]

John, alias John Barley of Hascombe, wheeler [DW/PA/7/6 f.108; 1559]

John of Kingston, gent., junior [PRO; PCC 1647]

John of Swk - French Church near London Bridge [DW/PA/5/1593/89]

Richard of Lambeth - Stockwell [PRO; PCC 1646]

Richard of Lambeth - Stockwell [PRO; PCC 1649]

Robert of Oxted [DW/PA/7/1 f.13; 1485] <Abs 42>

William of Wimbledon [PRO; PCC Admon 1608]

BALLARD (BALLARDE,BALLART)

Adrian of Christ Church, London; Mortlake [PRO; PCC 1640]

Christopher of Wandsworth [PRO; PCC Will 1615]

John of Oxted [PRO; PCC 1649]

Robert of Lambeth - Water Lambeth, yeoman [DW/PA/5/1576/151]

Robert of Swk St Olave; Bexley, Kent [DW/PA/7/6 f.219; 1561]

Simon of ... [Dutch] [DW/PA/7/7 f.507; DW/PA/5/1605/8] <Abs 949>

BALLDING *see* BALDWIN

BALLE *see* BALL

BALNOT

John of Thorpe [DW/PA/5/1552/24]

BALY *see* BAYLEY

BAMBER (BAMB'R)

Agnes of Byfleet, widow of Richard [DW/PA/5/1546/33] [*filed with husband's will*]

Richard of Byfleet, husbandman [DW/PA/5/1546/33]

BAMLETT (BAMLATT)

John of Effingham, husbandman [DW/PA/7/7 f.331; DW/PA/5/1601/7] <Abs 595>

Nicholas of Alfold, yeoman [DW/PA/7/12 f.515; DW/PA/5/1638/21]

Richard of Alfold, bachelor [PRO; PCC Admon 1626]

BAMPTON

Robert of Bermondsey [DW/PA/7/5 f.216; 1541]

BANASTER *see* BANNISTER

BANBRIDGE *see* BAINBRIDGE

BANCKES, BANCKS *see* BANKS
BANDERBRIGG
  Christian Earth of ... [DW/PA/7/8 f.72; 1609]
BANDY
  Agnes of Swk St Olave [DW/PA/7/2 f.48; 1497]
BANE, BANES *see* BAINES
BANESTER, BANESTRE, BANISTER *see* BANNISTER
BANKS (BANCKES,BANCKS,BANKES,BYNCKES)
  Agnes, alias Agnes Haman of Battersea, widow [DW/PA/5/1562/42]
  Francis of Lambeth - Water Lambeth, victualler [DW/PA/7/8 f.284; DW/PA/5/1613/7]
  John of Bermondsey [DW/PA/5/1593/121]
  John of Richmond [PRO; PCC Will 1590]
  Matthew of Swk St Olave [DW/PA/5/1603/9] <Abs U60>
  Peter of Bermondsey, matlayer [DW/PA/7/11 f.115; DW/PA/5/1624/7]
  Richard of Swk St Saviour, baker [DW/PA/7/12 f.182; DW/PA/5/1633/10]
  Richard of Streatham - Tooting Bec [PRO; PCC Will 1639]
  Thomas of Farnham [DW/PA/7/2 f.104; 1513]
BANNASTER, BANNESTER *see* BANNISTER
BANNETT *see* BENNETT
BANNISTER (BANASTER,BANESTER,BANESTRE,BANISTER,BANNASTER,BANNESTER, BANNYSTER,BANYSTER)
  Alice wife of John of Limpsfield [PRO; PCC 1620] <see Soame 809>
  Ann [*altered from Jane*] of All Hallows, [?]London; bequest to Chertsey [DW/PA/7/6 f.206; 1560]
  Bartholomew of Croydon, gent. [PRO; PCC Will 1626]
  Daniel of Rotherhithe [PRO; PCC Will 1631]
  Edward of Putney, esq. [PRO; PCC Will 1606]
  Edward of Swk St Olave, leatherdresser [DW/PA/5/1593/170]
  Emma of Worplesdon - Burpham [DW/PA/7/8 f.64; DW/PA/5/1609/10]
  George of Chertsey, tailor [DW/PA/5/1588/8]
  Gilbert of Lingfield - Dormansland, baker [DW/PA/7/11 f.59; DW/PA/5/1623/8]
  Henry of Chertsey, clerk of the king's works [PRO; PCC Will 1613]
  Henry of Guildford, yeoman, senior [DW/PA/5/1587/40]
  Henry of Guildford Holy Trinity, senior [DW/PA/5/1586/25]*
  Joan (later Joan Everarde) of Surrey [PRO; PCC Will 1551]
  John of Chertsey, husbandman [HRO; 1561 B14-15]
  John of Cranleigh [DW/PA/7/5 f.16; 1538] <Abs 25>
  John of Guildford [? HRO; 1567]
  John of Guildford Holy Trinity [DW/PA/7/7 f.557; DW/PA/5/1606/5] <Abs 1042>
  John, alias John Caron of Kingston [PRO; PCC Admon 1590]
  John of Limpsfield, yeoman, senior [DW/PA/7/12 f.76; DW/PA/5/1632/4]
  John of Shere, clerk [PRO; PCC Will 1516] <Abs SAC v.8 p.229>
  John of Swk St George, innholder [DW/PA/5/1592/52]
  Margaret of Worplesdon, widow [DW/PA/7/1 f.4; 1480] <Abs 11>
  Nicholas of Worplesdon [HRO; Reg. Fox 2 p.29; 1507]
  Richard of Limpsfield, yeoman [DW/PA/7/8 f.154; DW/PA/5/1611/7]
  Roger of Windlesham [DW/PA/7/2 f.144; 1520]
  Thomas of Bisley [DW/PA/7/9 f.270; 1618]
  Thomas of Thames Ditton, yeoman [PRO; PCC Will 1627]
  Thomas of Lambeth [DW/PA/7/8 f.282; DW/PA/5/1613/8]

BANNISTER (BANASTER,BANESTER,BANESTRE,BANISTER,BANNASTER,BANNESTER, BANNYSTER,BANYSTER) [*continued*]

Thomas of Swk St Saviour - Upper Ground, yeoman [DW/PA/7/7 f.34; DW/PA/5/1595/6] <Abs 70>

Thomas of Worplesdon, yeoman [DW/PA/5/1579/12]*

Valentine of Swk St Olave, carver [DW/PA/7/7 f.343; DW/PA/5/1601/8] <Abs 625>

William of Chertsey, yeoman [DW/PA/7/7 f.511; DW/PA/5/1605/9] <Abs 959>

William of Windlesham [DW/PA/7/6 f.203; 1560]

William of Windlesham, yeoman, senior [DW/PA/7/12 f.218; DW/PA/5/1633/15]

William of Worplesdon [DW/PA/5/1545/4]

William of Worplesdon, yeoman [DW/PA/7/9 f.69; DW/PA/5/1614/12]

BANNOCK (BANNOK)

John of ...., minstrel [DW/PA/7/2 f.94; 1513] <Abs SAC v.1 pp.183-184>

BANNYSTER *see* BANNISTER

BANWELL

Thomas of Frimley, blacksmith [DW/PA/7/8 f.253; DW/PA/5/1613/9]

BANYSTER *see* BANNISTER

BARBER (BARBAR,BARBOR,BARBOUR).

Edmund of Swk St Mary Magdalen [BM; Add.Ms 24,925 f.13v; 1544] <Abs 25>

Edward of Blechingley [PRO; PCC Admon 1582]

Edward of Blechingley [PRO; PCC Will 1584]

Edward, alias Edward a Strete of Shalford; Wonersh [DW/PA/7/4 f.82; 1534]

Nicholas of Croydon, weaver [LPL; 96/140; Will 1625]

Thomas of Ockham, gent. [PRO; PCC 1639]

Thomas of Ockham [PRO; PCC Admon 1640]

BARBON

Thomas of Charlwood; Lambeth [PRO; PCC Will 1507]

BARCLAY *see* BARKLEY, BARQUELEY

BARCROFT (BARCROFTE)

Edmund of Croydon, gent. [GL; Archdeaconry Court of London Will 1629]

John of Croydon; Swk St Olave [PRO; PCC Will 1616]

BARCSCHYRE *see* BERKSHIRE

BARDEN

John of Godstone [DW/PA/5/1591/43]

BARDESLIE

John of Lambeth - Kennington, yeoman [PRO; PCC Will 1627]

BARDSAIE

Edmund of Surrey [PRO; C146 9638; Will 1498]

BARDWELL

Mary, *or* Mary Bradwell of Rotherhithe, widow [PRO; PCC Will 1627]

BAREFOOTE

Roger of Swk St Saviour, tanner [DW/PA/7/10 f.160; DW/PA/5/1621/5]

BARETT *see* BARRETT

BAREW *see* BARROW

BAREY

James of Guildford Holy Trinity [DW/PA/7/5 f.32; 1538] <Abs 51>

BARGETT

Thomas of Swk St Margaret [DW/PA/7/5 f.126; 1539]

BARKER

Elizabeth of Bermondsey, widow [PRO; PCC 1646]

Gillian of Windlesham [DW/PA/7/12 f.356; DW/PA/5/1638/5]

BARKER [*continued*]
Griffin of Rotherhithe, tailor [DW/PA/7/7 f.296; DW/PA/5/1600/5] <Abs 531>
James of Tooting; Streatham, junior [PRO; PCC 1633]
John of Chiswick, Middlesex; Godalming [PRO; PCC Will 1595] <Abs SAC v.28 p.84>
John of Godalming [PRO; PCC Admon 1618]
Robert of Lambeth, citizen and cordwainer [PRO; PCC Will 1624]
Robert of Lambeth - Kentish St. [GL; Archdeaconry Court of London Will 1629]
Samuel of Pirbright [PRO; PCC Admon 1584]
Thomas of Kingston, gent. [PRO; PCC Will 1617]
William of Bermondsey, fellmonger [DW/PA/7/11 f.323; DW/PA/5/1625/10]
William of Swk St Olave, citizen and woodmonger [DW/PA/7/11 f.546; DW/PA/5/1629/5]

BARKESHERE *see* BERKSHIRE

BARKHAM
Brian of Dorking, yeoman [PRO; PCC Will 1620] <Soame 69>

BARKLEY
John of Swk St Margaret, clerk [DW/PA/7/2 f.50; 1496]
see also BARQUELEY

BARLE *see* BARLEY

BARLET
Nicholas of Swk St Margaret [DW/PA/7/2 f.52; 1497]

BARLEY (BARLE, BARLEE)
John of Bermondsey [PRO; PCC Will 1409]
John, alias John Ball of Hascombe, wheeler [DW/PA/7/6 f.108; DW/PA/5/1559/57]
John of Swk St Saviour - Clink Liberty, whitebaker [DW/PA/7/9 f.213; DW/PA/5/1617/6]
Robert of Lambeth [PRO; PCC Admon 1636]
William of Newington, skinner [PRO; PCC Will 1612]

BARLING
William of Bermondsey [PRO; PCC 1648]

BARLOW (BARLOWE)
James of ... [DW/PA/7/9 f.329; DW/PA/5/1620/3]
John of Chiddingfold, clerk [PRO; PCC 1640 *and* PCC Admon 1641]
William of Croydon, bishop of Lincoln [PRO; PCC Will 1613]

BARMWELL
Edward of Streatham, husbandman [DW/PA/7/10 f.95; DW/PA/5/1619/9]

BARNABY
George of Croydon, tailor [LPL; 96/147; Will 1618]
John of Croydon [LPL; 98/1 f.4v; Will 1629]
Mary, alias Mary Parbyn of Swk St Olave, widow [DW/PA/7/7 f.550; DW/PA/5/1606/68] <Abs 1031>
Thomas of Croydon, yeoman [LPL; 96/148; 98/1 f.68r; Will 1635]
William of Croydon [PRO; PCC 1649]
William of Swk St Saviour [DW/PA/7/7 f.526; 1607] <Abs 991>

BARNAM
Francis of Surrey, citizen and draper [PRO; PCC Will 1576]

BARNARD (BARNARDE, BARNERD)
George of Bermondsey, saddler [DW/PA/5/1579/20]*
Helen, alias Helen Netlenigham of Wandsworth [PRO; PCC Admon 1638]
John of Dorking [HRO; 1587 AD3]

BARNARD (BARNARDE,BARNERD) [*continued*]
John of Ewell [DW/PA/7/4 f.120; 1535]
Richard of Thorpe [HRO; Reg. Fox 3 p.66; 1515]
Thomas of Nutfield [PRO; PCC Will 1495]
Thomas of Send [DW/PA/5/1571/91]
William of Leigh, senior [*in* DW/PA/5/1544/5]

BARNARDISTON (BARNARDESTON)
George of Chertsey [PRO; PCC Admon 1571]
George of Chertsey, gent. [PRO; PCC Admon 1579]
George of Chertsey [PRO; PCC Admon 1583]

BARNBURY (BARNB'R,BARNBURE)
Agnes of Byfleet, widow of Richard [DW/PA/5/1546/33]
John of Send [DW/PA/7/1 f.17; 1485] <Abs 58>
Richard of Byfleet, husbandman [DW/PA/5/1546/33]

BARNE *see* BARNES

BARNERD *see* BARNARD

BARNES (BARNE)
Alexander of Guildford, tailor [DW/PA/7/11 f.592; DW/PA/5/1630/3]
Edmund of Swk St Olave, feltmaker [DW/PA/7/12 f.164; DW/PA/5/1633/6]
Henry of Lambeth [PRO; PCC Admon 1640]
Henry of Swk St Saviour [DW/PA/7/7 f.642; DW/PA/5/1608/7] <Abs 1205>
John of Croydon, tailor [LPL; 96/151; Will 1615]
John of Croydon, tailor [LPL; Reg. Abp Abbot i f.272; Will 1615]
John of Egham, yeoman [DW/PA/5/1562/71]
John of Epsom [PRO; PCC 1646]
John of Guildford St Mary, smith [DW/PA/5/1591/47]
John of Kingston [DW/PA/7/13 f.281; DW/PA/5/1643/10]
John of Lambeth, bachelor [PRO; PCC 1649]
John of Nutfield, husbandman [DW/PA/5/1570/40]
John of Sanderstead, tailor [DW/PA/7/9 f.134; DW/PA/5/1615/6]
Jonas of Rotherhithe, mariner (died overseas) [GL; Commissary Court of London Will 1625]
Ralph of Carshalton, husbandman [DW/PA/5/1574/17]
Ralph of Titsey [PRO; PCC 1635]
Ralph of Wimbledon, yeoman [LPL; 96/152; Will 1626]
Richard of Bermondsey, tanner [DW/PA/7/9 f.203; DW/PA/5/1616/7]
Richard of Wonersh - Tangley, esq. [PRO; PCC Will 1621]
Robert of Rotherhithe, shipwright [DW/PA/7/11 f.534; DW/PA/5/1629/7]
Robert of Shere [DW/PA/5/1568/7]
Robert of Sutton, husbandman [DW/PA/7/12 f.249; DW/PA/5/1636/8]
Roger of Kingston, ironmonger [PRO; PCC Will 1614]
Susan of Epsom, widow [DW/PA/7/12 f.295; DW/PA/5/1635/9]
Thomas of Guildford, tailor [PRO; PCC Will 1621]
Thomas of Guildford St Mary, blacksmith [HRO; 1578 B7]
Thomas of Newington [LPL; 98/1 f.74r; Will 1636]
William of Bentley, Hampshire, husbandman [DW/PA/7/13 f.51; DW/PA/5/1639/26]
William of Newington [LPL; 98/1 ff.74v (ren.),83v; Will 1636,1637]
William of Nutfield, senior [HRO; 1585 B5]
see also BRAON

BARNESLEY, BARNESLAY *see* BARNSLEY

BARNET *see* BARNETT

BARNETER
Walter of Wonersh [DW/PA/7/1 f.86; 1488] <Abs 288>

BARNETT (BARNET)
Thomas of Chertsey [DW/PA/7/11 f.96; DW/PA/5/1624/8]
William of Sutton, clerk [PRO; PCC Will 1451] <Abs, SAC v.52 pp.44-45>
BARNHAM *see* BARNAM
BARNSDALE
Faith of Wandsworth; St Sepulchre, London, widow of William [DW/PA/7/8 f.244; DW/PA/5/1613/10]
BARNSLEY (BARNESLEY,BARNESLAY)
Ann, alias Ann Norfolke of Lambeth [PRO; PCC Admon 1649]
Richard of Lambeth, gent. [PRO; PCC Will 1624]
Richard of Lambeth - Water Lambeth, gent. [PRO; PCC 1634]
Richard of Lambeth [PRO; PCC 1649]
BARNWELL *see* BARMWELL
BARON
John of Bermondsey, clerk and rector[DW/PA/5/1580/6] *and* [PRO; PCC Will 1580]
Richard of Farnham - Wrecclesham [DW/PA/7/1 f.17; 1485] <Abs 56>
William of Swk St Olave, brewer [DW/PA/7/2 f.79; 1502]
see also BRAON
BAROP
John of Swk St Olave [HRO; Reg. Fox 3 p.68; 1517]
BAROW *see* BARROW
BARQUELEY
Alexander, D.D. of Croydon, clerk [PRO; PCC Will 1552]
see also BARKLEY
BARRETT (BARETT,BARRAT)
Edmund of Cheam, sergeant of H.M. cellar [PRO; PCC 1631]
Gregory of Wandsworth, waterman [DW/PA/7/13 f.35; DW/PA/5/1639/18]
John of Croydon, gent. [PRO; PCC Will 1487]
John of Witley, senior, husbandman [DW/PA/5/1546/70]
John of Witley - Wheelerstreet, senior, yeoman [DW/PA/7/7 f.167; DW/PA/5/1597/9] <Abs 308>
John of Witley - Wheelerstreet; Godalming, yeoman [DW/PA/7/7 f.255; DW/PA/5/1599/4] <Abs 450>
John of Witley [PRO; PCC Admon 1637]
Margaret of Swk St Saviour, widow [DW/PA/7/10 f.213; DW/PA/5/1620/4]
Richard of Newington [LPL; 98/1 f.75r (ren.); 1636]
Richard of Swk St Olave; Canterbury Christ Church, Kent, tailor [DW/PA/5/1546/91]
Thomas of Witley [PRO; PCC Will 1560]
William of Bermondsey, fellmonger [DW/PA/7/12 f.84; DW/PA/5/1633/19]
BARRON *see* BRAON
BARROW (BAREW,BAROW,BARROWES)
Margaret of Lambeth, widow of Thomas Barbon [DW/PA/7/3 f.189; 1531]
Maud of Croydon [PRO; PCC Will 1448]
Richard of Swk St Olave, hosier [DW/PA/7/11 f.151; DW/PA/5/1625/11]
see also BURROWS
BARRY *see* BAREY
BARTELETT *see* BARTLETT
BARTELMWE *see* BARTHOLOMEW
BARTERAME
Richard of Swk St Margaret [DW/PA/7/5 f.75; 1539]

BARTHOLOMEW (BARTELMWE,BARTHELMEW,BARTHOLMEW,BARTILMEW,BARTLEMEW, BARTLMEWE,BARTOLLMEW,BARTYLLMEW)

John of Farnborough, Hampshire; Ash; Frimley, yeoman [DW/PA/7/10 f,287; DW/PA/5/1623/9]

John of Egham - Englefield, yeoman [DW/PA/5/1575/77]

John of Egham - Englefield, yeoman [DW/PA/7/7 f,504; DW/PA/5/1605/10] <Abs 943>

John of Egham - Englefield, yeoman [DW/PA/7/13 f,84; DW/PA/5/1640/14]

John of Frimley, senior [PRO; PCC Will 1595]

Peter of Swk St Olave, bachelor [DW/PA/7/12 f,368; DW/PA/5/1627/4]

Thomas of Egham, husbandman [DW/PA/7/6 f,16; DW/PA/5/1559/5]

William of Swk St George [? HRO; 1552]

BARTLEM

John of Swk St Saviour - Paris Garden Liberty [DW/PA/5/1606/6] <Abs U186>

Nicholas of Swk St Saviour - Paris Garden Liberty, waterman [DW/PA/7/11 f,135; DW/PA/5/1624/10]

BARTLEMEW *see* BARTHOLOMEW

BARTLETT (BARTELETT,BARTLET)

Andrew of Lambeth [PRO; PCC Admon 1648]

Anthony of Lambeth [PRO; PCC Admon 1618]

Joan of Cheam, spinster [PRO; PCC 1648]

John of Reigate [HRO; 1557 U50-51]

John of Reigate [DW/PA/7/6 f,268; 1560]

Juliana of Malden, widow [DW/PA/7/10 f,118; DW/PA/5/1620/5]

Katherine of Ockley [DW/PA/5/1621/6] <Abs U246>

Katherine of Reigate, widow [PRO; PCC Will 1559]

Richard of Malden, husbandman [DW/PA/7/13 f,252; DW/PA/5/1640/24]

Robert of Betchworth [DW/PA/5/1579/14]*

Thomas of Thorpe [DW/PA/7/4 f,27; 1533]

BARTLMEWE, BARTOLLMEW *see* BARTHOLOMEW

BARTON (BARTUN)

Abraham of Swk St Olave, bricklayer [DW/PA/7/12 f,69; DW/PA/5/1631/22]

John of Bramley, brewer [HRO; 1640 B6]

John of Woking, yeoman [DW/PA/5/1558/22]*

Robert of Woking [DW/PA/7/4 f,188; 1536]

William of Swk St Olave, baker [DW/PA/7/1 f,26; 1486] <Abs 85>

William of Woking, husbandman [DW/PA/5/1576/68]

see also ABARTON

BARTYLLMEW *see* BARTHOLOMEW

BARWICK (BARWICKE,BARWYKE)

Agnes of Swk St George, widow [DW/PA/7/10 f,259; DW/PA/5/1622/3]

Ambrose of Swk St Olave, servant to John Cooper, shoemaker [DW/PA/5/1569/71]

Henry of West Clandon [DW/PA/7/5 f,118; 1539]

John of Swk St George, brewer [DW/PA/7/7 f,430; DW/PA/5/1603/10] <Abs 811>

John of Swk St Olave, shoemaker [DW/PA/7/12 f,31; DW/PA/5/1631/14]

Joyce of Walton, maidservant, spinster [PRO; PCC Will 1564]

BASELEY

Thomas of Swk St Saviour [DW/PA/7/12 f,137; DW/PA/5/1632/15]

William of Lambeth, esq, [PRO; PCC Will 1574]

BASEMORE *see* BASSMORE

BASFORD

Henry of Swk St Olave, woodmonger [DW/PA/7/10 f,197; DW/PA/5/1621/7]

BASINGTON *see* BASSINGTON

BASKERVILE

Ann of Bermondsey - Bermondsey Monastery [PRO; PCC Will 1517]

BASSANO (BASSONO)

Andrea of Horne, gent. [PRO; PCC Will 1626]

Robert of Horne, gent. [PRO; PCC Will 1625]

BASSEMORE *see* BASSMORE

BASSETT (BASSATE,BASSET)

Alice of Swk St Mary Overy [DW/PA/5/1575/32]

Anthony of Caterham, husbandman [DW/PA/7/7 f.108; DW/PA/5/1596/4] <Abs 195>

Edward of Horne, husbandman [DW/PA/7/13 f.18; DW/PA/5/1639/14]

John, of Chelsham; Tatsfield; Cowden, Kent, yeoman, senior [DW/PA/5/1555/49]

John of Chelsham - Bedlested; Tatsfield; Caterham yeoman [DW/PA/5/1601/9] <Abs U30>

John of Oxted; Croydon, yeoman [DW/PA/7/7 f.52; DW/PA/5/1596/5] <Abs 99>

John of Sanderstead, yeoman [DW/PA/7/13 f.319; DW/PA/5/1646/5]

John of Swk St Olave, leatherdresser [DW/PA/7/12 f.520; DW/PA/5/1638/22]

Robert of Chelsham [PRO; PCC Admon 1636]

Robert of Coulsdon [DW/PA/7/5 f.59; 1539] <Abs 23>

Robert of Stoke next Guildford, clerk [HRO; Reg. Fox 3 p.67; 1516]

Stephen of Tandridge [PRO; PCC 1647]

Thomas of Beddington - Wallington [DW/PA/7/5 f.101; 1539]

Thomas of Coulsdon [DW/PA/7/5 f.97; 1539]

Thomas of Coulsdon; Caterham, husbandman [DW/PA/7/8 f.44; DW/PA/5/1609/18]

Thomas of Coulsdon [PRO; PCC 1648]

William of Guildford; Westerham, Kent [LPL; Reg. Abp Chichele i f.418; Will 1429]

BASSINGTON (BASINGDEN,BASYNGDEN,BASYNGTON)

Agnes of Camberwell, widow [DW/PA/5/1550/37]

Elizabeth of Camberwell - Peckham Rye, widow [BM; Add.Ms 24,925 f.13r; 1545] <Abs 23>

Richard of Camberwell, yeoman [HRO; 1569 B14-15]

Richard of Camberwell, tailor [DW/PA/7/7 f.438; DW/PA/5/1603/11] <Abs 829>

BASSMORE (BAISMORE,BASEMORE,BASSEMORE)

Edward of Streatham - Upper Tooting [DW/PA/7/13 f.22; DW/PA/5/1640/7]

John of Thames Ditton, wheelwright [DW/PA/7/7 f.584; DW/PA/5/1607/9] <Abs 1088>

John of Esher, husbandman [HRO; 1557 U29-30]

John of Esher, husbandman [HRO; 1606 B4] [*and*] [DW/PA/7/7 f.520; DW/PA/5/1606/7] <Abs 977>

Robert of Esher, husbandman [DW/PA/5/1591/72]

BASSONO *see* BASSANO

BASTABLE

Gregory of Swk St Saviour, waterman [DW/PA/7/12 f.83; DW/PA/5/1633/18]

BASYNGDEN, BASYNGTON *see* BASINGDEN

BAT *see* BATT

BATCHELER,BATCHELLOR,BATCHELOR *see* BACHELER

BATCOCK *see* BATTCOCK

BATE *see* BATES

BATELL *see* BATTLE

BATEMAN
  Gilbert of Streatham [DW/PA/7/4 f,26; 1533]
  Luke of Woking [PRO; PCC Will 1616]
  Martin of Swk, tailor [DW/PA/5/1587/91]
  Richard of Bermondsey [PRO; PCC Admon 1564]
BATES (BATE)
  Edward of Mitcham [PRO; PCC Admon 1596]
  Elizabeth of Swk St Mary Overy, widow [DW/PA/5/1558/23]*
  Humphrey of Swk St Saviour, waterman [DW/PA/7/10 f,210; DW/PA/5/1620/6]
  John of Swk St Olave [DW/PA/7/2 f,56; 1499]
  John of Richmond [PRO; PCC Admon 1622]
  Nicholas of Putney [LPL; 98/1 f,65r; Will 1635]
  Stephen of Long Ditton [DW/PA/7/3 f,174; 1531]
  Thomas of Chertsey, citizen and mercer, senior [PRO; PCC Will 1612]
  William of Bermondsey [PRO; PCC 1641]
BATHURSTE
  Richard of Camberwell, esq, [PRO; PCC 1632]
BATT (BAT,BATTE,BATTS)
  Agnes of Camberwell - Peckham, widow [DW/PA/5/1558/19]*
  Edward of Mickleham [DW/PA/7/13 f,273; DW/PA/5/1643/9]
  John of Epsom, husbandman [DW/PA/7/13 f,18; DW/PA/5/1639/17]
  Richard of Croydon - Addiscombe, yeoman [PRO; PCC Will 1607]
  Roger of Coulsdon [DW/PA/7/11 f,2; DW/PA/5/1622/4]
  Thomas, *or* Thomas Butt of Woking, yeoman [DW/PA/7/13 f,35;
    DW/PA/5/1639/12]
BATTCOCK (BATCOCK)
  John of Bramley, husbandman [DW/PA/7/12 f,218; DW/PA/5/1637/7]
  Robert of Wonersh, yeoman [DW/PA/7/13 f,139; DW/PA/5/1640/23]
BATTE *see* BATT
BATTIE
  Elizabeth of Bermondsey, widow [DW/PA/5/1588/81]
BATTLE (BATELL,BATTELL)
  Harry of Farnham [DW/PA/5/1579/18]*
  John of Farnham [DW/PA/7/5 f,213; 1541]
  John of Farnham [DW/PA/7/8 f,346; DW/PA/5/1612/11]
  Margery of Farnham, widow [DW/PA/7/4 f,104; 1535]
  Thomas of Rotherhithe, sailor [PRO; PCC Will 1578]
  William of Farnham [DW/PA/7/3 f,135; 1530]
BATTS *see* BATT
BAULDIN, BAULDING *see* BALDWIN
BAULE *see* BALL
BAVYNE (BAYNINE)
  John of Newdigate, rector [HRO; Reg, F p,541 *and* 1541 U5]
    <Abs SAC v,38 pp,103-104>
BAX (BAXE,BEXE)
  John of Capel, husbandman [DW/PA/7/11 f,361; DW/PA/5/1626/12]
  John of Shalford, tailor [DW/PA/5/1587/9]
  Margaret of Ockley, widow [DW/PA/7/12 f,283; DW/PA/5/1635/7]
  Mary, *or* Mary Black of Ockley [DW/PA/7/8 f,263; DW/PA/5/1611/12]
  Robert of Shalford, tailor [DW/PA/7/7 f,206; 1598] <Abs 366>
  Thomas of Capel, yeoman [DW/PA/7/8 f,118; DW/PA/5/1610/14]
BAXTER (BAXSTER)
  Andrew of Swk St Saviour, yeoman [DW/PA/7/11 f,286; DW/PA/5/1625/12]
  Edward of Newdigate [DW/PA/7/12 f,361; DW/PA/5/1637/19]

BAXTER (BAXSTER) [*continued*]
John of Godstone, yeoman [DW/PA/5/1578/50]
Lancelot of Walton on Thames, surveyor of H.M. Buttery [DW/PA/7/13 f.307; DW/PA/5/1643/17]
Thomas of Bermondsey; Cavendish, Suffolk [DW/PA/7/7 f.229; 1598]<Abs 404>
William of Dorking [DW/PA/7/6 f.211; 1560]

BAYARDE
Thomas of Mortlake, gent. [PRO; PCC Will 1591]

BAYCHELER *see* BACHELOR

BAYDON
Susan of Swk St Olave, widow [DW/PA/7/10 f.10; DW/PA/5/1619/12]

BAYFORD
Lewis, *or* or Lewis Bagford of Merton, yeoman [DW/PA/7/13 f.177; DW/PA/5/1641/15]

BAYLDON
Roger of Barnes - Barn Elms [PRO; PCC Will 1592]

BAYLES
Frances of Swk [DW/PA/7/8 f.114; DW/PA/5/1610/9]

BAYLEY (BAILEY,BAILY,BALE,BALEY,BALY,BAYLIE,BAYLYE,BELEY)
Agnes of Swk St Saviour [DW/PA/7/8 f.147; DW/PA/5/1611/8]
Hugh of Lambeth - Water Lambeth, Worplesdon, musician [PRO; PCC 1630] <Scroope 803>
Hugh of Swk St Olave, citizen and woodmonger [DW/PA/7/10 f.225; DW/PA/5/1621/4]
Joan of Swk St Olave, widow [DW/PA/7/12 f.209; DW/PA/5/1633/13]
John of Long Ditton - Tolworth, yeoman [DW/PA/7/9 f.298; 1618]
John of Egham [PRO; PCC 1641]
John of Morden, husbandman [DW/PA/7/7 f.345; DW/PA/5/1601/10] <Abs 630>
John of Newington, blacksmith [LPL; Reg. Abp Abbot i f.269; Will 1615]
Robert of Kingston, gent. [PRO; PCC Will 1618]
Robert of Richmond, waterman [DW/PA/7/8 f.240; DW/PA/5/1613/11]
Robert of Send, husbandman [DW/PA/5/1572/3]
Rowland of Chertsey, husbandman [DW/PA/7/13 f.33; DW/PA/5/1640/10]
Thomas of Horsell, tailor [DW/PA/7/8 f.19; DW/PA/5/1608/9]
Thomas of West Molesey, yeoman [DW/PA/7/8 f.354; DW/PA/5/1612/12]
Thomas of Ripley; Ockham; Stoke; Tollesbury, Essex, yeoman [DW/PA/7/6 f.40; DW/PA/5/1559/34]
(Sir) William of Surrey, knight and Lord Mayor of London [PRO; PCC Will 1537]
William of Wandsworth, butcher [DW/PA/7/10 f.70; 1618]

BAYNAM *see* BAINHAM

BAYNBRYCKE *see* BAINBRIDGE

BAYNINE *see* BAVIN

BAYS
William of Kingston, baker [DW/PA/5/1592/42]

BAYTON
Griffin of Swk St Olave, citizen and haberdasher [DW/PA/7/8 f.107; DW/PA/5/1610/10]

BEACHAM (BEACHAMPE,BEAUCHAMP,BECHAM,BECHUNT,BECHUNTE)
Edward of Chertsey, yeoman [DW/PA/7/11 f.434; DW/PA/5/1627/5]
Joan of Thorpe, widow [DW/PA/7/12 f.421; DW/PA/5/1637/11]
John of Chobham [DW/PA/7/1 f.84; 1488] <Abs 282>
John of Chobham [DW/PA/7/2 f.4; 1491]
John of Chobham, yeoman [DW/PA/7/12 f.344; DW/PA/5/1636/7]

BEACHAM (BEACHAMPE,BEAUCHAMP,BECHAM,BECHUNT,BECHUNTE) [*continued*]
John of Thorpe [BM; Add.Ms 24,925 f.25r; 1544] <Abs 64>
John of Thorpe, husbandman [DW/PA/5/1588/43]
Thomas of Chertsey, yeoman, senior [DW/PA/7/10 f.212; DW/PA/5/1620/7]
Thomas of Egham, esq. [LPL; Reg. Abp Morton f.253v; Admon 1488]
Thomas of Reigate [PRO; PCC Admon 1647]
William of Chobham, yeoman [DW/PA/5/1622/5] <Abs U252>
William of Thorpe, ?miller [HRO; 1582 B7]
BEACHE
William of Thames Ditton - Weston, husbandman [DW/PA/5/1588/32]
BEADLE (BEADELL,BEDELL,BEDILL,BEDLE,BEDYLL,BEEDELL,BEEDLE,BIDDLE,BIDLE)
Agnes of Chobham, widow of Alan [DW/PA/5/1562/68]
Alan of Windlesham, yeoman [DW/PA/7/7 f.54; DW/PA/5/1596/6] <Abs 104>
Alice, alias Alice Foster of Witley [PRO; PCC Admon 1649]
Arnold of 'Farnborough, Surrey' [CCAL; 1559 V^2 68y]
Daniel of Chobham, yeoman [DW/PA/7/13 f.430; DW/PA/5/1646/2]
Edward of Tooting, labourer [DW/PA/7/13 f.28; DW/PA/5/1640/8]
George of Chobham, tailor [DW/PA/7/13 f.145; DW/PA/5/1641/7]
Harry of Worplesdon [DW/PA/7/3 f.102; 1529]
Henry of Godstone, yeoman [HRO; Reg. Fox 3 p.57; 1510]
Henry of Godstone [DW/PA/5/1570/49]
Henry of Godstone [PRO; PCC Will 1572]
Henry of Guildford Holy Trinity, mercer [DW/PA/5/1575/25]
Henry of Horne, husbandman [DW/PA/7/11 f.297; DW/PA/5/1626/13]
Henry of Puttenham, rector [DW/PA/7/12 f.347; DW/PA/5/1636/14]
James of Guildford [GMR; RBI 335; 1607]
Joan of Godstone, wife of Henry [HRO; Reg. D p.55; 1527]
John of Camberwell - Dulwich [PRO; PCC Admon 1593]
John of Chobham [DW/PA/7/6 f.201; 1560]
John of Chobham, yeoman, senior [DW/PA/7/12 f.279; DW/PA/5/1635/6]
John of Chobham, yeoman, senior [DW/PA/7/13 f.285; DW/PA/5/1643/12]
John of Horne [DW/PA/5/1558/24]*
John of Kingston, husbandman [DW/PA/7/13 f.282; DW/PA/5/1643/11]
John of Lingfield; Tandridge, yeoman [DW/PA/5/1547/5]
Richard of Chobham, husbandman [DW/PA/7/5 f.200; 1540]
Richard of Witley [PRO; PCC Admon 1647]
Robert of Compton [DW/PA/5/1543/3]*
Thomas of Godstone [PRO; PCC Will 1507]
Thomas of Godstone; Lingfield [DW/PA/7/6 f.143; DW/PA/5/1559/236]
Thomas of Nutfield, yeoman [PRO; PCC Will 1619]
Thomas of Swk St Olave, citizen and tallow chandler [DW/PA/5/1592/71]
William of Guildford St Mary [DW/PA/7/5 f.144; 1540]
BEALE (BEALL,BEELE,BELE)
Henry of Bermondsey [DW/PA/7/4 f.208; 1537]
John of Malden [DW/PA/7/7 f.243; DW/PA/5/1599/5] <Abs 429>
Mary of Chessington; Kingston, widow [HRO; 1634 B2]
Richard of Beddington; Thames Ditton, labourer [DW/PA/7/10 f.46; 1619]
Richard of Malden, husbandman [DW/PA/5/1580/35]
Robert of Bentley, Hampshire, weaver [DW/PA/7/11 f.440; DW/PA/5/1628/6]
Roger of Kingston - Surbiton, yeoman [HRO; 1608 B8]
William of Bermondsey [DW/PA/5/1558/25]*
William of Egham [HRO; 1633 B6]
BEAMAN
Leonard of Newington [PRO; PCC 1649]

BEANE (BEENE,BENE,BEYN)
Alice of Kingston [DW/PA/7/5 f,161; 1540]
Christopher of Frensham [DW/PA/5/1569/74]
John of Worplesdon, husbandman [DW/PA/7/13 f,36; DW/PA/5/1639/19] <Abs U257>
Juliana of Godalming, widow [DW/PA/5/1570/64]
Peter of Kingston [DW/PA/7/1 f,9; 1485] <Abs 30>
Robert of Kingston, yeoman [DW/PA/7/5 f,64; 1539] <Abs 57>
William of Swk St George - *The White Lion* [DW/PA/7/11 f,438; DW/PA/5/1628/7]
BEAR (BEARE)
Mary of Bermondsey [DW/PA/7/13 f,221; DW/PA/5/1643/4]
BEARD (BEARDE)
John of Bermondsey, leatherdresser [PRO; PCC Will 1607] <Abs, SAC v,13 p,95>
John of Bermondsey, citizen and woodmonger [DW/PA/7/11 f,463; DW/PA/5/1628/8]
John of Caterham, yeoman [PRO; PCC Will 1623]
John of Rotherhithe [PRO; PCC Will 1590]
Richard of Frimley, gent, [PRO; PCC 1645]
Richard of Rotherhithe [PRO; PCC Admon 1607]
Stephen of Newington, husbandman [LPL; 96/197; 98/1 f,127r; Will 1641]
Thomas of Reigate [PRO; PCC Will 1557]
William of Worplesdon [HRO; 1578 B8]
BEARDWELL
William of Rotherhithe, mariner [DW/PA/7/8 f,392; DW/PA/5/1612/13]
BEARE *see* BEAR
BEAST, BEASTE *see* BEST
BEATON
Richard of ...., citizen and weaver [DW/PA/7/13 f,296; DW/PA/5/1644/6]
William of Lambeth - Water Lambeth, carpenter [DW/PA/5/1578/7]
BEAUCHAMP *see* BEACHAM
BEAUFORD
Henry, Cardinal bishop of Winchester; Wiltshire; Surrey; Somerset; Oxfordshire; Berkshire; Buckinghamshire [LPL; Reg, Abp Stafford f,111; Will 1447]
BEAULIEU *see* BEWLY
BEAVEN *see* BEVAN
BEAVER (BEVER)
John of Lambeth [DW/PA/5/1570/93]
Robert of Mitcham, husbandman [DW/PA/7/5 f,209; 1541]
William of Lambeth [DW/PA/7/4 f,160; 1536]
BEBEE
Robert of Bermondsey [PRO; PCC Admon 1649]
BECHAM,BECHUNT,BECHUNTE *see* BEACHAM
BECK (a BEKE,BECKE)
Bridget of Windlesham, widow [PRO; PCC 1648]
John of Swk St Olave [DW/PA/7/4 f,193; 1537]
William of Mortlake, labourer [PRO; PCC Will 1616]
William of Richmond, servant [GL; Commissary Court of London Will 1550]
BECKENSALL,BECKENSHALL *see* BECKINSALL

BECKETT (BACKETT,BECKET)
Agnes of Caterham, widow [DW/PA/7/12 f.313; DW/PA/5/1636/12]
Christopher of Lambeth - South Lambeth, yeoman [DW/PA/7/7 f.509; DW/PA/5/1605/11] <Abs 954>
Elizabeth of Bermondsey, widow [DW/PA/7/12 f.425; DW/PA/5/1637/13]
Thomas of Caterham [DW/PA/5/1578/20]
Thomas of Ockley [DW/PA/7/4 f.189; 1536]
William of Caterham, yeoman [DW/PA/7/12 f.137; DW/PA/5/1632/14]
William of Kingston, vicar and confessor of the king's household [PRO; PCC Will 1626]
BECKHAM (BEKEHAM)
John of Farnham, clerk and vicar [HRO; 1558 B32-33]
BECKINSALL (BECKENSALL,BECKENSHALL,BEKENSALL)
Elizabeth of Epsom, widow [DW/PA/7/12 f.508; DW/PA/5/1638/20]
Humphrey of Lambeth [DW/PA/5/1558/20]*
Humphrey of Lambeth [PRO; PCC Will *and* Admon 1560]
BECKMAN
Henry of Putney [LPL; 98/1 f.80v; Will 1637]
BECKNOLD *see* BICKNOLD
BEDDEN
Francis of Lambeth [PRO; PCC Admon 1648]
BEDELL *see* BEADLE
BEDEN
Richard of Surrey [PRO; *in* C146 7007; Will 1572]
BEDFANT
John of Thorpe [DW/PA/5/1588/71]
BEDFORD (BEDFURTH)
Agnes of Woking [DW/PA/7/5 f.198; 1540]
Richard of Godalming [DW/PA/7/3 f.126; 1530]
Robert of Bermondsey [PRO; PCC 1649]
BEDILL *see* BEADLE
BEDOE
Robert of Putney, gent. [PRO; PCC Will 1624]
BEDOME *see* BELDHAM
BEDON
Thomas of Swk St Olave; Enfield, Middlesex, husbandman [DW/PA/7/6 f.133; DW/PA/5/1559/138]
BEDYLL *see* BEADLE
BEECHER
Bridget of Limpsfield, widow [PRO; PCC 1640]
Elizabeth of Blechingley, spinster [DW/PA/7/11 f.585; DW/PA/5/1630/4]
Henry of Croydon, alderman [PRO; PCC Will 1570]
Richard of Blechingley; Chiddingstone, Kent; Penshurst, Kent, gent. [DW/PA/7/10 f.172; DW/PA/5/1619/10]
Richard of Croydon [LPL; 99/1 f.128r; (ren.) 1642]
BEECKMAN (BEECKMANS)
Henry of Swk St Thomas Hospital, tallow chandler [DW/PA/5/1581/33]
BEEDELL,BEEDLE *see* BEADLE
BEEDEN
Agnes of Send [DW/PA/7/10 f.21; DW/PA/5/1616/8]
BEELE *see* BEALE
BEEN *see* BEANE

BEESTON (BEESTONE,BYSTON)
John of Swk St George, bodicemaker [DW/PA/7/13 f,324; DW/PA/5/1643/18]
Thomas of Mitcham, gent, [PRO; PCC Will 1549]
Thomas of Swk St Olave, silk throwster [DW/PA/7/12 f,476; DW/PA/5/1638/12]
William of Lambeth, esq, [PRO; PCC 1639 *and* PCC Admon 1639]
William of Swk St Olave [DW/PA/5/1578/17]
BEGGS
Jane of Chertsey [DW/PA/7/6 f,44; DW/PA/5/1559/33]
BEKE *see* BECK
BEKEHAM *see* BECKHAM
BEKENSALL *see* BECKENSALL
BELCHER
George of Swk St Saviour, wine porter [DW/PA/7/8 f,406; DW/PA/5/1614/7]
Thomas of Newington [LPL; 98/1 f,89r (ren,); 1638]
BELCONE
William, alias William Belton of Swk St Saviour, yeoman [DW/PA/7/11 f,462; DW/PA/5/1628/9]
BELDAM (BEDOME,BELDHAM,BELDOM,BELDUM,BELLDAM)
Alan of Farnham - Wrecclesham [DW/PA/7/9 f,221; DW/PA/5/1617/7]
Edward of Send, maltman, junior [DW/PA/7/13 f,39; DW/PA/5/1639/20]
Elizabeth of Abinger, widow [DW/PA/7/10 f,88; DW/PA/5/1615/7]
George of Frensham, blacksmith [DW/PA/7/13 f,447; DW/PA/5/1646/4]
Joan of Farnham - Wrecclesham, widow [DW/PA/5/1624/11]
John of Ockley, husbandman [DW/PA/7/13 f,66; DW/PA/5/1639/27]
John of Worplesdon, husbandman [DW/PA/5/1558/26]*
Noah of Alfold [DW/PA/7/9 f,95; DW/PA/5/1616/9]
Richard of ,,, [DW/PA/7/7 f,615; DW/PA/5/1607/10] <Abs 1149>
Stephen of Great Bookham [DW/PA/7/3 f,172; 1531]
Thomas of Worplesdon [DW/PA/7/6 f,123; DW/PA/5/1559/211]
BELE *see* BEALE
BELEHEWE
Cicely of Swk St Olave, widow of Lawrence [HRO; Reg, Wyk 2 p,102; 1372]
BELEY *see* BAYLEY
BELL
Elizabeth of Kingston, widow [DW/PA/7/13 f,407; DW/PA/5/1645/4]
George of Swk St Saviour [DW/PA/7/9 f,131; DW/PA/5/1615/8]
George of Lambeth, senior [PRO; PCC Admon 1632]
George of Limpsfield [PRO; PCC Will 1596]
Henry of Kingston, victualler [DW/PA/7/13 f,36; DW/PA/5/1640/11]
Henry of Witley - Milford, esq, [PRO; PCC 1634] <Abs SAC v,18 pp,32-33 *and* v,33 p,39>
Humphrey of Stoke next Guildford [PRO; PCC 1638]
Joan of Rotherhithe, widow [PRO; PCC Will 1593]
John of ,,, [DW/PA/5/1593/105]
John, alias John Tanner of Godalming, tailor [DW/PA/7/10 f,67; 1618]
John of Newington [LPL; 98/1 f,1r; (ren,) 1629]
John of Thorpe [DW/PA/7/6 f,285; 1560]
Lewis of ,,, [DW/PA/7/7 f,558; DW/PA/5/1606/9] <Abs 1044>
Mary of Newdigate, widow [DW/PA/5/1561/53]
Matthew of Newdigate, rector [HRO; 1538 B11 *and* Reg, C p,249]
Nicholas of Newdigate, husbandman [DW/PA/7/6 f,231; 1561]
Parat, alias Parat Tanner of Godalming, widow [DW/PA/5/1587/120]
Richard of Newdigate, husbandman [DW/PA/7/4 f,69; 1534]

BELL [*continued*]
Robert of Wimbledon [PRO; PCC 1640]
Thomas, alias Thomas Tanner of Godalming, tailor [DW/PA/7/7 f.105; 1596] <Abs 188>
Thomas of Nutfield [PRO; PCC Will 1627]
BELLAMY (BELLAMYE)
John of Rotherhithe [PRO; PCC Admon 1631]
Richard of Swk St George, yeoman [DW/PA/5/1571/56]
BELLDAM *see* BELDAM
BELLINGHAM
Charles of Ewell, esq. [PRO; PCC Will 1618]
Rachel, alias Rachel Ceely of Kingston [PRO; PCC Admon 1598]
Thomas of Ewell [PRO; PCC Admon 1615]
BELLOGE
John of Ewell [GL; Archdeaconry Court of London Will 1405]
BELLOWE
Roger of Cobham, citizen and brewer [PRO; PCC Will 1614]
BELSON
Thomas of Wandsworth, yeoman [DW/PA/7/10 f.131; DW/PA/5/1620/8]
BELTON
William alias William Belcone of Swk St Saviour, yeoman [DW/PA/7/11 f.462; DW/PA/5/1628/9]
BELYNGHURSTE *see* BILLINGHURST
BENBOW (BENBE,BENBON)
John of Lambeth, citizen and leatherseller [DW/PA/7/8 f.26; DW/PA/5/1608/10]
BENBRICK (BENBRICKE,BENBRIGE,BONBROKE)
Edmund of Frimley; Dorset, yeoman [DW/PA/5/1593/75]*
Henry of Dunsfold [DW/PA/5/1576/29]
Joan of Swk St Saviour [DW/PA/7/7 f.430; DW/PA/5/1603/13] <Abs 813>
John of Swk St Saviour [DW/PA/7/7 f.437; DW/PA/5/1603/12] <Abs 827>
William of Swk St Olave, leatherdresser [DW/PA/7/12 f.305; DW/PA/5/1635/13]
see also BAINBRIDGE
BENE *see* BEANE
BENESE
Richard of Long Ditton, clerk [PRO; PCC Will 1547]
BENET *see* BENNETT
BENEVOLD
Henry of Farnham [DW/PA/7/1 f.101; 1489] <Abs 328>
BENGE
Agnes of Swk St George, widow [DW/PA/7/8 f.301; DW/PA/5/1613/12]
BENHAM
William of Streatham - Tooting Bec, carpenter [DW/PA/7/8 f.361; DW/PA/5/1612/14]
BENLIE *see* BENTLEY
BENN
Mary of Dorking, spinster [DW/PA/7/12 f.84; DW/PA/5/1633/21]
BENNETT (BANNET,BENET,BENETT,BENNET)
Agnes of Ewhurst, widow [DW/PA/7/12 f.364; DW/PA/5/1638/4]
Dorothy of Mortlake, widow [PRO; PCC 1642]
Edmund of Lambeth - Stockwell [DW/PA/7/7 f.72; 1539]
Edward of Walton on Thames, citizen and merchant tailor [PRO; PCC Will 1577]

BENNETT (BANNET,BENET,BENETT,BENNET) [*continued*]
Elizabeth of Lambeth, wife of Mr Robert, gent. [PRO; PCC Will 1610] <Abs. SAC v.24 p.65>
Elizabeth of Lambeth, wife of Robert, gent. [PRO; PCC Admon 1610]
Emming of Kingston, widow [DW/PA/7/13 f.105; DW/PA/5/1640/19]
John of Blechingley, butterman [DW/PA/7/2 f.106; 1516]
John of Farnham, mercer, senior [DW/PA/7/7 f.585; DW/PA/5/1607/11] <Abs 1090>
John of Farnham, sergeant at arms to the king[PRO; PCC 1631]
John, alias John Kyngeston of Kingston [PRO; PCC Will 1476]
John of Swk St Saviour, brazier [DW/PA/5/1578/108]
Margaret of Farnham, widow [HRO; 1599 B4]
Mary of Streatham, widow [PRO; PCC Admon 1640]
Nicholas of Bermondsey, citizen and leatherseller [PRO; PCC 1645]
Nicholas of Swk St Saviour, shipwright [DW/PA/7/12 f.128; DW/PA/5/1632/11]
Ralph of Morden [PRO; PCC Admon 1626]
Richard of Bermondsey, citizen and leatherseller [PRO; PCC 1637]
Richard of Betchworth, citizen and draper [PRO; PCC Will 1608] <Abs. SAC v.13 pp.185-186>
Richard of Chiddingfold [HRO; 1587 B9]
Richard of Hascombe [HRO; 1621 AD5]
Richard of Kingston, butcher [DW/PA/7/11 ff.156,353; DW/PA/5/1625/13 *and* DW/PA/5/1625/14]
Robert of Croydon [PRO; PCC 1649]
Thomas of Alfold, husbandman [DW/PA/7/13 f.207; DW/PA/5/1642/7]
Thomas of Camberwell; New Cross, Deptford, Kent, citizen and clothworker [DW/PA/7/12 f.179; DW/PA/5/1633/9]
Thomas of Capel [DW/PA/7/4 f.118; 1535]
Thomas of Guildford St Nicholas - Littleton [DW/PA/5/1558/27]*
Thomas of Kingston - Norbiton [PRO; PCC Will 1597]
Thomas of Lambeth - Water Lambeth [DW/PA/7/2 f.77; 1501]
Thomas of Lingfield, yeoman [DW/PA/7/12 f.32; DW/PA/5/1631/16]
Thomas of Swk St George, tailor [DW/PA/5/1578/107]
Thomas of Swk St Saviour, tailor [DW/PA/7/12 f.307; DW/PA/5/1635/14]
Thomas of Swk St Thomas, cordwainer [DW/PA/7/13 f.293; DW/PA/5/1643/16]
William of Bermondsey, glover [DW/PA/7/9 f.244; DW/PA/5/1617/8]
William of Bermondsey [PRO; PCC Admon 1636]
William of Farnham, haberdasher [HRO; 1611 AD7]
William of Godstone [DW/PA/5/1543/2]*
William of Kingston, weaver [DW/PA/7/6 f.225; 1561]
William of Kingston, senior, yeoman [DW/PA/7/9 f.30; DW/PA/5/1614/4]
William of Swk St Saviour, shoemaker [DW/PA/5/1593/163]

BENNOYER *see* BENOYER

BENNYNGE
William of Swk St Saviour, innholder [DW/PA/7/10 f.280; DW/PA/5/1622/6]

BENOYER (BENNOYER)
Robert of Swk St Olave, whitster [DW/PA/5/1624/12]
Robert of Swk St Olave - Horsleydown [DW/PA/7/13 f.257; DW/PA/5/1643/6]

BENSON
George of ...., yeoman of the king's kitchen [DW/PA/5/1550/19]
Joan of Kingston, widow [DW/PA/7/13 f.142; DW/PA/5/1645/5]
John of Kingston - Surbiton, fisherman [DW/PA/5/1593/99]
John of Lambeth - South Lambeth [PRO; PCC Admon 1625]

BENSON [*continued*]
Margaret of Putney - Roehampton, widow [PRO; PCC Will 1614]
Richard of Kingston, esq. [PRO; PCC Will 1540]
Robert of Kingston, gent. [PRO; PCC Will 1551]
Thomas of Kingston, gent. [DW/PA/5/1582/91]
Timothy of Putney - Roehampton, citizen and embroiderer [PRO; PCC 1636]
BENTLEY (BENLIE,BENTLIE,BENTLOW,BENTLY,BENTLYE,BENTTELEY)
Alice of Petersham, widow of John [DW/PA/7/8 f.5; DW/PA/5/1608/11]
John of Petersham [DW/PA/7/7 f.508; DW/PA/5/1605/12] <Abs 953>
John of Rotherhithe [PRO; PCC Admon 1604]
John of Wandsworth; Petersham, yeoman [DW/PA/7/10 f.68; 1618]
Luke of Ewhurst, victualler & alehouse keeper [HRO; 1639 B4]
Richard of Woodmansterne, husbandman [DW/PA/7/5 f.3; 1538] <Abs 127>
Richard of Wandsworth [DW/PA/5/1543/1]*
Robert of Chiddingfold [PRO; PCC Admon 1628]
Robert of Wandsworth, yeoman [DW/PA/7/9 f.127; DW/PA/5/1615/9]
Thomas of Chiddingfold [PRO; PCC Admon 1614]
Thomas of Chipstead [DW/PA/7/4 f.108; 1535]
Thomas of Swk St Saviour; Oxford St Michael, gent. [DW/PA/7/7 f.559; DW/PA/5/1606/10] <Abs 1045>
Walter of Wandsworth, husbandman [DW/PA/7/7 f.242; DW/PA/5/1598/7] <Abs 425>
William of Chiddingfold, husbandman [DW/PA/7/13 f.161; DW/PA/5/1641/10]
William of Titsey [DW/PA/5/1579/11]*
William of Woodmansterne, yeoman [DW/PA/7/7 f.586; DW/PA/5/1607/12] <Abs 1094>
BENWELL
Seath of Swk St Saviour, baker [DW/PA/7/10 f.40; DW/PA/5/1617/9]
BEPESSE
John of Swk St Margaret [DW/PA/7/4 f.207; 1537]
BERDE *see* BIRD
BERESFORD
Rowland of Bermondsey, gent. [PRO; PCC Will 1624]
Rowland of Bermondsey, gent. [PRO; PCC 1633]
BEREWYK *see* BERWICK
BERIMAN *see* BERRIMAN
BERKET *see* BURKETT
BERKSHIRE (BARCSCHYRE,BARKESHERE)
Robert of Alfold [DW/PA/7/5 f.133; 1539]
Thomas of Farnham, yeoman [DW/PA/7/13 f.147; DW/PA/5/1641/9]
BERKWITH
William of Bermondsey [PRO; PCC Will 1543]
BERNARD
Agnes of Betchworth [PRO; PCC Will 1535]
Richard of Swk [LPL; Reg. Abp Bourgchier f.51r; Admon 1464]
BERNERS *see* BOURGCHIER
BERRIMAN (BERIMAN,BERRYEMAN,BERRYMAN,BERYMAN,BURYMAN,BYRRIMAN)
Elizabeth of Chertsey, widow & farmer's wife [HRO; 1623 B3]
John of Thames Ditton [DW/PA/7/2 f.173; 1522]
John of Thames Ditton [DW/PA/7/6 f.136; DW/PA/5/1559/142]
Magdalen of Guildford St Mary, servant to Anthony Abbott [DW/PA/7/7 f.269; DW/PA/5/1599/6] <Abs 472>
Margaret of Kew; St Mary Aldermary, London [DW/PA/7/3 f.197; 1532]
Nicholas of Merrow, yeoman [DW/PA/5/1593/12]

BERRIMAN (BERIMAN,BERRYEMAN,BERRYMAN,BERYMAN,BURYMAN,BYRRIMAN) [*continued*]
Richard of Pyrford [DW/PA/7/2 f.102; 1515]
Richard of Bermondsey [PRO; PCC 1631]
Robert of Chertsey, husbandman [DW/PA/5/1587/77]
Thomas of Chertsey - Woodham; Worplesdon - Wyke, yeoman [DW/PA/7/12 f.489; DW/PA/5/1639/11]
Thomas of Worplesdon - Wyke [DW/PA/7/12 f.480; DW/PA/5/1638/15]
William of Chertsey [PRO; PCC Admon 1647]
William of Chertsey [PRO; PCC 1647]
William of Epsom, yeoman [DW/PA/5/1576/69]
William of Richmond; Thames Ditton - Weston [PRO; PCC Will 1525]

BERRY (BERRIE)
Anthony of Chipstead; Ewell; Headley [DW/PA/7/8 f.1; DW/PA/5/1608/12]
John of Guildford [DW/PA/7/12 f.10; DW/PA/5/1631/9]
John of Guildford St Nicholas, weaver, senior [DW/PA/7/7 f.323; DW/PA/5/1601/11] <Abs 579>
John of Guildford St Nicholas, senior [DW/PA/7/11 f.87; DW/PA/5/1624/9]
Robert of Bermondsey [DW/PA/5/1603/14] <Abs U61>
Robert of Esher, yeoman [DW/PA/7/13 f.204; DW/PA/5/1642/6]
Robert of Guildford St Nicholas, linen weaver [DW/PA/7/13 f.459; DW/PA/5/1647/2]

BERRYMAN *see* BERRIMAN

BERTES *see* NOPEN

BERWICK (BEREWYK,BERWYCKE)
Joan of Woking, widow [DW/PA/7/3 f.122; 1529]
John of Battersea, clerk [PRO; PCC Will 1402]

BERYMAN *see* BERRIMAN

BESBEECH
Elizabeth, alias Elizabeth Jemet of Lingfield [PRO; PCC Admon 1633]

BEST (BEAST,BEASTE,BESTE)
Aaron (widow, Ann) of Croydon, gent. [PRO; PCC 1635]
Alan of Godstone [DW/PA/5/1569/86]
Alan of Godstone; Lingfield, yeoman [DW/PA/7/8 f.262; DW/PA/5/1611/9]
Alan of Sutton [DW/PA/5/1581/63]
Ann of Coulsdon, spinster [PRO; PCC Admon 1647]
Ann of Swk St Saviour, wife of Francis [DW/PA/7/8 f.392; DW/PA/5/1612/15]
Charles of Thames Ditton, husbandman [DW/PA/7/8 f.354; DW/PA/5/1612/16]
Christopher of Merstham [PRO; PCC Will 1547]
Christopher of Merstham [PRO; PCC Will 1561]
Christopher of Merstham [PRO; PCC Admon 1569]
Henry of Sanderstead; Coulsdon - Waddington, yeoman [DW/PA/7/8 f.127; DW/PA/5/1610/16]
James of Blechingley, cordwainer [DW/PA/7/4 f.63; 1534]
Joan of Chaldon, widow of Richard [DW/PA/7/2 f.136; 1519]
Joan of Charlwood [LPL; 98/1 f.118v; Will 1640]
Joan of Gatton, widow [HRO; 1568 B18-20]
John of ... [*in* DW/PA/5/1571/22]
John of Banstead - Tadworth [DW/PA/7/7 f.318; DW/PA/5/1600/6] <Abs 567>
John of Beddington, yeoman [PRO; PCC Will 1620] <Soame 630>
John of Caterham [DW/PA/7/4 f.5; 1532]
John of Chipstead [PRO; PCC 1649]
John of Croydon [LPL; 98/1 f.6r; Will 1630]
John of Croydon [LPL; 96/225; 98/1 f.119v; Will 1640]
John of Thames Ditton [DW/PA/7/4 f.179; 1536]

BEST (BEAST,BEASTE,BESTE) [*continued*]
John of East Horsley [PRO; PCC 1634]
John of Putney, husbandman [LPL; 96/224; Will 1616]
John of Sutton [DW/PA/7/6 f.271; 1560]
John of Sutton [DW/PA/5/1576/72]
John of Sutton, yeoman [DW/PA/7/13 f.173; DW/PA/5/1641/14]
Joyce of ... [*in* DW/PA/5/1571/22]
Margaret of Lingfield, spinster [PRO; PCC Admon 1633]
Nicholas of Nutfield [DW/PA/5/1579/15]*
Richard of Camberwell [DW/PA/7/3 f.158; 1530]
Richard of Chaldon [DW/PA/7/2 f.119; 1518]
Richard of Chipstead [DW/PA/7/4 f.135; 1536]
Richard of Reigate, yeoman [DW/PA/7/8 f.132; DW/PA/5/1610/17]
Richard of Streatham [DW/PA/5/1570/97]
Robert of Camberwell - Dulwich [DW/PA/7/11 f.222; DW/PA/5/1620/9]
Robert of Camberwell - Dulwich, yeoman [DW/PA/7/9 f.341; 1621]
Robert of Chipstead, senior [DW/PA/5/1550/24]
Robert of Coulsdon, yeoman [DW/PA/7/12 f.206; DW/PA/5/1634/5]
Roger of Chipstead, yeoman [DW/PA/7/9 f.129; DW/PA/5/1615/10]
Thomas of Carshalton [DW/PA/7/5 f.93; 1539]
Thomas of Chipstead; Merstham; Gatton; Chaldon [DW/PA/7/5 f.46; 1538] <Abs 21>
Thomas of Coulsdon, yeoman [DW/PA/5/1572/19]
Thomas of Coulsdon [PRO; PCC 1648]
Thomas of Kingston [PRO; PCC Admon 1603]
Thomas of Merstham, gent., senior [PRO; PCC 1633]
Thomas of Pirbright, yeoman [PRO; PCC Will 1599]
Thomas of Walton on the Hill, yeoman [DW/PA/7/13 f.76; DW/PA/5/1640/13]
William of Chipstead [DW/PA/7/3 f.108; 1529]
William of Chipstead, yeoman [DW/PA/5/1587/59]
William of Chipstead, yeoman [DW/PA/7/10 f.299; DW/PA/5/1617/27]
William of Lingfield - Blockfield, yeoman [DW/PA/5/1580/2]
William of Nutfield; Blechingley; Merstham, yeoman [DW/PA/7/7 f.380; DW/PA/5/1602/7] <Abs 705>
William of Limpsfield; Caterham, yeoman [DW/PA/7/7 f.562; DW/PA/5/1606/8] <Abs 1050>
William of Streatham [? HRO; 1529]

BESWICKE (BESTWICK)
Henry of Walton on Thames - Oatlands, servant to Queen Ann [PRO; PCC Admon 1617]

BETHELL
Catherine of Swk St Olave [DW/PA/7/11 f.165; DW/PA/5/1625/15]

BETSWORTH (BETTISWORTHE)
Alice of Frensham - Pitfold, widow [PRO; PCC Will 1621]
Peter of Reigate [PRO; PCC Will 1589]
Richard of Wanborough [HRO; 1638 AD21]
Thomas of Lambeth - Water Lambeth, waterman [DW/PA/7/8 f.333; DW/PA/5/1614/6]

BETT,BETTE *see* BETTS

BETTERTON
John of Swk St George, yeoman [DW/PA/7/7 f.523; DW/PA/5/1606/11] <Abs 984>

BETTES *see* BETTS

BETTISWORTHE *see* BETSWORTH

BETTS (BETT,BETTE,BETTES)
George of Swk; Stretford Langthorne, Essex [DW/PA/5/1593/168]
Henry of Camberwell - Peckham, carpenter [DW/PA/7/8 f,19; DW/PA/5/1608/13]
John of Croydon, yeoman [PRO; PCC Will 1605] <Abs, SAC v,12 p,92>
John of Dorking [DW/PA/7/2 f,47; 1496]
John of Farnham [DW/PA/7/11 f,295; DW/PA/5/1626/14]
John of Fetcham [HRO; 1567 B15-16]
John of Fetcham [HRO; 1568 B21]
Richard of Blechingley, yeoman [DW/PA/7/13 f,313; DW/PA/5/1644/8]
Robert of St Mary Aldermanbury, London, citizen and brewer [DW/PA/5/1552/26]
William of Swk St Olave, beltmaker [DW/PA/7/11 f,600; DW/PA/5/1630/5]

BEVAN (BEAVEN,BEVENNE,BEVENS,BEVIN)
David of Merton, labourer [DW/PA/7/10 f,72; 1619]
John of Godstone [DW/PA/7/10 f,189; DW/PA/5/1621/8]
John of Lingfield [PRO; PCC Will 1596]
William of ,,, [DW/PA/7/8 f,57; DW/PA/5/1609/19]

BEVER *see* BEAVER

BEVERLEY
John of Merstham [PRO; PCC Will 1449]
John of Nutfield [PRO; PCC Will 1496]
William of St John the Baptist Walbrook, London, citizen and skinner [DW/PA/5/1547/14]

BEVIN *see* BEVAN

BEWLY
Thomas of Kingston - Ham [PRO; PCC Will 1621]

BEX,BEXE *see* BAX

BEXLEY
Winifred of Capel, widow [DW/PA/7/11 f,65; DW/PA/5/1623/10]

BEYGEN (de BEYGEN)
Adrian of Swk St Olave [DW/PA/7/3 f,150; 1530]

BEYN *see* BEANE

BIBSWORTH
Edward of Swk St Thomas, citizen and haberdasher [DW/PA/7/10 f,102 DW/PA/5/1621/9]

BICKER (BYKER)
Thomas of Swk [HRO; Reg, Wyk 2 p,171; 1378]

BICKERDIKE (BYKERDYKE)
John of Walton on Thames, vicar [HRO; 1546 B35-36]

BICKERSTAFF (BICKERSTAFFE,BYCKERSTAFE)
Anthony of Croydon [PRO; PCC Admon 1600]
Haward of Godstone [PRO; PCC 1649]
Robert of Cobham [DW/PA/5/1568/12]
Robert of Walton on Thames, gent, [DW/PA/7/13 f,95; DW/PA/5/1641/22]
William of Kingston, waterman [DW/PA/7/8 f,226; DW/PA/5/1612/17]

BICKNALL,BICKNELL *see* BIGNALL

BICKNER (BIKNER,BYCKNER)
John of St Albans, Hertfordshire; Puttenham, one of the grooms of (Rt Hon) Earl of Essex, Lord High Marshall of England [DW/PA/7/7 f,302; DW/PA/5/1600/7] <Abs 540>
Nicholas of Alfold [DW/PA/7/11 f,453; DW/PA/5/1628/10]
Thomas of Wonersh [DW/PA/7/3 f,103; 1529]

BICKNOLD,BICKNOLDE,BICKNOLL *see* BIGNALL

BICKTON
  Gilbert of Windlesham - Bagshot [PRO; PCC Admon 1620]
BIDDELL,BIDDLE,BIDLE *see* BEADLE
BIERS *see* BYERS
BIFFINE
  John of Camberwell - Peckham Rye, husbandman [PRO; PCC Will 1626]
BIGGINS
  John of Swk St George; St Botolph Bishopsgate, London,victualler
    [DW/PA/5/1605/6] <Abs U129>
BIGGS
  Helen of Swk St George, widow [DW/PA/7/11 f,351; DW/PA/5/1625/16]
  John, alias John Bix of Putney [PRO; PCC Admon 1624]
BIGLEY
  Elizabeth of Cobham, widow [PRO; PCC Admon 1563]
  George of Cobham [PRO; PCC Will 1558]
BIGNALL (BECKNOLD,BICKNALL,BICKNELL,BICKNOLD,BICKNOLDE,BICKNOLL,BIGNOLL,
    BYCKNALL,BYCKNOLDE,BYCKNOLL,BYCONYLL,BYGGNOLD,BYGNALL,BYKNALDE)
  Alice of Farnham, widow [DW/PA/5/1558/41]*
  Ellen of Chiddingfold, spinster [DW/PA/5/1592/83]*
  Fulk of Lambeth, widower [PRO; PCC Admon 1648]
  George of Godalming - Catteshall, senior [DW/PA/7/12 f,329;
    DW/PA/5/1636/5]
  Harry of Wonersh [DW/PA/5/1558/37]*
  Helen of Chiddingfold [DW/PA/5/1592/82]
  Henry of Wonersh, husbandman [DW/PA/7/7 f,583;DW/PA/5/1607/13] <Abs 1086>
  James of Cobham, tanner [DW/PA/5/1557/136]
  James of Esher, tanner [DW/PA/7/11 f,308; DW/PA/5/1626/15]
  John of Chiddingfold, tanner [DW/PA/7/6 f,60; DW/PA/5/1559/60]
  John of Cobham [HRO; 1528 B10]
  John of Epsom; Cobham, husbandman [DW/PA/5/1557/17]
  John of Farnham, husbandman [DW/PA/7/10 f,61; 1618]
  John of Farnham [PRO; PCC 1647]
  John of Godalming [DW/PA/7/3 f,186; 1531]
  John of Puttenham [HRO; 1561 B24-25]
  John of Shere, weaver [DW/PA/7/13 f,121; DW/PA/5/1640/20]
  John of Wonersh - Shamley, yeoman [DW/PA/7/7 f,611; DW/PA/5/1607/14]
    <Abs 1142>
  Margaret of Godalming, widow of John [DW/PA/7/3 f,185; 1531]
  Margaret of Cobham, widow [DW/PA/7/4 f,32; 1533]
  Richard of Weybridge [PRO; PCC 1648]
  Robert of Ewell, tailor [DW/PA/5/1581/5]
  Robert of Farnham, chirurgeon [PRO; PCC 1648]
  Robert of Swk St Olave [DW/PA/7/12 f,223; DW/PA/5/1634/9]
  Thomas of Chiddingfold [DW/PA/5/1579/13]*
  Thomas of Frensham [HRO; 1578 B12]
  Thomas of Godalming [PRO; PCC Admon 1647]
  Thomas of Godalming, dyer [DW/PA/7/13 f,485; DW/PA/5/1648/4]
  Thomas of Shalford, yeoman [DW/PA/5/1586/43]*
  Thomas of Wonersh, tanner [DW/PA/7/8 f,132; DW/PA/5/1610/18]
  William of Mickleham; Wimborne Minster, Dorset, Official of the Court of Canterbury,,
    Canon of Wells, Prebendary of Lincoln and London; Oxford University [LPL; Reg, Abp Stafford f,
    Will 1448]
  William of Shalford [DW/PA/5/1550/18]
  see also BAGNALL

BIGROVE
  John of Camberwell [DW/PA/7/11 f.4; DW/PA/5/1622/7]
BIKNER *see* BICKNER
BILBEE
  Thomas of St Martha's - Chilworth [DW/PA/7/12 f.409; DW/PA/5/1637/10]
BILL
  (Lady) Jane, alias (Lady) Jane Bludder of Reigate [PRO; PCC Admon 1646]
  John of Newington, gent. [PRO; PCC Will 1589]
BILLINGE
  Friswith of Swk St George - Kent Street, widow [DW/PA/7/10 f.220; DW/PA/5/1621/10]
BILLINGHURST (BELYNGHURSTE,BILLINGHURSTE,BYLLYNGHURST,BYLLYNGHURSTE, BYLLYNGHYRST)
  George of Puttenham, senior, yeoman [PRO; PCC Will 1629]
  Henry of Godalming [*in* DW/PA/5/1544/4]
  Henry of Guildford St Nicholas - Littleton; Kingsley, Hampshire, yeoman [DW/PA/7/10 f.269; DW/PA/5/1622/8]
  Isabel of Godalming [DW/PA/7/4 f.213; 1537]
  John of Chiddingfold; Haslemere - Puckshot [DW/PA/5/1580/56]
  John of Guildford St Nicholas - Littleton, yeoman [DW/PA/7/13 f.198; DW/PA/5/1641/17]
  John of Haslemere, yeoman [DW/PA/7/11 f.100; DW/PA/5/1624/13]
  John of Haslemere, senior, weaver [DW/PA/7/13 f.56; DW/PA/5/1640/12]
  John of Puttenham - Rodsell [*in* DW/PA/5/1546/24]
  John of Puttenham [DW/PA/7/11 f.307; DW/PA/5/1626/16]
  John of Puttenham, yeoman [DW/PA/7/12 f.377; 1637]
  John of Witley - Mousehill; Godalming, husbandman [DW/PA/7/9 f.87; DW/PA/5/1615/11]
  Margaret of Guildford St Nicholas - Littleton [HRO; 1612 B8]
  Margaret of Haslemere, widow [PRO; PCC 1641]
  Nicholas of Puttenham, yeoman [DW/PA/7/7 f.220; DW/PA/5/1598/8] <Abs 388>
  Richard of Alfold, yeoman [DW/PA/7/11 f.205; DW/PA/5/1625/17]
  Richard of Godalming - Lydling, husbandman [DW/PA/5/1592/55]
  Robert of Puttenham [DW/PA/5/1546/57]
  Robert of Haslemere - Haslehurst, senior, yeoman [DW/PA/7/8 f.54; DW/PA/5/1609/20]
  Robert of Haslemere - Haslehurst; Thursley, yeoman [DW/PA/7/9 f.168; DW/PA/5/1616/10]
  Thomas of Guildford St Nicholas - Littleton [DW/PA/5/1593/200]
  Thomas of Haslemere - Oaks, clothworker [DW/PA/7/8 f.345; 1612]
  Thomas of Haslemere, weaver [DW/PA/7/10 f.275; 1621]
  Thomas of Puttenham [HRO; 1630 AD10]
  William of Godalming - Shackleford; Shalford; Dunsfold; Hascombe [DW/PA/7/6 f.165; DW/PA/5/1559/164]
  William of Haslemere [DW/PA/5/1561/55]
  William of Puttenham - Rodsell, husbandman [DW/PA/7/2 f.188; 1523]
BINCKS *see* BINKS
BIND (BYND,BYNDE)
  James of Carshalton, gent. [DW/PA/7/11 f.210; DW/PA/5/1625/35]
  Robert of Swk, horner [HRO; Reg. Edn 2 p.16; 1348]
BINDELOSSE *see* BYNDELOSSE
BINDING (BYNDYNG)
  Richard of Chertsey, yeoman [DW/PA/5/1572/15]

BINE (BYNE)
Frances, alias Frances Bowyer of Lingfield [PRO; PCC Admon 1630]
Thomas of Camberwell, gent, [PRO; PCC Will 1613]
BINGHAM
Ann of Rotherhithe, widow [PRO; PCC 1630] <Scroope 1300>
BINGLEY (BYNGLEY)
Thomas of Croydon, bachelor [LPL; 96/453; Will 1629]
BINKS (BINCKS,BYNCKES)
George of Bermondsey [PRO; PCC Will 1621]
John of Richmond [PRO; PCC Will 1590]
Nathaniel of Bermondsey [PRO; PCC 1631]
BINNS (BYNNES)
Richard of Thames Ditton - Weston [DW/PA/5/1587/124]
BINSTEAD
Edward of Swk St Saviour - Winchester House [HRO; 1606 AD4]
BIRCH (BIRCHE,BYRCHE)
Alice of Swk St Saviour, widow [DW/PA/7/8 f,258; DW/PA/5/1617/28]
George of Witley, vicar [HRO; 1569 B31-32]
James of Egham - Stroud, yeoman [DW/PA/7/13 f,252; DW/PA/5/1641/23]
John of Ockham; Ripley; East Horsley; Wisley; Thorpe; Effingham; Pyrford; Byfleet, baron of the Exchequer [PRO; PCC Will 1581]
Robert of Ockham [PRO; PCC Will 1525]
BIRCHALL *see* BURCHALL
BIRCHARD *see* BURCHARD
BIRCHE *see* BIRCH
BIRCHET *see* BURCHETT
BIRD (BERDE,BIRDE,BURD,BURDE,BYRD)
Edward of Fetcham [DW/PA/7/12 f,188; DW/PA/5/1641/13]
Elizabeth of Rotherhithe, widow [DW/PA/7/11 f,319; DW/PA/5/1626/17]
George of Thames Ditton - Claygate; Stoke Dabernon - Oxshott, husbandman [DW/PA/7/8 f,188; DW/PA/5/1610/23]
Henry of Tooting, parson and M,A, [DW/PA/7/9 f,340; DW/PA/5/1620/10]
Joan of Croydon, widow [LPL; 96/246; Will 1643]
John of Caterham [DW/PA/7/9 f,261; DW/PA/5/1617/10]
John of Epsom - Horton, yeoman [DW/PA/7/8 f,258; DW/PA/5/1611/10]
John of Stoke Dabernon [DW/PA/5/1576/130]
John of Swk St Olave, waterman [DW/PA/7/11 f,402; DW/PA/5/1627/15]
Margaret of Lambeth, widow [DW/PA/7/11 f,171; DW/PA/5/1625/18]
Nicholas of Richmond, senior [PRO; PCC Admon 1596]
Nicholas of Richmond, esq, [PRO; PCC 1642]
Richard of Horsell [DW/PA/7/2 f,86; ?1503]
Richard of West Molesey, bachelor [DW/PA/5/1588/9]
Robert of Swk St Saviour; Swk St Mary Overy [DW/PA/7/7 f,429; DW/PA/5/1603/15] <Abs 806>
Simon of Swk St Saviour, waterman [DW/PA/7/8 f,298; DW/PA/5/1613/13]
Thomas of Epsom, carpenter [DW/PA/7/10 f,290; DW/PA/5/1623/11]
William of Richmond [PRO; PCC Admon 1639]
William of Swk St Saviour, brewer [DW/PA/5/1582/62]
see also BURT
BIRDWELL (BURDWYLL)
Harry of Swk St Olave [DW/PA/5/1561/18A]
see also BURDEVILL
BIRKBECK *see* BURBECK
BIRKESTE *see* BUCKHURST

BIRKINSHAW (BURCHINSHAW)
  Joan of Swk St Olave, widow [DW/PA/7/12 f.460; DW/PA/5/1639/10]
BIRKS *see* BURKE
BIRLE *see* BURLE
BIRSTIE
  Robert of Tatsfield, yeoman [PRO; PCC Will 1618]
BIRT,BIRTE *see* BURT
BIRTCHLEY
  Peter of Swk St Saviour, yeoman [DW/PA/5/1593/134]
BISBRIDGE (BISBRIGE)
  Robert of Wonersh [DW/PA/7/1 ff.82,86; 1488] <Abs 272,289>
BISHE (BYSSH,BYSSHE)
  John of Burstow, senior, gent. [PRO; PCC Will 1494]
  John of Burstow [PRO; PCC Will 1522]
  John of Burstow, gent. [PRO; PCC Will 1568]
  Robert of Worth, Sussex [DW/PA/7/4 f.161; 1536]
  William of Godstone, sheather [DW/PA/5/1591/104]
BISHOP (BISHOPP,BISSHOP,BISSHOPP,BUSHOP,BYSHOP,BYSHOPE,BYSHOPP,BYSSHOPP,
    BYSSHYPE)
  Elizabeth of Thames Ditton - Claygate, widow [DW/PA/7/10 f.189;
    DW/PA/5/1620/11]
  Frances of Bermondsey, widow [DW/PA/7/12 f.50; DW/PA/5/1631/18]
  Jeremy of Bermondsey, mariner [DW/PA/7/13 f.349; 1644]
  John of Thames Ditton - Claygate [DW/PA/7/5 f.207; 1541]
  John of Farnham, servant to the bishop [HRO; Reg. Way 2 p.144; 1470]
  John of Nutfield, yeoman [DW/PA/7/13 f.269; DW/PA/5/1644/7]
  Mary of Dorking, widow [HRO; 1594 AD5]
  Matthew of Leigh [HRO; 1583 B11]
  Richard of Chertsey [HRO; 1524 B12]
  Richard of Merrow [DW/PA/7/1 f.6; 1484] <Abs 19>
  Robert of Abinger, husbandman [PRO; PCC Will 1612]
  Robert of Bermondsey [PRO; PCC Will 1551]
  Robert of Seale [DW/PA/5/1571/26]
  Susan of Kingston, widow [DW/PA/7/13 f.326; 1644]
  Thomas of Bermondsey, leatherseller [DW/PA/7/5 f.184; 1540]
  Thomas of Thames Ditton [DW/PA/5/1569/75]
  Thomas of Thames Ditton - Claygate, yeoman [PRO; PCC Will 1609] <Abs.
    SAC v.23 p.135>
  Thomas of Kingston, gent. [PRO; PCC 1638]
  William of Charlwood, husbandman [LPL; 96/253; Will 1627]
  William of Thames Ditton, junior, husbandman [DW/PA/7/4 f.102; 1535]
  William of Kingston [PRO; PCC Admon 1649]
  William of Leigh [DW/PA/7/12 f.378; DW/PA/5/1637/6]
  William of Reigate [PRO; PCC 1640]
BISLEY
  Jasper of Walton on Thames, fisherman [DW/PA/7/13 f.29; DW/PA/5/1639/16]
BISSAKER
  Thomas of Lambeth, innholder [PRO; PCC Will 1577]
BISSELL
  Cicely of Wandsworth, widow [DW/PA/7/11 f.453; DW/PA/5/1628/11]
  William of Wandsworth, victualler [DW/PA/7/11 f.367; DW/PA/5/1626/18]
BISSET (BYSSETT)
  Alice of Limpsfield [DW/PA/7/1 f.85; 1488] <Abs 284>
  Alice of Limpsfield [DW/PA/7/2 f.34; 1488]

BISSETER (BYSYTTER)
  (Sir) Stephen of Swk St Saviour, knight [DW/PA/7/6 f.171; DW/PA/5/1559/156]
BISSHOP,BISSHOPP *see* BISHOP
BITACKE
  Emma of Lambeth [PRO; PCC Admon 1647]
BITHELL *see* BOTHELL
BITHEWOOD (BITHWOOD,BYTHEWOOD)
  John of Great Bookham, husbandman [DW/PA/7/7 f.466; DW/PA/5/1603/16A] <Abs 879>
  John of Walton on Thames, yeoman [DW/PA/7/12 f.502; 1638]
  Lawrence of East Clandon, senior, yeoman [DW/PA/7/13 f.39; DW/PA/5/1639/21]
  Richard of Effingham, blacksmith [PRO; PCC Will 1614]
  Richard of East Horsley, bachelor [PRO; PCC Admon 1641]
  William of Effingham, husbandman [DW/PA/5/1568/61]
  see also ATWOOD,WOOD
BITTENDEN
  John, alias John Ellis of Thursley, husbandman [DW/PA/7/7 f.289; DW/PA/5/1599/91] <Abs 517>
BITTENSON
  Ann of Lambeth, widow [DW/PA/7/7 f.309; DW/PA/5/1600/8] <Abs 551>
BITTERLEY
  Elizabeth of Woking [DW/PA/5/1579/19]*
BIX
  John, alias John Biggs of Putney [PRO; PCC Admon 1624]
BIXLEY (BIXLY,BYXLEY)
  Edward of West Horsley [DW/PA/7/4 f.76; 1534]
  Robert of West Horsley [DW/PA/7/3 f.173; 1531]
  William of Capel, tailor [DW/PA/7/7 f.470; DW/PA/5/1604/5] <Abs 886>
  William of East Clandon [PRO; PCC Admon 1649]
BIXON
  Martha of Swk St George, widow [DW/PA/7/13 f.404; DW/PA/5/1645/3]
BLABYE
  Tristram of Swk, gent. [HRO; 1595 AD6]
BLACK (BLACKE)
  Mary, or Mary Bax of ? Ockley [DW/PA/7/8 f.263; 1612]
BLACKBOURNE (BLACKBORNE)
  John of Croydon, tailor [LPL; 96/260; 98/1 f.3r; Will 1625 *and* 1629]
  Margaret of Croydon, widow [LPL; 96/261; 98/1 f.2v; Will 1629]
  Walter of Bermondsey [PRO; PCC Admon 1645]
BLACKDEN (BLAKDEN)
  Cuthbert of Thames Ditton, sergeant of confectionery to the king [PRO; PCC Will 1540]
BLACKE *see* BLACK
BLACKELOCKE *see* BLACKLOCK
BLACKETT (BLACKET,BLAKETT)
  John of Swk St Saviour, parish clerk [DW/PA/5/1563/1]
  John of Swk St Saviour, parish clerk [DW/PA/7/7 f.197; DW/PA/5/1598/9] <Abs 357>
  Robert of Kingston [DW/PA/7/1 f.51; 1487] <Abs 168>
BLACKHOOD
  Thomas of Lambeth [DW/PA/7/4 f.63; 1534]

BLACKLOCK (BLACKELOCKE)
  William of Swk St Saviour [DW/PA/5/1558/28]*
BLACKMAN
  John of Long Ditton - Tolworth, senior [DW/PA/7/4 f.91; 1534]
  Richard of Leatherhead, mercer [DW/PA/7/13 f.501; DW/PA/5/1649/3]
BLACKSTONE
  Robert of Mortlake [LPL; 98/1 f.107r; Will 1639]
  Thomas of Mortlake [LPL; 98/1 f.86v; Will 1637]
BLACKWELL
  Michael of Godalming [PRO; PCC Admon 1632]
  Richard of Swk St Olave, citizen and woodmonger [DW/PA/7/13 f.104; DW/PA/5/1640/18]
BLAGDEN
  Tristram of Newington, esq. [PRO; PCC 1631]
BLAGE
  Richard of Tooting Graveney [DW/PA/5/1576/135]
  Richard of Worplesdon [DW/PA/7/4 f.166; 1536]
  William of Carshalton, yeoman [DW/PA/7/7 f.33; DW/PA/5/1595/7] <Abs 67>
BLAGRAVE
  Edward of Swk St George, gent. [DW/PA/7/13 f.470; DW/PA/5/1648/2]
  Richard of Woking, gent. [DW/PA/7/13 f.162; DW/PA/5/1642/11]
BLAK *see* BLAKE
BLAKDEN *see* BLACKDEN
BLAKE (BLAK)
  Alice of Esher, widow [DW/PA/7/9 f.90; DW/PA/5/1615/12] <Abs U205>
  Alice of Shere [DW/PA/7/1 f.91; 1490] <Abs 308>
  Ann of Ewhurst, spinster [PRO; PCC Admon 1634]
  Elizabeth of Walton on the Hill, widow [DW/PA/7/12 f.259; DW/PA/5/1634/16]
  Ferdinand of Swk St Saviour, baker [DW/PA/5/1592/111]
  Harry of Carshalton [DW/PA/5/1559/2]
  Harvey of Godalming, butcher [DW/PA/5/1570/65]
  Joan of Banstead - Tadworth, widow [DW/PA/5/1629/6]
  Joan of Carshalton - Wellington [DW/PA/7/12 f.259; DW/PA/5/1634/12]
  John of Banstead - Tadworth, yeoman [DW/PA/7/10 f.92; DW/PA/5/1616/14]
  John of Beddington [DW/PA/5/1580/25]
  John of Beddington [DW/PA/5/1587/97]
  John of Rotherhithe, mariner [PRO; PCC 1636]
  Juliana of Godalming, widow of Harry [DW/PA/5/1570/66]
  Richard of Beddington - Bandon [DW/PA/5/1596/8] <Abs U2>
  Richard of Ewhurst; Warnham, Sussex; Rudgwick, Sussex, yeoman [DW/PA/7/8 f.122; DW/PA/5/1610/19]
  Robert of Esher [DW/PA/7/7 f.561; DW/PA/5/1606/12] <Abs 1047>
  Thomas of Coulsdon [HRO; 1587 B12]
  Thomas of Swk St Olave [DW/PA/5/1576/51]
  Walter of ...., citizen and clothworker [DW/PA/5/1562/7]
  William of Carshalton - Wellington [DW/PA/7/11 f.197; DW/PA/5/1625/19]
  William of Charlwood [LPL; Reg. Abp Abbot i f.276; Will 1615]
  William of Dorking, husbandman [HRO; 1642 B5]
BLAKY
  William of Swk St Saviour; Cowlinge Head in Craven, Yorkshire, waterman [DW/PA/7/10 f.231; DW/PA/5/1621/11]
BLANCCHARD *see* BLANCHARD

BLANCH
  Edmund of Esher [DW/PA/5/1627/6]
BLANCHARD (BLANCCHARD,BLANCHET,BLANSHARDE)
  Alexander of Swk St Olave, joiner [DW/PA/5/1576/111]
  John of Newington [LPL; 98/1 f,90r; (ren,) 1638]
  Richard of Bentley, Hampshire [DW/PA/7/1 f,61; 1487] <Abs 203>
BLANCK *see* BLANK
BLAND
  Joan of Rotherhithe, widow [DW/PA/7/7 f,225; DW/PA/5/1598/10] <Abs 397>
BLANK (BLANCK,BLANKE)
  Elizabeth of Guildford Holy Trinity, widow [DW/PA/7/5 f,66; 1539] <Abs 52>
  Elizabeth of Swk St Olave; Warblington, Hampshire; Colby, Lincolnshire, widow [DW/PA/5/1557/68]
  Thomas of Guildford Holy Trinity [DW/PA/7/4 f,139; 1536] [GMR; *in* RB1 335]
  Thomas of Mitcham [PRO; PCC Will 1588]
BLANSHARDE *see* BLANCHARD
BLASDALE
  Elizabeth of Swk St Saviour [DW/PA/7/6 f,14; DW/PA/5/1559/11]
BLASDON (BLAYSDON)
  John of Kingston [DW/PA/7/3 f,198; 1532]
BLAST
  John of Crawley, Sussex; Surrey [LPL; Reg, Abp Stafford f,130; Will 1445]
BLAYSDON *see* BLASDON
BLEAKE
  Margery of Swk St Saviour, servant to Christopher Thomas, waterman [DW/PA/7/11 f,230; DW/PA/5/1625/20]
BLENCOE (BLINCOE)
  Mary, alias Mary Radford of Newington; Bermondsey; Waltham, Essex; Swk, widow [PRO; PCC Will 1627] [LBLAD; Surrey Deeds 1/1510; 1626]
  Nicholas of Newington, esq, [PRO; PCC Will 1625 *and* 1626]
BLENKINSOP (BLYNKYNSOP)
  ...rd of Farnham [*in* DW/PA/5/1544/8]
BLINCOE *see* BLENCOE
BLISSETT
  Richard of Swk St Saviour, waterman [DW/PA/5/1578/106]
BLITHMAN (BLYTHMAN)
  Richard of Chertsey, labourer [DW/PA/7/12 f,82; DW/PA/5/1633/17]
  William of Egham - Trumps, husbandman [DW/PA/7/11 f,599; DW/PA/5/1630/6]
BLONDELL *see* BLUNDELL
BLOOD
  Christina of Bermondsey, widow [HRO; Reg, Way 1 p,30; 1453]
BLOOME (BLOWME,BLOWNE,BLUME)
  John of ..., citizen and stationer [DW/PA/7/13 f,229; DW/PA/5/1642/9]
  John, alias John Gillam of Stoke next Guildford, yeoman [DW/PA/7/8 f,176; DW/PA/5/1610/64]
  Margaret of Swk St Saviour [DW/PA/7/8 f,71; DW/PA/5/1609/11]
  Roger, alias Roger Gilham of Stoke next Guildford, yeoman [HRO; 1614 B3]
  Thomas, alias Thomas Gillam of Worplesdon [DW/PA/7/12 f,222; DW/PA/5/1634/8]
  William of Stoke next Guildford, gardener [DW/PA/5/1591/22]
  William, alias William Gillam of Stoke next Guildford, tailor [DW/PA/5/1617/50] <Abs U215>

BLOUNDELL *see* BLUNDELL

BLOWER
- Thomas of Surrey [PRO; PCC Will 1551]

BLOWME,BLOWNE *see* BLOOME

BLOWYER
- John of Tournai, Netherlands, [DW/PA/7/9 f.73; DW/PA/5/1614/32]

BLOYE
- Agnes of Swk St Saviour, widow [DW/PA/5/1558/29]*

BLUDDER
- (Lady) Jane, alias (Lady) Jane Bill of Reigate [PRO; PCC Admon 1646]
- (Sir) Thomas of Reigate - Flanchford, knight [PRO; PCC Will 1619]

BLUME *see* BLOOME

BLUNDELL (BLONDELL,BLOUNDELL)
- ...rd of Wotton, husbandman [DW/PA/5/1563/17]
- Alice of Pyrford, widow [DW/PA/7/2 f.22; 1492]
- Alice of Wotton, widow [DW/PA/7/8 f.365; DW/PA/5/1612/18]
- Christian of Ewell, widow of Richard [DW/PA/5/1593/151]
- Christopher of Chessington, jun., bricklayer [DW/PA/7/13 f.460; DW/PA/5/1647/1]
- Francis of Fetcham [HRO; 1609 B11]
- George of Lingfield [DW/PA/5/1559/222]
- Joan of Fetcham, widow [DW/PA/7/12 f.446; DW/PA/5/1639/7]
- Joan of Malden; Chessington, widow [DW/PA/7/4 f.222; 1537]
- John of Blechingley, widow of Catherine [PRO; PCC 1642]
- John of Great Bookham [DW/PA/7/5 f.148; 1540]
- John of Great Bookham [LPL; Reg. Abp Parker i f.171r; Admon 1560]
- John of Clapham [PRO; PCC 1649]
- John of Fetcham, husbandman [DW/PA/5/1591/98]*
- John of Lingfield, husbandman [DW/PA/7/2 f.32; 1492]
- John of Lingfield [DW/PA/7/6 f.86; DW/PA/5/1559/240]
- John of Mickleham - West Humble, yeoman [DW/PA/7/9 f.217; DW/PA/5/1617/29]
- John of Wotton, husbandman [DW/PA/5/1561/31]
- Margaret of Mickleham - Byttam, widow [DW/PA/7/12 f.300; DW/PA/5/1635/11]
- Matthew of Dorking [DW/PA/7/6 f.213; 1560]
- Nicholas of Lingfield, sheather [DW/PA/7/11 f.313; DW/PA/5/1626/19]
- Nicholas of Wotton, yeoman [DW/PA/7/8 f.63; DW/PA/5/1609/21]
- Ralph of Ewell [DW/PA/5/1593/58]
- Ralph of Walton on Thames; Horsley [DW/PA/7/8 f.303; DW/PA/5/1613/14]
- Richard of Ewell [DW/PA/5/1593/52]
- Richard of Fetcham, husbandman [DW/PA/7/7 f.474; DW/PA/5/1604/6] <Abs 895>
- Richard of West Molesey [DW/PA/7/11 f.299; DW/PA/5/1626/20]
- Thomas of Croydon [PRO; PCC 1646]
- Thomas of Mickleham [DW/PA/5/1607/18] <Abs U191>
- William of Blechingley - Mitcheners, bricklayer [DW/PA/7/13 f.30; DW/PA/5/1640/9]
- William of Fetcham [DW/PA/7/12 f.299; DW/PA/5/1635/10]
- William of Lingfield, senior, carpenter [DW/PA/7/11 f.110; DW/PA/5/1624/14]
- William of Ripley, priest [HRO; 1545 B28]

BLUNDIEN
Thomas of Charlwood, yeoman [LPL; 96/283; Will 1624]
William of Charlwood, tailor [LPL; 96/282; Will 1624]
BLUNT (BLUNTT)
George of Swk St Olave, woodmonger [DW/PA/7/9 f.337; DW/PA/5/1620/12]
Robert of Swk St Olave, shoemaker [DW/PA/7/7 f.197; DW/PA/5/1598/11] <Abs 356>
BLY
Henry of Newington [LPL; 98/1 f.81v; (ren.) 1637]
BLYMAN
Richard of Chertsey - Lyne Green [DW/PA/7/9 f.149; DW/PA/5/1615/14]
BLYNKYNSOP *see* BLENKINSOP
BLYTHMAN *see* BLITHMAN
BOARD (BOORD,BOORDE,BORDE)
Elizabeth of Richmond, widow [DW/PA/7/12 f.200; DW/PA/5/1633/12]
James of Egham, fisherman [DW/PA/7/6 f.154; DW/PA/5/1559/223]
John of Egham, husbandman [GL; Commissary Court of London Will 1535]
John of Egham [DW/PA/7/6 f.176; DW/PA/5/1559/224]
Thomas of Croydon [PRO; PCC 1633]
Thomas of Egham [PRO; PCC 1648]
Thomas of Tandridge, gent. [PRO; PCC Will 1602]
BOARDMAN (BORDMAN)
John of Swk St Olave [DW/PA/7/5 f.182; 1540]
BOARER *see* BORER
BOATE
Catherine of Swk St Thomas Hospital, widow [DW/PA/7/7 f.375; DW/PA/5/1602/8] <Abs 693>
BOBRACKE,BOBRAICKE *see* BOWBRICK
BOCAM *see* BOOKHAM
BOCAR,BOCCHER,BOCHER *see* BUTCHER
BOCKFOLD *see* BOXALL
BODARDE
John of Lambeth; Houghton, Bedfordshire [DW/PA/7/3 f.196; 1532]
BODDAM
Sarah of Newington, widow [LPL; 96/287; Will 1625]
BODE
John of Richmond [PRO; PCC Admon 1624]
BODELEY
Francis of Streatham, citizen and fishmonger [PRO; PCC Will 1566] <Abs. SAC v.52 p.43>
BODGE
Ellis of Newington [LPL; 96/291; 98/1 f.69v; Will 1635]
BODGER
Robert of Camberwell - Dulwich [DW/PA/7/9 f.164; DW/PA/5/1616/6]
BODHAM
Francis of Swk St Olave, shipwright [DW/PA/7/10 f.120; DW/PA/5/1620/13]
BOGGIN (BOGYN)
William of Limpsfield [DW/PA/7/5 f.194; 1540]
BOHUN (BOHUNE)
John of Bermondsey, citizen and haymonger [GL; Commissary Court of London Will 1394]
Lawrence of Lambeth, Doctor of Physic [PRO; PCC Will 1622]
BOICE
Christopher of West Clandon [HRO; 1605 AD5]

BOKER *see* BOOKER
BOLINGE,BOLLING *see* BULLEN
BOLNEY
James of Blechingley [PRO; PCC Will 1536]
BOLSOM
Richard of Albury, bachelor [PRO; PCC Admon 1645]
BOLT
Phide of Swk St Olave [DW/PA/5/1579/10]*
BOLTBY
John of Bermondsey, late servant to Prince Charles, duke of York [DW/PA/7/10 f.119; DW/PA/5/1620/14]
BOLTON (BOULTON)
Cicely of Kingston; Thames Ditton - Claygate, widow [DW/PA/7/6 f.9; DW/PA/5/1559/7]
Clement of Swk St Saviour, waterman [DW/PA/7/11 f.541; DW/PA/5/1629/8]
John of Swk St Margaret [DW/PA/7/2 f.55; 1499]
John, alias John Botton of Streatham, yeoman [DW/PA/7/5 f.46; 1538]
Lawrence of Surrey [GL; Archdeaconry Court of London Will 1611]
Margaret of Mitcham, widow [DW/PA/7/13 f.29; DW/PA/5/1639/15]
BONAM *see* BONHAM
BONBROKE *see* BENBRICKE
BONCEY *see* BONSEY
BOND (BONDE,BONND)
Agnes of Shere [DW/PA/7/1 f.90; 1489] <Abs 304>
Anthony of Egham, gent. [DW/PA/5/1576/118] <Abs SAC v.28 pp.55-56>
James of Thorpe, esq. [PRO; PCC Will 1598] <Abs SAC v.30 p.9>
Jane of Swk St Thomas [DW/PA/7/13 f.492; DW/PA/5/1649/2]
John of Thorpe, gent. [DW/PA/5/1579/21]*
John of Tooting Graveney, gent. [DW/PA/7/7 f.246; DW/PA/5/1599/7] <Abs 436>
John of Tooting [PRO; PCC Admon 1613]
Phillip of Swk St Thomas, clerk [DW/PA/7/13 f.142; DW/PA/5/1641/4]
William of Swk St Olave, minister [DW/PA/5/1576/93]
William of Thorpe; Richmond; Kingston [DW/PA/7/3 f.157; 1530]
BONDELL
William of Chertsey [DW/PA/7/3 f.109; 1529]
BONE
Dorothy of Camberwell - Dulwich [DW/PA/7/12 f.53; DW/PA/5/1631/20]
John of Carshalton [DW/PA/7/11 f.552; DW/PA/5/1629/9]
Nicholas of Surrey [PRO; PCC Will 1523]
BONER *see* BONNER
BONGONS
Elizabeth Vleeschauwers of ...., widow of Giles [DW/PA/5/1576/140]
BONHAM (BONAM)
Leonard of Tooting Graveney [DW/PA/7/11 f.429; DW/PA/5/1627/7]
Thomas of Tooting Graveney, mealman [DW/PA/5/1558/33]*
BONION (BONYON)
John of Chobham, yeoman [DW/PA/5/1565/9]
John of Chobham, yeoman [HRO; 1565 B21-22]
BONND *see* BOND
BONNE
John of Swk St Saviour [DW/PA/5/1592/75]

BONNER (BONER)
Joan of Richmond, widow [DW/PA/7/12 f.490; DW/PA/5/1638/16]
John of Kingston; Long Ditton; Thames Ditton, husbandman [DW/PA/7/4 f.176; 1536]
Nicholas of Addington, husbandman [HRO; 1529 B6]
Rachel of Rotherhithe, widow [DW/PA/7/11 f.401; DW/PA/5/1627/9]
Richard of Rotherhithe [PRO; PCC Admon 1636]
William of Lambeth - Lambeth South [PRO; PCC Will 1586]
William of Richmond; Bridge House, Swk, citizen and carpenter [PRO; PCC 1630] <Scroope 697>
BONNICK *see* BONWICK
BONSEY (BONCEY,BONSSE,BONSYE)
Alice of Bisley, widow [DW/PA/7/9 f.77; DW/PA/5/1614/34]
Alice of Ockham, widow [DW/PA/5/1578/3]
Edmund of Bisley, husbandman [DW/PA/7/8 f.277; DW/PA/5/1613/15]
Elizabeth of Kingston, widow [DW/PA/7/7 f.560; DW/PA/5/1606/14] <Abs 1046>
Helen of Walton on Thames, widow [PRO; PCC Will 1622]
John of Byfleet, husbandman [DW/PA/7/12 f.456; DW/PA/5/1638/7]
John of Chertsey, yeoman [DW/PA/7/13 f.17; DW/PA/5/1640/6]
Richard of Bisley, husbandman [DW/PA/7/3 f.154; 1530]
Richard of Horsell, yeoman [DW/PA/7/8 f.272; DW/PA/5/1613/16]
Richard of Kingston, shoemaker [DW/PA/7/7 f.331; DW/PA/5/1601/12] <Abs 597>
BONWICK (BONNICK,BONWICKE,BONYCKE)
Alice of Horley, widow, senior [HRO; 1637 B6]
Eleanor of Horley, widow [DW/PA/7/12 f.472; DW/PA/5/1638/9]
Henry of Epsom, labourer [DW/PA/5/1572/11]
Henry of Horley [DW/PA/7/11 f.139; DW/PA/5/1624/15]
John of Horley; Buxted, Sussex [DW/PA/5/1555/50]
John of Horley, senior, yeoman [HRO; 1631 B10]
Peter of Horley [HRO; 1573 B14]
Richard of Lingfield [DW/PA/5/1591/112]
BONYON *see* BONION
BOOGS
John of Betchworth, yeoman [DW/PA/7/13 f.285; DW/PA/5/1643/13]
BOOKER (BOKER)
John of Burstow [PRO; PCC Admon 1626]
Richard of Ockley [DW/PA/5/1561/54]
BOOKHAM (BOCAM,BOWCOMBE,BUCKHAM)
Henry of Swk St Saviour, woodmonger [DW/PA/7/8 f.66; DW/PA/5/1609/14]
Joan of Elstead [*in* DW/PA/5/1558/30]*
John of Farnham, tailor [DW/PA/7/6 f.47; DW/PA/5/1559/1]
John of Farnham, senior, yeoman [DW/PA/7/13 f.64; DW/PA/5/1642/5]
William of Elstead, senior, yeoman [DW/PA/7/13 f.156; DW/PA/5/1641/12]
William of Frensham - Hillside, husbandman [DW/PA/5/1558/31]*
BOONDELL *see* BUNDLE
BOONE (BOUNE,BOWNE)
Alan, alias Alan Stasey of Reigate, mason [DW/PA/7/7 f.447; DW/PA/5/1603/16B] <Abs 847>
Guillam of Richmond, coachman to king James [PRO; PCC Will 1617]
Humphrey of ? Camberwell [DW/PA/5/1561/2]
Leonard of Bermondsey [PRO; PCC 1648]
Robert of Shere, bachelor [DW/PA/7/13 f.49; DW/PA/5/1639/23]

BOORD,BOORDE *see* BOARD
BOORER *see* BORER
BOORNE *see* BOURNE
BOOTE
Elizabeth of Swk [DW/PA/5/1561/12]
BOOTH (BOOTHE,BOWTH)
Gilbert of Surrey [PRO; 1568 Will]
John of ...., citizen and merchant tailor [DW/PA/7/12 f.452; 1638]
John of Beddington, yeoman [PRO; PCC Will 1613]
Joshua of ...., citizen and merchant tailor [DW/PA/7/12 f.454; DW/PA/5/1639/9]
Juliana of Thames Ditton, widow of John, gent. [DW/PA/5/1586/16]
Reynold of ... [brother in Cheshire] [DW/PA/7/7 f.462; DW/PA/5/1603/16C] <Abs 874>
BOOTHBY (BOTHBY)
Robert of Thames Ditton - Weston [PRO; PCC 1649]
Robert of Thames Ditton - Weston [PRO; PCC 1642]
Thomas of Swk St George, carpenter [DW/PA/7/4 f.38; 1533]
BOOTHE *see* BOOTH
BORCHAT *see* BURCHETT
BORDE *see* BOARD
BORDEN (BOURDEN)
Katherine of Swk St Mary Overy [DW/PA/7/6 f.178; DW/PA/5/1559/159]
Thomas of Swk St Saviour [DW/PA/5/1569/34]
BORDMAN *see* BOARDMAN
BORER (BOARER,BOORER,BOWERER,BOWRER)
Elizabeth of Horsley, widow [DW/PA/7/10 f.31; DW/PA/5/1616/13]
George of Bermondsey, citizen and dyer [PRO; PCC 1646]
Henry of Kingston, senior, yeoman [DW/PA/7/7 f.75; DW/PA/5/1596/9] <Abs 138>
Henry of Kingston - Norbiton, senior, mercer [DW/PA/7/9 f.245; DW/PA/5/1617/30]
John of Wotton, yeoman [DW/PA/5/1591/41]
Nicholas of Godstone, husbandman [DW/PA/5/1627/8]
Thomas of East Grinstead, Sussex, yeoman [SRO; 303/13/1; 1631]
Thomas of Wotton, husbandman [DW/PA/7/12 f.433; DW/PA/5/1637/16]
Walter of Ockley [PRO; PCC Admon 1649]
William of Burstow [PRO; PCC Will 1596]
BORMAN *see* BOURMAN
BORNAM *see* BURNHAM
BORNE *see* BOURNE
BORODALE *see* BORROWDALE
BOROUGH,BOROWE,BOROWGHT,BOROWGHWELL *see* ABURROW,BORROWE,BURROWS
BORRE
Derek, alias Derek Peterson of Swk St Olave, coppersmith [DW/PA/7/4 f.51; 1533]
BORROWDALE (BORODALE,BORRADELL)
John of Sutton, husbandman [DW/PA/7/7 f.638; DW/PA/5/1608/16] <Abs 1195>
Robert of Leatherhead, yeoman [DW/PA/7/12 f.116; DW/PA/5/1632/8]
BORROWE (BOROWE,BORROW)
Richard of Swk St Olave, hatmaker [DW/PA/5/1563/106]
Thomas of Abinger, hat maker, gent. [PRO; PCC Will 1530]
see also ABURROW,BURROWS
BORTEN *see* BOUGHTON

BORYLL *see* BURRELL
BOSQUILLON
Peter of London, parchment maker [DW/PA/5/1563/14]
BOSSE
Francis of Swk St Saviour, woodmonger [DW/PA/7/8 f.261; DW/PA/5/1611/11]
Joan of Swk St Saviour, widow [DW/PA/7/10 f.268; DW/PA/5/1622/9]
BOSTOCK (BOSTOCKE,BOSTOKE)
Jane of Tandridge, widow of Richard esq.; Crowhurst [DW/PA/7/8 f.373; DW/PA/5/1612/19]
Joan of Weybridge, spinster [PRO; PCC 1636]
Richard of Tandridge, esq. [PRO; PCC Will 1606] <Abs. SAC v.12 p.100>
Thomas of Swk St Margaret [DW/PA/7/4 f.52; 1533]
BOSWELL
Andrew of Battersea [PRO; PCC 1646]
BOSYATE
George of Kingston [DW/PA/7/5 f.56; 1539] <Abs 59>
BOTELAR *see* BUTLER
BOTELEY *see* BOTLEY
BOTERYE
William of Rotherhithe [DW/PA/5/1575/26]
BOTHBY *see* BOOTHBY
BOTHE
John of Thames Ditton, gent. [PRO; PCC Will 1547]
BOTHELL (BITHELL)
Edward of Swk St Saviour [DW/PA/7/7 f.524; DW/PA/5/1606/13] <Abs 986>
Ephraim of Dorking [PRO; PCC 1638]
John of Dorking, glover [DW/PA/7/10 f.184; DW/PA/5/1619/11]
John of Dorking [PRO; PCC 1639]
Susan of Dorking, widow [PRO; PCC 1649]
BOTLEY (BOTELEY,BOTTELAY,BOTTELEY,BOTTLEY)
Catherine of Lingfield, widow [DW/PA/7/12 f.362; DW/PA/5/1637/17]
Christiana of Lingfield,widow [HRO; 1558 B62-63]
Edward of Limpsfield; Crowhurst, yeoman [DW/PA/7/9 f.155; DW/PA/5/1615/15]
John of Limpsfield [DW/PA/7/1 f.87; 1489] <Abs 294>
John of Lingfield, yeoman [DW/PA/7/12 f.311; DW/PA/5/1636/9]
John of Oxted [DW/PA/7/4 f.196; 1537]
Richard of Limpsfield; Oxted [DW/PA/7/7 f.191; DW/PA/5/1598/12] <Abs 346>
Robert of Crowhurst [PRO; PCC Will 1552]
Thomas of Crowhurst, husbandman [DW/PA/7/13 f.79; DW/PA/5/1641/21]
Thomas of Oxted, yeoman [HRO; 1606 B6]
Thomas of Oxted [DW/PA/7/7 f.523; DW/PA/5/1606/15] <Abs 983>
William of Limpsfield [DW/PA/7/6 f.119; DW/PA/5/1559/212]
BOTOLPH *see* BUTTOLPHE
BOTTELAY,BOTTELEY *see* BOTLEY
BOTTING (BOTTINGE)
Hugh of Horne [PRO; PCC Will 1566]
John of Ewhurst [PRO; PCC 1648]
Thomas of Wotton [PRO; PCC Admon 1647]
BOTTLEY *see* BOTLEY
BOTTOMLYE
Richard of Carshalton, yeoman [HRO; 1585 B12]

BOTTON
John of Streatham, yeoman [DW/PA/7/5 f.46; 1538] <Abs 114>
BOTTY (BOTYE)
John of Swk St Mary Magdalen Overy [DW/PA/7/4 f.132; 1536]
BOUGEY
John of Bermondsey [PRO; PCC Will 1501]
BOUGHTON (BORTEN,BOUGHTONE,BOWGHTON,BOWTEN,BOWTON)
Anthony of Ewell [DW/PA/7/12 f.210; DW/PA/5/1633/14]
Henry of Chobham, yeoman [DW/PA/7/11 f.591; DW/PA/5/1630/7]
Joan of Send, widow [DW/PA/7/5 f.52; 1538] <Abs 76>
John of Capel [DW/PA/5/1592/53]
John of Dunsfold [DW/PA/5/1562/10]
John of East Horsley, yeoman [LPL; 96/309; Will 1628]
John of Wotton, husbandman [HRO; 1600 B4]
Robert of Ockley [DW/PA/7/6 f.279; 1560]
Robert of Send; Godalming; Woking; Wonersh; Walton on Thames; yeoman [DW/PA/5/1605/7] <Abs U127>
Thomas of Send [HRO; 1528 B9]
Thomas of Send and Ripley, yeoman [DW/PA/7/9 f.102; DW/PA/5/1614/39]
William of Battersea [PRO; PCC Admon 1636]
William of Send; Wonersh; Ripley [DW/PA/7/7 f.635; DW/PA/5/1608/17] <Abs 1188>
William of Swk St Thomas [DW/PA/7/8 f.180; DW/PA/5/1611/20]
BOULAND
John of Streatham [DW/PA/7/11 f.411; DW/PA/5/1627/10]
BOULTER
Ursula of Swk St George, spinster [DW/PA/7/12 f.267; DW/PA/5/1635/3]
William of Barnes, gent. [PRO; PCC 1631]
BOULTON *see* BOLTON
BOUNE *see* BOONE
BOURCHIER (BOURGCHIER,BOWCHER,BURCHIER)
Elizabeth of Richmond, gent. [PRO; PCC Will 1564]
(Sir) John of Barnes, knight [PRO; PCC Will 1533]
(Sir) John of Barnes; Chertsey, knight [PRO; PCC Will 1474]
(Sir) John of Lambeth, knight [PRO; PCC Admon 1626]
(Sir) John of Lambeth, knight [PRO; PCC Admon 1635]
Roger of Chertsey [PRO; PCC Will 1507]
BOURDEN *see* BORDEN
BOURMAN
John of London, citizen and mercer [DW/PA/7/13 f.328; 1644]
Richard of Mortlake, bachelor [PRO; PCC Admon 1607]
BOURNE (BOORNE,BORNE)
Ann of Leatherhead - Pachesham, widow [DW/PA/7/8 f.8; DW/PA/5/1608/14]
Beatrice of Swk St Saviour, spinster [DW/PA/5/1592/20]
Beatrice of Swk, sp. [DW/PA/5/1592/93]
Elizabeth of Epsom, widow [DW/PA/7/12 f.122; DW/PA/5/1632/9]
James of Great Bookham, yeoman [DW/PA/7/12 ff.41,45; DW/PA/5/1631/17]
James of Swk St Olave, ironmonger [DW/PA/7/7 f.49; DW/PA/5/1595/8] <Abs 91>
John of Mortlake [LPL; 98/1 f.117r; (ren.) 1640]
John of Reigate, innholder [DW/PA/5/1570/28]
John of Richmond, barber [DW/PA/7/10 f.280; DW/PA/5/1622/10]
Nicholas of Swk St Olave, citizen and grocer [DW/PA/7/11 f.25; DW/PA/5/1623/12]

BOURNE (BOORNE,BORNE) [*continued*]
  Ralph of Walton on Thames [PRO; PCC Admon 1589]
  Robert of Epsom; Ewell, husbandman [DW/PA/7/8 f.26; DW/PA/5/1608/15]
  Thomas of Bermondsey, gent. [PRO; PCC 1637]
  William of Betchworth; Middle Temple, Middlesex, esq.
    [PRO; PCC Will 1606] <Abs. SAC v.12 p.106>
  William of Chertsey, baker [DW/PA/7/10 ff.142,278; DW/PA/5/1620/15]
  William, alias William Tagborn of Croydon [LPL; 96/2531; Will 1617]
  see also ABOURNE,ABURNE,BOONE(BOWNE),BYRNE
BOUTCHINGE *see* BUTCHIN
BOVER
  Eleanor, alias Eleanor Bowtell of Egham, widow [DW/PA/5/1592/8]
BOVINGTON
  Robert of Swk St Olave, bricklayer [DW/PA/7/11 f.229; DW/PA/5/1625/21]
BOWBRICK (BOBRACKE,BOBRAICKE,BOWBROKE,BOWBROOKE)
  Isaac of Dunsfold, widow [DW/PA/7/6 f.242; 1560]
  John of Alfold, yeoman [DW/PA/7/9 f.319; DW/PA/5/1619/13]
  William of Dunsfold, husbandman [*in* DW/PA/5/1557/88]
BOWCHER *see* BOURCHIER
BOWCOMBE *see* BOOKHAM
BOWDEN (BOWDONE)
  Agnes of Battersea, widow [DW/PA/5/1592/88]
  John of Bermondsey [PRO; PCC Admon 1592]
  William of Clapham [DW/PA/7/8 f.29; DW/PA/5/1608/18]
  William of Godalming [DW/PA/7/2 f.42; 1492]
BOWDOCKE
  Bartholomew of Albury, yeoman [DW/PA/7/13 f.344; 1644]
BOWDONE *see* BOWDEN
BOWDOX
  Bartholomew of Albury, parson [HRO; 1582 AD3]
BOWELANDE *see* BOWLAND
BOWELL
  Edward of Dorking [PRO; PCC Admon 1647]
  Isabella of Reigate [DW/PA/5/1576/16]
  John of Capel [PRO; PCC Admon 1635]
  John of Reigate, yeoman [DW/PA/7/6 f.131; DW/PA/5/1559/132]
  Richard of 'Shethingdon', Surrey [PRO; PCC Will 1478]
  William of Capel [PRO; PCC Will 1599]
  William of Capel [PRO; PCC Will 1615]
BOWEN
  Agnes of ..., widow of Martin [*French*] [DW/PA/7/8 f.61; DW/PA/5/1609/22]
  Martin of ... [*French*] [DW/PA/7/8 f.62; DW/PA/5/1609/23]
BOWER
  Sarah of Swk St Saviour - Clink Liberty, widow [DW/PA/7/7 f.521;
    DW/PA/5/1606/16] <Abs 978>
  Thomas of Newington, gent. [PRO; PCC Will 1617]
  William of Swk St Mary Magdalen Overy [DW/PA/7/2 f.86; 1503]
BOWERER *see* BORER
BOWES
  Martin of Battersea [PRO; PCC Admon 1573]
BOWETT
  Thomas of Newdigate, gent. [PRO; PCC Admon 1574]
BOWLAND (BOWLANDE)
  John of Malden, yeoman [DW/PA/5/1558/32]

BOWLAND (BOWLANDE) [*continued*]
John of Rotherhithe, labouring man [DW/PA/5/1578/92]
BOWLER
Bartholomew of Godalming, clothier [DW/PA/7/7 f.586; DW/PA/5/1607/15] <Abs 1091>
Thomas of Limpsfield, yeoman [LPL; Reg. Abp Abbot i f.280; Will 1616]
BOWLETT
Thomas of Reigate [DW/PA/7/11 f.446; DW/PA/5/1628/13]
BOWLEY
Robert of Malden, husbandman [PRO; PCC Will 1628]
BOWLING
Juliana of Kingston, widow [DW/PA/7/12 f.272; DW/PA/5/1635/5]
BOWLSHAM
Peter of Haslemere [DW/PA/5/1588/7]
BOWLSON
John of Clapham, husbandman [DW/PA/7/7 f.633; DW/PA/5/1608/19] <Abs 1183>
BOWMAN
Hugh of Swk St Saviour, shipwright [DW/PA/7/7 f.315; DW/PA/5/1600/10] <Abs 561>
John of Merstham, yeoman [PRO; PCC Will 1629] [SRO; 212/70/3; 1629]
Richard of Merstham [PRO; PCC 1649]
Thomas of Merstham, yeoman [LPL; 96/321; Will 1626]
BOWMER
Edward of the Ship *Royal Navy*, sailor [DW/PA/7/13 f.368; 1644]
BOWNE *see* BOURNE
BOWNEY *see* BURNEY
BOWRE *see* BOWYER
BOWRER *see* BORER
BOWRES
Henry of Kingston [HRO; 1526 B5]
BOWSER
John of Mitcham, citizen and vintner [PRO; PCC Will 1615]
BOWTELL
Eleanor, alias Eleanor Bover of Egham, widow [DW/PA/5/1592/8]
BOWTEN *see* BOUGHTON
BOWTH *see* BOOTH
BOWTON *see* BOUGHTON
BOWYER (BOWRE,BOYER)
Agnes of Wimbledon, widow [PRO; PCC Admon 1579]
Benjamin of Camberwell, esq. [PRO; PCC Will 1618]
(Sir) Edmund of Camberwell, knight [PRO; PCC Will 1627]
Edmund of Camberwell [PRO; PCC Admon 1630]
Emma of Camberwell, widow [DW/PA/7/11 f.133; DW/PA/5/1624/16]
Frances, alias Frances Byne of Lingfield [PRO; PCC Admon 1630]
Joan, alias Joan Lane of Bermondsey - Bermondsey Street, widow [DW/PA/7/12 f.266; DW/PA/5/1635/58]
John of Camberwell, esq. [PRO; PCC Will 1570] [LBLAD; Surrey Deeds 1/6703; 1569]
John of Camberwell [DW/PA/7/11 f.363; DW/PA/5/1626/21]
John of Camberwell; Lambeth [PRO; PCC Admon 1636]
John of Mortlake [PRO; PCC Admon 1596]
Nicholas of Bermondsey [DW/PA/7/3 f.97; 1529]
Niman of Swk St Olave, mariner [DW/PA/7/8 f.228; DW/PA/5/1612/20]
Richard of Kingston [SRO; KB26/1; 1574]

BOWYER (BOWRE,BOYER) [*continued*]
  Simon of Thorpe [PRO; PCC Admon 1597]
  Thomas of Wandsworth [PRO; PCC Will 1504]
  William of Bermondsey, citizen and white baker [DW/PA/7/13 f.292; DW/PA/5/1643/15]
  William, alias William Bowyer of Byfleet [PRO; PCC Will 1605] <Abs. SAC v.12 p.86>
  William of Charlwood, gent. [PRO; PCC 1632]
  William of Wimbledon, gent. [PRO; PCC Will 1570]
  William of Wimbledon [PRO; PCC Admon 1578]
BOXALL (BOCKFOLD,BOXALD,BOXFOLD,BOXFOLLD,BOXOLL,BOXSALL,BOXSOLD,BOXSOULE)
  Agnes of Elstead, widow [DW/PA/7/7 f.181; DW/PA/5/1597/11] <Abs 333>
  Harry of Haslemere, labourer [DW/PA/7/3 f.99; 1529]
  Henry of Elstead, husbandman [HRO; 1573 B15]
  Henry of Elstead; Thursley, yeoman [DW/PA/7/9 f.177; DW/PA/5/1616/12]
  Joan, alias Joan Edmeade of Windlesham, widow [PRO; PCC Admon 1648]
  Joan, alias Joan Edmunds of Windlesham [PRO; PCC Admon 1649]
  John of Elstead - Ridgeway [DW/PA/7/13 f.94; DW/PA/5/1640/17]
  John of Frensham; Haslemere; Linchmere, Sussex [DW/PA/7/5 f.119; 1539]
  John of Frensham, husbandman [DW/PA/5/1588/53]
  John of Shere, husbandman [DW/PA/7/8 f.382; DW/PA/5/1612/21]
  John of Thursley - 'Hantes' [BM; Add.Ms 27,740; 1505]
  John of Thursley [PRO; PCC Will 1597]
  John of Thursley - Smallbrook, yeoman [DW/PA/7/7 f.212; DW/PA/5/1598/13] <Abs 379>
  Magdalen of Elstead, widow [HRO; 1587 B13]
  Market of Frensham, widow [DW/PA/5/1568/39]
  Thomas of Godalming [PRO; PCC Admon 1615]
  William of Thursley [DW/PA/7/1 f.11; 1484] <Abs 37>
  William of Thursley, yeoman [DW/PA/5/1568/34]
  William of Thursley [DW/PA/7/12 f.312; DW/PA/5/1636/11]
BOYD
  Thomas of Bermondsey, gardener [DW/PA/7/12 f.32; DW/PA/5/1631/15]
BOYDELL
  George of Kingston [PRO; PCC Admon 1598]
BOYER *see* BOWYER
BOYES *see* BOYS,du BOYES
BOYLETT (BOYLET)
  Bridget of Ash, widow [DW/PA/7/7 f.392; DW/PA/5/1603/17] <Abs 729>
  George of Ash, senior [DW/PA/7/11 f.138; DW/PA/5/1624/17]
  Joan of Ash, widow [DW/PA/7/12 f.260; DW/PA/5/1634/13]
  John of Ash [HRO; 1590 B7]
  John of Ash, yeoman [DW/PA/7/12 f.444; DW/PA/5/1639/5]
  John of Ash [PRO; PCC Admon 1639]
  John of Ash [PRO; PCC 1639 Sentence]
  John of Worplesdon, bricklayer [DW/PA/7/8 f.163; DW/PA/5/1611/12]
  Thomas of Woking, mason [HRO; 1623 AD6]
BOYNTON
  William of Guildford [PRO; PCC Will 1539]
BOYS
  Anthony of Coulsdon; Nutfield; Merstham, clerk [DW/PA/7/8 f.195; DW/PA/5/1610/21]
  Elizabeth of Beddington, widow [PRO; PCC Will 1600]
  Elizabeth of Epsom, spinster [PRO; PCC Will 1618]

BOYS [*continued*]
John of Croydon, gent. [PRO: PCC Will 1611] <Abs. SAC v.35 p.33-34>
John of Rotherhithe, gent. [PRO: PCC Admon 1611]
John of Send [DW/PA/7/2 f.7; 1491]
(Sir) John of Harrow Hill, Middlesex; Swk Stews Side, knight [LPL: Reg. Abp Stafford f.163; Will 1448]
Richard of Dorking, clerk [PRO: PCC Will 1517]
see also du BOYS

BRABORNE (BRABAN,BRABAND,BRABOREN,BRABOURN,BRABRN,BRABURNE,BRAYBORN)
Alice of Farnham [PRO: PCC Will 1546]
Henry of Albury [HRO: 1641 B9]
Henry of Farnham [PRO: PCC Will 1553]
Henry of Farnham, yeoman [DW/PA/7/8 f.216; 1612]
Jane of Farnham, widow [DW/PA/7/7 f.585; DW/PA/5/1607/16] <Abs 1089>
Joan of Pirbright, widow [DW/PA/5/1558/34]*
John of Bramley, tanner [DW/PA/7/9 f.284; 1618]
John of Bramley, tanner [DW/PA/7/12 f.307; DW/PA/5/1635/15]
John of Farnham, senior [DW/PA/7/5 f.29; 1538]
John of Farnham [DW/PA/7/5 f.111; 1539] <Abs 33>
John of Farnham, tanner [DW/PA/5/1587/8]
John of Farnham, saddler [DW/PA/7/11 f.97; DW/PA/5/1624/18]
Robert of Farnham [PRO: PCC Will 1563]
Robert of Windlesham - Bagshot, innholder [DW/PA/7/8 f.68; DW/PA/5/1609/12]
Thomas of Farnham [DW/PA/7/2 f.125; 1518]
Thomas of Farnham [DW/PA/7/5 f.35; 1538] [*regrant of 1518 will*] <Abs 34>
Thomas of Farnham, junior, baker [DW/PA/7/11 f.347; DW/PA/5/1625/22]
Thomas, alias Thomas Brabant of Farnham, yeoman [DW/PA/7/11 f.602; DW/PA/5/1630/8]

BRABROOKE
John of Swk St Saviour [DW/PA/7/7 f.388; DW/PA/5/1602/9] <Abs 720>
Richard, alias Richard Bravebrooke of Swk St Olave [DW/PA/5/1620/16] <Abs U240>

BRACEBRIGGE
William of Sheen [PRO: PCC Will 1499]

BRACEWELL (BRASWELL)
John of Swk St Saviour, waterman [DW/PA/7/6 f.259; 1560]

BRACKAN
Thomas of Newington, yeoman [LPL: 96/328; Will 1625]

BRACKLEY (BRAKLAY)
Hugh of Rotherhithe [PRO: PCC Will 1561 *and* 1562]
Thomas of Kingston [DW/PA/7/1 f.193; 1488]

BRADBORNE (BRADBORN)
Jane of Swk St Saviour, spinster [DW/PA/5/1586/30]
Thomas of Kingston [PRO: PCC Admon 1599]

BRADBRIDGE (BRADBRIGG,BRADBRYGE)
John of Surrey, gent. [PRO: PCC Will 1503]
Richard of Farnham, husbandman [DW/PA/7/5 f.133; 1539]
Thomas of Lambeth, gent. [PRO: PCC Will 1624]
Thomas of Reigate, gent. [PRO: PCC Will 1477]

BRADFOLD (BRADEFOLDE,BRADFOLDE)
Henry of Chiddingfold [PRO: PCC Admon 1594]
John of Chiddingfold, husbandman [DW/PA/5/1588/49]
John of Godalming, senior, clothier [DW/PA/5/1588/68]

BRADFOLD (BRADEFOLDE, BRADFOLDE) [*continued*]
John of Haslemere; Thursley, husbandman [DW/PA/7/9 f.116; DW/PA/5/1615/18]
Thomas of Chiddingfold [*in* DW/PA/5/1555/14]
Thomas of Chiddingfold, gent. [PRO; PCC 1639]

BRADFORD
Elizabeth of Addington [PRO; PCC 1648]

BRADIE *see* BRADY

BRADLEY (BRADLEYE)
Jane *or* Joan Bradley of Swk St Olave [DW/PA/7/5 f.100; 1539]
John of Swk St Saviour [BM; Add.Ms 24,925 f.7v; 1544] <Abs 12>
John of Swk St Saviour - Upper Ground, waterman [DW/PA/7/11 f.267; DW/PA/5/1625/23]
Richard of Guildford [PRO; PCC Admon 1617]
Robert of Chobham, husbandman [DW/PA/7/1 f.16; 1485] <Abs 53>
Thomas of Newington - Walworth [PRO; PCC Admon 1637]

BRADMORE
Robert of Rotherhithe [PRO; PCC 1647]

BRADSHAW (BRADSHAWE)
Ann of Swk St Saviour, widow [DW/PA/7/7 f.513; DW/PA/5/1605/13] <Abs 963>
Hercules of Battersea [PRO; PCC 1636]
John of Bermondsey [PRO; PCC Admon 1646]
Margery of Ockham; ? Shere - Wickhams [DW/PA/7/10 f.201; DW/PA/5/1621/12] <Abs U247>
Robert of Kingston, cooper [DW/PA/5/1563/19]

BRADSTON
Alice of Ash, widow of Richard Bradston, and of Richard Hiller [DW/PA/7/2 f.14; 1491] [*two copies*]

BRADWAY (BRADWAIE)
Abraham of Newington, senior [PRO; PCC 1637]
Ann of Newington, widow of Abraham [PRO; PCC 1645]

BRADWELL
Mary, alias Mary Bardwell of Rotherhithe, widow [PRO; PCC Will 1627]

BRADY (BRADIE)
Nicholas of Lambeth [PRO; PCC Admon 1608]

BRAESE
John of Lambeth [DW/PA/7/6 f.54; DW/PA/5/1559/121]

BRAGG
Alice of Swk St George [DW/PA/7/7 f.337; DW/PA/5/1601/13]

BRAIE *see* BRAY

BRAINE (BRAYNE)
Andrew of Wandsworth, mealman [PRO; PCC Will 1602] <Abs, SAC v.10, p.310> [*and*] [DW/PA/5/1602/10] <Abs U42>
Andrew of Wandsworth
Joan of Wandsworth [DW/PA/7/11 f.292; DW/PA/5/1626/22]

BRAITHWAITE (BRATHAT, BRAYTHATE, BRAYTHWAITE)
Gawen of Swk St Olave, tapster [DW/PA/5/1582/7]
Robert of Bermondsey [PRO; PCC Will 1609]

BRAKLAY *see* BRACKLEY

BRAMLEY
John of Egham - Egham Wick, yeoman [HRO; 1639 B6]

BRAMPTON (BRAMTON)
John of Mitcham, husbandman [DW/PA/5/1552/13]
John of Swk [LPL; Reg. Abp Bourgchier f.39v; Admon 1456]

BRAMPTON (BRAMTON) [*continued*]
  Richard of Richmond, gent. [DW/PA/7/3 f.149; 1520]
  Thomas of Richmond, gent. [PRO; PCC Will 1528]
BRAMSON
  Ann of Leatherhead, widow [DW/PA/7/9 f.77; DW/PA/5/1614/35]
  John of Leatherhead, yeoman [DW/PA/7/7 f.416 *and* DW/PA/7/8 f.283; DW/PA/5/1603/18 *and* DW/PA/5/1613/17] <Abs 780 of DW/PA/7/7 entry>
BRAMSTON
  John of Blechingley [DW/PA/7/1 f.84; c1488] <Abs 280>
BRAMTON *see* BRAMPTON
BRANCHE
  Robert of Surrey, girdler [PRO; PCC Will 1567]
BRAND
  Jacob of Swk St Saviour, beer brewer [DW/PA/5/1586/7]
  Katherine of Ockley [HRO; 1581 AD8]
  Richard of Dorking, tanner [DW/PA/7/10 f.18; DW/PA/5/1616/15]
BRANDON
  Charles, duke of Suffolk, of Surrey [PRO; PCC Will 1547]
  Edward of Lambeth - Marsh Lambeth [PRO; PCC Admon 1633]
  Richard of Swk St Mary Overy, hosier [DW/PA/7/2 f.106; 1516]
BRANSTONE
  Robert of ... [DW/PA/5/1603/19] <Abs U62>
BRAON
  Thomas, alias Thomas Bracon,Barron,Baron,Barne, senior of Guildford St Mary; Godalming [BM; Add.Ms 24,925 f.18v; 1542] <Abs 43>
BRASIER
  Denise of Sutton, spinster, servant of R. Cordell [HRO; 1619 B10]
  John of Morden; Tatsfield; Cudham, Kent [DW/PA/7/10 f.86; DW/PA/5/1615/22]
BRASSETT
  John of Long Ditton - Tolworth, husbandman [DW/PA/7/10 f.2; DW/PA/5/1616/16]
BRASWELL *see* BRACEWELL
BRATFORD
  William of Croydon [LPL; 98/1 ff.98v,108r; Will 1638 *and* 1639]
BRATHAT *see* BRAITHWAITE
BRATHER
  William of Swk St Saviour [DW/PA/5/1593/76]
BRATHERTON *see* BROTHERTON
BRAVEBROOKE
  Richard, alias Richard Brabrooke of Swk St Olave [DW/PA/5/1620/16] <Abs U240>
BRAWNE
  (Sir) Hugh of Newington, knight [PRO; PCC Will 1615]
BRAY (BRAIE,BRAYE)
  Ann of Horley, widow [DW/PA/5/1569/24]
  Christopher of Horley; Horne; Charlwood [DW/PA/7/6 f.155; DW/PA/5/1559/221]
  Christopher of Horley [DW/PA/5/1586/12]
  (Sir) Edward of Cranleigh, knight [PRO; PCC Will 1558; GMR; 85/13/179]
  (Sir) Edward of Shere, knight [PRO; PCC Will 1581; GMR; 85/13/236]
  Edward of Shere [PRO; PCC Admon 1635]
  Henry of Reigate, tanner [HRO; 1586 B8]
  (Dame) Jane of Surrey [PRO; PCC Will 1579; GMR; 85/13/215]

BRAY (BRAIE,BRAYE) [*continued*]
John, senior of Horley [PRO; PCC Will 1558]
John of Leigh [DW/PA/7/3 f.184; 1531]
Owen of Chobham [PRO; PCC Will 1568]
Richard of Ewell; Merstham; Epsom; Cheam; Horley; Charlwood; Leigh [DW/PA/7/6 f.293; 1560]
Sander of Ewell [PRO; PCC Admon 1593]
Thomas of Burstow [PRO; PCC Admon 1560]
Thomas of Croydon [LPL; 98/1 f.120v; Will 1641]
Thomas of Croydon [PRO; PCC Will 1641]
William of Pyrford [PRO; PCC Admon 1647]

BRAYBORN *see* BRABORNE

BRAYBROKE
Nicholas of Horsley; Bideford, Devon, canon of St Paul's and Exeter, formerly archdeacon of Cornwall [LPL; Reg. Abp Arundel i f.165; Will 1399]

BRAYNE *see* BRAINE

BRAYTHAT,BRAYTHWAITE *see* BRAITHWAITE

BREAME
Richard of Wandsworth [PRO; PCC Will 1610] <Abs. SAC v.24 p.58 *and* v.33 p.24>
Richard of Wandsworth, gent. [PRO; PCC Will 1619]

BREE
Joab of Newington [LPL; 98/1 f.130v; Will 1642]

BREECHER
Thomas of Limpsfield [PRO; PCC 1649]

BREENE *see* BRIAN

BREGNELL *see* BRIDGELL

BREMOND
Robert of Swk, chaplain [LPL; Reg. Abp Morton f.79v; Admon 1492]

BREMYSDEN *see* BRUMSDEN

BREND (BRENDE,BROND)
John of West Molesey, gent. [PRO; PCC Will 1627]
Judith of West Molesey, spinster [PRO; PCC Will 1599]
Nicholas of West Molesey, esq. [PRO; PCC Will 1601] <Abs. SAC v.10 p.302 *and* v.30 p.98>
Thomas of West Molesey, gent. [PRO; PCC Will 1599] <Abs SAC v.30 pp.97-98>
William of Blechingley, gent. [PRO; PCC Will 1610] <Abs. SAC v.24 p.64>

BRENLEY
William, alias William Brinley of ... [DW/PA/5/1601/14] <Abs U31>

BRENNOK
William of Swk St Margaret [DW/PA/7/2 f.84; 1502]

BRENT
Joan of Carshalton, widow [Kent Archives Office; Rochester Consistory Court v.245; 1492] <Abs SAC v.27; Arch.Cantiana v.29>

BRERETON
Richard of Rotherhithe [PRO; PCC Admon 1633]
Theophilus of Mitcham, esq. [PRO; PCC 1639]

BRETT
Lawrence of Swk St George [DW/PA/7/12 f.311; DW/PA/5/1636/10]
Robert of Croydon, innholder [LPL; 96/336; Will 1647]

BRETTON
Christopher of Camberwell - Peckham Rye [DW/PA/5/1588/2]

BREWARTH
John of Bermondsey, victualler [DW/PA/7/11 f.211; DW/PA/5/1625/24]
BREWEN
John of Farnham, esq. [PRO; PCC Will 1544]
BREWER (BRUER,BRWAR)
Agnes of Farnham [DW/PA/7/11 f.393; DW/PA/5/1626/23]
Hilliard of Swk St Olave [DW/PA/5/1579/17]*
John, alias John Molyneux of Windlesham - Bagshot [PRO; PCC Will 1548]
BREWES
Lancelot of Swk St Olave [DW/PA/7/12 f.311; DW/PA/5/1637/18]
BREWTON
Frances, alias Frances Stapley, of ...., widow [PRO; PCC Admon 1641]
BRIAN (BRIEN,BRYAN,BRYAND,BRYANDE)
Charles of Swk St Saviour - Old Paris Garden Liberty [DW/PA/7/11 f.58; DW/PA/5/1623/13]
Elizabeth, alias Elizabeth Grisbrooke of Blechingley [PRO; PCC Admon 1643]
Garret, alias Garret Breene of Wandsworth, servant to the Queen [PRO; PCC Will 1609] <Abs. SAC v.23 p.133>
Garret of Wandsworth [PRO; PCC Will 1614]
John, alias John Scrofton of Lingfield [PRO; PCC Will 1602] <Abs. SAC v.10 pp.305-306]
John, alias John Scrofton of Lingfield [PRO; PCC 1649]
Richard of Rotherhithe, sailor [DW/PA/7/7 f.293; DW/PA/5/1600/9] <Abs 525>
Richard, alias Richard Strafton of Lingfield, weaver [DW/PA/7/13 f.88; DW/PA/5/1640/15]
Robert of Mortlake [PRO; PCC Admon 1633]
Thomas of Swk St Saviour, waterman [DW/PA/7/12 f.320; DW/PA/5/1636/4]
William, alias William Scrofton of Lingfield, weaver [DW/PA/7/13 f.91; DW/PA/5/1640/16]
William of Swk St Olave, coroner [DW/PA/7/2 f.75; 1501]
BRICE
Mabel of Chiddingfold, widow [DW/PA/7/12 f.51; DW/PA/5/1631/19]
BRICKDAILE
John of Swk St Saviour, saddler [DW/PA/5/1558/35]*
BRICKETT (BRIKETT)
Christopher of Swk St Olave, ale brewer [HRO; Reg. CCB 20 p.2; 1563] [*and*] [DW/PA/5/1563/52 *and in* DW/PA/5/1563/64]
BRICKLETON
Richard of Shalford; Guildford St Mary, yeoman [DW/PA/7/9 f.153; DW/PA/5/1615/16]
BRICKMAN (BRYKEMAN)
Richard of Bermondsey, gardener [HRO; Reg. Wyk 2 p.227; 1386]
BRICKSTOCK *see* BRIGSTOCK
BRICQUEMAN
Phillip of ... [*French Church*] [DW/PA/5/1563/15]
BRIDGE *see* BRIDGES
BRIDGELL (BREGELL,BREGNELL)
John of Blechingley [SRO; 2247/1/48/48; 1528]
Richard of Blechingley [PRO; PCC Admon 1625]
Thomas of Blechingley [DW/PA/7/4 f.33; 1533]
BRIDGEMAN *see* BRIDGMAN

BRIDGER (BRYGER,BRYGGER)
Elizabeth of Wandsworth [PRO; PCC Admon 1649]
Harry of Godalming [DW/PA/7/2 f.165; 1521]
Joan of Godalming, widow [DW/PA/7/12 f.473; DW/PA/5/1638/10]
Margery of Godalming; Slimbridge, Gloucestershire, widow [DW/PA/5/1602/11] <Abs U43>
Richard of Betchworth, yeoman [DW/PA/7/7 f.148; DW/PA/5/1597/12] <Abs 276>
Richard of Guildford; Stoke next Guildford; Shalford, clothier [DW/PA/7/10 f.207; DW/PA/5/1620/17]
Richard of Kingston, gent. [PRO; PCC 1637]
Robert of Stoke [DW/PA/7/3 f.126; 1530]
Thomas of Wandsworth, weaver [DW/PA/7/12 f.4; DW/PA/5/1631/8]

BRIDGES (BRIDGE,BRIGES)
Edmund of Swk St George, glover [DW/PA/7/13 f.264; DW/PA/5/1643/8]
Elizabeth of Clapham, widow [PRO; PCC 1633]
Francis of Clapham, citizen and salter [PRO; PCC 1642]
John of West Horsley, yeoman [DW/PA/7/12 f.477; 1638]
William of Bermondsey, yeoman [PRO; PCC Will 1618]
William of Lambeth - South Lambeth [PRO; PCC Admon 1593]
see also BRIGGS for BRIGGE

BRIDGEWATER
(Lady) Katherine of Lambeth (formerly wife of (Sir) Rees ap Thomas, knight) [PRO; PCC Will 1554]

BRIDGMAN (BRIDGEMAN,BRIGMAN)
John of Wandsworth [DW/PA/5/1587/75]
Margaret of Swk St Olave, widow [HRO; 1591 B8] [*and*] [DW/PA/5/1591/55]
Robert of Esher [PRO; PCC Admon 1649]
Thomas of Swk St Olave [HRO; 1591 B8]

BRIDON
John of Melchborne, Bedfordshire; Colchester, Essex, friar [DW/PA/7/1 f.52; 1487] <Abs 171>

BRIEN *see* BRIAN

BRIGDEN
Alice of Ewhurst, widow of Richard [PRO; PCC Will 1611]

BRIGGS (BRIGGE,BRIGGES,BRYGGS,BRYGYS)(for BRIGES *see* BRIDGES)
Jacob of Farnham, innholder [DW/PA/7/9 f.25A; DW/PA/5/1614/5]
John of Swk St Thomas [DW/PA/5/1568/21]
Matthew of Mickleham, husbandman [HRO; 1614 B4]
Richard of Swk St Olave [DW/PA/7/3 f.135; 1530]
Stephen of Great Bookham, butcher [DW/PA/7/13 f.129; DW/PA/5/1640/22]
Thomas of Mickleham, senior [DW/PA/5/1576/21]
Thomas of Swk St Olave [DW/PA/7/5 f.36; 1538] <Abs 102>

BRIGGSMAN
Katherine of West Molesey [DW/PA/7/1 f.44; 1486] <Abs 145>

BRIGHAM
Emlin of Lambeth, widow [PRO; PCC 1637]
Richard of Lambeth, esq. [PRO; PCC 1636]

BRIGHT
Richard of Ewell, yeoman [DW/PA/5/1587/10]

BRIGHTLIN
Stephen of Swk St Saviour, tailor [DW/PA/7/11 f.360; DW/PA/5/1625/25]

BRIGHTRIDGE (BRITRIDGE,BRYGHTRED)
Ann of Kingston, widow [PRO; PCC 1641]
Elizabeth of Walton on Thames, widow [DW/PA/7/12 f.92; DW/PA/5/1633/16]
Richard of Guildford Holy Trinity [DW/PA/7/1 f.84; 1488] <Abs 279>
William of Thames Ditton - Ember Mill [DW/PA/7/8 f.110; DW/PA/5/1610/11]
William of Kingston, yeoman [DW/PA/7/13 f.245; DW/PA/5/1640/25]
William of Malden, yeoman [DW/PA/7/11 f.188; DW/PA/5/1625/26]
BRIGHTWELL
Robert of Newington [LPL; 98/1 f.42r; Will 1633]
BRIGMAN *see* BRIDGMAN
BRIGSTOCK (BRICKSTOCK,BRIGSTOCKE)
John of Croydon, senior, brewer [PRO; PCC Will 1627]
Richard of Croydon [PRO; PCC Will 1604] <Abs, SAC v.11 p.289>
Robert of Croydon, yeoman [PRO; PCC Will 1619]
BRIKETT *see* BRICKETT
BRILMAN (BRILMANS)
Mary of Swk St Olave, widow [DW/PA/7/7 f.330; DW/PA/5/1601/15] <Abs 592>
BRIMSTED
Edward of Godstone, tailor [DW/PA/7/7 f.121; DW/PA/5/1597/13] <Abs 223>
Richard of Gatton, yeoman [DW/PA/7/8 f.237; DW/PA/5/1613/18]
BRINK (BRYNKE)
Peter of Swk St George [DW/PA/7/5 f.183; 1540]
BRINKHURST (BRYNKEHURST)
John of Kingston [DW/PA/7/5 f.63; 1539] <Abs 58>
Richard of Kingston, vintner [DW/PA/7/3 f.113; 1529]
BRINLEY
William, alias William Brenley of ... [DW/PA/5/1601/14]
BRINTON (BRYNTON)
Mary of Swk, widow [DW/PA/7/8 f.375; DW/PA/5/1612/25]
BRISBY
Thomas of Wandsworth [PRO; PCC Admon 1649; former grant 1630]
BRISCOE (BRUSCOE)
Ralph of Richmond, one of H.M.'s yeomen of the chamber [DW/PA/5/1581/41]
BRISKEN (BRISKYN)
Jane of Wandsworth, spinster [PRO; PCC Will *and* Admon 1598]
BRISKET
Jane of Malden, widow [PRO; PCC Admon 1613]
BRISKYN *see* BRISKEN
BRISLEY
Joan of Wandsworth, widow [DW/PA/7/13 f.90; DW/PA/5/1640/26]
Thomas of Wandsworth [PRO; PCC 1639]
BRISTOW (BRISTOE,BRISTOWE,BROUSTWO,BRUSTOW,BRYSTOW)
Agnes of Capel, widow [DW/PA/7/13 f.499; DW/PA/5/1649/1]
Alice of Horley [DW/PA/7/11 f.221; DW/PA/5/1620/18]
Benjamin of Leigh, yeoman [DW/PA/7/13 f.410; DW/PA/5/1646/6]
Eustace of Horley, yeoman [PRO; PCC Will 1607] <Abs, SAC v.12 pp.205-6>
Gilbert of Dorking, yeoman [DW/PA/7/10 f.152; DW/PA/5/1619/14]
<Abs U236>
Henry of ... [LPL; 96/3389; Will 1628]
Henry of Farnham [DW/PA/7/4 f.66; 1534]
Henry of Farnham, farmer [HRO; 1633 AD17]
Henry of Hambledon, husbandman [DW/PA/7/12 f.30; DW/PA/5/1631/13]
Henry of Horley, yeoman [DW/PA/7/11 f.223; DW/PA/5/1620/19]
Henry of Wotton, yeoman [DW/PA/7/7 f.174; DW/PA/5/1597/14] <Abs 320>

BRISTOW (BRISTOE,BRISTOWE,BROUSTWO,BRUSTOW,BRYSTOW) [*continued*]
Joan of Leigh, widow [DW/PA/7/8 f.34; DW/PA/5/1609/24]
John of ...., citizen and freeman of London [DW/PA/7/7 f.450; DW/PA/5/1603/20] <Abs 853>
John of Ash [DW/PA/7/5 f.223 *and* DW/PA/7/6 f.260; 1541]
John of Charlwood, clerk [PRO; PCC 1637]
John of Cranleigh; Rudgwick, Sussex; Okewood Chapel; Ewhurst; Kingston; Worplesdon; Warnham, Sussex [PRO; PCC Will 1596]
John of Cranleigh, husbandman [DW/PA/5/1596/10] <Abs U3>
John of Dorking, wheeler [DW/PA/7/11 f.424; DW/PA/5/1627/11]
John of Dorking, yeoman [DW/PA/7/12 f.447; DW/PA/5/1639/8]
John of Farnham - Dippenhall [DW/PA/7/1 f.16; 1485] <Abs 54>
John of Frensham, clothworker [DW/PA/5/1588/77]
John of Horley, husbandman [DW/PA/7/7 f.386; DW/PA/5/1602/12] <Abs 715>
John of Leigh [DW/PA/7/3 f.171; 1531]
John of Wotton, husbandman [HRO; 1587 B14]
Lawrence of Horley [DW/PA/7/6 f.148; DW/PA/5/1559/227]
Margaret of Dorking - Westcott, widow [DW/PA/7/13 f.189; DW/PA/5/1641/18]
Nicholas of Capel, yeoman [DW/PA/7/13 f.473; DW/PA/5/1648/3]
Richard of Horley [DW/PA/7/4 f.33; 1533]
Richard of Horley; Charlwood; Lingfield [DW/PA/5/1550/82]
Richard of Newdigate, husbandman [DW/PA/7/7 f.381; DW/PA/5/1602/13] <Abs 707>
Richard of Frimley, yeoman [DW/PA/7/9 f.218; DW/PA/5/1617/31]
Richard of Horley [DW/PA/7/13 f.396; DW/PA/5/1645/2]
Robert of Horley [PRO; PCC Will 1561]
Robert of Frimley [DW/PA/5/1576/144]
Thomas of Frimley, yeoman [DW/PA/5/1576/108]
Thomas of Horley; Worth, Sussex [DW/PA/7/6 f.149; DW/PA/5/1559/228]
Thomas of Ripley, labourer [DW/PA/7/7 f.19; DW/PA/5/1595/9] <Abs 40>
Thomas of Sutton [DW/PA/7/11 f.365; DW/PA/5/1626/24]
Tobias of Wotton [DW/PA/7/12 f.129; DW/PA/5/1632/12]
Walter of Horley, senior [PRO; PCC Will 1633]
William of Dorking, yeoman [DW/PA/5/1627/12]
William of Frensham, yeoman [DW/PA/5/1586/1]
William of Leigh, yeoman [DW/PA/5/1592/104]

BRITRIDGE *see* BRIGHTRIDGE

BRITTON (BRITTEN,BRYTYAN)
George of Newington [LPL; 98/1 f.80r; (ren.) 1637]
Richard of Mitcham [DW/PA/7/1 f.46B; 1487] <Abs 155>
Thomas of Blechingley [PRO; PCC 1633]

BROAD (BROADE,BRODE)
Joan of Rotherhithe, widow [PRO; PCC Admon 1648]
John of Capel [DW/PA/5/1569/31]

BROADBRIDGE (BRODBRIDGE,BRODBRYDGE,BRODEBRIG)
James of Worplesdon; Farnham, yeoman [DW/PA/7/13 f.220; DW/PA/5/1642/8]
Robert of Guildford, senior [PRO; PCC Will 1603] <Abs, SAC v.11 pp.106-7>
Thomas of Compton; Wonersh, labourer [DW/PA/7/6 f.96; DW/PA/5/1559/59]
William of Farnham - Tilford [HRO; 1576 B14]

BROADE *see* BROAD

BROADHURST (BRODEHURST)
Nicholas of Swk St Olave, citizen and haberdasher [DW/PA/7/11 f.394; DW/PA/5/1626/26]

BROCAS (BROCKAS)
  Edmund of Chobham, yeoman [DW/PA/7/11 f,294; DW/PA/5/1626/25]
  (Dame) Joan, alias Joan Aderle of Peper Harow [PRO; PCC Will 1487] <Abs SAC v,31 p,110>
BROCKELL
  William of Chessington; Thames Ditton, yeoman [DW/PA/7/6 f,143; DW/PA/5/1559/239]
BROCKET (BROCKETT,BROGAT,BROKETT)
  Frances of Walton, yeoman [DW/PA/5/1571/1]
  George of Dorking [DW/PA/7/4 f,142; 1536]
  Richard of Dorking [DW/PA/7/4 f,182; 1536]
  William of Dorking [DW/PA/7/4 f,188; 1536]
  William of Limpsfield [PRO; PCC Admon 1625]
BROCKHALL (BROCKHOLE,BROCKHOLL)
  Anthony of Wimbledon [PRO; PCC 1633]
  George of Thames Ditton, yeoman [PRO; PCC Will 1605] <Abs, SAC v,12 p,91>
  Thomas of Cobham, yeoman [DW/PA/5/1561/88]
BROCKWELL
  George of Wimbledon, yeoman [PRO; PCC Will 1615]
  John of Walton on Thames [PRO; PCC 1647]
BRODBRIDGE,BRODBRYDGE,BRODEBRIG *see* BROADBRIDGE
BRODE,BRODEHURST *see* BROAD,BROADHURST
BRODERTON *see* BROTHERTON
BRODRICK
  (Sir) Thomas of Wandsworth, knight [PRO; PCC 1646]
BROE
  John of Streatham, yeoman [DW/PA/7/12 f,176; DW/PA/5/1633/8]
BROGAT *see* BROCKETT
BROGDEN
  Elizabeth of Swk St Olave, widow [DW/PA/7/12 f,133; DW/PA/5/1624/19]
BROK,BROKE; BROKER; BROKESHED *see* BROOKE; BROOKER; BROOKSHEAD
BROKETT *see* BROCKETT
BROMBE (BRUMBE)
  Gillian of Seale, widow of William [DW/PA/5/1557/24]
  William of Seale [DW/PA/5/1557/23]
BROME *see* BROOM
BROMEFEILD *see* BROOMFIELD
BROMEHAM *see* BROMHAM
BROMELAWE *see* BROOMLAW
BROMELEY *see* BROMLEY
BROMELL *see* BROOMHALL
BROMESGROVE *see* BROMSGROVE
BROMFIELD (BROMEFIELD,BROMFEILD,BROOMFIELD,BRUMFEILDE)
  Agnes of Warlingham,spinster [DW/PA/7/7 f,369; DW/PA/5/1602/15]<Abs 677>
  Charles of Horne, yeoman [DW/PA/7/11 f,573; DW/PA/5/1630/9]
  Grace of Swk St Saviour, widow of Thomas of Sevenoaks, Kent, yeoman [DW/PA/7/12 f,63; DW/PA/5/1631/21]
  Henry of Guildford St Nicholas - Artington; Shalford; Peper Harow [DW/PA/7/7 f,498; DW/PA/5/1605/14] <Abs 935>
  Hugh of Lambeth, one of H,M,'s yeomen of the guard [PRO; PCC Will 1609] <Abs, SAC v,23 p,139>
  James of Bramley, husbandman [DW/PA/7/13 f,178; DW/PA/5/1641/16] [*and*] [SRO; 212/15/4]
  James of Guildford St Nicholas [PRO; PCC Will 1585]

BROMFIELD (BROMEFIELD,BROMFEILD,BROOMFIELD,BRUMFEILDE) [*continued*]
Magdalen of Guildford St Nicholas, widow [HRO; 1590 B8]
Richard of Guildford St Nicholas - Littleton, senior, yeoman [DW/PA/7/12 f.161; DW/PA/5/1633/5]
Robert of Blechingley; Horne, yeoman [DW/PA/7/7 f.47; DW/PA/5/1595/11] <Abs 88>
Robert of Burstow, husbandman [LPL; 96/354; Will 1635]
Rowland of Blechingley [DW/PA/7/10 f.79; DW/PA/5/1619/15] [*and*] [SRO; 212/12/1-4]
Susan of Guildford St Nicholas, widow [PRO; PCC 1648]
BROMHALL (BROMEHALL,BROMELL)
George of Abinger, yeoman [DW/PA/7/9 f.70; DW/PA/5/1614/11]
John of Elstead, husbandman [DW/PA/5/1575/29]
Lionel of Walton on Thames - Hersham [DW/PA/7/5 f.82; 1539]
BROMHAM (BROMEHAM,BRUMHAM)
Cicely of Godalming [DW/PA/7/7 f.637; DW/PA/5/1608/20] <Abs 1193>
Elizabeth of Dorking, spinster [DW/PA/7/13 f.144; DW/PA/5/1641/6]
George of Dunsfold [PRO; PCC 1644]
John of ... [DW/PA/5/1550/7]
John of Dunsfold [DW/PA/7/7 f.394; DW/PA/5/1603/21] <Abs 731>
Noah of Dunsfold, yeoman [DW/PA/7/10 f.121; DW/PA/5/1620/20]
Roger of Dunsfold, bachelor [PRO; PCC Admon 1634]
Thomas of Puttenham - Shoelands [PRO; PCC Admon 1607]
William of Godalming; Elstead, mercer [DW/PA/7/6 f.184; DW/PA/5/1559/165]
BROMLEY (BROMELEY)
George of Lambeth [PRO; PCC Admon 1622]
Joan of Swk St Saviour, wife of John, butcher [DW/PA/7/7 f.275; DW/PA/5/1599/8] <Abs 486>
John of Limpsfield [DW/PA/7/4 f.195; 1537]
Richard of Kingston; Easthampstead, Berkshire; Wokingham, Berkshire [DW/PA/7/7 f.91; 1596] <Abs 168>
William of Long Ditton, examiner of the Court of Chancery [GL; Commissary Court of London Will 1558]
BROMWELL
Isaac of Rotherhithe [PRO; PCC Admon 1649]
BRONKE
Abraham van der of Swk St George [DW/PA/7/11 f.322; DW/PA/5/1625/257]
BRONN *see* BROWN
BROOKE (BROK,BROKE,BROOK,BROOKES,BROWKES)
Ann of Chertsey, widow [DW/PA/7/12 f.84; DW/PA/5/1633/20]
(Dame) Ann of Croydon; Kensington, Middlesex, wife of (Sir) John, knight [PRO; PCC Will 1625]
(Dame) Ann of Streatham - Tooting Bec [PRO; PCC Will 1547]
Elizabeth of Camberwell, spinster [PRO; PCC Will 1620] <Soame 1267>
Elizabeth of Swk St Olave, widow [DW/PA/7/8 f.381; DW/PA/5/1612/22]
George of Horsell [DW/PA/7/1 f.14; 1485] <Abs 47>
Henry of Chertsey, yeoman [DW/PA/7/11 f.55; DW/PA/5/1624/20]
Henry of Swk St George, yeoman [DW/PA/5/1587/113]
Joan of Beddington, widow [*in* DW/PA/5/1574/26]
John of Chertsey, husbandman [DW/PA/7/7 f.126; DW/PA/5/1597/15] <Abs 231>
Maud of Oxted, widow [DW/PA/5/1568/79]
Oliver of Rotherhithe (died overseas) [PRO; PCC Admon 1639]
Ralph of Swk St George, yeoman [DW/PA/7/11 f.190; DW/PA/5/1624/21]
Randall of Tooting [DW/PA/7/4 f.53; 1533]

BROOKE (BROK,BROKE,BROOK,BROOKES,BROWKES) [*continued*]
(Sir) Richard of Putney, knight and chief baron of the Exchequer [PRO: PCC Will 1529] <Abs SAC v.31 p.122>
Richard of Chertsey [DW/PA/7/2 f.153; 1530]
Richard of Limpsfield [DW/PA/5/1557/17]
Thomas of Putney - Roehampton [PRO: PCC Admon 1599]
Thomas of Swk St George [DW/PA/5/1587/112]
William of Esher [DW/PA/5/1561/45]*
William of Farnham, yeoman [HRO: 1605 AD6]
William of Swk St Saviour, locksmith [DW/PA/7/12 f.502; DW/PA/5/1638/18]
see also ABROOKE,VANDERBROOKE
BROOKER (BROKER,BRUCKER)
... [*a man*] of Crowhurst [DW/PA/5/1562/15]
Ann of Tandridge, spinster [DW/PA/7/12 f.168; DW/PA/5/1633/7]
George of Charlwood [LPL: 98/1 ff.57r-57v; Will 1634]
Isabel of Carshalton, widow [DW/PA/7/1 f.65; 1487] <Abs 217>
John of ... [DW/PA/7/7 f.557; DW/PA/5/1606/17] <Abs 1041>
John of Oxted, yeoman [DW/PA/7/11 f.426; DW/PA/5/1627/13] [*and*] LBLAD: Surrey Deeds 1/4083; 1627]
John of Oxted [PRO: PCC 1631]
Joshua of West Horsley, yeoman [DW/PA/7/11 f.485; DW/PA/5/1628/14]
Nicholas of East Clandon, yeoman [DW/PA/7/12 f.237; DW/PA/5/1634/15]
Richard, senior of Oxted [BM: Add.Ms 24,925 f.21r; 1544] <Abs 49>
Richard of Oxted [PRO: PCC Will 1563]
Robert of Shere, shoemaker [DW/PA/5/1575/21]
Thomas of East Clandon, yeoman [DW/PA/7/12 f.96; DW/PA/5/1632/5]
Thomas of Lingfield [DW/PA/5/1562/38]
Thomas of Richmond, merchant tailor [DW/PA/7/12 f.227; DW/PA/5/1634/10]
BROOKES *see* BROOK
BROOKSBY (BROWKSBEY)
Margery, alias Margery Chydley of London [DW/PA/5/1572/2]
BROOKSHEAD (BROKESHED)
John of Chobham; Windlesham, yeoman [DW/PA/7/6 f.281; 1560]
BROOM (BROME,BROOME)
John of Rotherhithe, mariner [PRO: PCC 1645]
John of Swk St Olave, labourer, and citizen and white baker [DW/PA/7/9 f.98; DW/PA/5/1614/38]
Sense of Tooting, widow [PRO: PCC 1647]
Stephen of Tooting, vintner [DW/PA/7/11 f.587; DW/PA/5/1630/10]
BROOMEFIELD *see* BROMFIELD
BROOMLAW (BROMELAW)
(Sir) Edmund of Ditton, knight *or* clerk ? [PRO: PCC Will 1523]
BROMSGROVE (BROMESGROVE)
John of Guildford [PRO: PCC Will 1431]
BROND *see* BREND
BROTHERTON (BRATHERTON,BRODERTON,BROTHERTONN)
Eleanor of Buckland, widow [DW/PA/7/7 f.378; DW/PA/5/1602/14] <Abs 700>
John of Buckland, husbandman [DW/PA/7/7 f.342; DW/PA/5/1601/16] <Abs 622>
Roger of Swk St Olave [DW/PA/5/1578/82]
Thomas of Walton on Thames, gent. [DW/PA/5/1580/37]
William of Walton on Thames [DW/PA/7/8 f.337; DW/PA/5/1612/24]
William of Walton on Thames, gent. [PRO: PCC Will 1612]

BROUGHTON
  Humphrey of East Horsley, gent. [PRO; PCC Will 1566]
  Richard of Mitcham, esq. [PRO; PCC 1633]
BROUN; BROUNRICK *see* BROWN; BROWNRIGG
BROUSTWO *see* BRISTOW
BROWKES; BROWKSBEY *see* BROOKE; BROOKSBY
BROWN (BRONN,BROUN,BROWNE,BRUYN)
  Agnes of Betchworth [PRO; PCC Will 1535]
  Agnes of Egham, widow [DW/PA/7/5 f.147; 1540]
  Agnes of Swk St Mary Overy, widow of Richard, barber [DW/PA/7/2 f.54; 1497]
  Alexander of Lambeth; St Vedast, London [LPL; Reg. Abp Stafford f.126; Will 1444]
  Ann of Dorking, gentlewoman, widow [DW/PA/7/7 f.261; DW/PA/5/1599/9] <Abs 463>
  Ann of Lambeth - Lambeth Marsh [PRO; PCC Will 1590]
  Arthur of Egham [DW/PA/5/1546/36]
  Bridget of Betchworth, widow [PRO; PCC Will 1627]
  Catherine of Chaldon, spinster [PRO; PCC 1641]
  Charles of Betchworth [PRO; PCC Admon 1608]
  Christian of Dorking, spinster [DW/PA/7/7 f.425; DW/PA/5/1603/22] <Abs 794>
  Daniel of Bentley, Hampshire, husbandman [DW/PA/7/13 f.51; DW/PA/5/1639/24]
  Dionisia of Egham, widow [DW/PA/7/2 f.5; 1491]
  Edith, alias Edith Croyser of Stoke Dabernon [PRO; PCC Will 1418]
  Eleanor of Swk St Olave, widow [DW/PA/7/10 f.9; DW/PA/5/1619/16]
  Elizabeth of Banstead, wife of William [DW/PA/7/3 f.116; 1529]
  Elizabeth (formerly Hawkins) of Banstead [PRO; PCC Will 1540]
  (Dame) Elizabeth (formerly Poyngis) of Dorking [PRO; PCC Will 1488]
  Elizabeth of Lambeth, widow [PRO; PCC 1649]
  Elizabeth, alias Elizabeth Nicholls of Swk St Thomas Hospital [DW/PA/7/13 f.229; DW/PA/5/1642/65]
  Frances of Newington [LPL; 96/367; Will 1635]
  George of Cobham, senior, smith [DW/PA/7/11 f.199; DW/PA/5/1625/27]
  (Lady) Helen of Dorking - Betchworth Castle, widow of (Sir) Thomas, knight [PRO; PCC Will 1601] <Abs. SAC v.10 pp.299-300>
  Henry of Bermondsey [PRO; PCC Admon 1588]
  Henry of Betchworth, esq. [PRO; PCC Will 1549]
  Henry of Merrow [DW/PA/7/11 f.164; DW/PA/5/1625/28]
  Henry of Swk St Saviour, junior, esq. [DW/PA/7/7 f.274; DW/PA/5/1599/10] <Abs 483>
  Joan of Thames Ditton - Weston, widow [DW/PA/5/1555/73]
  John of Ashtead, esq., sergeant of H.M.'s woodyard [PRO; PCC Will 1612]
  John of Great Bookham; Little Bookham; Ashtead, gent. [PRO; PCC Will 1625 *and* 1626] [*and*] [LBLAD; Surrey Deeds 1/1272; 1625]
  John of Chertsey - Woodham [DW/PA/7/12 f.452; DW/PA/5/1638/6]
  John of Cranleigh; Alfold [HRO; 1575 AD10]
  John of Dorking [PRO; PCC Will 1558]
  John of Egham, husbandman [DW/PA/7/4 f.207; 1520]
  John of Farnham, tailor [DW/PA/7/12 f.30; DW/PA/5/1631/12]
  John of Horsell [DW/PA/5/1576/117]
  John of Kingston [PRO; PCC Will 1490]
  John of Malden, yeoman [DW/PA/7/9 f.11; DW/PA/5/1615/17]

BROWN (BRONN,BROUN,BROWNE,BRUYN) [*continued*]

John of Rotherhithe [DW/PA/7/12 f.370; DW/PA/5/1627/14]
John of Rotherhithe [PRO; PCC 1646]
John of Swk, servant to Sir John Cuttes, knight of Grub Street [DW/PA/5/1592/95]*
John of Swk St George, pintmaker [DW/PA/7/13 f.112; DW/PA/5/1639/28]
John of Swk St Margaret, waterman [DW/PA/7/2 f.63; 1498]
John of Swk St Margaret, tailor [DW/PA/7/2 f.62; 1500]
John of Swk St Olave [DW/PA/7/2 f.61; 1500]
John of Swk St Olave; Shoreham, Sussex, ship's carpenter [DW/PA/7/9 f.92; DW/PA/5/1616/17]
John of Swk St Saviour, farrier [DW/PA/7/8 f.156; DW/PA/5/1611/13]
John of Wonersh [PRO; PCC Will 1594]
John of Wonersh, gent. [PRO; PCC Will 1594]
Katherine of Leatherhead, gentlewoman [DW/PA/7/7 f.238; DW/PA/5/1598/14] <Abs 418>
Katherine of Leatherhead [PRO; PCC Will 1599]
Lawrence of Swk St Olave [DW/PA/7/11 f.198; DW/PA/5/1625/29]
Lionel of Newington [PRO; PCC 1646]
Margaret of Mitcham, widow [DW/PA/7/6 f.286; 1560]
(Dame) Martha of Kingston [PRO; PCC 1645]
Mary of Malden, widow [DW/PA/7/12 f.227; DW/PA/5/1634/11]
(Sir) Matthew of Betchworth - West Betchworth , knight [PRO; PCC Will 1557]
(Sir) Matthew of Dorking - Betchworth Castle, knight [PRO; PCC Will 1608] <Abs, SAC v.12 p.108>
Matthew of Dorking - Betchworth Castle, bachelor [PRO; PCC Admon 1629]
Nicholas of Elstead - North Elstead, yeoman [DW/PA/7/12 f.391; DW/PA/5/1637/9]
Nicholas of Keisborough in the Isle [*? of Wight*] [DW/PA/7/11 f.367; DW/PA/5/1626/27]
Nicholas of Rotherhithe [PRO; PCC Will 1589]
Owen of Dorking, gent. [DW/PA/5/1575/64]
Ralph of Hambledon, parson [DW/PA/7/12 f.26; DW/PA/5/1631/11]
Randolph of Chessington; Malden, husbandman [HRO; 1608 AD10]
Richard of Chipstead; Banstead, yeoman [DW/PA/7/9 f.34; DW/PA/5/1614/3]
Richard of Dorking, esq. [DW/PA/7/9 f.79; DW/PA/5/1614/37]
Richard of Egham [DW/PA/5/1546/48]
Richard of Egham, yeoman of the guard [DW/PA/5/1558/38]*
Richard of Lambeth, servant [DW/PA/7/2 f.2; 1490]
Richard of Mitcham [DW/PA/5/1555/82]
Richard of Peper Harow [DW/PA/7/3 f.146; 1530]
Richard of Reigate [DW/PA/7/4 f.10; 1532]
Richard of Swk St Mary Overy, barber [DW/PA/7/2 f.53; 1497]
Richard of Swk St Olave, feltmaker, senior [DW/PA/7/8 f.373; DW/PA/5/1612/23]
Richard of Swk St Saviour - Paris Garden Liberty, shipwright [DW/PA/7/9 f.14; DW/PA/5/1616/18]
Richard of Streatham - Tooting Bec, yeoman [DW/PA/7/7 f.35; DW/PA/5/1595/10] <Abs 72>
Richard of Wandsworth, yeoman [DW/PA/7/13 f.361; 1644]
Richard of Wandsworth [PRO; PCC 1645]
Richard of Witley - Milford [PRO; PCC 1638]
Robert of Croydon [PRO; PCC Admon 1596]

BROWN (BRONN,BROUN,BROWNE,BRUYN) [*continued*]

Robert of Guildford Holy Trinity [PRO; PCC 1649]
Robert of Lambeth [PRO; PCC Will 1573]
Robert of Lambeth, bachelor [PRO; PCC Admon 1647]
Robert of Merton [DW/PA/7/4 f,56; 1533]
Robert of Swk St George, bricklayer [DW/PA/7/10 f,247; DW/PA/5/1622/11]
Robert of Swk St Olave, feltmaker [DW/PA/7/10 ff,144,237; DW/PA/5/1620/21]
Robert of Weybridge, butcher [DW/PA/7/7 f,558; DW/PA/5/1606/18] <Abs 1043>
(Sir) Thomas of Dorking - Betchworth Castle, knight [PRO; PCC Admon 1597]
Thomas of Blechingley [PRO; PCC 1639]
Thomas of Cobham, miller [DW/PA/7/12 f,389; DW/PA/5/1637/8]
Thomas of Dorking, yeoman [DW/PA/7/7 f,144; DW/PA/5/1597/16] <Abs 264>
Thomas of Newington [PRO; PCC Admon 1572]
Thomas of Swk St Saviour, farrier [DW/PA/7/9 f,286; 1618]
Walter of Ashtead [DW/PA/7/10 f,12; DW/PA/5/1619/17]
Walter of Dorking, esq. [PRO; PCC Will 1595]
Walter of Dorking [PRO; PCC 1641]
Walter of Swk St Olave, hosier [DW/PA/5/1563/113]
William of Banstead [DW/PA/7/3 f,115; 1529]
William of Dorking, esq. [PRO; PCC Admon 1645]
William of Egham, yeoman [DW/PA/7/4 f,119; 1535]
William of Kingston, weaver [DW/PA/7/7 f,561; DW/PA/5/1606/19] <Abs 1049>
William of Horley, clerk pastor [DW/PA/7/8 f,268; DW/PA/5/1613/19]
William of Lambeth, tanner [DW/PA/7/12 f,445; DW/PA/5/1639/6]
William of Putney [PRO; PCC Admon 1606]
William of Reigate [DW/PA/5/1558/36]*
William of Swk St Margaret, yeoman of the guard, innholder [DW/PA/7/2 f,148; 1520]
William of Stoke next Guildford [PRO; PCC Admon 1615]

BROWNBREAD (BROWNEBREDE)

Christopher, alias Christopher Ambre of Farnham [LPL; Reg, Abp Morton f,252v; Admon 1487]

BROWNCARDE

Harman of Swk St Olave, blacksmith [DW/PA/5/1563/90]

BROWNEBREDE *see* BROWNBREAD

BROWNENTE *see* BROWNWEND

BROWNERIGGE; BROWNESWORDE; BROWNEWENDE *see* BROWNRIGG; BROWNSWORD; BROWNWEND

BROWNING (BROWNINGE)

Elizabeth of ..., widow [DW/PA/7/9 f,196; DW/PA/5/1616/19]
Henry of Wandsworth, yeoman [DW/PA/7/13 f,114; DW/PA/5/1639/29]

BROWNRIGG (BROUNRICK,BROWNERIGGE,BROWNRICKE,BROWNRIGGE)

Elizabeth of Swk St Saviour, widow [DW/PA/7/8 f,307; DW/PA/5/1613/20]
John, alias John Wylson of Godalming [DW/PA/5/1582/54]
John of Furness, Lancashire, citizen and vintner [DW/PA/7/7 f,353; DW/PA/5/1601/18] <Abs 648>

BROWNSWORD (BROWNESWORDE)

Beatrice of Swk St Olave; Bathhampton, Somerset, widow [DW/PA/7/8 f,73; DW/PA/5/1609/13]

BROWNWEND (BROWNENTE,BROWNEWENDE)

Jane of Long Ditton; Banstead; Southampton, Hampshire, widow [DW/PA/5/1601/17] <Abs U32>
John of Long Ditton, rector [HRO; 1599 B6]

BROWNWEND (BROWNENTE,BROWNEWENDE) [*continued*]
Richard of Banstead; Ashtead; Walton on the Hill; Headley; Nutfield, vicar [DW/PA/5/1604/7] <Abs U98>
Samuel of Nutfield [PRO; PCC Admon 1612]
BROWSE
Robert of Croydon, husbandman [PRO; PCC Will 1625]
BROXSTED
John of Chobham, husbandman [DW/PA/7/6 f.187; DW/PA/5/1559/193 *and* DW/PA/5/1559/195]
BRUCKER *see* BROOKER
BRUER *see* BREWER
BRUMBE *see* BROMBE
BRUMHAM *see* BROMHAM
BRUMSDEN (BREMYSDEN)
William of Effingham [DW/PA/7/5 f.84; 1539]
BRUSCOE *see* BRISCOE
BRUSHE
Joan of Mortlake, widow [PRO; PCC 1648]
BRUSSHER
John of Abinger, tanner [DW/PA/5/1582/36]
BRUSTOWE *see* BRISTOW
BRUYN *see* BROWN
BRVIER
Jan of [*Swk*]; Cambrai, France [*French Church*] [DW/PA/5/1593/197]
BRWAR *see* BREWER
BRYAN *see* BRIAN
BRYDGER,BRYGER,BRYGGER *see* BRIDGER
BRYGGES,BRYGGS *see* BRIGGS
BRYGHTRED *see* BRIGHTRIDGE
BRYGSMAN *see* BRIGGSMAN
BRYGYS *see* BRIGGS
BRYKEMAN *see* BRICKMAN
BRYNKE; BRYNKEHURST *see* BRINK; BRINKHURST
BRYNTON *see* BRINTON
BRYSTOW *see* BRISTOW
BUBRICK (BUBBREKE)
Ann of Alfold, widow [DW/PA/7/12 f.365; DW/PA/5/1637/5]
BUCHAM *see* BOOKHAM
BUCHER *see* BUTCHER
BUCK (BUCKE)
John of Alfold, husbandman [DW/PA/7/13 f.51; DW/PA/5/1639/25]
John of Wandsworth, miller [PRO; PCC Will 1625]
Peter of Lambeth, widower [PRO; PCC Admon 1649]
Robert of Swk St Saviour [DW/PA/7/11 f.322; DW/PA/5/1625/30]
Thomas of Egham, citizen and cutler [PRO; PCC Will 1567]
William of Croydon - Whaddon [LPL; 96/385; Will 1629]
BUCKBERRY (BUCKBERIE)
Jaquamine of Swk St Saviour, widow [DW/PA/7/8 f.158; DW/PA/5/1611/14]
Seth of ..., citizen and vintner [DW/PA/7/8 f.49; DW/PA/5/1609/25]
BUCKELL *see* BUCKLE
BUCKERDICKE
Christopher of ?Kingston [SRO; KE1/7/3; 1599] [*inventory only*]
BUCKETT
Susan of Kingston [DW/PA/7/13 f.255; DW/PA/5/1643/5]

BUCKFOLDE
Stephen of Esher; Mortlake, gent. [PRO; PCC Will 1592]
BUCKHAM *see* BOOKHAM
BUCKHURST (BIRKESTE)
William of Thursley; Witley [DW/PA/7/1 f.94; 1489] <Abs 311>
BUCKINGHAM
Christopher of Putney [LPL; 98/1 f.116v; Will 1638]
BUCKLAND (BUCLANDE,BUCLANDE,BUCLOND,BUKLAND)
Edward of Kingston [PRO; PCC Will 1559]
Edward of Kingston, senior, clerk [PRO; PCC Will 1620] <Soame 64>
Edward of Kingston; Sunbury, Middlesex; Shepperton, Middlesex, senior, clerk [PRO; PCC Will 1619] [*and*] [DW/PA/7/10 f.75; DW/PA/5/1619/18] [*and*] [SRO; KB28/2-3]
Joan of Limpsfield, widow [DW/PA/7/2 f.161; 1521]
Mary of Kingston, widow [DW/PA/7/12 f.453; 1638]
Peter of Kingston; Middlesex [HRO; 1582 B13] [*and*] [SRO; KB28/1; 1582]
Peter of Swk St Mary Overy, waterman [DW/PA/5/1593/199]
Robert of Limpsfield, husbandman [*in* DW/PA/5/1574/26]
Thomas of Kingston, yeoman [HRO; Reg. D p.51 *and* 1522 B12]
Thomas of Limpsfield, yeoman [DW/PA/5/1605/15] <Abs U130>
William of Oxted, tailor [DW/PA/5/1578/8]
BUCKLE (BUCKELL)
Alice of Farnham, widow [DW/PA/5/1582/34]
Andrew of Bentley, Hampshire, yeoman [DW/PA/7/12 f.110; DW/PA/5/1632/7A]
Cuthbert of Mitcham [PRO; PCC Will 1594]
John of Bentley, Hampshire [DW/PA/5/1588/50]
Richard of Farnham, gent. [DW/PA/7/9 f.16; DW/PA/5/1616/20]
Thomas of Bentley, Hampshire [DW/PA/7/8 f.160; DW/PA/5/1611/15]
BUCKLEDGE
Andrew of St Giles (? Camberwell), yeoman [DW/PA/7/11 f.176; 1625]
BUCKLEY
Hugh of Farnham [DW/PA/7/10 f.185; DW/PA/5/1620/22]
John of Bermondsey [PRO; PCC 1631]
William of Swk St Thomas, citizen and carpenter [DW/PA/7/8 f.407; DW/PA/5/1614/8]
BUCKNELL
William of Wimbledon [LPL; 98/1 f.96r; Will 1638]
BUCKQUAY
Harman of Putney [LPL; 98/1 f.128v; Will 1642]
BUCKRIDGE
Joan of Swk St Olave, widow [DW/PA/7/13 f.293; DW/PA/5/1644/5]
BUCKTON
James of Lambeth [DW/PA/7/11 f.23; DW/PA/5/1623/14]
BUCKWELL (BUKWELL)
Clement of Walton on Thames, husbandman [DW/PA/5/1576/53]
Ellen of Walton on Thames, widow [DW/PA/7/10 f.282; DW/PA/5/1622/12]
John of Weybridge [PRO; PCC Will 1618]
Thomas of Walton on Thames [DW/PA/7/4 f.67; 1534]
Thomas of Walton on Thames [DW/PA/7/6 f.192; DW/PA/5/1559/189]
William of Byfleet; Walton on Thames, yeoman [DW/PA/7/9 f.315; DW/PA/5/1619/20]
William of Walton on Thames, senior, yeoman [DW/PA/5/1593/34]
William of Walton on Thames, yeoman [DW/PA/7/10 f.95; DW/PA/5/1619/19]
BUCLANDE,BUCLOND *see* BUCKLAND

BUDD (BUDDE)
Henry of Lambeth, senior, yeoman [DW/PA/7/13 f.345; 1644]
Robert of Seale, husbandman [DW/PA/7/8 f.351; DW/PA/5/1612/26]
William of Seale - Tongham [DW/PA/7/8 f.32; DW/PA/5/1608/26]
BUDDER
Henry of Camberwell, senior, yeoman [DW/PA/7/11 f.445; DW/PA/5/1628/15]
James of Mortlake [PRO; PCC Admon 1633]
BUDGEN
John of Battersea [PRO; PCC Admon 1647]
Richard of Kingston, tanner [DW/PA/7/13 f.149B; DW/PA/5/1641/11]
BUFFORD
William of Merton [PRO; PCC Will 1487]
BUGBY
William of Swk St Olave [DW/PA/7/10 f.196; DW/PA/5/1621/13]
BUISHFIELD *see* BUSHFIELD
BUISINE
Andrew of Bermondsey [PRO; PCC 1637]
BUKLAND; BUKWELL *see* BUCKLAND; BUCKWELL
BULCHILL *see* BALCHILD
BULKLEY (BULKELEY)
Agnes (formerly Agnes Grey) of Lambeth [PRO; PCC Will 1523]
Richard of Morden [PRO; PCC Admon 1633]
BULL
John of Newington [PRO; PCC Will 1577]
Thomas of Swk St Olave, waterman [DW/PA/7/11 f.441; DW/PA/5/1628/16]
William of Swk St Olave [DW/PA/7/13 f.258; DW/PA/5/1643/7]
BULLEN (BOLINGE,BOLLING,BULLENN,BULLEYN,BULLIN,BULLINGE,BULLYNG)
Henry, senior of Woking - Sutton, yeoman [DW/PA/7/12 f.429; DW/PA/5/1637/15]
John of Rotherhithe [PRO; PCC Will 1595]
Juliana of West Clandon [DW/PA/5/1591/23]
Nicholas of Egham, husbandman [DW/PA/7/12 f.115; DW/PA/5/1632/7B]
Phillis of Wonersh, widow [DW/PA/5/1592/56]
Thomas of Woking - Sutton, husbandman [DW/PA/7/12 f.308; DW/PA/5/1635/16]
William of Byfleet [DW/PA/7/2 f.22; 1491]
William of Egham, collarmaker [DW/PA/7/7 f.469; DW/PA/5/1604/8] <Abs 884>
BULLERDINE
Isabel of Swk St Olave; Swk St Mary Overy, widow [DW/PA/7/8 f.146; 1611]
BULLEY
William of Swk St George, wireworker [DW/PA/7/11 f.321; DW/PA/5/1626/28]
BULLEYN,BULLIN,BULLINGE,BULLYNG *see* BULLEN
BULWORTH (BULWORTHE)
John of East Molesey, husbandman [DW/PA/5/1555/9]
Margaret of East Molesey [DW/PA/7/4 f.205; 1537]
BUN
Thomas of Richmond, yeoman [PRO; PCC Will 1613]
BUNCKLEY *see* BUNKLEY
BUNDLE (BOONDELL)
Richard of Chertsey, yeoman [DW/PA/5/1561/50]
Robert of Thames Ditton [HRO; 1571 B30]
BUNGEY
Jonas of Dorking, widower [PRO; PCC Admon 1626]
BUNKLEY (BUNCKLEY)
William of Rotherhithe, mariner [PRO; PCC 1648]

BUNT
Thomas of Swk St Saviour, baker [DW/PA/7/9 f.291; 1618]
BUNTING (BUNTYNE,BUNTYNG)
...hew (? Matthew) of Swk St Saviour [DW/PA/5/1557/11]
BUNYAN *see* BONION
BURBECK (BIRKBECK)
Bernard of Swk St Olave [DW/PA/7/7 f.427; DW/PA/5/1603/23] <Abs 798>.
BURCASSE
John of Witley [DW/PA/5/1582/61]
BURCESTRE
(Sir) John of Swk, knight [PRO; PCC Will 1466] <Abs SAC v.1 pp.195-197>
(Sir) William of Swk St Olave, knight [PRO; PCC Will 1407] <Abs SAC v.1 pp.192-193>
BURCHALL (BIRCHALL,BURCHELL)
John of Guildford, clothier [PRO; PCC Will 1600]
Richard of Guildford St Mary [DW/PA/7/11 f.526; DW/PA/5/1629/10]
Thomas of Croydon [PRO; PCC Admon 1567]
William of Croydon [PRO; PCC Admon 1570]
BURCHETT (BIRCHARD,BIRCHET,BORCHAT,BURCHATT,BYRCHAT,BYRCHATE,BYRCHED, BYRCHET,BYRCHETT)
Ambrose of Chobham [DW/PA/5/1570/95]
Edward of Guildford, shoemaker [DW/PA/7/12 f.296; DW/PA/5/1634/14]
James of Kingston - Ham [PRO; PCC Admon 1632]
John of Chobham [DW/PA/5/1576/71]
John of Horsell [DW/PA/7/4 f.92; 1534]
Margery of Chobham [DW/PA/5/1570/100]
Richard of Chobham [DW/PA/7/6 f.64; DW/PA/5/1559/39]
Richard of Chobham, husbandman [DW/PA/7/13 f.126; DW/PA/5/1640/21]
Robert of Abinger [DW/PA/7/5 f.221; 1541]
Robert of Chobham, husbandman [DW/PA/5/1557/13]
Thomas of West Molesey, blacksmith [PRO; PCC Will 1628]
William of West Horsley [*in* DW/PA/5/1546/75]
William of Abinger, yeoman [DW/PA/7/7 f.136; DW/PA/5/1597/10] <Abs 250>
BURCHIER *see* BOURCHIER
BURCHINSHAW *see* BIRKINSHAW
BURDE *see* BIRD
BURDEN *see* BURDON
BURDEVILL
Rowland of Warnham, Sussex, grocer [DW/PA/7/4 f.31; 1533]
see also BIRDWELL
BURDON (BURDEN)
Henry of Swk St Margaret, saddler [DW/PA/7/4 f.121; 1535]
Robert of Windlesham [DW/PA/7/1 f.77; 1487] <Abs 252>
Stephen of Swk St Margaret, innholder [DW/PA/7/2 f.87; 1503]
William of Swk St Olave, yeoman [DW/PA/7/2 f.124; 1518]
BURDWYLL *see* BURDEVILL,BIRDWELL
BURGATE (BURGATT,BURGETT)
John of Horne [PRO; PCC 1635]
Thomas of Horne, husbandman [DW/PA/7/12 f.206; DW/PA/5/1634/6]
William of Lingfield, husbandman [PRO; PCC Will 1618]
BURGESS (BURGEIS,BURGES,BURGIES,BURGIS,BURGYS)
Elizabeth of Kingston [PRO; PCC Admon 1626]
Henry of Thursley [DW/PA/5/1591/31]
Joan of Kingston, widow [HRO; 1558 B89-90]

BURGESS (BURGEIS,BURGES,BURGIES,BURGIS,BURGYS) [*continued*]
Joan of Horsell, late wife of Walter [*in* DW/PA/5/1544/4]
John of the Ship *Harte* [DW/PA/7/11 f.376; DW/PA/5/1626/29]
John of Bisley [DW/PA/7/5 f.201; 1540]
John of Little Bookham, yeoman [DW/PA/7/7 f.287; DW/PA/5/1599/92] <Abs 512>
John of Guildford St Mary [DW/PA/7/2 f.202; 1524]
John of Horley [PRO; PCC 1632]
John of Horsell [DW/PA/7/1 f.49; 1487] <Abs 162>
John of Horsell [DW/PA/7/1 f.64; 1487] <Abs 214>
John of West Horsley; Great Bookham, yeoman [DW/PA/7/12 f.376; DW/PA/5/1638/13]
John of Walton on Thames [PRO; PCC 1633]
Martin of Stoke next Guildford [DW/PA/7/11 f.296; DW/PA/5/1626/30]
Peter of Kingston, yeoman [DW/PA/5/1557/96]
Thomas, alias Thomas Peryn of Chiddingfold [DW/PA/5/1586/3]*
Thomas of Horley, yeoman [DW/PA/7/11 f.108; DW/PA/5/1624/22]
Thomas of Swk St Olave, feltmaker [DW/PA/7/10 f.278; DW/PA/5/1621/14]
William of Limpsfield [PRO; PCC Admon 1589]
William of Limpsfield [PRO; PCC Will 1590]
William of Wandsworth [DW/PA/7/4 f.53; 1533]

BURGETT *see* BURGATE

BURGH (BURGHE,de BURGH)
(Lady) Catherine of Lingfield - Starborough Castle, widow [PRO; PCC Admon 1622]
John of Beddington - Wallington [BM; Addtl MS 23,177; 1437]
Thomas of Swk St Thomas [HRO; Reg. Wyk 2 p.177; 1379] <Abs SAC v.3 pp.210-212>
(Lord) William of Lingfield - Starborough Castle [PRO; PCC Admon 1584]

BURISH
Edward of Carshalton, citizen and mercer [PRO; PCC 1635]

BURKE (BIRKS,BYRKES)
George of Rotherhithe, mariner [DW/PA/7/10 f.2; DW/PA/5/1616/11]
Thomas of Richmond [PRO; PCC Will 1525]

BURKETT (BERKET)
Miles of Lambeth [DW/PA/7/8 f.127; DW/PA/5/1610/15]

BURLACE
John of Farnham, gent. [DW/PA/7/8 f.105; DW/PA/5/1615/19]

BURLE (BIRLE,BURLL,BYRLE,BYRLLE)
Alice of Witley - Milford, widow [DW/PA/7/12 f.474; DW/PA/5/1638/11]
Edward of Witley - Birtley [DW/PA/5/1579/22]*
Edward of Witley, husbandman [DW/PA/7/12 f.205; DW/PA/5/1634/4]
Henry of Hascombe [DW/PA/7/3 f.152; 1530]
John of ... [DW/PA/7/8 ff.38,84; DW/PA/5/1609/15]
John of Thursley [DW/PA/5/1580/62]
Margaret of Worplesdon, widow [DW/PA/7/9 f.79; DW/PA/5/1614/36]
Nicholas of Godalming, yeoman [DW/PA/7/8 f.140; DW/PA/5/1610/22]
Richard of Wonersh [PRO; PCC 1647]
Thomas of Farnham, ostler [DW/PA/5/1558/40]*
Thomas of Shalford [DW/PA/7/3 f.183; 1531]
Thomas of Witley - Milford, yeoman [DW/PA/7/12 f.478; DW/PA/5/1638/14]
William of Cranleigh [DW/PA/5/1576/5]
William of Hascombe [HRO; 1567 B19-20]
William of Hascombe, yeoman [DW/PA/7/12 f.456; DW/PA/5/1638/8]

BURLE (BIRLE,BURLL,BYRLE,BYRLLE)
  William of Witley - Milford, yeoman [DW/PA/7/7 f.219; DW/PA/5/1598/15] <Abs 387>
BURLEY (BURLY,BYRLEY)
  Agnes of Wotton [DW/PA/7/6 f.27; DW/PA/5/1559/28]
  John of Mortlake [LPL; 98/1 f.71v; Will 1635]
  John of Swk St Olave, brewer [DW/PA/7/11 f.92; DW/PA/5/1624/23]
  John of Wonersh [PRO; PCC Will 1551]
  John of Wotton, husbandman [DW/PA/5/1558/39]*
  Nicholas of Pyrford, gent. [DW/PA/7/13 f.375; 1644]
  Ralph of Wotton, husbandman [DW/PA/5/1580/61]
  Stephen of Dunsfold [DW/PA/7/4 f.85; 1534]
  Susan of Chertsey - Woodham; Walton on Thames, widow [DW/PA/7/7 f.337; DW/PA/5/1601/19] <Abs 609>
  William of Barnes, clerk [PRO; PCC Will 1510]
  William, alias William Mychell of Bermondsey [DW/PA/7/3 f.97; 1529]
BURN *see* BYRNE
BURNAT *see* BURNETT
BURNE *see* BYRNE
BURNEHAM *see* BURNHAM
BURNELL
  William of Lambeth [PRO; PCC 1646]
BURNER
  Reynold of Leatherhead [DW/PA/7/1 f.35; 1486] <Abs 118>
BURNES *see* BYRNE
BURNETT (BURNAT,BURNET)
  John of Dorking, husbandman [DW/PA/5/1588/33]
  Margery of Walton on Thames, widow [DW/PA/7/13 f.190; DW/PA/5/1641/19]
  Robert of Dorking, husbandman [DW/PA/7/12 f.337; DW/PA/5/1636/6]
  Stephen of Dorking, yeoman [DW/PA/7/11 f.275; DW/PA/5/1625/33]
BURNEY (BOWNEY)
  Richard of Swk St Saviour, barber chirurgeon [DW/PA/7/13 f.445; DW/PA/5/1646/3]
BURNHAM (BORNAM,BURNEHAM)
  Henry of Chobham, labourer [DW/PA/7/13 f.195; DW/PA/5/1641/20]
  (Sir) John of Swk St Thomas Hospital, knight *or* clerk [LPL; Reg. Abp Morton f.79v; Admon 1492]
  Parnell of ... [DW/PA/7/9 f.282; 1618]
  William of Leatherhead, yeoman [PRO; PCC Will 1626]
BURRE
  Richard of Blechingley [DW/PA/5/1580/14]
BURREL (BORYLL)
  Cuthbert of ...., citizen and vintner [DW/PA/5/1576/85]
BURROWS (BORROWES,BURROWE,BURROWES)
  Adam of Swk St Saviour, gold wire drawer [DW/PA/7/12 f.229; DW/PA/5/1634/17]
  Ann of Chelsham; Farleigh, widow [DW/PA/7/9 f.317; DW/PA/5/1619/21]
  Robert of Farleigh [PRO; PCC Admon 1618]
  see also ABURROW,BORROW
BURSTOW (BURSTOWE)
  Henry of Betchworth [DW/PA/5/1593/82]
  John of Charlwood [PRO; PCC Will 1535]
  John, junior of Horley [DW/PA/7/2 f.28; 1487]
  John of Horley [DW/PA/5/1582/64]

BURSTOW (BURSTOWE) [*continued*]

Robert of Horley [DW/PA/7/2 f.135; 1519]

Robert of Horley, yeoman [DW/PA/7/8 f.49; DW/PA/5/1609/27]

Thomas of Godstone [PRO; PCC 1649]

Thomas of Horley [DW/PA/5/1580/47]

see also BRISTOW

BURT (BIRT,BIRTE,BURTE,BURTT,BYRTE)

Elizabeth of Pyrford, widow [DW/PA/7/12 f.220; DW/PA/5/1634/7]

George, alias George Loveland of Worplesdon, husbandman [HRO; 1582 B15]

Henry of Pyrford, husbandman [DW/PA/7/12 f.147; DW/PA/5/1633/4]

Jasper of Kingston, chandler [DW/PA/7/11 f.171; DW/PA/5/1625/32]

Joan of Reigate, widow [DW/PA/7/2 f.61; 1499]

John of Pyrford, yeoman [DW/PA/7/9 f.123; DW/PA/5/1615/13]

John of Woking, yeoman [DW/PA/7/6 f.210; 1560]

John of Woking, yeoman [DW/PA/7/13 f.290; 1643]

John of Woking, yeoman [DW/PA/7/13 f.293; DW/PA/5/1643/14]

John of Woking [PRO; PCC 1649]

Katherine of Woking - Sutton, widow [DW/PA/7/12 f.10; DW/PA/5/1631/10]

Richard of Dunsfold [DW/PA/5/1592/54] <Abs SAC v.32 p.4>

Richard of Woking - Sutton, tallow chandler [DW/PA/7/7 f.361; DW/PA/5/1602/16] <Abs 663>

Richard of Woking - Sutton, husbandman [DW/PA/7/7 f.378; DW/PA/5/1626/31]

Thomas of Dorking, cordwainer [DW/PA/7/13 f.231; DW/PA/5/1642/10]

Thomas of Pyrford, husbandman [HRO; 1639 B8]

Thomas of Reigate [PRO; PCC Will 1506]

Thomas of Woking - Sutton; Kingston [DW/PA/7/7 f.100; DW/PA/5/1596/7] <Abs 182>

William of Surrey, yeoman [PRO; PCC Will 1587]

William of Woking [DW/PA/7/7 f.282; DW/PA/5/1599/11] <Abs 504>

see also BIRD

BURTON

Alice, alias Alice Scudamore of Surrey [PRO; PCC Admon 1648]

Alice of Barnes, widow [PRO; PCC Will 1627]

Ann of Carshalton, widow of Richard, esq. [DW/PA/7/8 f.297; DW/PA/5/1613/21]

Daniel of Putney, yeoman [PRO; PCC Will 1622]

Edward of Lambeth, gent. [PRO; PCC Will 1610] <Abs. SAC v.24 p.69>

Eleanor of Carshalton, widow of Nicholas [PRO; PCC Admon 1566]

Harry of Kingston; Higham Ferrers, Northamptonshire, yeoman [DW/PA/7/3 f.201; 1532]

Henry of Carshalton, son of (Sir) Henry, knight [DW/PA/7/11 f.526; DW/PA/5/1630/11]

(Sir) Henry of Carshalton, knight [PRO; PCC 1646]

Humphrey of Send [DW/PA/5/1591/67]

James of Swk St Saviour, victualler [DW/PA/7/13 f.200; 1642]

John of Woking [PRO; PCC Admon 1649]

Lancelot of Swk St Olave, shipwright [DW/PA/5/1563/94]

Margaret of Swk St Saviour - Paris Garden Liberty, widow [DW/PA/7/7 f.440; DW/PA/5/1603/24] <Abs 832>

Mercy of Carshalton [DW/PA/7/1 f.54; 1487] <Abs 181>

Nicholas of Carshalton, esq. [PRO; PCC Will 1559]

Nicholas of Carshalton, gent. [DW/PA/7/11 f.480; DW/PA/5/1628/17]

Richard of Carshalton, gent. [DW/PA/7/5 f.229; 1541]

Richard of Carshalton, esq. [PRO; PCC Will 1589]

BURTON [*continued*]

Roger of Walton on Thames [DW/PA/5/1578/10]

Thomas of Bermondsey [PRO; PCC Will 1585]

Walter of East Clandon [PRO; PCC Will 1611] <Abs, SAC v,35 pp,30-31>

Walter of Swk St Saviour, servant to H,M, the Queen [DW/PA/7/7 ff,121, 139; DW/PA/5/1597/17] <Abs 224,256>

William of Newington; St Magnus, London, citizen and fletcher [LPL; Reg, Abp Arundel ii f,204; Will 1414]

William of Woldingham; Brasted, Kent, blacksmith [DW/PA/7/12 f,502; DW/PA/5/1638/19]

Winifred of Carshalton wife of (Sir) Henry (and late widow of John Theaker of Cooke, Yorkshire) [DW/PA/7/11 f,15; DW/PA/5/1623/15] [*and*] [PRO; PCC Will 1611] <Abs, SAC v,35 p,41>

BURWELL

William of Croydon [PRO; PCC Will 1523]

BURY (BURYE)

Robert of Merrow, clerk parson [DW/PA/7/9 f,339; DW/PA/5/1620/23]

BURYMAN *see* BERRIMAN

BURYN (van BURIN)

William of Swk [DW/PA/5/1579/16]*

BUSBRIDGE

Richard of Camberwell [PRO; PCC Will 1597]

see also BUSTBRIDGE

BUSBY

Edward of Wandsworth [DW/PA/5/1593/65]

BUSCOE (? BUSTON)

John of Horsell [DW/PA/5/1550/2]

BUSH (BUSHE,BUSSHE)

Hugo of Swk St Margaret, goldsmith [DW/PA/7/2 f,58; 1499]

John of Kingston, yeoman [DW/PA/5/1561/56]

Maria of Swk St Olave [DW/PA/7/11 f,529; DW/PA/5/1630/12]

Matthew of Swk St Thomas; Paddington, Middlesex, silk weaver [DW/PA/7/9 f,334; DW/PA/5/1620/24]

Thomas of Chertsey, husbandman [HRO; 1595 AD10]

William of Cobham, faggot binder [DW/PA/7/10 f,280; DW/PA/5/1622/13]

William of Swk St George, yeoman, senior [DW/PA/7/11 f,569; DW/PA/5/1630/13]

BUSHELL

Mary of Tooting, widow [PRO; PCC Admon 1617]

BUSHFIELD (BUISHFEILD)

Godfrey of Swk St Olave, brewer [DW/PA/7/7 f,638; DW/PA/5/1608/21] <Abs 1194>

BUSHOP *see* BISHOP

BUSS

Thomas of Croydon [LPL; 98/1 f,28v; Will 1631]

BUSSHE *see* BUSH

BUST

Robert of Titsey, parson [DW/PA/5/1580/43]

BUSTBRIDGE

Elizabeth of Godalming, widow [DW/PA/5/1563/26]

see also BUSBRIDGE

BUSTON (? or BUSCOE)

John of Horsell [DW/PA/5/1550/2]

BUTCHER (BOCAR,BOCCHER,BOCHER,BUCHER)
Avery of Swk St Saviour, citizen and grocer [DW/PA/5/1602/17] <Abs U44>
Avis of Egham, widow [DW/PA/7/5 f.13; 1538] <Abs 31>
George of Newdigate; Crawley, Sussex [DW/PA/7/8 f.150; DW/PA/5/1611/17]
Henry, alias Harry of Kingston; Richmond, bricklayer [DW/PA/7/6 f.49; DW/PA/5/1559/46]
Henry, alias Henry Chittie of Godalming [PRO; PCC Will 1559]
John of ... [LPL; 96/3481; Will 1645]
John of Beddington, servingman [PRO; PCC Will 1609] <Abs. SAC v.23 p.135>
John of Egham, yeoman [DW/PA/7/5 f.13; 1538] <Abs 30>
John, alias John Chetie of Godalming [PRO; PCC Will 1546]
John, alias John Chitty of Godalming - Catteshall, yeoman [HRO; 1629 B9]
John, alias John Taylor of Haslemere; Peper Harow [DW/PA/7/1 f.77; 1488] <Abs 254>
John of Send, labourer [*in* DW/PA/5/1559/29]
Robert of Bermondsey, fellmonger [DW/PA/7/11 f.166; DW/PA/5/1625/34]
Robert, alias Robert Chyttie of Godalming, baker [DW/PA/5/1568/13]
Thomas of Capel, stonehealer [DW/PA/7/9 f.144; DW/PA/5/1615/23]
Thomas of Chiddingfold [DW/PA/7/4 f.213; 1537]
Thomas of Croydon [LPL; 96/443; Will 1637]

BUTCHIN (BOUTCHINGE,BUTCHINGE)
John of Godstone, tailor [DW/PA/7/12 f.130; DW/PA/5/1632/13]
William of Nutfield, husbandman [DW/PA/7/7 f.584; DW/PA/5/1607/17] <Abs 1087>
William of Nutfield, yeoman [DW/PA/7/12 f.140; DW/PA/5/1633/22]

BUTLER (BOTELAR,BUTTLER)
Christopher of Lambeth - Lambeth Marsh, yeoman [PRO; PCC Will 1618]
Edward of Surrey [PRO; PCC Will 1584]
Francis of Croydon, gent. [PRO; PCC 1648]
Hugh of Banstead [PRO; PCC Admon 1612]
James, earl of Ormond, of Shere [LPL; Reg. Abp Courtenay f.217; Will 1386] <Abs SAC v.8 pp.223-224>
Katherine of Ewhurst, widow [DW/PA/5/1605/17] <Abs U131>
Mary of Putney - Roehampton, widow [LPL; 98/1 f.106v; Will 1639]
Mary of Swk St Olave, widow [DW/PA/7/11 f.573; DW/PA/5/1630/14]
Nicholas of Newington [LPL; 98/1 f.11r; Will 1630]
Richard, alias Richard Smyth of Battersea [PRO; PCC Will 1513]
Richard of East Clandon; Guildford St Mary; West Clandon, yeoman [DW/PA/7/9 f.52; DW/PA/5/1614/10]
Richard of Clapham, husbandman [DW/PA/7/12 f.122; DW/PA/5/1632/10]
Richard of Ewhurst, husbandman [DW/PA/5/1561/32]
Robert of Cranleigh, husbandman [DW/PA/7/9 f.121; DW/PA/5/1615/20]
Thomas of Swk St Mary Overy; Swk St Mary Magdalen [DW/PA/7/4 f.168; 1536]
Thomas of Send, yeoman [DW/PA/7/11 f.582; DW/PA/5/1630/15]
Thomas of Thorpe [PRO; PCC Will 1590]
Walter, senior of Cranleigh, yeoman [DW/PA/7/7 f.498; DW/PA/5/1605/16] <Abs 934>
William of ... [DW/PA/7/5 f.48; 1538] <Abs 107>
William of Ockley [DW/PA/7/7 f.41; DW/PA/5/1595/12] <Abs 80>
William of Ockley [PRO; PCC 1641]
William of Ockley [PRO; PCC Admon 1642]
William of Putney - Roehampton [LPL; 98/1 f.54v; Will 1634]
William of Rotherhithe, mariner [PRO; PCC Will 1599]

BYCKNER *see* BICKNER
BYERS
John of Esher [DW/PA/7/1 f,54; 1487] <Abs 180>
Richard of Walton on Thames, yeoman [DW/PA/7/5 f.210; 1541]
Robert of Walton on Thames [PRO; PCC Will 1521]
BYGGNOLD,BYGNALL *see* BIGNALL
BYHURST
John, alias John Pykeryng of Ewell, yeoman [DW/PA/7/2 f,184; 1522]
BYKENOLLE,BYKNALDE *see* BIGNALL
BYKER *see* BICKER
BYKERDYKE *see* BICKERDIKE
BYNCKES *see* BINKS
BYND,BYNDE *see* BIND
BYNDELOSSE
Christopher of Swk [DW/PA/5/1574/8]
BYNDYNG *see* BINDING
BYNE *see* BINE
BYNGLEY *see* BINGLEY
BYNNES *see* BINNS
BYRCHAT,BYRCHATE,BYRCHED,BYRCHET,BYRCHETT *see* BURCHETT
BYRD *see* BIRD
BYRKES *see* BURKE
BYRLEY *see* BURLEY
BYRNE (BURNE,BURNES)
Harry of Ockley, husbandman [DW/PA/5/1552/3]
Richard of Dorking [DW/PA/7/2 f,142; 1520]
Robert of Dorking [DW/PA/7/2 f,152; 1521]
Sancta, alias Senge Byrne of Carshalton [DW/PA/7/11 f,514; DW/PA/5/1629/11]
BYRRIMAN *see* BERRIMAN
BYRTE *see* BURT
BYSHOP,BYSHOPE,BYSHOPP *see* BISHOP
BYSSETT *see* BISSET
BYSSH *see* BISH
BYSSHOPP,BYSSHYPE *see* BISHOP
BYSSYTT *see* BISSET
BYSTON *see* BEESTON
BYSYTTER *see* BISSETER
BYTHEWOOD *see* BITHEWOOD
BYWATER
William of Swk St Olave, cooper [DW/PA/7/12 f,303; DW/PA/5/1635/12]
BYWORTH (BYWORTHE)
John of Farnham, clothworker [PRO; PCC Will 1623]
John of Lambeth, weaver [GL; Archdeaconry Court of London Will 1571]
Petronell of Farnham, widow [PRO; PCC Will 1628]
BYXLEY *see* BIXLEY

CABLE
John of ... [DW/PA/7/7 f,543; DW/PA/5/1606/20] <Abs 1019>
CACHEN
John of Swk St Olave; Tournai, Belgium [DW/PA/7/7 f,122; DW/PA/5/1597/19] <Abs 226>

CACKETT,CACOTT *see* COCKETT

CADE

Robert of Oxted, gent. [PRO; PCC Will 1625]

Thomas of Swk St Saviour, baker [DW/PA/5/1593/106]

Walter of Reigate, citizen and haberdasher [PRO; PCC Will 1621]

CADMAN

Lucretia of Swk St Olave, widow [DW/PA/7/13 f.304; DW/PA/5/1642/19]

CAESAR (CAYSER,KEYSAR)

Robert of Epsom, widower [PRO; PCC Admon 1641]

William of Swk St Olave, cooper [DW/PA/7/2 f.127; 1518]

CAGE

Richard of Thames Ditton, gent. [PRO; PCC 1636]

CAKETT *see* COCKETT

CALAY

Philpot, alias Philpot Lucere of ... [*French church*], widow [DW/PA/5/1576/103]

CALCOTT

James of Lambeth [PRO; PCC Will 1558]

CALDWELL (CALDWALL,CAWDWELL)

Edward of Swk St Saviour, yeoman [DW/PA/7/12 f.477; DW/PA/5/1638/30]

Lawrence of Battersea, esq., citizen and vintner [PRO; PCC Will 1626]

Lawrence of Battersea, esq., citizen and vintner [PRO; PCC 1649]

see also CORDWELL

CALET

James of Swk St Olave, citizen and haberdasher [DW/PA/5/1558/42]*

CALINGHAM *see* CALLINGHAM

CALLARD

Thomas of Dorking, yeoman [DW/PA/7/11 f.159; DW/PA/5/1624/24]

CALLEN

James of Richmond [PRO; PCC Will 1593]

CALLINGHAM (CALINGHAM,CALLENGHAM,COLLINGHAM)

John of Godalming, yeoman [HRO; 1610 AD10]

Oliver of Compton - Polsted, yeoman [DW/PA/7/11 f.184; DW/PA/5/1625/36]

Phillipa of Ewhurst; Albury, widow [DW/PA/7/10 f.105; DW/PA/5/1621/15]

Thomas of Compton, husbandman [DW/PA/7/7 f.324; DW/PA/5/1601/20] <Abs 581>

CALLTROPP

Thomas of Lambeth - Lambeth Marsh, gent. [DW/PA/5/1593/179]

CALTON

Nicholas of Camberwell - Dulwich [PRO; PCC Will 1576]

CALVERLEY

Alice of Swk St George [DW/PA/7/2 f.89; 1503]

Joan of Tooting [DW/PA/5/1579/25]*

John of Swk St Margaret [HRO; Reg. Way 2 p.163; 1473]

CALVERT

Ann of Swk St Saviour, widow [DW/PA/7/13 f.111; DW/PA/5/1640/33]

CAMBREE

Thomas of Newington [LPL; 98/1 f.20r (ren.); 1630]

CAMBYLL *see* CAMPBELL

CAMERON

John of Swk St Olave [*French*] [DW/PA/5/1603/25] <Abs U63>

CAMFIELD (CAMFFIELD,CAMFILD)

Edward of Lingfield [DW/PA/5/1562/19]

John of Lingfield [DW/PA/5/1558/43]*

CAMOCK
William of Wimbledon [PRO; PCC Admon 1593]
CAMPBELL (CAMBYLL)
Richard of Swk St Mary Overy [DW/PA/7/4 f.13; 1532]
CAMPION *see* CHAMPION
Christopher of Tooting, mealman [DW/PA/7/10 f.63; 1618]
John of Swk St George, citizen and brewer [DW/PA/7/9 f.199; DW/PA/5/1616/21]
Richard of Swk St Saviour [DW/PA/5/1569/23]
William of ... [DW/PA/5/1596/11] <Abs U4>
CANCELLER *see* CHANCELLOR
CANDISHE
Margaret of ..., widow [DW/PA/5/1592/80]
CANDY
Richard of Swk St Olave, waterman [DW/PA/5/1591/103]
CANE (CAYNE)
John of Farnham - Wrecclesham [DW/PA/7/1 f.80; 1487] <Abs 263>
CANNON (CANNAN)
Isaac of Clapham [PRO; PCC 1643]
John of Clapham [PRO; PCC 1642]
Peter of Swk St Thomas, combmaker [DW/PA/7/12 f.84; DW/PA/5/1633/36]
Richard of Newington [PRO; PCC Admon 1640]
CANTES
Josina of Swk, widow [DW/PA/7/9 f.75; DW/PA/5/1614/15]
CANTHARTHOP
Thomas, alias Thomas Cuntasthorp of Streatham, rector [HRO; Reg Wyk 2 p.186; 1380]
CANTLOWE
Geoffrey of Ewell [PRO; PCC Will 1509]
CANWAY *see* CONWAY
CAPELEN *see* CAPLIN
CAPON (CAPEN)
Edith of Swk St Olave, widow [DW/PA/7/13 f.169; DW/PA/5/1641/33]
Richard of Swk St Margaret, citizen and stock fishmonger [DW/PA/7/4 f.133; 1536]
CAPLIN (CAPELEN)
Thomas of Dunsfold [DW/PA/7/12 f.27; DW/PA/5/1631/28]
William of Chiddingfold [DW/PA/7/13 f.158; DW/PA/5/1641/31]
CAPPE
Harry of Farnham, joiner [DW/PA/5/1563/3]
CAPPER
Henry of Clapham, labourer [DW/PA/7/7 f.421; DW/PA/5/1603/26] <Abs 788>
CAR *see* CARR
CARDEN
Edward of Bermondsey, leatherseller [DW/PA/7/7 f.106; 1597] <Abs 190>
John of Mitcham, and Ship *Blessing* [PRO; PCC Will 1629]
CARDY
John of Swk St George, victualler [DW/PA/5/1576/134]
CARENT
Margaret of Beddington [PRO; PCC Will 1501]
CAREW (CAREWE, CARREU, CARREWE)
Elizabeth of Beddington - Wallington [PRO; PCC Will 1546]
(Sir) Francis of Beddington, knight [PRO; PCC Will 1611] <Abs, SAC v.35 pp.37-39> [*and*] [SRO; 281/5/1; 1611]

CAREW (CAREWE,CARREU,CARREWE) [*continued*]
John of Wandsworth, gent. [PRO; PCC Will 1507]
Margaret of Beddington [PRO; PCC Will 1501]
Nicholas of Beddington, senior [LPL; Reg. Courteney f.232; Will 1390]
Nicholas of Beddington [PRO; PCC Will 1432] <Abs SAC v.25 pp.62-63>
Nicholas of Beddington, senior, esq. [PRO; PCC Will 1458]
Nicholas of ...., esq. [LPL; Reg. Abp Bourgchier f.52v; Admon 1466]
Nicholas of Rotherhithe, gent. [PRO; PCC Will 1627]
(Sir) Richard of Beddington, knight [PRO; PCC Will 1522] <Abs. SAC v.52 pp.35-36>
CAREY
William of Burstow [LPL; 96/467; Will 1640]
William of Rotherhithe, sailor [DW/PA/5/1596/12] <Abs U5>
CARILL *see* CARRILL
CARINGHAM
Richard of Bramley, senior, yeoman [DW/PA/7/7 f.621; DW/PA/5/1607/20 *and* DW/PA/5/1607/21] <Abs 1158>
CARLELL *see* CARLISLE
CARLES
Ralph of Kingston [DW/PA/7/8 f.151; DW/PA/5/1611/33]
CARLETON
Edmund of Charlwood, husbandman [LPL; 96/470; Will 1616]
Edward of Chertsey; Chobham, gent. [DW/PA/7/10 f.65; 1618]
John of Surrey, gent. [PRO; PCC Will 1551]
John of Esher [HRO; Reg. Way 1 p.56; 1458]
John of Kingston [PRO; PCC Will 1502]
(Lady) Lucy of Thames Ditton [PRO; PCC Admon 1648]
CARLISLE (CARLELL,CARLYSLE)
Christopher, alias Norroy, king of Arms, of Richmond, herald [PRO; PCC Will 1511]
Christopher of Bermondsey [DW/PA/7/7 f.16; DW/PA/5/1595/14] <Abs 34>
CARLTON *see* CARLETON
CARLYSLE *see* CARLISLE
CARNOE
John of Bermondsey, clerk - master of arts and curate [DW/PA/7/8 f.100; DW/PA/5/1614/19]
CAROLL *see* CARRILL
CARON (CAROEN, de CARON)
Ann de, alias Ann van Delden of Lambeth - South Lambeth [PRO; PCC Admon 1635]
John, alias John Bannister of Kingston [PRO; PCC Admon 1590]
(Sir) Noel of Lambeth [PRO; PCC Admon 1627]
Phillip de of Lambeth [PRO; PCC Admon 1627]
CARPENTER (CARPENTAR,CARPYNTER)
Agnes of Godalming, widow [DW/PA/5/1546/43]
Alice of Witley [DW/PA/7/5 f.145; 1540]
Edward of Lambeth, gent. [PRO; PCC 1638]
Elizabeth of Guildford St Nicolas, widow [DW/PA/5/1558/44]*
Gregory of Merton, yeoman [DW/PA/7/12 f.6; DW/PA/5/1631/23]
Henry of Godalming [DW/PA/7/1 f.30; 1485] <Abs 102>
Henry of Merton, yeoman [DW/PA/7/8 f.332; DW/PA/5/1614/26]
Henry of Witley [? HRO; 1521]
James of Newington, cook [LPL; 96/471; Will 1644]
John of Cranleigh [DW/PA/7/3 f.169; 1531]

CARPENTER (CARPENTAR,CARPYNTER) [*continued*]

John of Esher, husbandman [DW/PA/7/8 f.258; DW/PA/5/1611/34]
John of Kingston, husbandman [DW/PA/7/7 f.178; DW/PA/5/1597/20]<Abs 330>
John of Merton, yeoman [PRO; PCC Will 1611] <Abs, SAC v.35 p.47>
John of Swk St Saviour - Clink Liberty, victualler [DW/PA/7/13 f.436; DW/PA/5/1646/8]
John of Wonersh - Byrdgome [DW/PA/7/12 f.315; DW/PA/5/1626/32]
Katherine of Cranleigh, widow of Peter [DW/PA/5/1562/81]
Millicent of Cobham, widow [DW/PA/7/7 f.293; DW/PA/5/1600/11] <Abs 523>
Richard of Godalming - Farncombe [DW/PA/7/5 f.120; 1539]
Richard *or* Robert of Godalming, weaver [HRO; 1571 B34]
Robert of Cranleigh [DW/PA/7/4 f.81; 1534]
Robert *or* Richard of Godalming, weaver [HRO; 1571 B34]
Simon of Cheam [PRO; PCC Admon 1617]
Susan of Swk St Saviour [DW/PA/7/12 f.431; DW/PA/5/1627/16]
Sybil of Merton; Feltham, Middlesex; Cheam [DW/PA/7/6 f.256; 1560]
Thomas of Godalming - Farncombe, weaver [DW/PA/5/1558/45]*
Thomas of Merton [PRO; PCC Will 1558]
Thomas of Wonersh - Willinghurst, yeoman [HRO; 1638 B10]
William of Godalming - Farncombe, husbandman [DW/PA/5/1576/70]
William of Kingston, clerk [PRO; PCC Will 1508]
William of Wonersh [HRO; 1531 B3-4]
William of Wonersh [DW/PA/7/4 f.3; 1531]

CARR (CAR,CARRE,CURR)

James of Weybridge [DW/PA/7/12 f.472; DW/PA/5/1638/29]
Thomas of Mickleham [DW/PA/7/12 f.343; DW/PA/5/1636/20]
Thomasine of Swk St Saviour, widow [DW/PA/5/1593/86]

CARREU,CARREWE *see* CAREW

CARRICKE

Richard of Tooting, esq. [PRO; PCC Will 1627]

CARRILL (CARILL,CAROLL,CARRELL,CARYLL)

Henry of Wonersh - Great Tangley, gent. [PRO; PCC Will 1616]
John of Surrey, sergeant at law [PRO; PCC Will 1523]
John of Bramley, gent. [HRO; 1638 B8]
John of Wonersh - Great Tangley, gent. [PRO; PCC Will 1612]
Margaret of Rotherhithe [PRO; PCC Admon 1648]
Mary of Richmond [PRO; PCC Will 1621]
Richard of Shalford, citizen and mercer [PRO; PCC Will 1576]
Simon of Wonersh - Great Tangley, gent. [DW/PA/7/9 f.302; DW/PA/5/1619/22]

CARRINGHAM (CARYNGHAME)

Ralph of Godalming - Catteshall [DW/PA/5/1582/15]

CARRINGTON (CARRINGTONN)

Robert of Swk St Olave, feltmaker [DW/PA/7/13 f.3; DW/PA/5/1639/35]

CARROW (CAROWE)

Ellen of Swk St Olave, widow [DW/PA/5/1576/43]

CARTE

Simon of Swk St Saviour, waterman [DW/PA/7/7 f.2; DW/PA/5/1595/15] <Abs 3>

CARTER (CARTAR,KARTER,le CARTERE)

Agnes of Chobham [DW/PA/5/1557/50]
Alan of Bisley, husbandman [DW/PA/5/1563/110]
Alice of Mortlake [PRO; PCC Admon 1619]
Christopher of Malden, husbandman [DW/PA/7/12 f.267; DW/PA/5/1625/37]

CARTER (CARTAR,KARTER,le CARTERE) [*continued*]

Elizabeth of Swk St George, widow [DW/PA/7/12 f.62; DW/PA/5/1631/32]
Harry of Woking, husbandman [DW/PA/5/1563/108]
Henry of Chobham, yeoman [DW/PA/7/13 f.357; 1644]
Henry of Cobham [PRO; PCC Admon 1646]
Henry of Swk St Olave, waggoner [DW/PA/7/13 f.284; DW/PA/5/1643/24]
Joan of Dorking - Stub's, widow of John [HRO; Reg. Edn 2 p.10; 1347]
Joan of Kingston [DW/PA/7/6 f.2; 1559]
John of Chertsey [PRO; PCC Will 1596]
Reynold of Ockley, gent. [PRO; PCC Will 1588]
Roger of Carshalton [HRO; Reg. Way 2 p.149; 1471]
Thomas of Carshalton, senior [PRO; PCC Will 1530]
Thomas of Thames Ditton [DW/PA/7/6 f.246; 1560]
Thomas of Kingston - Tillehouse, brickmaker [DW/PA/7/7 f.573; DW/PA/5/1606/21] <Abs 1071>
Thomas of Leatherhead [PRO; PCC Will 1558]
Thomasine of Capel, widow [DW/PA/7/11 f.578; DW/PA/5/1630/16]
William of Ashtead, husbandman [DW/PA/7/8 f.142; DW/PA/5/1611/35]
William of Capel [DW/PA/7/5 f.106; 1539]
William of Capel [DW/PA/7/10 f.94; DW/PA/5/1616/22]
William of Guildford St Nicolas, husbandman [HRO; 1617 B11]
William of Reigate, blacksmith [DW/PA/7/12 f.604; DW/PA/5/1630/17]
William of Swk St George, white baker [DW/PA/7/11 f.428; DW/PA/5/1627/17]
William of Swk St Margaret, corser [*horse dealer*] [DW/PA/7/4 f.122; 1535]
William of Swk St Olave, whitster [DW/PA/7/13 f.27; DW/PA/5/1639/36]

CARTWRIGHT

Elizabeth of Leatherhead, widow [DW/PA/7/8 f.259; DW/PA/5/1611/36]
Francis of Swk St Olave, feltmaker [DW/PA/7/9 f.44; DW/PA/5/1614/29]
Henry of East Molesey [HRO; 1601 B14]
Thomas of Newington [PRO; PCC Admon 1611]

CARVER (KARVER)

Edward of Godstone [DW/PA/7/2 f.95; 1513]
John of Thursley [PRO; PCC Admon 1649]
William of Swk St Olave, sailor [DW/PA/5/1569/48]

CARYLL *see* CARRILL

CASALL *see* CASSALL,CASTLE

CASE

William of Bermondsey, mariner [PRO; PCC 1641]

CASEY

John of Swk St Saviour, citizen and merchant tailor [DW/PA/5/1557/62]

CASINGHURST (CASINGHERST,CASINGHURSTE,CASSINGHERST)

Edward of Camberwell - Dulwich [DW/PA/5/1570/89]
John of Camberwell - Dulwich [DW/PA/7/5 f.206; 1540]
John of Camberwell - Upper Dulwich, husbandman [DW/PA/5/1570/87]
John of Camberwell - Dulwich [DW/PA/7/12 f.226; DW/PA/5/1634/21]
Robert of Limpsfield [PRO; PCC Admon 1614]

CASEY

Ellen of Swk St Saviour, widow of John, citizen and merchant tailor [DW/PA/5/1558/46]*

CASSALL (CASALL)

Alice of Swk St George, widow of Humphrey [DW/PA/5/1593/116]
Humphrey of Swk; Croydon, glover [DW/PA/5/1593/117]
see also CASTLE

CASSEN
  Robert of Swk St George, miller [DW/PA/5/1593/132]
CASSINGHERST *see* CASINGHURST
CASTELAIN *see* CHASTILEYN
CASTELL *see* CASTLE
CASTELTON *see* CASTLETON
CASTLE (CASTELL,CASTILE)
  Elizabeth of Horsell, widow of James, gent, [DW/PA/5/1558/48]*
  Humphrey of Swk St Olave, feltmaker [DW/PA/7/12 f,510; DW/PA/5/1639/31]
  James of Horsell, gent, [DW/PA/5/1558/47]*
  William of Bermondsey [PRO; PCC Admon 1649]
  William of Swk St Saviour - Paris Garden [DW/PA/5/1575/51]
    see also CASSALL
CASTLEMAN
  Nicholas of Reigate, mercer [DW/PA/7/12 f,31 (*note of 1626 appended*);
    DW/PA/5/1623/17]
CASTLETON (CASTELTON)
  John of Long Ditton [PRO; PCC Will 1546]
  Robert of Long Ditton [PRO; PCC Will 1527] <Abs SAC v,27 pp,64-65>
  William of Long Ditton, gent, [PRO; PCC Will 1492]
CASTILE *see* CASTLE
CASTILION
  Valentine of Godalming, gent, [DW/PA/7/13 f,149B; DW/PA/5/1641/27]
CATERIKE *see* CATTERICK
CATERINGHAM (CATRINGHAM,KETERYNGHAM)
  George of Send, bachelor [PRO; PCC Admon 1620]
  John of Limpsfield, rector [HRO; Reg, Wyk 2 p,171; 1378]
  Robert of Guildford St Mary [DW/PA/7/8 f,338; DW/PA/5/1612/27]
CATESBY (KATESBYE)
  Elizabeth of Swk St Olave, spinster [DW/PA/5/1561/49]
  George of Lambeth, gent, [PRO; PCC Will 1592]
CATHERNES *see* KATHERNES
CATHY *see* CATY
CATLANDE
  Thomas of Newdigate, husbandman [DW/PA/7/8 f,150; DW/PA/5/1611/37]
CATRECE *see* CATTERICK
CATRINGHAM *see* CATERINGHAM
CATT (CATTE)
  Francis of Betchworth - Brockham [DW/PA/7/9 f,221; DW/PA/5/1617/11]
  Margaret of Betchworth - Brockham, widow [DW/PA/7/10 f,123;
    DW/PA/5/1620/26]
  Robert of Reigate; Betchworth, yeoman [*in* DW/PA/5/1563/65]
CATTARUS (CATTERUS)
  William of Swk St Olave, citizen and haberdasher [DW/PA/5/1558/49]*
  William of ... 'in this savage place' [DW/PA/7/9 f,262; DW/PA/5/1617/12]
CATTE *see* CATT
CATTERICK (CATERIKE,CATRECE)
  John of Oxted [DW/PA/5/1568/72]
  Robert of Guildford Holy Trinity [DW/PA/7/3 f,120; 1529]
CATTERUS *see* CATTARUS
CATY (CATHY)
  John of Reigate [DW/PA/7/2 f,185; 1522]
  Thomas of Reigate, husbandman [DW/PA/7/4 f,30; 1533]
CAUSTEN,CAUSTON *see* CAWSTEN

CAUTE (CAUT,CAWT,CAWTE)
  John of Blechingley [HRO; 1561 B27-28]
  Stephen of Ash, blacksmith [DW/PA/7/8 f.33; DW/PA/5/1609/28]
  William, alias William Cawood of Frimley [PRO; PCC Admon 1596]
CAVELL
  Humphrey of Surrey [PRO; PCC Will 1558]
  Richard of Richmond [PRO; PCC Admon 1621]
CAVERLEY (KAVERLEY)
  P'se (? Piers) of Swk St Saviour, citizen and bowyer [DW/PA/7/6 f.139; DW/PA/5/1559/235]
  William of Horley; Leigh [DW/PA/7/5 f.88; 1539]
CAWARDEN
  (Dame) Elizabeth of Blechingley, widow [PRO; PCC Will 1560]
  (Sir) Thomas of Blechingley, knight [PRO; PCC Will 1559] <Abs SAC v.5 pp.258-260>
  William of Blechingley, esq. [DW/PA/5/1561/28]
CAWDEREY (CAWDREY)
  Gilbert of Lambeth, gent. [PRO; PCC Will 1596]
  Henry of Swk St Saviour, citizen and plumber [DW/PA/7/10 f.163; DW/PA/5/1621/16]
  see also CORDREY
CAWDWELL *see* CALDWELL
CAWLEY (CAULY)
  Joan of Leigh, spinster [HRO; 1628 B13]
  William of Charlwood [LPL; 98/1 f.116r; Will 1640]
CAWOOD (CAWOD,CAWOODE)
  John of Surrey [PRO; PCC Will 1509]
  William of Frimley [PRO; PCC Will 1591]
  William of Frimley [PRO; PCC Admon 1596]
CAWSEY
  Peter of Putney, gent. [PRO; PCC Will 1624]
CAWSON
  John of Swk St Olave, merchant tailor [DW/PA/5/1605/18] <Abs U132>
CAWSTEN (CAUSTEN,CAUSTON,CAWSTON,COSTEN,COSTON)
  Henry of Addington, husbandman [DW/PA/5/1561/14]
  Henry of Oxted, yeoman [DW/PA/7/12 f.212; DW/PA/5/1633/33]
  John of Lambeth - South Lambeth, yeoman [DW/PA/5/1570/91]
  John of Guildford St Nicolas - Littleton [DW/PA/7/7 f.107; DW/PA/5/1596/16] <Abs 192>
  John of Mitcham, husbandman [DW/PA/7/11 f.116; DW/PA/5/1624/25]
  John of Wanborough - Flexford [DW/PA/5/1562/41]
  Nicholas of Swk St Saviour; Addington, merchant tailor [DW/PA/5/1593/51]
  Robert of Battersea - Penge, husbandman [DW/PA/7/12 f.419; DW/PA/5/1637/29]
  Thomas of Godalming - Eashing [DW/PA/7/10 f.22; DW/PA/5/1616/28]
  William of Compton, glover [DW/PA/7/7 f.325; DW/PA/5/1601/29] <Abs 582>
  William of Oxted, senior, gent. [DW/PA/7/12 f.516; DW/PA/5/1638/36]
  William of Woking, yeoman [PRO; PCC Will 1614]
  William of Woking; Chertsey, yeoman [DW/PA/7/9 f.67; DW/PA/5/1614/13]
CAWT,CAWTE *see* CAUT
CAYNE *see* CANE
CAYSER *see* CAESAR

CECIL
  (Sir) Edward, Viscount Wimbledon, of Putney [PRO; PCC 1638]
CEELY,CELYE *see* SEELEY
CHADDESLEY
  William of Merton, chaplain [GL; Commissary Court of London Will; 1375]
CHAFFYN
  Edmund of Battersea [PRO; PCC Will 1523]
CHALCROFT (CHALCROFTE)
  Robert of Sutton, husbandman [DW/PA/7/11 f,581; DW/PA/5/1630/18]
  Thomas of Chiddingfold, yeoman [PRO; PCC Will 1608]<Abs, SAC v,12 p,106>
CHA'LER *see* CHANDLER
CHALKE
  John of Chiddingfold [PRO; PCC Admon 1601]
  John of Chiddingfold, yeoman [DW/PA/7/12 f,22; DW/PA/5/1631/26]
  John of Cranleigh, yeoman [DW/PA/7/7 f,49; DW/PA/5/1595/16] <Abs 92>
CHALLONER (CHALLENDOR,CHALLNER,CHALNER)
  Edward of Peper Harow [DW/PA/7/3 f,143; 1530]
  Henry of Bermondsey [PRO; PCC Admon 1583]
  Henry, senior of Wonersh [PRO; PCC Will 1579]
CHAMBER *see* CHAMBERS
CHAMBERLAIN (CHAMBERLAYN,CHAMBERLAYNE,CHAMBERLAYNIS,CHAMBERLEN,CHAMBERLEYN, CHAMBERLIANE)
  Agnes of Betchworth [PRO; PCC Will 1535]
  Joan of Betchworth [DW/PA/7/2 f,25; 1492]
  John of Wandsworth [PRO; PCC Will 1595]
  Robert of Betchworth [DW/PA/7/1 f,27; 1486] <Abs 87>
  William of Buckland, senior [PRO; PCC Will 1532]
  William of Lambeth, a Queen's ordinary waterman [DW/PA/5/1569/63]
  William of Swk St Saviour, carman [DW/PA/7/8 f,124; DW/PA/5/1610/24]
CHAMBERS (CHAMBER,CHAMBRE)
  ..., of Swk St Olave [DW/PA/5/1557/2]
  Adrian of Rotherhithe [DW/PA/7/12 f,51; DW/PA/5/1631/30]
  Edmund of Swk St Olave, waterman [DW/PA/7/13 f,166; DW/PA/5/1642/13]
  Elizabeth of Kingston - the Castle [DW/PA/7/11 f,481; DW/PA/5/1628/18]
  Henry of Kingston, innholder [DW/PA/7/11 f,484; DW/PA/5/1628/19]
  Henry of Wonersh - Barnett, yeoman [DW/PA/7/11 f,509; DW/PA/5/1629/12]
  Robert of Bermondsey, citizen and leatherseller [DW/PA/7/11 f,241; DW/PA/5/1625/38]
  William of Swk St Saviour; Swk St George; Bermondsey; Swk St Olave; Battersea, citizen and armourer [DW/PA/7/5 f,178; 1540]
CHAMBLETT
  Mary of Camberwell, widow [DW/PA/7/5 f,62; 1539] <Abs 15>
CHAMLEY
  John of Blechingley [DW/PA/7/5 f,50; c1538] <Abs 12>
CHAMPFLOUR
  John of Alton, Hampshire; Guildford, esq. [LPL; Reg. Abp Arundel ii f,103; Will 1408]
CHAMPION (CHAMPYON)
  Arnold of Godalming, yeoman [DW/PA/5/1562/77]
  Arnold of Godalming, clothier [DW/PA/5/1581/13]
  Edward of Farnham [DW/PA/7/1 f,45; 1486] <Abs 146>
  John of Guildford - Artington, blacksmith [DW/PA/7/10 f,295; DW/PA/5/1622/14]
  John of Stoke next Guildford, widower [PRO; PCC Admon 1639]

CHAMPION (CHAMPYON) [*continued*]

Richard of Godalming - Binscombe, senior [DW/PA/7/2 f,37; 1493]

Richard of Hassenbrook, Essex; Godalming, esq. [PRO; PCC Will 1600] <Abs Emmison p.65]

(Sir) Richard of Guildford, knight & alderman [PRO; PCC Will 1568]

Robert of Godalming [DW/PA/7/4 f,226; 1537]

Robert of Godalming - Binscombe [DW/PA/7/11 f,192; DW/PA/5/1624/26]

Thomas of Farnham, cordwainer [DW/PA/7/5 f,14; 1538] <Abs 35>

Walter of Godalming [PRO; PCC Will 1533]

see also CAMPION

CHAMPNEY (CHAMPNEIS,CHAMPNEYS,CHAPNIE)

Lawrence of Camberwell, yeoman [DW/PA/7/10 f,41; DW/PA/5/1617/13]

Margaret of Swk St Thomas, widow [DW/PA/7/10 f,149; 1622]

CHAMPYON *see* CHAMPION

CHANCELLOR (CANCELLER)

Thomas of Surrey, esq. [PRO; PCC Will 1509]

CHANDLER (CHA'LER,CHANDELER,CHANTLER,CHAUNDELER,CHAUNDELOR,CHAUNDLER, CHAUNLER,CHAYNLEARE)

Agnes of Cranleigh [DW/PA/5/1592/124]

Agnes of Haslemere [HRO; 1575 B10]

Alice of Wonersh, widow of John [DW/PA/7/9 f,236; DW/PA/5/1617/14]

Bennett of Swk St Saviour, widow [DW/PA/7/12 f,457; DW/PA/5/1638/26]

Edward of Witley - Brook, husbandman [DW/PA/7/12 f,367; DW/PA/5/1638/25]

George of Guildford [PRO; PCC 1647]

Harry of Frensham, husbandman [DW/PA/5/1563/10]

Henry of Farnham [DW/PA/7/5 f,79; 1539]

Henry of Hambledon, husbandman [DW/PA/7/4 f,212; 1537]

Jane of Guildford Holy Trinity, widow [PRO; PCC 1648]

Joan of Newdigate; Horsham, Sussex, widow [DW/PA/5/1593/48]

Jocose of Newington, widow [PRO; PCC Will 1620]

John of Cranleigh, husbandman [DW/PA/7/11 f,188; DW/PA/5/1625/42]

John of Farnham - Runfold; Seale, yeoman [DW/PA/7/10 f,133; DW/PA/5/1620/27]

John of Godalming, clothworker [DW/PA/7/8 f,307; DW/PA/5/1613/22]

John of Guildford, tanner [DW/PA/7/13 f,379; 1644]

John of Haslemere [DW/PA/5/1569/6]

John of Newdigate, yeoman [DW/PA/5/1579/26]*

John of Peper Harow, yeoman [DW/PA/5/1587/13]

John of Shalford [DW/PA/7/5 f,81; 1539]

John of Wonersh [DW/PA/5/1604/10] <Abs U100>

Joyce of Newington, widow [PRO; PCC Admon 1619] <Soame 89>

Margaret of Shalford, widow [DW/PA/5/1582/29]

Margaret of Wonersh - Barnett, widow [DW/PA/7/12 f,141; DW/PA/5/1633/23]

Mary of Bramley, widow [PRO; PCC 1649]

Maud of Dunsfold; Shalford [DW/PA/7/3 f,179; 1531]

Nicholas of Swk St Saviour, waterman [DW/PA/7/11 f,572; DW/PA/5/1630/19]

Peter of Shalford [DW/PA/7/12 f,337; DW/PA/5/1636/24]

Peter of Swk St Olave, winer [DW/PA/5/1575/2]

Robert of Haslemere [DW/PA/7/6 f,224; 1561]

Robert of Haslemere, yeoman [DW/PA/5/1570/101]

Robert of Haslemere, husbandman [HRO; 1590 B12]

Robert of Peper Harow [DW/PA/7/11 f,475; DW/PA/5/1628/20]

Robert of Peper Harow [DW/PA/7/13 f,154; DW/PA/5/1641/29]

Thomas of Bisley, victualler [DW/PA/7/12 f,432; DW/PA/5/1637/33]

CHANDLER (CHA'LER, CHANDELER, CHANTLER, CHAUNDELER, CHAUNDELOR, CHAUNDLER, CHAUNLER, CHAYNLEARE) [*continued*]
Thomas of Bramley, husbandman [DW/PA/7/11 f.274; DW/PA/5/1625/41]
Thomas of Bramley, yeoman [DW/PA/7/12 f.511; DW/PA/5/1639/32]
Thomas of Chiddingfold, bachelor [DW/PA/5/1569/7]
Thomas of Cranleigh [DW/PA/7/5 f.157; 1540]
Thomas of Dunsfold; Shalford [DW/PA/7/3 f.167; 1531]
William of Shalford - Thorncombe, husbandman [DW/PA/5/1555/59]
William of Swk St Margaret, servant to Charles, duke of Suffolk [DW/PA/7/5 f.69; 1539] <Abs 85>
William of Windlesham - Bagshot; Windsor, Berkshire, victualler [DW/PA/7/7 f.324; DW/PA/5/1601/21] <Abs 580>
CHANGE *see* De CHANGE
CHANNELL *see* CHENNELL
CHANTLER *see* CHANDLER
CHAPEL (CHAPPYLL)
Edward of Swk St Saviour [DW/PA/5/1582/70]
CHAPER
Nathaniel of Farnham, bachelor [PRO; PCC Admon 1638]
Thomas of Farnham [HRO; 1627 B15]
CHAPLIN (CHAPLEYN)
John of Godalming [DW/PA/7/1 f.54; 1487] <Abs 178>
CHAPMAN (CHEPMAN)
Abraham of Camberwell [PRO; PCC Admon 1647]
Agnes of Swk St Saviour, late servant with Mrs Rutter [DW/PA/7/10 f.72; 1618]
Brian of Oxted [PRO; PCC Will 1593]
Christopher of Blechingley [DW/PA/5/1557/101]
Christopher of Godstone; Merstham, husbandman [DW/PA/5/1604/9] <Abs U99>
Edward of Lambeth [PRO; PCC Will 1591]
Elizabeth of Ditton [DW/PA/7/8 f.291; DW/PA/5/1613/23]
George of Lingfield [DW/PA/7/11 f.593; DW/PA/5/1630/20]
Gregory, alias Gregory Gatton of Surrey [? HRO; 1529]
Henry of Bermondsey [PRO; PCC 1647]
Henry of Chertsey; Chobham, draper [DW/PA/7/11 f.3; DW/PA/5/1622/15]
Henry of Swk St Olave, waterman [DW/PA/7/8 f.192; DW/PA/5/1610/25]
Isabel of Surrey, widow of William [DW/PA/7/12 f.320; DW/PA/5/1637/35]
Jane of Swk St Olave, widow [DW/PA/7/8 f.241; DW/PA/5/1613/24]
Joan of Blechingley, widow [DW/PA/7/8 f.213; 1613]
John, alias John Gatton of Albury, husbandman [DW/PA/7/9 f.296; 1618]
John of Chertsey, mercer [DW/PA/5/1591/74]
John, alias John Heynys of Farnham [DW/PA/7/1 f.60; 1407] <Abs 199>
John of Kingston - Ham Hatch, yeoman [DW/PA/5/1598/17] <Abs U15>
John of Lingfield, hoopmaker [DW/PA/7/8 f.342; DW/PA/5/1612/28]
John, alias John Gatton, senior of Shere [HRO; 1608 B32]
Martin of Kingston - Hatch [DW/PA/5/1593/148]
Oliver of Lambeth [PRO; PCC Admon 1647]
Phillip of Dorking; Oxted; Reigate, shoemaker [DW/PA/7/7 f.417; DW/PA/5/1603/27] <Abs 782>
Rebecca of Streatham, widow [PRO; PCC 1645]
Richard, alias Richard Gatton of Albury, yeoman [DW/PA/5/1612/65] <Abs U200>
Richard of Blechingley [DW/PA/7/11 f.111; DW/PA/5/1624/27]

CHAPMAN (CHEPMAN) [*continued*]
Richard, alias Richard Gatton of Great Bookham, husbandman [HRO: 1622 B8]
Richard of Kingston [DW/PA/7/5 f.141; 1540]
Richard, alias Richard Baker of Kingston - Ham [DW/PA/5/1568/3]
Richard of Kingston - Ham [PRO: PCC 1640]
Robert of Albury [DW/PA/5/1558/50]*
Robert of Croydon [PRO: PCC Admon 1615]
Stephen, alias Stephen Gatton of Surrey [? HRO: 1529]
Thomas, alias Thomas Baker of Kingston - Ham Hatch, yeoman [PRO: PCC Will 1600]
Thomas of Lingfield, husbandman [DW/PA/7/11 f.21; 1623]
Thomas of Lingfield, husbandman [DW/PA/7/11 f.40; DW/PA/5/1623/18]
Thomas of Merstham [PRO: PCC Will 1572]
Thomas of Rotherhithe [DW/PA/7/10 f.163; DW/PA/5/1621/17]
William, alias William Elwyl of Battersea [PRO: PCC Will 1403]
William, alias William Gatton of Thames Ditton [DW/PA/7/7 f.118; DW/PA/5/1597/21] <Abs 218>
William of Kingston, fisherman [DW/PA/5/1578/45]
William of Swk St Olave, carpenter [DW/PA/7/13 f.93; DW/PA/5/1640/31]

CHAPNIE *see* CHAMPNEY

CHAPPYLL *see* CHAPEL

CHARE
Henry of Bermondsey, citizen and leatherseller [PRO: PCC Will 1563]
John of Wandsworth, gent. [PRO: PCC 1649]
Margaret of Bermondsey [PRO: PCC Will 1526]
Robert of Bermondsey [PRO: PCC Will 1553]

CHARESMORE *see* CHASMORE

CHARINGTON *see* CHARRINGTON

Charles of Coulsdon, rector [HRO: Reg. Orl 1 p.11; 1334]

CHARLEWOOD *see* CHARLWOOD

CHARLEY
George of Richmond, senior [DW/PA/7/11 f.422; DW/PA/5/1627/19]
Peter of ...., citizen and draper [DW/PA/7/11 f.287; DW/PA/5/1625/40]

CHARLWOOD (CHARELWOOD,CHARLEWODE,CHARLEWOOD,CHERLEWODE)
Alexander of Walton on the Hill, yeoman [DW/PA/5/1558/51]*
Ann of Albury, spinster [PRO: PCC Admon 1649]
Daniel of Dorking, glover [DW/PA/7/12 f.104; DW/PA/5/1632/18]
George of Reigate, mealman [DW/PA/7/13 f.117; DW/PA/5/1639/40]
Henry of Surrey, tanner [HRO: 1587 AD11]
Henry of Sutton, labourer [HRO: 1602 AD8]
Jane, alias Jane Jackson of Croydon [PRO: PCC Admon 1615]
John of Croydon [LPL: 98/1 f.80v; Will 1637]
John of Reigate [DW/PA/7/2 f.145; 1520]
John of Stoke Dabernon, husbandman [DW/PA/5/1607/22] <Abs U193>
John of Walton on the Hill, yeoman [DW/PA/5/1607/23] <Abs U194>
Margaret of Great Bookham, widow [HRO: 1591 B15]
Richard of Epsom, labourer [DW/PA/5/1570/50]
Richard of Leigh, husbandman [DW/PA/7/7 f.330; DW/PA/5/1601/22] <Abs 593>
Robert of Dorking, yeoman [DW/PA/7/11 f.234; DW/PA/5/1625/39]
Thomas of Croydon - Addiscombe [PRO: PCC 1630]
Thomas of Croydon, yeoman [LPL: 96/508; 98/1 f.9r; Will 1630]
Thomas of Walton, husbandman [DW/PA/5/1593/61]
William of Warlingham [DW/PA/5/1558/52]*

CHARM (CHARME)
Alice of Kingston, wife of Roger, citizen and cook [PRO; PCC Will 1615]
Roger of Kingston [PRO; PCC Will 1618]
Thomas of Thames Ditton - Marsh [DW/PA/7/7 f.606; DW/PA/5/1607/24] <Abs 1133>
CHARMAN (CHARMANE,CHARMON)
George of Dorking [PRO; PCC Admon 1648]
Jane of Wonersh [DW/PA/7/11 f.316; DW/PA/5/1626/34]
John of Capel [DW/PA/5/1557/128]
John of Farnham [DW/PA/7/1 f.71; 1487] <Abs 232>
Thomas of Godalming, smith [DW/PA/5/1558/54]*
CHARME *see* CHARM
CHARMON *see* CHARMAN
CHARNBERY
Joan of Lambeth, widow [PRO; PCC Will 1618]
CHARRINGTON (CHARINGTON,CHARYNGTON)
Alice of Charlwood, widow [PRO; PCC Will 1596]
Nicholas of Horley [DW/PA/5/1591/11]
Nicholas of Horley [DW/PA/7/11 f.405; DW/PA/5/1627/18]
CHARSELY
Thomas of Swk St Saviour, citizen and fishmonger [DW/PA/7/12 f.255; DW/PA/5/1634/26]
CHART (a CHARTE,CHARTE)
John of Burstow [PRO; PCC Will 1535]
John of Horne, husbandman [DW/PA/5/1558/53]*
Nicholas of Burstow; Tandridge [PRO; PCC Will 1592]
Thomas of Lingfield [PRO; PCC Will 1596]
see also Acharte
CHARTER
John of Chobham, husbandman [DW/PA/7/6 f.103; DW/PA/5/1559/61]
CHARYNGTON *see* CHARRINGTON
CHASMORE (CHARESMORE,CHASEMOORE,CHASEMORE,CHASMOUR,CHAYSMORE,JAYSMORE)
John of Abinger, yeoman [DW/PA/7/8 f.218; DW/PA/5/1612/29]
John of Horley [DW/PA/7/6 f.226; 1561]
Richard of Mickleham, labourer [DW/PA/7/9 f.128; DW/PA/5/1615/24]
Robert of Abinger [DW/PA/7/5 f.214; 1541]
Thomas of Effingham [DW/PA/5/1545/17]
Thomas of Ockley, husbandman [DW/PA/5/1617/15] <Abs U213>
William of Capel [DW/PA/7/4 f.110; 1535]
William of Capel, husbandman [DW/PA/7/8 f.342; DW/PA/5/1612/30]
CHASTILEYN (SHATTELYN)
Michael of Swk [*French*] [DW/PA/5/1571/44]
CHATTELTON
James of Swk St Saviour, weaver [DW/PA/7/8 f.30; DW/PA/5/1608/27]
CHATTERTON
Humphrey of ... [DW/PA/7/7 f.412; DW/PA/5/1603/28] <Abs 766>
CHAUNDELER,CHAUNDLER,CHAUNLER,CHAUNTELOR *see* CHANDLER
CHAYNELL *see* CHENNELL
CHAYNLEARE *see* CHANDLER
CHEASEMAN *see* CHEESEMAN
CHEEKE
Isabel of Thames Ditton [PRO; PCC Will 1601] <Abs, SAC v.10 pp.296-297 *and* v.27 p.83>
John of Thames Ditton, gent. [PRO; PCC Will 1590] <Abs SAC v.27 p.83>

CHEESEMAN (CHEASEMAN,CHEESMAN,CHEISSMAN,CHESEMAN,CHESMAN,CHISMAN,SCHESMON)

Bartholomew, alias Bartholomew Vivian of Leigh [DW/PA/5/1576/30]
Christopher of Leigh [DW/PA/7/7 f.2; DW/PA/5/1595/17] <Abs 6>
Edmund of Betchworth; Charlwood [DW/PA/7/7 f.346; DW/PA/5/1601/23] <Abs 632>
Edmund of Esher [PRO; PCC Admon 1642]
Edmund of Esher, yeoman [DW/PA/7/13 f.282; DW/PA/5/1643/22]
Harry of Reigate [DW/PA/7/2 f.102; 1514]
Harry, alias Harry Tanner of Tandridge [DW/PA/7/4 f.224; 1537]
Henry of Betchworth - Betchworth Park [PRO; PCC Admon 1635]
Joan of Reigate; Effingham, spinster [PRO; PCC Will 1581]
John of Leigh, yeoman [DW/PA/5/1569/58]
Oliver of Horley [PRO; PCC Will 1567]
Richard of Abinger [PRO; PCC 1647]
Richard of Coulsdon; Beddington - Wallington; Sanderstead; Warlingham; Caterham; Chaldon [DW/PA/7/4 f.78; 1534]
Richard of Shere [DW/PA/5/1557/25]
Robert, alias Robert Fevian of Buckland, priest and curate [DW/PA/5/1558/55]*
Robert of Leigh [DW/PA/7/1 f.31; 1486] <Abs 105>
Thomas of Shere [DW/PA/7/3 f.164; 1530]
Thomas of Walton on Thames, husbandman [DW/PA/7/12 f.458; DW/PA/5/1638/27]
Thomas of Walton on Thames, husbandman [DW/PA/7/12 f.519; 1638]
Thomas of Wotton [DW/PA/5/1559/13]
William of Thames Ditton, husbandman [DW/PA/5/1546/56]

CHELLSHAM,CHELSAM,CHELSAME *see* CHELSHAM

CHELSEA (CHELSEY)

Elizabeth of Swk St Olave, widow [DW/PA/5/1558/57]*

CHELSHAM (CHELSAM,CHELSAME,CHELLSHAM)

Agnes of Horley [*in* DW/PA/5/1546/23]
Edmund of West Clandon, husbandman [DW/PA/7/13 f.85; DW/PA/5/1640/30]
James of Ockley [DW/PA/7/11 f.213; DW/PA/5/1625/43]
John of Horley [DW/PA/7/4 f.117; 1535]
John of Horley [DW/PA/7/6 f.274; 1560]
John of Horley, joiner [DW/PA/7/7 f.525; DW/PA/5/1607/25 *and* DW/PA/5/1607/26] <Abs 990>
John of Kingston [PRO; PCC Admon 1610]
John of Leigh [DW/PA/7/1 f.31; 1486] <Abs 104>
John of Swk St Olave, baker [DW/PA/7/4 f.62; 1534]
Katherine of Leigh [DW/PA/7/4 f.142; 1536]
Richard of West Clandon, husbandman [DW/PA/7/9 f.341; DW/PA/5/1620/30]
Richard of Kingston, butcher [DW/PA/5/1620/29] <Abs U241>
Richard of Morden, husbandman [DW/PA/7/9 f.333; DW/PA/5/1620/28]
Robert of Kingston, beer brewer [PRO; PCC Will 1592]
Robert of Kingston, yeoman [DW/PA/7/11 f.13; DW/PA/5/1623/19]
William of Clapham, senior, citizen and mercer [PRO; PCC Will 1573]

CHELTNAM

George of Swk St Olave, victualler [DW/PA/7/11 f.166; DW/PA/5/1625/44]

CHENEY (CHENY,CHEYNEY)

John of Rotherhithe [PRO; PCC Admon 1618]
Juliana of Putney, widow [PRO; PCC Admon 1615]
Thomas of Newington, yeoman [PRO; PCC Will 1597]

CHENNELL (CHANNELL,CHAYNELL,CHENELL,CHENILL,CHEYNELL)
Agnes of Chobham, widow [HRO; 1578 B22]
Ann of Cranleigh, spinster [PRO; PCC 1646]
Edward of Ewhurst, yeoman [DW/PA/7/13 f.148; DW/PA/5/1641/26]
Elizabeth of Seale - Tongham, spinster [DW/PA/7/13 f.292; DW/PA/5/1643/25]
George of Ewhurst, yeoman [DW/PA/7/12 f.145; DW/PA/5/1633/24]
Henry of Albury [DW/PA/7/4 f.118; 1535]
Henry of Shere; Albury, yeoman [DW/PA/7/7 f.546; DW/PA/5/1606/22] <Abs 1025>
Henry of Chertsey, yeoman [DW/PA/7/9 f.83; DW/PA/5/1615/25]
Jane of Albury, widow [DW/PA/7/8 ff.357,367; DW/PA/5/1612/31]
Joan of Albury [DW/PA/7/4 f.118; 1535]
John of Godalming, clothier, senior [DW/PA/5/1587/11]
John of Seale, yeoman [DW/PA/7/12 f.312; DW/PA/5/1636/16]
John of Shere, yeoman [HRO; 1561 B35]
John of Shere - Gomshall, yeoman, senior [DW/PA/7/8 f.175; DW/PA/5/1610/26]
Richard of Byfleet [DW/PA/7/13 f.45; DW/PA/5/1639/38]
Richard of Wonersh, miller, senior [DW/PA/7/7 f.542; DW/PA/5/1606/23] <Abs 1018>
Richard of Wonersh, yeoman [DW/PA/7/11 f.22; DW/PA/5/1623/20]
Richard of Wonersh, husbandman [HRO; 1642 B6]
Robert of Ewhurst, tanner [DW/PA/7/13 f.238; DW/PA/5/1642/17]
Robert of Seale - Tongham, husbandman [DW/PA/7/12 f.237; DW/PA/5/1634/23]
Thomas of Albury [DW/PA/7/2 f.189; 1523]
Thomas of Albury - Pittance, yeoman [DW/PA/5/1587/105]
Thomas of Chertsey, yeoman [DW/PA/7/7 f.546; DW/PA/5/1606/24] <Abs 1024>
Thomas of Cranleigh, yeoman [PRO; PCC Will 1611] <Abs, SAC v.35 p.45>
Thomas of Cranleigh [DW/PA/7/12 f.363; DW/PA/5/1638/24]
Thomas of Shalford - Summersbury, yeoman, senior [DW/PA/7/10 f.229; DW/PA/5/1621/18]
Thomas of Shalford - Summersbury, husbandman [DW/PA/7/11 f.419; DW/PA/5/1626/35]
Thomas of Wonersh - Lee, yeoman [DW/PA/7/10 f.290; DW/PA/5/1623/21]
Walter of Ewhurst, yeoman [DW/PA/5/1561/33]
William of Albury, husbandman [DW/PA/7/12 f.109; DW/PA/5/1632/19]
William of Chobham, husbandman [DW/PA/5/1578/43]
William of Farnham [BM; Add.Ms 24,925 f.8r; 1545] <Abs 13>
William of Farnham - Wrecclesham [HRO; 1572 B18]
William of Haslemere, yeoman [DW/PA/5/1557/35]
William of Wonersh [HRO; 1561 B33-34]

CHENY *see* CHENEY

CHEPPES *see* CHIPPS

CHERCHER *see* CHURCHER

CHEREDIN
Thomas of Reigate, yeoman [DW/PA/7/8 f.2; DW/PA/5/1608/22]

CHERINGTON
Francis of Burstow, tailor [LPL; 96/521; Will 1625]

CHERLEWODE *see* CHARLWOOD

CHERRY (CHERYE)
Thomas of Swk St Olave, tailor [DW/PA/7/4 f.107; 1535]

CHERTSEY (CHERTESEYE)
  Robert of Chertsey [PRO; PCC Will 1555]
  Walter of Surrey [PRO; PCC Will 1443]
CHERYE *see* CHERRY
CHESEMAN, CHESMAN *see* CHEESEMAN
CHESTERTON
  John of Witley - Oxenford, gent. [PRO; PCC Will 1625]
CHESTON
  George of Swk St Thomas [DW/PA/5/1588/73]
CHESWICKE *see* CHISWICK
CHETEWYN *see* CHETWYN
CHETEY, CHITIE *see* CHITTY
CHETTELTON
  James, alias James Chattelton of Swk St Saviour, weaver [DW/PA/7/8 f.30; DW/PA/5/1608/27]
CHETTIE, CHETTYE *see* CHITTY
CHETWYN (CHETEWYN)
  John of Bermondsey - Bermondsey Abbey, esq. [PRO; PCC Will 1433]
  John of Swk St Olave, hatmaker [DW/PA/5/1570/33]
CHEWTER *see* CHUTER
CHEYNEY *see* CHENEY
CHEYNN
  Isabel of Richmond [PRO; PCC Will 1513]
CHIBBALL (CHIBALL, CHIBBALD)
  James of Bermondsey, citizen and leatherseller [PRO; PCC Will 1606] <Abs. SAC v.12 pp.194-195>
  Katherine of Swk St Saviour, spinster [DW/PA/7/12 f.212; DW/PA/5/1633/32]
CHIBORNE
  Catherine of Tooting, spinster [PRO; PCC Admon 1628]
CHICHELE
  Robert of St James Garlickhythe, London; Tandridge; Romford, Essex; Wimpole, Cambridgeshire; Higham Ferrers, Northamptonshire, citizen and grocer [LPL; Reg. Abp Chichele i f.467; Will 1439]
CHICKETT (CHYCKETT)
  Robert of Rotherhithe, sailor [DW/PA/5/1568/73]
CHIDLEY (CHYDLEY)
  Margery, alias Margery Browksbey of London [DW/PA/5/1572/2]
CHILD (CHILDE, CHYLD, CHYLDE)
  Alice of Ripley, widow [DW/PA/5/1591/91]
  Alvin of Bermondsey - St Saviour's Monastery, citizen of London [Bermondsey Abbey Register; 1082] <Abs SAC v.1 pp.190-191>
  Henry of Woking [DW/PA/7/6 f.78; DW/PA/5/1559/63]
  Jane of Weybridge; Byfleet, widow [DW/PA/7/9 f.255; DW/PA/5/1617/16]
  Joan of Woking, widow [DW/PA/7/12 f.209; DW/PA/5/1633/31]
  John of Leatherhead, yeoman [DW/PA/7/11 f.355; DW/PA/5/1625/45]
  John of Swk St Margaret [DW/PA/7/1 f.28; 1485] <Abs 91>
  John of Woking [DW/PA/7/2 f.170; 1522]
  John of Woking, yeoman [DW/PA/7/6 f.213; 1560]
  John of Woking, husbandman [DW/PA/7/12 f.255; DW/PA/5/1634/25]
  Margaret of Bisley, widow [DW/PA/5/1569/53]
  Maurice of Bermondsey [PRO; PCC Admon 1636]
  Morris of Bermondsey [DW/PA/7/12 f.398; DW/PA/5/1637/25]
  Richard of Farnham - Dippenhall [DW/PA/7/1 ff.70,80,81; 1488] <Abs 231, 265>

CHILD (CHILDE,CHYLD,CHYLDE) [*continued*]
  Robert of Send [DW/PA/5/1558/56]*
  Thomas of Surrey [PRO; PCC Will 1598]
  Thomas of Mitcham, mealman [DW/PA/7/11 f,552; DW/PA/5/1629/13]
  Thomas of Swk St George, fletcher [DW/PA/7/7 f,405; DW/PA/5/1603/29]
    <Abs 752>
  Thomas of Weybridge [PRO; PCC 1648]
  William of Bermondsey [DW/PA/5/1558/58]*
  William of Egham, senior [PRO; PCC 1645]
  William of Swk St George, yeoman [DW/PA/7/13 f,29; DW/PA/5/1639/37]
  William of Woking [DW/PA/7/5 f,199; 1540]
  William of Woking, yeoman [DW/PA/5/1571/15]
CHILDREN
  Susanna of Horley, widow [PRO; PCC 1632]
CHILLMAN *see* CHILMAN
CHILLMEADE *see* CHILMEADE
CHILMAN (CHILLMAN,CHILMANE)
  Christopher of Limpsfield, bachelor [PRO; PCC 1638]
  George of ... (proved at Kingston) [DW/PA/7/8 f,144; DW/PA/5/1611/38]
  John of Ashtead, husbandman [DW/PA/7/12 f,491; DW/PA/5/1638/34]
  Katherine of Ashtead, widow [DW/PA/7/13 f,122; DW/PA/5/1640/34]
  Margaret of Chipstead [DW/PA/5/1587/87]
  Margery of Walton on the Hill, widow [DW/PA/5/1593/103]
  Nicholas of Coulsdon, husbandman [DW/PA/5/1604/11] <Abs U101>
  Richard, alias Richard Chilmead of Chaldon; Lewisham, Kent, husbandman
    [DW/PA/5/1605/21] <Abs U133>
  Roger of Chipstead [PRO; PCC Admon 1648]
  Thomas of Headley [DW/PA/7/12 f,138; DW/PA/5/1632/24]
  William of Headley [PRO; PCC Admon 1648]
CHILMEADE (CHILLMEADE,CHILMAIDE,CHILMEED,CHYLMEDE)
  Alan of Ashtead, labourer [DW/PA/7/11 f,598; DW/PA/5/1630/21]
  Geoffrey of Godstone [PRO; PCC Admon 1626]
  George of Swk St Saviour, yeoman [DW/PA/5/1579/28]*
  John of Mitcham [DW/PA/7/4 f,224; 1537]
  John of Swk, cheesemonger [DW/PA/7/11 f,17; DW/PA/5/1623/22]
  Ralph of Mitcham, groom of the Stable [PRO; PCC Will 1597]
  Richard, alias Richard Chilman of Chaldon; Lewisham, Kent, husbandman
    [DW/PA/5/1605/21] <Abs U133>
CHILTON (CILTERNE,CITTERNE)
  Elizabeth of Swk St George, widow [DW/PA/7/8 f,35; DW/PA/5/1609/29]
  Richard of Barnes,citizen and freemason [PRO; PCC 1638]
CHIPPES *see* CHIPPS
CHIPPING (CHIPPINGE)
  Malachi of Blechingley, yeoman [PRO; PCC Will 1599]
  Robert of Little Bookham, yeoman [DW/PA/7/8 f,303; DW/PA/5/1613/25]
  Thomas of Nutfield, clerk and parson [DW/PA/5/1581/67]
CHIPPS (CHEPPES,CHIPPES,CHYPPS)
  Joan of Windlesham, widow [DW/PA/7/5 f,132; 1539]
  Thomas of Windlesham [DW/PA/7/5 f,30; 1538] <Abs 121>
  William of Egham - Millfield [DW/PA/7/11 f,568; 1630]
  William of Windlesham [DW/PA/5/1574/6]
CHIRCHEMAN *see* CHURCHMAN
CHISMAN *see* CHEESEMAN

CHISWICK (CHESWICKE,CHISWEEKE,CHISWICKE)
Agnes, alias Agnes Sedgewicke of Swk St Olave, widow [DW/PA/7/7 f.245; DW/PA/5/1599/60] <Abs 432>
Henry of Hambledon, husbandman [DW/PA/5/1586/44]*
John of Croydon, bachelor [LPL; 98/1 f.89v; Will 1638]
John of Godalming - Enton [DW/PA/5/1587/12]
Thomas of Tooting, husbandman [DW/PA/7/13 f.101; DW/PA/5/1640/32]
CHITTEN
John of Rotherhithe, mariner [PRO; PCC Will 1604] <Abs, SAC v.11 p.297>
CHITTY (CHETEY,CHETIE,CHETTIE,CHETTYE,CHETYE,CHITTEY,CHITTIE,CHITTYE, CHITYE,CHYTEE,CHYTTEY,CHYTIE,CHYTTY,CHYTTYE,CHYTYE)
Alice of Woking, widow [HRO; 1629 B8]
Edward of Croydon [PRO; PCC Will 1603] <Abs, SAC v.11 p.120>
George of Godalming, clothier [DW/PA/7/7 f.545; DW/PA/5/1606/25] <Abs 1023>
Henry of Ashtead, tailor [DW/PA/7/13 f.462; DW/PA/5/1647/3]
Henry of Great Bookham, husbandman [DW/PA/7/9 f.268; 1618]
Henry of Godalming [PRO; PCC Will 1559]
Henry of Godalming - Eashing, yeoman [HRO; 1585 B15]
Henry of Godalming, clothier [DW/PA/7/7 f.187; DW/PA/5/1598/18] <Abs 341>
Henry of Godalming, practitioner of physic [DW/PA/7/12 f.157; DW/PA/5/1633/26]
Henry of Shalford, yeoman [DW/PA/7/8 f.196; DW/PA/5/1610/28]
Henry of Shalford, yeoman [DW/PA/7/11 f.311; DW/PA/5/1626/36]
Henry of Shalford, thatcher [DW/PA/7/12 f.298; DW/PA/5/1635/20]
Henry of Wonersh - 'Crobbs', husbandman [DW/PA/7/8 f.193; DW/PA/5/1610/27]
John of Cranleigh, yeoman [DW/PA/7/13 f.223; DW/PA/5/1642/16]
John of Godalming - Farncombe [DW/PA/7/1 f.79; 1488] <Abs 261>
John, alias John Bocher of Godalming [PRO; PCC Will 1546]
John, alias John Coklys of Godalming - Winkworth [*in* DW/PA/5/1558/76]*
John of Godalming, weaver [DW/PA/5/1569/41]
John of Godalming - Eashing, husbandman [DW/PA/5/1579/23]*
John of Godalming - Hurtmore, yeoman [DW/PA/7/7 f.497; DW/PA/5/1605/19] <Abs 932>
John of Godalming, clothier [DW/PA/7/8 f.130; DW/PA/5/1610/29]
John, alias Butcher of Godalming - Catteshall, yeoman [HRO; 1629 B9]
John of Guildford St Mary, weaver [DW/PA/5/1593/13]
John of Witley - Mousehill, husbandman [DW/PA/5/1557/26]
Jonas of Godalming [PRO; PCC 1635]
Matilda of Godalming, widow [DW/PA/7/1 f.25; 1486] <Abs 81>
Richard of Frensham - Pitfold, yeoman [HRO; 1639 B11]
Robert of Godalming - Eashing [DW/PA/7/4 f.109; 1535]
Robert of Godalming [BM; Add.Ms 24,925 f.11r; 1544] <Abs 19>
Robert of Godalming, husbandman [DW/PA/7/6 f.213; 1560]
Robert, alias Robert Bocher of Godalming, clothier [DW/PA/5/1568/13]
Thomas of Godalming [DW/PA/7/2 f.171; 1521]
Thomas of Haslemere, husbandman [HRO; 1603 B10]
Thomas of Ockley [? HRO; 1570]
William of Elstead, weaver [DW/PA/7/7 f.397; DW/PA/5/1603/30] <Abs 735>
William of Godalming, husbandman [*in* DW/PA/5/1546/23]
William of Godalming - Eashing, husbandman [DW/PA/7/6 f.163; DW/PA/5/1559/62]

CHITTY (CHETEY,CHETIE,CHETTIE,CHETTYE,CHETYE,CHITTEY,CHITTIE,CHITTYE, CHITYE,CHYTEE,CHYTTEY,CHYTIE,CHYTTY,CHYTTYE,CHYTYE) [*continued*]
William of Godalming - Eashing, husbandman [HRO; 1564 B36]
William of Godalming, mercer [DW/PA/5/1579/27]*
William of Godalming; Witley, junior [HRO; 1580 AD11]
William of Godalming, clothier [HRO; 1587 AD14]
William of Godalming - Eashing, husbandman [DW/PA/7/9 f.4; DW/PA/5/1615/26]
William of Godalming - Burgate, yeoman [DW/PA/7/11 f.377; DW/PA/5/1626/33]
CHIVERS
Thomas of Rotherhithe (died overseas) [PRO; PCC Admon 1648]
CHOCTET
Richard of ... (at Chertsey) [DW/PA/7/3 f.108; 1529]
CHOLMELEY (CHOLMLEY,CHOLMLEYE,CHOMLY)
Henry of Blechingley [PRO; PCC Will 1547]
Humphrey of Bermondsey, citizen and innholder [DW/PA/7/11 f.228; DW/PA/5/1625/46]
Jasper of Newington - Walworth, esq. [PRO; PCC Will 1587]
John of Blechingley, gent. [DW/PA/5/1589/1]*
John of Blechingley, gent. [DW/PA/7/13 f.354; 1644]
Nicholas of Blechingley; Burstow, gent. [DW/PA/7/8 f.286; DW/PA/5/1613/26]
Richard of Blechingley [PRO; PCC Will 1558]
Richard of Blechingley [PRO; PCC 1632]
William of Newington, citizen and innholder [PRO; PCC 1648]
CHOMPART *see* COMFORT
CHORTHE
Robert of Kingston; Walton [DW/PA/7/10 f.106; DW/PA/5/1621/19]
CHOTER,CHOTTER,CHOULTER *see* CHUTER
CHOWNE
Elizabeth of Richmond, widow [PRO; PCC Will 1597]
CHOWNEY
John of Bermondsey [DW/PA/5/1582/89]
CHOWTER *see* CHUTER
CHRICHELOO *see* CRUTCHLOW
CHRISMAS *see* CHRISTMAS
CHRISTIAN
Evans of Swk St Saviour, cobbler [DW/PA/5/1586/22]
CHRISTIE
Susanna (widow of Richard Thicknesse) of Swk St Saviour, wife of Robert, citizen and saddler [DW/PA/7/13 f.316; DW/PA/5/1643/27]
CHRISTMAS (CHRISMAS,CHRYSMAS,CRISMAS,CRISTIMAS,CRISTMAS)
Alice of Guildford St Nicolas - Artington, widow [DW/PA/7/12 f.339; DW/PA/5/1636/25]
Henry of Worplesdon [DW/PA/5/1550/25]
Malyn of Carshalton [DW/PA/7/3 f.127; 1530]
Nicholas of Carshalton, husbandman [DW/PA/7/2 f.167; 1522]
Richard of Hambledon [DW/PA/7/10 f.246; DW/PA/5/1622/16]
Robert of Guildford St Mary [PRO; PCC Will 1584]
Thomas of Carshalton, collier [DW/PA/7/7 f.595; DW/PA/5/1607/33] <Abs 1114>
Thomas of Worplesdon, senior [PRO; PCC Will 1587]

CHRISTMAS (CHRISMAS, CHRYSMAS, CRISMAS, CRISTIMAS, CRISTMAS) [*continued*]

William of Worplesdon [DW/PA/5/1570/54]

William of Worplesdon, weaver [DW/PA/5/1576/112]

CHRISTOPHER

John of Richmond [DW/PA/5/1568/45]

Richard of Swk St Olave, ropemaker [DW/PA/7/13 f.402; DW/PA/5/1645/8]

CHROTHE *see* CHORTHE

CHROUCHER *see* CROUCHER

CHRYSMAS *see* CHRISTMAS

CHURCH (CHURCHE)

Agnes of Betchworth [PRO; PCC Will 1535]

Ralph of Swk St Saviour [DW/PA/7/7 f.633; DW/PA/5/1608/23] <Abs 1184>

Thomas of Bermondsey, bachelor [PRO; PCC 1633]

CHURCHAR *see* CHURCHER

CHURCHE *see* CHURCH

CHURCHER (CHERCHER, CHURCHAR)

James of Guildford [PRO; PCC Will 1622]

Thomas of Guildford [HRO; 1544 B21]

Thomas of Guildford St Mary, dyer [DW/PA/7/8 f.239; DW/PA/5/1613/27]

CHURCHMAN (CHIRCHEMAN)

William of Ewell, mason [GL; Commissary Court of London Will; 1451]

CHUTE

(Sir) George of Lambeth - Stockwell; Camberwell; Newington - Walworth; knight [PRO; PCC 1649 *and* PCC Admon 1649] [*and*] [LBLAD; Surrey Deeds 1/3936; 1647]

CHUTER (CHEWTER, CHOTER, CHOTTER, CHOULTER, CHOWTER, SHOTER, SHOWTER)

Adrian of Weybridge [HRO; 1602 B10]

Agnes of Wanborough [DW/PA/5/1557/111]

Henry of Cranleigh [DW/PA/7/7 f.187; DW/PA/5/1598/19] <Abs 343>

Joan of Cranleigh, widow [DW/PA/7/8 f.352; DW/PA/5/1612/32]

John of Swk St Saviour [DW/PA/5/1546/90]

John of Worplesdon, husbandman [DW/PA/7/7 f.358; DW/PA/5/1602/20] <Abs 655>

Robert of Wanborough [DW/PA/7/8 f.70; DW/PA/5/1609/106]

William of Cranleigh, yeoman [DW/PA/7/11 f.455; DW/PA/5/1628/21]

William of Windlesham [DW/PA/7/4 f.166; 1536]

CHYCKETT *see* CHICKETT

CHYDLEY *see* CHIDLEY

CHYLD, CHYLDE *see* CHILD

CHYLMEDE *see* CHILMEADE

CHYPPS *see* CHIPPS

CHYTIE, CHYTTEY, CHYTTY, CHYTTYE, CHYTYE *see* CHITTY

CICELY (SISLYE, SYSEYE, SYSLY)

Jane of Swk St Olave, widow [DW/PA/7/11 f.194; DW/PA/5/1625/224]

Simon of Merton [DW/PA/7/2 f.10; 1491]

William of Chobham [DW/PA/7/2 f.35; 1493]

CILLOCKE *see* SILLOCK

CILTERNE *see* CHILTON

CLABORNE

Sarah of Reigate, widow [PRO; PCC Admon 1626]

CLAMPORD (CLAMPARD, CLAMPERD, CLAMPORDE)

Jane of Shalford - Rushett, widow [DW/PA/7/8 f.369; DW/PA/5/1612/33]

John of Tandridge, yeoman [PRO; PCC Will 1615] <Abs, SAC v.12 pp.91-92>

Margaret of Oxted, widow [DW/PA/7/12 f.185; DW/PA/5/1633/28]

CLAMPORD (CLAMPARD,CLAMPERD,CLAMPORDE) [*continued*]
Richard of Oxted, yeoman [DW/PA/7/11 f,9; DW/PA/5/1622/17]
Robert of Wotton [PRO; PCC Admon 1588]
CLAPP
John of Swk St Thomas, citizen and cook [DW/PA/7/12 f,203; DW/PA/5/1634/18]
Margaret of Swk St Saviour, widow [DW/PA/7/13 f,369; 1644]
CLARE
Humphrey of St Benet Fink, London; Kingston, citizen and draper [PRO; PCC 1620] <Soame 794>
Joan of Bermondsey, widow [DW/PA/7/8 f,305; DW/PA/5/1613/28]
CLARK (CLARCKE,CLARKE,CLEARKE,CLERCKE,CLERK,CLERKE,le CLERCKE)
Agnes of Swk St Saviour - Liberty of Old Paris Garden, widow [DW/PA/7/9 f,267; 1618]
Alice of Mortlake, widow [PRO; PCC Will 1622]
Alice of Wandsworth, widow [DW/PA/7/7 f,262; DW/PA/5/1599/12] <Abs 466>
Ann, alias Ann Smyth of Egham, widow of Thomas Clarke [DW/PA/7/5 f,172; 1540]
Ann of Godalming, widow [DW/PA/7/12 f,335; DW/PA/5/1637/34]
Ann of Wandsworth, widow [PRO; PCC 1639]
Bartholomew of Clapham, Doctor of Law [PRO; PCC Will 1589]
Bartholomew of Clapham [PRO; PCC Admon 1594]
Christopher of Headcorn, Kent, clerk [DW/PA/5/1557/48]
Christopher of Swk St George [DW/PA/7/5 f,217; 1541]
Edward of Bermondsey, husbandman [DW/PA/7/12 f,314; DW/PA/5/1636/18]
Edward of Egham, yeoman [DW/PA/7/11 f,525; DW/PA/5/1630/22]
Eleanor of Clapham [PRO; PCC Will 1594 (two)]
Elizabeth of Thorpe [PRO; PCC Admon 1649]
Emma of Dorking, widow [DW/PA/7/7 f,597; DW/PA/5/1607/27] <Abs 1118>
Francis of Swk St George, wheelwright [DW/PA/5/1569/62]
George of Alfold; Hascombe, yeoman [DW/PA/7/8 f,22; DW/PA/5/1608/25]
George of Bermondsey, citizen and leatherseller [PRO; PCC 1647]
Gilbert of Egham, innholder [DW/PA/7/9 f,157; DW/PA/5/1616/23]
Gilbert of Egham, innholder [PRO; PCC Will 1616]
John of ...., blacksmith [DW/PA/7/11 f,545; DW/PA/5/1629/14]
John of Bermondsey [PRO; PCC Admon 1641]
John of Bermondsey [DW/PA/7/13 f,178; DW/PA/5/1641/34]
John of Cobham [PRO; PCC Admon 1646]
John, alias John Snypston of Croydon [PRO; PCC Will 1432]
John, alias John Smyth of Egham [DW/PA/7/1 f,23; 1485] <Abs 76>
John of Farnham, weaver [DW/PA/7/9 f,105; 1615]
John of Farnham - Dippenhall, yeoman [DW/PA/7/13 f,158; DW/PA/5/1641/30]
John of Farnham, gent. [PRO; PCC Will 1574]
John of Kingston, yeoman [DW/PA/5/1557/105]
John of Lambeth [DW/PA/7/11 f,111; DW/PA/5/1624/28A]
John of Merton, one of the proctors of the Arches [PRO; PCC Will 1572]
John le Clercke of Swk, combmaker [DW/PA/5/1571/7]
John of Swk St George, cook [DW/PA/5/1570/84]
John, alias John Curten of Swk St Olave [DW/PA/7/7 f,48; DW/PA/5/1595/22] <Abs 90>
John of Swk St Olave, joiner [DW/PA/7/12 f,346; DW/PA/5/1636/21]
John of Swk St Saviour, waterman [DW/PA/7/9 f,121; 1615]
John of Wandsworth [PRO; PCC Admon 1601]
John of Worplesdon, husbandman [DW/PA/5/1557/137]

CLARK (CLARCKE, CLARKE, CLEARKE, CLERCKE, CLERK, CLERKE, le CLERCKE) [*continued*]

Julian, alias Julian Nash of Bermondsey [PRO; PCC Admon 1649]
Margaret *or* Margery of Swk St George, widow [HRO; 1602 B11]
Margery of Woking, widow [DW/PA/7/5 f.175; 1540]
Margery of Chertsey, widow [DW/PA/5/1602/22] <Abs U46>
Martin of Camberwell, gent. [PRO; PCC Will 1629]
Mary of Worplesdon, widow [DW/PA/7/11 f.292; DW/PA/5/1626/37A]
Peter of Swk St Mary Overy, hosier [DW/PA/7/3 f.104; 1529]
Peter of Swk St Mary Overy, clockmaker [DW/PA/5/1593/174]
Reynold of Kingston [DW/PA/7/1 f.10; 1485] <Abs 31>
Richard of Swk St Olave, brewer [DW/PA/5/1546/25]
Richard of Swk St Saviour [DW/PA/5/1550/39]
Richard of Thorpe [PRO; PCC Admon 1649]
Robert of Bermondsey [PRO; PCC Will 1623]
Robert of Croydon [PRO; PCC Admon 1648]
Robert of Dorking; Guildford St Nicolas, currier [DW/PA/7/7 f.420; DW/PA/5/1603/31] <Abs 784>
Robert of Wandsworth, yeoman [DW/PA/5/1592/6]
Simon of Swk St Margaret [DW/PA/7/4 f.144; 1536]
Thomas of ... [DW/PA/7/8 f.138; DW/PA/5/1610/30]
Thomas of Bermondsey [PRO; PCC Will 1593]
Thomas of East Clandon, clerk [PRO; PCC Will 1545]
Thomas, alias Thomas Dyer of Egham [DW/PA/7/4 f.57; 1533]
Thomas of Egham [HRO; 1534 B9]
Thomas of Lambeth [PRO; PCC Will 1598]
Thomas of Lambeth, bachelor [PRO; PCC Admon 1628]
Thomas of Putney, yeoman [PRO; PCC Will 1627]
Thomas of Rotherhithe [PRO; PCC Admon 1618]
Thomas of Swk St Olave [DW/PA/7/8 f.61; DW/PA/5/1609/30]
Thomas of Swk St Thomas [DW/PA/7/11 f.436; DW/PA/5/1628/22]
Thomas of Worplesdon - Broadstreet, gent. [DW/PA/7/11 f.387; DW/PA/5/1626/38A]
Walter of a Ship [*unnamed*] [DW/PA/7/8 f.125; DW/PA/5/1610/31]
William of ... [DW/PA/7/4 f.203; 1537]
William of Battersea [PRO; PCC Will 1571]
William of Bermondsey [PRO; PCC Admon 1592]
William of Coulsdon, parson [DW/PA/5/1587/115]
William, alias William Smyth of Egham [PRO; PCC Will 1490]
William of Guildford St Nicolas [DW/PA/5/1558/59]*
William of Mortlake, esq. [PRO; PCC 1641]
William of Newington, chandler [LPL; 96/539; 98/1 f.125v; Will 1641]
William of Rotherhithe, mariner [DW/PA/7/9 f.218; DW/PA/5/1617/17]
William of Swk St Olave, chandler [DW/PA/7/7 f.305; DW/PA/5/1600/13] <Abs 545>
William of Swk St Olave [DW/PA/7/7 f.594; DW/PA/5/1607/28] <Abs 1111>

CLASCOCKE Agnes [*this is a mistranscription in Abs 197 of DW/PA/7/7* ('Register Herringman') *for Glascocke, q.v.*]

CLAVERLEY (CLAVERLY)

John of Chertsey [DW/PA/5/1581/9]
Thomas of Chertsey [BM; Add.Ms 24,925 f.22v; 1544] <Abs 54>
William, junior of Chertsey, husbandman [DW/PA/7/7 f.544; DW/PA/5/1606/26] <Abs 1020>
William of Chertsey, yeoman [DW/PA/7/8 f.51; DW/PA/5/1609/31]

CLAY (CLAYE)
Dionis of Lambeth, widow [PRO; PCC 1634]
Edmund of Lambeth - South Lambeth, gent. [PRO; PCC Will 1625]
George of Lambeth [PRO; PCC Admon 1625]
Hannah of Lambeth, spinster [PRO; PCC Admon 1633]
Martha of Lambeth, spinster [PRO; PCC Admon 1633]
Robert of Reigate, gardener [DW/PA/7/9 f.253; DW/PA/5/1617/18]
Sarah of Lambeth, spinster [PRO; PCC Admon 1633]

CLAYBROOK
Robert of Ockham, parson [HRO; 1573 AD8]

CLAYSON
Cornelius of Swk St Olave [DW/PA/7/2 f.52; 1497]
John of Swk St Olave, skinner [DW/PA/7/2 f.51; 1497]

CLAYTON (CLEATON)
George of Haslemere, chirurgeon [DW/PA/7/13 f.426; DW/PA/5/1646/12]
Paul of Swk St Olave, silk weaver [DW/PA/7/9 f.338; DW/PA/5/1620/31]

CLEAR (CLEARE,CLEERE,CLER',CLERE)
Agnes of Walton on Thames, widow [HRO; 1626 B23]
John of Walton on Thames - Hersham [DW/PA/7/5 f.173; 1540]
Joyce of Walton on Thames, widow [DW/PA/5/1593/203]
Lawrence of Frensham, husbandman [DW/PA/7/11 f.541; DW/PA/5/1629/15]
Rose of Walton on Thames - Hersham, widow [DW/PA/7/10 f.74; 1618]
Thomas of Lambeth [PRO; PCC Will 1544] <Abs SAC v.29 p.118>
Thomas of ... [DW/PA/7/9 f.195; DW/PA/5/1616/24]

CLEARKE *see* CLARK

CLEATON *see* CLAYTON

CLEMENTS (CLEMENT,CLEMENTE)
Edward of Merstham, husbandman [PRO; PCC Will 1616]
Elizabeth of Sutton [PRO; PCC 1649]
Giles of Guildford Holy Trinity, tailor [DW/PA/5/1592/29]*
Hugh of Kingston [PRO; PCC Will 1526]
John of Guildford, mason [HRO; 1612 B15]
John of Nutfield [DW/PA/7/6 f.245; 1560]
John of Nutfield, yeoman [DW/PA/7/12 f.427; DW/PA/5/1637/32]
Joseph of Guildford [DW/PA/7/12 f.383; DW/PA/5/1637/23]
Richard of Merstham [PRO; PCC Will 1549]
Richard, senior of Nutfield; Merstham; Gatton, carpenter [DW/PA/7/7 f.627; DW/PA/5/1608/24] <Abs 1172>
Robert of Dorking, tanner [DW/PA/5/1563/109]
Robert of Nutfield, wheelwright [DW/PA/7/7 f.138; DW/PA/5/1597/22] <Abs 253>
William of Rotherhithe [PRO; PCC 1646]
William of Swk St George [DW/PA/7/5 f.201; 1540]

CLER' *see* CLEAR

CLERCKE *see* CLARK

CLERE *see* CLEAR

CLERK,CLERKE *see* CLARK

CLERKENWELL (de CLERKENWELL)
Walter of Ewell, rector [HRO; Reg. Stra p.25; 1326]

CLEVE
Harry of Swk [DW/PA/5/1555/76]
Thomas of Reigate [PRO; PCC Will 1614]

CLEWER
William of Swk St Saviour, yeoman [DW/PA/7/8 f.157; DW/PA/5/1611/39]

CLIFFE
Robert, alias Robert Davies of Wandsworth, yeoman [DW/PA/5/1563/7]
William of London, pewterer [DW/PA/7/9 f.295; 1618]
CLIFFORD (CLYFFORD)
John of Swk St Margaret [DW/PA/7/3 f.111; 1529]
CLIFT
Henry of Swk St Saviour, butcher [DW/PA/7/13 f.224; DW/PA/5/1643/19]
CLIFTON (CLISTON,CLYFFTON,CLYFTON,CLYSTON)
Alice of Bermondsey, widow [DW/PA/7/13 f.124; DW/PA/5/1640/36]
Anthony of Kingston, servant to the Queen [DW/PA/5/1562/26]
Anthony of Worplesdon, yeoman [DW/PA/7/9 f.183; DW/PA/5/1616/25]
Bridget of Putney - Newlands, widow of William [PRO; PCC 1639]
Henry of Guildford, gent. [PRO; PCC Will 1608] <Abs. SAC v.12 p.107>
Henry of Lambeth, gent. [DW/PA/5/1546/83]
John of Ash, husbandman [DW/PA/7/7 f.497; DW/PA/5/1605/20] <Abs 933>
John of Egham; Clandon [DW/PA/7/6 f.201; 1560]
John of Puttenham, senior [HRO; 1584 B14]
John of Puttenham, widow [DW/PA/7/12 f.300; DW/PA/5/1635/22]
John of Worplesdon [DW/PA/7/12 f.271; DW/PA/5/1635/18]
John of Worplesdon (but died at Lincoln), lieut.colonel to the earl of Manchester's regiment [PRO; PCC 1646]
Margaret of Worplesdon [HRO; 1581 AD11]
Quivier of Richmond [PRO; PCC Admon 1592]
Richard of Godalming [DW/PA/5/1578/35]
Richard of Worplesdon [HRO; 1581 AD11]
Richard of Godalming, weaver [DW/PA/7/8 f.21; DW/PA/5/1608/26]
Robert of Puttenham, yeoman [DW/PA/7/12 f.256; DW/PA/5/1634/27]
Thomas of Stoke [DW/PA/7/6 f.166; DW/PA/5/1559/166]
Thomas of Thursley [HRO; 1619 AD21]
William of Albury [DW/PA/7/11 f.397; DW/PA/5/1627/20]
William of Putney - Newlands [PRO; PCC 1636]
William of Worplesdon [DW/PA/7/4 f.66; 1534]
CLINES (CLYNES)
Beatrice of Lambeth [PRO; PCC Admon 1623]
CLINTON
Ann of Newington - Walworth, widow [PRO; PCC 1649]
Elizabeth, Dowager Countess of Lincoln, widow of Edward, earl of Lincoln, of Woking [PRO; PCC Will 1589]
Margaret of Shalford [DW/PA/7/11 f.543; 1630]
CLOBERY
William of Kingston, merchant [PRO; PCC 1640]
CLONNE
Oliver of Bermondsey, citizen and draper [PRO; PCC Will 1563]
CLOPTON
William of Merton, esq. [PRO; PCC Will 1521]
CLOSSON
Godfrey of Swk St Olave, gunmaker [DW/PA/7/11 f.52; DW/PA/5/1623/23]
CLOUGH
Robert of Swk St Olave, vintner [DW/PA/7/13 f.152; DW/PA/5/1642/12]
CLOWES
John of East Horsley [PRO; PCC Admon 1642]
CLOWSER (CLOWZER)
Henry of Cranleigh, bachelor [PRO; PCC Admon 1630 *and* 1631]
John of East Horsley, husbandman [LPL; 96/556; 98/1 f.112r; Will 1640]

CLOWSER (CLOWZER) [*continued*]
Robert of Mickleham [PRO; PCC 1648]
CLOYDEN
Leonard of Swk St Olave - Horsleydown, silk weaver [DW/PA/5/1588/23]
CLUGGIS
Nicholas of Swk St Saviour, porter [DW/PA/7/10 f.189; DW/PA/5/1621/20]
CLYFFORD *see* CLIFFORD
CLYFFTON,CLYFTON *see* CLIFTON
CLYNES *see* CLINES
CLYSTON *see* CLIFTON
COALE,COANE *see* COLE,CONE
COATES (COTES)
Anthony of Swk St Saviour, gent. [DW/PA/7/9 f.265; 1618 *and* 1636]
James of Rotherhithe, shipwright [DW/PA/5/1587/7]
Katherine of Woodmansterne [DW/PA/7/2 ff.29,32; 1492]
Nicholas of Woodmansterne [DW/PA/7/1 f.32; 1485] <Abs 107>
Walter of Bentley, Hampshire [DW/PA/7/1 f.82; 1488] <Abs 273>
COATFIELD *see* COTEFIELD
COB *see* COBB
COBAT *see* COBBETT
COBB (COB,COBBE)
John of Ashtead [DW/PA/7/1 f.34; 1486] <Abs 115>
John of Ashtead [DW/PA/7/2 f.18; 1491]
Michael of Mortlake, esq. [PRO; PCC Will 1616]
William of Bermondsey [PRO; PCC Will 1459] [*and*] [HRO; Reg. Way 1 p.57; 1459]
William of Epsom [DW/PA/7/1 f.65; 1487] <Abs 218>
COBBEHAM *see* COBHAM
COBBETT (COBAT,COBBATT,COBBUT,COBET,COBHETT)
Alice of Guildford, widow [DW/PA/7/11 f.62; DW/PA/5/1623/24]
John of ... [DW/PA/7/13 f.373; 1644]
John of Bisley [HRO; 1592 B14]
John of Bisley, husbandman [DW/PA/7/12 f.104; DW/PA/5/1632/17]
John of Pirbright [DW/PA/5/1578/37]
John of Worplesdon [DW/PA/7/12 f.124; DW/PA/5/1632/21]
Richard of Bisley, husbandman [DW/PA/5/1550/41]
Richard of Bisley, husbandman [DW/PA/5/1576/86]
Robert of Bisley [DW/PA/7/7 f.591; DW/PA/5/1607/29] <Abs 1104>
Robert of Bisley, husbandman [DW/PA/7/8 f.371; DW/PA/5/1612/34]
Thomas of Bisley [HRO; Reg. Fox 2 p.29; 1507]
Thomas of Frimley, yeoman [HRO; 1621 AD19]
Thomas of Worplesdon, husbandman [DW/PA/7/7 f.65; 1596] <Abs 125>
Thomas of West Clandon, husbandman [DW/PA/7/9 f.325; DW/PA/5/1619/23]
Walter of Bisley [DW/PA/7/1 f.50; 1487] <Abs 165>
William of Pirbright, weaver [DW/PA/7/9 f.249; DW/PA/5/1617/19]
William of Guildford, clothier [DW/PA/7/10 f.149; DW/PA/5/1621/21]
COBET *see* de COBET
COBBY (COBEY)
John of Banstead, servant to Mr Francis Moyse [DW/PA/7/13 f.499; DW/PA/5/1649/4]
John, alias John Corne of Swk St Olave, woodmonger and citizen [DW/PA/5/1617/23]
COBDEN
John of Haslemere, gent. [PRO; PCC Will 1625]

COBEY *see* COBBY

COBHAM (COBBEHAM,COVEHAM,de Cobham)

Joan, Baroness de, lady of Swk St Mary Overy; Lingfield - Starborough Castle; Kent; Langley Burrell, Wiltshire [LPL; Reg. Abp Whittleseye f.114r; Will 1370] <Abs SAC v.2 pp.169-183 *and* v.3 pp.354-355>

John, alias John Melsham, senior of Cobham; Great Bookham [DW/PA/7/10 f.144; 1621]

Reginald de, master of Lingfield - Starborough; Kings Walden, Hertfordshire [LPL; Reg. Abp Arundel i ff.203,212; Will 1403] <Abs SAC v.2 pp.183-186>

(Sir) Reginald de, lord of Lingfield - Starborough; Kent, knight [LPL; Reg. Abp Stafford f.142; Will 1446]

Richard of Lingfield - Starborough [DW/PA/7/4 f.23; 1532]

Robert of Rotherhithe; the Ship *Trades Increase*, cook [DW/PA/7/9 f.36; DW/PA/5/1614/31]

(Sir) Thomas of Lingfield - Starborough, , knight [PRO; PCC Will 1471] <Abs. SAC v.51 pp.83-84>

(Sir) William de, of Charlwood; Penshurst, Kent, knight [LPL; Reg. Abp Sudbury f.80; Will 1375]

COBROE

John of Swk St Olave, turner [DW/PA/5/1591/114]

COBSTICKE

Nathaniel of Farnham [DW/PA/7/13 f.446; DW/PA/5/1646/9]

COBURNE

Richard of Rotherhithe, mariner [PRO; PCC Will 1626]

Richard of Rotherhithe, mariner [PRO; PCC 1633]

COCHEAN

Boye of City of London; Swk St Olave; Cambrai - Noiell [DW/PA/7/7 f.49; DW/PA/5/1595/18] <Abs 93>

COCK *see* COCKE

COCKAINE (COKAINE,COKAYNE)

Henry of Lambeth - Lambeth Marsh, husbandman [DW/PA/7/11 f.109; DW/PA/5/1624/29B]

Thomas of Clapham, senior [PRO; PCC Admon 1619]

(Sir) William of Kingston - Coombe, knight [PRO; PCC Will 1627]

see also COGAN (COGAYNE)

COCKE (KOK)

Christopher of Lambeth, citizen and vintner [PRO; PCC 1641]

Henry Co'red alias Henry Kok of Merton [DW/PA/5/1546/32]

John of Rotherhithe, mariner [DW/PA/7/12 f.483; DW/PA/5/1638/31]

Richard of Chertsey, yeoman [PRO; PCC Will 1613]

Robert of Dunsfold [DW/PA/7/9 f.278; 1618]

Thomas of Swk St Olave, leatherseller [DW/PA/5/1563/104]

William of Effingham [DW/PA/5/1555/65]

see also COCK, COX

COCKETT (CACOTT,CAKETT,COCOCKE,COCOK,COCOTT,COKOCKE,COLCOCK,COLCOCKE, COLCOTT,COOCOKE)

Agnes of Sutton, widow of Alan, yeoman [DW/PA/5/1569/38]

Alan of Kingston, linen draper [PRO; PCC Will 1625]

Alan of Reigate, yeoman [DW/PA/5/1568/30]

Alan of Reigate; Ewell; Chipstead, yeoman [HRO; 1585 B16]

Ann of Thames Ditton, widow [DW/PA/7/12 f.28; DW/PA/5/1631/29]

Dorothy of Lambeth, spinster [PRO; PCC 1634]

Henry of Thames Ditton - Claygate, yeoman [DW/PA/5/1592/115]

COCKETT (CACOTT,CAKETT,COCOCKE,COCOK,COCOTT,COKOCKE,COLCOCK,COLCOCKE,
COLCOTT,COOCOKE) [*continued*]
John of Blechingley [HRO; 1561 B27-28]
John of Chipstead [PRO; PCC Will 1523]
John of Swk St Saviour, waterman [DW/PA/7/7 f.433; DW/PA/5/1603/32] <Abs 819>
John of Walton on the Hill; Dorking, yeoman [DW/PA/7/11 f.470; DW/PA/5/1628/23]
Joshua of Thames Ditton - Claygate [DW/PA/7/11 f.72; DW/PA/5/1623/27]
Mary of Dorking, spinster [DW/PA/7/11 f.266; DW/PA/5/1625/48]
Richard of Chipstead [? HRO; 1532]
Robert of Thames Ditton [DW/PA/5/1576/112]
Roger of Bermondsey [DW/PA/7/5 f.137; 1540]
Thomas of Blechingley, yeoman [DW/PA/7/7 f.452; DW/PA/5/1603/33] <Abs 856>
Thomas of Blechingley, yeoman [DW/PA/7/12 f.410; DW/PA/5/1637/27]
William of Lambeth [PRO; PCC Admon 1628]
William of Streatham; Chipstead; Gatton; Tooting [DW/PA/5/1547/20]

COCKLIS (COKLYS)
John, alias John Chitty of Godalming - Winkworth [*in* DW/PA/5/1558/76]*

COCKS *see* COX

COCKSALTER
William of Epsom - Horton [DW/PA/7/12 f.118; DW/PA/5/1632/20]

COCKSHUTT
Elizabeth of Sanderstead [PRO; PCC Admon 1648]

COCOTT *see* COCKETT

COCQ (le COCQ)
Jehenna le, alias Jehenna de dacchin, of Swk St Olave, wife of William du Pysre [DW/PA/5/1570/34]

CODD
Miles of Weybridge, parson [HRO; 1559 U57-58]

CODDING (CODDINGE,CODDYNG)
John of Swk St Olave, butcher [DW/PA/7/4 f.153; 1536]
William of Swk [CCAL; 1500 f.86r]

CODDINGTON *see* CUDDINGTON

CODDYNG *see* CODDING

CODE
Richard of Lambeth [PRO; PCC Will 1457]

CODINGTON *see* CUDDINGTON

CODLYNG
Thomas of Swk St Saviour [DW/PA/5/1593/162]

CODRELL
Thomas, alias Thomas Cowdry of Lambeth [DW/PA/5/1603/34] <Abs U64>

CODYNGTON *see* CUDDINGTON

COE
Hugh of Swk St Olave - Horsleydown, gardener [DW/PA/7/7 f.106; DW/PA/5/1596/13] <Abs 189>
Joan of Croydon, widow [PRO; PCC Will 1595]
William of Farnham [DW/PA/7/11 f.380; DW/PA/5/1626/37B]

COFEILD
William of Rotherhithe, mariner [DW/PA/7/12 f.336; DW/PA/5/1636/23]
see also Coffin alias Coffell

COFFIN
Edward of Blechingley, yeoman [DW/PA/7/11 f.12; DW/PA/5/1623/25]
George, alias George Coffell of Warlingham [PRO; PCC Admon 1621]
Martin of Swk St Olave, surgeon [DW/PA/5/1587/104]
COGAN (COGAYNE)
Ann of Swk St Saviour, widow [DW/PA/7/8 f.251; DW/PA/5/1613/29]
John of Lambeth [PRO; PCC Admon 1588]
Robert of Streatham, senior, citizen and clothworker [PRO; PCC Will 1616]
see also COCKAINE
COGDALE
John of Richmond [PRO; PCC Admon 1629]
COKAINE,COKAYNE *see* COCKAINE
COKE (COK)
Alice of Dorking, widow [DW/PA/5/1593/137]
Henry Co'red alias Henry Kok of Merton [DW/PA/5/1546/32]
John of Leigh [DW/PA/7/1 f.21; 1485] <Abs 70>
John of Tandridge [DW/PA/7/1 f.70; 1487] <Abs 229>
John of Wonersh [DW/PA/7/1 f.12; 1485] <Abs 40>
Paul of Tandridge [DW/PA/5/1562/74]
Peter of Swk St Olave, cooper [DW/PA/5/1569/32]
Richard of Albury [DW/PA/5/1561/34]
Richard of Sutton, senior [PRO; PCC Will 1494] <Abs. SAC v.52 pp.45-46>
Thomas of Kingston [DW/PA/7/3 f.167; 1531]
Thomas of Pirbright [DW/PA/5/1570/104]
Valentine of Guildford, yeoman [DW/PA/5/1591/77]
William of Swk St Olave, smith [DW/PA/7/2 f.44; 1494]
William of Worplesdon, yeoman [DW/PA/5/1561/67]
COKER
Arnold of Limpsfield [PRO; PCC Admon 1587]
William of Limpsfield [PRO; PCC Admon 1635]
William of Limpsfield [PRO; PCC 1636]
William of Newington, citizen of London [PRO; PCC Will 1603]
William of Newington [PRO; PCC Will 1605]
COKKES *see* COX
COKLYS *see* COCKLIS
COKOCKE *see* COCKETT
COLBRAND
Walsingham of Lingfield, spinster [PRO; PCC 1645]
COLBROKE
John of Shalford [PRO; PCC Admon 1562]
COLCOCK,COLCOCKE,COLCOTT *see* COCKETT
COLDALE
John of Frensham, clerk [PRO; PCC Will 1501]
COLDHAM
John of Waverley, esq. [DW/PA/7/12 f.516; DW/PA/5/1638/35]
Richard of Waverley, esq. [DW/PA/7/12 f.529; DW/PA/5/1639/33]
COLE (a COWLES,COALE,COLES,COLLE,COLLES,COOLES,COULES,COWLES)
Ann of Swk St Saviour, widow [DW/PA/7/12 f.9; 1631]
Anthony of Rotherhithe, mariner [PRO; PCC 1641]
Edward of Lingfield [PRO; PCC Will 1558]
Elizabeth of Epsom, widow of Robert [DW/PA/7/7 f.475; DW/PA/5/1604/12] <Abs 897>
Elizabeth of Ewhurst, widow [DW/PA/7/13 f.158; DW/PA/5/1641/32]

COLE (a COWLES,COALE,COLES,COLLE,COLLES,COOLES,COULES,COWLES) [*continued*]
Frances of Petersham, widow [PRO; PCC 1633]
George of Petersham [PRO; PCC Will 1624]
Henry of Carshalton, husbandman [HRO; 1595 B8]
John of Egham - Hythe, yeoman [PRO; PCC Will 1617]
John of Ewhurst (but died in Ireland) [PRO; PCC 1647]
John of Ewhurst [PRO; PCC 1649]
John of Frimley, husbandman [DW/PA/5/1557/138]
John of Limpsfield [HRO; 1558 B140-141]
John of Puttenham; Chiddingfold, yeoman [DW/PA/7/9 f.72; DW/PA/5/1614/14]
John of Richmond [PRO; PCC 1633]
Margaret of Cobham, widow [DW/PA/7/9 f.258; DW/PA/5/1614/30]
Matthew of Swk St Thomas, carpenter [DW/PA/7/13 f.32; DW/PA/5/1640/27]
Michael of Kingston; Oxted, yeoman [PRO; PCC Will 1601] <Abs. SAC v.10 pp.301-302>
Ralph of Ewhurst, tailor [DW/PA/7/13 f.59; DW/PA/5/1640/28]
Reynold of Carshalton, yeoman [DW/PA/5/1588/56]
Robert of Chertsey, butcher [DW/PA/7/7 f.104; DW/PA/5/1596/14] <Abs 187>
Robert of Ewhurst, husbandman [DW/PA/5/1572/13]
Robert of Mortlake, yeoman [PRO; PCC Will 1626]
Roger of Cobham, butcher [DW/PA/7/8 f.274; DW/PA/5/1612/35]
Roger of Swk St Saviour [DW/PA/5/1570/96]
Thomas of Carshalton, gent. [DW/PA/5/1580/19]
Thomas of Ockley [PRO; PCC 1648]
Thomasine of Rotherhithe, widow [PRO; PCC Admon 1637]
William of Croydon, yeoman [LPL; 96/563; 98/1 f.117v; Will 1640]
William of Egham; North Molton, Devon; Chertsey; Kemmerton, Gloucestershire [PRO; PCC 1630] <Scroope 815>

COLEBRAND *see* COLBRAND

COLEBROOK *see* COLBROKE

COLEBURNE
Henry of Swk St Saviour, yeoman [DW/PA/7/13 f.191; DW/PA/5/1641/36]

COLEMAN (COLLMAN,COLMAN)
Frederick of Swk St Olave, feltmaker [DW/PA/5/1579/29]
Frederick of Swk St Olave, feltmaker [DW/PA/5/1579/29]* [duplicated]
Gilbert of Swk St Saviour, bricklayer [DW/PA/7/12 f.311; DW/PA/5/1636/15]
Hugh of Newington, glover [LPL; 96/571; Will 1627]
Richard of Esher, clerk [PRO; PCC Will 1430]
Richard of Swk St Olave [DW/PA/5/1592/14]*
William of Newington [LPL; 98/1 f.17v; Will 1630]

COLERERE *see* COLLIER

COLES *see* COLE

COLFE
Richard of Swk St Olave, brushmaker [DW/PA/5/1593/172]

COLIER *see* COLLIER

COLIN *see* COLLINS

COLLANT
Adrian of Mitcham, whitster [DW/PA/7/9 f.341; DW/PA/5/1620/32]

COLLAPP
Nicholas of Swk St Thomas, citizen and weaver [DW/PA/7/13 f.283; DW/PA/5/1643/23B]

COLLCOTT *see* COCKETT

COLLE *see* COLE
COLLEN, COLLENCE, COLLENS *see* COLLINS
COLLER *see* COLLIER
COLLETT (COLLET)
  Elizabeth of Newington, widow [PRO; PCC Will 1568]
  Humphrey of Banstead [PRO; PCC Will 1558]
  Thomas of Blechingley [PRO; PCC Admon 1609]
  Thomas of Blechingley, gent. [DW/PA/7/9 f.229; DW/PA/5/1617/20]
COLLEY (COLLYE)
  Elizabeth of Seale, widow [*in* DW/PA/5/1558/186]*
  Joan of Swk - Bankside [DW/PA/5/1592/50]
  Nicholas of Seale [HRO; 1609 AD21]
COLLIER (COLERERE, COLIER, COLLER, COLLYER, COLYAR, COLYER)
  Agnes of Woking, widow [DW/PA/5/1552/6]
  Agnes of Woking, widow [DW/PA/5/1558/64]*
  Alice of Worplesdon, widow [DW/PA/5/1580/29]
  Anthony of ...., citizen of London [*proved on 26 Feb 1593, in DW/PA/5/ series according to Campbell Cooke slips, but no will in series, 1988*]
  Christopher of Swk St Saviour, farrier [DW/PA/7/8 f.332; DW/PA/5/1614/25]
  Edward of Byfleet, shearman [DW/PA/5/1582/27]
  Edward of Byfleet, shearman [DW/PA/7/7 f.13; DW/PA/5/1595/28] <Abs 29>
  Edward of Pirbright, yeoman [DW/PA/7/7 f.253; DW/PA/5/1599/13] <Abs 445>
  George of Lambeth, yeoman [DW/PA/7/10 f.281; DW/PA/5/1622/18]
  George of Worplesdon, yeoman [HRO; 1579 B8]
  Harry of Ewell - Ewell Court [PRO; PCC Will 1559]
  Henry of Chertsey [PRO; PCC Admon 1587]
  Henry of Ewell, gent. [DW/PA/7/11 f.3; DW/PA/5/1622/19]
  Henry of Woking [? HRO; 1579]
  Henry, senior of Woking, yeoman [DW/PA/7/12 f.236; DW/PA/5/1634/22]
  Henry, senior of Woking, husbandman [HRO; 1640 B15]
  James of Woking, shearman [*in* DW/PA/5/1558/166]
  James of Woking, miller [DW/PA/7/13 f.346; 1644]
  Joan of Woking, widow [DW/PA/7/3 f.165; 1530]
  John of Beddington [PRO; PCC Admon 1649]
  John of Swk St Margaret, cooper [HRO; Reg. Wyk 2 p.242; 1388]
  John of Woking, husbandman [DW/PA/7/7 f.590; DW/PA/5/1607/30] <Abs 1102>
  John of Woking [DW/PA/7/11 f.131; DW/PA/5/1624/28B]
  John of Woking, yeoman [DW/PA/7/13 f.499; DW/PA/5/1649/5]
  Juliana of Pirbright, widow of John [DW/PA/7/1 f.46B; 1486] <Abs 152>
  Juliana of Ockham [DW/PA/7/2 f.36; 1493]
  Margaret of Pirbright, widow [HRO; 1551 U49-50]
  Margaret of Woking - Goldsworth, widow [DW/PA/7/11 f.596; DW/PA/5/1630/24]
  Mary of Swk [*proved on 4 Mar 1593, in DW/PA/5/ series according to Campbell Cooke slips, but no will in series, 1988*]
  Mary of Swk, widow of Anthony [DW/PA/7/8 f.85; DW/PA/5/1609/32]
  Nathaniel of Ewell, gent. [DW/PA/7/11 f.38; DW/PA/5/1623/26]
  Richard of Pirbright, yeoman [DW/PA/7/6 f.4; DW/PA/5/1559/4]
  Richard of Albury [DW/PA/5/1571/27]
  Richard of Woking, yeoman [DW/PA/5/1558/65]*
  Richard of Woking, husbandman [DW/PA/5/1568/60]
  Robert of Pirbright [DW/PA/7/9 f.168; DW/PA/5/1616/26]
  Robert of Shere, yeoman [DW/PA/7/12 f.353; DW/PA/5/1636/27]

COLLIER (COLERERE,COLIER,COLLER,COLLYER,COLYAR,COLYER) [*continued*]
Stephen of Frimley, weaver [HRO; 1618 B14]
Thomas of Pirbright [DW/PA/5/1561/35]
Thomas of Witley, yeoman [DW/PA/7/13 f.447; DW/PA/5/1646/10]
Thomas of Worplesdon [DW/PA/7/5 f.215; 1541]
William of Reigate, tailor [DW/PA/7/4 f.9; 1532]
William of Woking - Goldsworth, yeoman, senior [DW/PA/7/7 f.596; DW/PA/5/1607/31] <Abs 1117>
COLLIN *see* COLLINS
COLLINGBORNE
Henry of Blechingley [DW/PA/5/1561/18B]
COLLINGHAM *see* CALLINGHAM
COLLINGWORTHE
William of Little Bookham, parson [DW/PA/5/1568/5]
COLLINS (COLIN,COLLEN,COLLENCE,COLLENS,COLLIN,COLLYN,COLLYNE,COLLYNS,COLYN, van COLLEN)
Alice of Betchworth, yeoman, widow of Nicholas [PRO; PCC Will 1628]
Anthony of Swk St Olave, joiner [DW/PA/5/1569/76]
Ann of Seale - Tongham [DW/PA/7/13 f.366; 1644]
Edward of St Martha's [PRO; PCC Admon 1636]
George of Betchworth - Brockham, yeoman [DW/PA/7/7 f.387; DW/PA/5/1602/21] <Abs 717>
George of St Martha's [DW/PA/7/13 f.365; 1644]
Henry of Kingston - Ham, yeoman [DW/PA/7/13 f.262; DW/PA/5/1643/21]
Henry of Lingfield [PRO; PCC 1645]
Henry of Thursley [DW/PA/5/1557/131]
James of Sutton, yeoman [DW/PA/7/13 f.82; DW/PA/5/1640/29]
John of Ditton - Wood Ditton [PRO; PCC Will 1564]
John of Elstead, husbandman [DW/PA/7/7 f.357; DW/PA/5/1602/23] <Abs 653>
John of Hambledon, bricklayer [DW/PA/7/11 f.528; DW/PA/5/1630/23]
John of Newdigate, husbandman, senior [DW/PA/7/12 f.116; 1632]
John of Swk St Saviour, yeoman [DW/PA/5/1558/63]*
Marian of Wandsworth, widow of Thomas [DW/PA/7/12 f.71; DW/PA/5/1632/16]
Mark of Kingston, mercer [DW/PA/5/1593/4]
Maud of Mitcham, wife of Thomas [HRO; Reg. Fox 3 p.64; 1513]
Nicholas of Betchworth, yeoman [PRO; PCC Will 1627]
Nicholas of Godalming - Enton, husbandman [DW/PA/7/10 f.47; 1618]
Oliver of Alfold, tailor [PRO; PCC Will 1610]
Oliver of Cranleigh [DW/PA/7/5 f.43; 1538] <Abs 26>
Richard of Godalming - Enton, yeoman [HRO; 1628 B18]
Richard of ... (proved at Guildford) [DW/PA/5/1568/59]
Richard of Godalming [GMR; 5/2/143; 1649]
Robert of Betchworth [DW/PA/7/1 f.52; 1487] <Abs 172>
Robert of Betchworth - Brockham [DW/PA/5/1546/85]
Robert of Swk St Olave [DW/PA/5/1544/12]
Stephen of Richmond ('Kinge's Schene') [DW/PA/7/2 f.31; 1491]
Thomas of Capel; Ockley, yeoman [DW/PA/7/9 f.119; 1615]
Thomas of Seale - Tongham [DW/PA/5/1558/60]*
Thomas of Sutton, yeoman [DW/PA/7/13 f.501; DW/PA/5/1649/6]
Thomas of Walton on Thames - Apps Court [PRO; PCC Admon 1616]
Thomas of Wandsworth, mealman [DW/PA/7/11 f.427; DW/PA/5/1627/21]
Thomas of Witley, husbandman [DW/PA/7/13 f.132; DW/PA/5/1640/37]
William van Collen of ... [DW/PA/7/4 f.131; 1535]

COLLINS (COLIN,COLLEN,COLLENCE,COLLENS,COLLIN,COLLYN,COLLYNE,COLLYNS,COLYN, van COLLEN) [*continued*]

William (son of Henry) of Lingfield, yeoman [DW/PA/7/12 f.22; DW/PA/5/1631/25]
William of Richmond, husbandman [DW/PA/5/1582/37]
William of Rotherhithe [PRO; PCC Admon 1601]
William of Seale [DW/PA/5/1576/119]
William of Seale - Tongham, yeoman [DW/PA/7/8 f.197; DW/PA/5/1610/32]
William of Thursley, yeoman [HRO; 1561 B36-37]

COLLIS (a COLLYS,COLLYS)

Henry of Ewhurst [DW/PA/7/2 f.17; 1491]
Richard of Ewhurst [DW/PA/7/6 f.121; DW/PA/5/1559/161]
Robert of Ewhurst [DW/PA/7/1 f.52; 1487] <Abs 173>

COLLMAN *see* COLEMAN

COLLSON *see* COLSON

COLLTE *see* COLTE

COLLTON (COLTON)

John of Cobham, husbandman [HRO; 1585 B18]
William of Ripley, innholder [DW/PA/7/13 f.224; DW/PA/5/1643/20]

COLLYAR *see* COLLIER

COLLYE *see* COLLEY

COLLYER *see* COLLIER

COLLYN,COLLYNC,COLLYNS *see* COLLINS

COLLYS *see* COLLIS

COLMAN *see* COLEMAN

COLONIA (de COLONIA)

Peter (Petrig) de, of Swk St Thomas, chirurgeon [DW/PA/5/1550/103]

COLPAS (COLPIS,COPIS)

Elizabeth of Guildford St Nicolas; Guildford St Mary [DW/PA/7/9 f.112; DW/PA/5/1615/40]
Jane of ... (mentions 'Costers Miel, Sussex') [DW/PA/7/11 f.210; DW/PA/5/1625/49]
John of Dunsfold, yeoman [PRO; PCC Will 1616]
Thomas of Guildford St Nicolas [HRO; 1604 AD15]

COLSEY

Henry of Mitcham, yeoman [DW/PA/7/9 f.305; DW/PA/5/1619/24]

COLSON (COLLSON,COULSON)

Christopher of Lambeth, citizen and dyer [GL; Archdeaconry Court of London Will 1644]
Joan of Swk St Mary Overy; Swk St Saviour, widow [DW/PA/7/6 f.236; 1561]
John of Rotherhithe [DW/PA/5/1550/40]
Robert of Swk St Saviour, innholder [DW/PA/5/1556/16]*
Thomas of Bermondsey, drayman [DW/PA/7/9 f.220; DW/PA/5/1617/22]

COLSTONE (COULSTON)

Gabriel of Wimbledon, bachelor [PRO; PCC Admon 1639]
Thomas of Swk St Olave [BM; Add.Ms 24,925 f.15v; 1543] <Abs 32> [*and*] <Abs SAC v.1 pp.200-201>

COLTE (COLLTE)

Thomas of Waltham Holy Cross, Essex; Battersea, gent. [PRO; PCC Will 1559] <Abs Emmison pp.184-185>

COLTON *see* COLLTON

COLYAR,COLYER *see* COLLIER

COLYN *see* COLLINS

COMBE *see* COMBES

COMBER (COOMBER)

Edward of Lingfield, labourer [DW/PA/7/12 f,380; DW/PA/5/1637/21]

Elizabeth of Dorking, widow of William, gent, [DW/PA/7/11 f,454; DW/PA/5/1628/24]

Jane of Dorking, widow of John [PRO; PCC 1642]

John, alias John Kember of Camberwell [PRO; PCC 1649]

John of Dorking, innholder [DW/PA/7/12 f,387; DW/PA/5/1637/24]

John of Lingfield [DW/PA/7/8 f,115; DW/PA/5/1610/33]

Thomas of Lingfield, yeoman [DW/PA/7/13 f,249; DW/PA/5/1640/39]

William of Charlwood [PRO; PCC Admon 1638]

William of Dorking, gent, [DW/PA/7/11 f,156; DW/PA/5/1624/29A]

COMBES (COMBE,COMBS,COMBYS,COME,COMES,COOMBE,COOMES)

Joan of Malden, widow [DW/PA/7/8 f,308; DW/PA/5/1613/30]

John of Woking - Sutton [DW/PA/7/10 f,187; DW/PA/5/1620/33]

John of Farnham, husbandman [DW/PA/7/12 f,26; DW/PA/5/1631/27]

John of Frensham [DW/PA/5/1557/123]

John of Frensham - Pitfold, yeoman [DW/PA/7/12 f,380; DW/PA/5/1637/22]

John of Kingston - Wick, smith [GL; Commissary Court of London Will 1411]

Thomas of Frensham, yeoman [DW/PA/7/11 f,189; DW/PA/5/1624/32]

Thomas of Frensham - Pitfold, yeoman [DW/PA/7/12 f,421; DW/PA/5/1637/30]

Thomas of Wisley, husbandman [DW/PA/7/11 f,506; DW/PA/5/1629/17]

William of Malden, husbandman [DW/PA/7/7 f,115; DW/PA/5/1597/23] <Abs 213>

William of Stoke next Guildford [DW/PA/7/1 f,62; 1487] <Abs 207>

William of Stoke next Guildford, gent, [PRO; PCC Will 1503] <Abs, SAC v,51 p,93>

COMFORT (CHOMPART,COMPARDE,COMPORDE,COMPORT,COMPORTE,COMPORTH)

Harry of Addington [DW/PA/7/4 f,215; 1537]

Henry of Farleigh [PRO; PCC Admon 1624]

Henry of Warlingham [DW/PA/5/1592/17]

Joan of Caterham, widow [DW/PA/7/11 f,5; DW/PA/5/1622/20]

John of Addington, yeoman [DW/PA/5/1601/24] <Abs U33>

John of Addington, husbandman [DW/PA/7/11 f,339; DW/PA/5/1625/50]

John of Addington, yeoman [DW/PA/7/11 f,475; DW/PA/5/1628/25] [*and*] [SRO; 449/1]

John of Battersea - Penge; Beckenham, Kent, husbandman [DW/PA/7/3 f,107; 1529]

John of Burstow [PRO; PCC Admon 1649]

John of Croydon - Combe [PRO; PCC Will 1617]

John of Croydon, barber surgeon [LPL; 96/605; Will 1617]

John of Croydon [LPL; 98/1 f,122r; Will 1641]

John of Farleigh [DW/PA/7/1 f,48; 1482] <Abs 160>

John of Farleigh [DW/PA/7/1 f,58; 1487] <Abs 191>

John of Godstone; Lingfield; Tandridge; Oxted; Limpsfield [DW/PA/7/4 f,49; 1533]

John of Godstone [DW/PA/5/1546/54]

John of Sanderstead [DW/PA/7/8 f,291; DW/PA/5/1613/31]

John of Warlingham [DW/PA/5/1563/24]

Michael of Sanderstead, yeoman [DW/PA/7/13 f,283; DW/PA/5/1643/23A]

Morris of Godstone [DW/PA/7/3 f,149; 1530]

Nicholas of Warlingham [DW/PA/7/3 f,151; 1530]

Richard of Limpsfield, husbandman [DW/PA/7/10 f,191; DW/PA/5/1621/22]

Thomasine of Warlingham, widow [DW/PA/7/7 f,11; DW/PA/5/1595/27]<Abs 24>

COMFORT (CHOMPART,COMPARDE,COMPORDE,COMPORT,COMPORTE,COMPORTH) [*continued*]
William of Burstow [LPL; 98/1 f,112r; Will 1640]
William of Godstone; Lingfield, yeoman [DW/PA/7/7 f,332; DW/PA/5/1601/25 *and* DW/PA/5/1601/26] <Abs 598>
William of Tandridge [PRO; PCC Will 1557]
COMINGHAM
Richard of Swk St Saviour; Newport Pagnell, Buckinghamshire, joiner [DW/PA/7/10 f,81; DW/PA/5/1619/25]
COMLEY
John of Coulsdon, bachelor [PRO; PCC Admon 1611]
COMPARDE,COMPORT,COMPORTE,COMPORTH *see* COMFORT
COMPTON (COMTUN,de COMPTON)
Nicholas of Guildford, gent, [PRO; PCC Will 1504]
Peter de, of Swk, clerk [HRO; Reg, Stra pp,83,86; 1333]
Robert of Swk St Saviour [DW/PA/5/1579/24]*
Thomas of Godalming [PRO; PCC Will 1606] <Abs, SAC v,12 pp,104-105>
CONAWAY *see* CONWAY
CONBYE *see* TU'BYE
CONE (COANE)
John of ..., dyer of London [DW/PA/7/7 f,544; DW/PA/5/1606/27] <Abs 1021>
CONGHURST *see* SONGHURST
CONINGHAM *see* COMINGHAM
CONNER
Brian of Blechingley, widower [PRO; PCC Admon 1645]
Brian of Blechingley [PRO; PCC 1647]
John of Frimley [DW/PA/5/1562/78]
CONNEY (CONNY,CONNYE)
Giles of Walton on Thames [DW/PA/5/1570/102]
John of Kingston, grocer [DW/PA/7/11 f,523; DW/PA/5/1629/19]
John of Walton on Thames, junior, mercer [HRO; 1611 B20]
John of Walton on Thames, mercer [DW/PA/7/8 f,255; DW/PA/5/1611/40]
William of Walton on Thames [PRO; PCC Will 1536]
CONNIGRAVE
William of Bermondsey, citizen and leatherseller [PRO; PCC 1636]
CONRED *see* CO'RED
CONSETT (CONSET)
Henry of Barnes [PRO; PCC Admon 1636]
Thomas of Barnes, waterman [LPL; 98/1 f,14r; Will 1630]
Thomas of Barnes, waterman [LPL; 96/613; 98/1 ff,98v,106r; Will 1638 *and* 1639]
CONSTABLE (CONSTABULL,CUNSTABLE,CUSTABLE)
Edmund of Ockley [DW/PA/7/7 f,20; DW/PA/5/1595/29] <Abs 42>
Edward of Swk St Olave, barber chirurgeon [DW/PA/7/13 f,151; DW/PA/5/1641/28]
Frusan of Capel, widow of John [PRO; PCC 1649]
James of Capel [DW/PA/5/1569/19]
James of Kingston, yeoman [DW/PA/5/1570/20]
John of Abinger [DW/PA/7/5 f,66; 1539] <Abs 1>
John of Ashtead [DW/PA/7/2 f,98; 1514]
John of Capel [DW/PA/7/6 f,244; 1560]
John of Capel, yeoman [DW/PA/7/12 f,488; DW/PA/5/1638/33]
John of Capel - Aldhurst [PRO; PCC 1644]
John of Capel - Aldhurst [PRO; PCC 1647]

CONSTABLE (CONSTABULL, CUNSTABLE, CUSTABLE) [*continued*]
  John of Charlwood [LPL; 98/1 ff.96v,107v; Will 1638 *and* 1639]
  John of Newdigate, yeoman [DW/PA/7/12 f.316; DW/PA/5/1636/19]
  John of Ockley [? HRO; 1570]
  John of Ockley, yeoman [DW/PA/7/12 f.499; DW/PA/5/1639/30]
  Joseph of Rotherhithe, mariner [PRO; PCC 1641]
  Richard of Capel, husbandman [DW/PA/7/12 f.244; DW/PA/5/1634/24]
  Richard of Mickleham [DW/PA/7/1 f.28; 1486] <Abs 90>
  Richard of Abinger, yeoman [HRO; 1603 AD12]
  Rose of Swk St Olave, widow [DW/PA/7/12 f.484; DW/PA/5/1638/32]
  Thomas of Alfold, husbandman [HRO; 1590 B14]
  Thomas of Mitcham [DW/PA/5/1578/84]
  Thomas of Ockley [DW/PA/5/1576/49]
  Thomas of Ockley - 'Brits', husbandman [DW/PA/7/12 f.355; DW/PA/5/1638/23]
  William of Abinger [PRO; PCC 1648]
  William of Capel, yeoman [DW/PA/7/10 f.109; DW/PA/5/1619/26]
  William of Capel, senior, yeoman [DW/PA/7/10 f.111; DW/PA/5/1619/27]
CONSTANT
  Ann of Barnes, widow [LPL; 96/622; Will 1643]
CONVERSE
  William, alias William Kelshull of Bermondsey [PRO; PCC Will 1432]
  William of Swk St Saviour, citizen and cook [DW/PA/7/13 f.404; DW/PA/5/1645/9]
CONWAY (CANWAY, CONAWAY, CONWEY, CONWEYE)
  Christopher of Swk St Olave [DW/PA/7/4 f.124; 1535]
  Frances of Kingston, widow [DW/PA/5/1624/30]
  Frances of Kingston, widow [PRO; PCC Will 1625]
  Henry of Bermondsey [PRO; PCC Will 1539]
  John of Swk St Olave, tiler [DW/PA/7/4 f.207; 1537]
  Richard, alias Richard Griffen of Guildford, brazier [DW/PA/7/12 f.213; DW/PA/5/1633/34]
  Thomas of Kingston, yeoman usher of H.M.'s chamber [PRO; PCC Will 1607] <Abs. SAC v.12 pp.98-99>
  William of Swk St George [DW/PA/5/1559/25]
CONY
  John of Walton on Thames, yeoman [DW/PA/7/5 f.133; 1539]
COOCHMAN *see* COUCHMAN
COOCOKE *see* COCKETT
COOK (COOKE, COUKE, KOOKE)
  Agnes of Effingham, widow [HRO; 1604 B15]
  Agnes of Reigate, widow [DW/PA/5/1571/60]
  Alexander of Petersham [DW/PA/5/1570/22]
  Ann of Worplesdon, late servant to John Gylberte [DW/PA/7/7 f.137; DW/PA/5/1597/24] <Abs 252>
  Edward of Chertsey [PRO; PCC Admon 1595]
  Edward of Lingfield [DW/PA/5/1592]
  Edward of Richmond, of the household of (Sir) James Crofts, Comptroller of the Queen's Household, knight [PRO; PCC Admon 1577]
  Francis of Lambeth, merchant tailor [PRO; PCC Will 1625]
  Henry of Horsell, yeoman [DW/PA/7/8 f.275; DW/PA/5/1612/36]
  Henry of Effingham, yeoman [DW/PA/7/13 f.427; DW/PA/5/1646/7]
  Henry of Reigate [PRO; PCC Admon 1647]
  Joan of Kingston, widow [DW/PA/5/1593/33]

COOK (COOKE,COUKE,KOOKE) [*continued*]

John of Chertsey, clothworker [PRO; PCC Will 1622]
John of Cranleigh, husbandman [DW/PA/5/1558/67]*
John of Cranleigh, forester, senior [DW/PA/7/10 f.146; DW/PA/5/1621/23]
John of Crowhurst, husbandman [DW/PA/7/10 f.152; DW/PA/5/1619/28]
John of Effingham [PRO; PCC 1647]
John of Ewell [DW/PA/5/1576/19]
John of Guildford Holy Trinity [DW/PA/7/3 f.180; 1531]
John of Kingston, tailor [DW/PA/7/12 f.415; DW/PA/5/1637/28]
John of Lingfield, weaver [DW/PA/5/1558/68]*
John of Rotherhithe, mariner [DW/PA/7/7 f.293; DW/PA/5/1600/14] <Abs 524>
John of Swk St Saviour, glover [DW/PA/7/12 f.247; DW/PA/5/1635/17]
John of Walton on Thames, parish clerk [HRO; 1596 B13]
John of Walton on the Hill [DW/PA/7/7 f.88; 1596] <Abs 162>
John of Woking, husbandman [DW/PA/7/6 f.282; 1560]
Joyce of Kingston, widow of Thomas, citizen and haberdasher [PRO; PCC 1636]
Katherine, alias Katherine Saxbye of Lingfield [DW/PA/7/10 f.84; DW/PA/5/1615/88]
Margaret of Worplesdon, widow [DW/PA/5/1558/66]*
Matthew of Kingston, brewer [DW/PA/7/10 f.141; DW/PA/5/1621/24]
Nicholas of Camberwell - Peckham Rye [DW/PA/7/7 f.532; DW/PA/5/1606/28] <Abs 1001>
Nicholas of Walton on the Hill [DW/PA/7/9 f.257; DW/PA/5/1617/21]
Nicholas of Reigate [PRO; PCC 1642]
Oliver of Long Ditton - Tolworth, husbandman [DW/PA/7/7 f.322; DW/PA/5/1601/27] <Abs 576>
Phillip of Putney, widow [PRO; PCC Admon 1648]
Richard of Sutton, yeoman [DW/PA/7/2 f.94; 1513]
Richard of Swk St Margaret [DW/PA/7/2 f.152; 1521]
Richard of Ewhurst, blacksmith [DW/PA/7/13 f.394; DW/PA/5/1645/6]
Richard of Reigate, husbandman [DW/PA/7/13 f.183; DW/PA/5/1641/35]
Robert of Effingham, yeoman [DW/PA/7/7 f.376; DW/PA/5/1602/24] <Abs 696>
Robert of Walton on the Hill [DW/PA/7/12 f.186; DW/PA/5/1633/29]
Robert of Woking, innholder [DW/PA/7/10 f.157; DW/PA/5/1621/25]
Robert of Worplesdon [*in* DW/PA/5/1546/75]
Roger of Chertsey [PRO; PCC Admon 1597]
Roger of Effingham, clerk [DW/PA/7/8 f.148; DW/PA/5/1611/41]
(Sir) Thomas of Surrey, knight and citizen of London [PRO; PCC Will 1478]
Thomas of West Clandon [DW/PA/7/5 f.84; 1539]
Thomas of Epsom, yeoman [DW/PA/7/11 f.579; DW/PA/5/1630/25]
Walter of Ewhurst [DW/PA/7/3 f.200; 1532]
William of Ashtead, ploughwright [DW/PA/7/10 f.133; DW/PA/5/1620/34]
William of Epsom, yeoman [HRO; 1632 B11]
William of Richmond [PRO; PCC Will 1505]
William of Swk St Olave, tanner [HRO; Reg. Fox 3 p.66; 1515]
William of Tandridge [PRO; PCC Admon 1649]
William of Woking - Sutton [GL; Commissary Court of London Will 1443]
William of Worplesdon [DW/PA/7/8 f.71; DW/PA/5/1609/33]
see also COCK

COOKSON (CUCKSON)

John of Swk, yeoman [DW/PA/7/7 f.271; DW/PA/5/1599/16] <Abs 476>

COOLEDGE
John of Lambeth, yeoman [PRO; PCC Will 1621]
Robert of Swk, tailor [DW/PA/7/12 f.204; DW/PA/5/1634/19]
COOLES *see* COLE
COOMBE *see* COMBES
COOMBER *see* COMBER
COOMES *see* COMBES
COOPAH (COOPAL)
Neelken of ...., wife of Giles Govaert, harness maker (he born at Antwerp, Belgium) [DW/PA/5/1558/119]*
COOPE
Stephen of Surrey, esq. [PRO; PCC Will 1534]
William of Rotherhithe, mariner [DW/PA/7/11 f.524; DW/PA/5/1630/26]
COOPER (COUPER,COWEPAR,COWPER,CUPER)
Alice of Godalming; Witley, widow of Thomas [DW/PA/7/8 f.222; DW/PA/5/1612/89]
Alice of Guildford St Mary, widow of Harry [DW/PA/7/4 f.67; 1534]
Alice of Oxted, widow [DW/PA/5/1570/53]
Anthony of Frimley [PRO; PCC Will 1596]
Barbara of Swk St Olave, widow of Francis Cuper alias Gems [DW/PA/7/2 f.85; 1502]
Barbara, alias Barbara Astry of Titsey [PRO; PCC Admon 1648]
Benjamin of East Horsley, yeoman [PRO; PCC Will 1621]
Christopher of London [DW/PA/5/1593/150]
Dionis of Oxted, widow [DW/PA/7/2 f.37; 1493]
Dionisia of Oxted, widow [DW/PA/7/2 f.35; 1497]
Edith of Guildford [PRO; PCC Will 1521]
Edward of Swk St Olave, wine porter [DW/PA/7/11 f.191; DW/PA/5/1625/51]
Elizabeth of Capel, widow [DW/PA/7/12 f.192; DW/PA/5/1633/30]
Elizabeth of Horley, widow [DW/PA/5/1561/78]
Emma of Swk St Olave, widow [DW/PA/7/5 f.10; 1538] <Abs 104>
Henry of Battersea, yeoman [DW/PA/7/10 f.72; 1618]
Henry of Battersea, yeoman [DW/PA/7/12 f.267; DW/PA/5/1634/29]
Henry of Guildford St Mary [DW/PA/7/2 f.171; c1521]
Henry of Newington [LPL; 96/632; Will 1629]
Henry of Swk St George, tailor [DW/PA/7/7 f.405; DW/PA/5/1603/35] <Abs 753>
James of Reigate, labourer [DW/PA/5/1570/26]
Jane of Swk St Olave, widow [DW/PA/7/10 f.161; 1622]
Joan of Surrey [PRO; PCC Will 1552]
Joan, alias Joan Attwell of Bentley, Hampshire, widow [DW/PA/7/11 f.318; DW/PA/5/1626/9]
John of Battersea - Penge [DW/PA/7/5 f.122; 1539]
John of Bentley, Hampshire, ploughwright [DW/PA/7/8 f.216; DW/PA/5/1612/37]
John of Capel [PRO; PCC Admon 1591]
John of Capel, sergeant at law [PRO; PCC Will 1593]
John of Frimley, yeoman [DW/PA/5/1561/82]
John of Reigate, mercer [DW/PA/7/1 f.74; 1487] <Abs 242>
John of Reigate - Linkfield [DW/PA/7/3 f.131; 1530]
John of Reigate, weaver [DW/PA/5/1582/14]
Joseph of Bermondsey, citizen and leatherseller [PRO; PCC 1636]
Juliana of Leatherhead, widow [PRO; PCC Will 1621]

COOPER (COUPER,COWEPAR,COWPER,CUPER) [*continued*]

Michael of Rotherhithe [PRO; PCC Admon 1616]
(Sir) Richard of Capel - Temple Elfande, knight [PRO; PCC Will 1625]
Richard, alias Richard Stenynge of Cranleigh; Rudgwick, Sussex [DW/PA/7/9 f.99; DW/PA/5/1614/18]
Richard, alias Richard Gilbert of Egham [DW/PA/7/1 f.72; 1487] <Abs 238>
Richard, alias Richard Steaninge of Haslemere; Lurgashall, Sussex, yeoman [DW/PA/7/8 f.71; DW/PA/5/1609/34]
Richard of Leatherhead [PRO; PCC Admon 1627]
Robert of Albury; Shere; Rusper, Sussex, clerk and parson [DW/PA/7/8 f.182; DW/PA/5/1610/34]
Robert of Horley, yeoman [DW/PA/7/8 f.351; DW/PA/5/1612/38]
Robert of Horley, yeoman [DW/PA/7/8 f.382; DW/PA/5/1612/39]
Robert of Oxted [DW/PA/5/1550/68]
Roger of Rotherhithe, mariner [DW/PA/7/13 f.297; DW/PA/5/1643/26]
Samuel of Bermondsey [PRO; PCC Admon 1637]
Stephen of ... [DW/PA/7/2 f.194; 1523]
Thomas, alias Thomas Stayning of Dorking [PRO; PCC Admon 1626]
Thomas of Farnham, gent. [DW/PA/7/13 f.364; 1644]
Thomas of Guildford; Godalming, Zgent. [PRO; PCC Will 1596]
Thomas of Horley [PRO; PCC Will 1499]
Thomas of Horley [DW/PA/5/1550/85]
Thomas of Tandridge - 'Hodge a Horne'; Burstow, pailmaker [DW/PA/7/8 f.46; DW/PA/5/1609/35]
Thomas, alias Thomas Marline of Worplesdon - Burpham, yeoman [DW/PA/7/8 f.234; DW/PA/5/1612/97]
Thomas, alias Thomas Marlyn of Worplesdon - Burpham, husbandman [DW/PA/7/12 f.284; DW/PA/5/1635/68]
Walter of Kingston [DW/PA/5/1561/62]
William of Surrey [PRO; PCC Will 1550]
William of Bermondsey [PRO; PCC Will 1593]
William of Chertsey; Steventon, ?Hampshire or Berkshire [DW/PA/7/7 f.33; DW/PA/5/1595/19 *and* DW/PA/5/1595/20] <Abs 69>
William of Guildford [PRO; PCC Will 1521]
William of Horley [DW/PA/5/1591/51]
William of Lambeth [PRO; PCC Admon 1601]
William of Oxted [DW/PA/5/1561/68]
William of Oxted [DW/PA/5/1569/49]
William of Oxted, yeoman [DW/PA/7/8 f.227; DW/PA/5/1617/24]
William of Swk St Saviour, porter [DW/PA/7/11 f.557; DW/PA/5/1630/27]

COOPLAND *see* COPELAND

COPE (COPP)

John of Betchworth [DW/PA/7/5 f.3; 1538] <Abs 11>
Thomas of Betchworth [DW/PA/7/7 f.152; DW/PA/5/1597/25] <Abs 286>

COPELAND (COOPLAND)

Ellen Gresham, formerly Ellen Copeland of Puttenham [PRO; PCC Will 1553]
Harry of Swk St Olave [DW/PA/7/2 f.89; 1504]

COPIS *see* COLPIS

COPLEY (COPLEYE,COPPELEY,COPPLEY)

(Lady) Elizabeth of Gatton, widow [PRO; PCC Will 1559] <Abs SAC v.11 pp.154-156>
(Sir) Roger of Gatton, knight [PRO; PCC Will 1549]
Thomas of Gatton, esq. and knight [PRO; PCC Will 1584] <Abs SAC v.22 pp.164-167>

COPLEY (COPLEYE,COPPELEY,COPPLEY) [*continued*]
Ursula of Oxted, gent. [PRO; PCC 1648]
COPOUD
Joan of Swk St Saviour, widow [DW/PA/5/1558/69]*
COPP *see* COPE
COPPELEY *see* COPLEY
COPPER
Alice of Farnham; New Alresford, Hampshire, wife of Thomas [DW/PA/7/4 f.98; 1534]
COPPEY
William of Swk St Olave, victualler [DW/PA/7/12 f.161; DW/PA/5/1633/38]
COPPIN
Thomas of Swk St Saviour [DW/PA/5/1579/30]*
COPPINGER
Cicely (formerly Cicely Long) of Surrey, widow [PRO; PCC Will 1559]
COPPLEY *see* COPLEY
COPPOOLL
Ralph of Swk St Saviour, skinner [DW/PA/5/1547/25]
COPPSELL
Harry of Lingfield [DW/PA/5/1558/70]*
CORBETT (CORBIT)
John of Lambeth, yeoman [DW/PA/5/1593/185]
Margaret of Swk St Olave, widow [DW/PA/7/13 f.349; 1644]
Richard of Farnham [PRO; PCC Will 1626]
Richard of Swk St George [DW/PA/7/8 f.28A; DW/PA/5/1608/28]
CORBIN
George of Swk St George, gent. [DW/PA/7/10 f.198; DW/PA/5/1621/27] <Abs U248>
CORBIT *see* CORBETT
CORBRIDGE
William of Rotherhithe [PRO; PCC 1648]
CORBYE
Thomas of Worplesdon [PRO; PCC Will 1558]
CORDELL *see* CORDWELL
CORDEN
William of Swk St Saviour, citizen and tallow chandler [DW/PA/7/10 f.168; DW/PA/5/1621/28]
CORDER
Arthur of Mitcham, husbandman [DW/PA/7/13 f.200; DW/PA/5/1642/15]
CORDIWEN
John of Swk St Olave, joiner [DW/PA/5/1623/28]
CORDREY (CORDRAY)
John of Egham [PRO; PCC Will 1541] <Abs SAC v.47 p.27>
Read of Surrey [PRO; PCC Will 1644]
Read of Kingston [PRO; PCC 1645]
see also CAWDEREY
CORDWELL (CORDELL)
Dionisis of Swk St Thomas, widow [DW/PA/7/10 ff.148,276; DW/PA/5/1621/30]
Edmund of Swk St Olave, citizen and skinner [DW/PA/5/1627/22]
Robert of Sutton; Swk St Saviour; Walton on the Hill, clerk etc. [DW/PA/7/10 f.167; DW/PA/5/1621/29]
Samuel of Lambeth [PRO; PCC 1648]
see also CALDWELL

CO'RED
Henry, alias Henry Kok of Merton [DW/PA/5/1546/32]
CORFE
Henry of Ewell [DW/PA/7/10 f.115; DW/PA/5/1620/35]
CORKIN
Anthony of Cranleigh, parson [DW/PA/7/6 f.222; 1561]
CORKS
Richard, alias Richard Levat of Great Bookham; Effingham, tailor [DW/PA/7/10 f.109; DW/PA/5/1619/30]
CORNE
John, alias John Covey of Swk St Olave, citizen and woodmonger [DW/PA/5/1617/23] <Abs U214>
Thomas of Swk St Saviour, oarmaker [DW/PA/7/12 f.140; DW/PA/5/1632/25]
CORNEFORDE *see* CORNFORD
CORNER
Matthew of Swk St Olave, brewer [DW/PA/7/7 f.345; DW/PA/5/1601/28] <Abs 629>
CORNEWALLIS *see* CORNWALLIS
CORNEY
Alice of Lambeth - Water Lambeth; Yorkshire [DW/PA/7/7 f.62; DW/PA/5/1596/15] <Abs 119>
Frances of Swk St Saviour, victualler [DW/PA/7/9 f.13; DW/PA/5/1616/27]
James of Buckland [PRO; PCC 1640]
CORNFORD (CORNEFORDE, de CORNEWAYLE)
Isabel of West Molesey, widow of James [DW/PA/7/7 f.283; DW/PA/5/1599/14] <Abs 507>
James of West Molesey; Kendal, Westmorland, yeoman [DW/PA/7/7 f.97; 1596] <Abs 179>
Joan of Swk St Olave, wife of John, glover [HRO; Reg. Wyk 2 p.81; 1372]
CORNWALLIS (CORNEWALLEIS, CORNEWALLIS)
Francis of Camberwell - Peckham, esq. [PRO; PCC Will 1570]
Katherine of East Horsley, widow [PRO; PCC Will 1626]
(Lady) Katherine of East Horsley, widow [PRO; PCC 1632]
Thomas of East Horsley, esq. [PRO; PCC Will 1597]
Thomas of East Horsley [PRO; PCC Will 1598]
CORTE *see* COURT
CORTES *see* CURTIS
CORTEMYLL *see* COURTMELL
CORTEYS *see* CURTIS
CORTNESHE *see* COURTNESH
CORTYS *see* CURTIS
COSIN *see* COUSINS
COSSE
John of Farnham, weaver [DW/PA/7/5 f.40; 1538] <Abs 36>
COSSENS *see* COUSINS
COSSEY
Richard of Swk St Saviour, citizen and haberdasher [DW/PA/5/1624/31]
Thomasine of Swk St Saviour, widow [DW/PA/7/11 f.374; DW/PA/5/1626/38B]
COSTEN *see* CAWSTEN
COSTHE
Thomas of Swk St Olave, barber surgeon [DW/PA/7/5 f.224; 1541]
COSTON *see* CAWSTEN
COTEFEILD
William of ...., waterman [DW/PA/7/11 f.224; DW/PA/5/1625/52]

COTELOND
John of Swk [HRO; Reg. Wyk 2 p.188; 1380]
COTER *see* COTTER
COTES *see* COATES
COTLEN
John of Croydon, brother of Trinity Hospital [LPL; 96/658; Will 1629]
COTON *see* COTTON
COTTELL
George of Walton on Thames, husbandman [DW/PA/7/11 f.553; DW/PA/5/1629/20]
Henry of Leigh, yeoman [DW/PA/5/1579/31]*
John of Walton on Thames; Ockham; Weybridge [DW/PA/7/4 f.110; 1535]
John of Shere, yeoman [DW/PA/7/6 f.215; 1560]
Ralph of Swk St George, broom-man [DW/PA/7/11 f.433; DW/PA/5/1627/23]
William of Walton on Thames [DW/PA/7/4 f.100; 1534]
COTTEN *see* COTTON
COTTER (COTER)
Richard of Dorking [DW/PA/7/1 f.44; 1486] <Abs 142>
COTTERELL (COTTRELL,COTTRYLL)
Anthony of Newington [PRO; PCC Admon 1649]
Crispin of Petersham [PRO; PCC Admon 1649]
Richard of Windlesham - Bagshot [PRO; PCC Will 1583]
Richard of Windlesham - Bagshot; Chobham [PRO; PCC Will 1583]
Rose of Windlesham, widow [DW/PA/7/9 f.96; DW/PA/5/1614/16]
COTTEY (COTTIE,COTTYE)
Martin of Morden, yeoman [DW/PA/7/8 f.160; DW/PA/5/1611/42]
Robert of Lingfield [DW/PA/5/1558/72]*
Thomas of Blechingley, yeoman [DW/PA/7/12 f.134; DW/PA/5/1632/23]
COTTINGHAM (COTYNGHAM)
Bartholomew of Clapham [DW/PA/7/13 f.395; DW/PA/5/1645/7]
John of Surrey, poulterer [PRO; PCC Will 1560]
Thomas of Esher [DW/PA/7/5 f.164; 1540]
COTTMAN
Nicholas of Swk St Saviour [HRO; Reg. CCB 20 p.7; 1563]
Nicholas of ... [DW/PA/5/1563/70] [*and*] [*in* DW/PA/5/1563/65]
William of Rotherhithe, mariner [PRO; PCC Will 1624]
COTTON (COTON,COTTEN)
Ann of Farnham, widow [DW/PA/7/8 f.202; DW/PA/5/1611/43]
Christopher of Chertsey, gent. [DW/PA/5/1591/56]
Ellen of Rotherhithe, widow [DW/PA/7/8 f.149; DW/PA/5/1611/44]
John of Farnham, gent. [PRO; PCC Will 1603] <Abs. SAC v.11 pp.112-113>
Margaret of Surrey, wife of John, esq. [PRO; PCC Will 1582]
Margaret of Chertsey, gent. [PRO; PCC Will 1592]
Robert of Swk St George [DW/PA/5/1591/17]
Robert of Walton on Thames - Oatlands, gent., yeoman of H.M.'s removing wardrobe [PRO; PCC Will 1591 *and* 1592] <Abs SAC v.32 p.74>
Thomas of Farnham, gent. [PRO; PCC Will 1591]
William of Swk St Olave; Shoreditch, Middlesex, feltmaker [DW/PA/5/1596/17] <Abs U6>
COTTRELL,COTTRYLL *see* COTTERELL
COTTYE *see* COTTEY
COUCHE
Gertrude of Swk St Olave, widow [DW/PA/7/7 f.147; DW/PA/5/1597/26] <Abs 271>

COUCHMAN (COOCHMAN)
  Edward of Clapham, parson [PRO; PCC Will 1603] <Abs, SAC v.11 p.122>
COUCKE *see* COOK
COULES *see* COLE
COULSON *see* COLSON
COULSTONE *see* COLSTONE
COULTER (CULTOR)
  William of Guildford Holy Trinity [DW/PA/7/2 f.117; 1517]
COUPER *see* COOPER
COURT (CORTE,COURTE,COWRTE)
  Isebrand of ... (proved at Lambeth) [DW/PA/7/4 f.6; 1532]
  Margaret of Thursley, servant to Joan Bayly, spinster [DW/PA/5/1593/14]
  Thomas of Thursley [DW/PA/5/1569/81] (*two wills*)
  Thomas of Thursley [DW/PA/5/1571/50]
COURTENESHE *see* COURTNESH
COURTES *see* CURTIS
COURTHOPP
  John of Lingfield, esq. [PRO; PCC Will 1616] [*and*] [SRO; 204/3/9]
COURTMELL (CORTEMYLL)
  Joan of Shere, widow [DW/PA/7/1 f.62; 1487] <Abs 206>
  Joan of Godalming, widow [DW/PA/7/5 f.6; 1538] <Abs 45>
  Thomas of Godalming [HRO; 1533 B11]
COURTNESH (CORTNESHE,COURTENESHE,COURTNISHE,CURTNESHE)
  John of Chiddingfold, yeoman [PRO; PCC Will 1628]
  Richard of Compton [DW/PA/7/5 f.157; 1540]
  Thomas of Godalming [PRO; PCC Will 1559]
  William of Chiddingfold, husbandman [DW/PA/7/12 f.256; DW/PA/5/1634/28]
  William of Farnham [DW/PA/5/1582/95]
COURTNEY (COWRTENAYS)
  Arnold of Guildford St Mary [HRO; Reg. Fox 2 p.30; 1508]
  William of Chertsey [DW/PA/5/1543/6]*
COURTNISHE *see* COURTNESH
COUSALT
  Walter of Swk St Saviour - Upper Ground, waterman [DW/PA/7/11 f.555; DW/PA/5/1629/18]
COUSINS (COSIN,COSSENS,COUSSINS)
  Edward of Lambeth, gent. [PRO; PCC 1637]
  Elizabeth of Surrey [PRO; PCC 1643]
  Henry of Swk St Saviour, waterman [DW/PA/7/13 f.252; DW/PA/5/1641/25]
  Joseph of Camberwell - Peckham, gent. [PRO; PCC 1633]
  Thomas of Rotherhithe, mariner [PRO; PCC 1649]
COVEHAM *see* COBHAM
COVENTRY
  Lucy, alias Lucy Powell of Tooting, spinster [DW/PA/7/13 f.162; 1641]
COVERT
  Ann of Godstone, widow of Humphrey [DW/PA/7/12 f.272; DW/PA/5/1635/19]
  Anthony of Hascombe, esq. [PRO; PCC 1631]
  Dulcibell, alias Dulcibell Vyne of Shalford [PRO; PCC Admon 1599]
  Emma of Hascombe, widow [PRO; PCC Admon 1638]
  Francis of Chaldon, Doctor of Law [PRO; PCC Admon 1609]
  Humphrey of Lambeth, captain [PRO; PCC Will 1614]
  Isabel of Chaldon [PRO; PCC Will 1401]
  John of Mickleham, gent. [PRO; PCC Will 1628]
  Thomas of Lambeth, esq. [PRO; PCC Will 1608] <Abs, SAC v.13 pp.192-193>

COVEY (COVIE)
  John, alias John Corne of Swk St Olave, citizen and woodmonger [DW/PA/5/1617/23] <Abs U214>
COWDREY (COWDRY,COWDRYE)
  Gilbert of Lambeth, gent. [PRO; PCC Will 1596]
  Thomas, alias Thomas Codrell of Lambeth [DW/PA/5/1603/34]
  William of Farnham [DW/PA/5/1557/139]
COWICKE (COWYKE)
  John of Ewhurst [DW/PA/5/1558/73]*
  Thomas of Ewhurst [DW/PA/5/1556/3]
  William, senior of Ewhurst [DW/PA/7/5 f.17; 1538] <Abs 32>
COWLES *see* COLE
COWLEY
  John of Effingham, blacksmith [DW/PA/7/12 f.299; DW/PA/5/1635/21]
COWNDEN
  John of Newington - Walworth, gent. [PRO; PCC Will 1612]
COWPER *see* COOPER
COWRTENAYS *see* COURTNEY
COX (COCKES,COCKS,COKES,COKKES,COXE)
  Alice of Swk St Saviour, widow [DW/PA/7/11 f.186; DW/PA/5/1625/47]
  Alice of Wonersh, late wife of John, yeoman [DW/PA/7/12 f.313; DW/PA/5/1636/17]
  Edward of Dorking, yeoman [DW/PA/5/1593/90]
  Elizabeth of Shere [DW/PA/7/10 f.185; DW/PA/5/1620/36]
  Francis of Bermondsey [PRO; PCC Admon 1638]
  George of Lambeth [PRO; PCC Admon 1633]
  James of Stoke next Guildford, yeoman [PRO; PCC Will 1622]
  Joan of Newington - Walworth, widow [LPL; 96/676; Will 1614]
  John of London, mariner [DW/PA/7/11 f.68; DW/PA/5/1623/29]
  John of Cranleigh, yeoman [DW/PA/7/8 f.396; DW/PA/5/1612/40]
  John of Ewhurst [DW/PA/7/2 f.13; 1491]
  John of Farnham, shoemaker [DW/PA/7/7 f.185; DW/PA/5/1598/20] <Abs 336>
  John of Guildford St Nicolas, shearman [DW/PA/7/10 f.139; DW/PA/5/1620/34]
  John of Swk St Olave, citizen and leatherseller [DW/PA/5/1546/41]
  John of Swk St Saviour [DW/PA/7/7 ff.418,432; DW/PA/5/1603/36] <Abs 783>
  Katherine of Tooting, widow [DW/PA/7/10 f.50; 1618]
  Peter of Worplesdon, yeoman [DW/PA/7/10 f.61; 1618]
  Richard of Stoke next Guildford, yeoman [PRO; PCC Will 1610] <Abs. SAC v.24 p.63>
  Robert of Swk St George, labourer [DW/PA/7/11 f.184; DW/PA/5/1625/53]
  Sarah of Cobham, widow of Ralph, citizen and saddler [PRO; PCC 1632]
  Thomas of Chiddingfold, shoemaker [HRO; 1557 U153]
  Thomas of Long Ditton - Tolworth, husbandman [DW/PA/7/8 f.79; DW/PA/5/1609/36]
  Thomas of Long Ditton - Tolworth [PRO; PCC 1649]
  Thomas of Thames Ditton, senior [DW/PA/7/7 f.271; DW/PA/5/1599/15] <Abs 478>
  Thomas of Merton, labourer [DW/PA/7/12 f.399; DW/PA/5/1637/26]
  Thomas of Pirbright, smith [DW/PA/7/9 f.322; DW/PA/5/1619/29]
  Thomas of Rotherhithe [PRO; PCC 1645]
  Thomas of Swk St George, victualler [DW/PA/5/1576/46]
  Thomas of Swk St Saviour - Bankside, waterman [DW/PA/7/7 f.508; DW/PA/5/1605/23] <Abs 951> [*and*] <Abs U135>

COX (COCKES,COCKS,COKES,COKKES,COXE) [*continued*]

Thomas of Worplesdon; Stoke next Guildford; Guildford, yeoman [DW/PA/5/1605/22] <Abs U134>

Thomas of Worplesdon - Burpham, yeoman [DW/PA/7/9 f.200;DW/PA/5/1616/29]

William of Albury; Guildford St Nicolas [DW/PA/7/9 f.258; DW/PA/5/1617/25]

William of Guildford Holy Trinity [DW/PA/7/8 f.179; DW/PA/5/1610/35]

William of Mitcham, gent. [PRO; PCC Will 1615] [*and*] [DW/PA/7/9 f.89; 1615]

William, alias William Haynes of Ockley, yeoman [DW/PA/7/10 f.261; DW/PA/5/1622/39]

William of Putney - Roehampton, husbandman [PRO; PCC Will 1599]

see also COCK,COOK,CORKS

COYTE

William of Farnham [HRO; Reg. Fox 3 p.65; 1515]

CRABB (CRAB,CRABBE)

Henry of St Gregory, London; Swk St Saviour - Bankside; Cranleigh, citizen and merchant tailor [PRO; PCC 1620] <Soame 1289>

John of Cranleigh, yeoman [PRO; PCC Will 1628]

John of Wotton [DW/PA/7/3 f.137; 1530]

Nicholas of Wotton [DW/PA/7/2 f.21; 1491]

see also PAGE

CRADDOCKE

Edward of Newington [PRO; PCC Admon 1637]

Richard of Charlwood, husbandman [LPL; 96/687; Will 1616]

CRAEN *see* CRANE

CRAFT

Daniel of Swk St George [DW/PA/7/9 f.140; 1615]

CRAGG (CRAGGE)

Ann of Guildford, widow [DW/PA/7/12 f.341; DW/PA/5/1636/26]

Anthony of Swk St Olave, baker [DW/PA/7/12 f.354; DW/PA/5/1637/20]

Rowland of Guildford, innholder [DW/PA/7/12 f.148; DW/PA/5/1633/25]

CRANE (CRAEN)

Anthony of Molesey, master of the Queen's Household [PRO; PCC Will 1583]

John of Guildford Holy Trinity [DW/PA/7/12 f.7; DW/PA/5/1631/24]

John of Swk St Olave [DW/PA/7/8 f.88; DW/PA/5/1609/37]

Millicent of Guildford, widow [DW/PA/7/12 f.181; DW/PA/5/1633/37]

Rowland of Farnham, saddler [HRO; 1563 B49]

CRANFORD

Richard of Shalford, husbandman [DW/PA/7/9 f.215; DW/PA/5/1617/26]

CRANKER

Christopher of Swk St Saviour [DW/PA/7/11 f.546; DW/PA/5/1629/21]

CRANLEY (CRANLY,CRAWLEY)

Alexander of Swk St Olave, yeoman [DW/PA/5/1547/21]

Edward of Ash, husbandman [HRO; 1597 B18]

John of Cranleigh; Godalming; Hascombe, yeoman [DW/PA/7/8 f.111; DW/PA/5/1610/36]

John of Dunsfold [PRO; PCC Will 1557]

Robert of Worplesdon [DW/PA/7/6 f.251; 1560]

Roger of Chiddingfold, yeoman [DW/PA/5/1593/180A]*

CRASSE *see* CROSSE

CRAVET

Thomas of Chertsey, servant to the Queen [PRO; PCC Will 1598]

CRAWLEY *see* CRANLEY

CRAYFORD
Nicholas of Carshalton, gent. [DW/PA/5/1591/53]
William of Rotherhithe [PRO; PCC Admon 1627]
CREANER (CREAMER)
Jane of Swk St George, widow [DW/PA/7/9 f.166; DW/PA/5/1616/30]
Jasper of Swk St George, cordwainer [DW/PA/7/8 f.407; DW/PA/5/1614/28]
CREASEY (CRESSEY,CREYSIE)
Edward (son of John late of West Horsley, husbandman) of Merrow; West Clandon [DW/PA/5/1593/15]
John of West Horsley, husbandman [HRO; 1581 B28]
CREDY
John of Surrey, esq. [PRO; PCC Will 1426]
CREED
William of Mitcham, mealman [DW/PA/7/12 f.175; DW/PA/5/1633/27]
CRESSELL *see* CRESWELL
CRESSEY *see* CREASEY
CRESSWICK
William of Camberwell - Peckham [GL; Commissary Court of London Will 1407]
CRESTON
Henry of Kingston, carpenter [*in* DW/PA/5/1546/10]
CRESWELL (CRESSELL,CRESSWELL,CROSWELL,CRUSSELL)
Christopher of Cranleigh [PRO; PCC 1646]
Edward of Egham [PRO; PCC Admon 1623]
Edward of Farnham, tailor [DW/PA/5/1585/4]*
George of Lambeth [PRO; PCC 1636]
Hugh of Farnham [HRO; Reg. D p.99; 1528]
Jane of Warlingham, widow [DW/PA/7/11 f.89; DW/PA/5/1623/31]
John of Swk St Saviour, yeoman [DW/PA/7/12 f.425; DW/PA/5/1637/31]
John of Worplesdon [DW/PA/7/4 f.104; 1535]
Matthias of Lambeth [PRO; PCC Admon 1630]
Richard of Ash, husbandman [DW/PA/7/4 f.101; 1534]
Richard of Kingston [PRO; PCC Will 1560]
Richard of Swk St Olave, cooper [DW/PA/7/11 f.155; DW/PA/5/1625/55]
Richard of Warlingham, yeoman [DW/PA/5/1620/37] <Abs U242>
Thomas of Kingston, wheelwright [HRO; 1585 B23]
Walter of West Horsley; Cranleigh; Guildford [PRO; PCC Will 1593]
William of Cranleigh, bachelor [PRO; PCC Admon 1623]
William of Farnham, gent. [DW/PA/5/1558/74]*
William of Guildford St Nicholas - Littleton, husbandman [DW/PA/5/1575/65]
William of Kingston, wheelwright [DW/PA/5/1561/70]
CREW (CREWE,CREWES,CREWZE,CRUE)
Geoffrey of Lambeth, gent. [PRO; PCC 1645]
James of Bermondsey [PRO; PCC Will 1591]
Jeremy of Swk St Saviour, needlemaker [DW/PA/7/8 f.273; DW/PA/5/1612/41]
Thomas of Windlesham, labourer [HRO; 1591 B17]
Thomas of Windlesham, husbandman [DW/PA/7/8 f.120; DW/PA/5/1610/37]
CREYSER *see* CROYSER
CRIDLANDE
William of London; Lidyeard St Lawrence, Somerset; Taunton, Somerset [DW/PA/5/1593/84]
CRIER *see* CRYER
CRIMES *see* CRYMES

CRIPPS (CRIPPES,CRIPPZ)
Henry of Rotherhithe [PRO; PCC Admon 1609]
John of Swk St Olave [DW/PA/7/6 f.227; 1561]
Thomas of Addington [PRO; PCC Will 1616]
Vaughan of Richmond, spinster [DW/PA/7/12 f.52; DW/PA/5/1631/31]
CRISPE
Margaret of Swk St Saviour, widow [DW/PA/7/12 f.459; DW/PA/5/1638/28].
CRISMAS,CRISTIMAS,CRISTMAS *see* CHRISTMAS
CROCHAR,CROCHER *see* CROUCHER
CROCKE
Christopher of Swk St Olave, beltmaker [DW/PA/7/11 f.207;
DW/PA/5/1625/54]
CROCKER (CROKKER)
Richard of Walton on Thames [HRO; Reg. Way 1 p.27; 1453]
CROCKFORD (CROCKFORDE,CROKEFORDE)
Agnes of Chertsey, spinster [DW/PA/7/10 f.123; DW/PA/5/1620/38]
Henry of Chertsey, husbandman [DW/PA/7/13 f.122; DW/PA/5/1640/35]
John of Chertsey, widower [DW/PA/7/5 f.40; 1538] <Abs 18>
John of Chertsey [DW/PA/7/7 f.545; DW/PA/5/1606/29] <Abs 1022>
Maurice of Chertsey, yeoman [DW/PA/7/13 f.163; DW/PA/5/1642/14]
Richard of Thorpe, yeoman [DW/PA/7/12 f.328; DW/PA/5/1636/22]
Robert of Chertsey [DW/PA/7/6 f.263; 1560]
CROFT (CROFTE)
John of Guildford Holy Trinity [DW/PA/7/1 f.2; 1484] <Abs 6>
John of Streatham, gent. [PRO; PCC Will 1584]
CROFTER
Edward of Godalming [DW/PA/7/13 f.320; 1644]
Thomas of Stoke Dabernon, tailor [DW/PA/7/6 f.182; DW/PA/5/1559/213]
CROFTON
Parnell of Wonersh [DW/PA/5/1582/38]
CROKES *see* CROOKE
CROKKER *see* CROCKER
CROMER
George of Ockham, gent. [PRO; PCC 1631]
CROMPE *see* CRUMP
CROMPTON
Joyce of Swk St Saviour, widow [DW/PA/7/9 f.193; 1616]
CRONEY
Anthony, senior of Guildford, tailor [DW/PA/7/7 f.594;
DW/PA/5/1607/33] <Abs 1110>
CROOCHER *see* CROUCHER
CROOKE (CROKES)
George of Camberwell [DW/PA/7/6 f.8; DW/PA/5/1559/10]
Hugh of Bermondsey [DW/PA/7/12 f.90; DW/PA/5/1633/35]
Margaret, alias Margaret Miller of ... [DW/PA/7/12 f.379; 1637]
Thomas of Bermondsey [PRO; PCC 1648]
William of ..., one of H.M.'s yeomen waiters within the Tower of London
[DW/PA/7/10 f.122; DW/PA/5/1620/39]
CROP
Eusebius of Surrey [? HRO; 1551]
CROS *see* CROSS, DU CROS
CROSBY (CROSBIE)
Ann of Rotherhithe, widow [DW/PA/7/11 f.554; DW/PA/5/1629/22]
Henry of Rotherhithe [PRO; PCC Admon 1626]

CROSBY (CROSBIE) [*continued*]
John of Swk St Mary Magdalen, weaver [DW/PA/7/7 f.153; DW/PA/5/1597/28] <Abs 287>

CROSLEY
John of Byfleet, clerk [PRO; PCC Admon 1638]
Katherine, alias Old Katherine of Send, spinster [DW/PA/7/9 f.329; DW/PA/5/1620/40]

CROSS (CROS,CROSE,CROSSE,CROUSSE)
Agnes of Petersham [DW/PA/7/10 f.164; DW/PA/5/1621/31]
(Lady) Dorothy of Merton - Merton Abbey, widow of (Sir) Robert, knight [PRO; PCC Will 1623]
Elizabeth of Swk St Thomas, widow [DW/PA/5/1570/41]
Ellen of Swk St Saviour, widow of John, brewer [DW/PA/5/1557/14]
Frideswide of Great Bookham, widow [DW/PA/7/10 f.77; DW/PA/5/1619/31]
Harry of Worplesdon [DW/PA/7/2 f.167; 1521]
Henry of Battersea [GL; Commissary Court of London Will 1483]
Henry of Battersea [PRO; PCC Will 1494]
Jane of Chiddingfold [PRO; PCC Will 1601]
John of Mitcham, husbandman [DW/PA/7/11 f.82; DW/PA/5/1623/30]
John of Swk St Saviour, brewer [DW/PA/5/1555/36]
Richard of Mitcham, gent. [PRO; PCC 1645]
Richard of Wandsworth, miller [PRO; PCC Will 1613]
Richard of Worplesdon [DW/PA/5/1587/99]
Robert of Guildford St Mary, shearman [DW/PA/5/1575/19]
Robert of Stoke Dabernon [HRO; 1587 B24]
Roger of Egham - Englefield [HRO; 1595 B10]
Thomas of Shalford; Guildford, yeoman [DW/PA/7/7 f.412; DW/PA/5/1603/37] <Abs 765>
Thomas of Worplesdon [DW/PA/7/6 f.169; *in* DW/PA/5/1559/174]
William of Great Bookham, gent. [PRO; PCC Will 1613]
William of Richmond; London, merchant [PRO; PCC Will 1647]
William of Wandsworth, yeoman [DW/PA/7/8 f.340; DW/PA/5/1612/42]
William of Worplesdon, yeoman [DW/PA/5/1568/25]

CROSSKEYS
Daniel of Chipstead [PRO; PCC 1649]

CROSWELL *see* CRESWELL

CROUCH (CROWCHE)
Thomas of Lambeth, husbandman [DW/PA/5/1582/68]

CROUCHER (CHROUCHER,CROCHAR,CROCHER,CROOCHER,CROUCHAR,CROWCHAR,CROWCHER, CRUCHER,KRWTCHERE)
Ann of Swk St Saviour, widow [DW/PA/7/7 f.416; DW/PA/5/1603/38] <Abs 777>
John of West Horsley [DW/PA/5/1562/36]
John of Effingham; Swk - White Lion Prison, husbandman [DW/PA/7/9 f.97; DW/PA/5/1614/17]
John of West Horsley, wheeler [DW/PA/7/7 f.170; DW/PA/5/1597/27] <Abs 313>
John of Leatherhead [DW/PA/7/3 f.187; 1531]
John of Merrow [DW/PA/7/1 f.3; 1484] <Abs 7>
Phillip of Effingham [DW/PA/7/4 f.27; 1533]
Ralph of Great Bookham, husbandman [DW/PA/7/8 f.133; DW/PA/5/1610/38]
Richard of Ashtead [DW/PA/7/4 f.18; 1532]
Robert of Cobham [DW/PA/7/4 f.61; 1533]
Simon of Swk St Olave [DW/PA/7/4 f.203; 1537]
Stephen of East Clandon, tailor [DW/PA/7/8 f.197; DW/PA/5/1610/39]

CROUCHER (CHROUCHER,CROCHAR,CROCHER,CROOCHER,CROUCHAR,CROWCHAR,CROWCHER,
CRUCHER,KRWTCHERE) [*continued*]

Thomas of Croydon [PRO; PCC Will 1457]

Thomas of West Horsley [DW/PA/5/1581/16]

William of Farnham [DW/PA/7/1 f.88; 1489] <Abs 298>

William of Send, yeoman [DW/PA/7/13 f.69; DW/PA/5/1639/39]

William of Swk St Saviour, waterman [DW/PA/7/7 f.437; DW/PA/5/1603/39] <Abs 828>

CROUSSE *see* CROSS

CROUSTE *see* CRUST

CROVER

Francis of Rotherhithe (died overseas) [PRO; PCC Admon 1647]

CROWCHE,CROWCHAR,CROWCHER *see* CROUCH,CROUCHER

CROWE

John of Stoke next Guildford, clerk, rector [DW/PA/7/12 f.163; DW/PA/5/1633/39]

CROWSTE *see* CRUST

CROWTHER

Ann, alias Ann Maltbie, alias Ann Pybus of Lambeth [PRO; PCC Admon 1647]

CROYSER (CREYSER)

Edith Bruyn, formerly Edith Croyser of Stoke Dabernon [PRO; PCC Will 1418] <Abs. SAC v.51 p.92>

(Sir) William of Stoke Dabernon; Hertfordshire; Bedfordshire, knight [LPL; Reg. Abp Courtenay f.222; Will 1387] [*and*] [HRO; Reg. Wyk 2 p.231; 1387]

William of Stoke Dabernon, esq. [PRO; PCC Will 1416] <Abs. SAC v.51 p.92>

CRUCHAR *see* CROUCHER

CRUE *see* CREW

CRUMLIN

John of Godstone [PRO; PCC Admon 1602]

CRUMP (CROMPE,CROMPLE)

Thomas of Swk St Saviour, waterman [DW/PA/7/7 f.547; DW/PA/5/1606/30] <Abs 1026>

CRUMPLY

Edward of Frimley, bachelor [PRO; PCC Admon 1645]

CRUSSELL *see* CRESWELL

CRUST (CROUSTE,CROWSTE,CRUSTE)

Arthur of Epsom, labourer [DW/PA/7/8 f.23; DW/PA/5/1608/29]

Christopher of Leigh, yeoman [DW/PA/7/7 f.191; DW/PA/5/1598/21] <Abs 347>

Hugh of Chelsham, labourer [DW/PA/7/8 f.13; DW/PA/5/1608/20]

John of Leigh, yeoman [DW/PA/5/1586/13] (*former grant of 1585 revoked*) [*and*] [SRO; 79/3/1,2; 1586]

John of Leigh, yeoman [DW/PA/5/1591/102] (*former grants revoked*)

William of Ewell, carpenter [DW/PA/7/10 f.87; DW/PA/5/1615/146]

William of Leigh [DW/PA/7/2 f.166; 1522]

William of Leigh, yeoman [DW/PA/5/1555/53]

CRUTCHLOW (CHRICHELOO)

William of Worplesdon, shearman [DW/PA/5/1587/14]

CRYER

Agnes of Swk St George, widow of William, wheelwright [DW/PA/5/1571/74]

John of Chipstead, clerk [PRO; PCC Will 1586]

William of ... (*property in* Lewisham, Kent) [DW/PA/5/1571/13]

CRYMES
  (Sir) Thomas of Camberwell - Peckham, knight [DW/PA/7/13 f.339; 1644]
CUCKNEY
  Henry of Kew [PRO; PCC Will 1624]
CUCKSON *see* COOKSON
CUCKVCK
  Richard of Newington, yeoman [PRO; PCC Will 1613]
CUDDINGTON (CODDINGTON,CODINGTON,CODYNGTON)
  Ann of Cuddington [PRO; PCC Will 1500]
  Edward of Ewell, yeoman [DW/PA/5/1605/24] <Abs U136>
  John of Adisham, Kent, rector; Whitefriars, London; Henfield, Sussex; Hastings, Sussex; Cuddington; Bottesford, Leicestershire [LPL; Reg. Abp Whittleseye f.107; Will 1369]
  John of Cuddington; Ewell; Chobham, esq. [DW/PA/7/4 f.120; 1535]
  John of Reigate [DW/PA/7/4 f.114; 1535]
  John of Reigate; Leigh, yeoman [DW/PA/7/10 f.125; DW/PA/5/1620/41]
  John of Reigate - Sidlow Mill, yeoman [DW/PA/5/1627/24]
  Ralph of Cuddington [LPL; Reg. Abp Chichele i f.349; Will 1421]
  Richard of Horley, yeoman [PRO; PCC Will 1599]
  Thomas of Ewell, husbandman [DW/PA/5/1555/51] (2 copies)
  Thomas, senior of Ewell, husbandman [DW/PA/7/8 f.142; DW/PA/5/1611/45]
  William of Ewell, gent. [PRO; PCC Will 1482]
  William of Ewell, yeoman [DW/PA/7/9 f.188; DW/PA/5/1616/31]
    see also QUIDDINGTON,QUITTINGTON
CUDGELL
  Nicholas of Chiddingfold [DW/PA/7/10 f.99; DW/PA/5/1619/32]
CULLEN (CULLEYN)
  James of Lambeth [PRO; PCC Admon 1589]
  Maurice of Swk St Margaret, waterman [DW/PA/7/1 f.30; 1486] <Abs 101>
  Richard of Wandsworth, merchant [PRO; PCC 1645]
CULLY
  William of Kingston [HRO; Reg. Stra p.28; 1327]
CULPEPPER (CULPEPER)
  Joan of Horne, widow [DW/PA/5/1558/75]*
  Richard of Surrey, esq. [PRO; PCC Will 1516]
CULSTOCK (CULSTOKE)
  John of Swk St Olave, hosier [DW/PA/7/5 f.183; 1540]
CULTOR *see* COULTER
CULVER
  Peter of Christ Church, London; Swk St Saviour - Paris Garden Liberty and Bankside, butcher [GL; Commissary Court of London Will 1613]
CULVERWELL
  Nicholas of Richmond, citizen and haberdasher [PRO; PCC Will 1569]
CUMBER
  Ann of Lingfield, widow [DW/PA/7/13 f.139; DW/PA/5/1640/38]
CUNSTABLE *see* CONSTABLE
CUNTASTHORP
  Thomas, alias Thomas Cantharthorp of Streatham, rector [HRO; Reg. Wyk 2 p.186; 1380]
CUPER *see* COOPER
CURE
  Thomas of Newington [PRO; PCC Admon 1637]
CURFEW (KERFEWE)
  Edward of ... [DW/PA/7/9 f.326; DW/PA/5/1619/74]

CURLE
Christopher of Swk St Olave, citizen and cutler [DW/PA/5/1569/45]
CURLEW (CURLEWE,CURLO)
John of Swk St Olave, miller [DW/PA/7/1 f.24; 1486] <Abs 80>
John of Swk St Saviour; Swk St Olave [DW/PA/7/4 f.214; 1537]
William of Bermondsey [PRO; PCC Will 1504]
CURR *see* KERR
CURSELL
John of Mortlake [DW/PA/7/2 f.34; 1492]
CURSON
Agnes of Camberwell - 'Dimocke'[DW/PA/7/7 f.39; DW/PA/5/1595/21] <Abs 77>
Christopher of Camberwell - Dulwich [HRO; 1593 B18]
(Sir) Robert of Bermondsey, knight [PRO; PCC Will 1550]
CURTEN
John, alias John Clarke of Swk St Olave [DW/PA/7/7 f.48; DW/PA/5/1595/22] <Abs 90>
CURTIS (CORTES,CORTEYS,CORTYS,COURTES,CURTEIS,CURTES,CURTESSE,CURTEYS, CURTISSE,CURTYSE)
Ellen Jennyn, formerly Ellen Curteys of Clapham [PRO; PCC Will 1553]
Henry of Guildford St Mary [DW/PA/7/1 f.90; 1489] <Abs 302>
Humphrey of Croydon, senior, husbandman [LPL; 96/705; Will 1624]
John of Esher [DW/PA/5/1578/33]
John of Clapham [PRO; PCC Will 1540]
Piers of Kingston [PRO; PCC Will 1505]
Richard of Swk St Olave [DW/PA/7/13 f.311; DW/PA/5/1646/11]
Robert of Swk St Saviour [DW/PA/5/1568/50]
Robert' of Guildford Holy Trinity, rector [HRO; Reg.Stra pp.52-53; 1330]
' *Only initial is given in register, full name supplied from clergy list.*
Susan of Croydon, widow [LPL; 96/706; Will 1624]
Thomas, alias Thomas Perry of Ewell [PRO; PCC Will 1595 *and* 1596]
Thomas of Lambeth [PRO; PCC Admon 1589]
Thomas of Puttenham [DW/PA/7/8 f.177; DW/PA/5/1610/40]
Thomas of Puttenham [DW/PA/7/12 f.107; DW/PA/5/1632/18]
Thomas of Swk St Saviour, oarmaker [DW/PA/5/1588/62]
Walter of ... [LPL; 96/3871; Will 1627]
William of West Molesey, yeoman [DW/PA/7/13 f.240; DW/PA/5/1642/18]
CURTNESHE *see* COURTNESH
CURWEN (KYRWYN)
Robert of Wandsworth, yeoman [DW/PA/5/1563/7]
CUSSETT
John of Camberwell [DW/PA/7/1 f.39; 1486] <Abs 125>
CUSTANCE (CUSTONS)
Edmund of Camberwell - Dulwich, husbandman [DW/PA/7/8 f.333; DW/PA/5/1614/27]
John of Mitcham; Carshalton, husbandman [DW/PA/7/5 f.95; 1539]
CUTFIN (CUTTEFYN)
Ralph of Tooting [DW/PA/7/2 f.41; 1493]
CUTHBERTE
William of Swk St Saviour; Swk St George; Mitcham; Nutfield, butcher [DW/PA/5/1604/13]
CUTLE *see* CUTTLE
CUTLER (CUTTLER)
Elizabeth of Long Ditton, widow [DW/PA/7/13 f.427; DW/PA/5/1643/28]
George of Kingston, gent. [PRO; PCC 1643]

CUTLER (CUTTLER) [*continued*]
John of Long Ditton, shoemaker [DW/PA/7/11 f.540; DW/PA/5/1629/23]
John of Swk St Olave, citizen and woodmonger [DW/PA/7/12 f.223; DW/PA/5/1634/20]
John of Swk St Saviour - Old Paris Garden Liberty [DW/PA/7/11 f.543; DW/PA/5/1629/24]
John of Worplesdon - Spicers; Swk St George, clerk and parson [DW/PA/5/1593/16]
Katherine of Swk St Olave, widow [DW/PA/7/13 f.120; DW/PA/5/1641/24]
Robert of Swk St Saviour [DW/PA/7/7 f.641; DW/PA/5/1608/31] <Abs 1201>
CUTSON
William of Banstead, vicar [DW/PA/7/5 f.11; 1538] <Abs 5>
CUTT (CUTTE,CUTTS)
Elizabeth of Barnes [PRO; PCC Admon 1638]
Henry of Chertsey, yeoman [DW/PA/5/1588/72]
John of Chertsey, yeoman [DW/PA/7/11 f.95; DW/PA/5/1624/33]
John of Thorpe [DW/PA/7/2 f.191; 1523]
John of Windlesham - Bagshot [PRO; PCC Admon 1564]
Richard of Chertsey, husbandman [DW/PA/7/12 f.133; DW/PA/5/1632/22]
William of Chertsey, husbandman [HRO; 1596 B14]
CUTTEFYN *see* CUTFIN
CUTTLE (CUTLE)
Walter of Carshalton, husbandman [DW/PA/7/8 f.115; DW/PA/5/1610/41]
CUTTLER *see* CUTLER
CUTTS *see* CUTT
CUYPERS
Rieynerus of Swk St Olave [DW/PA/7/2 f.67; 1500]
CYMONDE *see* SIMMONDS

DABES
Agnes of Swk, widow of Thomas [DW/PA/5/1575/72]
Thomas of Swk St Saviour [DW/PA/5/1558/77]*
see also DIBBS
DABORN (DABORNE,DABYRNE,DALBORN,DAWBENE,DAWBER,DAWBORN,DAWBORNE)
Augustine of Newington [LPL; 98/1 ff.49v,64r; Will 1633 *and* 1634]
Edmund of Esher [DW/PA/5/1581/58]
Edward of Wandsworth; Putney [DW/PA/7/6 f.172; DW/PA/5/1559/157]
Elizabeth of Swk St Olave, widow [DW/PA/7/7 f.563; DW/PA/5/1606/33] <Abs 1052>
Elizabeth of Worplesdon [DW/PA/7/12 f.308; DW/PA/5/1635/25]
Henry of Worplesdon [DW/PA/7/13 f.46; DW/PA/5/1639/46]
James of Esher, husbandman [DW/PA/7/11 f.183; DW/PA/5/1625/61]
Joan of Newington, widow [LPL; 96/736; 98/1 f.88v; Will 1638]
John of Guildford, senior [PRO; PCC Will 1549]
John of Guildford [PRO; PCC Will 1558]
John of Leatherhead, mercer [DW/PA/5/1588/76]
Richard of Woking, husbandman [DW/PA/5/1580/63]
Robert of Swk [*in* DW/PA/5/1563/13]
Robert of Worplesdon, husbandman [HRO; 1594 B13]
Thomas of Chobham, labourer [DW/PA/7/7 f.16; DW/PA/5/1595/23] <Abs 35>
Thomas of Cobham [DW/PA/7/2 f.143; 1520]
Thomas of Waverley [PRO; PCC Will 1494]

DABORN (DABORNE,DABYRNE,DALBORN,DAWBENE,DAWBER,DAWBORN,DAWBORNE)[*continued*]

Thomas of Worplesdon, yeoman [DW/PA/7/10 f.252; DW/PA/5/1622/21]

William of Rotherhithe [PRO; PCC Admon 1604]

DACCHIN *see* DE DACCHIN

DACKOMB (DACKOMBE)

Christian of St Martha's - Chilworth [PRO; PCC Will 1471]

Nicholas of Sheen, widow [PRO; PCC Admon 1640]

DADSOME

George of Ashtead [DW/PA/7/11 f.568; DW/PA/5/1630/28]

DAGANEY

Richard of Egham [DW/PA/7/1 f.68; 1487] <Abs 224>

DAGAT

Robert of Swk St Margaret [DW/PA/7/4 f.73; 1534]

DAGNOLL

Thomas of Bermondsey, glover [DW/PA/7/11 f.206; DW/PA/5/1625/56]

DAKIN

Thomas of Seale, curate [HRO; 1574 B62]

see also DEACON

DALAMER

John of Lambeth, waterman [DW/PA/7/2 f.65; 1500]

DALBORN *see* DABORN

DALE

John of Dorking, yeoman [DW/PA/7/11 f.382; DW/PA/5/1626/39]

Robert of Chertsey, servant to the Queen [HRO; 1527 B8]

DALEY *see* DALLEY

DALLE *see* DE LA DALLE

DALLENDER (DALLYNDER)

Edward of Buckland, gent. [PRO; PCC Will 1628]

John of Buckland; Leigh, gent. [DW/PA/7/9 f.220; DW/PA/5/1617/32]

Richard of Leigh, gent. [PRO; PCC 1638]

Roger of Buckland; Reigate; Betchworth [DW/PA/7/7 f.238; DW/PA/5/1598/24] <Abs 420>

William of Buckland, esq. [PRO; PCC Will 1618]

DALLEY (DALLY,DALY,DAYLY,DOLBYE,DOLLEY,DOLY,DOWLEY,DULLEY)

Bernard of Kingston, blacksmith [DW/PA/7/10 f.96; DW/PA/5/1619/33]

Daniel of Horsell, tailor [DW/PA/7/12 f.169; DW/PA/5/1633/43]

James of Esher, husbandman, junior [DW/PA/5/1557/132]

James of Esher [DW/PA/5/1563/6]

James of Esher [DW/PA/7/7 f.261; DW/PA/5/1599/17] <Abs 464>

James of Horsell, tailor [HRO; 1623 B13]

Jane of Newington, widow [PRO; PCC Admon 1628]

Joan of Chobham [DW/PA/7/6 f.64; DW/PA/5/1559/37]

John (grandson of James) of Horsell, servant to John Potter [DW/PA/7/9 f.89; DW/PA/5/1615/29]

John of Swk St Saviour [DW/PA/7/13 f.469; DW/PA/5/1648/5]

John of Walton on Thames - Apps, husbandman [DW/PA/5/1575/58]

John of Walton on Thames [DW/PA/7/7 f.562; DW/PA/5/1606/31] <Abs 1051>

Richard of Esher [HRO; Reg. Way 1 pp.74, 76; 1462]

Richard of Pyrford [DW/PA/7/5 f.173; 1540]

Richard of Walton on Thames, husbandman [DW/PA/7/10 f.164; DW/PA/5/1621/32]

Robert of Thames Ditton - Claygate [DW/PA/7/11 f.129; DW/PA/5/1624/34]

Robert of West Molesey, tailor [DW/PA/7/7 f.59; DW/PA/5/1596/19] <Abs 112>

DALLEY (DALLY,DALY,DAYLY,DOLBYE,DOLLEY,DOLY,DOWLEY,DULLEY) [*continued*]
Thomas of Great Bookham, shepherd [DW/PA/7/10 f.265; DW/PA/5/1622/22]
Thomas of Fetcham [DW/PA/7/13 f.289; DW/PA/5/1643/29]
Thomas of East Molesey [*in* DW/PA/5/1545/10]
Thomas of Walton on Thames - Hersham, yeoman [HRO; 1604 B17]
Thomas of Walton on Thames - Hersham [DW/PA/7/11 f.109; DW/PA/5/1624/35]
William of Barnes [LPL; 96/714; 98/1 f.73r; Will 1636]

DALLING (DALLYN,DOLLINGE,DOLLYN,DOLWYN)
Ann of Kingston, widow [DW/PA/5/1580/50]
Christopher of Chobham, husbandman [DW/PA/5/1558/86]*
Joseph of Barnes [PRO; PCC Will 1620] <Soame 737>
William of Egham, labourer [DW/PA/5/1563/63]
William of Kingston; Swk, carpenter [DW/PA/7/4 f.214; 1537]
William of Leatherhead [DW/PA/7/8 f.4; DW/PA/5/1608/32]

DALLISON
Martin of ...., citizen and wax chandler [DW/PA/7/11 f.149; DW/PA/5/1625/57]

DALLY *see* DALLEY

DALLYN *see* DALLING

DALLYNDER *see* DALLENDER

DALTON (DAWLTON)
Elizabeth of Ockley, widow [DW/PA/7/8 f.231; DW/PA/5/1612/43]
Elizabeth of Swk St Saviour, widow [DW/PA/7/7 f.527; DW/PA/5/1606/32] <Abs 994>
George of Swk St Saviour, citizen and joiner [DW/PA/7/11 f.369; DW/PA/5/1626/40]
Henry of Swk St Saviour; Enfield, Middlesex; Lambeth - Lambeth Dean, Norwood; St Giles Cripplegate, London, citizen and joiner,, senior [DW/PA/5/1605/25] <Abs U137>
Joan of Ockley, widow [DW/PA/7/12 f.107; DW/PA/5/1632/27]
Peter of Abinger, yeoman [DW/PA/5/1607/34] <Abs U195>
Peter of Lambeth, groom of the privy larder of the king [DW/PA/7/4 f.131; 1535]
Ralph of Abinger [PRO; PCC Will 1494]
Ralph of Abinger [DW/PA/7/2 f.101; 1514]
Ralph of Abinger, yeoman, senior [DW/PA/5/1570/42]
Ralph of Abinger, yeoman [DW/PA/7/12 f.11; DW/PA/5/1631/33]
Ralph of Dorking, yeoman [DW/PA/7/12 f.26; DW/PA/5/1631/34]
Ralph of Dorking [PRO; PCC 1633]
Ralph of Ewhurst; Ockley; Abinger; Cranleigh; Wisborough Green, Sussex [DW/PA/7/7 f.360; DW/PA/5/1602/26] <Abs 661>
Richard of Abinger [BM; Add.Ms 24,925 f.19v; 1544] <Abs 45>
Richard of Abinger, yeoman [DW/PA/5/1570/80]
Richard of Dorking, yeoman [DW/PA/7/12 f.423; DW/PA/5/1637/37]
Richard of Ewhurst; Ockley; Abinger, yeoman [DW/PA/7/9 f.180; DW/PA/5/1616/32]
Richard of Leatherhead, yeoman [DW/PA/7/13 f.206; DW/PA/5/1642/24]
Robert of Abinger, yeoman [DW/PA/7/13 f.87; DW/PA/5/1640/41]
Thomas of Godalming, tailor [DW/PA/7/10 f.284; DW/PA/5/1623/32]
Thomas of Newington, bachelor [PRO; PCC Admon 1631]
Thomas of Ockley, tailor [DW/PA/7/11 f.510; DW/PA/5/1629/25]
William of Ockley [HRO; 1633 A027]
William of Swk St Saviour [DW/PA/7/7 f.17; DW/PA/5/1595/24] <Abs 36>

DALWIN (DALWEN)
  Charles of Swk St Saviour [DW/PA/7/12 f.138; DW/PA/5/1632/31]
  William of Egham [HRO; Reg. CCB 20 p.3; 1563]
DALY *see* DALLEY
DAM'BEN *see* DAWBUYE
DAMPORT (DAMPORTE)
  Henry of Richmond [PRO; PCC Admon 1580]
  James of Lambeth [PRO; PCC Will 1471]
  Thomas of Kingston, tailor, senior [DW/PA/7/7 f.8; DW/PA/5/1595/25] <Abs 19>
  Thomas of Kingston [PRO; PCC 1648]
  William of Tooting [PRO; PCC Admon 1624]
DANASTER
  John of Chobham [PRO; PCC Will 1504]
DANBECHIES
  John of London [DW/PA/5/1563/14]
DANBY
  William of Limpsfield, parson [DW/PA/5/1572/8]*
DANCER (DANSIR,DAWNCER)
  Giles of Swk St Saviour, waterman [DW/PA/7/10 f.264; DW/PA/5/1622/23]
  William of Swk St Saviour [DW/PA/5/1576/41]
DANE (DAYNE)
  George of Limpsfield, senior [PRO; PCC 1633]
  John of Horne [PRO; PCC 1649]
  John of Lingfield - Prinkham, yeoman [PRO; PCC Will 1624]
  Katherine of Lingfield, spinster [DW/PA/7/12 f.258; DW/PA/5/1634/34]
  Mary of Horne [DW/PA/7/11 f.172; DW/PA/5/1625/58]
  Richard of Lingfield [DW/PA/7/3 f.180; 1531]
  Robert of Lingfield [DW/PA/5/1569/29]
  Robert of Lingfield, yeoman [DW/PA/5/1604/14] <Abs U103>
  Thomas of Burstow [LPL; 96/720; Will 1617]
  Thomas of Lingfield [BM; Add.Ms 24,925 f.10r; 1544] <Abs 18>
  Thomas of Lingfield - Waterside, yeoman [DW/PA/7/7 f.198; DW/PA/5/1598/25] <Abs 359>
DANFORD
  Catherine, alias Catherine Davenport of Ditton, widow [PRO; PCC Admon 1643]
  Edmund, alias Edmund Davenport of Thames Ditton [PRO; PCC 1640]
  Rebecca, alias Rebecca Davenport of Ditton, spinster [PRO; PCC Admon 1643]
DANIELS (DANIELL,DANNIELL,DANYELL,DAYNNELL)
  Gerard of Walton on Thames [PRO; PCC Will 1513]
  Joan of Swk St Olave, widow [DW/PA/7/8 f.161; DW/PA/5/1611/18]
  John of Walton on Thames, gent. [PRO; PCC Will 1467]
  Nicholas of Lambeth, yeoman of H.M.'s guard [DW/PA/5/1586/40]*
  Thomas of Swk St Margaret [DW/PA/7/4 f.132; 1536]
DANNETT *see* DONNETT
DANNIELL *see* DANIELS
DANNOW
  Ann of Lambeth [PRO; PCC Admon 1642]
DANSIR *see* DANCER

DANVELL (DANVILE)
William, alias William Taileur of Weybridge - Dorney; New Windsor, Berkshire, gent. [PRO; PCC 1640]
DANYELL *see* DANIELS
DAQUIA
Signarano of Lambeth, bachelor [PRO; PCC Admon 1647]
DARBISHIRE *see* DERBYSHIRE
DARBYE *see* DERBY
DARE (DARIE,DARY,DARYE,DAYER,DAYRE,DAYRIE,DORRY,DORY)
Agnes of Elstead, widow [HRO; 1581 B30]
Blanch of Dorking - Logmore, widow [DW/PA/7/10 f.188; DW/PA/5/1620/42]
Harry of Elstead, victualler [DW/PA/5/1576/102]
Joan of Leigh, widow [DW/PA/7/12 f.305; DW/PA/5/1635/24]
John, alias John Eyere of Ash, yeoman, senior [DW/PA/5/1582/40]
Matthew of Ash, yeoman [DW/PA/7/13 f.108; DW/PA/5/1640/44]
Matthew of Leigh, husbandman, senior [HRO; 1610 B18]
Millicent of Guildford St Nicolas, widow [DW/PA/5/1578/13]
Robert of Reigate, weaver [DW/PA/7/8 f.248; DW/PA/5/1613/32]
Thomas of Ash [DW/PA/5/1578/46]
Thomas of Wonersh [DW/PA/7/2 f.100; 1515]
William of Dorking - Logmore, yeoman [DW/PA/7/8 f.372; DW/PA/5/1612/44]
William of Dorking, yeoman [HRO; 1642 B13]
DARELL *see* DARRELL
DARKE
John of Swk St Saviour [DW/PA/5/1546/64]
DARKING (DARKYNG)
John of Guildford Holy Trinity, yeoman of H.M.'s chamber [DW/PA/5/1558/84]*
DARLASON *see* DARLISON
DARLEY (DARLAYE)
Elizabeth of Tandridge [PRO; PCC Admon 1633]
Thomas of Swk St Margaret [DW/PA/7/4 f.74; 1534]
DARLING (DARLINGE)
Winifred of Swk St George, widow [DW/PA/7/7 f.607; DW/PA/5/1607/35] <Abs 1135>
DARLISON (DARLASON,DARLYNSONNE)
Elizabeth of Swk St Saviour, widow [DW/PA/5/1592/32]
Richard of Swk St Saviour [DW/PA/5/1576/149]
Thomas of Swk St George, blacksmith [DW/PA/7/7 f.403; DW/PA/5/1603/40] <Abs 747>
DARNSELL
John of Swk, chaplain (? 'Cap*') [LPL; Reg. Abp Morton f.79v; Admon 1492]
DARRELL (DARELL)
Christopher of Surrey, citizen and merchant tailor [PRO; PCC Will 1581]
Edward of Mitcham, gent., clerk of Chancery to the Queen [PRO; PCC Will 1573]
Henry of Newdigate - Ewood, senior [PRO; PCC Admon 1618]
Richard of Swk St Saviour, vintner [DW/PA/7/7 f.401; DW/PA/5/1603/41] <Abs 743>
DARY *see* DARE
DAUBENEY
(Lady) Katherine, countess of Bridgewater, formerly wife of (Sir) Rees ap Thomas, knight) of Lambeth [PRO; PCC Will 1554]

DAUSON *see* DAWSON
DAUSTYN
William of Swk St Olave, silk weaver [DW/PA/7/11 f,586; DW/PA/5/1630/29]
DAVENAUNTE
John of Croydon [PRO; PCC Will 1596]
DAVENPORT (DAVENPORTE)
Catherine, alias Catherine Danford of Ditton, widow [PRO; PCC Admon 1643]
Edmund, alias Edmund Danford of Thames Ditton [PRO; PCC 1640]
Henry of Richmond, gent,, senior [PRO; PCC Admon 1580]
Rebecca, alias Rebecca Danford of Ditton, spinster [PRO; PCC Admon 1643]
DAVEY *see* DAVY
David, Griffin ap David ap Eign of Richmond [PRO; PCC Will 1501]
DAVIE *see* DAVY
DAVIS (DAVIES,DAVYES)
Agnes of East Clandon; Wonersh, widow of Arthur [DW/PA/7/9 f,335; DW/PA/5/1620/43]
Amy of Kingston, widow [PRO; PCC 1643]
Edward of Lambeth [PRO; PCC Will 1611] <Abs, SAC v,35 p,40>
Edward of Swk St Saviour [DW/PA/7/10 f,107; DW/PA/5/1619/34]
Elizabeth of Carshalton; Sutton, widow [GL; Archdeaconry Court of London Will 1636]
Evan of Swk St Mary Overy, pewterer [DW/PA/7/9 f,278; 1619]
Evan of Bermondsey [PRO; PCC 1641]
Evans of Swk St Olave [DW/PA/5/1582/107]
Griffin of Swk St George [DW/PA/5/1592/30]
Hugh of Swk St Saviour, waterman [DW/PA/7/8 f,56; DW/PA/5/1609/39]
Isabel of Lambeth, widow [DW/PA/5/1579/33]*
John of ,,,, chandler, citizen and haberdasher [DW/PA/7/11 f,512; DW/PA/5/1629/27]
John of Swk St Olave, feltmaker [DW/PA/5/1593/146]
John of Swk St Olave, victualler [DW/PA/7/7 f,524; DW/PA/5/1607/36] <Abs 988>
John of Guildford 1596 [*This is error in Abs 113 of DW/PA/7/7 for Davie*]
Judith of Swk St George, widow [DW/PA/7/11 f,184; DW/PA/5/1625/60]
Katherine of Lambeth, widow of Edward, innkeeper [DW/PA/7/9 f,315; DW/PA/5/1619/35]
Mary of Swk St Saviour, widow [DW/PA/7/8 f,352; DW/PA/5/1612/45]
Nicholas of Swk St Olave [DW/PA/7/8 f,378; DW/PA/5/1612/46]
Richard, alias Richard Davye of Shere, sawyer [HRO; 1596 B17]
Richard of Shere, husbandman [DW/PA/5/1621/33]
Richard of Swk St Olave, victualler [DW/PA/7/10 f,200; DW/PA/5/1621/34A]
Robert of Croydon [PRO; PCC Will 1618]
Robert, alias Robert Cliffe of Wandsworth, yeoman [DW/PA/5/1563/7]
Roger of Lambeth, waterman [DW/PA/5/1579/32]*
Susan of Swk St Olave, widow [DW/PA/7/12 f,170; DW/PA/5/1633/44]
Thomas of West Molesey, labourer [DW/PA/7/11 f,565; DW/PA/5/1630/30]
Thomas of Swk St Olave, labourer [DW/PA/7/12 f,46; DW/PA/5/1632/28]
Walter of Rotherhithe (died overseas) [PRO; PCC Admon 1649]
Walter of Swk St George, tailor [DW/PA/7/12 f,119; DW/PA/5/1632/30]
William of Cheam [PRO; PCC Will 1628]
William of Clapham, labourer [DW/PA/7/8 f,58; DW/PA/5/1609/38]
DAVY (DAVEY,DAVIE,DAVYE)
,,, (male) of Woking [DW/PA/5/1558/78]*
Arthur of East Clandon, yeoman [HRO; 1619 B19]

DAVY (DAVEY,DAVIE,DAVYE) [*continued*]

Edmund of Lambeth [DW/PA/7/3 f.141; 1530]

Edmund of Stoke Dabernon - Oxshott, husbandman [DW/PA/7/11 f.535; DW/PA/5/1629/26]

Edward of Chobham [HRO; 1639 AD58]

Elias of Croydon [PRO; PCC Will 1455]

Henry of Swk St Saviour [DW/PA/5/1563/123]*

Joan of Albury - Farley Green, widow [DW/PA/5/1593/18]

Joan of Stoke Dabernon, widow [HRO; 1604 B18]

John of Bermondsey, citizen and draper [GL; Archdeaconry Court of London Will 1612]

John of Blechingley [DW/PA/7/2 f.25; 1492]

John of Chobham, tanner [DW/PA/7/7 f.187; DW/PA/5/1598/22] <Abs 342>

John of Croydon [PRO; PCC Admon 1560]

John of Guildford, weaver [DW/PA/7/7 f.59; 1596] <Abs 113> [*In abstract, mistranscribed as Davis.*]

Lucy of Walton on Thames, widow [DW/PA/7/9 f.191; DW/PA/5/1616/33]

Peter of Guildford, tailor [DW/PA/5/1578/76]

Peter of Send, priest [HRO; 1561 B43-44]

Richard of Shere, sawyer [HRO; 1596 B17]

Richard of Walton on Thames, husbandman [DW/PA/7/7 f.372; DW/PA/5/1602/27] <Abs 685>

Richard of Woking [DW/PA/7/7 f.301; DW/PA/5/1600/24] <Abs 539>

Roger of Kingston - Coombe [PRO; PCC Will 1496]

Roger of Stoke Dabernon [DW/PA/7/7 f.349; DW/PA/5/1601/30] <Abs 641>

DAVYLL

Harry of ... [DW/PA/7/4 f.87; 1534]

DAWBENE,DAWBENER,DAWBER,DAWBERNE,DAWBORN,DAWBORNE *see* DABORN

DAWBUYE (DAM'BEN)

Giles of Swk St Olave, citizen and painter [DW/PA/5/1569/17]

DAWE (DAW,DAWES,DAWSE)

(Sir) Abraham of Putney, knight, citizen and skinner [PRO; PCC 1640]

Brian of Lingfield, husbandman [DW/PA/5/1578/24]

Christopher of Ewell [DW/PA/7/4 f.146; 1536]

George of Lingfield, yeoman [DW/PA/7/7 f.134; DW/PA/5/1597/32] <Abs 246>

Joan of Ripley, widow [DW/PA/5/1587/15]

John of ... [DW/PA/7/7 f.371; DW/PA/5/1602/25] <Abs 683>

John of Send, husbandman [DW/PA/7/11 f.382; DW/PA/5/1626/41]

John of Worplesdon [DW/PA/7/6 f.69; DW/PA/5/1559/64]

(Lady) Judith of Putney [PRO; PCC Admon 1642]

Nicholas of Wimbledon, bachelor [PRO; PCC Will 1625]

Richard of Battersea - Penge; Beckenham, Kent [DW/PA/7/1 f.78; 1488] <Abs 255>

Thomas of ... (proved at Guildford) [DW/PA/5/1591/36]

William of Rotherhithe [DW/PA/7/13 f.126; DW/PA/5/1640/47]

William of Swk St Olave, cutler [DW/PA/7/11 f.117; DW/PA/5/1624/36]

DAWKINS (DAWKNIES)

Thomas of ... (? near Egham) [DW/PA/7/8 f.380; DW/PA/5/1612/47]

DAWLTON *see* DALTON

DAWNCER *see* DANCER

DAWSE *see* DAWE

DAWSON (DAUSON)

Christopher of Swk St Olave, citizen and turner [*Flemish churchyard*][DW/PA/5/1603/42] <Abs U65>

DAWSON (DAUSON) [*continued*]
John of Kingston [DW/PA/7/1 f.72; 1487] <Abs 237>
John of Swk St Saviour, waterman [DW/PA/7/11 f.183; DW/PA/5/1625/62]
Ralph of Rotherhithe, rector [PRO; PCC Will 1611]
Thomas of Swk St Saviour, cutler [DW/PA/7/7 f.614; DW/PA/5/1607/37] <Abs 1146>
Thomas of Swk St Saviour, alebrewer [DW/PA/7/12 f.171; DW/PA/5/1633/45]
Thomas of Swk St Saviour, porter [DW/PA/7/12 f.417; DW/PA/5/1638/37]

DAWTON
Emery of Abinger; Leatherhead [DW/PA/5/1550/51]

DAWY *see* DAVY

DAY (DAYE,DEY,DEYE)
Ann of Swk St Olave, widow [DW/PA/7/7 f.245; DW/PA/5/1599/18] <Abs 433>
Edward of Shalford [DW/PA/7/11 f.499; DW/PA/5/1629/28]
Edward of Worplesdon, tailor [DW/PA/5/1588/59]
Elizabeth of Lambeth, widow [DW/PA/5/1587/73]
Ellen of Chertsey, widow [DW/PA/7/13 f.342; 1644]
John of Egham, husbandman [DW/PA/5/1558/83]
John of Swk; Gosport, Hampshire, sailor [DW/PA/7/11 f.61; DW/PA/5/1623/33]
Richard of Thames Ditton [DW/PA/7/5 f.164; 1540]
Thomas of Chelsham, yeoman, senior [DW/PA/7/13 f.397; DW/PA/5/1646/13]
Thomas of Egham - Rusham, yeoman [DW/PA/7/7 f.563; DW/PA/5/1606/34] <Abs 1053>
Thomas of Frensham - Shottermill, tanner [DW/PA/5/1622/24]
Thomas of Kingston [DW/PA/7/2 f.39; 1493]
William of Chertsey [DW/PA/7/3 f.172; 1531]

DAYER *see* DARE

DAYLY *see* DALLEY

DAYNNELL *see* DANIELS

DAYRE,DAYRIE *see* DARY

DEACON (DEAKON,DEKON)
Edward of Petersham, labouring man [DW/PA/7/10 f.113; DW/PA/5/1619/36]
Harry of Leatherhead [DW/PA/7/5 f.114; 1539]
Joan of Walton on Thames, widow [DW/PA/5/1591/84]
Joan of Wotton; Walton on Thames [DW/PA/7/8 f.199; DW/PA/5/1610/42
Thomas of Ockham, yeoman [DW/PA/7/13 f.123; DW/PA/5/1640/46]
Thomas of Richmond [PRO; PCC Will 1597]
Thomas of Walton on Thames, blacksmith [DW/PA/7/8 f.134; DW/PA/5/1610/43]
William of Ockham [HRO; 1603 B14]

DEAKES
John of St Martin in the Fields, Middlesex [SRO; 43/39/7; 1620]

DEANE (a DEANE,atte DENNE,DENE)
Alice of Alfold, widow [DW/PA/7/8 f.99; DW/PA/5/1610/44]
Elizabeth, alias Elizabeth Pigott of Newington, widow [PRO; PCC Admon 1629]
Elizabeth of Swk St George [DW/PA/7/11 f.550; DW/PA/5/1629/29]
Gunnilda of Newdigate [BM; Add.Ms 17,295; 1318]
Henry of Blechingley (died overseas) [PRO; PCC Admon 1636]
Henry of Swk St George, brewer [DW/PA/7/11 f.138; DW/PA/5/1624/37]
Joan of Guildford [DW/PA/7/11 f.451; DW/PA/5/1628/26]
John of Fetcham; Leatherhead [DW/PA/7/3 f.145; 1530]
Margery of Fetcham, widow [DW/PA/5/1571/87]
Richard of Abinger, clerk and rector [PRO; PCC Will 1558]

DEANE (a DEANE,atte DENNE,DENE) [*continued*]
Richard, alias Richard Farley of Albury [DW/PA/5/1561/37]
Richard of Alfold, husbandman [HRO; 1598 AD17]
Richard of Wandsworth, husbandman, senior [DW/PA/7/13 f.377; 1644]
Robert of Chobham, husbandman [DW/PA/7/10 f.195; DW/PA/5/1621/34B]
Robert of Richmond, yeoman [PRO; PCC 1630] <Scroope 1030>
Thomas of Bermondsey [PRO; PCC 1639]
Thomas of Fetcham [DW/PA/5/1579/7]*
Thomas of Guildford St Mary, bachelor [PRO; PCC Admon 1649]
William of Newdigate [DW/PA/7/9 f.39; DW/PA/5/1614/21]
William of Swk St Olave, cordwainer [DW/PA/5/1591/54]
see also ADEANE
DEARE (DEERE)
Joan of Richmond, widow [PRO; PCC Will 1623]
John, alias John Fire of ... [DW/PA/7/7 f.79; 1596] <Abs 144>
DEARING (DEAREINGE,DEARINGE,DEERING,DEERINGE,DERING,DERYNGE)
Alice of Newington, spinster [PRO; PCC Will 1621]
John of Swk St Saviour, yeoman of H.M. chamber [DW/PA/5/1578/88]
Robert of Croydon [PRO; PCC Admon 1643]
Thomas of Swk St Olave [DW/PA/7/10 f.187; DW/PA/5/1620/44]
William of Shalford, yeoman [HRO; 1596 B21]
de ARTEM *see* ARTEM
DE ARUNDEL
William of Mickleham [PRO; E327 771; 1295]
DE ASCH in BRABANCIA
Ludocus of Swk St Olave [DW/PA/7/2 f.66; 1500]
DEBES *see* DIBBS
DE BEYGEN *see* BEYGEN
DEBONSOLIS
Thomas, alias Thomas Butsall of Ewell [PRO; PCC Will 1612]
DEBUNCORTE
Bartholomew of Dunsfold [DW/PA/7/7 f.257; DW/PA/5/1599/19] <Abs 453>
de BURGH
John of Beddington - Wallington [BM; Add.Ms 23,177; 1437]
DE CARON
Ann, alias Ann Vandelden of Lambeth - South Lambeth [PRO; PCC Admon 1635]
DE CHANGE
Pieter, alias Pieter Chanbye of ... [DW/PA/5/1593/113]
DE COBET
Pieter of Swk St Olave, silk weaver [DW/PA/5/1593/141]
DE COLONIA
Petrig of Swk St Thomas, chirurgeon [DW/PA/5/1550/103]
DE DACCHIN
Jehenne, alias Jehenne Le cocq of Swk St Olave wife of William Dupysre [DW/PA/5/1570/34]
DEE
Richard of Lambeth [PRO; PCC Will 1593]
DEERE *see* DEARE
de EUCK *see* EUCK
DEFFORDE
Thomas of Newington [PRO; PCC Will 1497]

DE FRETON
  Roger, dean of Chichester; canon of York; of Ratlesden, Suffolk; Dorking; Aldingbourne, Sussex; St Bride, London [LPL; Reg. Abp Courtenay ff.195,203; Will 1383]
DEFTE
  Stephen of Swk St George [DW/PA/7/8 f.8; DW/PA/5/1608/35]
de EIICK
  Francis of Swk St Olave [DW/PA/7/3 f.159; 1530]
DE GRACE *see* FARDYNG DE GRACE
DE HONE
  Calix of ... [*French*] [DW/PA/5/1571/29]
DEKON *see* DEACON
DE LA DALLE (DEL DALLE)
  Daniel of Swk St Thomas [DW/PA/5/1578/5]
DELAHAY
  George of Reigate, esq. [PRO; PCC Will 1609] <Abs. SAC v.23 pp.136-137>
  William of Kingston [DW/PA/7/11 f.136; DW/PA/5/1624/38]
DE LANNAY *see* LANNAY
DE LANO *see* LANO
DE LA POOLE
  Margaret of Bermondsey - Bermondsey Monastery [PRO; PCC Will 1473]
DEL DALLE *see* DE LA DALLE
DELDEN (van DELDEN)
  Ann, alias Ann Dè Caron of Lambeth - South Lambeth [PRO; PCC Admon 1635]
DELDESDEN *see* DELS DE ALE
DE LESTRE
  Anthony of ... [DW/PA/5/1569/73]
DELEWOOD
  Robert, alias Robert Wood of Carshalton, weaver [DW/PA/7/7 f.52; DW/PA/5/1596/18] <Abs 98>
de LINSELL
  Allard of Swk St Olave; London (born at Blandin, near Tournai, France) [*French*] [DW/PA/7/13 f.414; DW/PA/5/1645/32
DELL
  Elizabeth of Bermondsey, widow [PRO; PCC Will 1626]
  Phillip of Wandsworth, cordwainer [DW/PA/7/13 f.12; DW/PA/5/1640/40]
DELLAR (DELLER)
  James of Long Ditton - Tolworth [Admon *in* DW/PA/5/1559/30]
  James of Long Ditton [DW/PA/7/3 f.173; 1531]
  John of Long Ditton - Tolworth [DW/PA/7/4 f.223; 1537]
  William of Walton on Thames - Pains Hill [DW/PA/7/5 f.46; 1538] <Abs 119>
DEL MALAISE
  Jermain of Swk St Olave; London [DW/PA/7/11 f.412; DW/PA/5/1627/25]
DELS DE ALE (DELDESDEN)
  John of Blechingley [DW/PA/5/1582/102]
DELVE
  Thomas of Lambeth - South Lambeth, labourer [DW/PA/5/1555/27]
DELVER
  Thomas of Tatsfield, yeoman, senior [PRO; PCC Will 1618]
DE MAECHT
  Phillip of Mortlake [LPL; 98/1 f.102r; Will 1639]
DE MAYER (DE MEYER)
  Arnold of Swk St George, silk weaver [DW/PA/7/11 f.204; DW/PA/5/1625/63]

DE MAYER (DE MEYER) [*continued*]
John of Swk St Thomas, weaver [DW/PA/7/11 f.223; DW/PA/5/1620/45] <Abs U243>
see also MEIR (DE MEIER)

DE MEILEMEESTER
William of Oudenarde, Belgium [DW/PA/5/1593/47]

DEMES
Richard of Petersham; Richmond [DW/PA/7/3 f.187; 1531]

DEMEYER *see* DE MAYER

DE MOULYM
Simon of ... (mother of Troy, France) [*French*] [DW/PA/5/1593/191]

DENAM *see* DENHAM

DE NAVARRE
Daniel of Swk St Olave [DW/PA/7/8 f.87; DW/PA/5/1609/40]

DENBY (DENBIE,DENNBE,DENBYE)
Joan of Chertsey, widow [DW/PA/7/9 f.189; DW/PA/5/1616/34]
Maurice of Chertsey [PRO; PCC Will 1590]
Richard of Caterham, yeoman [DW/PA/7/12 f.407; DW/PA/5/1637/36]
William of Buckland [PRO; PCC Admon 1648]
William of East Molesey, miller [DW/PA/7/6 f.4; DW/PA/5/1559/241]

DENDEN (vanden DENDEN)
Alexander of Swk St George; London, merchant stranger [DW/PA/7/13 f.273; DW/PA/5/1644/19]

DENDY (DENDI,DENDIE,DENDYE)
George of Abinger, husbandman [DW/PA/7/11 f.16; DW/PA/5/1623/35]
George of Ewhurst, senior [DW/PA/7/11 f.417; DW/PA/5/1626/42]
George of Ewhurst, senior [DW/PA/5/1576/37]
George of Ewhurst, yeoman, junior [DW/PA/5/1591/24]
John of Dorking, tailor [DW/PA/5/1602/29] <Abs U47>
John of Ewhurst [DW/PA/7/5 f.212; 1541]
John of Ewhurst, gent. [DW/PA/5/1561/17]
John of Ewhurst, yeoman, senior [DW/PA/7/12 f.330; DW/PA/5/1636/30]
Margaret of Abinger, servant [DW/PA/7/8 f.203; DW/PA/5/1611/19]
Nicholas of Cranleigh [DW/PA/5/1570/88]
Nicholas of Ewhurst [PRO; PCC Admon 1588]
Ralph of Ewhurst, yeoman [PRO; PCC Will 1599]
Richard of Ewhurst, senior [DW/PA/7/4 f.124; 1535]
Richard of Ewhurst, tailor [DW/PA/7/5 f.156; 1540]
Richard of Ewhurst, husbandman [DW/PA/7/7 f.211; DW/PA/5/1598/26] <Abs 377>
Richard of Ewhurst - Downhurst, yeoman [DW/PA/7/12 f.112; DW/PA/5/1632/29]
Richard of Horley [DW/PA/7/11 f.112; DW/PA/5/1624/39]
Robert of Dorking, tailor [DW/PA/7/11 ff.200,323; DW/PA/5/1625/64]
Robert of Godalming [DW/PA/7/9 f.247; DW/PA/5/1617/33]
Thomas of Abinger [DW/PA/5/1575/33]
Thomas of Buckland [DW/PA/5/1568/49]
Thomas of Cranleigh [DW/PA/7/4 f.48; 1533]
Thomas of Ewhurst, wood broker [DW/PA/5/1568/35]
Thomas of Ewhurst, yeoman [HRO; 1621 B11]
Thomas of Worplesdon, yeoman [DW/PA/7/11 f.14; DW/PA/5/1623/36]
William of Dorking, baker [DW/PA/7/13 f.465; DW/PA/5/1648/6]

DENE *see* DEANE

DENERST *see* DENHURST
DENET *see* DENNATT
DENHAM (DENAM,DYNHAM)
Anthony of Swk St George, victualler [DW/PA/7/13 f,163; DW/PA/5/1642/21B]
George of Lambeth [PRO; PCC Admon 1594]
Joan of Thorpe, widow [PRO; PCC Will 1589] <Abs SAC v,30 p,2>
(Sir) John of Egham, knight [PRO; PCC 1639]
John of Farnham, shearman [DW/PA/5/1582/39]
John of Farnham - Castle Street, draper [GL; Archdeaconry Court of London Will 1596]
Oliver of Farnham, clerk and archdeacon of Surrey [PRO; PCC Will 1500]
William of Thorpe, goldsmith [PRO; PCC Will 1583] <Abs SAC v,30 p,2 *and* v,33 p,6>
DENHURST (DENERST)
Thomas of Thorpe [HRO; 1531 B5]
DENIER,DENIOR *see* DENYER
DENIS *see* DENNIS
DENNATT (DENET,DYNNOTTE)
John of Chertsey [DW/PA/7/1 f,26; 1486] <Abs 86>
John of Ripley [DW/PA/7/4 f,119; 1535]
Robert of Godstone, yeoman [DW/PA/7/11 f,457; DW/PA/5/1628/27]
DENNBE *see* DENBY
DENNE
Vincent of Newington, Doctor of Law [PRO; PCC Will 1591]
DENNES *see* DENNIS
DENNETT *see* DENNATT
DENNING (DENYNGE)
John of Kingston [DW/PA/7/11 f,355; DW/PA/5/1625/65]
DENNIS (DENNES,DENNYS,DENYS,DEYNYS)
Charles of Godstone [PRO; PCC 1633]
Elizabeth (dau,of Richard of Lambeth, esq,), spinster [PRO; PCC Will 1604]
Joachim of Swk St Olave [DW/PA/5/1563/114]
Martin of Caterham, husbandman [DW/PA/7/13 f,200; DW/PA/5/1642/23]
Michael of Cheam, gent, [PRO; PCC Will 1518] <Abs SAC v,26 p,60>
Thomas of Burstow [PRO; PCC Will 1590]
William, canon of York; parson of St Bride's, London; Beddington; Walton; Brigsley, Lincolnshire [LPL; Reg, Abp Arundel i f,244; Will 1407]
William of Camberwell, gent, [PRO; PCC Will 1627]
DENNY (DENY)
John of Chobham [DW/PA/7/1 f,87; 1488] <Abs 292>
Thomas of Lambeth - Stockwell; Lambeth - South Lambeth; Wandsworth; Battersea, citizen and fishmonger [GL; Commissary Court of London Will 1401]
DENNYER *see* DENYER
DENNYS *see* DENNIS
DE NORBON *see* NORBON
DENT
Edmund of Lambeth - Stockwell, yeoman [DW/PA/7/7 f,642; DW/PA/5/1608/34] <Abs 1206>
DENTETHE
John of Horley [DW/PA/5/1591/44]

DENTON
Elizabeth of West Horsley [DW/PA/7/8 f.256; DW/PA/5/1611/20]
John of Bermondsey, brewer [DW/PA/5/1550/78]
DENY *see* DENNY
DENYER (DENIER,DENIOR,DENNYER,DENYAR,DENYARE,DENYOR)
Alice of Hambledon, widow [DW/PA/7/12 f.143; DW/PA/5/1633/40]
Elizabeth of Thursley [BM; Add.Ms 24,925 f.23v; 1544] <Abs 58>
Francis of Godalming - Vann; Chiddingfold - Pockford, yeoman [HRO; 1611 B21]
Francis of Hambledon [DW/PA/7/11 f.502; DW/PA/5/1629/30]
George of Godalming [DW/PA/7/8 f.20; DW/PA/5/1608/33]
Henry of Godalming, clothier [DW/PA/7/8 f.394; DW/PA/5/1612/48]
Henry of Hambledon, husbandman [DW/PA/7/13 f.95; DW/PA/5/1640/42]
Henry of Thursley, husbandman [DW/PA/5/1558/79]*
Henry of Witley, yeoman [DW/PA/7/12 f.66; DW/PA/5/1631/37]
John of Farnham [PRO; PCC Will 1563]
John of Godalming, senior [DW/PA/7/11 f.500; DW/PA/5/1629/31]
John of Godalming [PRO; PCC 1633]
Nicholas of Godalming, maltman [DW/PA/7/11 f.349; DW/PA/5/1625/66]
Thomas of Godalming, weaver, senior [DW/PA/7/9 f.79; DW/PA/5/1614/23]
Thomas of Hambledon [DW/PA/7/8 f.395; DW/PA/5/1612/49]
Thomas of Thursley [DW/PA/5/1561/83]
Thomas of Thursley, yeoman [DW/PA/7/11 f.421; DW/PA/5/1627/28]
William of Frensham [DW/PA/7/5 f.121; 1539]
William of Godalming - Tuesley, yeoman [DW/PA/7/13 f.25; DW/PA/5/1639/45]
William of Hambledon [PRO; PCC 1649]
DENYNGE *see* DENNING
DENYS *see* DENNIS
DE PAN (DE PAU)
Margaret of Swk St Olave, widow of Gilbert Tout le Monde [*French*] [DW/PA/5/1593/144]
DE QUENEULLE
Joan, alias Joan de Lannay of ...., widow of Francis [*French*] [DW/PA/7/7 f.43; DW/PA/5/1595/26] <Abs 84>
DERBY (DARBYE,DERBE,DERBYE)
John of Walton on the Hill, yeoman [DW/PA/7/11 f.328; DW/PA/5/1625/59]
Marione of Godstone [DW/PA/7/2 f.17; 1491]
Richard of Godstone [DW/PA/7/1 f.58; 1487] <Abs 192>
Robert of Godstone [DW/PA/7/5 f.190; 1540]
DERBYSHIRE (DARBISHIRE)
Mary of Battersea, widow [PRO; PCC Admon 1647]
DEREMOUNDE
Fyrmundus of Bermondsey, whitster [DW/PA/7/2 f.66; 1500]
DERICKE *see* DERRICK
DERIE *see* DERRY
DERING,DERINGE *see* DEARING
DERNFORD *see* DURNFORD
DERRICK (DERICKE,DERRICKE,DERYCK)
Agnes, alias Agnes Gilberdson of Guildford [Holy Trinity], widow [DW/PA/5/1568/53]
Alexander of Swk St Olave, hatmaker [DW/PA/5/1570/21]
Andrew, alias Andrew Gilbertsonne of Guildford [Holy Trinity], bricklayer [DW/PA/5/1570/63]

DERRICK (DERICKE,DERRICKE,DERYCK) [*continued*]
John, alias John Gilbertson of Guildford - *White Hart*, innholder [DW/PA/7/8 f,42; 1607]
John, alias John Gilbertson of Guildford Holy Trinity; Guildford St Mary; St Giles in the Fields, Middlesex, senior [DW/PA/7/8 f,242; DW/PA/5/1613/55]
John of Swk St Olave, feltmaker [DW/PA/5/1570/18]
Richard, alias Richard Gilberdsonne of Guildford [Holy Trinity] [DW/PA/5/1563/5]
Richard, alias Richard Gilbertson of Guildford Holy Trinity; Guildford St Mary; Stoke next Guildford - Slyfield Green [DW/PA/7/7 f,354; DW/PA/5/1602/33] <Abs 650>
William of Bermondsey, brewer and alien [DW/PA/7/8 f,312; DW/PA/5/1613/33]

DERRICKSON (DERICSONE)
John of Swk St Olave, beer brewer [DW/PA/5/1587/54]

DERRY (DERIE)
Edward of Swk St Saviour, carman [DW/PA/7/7 f,374; DW/PA/5/1602/28] <Abs 690>

DE RUPRIBUS
Luke of Epsom, rector and archdeacon of Surrey [PRO; E210 11304 - *no date, but he was archdeacon 1230-1239*]

DERYNGE *see* DEARING

de SANCTO MICHAELE
Lawrence of Surrey [PRO; E315/46 78; 1282]

DESNOTZ
Phillip of Swk [DW/PA/5/1581/66]

DETHICKE
Humphrey of Weybridge, esq, [PRO; PCC Admon 1642] <Abs SAC v,33 pp,34-35>

DE VOECHT
Diericke of Swk, surgeon [DW/PA/5/1578/26]

DEW (DEWE,DUE)
Alice of Cobham, widow [DW/PA/7/8 f,408; DW/PA/5/1614/20]
James of Lambeth [DW/PA/7/10 f,45; 1618]
John of Cobham, husbandman [DW/PA/7/7 f,4; DW/PA/5/1595/33] <Abs 10>
Margaret of Fetcham [DW/PA/7/12 f,241; DW/PA/5/1634/33]
Richard of Ashtead [DW/PA/7/4 f,99; 1534]

DEWALLE
Joan of Swk St Olave, widow [DW/PA/5/1563/47]

de WALWORTH
(Sir) William of Newington - Walworth, knight [PRO; PCC Will 1385]

DEWBURY (DEWBERIE,DEWBURYE)
Bartholomew of Beddington [DW/PA/5/1558/82]
Richard of Clapham [DW/PA/7/7 f,32; DW/PA/5/1595/30] <Abs 65>

DEWDNEY (DEWDNEYE,DEWEDNEY,DUDENEY,DUDENY,DUEDNEY)
Elizabeth of Betchworth [DW/PA/5/1568/28]
John of Abinger, yeoman [PRO; PCC Will 1600]
John of Ewhurst [DW/PA/5/1569/5]
Robert of Ewhurst, labourer [DW/PA/5/1576/58]
Robert of Ewhurst [PRO; PCC Admon 1580]
Thomas of Reigate, tailor [DW/PA/5/1576/148]

DEWE *see* DEW

DEWELL
Thomas of Walton on Thames [DW/PA/7/11 f,318; DW/PA/5/1626/43]

DE WILLEMS
  Adltgen of Swk St Olave, widow of Christopher [DW/PA/7/12 f.497; DW/PA/5/1638/155]
DEWSBURY *see* DUSBURYE
DEYBLE *see* DIBBLE
DEYE *see* DAY
DEYNYS *see* DENNIS
DIAPER
  Thomas of Stoke Dabernon [PRO; PCC 1632]
DIBBLE (DEYBLE,DIBLE,DYBLE)
  Alice of Long Ditton, widow [DW/PA/7/9 f.237; DW/PA/5/1617/34]
  Simon of Long Ditton; Thames Ditton, waterman [DW/PA/5/1603/43] <Abs U66>
  Thomas of Dorking, yeoman [HRO; 1608 B23]
  Thomas of Esher [BM; Add.Ms 24,925 f.22r; 1544] <Abs 51>
  William of Newdigate, yeoman [HRO; 1588 B17] [*and*] [DW/PA/5/1588/27]
DIBBS (DEBES)
  Alice of Wotton, widow [DW/PA/7/12 f.268; DW/PA/5/1635/23]
  James of Molesey [PRO; PCC Admon 1620]
  Lawrence of ... [DW/PA/7/11 f.65; DW/PA/5/1623/34]
  Richard of Walton on Thames, yeoman [DW/PA/7/11 f.217; DW/PA/5/1625/67]
  see also DABES
DICKENSON (DICONSON,DYCKYNSONE)
  Charles of Swk St Saviour, silk weaver [DW/PA/7/9 f.310; DW/PA/5/1619/37]
  Margaret, alias Margaret Shipley of Wandsworth [PRO; PCC Admon 1634]
  Peter of Weybridge, bricklayer [DW/PA/5/1563/13]
  Richard of Swk St Saviour; Swk St Mary Overy [DW/PA/7/9 f.163; DW/PA/5/1616/35]
  Richard of Swk St Saviour - Liberty of the Clink, victualler [DW/PA/7/9 f.188; DW/PA/5/1616/36]
  Robert of Ash [DW/PA/7/2 f.102; 1514]
DICKER (DYCKAR,DYKAR)
  Agnes of Carshalton [DW/PA/5/1557/16]
  Hugh of Carshalton [*in* DW/PA/5/1555/14]
DICKERMAN
  Abraham of Swk St George, cook [DW/PA/7/13 f.199; DW/PA/5/1642/22]
DICKLING (DICKLINGE)
  John of Swk St George, carpenter [DW/PA/5/1558/80]*
  Margaret of Swk St George, widow [DW/PA/5/1558/81]*
DICONSON *see* DICKENSON
DIDDLESFORD (DIDDELSFOLD,DIDLESFOLD,DUDLESFOLD,DYDELSFOLD)
  Ann of Hascombe, widow [PRO; PCC Will 1628]
  Evershed of Alfold, gent. [PRO; PCC Admon 1651]
  John of Alfold [PRO; PCC Will 1558]
  John of Alfold, yeoman [DW/PA/7/12 f.527; DW/PA/5/1636/29]
  Richard of Alfold; Pulborough - Charmanbrook, Sussex; Rudgwick, Sussex; Wisborough Green, Sussex [DW/PA/5/1593/6]
  William of Alfold [PRO; PCC 1648]
DIDLESDON (DIDDLESDON,DIDELLDOM,DYDLESDON,DYLLSDONE)
  Elizabeth of Merrow, servant [DW/PA/5/1572/5]
  Hugh of Pyrford [DW/PA/7/4 f.147; 1536]
  John of Pyrford; Send, yeoman [DW/PA/7/7 f.228; DW/PA/5/1598/27] <Abs 403>

DIDLESDON (DIDDLESDON,DIDELLDOM,DYDLESDON,DYLLSDONE) [*continued*]

John of Woking [PRO; PCC Will 1615]

Richard of Pyrford, yeoman [DW/PA/5/1570/79]

DIDLESFOLD *see* DIDDLESFORD

DIEMEN (van DYMEN)

John of Swk St Olave; Utrecht, Netherlands, 'kerner' [DW/PA/7/4 f.124; 1535]

DIEPENRIECK (van DIEPENRIECK)

Giles of ... [*Dutch*] [DW/PA/7/9 f.310; DW/PA/5/1619/122]

DIER *see* DYER

DIGBIE

George of Barnes, esq. [PRO; PCC Will 1627]

DIGG *see* DIGGS

DIGGON (DYGKYN,DYGYN)

Daniel of Godstone [PRO; PCC Admon 1610]

Joan of Horne; Lingfield, widow [DW/PA/7/9 f.299; 1618]

John of Lingfield, yeoman, senior [DW/PA/7/9 f.249; DW/PA/5/1617/35]

Thomas of Horne; Lingfield; Crawley, Sussex, yeoman [DW/PA/7/9 f.238; DW/PA/5/1617/36]

Thomas of Frensham [DW/PA/5/1550/58]

William of Frensham [DW/PA/7/3 f.170; 1531]

see also DIRKIN

DIGGS (DIGG)

Roger of Adisham, Kent; Chipstead [LPL; Reg. Abp Sudbury f.79; Will 1378]

DIGHTON

Gilbert of Lambeth - Lambeth Marsh [PRO; PCC Admon 1579]

DIKES *see* DYKE

DILCOKE

Nicholas of Carshalton, husbandman [DW/PA/7/10 f.176; DW/PA/5/1620/46]

DILKES

Eleanor of Swk St Olave, widow [DW/PA/7/12 f.204; DW/PA/5/1634/31]

DIMBLY

Roger of Bermondsey, citizen and leatherseller [DW/PA/7/11 f.326; DW/PA/5/1625/68]

DIMES *see* DYMES

DIMMING (DYMMINGE)

Joan of Frensham, widow [DW/PA/7/7 f.320; DW/PA/5/1600/22] <Abs 573>

John of Farnham, yeoman [DW/PA/7/7 f.26; DW/PA/5/1595/31] <Abs 56>

DIMMOCK (DYMOCK,DYMOCKE)

Robert of Swk St Olave, shipwright [DW/PA/5/1587/117]

Robert of Tooting Graveney, esq. [PRO; PCC Will 1593]

DINES (DYNES)

John of Lambeth [PRO; PCC 1642]

John of Wandsworth, bricklayer [DW/PA/7/12 f.203; DW/PA/5/1634/30]

William of Godalming, husbandman [HRO; 1601 B21]

DINGLEY (DYNGLEY)

Robert of Kingston, butcher [DW/PA/7/5 f.92; 1539]

Thomas of Kingston [PRO; PCC Will 1503; CCAL; 1503 f.260r]

DINNINGE (DYNNINGE) Joan 1601 [*This is an error of transcription for Dimming in the printed calendar of DW/PA/7/7* .]

DIRDOE

James of Windlesham - Bagshot [PRO; PCC 1634]

DIRKIN (DIRKYN,DORKIN,DURKIN)
Edward of Horley [DW/PA/7/8 f.50; DW/PA/5/1609/42]
Margery of Horley [DW/PA/7/8 f.376; DW/PA/5/1612/51]
Richard of Blechingley, keeper [PRO; PCC Will 1608] <Abs, SAC v.13 p.194>
Richard of Blechingley, keeper [DW/PA/7/8 f.5; DW/PA/5/1608/39]
see also DIGGON
DIRREY (DYRREY)
William of St Katherine Creechurch, London; Ewell, silk weaver [GL; Commissary Court of London Will 1611]
DIRRIFALL
John of Rotherhithe [PRO; PCC Admon 1591]
DISHER (DISCHER,DISTHAR,DYSCHERE,DYSSHER)
John of Lambeth [DW/PA/5/1576/110]
John of Merrow [HRO; Reg. Wyk 2 p.189; 1351]
William of Lambeth, husbandman [DW/PA/5/1555/28]
DISON *see* DYSON
DISTHER *see* DISCHER
DIXON (DIXSON,DYCKESON,DYCKSONE,DYXSON,DYXSONE)
Edward of Swk St Olave [DW/PA/7/3 f.141; 1530]
George of Swk St Olave, fellmonger [DW/PA/5/1557/64]
George of Swk St Olave; Windermere, Westmorland, drayman [DW/PA/7/8 f.13; DW/PA/5/1608/36]
James of Swk St Olave [DW/PA/5/1561/73]
James of Wandsworth, citizen and fishmonger [PRO; PCC Will 1592]
Joan of Weybridge; Thorpe, widow [DW/PA/7/10 f.107; DW/PA/5/1619/38]
Joan of Weybridge, widow [DW/PA/5/1624/40]
John of Leigh, Essex; Rotherhithe [PRO; PCC Admon 1632]
John of Swk St George, yeoman [DW/PA/5/1569/27]
John of Swk St Saviour [DW/PA/5/1543/11]*
Margaret of Swk St Thomas, widow of James [DW/PA/7/11 f.478; DW/PA/5/1628/28]
Robert of Mitcham [PRO; PCC Admon 1647]
William of Oxted [DW/PA/7/6 f.200; 1560]
William of Swk St Margaret [DW/PA/7/3 f.112; 1529]
William of Swk St Olave, joiner [DW/PA/5/1563/103]
Zachary of Swk St Olave, feltmaker [DW/PA/7/10 f.199; DW/PA/5/1621/35]
DOBBINS
Joseph of Rotherhithe [PRO; PCC Admon 1629]
Jane of Newington, widow [LPL; 96/761; 98/1 f.39r; Will 1632]
Richard of Lambeth [PRO; PCC 1634]
Robert of Lambeth [PRO; PCC Admon 1631]
William of Ockley, parson [HRO; 1586 B16]
DODD (DOD,DODDE)
Agnes of Swk St Olave - Horsleydown, widow [DW/PA/7/7 f.639; DW/PA/5/1608/37] <Abs 1198>
Elizabeth of Lambeth [PRO; PCC Admon 1600]
James of Tandridge; Horley; Charlwood [PRO; PCC Will 1595]
James of Tandridge, yeoman [DW/PA/7/11 f.266; DW/PA/5/1625/69]
James of Tandridge [PRO; PCC 1642]
John of Croydon - Waddon, yeoman [PRO; PCC Will 1609] <Abs, SAC v.23 p.145>
John of Godstone, petty chapman [DW/PA/5/1624/41]

DODD (DOD,DODDE) [*continued*]

John of Swk St Olave, cooper in the Ship *James Royal* [DW/PA/5/1621/36] <Abs U250>

John of Tandridge, gent. [PRO; PCC 1642]

Mary, alias Mary Meantis of Oxted, widow [PRO; PCC Admon 1648]

Michael of Caterham, husbandman [DW/PA/7/8 f.126; DW/PA/5/1610/45]

Phillip of Lambeth, brewer [DW/PA/7/7 f.319; DW/PA/5/1600/21] <Abs 570>

Phillip of Lambeth, brewer [PRO; PCC Will 1601] <Abs, SAC v.10 p.144>

Randall of Tandridge [PRO; PCC Admon 1648 *and* grant revoked 1649]

Thomas of Lingfield, yeoman [DW/PA/7/2 f.108; 1516]

William of Croydon; Tandridge [PRO; PCC Will 1543]

DODDRIDGE

Ann of Egham; Thorpe, widow [PRO; PCC 1630] <Scroope 964>

(Sir) John of Egham, knight [PRO; PCC Will 1638]

DODGESON *see* DODSON

DODGIN

Richard of Bermondsey [DW/PA/7/13 f.100; DW/PA/5/1640/43]

DODMER

John of Putney [PRO; PCC Will 1571]

Ralph of Putney, esq. [PRO; PCC Will 1558]

DODSON (DODGESON)

Ellen of Kingston, widow of William, cooper [DW/PA/7/12 f.264; DW/PA/5/1634/36]

James of Kingston, yeoman [DW/PA/5/1574/12]

Lambert of Kingston, cooper [DW/PA/7/10 f.48; 1618]

Miles of Swk St Olave, citizen and merchant tailor [DW/PA/5/1593/128]

Richard of Lambeth, labourer [DW/PA/5/1568/44]

Rowland of Swk St Thomas, labourer [DW/PA/7/11 f.468; DW/PA/5/1629/29]

Thomas of Newington [LPL; 98/1 f.123v; Will 1641]

William of Kingston [DW/PA/7/11 f.118; DW/PA/5/1624/42]

DODYN

Goraths of Swk St Olave [HRO; Reg. Way 2 p.160; 1473]

DOEMERIGHTE

Peter of Swk St Olave, yeoman [DW/PA/7/9 f.143; DW/PA/5/1615/28]

DOFFELL *see* DUFFELL

DOGGETT

James of Lingfield, husbandman [DW/PA/7/12 f.259; DW/PA/5/1634/35]

John of Oxted, husbandman [PRO; PCC Will 1618]

Nicholas of Horne [PRO; PCC 1647]

DOGGWELL

Nicholas of Walton on Thames, faggot binder [DW/PA/5/1576/74]

DOLBYE *see* DALLEY

DOLETT

John of Buckland [DW/PA/7/1 f.73; 1487] <Abs 241>

DOLLARD

Mary of Newington [LPL; 98/1 f.95r; Will 1638]

DOLLEY *see* DALLEY

DOLLINGE, DOLLYN *see* DALLING

DOLMAN

Walter of Cranleigh [PRO; PCC Will 1449]

DOLPHE

William of Swk St Margaret, waterman [DW/PA/7/3 f.182; 1531]

DOLWYN *see* DALLING

DOLY *see* DALLEY

DOMERIGHT *see* DOEMERIGHTE
DONECAN
  Thomas of ? Surrey, clerk [PRO; PCC Will 1461]
DONMOW
  Thomas of Swk St Margaret [DW/PA/7/4 f.60; 1533]
DONNE *see* DUNN
DONNESTALE *see* DUNSTALL
DONNETT (DANNETT,DONET)
  (Dame) Jane of Merstham [PRO; PCC Admon 1577]
  Thomas of Cobham [PRO; PCC Admon 1605]
  William of Chertsey - Hardwick [DW/PA/7/2 f.98; 1514]
DONWELL
  James of Swk St Saviour [DW/PA/5/1547/23]
DOPPEN
  Peter of Swk St Olave; Dusseldorf, Germany [DW/PA/5/1547/16]
DORANT *see* DURRANT
DORINGTON
  William of Tandridge [DW/PA/5/1570/67]
DORKIN *see* DIRKIN
DORMER
  Michael of Tooting, widower [PRO; PCC Admon 1647]
  Phillipa of Clapham, widow [PRO; PCC Will 1603]
DORMYN
  John of Swk St Olave, porter [DW/PA/7/12 f.164; DW/PA/5/1633/41B]
DORRANT *see* DURRANT
DORRELL
  John of Morden, husbandman [DW/PA/7/11 f.114; DW/PA/5/1624/43]
DORRY *see* DARE
DORSTEN
  Conrad of Swk, brewer [DW/PA/7/7 f.6; DW/PA/5/1595/32] <Abs 16>
DORY *see* DARE
DOUGHTY (DOUGHTIE,DOWTYE)
  Richard of Swk St Saviour, clerk and curate [DW/PA/5/1555/46]
  Robert of Kingston, baker [DW/PA/5/1579/34]*
DOUGLAS (DOUGLASSE,DOWGLAS,DUGLESSE,DUGLIS,DUGLISSE)
  Edward of Streatham - Tooting Bec [DW/PA/7/13 f.14; DW/PA/5/1639/43]
  George of Coulsdon, tailor [DW/PA/7/12 f.512; DW/PA/5/1638/38]
  Joan of Walton on Thames, widow [DW/PA/7/12 f.443; DW/PA/5/1639/41]
  Margaret, alias Margaret Heath, alias Margaret Fuller of Lingfield, widow [PRO; PCC Admon 1648 *and* PCC 1649]
  Margaret of Streatham - Tooting Bec, widow [DW/PA/7/13 f.167; DW/PA/5/1642/21A]
  Richard of Croydon [DW/PA/7/9 f.191; DW/PA/5/1616/37]
  Richard of Lingfield [PRO; PCC 1648]
DOVE
  Bartholomew of Newington [PRO; PCC Will 1556]
  Henry of Bermondsey, leatherdresser [DW/PA/7/11 f.566; DW/PA/5/1630/31]
  John of Camberwell; Lambeth [DW/PA/7/4 f.41; 1533]
  John of Camberwell - Dulwich [PRO; PCC Admon 1593]
  John of Rotherhithe, baker [DW/PA/5/1591/58]
  Richard of Newington [LPL; 98/1 f.92r; Will 1638]
  Vincent of Newington - Walworth [PRO; PCC Will 1587]

DOVEY
  Humphrey of ...., junior citizen and plasterer [DW/PA/7/12 f.439; DW/PA/5/1637/38]
DOWELL (DOWLLE)
  Robert of Bermondsey [PRO; PCC 1642]
  Robert of Walton on Thames [BM; Add.Ms 24,925 f.25v; 1544] <Abs 65>
  William of Swk St Olave, gent. [DW/PA/7/13 f.298; DW/PA/5/1643/30]
    see also DALLEY
DOWEN *see* DOWNES
DOWGLAS *see* DOUGLAS
DOWLEY *see* DALLEY
DOWMAN
  John of Surrey, archdeacon of Suffolk [PRO; PCC Will 1526]
DOWMINGE *see* DOWNING
DOWNES (DOWEN,DOWNE)
  Elizabeth of Kingston, widow [DW/PA/7/6 f.229; 1561]
  Henry, *or* Henry Donne of Lambeth, yeoman [DW/PA/7/8 f.184; DW/PA/5/1610/46]
  John of Kingston [DW/PA/7/4 f.34; 1533]
  Mary of Chertsey; London [PRO; PCC 1634]
  Richard of Swk St Saviour, waterman [DW/PA/7/12 f.319; DW/PA/5/1636/28]
  Robert, alias Robert Adowne of Leatherhead [PRO; PCC 1632]
  William of Surrey, citizen and merchant tailor [PRO; PCC Will 1589]
    see also ADOWNE
DOWNING (DOWMINGE,DOWNINGE)
  James of Swk St Saviour, yeoman [DW/PA/7/9 f.299; DW/PA/5/1619/39] <Abs U237>
  John of Beddington [PRO; PCC 1637]
  William of Carshalton, shepherd [HRO; 1589 AD21]
  William of Guildford Holy Trinity, miller [DW/PA/7/9 f.185; DW/PA/5/1616/38]
  William of Rotherhithe [PRO; PCC Admon 1600]
DOWSE
  Nicholas of Ewell, husbandman, senior [DW/PA/7/13 f.15; DW/PA/5/1639/44]
DOWTYE *see* DOUGHTY
DRAKE
  Francis of Esher, esq. [PRO; PCC Admon 1634 *and* PCC 1634, and sentence]
  Henry of Reigate [PRO; PCC Admon 1610]
  Henry of Reigate [PRO; PCC 1646]
  Richard of Esher, esq. [PRO; PCC Will 1604] <Abs, SAC v.11 p.132>
DRANNFYLD
  James of Swk [DW/PA/5/1568/48]
DRAPER (DRAPIER)
  Edward of Woking [DW/PA/5/1561/22]
  Elizabeth of Camberwell [PRO; PCC Will 1557] [*and*] [LBLAD; Surrey Deeds 1/6702; 1554]
  Elizabeth of Camberwell [PRO; PCC Will *and* Admon 1628]
  George of East Horsley, gardener [LPL; 96/781; 98/1 f.121r; Will 1641]
  George of Wandsworth [DW/PA/5/1568/81]
  Henry of Camberwell [PRO; PCC Will 1558] [*and*] [LBLAD; Surrey Deeds 1/6755; 1558]
  Joan of Egham; Thorpe, widow [PRO; PCC Will 1596] <Abs SAC v.30 pp.8-9>
  John of Farnham, wheelmaker, senior [DW/PA/7/9 f.230; DW/PA/5/1617/37]
  Katherine of Lingfield - Ford, widow [PRO; PCC Will 1619]

DRAPER (DRAPIER) [*continued*]

Matthew of Camberwell, gent. [PRO; PCC Will 1577]

Nathaniel of Ippollitts, Hertfordshire, citizen and haberdasher [DW/PA/7/11 f.327; DW/PA/5/1625/70]

Robert of Camberwell, gent. [PRO; PCC Will 1547]

Robert of Kingston, husbandman [DW/PA/7/13 f.111; DW/PA/5/1640/45]

Thomas of Camberwell [PRO; PCC Will 1558]

William of Camberwell [PRO; PCC Will 1559]

DRAX

Richard of Thames Ditton [PRO; PCC Will 1457]

DRAY (DREY)

John of Cranleigh; Ewhurst [DW/PA/7/1 f.87; 1488] <Abs 293>

DRENCHER

Richard, alias Richard Lincoln of Limpsfield, husbandman [PRO; PCC Will 1618]

Robert of Limpsfield [DW/PA/5/1555/54]

William, alias William Lyncon of Limpsfield, yeoman [DW/PA/5/1580/57]

DREW (DREWE,DRUE)

Humphrey of Chertsey, yeoman [DW/PA/7/10 f.249; DW/PA/5/1622/25]

James of Carshalton, tailor [DW/PA/5/1592/92]

Jane of Swk St Saviour, widow [DW/PA/7/9 f.215; DW/PA/5/1617/38]

John of Bermondsey [DW/PA/5/1561/5]

John of Chertsey - Addlestone [DW/PA/7/8 f.205; DW/PA/5/1611/21]

John of Farleigh [DW/PA/7/1 f.59; 1487] <Abs 197>

John of Walton on the Hill; Headley [DW/PA/7/2 f.20; 1491]

Richard of Swk St Olave [DW/PA/7/4 ff.53,58; 1533]

Robert of Carshalton [PRO; PCC 1638]

Robert of Limpsfield [SRO; 18/1/36; 1555]

Roger of Surrey [PRO; PCC Will 1589]

Susan of Chertsey, widow of William of London, gent. [PRO; PCC 1643]

Thomas of Chertsey [HRO; 1583 AD18]

William of Chertsey; St Giles in the Fields, Middlesex [PRO; PCC 1638]

William of Thorpe, thatcher [DW/PA/7/8 f.159; DW/PA/5/1611/22]

William of Thorpe, senior [DW/PA/7/12 f.333; DW/PA/5/1636/31]

DREY *see* DRAY

DRING

Elizabeth of Wandsworth, widow [DW/PA/7/13 f.306; DW/PA/5/1643/31]

Jasper of Wandsworth [PRO; PCC 1634]

DRINKWATER (DRYNKWATER)

John of Camberwell - Peckham [PRO; *in* C146 9498; 1443]

DRIVER

John of Lingfield [PRO; PCC 1646]

Nicholas of West Molesey, clerk [PRO; PCC Admon 1632]

Thomas of Battersea [PRO; PCC 1649]

DROUGHT

William of Swk St Saviour, white baker [DW/PA/7/7 f.195; DW/PA/5/1598/23] <Abs 354>

DRUE *see* DREW

DRYBUTTER

Michael of Bermondsey, fuller & setter [DW/PA/7/12 f.450; DW/PA/5/1639/42]

DRYLAND (DRYLING)

John, alias John Dryling of Swk St Saviour, shipwright [DW/PA/7/9 f.74; DW/PA/5/1614/22]

DRYNKWATER *see* DRINKWATER

DUBBER

Edward of Bermondsey [PRO; PCC Admon 1623]

Elizabeth of Betchworth, wife of Richard, gent, (and widow of Richard Woodman) [DW/PA/7/12 f,165; DW/PA/5/1633/42]

du BOYES

Francis of London; Farme, near Armentieres, Flanders [*French*] [DW/PA/7/9 f,135; DW/PA/5/1615/41]

DUCK

Edmund of Wandsworth [PRO; PCC Admon 1647]

Robert of Bermondsey [PRO; PCC 1641]

DUCKER

Henry of Compton [DW/PA/7/12 f,93; DW/PA/5/1632/26]

John of Compton - Polsted, husbandman [DW/PA/7/8 f,276; DW/PA/5/1612/52]

DUCKMAN (DUKMAN)

Cicily of Wandsworth [PRO; PCC Will 1526]

Richard of Wandsworth [PRO; PCC Will 1526]

see also DUKMONTON

DU CROS

James of ,,, (*French church*) [DW/PA/7/11 f,82; DW/PA/5/1623/37]

DUDELEY,DUDELEYE *see* DUDLEY

DUDENEY,DUDENY *see* DEWDNEY

DUDLESFOLD *see* DIDDLESFORD

DUDLEY (DUDELEY,DUDELEYE,DUDLE,DUDLY)

Alice (formerly Gibson) of Rotherhithe [PRO; PCC Will 1556]

Ann of Swk St Saviour, widow [DW/PA/5/1587/102]

David of Dorking, wheelwright [PRO; PCC 1646]

Edward of Great Bookham [*in* DW/PA/5/1544/5]

John of Great Bookham [DW/PA/7/2 f,185; 1523]

John of Great Bookham, yeoman [DW/PA/7/12 f,29; DW/PA/5/1631/36]

Lettice of Great Bookham, widow [DW/PA/7/13 f,150; DW/PA/5/1642/20]

Miles of Dorking, yeoman [DW/PA/7/7 f,132; DW/PA/5/1597/30] <Abs 242>

Miles of Dorking - Milton [PRO; PCC Will 1597]

Miles of Dorking, yeoman [DW/PA/7/13 f,174; DW/PA/5/1641/38]

Richard of Great Bookham, husbandman, senior [DW/PA/7/11 f,424; DW/PA/5/1627/27]

Richard of Great Bookham, husbandman, senior [DW/PA/7/12 f,371; 1627]

Roger of ,,, [DW/PA/5/1614/24] <Abs U203>

Walter of Albury [DW/PA/5/1575/68]

William of Dorking - Milton, yeoman [DW/PA/7/8 f,339; DW/PA/5/1612/50]

DUDSON (DUTSON)

William, alias William Dutson of Thames Ditton [PRO; PCC Will 1600]

DUE *see* DEW

DUEDNEY *see* DEWDNEY

DUFFELL (DOFFELL,DUFFET)

Dorothy, alias Dorothy Duffet of Swk St Olave [DW/PA/7/7 f,130; DW/PA/5/1597/31] <Abs 239>

Robert of ,,, [DW/PA/7/7 f,134; DW/PA/5/1597/29] <Abs 245>

DUGGEN

Owen of Clapham, husbandman [DW/PA/7/7 f,431; DW/PA/5/1603/44] <Abs 816>

DUGGLEY

Richard of Tandridge [DW/PA/5/1582/65]

DUGLIS,DUGLISSE *see* DOUGLAS

DU GORDON
  Roger of Swk St Olave - Gleave Alley [DW/PA/7/7 f.632; DW/PA/5/1608/38] <Abs 1181>
DUKE
  James of Bermondsey [PRO; PCC Will 1502]
  Robert of Bermondsey [PRO; PCC Will 1507]
  William, alias William Winter, alias William Fuller of Chertsey [PRO; PCC Will 1414]
  William of Richmond [PRO; PCC 1649]
DUKEQUESNOY
  Peter of Mortlake [PRO; PCC Will 1610] <Abs, SAC v.24 p.61>
DUKMAN *see* DUCKMAN
DUKMONTON
  Thomas of Coulsdon [PRO; PCC Will 1446]
DULLEY *see* DALLEY
DUMBRELL
  Edward of Morden, labourer [DW/PA/5/1587/79]
DUNCE (DUNSSE)
  Henry, alias Henry Dunsehurst of Godalming - Hurtmore [DW/PA/7/12 f.146; DW/PA/5/1633/41A]
  Richard, alias Richard Dunshurst of Godalming - Hurtmore, weaver [DW/PA/5/1593/7]
DUNCUMBE
  George of Albury, esq. [PRO; PCC 1647]
DUNKIN
  Joan of Newington, widow [LPL; 98/1 f.118r; Will 1640]
DUNLEY
  Bennett of Rotherhithe [PRO; PCC Admon 1594]
DUNMOLE
  Thomas of Swk St Olave [DW/PA/7/4 f.94; 1534]
DUNN (DONNE)
  Alice of Putney - Mortlake Park [PRO; PCC Will 1604]
  Henry, *or* Henry Downe of Lambeth, yeoman [DW/PA/7/8 f.184; DW/PA/5/1610/46]
DUNSHURST (DUNSEHURST,DUNSHIRST)
  Henry, alias Henry Dunce of Godalming [DW/PA/7/12 f.146; DW/PA/5/1633/41A]
  John of Cobham [DW/PA/7/1 f.33; 1486] <Abs 111>
  Richard, alias Richard Dunsse of Godalming - Hurtmore; Godalming - Eashing, weaver [DW/PA/5/1593/7]
DUNSTALL (DONNESTALE)
  Bernard of Cranleigh, yeoman [HRO; 1618 AD20]
  John, alias John Tonstall of Swk St Saviour, tailor [DW/PA/5/1582/92]
DUNWELL
  Richard of Kingston, saddler [DW/PA/7/7 f.30; DW/PA/5/1595/34] <Abs 64>
DU PRES
  Nicholas of ... [DW/PA/5/1568/70]
DUPYSRE *see* DE DACCHIM
DURANT *see* DURRANT
DURDEN (DURDYN)
  Richard of Great Bookham [DW/PA/7/4 f.34; 1533]
  Richard of Walton on Thames - Hersham [DW/PA/7/13 f.152; DW/PA/5/1641/37]
DURGATE
  John of Bramley, husbandman [HRO; 1608 B24]

DURKIN *see* DIRKYN
DURNFORD (DERNFORD)
  Richard of Reigate [DW/PA/7/1 f.99; 1489] <Abs 323>
DURRANT (DORANT,DORRANT,DURANT,DURRENTE,DYRRANT)
  Joan of Oxted, widow [DW/PA/7/10 f.97; DW/PA/5/1619/40]
  John of Limpsfield, senior [PRO; PCC Will 1504]
  John of Newington [LPL; 98/1 f.100r; Will 1638]
  John of Tandridge [DW/PA/5/1583/3]*
  Mary of Swk St Olave; Bermondsey, widow [DW/PA/7/7 f.510; DW/PA/5/1605/26] <Abs 957>
  William of East Molesey [DW/PA/7/7 f.345; DW/PA/5/1601/31] <Abs 631>
  William of Limpsfield [PRO; PCC 1633]
DUSBURYE
  John of Swk St Olave, feltmaker [DW/PA/5/1592/121]
DUTSON
  William, alias William Dudson of Thames Ditton [PRO; PCC Will 1600]
DUTTON
  Francis of Swk, gent. [DW/PA/5/1593/181]
  John of Swk St George [DW/PA/7/4 f.26; 1533]
DYAR *see* DYER
DYBLE *see* DIBBLE
DYCKAR *see* DICKER
DYCKYNSONE *see* DICKENSON
DYDELSFOLD *see* DIDDLESFORD
DYDLESDON *see* DIDLESDON
DYE
  John of Swk St Olave [DW/PA/7/5 f.59; 1539] <Abs 98>
  Robert of Richmond, yeoman [DW/PA/7/10 f.13; DW/PA/5/1616/39]
DYER (DIER,DYAR)
  Anthony of East Molesey [PRO; PCC Admon 1626]
  John of Elstead; Godalming [*in* DW/PA/5/1544/9]
  Richard of Farnham [DW/PA/7/1 f.60; 1487] <Abs 201>
  Richard of Kingston [DW/PA/7/2 f.98; 1514] <Abs SAC v.8 pp.115-116>
  Richard of Kingston [PRO; PCC Admon 1596]
  Thomas of Bermondsey [DW/PA/7/12 f.370; DW/PA/5/1627/26]
  Thomas, alias Thomas Clarke of Egham [DW/PA/7/4 f.57; 1533]
  Thomas of Godalming [*in* DW/PA/5/1546/75]
  William of Bermondsey, chandler [DW/PA/7/8 f.147; DW/PA/5/1611/23]
DYGKYN,DYGYN *see* DIGGON
DYKAR *see* DICKER
DYKE (DIKES)
  Thomas of Thames Ditton [DW/PA/7/12 f.208; DW/PA/5/1634/32]
DYLLSDONE *see* DIDLESDON
DYMEN *see* DIEMEN
DYMES (DIMES)
  Agnes of Petersham, widow [DW/PA/7/8 f.62; DW/PA/5/1609/41]
  Joan of Witley - Brook, widow [DW/PA/7/12 f.177; DW/PA/5/1633/46]
  John of Witley - Brook, yeoman [DW/PA/7/12 f.28; DW/PA/5/1631/35]
DYMMINGE *see* DIMMING
DYMOCK,DYMOCKE *see* DIMMOCK
DYNES *see* DINES
DYNGLEY *see* DINGLEY
DYNHAM *see* DENHAM
DYNNOTTE *see* DENNATT

DYRRANT *see* DURRANT
DYRREY *see* DIRREY
DYSCHER *see* DISHER
DYSON (DISON)
  Ralph of Weybridge, gent. [PRO; PCC Will 1625]
DYSSHER *see* DISHER
DYWES
  Alexander of Swk St Olave, sojourner [DW/PA/7/4 f.98; 1534]
DYXSON,DYXSONE *see* DIXON

EADE *see* EDE
EAGER (EAGRE,EGEAR,EGER,EGGAR,EGGER)
  Alice of Abinger, widow [DW/PA/5/1557/140]
  Elizabeth of Kingston [PRO; PCC Admon 1579]
  Henry of Ewhurst [PRO; PCC Will 1585]
  Henry of Shere [DW/PA/7/6 f.180; DW/PA/5/1559/215]
  John of Albury [DW/PA/7/3 f.102; 1529]
  John of Richmond, tailor [DW/PA/5//1546/84]
  John of Shere, husbandman [DW/PA/5/1576/55]
  Maud of Bentley, Hampshire [DW/PA/7/2 f.193; 1523]
  Thomas of Dorking [DW/PA/7/4 f.18; 1532]
  William of Shere [BM; Add.Ms 24,925 f.17r; 1544] <Abs 37>
EAGLE (EAGLES,EGELL,EGLES)
  Ann of Kingston [PRO; PCC Admon 1588]
  Jasper, alias Jasper Eales of Weybridge, vintner [DW/PA/7/7 f.486; DW/PA/5/1604/15] <Abs 916>
  Richard of Alton, Hampshire; Farnham, tanner [DW/PA/7/13 f.400; DW/PA/5/1645/11]
  Thomas of Putney, widower [LPL; 98/1 f.88r; Will 1638]
  Thomas of Weybridge, innholder [PRO; PCC Will 1620] <Soame 383>
EAGLESFIELD (EGLESFELD,EGLESFELDE)
  Christopher of Bermondsey [PRO; PCC Will 1546]
  John of ... [DW/PA/5/1546/39]
  John of Swk St Olave, yeoman [DW/PA/7/6 f.127; DW/PA/5/1559/208]
EAGRE *see* EAGER
EALES (EAYLES,EELES)
  Jasper, alias Jasper Eagles of Weybridge, vintner [DW/PA/7/7 f.486; DW/PA/5/1604/15] <Abs 916>
  John, alias John Hilder of Ewell, bachelor [DW/PA/7/13 f.401; DW/PA/5/1645/12] [*and*] [PRO; PCC Admon 1645]
  Thomas of Horsell, husbandman [DW/PA/7/9 f.250; DW/PA/5/1617/42]
  William, alias William Hilder of Ashtead, husbandman [DW/PA/7/9 f.261; DW/PA/5/1617/73]
  William of East Molesey, yeoman [DW/PA/7/8 f.125; DW/PA/5/1610/47]
    see also ELLIS *for* ELES
EALING (EELING,ELINS)
  John of Farnham, blacksmith [DW/PA/7/6 f.238; 1560]
  Thomas of Mortlake, yeoman [LPL; 96/850; 98/1 f.5r; Will 1626 *and* 1629]
EARLE (EARLES,ERLE,ERLES)
  Catherine of Malden, spinster [DW/PA/7/9 f.180; DW/PA/5/1616/40]
  Michael of Charlwood, parson [PRO; PCC Will 1615]
  Richard of Frensham, yeoman [DW/PA/7/6 f.218; 1561]

EARLE (EARLES,ERLE,ERLES) [*continued*]
Thomas of Burstow [LPL: 98/1 f.57v; Will 1634]
Thomas of Wandsworth, mealman [DW/PA/7/12 f.195; DW/PA/5/1633/48]
William of Godalming; Witley [DW/PA/7/1 f.97; 1489] <Abs 319>
EARLY (EAYRLAY,ERLEYE,ERLY)
Agnes of Swk St Saviour, widow [DW/PA/5/1592/13]
John of Bermondsey [PRO; PCC Admon 1647]
Nicholas of Kingston, yeoman [DW/PA/5/1550/86]
Peter of Bermondsey, citizen and woodmonger [DW/PA/7/13 f.301; DW/PA/5/1643/33]
Thomas of Kingston [PRO; PCC Will 1541]
EARTH BANDERBRIGG
Christian of Ewell, widow [DW/PA/7/8 f.72; DW/PA/5/1609/17]
EASDOWNE *see* EASTDOWN
EASON
Thomas of Swk St Saviour, brewer [DW/PA/7/13 f.64; DW/PA/5/1641/39]
EAST (EST)
Arthur of Ockley [DW/PA/7/8 f.324; DW/PA/5/1611/24]
Gilbert, alias Gilbert Yeast of Swk St Saviour, cordwainer [DW/PA/7/11 f.1; DW/PA/5/1622/112]
John of Clapham [PRO; PCC Admon 1648]
Matthew of Swk St Olave, barber surgeon [DW/PA/7/8 f.9;DW/PA/5/1608/40]
William of Croydon; Newington [GL; Commissary Court of London Will 1421]
EASTDOWN (EASDOWNE)
George of Swk St Olave, victualler [DW/PA/7/11 f.437; DW/PA/5/1628/30]
EASTED (EYSTED,ISTEED,ISTED,YESTED,YSTED)
Harry of Effingham, yeoman [DW/PA/7/12 f.205; DW/PA/5/1634/58]
Margaret of Nutfield, widow [DW/PA/7/7 f.240; DW/PA/5/1598/94] <Abs 422>
Nicholas of Nutfield [DW/PA/7/7 f.29; DW/PA/5/1595/52] <Abs 61>
Phillip of Worplesdon [DW/PA/7/8 f.361; DW/PA/5/1612/55]
Richard of Leigh [DW/PA/7/8 f.353; DW/PA/5/1612/83]
Richard of Nutfield, yeoman [HRO; Reg. CCB 20 p.12; 1563] [*and*] [DW/PA/5/1563/80]
Samuel of Blechingley [PRO; PCC Admon 1649]
Thomas of Lingfield [DW/PA/5/1575/75]
Thomas, alias Thomas Ashted of Nutfield, yeoman [HRO; 1571 B62]
Thomas of Nutfield, yeoman [DW/PA/5/1574/11]
Thomas of Nutfield, yeoman [PRO; PCC Will 1575]
Thomas of Nutfield, yeoman [DW/PA/5/1576/150]
Thomas of Nutfield; Blechingley; Burstow, yeoman [DW/PA/7/10 f.206; DW/PA/5/1620/69]
William of Blechingley [DW/PA/7/4 f.11; 1532]
EASTLAND (EASTELAND,ESLAND,ESTLAND,ESTLONDE)
Alice of Godstone, widow [DW/PA/5/1547/15]
Caleb of Lingfield, carpenter [DW/PA/7/10 f.264; DW/PA/5/1622/26] [*and*] [PRO; PCC Will 1623]
Edward, alias Edward Lander of Godstone, yeoman [DW/PA/5/1591/10]
Erasmus, alias Erasmus Lander of Tandridge, yeoman [DW/PA/7/8 f.320; DW/PA/5/1611/25]
Erasmus, alias Erasmus Lander of Tandridge, yeoman [DW/PA/7/12 f.490; DW/PA/5/1638/40]
Henry, alias Henry Launder of Tandridge; Lingfield [PRO; PCC Will 1597]
Joan, alias Joan Launder of Tandridge, widow [PRO; PCC Will 1586]
John, alias John Lander of Crowhurst [DW/PA/5/1592/41]

EASTLAND (EASTELAND,ESLAND,ESTLAND,ESTLONDE) [*continued*]
John of Godstone [DW/PA/7/2 f.38; 1493]
John of Oxted, seedsman [DW/PA/5/1561/90]
John, alias John Launder of Tandridge, yeoman [DW/PA/7/11 f.102; DW/PA/5/1624/68]
Katherine, alias Katherine Launder of Tandridge; Lingfield [HRO; 1597 B24] [*and*] [DW/PA/7/7 f.120; DW/PA/5/1597/33] <Abs 221>
Oliver, alias Oliver Lander of Oxted; Crowhurst, yeoman [DW/PA/7/9 f.289; 1618]
Richard of Swk St Olave, cooper [DW/PA/7/11 f.177; DW/PA/5/1625/71]
Richard, alias Richard Launder of Tandridge, yeoman [DW/PA/5/1570/5]
Thomas, alias Thomas Launder of Godstone [DW/PA/7/6 f.221; 1561]
EASTLANDER
Edward of Croydon [LPL; 98/1 f.28r; Will 1631]
EASTMAN (ESTMENT)
John of Guildford [DW/PA/5/1561/47]
John of Puttenham [DW/PA/7/3 f.139; 1530]
Thomas of Guildford Holy Trinity; Guildford St Mary; Guildford St Nicolas, shoemaker [DW/PA/7/10 f.296; DW/PA/5/1622/27]
EASTON (ESTIN,ESTON)
Agnes of Shalford, widow [DW/PA/7/6 f.209; 1560]
Alice of Lambeth [PRO; PCC 1640]
James of Lambeth, yeoman [DW/PA/5/1578/109]
Lucy of Swk St Olave; Bermondsey; Antwerp, Belgium [DW/PA/5/1596/21] <Abs U7>
Richard of Camberwell - Peckham, husbandman [DW/PA/7/9 f.41; DW/PA/5/1614/46]
Robert of Swk St Olave, waterman [DW/PA/7/2 f.77; 1502]
William of Lambeth - South Lambeth, gent. [PRO; PCC Will 1585]
William of Swk St George, colour grinder [DW/PA/7/10 f.176; 1620]
EASTOWE
Samuel of Newington [PRO; PCC Admon 1628]
EASTWICK (ESTWICKE)
Thomas of Lambeth [PRO; PCC Will 1584]
EASTWOOD
Alice of Titsey, widow [PRO; PCC Will 1611] <Abs. SAC v.35 p.32>
EATON (ETON)
Alice of West Molesey, widow [DW/PA/7/2 f.150; 1521]
Ann of Lambeth, widow [DW/PA/7/8 f.217; DW/PA/5/1612/53]
Edward of Swk St Thomas, weaver [DW/PA/7/11 f.151; DW/PA/5/1625/72]
George of Swk St Olave, woolcomber [DW/PA/7/11 f.322; DW/PA/5/1625/73]
John of Bermondsey, bucklemaker [DW/PA/5/1563/81]
John of Ewell [DW/PA/7/12 f.213; DW/PA/5/1633/49]
John of Lambeth, fisherman [DW/PA/7/8 f.140; DW/PA/5/1611/26]
John of Swk St Olave; the Ship *The Peter of London* [DW/PA/7/12 f.91; DW/PA/5/1633/53]
Robert of Blechingley [DW/PA/7/6 f.188; DW/PA/5/1559/200]
Robert of Ewhurst, husbandman [DW/PA/7/12 f.125; DW/PA/5/1632/34]
Thomas of Bermondsey, smith [DW/PA/5/1568/87]
Thomas of Croydon, metalman [LPL; 96/814; 98/1 f.67v; Will 1635]
Thomas of Lambeth - Stockwell, yeoman [DW/PA/5/1543/8]*
William of Epsom, yeoman [DW/PA/5/1588/4]
EAVES *see* EVES
EAYLES *see* EALES

EAYRLAY *see* EARLY

EBB

Katherine of Swk St Olave, widow [DW/PA/7/11 f.480; DW/PA/5/1628/31]

EBDALL

Godfrey of Sheen [PRO; PCC Admon 1592]

EBRON

Alice of Ewhurst, widow [DW/PA/5/1571/35]

EBSON

Joan of Battersea, widow [DW/PA/7/9 f.242; DW/PA/5/1617/39]

EDE (EADE,EDD,EDES,EEDE,UDE)

Agnes of Reigate, widow [DW/PA/7/6 ff.88, 229; DW/PA/5/1559/65]

Edward of Godalming; Witley [DW/PA/7/3 f.202; 1532]

Edward of Godalming, shearman [DW/PA/5/1568/62]

Elizabeth of Guildford St Mary; Worplesdon, widow of Thomas [DW/PA/7/8 f.167; DW/PA/5/1610/50]

Henry of Ash; Chiddingfold, yeoman [HRO; 1597 B23]

Henry of Dunsfold, yeoman [DW/PA/7/11 f.418; DW/PA/5/1626/44]

Joan of Witley, widow [DW/PA/7/7 f.23; DW/PA/5/1595/35] <Abs 48>

John of Abinger, yeoman [DW/PA/7/12 f.276; DW/PA/5/1635/26]

John of Nutfield [DW/PA/7/7 f.129; DW/PA/5/1597/34] <Abs 238>

John of Puttenham [DW/PA/7/4 f.200; 1537]

John of Witley, yeoman [DW/PA/7/7 f.285; DW/PA/5/1599/93] <Abs 509>

Katherine of Godalming, widow [DW/PA/7/3 f.200; 1532]

Oliver of Shalford, husbandman [DW/PA/7/13 f.136; DW/PA/5/1640/50]

Peter of Dunsfold, yeoman [DW/PA/5/1569/8] <Abs SAC v.32 p.4>

Peter of Godalming; Hascombe, yeoman [DW/PA/7/9 f.213; DW/PA/5/1616/41]

Richard of Farnham [DW/PA/7/4 f.85; 1534]

Richard of Ripley [PRO; PCC Will 1534]

Richard of Witley [DW/PA/7/2 f.113; 1517]

Richard of Witley, yeoman [DW/PA/7/10 f.23; DW/PA/5/1616/42] <Abs U208>

Richard of Wotton [HRO; 1592 AD29]

Robert of Lingfield, yeoman [DW/PA/5/1578/27]

Stephen of Haslemere [DW/PA/5/1558/91]*

Thomas of Chiddingfold, husbandman [DW/PA/7/12 f.75; DW/PA/5/1632/32]

Thomas of Guildford St Mary; Worplesdon; Shalford, clothier [DW/PA/7/8 f.45; DW/PA/5/1609/43]

Thomas of Newdigate, husbandman [DW/PA/7/7 f.338; DW/PA/5/1601/32] <Abs 612>

Thomas of Swk St Thomas, grazier [DW/PA/7/7 f.528; DW/PA/5/1606/35] <Abs 996>

Thomas of Thursley, weaver [DW/PA/5/1635/27] <Abs U253>

Thomas of Weybridge; Haslemere, husbandman [DW/PA/7/9 f.214; DW/PA/5/1617/40]

Thomas of Witley, husbandman [DW/PA/7/4 f.187; 1536]

William of Ash, servant to Henry Eed [DW/PA/7/13 f.290; DW/PA/5/1643/32]

William of Bentley, Hampshire, bricklayer [DW/PA/7/9 f.204; DW/PA/5/1616/43]

William of Chiddingfold [PRO; PCC 1639]

William, alias William Ade of Farnham [PRO; PCC Will 1529]

William of Farnham - Wrecclesham, husbandman [HRO; 1573 B42]

William of Godalming - Munstead [DW/PA/7/12 f.14; DW/PA/5/1631/39]

William of Hambledon; Godalming, husbandman [DW/PA/7/8 f.162; DW/PA/5/1611/27]

EDEN
Margaret of Richmond [DW/PA/7/12 f.371; DW/PA/5/1627/30]
William, alias William Sampson of Newington, mariner [PRO; PCC Will 1625]
EDENBRASSE
Richard of Leatherhead; Kingston [DW/PA/7/6 f.292; 1560]
EDES *see* EDE
EDGAR
Thomas of Bermondsey, esq. [PRO; PCC Will 1547]
EDGE
Giles of Ewell, yeoman [DW/PA/5/1557/18]
EDGECOMBE
John of Bermondsey - Bermondsey Abbey, esq. [PRO; PCC Will 1533]
EDGELEY (EGELEY)
John of Bentley, Hampshire [DW/PA/7/4 f.206; 1537]
EDGERTON (EGERTON)
Reynold of Kingston, fisherman [DW/PA/7/8 f.25; DW/PA/5/1608/41]
Richard of Swk St Olave, bricklayer [DW/PA/7/11 f.440; DW/PA/5/1628/32]
EDGINTON (EDYNDON)
William of Swk; Wappenham, Northamptonshire; Edington, Wiltshire, bishop of Winchester [LPL; Reg. Abp Langham f.110; Will 1366]
EDLIN (EDLEN)
Ann of Addington, widow [PRO; PCC 1634]
Henry of Addington, yeoman [DW/PA/7/12 f.117; DW/PA/5/1632/33]
Oliphe of Croydon, yeoman [LPL; 96/828; 98/1 f.72v; Will 1636]
EDMEAD (EDMEADE,EDMEADS,EDMED,EDMEDE,EDMEID,EDMETT,EDMYDE)
George of Horsell, husbandman [DW/PA/7/13 f.135; DW/PA/5/1640/49]
Henry of Horsell [DW/PA/7/3 f.160; 1530]
James of Chobham, husbandman [DW/PA/7/7 f.150; DW/PA/5/1597/35] <Abs 281>
Joan, alias Joan Boxall of Windlesham, widow [PRO; PCC Admon 1648]
John of Horsell - Parley; Pyrford - Walsham, carpenter, senior [DW/PA/7/10 f.27; DW/PA/5/1615/42]
John of Horsell, yeoman [DW/PA/7/12 f.142; DW/PA/5/1633/47]
John of Stoke, husbandman [DW/PA/7/13 f.149A; DW/PA/5/1641/40]
Richard of Chobham, husbandman [HRO; 1597 B27]
Richard of Horsell [DW/PA/7/2 f.8; 1491]
Richard of Horsell, carpenter [DW/PA/5/1569/60]
Richard of Horsell, husbandman [DW/PA/5/1571/16]
Richard of Horsell, yeoman [HRO; 1600 B16]
Robert of Cobham, husbandman [DW/PA/7/9 f.187; DW/PA/5/1616/44]
Robert of Horsell [DW/PA/7/5 f.112; 1539]
William of Chobham, husbandman [DW/PA/7/6 f.44; DW/PA/5/1559/38]
EDMOND,EDMONDES,EDMONDS *see* EDMUNDS
EDMONDSON,EDMONDSONE *see* EDMUNDSON
EDMUNDS (EDMOND,EDMONDES,EDMONDS,EDMUNDES)
Agnes of Kingston, widow [DW/PA/7/6 f.257; 1560]
Dorothy of East Molesey, widow of (Sir) Christopher, knight [PRO; PCC Will 1615]
George of ...; York, Yorkshire [DW/PA/5/1575/56]
Joan, alias Joan Boxall of Windlesham [PRO; PCC Admon 1649]
John of Blechingley, husbandman [DW/PA/7/12 f.81; DW/PA/5/1633/51]
John of Kingston, husbandman [DW/PA/7/9 f.293; 1618]
John of Kingston, husbandman [DW/PA/7/13 f.192; DW/PA/5/1642/25]

EDMUNDS (EDMOND,EDMONDES,EDMONDS,EDMUNDES) [*continued*]
  Reginald of Rotherhithe (but died overseas) [PRO; PCC Admon 1632]
  Reynold of Kingston [DW/PA/7/10 f.172; DW/PA/5/1619/41]
  Richard of ... [DW/PA/7/8 f.185; DW/PA/5/1610/48]
  Robert of Chobham [PRO; PCC Admon 1649]
  Thomas of Egham, bricklayer [DW/PA/7/11 f.519; DW/PA/5/1629/32]
  Thomas of Egham [PRO; PCC 1639]
  Thomas of St Mary Aldermanbury, London; Horsell, citizen and carpenter [GL; Commissary Court of London Will 1619]
  William of Kingston, gardener [DW/PA/7/12 f.504; 1638]
  William of Shalford, tanner [DW/PA/5/1576/54]
  William of Windlesham [PRO; C146 8186 (*no date given but* c.1570)]

EDMUNDSON (EDMONDSON,EDMONDSONE,EMANSON,EMENSON)
  Gawain of Swk St Olave [HRO; Reg. Fox 3 p.57; 1511]
  John of Bermondsey [DW/PA/7/6 f.148; DW/PA/5/1559/229]
  John of Lambeth [DW/PA/7/4 f.190; 1536]
  Thomas of Swk, waterman [DW/PA/5/1592/7] [*two copies, one* *]

EDMYDE *see* EDMEAD

EDNAM
  John of Swk St Thomas [DW/PA/5/1578/32]

EDSAW (EDSA,EDSALL,EDSAR,EDSAWE,EDSEY,EDSHALL,EDSHAW,EDSHAWE)
  Ellen of Windlesham, widow [DW/PA/7/13 f.398; DW/PA/5/1645/10]
  Henry of Pyrford [DW/PA/7/1 f.53; 1487] <Abs 176>
  Joan of Ewhurst [DW/PA/5/1557/87]
  Joanna of Fetcham, widow [DW/PA/5/1545/10]*
  John of Ewhurst, yeoman [DW/PA/7/9 f.152; DW/PA/5/1610/52]
  John of Ewhurst, husbandman [HRO; 1624 B18]
  John of Fetcham [PRO; PCC Will 1544]
  John of Thorpe [DW/PA/5/1563/87]
  Richard of Fetcham [DW/PA/7/7 f.564; DW/PA/5/1606/36] <Abs 1054>
  Richard of Stoke Dabernon [DW/PA/5/1568/42]
  Robert of Ashtead [DW/PA/7/6 f.89; DW/PA/5/1559/66]
  Robert of Ockley [PRO; PCC Admon 1640]
  Thomas of Ewhurst; Rudgwick, Sussex [DW/PA/7/9 f.86; DW/PA/5/1615/43]
  Thomas of Fetcham [DW/PA/5/1605/27] <Abs U138>
  Thomas of Leatherhead, husbandman [DW/PA/7/8 f.284; DW/PA/5/1613/34]
  Thomas of Windlesham, yeoman [*in* DW/PA/5/1555/68]
  Thomas of Windlesham, husbandman, senior [DW/PA/7/7 f.471; DW/PA/5/1604/16] <Abs 890>
  Thomas of Windlesham, yeoman, senior [DW/PA/7/12 f.260; DW/PA/5/1634/40]
  Thomas of Windlesham - Bagshot [DW/PA/7/13 f.188; DW/PA/5/1641/42]
  Walter of Bentley, Hampshire [DW/PA/7/4 f.56; 1533]
  Walter of Worplesdon [HRO; 1557 U217-218]

EDWARDS (EDWARD,EDWARDE,EDWARDES)
  Adam of Bentley, Hampshire [DW/PA/7/12 f.204; DW/PA/5/1634/37]
  Agnes of Charlwood, widow [PRO; PCC 1633]
  Agnes of Swk St George - Kent Street, widow [DW/PA/7/11 f.182; DW/PA/5/1625/75]
  Arnold of Godalming, yeoman [DW/PA/7/9 f.9; DW/PA/5/1615/30]
  David of Rotherhithe [PRO; PCC 1647]
  Elizabeth of Guildford St Mary, widow [DW/PA/7/12 f.273; DW/PA/5/1635/29]
  George of Walton on Thames [DW/PA/7/8 f.180; DW/PA/5/1610/49]
  Henry of Godalming - Lodkin, husbandman [DW/PA/7/13 f.422; DW/PA/5/1645/15]

EDWARDS (EDWARD,EDWARDE,EDWARDES) [*continued*]
Henry of Witley [HRO; 1597 B29]
Hugh of Barnes, maltster [LPL; 96/845; 98/1 f.70r; Will 1635]
Hugh of Kingston [DW/PA/7/1 f.31; 1486] <Abs 106>
Hugh of Swk St Saviour [DW/PA/7/9 f.265; 1618]
James of Newdigate [DW/PA/7/10 f.92; DW/PA/5/1615/44]
James of Swk St Olave [DW/PA/7/2 f.52; 1497]
Jane of Godalming, widow [HRO; 1639 B25]
John of Chertsey [PRO; PCC Admon 1604]
John of Lambeth - South Lambeth, gent. [PRO; PCC Will 1622]
John of Newington [PRO; PCC 1647]
John of Shalford - Rushett; Witley; Bramley, yeoman [DW/PA/7/9 f.84; DW/PA/5/1615/45]
John of Tandridge, weaver [DW/PA/7/10 f.166; DW/PA/5/1621/37]
Juliana of Newington, widow [LPL; 96/846; 98/1 f.109r; Will 1639]
Katherine of Dunsfold [PRO; PCC Admon 1647]
Margaret of Wotton; Ewhurst; Warnham, Sussex; Oakwood, widow [DW/PA/7/7 f.442; DW/PA/5/1603/45] <Abs 835>
Morgan of London, citizen and joiner [DW/PA/7/8 f.27; DW/PA/5/1608/42]
Nicholas of Compton, husbandman [DW/PA/7/8 f.248; DW/PA/5/1613/35]
Nicholas of Godalming, mercer [PRO; PCC Will 1604] <Abs, SAC v.11 p.136>
Ralph of Stoke next Guildford; Worplesdon, gent. [DW/PA/7/10 f.150; DW/PA/5/1621/38]
Samuel of Godalming, butcher [DW/PA/7/11 f.84; DW/PA/5/1623/38]
Susanna of Godalming, widow [DW/PA/7/12 f.81; DW/PA/5/1633/50]
Thomas of Charlwood, butcher [LPL; 96/847; 98/1 f.120v; Will 1641]
Thomas of Chobham [DW/PA/5/1593/193]
Thomas of Thames Ditton, husbandman [DW/PA/7/7 f.386; DW/PA/5/1602/30] <Abs 714>
Thomas of Ewhurst [PRO; PCC Will 1590]
Thomas, alias Thomas Wylld of Farnham [DW/PA/7/6 f.189;DW/PA/5/1559/204]
Thomas of Swk St George [DW/PA/5/1593/108]
William of Bermondsey [PRO; PCC Admon 1597]
William of Bermondsey [PRO; PCC Admon 1600]
William of Lambeth [PRO; PCC Admon 1634]
William of Swk St Saviour, tailor [DW/PA/7/12 f.35; DW/PA/5/1631/40]
William of Witley - Mousehill; Witley - Milford, husbandman [HRO; 1613 B22]

EDWIN
John of Wandsworth [HRO; 1585 AD22]

EDYNDON *see* EDGINTON
EEDE *see* EDE
EEICK *see* EYCK
EELES *see* EALES
EELING *see* EALING
EGEAR *see* EAGER
EGELEY *see* EDGELEY
EGELL *see* EAGLE
EGER *see* EAGER
EGERTON *see* EDGERTON
EGGAR *see* EAGER

EGGEN
Cornelius of Swk St Olave; Falkenburg [? *country*], cooper [HRO; 1588 B21]

EGGER *see* EAGER

EGLES *see* EAGLE
EGLESFELDE *see* EAGLESFIELD
EGLIONBEE
  Cecilia, alias Cecilia Lake of Godalming - Enton [PRO; PCC Admon 1611]
Eign *see* ap David ap Eign
EIICK *see* EYCK
ELBORNE
  Thomas of Malden [DW/PA/5/1605/28] <Abs U139>
ELDER
  John of Great Bookham [GL; Commissary Court of London Will 1543]
ELDRIDGE (ELDREDGE)
  Brian of Chertsey [PRO; PCC 1640]
  John of Farnham - 'Meadmill', miller [DW/PA/7/13 f.168; 1641]
  John of Farnham, senior [DW/PA/7/13 f.169; DW/PA/5/1642/26]
  Thomas of Thursley, miller [DW/PA/7/11 f.265; DW/PA/5/1625/74]
ELEANOR (ELLYNOR)
  John of Walton on Thames [DW/PA/7/5 f.220; 1541]
ELES *see* ELLIS
ELETES *see* ELLIOTT
ELFORD
  John of Swk, yeoman [DW/PA/7/10 f.14; DW/PA/5/1616/45]
ELHORNE
  Thomas of Swk St Saviour, waterman [DW/PA/7/10 f.134; DW/PA/5/1620/47]
ELIEDE *see* ELLIOT
ELINCK
  Hubert of Swk [DW/PA/5/1574/16]
ELINS *see* EALING
ELIOT,ELIOTT *see* ELLIOTT
ELLES *see* ELLIS
ELLIETT *see* ELLIOTT
ELLINGBRIDGE (ELLYNGBRIGE,ELMERUGGE,ELYNGBRIGGE)
  Ann of Merstham, widow [LPL; Reg. Abp Warham f.20; 1517]
    <Abs SAC v.30 p.87>
  Thomas of Carshalton, esq. [PRO; PCC Will 1497]
  Thomas of Merstham, gent. [PRO; PCC Will 1507] <Abs SAC v.30 p.87>
  Thomas of Merstham [LPL; Reg. Abp Warham f.15; Will 1510]
ELLINGWORTH
  Robert of Bermondsey, bachelor [PRO; PCC Will 1618]
ELLIOTT (ELEATT,ELETES,ELIEDE,ELIOT,ELIOTT,ELLIETT,ELLOATE,ELLYOTT,ELYATTE,
    ELYEATT,ELYET,ELYETT,ELYOT,ELYOTT,HELYT)
  Anthony of Godalming [PRO; PCC Admon 1613]
  Arnold of Dunsfold, freemason [DW/PA/5/1592/58] <Abs SAC v.32 p.4>
  Catherine of Banstead [PRO; PCC Admon 1631]
  Edmund of Shalford [DW/PA/7/1 f.71; 1487] <Abs 234>
  Edmund of Swk St Saviour, yeoman [DW/PA/7/11 f.433; DW/PA/5/1627/31]
  George of Dorking, husbandman [DW/PA/7/9 f.70; DW/PA/5/1614/45]
  George of Godalming, gent. [PRO; PCC 1642]
  George of Limpsfield, esq. [PRO; PCC 1645]
  Gregory of Shalford, husbandman [DW/PA/7/8 f.166; DW/PA/5/1610/51]
  Henry of Hambledon, yeoman [DW/PA/5/1588/10]
  Henry of Shalford [DW/PA/7/1 f.1; 1484] <Abs 3>
  Henry of Shere [DW/PA/5/1557/27]
  Isabel of Shalford [DW/PA/7/1 ff.86,91; 1487] <Abs 290>
  James of Godalming, gent. [PRO; PCC Will 1626]

ELLIOTT (ELEATT,ELETES,ELIEDE,ELIOT,ELIOTT,ELLIETT,ELLOATE,ELLYOTT,ELYATTE, ELYEATT,ELYET,ELYETT,ELYOT,ELYOTT,HELYT) [*continued*]

James of Richmond, groom of H.M.'s Privy Chamber [PRO; PCC 1634]
Joan of Epsom, widow [DW/PA/5/1558/89]*
Joan of ..., widow of William [DW/PA/5/1605/29] <Abs U140>
Joan of Chobham [DW/PA/5/1550/88]
John of Albury, gent. [PRO; PCC Will 1595]
John of Godalming - Catteshall; Albury, shearman [DW/PA/5/1552/25]
John of Godalming [PRO; PCC Will 1553]
John of Godalming, gent. [DW/PA/7/7 f.180; DW/PA/5/1597/36] <Abs 331>
John of Godalming, gent. [DW/PA/7/7 f.598; DW/PA/5/1607/38] <Abs 1121>
John of Godalming, gent. [PRO; PCC Will 1628]
John of Guildford St Nicolas [DW/PA/7/1 f.43; 1486] <Abs 140>
John of West Horsley - Woodcote, yeoman [DW/PA/7/10 f.222; DW/PA/5/1621/40]
John of Shalford [DW/PA/7/4 f.35; 1533]
John of Worplesdon, weaver [DW/PA/7/7 f.257; DW/PA/5/1599/20] <Abs 452>
Juliana of Albury, widow [DW/PA/7/3 f.152; 1530]
Juliana of Godalming - Catteshall, widow [HRO; 1571 B59]
Lawrence of West Clandon, husbandman [HRO; 1582 B29]
Lawrence of Godalming, esq. [PRO; PCC Will 1619]
Margery of Godalming, widow [DW/PA/5/1558/87]*
Martha of Godalming, spinster [PRO; PCC 1630] <Scroope 1219>
Nicholas of Ditton, gent. [PRO; PCC Will 1547]
Nicholas of Hambledon [DW/PA/5/1587/16]
Nicholas of Leatherhead, labourer [DW/PA/7/9 f.273; 1618]
Nicholas of Shalford [DW/PA/7/4 f.200; 1537]
Rachel of Reigate, widow [DW/PA/7/12 f.522; DW/PA/5/1635/30]
Richard of Albury, gent., senior [DW/PA/5/1581/31]
Richard of Dorking, husbandman [DW/PA/5/1581/60]
Richard of Godalming [DW/PA/7/1 f.45; 1486] <Abs 148>
Richard of Dunsfold, weaver [DW/PA/5/1592/101]
Richard of Godalming [DW/PA/7/9 f.200; DW/PA/5/1616/46]
Richard of Godalming [DW/PA/7/13 f.233; DW/PA/5/1642/28]
Richard of Reigate, esq. [PRO; PCC Will 1614]
Richard of Sutton, priest [PRO; PCC Will 1543] <Abs. SAC v.52 p.48>
Robert of Compton [*in* DW/PA/5/1558/166]*
Robert of Godalming - Farncombe, weaver [DW/PA/7/8 f.27; DW/PA/5/1608/43]
Robert of Godalming [DW/PA/7/11 f.224; DW/PA/5/1625/76]
Robert of Shalford, yeoman [HRO; 1595 B14]
Robert of Sutton, husbandman [DW/PA/5/1591/68]
Robert of Windlesham - Bagshot, tanner [DW/PA/7/7 f.112; DW/PA/5/1596/22] <Abs 205>
Robert of Witley, husbandman [DW/PA/7/13 f.417; DW/PA/5/1645/14]
Roger of Godalming - Catteshall, yeoman [DW/PA/7/10 f.216; DW/PA/5/1621/39]
Sarah of Ewhurst [PRO; PCC 1647]
Stephen of Dunsfold, yeoman [DW/PA/5/1558/92]*
Stephen of Shalford [DW/PA/7/2 f.45; c.1495]
Thomas of Bramley, gent. [PRO; PCC Will 1548]
Thomas of West Clandon; East Clandon, husbandman [DW/PA/7/8 f.232; DW/PA/5/1612/54]
Thomas of Dorking, bricklayer [DW/PA/5/1575/49]
Thomas of Limpsfield, carpenter [DW/PA/7/9 f.122; DW/PA/5/1615/46]

ELLIOTT (ELEATT,ELETES,ELIEDE,ELIOT,ELIOTT,ELLIETT,ELLOATE,ELLYOTT,ELYATTE, ELYEATT,ELYET,ELYETT,ELYOT,ELYOTT,HELYT) [*continued*]

Thomas of Send, carpenter [DW/PA/7/8 f.285; DW/PA/5/1613/36]
Thomas of Shalford [DW/PA/7/3 f.142; 1530]
Thomas of Shalford [PRO; PCC 1639]
Thomas of Shere [PRO; PCC Will 1589]
Thomas of Windlesham - Bagshot [DW/PA/7/4 f.166; 1536]
William of Dorking [HRO; 1531 B7]
William of Epsom [DW/PA/5/1561/9]
William of Godalming, gent. [DW/PA/7/13 f.134; DW/PA/5/1640/48]
William of Guildford St Nicolas [DW/PA/7/1 f.43; 1486] <Abs 139>
William of Lambeth [PRO; PCC Will 1533]
William of Shalford, husbandman [DW/PA/7/11 f.540; DW/PA/5/1629/33]
William of Shalford, husbandman [DW/PA/7/13 f.449; DW/PA/5/1646/16]
William of Shere, yeoman [DW/PA/7/13 f.45; DW/PA/5/1639/51]
Zachariah of Godalming, clothier [DW/PA/7/11 f.199; DW/PA/5/1625/77]

ELLIS (ELES,ELLES,ELLYS,ELYS,HELIS)

Anthony of East Molesey [PRO; PCC Will 1576]
Christopher of Cobham [DW/PA/5/1550/83]
Edmund of Reigate, husbandman [DW/PA/7/12 f.340; DW/PA/5/1636/36]
Edward of Swk St Saviour; Oswestry, Shropshire, leatherdresser [DW/PA/7/9 f.28; DW/PA/5/1614/44]
Edward, alias Edward Knight of Ewhurst [DW/PA/7/11 f.527; DW/PA/5/1630/65]
Edward of Horne [PRO; PCC Will 1549]
Edward of Lingfield [PRO; PCC Will 1584]
Edward of Rotherhithe [PRO; PCC Will 1596]
Francis of Croydon, yeoman [LPL; 96/861; Will 1618]
John of Dorking, baker [DW/PA/7/11 f.411; DW/PA/5/1627/33]
John, alias John Knight of Ewhurst, yeoman [DW/PA/7/8 f.196; DW/PA/5/1610/79]
John, alias John Knight of Ewhurst, husbandman [DW/PA/5/1627/66]
John of Farnham - Tilford [DW/PA/7/7 f.642; DW/PA/5/1608/55] <Abs 1207>
John of Horsell, esq. [PRO; PCC Will 1584]
John of Lingfield [DW/PA/7/8 f.87; DW/PA/5/1609/44]
John (son of Ellis ap Teller) of Swk St Saviour, victualler [DW/PA/7/9 f.116; DW/PA/5/1615/47]
John, alias John Bittenden of Thursley, husbandman [DW/PA/7/7 f.289; DW/PA/5/1599/91] <Abs 517>
John of Swk St Saviour [DW/PA/5/1578/80]
Margaret of Rotherhithe, widow [PRO; PCC Will 1611] <Abs, SAC v.35 p.40>
Ralph, alias Ralph Knight of Ewhurst, yeoman [DW/PA/7/12 f.395; DW/PA/5/1637/65]
Richard of Great Bookham [DW/PA/7/2 f.109; 1517]
Richard of Horne [DW/PA/7/2 f.36; 1493]
Richard of Mickleham, clerk and rector [DW/PA/7/8 f.298; DW/PA/5/1613/37]
Richard of Swk St George [DW/PA/7/12 f.319; DW/PA/5/1636/32]
Thomas of Burstow [PRO; PCC Will *and* Admon 1582]
Thomas of Swk St Olave, servant of Sampson Cleyton, baker [DW/PA/7/3 f.118; 1529]
William of Chipstead [DW/PA/7/2 f.123; 1518]
William of East Molesey, husbandman [DW/PA/5/1557/66]

ELLOATE *see* ELLIOTT

ELLSTEED *see* ELSTEAD
ELLYNGBRIGE *see* ELLINGBRIDGE
ELLYNOR *see* ELEANOR
ELLYOTT *see* ELLIOTT
ELLYS *see* ELLIS
ELMAN
Joan of Lingfield, widow [DW/PA/7/13 f.41; DW/PA/5/1639/50]
ELMER
Amy of Beddington, widow [DW/PA/7/7 f.234; DW/PA/5/1598/28] <Abs 411>
Christopher of Weybridge, yeoman [DW/PA/7/13 f.77; DW/PA/5/1641/41]
Richard of Beddington [DW/PA/5/1593/190]
Richard of Swk St Olave, feltmaker [DW/PA/7/9 f.259; DW/PA/5/1617/41]
ELMERUGGE *see* ELLINBRIDGE
ELMES
Elizabeth of Surrey [PRO; PCC Will 1526]
ELMORE
Ann of Weybridge, widow [DW/PA/7/11 f.128; DW/PA/5/1624/44]
ELRINGTON (ELRYNGTON)
(Sir) John of Surrey, knight [PRO; PCC Will 1483]
Thomas of Abinger; Shere, esq. [PRO; PCC Will 1566]
William of ... [GMR; 97/13/1112; Will 1606]
ELSEY (ELSAYE)
Ann of Merstham, widow [LPL; 96/866; 98/1 f.81v; Will 1637]
John of Betchworth [DW/PA/5/1591/45]
John of Leigh [DW/PA/5/1558/86]*
John of Mortlake, yeoman [LPL; 96/865; Will 1628]
Nicholas of Merstham [PRO; PCC 1649]
ELSMORE
Richard of Rotherhithe, gent. [DW/PA/7/12 f.521; DW/PA/5/1638/41]
Richard of Rotherhithe, yeoman [DW/PA/7/13 f.171; DW/PA/5/1641/43]
ELSON
Henry, alias Henry Nelson of Swk St Olave [DW/PA/5/1582/105]
ELSTEAD (ELLSTEED,ELSTED,ELSTEED)
Henry of Worplesdon [? HRO; 1622]
John of Worplesdon, pailmaker [DW/PA/5/1588/25]
Robert of Worplesdon, husbandman [DW/PA/7/12 f.12; DW/PA/5/1631/38]
Humphrey of Ewell [PRO; PCC Will 1505]
ELTON
Edward of Bermondsey, clerk [PRO; PCC Will 1624]
Richard of Lambeth - Lambeth Marsh [PRO; PCC 1649]
ELVERSTON
Randolph of Putney [LPL; 98/1 f.61r; (ren.) 1637]
ELVIN (ELVEN,ELVYN)
Andrew of Reigate [DW/PA/7/12 f.231; DW/PA/5/1634/38]
John, alias John Amyas of Horley [PRO; PCC Will 1591 (*two*)]
John, alias John Amyas of Horley, yeoman [DW/PA/5/1591/59]
John, alias John Amyas of Reigate, junior [DW/PA/7/11 f.473; DW/PA/5/1628/33]
Matilda of Nutfield, widow [HRO; Reg. CCB 20 p.13; 1563]
Richard of Reigate [DW/PA/7/5 f.162; 1540]
Robert of Nutfield [PRO; PCC Admon 1603]
William of Horne [HRO; 1566 B68-69]
William of Reigate, yeoman husbandman [DW/PA/5/1557/19]
see also ALWYN

ELWARD
Robert of Lambeth [PRO; PCC Will 1554]
ELWICKE (ELWOLD,ELWYL)
Elizabeth of Battersea [PRO; PCC 1646]
Leonard of Ewell [DW/PA/7/9 f.294; 1619]
Lucy of Battersea [PRO; PCC Admon 1646]
Sarah of Battersea [PRO; PCC 1644]
Timothy of Putney [PRO; PCC Admon 1641]
William Elwyl alias William Chapman of Battersea [PRO; PCC Will 1403]
ELY (ELYE)
John of Guildford St Nicolas - Artington [DW/PA/5/1592/3]
Nicholas West, bishop of, of Putney [PRO; PCC Will 1534]
Richard of Swk St Margaret [HRO; Reg. Way 1 p.54; 1458]
ELYATTE *see* ELLIOTT
ELYE *see* ELY
ELYEATT,ELYET,ELYETT *see* ELLIOTT
ELYNGBRIG,ELYNGBRIGGE *see* ELLINGBRIDGE
ELYOT,ELYOTT *see* ELLIOTT
ELYS *see* ELLIS
EMANSON *see* EDMUNDSON
EMBERTON
William of Barnes, waterman [LPL; 96/872; 98/1 f.115r; Will 1640]
EMENSON *see* EDMUNDSON
EMERSON *see* EMMERSON
EMERY
Peter of Swk St Saviour - Liberty of the Clink, waterman [DW/PA/7/8 f.303; DW/PA/5/1613/39]
EMETE,EMETT *see* EMMETT
EMME
Simon of Richmond - Kings Sheen [DW/PA/7/5 ff.81,84; 1488] <Abs 266,281>
EMMERSON
Humphrey of Swk St Saviour, gent. [DW/PA/5/1603/47] <Abs U67>
EMMETT (EMETE,EMETT,EMMET,EMOTT)
Nicholas of Cobham [DW/PA/5/1578/6]
Richard of Chobham, husbandman [DW/PA/5/1571/10]
Richard of Chobham, yeoman, senior [DW/PA/7/13 f.207; DW/PA/5/1642/27]
Thomas of Thames Ditton, tanner [DW/PA/7/13 f.248; DW/PA/5/1641/44]
William of Chobham [DW/PA/7/6 f.21; DW/PA/5/1559/18]
William of Cobham [PRO; PCC Admon 1646]
EMMONS
Stephen of Swk St Saviour, butcher [DW/PA/7/12 f.320; DW/PA/5/1636/33]
EMNTYNAT *see* ENTICKNAP
EMOTT *see* EMMETT
EMPNAT *see* ENTICKNAP
EMPSON (EMSON)
John of Swk St Saviour; Hornsey, Middlesex; Grays Inn, Middlesex, victualler [DW/PA/5/1605/30] <Abs U141>
William of Egham [HRO; 1551 U51-52]
William of Rotherhithe; Bermondsey [PRO; PCC Will 1603 *and* 1604]
ENDERBY (ENDERBIE)
Alice of Bermondsey, widow [DW/PA/7/11 f.229; DW/PA/5/1625/78]
Daniel of Bermondsey, weaver [DW/PA/5/1627/29]
ENFEILD
William of Swk St Saviour, waterman [DW/PA/7/10 f.96; DW/PA/5/1619/42]

ENGLAND
George of Swk St Saviour, cordwainer [DW/PA/7/12 f.336; DW/PA/5/1636/35]
Stephen of Swk St George, citizen and painter stainer [DW/PA/7/7 f.641; DW/PA/5/1608/44] <Abs 1203>
ENGLER (INGLER,YNGLAR)
Thomas of Reigate - 'Linckefeld' [DW/PA/5/1575/90]
William of Betchworth, gent. [DW/PA/7/13 f.19; DW/PA/5/1639/49]
ENGLISH (ENGLISHE)
Christopher of Swk St Olave, cooper [DW/PA/7/7 f.402; DW/PA/5/1603/46] <Abs 744>
George of Cranleigh [PRO; PCC Admon 1636]
John of Cranleigh, yeoman [DW/PA/7/12 f.234; DW/PA/5/1634/39]
Katherine of Swk St Olave, widow [DW/PA/7/7 f.517; DW/PA/5/1613/38] <Abs 971> [*The will is dated 1603, and may be filed in 1613 in error.*]
ENMY
Gilbert of Lambeth [DW/PA/5/1578/83]
ENSALL *see* ANSELL
ENSCOMBE *see* ANSCOMBE
ENSOLL *see* ANSELL
ENSTY *see* ANSTY
ENTICKNAP (ANTEKEP,AWYKELDER,EMNTYNAT,EMPNAT,ENTNAP,ENTNEPP,ENTYCNAP)
Ann of Chiddingfold, spinster [PRO; PCC Admon 1649]
Harman, alias Harman Witley of Stoke next Guildford, beer brewer [*in* DW/PA/5/1551/1]
Richard of Godalming, husbandman [DW/PA/7/12 f.513; DW/PA/5/1639/47]
Thomas of Chiddingfold [DW/PA/5/1558/90]
Thomas of Chiddingfold, yeoman [DW/PA/7/12 f.435; DW/PA/5/1637/39]
Thomas of Thursley, junior [DW/PA/7/12 f.308; DW/PA/5/1635/28]
Thomas of Thursley [HRO; 1642 B15]
William of Chiddingfold [DW/PA/7/1 f.100; 1490] <Abs 327>
ERBERY
William of Swk St Olave [DW/PA/7/12 f.466; DW/PA/5/1638/39]
ERCKELE
'Joannes' of ...; 'Bellecoli', Flanders [*German Church - in Latin*] [DW/PA/5/1563/102]
ERELL *see* ERROLL
ERITH (ERYTHE)
John of Wandsworth [PRO; PCC Will 1506]
ERLE,ERLES *see* EARL
ERLEYE,ERLY *see* EARLY
ERNESBIE
Griffin of Colchester, Essex; Lambeth, clothier [PRO; PCC Will 1591] <Abs Emmison pp.284-285>
ERRINGTON
Anthony of Morden; Newcastle on Tyne, Northumberland [PRO; PCC 1648]
ERROLL (ERELL)
Joyce of Farnham, widow [DW/PA/7/7 f.57; DW/PA/5/1596/20] <Abs 109>
ERYTHE *see* ERITH
ESCOTT
George of Bermondsey [PRO; PCC Admon 1647]
Nathaniel of Rotherhithe (but died overseas) [PRO; PCC Admon 1641]
ESLAND *see* EASTLAND

ESLIN
William of Swk St George, colour grinder [DW/PA/7/9 f.305; DW/PA/5/1619/43]
ESSELL
Richard of Guildford Holy Trinity [BM; Add.Ms 24,925 f.18v; c1544] <Abs 42>
ESSEX
(Sir) William of Surrey, knight [PRO; PCC Will 1548]
EST *see* EAST
ESTED *see* EASTED
ESTIN *see* EASTON
ESTLAND,ESTLONDE *see* EASTLAND
ESTMENT,ESTMUNDE *see* EASTMAN
ESTON *see* EASTON
ESTWICKE *see* EASTWICK
ETHERIDGE (ETHEREDGE,ETHERIDG)
Thomas of Swk St Saviour, citizen and ale brewer [DW/PA/5/1581/51]
Thomas of Streatham, victualler [DW/PA/7/8 f.264; DW/PA/5/1611/28]
ETON *see* EATON
EUSTACE
Geoffrey of Newington [PRO; PCC Will 1625]
see also HEWSTICE
EUSTON (EUSTONN,EWSTON)
Walter of Bermondsey, rector [HRO; Reg. Way 1 f.16; 1448]
William of Warlingham [DW/PA/7/1 f.19; 1485] <Abs 64>
EVANS (EVANCE,YVANS)
Barbara of Swk St Olave, widow [DW/PA/7/11 f.585; DW/PA/5/1630/32]
Charles of Horne, gent. [PRO; PCC Will 1603] <Abs, SAC v.11 pp.110-111>
Elizabeth of Lambeth - Lambeth Marsh, widow [PRO; PCC Will 1622]
Golawayes of Newington [LPL; 98/1 f.84v; (ren.) 1637]
Henry of Swk St Olave, silk weaver [DW/PA/7/10 f.182; DW/PA/5/1620/48]
Humphrey of Swk St Saviour, fisherman [DW/PA/5/1571/14]
Jeremy of Swk St Saviour [DW/PA/7/13 f.395; DW/PA/5/1645/17]
John of Kingston, gent. [PRO; PCC 1642]
John of Newington, widower [PRO; PCC Admon 1639]
John of Swk St George, victualler [DW/PA/5/1581/50]
John of Swk St George [DW/PA/5/1604/17] <Abs U104>
Magdalen of Swk St Olave, spinster [DW/PA/7/7 f.349; DW/PA/5/1601/33] <Abs 640>
Meredith of Swk St Olave, feltmaker [DW/PA/7/8 f.44; DW/PA/5/1609/45]
Richard of Mortlake [PRO; PCC Will 1601]
Richard of Newington [LPL; 98/1 f.101v; (ren.) 1639]
Richard of Rotherhithe, waterman [DW/PA/7/11 f.570; DW/PA/5/1630/33]
Robert of ...., citizen and grocer [DW/PA/7/12 f.323; DW/PA/5/1636/34]
Susan of Richmond, widow [DW/PA/7/8 f.144; DW/PA/5/1611/29]
Thomas of Leatherhead, yeoman [PRO; PCC Will 1626]
Thomas of Swk St Saviour, fisherman [DW/PA/5/1552/22]
William of Newington [PRO; PCC Will 1590]
William of Rotherhithe [PRO; PCC Admon 1638]
EVATTES
Henry of Swk St Thomas Hospital [DW/PA/5/1575/6]
EVE *see* EVES
EVELYN (EVELING)
Frances of Kingston, widow [PRO; PCC Admon 1649]

EVELYN (EVELING) [*continued*]

George of Wotton [PRO; PCC Will 1603] <Abs, SAC v.11 p.111>

George of Wotton, esq. [PRO; PCC Will 1606]

Henry of East Clandon, husbandman [DW/PA/7/10 f.187; DW/PA/5/1620/49]

John of Streatham, gent. [DW/PA/7/11 f.397; DW/PA/5/1627/35]

Richard of Wotton, esq. [PRO; PCC 1641]

Thomas of Long Ditton, esq. [PRO; PCC Will 1617]

EVERED (AVERED,EVERARD,EVERARDE,EVERETT,EVERIDGE,EVERYT)

Elizabeth of Guildford Holy Trinity, widow [DW/PA/7/13 f.441; DW/PA/5/1646/15]

Elizabeth of Swk St Saviour [DW/PA/7/6 f.222; 1561]

Joan (formerly Joan Banister) of Surrey [PRO; PCC Will 1551]

Joan of Kingston, widow [DW/PA/7/8 f.172; DW/PA/5/1610/8]

Nicholas of Mitcham [DW/PA/7/7 f.350; DW/PA/5/1601/34] <Abs 645>

William of Kingston, carpenter [DW/PA/7/8 f.36; DW/PA/5/1609/9]

see also EVERSHED

EVERS

Hugh of Swk St Margaret [DW/PA/7/5 f.61; 1539] <Abs 86>

EVERSEDE,EVERSEED *see* EVERSHED

EVERSFIELD (EVERSFELD)

Nicholas of Seale - Poyle [PRO; PCC Will 1552]

EVERSHED (EVERSEDE,EVERSEED,EVERSYDE,EVESEED)

Edmund of Abinger, yeoman [DW/PA/5/1558/88]*

John of Ockley [PRO; PCC Will 1564]

Mary of Swk St Thomas, spinster [DW/PA/7/7 f.641; DW/PA/5/1608/45] <Abs 1202>

Richard of Charlwood, yeoman [LPL; 96/886; 98/1 f.118r; Will 1640]

Thomas of Newdigate; Rusper, Sussex [DW/PA/7/7 f.468; DW/PA/5/1604/18] <Abs 883>

see also EVERED

EVERYT *see* EVERETT

EVES (EVE,EYVES)

Artemisia of Swk St Olave, widow [DW/PA/7/8 f.279; DW/PA/5/1613/40]

John of Bermondsey, tailor [DW/PA/5/1639/48] <Abs U258>

Robert of Swk St Saviour, chandler [DW/PA/7/10 f.47; 1619]

EWARD

David of Bermondsey [DW/PA/7/3 f.110; 1529]

EWELL

John of Walton [*Probably Walton on the Hill, as proved at Reigate.*] [DW/PA/7/3 f.151; 1530]

EWEN (EWINE,EWYN)

John of Camberwell [DW/PA/7/13 f.409; DW/PA/5/1645/13]

John of Swk St Margaret, coroner [DW/PA/7/2 f.76; 1501]

Nicholas of Swk St Margaret [DW/PA/7/2 f.69; 1500]

Rebecca of Camberwell, widow [DW/PA/7/13 f.428; DW/PA/5/1646/14]

EWER (EWERS)

Alice of Malden [PRO; PCC Will 1592]

Alice of Egham [DW/PA/7/10 f.170; DW/PA/5/1621/41]

Richard of Chelsea - Little Chelsea, Middlesex, yeoman [DW/PA/7/12 f.528; 1637]

Richard of Putney [LPL; 98/1 f.77v; (ren.) 1636]

Roger of Malden [PRO; PCC Will 1592]

EWHURST (EWHERST,EWHORSTE)

James of Horley [PRO; PCC Admon 1571]

EWHURST (EWHERST,EWHORSTE) [*continued*]
Joan of Horley, widow [DW/PA/5/1571/3]
Robert of Horley [DW/PA/7/9 f.189; DW/PA/5/1616/47]
EWINE *see* EWEN
EWSTON *see* EUSTON
EWYN *see* EWEN
EXALL (EXFEILDE,EXEFOULDE,EXFOLD,EXFOULDE,EXHOLDE,EXOLD,EXOLDE,EXOLLDE, EXSOLDE)
Ann of Guildford St Mary, widow [DW/PA/7/2 f.101; 1514]
Edward of Worplesdon; Puttenham, yeoman [DW/PA/7/12 f.359; DW/PA/5/1636/37]
Elizabeth of Godalming, widow [DW/PA/5/1562/80]
Henry of Worplesdon; Ash, yeoman [DW/PA/5/1555/66]
John of Ash, husbandman [DW/PA/7/6 f.207; 1560]
Margaret of Guildford St Mary [DW/PA/7/2 f.100; 1514]
Richard of Ash, husbandman [DW/PA/7/5 f.212; 1541]
Richard of Frimley, husbandman [HRO; 1582 B30]
Richard of Worplesdon [DW/PA/7/1 f.61; 1487] <Abs 204>
Richard of Worplesdon [DW/PA/7/2 f.9; 1491]
Robert of Kingston, butcher [DW/PA/7/4 f.77; 1534]
Robert of Swk St George; Guildford St Nicolas [PRO; PCC Admon 1595]
Robert of Worplesdon [DW/PA/7/4 f.68; 1534]
EXNING
John of Lambeth - Water Lambeth [PRO; PCC Will 1570]
EXOLD,EXOLDE,EXOLLDE,EXSOLDE *see* EXALL
EYCHCOKE *see* HITCHCOCK
EYCK (de EUCK)
Francis of Swk; 'St Odulph' [DW/PA/7/3 f.159; 1530]
EYE
John of Godalming [HRO; 1520 B11]
EYER,EYERE *see* EYRES
EYMERS *see* AYLMER
EYRES (AYRE,AYRES,EYER,EYERS)
John, alias John Dayer of Ash, yeoman, senior [DW/PA/5/1582/40]
Richard of Bermondsey, citizen and leatherseller [PRO; PCC 1648]
Richard of Swk St Olave [DW/PA/7/13 f.423; DW/PA/5/1645/16]
Robert of Reigate, clerk [DW/PA/7/5 f.151; 1540]
Robert of Swk St Saviour, waterman [DW/PA/7/9 f.80; DW/PA/5/1614/2]
Thomas of Battersea; Dorking [PRO; PCC Will 1547]
Thomas of Lambeth, yeoman [PRO; PCC 1630] <Scroope 1022>
EYSTED *see* EASTED
EYVES *see* EVES
EZERYE
John of Camberwell - Dulwich [DW/PA/5/1587/85]

FABIAN (FABYAN)
John of Thorpe, gent., senior [PRO; PCC Will 1618]
John of Thorpe, gent. [PRO; PCC 1631]
FACE
Robert of Swk St Saviour [HRO; 1606 B18] [*and*] [DW/PA/7/7 f.529; DW/PA/5/1606/37] <Abs 997>

FACHEN (FAUCHIN)
Edward of Frensham - Pitfold, yeoman [PRO; PCC Will 1628]
FACY
John of Newington - Walworth [PRO; PCC Will 1550]
FAGGETTER (FAGAT'R,FAGATTERE,FAGITER)
Henry of Ash, blacksmith [DW/PA/7/13 f.445; DW/PA/5/1646/20]
Richard of Guildford Holy Trinity, smith [*in* DW/PA/5/1557/88]
Richard of Pirbright [HRO; 1573 B43]
FAIRBANK (FAIRBANCK,FAIRBANCKE,FAYREBANCK)
Edward of Kingston, gent. [DW/PA/7/10 f.90; DW/PA/5/1615/31]
Joseph of Kingston, gent. [DW/PA/7/13 f.159; DW/PA/5/1641/50]
Mary of Kingston, widow [DW/PA/7/13 f.404; DW/PA/5/1645/19]
FAIRBROTHER (FAYREBROTHER,FENROTHER)
Richard of Shere, glover [DW/PA/7/12 f.16; DW/PA/5/1631/44]
Robert of Kingston [PRO; PCC Will 1524]
FAIRCHILD (FAIRECHILD,FAYERCHILD,FAYRCHILD,FAYRECHILD,FAYRECHYLDE)
Beatrice of Ockham, widow [*in* DW/PA/5/1558/166]*
George of Walton on Thames [DW/PA/5/1570/43]
Oliver of Ockham, yeoman [DW/PA/5/1558/105]*
Oliver of Stoke Dabernon [HRO; 1604 B22]
Thomas of Stoke Dabernon, husbandman [HRO; 1620 B10]
FAIRCLOTH
Lawrence of Newington [LPL; 98/1 ff.75r,87r; Wills 1636 *and* 1637]
FAIRECHILD *see* FAIRCHILD
FAIRFIELD (FAYREFELD,FAYRFYELDE)
John of Swk St Saviour, butcher [DW/PA/7/7 f.146; DW/PA/5/1597/37] <Abs 268>
John of Streatham [PRO; PCC Will 1488] <Abs. SAC v.52 pp.33-34>
FAIRMAN (FAIREMAN,FAYRMAN,FEAREMAN,FERMAN)
Henry of Swk St George [DW/PA/7/4 f.107; 1535]
Rebecca of Swk St Olave [DW/PA/7/11 f.205; DW/PA/5/1625/83]
Robert of Swk St George [DW/PA/7/4 f.144; 1536]
Thomas of London, citizen and carpenter [DW/PA/5/1575/83]
Thomas of Swk St Saviour, yeoman [DW/PA/7/11 ff.174,324; DW/PA/5/1625/81]
see also FARMAN
FAIRWEATHER (FAYREWETHER)
Richard of Rotherhithe [PRO; PCC Will 1588]
FAIRY *see* FARY
FALCONER,FALKNER *see* FAULKNER
FALLOWES
John, alias John Follis of Newington, yeoman [LPL; 96/890; Will 1625]
FALLOWFIELD (FALLOWFEILD,FALLOWFELD)
Richard of Bermondsey, leatherseller [DW/PA/7/8 f.149; DW/PA/5/1611/31]
William of Seale, junior [PRO; PCC Admon 1611]
FANE
Anthony of Kingston (3rd son of Francis, earl of Westmorland) [PRO; PCC 1642]
FANNER
Edward of Rotherhithe [PRO; PCC Admon 1617]
FARDING (FARDYNG de GRACE)
Edmund of Bermondsey [PRO; PCC 1646]
Mome Farding de Grace of Swk St Mary Overy [DW/PA/7/5 f.11; 1538] <Abs 92>
FAREBANK *see* FAIRBANK

FARELYE *see* FARLEY
FARENDEN, FARENDON *see* FARRINGDON
FARLEY (FARELYE, FARLE, FARLEYE, FARLIE, FARLYE, FARNLEY, FAYRLEY)
  Edward of West Horsley, weaver [DW/PA/7@/8 f.10; DW/PA/5/1608/46]
  Edward of Kingston - Surbiton, carpenter [DW/PA/7/7 f.516; DW/PA/5/1605/31] <Abs 970>
  Edward of Newington [LPL; 98/1 f.38r (ren.); 1632]
  Edward of Woking, yeoman [DW/PA/7/13 f.23; DW/PA/5/1639/54]
  Harry of Albury; Ewhurst [DW/PA/7/6 f.102; DW/PA/5/1559/67]
  John of Effingham, husbandman [*in* DW/PA/5/1558/95]*
  John of West Horsley, husbandman [DW/PA/5/1570/68]
  John of West Horsley, husbandman [DW/PA/5/1576/126]
  John of West Horsley, yeoman [DW/PA/7/11 f.410; DW/PA/5/1627/36]
  John of Kingston - Surbiton, carpenter [DW/PA/7/9 f.326; DW/PA/5/1619/44]
  Juliana of Woking - Sutton, widow [DW/PA/5/1587/17]
  Margaret of Shalford [DW/PA/5/1558/94]*
  Richard, alias Richard Deane of Albury [DW/PA/5/1561/37]
  Richard of Guildford Holy Trinity [DW/PA/7/2 f.173; 1522]
  Silvester of Send; West Horsley [DW/PA/7/3 f.178; 1531]
  Thomas of Albury [DW/PA/7/1 f.53; 1487] <Abs 175>
  Thomas of Albury - Farley Green, yeoman [HRO; 1605 B24]
  Thomas of Ewhurst [DW/PA/7/11 f.392; DW/PA/5/1626/45]
  Thomas of Walton on Thames [DW/PA/7/11 f.369; DW/PA/5/1627/37]
  Thomas of Wonersh, husbandman [DW/PA/5/1591/30]
  William of Send, husbandman [HRO; 1637 B18]
FARLIMAN
  John of Mitcham, carpenter [DW/PA/7/12 f.269; DW/PA/5/1635/32]
FARLYE *see* FARLEY
FARMAN
  James of Swk St Olave, haberdasher [DW/PA/7/11 f.155; DW/PA/5/1625/82]
  Martin of Swk St George [DW/PA/7/5 f.48; 1538] <Abs 83>
    see also FAIRMAN
FARMER
  John of Chertsey [DW/PA/7/12 f.1; DW/PA/5/1631/41]
  John of Swk St Saviour, bachelor [DW/PA/7/12 f.369; DW/PA/5/1627/32]
  William of Merton [PRO; PCC Admon 1607]
FARNDEN (FARNEDEN, FARNDON, FERNEDEN, FERNDEN)
  George of Haslemere, yeoman [DW/PA/7/6 f.122; DW/PA/5/1559/167]
  James of Thursley, husbandman [DW/PA/7/12 f.299; DW/PA/5/1635/36]
  Richard, alias Richard Varden of Haslemere, husbandman [HRO; 1609 B28]
  Robert of Haslemere, yeoman [DW/PA/7/7 f.294; DW/PA/5/1600/20] <Abs 527>
  Robert of Haslemere, yeoman [DW/PA/7/8 f.240; DW/PA/5/1613/41]
  Thomas of Elstead [DW/PA/7/11 f.539; DW/PA/5/1629/34]
    see also FINDEN
FARNHAM
  John of Bisley [HRO; 1585 B26]
FARNHURST (FARNES, VERNEST)
  John of Guildford St Nicolas [DW/PA/7/1 f.3; 1484] <Abs 8>
  John of Newdigate [DW/PA/7/1 f.25; 1486] <Abs 83>
FARNLEY *see* FARLEY
FARR
  Anthony of Swk St Olave, waterman [DW/PA/7/8 f.; DW/PA/5/1611/30]
  Helen of Newington, widow [LPL; 96/899; Will 1617]

FARR [*continued*]
John of Bermondsey, shipwright [DW/PA/7/13 f.144; DW/PA/5/1641/46]
John of Swk, smith [DW/PA/7/13 f.127; DW/PA/5/1640/55]
Richard of Shalford; Dunsfold, husbandman [DW/PA/7/8 f.195; DW/PA/5/1610/53]
FARRALL *see* FARRELL
FARRAND *see* FERRAND
FARRAR *see* FERRERS
FARRELL (FARRALL,FARRAWLE)
George of Windlesham [PRO; PCC Will 1605] <Abs, SAC v.12 p.88>
John, alias John Toddie of Windlesham - Bagshot [HRO; 1593 AD88]
Thaddeus of Windlesham - Bagshot, innholder [PRO; PCC Will 1583]
FARRIER
William of Swk St Saviour, porter [DW/PA/7/7 f.343; DW/PA/5/1601/35] <Abs 626>
FARRINGDON (FARENDON,FARYNGTON,FERRENDEN)
Alice of Farnham, widow [DW/PA/7/6 f.258; 1560]
Elizabeth of Frensham - Pitfold [DW/PA/7/11 f.473; DW/PA/5/1628/34]
John, alias John Varndell of Haslemere [PRO; PCC 1632]
John of West Molesey, yeoman [PRO; PCC Will 1605] <Abs, SAC v.12 p.95>
Ralph of Swk St Margaret, grocer [DW/PA/7/2 f.134; 1519]
FARROR *see* FERRERS
FARTHING
Christopher of Croydon [LPL; 96/901; 98/1 f.5v; Will 1629]
FARY
Richard of Surrey, yeoman [PRO; PCC Will 1581]
FARYNGTON *see* FARRINGDON
FASSAT *see* FAWCETT
FATHERS (FATHERE)
Ann of Swk St George, widow [DW/PA/7/12 f.285; DW/PA/5/1635/35]
Bridget of Swk St George, widow [DW/PA/7/11 f.178; DW/PA/5/1625/79]
FAUCET,FAUCETT *see* FAWCETT
FAUCHIN *see* FACHEN
FAUCKES *see* FULKE
FAULASFAN *see* FULLFINE
FAULKNER (FALCONER,FALKNER,FAWCONER,FAWKENER)
Hugh of Chertsey [PRO; PCC Will 1494]
Michael, alias Michael Foster of Newington, yeoman [PRO; PCC Will 1602] <Abs, SAC v.10 p.311>
Nicholas of Swk St Margaret [DW/PA/7/5 f.127; 1539]
Robert of Bermondsey [PRO; PCC Admon 1599]
Robert of Bisley, clerk [PRO; PCC Will 1512]
Simon of Battersea [DW/PA/7/12 f.519; DW/PA/5/1638/50]
FAVELL
Anthony of ...; Arras, France [DW/PA/7/11 f.391; DW/PA/5/1626/46]
FAWCETT (FASSAT,FAUCET,FAUCETT,FAVERTT,FAWCET,FAWSETT)
Edmund of Swk St Olave [DW/PA/5/1578/97]
Richard of Bermondsey [PRO; PCC Admon 1614]
Richard of Swk St Olave [DW/PA/7/11 f.165; DW/PA/5/1625/80]
Sarah of Swk St Olave, widow [DW/PA/7/12 f.155; DW/PA/5/1633/53]
Thomas of the Ship *Hart*, sailor [DW/PA/7/11 f.367; DW/PA/5/1626/47]
Thomas of Bermondsey [DW/PA/7/7 f.143; DW/PA/5/1597/38] <Abs 262>
FAWCONER,FAWKENER *see* FAULKNER
FAWSETT *see* FAWCETT

FAYERCHILD,FAYRCHILD *see* FAIRCHILD
FAYREBANCK *see* FAIRBANK
FAYREBROTHER *see* FAIRBROTHER
FAYRECHILD,FAYRECHYLDE *see* FAIRCHILD
FAYREFELD *see* FAIRFIELD
FAYREWETHER *see* FAIRWEATHER
FAYRLEY *see* FARLEY
FAYRMAN *see* FAIRMAN
FEAR *see* FERE
FEAREMAN *see* FAIRMAN
FEAREWALL
John of Camberwell, clerk [PRO; PCC Will 1556]
FEARINGE
Thomas of Camberwell - Dulwich [DW/PA/7/7 f.147; DW/PA/5/1597/39] <Abs 272>
FEARMAN *see* FAIRMAN
FEARNE *see* FERNE
FEATHERSTONE (FETHERSTON,FETHERSTONE)
Arthur of Burstow, gent. [PRO; PCC Will 1627]
Katherine of Burstow, widow [PRO; PCC Will 1627]
Leonard of Fetcham, clerk [DW/PA/7/11 f.302; DW/PA/5/1626/48]
FEATLEY
Daniel of Lambeth, clerk [PRO; PCC 1645]
FEE
William of Swk St Olave, citizen and leatherseller [DW/PA/5/1582/25]
FEELDE *see* FIELD
FEELDER,FEILDER *see* FIELDER
FEILDOWSE *see* FIELDHOUSE
FELD,FELDE *see* FIELD
FELDER,FELD'R *see* FIELDER
FELL
Leonard of Bermondsey, citizen and leatherseller [DW/PA/7/10 f.4; DW/PA/5/1619/45]
Peter of Lambeth, glazier [DW/PA/5/1623/39]
Thomas of Swk St George, bachelor, servant to Stephen England [DW/PA/5/1579/9]*
see also AFFELL
FELLMORE
Andrew of Farnham, servant [HRO; 1599 B16]
FELLOWE
Richard of Esher [HRO; 1588 AD24]
Thomas of Croydon [PRO; PCC 1631]
FELTON
John of Croydon [PRO; PCC Admon 1641]
Katherine of Croydon, spinster [PRO; PCC Admon 1618]
Richard of Dorking, husbandman [DW/PA/7/8 f.142; DW/PA/5/1611/32]
Thomas of Betchworth, tailor [DW/PA/7/10 f.171; DW/PA/5/1621/43]
FELTWELL
John of Swk St Olave, citizen and clothworker [DW/PA/7/8 f.194; DW/PA/5/1610/55]
FELYPE *see* PHILLIPS
FEMEL (FEMELL)
Henry of Rotherhithe, merchant [PRO; PCC 1638]
Henry of Rotherhithe [PRO; PCC Admon 1643]

FEN *see* FENN

FENDALL

Thomas of Kingston, butcher [DW/PA/7/8 f.406; DW/PA/5/1614/41]

FENN (FEN,FENE,FENNE)

Anthony of Byfleet, yeoman [HRO; 1603 B15]

Christopher of West Horsley [PRO; PCC 1631]

Henry of Horsell, husbandman [DW/PA/7/13 f.37; DW/PA/5/1639/58]

Joan of West Horsley, widow [DW/PA/7/7 f.208; 1598] <Abs 370>

John of Chertsey, yeoman, senior [SRO; 215/6/1; 1598] [*and*] [DW/PA/7/7 f.232; DW/PA/5/1598/29] <Abs 410>

John of West Clandon [DW/PA/7/3 f.201; 1532]

John of West Horsley, yeoman [DW/PA/7/10 f.38; DW/PA/5/1617/43]

Juliana of Chertsey, widow [PRO; PCC Will 1615]

Nicholas of West Horsley, yeoman [DW/PA/7/7 f.86; 1596] <Abs 157>

Nicholas of Wandsworth, bachelor [PRO; PCC Admon 1632]

Ralph of West Clandon, husbandman [DW/PA/5/1578/67]

Robert of Pyrford, husbandman *or* yeoman [HRO; 1585 B27]

Thomas of Chertsey, tilemaker [DW/PA/7/7 f.163; DW/PA/5/1597/40] <Abs 301>

William of West Horsley, yeoman [DW/PA/5/1592/16]

FENNALE *see* FENNELL

FENNE *see* FENN

FENNELL (FENNALE)

Elizabeth of Newington [LPL; 96/920; 98/1 f.47v; Will 1633]

Margery of Newington, widow [LPL; 98/1 f.75r; Will 1636]

Richard of Newington [LPL; 98/1 f.49v; Will 1633]

Thomas of Horne, yeoman [DW/PA/5/1593/187]

FENNER (FENNOR)

Henry of Horne, husbandman [DW/PA/7/10 f.181; DW/PA/5/1620/50]

James of Walton on Thames, yeoman [DW/PA/7/13 f.372; 1644]

James of Walton on Thames [PRO; PCC 1645]

John of Surrey [PRO; PCC Will 1513]

John of Reigate [DW/PA/5/1582/41]

Robert of Walton on Thames, tailor [DW/PA/7/7 f.260; DW/PA/5/1599/21] <Abs 462>

Thomas of Burstow, bachelor [PRO; PCC Admon 1638]

Thomas of Horne; Burstow; Horley; Worth, Sussex, senior [DW/PA/7/7 f.351; DW/PA/5/1601/37 *and* DW/PA/5/1601/38] <Abs 647>

Thomas of Horne, yeoman, senior [PRO; PCC Will 1603] <Abs, SAC v.11 p.112>

Thomasine of Godstone, widow [DW/PA/7/13 f.39; DW/PA/5/1640/56]

FENROTHER *see* FAIRBROTHER

FENTON

John of Streatham, husbandman [DW/PA/7/11 f.479; DW/PA/5/1628/35]

FERE

John of Bermondsey [HRO; Reg. Fox 3 p.67; 1517]

FERIBY

John of Chertsey; Beaumont, Essex; Swallowfield, Berkshire; Gloucestershire; Heythrop, Oxfordshire; Thames Street, London, esq. [LPL; Reg. Abp Chichele i f.473; Will 1441]

FERMAN *see* FAIRMAN

FERNDELL (FERNEDELL)

Joan of Haslemere, widow [DW/PA/5/1578/68 *and* DW/PA/5/1578/70]*

FERNDEN *see* FARNDEN

FERNE (FEARNE)
James of Streatham [DW/PA/7/12 f.507; DW/PA/5/1638/49]
Matthew of Lambeth - Stockwell, a minor [PRO; PCC Admon 1649]
Richard of Swk St George [DW/PA/7/11 f.285; DW/PA/5/1625/84]
William of Lambeth - Stockwell [PRO; PCC 1648]
FERNEDALL,FERNEDEN *see* FERNDEN
FERNLY
Elizabeth of Croydon - Trinity Hospital, almswoman and widow [LPL; 96/925; Will 1623]
FERNYALL
Andrew of Newington, citizen and skinner [PRO; PCC 1631]
FERRAND (FARRAND,FERRANT)
John of Send [DW/PA/7/7 f.288; DW/PA/5/1599/94] <Abs 515>
John of Send, husbandman [DW/PA/7/13 f.281; DW/PA/5/1643/36]
Mary of Mitcham, widow of William [PRO; PCC 1645]
Samuel of Chelsham, widower [PRO; PCC Admon 1649]
William of Mitcham, Doctor of Law [PRO; PCC Will 1615]
FERRENDEN *see* FARRINGDON
FERRERS (FARROR,FERRES,FERRIS,FERROUR)
Edward of Barnes, esq. [PRO; PCC 1639]
Harry of Wandsworth [DW/PA/7/5 f.33; 1538] <Abs 120>
John of Mortlake, esq. [PRO; PCC 1638]
Nicholas of Swk St Olave [DW/PA/5/1576/36]
Robert, alias Robert Smyth of Woking [DW/PA/7/1 f.87; 1489] <Abs 295>
William of St Michael Cornhill, London; Chertsey, citizen of London [LPL; Reg. Abp Kempe f.295; Will 1453]
FERRIBY *see* FERIBY
FERRIS,FERROUR *see* FERRERS
FERRYMAN *see* FERYMAN
FERYAN
Nicholas of Swk St Saviour, pinmaker [DW/PA/5/1605/32] <Abs U142>
FERYMAN
William of Kingston, yeoman [DW/PA/5/1550/20]
FETHESTON,FETHERSTONE *see* FEATHERSTONE
FETTERPLACE
James of Battersea, waterman [DW/PA/7/10 f.53; 1618]
FEVERELL
William of Swk St Olave, shipwright [DW/PA/7/12 f.442; DW/PA/5/1638/48]
FEVIAN *see* VIVIAN
FEW
Robert of East Molesey [DW/PA/5/1568/76]
FEYLD,FEYLDE *see* FIELD
FEYLDER *see* FIELDER
FEYLYSCHKYRKE *see* PHILLICHURCH
FIELD (FEELD,FEELDE,FEILD,FEILDE,FELD,FEYLD,FEYLDE,FILDE,FYLD)
Christopher of Chobham, yeoman [DW/PA/5/1605/34] <Abs U144>
Eden of Frensham, wife of Oliver [HRO; 1576 B22]
Edmund of Shalford - Smithbrook; Hascombe; Bramley, yeoman [DW/PA/7/9 f.49; DW/PA/5/1614/43]
Elizabeth of Chobham, widow [DW/PA/7/7 f.359; DW/PA/5/1602/31] <Abs 658>
Henry of Chobham, yeoman [HRO; 1595 B16]
Henry of Chobham [PRO; PCC Admon 1648]
Henry of Shalford; Hascombe [HRO; 1586 B21]

FIELD (FEELD,FEELDE,FEILD,FEILDE,FELD,FEYLD,FEYLDE,FILDE,FYLD) [*continued*]
James of Bramley; Hascombe, husbandman [DW/PA/7/7 f.331; DW/PA/5/1601/36] <Abs 596>
James of Bramley [PRO; PCC Will 1601] <Abs, SAC v.10 p.146>
Jane of Shalford - Smithbrook; Hascombe [DW/PA/7/10 f.3; DW/PA/5/1616/48]
Joan of Chobham, widow [DW/PA/5/1562/28]
Joan of Thames Ditton, widow of Ralph [DW/PA/7/13 f.196; DW/PA/5/1641/54] [*and*] [SRO; 212/38/1; 1641]
Joan of Frensham - Mytchett, widow [DW/PA/5/1558/109]
Joan of Puttenham, widow [DW/PA/5/1591/38]
John of Bisley, husbandman [DW/PA/7/7 f.255; DW/PA/5/1599/22] <Abs 449>
John of Chertsey - Botleys, husbandman, senior [PRO; PCC Will 1614]
John of Chertsey, labourer [DW/PA/7/10 f.43; 1618]
John of Egham - Bakeham, husbandman [DW/PA/5/1572/4]
John of Egham [DW/PA/7/8 f.251; DW/PA/5/1613/42]
Nicholas of Chertsey; Chobham [DW/PA/7/8 f.184; DW/PA/5/1610/54]
Richard, alias Richard Anstye of Charlwood, servant to Edmund Jordan, esq. [LPL; 96/66; Will 1629]
Robert of Lambeth [DW/PA/7/11 f.107; DW/PA/5/1624/45]
Sarah of Lambeth, widow [DW/PA/7/11 f.113; DW/PA/5/1624/46]
Thomas of Camberwell; the Ship *Rose*, sailor [PRO; PCC Will 1624]
Thomas of Farnham - Tilford; Frensham, yeoman [DW/PA/7/7 f.253; DW/PA/5/1599/23] <Abs 446>
Thomas, alias Thomas Anstye of Limpsfield, bachelor [PRO; PCC Admon 1646]
Thomas, alias Thomas Ryppley of Send [DW/PA/5/1558/104]*
Thomas of Walton on Thames - Hersham, weaver [DW/PA/5/1637/40] <Abs U256>
Walter of Chobham [DW/PA/7/2 f.157; 1521]
Walter of Chobham, husbandman, senior [DW/PA/7/11 f.129; DW/PA/5/1624/47]
see also ATTFIELD

FIELDER (FEELDER,FEILDER,FELDER,FEYLDER,FILDER,FYLDER)
Alice of Ripley, widow [DW/PA/5/1586/42]*
Edward of Caterham, husbandman [DW/PA/7/13 f.162; DW/PA/5/1642/33]
Edward of Walton on Thames - Hersham [PRO; PCC 1649]
Harry of Send [DW/PA/5/1550/15]
John of Esher [DW/PA/7/7 f.12; DW/PA/5/1595/36] <Abs 26>
John, alias John Fludder of Godalming, senior [DW/PA/7/4 f.151; 1536]
John of Haslemere, yeoman [DW/PA/7/10 f.259; DW/PA/5/1622/28]
John of Leatherhead [DW/PA/7/4 f.95; 1534]
John of Send [DW/PA/5/1552/9]
John of Walton on Thames - Hersham, yeoman [HRO; 1592 B20]
Mary of Farnham, widow [PRO; PCC Will 1624]
Richard of Beddington [DW/PA/7/9 f.156; DW/PA/5/1615/48]
Richard of Kingston - Surbiton, husbandman [DW/PA/7/7 f.241; DW/PA/5/1598/30] <Abs 424>
Robert of Farnham [PRO; PCC Will 1561]
Robert of Farnham, junior [PRO; PCC Admon 1562]
Robert of Farnham, senior [PRO; PCC Admon 1562]
Roger of Esher; Thames Ditton, senior [DW/PA/7/9 f.242; DW/PA/5/1617/44]
Samuel of Malden [DW/PA/7/10 f.78; DW/PA/5/1619/46]
Walter of Leatherhead [DW/PA/7/3 f.187; 1531]
William of Sanderstead, mason [DW/PA/7/2 f.108; 1516]

FIELDHOUSE (FEILDOWSE)
Dorothy of Swk - Fowle Lane, widow [DW/PA/7/10 f.238; DW/PA/5/1621/42]

FIELDING (FYLDING)
  Richard of Swk St Saviour [HRO; 1573 B45]
FIETT
  Ann, alias Ann Arnold of Croydon [PRO; PCC Admon 1597]
FIFE (FYFFE,FYFTE,PHIFE)
  Robert of Mitcham [DW/PA/7/2 f.1; 1490]
  Thomas of Kingston; Hampton, Middlesex, innholder [DW/PA/5/1547/6]
  William of Swk St Thomas, weaver [DW/PA/7/13 f.191; DW/PA/5/1641/110]
FIGG (FYGE,FYGGE)
  Henry of Frensham, husbandman [DW/PA/7/11 f.411; DW/PA/5/1627/38]
  John of Farnham [DW/PA/5/1607/39] <Abs U196>
  John of Farnham, yeoman [HRO; 1639 B29]
  John of Farnham [DW/PA/7/13 f.434; DW/PA/5/1646/18]
  John of Haslemere; Frensham [DW/PA/7/5 f.172; 1540]
  Margaret of Farnham, widow [DW/PA/7/8 f.110; DW/PA/5/1610/56]
  Robert of Shere [DW/PA/5/1558/102]*
  Sarah of Guildford, widow [PRO; PCC 1633]
  Thomas of Shalford [DW/PA/7/2 f.180; 1522]
  William of Guildford, clothier [DW/PA/7/11 f.46; DW/PA/5/1623/40]
FILDE *see* FIELD
FILDER *see* FIELDER
FILEWOOD (PHILEWOODE)
  Paul of Swk St Olave, feltmaker [DW/PA/5/1593/206]
FILLCOTT (FYLCOTE)
  Joan of St Mary Aldermary, London; Nutfield; Hollingbourne, Kent [LPL; Reg. Abp Kempe f.295; Will 1453]
FILLIAN (FYLYAN)
  Henry of Streatham; Clapham; Sutton [DW/PA/7/4 f.54; 1533]
FILIPPIS *see* PHILLIPS
FILLPOTT *see* PHILPOTT
FILPE *see* PHILLIPS
FINCH (FINCHE,FYNCHE,FYNTCHE,FYNYSSHE)
  Ann of Wandsworth [PRO; PCC Will 1623]
  Christopher of Worplesdon, yeoman [DW/PA/7/12 f.250; DW/PA/5/1635/31]
  Daniel of Bermondsey, mariner [PRO; PCC Will 1620] <Soame 325>
  Henry of Swk St Saviour, victualler [DW/PA/7/12 f.203; DW/PA/5/1634/41]
  Henry of Walton on Thames [DW/PA/7/13 f.142; DW/PA/5/1641/45]
  James of Horley [DW/PA/5/1555/55]
  John of Richmond, groom of the Prince's Wardrobe [PRO; PCC Will 1618]
  John of Swk St Olave, citizen and bowyer [DW/PA/5/1568/51]
  Matthew of Kingston - Ham, gent. [PRO; PCC Will 1616]
  Nicholas of Dorking, shearman [DW/PA/7/7 f.603; DW/PA/5/1607/40] <Abs 1128>
  Richard of Reigate [DW/PA/7/5 f.41; 1538] <Abs 71>
  Robert of Pirbright, citizen and white baker [PRO; PCC 1642]
  Rowland of Swk St George [*Listed in *, but no original will now, see* DW/PA/7/7 f.305; 1600] <Abs 547>
  Samuel of Croydon, clerk and vicar [LPL; 96/931; Will 1616]
  Thomas of Lambeth [PRO; PCC Admon 1599]
  Thomas of Swk St Olave, yeoman [DW/PA/5/1601/39] <Abs U34>
  Walter of Croydon, gent. [PRO; PCC Will 1626]
  William of Chertsey [PRO; PCC Admon 1585]
FINCKHORNE *see* FINKHORN

FINDEN (FINDON,FINTON,FYNDEN,VARDEN,VIGNION,VINDON)
Henry of Alfold; Wonersh; Lambeth; Brentford, Middlesex, yeoman [DW/PA/7/8 f.69; DW/PA/5/1609/81]
John of Alfold [PRO; PCC Admon 1609]
John of Effingham [DW/PA/7/12 f.10; DW/PA/5/1631/42]
John of Wonersh - Whipley, yeoman [DW/PA/7/8 f.238; DW/PA/5/1613/43]
Lawrence of Effingham, husbandman [HRO; 1571 B190]
Lawrence of Effingham, yeoman [DW/PA/7/11 f.476; DW/PA/5/1628/36]
Margery of Alfold, widow [PRO; PCC Admon 1624]
Richard of Effingham [HRO; 1605 AD25]
Richard of Haslemere, husbandman [HRO; 1609 B28]
Thomas of Wonersh [DW/PA/5/1591/78]
William of Swk St Olave, yeoman [DW/PA/7/11 f.591; DW/PA/5/1630/34]
see also FARNDEN
FINES
Robert of Swk St Saviour, blacksmith [DW/PA/7/12 f.350; DW/PA/5/1636/39]
FINGES (FYNGES)
Giles of Tandridge, carpenter [HRO; 1573 B47]
FINKHORNE (FINCKHORNE)
Mary of Frensham, widow [DW/PA/7/10 f.288; DW/PA/5/1623/43]
FINNEY (FYNNEY)
William of Swk St Saviour [DW/PA/5/1576/156]
FINNIMORE (FYNYMORE)
Edmund of Wandsworth, gent. [PRO; PCC 1634]
FINTON *see* FINDEN
FIRE (FYER)
Joan, alias Joan Deare of Richmond, widow [PRO; PCC Will 1623]
John, alias John Deere of ... [DW/PA/7/7 f.79; 1596] <Abs 144>
FISH
Edward of Bermondsey [PRO; PCC 1633]
John of Frensham, yeoman [DW/PA/7/12 f.514; DW/PA/5/1639/56]
John of Frensham, weaver [DW/PA/7/13 f.157; DW/PA/5/1641/49]
Peter of Chertsey - Sayes [PRO; PCC 1634]
FISHER (FISSHER,FYSCHAR,FYSHER)
Agnes of Swk St Saviour, widow [DW/PA/7/12 f.228; DW/PA/5/1634/44]
Andrew of Lambeth - South Lambeth, gent. [PRO; PCC Will 1606]
Arthur of Lambeth, gent. [PRO; PCC 1639]
Elizabeth of Sheen; Kingston [PRO; PCC Admon 1625]
Hugh of Bermondsey [DW/PA/7/6 f.244; 1560]
Joan of Bermondsey, widow [DW/PA/5/1546/19]
John of Epsom [DW/PA/5/1587/110]
John of Ewell, yeoman [DW/PA/5/1587/32]
John of Ewell, yeoman [HRO; 1587 B32]
Mary of Bermondsey, widow [GL; Archdeaconry Court of London Will 1612]
Richard of Bermondsey [PRO; PCC Will 1553]
Richard of Charlwood [PRO; PCC Admon 1590]
Richard of West Molesey [PRO; PCC Admon 1594]
Robert of Rotherhithe, gent. [PRO; PCC Will 1602] <Abs, SAC v.10 p.306>
Silvester of Wandsworth, wheelwright [DW/PA/7/7 f.242; DW/PA/5/1598/32] <Abs 426>
Thomas, alias Thomas Taner of Thames Ditton [DW/PA/5/1581/38]
Thomas of Molesey, gent. [PRO; PCC Will 1591]
Thomas of Swk St Olave, porter [DW/PA/7/11 f.207; DW/PA/5/1625/85]

FISHER (FISSHER,FYSCHAR,FYSHER) [*continued*]
  Thomas of Swk St Saviour, citizen and woodmonger [DW/PA/7/12 f.15; DW/PA/5/1631/43]
  William, alias William Parsson of Lingfield - Dormansland [DW/PA/7/3 f.199; 1532]
  William of Swk St Olave, blacksmith [DW/PA/7/7 f.411; DW/PA/5/1603/49] <Abs 763>
FISHWICK (FISHWEKE)
  Elizabeth of Lambeth, widow [DW/PA/5/1591/100]
FITCH
  Robert of Weybridge [DW/PA/7/13 f.437; DW/PA/5/1646/19]
  Thomas of Bermondsey [DW/PA/7/13 f.429; DW/PA/5/1646/17] [*and*] [PRO; PCC Admon 1646]
FITTON (PHITTON)
  George of Cobham [PRO; PCC Admon 1617]
FITZ
  Isabel of Addington [PRO; PCC Will 1544]
FITZGERALD
  Frances of Walton on Thames [PRO; PCC Will 1619]
  Thomas of Walton on Thames [PRO; PCC Will 1618]
FITZHARRY *see* FREEHARRY
FITZROBERT
  Robert of St Mary Aldermary, London; St Mildred Bread Street, London; All Hallows, London; Putney; Barnes [LPL; Reg. Abp Chichele i f.445; Will 1434]
FITZWARREN (PHIGHWARREN)
  Stephen of Lingfield, parson [HRO; 1546 B74]
FITZWATER
  Thomas of Kingston - Ham [DW/PA/7/13 f.308; DW/PA/5/1643/37]
FITZWILLIAMS (FITZWILLIAM)
  (Dame) Jane of Chertsey, widow of (Sir) William [PRO; PCC Will 1585]
  William of Surrey, earl of Southampton [PRO; PCC Will 1542]
  William of Mitcham; Tooting, esq. [PRO; PCC Will 1597] <Abs SAC v.33 p.13>
FLAMANCKE
  Hugh of Battersea [PRO; PCC Admon 1641]
FLANNSELL
  John of Swk St Olave, tailor [DW/PA/7/9 f.173; DW/PA/5/1616/49]
FLASKETT
  Elizabeth of Swk St George, widow [DW/PA/5/1580/21]
FLATHTERFORD *see* FLATTERFORD
FLATTER *see* FLAYTER,FLUDDER
FLATTERFORD (FLATHTERFORD)
  William of Thames Ditton [DW/PA/7/5 f.18; 1538] <Abs 117>
FLAUNE
  Mark of Bermondsey (died overseas), bachelor [PRO; PCC Admon 1633]
FLAUNSELL *see* FLANNSELL
FLAYTER
  Matthew of Kingston, yeoman [DW/PA/7/8 f.207; DW/PA/5/1612/56]
  Thomas of Kingston, yeoman [DW/PA/7/12 f.199; DW/PA/5/1633/55]
FLEET (FLETE,FLOOTE)
  Martin of Croydon [GL; Commissary Court of London Will 1407]
  Thomas of Warlingham, husbandman [DW/PA/7/9 f.175B; DW/PA/5/1616/50]
  William of Lambeth [PRO; PCC Will 1421]

FLEMING (FLEMINGE,FLEMYNG,FLEMYNGE,FLEMMYNG)
Dennis of Camberwell, esq. [PRO; PCC 1639]
Isabella (formerly Isabella Leigh) of Addington [PRO; PCC Will 1544]
James of Bermondsey [DW/PA/7/5 f.137; 1540]
Nicholas of Rotherhithe, cooper [DW/PA/7/11 f.272; DW/PA/5/1625/86]
Richard of Newington [PRO; PCC Will 1595]
(Sir) Thomas of Surrey, knight [PRO; PCC Will 1466]

FLETCHER
Henry of Swk St Saviour [DW/PA/5/1575/50]
Joan of Bermondsey, widow [DW/PA/7/13 f.223; DW/PA/5/1643/34]
John of Lambeth [PRO; PCC Will 1578]
John of Mitcham [DW/PA/7/8 f.10; DW/PA/5/1608/47]
Nicholas of Camberwell - Peckham, yeoman [DW/PA/7/7 f.519; DW/PA/5/1606/38] <Abs 974>
Ralph of Richmond, esq. [PRO; PCC Will 1608] <Abs. SAC v.13 p.195>
Thomas of Bermondsey, citizen and leatherseller [DW/PA/7/11 f.560; DW/PA/5/1630/35]
Thomas of Swk St Saviour, porter [DW/PA/5/1576/136]
Thomas of Sutton [DW/PA/7/12 f.369; DW/PA/5/1627/39]
William of Kingston, yeoman [DW/PA/7/4 f.65; 1534]
William of Swk St Olave, waterman [DW/PA/5/1592/91]
William of Swk St Saviour, brewer [DW/PA/7/10 f.184; DW/PA/5/1619/47]

FLETE *see* FLEET

FLINT (FLYNT,FLYNTE,FLYNTT)
John of Ash [DW/PA/5/1563/27]
Nicholas of Headley [PRO; PCC 1649]
Richard of Cobham, yeoman [DW/PA/7/13 f.191; DW/PA/5/1641/53]
William of Gatton, freemason [DW/PA/5/1580/49]
William of Gatton, freemason, builder of Gatton Church [PRO; PCC Will 1589]
William of Horley [PRO; PCC Admon 1639]
William of Swk St George, gent. [DW/PA/7/8 f.157; DW/PA/5/1611/46]

FLOATE
Richard of Bisley, yeoman [DW/PA/7/12 f.271; DW/PA/5/1635/33]

FLODDER *see* FLUDDER

FLOOD *see* FLUDD

FLOOTE *see* FLEET

Florens son of Peter of Swk St Olave [DW/PA/7/4 f.218; 1537]

FLOWDDERE *see* FLUDDER

FLOWDE *see* FLUDD

FLOWER
William of Bermondsey [PRO; PCC Will 1627]

FLOWKE
John of Swk St Saviour [DW/PA/7/7 f.18; DW/PA/5/1595/37] <Abs 39>

FLOYD
Jane of Battersea, spinster [PRO; PCC Admon 1641]

FLUDD (FLOOD,FLOUD,FLOWDE,FLUD,FLUDDE)
Bridget of Mortlake, widow [PRO; PCC Admon 1626]
Edward of Godalming [DW/PA/7/3 f.193; 1531]
Fulco of Richmond [PRO; PCC Admon 1614]
Henry of Cheam, gent. [LPL; 96/955; Will 1643]
James of Newington, Doctor of Divinity [PRO; PCC Will 1626]
John of Reigate; Charlwood, gent. [DW/PA/7/7 f.69; 1596] <Abs 131>
Robert of Cranleigh, yeoman [DW/PA/5/1591/87]

FLUDD (FLOOD,FLOUD,FLOWDE,FLUD,FLUDDE) [*continued*]
Rowland of Swk St Saviour, waterman [DW/PA/7/8 f,9; DW/PA/5/1608/48]
Thomas of Clapham, bachelor [PRO; PCC Admon 1649]
FLUDDER (FLODDER,FLODER,FLOWDDERE,FLUTTER)
Grace of Godalming - Lydling, spinster [DW/PA/7/12 f,434;DW/PA/5/1637/42]
Henry of Witley - Birtley [HRO; 1603 B17]
John of Farnham, junior [HRO; Reg, Way 1 p,64; 1460]
John, alias John Felder of Godalming, senior [DW/PA/7/4 f,151; 1536]
John of Godalming - Eashing, yeoman [HRO; 1603 B16]
Richard of Farnham [PRO; PCC Will 1510]
Richard of Witley - Milford, husbandman [DW/PA/7/13 f,159; DW/PA/5/1641/51]
William, alias William Freebarne of Farnham - Tilford, husbandman [DW/PA/5/1568/33]
William of Godalming - Lydling, husbandman [DW/PA/7/8 f,183; DW/PA/5/1610/57]
see also FLAYTER
FLUELLEN
Elizabeth of Newington, widow [PRO; PCC Will 1595]
see also LLEWLELLYN
FLUET
Humphrey of East Molesey [PRO; PCC Will 1590]
FLUTTER *see* FLUDDER
FLYNT,FLYNTE,FLYNTT *see* FLINT
FOATE
Joan of Swk St Olave, spinster [DW/PA/5/1593/68]
FOG
(Lady) Mary of Farleigh [PRO; PCC Admon 1614]
FOILER (FOYLER)
Thomas of Reigate [DW/PA/7/3 f,188; 1531]
FOLENTYNE *see* VALENTINE
FOLKIS *see* FULKE
FOLLIS
John, alias John Fallowes of Newington, yeoman [LPL; 96/890; Will 1625]
FONACE
Giles of ,,, [*French Church of London and Norwich*] [DW/PA/5/1592/78]
FOOKES *see* FULKE
FOORDE *see* FORD
FOOT (FOOTE,FOOTTE)
George of Streatham, labouring man [DW/PA/7/7 f,305; DW/PA/5/1600/19] <Abs 546>
George of Thorpe, labourer [DW/PA/5/1580/54]
FORBENCH (FORBUNCHE)
Isabella of Lambeth [DW/PA/7/12 f,306; DW/PA/5/1635/37]
Richard of Ripley, Chertsey, gent, [PRO; PCC Will 1620] <Soame 801>
FORD (FOORDE,FORDE)
Alice of Swk St Olave, widow [DW/PA/7/11 f,270; DW/PA/5/1625/87]
Ann of Guildford, widow [DW/PA/7/11 f,313; DW/PA/5/1626/49]
Erasmus of Thames Ditton; Kingston; Chessington, gent, [DW/PA/7/5 f,21; 1538] <Abs 21> [*and*] <Abs SAC v,27 p,71>
Humphrey of ,,, [DW/PA/7/5 f,4; 1538] <Abs 105>
John of Godalming, weaver [DW/PA/7/8 f,78; DW/PA/5/1609/78]
John of Swk St George [DW/PA/7/5 f,62; 1539] <Abs 84>
John of Wandsworth, wharfinger [DW/PA/7/12 f,82; DW/PA/5/1633/56]

FORD (FOORDE,FORDE) [*continued*]
Lawrence of Swk St Olave, skinner [DW/PA/7/4 f,72; 1534]
Luke of East Molesey [PRO; PCC Will 1604]
Nicholas of Stoke next Guildford, clothworker [DW/PA/7/12 f,205; DW/PA/5/1634/42]
Richard of Guildford, shoemaker [HRO; 1561 B64-65]
Richard of Guildford [PRO; PCC 1647]
Richard of Guildford St Mary; Guildford St Nicolas; Guildford Holy Trinity, brewer [DW/PA/7/9 f,21; DW/PA/5/1614/40] [*and*] [LBLAD; Surrey Deeds 1/404; 1614]
Richard of Guildford St Nicolas, gent,[DW/PA/7/10 f,293; DW/PA/5/1622/29]
Richard of Swk St Olave, feltmaker [DW/PA/7/11 f,49; DW/PA/5/1623/41]
Thomas of Guildford, gent, [PRO; PCC 1646]
William of Swk St George; Newington - Walworth [DW/PA/5/1543/7]*
FORDER
John of Bentley, Hampshire, husbandman [DW/PA/7/6 f,265; 1560]
John of Rotherhithe, carpenter [DW/PA/7/8 f,299; DW/PA/5/1613/44]
Richard of Blechingley [PRO; PCC 1636]
William of Farnham [DW/PA/7/4 f,97; 1534]
FOREMAN (FORMAN)
Simon of Lambeth [PRO; PCC Admon 1611]
Thomas of Limpsfield, yeoman [DW/PA/7/11 f,612; DW/PA/5/1630/36]
Thomas of Swk St Saviour, spurrier [DW/PA/5/1561/51]
Thomas of Swk St Saviour, brewer [DW/PA/7/11 f,314; DW/PA/5/1626/50]
FOREST *see* FORREST
FORMAN *see* FOREMAN
FORREST (FOREST)
Agnes of Barnes - Barn Elms [PRO; PCC Admon 1581]
Boniface of Barnes - Barnes Court, shoemaker [GL; Archdeaconry Court of London Will 1559]
George of Lancing, Sussex [DW/PA/5/1562/25]
John of Abinger, gent, [PRO; PCC Will 1598]
Richard of Newington [LPL; 98/1 f,13r (ren,); 1630]
William of Swk St Olave, porter [DW/PA/7/13 f,97; DW/PA/5/1640/51]
FORRINGTON
Katherine of Rotherhithe, widow [PRO; PCC 1631]
FORSTER *see* FOSTER
FORTE
John of Swk St Margaret, carpenter [DW/PA/7/1 f,27; 1486] <Abs 88>
Margaret of Swk St Thomas, widow [DW/PA/7/13 f,236; DW/PA/5/1642/34]
FORTERY
Samuel of Richmond; London, merchant [PRO; PCC 1647]
FORTHE
Robert of Streatham, doctor of law [PRO; PCC Will 1595]
FOSBERY
Richard of Camberwell, servingman [PRO; PCC Will 1603] <Abs, SAC v,11 p,129>
FOSSE
Thomas of Egham - Fosters [DW/PA/7/11 f,413; DW/PA/5/1627/40]
FOSTER (FORSTER,FOSTYR)
Agnes of Newington, widow [PRO; PCC Admon 1591]
Alice of Bermondsey [PRO; PCC Will 1535]
Alice, alias Alice Beadle of Witley [PRO; PCC Admon 1649]
Elizabeth of Camberwell, widow [PRO; PCC Will 1617]

FOSTER (FORSTER,FOSTYR) [*continued*]
  Elizabeth of Camberwell, widow [PRO; PCC 1642]
  Henry of Kingston, glover [DW/PA/5/1558/107]*
  Henry of Lambeth - Water Lambeth, waterman [DW/PA/7/7 f.107; DW/PA/5/1596/23] <Abs 194>
  James of Swk St Olave [DW/PA/7/5 f.94; 1539]
  Joan of Kingston [DW/PA/7/1 f.51; 1488] <Abs 169>
  John of Capel [DW/PA/7/1 f.6; 1484]
  John of Farnham - Wrecclesham, yeoman [HRO; 1597 B31]
  John of Newington - Walworth, yeoman [PRO; PCC Will 1627]
  Katherine of Swk St George, spinster [DW/PA/7/11 f.239; DW/PA/5/1625/88]
  Mary of Lambeth, widow [DW/PA/7/7 f.434; DW/PA/5/1603/50 *and* DW/PA/5/1603/51] <Abs 820>
  Michael, alias Michael Falkner of Newington, yeoman [PRO; PCC Will 1602] <Abs, SAC v.10 p.311>
  Nicholas of Camberwell - Dulwich [DW/PA/7/11 ff.442,473; DW/PA/5/1628/37 *and* DW/PA/5/1628/38]
  Nicholas of Cobham, yeoman [DW/PA/7/11 f.443; DW/PA/5/1628/39]
  Nicholas of Lambeth, yeoman [DW/PA/7/11 f.572; DW/PA/5/1630/37]
  Phillipa of Camberwell - Dulwich, widow [DW/PA/7/13 f.28; DW/PA/5/1639/55]
  Ralph of Lambeth [BM; Add.Ms 24,925 f.13v; 1544] <Abs 24>
  Richard of Kingston [PRO; PCC Will 1496]
  Richard of Puttenham, yeoman [DW/PA/5/1558/103]*
  Robert of Cobham, tailor [DW/PA/7/10 f.289; DW/PA/5/1623/42]
  Robert of Lambeth, yeoman [PRO; PCC Will 1603]
  Robert of Worplesdon, husbandman [DW/PA/7/11 f.316; DW/PA/5/1626/51]
  Roger of Lambeth, victualler [HRO; 1595 AD18]
  Roger of Swk St George, yeoman [DW/PA/5/1578/61]
  Sarah of Cobham, spinster [PRO; PCC Admon 1649]
  Stephen of Farnham - Badshot, husbandman [DW/PA/7/6 f.214A; 1560]
  Thomas of Bermondsey, citizen [PRO; PCC Will 1525]
  Thomas of Kingston, senior [DW/PA/7/1 f.8; 1484] <Abs 25>
  Thomas of Kingston [DW/PA/7/5 f.209; 1541]
  Thomas of Rotherhithe (died overseas) [PRO; PCC Admon 1638]
  William of Compton [PRO; PCC Will 1558]
  William of Swk St George; Shevington, Lancashire [DW/PA/5/1579/35]*
  William of Swk St George [DW/PA/5/1581/21]
  William of Wanborough [HRO; 1578 B37]
FOUKE,FOUKES *see* FULKE
FOUL *see* FOWLE
FOULGIER
  William of Rotherhithe [PRO; PCC Admon 1649]
FOULKES *see* FULKE
FOULL *see* FOWLE
FOULMER *see* FOWLEMER
FOUNDER *see* FOWNDER
FOUNTAIN (FOUNTAINE,FOWNTAYNE)
  John of Rotherhithe [PRO; PCC Will 1569]
  Richard of Rotherhithe (died overseas) [PRO; PCC Admon 1638]
FOWLAR *see* FOWLER
FOWLE (FOUL,FOULL,FOWLES)
  Anthony of Swk St Thomas, blacksmith [DW/PA/7/8 f.400; DW/PA/5/1612/57]
  Edward of Newington [LPL; 96/971; Will 1616]

FOWLE (FOUL,FOULL,FOWLES) [*continued*]
John of Oxted [DW/PA/5/1561/24]
Meshach of Lambeth [PRO; PCC Admon 1616]
Robert of Croydon, butcher [LPL; 96/974; 98/1 f.53r; Will 1633]
Robert of Oxted, husbandman [HRO; 1596 B25]
William of Mitcham; Camberwell [PRO; PCC Will 1547]

FOWLEMER
Richard, alias Richard Tepelene of Lambeth; Kingston [PRO; PCC Will 1429]

FOWLER (FOWLAR,FOWLLER)
Ann of Croydon, widow [LPL; 96/972; Will 1644]
Frances of Petersham, widow [DW/PA/7/12 f.40; DW/PA/5/1631/46]
John of Alfold, husbandman [DW/PA/7/8 f.39; DW/PA/5/1609/79]
John of East Clandon [PRO; PCC Admon 1641]
John of East Clandon, gent. [PRO; PCC 1641]
John of Kingston - Ham, yeoman [DW/PA/7/9 f.154; DW/PA/5/1615/49]
Ralph of Wandsworth, husbandman [DW/PA/7/12 f.18; DW/PA/5/1631/45]
Richard of Thames Ditton, esq. [DW/PA/7/11 f.571; DW/PA/5/1630/38]
Richard of Swk St George, woollen draper [DW/PA/7/11 f.197; DW/PA/5/1625/89]
Robert of Bermondsey [PRO; PCC Admon 1620]
Robert of West Clandon, citizen and carpenter [GL; Archdeaconry Court of London Will 1551]
Robert of Kingston - Ham, yeoman [DW/PA/5/1569/13]
Robert of Kingston - Ham, yeoman [DW/PA/5/1578/103]
Thomas of Petersham; Kingston, fisherman [DW/PA/5/1558/98]*
William of Kingston - Ham, yeoman [DW/PA/5/1557/65]
William of Kingston, weaver [DW/PA/5/1571/78]
William of Kingston - Ham [DW/PA/7/8 f.219; DW/PA/5/1612/58]
William of Petersham, yeoman [DW/PA/7/11 f.490; DW/PA/5/1628/40]

FOWLES *see* FOWLE

FOWLMER *see* FOWLEMER

FOWNDER
Stephen of Croydon [PRO; PCC Admon 1591]

FOWNTAYNE *see* FOUNTAIN

FOWRNES *see* FURNESS

FOX (FOXE)
Edward of Leatherhead [PRO; PCC Admon 1649]
Favor of Camberwell - Dulwich, yeoman [DW/PA/7/12 f.388; DW/PA/5/1638/42]
Henry of Farnham, shearman [DW/PA/7/7 f.340; DW/PA/5/1601/40] <Abs 617>
James of Kingston, yeoman [DW/PA/7/11 f.375; DW/PA/5/1626/52]
John of Chobham, servant to Henry Lee [DW/PA/5/1605/33] <Abs U143>
John of Lambeth [PRO; PCC Will 1604]
Mabel of Kingston [PRO; PCC Will 1592]
Margaret of Swk, widow [HRO; Reg. D p.53; 1520]
Nicholas of Kingston, blacksmith [DW/PA/7/9 f.40; DW/PA/5/1614/42]
Peter of Swk St Olave, seaman [DW/PA/7/13 f.322; DW/PA/5/1643/38]
Ralph of Kingston - Surbiton, yeoman [DW/PA/7/13 f.187; DW/PA/5/1642/32]
Richard of Kingston, innholder [DW/PA/5/1574/41]
Richard of Kingston, innholder [DW/PA/5/1593/167]
Richard of Putney [PRO; PCC Admon 1622]
Richard of Swk St Saviour, citizen and cook [DW/PA/5/1593/118]
Robert of Egham, husbandman [DW/PA/7/12 f.314; DW/PA/5/1636/38]
Swithin of Kingston - Surbiton, husbandman [DW/PA/7/6 f.216; 1560]

FOX (FOXE) [*continued*]
Thomas of Kingston - Surbiton, yeoman [HRO; 1573 B48]
William of Camberwell - Peckham, yeoman [DW/PA/7/9 f.330; DW/PA/5/1620/51]
William of Camberwell - Peckham [DW/PA/7/11 f.556; DW/PA/5/1630/39]
William of Walton on Thames, vicar [HRO; Reg. Way 1 p.27; 1453]
FOXWELL (FOXEWELL)
Thomas of Swk St Saviour [DW/PA/7/6 f.266; 1560]
FOYCE
Mary, alias Mary Parson of Guildford [PRO; PCC Admon 1646]
FOYLER *see* FOILER
FRAILE (FRAYLE)
Joan of Woking, widow [DW/PA/7/8 f.169; DW/PA/5/1610/58]
Richard of Woking, yeoman [HRO; 1593 AD34]
FRANCIS (FRANCEIS,FRANCES,FRANCESS,FRANCYS,FRANSH,FRAUNCES,FRAUNCESE, FRAUNCEYS,FRAUNCIS,FRAUNSYS)
Agnes of ... [DW/PA/7/12 f.102; DW/PA/5/1632/35]
Edmund of Bermondsey [GL; Archdeaconry Court of London Will 1397]
Henry of Shere [DW/PA/7/1 f.53; 1487] <Abs 177>
John of Esher [DW/PA/7/5 f.208; 1541]
John of Ockham [DW/PA/7/1 f.83; 1488] <Abs 277>
John of Ockham, yeoman [DW/PA/7/13 f.5; DW/PA/5/1639/52]
John of Shalford - Smithbrook, husbandman [HRO; 1610 B27]
John of Shere [DW/PA/7/2 f.126; 1518]
Juliana of Shalford - Thorncombe Street, widow [DW/PA/7/12 f.264; DW/PA/5/1634/45]
Mary of Shalford, spinster [DW/PA/7/13 f.361; 1644]
Michael of Swk St Saviour, starchmaker [DW/PA/7/11 f.562; DW/PA/5/1630/40]
Nicholas of Godalming [HRO; 1627 B28]
Nicholas of Send [PRO; PCC Admon 1648]
Nicholas of Shalford - Thorncombe Street, yeoman [DW/PA/7/12 f.224; DW/PA/5/1634/43]
Oliver of Shere, tailor [DW/PA/5/1582/42]
Ralph of Richmond [DW/PA/7/2 f.187; 1523]
Richard of Chiddingfold, husbandman [PRO; PCC Will 1627]
Richard of Newdigate [DW/PA/7/9 f.188; DW/PA/5/1616/51]
Robert of Chatham, Kent; Gosport, Hampshire; Alverstoke, Hampshire [DW/PA/5/1643/35] <Abs U261>
Robert of Clapham, rector [HRO; Reg. Wyk 2 p.248; 1390]
Thomas of Kingston - Ham, husbandman [DW/PA/7/4 f.9; 1532]
Thomas of Kingston [PRO; PCC Admon 1649]
Thomas of Send, yeoman [DW/PA/5/1569/4]
Thomas, alias Thomas Franks of Ripley, labourer [DW/PA/7/7 f.32; DW/PA/5/1595/39] <Abs 66>
Thomas of Wonersh, blacksmith [DW/PA/7/11 f.441; DW/PA/5/1628/41]
William of Lingfield, yeoman [DW/PA/5/1558/100]*
William of Ripley, labourer [DW/PA/7/7 f.3; DW/PA/5/1595/38] <Abs 7>
William of Send [DW/PA/7/7 f.252; DW/PA/5/1599/24] <Abs 443>
William of Send [DW/PA/7/9 f.179; DW/PA/5/1616/52]
William of Shere [DW/PA/7/1 f.7; 1486] <Abs 24>
see also FRANKS; FRENCH
FRANCK,FRANCKE,FRANCKIS,FRANCKS *see* FRANKS
FRANCKLIN,FRANCKLYN,FRANCKLYNE *see* FRANKLIN

FRANCYS *see* FRANCIS
FRANK,FRANKE *see* FRANKS
FRANKLIN (FRANCKLIN,FRANCKLYN,FRANCKLYNE)
Geoffrey of Swk St Olave, feltmaker [DW/PA/7/7 f.636; DW/PA/5/1608/49] <Abs 1191>
Margery of Lambeth, widow [DW/PA/5/1592/74]
Nicholas of Swk St Olave [DW/PA/7/8 f.393; DW/PA/5/1612/59]
Richard of Farnham, shoemaker [HRO; 1603 B21]
Robert of Rotherhithe (died in Bristol) [PRO; PCC Admon 1642]
Robert of Rotherhithe, bachelor [PRO; PCC 1645]
William of Farnham, shoemaker [DW/PA/7/9 f.19; DW/PA/5/1616/53]
William of Swk St Thomas, currier [DW/PA/7/12 f.61; DW/PA/5/1631/47]
FRANKS (FRANCK,FRANCKE,FRANCKIS,FRANCKS,FRANK,FRANKE,FRANKYS)
Agnes of Ashtead, widow [*also, in* DW/PA/5/1558/30 *and* [DW/PA/5/1558/106]*
Elizabeth of Walton on the Hill, widow [DW/PA/5/1562/43]
George of Ewhurst, yeoman [DW/PA/7/8 f.277; DW/PA/5/1613/45]
George of Walton [DW/PA/7/11 f.148; DW/PA/5/1625/90]
Humphrey of Swk St Saviour, clerk schoolmaster of the Free School [DW/PA/7/12 f.380; DW/PA/5/1637/41A]
John of Burstow [PRO; PCC Will 1596]
John of Coulsdon [DW/PA/5/1587/114]
John of Newington [LPL; 96/981; Will 1625]
Richard of Ockham [DW/PA/5/1557/43]*
Richard of Rotherhithe [PRO; PCC Admon 1635]
Robert of Bermondsey, yeoman [PRO; PCC Will 1608] <Abs, SAC v.13 p.193>
Robert of Walton on the Hill, husbandman [HRO; 1631 AD27]
Thomas of Surrey, esq., senior [PRO; PCC Will 1560]
Thomas of Burstow; Horne [PRO; PCC Will 1595]
Thomas of Ripley, labourer [DW/PA/7/7 f.32; DW/PA/5/1595/39] <Abs 66>
Thomas of Walton on the Hill, husbandman [DW/PA/5/1562/46]
William of Cheam [PRO; PCC Will 1573]
William of Richmond, linen draper [PRO; PCC Wills 1597 *and* 1599]
William of Richmond [PRO; PCC Admon 1599]
William of Walton, husbandman [DW/PA/7/10 f.37; DW/PA/5/1617/45]
see also FRANCIS
FRANSH *see* FRANCIS
FRANSHAM *see* FRENSHAM
FRAUNCES,FRAUNCESE,FRAUNCIS,FRAUNSYS *see* FRANCIS
FRAY (FRAYE)
Elizabeth of Carshalton, widow [DW/PA/7/4 f.48; 1533]
John of Charlwood [PRO; PCC Admon 1613]
John of Croydon - Waddon [LPL; 98/1 f.105v; Will 1639]
Katherine of Carshalton, widow [DW/PA/7/11 f.373; DW/PA/5/1626/53]
Robert of Carshalton [HRO; 1584 B26]
William of Carshalton, yeoman [DW/PA/5/1576/28]
William of Carshalton, husbandman [DW/PA/7/9 f.268; 1618]
FRAYLE *see* FRAILE
FREAK (FREAKE,FREKE)
Ellen of Godalming, widow [DW/PA/7/11 f.207; DW/PA/5/1625/91]
Katherine of Swk St Olave, widow [DW/PA/5/1587/95]
Richard of Swk St Olave, waterman [DW/PA/5/1587/94]
Thomas of Cobham [PRO; PCC Will 1415]
FREAR *see* FREER

FREEBARNE

William, alias William Flowddere of Farnham - Tilford, husbandman [DW/PA/5/1568/33]

FREEHARRY (FYEHARRYE)

Joan, alias Joan Harrye of Kingston - Ham, widow [DW/PA/5/1576/56]

FREEK *see* FREAKE

FREELAND (FREELANDE,FRELAND,FRELANDE,FRELOND,FRELONDE,FRILOND)

Christian of Pyford; Ockham, widow [HRO; 1617 B20]

Edward of Ockham, husbandman [DW/PA/5/1578/16]

Edward of Ockham, husbandman [DW/PA/5/1605/35] <Abs U145>

George of Ockham, tailor [DW/PA/7/13 f.126; DW/PA/5/1640/54]

George of Swk St Saviour [DW/PA/7/7 f.226; DW/PA/5/1598/31] <Abs 399>

Henry of Wisley - Hyde, yeoman [DW/PA/7/12 f.274; DW/PA/5/1635/34]

John of Thames Ditton - Claygate [DW/PA/5/1591/13]

John of Ockham, yeoman [DW/PA/7/4 f.91; 1534]

John of Ockham, yeoman [DW/PA/5/1558/108]*

John of Ockham; Pyrford, husbandman [DW/PA/7/8 f.117; DW/PA/5/1610/59]

John of Pyrford; Ockham, yeoman [DW/PA/7/8 f.350; DW/PA/5/1612/60]

Margaret of Ockham, widow [BM; Add.Ms 24,925 f.24v; 1544] <Abs 62>

Matthew of Walton on Thames, husbandman [HRO; 1625 B16]

Richard of Farnham, maltster [DW/PA/7/13 f.377; 1644]

Robert of Ockham, sawyer *or* husbandman [HRO; 1585 B28]

Thomas of Mitcham [HRO; Reg. Fox 3 p.67; 1515]

Thomas of Ockham [DW/PA/7/3 f.179; 1531]

Thomas of Windlesham, husbandman [HRO; 1585 B29]

Walter of Aldington, Kent; Ockham, rector [LPL; Reg. Abp Sudbury f.83; Will 1376]

William of Horsell, husbandman [DW/PA/7/11 f.421; DW/PA/5/1626/54]

William of Ockham [DW/PA/7/2 f.15; 1491]

William of Ockham, carpenter [*in* DW/PA/5/1558/186]*

William of Ockham; Reigate, yeoman [DW/PA/7/6 f.105; DW/PA/5/1559/68]

William of Ockham, husbandman [DW/PA/7/13 f.396; DW/PA/5/1645/18]

FREEMAN (FREMAN)

Ann of Swk St Saviour, widow of Robert, gent. [HRO; 1571 B67]

Edward of Lambeth [PRO; PCC Admon 1642]

Henry of ...., citizen and tallow chandler [DW/PA/7/11 f.593; DW/PA/5/1630/41]

Hugh of Lambeth, waterman [DW/PA/7/9 f.165; DW/PA/5/1616/54]

John of Kingston, yeoman [DW/PA/7/12 f.351; DW/PA/5/1636/40]

Robert of Swk St Olave [DW/PA/7/5 f.45; 1538] <Abs 101>

Robert of Swk St Saviour [DW/PA/5/1578/12]

Robert of Swk St Saviour [DW/PA/7/13 f.272; 1644]

Simon of Little Bookham, yeoman [DW/PA/7/13 f.100; DW/PA/5/1640/52]

Thomas of Bermondsey, citizen and leatherseller [PRO; PCC Will 1581]

Thomas of Newington [PRO; PCC Admon 1626]

William of Swk St Olave [Southwark Local Studies Library Deed 1550; 1648]

FREEMANTLE

Reginald of Farnham, husbandman [HRO; 1624 AD40]

FREER (FREAR,FREYRE)

Denise of Camberwell - Peckham, widow [DW/PA/5/1546/77]

John of Byfleet, clerk and parson [DW/PA/5/1568/78]

FREIND *see* FRIEND

FREKE *see* FREAKE

FRELAND,FRELANDE,FRELOND,FRELONDE *see* FREELAND

FREMAN *see* FREEMAN
FREMLIN
Thomas of Wandsworth [PRO; PCC Admon 1601]
FRENCH (FRENSHE)
Hugh of Send, vicar [DW/PA/7/9 f.205; DW/PA/5/1616/55]
John of Pyrford [DW/PA/7/1 f.23; 1485] <Abs 77>
William of Pyrford, husbandman [DW/PA/5/1557/141]
see also FRANCIS
FRENCHWOMAN (FRENSHEWOMAN)
Gylmet of Bermondsey, capper [DW/PA/7/1 f.41; 1486] <Abs 132>
FRENDE *see* FRIEND
FRENSHAM (FRANSHAM)
Edward of Farnham [DW/PA/7/5 f.14; 1538] <Abs 37>
Elizabeth of Farnham, widow [DW/PA/7/5 f.117; 1539]
John of Farnham [DW/PA/5/1569/54]
William of Farnham, yeoman [DW/PA/5/1627/41]
FRENSHE *see* FRENCH
FRENSHEWMAN *see* FRENCHWOMAN
FRESTON
John of Putney, servant [PRO; PCC Will 1602] <Abs, SAC v.10 p.309>
FRETON (de FRETON)
Roger, dean of Chichester; canon of York; Rattlesden, Suffolk; Dorking; Aldingbourne, Sussex; St Bride, London [LPL; Reg. Abp Courtenay ff.195,203; Will 1383]
FREYRE *see* FREER
FRICE (FRITE)
John of Swk St Margaret, carpenter [DW/PA/7/1 f.27; 1486] <Abs 88>
FRIDAY (FRYDAYE)
Edward of Ash; Egham, husbandman [BM; Add.Ms 24,925 f.4v; 1544] <Abs 7>
FRIEND (FREIND,FRENDE)
John of Bermondsey, gent. [PRO; PCC Will 1609] <Abs, SAC v.23 p.142>
Richard of Thorpe, yeoman [DW/PA/7/13 f.166; DW/PA/5/1641/52]
Robert of Bermondsey [PRO; PCC 1639]
Thomas of Rotherhithe [PRO; PCC Admon 1649]
FRIER *see* FRYER
FRIGGEN
Agnes of ...., widow of Martin Bowen [*French*] [DW/PA/7/8 f.61; DW/PA/5/1609/22]
FRILOND *see* FREELAND
FRIMLEY
Mary, alias Mary Hampton of Putney, wife of John Hampton [LPL; 98/1 f.84r; Will 1637]
FRING (FRYNG)
John of Swk St Olave, weaver [DW/PA/5/1576/33]
FRISBY (FRISBIE,FRYSBEY,FRYSBYE)
Agnes, alias Agnes Wallis of Croydon [LPL; 98/1 f.53v; Will 1634]
Elizabeth of Croydon, widow [LPL; 96/1001; Will 1627]
Henry of Chaldon [PRO; PCC Admon 1649]
Henry of Croydon, yeoman [LPL; 96/999; Will 1615]
John of Lambeth, labourer [DW/PA/5/1576/155]
John of Morden, husbandman [DW/PA/7/6 f.51; DW/PA/5/1559/117]
Richard of Croydon, husbandman [LPL; 96/1002; Will 1627]
Robert of Croydon, bachelor [LPL; 98/1 f.130v; Will 1642]
Thomas of Carshalton, yeoman [DW/PA/5/1592/114]

FRISBY (FRISBIE,FRYSBEY,FRYSBYE) [*continued*]
William of Croydon, baker [LPL; 96/1000; Will 1624]
William of Reigate [DW/PA/7/7 f.444; DW/PA/5/1603/52] <Abs 840>
FRITE (FRICE)
John of Swk St Margaret [DW/PA/7/1 f.27; 1486] <Abs 88>
FRITH (FRITHE)
Ann of Mitcham [PRO; PCC Admon 1599]
George of Mitcham, husbandman [HRO; 1597 B32]
George of Mitcham, husbandman [DW/PA/7/7 f.123; DW/PA/5/1597/41] <Abs 228>
George of Mortlake, yeoman [PRO; PCC Will 1616]
George of Mortlake, yeoman [LPL; 96/1004; Will 1629]
John of Caterham, husbandman [DW/PA/7/11 f.90; DW/PA/5/1624/48]
Joyce, alias Joyce Richbell of Reigate, widow [PRO; PCC Admon 1619]
Lettice of Mortlake, widow [PRO; PCC 1640]
Miles of Mortlake, yeoman [PRO; PCC Will 1628]
Millicent of Swk St Olave, widow [DW/PA/7/8 f.80; DW/PA/5/1609/80]
William of Swk St Olave, citizen and turner [DW/PA/7/7 f.150; DW/PA/5/1597/42] <Abs 279>
FROMONDE (FROMANS,FROMONDES,FROMONDS,FROMONS,FROMOUNDES)
Bartholomew of Cheam; Ewell; Epsom, gent. [PRO; PCC Will 1579] <Abs SAC v.26 pp.64-65>
Bartholomew of Cheam, esq. [PRO; PCC Admon 1642]
Eleanor of Mitcham, widow [DW/PA/5/1588/42]
Henry of Cheam; Ewell; Epsom, gent. [PRO; PCC Will 1597]
John of Carshalton, gent. [PRO; PCC Will 1580]
John of Carshalton [PRO; PCC Admon 1597]
Thomas of Cheam, bachelor [PRO; PCC Admon 1614]
William of Cheam, gent. [PRO; PCC Will 1607] <Abs. SAC v.12 pp.206-207>
FROOME
Frances of Lambeth, widow [PRO; PCC Will 1622 *and* 1623]
FROST
Francis of Ockham [PRO; PCC 1633]
John of Farnham, husbandman labourer [DW/PA/7/3 f.122; 1529]
John, alias John Vause of Swk St Saviour, butcher [DW/PA/7/12 f.156; DW/PA/5/1633/120]
Mark of Albury; Wonersh, tanner [DW/PA/7/10 f.257; DW/PA/5/1622/30]
Robert of Farnham, glazier [DW/PA/7/11 f.423; DW/PA/5/1627/42]
FROWYK
Thomas of Betchworth - Brockham, esq., senior [PRO; PCC Will 1448]
FRY (FRYE)
Agnes of Puttenham [PRO; PCC Will 1502]
Audrey of Battersea [DW/PA/7/11 f.497; DW/PA/5/1629/35]
Nicholas, alias Nicholas Russell of Albury [DW/PA/5/1550/30]
Robert of Chiddingfold, tanner [DW/PA/7/10 f.1; DW/PA/5/1616/56]
Thomas of Stoke Dabernon, husbandman [DW/PA/7/13 f.186; DW/PA/5/1642/29]
Walter of Chertsey [PRO; PCC Will 1475]
FRYDAYE *see* FRIDAY
FRYE *see* FRY
FRYER (FRIER)
Constance of Lambeth, widow [PRO; PCC 1639]
John of Swk St Olave, shipmaster [DW/PA/5/1588/58]
Lawrence of Ewhurst, glassfounder [DW/PA/7/8 f.301; DW/PA/5/1613/46]
Nicholas of Swk St Olave [DW/PA/7/11 f.201; DW/PA/5/1625/92]

FRYER (FRIER) [*continued*]
  Robert of Bermondsey, citizen and goldsmith [PRO; PCC Will 1576]
  Thomas of Lambeth [DW/PA/7/13 f.46; DW/PA/5/1639/57]
FRYNG *see* FRING
FRYSBEE,FRYSBEY,FRYSBYE *see* FRISBY
FUDDS
  Jane of Richmond, widow [PRO; PCC 1640]
FULKE (FAUCKES,FOLKIS,FOOKES,FOUKE,FOUKES,FOULKES,FULCKE,FULK,FULKES,FULKS)
  Edward of Bermondsey [PRO; PCC Will 1622]
  Elizabeth of Chilworth [PRO; PCC 1633]
  Jasper of West Horsley, yeoman [DW/PA/7/10 f.179; DW/PA/5/1620/52] [*and*] [GMR; 54/1/62]
  Jasper of Ash, yeoman [DW/PA/7/13 f.150; DW/PA/5/1641/47]
  John of Egham [DW/PA/5/1579/36]*
  John of West Horsley, yeoman [DW/PA/7/13 f.8; DW/PA/5/1639/53] [*and*] [GMR; 54/1/64]
  Lewis of Swk St Saviour - Bankside, porter [DW/PA/7/10 f.81; DW/PA/5/1619/48]
  Roger of Chessington, labourer [DW/PA/5/1568/29]
  Thomas of Surrey [PRO; PCC Will 1602]
FULL
  Hugh of Bermondsey, citizen and draper [PRO; PCC Will 1578]
  Stephen of New Windsor, Berkshire; London, citizen and merchant tailor [DW/PA/5/1558/101]*
FULLER
  Alice of Leigh, widow [DW/PA/7/9 f.185; DW/PA/5/1616/57]
  Ann of Worplesdon [DW/PA/7/9 f.271; 1618]
  Barbara of Wotton, widow [DW/PA/7/12 f.160; DW/PA/5/1633/54]
  Bostock of Tandridge, esq. [PRO; PCC Will 1626]
  Edward of East Clandon, yeoman [DW/PA/7/13 f.221; DW/PA/5/1642/31]
  Edward Bostock of Tandridge [DW/PA/7/12 f.422; DW/PA/5/1637/41B]
  Eliza of Dunsfold, widow [DW/PA/7/10 f.72; 1618]
  Elizabeth of Stoke next Guildford, spinster [HRO; 1584 B28]
  James of Leigh, yeoman [DW/PA/7/9 f.126; DW/PA/5/1615/50]
  John of Dorking, carpenter [HRO; 1595 B18]
  John of Dunsfold; Warnham, Sussex [DW/PA/7/8 f.381; DW/PA/5/1612/61]
  John of Worplesdon, husbandman [DW/PA/7/13 f.154; DW/PA/5/1641/48]
  Margaret, alias Margaret Douglas, alias Margaret Heath of Lingfield, widow [PRO; PCC Admon 1648]
  Robert of East Clandon, husbandman [DW/PA/7/8 f.244; DW/PA/5/1613/47]
  Robert of Dorking, carpenter [HRO; 1633 B18]
  Robert of Ockham, carpenter [DW/PA/5/1575/16]
  Thomas of Dorking [DW/PA/7/11 f.430; DW/PA/5/1627/43]
  Thomas of Dunsfold, weaver [DW/PA/7/13 f.215; DW/PA/5/1642/30]
  Thomas of Wotton, yeoman [DW/PA/5/1627/44]
  William, *or* William Duke of Chertsey [PRO; PCC Will 1414]
  William of Farnham, senior [DW/PA/7/1 f.44; 1486] <Abs 143>
  William of Kingston [DW/PA/7/11 f.393; DW/PA/5/1626/55]
  William of Reigate [PRO; PCC 1649]
FULLFINE (FAULASFAN,FULLVEN,VOLVAN,VOULPHAM,VULVAN)
  Alice, alias Alice Haunce of Swk St Thomas Hospital [DW/PA/5/1555/35]
  Ann of Witley, widow [DW/PA/7/11 f.565; DW/PA/5/1630/42]
  Harry of Guildford Holy Trinity [DW/PA/7/4 f.230; 1537]
  John of Camberwell [DW/PA/5/1558/293]*

FULLFINE (FAULASFAN,FULLVEN,VOLVAN,VOULPHAM,VULVAN)
John of Witley, yeoman [HRO; 1623 B19]
Richard of Witley [DW/PA/7/8 f.56; DW/PA/5/1609/120]
Stephen Voulpham, alias Stephen Fulfan of Wotton, husbandman [DW/PA/5/1581/12]

FULLSTONE
Joan of Frensham, widow [HRO; 1579 B17]
Thomas of Frensham [HRO; 1573 B52]
William of Frensham [HRO; 1581 B46]

FULLVEN *see* FULLFINE

FULMER
John of Swk St Margaret [DW/PA/7/4 f.37; 1533]

FURBIE
Phillip of Dorking, yeoman [DW/PA/7/10 f.186; DW/PA/5/1620/53]

FURLEY
Matthew of Guildford St Nicolas, yeoman [PRO; PCC 1649]

FURLONGER
Alice of Chiddingfold, widow [HRO; 1587 B37]
Elizabeth of Cranleigh, spinster [DW/PA/7/13 f.110; DW/PA/5/1640/53]
John of Bramley [PRO; PCC Admon 1633]
Robert of Alfold 'going forth to the king's wars' [*in* DW/PA/5/1544/4]
William of Cranleigh, yeoman [DW/PA/7/11 f.341; DW/PA/5/1625/93]

FURNESS (FOWRNES)
John of Battersea [DW/PA/7/2 f.39; 1493]
see also FONACE

FYFE,FYFFE,FYFTE *see* FIFE

FYGE,FYGGE *see* FIGG

FYLCOTE *see* FILLCOTT

FYLD *see* FIELD

FYLDER *see* FIELDER

FYLDING *see* FIELDING

FYLLPOTT,FYLPOT *see* PHILPOTT

FYLPE *see* PHILLIPS

FYLYAN *see* FILLIAN

FYLYCHURCH *see* PHILLICHURCH

FYNCH,FYNCHE,FYNTCHE,FYNYSSHE *see* FINCH

FYNDEN *see* FINDEN

FYNGES *see* FINGES

FYNNEY *see* FINNEY

FYNYMORE *see* FINNIMORE

FYSHER *see* FISHER

GAD *see* GADD

GADBURY
Lucretia of Compton, widow [DW/PA/7/7 f.610; DW/PA/5/1607/41] <Abs 1141>

GADD (GAD)
Alice of Worplesdon [PRO; PCC Admon 1647]
Alice of Worplesdon [PRO; PCC Admon 1649]
Anthony of Worplesdon [PRO; PCC Admon 1649]
Elizabeth of East Horsley, widow [PRO; PCC Will 1619]
Henry of West Clandon, husbandman [DW/PA/5/1558/110]*
Richard of Shere, husbandman [DW/PA/7/12 f.235; DW/PA/5/1634/49]

GADDESDON (GADDISTON,GODESDEN)
John of Woking [DW/PA/7/1 f.19; 1485] <Abs 62>
William of Farnham [DW/PA/7/3 f.178; 1531]
GADEN
Ralph of East Clandon [DW/PA/7/3 f.195; 1531]
GADSON
Abraham of Horne, husbandman [DW/PA/7/12 f.278; DW/PA/5/1636/44]
John of Tandridge, husbandman [DW/PA/7/7 f.274; DW/PA/5/1599/25] <Abs 484>
GAGE
(Sir) Edward of Horne - Hedgecourt, knight [PRO; PCC Will 1568]
Urithe, widow of James (sometime wife of Richard Milles) of Malden [PRO; PCC Will 1583]
William of Burstow, esq. [PRO; PCC Will 1497]
GAINSBOROUGH (GANSBOROWGHT,GAYNSBOROWE)
Joan of Swk St Saviour, widow [DW/PA/5/1558/115]*
William of Swk St George [DW/PA/7/4 f.77; 1534]
GAINSFORD (GAINSFORDE,GAYNESFORD,GAYNESFORDE,GAYNESSFORD,GAYNSFORDE)
Erasmus of Crowhurst, esq. [DW/PA/5/1581/23]
Henry of Carshalton, esq. [PRO; PCC Will 1545]
Jane of Richmond [PRO; PCC Will 1559]
Jane of Richmond, widow [PRO; PCC Admon 1560]
John of Crowhurst, esq., senior [PRO; PCC Will 1450]
John of Crowhurst, esq., senior [PRO; PCC Will 1464] <Abs SAC v.27 pp.32-33>
(Sir) John of Crowhurst [PRO; PCC Will 1540]
John of Lingfield - Ford, gent. [PRO; PCC Will 1580]
Margaret of Carshalton [PRO; PCC Will 1503; CCAL; 1503 f.251r] <Abs SAC v.26 p.31>
Nicholas of Carshalton, esq. [PRO; PCC Will 1498] <Abs SAC v.26 pp.30-31>
Robert of Carshalton, squire [DW/PA/7/2 f.163; 1521]
Robert of Carshalton, gent. [DW/PA/5/1558/114] [*For further grant see will of Elizabeth Gander.*]
Robert of Swk St George; Wandsworth; St Katherine by the Tower, Middlesex, gent. [DW/PA/5/1593/45]
Thomas of Crowhurst, esq. [PRO; PCC Will 1551]
Thomas of Lingfield, esq. [PRO; PCC Will 1587]
(Sir) William of Lingfield - Ford, knight [PRO; PCC Will 1608] <Abs. SAC v.13 p.181>
William of Lingfield [PRO; PCC Admon 1649]
William of Newington [PRO; PCC Will 1607] <Abs. SAC v.12 p.98>
GAIRSTANG *see* GARSTANG
GAITTER *see* GATER
GALE
Elizabeth of Wandsworth [PRO; PCC Will 1545] <Abs SAC v.33 p.23>
Margaret of Bermondsey, widow [DW/PA/7/11 f.539; DW/PA/5/1629/36]
Robert of Swk St Saviour, shipwright [DW/PA/7/9 f.323; DW/PA/5/1619/49]
Thomas of Wandsworth [PRO; PCC Will 1540] <Abs SAC v.33 p.23>
GALL
Robert of Swk St George [DW/PA/7/7 f.615; DW/PA/5/1607/42] <Abs 1150>
GALLAMORE
William of Lambeth, yeoman [PRO; PCC Will 1600]
GALLANT (GALLANDE)
Isabel of Reigate [DW/PA/7/4 f.31; 1533]

GALLANT (GALLANDE) [*continued*]
Thomas of Farnham [PRO; PCC Admon 1645]
GALLAPINE
Robert of Rotherhithe, waterman [DW/PA/5/1593/56]
GALLAWAIE,GALLAWAYE *see* GALLOWAY
GALLIARDELLO
Margery of Camberwell, widow [DW/PA/7/8 f.178; DW/PA/5/1610/60]
GALLOP (GOLLOP)
John of Betchworth, yeoman [DW/PA/7/8 f.57; DW/PA/5/1609/82]
GALLOWAY (GALLAWAIE,GALLAWAYE)
Frances, alias Frances Whyte of Swk St Saviour, widow [DW/PA/5/1572/10]
Geanes, alias Geanes Agalliaway of Morden [DW/PA/5/1575/63]
GALYS *see* GILES
GAMLYN
John of Holme Hale, Norfolk; Swk St Saviour, tailor [DW/PA/5/1593/154]
GANDER (GANDAR,GANYCHE)
Alice of Thursley, widow [DW/PA/7/6 f.210; 1560]
Elizabeth of Sutton, husbandman [DW/PA/5/1558/112]
John of Reigate [DW/PA/7/3 f.187; 1531]
John of Thursley [DW/PA/7/6 f.152; DW/PA/5/1559/168]
Nicholas of Reigate, yeoman, senior [DW/PA/5/1591/5]
Richard of Croydon, husbandman [LPL; 96/1011; 98/1 f.51v; Will 1633]
Richard of Reigate, yeoman [DW/PA/7/8 f.114; DW/PA/5/1610/61]
Roger of Reigate [DW/PA/7/11 f.472; DW/PA/5/1628/42]
GANDY *see* GAUDY
GANYCHE *see* GANDER
GANESFORD *see* GAINSFORD
GANSBOROWGHT *see* GAINSBOROUGH
GAPPER
Isaac of Swk St Saviour, waterman [DW/PA/7/12 f.345; DW/PA/5/1636/47]
GARARD *see* GERRARD
GARDENER (GARDINER,GARDNER,GARDYNER)
Christopher of Leatherhead [PRO; PCC Will 1608]
Edward of Newdigate [DW/PA/5/1647/4] <Abs U262>
Edward of Newdigate [PRO; PCC 1647]
(Dame) Frances of Camberwell - Peckham, widow [PRO; PCC 1638]
Giles of Battersea [DW/PA/5/1578/34]
James of Guildford Holy Trinity; Guildford St Mary; Stoke next Guildford; Rusper, Sussex, butcher [DW/PA/7/7 f.124; DW/PA/5/1597/43] <Abs 229>
Joan of Chiddingfold, widow [DW/PA/7/1 f.96; 1489] <Abs 316>
John of Great Bookham [DW/PA/7/2 f.120; 1518]
John of Great Bookham, yeoman [DW/PA/5/1593/17]
John of Great Bookham, , yeoman [DW/PA/7/13 f.218; DW/PA/5/1642/36]
John of Chiddingfold [DW/PA/7/3 f.108; 1529]
John, alias John Lamberd of Cranleigh, ironmaker [DW/PA/5/1593/176]
John of Lambeth, yeoman [DW/PA/5/1604/19] <Abs U105>
John of Newdigate, tanner [DW/PA/7/8 f.172; DW/PA/5/1610/62]
John of Ockham, husbandman [DW/PA/7/6 f.98; DW/PA/5/1559/69]
John of Putney [PRO; PCC Will 1509]
John of Wandsworth, citizen and cutler [PRO; PCC Will 1608] <Abs, SAC v.13 p.177>
John of Woking, vicar [HRO; Reg. Way 1 p.95; 1468]

GARDENER (GARDINER,GARDNER,GARDYNER) [*continued*]
Margery of Wandsworth, widow [PRO; PCC Will 1616]
Morgan, alias Morgan Hoggyns of Walton on Thames - Apps [DW/PA/7/5 f,156; 1540]
Oliver of Capel [PRO; PCC Admon 1611]
Ralph of Great Bookham, yeoman [DW/PA/7/7 f,479; DW/PA/5/1604/20] <Abs 904>
Richard of Bermondsey [PRO; PCC Will 1551]
Richard of Bermondsey [PRO; PCC Admon 1593]
Richard of Lambeth [PRO; PCC 1647]
Richard of Leatherhead [PRO; PCC Admon 1595]
Richard of Leatherhead [PRO; PCC Admon 1607]
Richard of Send, saddler [DW/PA/7/11 f,223; 1620]
Richard of Swk St Saviour [DW/PA/7/12 f,352; DW/PA/5/1636/48]
Richard of Swk St Saviour [DW/PA/7/13 f,367; 1644]
Richard of Streatham, citizen and armourer [PRO; PCC Will 1618]
Robert of Leatherhead, sergeant of the Queen's cellar, esq. [PRO; PCC Will 1571] <Abs SAC v,29 p,133>
Robert of Swk St Margaret - Bankside, yeoman [DW/PA/7/5 f,53; 1538] <Abs 87>
Roger of Reigate, yeoman [DW/PA/7/7 f,30; DW/PA/5/1595/41] <Abs 62>
Thomas of Burstow, esq, [PRO; PCC 1642]
(Sir) Thomas of Camberwell - Peckham, knight [DW/PA/7/12 f,133; DW/PA/5/1632/38]
Thomas of Charlwood [PRO; PCC 1633]
Thomas of Newdigate [DW/PA/5/1561/74]
William of Albury; Wem, Shropshire, bachelor [PRO; PCC 1645]
William of Bermondsey [PRO; PCC Will 1599]
William of Bermondsey; Dorking [PRO; PCC Will 1597]
(Sir) William of Godstone - Lagham; Ewell; Swk St Olave, knight [PRO; PCC Will 1622] [*and*] [LBLAD; Surrey Deeds 1/1359; 1618]
William of Windlesham, carpenter [PRO; PCC Will 1617]
see also GARSSENER

GARETT *see* GARRETT

GARFORD
Richard of Swk St Olave, aquavita seller [HRO; 1586 B23]

GARLAND (GARLANDE)
Alice of Shere, widow of Thomas [DW/PA/7/8 f,214; DW/PA/5/1612/62]
Francis of Newington [PRO; PCC Will 1618]
John of Croydon [GL; Commissary Court of London Will 1446]
John of Leatherhead [DW/PA/7/2 f,13; 1491]
John of Swk, innholder [DW/PA/5/1563/69 *and, in* DW/PA/5/1563/64]
John of Swk St Saviour [HRO; Reg, CCB 20 p,3; 1563]
Juliana of Long Ditton, widow [DW/PA/7/1 f,78; 1488] <Abs 257>
Robert of Leatherhead [DW/PA/7/6 f,157; DW/PA/5/1559/150]
Thomas of Shere [DW/PA/7/8 f,188; DW/PA/5/1610/63]
William of Long Ditton [DW/PA/7/1 f,79; 1488] <Abs 260>

GARMAN
John of Woking, yeoman [HRO; 1614 AD34]

GARNARD
John of Farnham [DW/PA/7/5 f,41; 1538] <Abs 38>

GARNER
John of ... [DW/PA/7/7 f,107; DW/PA/5/1596/24] <Abs 193>

GARNETT (GARNET,GRANET)

Hugh of Newington [DW/PA/7/7 f,415; DW/PA/5/1603/54] <Abs 774>

John of Newington [LPL; 98/1 f,27v; Will 1631]

Robert of Swk St George, fishmonger [DW/PA/5/1563/116]

Thomas of Swk St Mary Magdalen; Cheshunt, Hertfordshire, citizen and armourer [DW/PA/7/2 f,71; 1500]

Thomas of Newington; the Ship *Royal Mary* [LPL; 96/1022; 98/1 f,3v; Will 1629]

Thomas of Woking, yeoman [DW/PA/5/1555/26]

GARRETT (GARETT)

Elizabeth of Swk St Olave, widow [DW/PA/7/7 f,509; DW/PA/5/1605/37] <Abs 956>

James of Swk St Olave [DW/PA/7/7 f,151; DW/PA/5/1597/44] <Abs 283>

Joseph of Kingston, brickmaker [DW/PA/7/10 f,234; DW/PA/5/1621/44]

Stephen of Newdigate [PRO; PCC Will 1489]

GARRETSON

John of Swk St Olave, joiner [DW/PA/5/1568/52]

GARSSENER

John of Richmond, husbandman [DW/PA/5/1580/41]

see also GARDENER

GARSTANG (GAIRSTANG,GARSTAN,GARSTANGE)

John of Bermondsey [PRO; PCC Will 1477]

Richard of Swk St Mary Overy; Swk St Margaret [DW/PA/7/2 f,138; 1520]

Robert of Farnham - Wrecclesham [DW/PA/7/1 f,80; 1487] <Abs 262>

GARTH (GEARTHE,GOWYTH)

Beatrice of Morden, widow [PRO; PCC 1648]

Edward of Kingston [PRO; PCC Will 1555]

George of Morden, esq, [PRO; PCC Will 1627]

Joan of ..., widow [DW/PA/7/10 f,85; DW/PA/5/1615/33]

Richard of St Dunstan in the West, London; Morden [PRO; PCC Will 1598]

Richard of Morden, esq, [PRO; PCC 1640]

Robert of Morden, esq, [PRO; PCC Will 1613]

William of Merton [DW/PA/7/3 f,177; 1531]

GARTON

Robert of Camberwell - Peckham [DW/PA/7/8 f,331 *and* DW/PA/7/9 f,74; DW/PA/5/1614/47]

Thomas of Bermondsey [DW/PA/7/3 f,162; 1530]

GARWAY (GARWAYE)

(Dame) Elizabeth of Weybridge [PRO; PCC 1636]

Thomas of Mortlake, gent, [PRO; PCC Will 1625]

see also GORWAY

GARY (GURREY,GURRY)

Ann of Swk St George, widow [DW/PA/7/13 f,258; DW/PA/5/1643/42]

Christopher of Swk St George, citizen and lorimer [DW/PA/7/12 f,419; DW/PA/5/1637/44]

Luke of Bentley, Hampshire [DW/PA/7/4 f,73; 1532] [cf, Luke Gray]

see also GEERY

GASCON

William of Lambeth [PRO; PCC Will 1541]

GASE (GASSE,GAYSCE)

Agnes of Cobham, widow [DW/PA/5/1593/130]

John of Haslemere [DW/PA/7/2 f,44; 1494]

John of Haslemere; Witley; Bosham, Sussex [DW/PA/7/2 f,166; 1521]

John of Haslemere [DW/PA/5/1558/116]*

GASE (GASSE,GAYSCE) [*continued*]
John of Haslemere, yeoman [DW/PA/7/10 f,219; DW/PA/5/1621/45]
GASKER
Jane of Swk St George, widow [DW/PA/7/7 f,261; DW/PA/5/1599/26] <Abs 465>
GASNER (GASTER,GASTNER)
Alice of Croydon, widow [PRO; PCC Will 1626]
Geoffrey of Croydon, yeoman [PRO; PCC Will 1624]
James of Richmond [PRO; PCC Admon 1630]
Richard of Richmond [PRO; PCC Admon 1623]
Susan of Richmond, widow [DW/PA/7/12 f,162; DW/PA/5/1633/59]
GASSE *see* GASE
GASSON (GASTON)
John of Shalford [HRO; 1557 U250; Reg, D3/59]
John of Shalford, husbandman [DW/PA/7/8 f,365; DW/PA/5/1612/63]
Thomas of Shalford, yeoman [DW/PA/7/7 f,126; DW/PA/5/1597/45] <Abs 230>
William of Shalford - East Shalford, yeoman [DW/PA/5/1624/49]
GASTER,GASTNER *see* GASNER
GASTON *see* GASSON
GASTRELL
Edmund of Shere, gent, [PRO; PCC Will 1626]
George of St Dunstan, London; Axwell House, Durham; Shere - Towerhill [GL; Commissary Court of London Will 1617]
GATACRE
Thomas of Newington, parson [PRO; PCC Will 1593]
GATE *see* AGATE,ATGATE,GATES
GATER (GAITTER)
Joan of Kingston, widow [DW/PA/7/11 f,124; DW/PA/5/1624/50]
William of Banstead [DW/PA/7/12 f,483; DW/PA/5/1638/55]
GATES (GATIS)
Henry of Ockley, sawyer [DW/PA/5/1603/53] <Abs U69>
James of Betchworth [HRO; 1622 AD27]
James of Rotherhithe, house carpenter [DW/PA/7/7 f,600; DW/PA/5/1607/43] <Abs 1122>
John of Malden, yeoman [DW/PA/7/7 f,375; DW/PA/5/1602/32] <Abs 694>
John of Send, priest and vicar [PRO; PCC Will 1558]
Richard of Frimley [DW/PA/7/9 f,236; DW/PA/5/1617/46]
Robert of Walton on Thames - Apps [DW/PA/7/1 f,49; 1487] <Abs 163>
Thomas of Bermondsey [PRO; PCC 1639]
Thomas of Reigate, labourer [DW/PA/7/8 f,351; DW/PA/5/1612/64]
Walter of Swk St Olave, whitster [DW/PA/7/10 f,89; DW/PA/5/1615/32]
William of Reigate [DW/PA/7/2 f,198; 1524]
see also AGATE,ATGATE
GATTON (GAUTTON)
Gregory, alias Gregory Chepman of Surrey [? HRO; 1529]
John, alias John Chapman of Albury, husbandman [DW/PA/7/9 f,296; 1618]
John of Lambeth, hair weaver [PRO; PCC Will 1625]
John of Petersham [PRO; PCC 1647]
John, alias John Chapman of Shere, senior [HRO; 1608 B32]
Richard, alias Richard Chapman of Albury, yeoman [DW/PA/5/1612/65] <Abs U200>
Richard, alias Richard Chapman of Great Bookham, husbandman [HRO; 1622 B8]
Stephen, alias Stephen Chapman of Surrey [? HRO; 1529]
Thomas of Albury [? HRO; 1529]

GATTON (GAUTTON) [*continued*]

William, alias William Chapman of Thames Ditton [DW/PA/7/7 f.118; DW/PA/5/1597/21] <Abs 218>

William of Ewhurst [DW/PA/7/4 f.109; 1535]

GAUDYE

John of Swk St Olave, feltmaker [DW/PA/7/7 f.220; 1598] <Abs 389>

GAUGE *see* GAWGE

GAUTTON *see* GATTON

GAUSTONE

William of Walton on the Hill [HRO; Reg. Fox 2 p.33; 1508]

GAVELL

Edmund of Weybridge - 'Evernes', esq. [PRO; PCC Will 1612]

Francis of Cobham, gent. [PRO; PCC Will 1611] <Abs. SAC v.35 p.34>

Mary of Cobham, widow [DW/PA/7/13 f.21; DW/PA/5/1639/61]

Robert of Cobham; Buckland; Reigate; Hundon, Suffolk; Stoke by Clare - College, Suffolk, gent. [DW/PA/7/7 f.36; DW/PA/5/1595/40] <Abs 73>

Robert of Ripley, gent. [PRO; PCC 1649]

Vincent of Cobham, esq. [PRO; PCC 1648]

Vincent of Cobham [PRO; PCC Admon 1648]

GAVYNE

Thomas of Swk St Saviour, plasterer [DW/PA/5/1578/44]

GAWEN *see* GAWYN

GAWGE

John of Wimbledon [PRO; PCC Will 1540]

GAWSEM

Ann, alias Ann Salford of Barnes [PRO; PCC Will 1509]

GAWTON

John of Nutfield [PRO; PCC 1649]

John of Warlingham [DW/PA/5/1558/113]

Magdalen of Blechingley; Merstham, widow [DW/PA/7/7 f.565; DW/PA/5/1606/39] <Abs 1057>

Richard of Nutfield, husbandman [DW/PA/5/1557/102]

Susanna of Nutfield [PRO; PCC Admon 1649]

William of Nutfield; Swk St Olave, senior [PRO; PCC Will 1593]

GAWYN (GAWEN, GOWEN, GOWENE)

Daniel of Cheam [LPL; 96/1032; 98/1 f.101v; Will 1639]

Elizabeth of Betchworth - Brockham [DW/PA/7/10 f.250; DW/PA/5/1622/37]

James of Guildford, glazier [DW/PA/7/7 f.484; DW/PA/5/1604/21] <Abs 912>

James of ... [DW/PA/7/9 f.291; 1618]

John of Swk St George, collier [DW/PA/5/1593/74]

Thomas of Banstead [DW/PA/7/7 f.436; DW/PA/5/1603/55] <Abs 825>

GAY (GAYE)

John of Swk St Saviour, waterman [DW/PA/7/10 f.188; DW/PA/5/1620/54]

Mary of Kingston, maid servant of R. Bifield [HRO; 1625 B18]

GAYNSBOROWE *see* GAINSBOROUGH

GAYNESFORD, GAINESFORDE, GAYNESSFORD, GAYNSFORD, GAYNSFORDE *see* GAINSFORD

GAYRE

Thomas, *or* Thomas Guyn of Swk St George, baker [DW/PA/7/12 f.397; DW/PA/5/1638/52]

see also GEYRES

GAYSCE *see* GASE

Thomas of Petersham, husbandman [DW/PA/7/12 f.480; DW/PA/5/1638/54]

GEALE (GELE,JEALE,JELE,JELLE)
Anthony of Reigate [DW/PA/7/11 f,452; DW/PA/5/1628/62]
George of Frensham, yeoman [DW/PA/7/11 f,86; DW/PA/5/1623/44]
James of Epsom, labourer [HRO; 1608 B33]
Joan of Richmond, widow [DW/PA/7/11 f,206; DW/PA/5/1625/94]
John of Nutfield - Woolborough [DW/PA/7/5 f,87; 1539]
John of Richmond, yeoman [DW/PA/7/11 f,16; DW/PA/5/1623/45]
Nicholas of Charlwood, yeoman, senior [LPL; 96/1451; Will 1614]
Richard of Chaldon, husbandman [DW/PA/7/8 f,97; DW/PA/5/1609/92]
Richard of Dorking [PRO; PCC Will 1593]
Richard of Nutfield [DW/PA/5/1571/94]
Robert of Byfleet, day labourer [HRO; 1575 AD26]
Thomas of Abinger, yeoman [DW/PA/7/13 f,19; DW/PA/5/1639/60]
William of Chaldon [DW/PA/7/12 f,301; DW/PA/5/1636/43]
William of Dorking [DW/PA/7/4 f,202; 1537]
William of Horley [DW/PA/5/1568/71]
William of Nutfield0; Reigate, yeoman [DW/PA/7/8 f,88; DW/PA/5/1609/93]
GEARING (GERYNG)
William of Egham; Berkshire [DW/PA/7/4 f,26; 1532]
GEARTHE *see* GARTH
GEE
Edmund of West Horsley [DW/PA/7/12 f,368; DW/PA/5/1627/45]
George of Titsey, husbandman [PRO; PCC Will 1619]
GEERY (GERRY)
Eleanor of Shalford - West Shalford [PRO; PCC 1636]
John, alias John Gery of Merstham, yeoman [LPL; 96/1036; 98/1 f,78r; Will 1636]
see also GARY
GEFFRESON *see* JEFFERSON
GEFFREY *see* JEFFRIES
GEFSON *see* JEFFERSON
GELE *see* GEALE
GELYE *see* JELLEY
GEMS *see* Barbara COOPER & Francis JAMS
GENCE *see* GENT
GENNER *see* JENNER
GENNYNS *see* JENNINGS
GENT (GENCE,JENT)
James of Godstone; Oxted, gent, [PRO; PCC Will 1593]
John of Chertsey, husbandman [DW/PA/7/9 f,122; DW/PA/5/1615/72]
John of Swk St Olave, miller [DW/PA/7/9 f,276; 1618]
GEORGE
Cornelius of Bermondsey, silk weaver [PRO; PCC Will 1625]
John of Woking, victualler [DW/PA/7/12 f,312; DW/PA/5/1636/46]
GERRARD (GARARD)
John of Dorking [PRO; PCC Will 1476]
GERRY *see* GEERY
GERVICE *see* JERVIS
GERY *see* GEERY
GERYNG *see* GEARING
GESTLYN
Thomas of Kingston [DW/PA/7/3 f,112; 1529]

GEYRES

John of Swk St Saviour - Liberty of the Clink, waterman [DW/PA/7/9 f.117; DW/PA/5/1615/51]

GIBBONS (GIBBINS,GIBBON,GUYBON,GYBENES,GYBONS)

Agnes of Betchworth [PRO; PCC Will 1535]

Agnes of Chertsey [PRO; PCC Will 1458]

Agnes of Wandsworth, widow [DW/PA/7/11 f.3; DW/PA/5/1622/31]

Francis of London, citizen and woodmonger [DW/PA/7/11 f.69; DW/PA/5/1623/46]

Simon of Putney, citizen and goldsmith [PRO; PCC 1645]

Thomas of Wandsworth, husbandman [DW/PA/5/1588/74]

William of London, clothworker [DW/PA/7/9 f.231; DW/PA/5/1617/47]

GIBBS (GIBBES,GYBBS,GYBBYS)

Alice of Byfleet, widow of Edward [DW/PA/7/5 f.109; 1539]

Edward of Byfleet [DW/PA/7/4 f.25; 1532]

Ellen of Cheam, widow [PRO; PCC Will 1613]

Francis of Swk St Thomas, citizen and currier [DW/PA/7/13 f.149A; DW/PA/5/1641/58]

Jane of Swk St Thomas, wife of Francis citizen and currier [DW/PA/7/13 f.184; DW/PA/5/1641/62]

John of Cheam [PRO; PCC Admon 1601]

GIBLETT (GYBLETT,GYBLOTT)

William of Bermondsey [PRO; PCC Will 1464]

William of Swk St Olave [DW/PA/5/1582/6]

GIBSON (GYBSON,GYBSONE)

Alice of Lambeth [PRO; PCC Admon 1585]

Alice (Alice Dudley, formerly Alice Gibson) of Rotherhithe [PRO; PCC Will 1556]

Anthony of Egham [DW/PA/7/12 f.28; DW/PA/5/1631/49]

Cuthbert of Newington - Walworth [PRO; PCC 1642]

Henry of Egham, husbandman [DW/PA/7/9 f.320; DW/PA/5/1619/50]

Joan of Thames Ditton, widow [DW/PA/7/12 f.52; DW/PA/5/1631/50]

John of Lambeth, chapman [DW/PA/7/7 f.77; DW/PA/5/1596/45] <Abs 141>

John of Newington [PRO; PCC Admon 1638]

John of Streatham [DW/PA/5/1568/2]

Phillip of Rotherhithe [PRO; PCC Will 1552]

Phillippa of Rotherhithe [PRO; PCC Admon 1561]

Richard of Richmond [PRO; PCC Admon 1649]

Robert of Swk St Olave, tailor [DW/PA/7/1 f.39; 1486] <Abs 127>

Susan, alias Susan Marsh of Newington - Walworth [PRO; PCC Admon 1647]

Thomas of Camberwell - Peckham, yeoman [DW/PA/7/6 f.287; 1560]

Thomas of Egham - Englefield [DW/PA/5/1575/10]

Thomas of Swk St Thomas [DW/PA/7/13 f.74; DW/PA/5/1640/59]

William of Egham, yeoman [DW/PA/7/9 f.215; DW/PA/5/1617/48]

William of Swk St Olave, waterman [DW/PA/7/10 f.261; DW/PA/5/1622/32]

William of Wandsworth - All Hallows [HRO; 1529 B12]

GIE *see* GUY

GILBERD,GILBERDSON *see* GILBERT,GILBERTSON

GILBERT (GILBERD,GILBERTE,GYLBERTE)

Daniel of Carshalton, labourer [DW/PA/7/7 f.503; DW/PA/5/1605/38] <Abs 941>

John of Worplesdon; Chiddingfold, yeoman [DW/PA/7/8 f.33; DW/PA/5/1609/83]

Nicholas of Crowhurst [DW/PA/5/1604/23] <Abs U107>

GILBERT (GILBERD,GILBERTE,GYLBERTE) [*continued*]
Richard, alias Richard Cowper of Egham [DW/PA/7/1 f.72; 1487] <Abs 238>
Robert of Lingfield; Crowhurst, tailor [DW/PA/5/1605/36] <Abs U146>
Thomas of Bermondsey, citizen and leatherseller [PRO; PCC Will 1619]
Thomas of Worplesdon, yeoman [DW/PA/7/5 f.196; 1540]

GILBERTSON (GILBERDSON,GILBERDSONNE,GILBERTSONNE)
Agnes, alias Agnes Derrick of Guildford, widow [DW/PA/5/1568/53]
Andrew, alias Andrew Derrick of Guildford, bricklayer [DW/PA/5/1570/63]
John, alias John Derrick of Guildford - *White Hart*, innholder [DW/PA/7/8 f.42; DW/PA/5/1607/44]
John, alias John Derrick of Guildford Holy Trinity; Guildford St Mary; St Giles in the Fields, Middlesex, gent., senior [DW/PA/7/8 f.242; DW/PA/5/1613/55]
Richard, alias Richard Deryck of Guildford [DW/PA/5/1563/5]
Richard, alias Richard Derricke of Guildford Holy Trinity; Guildford St Mary; Stoke next Guildford, bricklayer [DW/PA/7/7 f.354; DW/PA/5/1602/33] <Abs 650>

GILBOURNE
William of Tandridge [PRO; PCC Admon 1642]

GILDING (GILDEN,GILDINGE,GILDINGS,GILLDYNE)
Ellen of Swk St Saviour, widow [DW/PA/7/8 f.305; DW/PA/5/1613/56]
Francis of Swk St Saviour, cordwainer [DW/PA/7/11 f.242; DW/PA/5/1625/95]
Katherine of Swk St Saviour, widow of Francis [DW/PA/7/11 f.399; DW/PA/5/1627/47]
Roger of Swk St Saviour; Swk St George, innholder [DW/PA/5/1604/22] <Abs U106>

GILES (GALYS,GILE,GILLES,GYELES,GYLE,GYLES,GYLIS,GYLLES,GYLYS)
... [*man, brother of William*] of Worplesdon [DW/PA/5/1558/124]*
Arnold of Swk St Olave [DW/PA/5/1581/56]
Elizabeth of Worplesdon, widow [DW/PA/5/1571/92]
George of Lingfield, junior [PRO; PCC Will 1589]
George of Lingfield [PRO; PCC Will 1596]
Henry of Chertsey, gent. [DW/PA/5/1576/141 *and* DW/PA/5/1576/142]
Henry of Mitcham, labourer [DW/PA/5/1588/39]
Hugh of Mitcham [DW/PA/7/4 f.179; 1536]
Joan of Mitcham, widow of Richard [DW/PA/7/4 f.216; 1537]
John of Charlwood, clerk [PRO; PCC Will 1428]
John of Chertsey, gent. [HRO; 1512 B8]
John of Kingston [DW/PA/7/3 f.207; 1532]
John of Kingston, husbandman [DW/PA/5/1575/31]
John of Swk St Olave, cooper [DW/PA/7/5 f.59; 1539] <Abs 99>
John of Windlesham [DW/PA/7/13 f.309; DW/PA/5/1643/45]
John of Worplesdon, citizen and joiner [GL; Archdeaconry Court of London Will 1598]
John of Woking, blacksmith [DW/PA/7/13 f.130; DW/PA/5/1640/63]
Margaret of Chertsey, widow [DW/PA/7/5 f.197; 1540]
Mary of Lingfield, spinster [PRO; PCC Will 1623]
Ralph of Pirbright, tailor [DW/PA/7/10 f.38; DW/PA/5/1617/53]
Reginald of Walton on Thames - Oatlands [PRO; PCC Admon 1612]
Richard of West Horsley, yeoman [HRO; 1622 B18]
Richard of Mitcham; Mickleham, husbandman [DW/PA/7/4 f.204; 1537]
Richard of Pyrford, carpenter [DW/PA/5/1591/3]
Robert of Chertsey, bargeman [DW/PA/7/7 f.40; DW/PA/5/1595/44] <Abs 79>
Robert of Mitcham, yeoman [DW/PA/7/7 f.369; DW/PA/5/1602/34] <Abs 678>

GILES (GALYS,GILE,GILLES,GYELES,GYLE,GYLES,GYLIS,GYLLES,GYLYS) [*continued*]
Robert of Send [DW/PA/5/1550/111]
Stephen of Woking [DW/PA/7/3 f.170; 1531]
Thomas of Bermondsey, leatherdresser [DW/PA/7/12 f.362; DW/PA/5/1637/43]
Thomas of East Clandon, labourer [HRO; 1614 B30]
Thomas of Egham, husbandman [DW/PA/5/1558/111]*
Thomas of Send [*in* DW/PA/5/1544/9]
Thomas of Send [DW/PA/7/6 f.163; DW/PA/5/1559/72]
Thomas of Swk St Thomas [DW/PA/7/9 f.311; DW/PA/5/1619/53]
Thomas of Worplesdon, yeoman, senior [DW/PA/7/12 f.48; DW/PA/5/1632/37]
Thomas of Worplesdon [DW/PA/7/12 f.221; DW/PA/5/1634/47]
William of ... [GMR; 97/13/1110; 1576]
William of Bermondsey [DW/PA/7/12 f.498; DW/PA/5/1638/57]
William of West Horsley [HRO; 1586 B24]
William of West Horsley [HRO; 1587 AD27]
William of Mitcham [DW/PA/5/1543/9]*
William of Woking - Mayford; Frimley; Little Marlow, Buckinghamshire; Pyrford; Bisley; Woking - 'Styles', yeoman, senior [DW/PA/5/1593/81]
William of Worplesdon [DW/PA/7/5 f.44; 1538] <Abs 128>
see also GILL

GILGRASSE
William of Tooting Graveney [DW/PA/7/11 f.579; DW/PA/5/1630/43]

GILHAM *see* GILLAM

GILKIN (GYLKYN)
Emery of Guildford St Mary [DW/PA/7/5 f.177; 1540]
John of Cranleigh [DW/PA/5/1592/59]

GILL (GILLE,GYLL)
Henry of Godalming [PRO; PCC 1645]
Mark of Swk St Olave, chandler [DW/PA/7/11 f.273; DW/PA/5/1625/96]
Richard of Swk St George [DW/PA/7/5 f.74; 1539]
William of Frensham, yeoman [DW/PA/7/12 f.303; DW/PA/5/1635/39]

GILLAM (GILHAM,GILLEAMS)
Agnes of Stoke next Guildford - Aldham, widow [DW/PA/7/10 f.53; 1618]
John of Richmond, gent, practised in physic [DW/PA/7/11 f.80; DW/PA/5/1623/47]
John, alias John Blowme of Stoke next Guildford, yeoman [DW/PA/7/8 f.176; DW/PA/5/1610/64]
Katherine of Stoke next Guildford, widow [DW/PA/7/9 f.220; DW/PA/5/1617/49]
Katherine of Guildford, widow of John [LBLAD; Surrey Deeds 1/419; 1649]
Richard of Swk St Olave, waterman [DW/PA/7/11 f.398; DW/PA/5/1627/46]
Roger, alias Roger Blowne of Stoke next Guildford, yeoman [HRO; 1614 B31]
Thomas, alias Thomas Blume of Worplesdon [DW/PA/7/12 f.222; DW/PA/5/1634/8]
William of Chiddingfold, blacksmith [DW/PA/7/8 f.96; DW/PA/5/1609/84]
William of Chiddingfold, blacksmith [DW/PA/7/11 f.47; 1623]
William, alias William Bloome of Stoke next Guildford, tailor [DW/PA/5/1617/50] <Abs U215>
William of Stoke next Guildford [PRO; PCC Admon 1647]
see also GILES,GWILLIAMS

GILLDYNE *see* GILDING

GILLE *see* GILL

GILLEAMS *see* GILLAM

GILLES *see* GILES

GILLETT
  Elizabeth of Dorking [DW/PA/7/10 f,283; 1623]
GILLMYN *see* GILMAN
GILLPEN *see* GILPIN
GILMAN (GILLMYN,GILMIN,GILMYN,GYLLMYN,GYLMIN,GYLMYN)
  Alice of Reigate, widow [DW/PA/5/1580/46]
  Anthony of Reigate [PRO; PCC Will 1575]
  Anthony of Kingston [PRO; PCC Will 1628]
  Charles of Nutfield, gent, [PRO; PCC 1631]
  Dorothy of Nutfield, widow [DW/PA/7/12 f,134; DW/PA/5/1632/39]
  John of Richmond, esq, [PRO; PCC Will 1558]
  Richard of Blechingley, gent, [HRO; 1571 B80]
  Richard of Reigate [DW/PA/5/1558/125]*
GILPIN (GILLPEN,GILPEN)
  Ann of Croydon, wife of John gent, [LPL; 96/1053; Will 1616]
  John of Croydon, gent, [PRO; PCC Will 1621]
  John of Kingston, tailor, senior [DW/PA/7/11 f,384; DW/PA/5/1626/56]
  Robert of Kingston, tailor [DW/PA/7/11 f,252; DW/PA/5/1625/97]
GINGE (GYNDGE)
  John of Swk St Saviour [DW/PA/7/11 f,227; DW/PA/5/1625/106]
GINNOW (GYNNOWE)
  Thomas of Oxted [DW/PA/7/5 f,192; 1540]
GISBIE
  Thomas of Richmond, groom of the stable to the prince [DW/PA/7/10 f,115; DW/PA/5/1620/55]
GISORS (GYSORS)
  John of Bermondsey, gent, [PRO; PCC Will 1510]
GITTINGS (GITTENS,GITTYNS,GYTTINS)
  Richard of Cheam, servant to Lord Lumley [PRO; PCC Will 1606] <Abs, SAC v,12 pp,99-100>
  Richard of Cheam [PRO; PCC Admon 1606]
  Robert of Godstone [PRO; PCC Admon 1589]
GLADING
  William of Putney [LPL; 98/1 f,54v; Will 1634]
GLASCOCK (GLASCOCKE) [*Clascocke in the abstract of DW/PA/7/7 f,109 is a mistranscription*]
  Agnes of Swk St Saviour, widow [DW/PA/7/7 f,109; DW/PA/5/1596/25] <Abs 197>
  Mary of Camberwell - Peckham [PRO; PCC 1631]
  Robert of Mortlake, gent, [PRO; PCC 1631]
  William of Wandsworth, yeoman [DW/PA/5/1582/3]
  William of Wandsworth, gent, [PRO; PCC 1640]
GLASEN
  John of Stisted, Essex; Swk, rector [LPL; Reg, Abp Arundel ii f,107; Will 1409]
GLASMONDE
  Robert of Lambeth, clerk [PRO; PCC Will 1558]
GLASSINGTON
  John of Woodmansterne, yeoman [DW/PA/7/12 f,194; DW/PA/5/1633/63]
GLEASTE
  James of Swk St Olave; Ormskirk, Lancashire [DW/PA/5/1605/39] <Abs U147>
GLEED
  Stephen of Newington [LPL; 96/1060; Will 1628]

GLEGG

Ralph of Swk St Olave [DW/PA/5/1555/77]

GLENE

Hugh of Bisley [PRO; PCC Will 1445]

GLENTON (GLENTONE)

Martin of Swk St George [DW/PA/5/1582/72]

William of Swk St Thomas Hospital [DW/PA/5/1578/89]

GLOSTER

John of Swk St Saviour [DW/PA/5/1625/98]

GLOVER

Alice of Farnham - Badshot, widow [DW/PA/7/13 f.316; 1643]

Elizabeth of Chobham, widow [DW/PA/7/9 f.309; DW/PA/5/1619/51]

Emma of Tatsfield, widow [DW/PA/5/1570/55]

George of Guildford St Mary, clothier [HRO; 1561 B72-74]

George of Guildford St Mary [GMR; E List 370; (*no date*)]

James of Bermondsey [PRO; PCC Will 1593]

James of Wimbledon, clerk [LPL; 96/1063; Will 1649]

Joan, alias John Parson of Godalming [DW/PA/7/4 f.232; 1537]

John of Battersea, labourer [DW/PA/7/7 f.564; DW/PA/5/1606/40] <Abs 1055>

John of Newington - the Lock Hospital [PRO; PCC Will 1613]

Mark of Godstone, bachelor [PRO; PCC Admon 1625]

Nicholas of Tatsfield, husbandman [DW/PA/5/1570/15]

Richard of Battersea [PRO; PCC Admon 1647]

Richard of Chobham, bachelor, junior [PRO; PCC Admon 1620]

Richard of Croydon [PRO; PCC Will 1459]

Richard of Kingston [DW/PA/7/13 f.79; DW/PA/5/1641/56]

Thomas of Caterham, husbandman [DW/PA/7/9 f.295; 1618]

Thomas of Kingston - Hook [DW/PA/7/11 f.319; DW/PA/5/1626/57]

Thomas of Swk St Margaret [DW/PA/7/5 f.134; 1539]

William of Bermondsey, leatherdresser [DW/PA/7/11 f.527; DW/PA/5/1630/44]

William of Swk St Saviour, waterman [DW/PA/7/9 f.118; DW/PA/5/1615/52]

GLYN

Jenkin of Egham [PRO; PCC Will 1557]

GOADE

Jane of Dorking, widow of Christopher [PRO; PCC Will 1601]

Lewis of Chertsey, yeoman [PRO; PCC Will 1598]

GODDARD (GODARD,GODDERD,GODERD)

Agnes of West Horsley, widow [DW/PA/5/1563/28]

Anthony of West Horsley, yeoman [DW/PA/7/4 f.229; 1537]

Clement of Dorking [DW/PA/7/4 f.181; 1536]

Edward of West Horsley, yeoman [DW/PA/7/13 f.117; DW/PA/5/1639/64]

Elizabeth of Cobham, widow [HRO; 1595 AD21]

Francis of Swk St Olave, tanner [DW/PA/7/11 f.362; DW/PA/5/1626/58]

Isabella of West Horsley [HRO; 1619 B30]

John of Cobham, carpenter [DW/PA/7/12 f.226; DW/PA/5/1634/48]

John of West Horsley, husbandman, senior [DW/PA/5/1578/71]

John of West Horsley, husbandman [DW/PA/7/7 f.357; DW/PA/5/1602/35] <Abs 654>

John of Abinger; West Horsley [DW/PA/7/10 f.187; DW/PA/5/1620/56]

John of Walton on Thames, fisherman [DW/PA/7/12 f.20; DW/PA/5/1631/48]

Lawrence of Send, husbandman [DW/PA/7/12 f.152; DW/PA/5/1633/58]

Richard of Cobham [DW/PA/5/1576/146]

Robert of West Horsley [DW/PA/5/1563/29]

Thomas of West Horsley, yeoman [DW/PA/7/13 f.228; DW/PA/5/1643/40]

GODDARD (GODARD,GODDERD,GODERD) [*continued*]

William of West Horsley, yeoman [DW/PA/7/12 f,418; DW/PA/5/1637/47]

GODDINS

Joan of Dorking, spinster [PRO; PCC 1649]

GODESDEN *see* GADDESDON

GODEWYK (de GODEWYK)

John of Cliffe, Kent, rector; Croydon; Rushworth, Norfolk [LPL; Reg, Abp Arundel i f,156; Will 1397]

GODFREY (GODFRAY,GODFRY)

Henry of Newington [LPL; 98/1 ff,68v-69r; Will 1635]

Mary of Wimbledon, spinster [PRO; PCC Admon 1628]

Robert of Lambeth [PRO; PCC Admon 1648]

Samuel of Croydon [LPL; 98/1 f,37v; Will 1632]

Thomas of Chertsey, carpenter [DW/PA/7/5 f,170; 1540]

Thomas of Swk St George, brewer [DW/PA/7/2 f,36; 1493]

William of Lambeth, gardener [DW/PA/7/11 f,415; DW/PA/5/1627/48]

William of Send [DW/PA/7/1 f,18; 1485] <Abs 59>

GODHELP (GODHELPE)

Edward of Esher, hoopmaker [DW/PA/7/12 f,356; DW/PA/5/1638/51]

James of Cobham, yeoman [DW/PA/5/1575/73]

Juliana of Wonersh, widow [DW/PA/7/7 f,565; DW/PA/5/1606/50] <Abs 1058>

GODLEY (GODLEIGH,GODLYF)

Richard of Crowhurst [PRO; PCC Admon 1561]

Richard of Crowhurst [PRO; PCC Will 1565]

GODMAN (GODEMAN,GOODMYN)

Agnes of Battersea [PRO; PCC Admon 1580]

Ann of Leatherhead, widow of Thomas [PRO; PCC 1640]

George of Mitcham, yeoman [DW/PA/7/11 f,446; DW/PA/5/1628/43]

Margaret of Leatherhead [PRO; PCC Will 1596]

Richard of Great Bookham [DW/PA/7/4 f,129; 1535]

Richard of Leatherhead [DW/PA/5/1543/151]*

Thomas of Leatherhead [PRO; PCC Will 1559]

William, alias William Skynner of Egham, yeoman [DW/PA/7/6 f,272; 1560]

see also GOODMAN

GODSALL

Martha of West Horsley [PRO; PCC 1633]

GODWARD

George of Merrow, husbandman [DW/PA/7/11 f,435; DW/PA/5/1628/44]

GODWIN

Benjamin of Battersea, blacksmith [DW/PA/7/12 f,205; DW/PA/5/1634/46]

see also GOODWIN

GOFF (GOFFE)

Samuel of Guildford, linen draper [DW/PA/7/12 f,257; DW/PA/5/1635/38]

Thomas of East Clandon, parson [DW/PA/7/11 f,544; DW/PA/5/1629/37]

Thomas of Swk St Olave, citizen and fishmonger [HRO; 1590 B18]

Walter of Rotherhithe [PRO; PCC Admon 1591]

William of Carshalton, husbandman [DW/PA/7/11 f,63; DW/PA/5/1623/48]

see also GOUGH

GOFTON

(Dame) Katherine of Lambeth - Stockwell, widow [PRO; PCC 1634]

GOGHE *see* GOUGH

GOLD (GOLDE)

Giles of Dunsfold, yeoman [DW/PA/7/11 f,92; DW/PA/5/1624/51]

John of Alfold [PRO; PCC 1649]

GOLD (GOLDE) [*continued*]
Richard of Swk St Saviour [DW/PA/5/1546/88]
William of Dunsfold [DW/PA/7/9 f.243; DW/PA/5/1617/51]
see also GOULD
GOLDER (GOLLDER)
Thomas of Swk St George, cordwainer [DW/PA/7/11 f.58; DW/PA/5/1623/49]
GOLDING (GOULDING)
Edward of Rotherhithe, mariner [PRO; PCC Admon 1590]
Robert of ...., in the Ship *Globe* sailor [DW/PA/7/10 f.196; DW/PA/5/1621/49]
GOLDOCK (GOULDOCK)
Henry of Egham [DW/PA/5/1545/14]
Robert of Chertsey [HRO; 1620 AD52]
GOLDSMITH (GOLDESMYTHE, GOULDSMITHE, GOULDSMYTH)
Edward of Cheam [PRO; PCC Will 1587]
James of Surrey [PRO; PCC Will 1548]
James of Woldingham, weaver [DW/PA/7/7 ff.428,459; DW/PA/5/1603/56] <Abs 804,865>
Richard of Swk St Saviour, draper [DW/PA/7/7 f.402; DW/PA/5/1603/57] <Abs 745>
GOLDSTONE (GOULDSTONE)
Seth of Richmond, yeoman [DW/PA/7/10 f.6; DW/PA/5/1619/52]
GOLDWELL (GOULDWELL)
Ann of Lambeth - Brockwells, widow [PRO; PCC 1640]
John of Surrey [PRO; PCC Will 1466]
Matthew of Lambeth - Brockwells [PRO; PCC 1637]
Olave of Croydon [PRO; PCC Admon 1605]
Richard of Croydon - Bensham, yeoman [PRO; PCC Will 1615]
Richard of Croydon [PRO; PCC 1640]
William of Lambeth, gent. [PRO; PCC 1633]
GOLDWYE (GOLDWYER, GOWLDWYER)
Daniel of Headley [DW/PA/7/7 f.109; 1597] <Abs 198>
Grace of Kingston [PRO; PCC Admon 1647]
Thomas of Mitcham, yeoman [DW/PA/7/11 f.530; DW/PA/5/1629/38]
GOLIGHTLIE (GOLIGHTLY)
Joan of Farnham, widow [HRO; 1620 B14]
John of Farnham [PRO; PCC Admon 1601]
GOLLDER *see* GOLDER
GOLLOP
John *or* John Gallop of Betchworth, yeoman [DW/PA/7/8 f.57; DW/PA/5/1609/82]
GOMPORT (GUMPORT)
Henry of Swk St Saviour; London, stranger [HRO; 1585 B33]
John of Newington [PRO; PCC Will 1583]
GONAT
Nicholas of Abinger, forgeman [DW/PA/5/1624/52]
GONNE (GONN, GUNE)
Harry of Horley [DW/PA/5/1568/77]
Thomas of Ewell [DW/PA/7/7 f.193; DW/PA/5/1598/34] <Abs 352>
Thomas of Ewell [DW/PA/7/11 f.79; DW/PA/5/1623/50]
Thomas of Swk St Olave, mason [DW/PA/7/2 f.62; 1500]
William of Coulsdon, husbandman [DW/PA/7/10 f.269; DW/PA/5/1622/33]
GONNELL
William of Lambeth - Kennington, clerk [PRO; PCC Will 1560]

GONNER *see* GUNNER
GONNYS *see* JONES
GOOD (GOODE)
Elizabeth of Malden, widow [PRO; PCC 1649]
Joan of Malden, widow of James, doctor of physic [PRO; PCC Will 1589]
John of Kingston, baker [DW/PA/7/2 f.117; 1517]
John of Kingston, gent. [PRO; PCC Will 1586]
John of Malden, esq. [PRO; PCC Will 1627]
Robert of Coulsdon [PRO; PCC Will 1558]
GOODALE
Edward of Kingston [DW/PA/7/10 f.264; DW/PA/5/1622/34]
John of Swk St Olave [HRO; Reg. Way 1 pp.38-39; 1455]
Timothy of Kingston, tailor [DW/PA/7/13 f.116; DW/PA/5/1640/58]
GOODCHILD (GOODCHILDE)
Hugh of Shere [DW/PA/7/8 f.78; DW/PA/5/1609/85]
John of Kingston [PRO; PCC Admon 1593]
Margery of Chessington, widow [DW/PA/5/1571/82]
Pleasant of Kingston, widow [PRO; PCC Will 1593]
Richard of Kingston [PRO; PCC Admon 1560]
Thomas of Chessington; Barnes, husbandman [DW/PA/7/6 f.70; DW/PA/5/1559/70]
GOODDIER *see* GOODIER
GOODE *see* GOOD
GOODENOUGH *see* GOODINOUGH
GOODFELLOWE
Thomas of Newington, yeoman [PRO; PCC Will 1625]
GOODGROOM (GOODGROME,GOODGROOME)
Frances, alias Frances Langbridge of Richmond [PRO; PCC Admon 1647]
Henry of Richmond [PRO; PCC Admon 1648]
John of Chertsey [PRO; PCC Admon 1591]
John of Richmond, ferryman [DW/PA/7/8 f.160; DW/PA/5/1611/47]
Margaret of Richmond, widow [DW/PA/7/8 f.265; DW/PA/5/1611/48]
Richard of Richmond [PRO; PCC Admon 1625]
GOODIER (GOODDIER,GOODYERE,GOOGIER)
Henry of Bermondsey, esq. [PRO; PCC Will 1556]
John of Alfold [PRO; PCC Will 1626]
Mary of Farnham, widow [DW/PA/7/12 f.235; DW/PA/5/1634/50]
GOODINOUGH
Robert of Putney, servant [LPL; 96/1085; 98/1 f.66v; Will 1635]
GOODLIFE *see* GODLYF
GOODMAN
Beatrice of Camberwell [PRO; PCC Admon 1619]
Gabriel of Surrey and several other counties, Doctor of Divinity [PRO; PCC Will 1601]
Isabel of Walton on Thames, widow [DW/PA/5/1575/48]
Joan of Bermondsey, widow [DW/PA/7/12 f.500; DW/PA/5/1638/58]
Peter of Swk St Olave [DW/PA/7/11 f.457; DW/PA/5/1628/45]
see also GODMAN
GOODRIDGE (GOODRICHE,GOODRYD)
John of Mortlake [PRO; PCC Will 1492]
Juliana of Swk St Saviour [DW/PA/7/11 f.506; DW/PA/5/1629/39]
Maurice of Lambeth [DW/PA/7/4 f.220; 1537]
William of Swk St Saviour, silk weaver [DW/PA/7/9 f.160; DW/PA/5/1616/58]

GOODWALL
William of Godalming [DW/PA/7/10 f.218; DW/PA/5/1621/47]
GOODWIN (GOODWINE,GOODWYN,GOODWYNE,GYDWYN)
Alice of Guildford St Nicolas, widow [LBLAD; Surrey Deeds 1/1066; 1646]
Benn of Dorking [PRO; PCC Admon 1648]
Edward of Dorking, senior [DW/PA/7/7 f.388; DW/PA/5/1602/37] <Abs 719>
Edward of Horne, gent. [PRO; PCC Will 1627]
Henry, alias Henry Sawnders of ... [DW/PA/7/7 f.389; DW/PA/5/1603/58] <Abs 721>
Henry, alias Henry Saunders of Egham [DW/PA/7/12 f.489; DW/PA/5/1638/56]
Henry of Horne [PRO; PCC 1638]
John, alias John Sander of Egham - Hythe [DW/PA/7/4 f.186; 1536]
John, alias John Sander of Egham - Hythe, yeoman [DW/PA/5/1579/39]*
John of Guildford St Nicolas [DW/PA/7/10 f.227; DW/PA/5/1621/48]
John of Guildford St Nicolas, maltster [DW/PA/7/11 f.581; DW/PA/5/1630/45]
John of Horne, gent. [PRO; PCC Will 1619]
John of Westminster, Middlesex; Hampshire; Swk - King's Bench Prison, prisoner [DW/PA/5/1598/33] <Abs U16>
John of Swk St Olave, joiner [DW/PA/7/11 f.71; 1623]
John of Swk St Saviour, tapster [DW/PA/7/8 f.156; DW/PA/5/1611/49]
Magdalen of Cranleigh, spinster [DW/PA/7/7 f.183; 1598] <Abs 334>
Mary of Newington, widow [PRO; PCC Will 1608] <Abs. SAC v.13 p.186>
Robert, alias Robert Saunders of Egham - Hythe [PRO; PCC 1647]
Stephen of Tooting Graveney [DW/PA/7/2 f.29; 1499]
Walter of Bermondsey [PRO; PCC Will 1627]
William of Bermondsey [PRO; PCC Will 1554]
see also GODWIN
GOODYER *see* GOODIER
GOOFE
Thomas of Swk St Margaret [? HRO; 1529]
GOOLE
John of Swk St Saviour, servingman [DW/PA/5/1558/117]*
GOOLLY
John(?) of Cobham [*in* DW/PA/5/1544/7]
see also GULLYE
GOONE
William of Beddington [DW/PA/5/1563/85]
GOORD'N *see* JORDAN
GOORINGE *see* GORING
GOOSE
Ann of Ewell, widow [DW/PA/7/13 f.196; DW/PA/5/1641/64]
Robert of Walton on the Hill, husbandman [DW/PA/7/13 f.397; DW/PA/5/1645/21]
GOOTHERUM *see* GUDRUM
GORDON (du GORDON)
Roger of Swk St Olave - Gleave Alley [DW/PA/7/7 f.632; DW/PA/5/1608/38] <Abs 1181>
GORE
Margery of Swk St George [DW/PA/5/1592/47]
GORGAINE
Joan of Deptford, Kent; Swk St Saviour, widow [DW/PA/7/11 f.11; DW/PA/5/1622/35]

GORING (GOORINGE,GORINGE,GORYNG,GORYNGE)
Ann of Worplesdon, widow [*in* DW/PA/5/1555/67]
Elizabeth of Dorking, widow [DW/PA/7/13 f.197; DW/PA/5/1641/66]
Elizabeth of Frimley [DW/PA/5/1550/42]
(Sir) Henry of Surrey; Sussex, knight [PRO; PCC Will 1595]
Henry of Chertsey, labourer [DW/PA/7/7 f.177; DW/PA/5/1597/46] <Abs 327>
Hugh of Ash; Farnham - Wrecclesham [DW/PA/7/9 f.264; 1618]
John of Horsell, senior [HRO; 1629 B16]
John of Thorpe, husbandman [DW/PA/5/1562/52]
John of Thorpe, husbandman [DW/PA/7/13 f.93; DW/PA/5/1640/62]
John of Worplesdon, yeoman [HRO; 1591 B25]
Nicholas of Morden, labourer [DW/PA/5/1558/118]
Ralph of Thorpe [DW/PA/7/13 f.250; DW/PA/5/1641/55]
Robert of Bisley [DW/PA/5/1570/98]
Robert of Horsell, husbandman [DW/PA/7/6 f.123; DW/PA/5/1559/210]
Thomas of Bisley [DW/PA/7/6 f.3; DW/PA/5/1559/3]
Thomas of Thorpe [DW/PA/7/4 f.96; 1534]
Thomas of Thorpe [DW/PA/5/1556/7]
(Sir) William of Carshalton, knight [PRO; PCC Will 1555]
William of Godalming, blacksmith [DW/PA/7/13 f.155; DW/PA/5/1641/59]
William of Thorpe, yeoman, senior [HRO; 1615 B18]
William of Thorpe - Thorpe Lea, yeoman [DW/PA/7/13 f.489; DW/PA/5/1648/8]

GORLINGE
Godfrey of Swk St Saviour, pinmaker [DW/PA/7/7 f.463; DW/PA/5/1603/60] <Abs 877>

GORNE
Abraham *or* Abraham Gurney of Bermondsey [PRO; PCC Will 1625]

GORWAY (GOROWAYE)
Joan of Chertsey [DW/PA/7/6 f.194; 1560]
John of Chertsey [DW/PA/7/6 f.140; DW/PA/5/1559/143]

GOSBY
William of Kingston, smith [DW/PA/7/4 f.27; 1533]

GOSDEN
Henry of Wonersh [DW/PA/7/7 f.446; DW/PA/5/1603/61] <Abs 845>
John of Esher [PRO; PCC Admon 1649]
John of Wonersh, yeoman [HRO; 1575 B28]
John of Wonersh - Hyde, yeoman [DW/PA/7/9 f.12; DW/PA/5/1615/53]
Joseph of Shalford, husbandman [DW/PA/7/13 f.67; DW/PA/5/1639/63]
Richard of Elstead, yeoman [DW/PA/7/7 f.448; DW/PA/5/1603/62] <Abs 848>
Richard of Esher [DW/PA/7/10 f.262; DW/PA/5/1622/36]

GOSLING
Thomas of Rotherhithe, senior [PRO; PCC 1647]

GOSSE
David of Swk St Olave, mariner [DW/PA/7/9 f.186; DW/PA/5/1616/59]

GOSSEDGE
Robert of Swk St George, victualler [DW/PA/5/1571/39]

GOSTWICKE
Ann, alias Ann Hooke of Bramley [PRO; PCC Admon 1637]

GOTHERSON
Nicholas of Swk St George, farrier [DW/PA/7/12 f.322; DW/PA/5/1636/42]

GOTT
Bridget of Blechingley, widow of Thomas of Grays Inn, Middlesex [PRO; PCC 1648]

GOTT [*continued*]

Henry of Swk St George, victualler [DW/PA/7/11 f,325; DW/PA/5/1625/99]
Robert of Lambeth - Lambeth Marsh, gent, [PRO; PCC 1638]

GOUGH (GOGHE,GOUGHE,GOWGH,GOWGHE)

Agnes of West Horsley, widow [DW/PA/5/1591/47]
Christopher of West Horsley, gent, [PRO; PCC Will 1587]
Christopher of Woking, husbandman [DW/PA/7/13 f,378; 1644]
Eleanor of Swk St Saviour, wife of John of London, tailor, late wife of John Butler, tailor) [DW/PA/7/7 f,547; DW/PA/5/1606/49] <Abs 1027>
Geoffrey of Swk St Mary Overy, yeoman of the guard [DW/PA/7/2 f,148; 1520] <Abs SAC v,1 pp,184-185>
Joan of Swk St Margaret, widow [DW/PA/7/3 f,123; 1530]
John of Putney gentleman [PRO; PCC 1630] <Scroope 1018>
Lawrence of East Clandon, husbandman [DW/PA/5/1557/28]
Robert of Windlesham, husbandman [DW/PA/5/1570/56]
William of Lambeth [PRO; PCC Admon 1619]
see also GOFF

GOULD

Ann of Long Ditton, widow [DW/PA/7/11 f,483; DW/PA/5/1628/46]
William of Lambeth - Water Lambeth [PRO; PCC Will 1626]
William of Swk St Saviour [DW/PA/7/11 f,219; DW/PA/5/1625/100]
see also GOLD

GOULDING,GOULDOCK *see* GOLDING,GOLDOCKE

GOULDSMITHE,GOULDSMYTH *see* GOLDSMITH

GOULDSTONE *see* GOLDSTONE

GOULDWELL *see* GOLDWELL

GOWLDWYER *see* GOLDWYRE

GOUNTER *see* GUNTER

GOVAERT

Giles of ..., Antwerp, Belgium, harness maker (and Neelken Coopah, his wife) [DW/PA/5/1558/119]*

GOWEN,GOWENE *see* GAWEN

GOWER

John of Swk St Mary Overy, poet, esq, [LPL; Reg,Abp Arundel i f,256; Will 1408] <Abs SAC v,1 pp,193-194, *see also* Gentleman's Magazine, 1835>
Lawrence of Lambeth - Kennington [PRO; PCC Will 1543]
Thomas of Clapham, esq, [PRO; PCC Will 1458]

GOWLDWYER *see* GOLDWYRE

GOWYTH *see* GARTH

GRACE

James of Kingston [PRO; PCC Admon 1637]
Matthew of Swk, citizen and joiner, , senior [DW/PA/7/12 f,436; DW/PA/5/1637/49]
Thomas of Kingston, blacksmith [HRO; 1600 B21]
William of Swk St George, clothworker [DW/PA/7/13 f,210; DW/PA/5/1642/35]
see also FARDYNG de GRACE

GRACEBROKE

Thomas of Swk St Saviour [HRO; Reg, CCB 20 p,10; 1563]

GRACIOUTT

Agnes of Ash, widow [DW/PA/5/1582/43]

GRAFFHAM (GRAFFAM,GRASSAM,GROFFHAM)

John of Albury [? HRO; 1567]
John of Albury, yeoman, senior [DW/PA/7/13 f,167; DW/PA/5/1641/60]

GRAFFHAM (GRAFFAM,GRASSAM,GROFFHAM) [*continued*]
  John of Dorking [PRO; PCC Admon 1604]
  Juliana of Albury, widow [DW/PA/5/1575/53]
  Robert of Albury, yeoman [DW/PA/5/1588/11]
  Thomas of Albury [DW/PA/5/1558/120]*
  Thomas of Albury [DW/PA/7/6 f.264; 1560]
  Walter of Wonersh [DW/PA/7/3 f.138; 1530]
GRAIE *see* GRAY
GRAINE
  Clement of Bermondsey, citizen and leatherseller [DW/PA/7/10 f.44; 1618]
GRAME
  Thomas of Blechingley [DW/PA/5/1575/62]
GRANAT *see* GRAVETT
GRANDISON
  Jane St.John, viscountess of Battersea [DW/PA/7/11 f.601;
    DW/PA/5/1630/46]
  Oliver *and* Jane, viscount and viscountess, of Battersea [PRO; PCC 1631]
GRANGE
  Thomas, alias Thomas Strange of Stoke Dabernon, yeoman [DW/PA/7/9
    f.204; DW/PA/5/1616/131]
GRANGER
  John of Swk St George, yeoman [DW/PA/5/1568/74]
  Robert of Swk St Saviour - Bankside, yeoman [DW/PA/5/1575/45]
  Thomas of Bermondsey, bachelor [PRO; PCC Admon 1636]
GRANT (GRAUNT,GRAUNTE)
  Adrian of Windlesham - Bagshot [*in* DW/PA/5/1557/75]
  Christopher of Windlesham, smith [DW/PA/5/1582/44]
  John of Bermondsey [PRO; PCC Will 1495]
  John of Swk St Olave, feltmaker [HRO; 1587 B38] [*and*] [DW/PA/5/1587/35]
GRAPE
  Richard of Long Ditton [CCAL; 1500 f.59v]
GRASBOROUGHE
  John of Croydon [PRO; PCC Will 1560]
GRASSAM *see* GRAFFHAM
GRASTYE
  Alice of Ewell, wife of Richard, yeoman [DW/PA/7/7 f.9;
    DW/PA/5/1595/42] <Abs 21>
GRATEHURST *see* GREETHURST
GRAUNT *see* GRANT
GRAVAT *see* GRAVETT
GRAVE (GRAVES)
  John of Mitcham [DW/PA/5/1578/54]
  Sarah, alias Sarah Greaves of Guildford, widow [PRO; PCC 1640]
  Thomas of Bermondsey [PRO; PCC Admon 1624 *and* Will 1625]
GRAVETT (GRAVAT,GRAVELL,GRAVET,GRAVETTE,GRAVEYTT,GREVET,GREVETT,GRIVELL,
    GRYUELL)
  Anthony of Sutton [PRO; PCC Will 1568] <Abs, SAC v.52 pp.48-49>
  Edward of Woking [DW/PA/5/1555/79]
  Henry of Chertsey, yeoman [DW/PA/5/1552/28]
  Henry of Kingston, gent. [PRO; PCC Will 1575]
  John of Chertsey, widower, senior [DW/PA/7/4 f.140; 1536]
  John of Chertsey, gent. [DW/PA/5/1561/11]
  Nicholas of Woking [DW/PA/7/3 f.202; 1532]
  Richard of Thursley, husbandman [DW/PA/7/11 f.167; DW/PA/5/1625/104]

GRAVETT (GRAVAT,GRAVELL,GRAVET,GRAVETTE,GRAVEYTT,GREVET,GREVETT,GRIVELL, GRYUELL) [*continued*]
  Richard of Woking, yeoman [DW/PA/7/6 f,106; DW/PA/5/1559/71]
  Thomas of Chertsey [PRO; PCC Will 1529]
  William of Chertsey - Addlestone, yeoman [DW/PA/5/1561/6]
  William of Chiddingfold, yeoman [PRO; PCC Will 1627]
GRAY (GRAIE,GRAYE,GREY)
  Agnes Bulkeley, formerly Agnes Grey of Lambeth [PRO; PCC Will 1523]
  Alexander of Rotherhithe, waterman [DW/PA/7/7 f,612; DW/PA/5/1606/46] <Abs 1144>
  Alexander of Swk St Olave, citizen and innholder [DW/PA/7/13 f,391; DW/PA/5/1645/20]
  (Sir) Andrew of Rotherhithe, knight [PRO; PCC Admon 1633]
  Christopher of Wandsworth [PRO; PCC Will 1577]
  George of Stoke Dabernon [DW/PA/7/3 f,195; 1531]
  Henry of Chertsey, yeoman [DW/PA/7/7 f,109; DW/PA/5/1596/26] <Abs 196>
  Henry of Swk St Saviour; Bermondsey, shopkeeper; lorimer [HRO; 1587 B39]
  Luke of Bentley, Hampshire [DW/PA/7/3 f,199; 1531] [*see also* Luke Gary]
  Margaret of Bermondsey, gentlewoman [PRO; PCC Will 1618]
  Rice of Swk St Olave [DW/PA/7/11 f,230; DW/PA/5/1625/101]
  Thomas of Streatham [PRO; PCC 1633]
  William of Rotherhithe [DW/PA/7/9 f,333; DW/PA/5/1620/57]
  William of Rotherhithe, seaman [DW/PA/7/12 f,321; DW/PA/5/1636/41]
GRAYNE *see* GRAINE
GRAYSHOTT
  John of Frensham, husbandman [DW/PA/7/6 f,248; 1560]
GREAT (GREET,GRETE)
  Juliana of Farnham [PRO; PCC Will 1510]
  Richard of Farnham [DW/PA/7/1 f,24; 1485] <Abs 79>
  Thomas of Frensham [PRO; PCC Will 1501]
  William of Farnham [PRO; PCC Will 1510]
GREAVES
  Sarah, alias Sarah Graves of Guildford, widow [PRO; PCC 1640]
GREDDIE
  Phillip of Bermondsey [PRO; PCC Admon 1605]
GREEN (atte GRENE,GREENE,GREN,GRENE)
  Ann, alias Ann Richardson of Barnes, widow [LPL; 98/1 f,81r; Will 1637]
  Audrey of Betchworth [DW/PA/7/13 f,43; DW/PA/5/1639/62]
  Eleanor of Kingston; Wargrave, Berkshire [DW/PA/5/1593/1]
  Elizabeth of Croydon, widow [LPL; 96/1107; Will 1617]
  Frances of Swk St Olave, widow [DW/PA/7/12 f,523; DW/PA/5/1636/45]
  Godfrey of Clapham, parson [DW/PA/7/9 f,126; DW/PA/5/1615/54]
  Henry of Newington [LPL; 98/1 f,1v; Will 1629] [*and*] [PRO; PCC Admon 1630]
  Joan of Farnham, widow of John [PRO; PCC Will 1585]
  Joan of Swk St Mary Overy [DW/PA/7/3 f,194; 1531]
  Joan of Farnham, widow of John of Basingstoke, Hampshire [HRO; 1585 B35]
  John of Barnes [LPL; 98/1 f,36r; Will 1632]
  John of Coulsdon [DW/PA/5/1557/21]
  John of Thames Ditton - Weston [DW/PA/7/11 f,494; DW/PA/5/1628/47]
  John of Farnham [PRO; PCC Admon 1589]
  John of Kingston, husbandman [DW/PA/5/1581/42]
  John of Oxted, husbandman [DW/PA/7/9 f,32; DW/PA/5/1614/48]

GREEN (atte GRENE, GREENE, GREN, GRENE) [*continued*]
John of Swk St Olave, priest and chaplain [DW/PA/5/1546/44]
John of Swk St Olave, citizen and draper [DW/PA/7/11 f.241; DW/PA/5/1625/102]
John of Swk St Olave, victualler [DW/PA/7/11 f.559; DW/PA/5/1630/47]
John of Swk St Olave, lighterman [DW/PA/7/13 f.191; DW/PA/5/1641/63]
John of Castle Combe, Wiltshire, rector; Swk St Saviour; Bromton St Peter [*? county*]; Lugwardine, Herefordshire; Dursley, Gloucestershire [LPL; Reg. Abp Stafford f.130; Will 1445]
John of Streatham [LPL; Reg. Abp Arundel ii f.163; Will 1412]
Luke of Swk St Olave, citizen and haberdasher [DW/PA/7/13 f.33; DW/PA/5/1640/57]
Mary of Banstead, widow [PRO; PCC 1640]
Michael of Egham, gent. [PRO; PCC Will 1576]
Nicholas of Camberwell [PRO; PCC Will 1557]
Nicholas of Swk St Saviour, victualler [DW/PA/7/9 f.120; DW/PA/5/1615/55]
Peter of West Molesey, husbandman [DW/PA/5/1562/76]
Phillip of Swk St Olave, yeoman [DW/PA/7/11 f.268; DW/PA/5/1625/103]
Richard of Oxted, husbandman [DW/PA/7/12 f.304; DW/PA/5/1635/40]
Robert of Thames Ditton - Claygate, husbandman [*in* DW/PA/5/1574/26]
Robert of Kingston [DW/PA/5/1545/2]
Rose of Caterham, widow [DW/PA/7/12 f.177; DW/PA/5/1633/60]
Thomas of Bermondsey [PRO; PCC 1640]
Thomas of Bermondsey - West Lane, waterman [DW/PA/7/13 f.197; DW/PA/5/1641/65]
Thomas of Coulsdon; Burstow; Horley, senior [DW/PA/7/8 f.231; DW/PA/5/1612/66]
Thomas of Coulsdon, yeoman [DW/PA/7/13 f.146; DW/PA/5/1641/57]
Thomas of Guildford St Mary [DW/PA/7/2 f.116; 1517]
Thomas of Kingston, faggotbinder [DW/PA/5/1570/9]
Thomas of Putney - Roehampton [PRO; PCC Admon 1640]
Thomas of Reigate, carpenter [DW/PA/7/6 f.118; DW/PA/5/1559/110]
Thomas of Warlingham; Coulsdon, husbandman [DW/PA/7/7 f.512; DW/PA/5/1605/41] <Abs 961>
Thomas of Wimbledon, bachelor of law [PRO; PCC Will 1508]
Walter of Chobham, labourer *or* yeoman [HRO; 1590 B19]
William of Addington [PRO; PCC Admon 1625]
William of Beddington [PRO; PCC Will 1425]
William of Bermondsey [HRO; Reg. Way 1 p.26; 1453]
William of Thames Ditton - Weston [DW/PA/5/1586/18]
William of Egham [PRO; PCC Admon 1592]
William of Ewell [PRO; PCC Admon 1583]
William of Farnham, clothier [PRO; PCC Will 1604] <Abs. SAC v.11 p.132>
William of Frensham [DW/PA/7/9 f.159; DW/PA/5/1616/60]
William of Frensham - Churt, weaver [HRO; 1629 B17]
William of Frensham - Churt, yeoman [DW/PA/7/13 f.435; DW/PA/5/1646/22]
William of Swk St Olave [DW/PA/5/1575/37]

GREENACRE (GRENACRE)
Idonya Hert, formerly Idonya Grenacre of Ripley [PRO; PCC Will 1402]

GREENE *see* GREEN

GREENEFIELD *see* GREENFIELD

GREENEGOE *see* GREENGO

GREENER
John of Godalming, weaver [DW/PA/7/7 f.566; DW/PA/5/1606/48] <Abs 1059>

GREENETRIE *see* GREENTREE
GREENEUPP *see* GREENUP
GREENEWAY *see* GREENWAY
GREENEWOOD *see* GREENWOOD
GREENFIELD (GREENEFIELD,GREENFEILD,GRENEFEILD,GRENEFELDE)
Charity of Bermondsey, servant to Mr Wayte [DW/PA/5/1603/67] <Abs U71>
Joan, alias Joan Tidy of Capel, widow [PRO; PCC Admon 1635]
Joan of Ockley, widow of Thomas [PRO; PCC Will 1625]
John of Leigh [PRO; PCC 1631]
Margaret of Witley, wife of Toby [DW/PA/7/11 f,437; DW/PA/5/1628/48]
Thomas of Capel [PRO; PCC 1642]
Thomas of Witley - Milford, husbandman [HRO; 1608 B34]
William of Capel, yeoman [PRO; PCC Will 1620] <Soame 1076>
GREENGO (GREENEGOE)
Phillip of Dunsfold, senior [DW/PA/7/11 f,383; DW/PA/5/1626/59]
GREENHILL
William of Putney, husbandman [LPL; 96/1112; Will 1623]
GREENHOW
Judith of Kingston, widow [DW/PA/7/13 f,426; DW/PA/5/1646/23]
Thomas of Kingston [DW/PA/7/13 f,265; DW/PA/5/1643/43]
GREENING (GRENNYNG,GRENYNG,GRENYNGE)
John of Farnham [DW/PA/7/3 f,206; 1532]
John of Reigate [DW/PA/7/2 f,40; 1494]
Robert of Farnham, yeoman [DW/PA/7/4 f,134; 1536]
Robert of Farnham [DW/PA/7/5 f,156; 1540]
William of Farnham [PRO; PCC Will 1558]
GREENRIDGE (GRENERIGGE,GRENRIG)
John of Camberwell [PRO; PCC Will 1489]
Margery of Camberwell - Peckham [PRO; PCC Will 1491]
GREENSMITH (GRENESMYTH)
William of Surrey [PRO; PCC Will 1571]
GREENSTEAD *see* GRINSTEAD
GREENTREE (GREENETRIE,GRENETREE,GRENETRYE,GRENTRE)
John of Walton on Thames - Apps, labouring man [DW/PA/7/7 f,165; DW/PA/5/1597/47] <Abs 305>
Katherine of Walton on Thames, widow [DW/PA/5/1558/121]*
Richard of Walton on Thames [DW/PA/7/4 f,25; 1532]
Robert of Walton on Thames [PRO; PCC Will 1552]
Robert of Walton on Thames, apprentice to a carpenter [GL; Archdeaconry Court of London Will 1553]
Thomas of Walton on Thames - Hersham [DW/PA/5/1558/122]*
William of Walton on Thames - Hersham, yeoman [DW/PA/7/7 f,81; 1596] <Abs 147>
GREENUP (GREENEUPP)
Alice of Swk St Olave, widow [DW/PA/7/13 f,468; DW/PA/5/1648/7]
Thomas of Swk St Olave, victualler [DW/PA/7/13 f,87; DW/PA/5/1640/61]
GREENWAY (GREENEWAY,GRENEWAY)
Margaret of Rotherhithe, widow [PRO; PCC 1631]
Thomas of Bermondsey [DW/PA/7/2 f,71; 1500]
Thomas of Rotherhithe, citizen and white baker [PRO; PCC 1630] <Scroope 1010>
GREENWELL
Ann of Morden, junior [DW/PA/7/12 f,184; DW/PA/5/1633/62]
Robert of Morden [PRO; PCC 1638]

GREENWICH (GRENEWYCH,GRENEWYCHE)
John of Kingston [DW/PA/7/2 f.136; 1519]
John of Kingston [DW/PA/7/5 f.153; 1540]
GREENWOOD (GREENEWOOD,GRENEWODE)
Richard of Swk St Olave, cooper aboard the Ship *Centaur* [DW/PA/7/7 f.350; DW/PA/5/1601/41] <Abs 642>
Thomas of Wandsworth; Sevenoaks, Kent [DW/PA/5/1543/10]*
GREET *see* GREAT
GREETHURST (GRATEHURST,GRETEHURST,GRETERSTE,GRETHURST,GRETHYRST,GRITTESTE)
Henry of Cranleigh [DW/PA/5/1582/2]
Phillip of Albury, yeoman [DW/PA/7/13 f.371; 1644]
Thomas of Shere; Wonersh, husbandman [DW/PA/7/7 f.391; DW/PA/5/1603/66] <Abs 727>
Thomas of Wonersh [DW/PA/5/1587/18]
Thomas of Wonersh - Hull, yeoman [DW/PA/7/9 f.342; DW/PA/5/1620/58]
Walter of Wonersh [DW/PA/7/3 f.140; 1530]
William of Guildford St Nicolas - Loseley, cook [DW/PA/7/13 f.11; DW/PA/5/1639/59]
GREGORY (GREGORIE,GRIGORIE)
Agnes of Dorking [PRO; PCC Admon 1647]
Anthony of Send; Farnham, husbandman [DW/PA/7/8 f.78; DW/PA/5/1609/86]
Elizabeth of Guildford St Nicolas, spinster [DW/PA/7/13 f.374; 1644]
George of Send, yeoman [DW/PA/7/12 f.365; DW/PA/5/1637/45]
Henry of Chertsey [DW/PA/7/9 f.289; 1618]
Joan of Bentley, Hampshire, widow [DW/PA/7/7 f.28; DW/PA/5/1595/43] <Abs 58>
John of Send, husbandman [DW/PA/7/13 f.253; DW/PA/5/1643/39]
Matilda of Esher, widow [HRO; Reg. Fox 3 p.58; 1511]
Nicholas of Battersea, yeoman [PRO; PCC Will 1615]
Nicholas of Wimbledon [PRO; PCC 1647]
Oliver of Battersea, yeoman [PRO; PCC Will 1629]
Paul of Swk St Olave [DW/PA/7/7 f.319; DW/PA/5/1600/17] <Abs 569>
Phillipa of Kew, widow [PRO; PCC Will 1586]
Thomas of Lambeth - Water Lambeth [DW/PA/7/13 f.76; DW/PA/5/1640/60]
GREIN
John of ... *Dutch*] [DW/PA/7/7 f.406; DW/PA/5/1603/63] <Abs 754>
GREN,GRENACRE *see* GREEN,GREENACRE
GRENE *see* GREEN
GRENEFEILD,GRENEFELDE *see* GREENFIELD
GRENERIGGE *see* GREENRIDGE
GRENESMYTH *see* GREENSMITH
GRENESTEADE *see* GRINSTEAD
GRENETREE,GRENETRYE *see* GREENTREE
GRENEWAY *see* GREENWAY
GRENEWODE *see* GREENWOOD
GRENEWYCH,GRENEWYCHE *see* GREENWICH
GRENNYNG *see* GREENING
GRENRIG *see* GREENRIDGE
GRENSTED *see* GRINSTEAD
GRENT
Roger of Lambeth; Henbury, Gloucestershire, gent. [PRO; PCC 1630] <Scroope 841>
see also GRINT
GRENTRE *see* GREENTREE

GRENYNG,GRENYNGE *see* GREENING

GRESHAM (GRESSAM,GRESSHAM)

Beatrice of Titsey, widow [PRO; PCC Will 1604] <Abs, SAC v,11 p,292 *and* v,33 p,11>

Edmund of Surrey and several counties, esq, [PRO; PCC Will 1586]

(Sir) Edward of Limpsfield, knight [PRO; PCC Admon 1647]

James son of William of Titsey [PRO; PCC Admon 1564 *and* 1576]

(Sir) John of Surrey, knight [PRO; PCC Will 1556]

(Sir) John of Titsey, knight [PRO; PCC Admon 1646]

Thomas of Newington, citizen and hatter [GL; Commissary Court of London Will 1473]

(Sir) Thomas of Titsey; Limpsfield; Tandridge; Woldingham; Bishopsgate, London knight [PRO; PCC 1630] <Scroope 775>

(Sir) William of Croydon, knight [PRO; PCC Admon 1624]

William of Titsey, esq, [PRO; PCC Will 1579] <Abs SAC v,33 pp,10-11>

GRETE *see* GREAT

GRETEHURST,GRETERSTE,GRETHURST,GRETHYRST *see* GREETHURST

GREVET,GREVETT *see* GRAVETT

GREY *see* GRAY

GREYF

John of Swk St George, blacksmith [DW/PA/7/1 f,30; 1486] <Abs 100>

GRIFFIN (GRIFFEN,GRIFFENG,GRIFFYN,GRYFFYN)

David of Swk St Margaret [DW/PA/7/4 f,162; 1536]

David of Swk St Saviour, waterman [DW/PA/5/1579/37]*

Edward of Abinger, clerk [DW/PA/7/12 f,384; DW/PA/5/1637/46]

Elizabeth of Swk St George, widow [DW/PA/7/8 f,222; DW/PA/5/1612/67]

George of Fetcham, yeoman [DW/PA/5/1603/65] <Abs U70>

George of Fetcham, yeoman [DW/PA/7/12 f,182; DW/PA/5/1633/61]

Henry of Walton on Thames, yeoman of the guard [DW/PA/7/7 f,313; 1600] <Abs 556>

Henry of Swk St Olave, dyer [DW/PA/7/10 f,100; DW/PA/5/1621/50]

Joan of Great Bookham; Fetcham, widow [DW/PA/7/7 f,62; DW/PA/5/1596/27] <Abs 117>

John of ,,, [LPL; 96/4447; Will 1624]

John of Bermondsey, mariner [DW/PA/7/10 f,191; DW/PA/5/1621/51]

John of Dorking [PRO; PCC Will 1554]

John of Fetcham [HRO; 1593 B30]

John of Rotherhithe, shipwright [DW/PA/7/11 f,414; DW/PA/5/1627/49]

Maurice of Swk St Saviour, victualler [DW/PA/7/11 f,467; DW/PA/5/1628/49]

Rees of Chobham [PRO; PCC Admon 1613]

Richard, alias Richard Conaway of Guildford, brazier [DW/PA/7/12 f,213; DW/PA/5/1633/34]

Richard of Swk St Saviour, waterman [DW/PA/7/7 f,479; DW/PA/5/1604/24] <Abs 903>

GRIFFITHS (GRIFFITH,GRYFFITH)

John of Kingston [PRO; PCC Will 1532]

John of Walton on Thames - Oatlands [PRO; PCC Admon 1647]

GRIGG (GRYGGE)

John, alias John Williams of Surrey, gent, [PRO; PCC Will 1561]

John of Blechingley [DW/PA/7/7 ff,458,467; DW/PA/5/1603/64] <Abs 863>

William of Compton, rector [HRO; Reg, Way 1 p,73; 1462]

GRIGORIE *see* GREGORY

GRIMES (GRYME, GRYMES)
Robert of Swk St Olave, rector [LPL; Reg, Abp Morton f,79v; Admon 1492]
Thomas of Bermondsey (died overseas) [PRO; PCC Admon 1649]
William of Swk St Olave, turner [DW/PA/7/13 f,254; DW/PA/5/1643/41]
GRIMSDITCH (GRYMSDITCHE)
Thomas of Haslemere [PRO; PCC Admon 1641]
William of Beddington, yeoman [DW/PA/7/11 f,425; DW/PA/5/1627/51]
GRIMSTONE (GRYMSTON)
Isabel of Bermondsey [PRO; PCC Will 1430]
GRINDALL
Edmund, archbishop of Canterbury, of Newington [PRO; PCC Will 1583]
GRINSTEAD (GRENESTEADE, GRENSTED, GRINSTED, GRYNSTEDE)
George of Swk St Margaret [DW/PA/7/4 f,214; 1537]
James of Reigate, labourer [DW/PA/5/1574/4]
Thomas of Reigate [HRO; Reg, CCB 20 p,2; 1563]
Thomas of Reigate, husbandman [DW/PA/5/1563/61 *and* DW/PA/5/1563/64]
GRINT
Alice of Kingston, wife of Edward [PRO; PCC Admon 1604]
see also GRENT
GRISBROOKE
Elizabeth, alias Elizabeth Bryan of Blechingley [PRO; PCC Admon 1643]
GRIST (GRYST)
Robert of East Clandon, yeoman [DW/PA/7/9 f,235; DW/PA/5/1617/52]
GRITTESTE *see* GREETHURST
GROCOCKE
Thomas of Newington [LPL; 98/1 f,2r; Will 1629]
GROFFHAM *see* GRAFFHAM
GROMEBRIDGE *see* GROOMBRIDGE
GROOM (GROOME)
Richard of Egham, yeoman [PRO; PCC Will 1627]
GROOMBRIDGE (GROMEBRIDGE)
George of Lingfield, husbandman [DW/PA/7/12 f,103; DW/PA/5/1632/36]
Nicholas of Lingfield, husbandman [DW/PA/7/12 f,244; DW/PA/5/1634/51]
William of Lingfield, yeoman [DW/PA/5/1593/202]
GROOME *see* GROOM
GROPE
Richard of Long Ditton [PRO; PCC Will 1500]
GROVE
Agnes of Chertsey, widow [PRO; PCC 1640]
Edward of Newington [LPL; 98/1 f,110r; Will 1639]
Elizabeth of Kingston, widow [DW/PA/7/13 f,334; 1644]
Ellen of Kingston, widow [DW/PA/5/1575/46]
Francis of Swk St Saviour [DW/PA/7/13 f,279; DW/PA/5/1643/44]
Joan of Ash [DW/PA/5/1599/27] <Abs V21>
John of Chertsey, yeoman [DW/PA/7/13 f,435; DW/PA/5/1646/21]
John of Lambeth [PRO; PCC Admon 1637]
John of Woking [PRO; PCC Will 1573]
Katherine, alias Katherine Morer of Kingston [PRO; PCC Admon 1570]
Margaret, formerly Margaret Wyncot of Mortlake [PRO; PCC Will 1513]
Richard of Cobham [DW/PA/5/1550/106]
Richard of Kingston [DW/PA/7/2 f,150; 1521] <Abs SAC v,8 pp,116-117>
Robert of Capel, yeoman [DW/PA/5/1568/20]
Robert of Egham; White Waltham, Berkshire; Thorpe, yeoman [DW/PA/7/8 f,325; DW/PA/5/1612/68]

GROVE [*continued*]
Roger of Mortlake [PRO; PCC Will 1504]
Thomas of Chertsey [PRO; PCC Will 1593]
Thomas of Kingston, yeoman [DW/PA/5/1579/38]*
William of Kingston [PRO; PCC Will 1551]
GROVER
Ann, alias Ann Webb of Compton, widow [DW/PA/7/12 f.424; DW/PA/5/1637/48]
Bartholomew of Esher [HRO; Reg. Way 1 p.74; 1462]
John of Surrey; Leicestershire; Middlesex [PRO; PCC Will 1595]
John of Farnham [DW/PA/7/4 f.9; 1532]
John of Frensham - Lowick [DW/PA/5/1591/35]
John of Kingston [PRO; PCC Will 1524]
Margery of Farnham, widow [DW/PA/7/6 f.217; 1561]
Miles of Molesey, gent. [PRO; PCC Will 1537]
Richard of Bentley, Hampshire [DW/PA/7/1 f.82; 1488] <Abs 274>
Richard of Godalming, tailor [DW/PA/5/1580/30]
Thomas of Godalming - Eashing [DW/PA/7/11 f.577; DW/PA/5/1630/48]
GRUBB (GRUBBE)
Elizabeth of Swk St Saviour, widow [DW/PA/7/13 f.172; DW/PA/5/1641/61]
Joan of Bermondsey, widow [DW/PA/7/11 f.429; DW/PA/5/1627/50]
John of Carshalton, husbandman [DW/PA/7/4 f.33; 1533]
Rowland of Cranleigh, weaver [DW/PA/7/11 f.329; DW/PA/5/1625/105]
GRUELL
Joan of Bermondsey [DW/PA/5/1547/26]
GRYFFITH *see* GRIFFITHS
GRYGGE *see* GRIGG
GRYMES *see* GRIMES
GRYMSDITCHE *see* GRIMSDITCH
GRYMSTON *see* GRIMSTONE
GRYNSTEDE *see* GRINSTEAD
GRYUELL *see* GRAVETT
GUDRUM (GOOTHERUM)
Ellen of Swk St Saviour, widow [DW/PA/7/7 f.444; DW/PA/5/1603/59] <Abs 842>
GUILDFORD (GULDEFORD,GYLFORDE)
Elizabeth of Godalming, widow [BM; Add.Ms 24,925 f23r.; 1544] <Abs 55>
(Dame) Mary widow of (Sir) John of Surrey, knight [PRO; PCC Will 1578]
Robert of Godalming, tailor [DW/PA/7/12 f.149; DW/PA/5/1633/57]
GUILLAM,GUILLAMS,GULHAM *see* GWILLIAMS
GULLYE
Robert of Pyrford [*in* DW/PA/5/1558/76]
GUMPORT *see* GOMPORT
GUNE *see* GONNE
GUNNER (GONNER,GUNARE)
Henry of Frimley, husbandman [DW/PA/7/12 f.468; DW/PA/5/1638/53]
John of Chobham, labourer [DW/PA/5/1558/69]
John of Frimley, bachelor [DW/PA/5/1591/66]
John of Frimley - Sturt Lane End [DW/PA/7/7 f.564; DW/PA/5/1606/47] <Abs 1056>
John of Frimley [PRO; PCC 1638]
Richard of Frimley, milliner [DW/PA/7/7 f.278; DW/PA/5/1599/28] <Abs 494>
Robert of Frimley, potter [HRO; 1637 B20]
Thomas of Frimley, yeoman [DW/PA/5/1587/19]
William of Ash [DW/PA/7/1 f.97; 1489] <Abs 320>

GUNSLEY
  Robert of Titsey, clerk [PRO; PCC Will 1618]
  Robert of Titsey, clerk [PRO; PCC 1648]
GUNTER (GOUNTER)
  Alice, alias Alice List of Newington [PRO; PCC Admon 1630]
  John of St Martha's - Chilworth, esq. [PRO; PCC Will 1510]
GURNARD
  John of Putney, husbandman [LPL; 96/1134; 98/1 f.57v; Will 1634]
  Robert of Banstead, blacksmith [DW/PA/7/11 f.306; DW/PA/5/1626/60]
GURNEY
  Abraham, *or* Abraham Gorne of Bermondsey [PRO; PCC Will 1625]
  Anthony of Clapham [PRO; PCC Admon 1649]
GURREY, GURRY *see* GARY
GUY (GIE, GUYE, GY, GYE)
  Ann of ...., spinster [DW/PA/7/11 f.60; DW/PA/5/1623/51]
  Ann of Bermondsey, wife of William [DW/PA/7/11 f.393; DW/PA/5/1626/61]
  Elizabeth of Thames Ditton, widow [DW/PA/5/1593/100]
  Henry of Elstead [DW/PA/7/4 f.29; 1533]
  Richard of Thursley, husbandman [DW/PA/7/4 f.212; 1537]
  Thomas of Godalming, weaver [DW/PA/5/1580/64]
  Thomas of Shalford; Witley - Milford; Godalming [DW/PA/7/5 f.7; 1538]
    <Abs 78>
  William of Bermondsey, citizen and carpenter [DW/PA/7/11 f.282;
    DW/PA/5/1626/62]
GUYBON *see* GIBBONS
GUYE *see* GUY
GUYLLAM *see* GWILLIAMS
GUYN
  Thomas, *or* Thomas Gayre of Swk St George, baker [DW/PA/7/12 f.397;
    DW/PA/5/1638/52]
GWILLIAMS (GUILLAM, GUILLAMS, GULHAM, GUYLLAM, GWILLIAM)
  Ann of Swk St Olave [DW/PA/7/11 f.471; DW/PA/5/1628/50]
  Elizabeth of Tooting, widow [PRO; PCC Admon 1632]
  Gillian of Swk St Saviour; Swk St George; Swk St Olave; Clapham; Swk St
    Thomas , widow [DW/PA/5/1602/36] <Abs U48>
  Thomas of Swk St Olave, yeoman of H.M. Chamber [DW/PA/5/1605/40]
    <Abs U148>
  Thomas of Tooting Graveney [PRO; PCC Admon 1624]
  William of Bermondsey [PRO; PCC Admon 1614]
  William of Swk St George, servant to Thomas Swannicke [*French*]
    [DW/PA/5/1582/4]
    see also GILLAM, WILLIAMS
GWITE
  Nicholas of Compton [? HRO; 1530]
GWYNN *see* GUYN
GY *see* GUY
GYBBS, GYBBYS *see* GIBBS
GYBENES *see* GIBBONS
GYBLETT, GYBLOTT *see* GIBLETT
GYBONS *see* GIBBONS
GYBSON, GYBSONE *see* GIBSON
GYDWYN *see* GOODWIN
GY, GYE *see* GUY
GYELES *see* GILES

GYLBERTE *see* GILBERT
GYLFORDE *see* GUILDFORD
GYLE,GYLES,GYLIS *see* GILES
GYLHAM *see* GILLAM
GYLKYN *see* GILKIN
GYLL *see* GILL
GYLLES *see* GILES
GYLLMYN *see* GILMAN
GYLMET *see* FRENSHWOMAN
GYLMIN,GYLYMYN *see* GILMAN
GYNDGE *see* GINGE
GYNKYNSON *see* JENKINSON
GYNNOWE *see* GINNOW
GYNYNGES *see* JENNINGS
GYSORS *see* GISORS
GYTTINS,GYTTYNS *see* GITTINGS

HABITTLE *see* HAYBITLE
HACKET
  Thomas of Surrey, citizen and dyer [PRO; PCC Will 1579]
HACKMAN
  James of Godalming, weaver [DW/PA/7/13 f,44; DW/PA/5/1639/75]
  Joan of Godalming, widow [PRO; PCC 1640]
  Lawrence of Godalming [DW/PA/7/12 f,438; DW/PA/5/1636/56]
  Lawrence of Godalming [PRO; PCC 1637]
HACKWORTHE
  Rowland of Swk St Saviour, victualler [DW/PA/7/11 f,199; DW/PA/5/1625/107]
HADBACH
  William of St John Clerkenwell, Middlesex; Lambeth [LPL; Reg, Abp Arundel ii f,104; Will 1408]
HADDINGTON
  Abraham of Farnham, husbandman [GL; Archdeaconry Court of London Will 1628]
HADDOCK (HADDOCKE)
  James of Walton on the Hill, clerk [PRO; PCC Will 1552]
  James of Reigate [PRO; PCC Will 1572]
HADNET (HUDNAT,HUDNETT)
  Daniel of Chertsey, husbandman [DW/PA/7/7 f,178; DW/PA/5/1597/54] <Abs 329>
  Humphrey of Swk St Saviour [BM; Add,Ms 24,925 f,3r; 1544] <Abs 2>
  Robert of Chertsey, husbandman [DW/PA/5/1569/59]
HAIGH
  Robert of Bermondsey [PRO; PCC 1649]
HAILE *see* HALE
HAILER (HAYLER)
  Thomas of Dorking - Swires, yeoman [DW/PA/7/13 f,429; DW/PA/5/1646/25]
  William of Godalming, yeoman [DW/PA/5/1607/55] <Abs U197>
HAINES *see* HAYNES
HALDYNG
  Nicholas of Farnham [CCAL; 1503 f,214r]
HALE (HAILE,HAILES,HALES,HALIS,HALS,HALYS)
  Henry of Chobham, yeoman [DW/PA/7/8 f,268; DW/PA/5/1613/48]
  Henry of Kingston, cordwainer [DW/PA/7/13 f,421; DW/PA/5/1645/26]

HALE (HAILE,HAILES,HALES,HALIS,HALS,HALYS) [*continued*]
Henry of Surrey [BM; Add.Ms 9,069; 1456 *and* 1458]
Henry of Wotton? ['Wodington'] [PRO; PCC Will 1457]
John of Chobham, yeoman [DW/PA/5/1571/17]
John of Kew [DW/PA/5/1578/90]
John of Kingston, yeoman [DW/PA/5/1581/28]
John of Swk [HRO; Reg. Wyk 2 pp.15,84; 1368]
Richard of Chobham, yeoman [DW/PA/7/12 f.29; DW/PA/5/1631/55]
Richard of Farnham - Hale [DW/PA/7/1 f.80; 1488] <Abs 264>
Richard of Kingston, wheelwright [DW/PA/5/1593/127]
Walter of Frensham [DW/PA/7/9 f.34; DW/PA/5/1614/50]
William of Bermondsey [PRO; PCC Will 1568]
William of Kingston, cordwainer [DW/PA/7/12 f.293; DW/PA/5/1635/48]
HALEY (HALIE)
John of Lambeth - South Lambeth, merchant [PRO; PCC Will 1624]
Nicholas of Newington [LPL; 98/1 f.74r; Will 1636]
Richard of Mortlake [LPL; 98/1 f.46r; Will 1633]
HALFEHEAD
John of Wimbledon [PRO; PCC 1649]
HALIS *see* HALE
HALL (HALLE,HAULE,HAULL,HAWELL,HAWLE,HAWLES,HAWLLE)
... of Reigate [DW/PA/5/1544/3]
Agnes of Epsom - Woodcote, widow [DW/PA/5/1558/137]*
Agnes of Ripley [PRO; PCC Admon 1597]
Alexander of Bermondsey [DW/PA/5/1547/8]
Christian of Egham, wife of William, gent. [PRO; PCC Will 1613]
Christine of Epsom, widow [DW/PA/7/5 f.220; 1541]
Edmund of Chobham [DW/PA/7/6 f.190; DW/PA/5/1559/197]
Edward of Putney [PRO; PCC Admon 1614]
Elizabeth of Newington [LPL; 96/1143; 98/1 f.108v; Will 1639]
Giles of Thorpe [DW/PA/7/4 f.84; 1534]
Isabel of Chobham, widow [DW/PA/7/6 f.179; DW/PA/5/1559/216]
Jane of Chertsey, widow [DW/PA/5/1562/47]
Jane of Swk St Saviour, widow [DW/PA/7/10 f.147; DW/PA/5/1621/52]
Joan of Camberwell - Dulwich [DW/PA/7/9 f.53; DW/PA/5/1614/51] <Abs U204>
Joan of Farnham - Runfold, innholder, widow [HRO; 1563 B79-80]
John of Surrey [PRO; PCC Will 1447]
John of Camberwell - Dulwich, yeoman [DW/PA/7/8 f.247; DW/PA/5/1613/49]
John of Cranleigh [PRO; PCC Will 1499]
John of Headley, junior [DW/PA/7/2 f.15; 1491]
John of Walton [HRO; Reg. Way 1 p.71; 1462]
John of Walton on Thames [PRO; PCC Will 1506]
Margaret of Swk St Saviour, widow [DW/PA/7/11 f.67; DW/PA/5/1623/52]
Mary of Leigh [PRO; PCC Admon 1640]
Nicholas of Streatham [DW/PA/7/8 f.5; DW/PA/5/1608/50]
Richard of Battersea [PRO; PCC Admon 1624]
Richard of Chertsey, husbandman [DW/PA/5/1588/13]
Rowland of East Horsley, yeoman [PRO; PCC Will 1617]
Simon of Dorking [PRO; PCC 1647]
Stephen of Ashtead [DW/PA/7/4 f.64; 1534]
Thomas of Surrey [PRO; PCC Will 1443]
Thomas of Charlwood [PRO; PCC Admon 1599]
Thomas of Chiddingfold [DW/PA/5/1588/12]
Thomas of Farnham [DW/PA/5/1552/27]

HALL (HALLE,HAULE,HAULL,HAWELL,HAWLE,HAWLES,HAWLLE) [*continued*]
  Thomas of Guildford, yeoman [DW/PA/5/1570/69]
  Thomas of Kingston [BM; Add.Ms 24,925 f.22v; 1544] <Abs 53>
  Thomas of Lambeth, clerk and parson [PRO; PCC Will 1563]
  Thomas of Leatherhead [HRO; 1529 B13]
  Thomas of West Molesey [PRO; PCC Admon 1645]
  Thomas of West Molesey, citizen and cooper [PRO; PCC 1645]
  Thomas of Putney, butcher [LPL; 96/1142; Will 1617]
  Thomas of Swk, glover [DW/PA/5/1587/67]
  William of ,,, [relatives in Lancashire], citizen and currier [DW/PA/5/1603/68] <Abs U72>
  William of Bermondsey, barber chirurgeon [DW/PA/7/11 f.547; DW/PA/5/1629/40]
  William of Thames Ditton, labourer [HRO; 1604 AD24]
  William of Kingston, yeoman [DW/PA/7/7 f.223; DW/PA/5/1598/35] <Abs 394>
  William of Merton, curate [DW/PA/5/1558/127]
  William of Reigate [DW/PA/7/2 f.93; 1510]
  William of Reigate [DW/PA/5/1544/3]
  William of Rotherhithe, gent. [PRO; PCC Will 1612]
  William of Windlesham [DW/PA/7/4 ff.74-75; 1534]
HALLAM *see* HALLUM
HALLAWAY *see* HOLLOWAY
HALLE *see* HALL
HALLIDAY (HALLYDAY)
  Adam of Richmond [DW/PA/7/4 f.1; 1532]
HALLIETT
  Thomas of Rotherhithe, gent. [PRO; PCC Will 1612]
HALLIN
  Roger of Betchworth - Brockham [DW/PA/7/7 f.625; DW/PA/5/1607/45] <Abs 1168>
HALLINGTON
  Richard of Rotherhithe, mariner [DW/PA/7/2 f.70; 1500]
HALLUM (HALLAM)
  Mary of ,,, [DW/PA/7/9 f.50; DW/PA/5/1614/52]
  Richard of Headley, esq. [PRO; PCC Will 1419]
HALLYDAY *see* HALLIDAY
HALMER
  Susan of Kingston, widow [PRO; PCC Admon 1639]
  William of Richmond, one of the Scalding House, Prince's man [PRO; PCC Will 1610] <Abs, SAC v.24 p.67>
HALS *see* HALE
HALSEY (HALSYE)
  John of Swk St Saviour, citizen and draper [DW/PA/7/7 f.417; DW/PA/5/1603/71 *and* DW/PA/5/1603/72 *and* DW/PA/5/1604/26] <Abs 781>
HALSTED
  Henry of Swk St Olave [DW/PA/5/1627/52]
HALSTON
  William of Swk St Olave, citizen and salter [DW/PA/5/1581/57]
HALYS *see* HALL
HAM (HAMME)
  Alexander of Ockham, junior [DW/PA/7/8 f.217; DW/PA/5/1612/69]
  Daniel of Ockham [DW/PA/7/8 f.166; DW/PA/5/1610/65]
  Matthew of Ockham, yeoman [DW/PA/7/13 f.84; DW/PA/5/1640/71]
  Robert of Ockham, yeoman [DW/PA/5/1558/128]*

HAM (HAMME) [*continued*]
  Thomas of Ockham, husbandman [DW/PA/7/8 ff.330,338; DW/PA/5/1612/70]
  William of Ockham, husbandman [DW/PA/5/1576/39]
HAMAN *see* HAMMOND
HAMBLEDON (HAMBLETON,HAMELDON,HAMLENDEN,HAMULDEN,HAMULDON)
  Joseph of Shalford; Dunsfold [DW/PA/7/13 f.156; DW/PA/5/1641/72]
  Maud of Witley [DW/PA/7/5 f.64; 1539] <Abs 122>
  Richard of Witley [DW/PA/7/1 f.46B; 1487] <Abs 153>
  Richard of Witley [? HRO; 1521]
  William of Godalming; Witley [DW/PA/7/6 f.161; DW/PA/5/1559/145]
HAMDEN
  Christopher of Lambeth - Stockwell, yeoman [DW/PA/7/7 f.92; 1596] <Abs 169>
  George of Coulsdon, clerk [PRO; PCC 1632]
  John, alias John Holmden of Chipstead, rector [DW/PA/7/12 f.45; DW/PA/5/1632/42]
HAME (van HAME)
  Henry of Swk St Margaret, cobbler [DW/PA/7/2 f.56; 1500]
HAMERTON
  William of Kingston [PRO; PCC Will 1500; CCAL; 1500 f.69r]
HAMLENDEN *see* HAMBLEDON
HAMLYN (HAMLEN,HOMELIN)
  Nicholas of Farnham [PRO; PCC Will 1503; CCAL; 1503 f.214r]
  Robert of Seale [DW/PA/7/2 f.38; 1493]
  Thomas of Guildford Holy Trinity, bricklayer [DW/PA/7/9 f.131; DW/PA/5/1615/57]
HAMME *see* HAM
HAMMERTON *see* HAMERTON
HAMMOND (HAMAN,HAMMON,HAMMONDE,HAMON,HAMOND,HAMONDE,HAWMONT)
  Agnes, alias Agnes Banckes of Battersea, widow [DW/PA/5/1562/42]
  Ann of Lambeth, widow [DW/PA/5/1603/69] <Abs U73>
  Charles of Kingston, chandler [DW/PA/7/9 f.61; DW/PA/5/1614/53]
  Christopher of Wandsworth [PRO; PCC Will 1602] <Abs, SAC v.10 p.304>
  Elizabeth of Stoke next Guildford - Stoughton [PRO; PCC Will 1592] <Abs SAC v.28 p.100>
  George of Thorpe, yeoman [PRO; PCC 1646]
  Harry of Guildford St Nicolas [DW/PA/7/6 f.170; *in* DW/PA/5/1559/174]
  Helen of Kingston [PRO; PCC Will 1559]
  Helen of Ashtead, widow of John [DW/PA/7/7 f.93; 1596] <Abs 170>
  Henry of Battersea [DW/PA/7/11 f.105; DW/PA/5/1624/53]
  Henry of Guildford St Nicolas [DW/PA/7/6 f.182; DW/PA/5/1559/170]
  Henry of Send; East Clandon; West Clandon; Godalming [DW/PA/7/10 f.203; DW/PA/5/1620/64 *includes admon of 1627*]
  James of Rotherhithe [PRO; PCC 1634]
  Jane of Dorking, widow [DW/PA/7/9 f.135; DW/PA/5/1615/56]
  Joan of Guildford [PRO; PCC Will 1558]
  Joan of Swk, widow [DW/PA/5/1570/24]
  John of Albury, smith [DW/PA/5/1569/82]
  John of Albury - Farley Green, yeoman [DW/PA/7/11 f.99; DW/PA/5/1624/54]
  John of Alfold [DW/PA/7/4 f.150; 1536]
  John of Alfold [DW/PA/5/1558/131]*
  John of Chelsham, yeoman [DW/PA/7/11 f.58; DW/PA/5/1623/53]
  John of Chertsey, doctor of medicine [PRO; PCC Will 1617]
  John of Kingston, cordwainer [DW/PA/7/13 f.446; DW/PA/5/1646/28]

HAMMOND (HAMAN,HAMMON,HAMMONDE,HAMON,HAMOND,HAMONDE,HAWMONT) [*continued*]
John of Lambeth, yeoman [PRO; PCC Will 1609] <Abs, SAC v,23 p,133>
John of West Molesey [PRO; PCC Will 1501; CCAL; 1500 f,50v]
John of Shere, weaver [DW/PA/7/8 f,142; DW/PA/5/1611/50]
John of Streatham - Tooting Bec [PRO; PCC Will 1551]
Richard of Albury - Farley Green, yeoman [HRO; 1625 B24]
Richard of Godalming [DW/PA/7/3 f,172; 1531]
Richard of Godalming - Binscombe, husbandman [DW/PA/5/1558/129]*
Richard of Godalming - Binscombe, yeoman [DW/PA/7/7 f,363; DW/PA/5/1602/38] <Abs 665>
Robert of 'Loseley' [? Ewhurst *or* Guildford St Nicolas], husbandman [DW/PA/7/7 f,502; DW/PA/5/1605/42 *and* DW/PA/5/1605/43] <Abs 939>
Robert of Alfold [DW/PA/7/6 f,145; DW/PA/5/1559/230]
Robert of Battersea [DW/PA/5/1561/8]
Robert of Chertsey [PRO; PCC Admon 1623]
Robert of Godalming - Farncombe, husbandman [*in* DW/PA/5/1558/76]
Robert of Kingston; Hampton, Middlesex; West Molesey, gent, [PRO; PCC Will 1557] <Abs SAC v,8 p,120>
Robert of Kingston [PRO; PCC Admon 1647]
Stephen of Shere [DW/PA/7/6 f,139; DW/PA/5/1559/141]
Thomas of Send ? [DW/PA/7/11 f,221; DW/PA/5/1620/65]
Thomas of Battersea - Penge [PRO; PCC Will 1601] <Abs, SAC v,10 pp,297-298>
Thomas of Chobham [DW/PA/7/6 f,47; DW/PA/5/1559/40]
Thomas of Mortlake, yeoman [PRO; PCC Will 1617]
Thomas of Shere [DW/PA/7/4 f,165; 1536]
Thomas of Wandsworth, gent, [DW/PA/7/13 f,235; DW/PA/5/1642/46]
William of Battersea - Penge, yeoman [PRO; PCC Will 1613]
William of Long Ditton, husbandman [DW/PA/7/12 f,82; DW/PA/5/1633/64]
William of Godalming [DW/PA/7/12 f,329; DW/PA/5/1637/50]
William of Guildford, baker [DW/PA/7/6 f,270; 1560]
William of Guildford, esq, [PRO; PCC Will 1575] <Abs SAC v,28 pp,99-100>
William of Kingston, gent, [PRO; PCC Will 1549]
William of Kingston [PRO; PCC Will 1592]
William of Lambeth [DW/PA/7/5 f,35; 1538] <Abs 62>

HAMNETT (HAMN'T)
Isabel of Shere [DW/PA/5/1545/8]
John of Morden, gent, [PRO; PCC 1643]

HAMON,HAMOND,HAMONDE *see* HAMMOND

HAMPSHIRE (HAMPSHYRE,HAMSHEERE,HAMSHERE)
John of West Horsley, husbandman [DW/PA/5/1582/16]
Matthew of Cobham, husbandman [DW/PA/5/1557/70]
Thomas of Albury [DW/PA/7/6 f,97; DW/PA/5/1559/73]
Thomas of Albury, yeoman [DW/PA/7/10 f,232; DW/PA/5/1621/53]

HAMPTON
Alice of Swk St Olave, widow [DW/PA/5/1570/35]
Joan of Godalming - Lydling, widow [HRO; 1584 B37]
Margaret of Kingston, widow [DW/PA/7/1 f,36; 1486] <Abs 121>
Mary, alias Mary Frimley, of Putney, wife of John [LPL; 98/1 f,84r; Will 1637]
Robert of Seale, husbandman [DW/PA/5/1592/112]
Thomas of Farnham - Tilford [DW/PA/5/1558/132]*
Thomas of Kingston, bargeman [DW/PA/5/1591/7]
Thomas of Seale [DW/PA/7/5 f,32; 1538] <Abs 74>

HAMPTON [*continued*]
Thomas of Seale - Hampton [DW/PA/7/7 f,622; DW/PA/5/1607/46] <Abs 1159>
William of Dunsfold [DW/PA/7/10 f,93; DW/PA/5/1615/34]
William of Esher, husbandman [DW/PA/7/10 f,153; DW/PA/5/1619/55]
William of Puttenham - Rodsell [DW/PA/7/8 f,285; DW/PA/5/1613/50]
William of Reigate, clerk [DW/PA/7/12 f,341; DW/PA/5/1636/53]
William of Seale - Hampton, senior [HRO; 1582 B41]
William of Seale, yeoman, senior [DW/PA/7/9 f,281; 1618]

HAMRIDGE (HAM'RYEG)
William of Thames Ditton - Weston [DW/PA/5/1558/133]*

HAMSHEERE,HAMSHERE *see* HAMPSHIRE

HAMULDEN,HAMULDON *see* HAMBLEDON

HANCEY (HANZEY)
Olberton, or Olberton Hanzey of Alfold [PRO; PCC Admon 1618]

HANCOCK (HANCOCKE,HANDCOCKE)
Richard of Kingston, gent, [PRO; PCC Will 1608] <Abs, SAC v,13 p,189>
Roger of Newington, citizen and draper [PRO; PCC 1645]
William of Egham [PRO; PCC Admon 1626]

HANFORD (HANFORTHE)
Edmund of Stoke Dabernon, husbandman [DW/PA/7/12 f,268; DW/PA/5/1635/44]
John of Stoke Dabernon, husbandman [DW/PA/5/1575/74]
William of Stoke Dabernon [DW/PA/7/13 f,465; DW/PA/5/1648/10]

HANHAMSTEDE
John of Egham [PRO; PCC Will 1424]

HANKINE
John of Thames Ditton, yeoman [DW/PA/7/8 f,109; DW/PA/5/1610/66]

HANNAM
Sarah, alias Sarah Kennady of Rotherhithe [PRO; PCC Admon 1646]

HANNAWAY
George of East Clandon - 'Kyrettes House', husbandman [HRO; 1590 B23]

HANNINGTON (HANYNGTON)
Christopher of Send - Newark [PRO; PCC Will 1490]

HANNOTT
James of Swk St Olave [DW/PA/7/11 f,259; DW/PA/5/1625/108]
Mary of Swk St Olave, widow of James [DW/PA/7/11 f,327; DW/PA/5/1625/109]

HANNS *see* HAUNCE

HANSERDE
Alice of Swk St Mary Magdalen; St Bride, London, widow of John [DW/PA/7/5 f,34; 1538] <Abs 108>

HANYNGTON *see* HANNINGTON

HANZEY (HANCEY)
Olberton, alias Olberton Hancey of Alfold [PRO; PCC Admon 1618]

HAPP
Robert of Swk St Olave, sizemaker [DW/PA/7/8 f,204; DW/PA/5/1611/51]

HAPPY
William of Croydon [LPL; 96/1160; Will 1627]

HARBARD *see* HUBBARD

HARBLETT
Margaret of Swk St Saviour, widow [DW/PA/5/1587/83]

HARBY
Mary of Mitcham; Clerkenwell, Middlesex [PRO; PCC 1646]

HARCOURT (HARCORTE,HARECOURT)
(Sir) Richard of Surrey, knight [PRO; PCC Will 1486]
William of Newington - Walworth [PRO; PCC Will 1604]

HARDES

Robert, alias Robert Hordes of Limpsfield [PRO; PCC Will 1560]

HARDEWYN *see* HARDWYN

HARDING (HARDINGE,HARDYNG,HARDYNGE)

Agnes of Frensham, widow [DW/PA/5/1568/24]

Alice of Frensham, spinster [HRO; 1605 B32]

Alice of Stoke next Guildford, widow of John [DW/PA/7/8 f.284; DW/PA/5/1613/51]

Bartholomew of Frensham, husbandman [HRO; 1567 U172]

Bartholomew of Frensham - Pitfold, husbandman [DW/PA/7/8 f.237; DW/PA/5/1613/52]

Bartholomew of Puttenham, yeoman [DW/PA/7/7 f.485; DW/PA/5/1604/29] <Abs 914>

Elizabeth of Farnham - Badshot, spinster [DW/PA/7/13 f.289; DW/PA/5/1643/47]

Harry of Ockley [DW/PA/7/5 f.154; 1540]

Henry of Frensham, yeoman [DW/PA/7/13 f.134; DW/PA/5/1640/80]

Isabel of Frensham - Spreakley [DW/PA/5/1552/5]

John of Abinger [DW/PA/7/5 f.40; 1538] <Abs 2>

John of Cobham [HRO; 1623 AD49]

John of Farnham, yeoman [PRO; PCC Will 1628]

John of Farnham - Tilford, yeo., jun. [DW/PA/7/13 f.1; DW/PA/5/1639/67]

John of Frensham, senior [DW/PA/5/1582/101]

John of Frensham - Spreakley; Binstead, Hampshire [DW/PA/7/7 f.423; DW/PA/5/1603/73] <Abs 791>

John of Frensham - Hale, yeoman [DW/PA/7/13 f.399; DW/PA/5/1645/25]

John of Horne, tanner [DW/PA/7/10 f.211; DW/PA/5/1620/66]

John of East Molesey [DW/PA/7/4 f.162; 1536]

John of Stoke next Guildford [HRO; 1610 B36]

John of Walton on Thames, husbandman [DW/PA/7/10 f.32; DW/PA/5/1615/58]

Lawrence of Stoke next Guildford, shearman [HRO; 1591 B28] [*and*] [DW/PA/5/1591/52]

Mary of Farnham - Tilford, widow [DW/PA/5/1578/69 *and* DW/PA/5/1578/72]*

Nicholas of Puttenham, yeoman [DW/PA/5/1627/53]

Oliver of Frensham [DW/PA/5/1550/94]

Oliver of Farnham - Tilford [DW/PA/5/1557/30]

Richard of Farnham [DW/PA/7/2 f.193; 1523]

Richard of Frensham - Dockenfield, yeoman [HRO; 1600 B24]

Richard of Godalming - Hurtmore [DW/PA/7/7 f.114; 1597] <Abs 211>

Richard of West Molesey [PRO; PCC Will 1611] <Abs, SAC v.35 p.39>

Robert of ... [GMR; 97/13/1109; 1500]

Robert of Cranleigh [PRO; PCC Will 1504] <Abs SAC v.27 p.24; *see also* v.6 p.21>

Robert of Cranleigh [PRO; PCC Will 1515]

Robert of Puttenham; Wanborough [DW/PA/7/6 f.265; 1560]

Simon of Frensham, yeoman [HRO; 1603 B26]

Thomas of Chiddingfold; Sidlesham, Sussex, innkeeper [DW/PA/7/9 f.276; 1618]

Thomas of Farnham - Tilford, husbandman [HRO; 1597 B39]

Thomas of Merrow, yeoman [DW/PA/7/12 f.377; DW/PA/5/1637/52]

William of Chelsham [PRO; PCC Will 1549]

William of Frensham - Spreakley [BM; Add.Ms 24,925 f.17v; 1542] <Abs 38>

William of Worplesdon - Wyke; Aldershot, Hampshire; Frensham; Horsley; Ash, gent. [DW/PA/5/1593/91]

HARDMAN *see* HARMAN
HARDWEN *see* HARDWYN
HARDWICKE
  Richard of Ewhurst [PRO; PCC 1647]
HARDWYN (HARDEWYN,HARDWEN,HARDYWYNE,HERDWEN)
  Agnes of West Horsley, widow [DW/PA/5/1582/78]
  Joan of Byfleet, widow [DW/PA/7/3 f,121; 1529]
  Joan of Byfleet, widow [DW/PA/5/1588/83]
  John of Binfield, Berkshire [DW/PA/5/1555/72]
  John of Byfleet [DW/PA/7/1 f,7; 1485] <Abs 22>
  John of Byfleet [DW/PA/7/5 f,195; 1540]
  Margery of Byfleet, widow [DW/PA/5/1558/134]*
  Richard of Byfleet [PRO; PCC Will 1553]
  Robert of Byfleet, yeoman [HRO; 1573 B63]
  Thomas of Byfleet [DW/PA/7/2 f,195; 1524]
HARDY (HARDYE)
  Geoffrey of Camberwell, servant to Peter Dawson, vicar [DW/PA/7/11 f,452; DW/PA/5/1628/51]
  John of Farnham, senior [PRO; PCC Will 1472]
  John of Farnham, senior [DW/PA/5/1565/2]*
  John of Farnham, senior [DW/PA/7/7 f,159; DW/PA/5/1597/48] <Abs 294>
  Percival of Farnham, cloth maker [DW/PA/7/4 f,126; 1535]
  Thomas of Swk St Saviour [DW/PA/5/1593/180B]*
HARDYNG *see* HARDING
HARDYWYNE *see* HARDWYN
HARE
  Melcah of Mitcham, widow [PRO; PCC 1630; Sentence 1631] <Scroope 1272>
  William of Esher [BM; Add.Ms 24,925 f,17r; 1544] <Abs 36>
HARECOURT *see* HARCOURT
HAREGOOD
  Jane of Swk St Saviour, widow [DW/PA/7/9 f,99; DW/PA/5/1614/54]
HARFELD *see* HARPER
HARFORD (HARFFORD)
  Christopher of Lambeth - Lambeth Marsh [DW/PA/5/1592/117]
  Francis of Battersea [DW/PA/7/7 f,398; DW/PA/5/1603/74] <Abs 738>
HARIP
  John of Swk St Olave, barber [HRO; Reg, Fox 3 p,68; 1517]
HARISON *see* HARRISON
HARLING (HARLINGE,HARLYNG,HARLYNGE,HORLINGE)
  John of Crowhurst, senior [PRO; PCC Will 1504]
  John of Crowhurst [PRO; PCC Will 1530]
  John of Tandridge [PRO; PCC 1649]
  Nicholas of Horne, yeoman [DW/PA/7/7 f,7; DW/PA/5/1595/46] <Abs 18>
  Richard of Lingfield [PRO; PCC Will 1601] <Abs, SAC v,10 p,149>
  Robert of Horne [DW/PA/5/1576/94]
  Roger of Newington, yeoman [LPL; 96/1167; Will 1628]
  Thomas of Horne, husbandman [DW/PA/7/10 f,45; 1618]
  William of Godstone, yeoman [DW/PA/5/1593/98]
  William of Horne [PRO; PCC 1643 *and* PCC Admon 1643]
HARLOWE
  Thomas of Clapham [PRO; PCC Admon 1612]
HARMAN (HARDMAN,HARMON,HARMONDE)
  Christopher of Wimbledon [PRO; PCC Will 1624]

HARMAN (HARDMAN, HARMON, HARMONDE) [*continued*]
Edward of Farnham, late keeper and servant to (Sir) George Moore, knight [DW/PA/7/8 f.274; DW/PA/5/1612/71]
Elizabeth of Tooting Graveney, widow of Guy, yeoman [DW/PA/5/1593/122]
Guy of Tooting Graveney, yeoman [DW/PA/5/1586/10]
Henry of Croydon, bachelor [PRO; PCC Admon 1647]
Henry of Ewell, yeoman [DW/PA/7/13 f.81; DW/PA/5/1641/69]
John of Rotherhithe, shipwright [DW/PA/5/1593/133]
John of Swk St Saviour, waterman [DW/PA/7/10 f.249; DW/PA/5/1622/38]
John of Wandsworth, innholder [DW/PA/5/1546/28]
Lambert of Swk, brewer [DW/PA/5/1579/45]*
Margaret, alias Margaret Atride of Ewhurst [PRO; PCC Admon 1649]
Margaret of Wimbledon, widow [LPL; 96/1168; Will 1617]
Nicholas of Kingston [DW/PA/5/1579/46]*
Richard of Bermondsey [PRO; PCC Admon 1625]
Richard of Mitcham, carpenter [DW/PA/5/1587/81]
Thomas of Betchworth, blacksmith [DW/PA/7/11 f.134; DW/PA/5/1624/56]
Thomas of Tooting Graveney, yeoman [DW/PA/5/1601/43]

HARMANSON (HARMANSONNE, HEMANSON)
Arnold of Swk St Olave [DW/PA/5/1547/18]
Derek of Swk St Olave, hatmaker [DW/PA/5/1546/87]
Henry of Swk St Thomas Hospital, bookseller [DW/PA/5/1546/12]

HARME (HARMES)
George of Esher, yeoman [DW/PA/7/11 f.114; DW/PA/5/1624/55]
George of Worplesdon [PRO; PCC Admon 1639]
John of Byfleet [DW/PA/5/1563/30]
John of Byfleet, tailor [DW/PA/7/8 f.138; DW/PA/5/1610/67]
John of Stoke Dabernon [DW/PA/5/1581/44]
Marianne of Stoke Dabernon, widow of John [DW/PA/5/1581/7]
Marianne of Thames Ditton, widow [DW/PA/7/9 f.170; DW/PA/5/1616/61]
Robert of Byfleet, yeoman, senior [DW/PA/7/7 f.450; DW/PA/5/1603/75] <Abs 854>
William of Thames Ditton, husbandman [DW/PA/7/8 f.31; DW/PA/5/1608/51]

HARMER
Anthony of Chertsey [PRO; PCC Admon 1623]

HARNEHAM
John of Lambeth, clerk [PRO; PCC Will 1473]

HARPE
John of Burstow [LPL; 98/1 f.44v; Will 1633]

HARPER (HARFELD)
Agnes of Wonersh [DW/PA/7/8 f.364; DW/PA/5/1612/72]
Henry of Camberwell [PRO; PCC Admon 1624]
Henry of Dunsfold, husbandman [HRO; 1601 B35]
Henry of Wonersh [DW/PA/7/7 f.638; DW/PA/5/1608/52] <Abs 1196>
John of Wonersh - Plonk's [DW/PA/5/1557/40]
John of Wonersh [DW/PA/5/1558/136] [*two copies - one**]
John *or* John Harfeld of Wonersh - Blundels [HRO; 1567 B64-65]
John of Wonersh, husbandman [DW/PA/7/7 f.279; DW/PA/5/1599/29] <Abs 496>
Lawrence of Wonersh, weaver [DW/PA/7/12 f.310; DW/PA/5/1635/53]
Richard of Godalming - Farncombe, weaver [DW/PA/7/7 f.281; DW/PA/5/1599/30] <Abs 501>
Susan of Guildford Holy Trinity, spinster [DW/PA/5/1591/25]
Thomas of Wonersh, weaver [DW/PA/7/13 f.448; DW/PA/5/1646/30]
William of Newington [PRO; PCC Will 1628]

HARPER (HARFELD) [*continued*]

William of Swk St Olave, baker [DW/PA/5/1576/32]
William of Swk St Saviour, cordwainer [DW/PA/7/11 f.214; DW/PA/5/1625/110]
William of Wonersh [DW/PA/7/7 f.533; DW/PA/5/1607/47] <Abs 1002>

HARRIDEN *see* HARRYDON

HARRINGTON

John, Lord Harrington, of Exton, Rutland; Kew [PRO; PCC Will 1614]

HARRIS (HARES, HARREIS, HARRIES, HARRYS)

Benjamin of Newington [PRO; PCC Admon 1621]
Dorothy of Newington, widow [PRO; PCC Will 1586]
Henry, alias Henry Bocher of Kingston; Richmond, bricklayer [DW/PA/7/6 f.49; DW/PA/5/1559/46]
Hugh of Putney, butcher [LPL; 96/1174; Will 1616]
Isaac of Cobham [PRO; PCC Admon 1649]
John of Swk St Mary Overy [DW/PA/7/2 f.49; 1497]
John of Lambeth, brewer [DW/PA/7/13 f.128; DW/PA/5/1640/78]
John of Swk St Saviour [DW/PA/7/10 f.22; DW/PA/5/1616/74]
Lawrence of Surrey [PRO; PCC Will 1508]
Lyde of Swk St Saviour, gunner [DW/PA/7/13 f.292; DW/PA/5/1643/50]
Margery of Newington, widow of Benjamin [PRO; PCC Will 1623]
Mary of Banstead [PRO; PCC 1647]
(Lady) Mary of Lambeth, widow [PRO; PCC Admon 1618]
Nathaniel of Blechingley, doctor of law [PRO; PCC Will 1625]
Phillip of Swk St Thomas [DW/PA/7/11 f.165; DW/PA/5/1625/111]
Richard of Chertsey - Lyne, esq. [PRO; PCC Will 1627]
Robert of Chertsey [DW/PA/7/12 f.25; DW/PA/5/1631/53]
Robert of Chipstead; Woodmansterne [PRO; PCC Will 1588]
Robert of Kingston, husbandman [DW/PA/7/3 f.132; 1530]
Robert, alias Robert Stacye of Kingston - Surbiton, husbandman [DW/PA/5/1555/42]
Thomas of Swk St Olave, freemason [DW/PA/5/1563/86]
William of Swk, scrivener [DW/PA/7/7 f.538; DW/PA/5/1606/45] <Abs 1010>
William of Newington [LPL; 96/1176; Will 1625]

HARRISON (HARISON, HARRYSON, HERRYSON)

Andrew of Swk St Saviour, shoemaker [DW/PA/7/13 f.454; DW/PA/5/1647/5]
Cornelius of Swk St Olave, shoemaker [DW/PA/7/7 f.611; DW/PA/5/1607/48] <Abs 1143>
Francis of Swk St Olave, feltmaker [DW/PA/5/1579/43]*
Gertrude of Swk St Olave, widow [DW/PA/7/3 f.130; 1530]
Henry of Swk St Saviour [CCAL; 1559 U^2 f.92v]
James of Newington [LPL; 96/1187; 98/1 f.49r; Will 1633]
Jane of Swk St George, widow [DW/PA/7/7 f.409; DW/PA/5/1603/76] <Abs 757>
Joan of Swk St Saviour, widow [DW/PA/5/1592/110]
John of Little Bookham [DW/PA/7/4 f.206; 1537]
John of Swk St Olave [DW/PA/7/4 f.32; 1533]
John of Camberwell - Peckham; Lincs. - Isle of Oxholme [DW/PA/5/1550/26]
John of Chertsey, waterman [DW/PA/7/8 f.68; DW/PA/5/1609/87]
John of Swk St Olave [DW/PA/7/12 f.51; DW/PA/5/1632/41]
John of Swk St Saviour, pointmaker [DW/PA/7/7 f.377; DW/PA/5/1602/39] <Abs 699>
John of Walton on Thames [DW/PA/7/12 f.309; DW/PA/5/1636/51]
Lucy of Swk St Olave, widow [DW/PA/7/8 f.141; DW/PA/5/1611/52]
Margaret of Battersea, widow [PRO; PCC 1642]

HARRISON (HARISON,HARRYSON,HERRYSON) [*continued*]
Mark of Swk St Saviour [DW/PA/7/12 f,76; DW/PA/5/1632/44]
Nicholas of Woking [DW/PA/7/5 f,173; 1540]
Peter of Mitcham, tallow chandler [DW/PA/7/11 f,431; DW/PA/5/1627/54]
Peter of Swk St Saviour [BM; Add.Ms 24,925 f,20r; 1544] <Abs 46>
Richard of Bermondsey [HRO; 1591 AD29]
Richard of Epsom [DW/PA/5/1552/19]
Richard of Wandsworth, yeoman [DW/PA/5/1588/42]
Robert of Ash [DW/PA/7/9 f,72; DW/PA/5/1614/55]
Robert of Ash, husbandman [DW/PA/7/12 f,189; DW/PA/5/1633/71]
Robert of Effingham, husbandman [DW/PA/7/7 f,135; DW/PA/5/1597/49] <Abs 247>
Robert of Fetcham [DW/PA/7/13 f,475; DW/PA/5/1648/12]
Stephen of Seale - Tongham [DW/PA/5/1562/82]
Thomas of Croydon [LPL; 98/1 f,39v; Will 1632]
Thomas of Molesey [PRO; PCC Admon 1566]
Thomas of Sutton [DW/PA/7/11 f,433; DW/PA/5/1627/55]
Thomas of Swk St Thomas, tailor [DW/PA/7/12 f,208; DW/PA/5/1634/53]
Thomas of Woking - Sutton, weaver [DW/PA/5/1562/66]

HARROLD
Christopher of Wandsworth, gent, [PRO; PCC Will 1595]

HARROW
John of Swk St George, porter [DW/PA/7/13 f,164; DW/PA/5/1642/38]

HARRY (HARRYE)
Joan, alias Joan Fye Harrye of Kingston - Ham, widow [DW/PA/5/1576/56]

HARRYDON
Joan of Swk St Olave, maidservant to Mr Allen, silkman [DW/PA/7/11 f,373; DW/PA/5/1626/63]

HARRYE *see* HARRY

HARRYS,HARRYSON *see* HARRIS,HARRISON

HARSET
Robert of Newington, clerk [PRO; PCC Will 1498]

HARSOLL
Hugh of Swk St Saviour, innholder [DW/PA/7/11 f,25; DW/PA/5/1623/59]

HART (HARTE,HEARTE,HERT,HERTE)
Elizabeth of Rotherhithe, widow [PRO; PCC 1635]
Henry of Horley [DW/PA/7/8 f,52; DW/PA/5/1609/88]
Idonya, formerly Idonya Grenacre, of Ripley [PRO; PCC Will 1402]
John of Bramley, tanner [DW/PA/7/13 f,16; DW/PA/5/1639/68]
John of Godstone, smith [DW/PA/7/7 f,222; DW/PA/5/1598/36] <Abs 393>
John, alias John Liverhart of Merton [PRO; PCC Admon 1627]
John of Swk St George [HRO; Reg, Way 2 p,151; 1472]
John of Windlesham [DW/PA/5/1552/17]
Juliana of Horne, widow [DW/PA/7/1 f,42; 1486] <Abs 136>
Luke of Windlesham [PRO; PCC 1649]
Thomas, alias Thomas Mathew of Albury, husbandman [DW/PA/7/10 f,283; DW/PA/5/1623/54]
Thomas of Godstone, blacksmith [DW/PA/7/8 f,279; DW/PA/5/1613/53]
Thomas of Horne [DW/PA/7/1 f,34; 1486] <Abs 116>
Thomas of Rotherhithe, mariner [PRO; PCC 1636]
Thomas of Rotherhithe (died overseas) [PRO; PCC Admon 1639]
Thomas of Windlesham, yeoman, senior [HRO; 1603 B28]
Thomas of Windlesham - Bagshot, yeoman [DW/PA/7/13 f,195; DW/PA/5/1641/78]

HART (HARTE,HEARTE,HERT,HERTE) [*continued*]
William of Bermondsey, wire drawer [DW/PA/7/8 f.347; DW/PA/5/1612/73]
William of Thames Ditton [DW/PA/7/5 f.36; 1538] <Abs 115>
William, alias William Liverhart of Merton [PRO; PCC Admon 1630]
William of Windlesham [DW/PA/5/1557/133]
HARTCOMBE *see* HERTCOMBE
HARTE *see* HART
HARTFORD
John of Swk St Olave [DW/PA/7/3 f.176; 1531]
Margaret of Lambeth [PRO; PCC Admon 1614]
HARTNESSE
Robert of Lambeth, tailor [DW/PA/7/7 f.607; DW/PA/5/1607/49] <Abs 1136>
HARTOPP (HARTOP)
John of Godstone, esq. [SRO; KB31/2,6] [*and*] [PRO; PCC Will 1608]
<Abs SAC v.13 pp.194-195>
Robert of Surrey [PRO; PCC Will 1555]
HARTWELL
Abraham of Lambeth [PRO; PCC Will 1607]
John of Grays Inn, Middlesex, gent. [*Parents buried at Lambeth*]
[PRO; PCC 1645]
(Sir) William of Surrey, knight] [PRO; PCC Will 1503]
HARVARD
John of Swk St Saviour, butcher [DW/PA/7/8 f.158; DW/PA/5/1611/53]
HARVEST (HARVISTE)
William of Godalming - Farncombe, shoemaker [DW/PA/7/9 f.148;
DW/PA/5/1615/59]
HARVEY (HARVIE,HARVY,HARVYE)
Agnes of Kingston, widow of Henry Thompson, citizen and white baker
[PRO; PCC Will 1605] <Abs, SAC v.12 pp.83-84>
Daniel of Croydon [PRO; PCC 1649]
Henry of Chessington, esq. [PRO; PCC Will 1590]
Henry of Newington [LPL; 96/1199; Will 1643]
Isaac of Rotherhithe (died overseas) [PRO; PCC Admon 1639]
John of Newington [LPL; 96/1198; 98/1 f.104r; Will 1639]
Matthew of Kingston - Coombe; London, merchant [PRO; PCC 1643]
Richard of Kingston - Hatch [DW/PA/5/1591/61]
Robert of Bermondsey; Stanton [*? county*] [DW/PA/7/8 f.319;
DW/PA/5/1611/54]
Robert of Godstone; Blechingley; Flitwick, Bedfordshire
[DW/PA/5/1593/3]
Robert of Swk St Saviour, waterman [DW/PA/5/1576/47]
Thomas of Kingston; Ditton, esq. [PRO; PCC Will 1601] <Abs, SAC v.10
pp.147-148>
William of Chessington, pensioner gent.of H.M. [PRO; PCC Will 1590]
William of Kingston - Ham [DW/PA/5/1568/84]
William of Kingston - Ham [DW/PA/5/1575/79]
HARVISTE *see* HARVEST
HARVY,HARVYE *see* HARVEY
HARWARD *see* HARWOOD
HARWELL
Alice of Streatham [GL; Commissary Court of London Will 1384]
HARWOOD (HARWARD,HARWOD)
Agnes of Guildford, widow [DW/PA/5/1591/60]
Ann, alias Ann Sutton of 'Kegworth, Surrey' [PRO; PCC Admon 1649]

HARWOOD (HARWARD,HARWOD) [*continued*]
Ann of Wandsworth, widow [DW/PA/7/13 f.21; DW/PA/5/1639/69]
Blanch of Putney [PRO; PCC Admon 1585]
Henry of Ash, yeoman [DW/PA/7/8 f.320; DW/PA/5/1611/55]
John of Godalming - Shackleford, farrier [DW/PA/7/13 f.494; DW/PA/5/1649/7]
Leonard of Camberwell - Peckham [PRO; PCC Admon 1613]
Nicholas of Banstead [DW/PA/7/5 f.142; 1540]
Ralph of St Mary Magdalen, London; Walton on Thames, citizen and blacksmith [PRO; PCC 1620] <Soame 982>
Richard of Kingston [PRO; PCC Admon 1646]
Robert of Kingston, draper [DW/PA/7/13 f.367; 1644]
Robert of Kingston [PRO; PCC 1646]
Thomas of Merrow, gent., senior [DW/PA/5/1581/64]
Thomas of Merrow, gent. [PRO; PCC Will *and* Admon 1595]
William of Cranleigh, cook [PRO; PCC 1643] [*and*] [SRO; 212/35/38]
William of Swk St George, yeoman [DW/PA/7/12 f.175; DW/PA/5/1633/70]
see also HAYWARD [*for* HAWARD]

HASELEY *see* HASLEY

HASLER
Ralph of Swk St Saviour, citizen and vintner [DW/PA/5/1593/149]

HASLETT
William of Dunsfold, sawyer [DW/PA/7/7 f.84; 1596] <Abs 153>
see also ASLETT

HASLEY (HASELEY,HASLEYE)
Christopher, alias Christopher Jaslyn of Reigate, yeoman [DW/PA/7/6 f.235; 1561]
Thomas of Crutched Friars, London; Fulham, Middlesex; Kingsbury, Middlesex; Great Haseley, Oxfordshire; Windlesham, knight, Submarshal of England [LPL; Reg. Abp Stafford f.174; Will 1449]

HASSALL
Robert of Bermondsey, citizen and farrier [PRO; PCC Will 1606] <Abs, SAC v.12 pp.100-101>

HASSARD *see* HAZARD

HASSAWE
Robert of Swk ? [DW/PA/5/1579/41]*

HASTED *see* HASLETT

HASTINGE
John of Dorking, cook [DW/PA/7/11 f.175; DW/PA/5/1625/112]

HASWELL (HUSWELL)
Edward of Coulsdon, husbandman [DW/PA/7/7 f.497; DW/PA/5/1604/30] <Abs 919>
John of Battersea - Penge; Beckenham, Kent, husbandman [DW/PA/7/10 f.284; DW/PA/5/1623/55]
John of Beddington, yeoman [DW/PA/7/13 f.81; DW/PA/5/1640/70]
John of Oxted [PRO; PCC 1640]
Thomas of Coulsdon, yeoman [DW/PA/7/13 f.24; DW/PA/5/1639/70]

HATCH
Ann of Swk St Olave, widow [DW/PA/7/12 f.358; DW/PA/5/1637/51]
Edward of Chipstead, yeoman [DW/PA/7/8 f.3; DW/PA/5/1608/53]
Elizabeth of Chipstead, widow [DW/PA/7/11 f.398; DW/PA/5/1627/56]
John of Ashtead, yeoman [DW/PA/7/13 f.72; 1640]
John of Croydon [PRO; PCC Will 1546]

HATCH [*continued*]

John of Walton on the Hill, husbandman [DW/PA/7/13 f.28; DW/PA/5/1639/71 *and* DW/PA/5/1640/69]

Miles of Addington [DW/PA/7/12 f.442; DW/PA/5/1638/61]

Robert of Ashtead, husbandman [DW/PA/7/12 f.245; DW/PA/5/1634/56]

Robert of Beddington, yeoman [DW/PA/7/12 f.444; DW/PA/5/1639/66]

Thomas of Chipstead [DW/PA/7/4 f.109; 1535]

HATCLIFFE *see* HATTCLIFF

HATE (HAYT)

John of Tandridge - Tillingdown [DW/PA/5/1546/40]

HATFEILD (HATFELDE,HATFFYLD,HATFYLLD)

Joan of Wandsworth [DW/PA/5/1557/92]

John of Ewell, tallow chandler [DW/PA/7/12 f.204; DW/PA/5/1634/52]

John of Wandsworth [DW/PA/5/1555/84]

Thomas of Newington [PRO; PCC Will 1592]

HATHEWELL *see* HATHWELL

HATHORNE *see* HEATHORN

HATHWELL (HATHEWELL,HATHWOLFE,HAYTHWELL)

Anthony of Chobham, yeoman [DW/PA/7/13 f.291; DW/PA/5/1643/49]

John of Chobham [PRO; PCC 1648]

John of Horsell, yeoman [DW/PA/5/1563/50]

John of Horsell [DW/PA/5/1563/51]

John of Horsell [DW/PA/7/11 f.551; DW/PA/5/1629/41]

Robert of Horsell [DW/PA/7/4 f.57; 1533]

Robert of Horsell, yeoman [DW/PA/7/7 f.510; 1606] <Abs 958>

Rose of Horsell, widow of Robert [DW/PA/7/11 f.121; DW/PA/5/1624/57]

Walter of Horsell [DW/PA/7/1 f.15; 1485] <Abs 49>

see also ATWELL; WELLS

HATKINSON *see* ATKINSON

HATON *see* HAYTON

HATRELL

Juliana of Esher [DW/PA/7/6 f.28; *in* DW/PA/5/1559/29]

HATROM

Balthazar of Swk, joiner [DW/PA/5/1582/10]

Katherine of Swk St Olave; Rotterdam, Holland, widow [*Dutch*] [DW/PA/7/8 f.322; DW/PA/5/1611/56]

HATT

George of Compton, gent. [DW/PA/5/1570/86]

HATTCLIFF (HATCLIFFE,HATTECLYF)

Isabel of Addington [PRO; PCC Will 1544]

Thomas of Surrey [PRO; PCC Will 1540] <Abs SAC v.7 p.84 *and* v.25 p.34>

William of Surrey [PRO; PCC Will 1480]

William of East Greenwich, Kent; Carshalton [PRO; PCC 1620] <Soame 880>

HATTER

Anthony of Swk St Saviour, chandler [DW/PA/7/7 f.110; DW/PA/5/1596/28] <Abs 200>

HATTON

Humphrey of Long Ditton - Tolworth [DW/PA/5/1558/135]*

John of London, saddler [DW/PA/5/1550/43]

John of Thorpe [PRO; PCC Will 1557]

Richard of Long Ditton - Tolworth, gent. [PRO; PCC Will 1577]

see also HAYTON [for HATON]

HAUCKES *see* HAWKES

HAUGHTON *see* HOUGHTON

HAUKEN *see* HAWKINS
HAULE,HAULL *see* HALL
HAUNCE (HANNS)
Alice, alias Alice Faulasfan of Swk St Thomas Hospital [DW/PA/5/1555/35]
John, alias John Marcellis, alias John Musselis of Rotherhithe [PRO; PCC Admon 1628]
Richard of Lambeth [PRO; PCC Admon 1640]
HAVARD
Walter of Lambeth, gent. [PRO; PCC Will 1504]
HAVELL
Joan of Swk St Saviour, widow [DW/PA/7/10 f.135; DW/PA/5/1620/67]
HAVERCAMPE
Peter of Barnes, gent. [PRO; PCC Wills 1625 *and* 1626]
HAVERJOHN
Ambrose of ... [DW/PA/7/11 f.83; DW/PA/5/1623/56]
HAWARD,HAWARDE *see* HAYWARD
HAWCES
Robert, alias Robert Hawkes of Swk St Saviour, waterman [DW/PA/7/11 f.530; DW/PA/5/1629/42]
HAWCOCKE
Edmund of Walton on Thames, tailor [DW/PA/7/7 f.490; 1605] (Abs 926)
HAWELL *see* HALL
HAWES
John of Lambeth [PRO; PCC Admon 1638]
William of Swk St Olave, carman [DW/PA/5/1593/73]
HAWFIELD (HAWFEILD)
George of Windlesham - Bagshot, senior [DW/PA/7/11 f.496; 1629]
Joan of Lambeth - Lambeth Marsh, widow [PRO; PCC 1640]
Robert of Swk St Saviour, sawyer [DW/PA/7/10 f.82; DW/PA/5/1619/57]
HAWKER
Nathaniel of Swk St Saviour - Bankside [DW/PA/7/12 f.256; DW/PA/5/1634/57]
HAWKES (HAUCKES)
Richard of Swk St Saviour [DW/PA/5/1593/66]
Robert, alias Robert Hawces of Swk St Saviour, waterman [DW/PA/7/11 f.530; DW/PA/5/1629/42]
Susan of Croydon, spinster [PRO; PCC Admon 1628]
HAWKESWORTH
William of Swk St Saviour, gent. [DW/PA/7/9 f.224; DW/PA/5/1617/69]
HAWKINS (HAUKEN,HAWKYNS)
Agnes of Clapham, widow [PRO; PCC 1637]
Austin of Chaldon [PRO; PCC Will 1450]
Ede of Windlesham, widow [DW/PA/5/1563/31]
Elizabeth, formerly Elizabeth Brown of Banstead [PRO; PCC Will 1540]
Joan of Thames Ditton, widow of John [DW/PA/7/9 f.233; DW/PA/5/1617/54]
Juliana of Godalming, widow [DW/PA/7/4 f.141; 1536]
Richard of Banstead [PRO; PCC Will 1526]
Richard of Swk St Olave, woodmonger [DW/PA/5/1627/59A]
Robert of West Molesey, blacksmith [DW/PA/7/13 f.227; DW/PA/5/1642/45]
Sense, formerly Sense Myllwarde of Rotherhithe [PRO; PCC Will 1549]
Thomas of Windlesham [DW/PA/5/1579/47]*
William of Kingston [PRO; PCC Will 1515]
William of Windlesham [DW/PA/7/11 f.334; DW/PA/5/1625/113]
HAWLE,HAWLLE,HAWLES *see* HALL

HAWLEY
Robert of Cobham; Weybridge; Walton on Thames, fishmonger [GL; Commissary Court of London Will 1540]
HAWMOND, HAWMONT *see* HAMMOND
HAWNDWERPP
Harry of Swk St Olave [DW/PA/5/1550/98]
HAWSERD
William of East Clandon [*in* DW/PA/5/1544/9]
HAWSON
Lawrence of Richmond [PRO; PCC Will 1555]
HAWTHORNE
Katherine of Bentley, Hampshire [DW/PA/5/1550/17]
HAWTREY
Ralph of London; Sanderstead, citizen and merchant tailor [PRO; PCC 1646]
HAY (HAYE)
Richard of Wandsworth [DW/PA/7/11 f.552; DW/PA/5/1629/44]
Simon of Fetcham, husbandman [DW/PA/7/13 f.502; DW/PA/5/1649/8]
see also HAYES
HAYBITLE
Robert of Effingham, yeoman [DW/PA/7/13 f.92; DW/PA/5/1640/73]
HAYBORNE (HEYBORNE)
Richard of Dorking; Betchworth [DW/PA/7/5 f.38; 1538] <Abs 27>
William of Betchworth, yeoman of the guard [BM; Add.Ms 24,925 f.4r; 1544] <Abs 6>
HAYDON (HAYDEN, HEDON, HEYDON)
Elizabeth of Lambeth [PRO; PCC Admon 1620]
Elizabeth of Lambeth - Lambeth Marsh, widow [PRO; PCC Will 1623]
John of Kingston - Norbiton, sawyer [DW/PA/5/1584/2]*
Richard of Lambeth, gardener [DW/PA/7/10 f.136; DW/PA/5/1620/59]
Richard of Wandsworth [PRO; PCC Will 1527]
Stephen of Fetcham, yeoman [DW/PA/7/10 f.31; DW/PA/5/1616/75]
HAYE *see* HAY; HAYES
HAYEMER
Robert of Kingston [DW/PA/7/2 f.121; 1518]
HAYES (HAYS, HAYSE, HEYES)
Agnes of West Molesey, widow [DW/PA/5/1580/13]
Ann of Wimbledon, widow [PRO; PCC 1639]
Godfrey of Swk St Olave; Swk St George, joiner [DW/PA/7/9 f.205; DW/PA/5/1616/62]
John of Headley [HRO; 1578 B44]
Thomas of Bramley [PRO; PCC Will 1503]
William of West Molesey [DW/PA/5/1576/81]
William of Wonersh, husbandman [DW/PA/7/7 f.326; DW/PA/5/1601/42] <Abs 585>
William of Wonersh, yeoman [DW/PA/7/9 f.148; DW/PA/5/1615/64] <Abs U206>
see also HAY
HAYHOLME
Thomas of Camberwell [DW/PA/7/1 f.57; 1487] <Abs 188>
HAYLER *see* HAILER
HAYNES (HAINE, HAINES, HAYN, HAYNE, HEYNES, HEYNYS)
Agnes of Wotton, widow [DW/PA/7/12 f.119; DW/PA/5/1632/49]
Alice of Chessington, widow [PRO; PCC Admon 1619]
Ann of Chessington, widow of William, esq. [PRO; PCC Will 1612]
George, alias George Radford of Newington [PRO; PCC Admon 1633]

HAYNES (HAINE,HAINES,HAYN,HAYNE,HEYNES,HEYNYS) [*continued*]

James of Swk St Saviour - Upper Ground, waterman [DW/PA/7/12 f,432; DW/PA/5/1637/58]

John, alias John Chapman of Farnham [DW/PA/7/1 f,60; 1487] <Abs 199>

John of Kingston, tailor [DW/PA/7/1 f,77; 1488] <Abs 251>

John of Ockley ? [DW/PA/5/1558/140]*

John of Swk St Margaret [DW/PA/7/4 f,88; 1534]

John of Wotton, yeoman [PRO; PCC Will 1610] <Abs, SAC v,24 p,63>

Matthew of Chessington [PRO; PCC Admon 1619]

Robert of Ockham, yeoman [DW/PA/5/1568/43]

Thomas of Guildford, innholder [PRO; PCC Will 1609] <Abs, SAC v,23 p,139>

William of Chessington, esq, [PRO; PCC Will 1611] <Abs, SAC v,35 pp,34-35>

William of Chessington [PRO; PCC Admon 1619]

William, alias William Coxe of Ockley, yeoman [DW/PA/7/10 f,261; DW/PA/5/1622/39]

William of Richmond [PRO; PCC Admon 1613]

William of Swk St Olave, citizen and pewterer [DW/PA/5/1561/66]

HAYSE *see* HAYES

HAYT *see* HATE

HAYTER

Henry of Kingston [PRO; PCC Will 1500; CCAL; 1500 f,56v]

William, *or* William Hayler of Godalming, yeoman [DW/PA/5/1607/55] <Abs U197>

HAYTHORNE *see* HEATHORN

HAYTHWELL *see* HATHWELL

HAYTON (HATON,HEIGHTON,HEYTON)

Beatrice of Merton [PRO; PCC Will 1433]

Joan of Croydon, widow [LPL; 96/1248; Will 1628]

John of Croydon, junior [PRO; PCC 1638]

John of Ewell, junior [DW/PA/7/1 f,66; 1487] <Abs 219>

John of Kingston, yeoman [DW/PA/7/4 f,175; 1536]

Richard of Kingston, gent, [PRO; PCC Will 1583]

Richard of Sutton [DW/PA/7/1 f,69; 1487] <Abs 226>

Thomas of Ewell, clerk [PRO; PCC Will 1396]

Thomas of Merton [LPL; Reg, Abp Chichele i f,423; Will 1431]

see also HATTON

HAYWARD (HAWARD,HAWARDE,HAWERD,HAYWARDE,HEWARD,HEYARDE,HEYWARD,HEYWARDE, HEYWOOD)

Alice of Woking - Goldworth [DW/PA/7/11 f,538; DW/PA/5/1629/45]

Edmund of London, citizen and apothecary [DW/PA/7/10 f,286; DW/PA/5/1623/58]

Elizabeth of Croydon, widow [LPL; 96/1225; Will 1643]

Francis of Newington [LPL; 98/1 f,37v; Will 1632]

Harry of Swk St Olave [DW/PA/7/4 f,235; 1538]

Henry of Limpsfield [DW/PA/5/1622/40]

Henry of Tandridge, gent, [PRO; PCC Will 1611] <Abs, SAC v,35 pp,35-36>

Joan of Farnham - Runfold, widow [DW/PA/5/1561/86]

Joan of Carshalton, widow [DW/PA/7/10 f,152; DW/PA/5/1619/58]

John of Egham, brickmaker, senior [DW/PA/7/13 f,181; DW/PA/5/1641/74]

John of Farnham, glazier [DW/PA/7/8 f,249; DW/PA/5/1613/54]

John of Kingston, husbandman [DW/PA/5/1568/26]

John of Mickleham [PRO; PCC 1648]

John of Oxted, husbandman [DW/PA/7/8 f,115; DW/PA/5/1610/68]

HAYWARD (HAWARD,HAWARDE,HAWERD,HAYWARDE,HEWARD,HEYARDE,HEYWARD,HEYWARDE, HEYWOOD) [*continued*]

John of Swk St Saviour, waterman [DW/PA/5/1571/45]
John of Tandridge, esq. [PRO; PCC 1631]
John of Warlingham, yeoman [DW/PA/7/13 f.374; 1644]
Juliana of Swk St Olave, widow [DW/PA/7/8 f.257; DW/PA/5/1611/57]
Mary of Caterham ? [DW/PA/7/8 f.166; DW/PA/5/1610/69]
Mary of Cobham, widow [PRO; PCC Admon 1632]
Michael of Blechingley, yeoman [DW/PA/7/7 f.465; DW/PA/5/1604/27] <Abs 878>
Michael of Croydon, brewer [LPL; 96/1223; 98/1 f.40v; Will 1632]
Michael of Woldingham [PRO; PCC Will 1544]
Michael of Woldingham; Tandridge; Oxted, yeoman [DW/PA/5/1599/31] <Abs U22>
Nicholas of Farnham - Runfold, husbandman [DW/PA/5/1557/29]
Richard of Ash [DW/PA/5/1580/65]
Richard of Bermondsey, leatherdresser [DW/PA/7/13 f.381; DW/PA/5/1645/22]
Richard of Oxted [PRO; PCC Will *and* PCC Admon 1608]
Richard of Tatsfield [PRO; PCC Will 1529]
Richard of Tatsfield, yeoman [PRO; PCC Will 1609] <Abs. SAC v.23 pp.146-147>
Richard of Woking, yeoman [DW/PA/5/1562/79]
Richard of Woldingham, yeoman, senior [DW/PA/7/12 f.242; DW/PA/5/1634/55]
Richard of Worplesdon [DW/PA/7/11 f.385; DW/PA/5/1626/66]
Robert of Frensham - Pitfold [DW/PA/5/1579/42]*
Robert of Frensham - Pitfold [PRO; PCC 1647]
Roger of Ash [PRO; PCC Admon 1636]
Samuel of Newington, parish clerk [LPL; 98/1 f.75r; Will 1636]
Sarah of Cobham, spinster [PRO; PCC Admon 1640]
Simon of Kingston - Surbiton, husbandman [DW/PA/5/1558/139]*
Susan of Farnham, widow [DW/PA/7/9 f.273; 1618]
Thomas of Cobham; Walton on Thames [PRO; PCC 1630] <Scroope 210>
Thomas of Egham, yeoman [DW/PA/5/1593/178]
Thomas of Farnham - Runfold, weaver [HRO; 1561 B90-91]
Thomas of Farnham - Wrecclesham, weaver [HRO; 1574 B94]
Thomas of Farnham - Moor Park [PRO; PCC 1649]
Thomas of Haslemere, trencher maker [HRO; 1619 AD52]
Thomas of Kingston, gent. [DW/PA/7/12 f.360; DW/PA/5/1636/55]
Thomas of Oxted [PRO; PCC Admon 1572]
Thomas of Oxted, brewer [PRO; PCC Will 1613]
Thomas of Swk St Olave [DW/PA/7/6 f.225; 1561]
Thomas of Tandridge [DW/PA/7/13 f.271; DW/PA/5/1643/46]
Thomas of Woking, yeoman [DW/PA/5/1562/67]
Thomas of Woldingham, yeoman [DW/PA/7/4 f.32; 1532 *or* 1533]
Thomas of Woldingham [PRO; PCC 1649]
Timothy of Swk St Olave [DW/PA/7/7 f.576; DW/PA/5/1606/44] <Abs 1075>
William of Chertsey, tilemaker [DW/PA/7/13 f.355; 1644]
William of Croydon, yeoman [LPL; 96/1224; 98/1 f.55v; Will 1634]
William of Egham, butcher [DW/PA/5/1624/58]
William of Frensham - Pitfold, yeoman [PRO; PCC Will 1618]
William of Frensham - Pitfold [PRO; PCC 1649]

HAYWARD (HAWARD,HAWARDE,HAWERD,HAYWARDE,HEWARD,HEYARDE,HEYWARD,HEYWARDE, HEYWOOD) [*continued*]

William of Haslemere; Farnhurst, Sussex; 'Tithing of Ambersome', Hampshire, bellowmaker [DW/PA/7/9 f,307; DW/PA/5/1619/63]

William of Oxted, yeoman [HRO; 1531 B9]

William of Woking, husbandman [DW/PA/5/1558/138]*

William of Woking [DW/PA/5/1571/28]

William of Woking, husbandman [DW/PA/5/1586/4]

William of Woking - Goldworth [DW/PA/7/11 f,511; DW/PA/5/1629/46]

William of Wonersh; Finchampstead, Berkshire [DW/PA/5/1605/45] <Abs U149>

see also HYWOOD

HAYWORTH (HEYWORTHE)

John of Deptford St Paul - Hatcham [PRO; PCC Will 1558]

HAZARD (HASSARD)

Ann of Mortlake, widow [PRO; PCC 1646]

Robert of Carshalton [PRO; PCC Admon 1624]

Robert of Carshalton [DW/PA/7/11 f,607; DW/PA/5/1630/49]

HEAD (HEADE,HED,HEDD,HEDDE,HEDE,HEEDE)

Edmund of Lingfield - Blockfield, yeo, [PRO; PCC Will 1620] <Soame 1158>

Francis of Swk St Saviour, labourer [DW/PA/7/13 f,427; DW/PA/5/1646/24]

George of ,,, [*but proved at* Guildford] [DW/PA/7/9 f,149;DW/PA/5/1615/60]

Harry of Ripley, husbandman [DW/PA/7/7 f,334; DW/PA/5/1601/46] <Abs 604>

Henry of Lingfield, collier [DW/PA/5/1587/42]

Henry of Lingfield, husbandman [DW/PA/7/9 f,241; DW/PA/5/1617/70]

Isabella of Swk St Margaret [CCAL; 1501 f,98r]

John of Woking [DW/PA/7/3 f,99; 1529]

Richard of Cobham [DW/PA/5/1563/119]

William of Woking, yeoman, senior [DW/PA/7/13 f,47; DW/PA/5/1639/76]

HEADIDGE (HEADIGE)

John of Egham, husbandman [DW/PA/7/12 f,95; DW/PA/5/1632/46]

Susanna of Egham, widow [HRO; 1637 B23]

HEADINGTON (HEDDINGTON)

John of Charlwood [PRO; PCC 1633]

HEALE (HELE)

Richard of ,,, [DW/PA/7/10 f,53; 1618]

Richard of Frimley; Egham [DW/PA/5/1557/4]

HEARTE *see* HART

HEATH (HEATHE,HEET,HETH,HETHE,HEYTHE)

Agnes of Bermondsey, widow of John [DW/PA/7/11 f,293; DW/PA/5/1626/65]

Agnes of Wonersh, widow [DW/PA/7/11 f,579; DW/PA/5/1630/50]

Alice of Reigate, widow [DW/PA/5/1578/11]

Bartholomew of Blechingley, shoemaker [DW/PA/5/1593/40]

Edmund of Lingfield, yeoman [DW/PA/7/13 f,160; DW/PA/5/1641/73]

Edward of Croydon [PRO; PCC Will 1595]

Edward of Reigate [DW/PA/5/1569/2]

Elizabeth of Limpsfield, widow [HRO; 1610 B38]

Elizabeth of Walton on Thames [DW/PA/7/12 f,334; DW/PA/5/1636/52]

Geoffrey of Banstead, husbandman [DW/PA/7/10 f,83; DW/PA/5/1615/33]

George of Coulsdon, yeoman [PRO; PCC Will 1619]

Henry of Woking, husbandman [DW/PA/7/13 f,101; DW/PA/5/1640/75]

James of Reigate, husbandman [DW/PA/7/7 f,384; DW/PA/5/1602/40] <Abs 711>

Joan of Nutfield [DW/PA/7/4 f,221; 1537]

Joan of Tandridge, widow [DW/PA/7/10 f,3; DW/PA/5/1616/63]

HEATH (HEATHE,HEET,HETH,HETHE,HEYTHE) [*continued*]

John of Beddington, husbandman [DW/PA/7/13 f.30; DW/PA/5/1640/66]
John of Bermondsey, gardener [DW/PA/7/13 f.130; DW/PA/5/1640/79]
John of Chertsey, baker [DW/PA/7/7 f.453; DW/PA/5/1603/77] <Abs 857>
John of Cobham, tailor [DW/PA/7/13 f.402; DW/PA/5/1645/27]
John of Dunsfold, husbandman [HRO; 1639 B38]
John of Epsom, widow [DW/PA/7/13 f.424; DW/PA/5/1646/29]
John of Horley [DW/PA/7/3 f.187; 1531]
John of Limpsfield [PRO; PCC Will 1491]
John of Limpsfield [DW/PA/7/2 f.191; 1517]
John of Limpsfield [PRO; PCC Will 1590]
John of Limpsfield, yeoman [DW/PA/7/8 f.21; DW/PA/5/1608/54]
John of Lingfield; Oxted [DW/PA/7/7 f.192; DW/PA/5/1598/38] <Abs 348>
John of Oxted [DW/PA/7/2 f.25; 1492]
John of Shalford, blacksmith [DW/PA/7/8 f.35; DW/PA/5/1609/89]
Joseph of Richmond [PRO; PCC Admon 1592]
Margaret of Caterham, widow [PRO; PCC Will 1628]
Margaret, alias Margaret Duglis of Lingfield, widow [DW/PA/7/13 f.474; DW/PA/5/1648/9]
Margaret, alias Margaret Fuller, alias Margaret Douglas of Lingfield, widow [PRO; PCC Admon 1648]
Margery of Guildford Holy Trinity, widow [DW/PA/7/7 f.215; DW/PA/5/1598/37] <Abs 383>
Nicholas of Chertsey, yeoman [DW/PA/7/5 f.117; 1539]
Richard of Coulsdon [PRO; PCC Will 1567]
Richard of Croydon, labourer [LPL; 96/1232; 98/1 f.55v; Will 1634]
Richard of Farleigh [PRO; PCC Will 1562 *and* PCC Admon 1563]
Richard of Reigate [PRO; PCC Will 1579]
Richard of Swk St Thomas [DW/PA/7/11 f.330; DW/PA/5/1625/114]
Richard of Weybridge [DW/PA/7/2 f.43; 1494]
Robert of Limpsfield, innholder [DW/PA/5/1576/22]
Robert of Merton [DW/PA/7/2 f.41; 1494]
Robert of Streatham [PRO; PCC Admon 1647]
Thomas of Coulsdon - Waddington; Coulsdon - Hooley [BM; Add.Ms 24,925 f.16r; 1544] <Abs 33>
Thomas *or* John of Dunsfold, husbandman [HRO; 1639 B38]
Thomas of Frensham, yeoman [DW/PA/7/8 f.139; DW/PA/5/1610/70]
Thomas of Guildford St Mary [DW/PA/5/1550/49]
Thomas of Limpsfield [PRO; PCC 1646]
Thomas of Morden, yeoman [DW/PA/7/12 f.407; DW/PA/5/1637/56]
Thomas of Swk St Saviour - Upper Ground, Paris Garden, waterman [DW/PA/5/1562/54]
Thomas of Swk St Saviour, butcher [DW/PA/7/13 f.314; DW/PA/5/1643/51]
William of Addington [DW/PA/5/1569/72]
William of Caterham, yeoman [PRO; PCC Will *and* Admon 1617]
William of Chobham, gent. [PRO; PCC Will 1569]
William of Dunsfold, tailor [HRO; 1628 B34]
William of Frensham [PRO; PCC Admon 1647]
William of Caterham; Warlingham; Coulsdon, yeoman [DW/PA/7/9 f.245; 1617]
William of Horley [DW/PA/7/1 f.79; 1488] <Abs 259>
William of Tandridge, yeoman [DW/PA/7/10 f.2; DW/PA/5/1617/71]
see also ATHEATH

HEATHER (HETHER)
George of Dorking, yeoman [DW/PA/5/1593/53]
George of Dorking; Leatherhead, yeoman [DW/PA/7/10 f.189; DW/PA/5/1620/60]
Joan of Worplesdon, widow [DW/PA/5/1581/46]
John of Abinger, husbandman [DW/PA/7/12 f.234; DW/PA/5/1634/54]
John of Worplesdon, yeoman [HRO; 1624 B29]
John of Worplesdon, yeoman [DW/PA/7/13 f.380; 1644] [*and*] [LBLAD; Surrey Deeds 1/2285; 1641]
Thomas of Dorking [DW/PA/5/1593/19]
William of Dorking [DW/PA/7/5 f.118; 1539]
William of Dorking, yeoman [DW/PA/7/9 f.163; DW/PA/5/1616/64]
William of Dorking [PRO; PCC Will 1623]
William *or* William Heathorne of Farnham - Tilford, yeoman [DW/PA/7/13 f.394; DW/PA/5/1645/23]
HEATHERLEY (HEATHERLY,HETHERLEY)
Helen of Mortlake, widow [PRO; PCC Will 1600]
John of Swk St George, senior [DW/PA/7/10 f.199; DW/PA/5/1621/55]
HEATHFIELD (HEATHFEILD,HEITHFEILD)
Anthony of Reigate, yeoman [DW/PA/7/13 f.248; DW/PA/5/1641/67]
Edmund of Betchworth, yeoman [DW/PA/7/7 f.579; DW/PA/5/1606/43] <Abs 1081>
Edmund of Betchworth - Brockham, mason [DW/PA/7/13 f.21;DW/PA/5/1640/64]
John of Headley; Betchworth, yeoman [DW/PA/7/9 f.336; DW/PA/5/1620/61]
Nicholas of Reigate [PRO; PCC Admon 1649]
Owen of Worplesdon, husbandman [DW/PA/7/12 f.247; DW/PA/5/1635/42]
Robert of Betchworth, carpenter [DW/PA/7/13 f.30; DW/PA/5/1639/74]
William of Walton on Thames [DW/PA/7/7 f.300; DW/PA/5/1600/16] <Abs 537>
HEATHORN (HATHORNE,HAYTHORNE,HEATHORNE)
Henry of Seale [HRO; 1636 B10]
Hugh of Farnham - Tilford, husbandman [DW/PA/5/1582/93]
James of Bentley, Hampshire, yeoman [DW/PA/7/10 f.100; DW/PA/5/1621/54]
Joan of Camberwell, widow [DW/PA/7/11 f.372; DW/PA/5/1626/64]
William *or* William Heather of Farnham - Tilford, yeoman [DW/PA/7/13 f.394; DW/PA/5/1645/23]
HEATS
James of Swk St George [DW/PA/7/4 f.1; 1532]
HEAVER (HEVER)
Margaret of Mitcham, widow [DW/PA/5/1571/90]
Peter of .. [DW/PA/7/10 f.97; DW/PA/5/1619/59]
Robert of Surrey [GL; Archdeaconry Court of London Will 1603]
William of Horley [DW/PA/7/7 f.366; DW/PA/5/1602/42] <Abs 671>
HEBB
Roger of Weybridge, shoemaker [DW/PA/7/10 f.108; DW/PA/5/1619/61]
HEBBERD,HEBERT *see* HUBBARD
HEBSON
Joan of Swk St Mary Magdalen; St Leonard Eastcheap, London, widow [CCAL; 1503 f.209r]
Richard of Battersea, yeoman [DW/PA/7/9 f.50; DW/PA/5/1614/56]
HECHISTE *see* HITCHHURST
HEDD *see* HEAD
HEDDINGTON *see* HEADINGTON
HEDE *see* HEAD

HEDGE (HEDGES)
... of ... [*see memo, of will in* DW/PA/5/1563/6]
Gillian of Windlesham, widow [HRO; 1609 B39]
Henry of Mitcham, yeoman [DW/PA/7/3 f.171; 1531]
Henry of Windlesham - Bagshot; Chobham, yeoman [DW/PA/7/7 f.83; 1596] <Abs 151>
John of Mitcham, yeoman, senior [BM; Add.Ms 24,925 f.12v; 1543] <Abs 22>
John of Mitcham; Merstham; Epsom, esq. [PRO; PCC Will 1620] <Soame 607>
Thomas of Swk St Saviour, butcher [DW/PA/7/12 f.302; DW/PA/5/1635/49]
HEDGEMAN (HEGEMAN)
Robert of Kingston [HRO; Reg. Wyk 2 p.159; 1377]
HEDGER (HEDGAR)
Harry of Thursley [HRO; 1561 B92-93]
Richard of Thursley, husbandman [HRO; 1571 B40]
Thomas of Ripley, yeoman [DW/PA/7/13 f.209; DW/PA/5/1642/40]
William of Horley [DW/PA/7/7 f.365; DW/PA/5/1602/41] <Abs 668>
HEDGES *see* HEDGE
HEDLYE
Christopher of Camberwell - Dulwich, yeoman [PRO; PCC Will 1624]
HEDON *see* HAYDON
HEEDE *see* HEAD
HEETH *see* HEATH
HEGEMAN *see* HEDGEMAN
HEIGHTON *see* HAYTON
HEITHFEILD *see* HEATHFIELD
HELE *see* HEALE
HELLIARD *see* HILLIARD
HELLIS *see* ELLIS
HELLONS (HELLOUS)
Agnes of Walton on Thames, widow of John [DW/PA/5/1558/142]*
Ann of Walton on Thames [DW/PA/5/1558/141]*
John of Walton on Thames, yeoman [DW/PA/5/1558/143]*
John of Walton on Thames, yeoman [HRO; 1592 B27]
HELLOWELL
Randall of Alfold, yeoman [DW/PA/7/8 f.409; DW/PA/5/1614/61]
HELLY (HELIE)
Joan of Swk St Saviour, widow [DW/PA/7/7 f.462; DW/PA/5/1603/78] <Abs 872>
William of Swk St Saviour, merchant tailor [DW/PA/7/7 f.431; DW/PA/5/1603/79] <Abs 814>
HELLYER
William of Thursley, husbandman [HRO; 1635 AD53]
HELMERAYE
William of Richmond [DW/PA/7/4 f.217; 1537]
HELYT (ELETES)
William of Epsom [DW/PA/5/1561/9]
see also ELLIOTT
HEMANSON *see* HARMANSON
HEMINGWAY (HEMINGWAYE, HEMYNGWAY, HEMYNGWAYE)
John of Cobham, gent. [PRO; PCC Will 1582]
Thomas of Cobham, senior [PRO; PCC Admon 1598]
Thomas of Cobham; Brentford, Middlesex; St Margaret Westminster, Middlesex, innholder [DW/PA/7/8 f.237; DW/PA/5/1613/63] [*and*] [LBLAD; Surrey Deeds 1/2847; 1613]

HEMSLEY

Michael of Swk St George, citizen and saddler [DW/PA/7/13 f.430; DW/PA/5/1646/26]

Richard of Newington [LPL; 96/1250; Will 1625]

HEMYNGWAY, HEMYNGWAYE *see* HEMINGWAY

HENDLE, HENDLEY *see* HENLEY

HENDON (HENDYN)

Nicholas of Frensham [DW/PA/7/3 f.109; 1529]

HENDRY (HENDRE)

Robert of Egham [PRO; PCC Admon 1617]

HENDYN *see* HENDON

HENEAGE

Thomas of Battersea [PRO; PCC 1641]

HENLEY (HENDLE, HENDLEY)

Henry of Camberwell, husbandman [DW/PA/5/1570/27B]

John of Camberwell - Peckham [DW/PA/7/1 f.23; 1485] <Abs 75>

John of Camberwell - Peckham [HRO; Reg. Fox 3 p.66; 1515]

Richard of Rotherhithe [PRO; PCC Will 1505]

Thomas of Camberwell - Dulwich [BM; Add.Ms 24,925 f.14v; 1544] <Abs 30>

Thomas of Swk St Olave, brewer [DW/PA/5/1563/118]

William of Camberwell [PRO; PCC Admon 1575]

William of Croydon [PRO; PCC Admon 1586]

HENNE

John of Newdigate, husbandman [DW/PA/5/1582/45]

William of Dorking, yeoman [PRO; PCC Will 1571]

HENNING

Jeremy of Bermondsey, farrier [DW/PA/7/9 f.292; 1618]

HENSBURY (HENSEBERYE)

Peter of Swk St Olave, locksmith [DW/PA/5/1570/16]

HENSHAW

Henry of Dorking [PRO; PCC 1635]

HENSLOW (HENSLOWE)

Ann of Camberwell - Dulwich, widow of Philip, esq. [DW/PA/7/10 f.37; DW/PA/5/1617/72] [*and*] [PRO; PCC Will 1617]

Phillip of Swk St Saviour, esq. [DW/PA/7/9 f.132; DW/PA/5/1615/61]

William of Lambeth [PRO; PCC Admon 1624]

HENSON

Tristram of Farnham, shearman [DW/PA/5/1558/144]

HENWOOD

John of Putney [LPL; 98/1 f.66r; Will 1635]

Richard of Barnes, yeoman [LPL; 96/1254; 98/1 f.101r; Will 1639]

HERALD

John of Lambeth, esq. [PRO; PCC Will 1416]

HERCEY, HERCY *see* HERSEY

HERD

Nicholas, alias Nicholas Hord of Swk St Olave; Sudbury, Derbyshire; St Gabriel Fenchurch, London; Barking, Essex; Wimbledon; Newington, innholder [DW/PA/7/4 f.233; 1538]

HERDWEN *see* HARDWYN

HERENDEN

Helen of Streatham, widow [PRO; PCC 1633]

Millicent of Long Ditton - Tolworth, widow [PRO; PCC Will 1581]

HERINGMAN *see* HERRINGMAN

HERITAGE *see* HERRITAGE

HERMAN
  Henry of Stoke next Guildford, rector [HRO; Reg, Edn 2 p,17; 1348]
HERON (HERNE)
  Ann of Croydon, gent, [PRO; PCC Will 1608] <Abs, SAC v,12 p,104>
  Elizabeth, alias Elizabeth Herne of Croydon, widow [PRO; PCC Will 1581]
  John of Croydon [PRO; PCC Will 1515]
  John of Tooting Graveney, mealman [BM; Add,Ms 24,925 f,3r; 1544] <Abs 1>
  (Dame) Mary of Croydon, widow of (Sir) Nicholas, knight [PRO; PCC Will 1580]
  (Sir) Nicholas of Croydon, knight [PRO; PCC Will 1568]
  Poynings of Croydon, esq, [PRO; PCC Will 1596]
  Thomas of Croydon, esq, [PRO; PCC Will 1544]
  William of Croydon - Addiscombe, esq, [PRO; PCC Will 1562]
  William of Tooting Graveney, husbandman [DW/PA/5/1571/95]
HERRETT (HERRET)
  Thomas of Camberwell [DW/PA/7/9 f,327; DW/PA/5/1619/62] <Abs U238>
  Thomas of Camberwell [DW/PA/7/11 f,544; DW/PA/5/1629/47]
HERRIARD
  Andrew of Surrey, citizen and tailor [GL; Archdeaconry Court of London Will 1416]
HERRINGMAN (HERINGMAN,HERYNGMAN)
  Bartholomew of Kingston - Surbiton, yeoman [DW/PA/7/7 f,1; DW/PA/5/1595/47] <Abs 1>
  Henry of Carshalton, esq, [PRO; PCC Admon 1631]
  John of Carshalton [PRO; PCC Admon 1645]
  John of Morden [PRO; PCC Will 1571]
  Thomas of Morden, yeoman [DW/PA/5/1558/145]
HERRITAGE
  Henry of ... [DW/PA/7/13 f,355; 1644]
HERRYSON *see* HARRISON
HERSEY (HERCEY,HERCY)
  Samuel of Newington, yeoman [PRO; PCC 1630] <Scroope 1243>
  Thomas of Chiddingfold [DW/PA/7/11 f,389; DW/PA/5/1626/72]
HERSHAM
  Thomas of Walton on Thames, weaver [DW/PA/7/12 f,378; 1637]
HERST *see* HURST
HERT *see* HART
HERTCOMBE
  John of Kingston, gent, [PRO; PCC Will 1488] <Abs SAC v,8 pp,110-111 and v,29 p,107>
HERTE *see* HART
HESLOPP
  Alexander of Croydon [PRO; PCC 1635]
  Oliver of Egham, husbandman [DW/PA/7/8 f,219; DW/PA/5/1612/74]
HETH,HETHE *see* HEATH
HETHER *see* HEATHER
HETHERLEY,HETHERLY *see* HEATHERLEY
HETHERSALL (HOTHERSALL)
  George of Mitcham, yeoman [DW/PA/7/9 f,5; DW/PA/5/1615/62]
  Thomas of Swk St Olave, brewers clerk [DW/PA/7/13 f,109; DW/PA/5/1640/77]
HEVET *see* HEWETT
HEVER *see* HEAVER
HEWARD *see* HAYWARD
HEWAT,HEWATT *see* HEWETT

HEWES *see* HUGHES
HEWET *see* HEWETT
HEWETSON (HEWETTSON,HEWYTSON)
  Christopher of Swk St Saviour, victualler [DW/PA/5/1602/44] <Abs U50>
  Robert of Kingston [PRO; PCC Will 1526]
HEWETT (HEWAT,HEWATT,HEWET,HEWYTT,HUAT,HUET,HUETT)
  Audrey of Newington - Walworth, widow [PRO; PCC Will 1627]
  Edmund of Dunsfold, yeoman [DW/PA/7/7 f,20; DW/PA/5/1595/51] <Abs 43>
  Elizabeth of Farnham, widow [DW/PA/7/10 f,3; DW/PA/5/1616/76]
  Elizabeth of Mitcham, widow [DW/PA/7/10 f,106; DW/PA/5/1621/57]
  Elizabeth of Wonersh, widow [DW/PA/7/10 f,170; DW/PA/5/1621/56]
  Henry of Horley [DW/PA/7/5 f,89; 1539]
  Henry of Horley, senior [DW/PA/7/7 f,50; DW/PA/5/1595/48] <Abs 94>
  Isabel of Chessington, widow [DW/PA/5/1586/6]
  John of Beddington - Wallington, citizen and cooper [GL; Commissary Court of London Will 1466]
  John of Cranleigh [? HRO; 1561]
  John of Farnham, yeoman [DW/PA/5/1587/49]
  John of Horne, husbandman [DW/PA/7/8 f,358; DW/PA/5/1612/75]
  John of Kingston, waterman [DW/PA/7/9 f,89; DW/PA/5/1615/63]
  John of Mitcham; Epsom, yeoman [DW/PA/7/7 f,577; DW/PA/5/1606/42] <Abs 1078>
  John of Newington - Walworth, citizen and grocer [PRO; PCC Will 1624]
  John of Pirbright, weaver [HRO; 1620 B19]
  Magdalen of Clapham [DW/PA/5/1569/68]
  Margaret of Farnham [HRO; 1639 B40]
  Margery of Kingston, widow [DW/PA/7/10 f,42; 1618]
  Nicholas of Dunsfold [DW/PA/7/12 f,144; DW/PA/5/1633/65]
  Nicholas of Horley, yeoman [DW/PA/5/1571/66]
  Ralph of Swk St Margaret [DW/PA/7/4 f,107; 1535]
  Robert of Bramley, husbandman [DW/PA/7/10 f,202; DW/PA/5/1620/62]
  Robert of Esher [DW/PA/5/1571/89]
  Robert of Mitcham, yeoman [DW/PA/7/12 f,467; DW/PA/5/1638/64]
  Robert of Shalford, husbandman, senior [DW/PA/5/1576/59]
  Samuel of Chobham, husbandman [HRO; 1614 B36]
  Stephen of Wonersh, clothier [DW/PA/7/13 f,28; DW/PA/5/1639/73]
  Thomas of Bramley, husbandman [DW/PA/7/12 f,443; DW/PA/5/1639/65]
  Thomas of Horley [DW/PA/7/3 f,207; 1532]
  Thomas of Wonersh [DW/PA/7/6 f,279; 1560]
  Thomas of Wonersh, yeoman [DW/PA/7/12 f,309; DW/PA/5/1635/52]
  Walter of Worplesdon [DW/PA/7/10 f,285; DW/PA/5/1623/57]
  William of Surrey etc,, citizen and clothworker [PRO; PCC Will 1599]
  William of Bramley, beer brewer [PRO; PCC Will 1595]
  William of Peper Harow [HRO; 1632 AD55]
  William of Swk St Olave; Chigwell, Essex, porter of the Bridge House [DW/PA/5/1550/49]
HEWETTSON *see* HEWETSON
HEWSE *see* HUGHES
HEWSTICE
  Elizabeth of Newington, widow [LPL; 96/1263; 98/1 f,70r; Will 1635]
HEWYTSON *see* HEWETSON
HEWYTT *see* HEWETT
HEXSTALL
  Henry of Blechingley [PRO; PCC Will 1492]

HEYARDE *see* HAYWARD
HEYBORNE *see* HAYBORNE
HEYDON *see* HAYDON
HEYES *see* HAYES
HEYNES,HEYNYS *see* HAYNES
HEYTHE *see* HEATH
HEYTON *see* HAYTON
HEYWARD,HEYWOOD *see* HAYWARD
HEYWORTHE *see* HAYWORTH
HIBBERD *see* HUBBARD
HICHEHURST *see* HITCHHURST
HICKES *see* HICKS
HICKMAN
Dixy of Kew [PRO; PCC Admon 1631]
Edward of Kingston [PRO; PCC Admon 1603]
HICKS (HICKES,HIX)
Francis of Bermondsey, shipwright [DW/PA/7/13 f,119; DW/PA/5/1641/70]
Thomas of Bermondsey [PRO; PCC Admon 1625]
Thomas of Morden [PRO; PCC 1634]
HIDE *see* HYDE
HIGGINS
Walter of Swk St Olave, mariner [DW/PA/7/12 f,273; DW/PA/5/1635/45]
HIGHAM
Jane of Wandsworth, widow [DW/PA/7/8 f,143; DW/PA/5/1611/58]
Robert of Wotton, parson [DW/PA/7/8 f,374; DW/PA/5/1612/76]
HIGHLORD
Judith, alias Judith Parham, alias Judith Lardge of Camberwell [PRO; PCC Admon 1627]
HIL *see* HILL
HILDER (HILDAR,HYLDER)
John of Great Bookham, shearman, junior [DW/PA/5/1588/35]
John of Great Bookham [DW/PA/7/4 f,178; 1536]
John of Great Bookham [DW/PA/7/12 f,370; DW/PA/5/1627/57]
John, alias John Eales of Ewell [PRO; PCC Admon 1645]
William, alias William Eles of Ashtead, husbandman [DW/PA/7/9 f,261; DW/PA/5/1617/73]
Zachary of Wonersh [PRO; PCC 1636]
HILL (atte HILLE,HIL,HILLE,HILLES,HILLS,HYLL,HYLLES,HYLLS)
Agnes of Bridewell, London; St Bride, London; Swk; Croydon; Writtle, Essex [GL; Commissary Court of London Will 1589]
Agnes of Swk St George [DW/PA/5/1582/88]
Alexander of Bermondsey [BM; Add,Ms 24,925 f,3v; 1544] <Abs 3>
Ann of Battersea, widow [DW/PA/7/13 f,72; DW/PA/5/1641/68]
Ann of Swk St Saviour, widow [DW/PA/5/1587/44]
Bernard of Kingston [PRO; PCC Will 1590]
Dennis of Bermondsey, whitster [DW/PA/5/1571/4]
Edmund of Croydon, citizen and woodmonger [PRO; PCC Will 1588]
Edmund of Shere [DW/PA/7/2 f,189; 1523]
Elizabeth of Guildford, widow [DW/PA/7/10 f,88; DW/PA/5/1615/36]
Elizabeth of Pyrford, widow [PRO; PCC 1640]
Elizabeth of Shalford [DW/PA/5/1569/9]
Elizabeth of Swk St Thomas, widow [DW/PA/5/1617/55] <Abs U216>
Elizeus of Kingston [PRO; PCC Admon 1620]
Frances of Swk St Thomas, widow [DW/PA/7/9 f,159; DW/PA/5/1616/65]

HILL (atte HILLE,HIL,HILLE,HILLES,HILLS,HYLL,HYLLES,HYLLS) [*continued*]
Geoffrey of Kingston, grocer [PRO; PCC Will 1615]
George of Kingston [PRO; PCC 1634]
Grace of Swk St Olave, widow [DW/PA/7/11 f,256; DW/PA/5/1625/115]
Harry of Ewhurst [DW/PA/5/1557/78]
Joan of Ewhurst [HRO; 1587 B45]
Joan of Swk St Olave, widow [DW/PA/5/1605/48] <Abs U151>
John of Surrey, citizen and fishmonger [GL; Commissary Court of London Will 1525]
John of Banstead [DW/PA/7/2 f,23; 1492]
John of Banstead [DW/PA/7/5 f,190; 1540]
John of Battersea [PRO; PCC Will 1550]
John of Betchworth [DW/PA/5/1584/3]*
John of Chiddingfold [PRO; PCC Will 1455]
(Sir) John of Thames Ditton, knight [PRO; PCC Will 1612]
John of Dunsfold, yeoman [DW/PA/7/13 f,198; DW/PA/5/1641/79]
John of Epsom, junior [DW/PA/7/1 f,68; 1487] <Abs 225>
John of Farnham [DW/PA/7/1 f,91; 1489] <Abs 307>
John of Guildford Holy Trin,[DW/PA/7/7 f,327; DW/PA/5/1601/47] <Abs 586>
John of Kingston, yeoman [PRO; PCC Will 1587]
John of Lambeth - Lambeth Marsh, citizen and skinner [PRO; PCC Will 1590]
John of Mitcham, tailor [DW/PA/7/9 f,152; DW/PA/5/1615/65]
John of Newington [PRO; PCC Will 1579]
John of Richmond [DW/PA/7/3 f,160; 1530]
John of Shere, husbandman [DW/PA/7/9 f,94; DW/PA/5/1616/66]
John of Swk St George [DW/PA/7/9 f,17; DW/PA/5/1616/67]
John of Streatham, husbandman [DW/PA/7/10 f,50; 1618]
Katherine of Dorking [PRO; PCC Will 1596]
Katherine of Dorking, widow and gent, [DW/PA/7/7 f,61; DW/PA/5/1596/29] <Abs 116>
Katherine of Kingston, widow [HRO; 1598 AD34]
Katherine of Swk St Olave - Stone Lane, widow of Thomas [DW/PA/7/7 f,413; DW/PA/5/1605/81] <Abs 768>
Lawrence of Swk St Olave; Banstead; Kingston, cordwainer [DW/PA/7/9 f,174; DW/PA/5/1616/68]
Margaret of Ewhurst, widow [DW/PA/5/1561/87]
Margery of Swk St Olave, widow [DW/PA/7/9 f,225; DW/PA/5/1617/74]
Nicholas of Ewhurst, husbandman [HRO; 1567 B51-52]
Nicholas of Horley - Horleyland [PRO; PCC Admon 1636]
Oliver of Wotton [DW/PA/5/1575/36]
Peter of Swk St Olave, joiner [DW/PA/7/11 f,249; DW/PA/5/1625/116]
Ralph of Ewhurst, yeoman [DW/PA/7/12 f,39; DW/PA/5/1631/56]
Richard of Camberwell - Peckham [PRO; PCC Will 1550]
Richard of Ewhurst, yeoman [DW/PA/5/1569/42]
Richard of Ewhurst, yeoman [DW/PA/5/1570/38]
Richard of West Horsley, weaver [DW/PA/7/10 f,272; DW/PA/5/1622/42]
Richard, alias Richard Atwater of Kingston, shoemaker [DW/PA/5/1605/4] <Abs U128>
Robert of Addington; Nutfield [DW/PA/7/7 f,636; DW/PA/5/1608/57] <Abs 1190>
Robert of Lingfield; Malden, yeoman [DW/PA/7/9 f,18; DW/PA/5/1616/69]
Robert of Nutfield [DW/PA/5/1580/42]
Robert of Swk St Saviour, citizen and merchant tailor [DW/PA/5/1568/23]

HILL (atte HILLE,HIL,HILLE,HILLES,HILLS,HYLL,HYLLES,HYLLS) [*continued*]
Roger of Streatham [PRO; PCC 1636]
Simon of Swk St Saviour, carpenter [DW/PA/7/12 f,406; DW/PA/5/1637/55]
Thomas of Bermondsey [DW/PA/5/1578/101]
Thomas of Betchworth, husbandman [DW/PA/7/6 f,131; DW/PA/5/1559/131]
Thomas of Camberwell [PRO; PCC Admon 1567]
Thomas of Croydon - Waddon [PRO; PCC Admon 1633]
Thomas of Ewhurst, yeoman [DW/PA/5/1558/157]*
Thomas of Ewhurst [DW/PA/5/1582/23]
Thomas of Lingfield - Starborough Castle [PRO; PCC Will 1601]
Thomas of Swk St George, tunman [DW/PA/7/11 f,36; 1623]
Thomas of Swk St George [DW/PA/7/10 f,283; 1623]
Thomas of Swk St Olave, citizen and armourer [DW/PA/7/7 f,435; DW/PA/5/1603/82] <Abs 823>
Walter of Ewhurst [DW/PA/5/1561/26]*
William of Dorking, yeoman [DW/PA/7/11 f,465; DW/PA/5/1628/53]
William of Epsom; Long Ditton; Banstead [DW/PA/7/4 f,60; 1533]
William of Guildford [PRO; PCC 1645]
William of Seale, husbandman, senior [DW/PA/5/1640/82] <Abs U259>
William of Shere [PRO; PCC Will 1558]
see also ATHILL [*Some early entries are confused with Hull and Athull.*]
HILLAR,HILLARE *see* HILLER
HILLARY (HILLARIE)
Elizabeth of Battersea [PRO; PCC Will 1592]
Sebastian of Battersea [PRO; PCC Will 1544]
Thomas of Battersea, gent. [PRO; PCC Will 1581]
HILLE *see* HILL
HILLER (HILLAR,HYLDE,HYLLAR,HYLLER)
Alice of Ash, widow of Richard Hiller and of Richard Bradston [DW/PA/7/2 f,14; 1491]
Alice of Horsell, widow [DW/PA/5/1555/75]
Ann of Albury [DW/PA/7/1 f,90; 1489] <Abs 303>
Elizabeth of Shere [PRO; PCC Admon 1649]
Ellen of Beddington, widow [DW/PA/7/8 f,204; DW/PA/5/1611/59]
John of Beddington, yeoman, junior [DW/PA/7/13 f,30; DW/PA/5/1640/67]
John of Chobham [DW/PA/7/6 f,105; DW/PA/5/1559/74]
John of Cobham, husbandman [DW/PA/7/11 f,506; DW/PA/5/1629/48]
John of Guildford [PRO; PCC Admon 1590]
John of Horsell - Sidewood, husb., jun. [DW/PA/7/1 f,20; 1485] <Abs 67>
John of Pyrford, yeoman [DW/PA/7/8 f,203; DW/PA/5/1611/60]
John of Ripley [DW/PA/7/3 f,98; 1529]
John of Shere [DW/PA/7/1 f,82; 1488] <Abs 271>
Matthew of Wandsworth [PRO; PCC Admon 1638]
Nicholas of Beddington [PRO; PCC 1638]
Nicholas of Chobham, yeoman [DW/PA/5/1580/66]
Richard of Albury, husbandman [HRO; 1583 AD35]
Richard of Chobham, yeoman, senior [DW/PA/7/1 f,12; 1485] <Abs 39>
Richard of Chobham; Horsell, yeoman [DW/PA/7/4 f,22; 1532]
Richard of Chobham, yeoman [DW/PA/5/1583/1]
Robert of Chipstead; Beddington, yeoman, senior [DW/PA/7/7 f,449; DW/PA/5/1603/83] <Abs 852>
Thomas of Beddington [DW/PA/7/7 f,106; DW/PA/5/1596/30] <Abs 191>
Thomas of West Horsley [DW/PA/5/1558/158]*
Thomas of Thursley [DW/PA/7/3 f,121; 1529]

HILLER (HILLAR,HYLDE,HYLLAR,HYLLER) [*continued*]
  William of Ash [DW/PA/7/5 f,147; 1540]
  William of Horsell [DW/PA/7/4 f,127; 1535]
  William of Horsell; Bisley [DW/PA/7/5 f,111; 1539]
HILLES *see* HILL
HILLIARD (HELLIARD)
  Robert of Bermondsey [PRO; PCC Admon 1641]
  William of Shere ? [DW/PA/7/7 f,633; DW/PA/5/1608/56] <Abs 1185>
HILTON (HILLTON)
  Edward of Putney, sailor in Ship *New Years Gift* [PRO; PCC Will 1616]
  John of Farnham - Dippenhall, yeoman [DW/PA/7/11 f,310; DW/PA/5/1626/67]
  Margery of Farnham, widow [DW/PA/7/12 f,114; DW/PA/5/1632/48]
HIND (HINDE,HYNDE)
  Augustine of Surrey [PRO; PCC Will 1554]
  Augustine of Richmond [PRO; PCC Will 1562]
  Edward of Mortlake, gent, [PRO; PCC Will 1602]
  Francis of Swk St Saviour, victualler [DW/PA/7/10 f,232; DW/PA/5/1621/58]
  Thomas of Chertsey, husbandman [DW/PA/7/7 f,78; 1596] <Abs 143>
  William of Lambeth - Kennington, esq, [PRO; PCC Admon 1649]
  William of Swk St Olave [DW/PA/7/7 f,430; DW/PA/5/1603/84] <Abs 810>
HINE (HYN)
  John of Farnham [PRO; PCC 1645]
  (Sir) Walter of Shere, knight] [DW/PA/7/1 f,55; 1487] <Abs 184>
HINKLEY (HINCKLEY)
  Robert of Kingston - Ham Hatch [PRO; PCC Admon 1646]
HINSLEY (HYNSLEY)
  Joan of Swk St Olave, widow [DW/PA/5/1575/3]
  Thomas of London, citizen and wax chandler [DW/PA/5/1575/47]
HINTON (HINTSON)
  Griffith of Swk St Saviour, waterman [DW/PA/7/13 f,193; DW/PA/5/1641/76]
  Henry of Camberwell, bachelor [PRO; PCC Admon 1616]
  Mary of Limpsfield, spinster [PRO; PCC Admon 1642]
  Sybil of Walton [PRO; PCC Admon 1642]
HIPKIN (HIPKYN)
  James of Cobham, husbandman [DW/PA/7/7 f,346; DW/PA/5/1601/48] <Abs 634>
  Robert of Cobham, labourer [DW/PA/7/8 f,399; DW/PA/5/1612/77]
HIPWELL
  Robert of Newington [LPL; 98/1 f,110v; Will 1638]
HIRE (HYER)
  George of Kingston, citizen and fishmonger [PRO; PCC 1635]
HITCHCOCK (EYCHCOKE,HISCHKOKE,HITCHCOK,HITCHCOX,HYCCECOKE,HYCHCOKE,
    HYCHECOKE,HYTCHECOCKE)
  ... of Farnham - Tilford, husbandman [DW/PA/5/1550/27]
  Ann of Farnham - Hale, widow [HRO; 1549 B59]
  Ann of Lambeth [PRO; PCC Will 1601] <Abs, SAC v,10 p,301>
  Francis of West Horsley [PRO; PCC Will 1568]
  Joan of Farnham - Tilford, widow [DW/PA/5/1555/25]
  John of Frensham, yeoman [DW/PA/5/1569/43]
  Richard of Farnham - Runfold, husbandman [DW/PA/5/1578/52]
  Robert of Farnham [DW/PA/7/3 f,117; 1529]
  Simon of Rotherhithe [PRO; PCC 1639]
  Thomas of Woldingham, carpenter [DW/PA/7/7 f,428; 1603] <Abs 803>
  William of Farnham - Tilford, husbandman [*in* DW/PA/5/1558/76]
  William of Horley [PRO; PCC 1632]

HITCHHURST (HECHISTE,HICHEHURST,HITCHEHURST,HITCHES,HITCHIS,HUTCHES,
HUTCHEST,HYCHESST,HYCHEST,HYCHURST,HYCHURSTE
George of Kingston [PRO; PCC 1640]
Humphrey of Ockham; East Horsley, husbandman [DW/PA/7/6 f.191; DW/PA/5/1559/203]
James of Walton on Thames; Cobham, husbandman [DW/PA/7/8 f.201; DW/PA/5/1611/61]
Jane of ... [DW/PA/7/13 f.377; 1644]
Jenkin of Newdigate [DW/PA/5/1547/7]
John of Cobham [DW/PA/7/4 f.8; 1532]
John of Cranleigh; Rudgwick, Sussex, husbandman [DW/PA/7/8 f.111; DW/PA/5/1610/71]
John of Kingston, cordwainer [DW/PA/7/10 f.129; DW/PA/5/1620/63]
John of Newdigate; Slaugham, Sussex [DW/PA/7/1 f.10; 1485] <Abs 32>
John of Woking, husbandman [DW/PA/7/13 f.363; 1644]
Mabel of Kingston, widow [DW/PA/7/11 f.141; DW/PA/5/1624/61]
Thomas of Cobham [DW/PA/7/2 f.155; 1521]
Thomas of Kingston, yeoman [DW/PA/7/7 f.244; DW/PA/5/1599/36] <Abs 431>
Thomas of Ripley [DW/PA/7/11 f.383; DW/PA/5/1626/68]
William of Cobham, husbandman [DW/PA/7/5 f.52; 1538] <Abs 24>

HITCHIN (HYTCHIN)
Agnes of Ewell, widow [DW/PA/7/9 f.78; DW/PA/5/1614/57]
John of Ewell [DW/PA/7/7 f.262; DW/PA/5/1599/32] <Abs 467>
John of Ewell [PRO; PCC Will 1599]

HITCHIS *see* HITCHHURST

HIWOOD *see* HYWOOD

HIX *see* HICKS

HOADE
William of Oxted [DW/PA/7/11 f.204; DW/PA/5/1625/117]

HOALTON
William rector of Oxted and Gatton; Tandridge; Limpsfield [DW/PA/7/7 f.237; DW/PA/5/1598/40] <Abs 417>

HOARD (HORD,HORDE,HORDES,HOURDE)
Alan of Ewell, gent. [PRO; PCC Will 1554] <Abs SAC v.28 pp.68-69>
Ann of Richmond, spinster [PRO; PCC Will 1621]
Arthur of Ewell; Fetcham; Berkshire [DW/PA/5/1593/63]
Edmund of Ewell, gent. [DW/PA/5/1574/27]
Nicholas of Swk St Olave; Sudbury, Derbyshire; St Gabriel Fenchurch, London; Barking, Essex; Wimbledon; Newington, senior, innholder [DW/PA/7/4 f.233; 1538]
Robert of Limpsfield [PRO; PCC Will 1560]

HOARE (HOORE,HORE,HORRE)
Alan of Ewell [PRO; PCC Will 1603]
Christopher of Coulsdon, husbandman [DW/PA/7/7 f.64; DW/PA/5/1596/37] <Abs 122>
Gabriel of Swk St Olave, shoemaker [DW/PA/7/10 f.209; DW/PA/5/1620/68]
John of Swk St Saviour [DW/PA/7/7 f.411; DW/PA/5/1603/86] <Abs 761>
Nicholas of Bermondsey [PRO; PCC Admon 1634]
Richard of Kingston [PRO; PCC 1642]
William of Swk St Saviour, tanner [DW/PA/5/1593/129]

HOBARD,HOBBARD,HOBBERD *see* HUBBARD

HOBBS (HOBBES,HOOBES)
John of Bermondsey [DW/PA/5/1592/11]
Richard of Streatham, smith [DW/PA/7/2 f.88; 1503]

HOBDAY
Elizabeth of Bermondsey, widow [DW/PA/7/11 f.264; DW/PA/5/1625/118]
John of Bermondsey, tanner [DW/PA/7/11 f.255; DW/PA/5/1625/119]
HOBEWEM
John of Limpsfield, husbandman [DW/PA/7/12 f.393; DW/PA/5/1638/59]
HOBSON
Ann of Woking; Farleigh; Ditton [PRO; PCC Will 1601] <Abs. SAC v.10 p.145>
Joan of Camberwell, widow [DW/PA/5/1546/82]
Roger of Camberwell - Peckham [DW/PA/5/1546/65]
William of ...., citizen and grocer [DW/PA/7/13 f.341; 1644]
William of Bermondsey, citizen and haberdasher [PRO; PCC Will 1581]
HOCH,HOCHE *see* HOOKE
HOCHER *see* HOOKER
HOCHYNSON *see* HUTCHINSON
HOCKE *see* HOOKE
HOCKETT
Jarvis of Rotherhithe, mariner [PRO; PCC Will 1645] [*and*] [DW/PA/7/13 f.340; 1644]
HOCKEY
John of Swk St George, cooper [DW/PA/5/1558/147]*
HOCKLEY
John of Swk St Thomas [DW/PA/7/11 f.556; DW/PA/5/1630/52]
Nicholas of Dunsfold, curate [DW/PA/7/12 f.462; 1638]
HODCHYN *see* HODGKIN
HODDESDEN
John of Streatham [PRO; PCC Admon 1602]
HODGEKINSON *see* HODGKINSON
HODGEKYN *see* HODGKIN
HODGES
John of East Molesey [HRO; 1556 B88-89]
Thomas of Staines, Middlesex [DW/PA/7/11 f.126; DW/PA/5/1624/59]
HODGESON *see* HODGSON
HODGKIN (HODCHYN,HODGEKYN,HODSKINS)
Arthur of Bermondsey, lastmaker [DW/PA/7/7 f.404; DW/PA/5/1603/85] <Abs 750>
Dorothy of Bermondsey, widow of Roger [DW/PA/7/7 f.137; DW/PA/5/1597/50] <Abs 251>
John of Swk St Olave, baker [DW/PA/5/1563/21]
HODGKINSON (HODGEKINSON,HODSKINSON)
Edward of Ewell [DW/PA/7/9 f.311; DW/PA/5/1619/64]
John of St Clement Eastcheap, London; Rotherhithe, citizen and butcher [GL; Commissary Court of London Will 1608]
HODGLAND *see* HOGELANDE
HODGSON (HODGESON,HOGESON)
Edmund of Guildford; Shalford, gent. [PRO; PCC Will 1593]
Edward of Leatherhead, registrar of Surrey [HRO; 1525 B1; Reg. D p.56]
Henry of Tooting [PRO; PCC 1641]
John of Ripley, citizen and upholder [PRO; PCC Will 1587]
Robert of Swk St Olave, victualler [DW/PA/7/11 f.577; DW/PA/5/1630/53]
HODLEY
George of Egham, widower [PRO; PCC Admon 1640]
HODSON *see* HUDSON

HODSULL
  Faith of Newington [LPL; 98/1 f,122v; Will 1641]
HOGA (de HOGA)
  John of Bermondsey [HRO; Reg, Fox 3 p,63; 1513]
HOGELANDE
  Thomas of Frensham [DW/PA/7/2 f,43; 1494]
HOGESON *see* HODGSON
HOGET,HOGETT,HOGETTE *see* HOGGETT
HOGG (HOGGE)
  Ann of Lambeth, widow [DW/PA/7/11 f,257; DW/PA/5/1625/120]
  Thomas of Seale - Tongham, clerk [DW/PA/7/10 f,175; DW/PA/5/1619/65]
HOGGETT (HOGET,HOGETT,HOGETTE,HOGGATT,HOGGET,HUGGETT)
  Anthony of Horne, clerk [PRO; PCC Will 1624]
  Anthony of Horne, clerk, senior [PRO; PCC 1647]
  Daniel of Petersham - Sudbrook, husbandman [DW/PA/5/1602/43] <Abs U49>
  George of Horne, yeoman [DW/PA/7/13 f,323; DW/PA/5/1643/52A]
  George of Horne [PRO; PCC Admon 1649]
  George of Lingfield [PRO; PCC Will 1584]
  Thomas of Oxted, yeoman [DW/PA/7/13 f,137; DW/PA/5/1640/81]
  Thomas of Horne [PRO; PCC 1649]
  William of Horne [PRO; PCC 1647]
HOGGYNS *see* HUGGINS
HOK,HOKE *see* HOOKE
HOKER *see* HOOKER
HOLBIDGE (HOLBYDGE)
  Richard, alias Richard Howlebeye of Swk St Saviour, waterman
    [DW/PA/5/1591/49]
HOLBORNE (HOLBEN)
  Anthony of Croydon [LPL; 98/1 f,31r; Will 1631]
  William of Wandsworth, smith [DW/PA/5/1546/94]
HOLBROOKE
  Henry of Egham [DW/PA/7/13 f,210; DW/PA/5/1642/41]
HOLBYDGE *see* HOLBIDGE
HOLDEN
  Agnes of Swk St Saviour, widow [DW/PA/5/1561/85]
  Alice of Camberwell, widow [PRO; PCC Will 1610] <Abs, SAC v,24 p,68>
  Nicholas of Camberwell, gent, [PRO; PCC Will 1607] <Abs, SAC v,12
    pp,202-203>
  Thomas of Battersea [DW/PA/7/5 f,20; 1538] <Abs 6>
HOLDSWORTH
  Seth of Bermondsey, citizen and leatherseller [PRO; PCC 1638]
HOLDWAY (HOLDWAIE)
  Richard of Swk St George, tailor [DW/PA/7/7 f,60; DW/PA/5/1596/31]
    <Abs 114>
HOLE (HOLL)
  Esabe of Farnham - Badshot, yeoman [DW/PA/7/12 f,151; DW/PA/5/1633/67]
  Joan of Betchworth, widow [DW/PA/7/6 f,131; DW/PA/5/1559/133]
  Joan of Farnham, widow [PRO; PCC 1638]
  John of Guildford St Mary, shoemaker [DW/PA/5/1550/35]
  Richard of Farnham, currier [DW/PA/7/7 f,361; DW/PA/5/1602/45] <Abs 662>
  Richard of Farnham, currier [DW/PA/7/10 f,99; DW/PA/5/1621/59]
  Thomas of Farnham, yeoman [DW/PA/7/12 f,23; DW/PA/5/1631/52]
    see also ATHILL; at HOLE; HOLLE

HOLFORD (HOLFORDE)
Benjamin of Lambeth [PRO; PCC Admon 1644]
Benjamin of Lambeth [PRO; PCC 1647] [*and*] [LBLAD; Surrey Deeds 1/4542; 1645 *Inventory only*]
Richard of Reigate [PRO; PCC Admon 1617]
William of Swk St Saviour, skinner [DW/PA/5/1587/84]
HOLGRAVE
Alice of Bermondsey [PRO; PCC Will 1487]
John of Bermondsey; Walton on the Hill [PRO; PCC Will 1487]
John of Epsom, gent. [PRO; PCC Will 1511]
William of Kingston [PRO; PCC Will 1503]
HOLIDAY *see* HOLLYDAY
HOLLAND (HOLANDE,HOLLANDE,HOLLANTE,HOLLOND,HOLLONDE)
Eleanor of Dorking, widow [DW/PA/7/9 f.7; DW/PA/5/1615/64]
Geoffrey of Walton on Thames [PRO; PCC Will 1563]
Joan of Swk St Saviour, widow [DW/PA/7/9 f.178; DW/PA/5/1616/70]
John of Dorking, yeoman [DW/PA/7/7 f.620; DW/PA/5/1607/50] <Abs 1157>
Margaret, alias Margaret Kermott of Wandsworth, widow [PRO; PCC 1639]
Ralph of Newington [PRO; PCC Will 1452]
Richard of Streatham [DW/PA/7/2 f.156; 1521]
Thomas of Chertsey, yeoman [DW/PA/7/5 f.146; 1540]
Thomas of Newington [PRO; PCC Admon 1576]
Thomas of Richmond [PRO; PCC 1647]
William of Croydon [PRO; PCC Will 1525]
William of Swk St Saviour, tailor [DW/PA/7/8 f.354; DW/PA/5/1612/78]
HOLLE
Richard of Swk St Olave [DW/PA/7/7 f.90; 1596] <Abs 165>
see also ATHILL; at HOLE; HOLE
HOLLIER
Christopher of Addington, glover [PRO; PCC Will 1623]
HOLLIMAN
John of Walton on Thames [HRO; 1620 B21]
HOLLINER (HOLYNAR)
Richard of Lambeth - Knights Hill [DW/PA/7/5 f.60; 1539] <Abs 61>
HOLLINGDALE
Richard of Dorking - 'Pyecombe' [PRO; PCC Will 1579]
HOLLIS (HOLLYS)
Edward of Dorking, yeoman [DW/PA/5/1575/38]
Jarram of Horsell [DW/PA/7/9 f.45; DW/PA/5/1614/58]
John of Farnham - Hale, senior [DW/PA/7/7 f.359; DW/PA/5/1602/47] <Abs 659>
William of Ewell, gardener [DW/PA/5/1571/69]
HOLLISTER
Maurice of Newington [PRO; PCC Admon 1616]
HOLLMAN *see* HOLMAN
HOLLOWAY (HALLAWAY,HOLLAWEE,HOLLOWAYE,HOLOWAY,HOLWAY)
Alexander of Crowhurst [DW/PA/7/11 f.458; DW/PA/5/1628/54]
Bernard of Chiddingfold [DW/PA/7/4 f.231; 1537]
Henry of Chiddingfold [DW/PA/5/1555/78]
Henry of Chiddingfold, yeoman [DW/PA/5/1580/67]
Henry of Chiddingfold - Pockford, yeoman [HRO; 1629 B24]
Isaac of Lambeth, gent. and merchant tailor [PRO; PCC Will 1616]
John of Farnham - Wrecclesham, yeoman [DW/PA/7/7 f.369; DW/PA/5/1602/48] <Abs 679>

HOLLOWAY (HALLAWAY,HOLLAWEE,HOLLOWAYE,HOLOWAY,HOLWAY) [*continued*]

John of Farnham - Wrecclesham, yeoman [HRO; 1632 B23]
John of Frensham, husbandman [DW/PA/7/7 f,209; DW/PA/5/1598/39] <Abs 372>
John of Godalming - Catteshall, husbandman [DW/PA/7/11 f,317; DW/PA/5/1626/69]
Richard of Thursley [DW/PA/7/12 f,364; DW/PA/5/1638/60]
Thomas of Bentley, Hampshire, butcher [DW/PA/7/12 f,487; DW/PA/5/1638/66]
Thomas of Chiddingfold, husbandman [DW/PA/5/1579/40]*
Thomas of Chiddingfold, husbandman, senior [DW/PA/7/7 f,111; DW/PA/5/1596/32 *and* DW/PA/5/1596/33] <Abs 203>
Thomas of Crowhurst [PRO; PCC Will 1558]
Thomas of Streatham [PRO; PCC Admon 1586]

HOLLYDAY

John of Rotherhithe, gent, [PRO; PCC Admon 1649]

HOLLYWELL

Robert of Lambeth [PRO; PCC Admon 1599]

HOLMAN (HOLLMAN,HOMAN)

Charles of Walton on the Hill, weaver [HRO; 1582 B48]
George of Godstone, citizen and grocer [PRO; PCC Will 1625] [*and*] [SRO; 2727/1/48/56] <Abs SAC v,28 p,91>
Henry of Chessington [PRO; PCC 1649]
John of Tandridge [DW/PA/7/4 f,11; 1532]
Matthew of Croydon [LPL; 98/1 f,32v; Will 1631]
Richard of Godstone, yeoman [PRO; PCC Will 1624]
Susan of Blechingley - Pendell, widow [PRO; PCC Will 1629]
Thomas of Godstone [DW/PA/7/1 f,69; 1487] <Abs 227>
William of Ewell [DW/PA/7/7 f,51; DW/PA/5/1596/36] <Abs 96>
William of Guildford [HRO; Reg, Way 1 p,76; 1463]
William of Guildford, shoemaker [DW/PA/7/13 f,213; DW/PA/5/1642/43]
William of Merstham [PRO; PCC Will 1532]

HOLMDEN (HOLMEDEN,HOMBEDENNE,HOMDEN)

Agnes of Limpsfield, widow [DW/PA/7/7 f,514; DW/PA/5/1605/44] <Abs 966>
Ann of Crowhurst, widow [PRO; PCC 1635]
Anthony of Lingfield, gent, [PRO; PCC Will 1607] <Abs, SAC v,12 pp,97-98>
George of ,,, [DW/PA/5/1555/2]
John of Addington [PRO; PCC Admon 1646]
John, alias John Hamden of Chipstead, rector [DW/PA/7/12 f,45; DW/PA/5/1632/42]
John of Croydon [PRO; PCC Will 1596]
John of Limpsfield [PRO; PCC Will 1550]
John of Limpsfield, husbandman [DW/PA/5/1591/16]
John of Limpsfield, yeoman [DW/PA/7/13 f,398; DW/PA/5/1645/24]
Reginald of Crowhurst, senior [PRO; PCC Will 1589]
Richard of Limpsfield; Cowden, Kent, chandler [DW/PA/7/8 f,353; DW/PA/5/1612/79]
Robert of Limpsfield [PRO; PCC 1649]
Thomas of Charlwood, senior [PRO; PCC Will 1566]
Thomas of Limpsfield, husbandman [DW/PA/7/11 f,306; DW/PA/5/1626/70]
William of Crowhurst, yeoman [DW/PA/5/1557/110]
William of Lingfield [DW/PA/7/2 f,125; 1516]
William of Limpsfield; Tatsfield, husbandman [DW/PA/7/7 f,4; DW/PA/5/1595/49] <Abs 12>

HOLMES (HOLMYS,HOMES)
  George of Guildford, clerk [PRO; PCC Admon 1647]
  Grace of Swk St Olave, servant to Mr William Beard, mariner [DW/PA/7/9 f.230; DW/PA/5/1617/75]
  John of Horley, yeoman, senior [DW/PA/7/13 f.217; DW/PA/5/1642/44]
  Leonard of Swk St Olave, carpenter [DW/PA/5/1552/16]
  Peter of Swk St George, writer of the Court letter [DW/PA/7/7 f.515; DW/PA/5/1605/46] <Abs 969>
  Robert of Chertsey, bargeman [DW/PA/7/10 f.69; 1618]
  Thomas of Bermondsey, bachelor [PRO; PCC Admon 1612]
  Thomas of Egham, yeoman [DW/PA/5/1557/134]
  Thomas of Walton on Thames [PRO; PCC 1649]
  William of Egham [PRO; PCC Will 1508]
HOLMEWOOD,HOLMWOOD *see* HOMEWOOD
HOLNEY
  William of Seale [PRO; PCC Admon 1648]
HOLPOOLE
  Jonathan of Wandsworth, weaver [DW/PA/7/11 f.524; DW/PA/5/1630/54]
HOLT (HOLTE,HOWLTE)
  Anthony of Mortlake [PRO; PCC Will 1603] <Abs, SAC v.11 p.110 *and* v.31 p.86>
  Elizabeth of Dunsfold, widow [DW/PA/7/13 f.26; DW/PA/5/1639/72]
  Elizabeth of Mortlake, widow of Anthony [PRO; PCC Will 1606] <Abs, SAC v.12 p.107 *and* v.31 p.86>
  Henry of Dunsfold, husbandman [DW/PA/7/12 f.78; DW/PA/5/1632/45]
  Isabella of Tooting [PRO; PCC Will 1538]
  John of Alfold [HRO; 1572 AD13]
  John of Chobham, husbandman [DW/PA/7/9 f.77; DW/PA/5/1614/59]
  John of Thorpe [PRO; PCC Admon 1610]
  John of Tooting [PRO; PCC Will 1536]
  John of Witley [DW/PA/7/3 f.173; 1531]
  John of Woking [DW/PA/7/13 f.99; DW/PA/5/1640/74]
  Lettice, alias Lettice Standen of Chertsey, widow [PRO; PCC 1640]
  Richard of Tooting Graveney [DW/PA/5/1550/10]
  Robert of Witley [HRO; 1576 B35]
  Thomas of Chertsey [PRO; PCC Will 1591]
  Thomas of Thames Ditton - Claygate [DW/PA/7/9 f.40; DW/PA/5/1614/60]
  William of Byfleet, yeoman [DW/PA/5/1571/58]
  William of Haslemere, shoemaker [HRO; 1634 B23]
  William of Thorpe, esq. [PRO; PCC Will 1603] <Abs, SAC v.11 p.128>
HOLTON *see* HOALTON
HOLWAY *see* HOLLOWAY
HOLWOOD (HOULLWODE,HOLYWOD)
  John of Kingston, husbandman [DW/PA/7/5 f.140; 1540]
  Robert of Godalming, husbandman [DW/PA/5/1558/148]*
HOLYNAR *see* HOLLINER
HOLYWOD *see* HOLWOOD
HOMAR
  Susan of Lingfield, widow [DW/PA/7/12 f.410; DW/PA/5/1637/57]
HOMBEDENNE,HOMDEN *see* HOLMDEN
HOMELIN *see* HAMLYN
HOMES *see* HOLMES

HOMEWOOD (HOLMEWOOD,HOLMWOOD,HOMEWOODE,HOMEWODE,HOMWOODE)
Bennet of Horne, yeoman [DW/PA/5/1572/25]
George of Charlwood [PRO; PCC Admon 1648]
Henry of Horne; Blechingley, tailor [HRO; 1597 B44]
John of Horley [DW/PA/7/4 f,44; 1533]
John of Reigate - Colley, yeoman [DW/PA/7/11 f,10; DW/PA/5/1622/43]
Richard of Horne; East Grinstead, Sussex; Blechingley, glover [DW/PA/7/7 f,130; DW/PA/5/1597/51] <Abs 240>
Thomas of Surrey [PRO; PCC Will 1509]
HONART (HOUART)
Mark of ... [*translated from French*] [DW/PA/7/8 f,230; DW/PA/5/1612/80]
HONE (de HONE,HONN,HONNE,HOON,WHONE,WOAN)
Abraham of Kingston, blacksmith [DW/PA/7/12 f,463; DW/PA/5/1638/62]
Celix of ... [*translated from the French*] [DW/PA/5/1571/29]
Garret of Swk St Saviour [DW/PA/5/1570/27A]
Geoffrey of Pyrford, husbandman [DW/PA/5/1571/70]
Geoffrey of Pyrford, yeoman [DW/PA/7/11 f,400; DW/PA/5/1627/58]
Jane of Swk St Saviour, spinster [DW/PA/7/12 f,490; DW/PA/5/1638/67]
John of Bisley; Horsell [HRO; 1594 B30]
John of Chobham [DW/PA/7/7 f,279; DW/PA/5/1599/33] <Abs 495>
John (John Woan) of Epsom, vicar [DW/PA/7/2 f,18; 1491]
John of Pyrford, husbandman and bachelor [DW/PA/5/1578/73]
John of Walton on Thames [DW/PA/7/11 f,438; DW/PA/5/1628/55]
Joseph of Bisley, yeoman [DW/PA/7/12 f,247; DW/PA/5/1636/49]
Peter of Chobham, husbandman [DW/PA/7/3 f,153; 1530]
Richard of Horsell [DW/PA/7/5 f,171; 1540]
Richard of Mitcham [DW/PA/7/10 f,167; DW/PA/5/1621/60]
Robert of Horsell [DW/PA/7/4 f,164; 1536]
Robert (Robert Whone) of Worplesdon, husbandman [DW/PA/7/12 f,3; DW/PA/5/1631/114]
Thomas of Horsell, husbandman [DW/PA/7/7 f,349; DW/PA/5/1601/49] <Abs 639>
William of Bisley [DW/PA/7/8 f,151; DW/PA/5/1611/62]
William of Horsell, husbandman [HRO; 1551 U110-111]
William of Horsell; Pyrford [DW/PA/7/12 f,252; DW/PA/5/1635/43]
William of Pirbright [DW/PA/7/1 ff,81,82; 1488] <Abs 267>
William of Pyrford [DW/PA/5/1591/1]
HONER (HONNER)
Cecily of Woking, widow [DW/PA/7/8 f,126; DW/PA/5/1610/72]
Edmund of Pyrford; Woking; Byfleet; Clandon, husbandman [DW/PA/5/1605/47] <Abs U150>
Elizabeth of Pyrford, widow of Edmund [DW/PA/7/7 f,515; DW/PA/5/1605/149] <Abs 968>
John of Woking, yeoman [DW/PA/7/6 f,240; 1560]
Margaret of Woking, spinster [HRO; 1638 B40]
Robert of Pyrford [DW/PA/5/1588/16]
Robert of Woking, yeoman [HRO; 1639 B43]
Thomas of Woking [DW/PA/7/9 f,219; DW/PA/5/1617/76] <Abs U223>
HONEYMAN (HONNYMAN)
Lettice of Walton on Thames - Hersham, widow [DW/PA/7/7 f,259; DW/PA/5/1599/34] <Abs 458>
HONN,HONNE *see* HONE
HONNER *see* HONER
HONTYNGFORTH *see* HUNTINGFORD

HOOD

Margaret of Swk St Saviour, widow [DW/PA/7/13 f.464; DW/PA/5/1647/6]

HOODLESSE

Francis of Oxted, gent. [DW/PA/7/12 f.400; DW/PA/5/1637/54]

HOOK (HOCH,HOCHE,HOCKE,HOK,HOKE,HOOCKE,HOOKE,HOOKES)

Agnes of Thames Ditton, widow [DW/PA/7/12 f.521; DW/PA/5/1638/69]
Alexander of Kingston [DW/PA/7/2 f.43; 1494]
Ann, alias Ann Gostwicke of Bramley [PRO; PCC Admon 1637]
Francis of Bermondsey (died overseas) [PRO; PCC Admon 1641]
Geoffrey of Long Ditton [PRO; PCC Admon 1460]
Henry of Peper Harow, husbandman [DW/PA/7/13 f.109; DW/PA/5/1640/76]
John of Chiddingfold [HRO; 1570 AD28]
John of Long Ditton [DW/PA/7/6 f.250; 1560]
John of Long Ditton - Tolworth, husbandman [DW/PA/7/7 f.348; DW/PA/5/1601/50] <Abs 638>
John of Thames Ditton - Weston [DW/PA/7/7 f.118; DW/PA/5/1597/53] <Abs 219>
John of Thames Ditton, labourer [DW/PA/7/9 f.298; 1618]
John of East Molesey, yeoman, senior [DW/PA/7/13 f.212; DW/PA/5/1642/42]
John of Shere, husbandman, senior [DW/PA/7/9 f.71; DW/PA/5/1614/62]
John of Tooting Graveney [PRO; PCC Admon 1618]
Margery of Godalming; Dunsfold, spinster [DW/PA/7/8 f.362; DW/PA/5/1612/81]
Peter of Thames Ditton [DW/PA/7/2 f.39; 1494]
Robert of Thames Ditton - Weston, labouring man [DW/PA/7/7 f.164; DW/PA/5/1597/52] <Abs 303>
Robert of Kingston - Surbiton [PRO; PCC 1648]
Robert of Swk St Olave, feltmaker [DW/PA/5/1578/48]
Robert of Swk St Saviour - Bankside, waterman [DW/PA/7/13 f.472; DW/PA/5/1648/11]
Robert of Witley - Milford [HRO; 1595 B28]
Stephen of Long Ditton - Tolworth, husbandman [DW/PA/7/9 f.209; DW/PA/5/1616/77]
Susan of Bermondsey, widow [DW/PA/7/11 f.571; DW/PA/5/1630/55]
Thomas of Alfold, yeoman [HRO; 1568 B113]
Thomas of Thames Ditton - Weston [DW/PA/7/8 f.158; DW/PA/5/1611/63]
Thomas of Dunsfold [DW/PA/7/1 f.50; 1487] <Abs 167>
Thomas of Epsom - Horton [DW/PA/7/1 f.98; 1489] <Abs 321>
Thomas of Godalming, clothier [DW/PA/7/7 f.254; DW/PA/5/1599/35] <Abs 448>
Thomas of Kingston - Hook, senior, bachelor [DW/PA/5/1555/8]
William of Long Ditton - Hook [DW/PA/7/1 ff.77-78; 1469] <Abs 253,256>
William of Godalming, clothier [DW/PA/7/7 ff.456,465; DW/PA/5/1604/25] <Abs 860>
William of Weybridge, gent. [PRO; PCC Will 1619]
William of Worplesdon [DW/PA/5/1571/52]

HOOKER (HOCHER,HOKER,HOOLKER)

Edward of Dorking, yeoman [DW/PA/7/11 f.56; DW/PA/5/1624/60]
Edward of Dorking, yeoman [DW/PA/7/13 f.432; DW/PA/5/1646/27]
Eleanor of Tooting, widow of John [PRO; PCC Will 1618]
John of Dorking, husbandman [DW/PA/7/6 f.220; 1561]
John of Dorking, husbandman [DW/PA/7/7 f.103; DW/PA/5/1596/34] <Abs 186>
John of Lambeth; Tooting, yeoman [PRO; PCC Will 1618]
John of Leigh - Denshott [DW/PA/5/1550/92]

HOOKER (HOCHER,HOKER,HOOLKER) [*continued*]
John of Reigate, senior [DW/PA/7/5 f,28; 1538] <Abs 70>
John of Reigate [DW/PA/7/11 f,9; DW/PA/5/1622/44]
John of Stoke next Guildford [DW/PA/7/2 f,179; 1522]
John of Shere - Sutton [DW/PA/7/12 f,129; DW/PA/5/1632/50]
Miles of Dorking, yeoman [DW/PA/7/7 f,382; DW/PA/5/1602/49] <Abs 709>
Richard of Puttenham, yeoman of Queen's Great Bakehouse [PRO; PCC Will 1571]
Thomas of Dorking [DW/PA/7/7 f,539; DW/PA/5/1606/41] <Abs 1013>
Walsingham of Betchworth, yeoman [PRO; PCC Will 1618]
William of Dorking, yeoman [DW/PA/7/11 f,600; DW/PA/5/1630/56]
William of Dorking, yeoman [DW/PA/7/8 f,270; DW/PA/5/1613/59]
William of Leigh [DW/PA/7/1 f,21; 1485] <Abs 71 - *where mistranscribed as* Lyker>
HOOKES *see* HOOK
HOOKEWAY
William, alias William Plommer of Swk St Mary Magdalen, barber [DW/PA/7/1 f,42; 1486] <Abs 134>
HOOLE
John of Dorking, husbandman [DW/PA/5/1558/146]*
HOOLKER *see* HOOKER
HOON *see* HONE
HOORE *see* HOARE
HOPE
George of ... [DW/PA/7/8 f,70; DW/PA/5/1609/90]
Ralph of Horne, gent, [PRO; PCC 1635]
HOPKINS (HOPKIN,HOPKYN,HOPKYNS)
John of Kingston - Ham [PRO; PCC Admon 1581]
John of Lingfield [DW/PA/5/1555/5]
John of Mitcham [PRO; PCC Will 1559]
Richard of Kingston [PRO; PCC Will 1586]
Robert of Guildford St Mary, quartermaster of the Ship *Solomon* [PRO; PCC Will 1620] <Soame 914>
Thomas of Newington, yeoman [PRO; PCC Will 1617]
William of Lingfield, yeoman [DW/PA/7/4 f,5; 1532]
William of Lingfield [DW/PA/5/1557/119] [inventory only]
William of Lingfield, husbandman [DW/PA/7/6 f,176; DW/PA/5/1559/151]
William of ...., chaplain to (Lady) Willoughby [DW/PA/5/1552/8]
William of Guildford St Mary; Guildford Holy Trinity; Guildford St Nicolas; Whitchurch, Hampshire; Stoke next Guildford, clothier [DW/PA/7/9 f,110; DW/PA/5/1615/67]
HORD,HORDE *see* HOARD
HORDEN
Audrey of Camberwell, widow [PRO; PCC Will 1579]
HORDES *see* HOARD
HORE *see* HOARE
HORLEY
Agnes of Charlwood, widow [PRO; PCC Admon 1568]
HORLINGE *see* HARLINGE
HORNE
Alice of Farnham [HRO; Reg, Fox 2 p,32; 1507]
Henry of Surrey [PRO; PCC Will 1544]
Henry of Farnham [PRO; PCC Will 1505] <Abs SAC v,28 p,80>
John of Swk St Saviour, saddler [DW/PA/7/12 f,304; DW/PA/5/1635/51]

HORNE [*continued*]
Robert of Rotherhithe [PRO; PCC Admon 1640]
Thomas of Swk St Saviour - The Axeyard [DW/PA/7/11 f,151; DW/PA/5/1625/122]
HORNER
John of Chiddingfold, husbandman [HRO; 1612 B44]
Phillip of Farnham - Downing Street, yeoman [DW/PA/5/1593/20]
HOROWBIN
Bartholomew of Croydon [PRO; PCC Admon 1648]
HORRE *see* HOARE
HORSEBRIDGE
Alice of Buckland [DW/PA/7/5 f,53; 1538] <Abs 14>
HORSEMAN
Arthur of Swk St Saviour, citizen and joiner [DW/PA/5/1603/70] <Abs U74>
HORSFORD
Robert of Farnham [PRO; PCC Admon 1634]
HORSHAM
Phillip of Wandsworth [PRO; PCC Admon 1603]
HORSLEY
Ann of Swk St Olave, widow [DW/PA/7/11 f,182; DW/PA/5/1625/123]
John of Newington [LPL; 98/1 f,131r; Will 1642]
HORSPOOLE
Simon of Rotherhithe, citizen and draper [PRO; PCC Will 1602]
HORTON (HORTEN)
Nicholas of Swk St Olave [DW/PA/7/3 f,114; 1529]
William of Egham [DW/PA/7/12 f,74; DW/PA/5/1632/43]
William of Newington [LPL; 98/1 f,17r; Will 1630]
see also HOUGHTON
HORWOOD (WHORWOD,WORWOOD)
Christopher of Wandsworth, yeoman [PRO; PCC Will 1575]
Nicholas of Swk St Saviour [DW/PA/5/1586/23]
William of Putney, esq, [PRO; PCC Will 1545]
see also WIRWOOD
HOSEY
Nicholas of Kingston [DW/PA/7/1 f,75; 1488] <Abs 246>
HOSIER (HOSYER)
Geoffrey of Swk St Thomas, curate [DW/PA/5/1601/51] <Abs U38>
William of Mickleham, rector [HRO; Reg, Way 1 p,86; 1465]
HOSKINS (HOSKYNS,HUSKINS)
Ann of Oxted, widow of Charles, citizen and merchant tailor [PRO; PCC Will 1601]
Charles of Oxted, gent,, senior [PRO; PCC Will 1598] [*and*] [SRO; 212/81/1]
Richard of Lambeth - Stockwell, victualler [DW/PA/7/13 f,289; DW/PA/5/1643/48]
(Sir) Thomas of Oxted, knight [PRO; PCC Admon 1616]
HOSSELL *see* HOUNSELL
HOSYER *see* HOSIER
HOTHERSALL *see* HETHERSALL
HOUART *see* HONART
HOUBLON
James of Swk St Olave, citizen and dyer [DW/PA/7/13 f,364; 1644]
Katherine of Swk St Olave, widow [DW/PA/7/13 f,351; 1644]

HOUGH
  George of Bermondsey [DW/PA/7/11 f.201; DW/PA/5/1625/124]
HOUGHTON (de HOUGHTON,HAUGHTON,HOWTON,HOWTYNG)
  Alice of Swk St George [DW/PA/7/9 f.326; DW/PA/5/1619/56]
  Ellen of Swk St Olave, widow [DW/PA/7/2 f.80; 1502]
  John of Cobham, rector [HRO; Reg. Orl 1 p.25; 1335]
  William of Mitcham [PRO; PCC Admon 1648]
  William of Swk St Saviour [DW/PA/7/11 f.152; DW/PA/5/1625/125]
    see also HORTON
HOULLWODE *see* HOLWOOD
HOUNDSON (HOUNDSONE,HOUNSON,HOWNSOME)
  Constance of Bramley, widow [DW/PA/7/11 f.475; DW/PA/5/1628/57]
  Edward of Shalford, dyer [DW/PA/7/13 f.89; DW/PA/5/1640/72]
  Rose of Frensham, widow [HRO; 1639 AD101]
  Thomas of Frensham - Churt, husbandman [DW/PA/7/12 f.274; DW/PA/5/1635/46]
HOUNSELL (HOSSELL)
  Roger of Rotherhithe, baker [DW/PA/7/7 f.429; DW/PA/5/1603/87] <Abs 809>
    see also ANSELL
HOUNSON *see* HOUNDSON
HOURDE *see* HOARDE
HOVE
  Juliana, alias Juliana Wolridge of Lingfield [PRO; PCC Admon 1649]
HOVER
  George of Dorking, husbandman, junior [DW/PA/5/1593/160]
HOW *see* HOWE; ATHOW
HOWARD (HOWARDE)
  Agnes of Lambeth, duchess of Norfolk [PRO; PCC Will 1545] <Abs SAC v.9 pp.427-428>
  Charity of Sheffield, Sussex; Surrey, wife of Charles [PRO; PCC Will 1618] <Abs SAC v.9 p.429>
  Charles of Reigate; Mickleham, earl of Nottingham [PRO; PCC Will 1642] <Abs SAC v.9 p.430>
  Dorothy of Surrey, wife of Edmund [PRO; PCC Will 1530] <Abs SAC v.3 p.174>
  (Sir) Edward of Westminster, Middlesex; Reigate; Windlesham - Bagshot; Lingfield, knight [PRO; PCC Will 1620] <Abs SAC v.9 p.430> <Soame 1259>
  (Lady) Frances of Battersea [PRO; PCC Will 1616] <Abs SAC v.9 pp.428-429>
  (Dame) Margaret of Streatham, widow [PRO; PCC Admon 1565]
  Thomas of Lambeth, duke of Norfolk [PRO; PCC Will 1524] <Abs SAC v.9 p.427>
  (Sir) William, Lord Howard of Effingham, of Reigate; Esher, Lord Chamberlain [PRO; PCC Will 1573] <Abs SAC v.9 p.423>
HOWCHER (HOWKER)
  John of Send [DW/PA/7/4 f.62; 1533]
  Richard of Farnham [DW/PA/7/3 f.103; 1529]
HOWCOTE
  Thomas of Swk St George [DW/PA/7/7 f.33; DW/PA/5/1595/50] <Abs 68>
HOWE (HOW,HOWES)
  Brian of East Molesey, clerk and curate [DW/PA/5/1561/52]
  George of Swk St George, citizen of London [DW/PA/7/11 f.219; DW/PA/5/1625/121]
  John of ... [DW/PA/7/10 f.63; 1618]

HOWE (HOW,HOWES) [*continued*]
John of Swk St George, fletcher [DW/PA/7/6 f,188; DW/PA/5/1559/201]
Thomas of Cobham [PRO; PCC Will 1559]
Thomas of Guildford, innholder [DW/PA/7/11 f,476; DW/PA/5/1628/56]
Thomas, alias Thomas Hewes of Swk St Saviour [DW/PA/7/10 f,99; DW/PA/5/1619/66]
William of Wandsworth, mealman [DW/PA/7/7 f,373; DW/PA/5/1602/50] <Abs 688>
see also ATHOWE; HOWSE

HOWELL
Thomas of Rotherhithe [DW/PA/5/1550/80]
see also ap HOWELL

HOWICK (HOWICKE,HOYCKE)
John of Witley, butcher, senior [DW/PA/7/8 f,42; DW/PA/5/1609/91]
Thomas of Elstead [HRO; 1588 B34]
Thomas of Elstead; Godalming - Farncombe, bucketmaker [DW/PA/7/7 f,446; DW/PA/5/1603/88] <Abs 844>

HOWKINS
Thomas of Swk St Saviour, hempdresser [DW/PA/7/13 f,194;DW/PA/5/1641/77]

HOWLAND
(Sir) Giles of Streatham, knight [PRO; PCC Will 1608]
(Sir) John of Streatham, knight [PRO; PCC 1649]

HOWLEBEYE
Richard, alias Richard Holbydge of Swk St Saviour, waterman [DW/PA/5/1591/49]

HOWLTE *see* HOLT

HOWSE
Thomas of London, citizen and embroiderer, senior [DW/PA/7/8 f,330; DW/PA/5/1613/60]
William of Swk St Saviour, barber [DW/PA/5/1591/106]
see also ATHOW; HOWE

HOWTON,HOWTYNG *see* HOUGHTON

HOYCKE *see* HOWICK

HUAT *see* HEWETT

HUBBARD (HARBARD,HEBBERD,HEBERT,HIBBERD,HOBARD,HOBBARD,HOBBERD,HUBBARDE, HUBBERD,HUBBERT,HUBBORD,HUBBOURDE)
Agnes of Blechingley, widow [DW/PA/7/5 f,36; 1538] <Abs 13>
Andrew of Streatham, husbandman [DW/PA/5/1556/12]
Edward of Newington, tailor [LPL; 96/1377; Will 1625]
Joan of Banstead, widow [DW/PA/7/3 f,124; 1530]
John of Great Bookham, yeoman [HRO; 1591 B40]
John of Great Bookham, yeoman [DW/PA/7/13 f,184; DW/PA/5/1641/75]
John of Farnham [DW/PA/7/5 f,40; 1538] <Abs 39>
John of Guildford St Nicolas [DW/PA/5/1588/15]
John of Oxted, tanner [DW/PA/5/1563/25]
John of Walton on the Hill, husbandman [DW/PA/7/8 f,2; DW/PA/5/1608/58]
Judith of Newington, widow of Edward, tailor [LPL; 96/1378; Will 1625]
Margery of Streatham, widow of Andrew [DW/PA/5/1556/11]
Richard of Blechingley [DW/PA/7/4 f,169; 1536]
Richard of Great Bookham - 'Bonnetts' [DW/PA/7/9 f,322; DW/PA/5/1619/60]
Richard of Caterham [PRO; PCC Admon 1606]
Richard of Dorking, dyer [DW/PA/7/12 f,297; DW/PA/5/1636/50]
Richard of Reigate, labourer [DW/PA/5/1580/52]
Thomas of Swk St George [DW/PA/7/11 ff,452,482; DW/PA/5/1628/58]

HUBBARD (HARBARD,HEBBERD,HEBERT,HIBBERD,HOBARD,HOBBARD,HOBBERD,HUBBARDE,
HUBBERD,HUBBERT,HUBBORD,HUBBOURDE) [*continued*]
Thomas of Streatham [DW/PA/5/1546/31]
Thomas of Walton on the Hill [DW/PA/5/1558/149]*
Thomas of Walton [DW/PA/5/1578/18] [proxy]
Thomas of Walton on the Hill [DW/PA/5/1579/44]*
William of Chipstead [DW/PA/5/1546/42]
HUBBERSTEY
James of Swk St Olave, feltmaker [DW/PA/7/10 f.33; DW/PA/5/1617/77]
<Abs U224>
HUBBERT *see* HUBBARD
HUCHENS,HUCHENSON *see* HUTCHINS,HUTCHINSON
HUCHINS *see* HUTCHINS
HUDDLESTONE (HUDDYLSTON,HURDLESTON)
Robert of Lambeth [PRO; PCC Admon 1565]
Thomas of Mitcham [PRO; PCC Will 1506]
HUDDSON *see* HUDSON
HUDDYLSTON *see* HUDDLESTONE
HUDNAT,HUDNETT *see* HADNET
HUDSON (HODSON,HUDDSON,HUDSHON)
Alice of Swk St Olave, widow [DW/PA/7/7 f.226; DW/PA/5/1598/41] <Abs 400>
Christopher of Mortlake [PRO; PCC Admon 1593]
Edmund of Swk St Olave [DW/PA/5/1588/28]
George of Little Bookham, parson [HRO; 1593 AD43]
Isabella of Putney, widow [LPL; 98/1 f.65r; Will 1635]
Joan of Swk St Olave [DW/PA/7/1 f.22; 1485] <Abs 74>
John of Great Bookham [DW/PA/7/1 f.11; 1485] <Abs 35>
John of Great Bookham [DW/PA/7/5 f.78; 1539]
John of Great Bookham - Polesden Lacy, yeoman [HRO; 1587 B47]
John of Limpsfield [DW/PA/5/1576/100]
Marianne of Tooting Graveney, widow [DW/PA/5/1575/78]
Miles of Mortlake, gent. [PRO; PCC Will 1608] <Abs. SAC v.12 pp.102-103>
Richard of Great Bookham, husbandman [DW/PA/5/1575/7]
Thomas of Mortlake [PRO; PCC Will 1592]
Thomas of Swk St Saviour, brewer [DW/PA/7/5 f.226; 1541]
Walter of Great Bookham [DW/PA/7/2 f.189; 1523]
William of Great Bookham, shearman [DW/PA/7/8 f.167; DW/PA/5/1610/73]
William of Cranleigh, labourer [DW/PA/5/1558/150]
William of Dorking, husbandman [DW/PA/7/12 f.105; DW/PA/5/1632/47]
HUEGHE
Pieter of ... [*translated from Dutch copy enclosed*] [DW/PA/5/1578/59]
HUES *see* HUGHES
HUETT *see* HEWETT
HUGGENS *see* HUGGINS
HUGGETT *see* HOGGETT
HUGGINS (HOGGYNS,HUGGENS,HUGGYNS)
Elizabeth of Bermondsey, servant to Alice Dunne, widow [DW/PA/5/1571/41]
John of Bermondsey, bachelor [PRO; PCC 1635]
Leonard of Swk [*Translated from Dutch*] [DW/PA/5/1592/99]
Margery, alias Margery Gardyner of Walton on Thames - Apps [DW/PA/7/5
f.156; 1540]
William of Shere [DW/PA/5/1563/2]
Hugh son of Hugh of Swk St Margaret [*Fresian*] [DW/PA/7/2 f.65; 1500]

HUGHES (a PEW, ap PUE, HEWES, HEWSE, HUES, HUGONIS)
Agnes of Kingston, widow [DW/PA/7/13 f.173; DW/PA/5/1642/37]
Alice of Swk St Olave, widow [DW/PA/7/7 f.161; DW/PA/5/1597/55] <Abs 299>
Edward of Newington [LPL; 98/1 f.13v; Will 1630]
Edward of Swk St Olave, bachelor [DW/PA/7/10 f.87; DW/PA/5/1615/37]
Elizabeth of Swk St Saviour, widow [DW/PA/7/11 f.203; DW/PA/5/1625/127]
Hugh ap John ap Pue of Swk St Olave; *? Clandils* [? Llandeilo], Radnorshire [DW/PA/7/7 f.489; DW/PA/5/1604/2] <Abs 924>
Humphrey of Swk St Saviour [DW/PA/7/12 f.255; DW/PA/5/1635/41]
Joan of Swk St Saviour - Paris Garden, widow of Richard [DW/PA/7/8 f.132; DW/PA/5/1610/74]
John of Haslemere - Imbhams [PRO; PCC 1648]
John of Swk St George [DW/PA/7/8 f.301; DW/PA/5/1613/58]
John of Swk St Olave, waterman [DW/PA/7/11 f.440; DW/PA/5/1628/52]
John of Swk St Saviour; Erith, Kent, butcher [DW/PA/7/6 f.9; DW/PA/5/1559/243]
Katherine of Swk St Thomas Hospital [DW/PA/7/10 f.270; DW/PA/5/1622/45]
Margaret of Wonersh, wife of Thomas a Pew [DW/PA/7/9 f.226; DW/PA/5/1617/4]
Owen of Kingston, vicar [PRO; PCC Will 1613]
Owen of Swk St Olave, feltmaker [DW/PA/7/7 f.613; DW/PA/5/1607/51]
Richard of Swk St Saviour, butcher [DW/PA/7/11 f.202; DW/PA/5/1625/126]
Robert of Swk St George, baker [DW/PA/7/11 f.179; DW/PA/5/1625/128]
Thomas of Kingston, yeoman [DW/PA/7/12 f.383; DW/PA/5/1637/53]
Thomas (Thomas Apew) of Wonersh, yeoman [HRO; 1613 B1]
Thomas, *or* Thomas Howes of Swk St Saviour [DW/PA/7/10 f.99; DW/PA/5/1619/56]
William of Swk - Borough [DW/PA/7/12 f.494; DW/PA/5/1638/68]
William of Swk St Olave, feltmaker [DW/PA/7/11 f.600; DW/PA/5/1630/51]

HUGHSON
Bartholomew of Ewhurst [PRO; PCC 1630]
Luke of Bermondsey, doctor [HRO; Reg. Fox 3 p.60; 1511]

HUGMAN
Thomas of Swk St Saviour, waterman [DW/PA/5/1588/29]

HUGONN
William of Newington [PRO; PCC Will 1418]

HUISHE
James of Walton on Thames [PRO; PCC Admon 1614]
William of Surrey and several counties, grocer [PRO; PCC Will 1590]

HULL (AT HULL)
Ann of Lambeth, widow [PRO; PCC Will 1617]
Christopher of Newington [LPL; 96/1390; 98/1 f.41r; Will 1632]
Edward of Peper Harow [DW/PA/7/3 f.111; 1529]
John of Battersea, gent. [PRO; PCC Admon 1648; PCC 1648]
John of Hambledon [PRO; PCC Will 1489]
John of Hambledon, gent. [DW/PA/7/5 f.42; 1538] <Abs 54>
Mary of Farnham, spinster [*but names children*] [DW/PA/7/9 f.244; DW/PA/5/1617/78]
Thomas of Godalming, gent. [DW/PA/7/11 ff.24,42; DW/PA/5/1623/60]
Walter of Thames Ditton, labourer [HRO; 1604 AD24]
[*Some early records confuse with* ATHILL; HILL.]

HUMBER
John of Swk, gunner [DW/PA/7/7 ff.425,458; DW/PA/5/1603/89] <Abs 795,864>

HUMBLE

Robert of Swk St Olave, feltmaker [DW/PA/5/1592/34]

HUMPHREYS (HUMFFREY, HUMFRAY, HUMFREY, HUMFREYE, HUMFREYS, HUMFRIES, HUMFRYE, HUMPHREY, HUMPRHIE, HUMPHRY, UMFREY, UMPFREY)

Alice, alias Alice Shawcrosse of Crowhurst [DW/PA/7/9 f.303; DW/PA/5/1619/54]

Andrew of Horne [DW/PA/7/7 f.243; DW/PA/5/1599/38] <Abs 430>

Andrew of Dorking, husbandman [DW/PA/7/13 f.489; DW/PA/5/1648/14]

Bartholomew of Effingham, husbandman [DW/PA/5/1601/44]

George of Charlwood, husbandman [LPL; 96/1392; Will 1623]

Jane of Kingston, widow [DW/PA/7/9 f.97; DW/PA/5/1614/63]

Jane of Kingston, spinster [PRO; PCC Will 1615]

John of Blechingley, yeoman [DW/PA/7/8 f.120; DW/PA/5/1610/75]

John of Effingham - Polesden, yeoman [DW/PA/7/12 f.28; DW/PA/5/1631/54]

John of Effingham [PRO; PCC 1647]

John of Godstone [PRO; PCC Admon 1583]

John of Horley [DW/PA/5/1555/33 *and* DW/PA/5/1555/6 (proxy)]

John of Lingfield - Felcourt, yeoman [DW/PA/5/1563/22]

John of Rotherhithe [PRO; PCC Admon 1576]

Nicholas of Epsom, yeoman [DW/PA/7/7 f.474; DW/PA/5/1604/31] <Abs 896>

Parnell of Swk St Olave, widow [DW/PA/7/12 f.345; DW/PA/5/1636/54]

Peter of Lingfield [PRO; PCC Will 1584]

Stephen of Crowhurst [PRO; PCC Admon 1612]

Thomas of Croydon, cooper [LPL; 96/1397; Will 1648]

Thomas of Epsom, yeoman [DW/PA/7/9 f.23; DW/PA/5/1614/64]

Thomas of Godstone [DW/PA/7/12 f.8; DW/PA/5/1631/51]

Thomas of Kingston [PRO; PCC Admon 1602]

Thomas of Newdigate [PRO; PCC 1638]

William of Capel [DW/PA/7/10 f.250; DW/PA/5/1622/46]

William of Lingfield [DW/PA/7/2 f.26; 1492]

HUNDELBY

Robert of Alford, Lincolnshire; London; Lambeth; Cliffe, Kent, clerk [LPL; Reg. Abp Arundel i f.236; Will 1406]

HUNNYMAN *see* HONEYMAN

HUNT (HUNTE, HUNTTE)

Agnes, alias Agnes Sewer of Croydon - Shirley, widow [PRO; PCC 1633]

Agnes of Send, widow [DW/PA/7/11 f.515; DW/PA/5/1629/49]

Alice of Bermondsey, spinster [PRO; PCC Admon 1627]

Alice of Swk St Olave, widow [DW/PA/7/13 f.143; DW/PA/5/1641/71]

Barbara of Swk St Saviour, widow [DW/PA/7/13 f.488; DW/PA/5/1648/13]

Christopher of Beddington - Wallington, husbandman [DW/PA/7/5 f.45; 1538] <Abs 8>

Christopher of Walton on Thames, of the king's woodyard [DW/PA/7/8 f.272; DW/PA/5/1613/61]

Dionis of Lambeth, widow [DW/PA/5/1558/153]*

Edmund of Chiddingfold [HRO; 1623 A057]

Edmund of Horley [PRO; PCC Admon 1635]

Edward of Ashtead, husbandman [DW/PA/5/1546/16]

Edward of West Horsley, yeoman [DW/PA/5/1592/60]

George of Camberwell, husbandman [PRO; PCC Admon 1648]

George of Chobham, yeoman [DW/PA/7/12 f.149; DW/PA/5/1633/66]

George of Shere, yeoman [DW/PA/7/8 f.278; DW/PA/5/1613/62]

Henry of Betchworth [DW/PA/7/1 f.34; 1486] <Abs 117>

Henry of Camberwell - Dulwich [DW/PA/7/6 f.299; 1560]

HUNT (HUNTE,HUNTTE) [*continued*]

James of Chobham, yeoman [DW/PA/7/11 f,436; DW/PA/5/1628/59]
James of Shere, yeoman [DW/PA/7/7 f,21; DW/PA/5/1595/54] <Abs 45>
Joan of Kingston, widow [DW/PA/7/11 f,564; DW/PA/5/1630/57]
Joan of Swk St Margaret, widow [DW/PA/7/5 f,123; 1539]
John of Abinger; Shere; Guildford, yeoman [DW/PA/5/1604/28] <Abs U108>
John of Abinger, yeoman [DW/PA/5/1627/59B]
John of Battersea, senior [DW/PA/7/12 f,165; DW/PA/5/1633/68]
John of Chertsey [DW/PA/7/2 f,91; 1505]
John of Cobham, husbandman [DW/PA/7/11 f,479; DW/PA/5/1628/60]
John of Swk St George, brewer's servant [DW/PA/7/10 f,79; DW/PA/5/1619/67]
John of Walton on Thames - Hersham, husbandman [DW/PA/5/1575/27]
John of Witley, yeoman [HRO; 1632 B27]
Margaret of Swk St George, widow [DW/PA/7/13 f,203; DW/PA/5/1642/39]
Nicholas of Camberwell, bachelor [PRO; PCC Admon 1614]
Nicholas of Camberwell, proctor of the Arches [PRO; PCC 1649]
Nicholas of Ockham, yeoman [PRO; PCC Will 1623]
Richard of Cobham [DW/PA/7/5 f,165; 1540]
Richard of Egham, citizen and girdler [PRO; PCC Will 1593]
Richard of Merton, gent, [PRO; PCC 1647]
Richard of Swk St Saviour - Clink Liberty, waterman [DW/PA/7/13 f,5; DW/PA/5/1640/65]
Richard of Walton on Thames - Hersham, senior [DW/PA/5/1558/151]*
Robert of ... [DW/PA/7/5 f,205; 1540]
Thomas of Battersea [DW/PA/7/13 f,38; DW/PA/5/1640/68]
Thomas of Beddington - Wallington, yeoman [DW/PA/7/5 f,54; 1538] <Abs 9>
Thomas of Dorking, innholder [DW/PA/7/11 f,317; DW/PA/5/1626/71]
Thomas of West Horsley, yeoman, junior [HRO; 1604 B32]
Thomas of West Horsley; Ockham; Shere, yeoman [DW/PA/7/7 f,495; DW/PA/5/1605/50] <Abs 929>
Thomas of Kingston - Hatch, citizen and woodmonger [PRO; PCC Will 1625]
Thomas of Lambeth, yeoman [DW/PA/5/1558/152]*
(Sir) Thomas of Lambeth - Lambeth Drive, knight, citizen and fishmonger [PRO; PCC Will 1617]
Thomas of Rotherhithe [PRO; PCC Will 1560]
Thomas of Swk St George [DW/PA/7/11 f,64; DW/PA/5/1623/61]
Thomas of Swk St Olave, joiner [DW/PA/7/7 f,338; DW/PA/5/1601/52] <Abs 610>
Thomasine of Dorking, widow [DW/PA/7/12 f,303; DW/PA/5/1635/50]
Walter of Long Ditton [DW/PA/7/2 f,8; 1490]
William of Egham [PRO; PCC 1638]
William of West Horsley; Ockley, yeoman [DW/PA/5/1555/69]
William of Shere [DW/PA/7/1 f,44; 1486] <Abs 144>
William of Swk St Margaret, sheather [DW/PA/7/2 f,74; 1501]
William of Swk St Saviour, silk weaver [DW/PA/7/11 f,210; DW/PA/5/1625/129]
William of Thursley, husbandman [DW/PA/7/12 f,505; 1638]

HUNTER

Edmund of Camberwell - Peckham, husbandman [DW/PA/7/7 f,641; DW/PA/5/1608/59] <Abs 1200>
Mabel of Camberwell, widow [DW/PA/7/10 f,39; DW/PA/5/1617/79]
Richard of Lambeth [PRO; PCC Admon 1637]
Thomas of Camberwell, esq, [PRO; PCC 1640]

HUNTER [*continued*]
William of Kingston, clerk [PRO; PCC Will 1544]
HUNTINGFORD (HONTYNGFORTH,HUNTINGEFORDE,HUNTYNGFORD,HUTYNGFFORD)
Gilbert of All Hallows Barking, London; Thursley - Hindhead
[GL; Commissary Court of London Will 1576]
John of Farnham [DW/PA/7/3 f.150; 1530]
Ralph of Thursley [DW/PA/5/1558/154]*
Richard of Frensham [DW/PA/7/5 f.39; 1538] <Abs 43>
Richard of Worplesdon, senior [DW/PA/7/12 f.486; DW/PA/5/1638/65]
William of Pirbright [DW/PA/7/2 f.44; 1494]
William of Worplesdon, husbandman [DW/PA/7/11 f.496; DW/PA/5/1629/50]
HUNTINGTON
George, alias George Hunton of Wonersh, clothier [DW/PA/5/1601/45]
HUNTLEY
Christine of Lingfield [DW/PA/7/4 f.45; 1533]
John of Beddington - Wallington [PRO; PCC Will 1625]
John of Woodmansterne; Godstone; Horne; Gatton; Tandridge;
Carshalton, gent. [DW/PA/7/7 f.119; DW/PA/5/1597/57] <Abs 220>
Margaret of Beddington - Wallington, widow [DW/PA/7/12 f.463;
DW/PA/5/1638/63]
Rose of Beddington - Wallington [PRO; PCC Will 1619]
Susan of Swk St Saviour, widow [DW/PA/7/12 f.190; DW/PA/5/1633/72]
Thomas of Swk St Saviour, waterman [DW/PA/5/1598/43] <Abs U17>
William of Woodmansterne, yeoman [DW/PA/5/1558/155]*
HUNTON
George, alias George Huntington of Wonersh, clothier [DW/PA/5/1601/45]
HURDLESTONE *see* HUDDLESTONE
HURLBATT
Juliana of Farnham, widow [DW/PA/7/2 f.147; 1520]
HURLING *see* HARLING
HURLSTON (HURLESTON)
Henry of Streatham, gent. [PRO; PCC Admon 1633]
Henry of Streatham, gent. [PRO; PCC 1646]
Thomas of Thames Ditton [PRO; PCC Admon 1621]
HURROK
Robert of Epsom [DW/PA/7/1 f.41; 1486] <Abs 133>
HURST (HERST,HURSTE)
Henry of Dunsfold; Alfold, yeoman [DW/PA/7/9 f.124; DW/PA/5/1615/68]
John of Alfold, yeoman [DW/PA/7/7 f.227; DW/PA/5/1598/42] <Abs 401>
John of Bermondsey [PRO; PCC Will 1500]
John of Chessington, collier [DW/PA/7/12 f.136; DW/PA/5/1632/51]
John of Wonersh [DW/PA/7/7 f.373; DW/PA/5/1602/52] <Abs 687>
Thomas of Egham [DW/PA/5/1581/30]
HUSBAND
Benjamin of Carshalton [PRO; PCC 1635]
Dinah of Streatham, widow [PRO; PCC Admon 1632]
Ralph of Streatham [PRO; PCC Admon 1613]
Thomas of Streatham [PRO; PCC Admon 1646]
HUSEY *see* HUSSEY
HUSKINS *see* HOSKINS
HUSSEY (HUSEY,HUSSIE)
Cicely of Kingston, widow [SRO; KB32/1; 1511]
Henry of Battersea, gent. [PRO; PCC Will 1611] <Abs, SAC v.35 p.40>
John of Kingston [PRO; PCC Will 1503; CCAL; 1503 f.188v]

HUSSEY (HUSEY,HUSSIE) [*continued*]
John of Richmond [DW/PA/7/7 f.145; DW/PA/5/1597/56] <Abs 266>
(Dame) Patience of Surrey [PRO; PCC 1643]
HUSTWAITE
Robert of London, pewterer [SRO; 3141/1; 1572]
HUTCHEN,HUTCHENS *see* HUTCHINS
HUTCHENSON *see* HUTCHINSON
HUTCHES,HUTCHEST *see* HITCHHURST
HUTCHINS (HUCHINS,HUTCHEN,HUTCHENS)
Cuthbert of Chertsey, tapster [PRO; PCC Will 1622]
Elizabeth of Swk St Olave, widow [DW/PA/7/12 f.275; DW/PA/5/1635/47]
John of Swk St Olave, weaver [DW/PA/7/12 f.166; DW/PA/5/1633/69]
Thomas of Swk St Olave [DW/PA/7/10 f.282 *and* DW/PA/7/11 f.39; DW/PA/5/1622/47]
William of Rotherhithe, waterman [DW/PA/7/12 f.56; DW/PA/5/1632/40]
William of Swk St Thomas [DW/PA/7/7 f.260; DW/PA/5/1599/37] <Abs 459>
HUTCHINSON (HOCHYNSON,HUCHENSON,HUTCHENSON)
Alice of Rotherhithe, widow [DW/PA/7/13 f.313; DW/PA/5/1644/9]
Henry of Thorpe [PRO; PCC 1649]
Thomas of Swk St Olave [DW/PA/7/4 f.153; 1536]
Thomas of Wandsworth [DW/PA/5/1543/14]*
HUTTON
John of Tooting Graveney [DW/PA/5/1562/12]
Margaret of Mortlake; Kingston, widow [LPL; 96/1417; 98/1 f.91r; Will 1638]
Richard of Swk St Olave; All Hallows the Less, London; All Hallows the Great, London, armourer [DW/PA/7/7 f.481; DW/PA/5/1604/32] <Abs 907>
Thomas of Bermondsey [PRO; PCC Will 1593]
William of Kingston, gent. [PRO; PCC 1631]
HUTYNGFFORD *see* HUNTINGFORD
HUXLEY
William of Newington [LPL; 96/1418; Will 1629]
William of Rotherhithe [PRO; PCC Will 1544]
HYCCECOKE,HYCHCOKE,HYCHECOKE *see* HITCHCOCK
HYCHESST,HYCHEST,HYCHURSTE *see* HITCHHURST
HYDE (HIDE)
Hugh of Wandsworth [DW/PA/7/7 f.460; DW/PA/5/1603/80] <Abs 867>
James of Epsom - Horton [DW/PA/5/1550/197]
Julian of Wotton [HRO; D2 A-1/83; 1547]
Lawrence of Little Bookham, husbandman [HRO; 1629 B22]
Robert of Epsom [DW/PA/7/3 f.191; 1531]
Thomas of Epsom - Horton [DW/PA/7/4 f.89; 1534]
William of Wotton [HRO; D2 A-1/83; 1547]
HYER *see* HIRE
HYLDE *see* HILLER
HYLL *see* HILL
HYLLAR,HYLLER *see* HILLER
HYLLES *see* HILL
HYN *see* HINE
HYND,HYNDE *see* HINDE
HYNSLEY *see* HINSLEY
HYSCHEKOKE,HYTCHECOCKE *see* HITCHCOCK
HYTCHIN *see* HITCHIN

HYWOOD
John of Chobham [DW/PA/7/7 f,9; DW/PA/5/1595/53] <Abs 20>

IBLE
Edward of Swk St Olave, shipwright [DW/PA/5/1588/24]
IBRY
William of Streatham, canon of St Paul's [PRO; PCC Will 1557] <Abs SAC v,52 pp,42-43>
IDLE (IDDOLKE,IDELL,IDOLL)
Charles of Swk St Olave [DW/PA/7/8 f,6; DW/PA/5/1608/60]
John of Swk St George, currier [DW/PA/5/1558/160]*
Margaret of Swk St George, widow of John [DW/PA/5/1558/159]*
Thomas, alias Thomas Iddolke, of Camberwell - Peckham Rye, yeoman [DW/PA/7/6 f,146; DW/PA/5/1559/237]
IFOLD (IFFOLD,IFOLDE,IFOULD,IFOULDE)
Cicely of Woking, widow [DW/PA/7/7 ff,6,68; DW/PA/5/1595/56] <Abs 15,129>
John of Dunsfold [DW/PA/5/1617/56] <Abs U217>
John of Dunsfold, bachelor [PRO; PCC Admon 1640]
Phillip of East Molesey, yeoman [DW/PA/5/1581/18]
Richard of Dunsfold; Sussex, yeoman [DW/PA/7/9 f,113; DW/PA/5/1615/69]
Thomas of Dunsfold; Kirdford, Sussex, yeoman [DW/PA/5/1605/51] <Abs U152>
Thomas of Dunsfold, junior [PRO; PCC 1635]
Thomas of Dunsfold [PRO; PCC 1640]
ILBERY
Richard of Swk St Saviour [DW/PA/5/1592/38]
ILLINGWORTH (ILLYNGWORTH)
(Sir) Richard of Surrey, knight, chief baron of the Exchequer [PRO; PCC 1476]
Richard of Mitcham, gent, [PRO; PCC Will 1511] <Abs SAC v,30 p,94>
William of Mitcham; St Margaret Pattens, London, gent, [DW/PA/7/5 f,20; 1538] <Abs 65>
ILMAN
Richard of Lingfield, blacksmith [DW/PA/7/10 f,244; DW/PA/5/1622/48]
INDE *see* JUDE
INFIELD (INFELDE,INYNGFELD,YNFELD)
James of Lingfield, yeoman [DW/PA/7/7 f,42; DW/PA/5/1595/55] <Abs 81>
Richard of West Hoathly, Sussex; Godstone; Tandridge; Burstow; Lingfield - Sugham; East Grinstead, Sussex [PRO; PCC 1620] <Soame 1259>
Thomas of Horne [PRO; PCC Will 1561]
INGERSONN
Richard of Swk St George, yeoman [DW/PA/5/1578/94]
INGES
Margaret of Swk [HRO; Reg, Way 2 p,152; 1472]
INGLE (INGELE,INGELLIE)
James, or James Jugellie, of Lambeth [DW/PA/7/10 f,26; DW/PA/5/1616/72]
Robert of Swk St Saviour, nailer [DW/PA/7/9 f,144; DW/PA/5/1615/70]
William of Swk St Saviour, husbandman [DW/PA/7/7 f,308; DW/PA/5/1600/15] <Abs 550>
INGLER *see* ENGLER
INGOLDSBY (INGOULDSBYE)
Francis of Bermondsey [DW/PA/7/11 ff,39,79; DW/PA/5/1623/62]

INGRAM
Anthony of Richmond [PRO; PCC Admon 1632]
John of Nursling, Hampshire [DW/PA/5/1558/161]
Thomas of Reigate [PRO; PCC Admon 1624]
William of Lambeth [PRO; PCC 1631]
INMAN
John of Oxted, labourer [DW/PA/5/1580/51]
INWOOD (INWARDE,INWOD,INWODE,INWOODE,INYWOOD,YNODE,YNWODD,YNWOOD)
Alice of Frensham [DW/PA/5/1558/162]*
Elizabeth of Compton, widow [DW/PA/5/1561/25]
Elizabeth of Witley, widow [DW/PA/5/1557/115]
George of Seale [DW/PA/7/7 f.484; DW/PA/5/1604/33] <Abs 910>
George of Wanborough [DW/PA/5/1563/32]
Harry of Send [DW/PA/7/5 f.6; 1538] <Abs 75>
Henry of Chertsey, yeoman [PRO; PCC Will 1606] <Abs, SAC v.12 pp.196-197 *and* v.33 p.29>
Joan of Weybridge, widow [PRO; PCC Will 1589] <Abs SAC v.33 p.29>
John of Farnham - Tilford [DW/PA/7/8 f.294; DW/PA/5/1613/64]
John of Farnham, clothier [DW/PA/7/10 f.66; (1618)]
John of Frensham [DW/PA/7/1 f.33; 1486] <Abs 112>
John of Frensham - Hylloke, husbandman [DW/PA/5/1562/33]
John of Frensham, weaver [DW/PA/5/1562/35]
John of Frensham, husbandman [DW/PA/7/7 f.586; DW/PA/5/1607/52] <Abs 1092>
John of Godalming [PRO; PCC Will 1567]
John of Godalming, yeoman [DW/PA/5/1591/93]
John of Send, yeoman [HRO; 1601 B39]
John of Send, yeoman [DW/PA/7/13 f.440; DW/PA/5/1646/31]
John of Woking, yeoman [DW/PA/5/1558/300]*
John of Woking; Guildford; Cranleigh; Wonersh [DW/PA/7/6 f.106; DW/PA/5/1559/75]
Oliver of Witley; Frensham, yeoman [*in* DW/PA/5/1557/75]
Richard of West Horsley, yeoman [DW/PA/7/11 f.494; DW/PA/5/1628/61]
Richard of Woking - Sutton, husbandman [DW/PA/7/7 f.83; 1596] <Abs 150>
Robert of Farnham - Tilford, weaver [DW/PA/5/1562/34]
Robert of Frensham, yeoman [DW/PA/7/7 f.172; DW/PA/5/1597/58] <Abs 315>
Robert of Woking [DW/PA/5/1587/61]
Thomas of Ash; Frensham; Aldershot, Hampshire, yeoman [DW/PA/7/7 f.587 DW/PA/5/1607/53] <Abs 1095>
Thomas of Godalming [DW/PA/7/5 f.177 1540]
Thomas of Send, yeoman [DW/PA/7/8 f.371 DW/PA/5/1612/82]
Thomas of Weybridge; Chertsey [PRO; PCC Will 1586] <Abs SAC v.33 p.28>
William of Farnham - Tilford, husbandman [DW/PA/5/1563/33]
William of Walton on Thames; Chertsey - Woodham, senior [LBLAD; Surrey Deeds 1/2740; 1635-1638]
INYNGFELD *see* INFIELD
IRELAND (IRELANDE,IRLAND)
George of Guildford [HRO; 1603 AD34]
George of Reigate, yeoman [DW/PA/7/7 f.397 DW/PA/5/1603/90] <Abs 737>
George of Rotherhithe [PRO; PCC Admon 1649]
James of Epsom, senior [PRO; PCC 1639]
John of Epsom, proctor of the Court of Arches [PRO; PCC Admon 1627]
John of Epsom [PRO; PCC Admon 1636]
Richard of Alfold - Sidney, yeoman [DW/PA/5/1593/57]

IRELAND (IRELANDE,IRLAND) [*continued*]
Robert of Bermondsey [PRO; PCC Will 1502]
Thomas of Swk St Olave, baker [DW/PA/7/6 f.217; 1561]
Tobias of Newington [PRO; PCC Admon 1612]
William of Horley [PRO; PCC 1649]

IREMONGER
William of Swk St Saviour, waterman [DW/PA/5/1582/74]

IRESTEAD
William of Blechingley, hoop shaver [DW/PA/7/13 f.152; DW/PA/5/1642/47]
see also EASTED

IRLAND *see* IRELAND

ISAAC (ISAACKE)
Edward of Streatham, esq. [PRO; PCC Will 1573]
William of Swk St Thomas [DW/PA/5/1586/31]

ISAM
Joan of Guildford St Nicolas; Old Windsor, Berkshire; Egham [DW/PA/7/4 f.158; 1536]
John of Horsell, yeoman [HRO 1573 B77]

ISHERWOOD
Ralph of Bermondsey [PRO; PCC Admon 1631]

ISLEY
Edward of Surrey [PRO; PCC Will 1528]

ISOTT
Thomas of Swk St Saviour, citizen and pewterer [DW/PA/7/11 f.258; DW/PA/5/1625/130]

ISSTED,ISTED, ISTEED *see* EASTED

IVATT
Phillipa of Ewell, widow [PRO; PCC Admon 1629]

IVE *see* IVES

IVEN
Henry of Newington [LPL; 98/1 f.7v; Will 1630]

IVER (IVERS) [*In most, if not all cases, this is a mistranscription of Juer, q.v.*]
Ann, or Ann Juers, of Esher, widow [DW/PA/7/12 f.52; DW/PA/5/1632/52]
Henry, or Henry Juer of Farnham [DW/PA/7/11 f.431; DW/PA/5/1627/63]
Henry, or Henry Juer of Wandsworth [DW/PA/7/12 f.321; DW/PA/5/1637/59]

IVERY
Richard of Effingham, labourer [DW/PA/7/12 f.27; DW/PA/5/1631/58]

IVES (IVE)
Isabel of Egham [GL; Commissary Court of London Will; 1432]
Joan of Sutton, widow [DW/PA/7/12 f.54; DW/PA/5/1632/53]
Nicholas of Surrey [PRO; PCC Will 1558]
Robert, or Robert Jues of ... [DW/PA/7/10 f.63; 1618]

IVEY
Paul of Lambeth - Lambeth Marsh, gent. [PRO; PCC Will 1605] <Abs. SAC v.12 pp.84-85>

IVORY *see* IVERY

JACK
Richard of Mortlake [PRO; PCC Admon 1581]

JACKMAN (JACMAN,JAKMAN)
Agnes of Hambledon, widow [DW/PA/7/13 f.275; DW/PA/5/1644/10]
Brian of Swk St Olave, citizen and grocer [DW/PA/7/7 f.138; DW/PA/5/1597/59] <Abs 255>

JACKMAN (JACMAN,JAKMAN) [*continued*]
John of Chiddingfold, husbandman [DW/PA/7/12 f.390; DW/PA/5/1637/61]
John of Hambledon [PRO; PCC Admon 1647]
John of Peper Harow, husbandman [DW/PA/7/7 f.23; DW/PA/5/1595/57] <Abs 49>
Reynold of Newdigate [DW/PA/7/13 f.40; DW/PA/5/1640/83]
Richard of Chiddingfold - Livinghurst, senior [DW/PA/5/1605/53] <Abs U153>
Richard of Shere [DW/PA/5/1558/169]*
Robert of Alfold [DW/PA/5/1570/82]
Robert of Hambledon, husbandman [DW/PA/7/12 f.219; DW/PA/5/1634/60]
William of Betchworth, husbandman [DW/PA/7/12 f.312; DW/PA/5/1636/58]

JACKSON (JACKSONE,JACKSONNE,JACSON,JACSONNE,JAKSON,JAXSON)
Christiana of Croydon, spinster [LPL; 98/1 f.110v; Will 1639]
Cresset of Swk St Olave, carpenter [DW/PA/7/13 f.261; DW/PA/5/1644/11]
Edward of Swk St Olave, cooper [DW/PA/7/10 f.51; 1618]
Elizabeth of Woodmansterne [DW/PA/7/7 f.443; DW/PA/5/1603/91] <Abs 837>
Frances of Lambeth, widow [DW/PA/7/12 f.468; DW/PA/5/1638/70]
Henry of Swk St George, citizen and chirurgeon , senior [DW/PA/7/13 f.344; 1644]
Hugh of Cranleigh, husbandman [DW/PA/5/1587/111]
Jane, alias Jane Charlwood of Croydon [PRO; PCC Admon 1615]
Joan of Swk St George, widow [DW/PA/5/1558/168]*
John of Battersea, husbandman [DW/PA/7/11 f.576; DW/PA/5/1630/58]
John of Swk St George [DW/PA/5/1550/11]
John of Swk St Saviour, butcher [DW/PA/7/12 f.117; DW/PA/5/1632/56]
Marianne of Swk St Olave [DW/PA/7/11 f.240; DW/PA/5/1625/131]
Mary of Swk St Olave, widow [DW/PA/7/9 f.317; DW/PA/5/1619/68]
Nicholas of Croydon - Ham [PRO; PCC Will 1579]
Richard of Swk St George, citizen and grocer [DW/PA/5/1557/49]
Robert of Croydon - Ham, yeoman, senior [PRO; PCC Will 1622]
Robert of Croydon [PRO; PCC 1631]
Robert of Croydon [PRO; PCC Admon 1629]
Roger of Lambeth - Water Lambeth, tailor [DW/PA/5/1579/52]*
Thomas of Lambeth [DW/PA/7/11 f.549; DW/PA/5/1629/51]
Thomas of Newington [PRO; PCC Will 1523]
Thomas of Richmond [DW/PA/7/11 f.340; DW/PA/5/1625/132]
Thomas of Swk St Olave, labourer [DW/PA/5/1593/171]
Thomas of Swk St Olave, yeoman [DW/PA/7/7 f.514; DW/PA/5/1605/52] <Abs 965>
William of Bermondsey [PRO; PCC Admon 1623]
William of Croydon - Norbury, yeoman [PRO; PCC Will 1607]
William of Epsom, bricklayer [DW/PA/5/1557/99]
William of Horne, curate [DW/PA/7/9 f.104; DW/PA/5/1614/65]

JACMAN *see* JACKMAN

JACOB
Robert of Rotherhithe [PRO; PCC Admon 1647]

JACOBI
William of Swk St Olave [DW/PA/7/5 f.85; 1539]

JACOPS
Peter of ... [*in Latin*] [DW/PA/5/1563/23]

JACSON,JACSONNE *see* JACKSON

JADWIN
Elizabeth of Newington, widow [PRO; PCC 1639]

JAGGER
  John of Tooting, curate and clerk [DW/PA/5/1579/50]*
JAGOE
  Edward of Rotherhithe (died overseas) [PRO; PCC Admon 1649]
  Prudence of Lambeth, widow [DW/PA/7/12 f.243; DW/PA/5/1634/62]
JAKMAN *see* JACKMAN
JAKSON *see* JACKSON
JAKYS *see* JAQUES
JAMES
  Abraham of Shalford, gent. [PRO; PCC Will 1619]
  Francis of Ewhurst, clerk [PRO; PCC Will 1621]
  Joan *or* Jane of Swk St Olave, widow [DW/PA/7/13 f.243; DW/PA/5/1646/32]
  John of Alfold [PRO; PCC 1647]
  Lawrence of Swk St George, gent. [DW/PA/7/11 f.408; DW/PA/5/1627/60]
  Nicholas of Croydon [PRO; PCC Will 1433]
  Richard of Send, yeoman [HRO; 1624 B35]
  (Sir) Roger of Reigate, knight [PRO; PCC 1637]
  Thomas of Reigate [PRO; PCC 1632]
  William of Swk St George, butcher [DW/PA/7/7 f.519; DW/PA/5/1606/51]
    <Abs 972>
JAMESON (JAMESSON)
  Otto of Swk St Olave, hatmaker [DW/PA/7/2 f.57; 1499]
JAMS
  Francis, alias Jacops Cuper of Swk St Olave [DW/PA/7/2 f.85; 1502]
JANSON (JANSSON)
  Derek of Swk St Olave, hatmaker [DW/PA/5/1563/78]
  Gerard of ... [DW/PA/5/1558/167]
  Henry of Swk St Olave [DW/PA/7/3 f.190; 1531]
  William of Swk St Olave, tailor [DW/PA/7/3 f.119; 1529]
JAQUES (JAKYS)
  John of Shere, master of arts [PRO; PCC Will 1517]
  Robert of Kingston [PRO; PCC Will 1515]
JARVIS
  John of Newington [PRO; PCC 1636]
    see also JERVIS
JASLYN
  Christopher (*or* Hasleye) of Reigate, yeoman [DW/PA/7/6 f.235; 1561]
    see also GESTLYN
JASON
  Frances of Cobham, widow [PRO; PCC 1640; PCC Admon 1640]
JAXSON *see* JACKSON
JAY (JAYE,JEYE)
  Anthony of Lambeth [PRO; PCC Admon 1608]
  Anthony of Lambeth [PRO; PCC Admon 1627]
  Benet of Waverley, gent. [PRO; PCC Will 1586]
  Elizabeth of Farnham - Badshot, widow [PRO; PCC Will 1594]
  Gregory of Swk St Saviour, barber chirurgeon [DW/PA/5/1569/14]
  Richard of Surrey [PRO; PCC Will 1467]
  Thomas of Swk St Thomas, joiner [DW/PA/7/8 f.170; DW/PA/5/1610/76]
JAYSMORE *see* CHASMORE
JEALE *see* GEALE
JEATER *see* JETTER
JEBLETT
  John of Dunsfold, husbandman [DW/PA/7/13 f.103; DW/PA/5/1641/80]

JEFF
  Richard of Camberwell [PRO; PCC Will 1584]
JEFFERSON (GEFFRESON,GEFSON,JEFSON)
  Agnes of Bermondsey, widow [DW/PA/7/9 f,130; DW/PA/5/1615/71]
  Joan of Guildford, widow [DW/PA/5/1562/14]
  John of Bermondsey [PRO; PCC Will 1609] <Abs, SAC v,23 p,145>
  William of Swk St Margaret, draper [DW/PA/7/4 f,219; 1537]
  William of Surrey, gent, [PRO; PCC Will 1542]
  William of Swk St Saviour, draper [DW/PA/5/1582/11]
JEFFRIES (GEFFREY,JEFFERAY,JEFFERY,JEFFERYES,JEFFRE,JEFFREY,JEFFREYES
    JEOFFREY)
  Ann of Newington, widow [LPL; 96/1452; 98/1 f,131v; Will 1642]
  Audrey of Newington, widow of William [GL; Archdeaconry Court of London
    Will 1633]
  John of Newington [LPL; 98/1 ff,116r,119r; Will 1640]
  John of Streatham, priest [GL; Commissary Court of London Will 1536]
  John of Streatham, priest [DW/PA/7/4 f,234; 1538]
  Susan of Richmond [PRO; PCC Admon 1624]
  Thomas of Little Bookham, rector [HRO; Reg, Way 2 p,146; 1470]
  William of Richmond, gent, [PRO; PCC Will 1622]
JEFSON *see* JEFFERSON
JELE *see* GEALE
JELLATT (JELLETT)
  Abraham of Dorking, joiner [DW/PA/7/12 f,295; DW/PA/5/1635/54]
  Elizabeth of Dorking, widow [DW/PA/7/12 f,315; DW/PA/5/1636/59]
  John of Horley [DW/PA/5/1555/4]
JELLE *see* JEALE
JELLEY (GELYE,JELLIE,JELLY,JELYE)
  Christopher of Swk St Olave, blacksmith [DW/PA/7/5 f,218; 1541]
  Henry of Worplesdon, husbandman [DW/PA/7/9 f,280; 1618]
  Jane of Reigate, widow [DW/PA/7/12 f,207; DW/PA/5/1634/59]
  Mary of Dorking, widow [DW/PA/7/8 f,383; DW/PA/5/1612/84]
  Richard of Shalford, husbandman, senior [DW/PA/5/1579/53]*
  Richard of West Clandon, husbandman [DW/PA/7/8 f,37; DW/PA/5/1609/94]
  Robert of Lambeth [PRO; PCC Admon 1647]
JELLIFE *see* JOLLIFFE
JELLY,JELYE *see* JELLEY
JEMET
  Elizabeth, alias Elizabeth Besbeech of Lingfield [PRO; PCC Admon 1633]
JEMPSON
  William of Newington [LPL; 98/1 f,33v; Will 1631]
JENCE *see* JENNE
JENDINGE
  John of Guildford Holy Trinity, shoemaker [DW/PA/7/13 f,472;
    DW/PA/5/1648/15]
JENECKE
  Phillip of Swk St Olave, waterman [DW/PA/7/7 f,89; 1596] <Abs 164>
JENENS,JENINES,JENINGES,JENINGS *see* JENNINGS
JENKES *see* JENKS
JENKINS (JENKIN)
  Hugh of Battersea [PRO; PCC Admon 1640]
  Robert of Croydon - Trinity Hospital [PRO; PCC Will 1626]
  Thomas of Morden [DW/PA/7/13 f,243; DW/PA/5/1645/28]

JENKINSON (GYNKYNSON,JENKYNSON)
  James of Croydon [PRO; PCC Will 1585]
  Joan of Swk St Olave [DW/PA/7/4 f,221; 1537]
  John of Croydon [LPL; 98/1 f,9v; Will 1630]
  William of Croydon, husbandman [LPL; 96/1460; Will 1626]
  William of Lambeth [DW/PA/7/4 f,87; 1534]
JENKS (JENKES)
  Richard of Croydon, yeoman [LPL; 96/1457; Will 1644]
JENMAN
  Alice of Clapham, wife of Richard, yeoman [DW/PA/7/13 f,220; DW/PA/5/1643/52B]
JENNER (GENNER,JENN')
  John of Lambeth; Westminster, Middlesex; North and South Wales; Genard Glen, Cardiganshire [DW/PA/7/5 f,12; 1538] <Abs 63>
  John of Stoke, yeoman [DW/PA/7/10 f,157; DW/PA/5/1621/61]
  Thomas of Leigh, husbandman [DW/PA/7/10 f,190; DW/PA/5/1621/46]
JENNINGS (GENNYNS,GYNYNGES,JENENS,JENINES,JENINGES,JENINGS,JENNINGES, JENNYN,JENYN,JENYNS)
  Bernard of Guildford [PRO; PCC Will 1552] <Abs, SAC v,52 pp,40-41>
  Bernard of Streatham [PRO; PCC Will 1550] <Abs, SAC v,52 p,40>
  Edward of Croydon, clerk [PRO; PCC Will 1508]
  Ellen (formerly Ellen Cortes) of Clapham [PRO; PCC Will 1553]
  Gabriel of Camberwell - Dulwich [PRO; PCC Admon 1607]
  Henry of Godalming [PRO; PCC Will 1589]
  Joan, alias Joan Marchaunte of Frimley; Shinfield, Berkshire [DW/PA/7/8 f,116; DW/PA/5/1610/86]
  John of Camberwell [DW/PA/7/12 f,377; DW/PA/5/1637/62]
  Matthew of Limpsfield, labourer [DW/PA/5/1580/58]
  Nicholas of Surrey [PRO; PCC Will 1532] <Abs, SAC v,52 pp,38-40>
  Richard of Kingston, fisherman [HRO; 1589 B31]
  Robert of Kingston, gent, [GL; Commissary Court of London Will 1554]
  Thomas of Surrey [PRO; PCC Will 1518]
  Thomas of Barnes [LPL; 98/1 ff,46v,66v; Wills 1633 *and* 1635]
JENT *see* GENT
JERBARD
  Thomas of Stoke next Guildford [PRO; PCC Will 1579]
JERMY
  (Lady) Elizabeth of Surrey, wife of (Sir) Isaac, knight [PRO; PCC 1645]
JERVIS (GERVICE,JERVES)
  Hugh of Streatham [PRO; PCC Will 1584]
  John of Rotherhithe, mariner [DW/PA/5/1545/15]
    see also JARVIS
JESOPP
  Henry of Godalming [PRO; PCC 1649]
  Robert of Newington [PRO; PCC Admon 1585]
JESTON
  Robert of Lambeth, haberdasher [PRO; PCC Will 1622]
JETTER
  Nicholas of Swk St George [DW/PA/7/5 f,34; 1538] <Abs 82>
JEVETT
  Thomas of Esher [DW/PA/7/5 f,37; 1538] <Abs 31>
JEWDRIE *see* JUDERY
JEWELL (JUELL)
  Bernard of Lingfield [DW/PA/7/4 f,101; 1535]

JEWELL (JUELL) [*continued*]
John of Limpsfield, yeoman [DW/PA/7/10 f,247; DW/PA/5/1622/49]
Richard of Oxted [PRO; PCC 1638]
Robert of Lingfield [DW/PA/5/1561/69]
Robert of Swk St George, yeoman [DW/PA/7/13 f,299; DW/PA/5/1643/53]
JEWER (JOURD,JOURE,JOWRE,JUER,JUERS,JURE)[*Sometimes mistranscribed as* IVER]
Alexander of Shalford [DW/PA/1558/170] [*Two copies - one* *]
Alice, *or* Alice Iver of Farnham, widow [HRO; 1563 B102-103]
Ann *or* Ann Ivers of Esher, widow [DW/PA/7/12 f,52; DW/PA/5/1632/52]
Benjamin of Farnham, miller [HRO; 1641 B26]
Christopher of Seale - Tongham [DW/PA/7/8 f,358; DW/PA/5/1612/85]
Henry *or* Henry Iver of Farnham [DW/PA/7/11 f,431; DW/PA/5/1627/63]
Henry *or* Henry Iver of Wandsworth [DW/PA/7/12 f,321; DW/PA/5/1637/59]
John of Farnham - Runfold, husbandman [HRO; 1576 B40]
John of Farnham - Badshot; Crondall, Hampshire, yeoman [DW/PA/7/9 f,314; DW/PA/5/1619/70]
John of Peper Harow, husbandman [DW/PA/7/8 f,301; DW/PA/5/1613/57]
John of Puttenham [HRO; Reg, CCB 20 p,11; 1563]
John of Puttenham [DW/PA/5/1563/76 *and in* DW/PA/1563/65]
John of Seale [DW/PA/5/1569/46]
John of Seale [DW/PA/5/1570/37]
John of Witley, millwright [DW/PA/7/10 f,243; DW/PA/5/1621/63]
Lettice of Frensham - Wrecclesham, spinster [DW/PA/7/11 f,60; DW/PA/5/1623/63]
Ralph of Seale [DW/PA/7/6 f,125; DW/PA/5/1559/171]
Richard of Peper Harow, husbandman, junior [HRO; 1619 B38]
Richard of Seale [DW/PA/7/3 f,139; 1530]
Richard of Seale, husbandman [DW/PA/5/1582/46]
Robert of Witley [DW/PA/5/1579/51]*
Stephen of Seale [DW/PA/7/5 f,80; 1539]
Thomas of Farnham - Runfold, yeoman [HRO; 1618 B33]
Thomas of Farnham, clothier [DW/PA/7/11 f,315; DW/PA/5/1626/74]
William of Seale [*in* DW/PA/5/1558/166]* [*There are two* William Jewer *of* Seale *wills in the document which bears this reference, one is shown as senior,*]
William of Seale [DW/PA/5/1558/163]*
William of Seale - Tongham [DW/PA/7/8 f,17; DW/PA/5/1608/63]
JEWERIE *see* JURY
JHONSONE *see* JOHNSON
JOANES (JOANS) *see* JONES
JOBSON (JOBBESON,JOBSONN)
Elizabeth of Swk St Saviour, widow [DW/PA/7/12 f,94; DW/PA/5/1632/54]
John of Kingston, yeoman [DW/PA/7/3 f,197; 1532]
John of Walton on Thames, fisher [DW/PA/7/7 f,320; DW/PA/5/1600/23] <Abs 571>
Thomas of Thorpe, yeoman [DW/PA/5/1576/132]
JOHANES *see* JONES
John, prior of Merton [LPL; Reg, Abp Morton f,80v; Admon 1492]
John, Henry son of, of Swk St Olave [DW/PA/7/4 f,219; 1537]
John, Edward ap John, alias Edward King of Bermondsey [PRO; PCC Will 1587]
John ap Hugh *see* APEW
JOHN (JOHNS)
Griffin of West Horsley, husbandman [DW/PA/7/7 f,207; DW/PA/5/1598/45] <Abs 369>

JOHN (JOHNS) [*continued*]
William of Swk St Thomas [DW/PA/5/1587/38]
JOHNES *see* JONES
JOHNS *see* JOHN
JOHNSON (JHONSON,JHONSONE,JOHNSONE,JOHNSONNE,JONSON)
Alice of Beddington [DW/PA/7/11 f,402; DW/PA/5/1627/62]
Alice of Bermondsey, widow [DW/PA/5/1557/47]
Anthony of Swk St Saviour; Normanton, Yorkshire, citizen and leatherseller [*in* DW/PA/5/1544/26]
Christopher of Wandsworth, mealman [DW/PA/7/7 f,474; DW/PA/5/1604/34] <Abs 894>
Cornelius of Kingston, cooper [DW/PA/7/7 f,500; DW/PA/5/1605/54] <Abs 936>
Edmund of Swk St Saviour, waterman [DW/PA/7/9 f,179; DW/PA/5/1616/78]
Elizabeth of Swk St Saviour, widow [DW/PA/5/1587/93]
Ellen of Swk St Saviour, widow [DW/PA/7/12 f,446; DW/PA/5/1639/78]
Geoffrey of Chipstead [PRO; PCC 1647]
George of ,,, [DW/PA/7/10 f,55; 1618]
Gilbert of ,,, [DW/PA/5/1587/58]
Harry of Swk St Olave, citizen and woodmonger [DW/PA/7/6 f,23; DW/PA/5/1559/6]
Henrick of Swk St Olave, brewer [DW/PA/5/1593/44]
Henry of London, citizen and cordwainer [DW/PA/5/1570/11]
Henry of Lambeth [DW/PA/7/11 f,7; DW/PA/5/1622/50]
Henry of Newington [? LPL; Will 1636] [*Though in an early list, this will does not appear in the index now at Lambeth Palace Library and would seem to be either a mistake, or lost,*]
Henry of Puttenham, clerk [DW/PA/7/7 f,58; DW/PA/5/1596/38] <Abs 110>
James of Chertsey [DW/PA/7/4 f,202; 1537]
James of Swk St Saviour [DW/PA/5/1580/22]
Joan of Puttenham [DW/PA/7/8 f,147; DW/PA/5/1611/64]
Joan of ,,, [DW/PA/7/9 f,212; DW/PA/5/1616/79]
John of ,,, [DW/PA/7/8 f,98; DW/PA/5/1609/95]
John of Banstead, tailor [DW/PA/7/9 f,245; DW/PA/5/1617/58]
John of Bramley, cooper [DW/PA/7/12 f,373; 1637]
John of Camberwell [DW/PA/7/9 f,36; DW/PA/5/1614/66]
John of London, citizen and cordwainer [DW/PA/5/1587/123]
John of Rotherhithe [PRO; PCC Will 1614]
John of Rotherhithe [PRO; PCC Admon 1617]
John of Rotherhithe, merchant [PRO; PCC Will 1622]
John of Swk St Olave, tailor [DW/PA/5/1569/56]
John of Swk St Saviour [DW/PA/7/11 f,207; DW/PA/5/1625/133]
Lancelot of Bermondsey, citizen and ale brewer [PRO; PCC Will 1592]
Leonard of Swk St Saviour, waterman [DW/PA/7/10 f,89; DW/PA/5/1615/38]
Margaret of Swk St Olave, widow [DW/PA/5/1555/83]
Margaret of Wonersh, widow [DW/PA/7/12 f,114; DW/PA/5/1632/55]
Martin of Swk St Olave, beer brewer [DW/PA/7/2 f,57; 1499]
Michael of Kingston [DW/PA/7/13 f,33; DW/PA/5/1639/79]
Nicholas of Bramley, husbandman [DW/PA/7/11 f,579; DW/PA/5/1630/59]
Nicholas of Leatherhead, yeoman [DW/PA/7/10 f,99; DW/PA/5/1619/69]
Nicholas of Swk St George, innholder [DW/PA/7/8 f,329; DW/PA/5/1613/65]
Owen of Swk St Thomas, citizen and bricklayer [DW/PA/5/1571/64]
Peter of Swk St Thomas Hospital [DW/PA/7/6 f,65; DW/PA/5/1559/45]
Ralph of ,,,, citizen and grocer [DW/PA/5/1602/55] <Abs U54>

JOHNSON (JHONSON,JHONSONE,JOHNSONE,JOHNSONNE,JONSON) [*continued*]
Ralph of Swk St George, blacksmith [DW/PA/5/1593/8]
Richard of Battersea, citizen and woodmonger [PRO; PCC Will *and* Admon 1645]
Richard of Croydon [PRO; PCC Admon 1579]
Richard of Rotherhithe [PRO; PCC Will 1593]
Richard of Wonersh, yeoman [DW/PA/7/7 f.586; DW/PA/5/1607/54] <Abs 1093>
Richard of Wonersh, yeoman [HRO; 1612 B50]
Robert of Swk St Mary Overy, citizen and clothworker [DW/PA/7/5 f.150; 1540]
Susan of Lingfield, widow [PRO; PCC Admon 1641]
Thomas of Bermondsey; Lewisham, Kent, whitster [DW/PA/7/2 f.67; 1500]
Thomas of Mitcham [DW/PA/7/1 f.35; 1486] <Abs 119>
Thomas of Swk St Margaret, tailor [DW/PA/7/2 f.69; 1500]
Thomas of Swk St Olave [? HRO; 1529]
Thomas of Swk St Olave [DW/PA/5/1576/147]
Thomas of Swk St Saviour, waterman [DW/PA/7/8 f.304; DW/PA/5/1613/66]
Walter of Newington [LPL; 96/1467; 98/1 f.74r; Will 1636]
William of Bramley, beer brewer [DW/PA/7/7 f.323; DW/PA/5/1601/53] <Abs 578>
William of Kingston, free mason [DW/PA/5/1550/21]
William of Kingston, sergeant of the mace [DW/PA/7/13 f.98; DW/PA/5/1640/84]
William of Swk St George [DW/PA/7/5 f.122; 1539]
William of Swk St Mary Magdalen next St Mary Overy Abbey [DW/PA/7/1 f.30; 1486] <Abs 99>
William of Swk St Olave [DW/PA/5/1582/94]

JOINER (JOYNER,JOYNOR)
Dorcas of Putney, spinster [PRO; PCC 1638]
Mary of Chessington, spinster [PRO; PCC Will 1617]

JOLLIFFE (JELLIFE,JOLYFF)
Alice, alias Alice March of Godalming - Tichbourne [PRO; PCC Admon 1648]
Henry of Godalming; Hambledon; Chiddingfold, husbandman [DW/PA/5/1546/59]
Joan of Godalming - Tichbourne, widow [DW/PA/5/1617/57] <Abs U218>
John of Godalming - Tichbourne; Chiddingfold; Hambledon, yeoman [DW/PA/5/1603/92] <Abs U75>
Thomas of Godalming - Tichbourne, yeoman [DW/PA/7/12 f.25; DW/PA/5/1631/57]

JOLLY
Edward of Dunsfold [HRO; 1604 B35]

JONES (GONNYS,JOANES,JOANS,JOHANES,JOHNES,JONYS,JOONE)
Agnes of Esher, widow [DW/PA/7/9 f.137; DW/PA/5/1615/73]
Alice of Swk St Saviour [DW/PA/7/11 f.371; DW/PA/5/1626/73]
Andrew of Kingston, glover [DW/PA/7/10 f.196; DW/PA/5/1621/62]
Ann of Wandsworth, widow [DW/PA/7/10 f.181; DW/PA/5/1620/70]
Avis of Horsell, widow [DW/PA/7/12 f.375; DW/PA/5/1637/60]
Christopher of Rotherhithe [PRO; PCC Admon 1622]
David of Croydon, shoemaker [PRO; PCC Will 1620] <Soame 677>
David of Reigate [PRO; PCC Will 1558]
David of Swk St Saviour, feltmaker [DW/PA/7/11 f.117; DW/PA/5/1624/62]
Edward of Horsell, clerk, senior [DW/PA/5/1627/61]
Edward of Swk St Saviour - Paris Garden, waterman [DW/PA/5/1579/49]*

JONES (GONNYS,JOANES,JOANS,JOHANES,JOHNES,JONYS,JOONE) [*continued*]
Elizabeth of Swk St Mary Overy; Ruabon, Denbighshire [DW/PA/7/9 f,161; 1617]
Ellen of Swk St Olave, widow [DW/PA/7/12 f,474; DW/PA/5/1639/77]
Evan of Newington [PRO; PCC Will 1624]
Fulk of Oxted [DW/PA/7/9 f,141; DW/PA/5/1615/74]
Henry of Lambeth [PRO; PCC Admon 1642]
Henry of Mitcham, yeoman [PRO; PCC Will 1608] <Abs, SAC v,13 p,191>
Henry of Reigate, shoemaker [DW/PA/7/13 f,479; DW/PA/5/1648/16]
Henry of Swk St Saviour, ale brewer [DW/PA/7/7 f,333; DW/PA/5/1601/54] <Abs 601>
Henry of Streatham; Brasted, Kent, yeoman [DW/PA/7/9 f,94; DW/PA/5/1616/80]
Isaac of Kingston, gent, [PRO; PCC 1647]
James of Chessington, yeoman [DW/PA/7/11 f,214; DW/PA/5/1625/134]
Jane of Swk St George [DW/PA/7/7 f,198; DW/PA/5/1598/46] <Abs 358>
John of Camberwell, yeoman [PRO; PCC 1630] <Scroope 864>
John of Nutfield [DW/PA/7/7 f,315; DW/PA/5/1600/25] <Abs 562>
John of Rotherhithe [PRO; PCC Admon 1632]
John of Swk St Thomas, carpenter [DW/PA/7/11 f,572; DW/PA/5/1630/60]
Katherine of Mitcham, widow of John [PRO; PCC 1633]
Katherine of Swk St Saviour - Bankside [DW/PA/7/11 f,391; DW/PA/5/1626/75]
Martha of Chessington, widow [DW/PA/7/12 f,176; DW/PA/5/1633/74]
Morgan of Swk St Olave, citizen and woodmonger [DW/PA/7/13 f,367; 1644]
Morgan of Swk St Olave, cook [DW/PA/7/13 f,411; DW/PA/5/1645/29]
Owen of Swk St Saviour, waterman [DW/PA/7/8 f,311; DW/PA/5/1613/67]
Richard of ,,, [DW/PA/5/1578/14]
Richard of Bermondsey [PRO; PCC 1640]
Richard of Headley, rector [HRO; Reg, Way 1 p,84; 1464]
Richard of Swk St Saviour, brewer [DW/PA/7/11 f,228; DW/PA/5/1625/135]
Thomas of Surrey [PRO; PCC Will 1619]
Thomas of Barnes, rector [LPL; 98/1 f,61v; Will 1634]
Thomas of Guildford Holy Trinity [DW/PA/7/4 f,165; 1536]
Thomas of Newington [PRO; PCC Will 1623]
Thomas of Newington - Walworth [LPL; 96/1484; Will 1626]
Thomas of Swk St Saviour, glover [DW/PA/5/1601/55] <Abs U55>
Thomas of Swk St Saviour, gent, [DW/PA/7/12 f,249; DW/PA/5/1636/57]
Thomas of Witley [GMR; 1225/4; Will 1521]
Thomas of Witley, esq, [DW/PA/5/1587/126]
Walter of Swk St Olave, hatbandmaker [DW/PA/7/7 f,645; DW/PA/5/1608/61] <Abs 1212>
William of Barnes [LPL; 98/1 f,35v; Will 1632]
William of Blechingley [DW/PA/7/9 f,71; DW/PA/5/1614/67]
William of Carshalton, gardener [PRO; PCC Will 1609] <Abs, SAC v,23 pp,141-142>
William of Newington [PRO; PCC Will 1597]
William of Nutfield, tailor [HRO; 1606 B32]
William, alias William Swayne of Swk St George, glover [DW/PA/5/1579/88]*
see also JOHN,JORNES

JOPPER
Agnes of Swk St Mary Magdalen, widow [DW/PA/7/7 f,641; DW/PA/5/1608/62] <Abs 1204>

JORDAN (GOORD'N,JORDAINE,JORDEN,JOURDEN,JOYRDAYN,JURDAN,JURDAYNE,JURDEYN)
Alice of Lambeth, widow [PRO; PCC 1648]
Andrew of Charlwood; Reigate [PRO; PCC Will 1584]
Catherine of Charlwood, widow of William [PRO; PCC Will 1627]
Edmund of Charlwood, gent., junior [LPL; 96/1500; Will 1643]
Helen of Swk St Saviour - Bankside, Upper Ground, widow [DW/PA/7/12 f.131; DW/PA/5/1632/57]
Henry of East Clandon [DW/PA/7/4 f.25; 1532]
James of Charlwood, yeoman [PRO; PCC Will 1611] <Abs. SAC v.35 p.33>
Joan of Reigate, widow [PRO; PCC Will 1593]
John of Charlwood [PRO; PCC Will 1512]
John of Charlwood; Horley [PRO; PCC Will 1587]
John of Charlwood [PRO; PCC Admon 1619]
John of Charlwood, yeoman [PRO; PCC Will 1628]
John of East Clandon [DW/PA/7/4 f.98; 1534]
John of East Clandon, yeoman [DW/PA/7/7 f.188; DW/PA/5/1598/44] <Abs 344>
Richard of Charlwood, tanner [PRO; PCC Will 1614]
Robert of Ashtead [DW/PA/7/9 f.211; DW/PA/5/1616/73]
Robert of Charlwood [PRO; PCC Admon 1607]
Stephen of East Clandon, husbandman [DW/PA/5/1570/13]
Thomas of Charlwood, gent. [PRO; PCC Will 1610]
Thomas of Horley, yeoman [DW/PA/5/1617/59] <Abs U219>
Thomas of Horley, yeoman [HRO; 1619 B37]
Thomas of Horley [PRO; PCC Admon 1622]
Thomas of Lambeth, yeoman [DW/PA/7/13 f.161; DW/PA/5/1642/48]
Thomas of Swk St Olave [DW/PA/5/1558/126]*
William of Ashtead [DW/PA/7/9 f.175B; DW/PA/5/1616/81]
William of Charlwood - Gatwick [PRO; PCC Will 1625]
William of Charlwood [PRO; PCC Admon 1641]
William of Horley [PRO; PCC Will 1596]

JORNES
Ambrose of Carshalton, husbandman [DW/PA/7/11 f.531; DW/PA/5/1629/52]
see also JONES

JOSEPH
John of Lambeth [PRO; PCC Admon 1639]
William of Lingfield [DW/PA/7/2 f.14; 1491]

JOSLIN *see* GESTLYN,JASLYN

JOSSON
John of Croydon [PRO; PCC Will 1524]

JOSSY
Robert of Cranleigh; Ewhurst - Baynards, esq. and yeoman [PRO; PCC Will 1627]

JOSUA
Richard of West Horsley, parson [DW/PA/7/8 f.43; DW/PA/5/1609/96]

JOUNGE
Catherine, alias Catherine Kidwell of Malden [PRO; PCC Admon 1641]

JOURDAN *see* JORDAN

JOURE,JOWRE *see* JEWER

JOWLES
John of Newington, esq. [PRO; PCC 1639]

JOY
John of Burstow [PRO; PCC 1642]

JOYCE
Ann of Walton on Thames, widow [DW/PA/7/13 f.226; DW/PA/5/1643/54]

JOYCE [*continued*]
Henry of Godalming, cordmaker [DW/PA/7/9 f,165; DW/PA/5/1616/82]
Henry of Guildford, innholder [DW/PA/7/13 f,355; 1644]
John of ... [DW/PA/7/11 f,80; DW/PA/5/1623/64]
John of Thorpe, husbandman [DW/PA/5/1574/21]
Richard of Swk St George, victualler [DW/PA/7/12 f,494; DW/PA/5/1638/71]
William of Swk St Saviour, waterman [DW/PA/5/1593/158]
JOYE *see* LOYE
JOYNER,JOYNOR *see* JOINER
JUBB
George of Croydon, victualler [LPL; 96/1503; 98/1 f,12v; Will 1641]
JUBY
Edward of Swk St Saviour, gent, [DW/PA/7/10 f,47; 1618]
JUDD (JUDDE,JUDE)
(Sir) Andrew of Surrey, knight and alderman [PRO; PCC Will 1558]
Thomas of Camberwell, husbandman [DW/PA/7/5 f,225; 1541]
JUDERY (JEWORIE,JUDRY)
Geoffrey of Sutton, husbandman [DW/PA/5/1571/62]
Roger of Sutton [DW/PA/7/12 f,231; DW/PA/5/1634/61]
JUDKYN
Thomas of Bermondsey, carman [DW/PA/7/9 f,89; DW/PA/5/1615/75]
JUDRY *see* JUDERY
JUELL *see* JEWELL
JUER,JUERS,JURE *see* JEWER
JUES
Robert, *or* Robert Ives of ... [DW/PA/7/10 f,63; 1618]
JUGELLIE
James, *or* James Ingellie of Lambeth [DW/PA/7/10 f,26; DW/PA/5/1616/72]
JUGES *see* INGES
JUPP
Michael of Ockley, husbandman [DW/PA/7/12 f,305; DW/PA/5/1635/55]
JURDAN,JURDAYNE,JURDEYN *see* JORDAN
JURY (JEWERIE)
Nicholas of Woking - Sutton [PRO; PCC 1646]
Nicholas of Woking; Horsham, Sussex, bachelor
[PRO; PCC 1648 *and* Admon 1648]
Richard of Blechingley [DW/PA/7/12 f,81; DW/PA/5/1633/73]
JUSTICE (JUSTIS)
Joan of Kingston [PRO; PCC 1645]
Judith of Egham, widow [HRO; 1636 B14]
Nicholas of Egham, weaver [HRO; 1629 B29]
Nicholas of Thorpe, weaver [DW/PA/7/13 f,121; DW/PA/5/1640/85]
JUSTINS
Agnes of Epsom, widow [DW/PA/5/1592/98]
JUX (JUXE)
John of Lambeth - Stockwell, husbandman [DW/PA/5/1558/165]*
Nicholas of Lambeth - Stockwell, yeoman [DW/PA/7/8 f,250;
DW/PA/5/1613/68]
JUXON
John of Mortlake, citizen and merchant tailor , gent, (Captain)
[LPL; 96/1508; Will 1644]
John of Mortlake, citizen and merchant tailor [PRO; PCC 1635]

KARTER,KARVER *see* CARTER,CARVER
KATE (KAYTE)
  Thomas of Farnham [PRO; PCC Will 1498]
  Thomas of Lambeth, widower [PRO; PCC Admon 1646]
KATESBYE *see* CATESBY
KATHERENES (KATHERENS)
  Gilbert of Swk St Saviour, carpenter [DW/PA/7/10 f,10; DW/PA/5/1619/71]
  Roger of Chertsey, waterman [DW/PA/7/10 f,165; 1621]
KAVERLEY *see* CAVERLEY
KAYES
  John of Godalming, husbandman [DW/PA/7/10 f,86; DW/PA/5/1615/39]
KAYTE *see* KATE
KEALING *see* KEELING
KEARE
  Richard of Swk St Saviour [DW/PA/7/10 f,197; DW/PA/5/1621/64]
KEATING (KETON,KEYTING)
  Joan of Swk St George, widow [DW/PA/7/5 f,224; 1541]
  Robert of Cobham, clerk, canon of Wells, Somerset [PRO; PCC Will 1429]
KEDGELL
  John of Swk St Olave, cook [DW/PA/7/13 f,362; 1644]
    see also KIDGELL
KEDYNG
  John of Croydon [PRO; PCC Will 1508]
KEELING (KEALING)
  Thomas of Bermondsey, citizen and butcher [GL; Commissary Court of London Will 1561]
  Thomas of Bermondsey, butcher [PRO; PCC Will 1568]
KEENE (KEEN,KENE,KENES,KYEN)
  Arthur of Newington [LPL; 96/1510; Will 1633]
  Eleanor of Haslemere, widow [DW/PA/7/13 f,201; DW/PA/5/1642/50]
  Frances of Putney, spinster [LPL; 96/1509; 98/1 f,34r; Will 1631]
  Henry of Godalming - Eashing, miller [DW/PA/7/6 f,169; *in* DW/PA/5/1559/174]
  Joan of Compton, widow [DW/PA/5/1570/51]
  Joan of Godalming - Eashing, wife of John [DW/PA/7/11 f,584; DW/PA/5/1630/61]
  Joan of Wonersh, widow of William [DW/PA/7/8 f,146; DW/PA/5/1611/65]
  John of Compton [HRO; 1570 B246]
  John of Godalming - Eashing [DW/PA/7/10 f,142; DW/PA/5/1620/71]
  John of Godalming - Eashing, miller [DW/PA/7/13 f,247; DW/PA/5/1640/89]
  John of Merrow, carpenter [HRO; 1617 B34]
  Joseph of Wonersh, shearman [HRO; 1612 B50]
  Nicholas of Dunsfold [DW/PA/7/8 f,189; DW/PA/5/1610/77]
  Richard of Swk St Olave, cooper [DW/PA/7/13 f,110; DW/PA/5/1640/87]
  Robert of Haslemere, husbandman [DW/PA/7/13 f,245; DW/PA/5/1640/88]
  Samuel of Woking, husbandman [DW/PA/7/12 f,372; 1637]
  Thomas of Godalming - Eashing [DW/PA/7/7 f,168; DW/PA/5/1597/60] <Abs 309>
  Thomas of Merrow, carpenter [HRO; 1639 B46]
  Thomas of Wonersh - Bridgeham, husbandman [DW/PA/7/8 f,294; DW/PA/5/1613/69]
  William of Witley - Milford, husbandman [DW/PA/7/6 f,175; DW/PA/5/1559/173]

KEGOW
  Alice of Epsom [DW/PA/7/2 f.45; 1495]
KELIK,KELLECK *see* KILLICK
KELLETT (KELETT,KELLEFETT,KELLET)
  Edward of Swk St Margaret [DW/PA/7/4 f.1; 1532]
  John of Surrey [PRO; PCC Will 1501]
  Matthew of Ripley, gent. [PRO; PCC Will 1556]
  Matthew of Rotherhithe, yeoman [PRO; PCC Will 1604] <Abs. SAC v.11 p.298>
  Richard of Egham, gent. [PRO; PCC Will 1596]
  Thomas of Lambeth, baker [DW/PA/7/9 f.50; DW/PA/5/1614/68]
  Walter of Swk St Margaret, citizen and barber [DW/PA/7/4 f.39; 1533]
  William of Camberwell, grocer [PRO; PCC Will 1616]
  William of Swk St Saviour; Lambeth - Lambeth Marsh, brewer [DW/PA/5/1552/23]
  William of Sutton, rector, clerk of the Chancery [PRO; PCC Will 1500; CCAL; 1500 f.67v] <Abs. SAC v.52 p.46>
KELLEY
  Arlington of Mortlake, gent. [PRO; PCC Will 1584]
  Henry of Swk St Saviour, yeoman [DW/PA/5/1587/55]
  Michael of Streatham [DW/PA/7/8 f.148; DW/PA/5/1611/66]
KELLYCKE *see* KILLICK
KELSEY
  John of Cranleigh, yeoman [DW/PA/5/1624/63]
  John of Ripley [DW/PA/5/1557/5]
  Thomas of Shere [PRO; PCC Will 1595]
KELSHULL
  Alice of Bermondsey - Bermondsey Monastery [PRO; PCC Will 1435]
  William, alias William Converse of Bermondsey [PRO; PCC Will 1432]
KELYKE *see* KILLICK
KEMBER (KEMKAR)
  Barbara of Weybridge [DW/PA/7/12 f.271; DW/PA/5/1635/57]
  Harry of West Horsley [DW/PA/7/6 f.49; DW/PA/5/1559/42]
  John, alias John Comber of Camberwell [PRO; PCC 1649]
  Robert of West Horsley [*in* DW/PA/5/1555/14]
  Roger of Walton on Thames, basketmaker [DW/PA/7/12 f.238; DW/PA/5/1634/64]
KEMBLE
  Maria of Swk St Saviour, widow [DW/PA/7/11 f.330; DW/PA/5/1625/136]
KEMP (KEMPE,KEMPP)
  Alice of Kingston - Surbiton [DW/PA/7/4 f.223; 1537]
  Frances of Rotherhithe [PRO; PCC Admon 1579]
  Frances of Rotherhithe, spinster [PRO; PCC Admon 1581]
  Henry of Banstead, husbandman [DW/PA/7/13 f.294; DW/PA/5/1643/56]
  Henry of Cranleigh, tailor [HRO; 1591 B45]
  James of Ewell [DW/PA/7/11 f.599; DW/PA/5/1630/62]
  Joan of Godstone, widow [DW/PA/5/1550/54]
  John of Surrey, parson [PRO; PCC Will 1587]
  John of Betchworth [DW/PA/7/2 f.203; 1524]
  John of Betchworth - Brockham, shoemaker [DW/PA/5/1582/100]
  John of Godstone [DW/PA/7/3 f.131; 1530]
  John of Godstone [DW/PA/5/1550/55]
  John of Godstone [HRO; 1553 U136] [*Inventory only*]
  John of Kingston, tailor [DW/PA/7/4 f.137; 1536]
  John of Swk St Saviour, waterman [DW/PA/7/12 f.227; DW/PA/5/1634/63]

KEMP (KEMPE,KEMPP) [*continued*]
Mary of Ewell, widow [DW/PA/7/13 f.469; DW/PA/5/1648/17]
Michael of Rotherhithe [PRO; PCC Admon 1568]
Richard of Cranleigh, tailor [HRO; 1604 B36]
Richard of Headley, yeoman [DW/PA/5/1562/18]
Robert of Betchworth, yeoman [DW/PA/7/9 f.308; DW/PA/5/1619/72]
Robert of Chertsey, husbandman [PRO; PCC Will 1597] [*and*] [DW/PA/5/1597/1] <Abs U11>
Thomas of Dorking, yeoman [DW/PA/5/1582/22]
William of Dorking, yeoman [DW/PA/5/1591/19]
William of Haslemere, shoemaker [PRO; PCC Will 1600]

KEMPFEILD
William of Thames Ditton, tailor [DW/PA/7/7 f.645; DW/PA/5/1608/64] <Abs 1213>

KEMPP *see* KEMP

KEMPSALL (KEMPSALE,KEMPSHALL,KEMSALL,KYMSOLL)
Denise of Walton on the Hill, widow [DW/PA/7/3 f.149; 1530]
Edward of Kingston, collarmaker [DW/PA/7/6 f.223; 1561]
George of Esher [HRO; 1623 AD59]
Henry of Battersea, yeoman [PRO; PCC Will 1623]
John of Compton - Eastbury, esq. [PRO; PCC Admon 1648]
John of Ewell - Kingswood, yeoman [DW/PA/5/1552/15]
Nicholas of Coulsdon [DW/PA/7/11 f.198; DW/PA/5/1625/137]
Richard of Chipstead [DW/PA/7/12 f.467; DW/PA/5/1638/72]
Richard of Lingfield, bachelor [DW/PA/7/10 f.175; DW/PA/5/1619/73]
Thomas of Chipstead, yeoman, senior [HRO; 1587 B50] [*and*] [DW/PA/5/1587/30]
Thomas of Epsom [PRO; PCC Admon 1611]
Thomas of Farleigh [PRO; PCC Will 1506]
William of Chipstead, yeoman [DW/PA/7/13 f.475; DW/PA/5/1648/18]
William of Ewell - Kingswood; Walton on the Hill [DW/PA/7/3 f.148; 1530]

KEMPSTER
William of Battersea, vintner [GL; Archdeaconry Court of London Will 1644]

KEMSALL *see* KEMPSALL

KENDALL
Richard of Newby Stones - Morland, Westmorland, wiredrawer [DW/PA/5/1576/82]
Thomas of Bermondsey [PRO; PCC Will 1552]
Thomas of Chaldon, husbandman [PRO; PCC Will 1617]
William of Richmond, marshal farrier to the king [PRO; PCC 1633]

KENDELMARSH
Henry of Swk St George [DW/PA/5/1575/57]

KENDRICKE
Ellen of Lingfield [PRO; PCC Will 1557]

KENE,KENES *see* KEENE

KENNADE,KENNARDESLIE,KENNADY *see* KENNEDY

KENNARD
John of Chaldon [PRO; PCC Admon 1649]

KENNEDY (KENNADE,KENNADY,KENNEDAIE,KENNARDESLIE)
(Sir) John of Barnes, knight [PRO; PCC Will 1622]
Patrick of Rotherhithe [PRO; PCC 1639]
Sarah, alias Sarah Hannam of Rotherhithe [PRO; PCC Admon 1646]

KENNEDY (KENNADE,KENNADY,KENNEDAIE,KENNARDESLIE) [*continued*]
  Thomas of Carshalton [PRO; PCC Will 1391]
  William of Newington, yeoman [PRO; PCC Will 1627]
KENNER
  Christopher of Bermondsey, citizen and leatherseller [DW/PA/7/11 f,178; DW/PA/5/1625/138]
KENNINGHAM (de KENYNGHAM)
  Thomas of Beddington [HRO; Reg, Stra p,83; 1333]
  William of Swk [DW/PA/5/1562/49]
KENRICK *see* KENWRICKE
KENT (KENTE)
  Elizabeth of Witley [? HRO; 1529]
  Hester, alias Hester Nubery of Farnham, spinster [DW/PA/7/12 f,329; DW/PA/5/1636/61]
  John, alias John Newbery of Farnham, glover [HRO; 1600 B37]
  John, alias John Newbery of Farnham, fellmonger [DW/PA/7/11 f,603; DW/PA/5/1630/63]
  John, alias John Nuberry of Farnham, fellmonger [DW/PA/7/12 f,330; DW/PA/5/1636/60]
  Margaret, alias Margaret Newburye of Farnham, widow [DW/PA/7/7 f,532; DW/PA/5/1607/56] <Abs 1000>
  Ralph of Swk, priest [HRO; Reg, Way 1 p,32; 1454]
  Thomas of Lambeth - Upper Ground, saddler [PRO; PCC 1630] <Scroope 1338>
  Thomas of Lingfield, esq, [PRO; PCC Will *and* Admon 1590]
KENTON
  Peter of Rotherhithe, mariner [PRO; PCC Will 1625]
KENWRICKE
  Thomas of Egham [PRO; PCC Admon 1621]
KENYNGHAM *see* KENNINGHAM
KERBIE,KERBY,KERBYE *see* KIRBY
KEREL,KERELL *see* KIRRELL
KERFEWE *see* CURFEW
KERFFIT
  Elizabeth of Ewell, widow [DW/PA/7/7 f,600; DW/PA/5/1607/57] <Abs 1123>
KERNE
  Elizabeth of Chiddingfold, widow of Robert [DW/PA/7/7 f,234; DW/PA/5/1598/47] <Abs 412>
  Robert of Chiddingfold, husbandman [DW/PA/7/7 f,169; DW/PA/5/1597/61] <Abs 311>
  William of Kingston, yeoman [DW/PA/7/2 f,203; 1525]
KERMOTT
  Margaret, alias Margaret Holland of Wandsworth, widow [PRO; PCC 1639]
KERR (CURR)
  James, *or* James Carr of Weybridge, gent, [DW/PA/7/12 f,472; DW/PA/5/1638/29]
KERRELL,KERRILL *see* KIRRILL
KERRINGTON
  Thomas of Newdigate, husbandman [DW/PA/7/8 f,282; DW/PA/5/1613/70]
KERSINGHALL
  Stephen of Newington [PRO; PCC Admon 1648]
KERSON
  Francis of Newington [LPL; 98/1 f,63r; Will 1634]
KERVER
  Henry of Farnham - Wrecclesham [PRO; PCC 1649]

KERWIN
Benjamin of Lambeth - Kennington [PRO; PCC Admon 1621]
KERYALL *see* KIRRELL
KETERYNGHAM *see* CATERINGHAM
KETMER
Richard of Frimley [DW/PA/7/1 f.60; 1487] <Abs 202>
KETON *see* KEATING
KETTELL
Raphael of Swk St Olave, citizen and fishmonger [DW/PA/5/1576/52]
KETTLWELL
Joan of Newington, widow [LPL; 96/1519; Will 1643]
KEY (KEYES,KEYS)
Frances *or* Francis of Lambeth [DW/PA/5/1579/56]*
John of Newington [LPL; 96/1520; Will 1625]
Thomas of Guildford St Nicolas, clerk parson [DW/PA/7/8 f.157; DW/PA/5/1611/67]
Thomas of Richmond, gent. [PRO; PCC Will 1611] <Abs, SAC v.35 p.37>
KEYFORD
Gilbert of Swk St George, tallow chandler [DW/PA/7/12 f.524; DW/PA/5/1635/56]
KEYMAR
Joan of Bermondsey, widow [PRO; PCC Will 1625]
KEYS *see* KEY
KEYSAR *see* CAESAR
KEYTING *see* KEATING
KIBBEE
Bartholomew of Swk St Olave - Horsleydown; on voyage to Spain, mariner [DW/PA/7/11 f.508; DW/PA/5/1629/53]
KICCHIN,KICHEN *see* KITCHEN
KIDD *see* KYD
KIDGELL
Henry of Newington, porter [LPL; 96/1523; 98/1 ff.74r-74v; Will 1636]
Nicholas of Chiddingfold [PRO; PCC 1646]
see also KEDGELL
KIDMAN
Anne of Lambeth; Croydon, etc., widow [PRO; PCC 1630] <Scroope 1015>
Edward of Lambeth - Water Lambeth [PRO; PCC Admon 1596]
KIDWELL (KIDWELLE,KYDWELL)
James of Streatham - Upper Tooting, mariner [PRO; PCC 1649]
Joan of Rotherhithe, wife of Richard [HRO; 1588 AD35]
Katherine, alias Katherine Jounge of Malden [PRO; PCC Admon 1641]
Nicholas of Kingston, yeoman of the Queens Chamber [DW/PA/7/7 f.201 *and* DW/PA/7/9 f.29; DW/PA/5/1598/48 *and* DW/PA/5/1614/70] <Abs 360>
Robert of Kingston, gent. [PRO; PCC 1643]
Thomas of Tooting, widower [PRO; PCC Admon 1649]
KIFFORD
Andrew of Swk St George, miller [DW/PA/7/13 f.322; DW/PA/5/1643/57]
KIGHTMAN
John of Swk St Saviour, blacksmith [DW/PA/5/1582/73]
KILLEFLEETE
Richard of Egham [PRO; PCC Will 1597]
KILLER
Phillip of Swk St Olave, citizen and woodmonger [DW/PA/7/8 f.318; DW/PA/5/1611/68]

KILLICK (KELIK, KELLECK, KELLYCKE, KELYKE, KILICK, KILLICE, KILLYCKE, KYLLICKE, KYLLIK, KYLLYK, KYLLYKE)
..., of Richmond [DW/PA/5/1569/1]
Alice of Fetcham, spinster [DW/PA/5/1593/39]
Amy of Nutfield, widow [DW/PA/5/1574/7]
Christopher of Blechingley [DW/PA/5/1576/109]
Joan of Blechingley, widow [DW/PA/5/1576/23]
John of Carshalton, miller [DW/PA/5/1624/64]
John of Epsom [DW/PA/7/1 f.56; 1487] <Abs 186>
John of Limpsfield [PRO; PCC Will 1610]
John of Nutfield [PRO; PCC Will 1439]
John of Nutfield - Kings, yeoman [DW/PA/7/6 f.90; DW/PA/5/1559/115]
John of Nutfield - Capenor [DW/PA/5/1579/54]*
John of Nutfield, yeoman [DW/PA/7/12 f.318; DW/PA/5/1637/63]
John of Reigate [DW/PA/7/11 f.314; DW/PA/5/1626/76]
John of Sutton, yeoman [DW/PA/7/13 f.97; DW/PA/5/1640/86]
Nicholas of Lambeth - Stockwell, yeoman [DW/PA/7/6 f.51; DW/PA/5/1559/118]
Nicholas of Reigate, shearman [DW/PA/5/1591/105]
Richard of Banstead, yeoman [DW/PA/7/7 f.48; DW/PA/5/1595/58] <Abs 89>
Richard of Farleigh, yeoman [DW/PA/7/11 f.374; DW/PA/5/1626/77]
Richard of Horley [DW/PA/5/1599/39] <Abs U23>
Richard of Mickleham, yeoman [DW/PA/7/10 f.291; DW/PA/5/1622/51]
Richard of Nutfield, yeoman [DW/PA/5/1578/36]
Robert of Blechingley, yeoman [DW/PA/5/1582/75]
Robert of Buckland [DW/PA/5/1558/173]
Robert of Effingham, husbandman [DW/PA/7/13 f.29; DW/PA/5/1639/80]
Robert of Nutfield [DW/PA/7/2 f.196; 1523]
Robert of Reigate, yeoman [DW/PA/7/9 f.211; DW/PA/5/1616/83]
Robert of Reigate [PRO; PCC 1648]
Thomas of Banstead, yeoman [DW/PA/5/1581/6]
Thomas of Gatton, labourer [DW/PA/7/11 f.549; DW/PA/5/1629/54]
Thomas of Lambeth [PRO; PCC Will 1551]
Thomas of Reigate, senior [DW/PA/7/11 f.456; DW/PA/5/1628/63]
Thomas of Reigate [PRO; PCC 1649]
William of Buckland [DW/PA/7/3 f.116; 1529]
William of Nutfield [DW/PA/7/6 f.144; DW/PA/5/1559/232]
William of Nutfield - Hathersham, yeoman [DW/PA/5/1586/15]
William of Nutfield - Warners, yeoman [DW/PA/7/8 f.52; DW/PA/5/1609/46]
William of Reigate, husbandman [DW/PA/7/10 f.108; DW/PA/5/1619/75]

KILLIGUE
Richard of Mitcham, gent. [PRO; PCC 1647]

KILLINGHALL
John of Guildford Holy Trinity [PRO; PCC 1648]

KILNER
Rowland of Croydon, yeoman [LPL; 96/1533; Will 1615]

KINDER
John of Walton on the Hill, clerk and parson [DW/PA/5/1572/26]

KINDES
Francis of Rotherhithe, servant to Mr Hills, mariner on the Ship *Ascension* [PRO; PCC Will 1606]

KINDRED *see* KINRED

KINE (KYNE)
Edward of Chertsey, butcher [DW/PA/5/1588/78]

KINE (KYNE) [*continued*]
Richard of Wonersh [DW/PA/5/1582/84]
KING (KINGE,KYINGE,KYNG,KYNGE)
Agnes of Ashtead [DW/PA/7/12 f,369; DW/PA/5/1627/64]
Ambrose of Egham [DW/PA/5/1568/6]
Ann of Reigate, widow [DW/PA/7/13 f,14; DW/PA/5/1640/90]
Anthony of Croydon [PRO; PCC Admon 1605]
Edward, alias Edward ap John of Bermondsey [PRO; PCC Will 1587]
Edward of Lambeth, oatmealmaker [DW/PA/7/11 f,53; DW/PA/5/1623/66]
Elizabeth of Battersea, widow [DW/PA/5/1579/55]*
Elizabeth of Cranleigh [DW/PA/7/1 f,88; 1489] <Abs 297>
Florence of Swk St Thomas [DW/PA/5/1586/21]
George of Banstead - Tadworth, yeoman [DW/PA/7/7 f,354; DW/PA/5/1601/56] <Abs 649>
George of Swk St Saviour, pursemaker [DW/PA/7/8 f,4; DW/PA/5/1608/65]
Henry of Tandridge; Ashtead [DW/PA/7/7 f,368; DW/PA/5/1602/56] <Abs 674>
Henry of Battersea, gardener [DW/PA/7/10 f,215; DW/PA/5/1621/65]
Henry of Streatham [PRO; PCC Will 1578]
Isabell of Lambeth, widow [DW/PA/5/1550/101]
James of Limpsfield [PRO; PCC Admon 1645]
Joan of Walton on Thames, widow [DW/PA/7/8 f,81; DW/PA/5/1609/47]
John of Beddington, clerk [PRO; PCC Will 1428]
John of Bermondsey, leatherdresser [PRO; PCC Will 1623]
John of Egham [PRO; PCC Will 1487]
John of Egham, yeoman [DW/PA/5/1586/8]
John of Epsom [DW/PA/7/3 f,167; 1531]
John of Fetcham, yeoman [DW/PA/7/7 f,344; DW/PA/5/1601/54] <Abs 628>
John of Limpsfield; Oxted [PRO; PCC Will 1592]
John of Reigate [DW/PA/7/2 f,112; 1517]
John of Ripley [DW/PA/7/11 f,580; DW/PA/5/1630/64]
John of Swk St George, clerk [DW/PA/5/1581/24]
John of Swk St Mary Overy, goldsmith [DW/PA/7/4 f,172; 1536]
John of Walton on Thames [DW/PA/7/7 f,385; DW/PA/5/1602/58] <Abs 712>
John of Warlingham, husbandman [DW/PA/7/12 f,53; DW/PA/5/1632/58]
Margery of Crowhurst, widow [DW/PA/7/12 f,167; DW/PA/5/1633/76]
Martin of Swk St Saviour, citizen and white baker [DW/PA/7/7 f,5; DW/PA/5/1595/59] <Abs 14>
Mary of Cobham, spinster [DW/PA/7/13 f,225; DW/PA/5/1642/52]
Mary of Ockley [PRO; PCC Admon 1604]
Nicholas of Blechingley, blacksmith [DW/PA/7/7 f,601; DW/PA/5/1607/59] <Abs 1125>
Nicholas of Kingston [PRO; PCC 1632]
Nicholas of Ockley [PRO; PCC Admon 1604]
Ralph of Streatham [PRO; PCC Will 1594]
Richard of Battersea, yeoman, senior [DW/PA/7/6 f,24; DW/PA/5/1559/27]
Richard of Cobham, yeoman [DW/PA/7/13 f,160; DW/PA/5/1642/49]
Richard of Cuddington [DW/PA/7/2 f,20; 1491]
Richard of Guildford St Mary [DW/PA/5/1569/65]
Richard of Kingston [DW/PA/7/1 f,51; 1487] <Abs 170>
Richard of Limpsfield, gent,, senior [DW/PA/7/11 f,293; DW/PA/5/1626/78]
Richard of Woking, mercer [DW/PA/7/12 f,329; DW/PA/5/1637/64]
Robert of Bermondsey [DW/PA/5/1593/135]
Robert of Cranleigh [DW/PA/7/1 f,76; 1488] <Abs 249>
Robert of Croydon [LPL; 98/1 f,63v; Will 1634]

KING (KINGE,KYINGE,KYNG,KYNGE) [*continued*]
  Robert of Reigate, yeoman [DW/PA/7/13 f.6; DW/PA/5/1640/91]
  Robert of Wimbledon [PRO; PCC Will 1533]
  Robert of Worplesdon, yeoman [DW/PA/7/8 f.101; DW/PA/5/1610/78]
  Robert of Worplesdon, yeoman [DW/PA/7/11 f.382; DW/PA/5/1626/79]
  Roger of Ashtead, husbandman [DW/PA/7/10 f.34; DW/PA/5/1617/60]
  Stephen of Rotherhithe (died overseas) [PRO; PCC Admon 1646]
  Stephen of Swk St George [DW/PA/7/11 f.165; DW/PA/5/1625/139]
  Thomas of Ashtead [DW/PA/7/3 f.98; 1529]
  Thomas of Clapham, parson [PRO; PCC Will 1591]
  Thomas of Horley [DW/PA/5/1550/87]
  Thomas of Kingston, shipwright [PRO; PCC Will 1617]
  Thomas of Swk St Saviour [DW/PA/7/7 f.413; DW/PA/5/1603/94] <Abs 769>
  Walter of Cranleigh, yeoman [DW/PA/7/12 f.178; DW/PA/5/1633/75]
  William of Ashtead, husbandman [DW/PA/5/1561/89]
  William of Banstead [DW/PA/7/2 f.132; 1519]
  William of Banstead [DW/PA/7/5 f.191; 1540]
  William of Egham, yeoman [DW/PA/5/1588/66]
  William of Newington [PRO; PCC Admon 1647]
  William of Reigate [DW/PA/7/2 f.3; 1490]
  William of Rotherhithe; Brightlingsea, Essex [DW/PA/5/1550/99]
  William of Tandridge, yeoman [DW/PA/7/11 f.413; DW/PA/5/1627/65]
  William of Windlesham [PRO; PCC Will 1474]
KINGDON
  Christopher of Camberwell, gent. [PRO; PCC 1639]
KINGESTON *see* KINGSTON
KINGSLAND
  Arthur of Camberwell - Dulwich, husbandman [DW/PA/7/10 f.110; DW/PA/5/1619/76]
  Robert of Camberwell - Dulwich, husbandman [DW/PA/7/8 f.250; DW/PA/5/1613/71]
KINGSMILL (KYNGESMYLL)
  William of Swk - *The Tabard*, dean of Winchester Cathedral, Hampshire [? HRO; 1548 B]
KINGSTON (KINGESTON,KINSTON,KYNGESTON,KYNGISTON,KYNGSTON)
  Anthony of Tooting Graveney, yeoman [DW/PA/5/1599/40]
  Henry of Lambeth - Lambeth Dean [DW/PA/5/1581/20]
  John of Kingston, citizen and mason [GL; Commissary Court of London Will 1457]
  John, alias John Benett of Kingston [PRO; PCC Will 1476]
  John of Kingston - Surbiton, yeoman [DW/PA/5/1574/34]
  Leonard of Kingston, husbandman [DW/PA/5/1557/6]
  Thomas of Kingston - Surbiton; Isleworth, Middlesex, yeoman [BM; Add.Ms 24,925 f.15r; 1544] <Abs 31>
  Thomas of Clapham, yeoman [DW/PA/7/8 f.79; DW/PA/5/1609/94]
KINRED
  Rose of Swk St Saviour, widow [DW/PA/7/10 f.264; DW/PA/5/1622/52A]
KINSMAN (KINMAN,KYNSMAN)
  Alice of Carshalton, widow [DW/PA/7/10 f.193; DW/PA/5/1621/66]
  John of Carshalton, husbandman [DW/PA/7/8 f.256; DW/PA/5/1611/69]
  Richard of Carshalton [PRO; PCC Admon 1610]
  William of Ewell [PRO; PCC Will 1638]
  William of Kingston [PRO; PCC Admon 1649]
KINSTON *see* KINGSTON

KIPLING (KYPLIN)
  Robert of Bermondsey, feltmaker [DW/PA/5/1578/79]
KIPPING (KYPPING)
  John of Lingfield [DW/PA/5/1571/79]
  Richard of Lingfield [PRO; PCC Will 1616]
KIRBY (KERBIE,KERBY,KERBYE,KYRKEBY)
  Anthony of Bermondsey; Suffolk; Guildford; Swk St George; Lewisham, Kent; Greenwich, Kent; Yorkshire; Westminster, Middlesex; Horsleydown [DW/PA/5/1596/35] <Abs U8>
  Anthony of Lambeth [PRO; PCC Admon 1649]
  Elizabeth of Betchworth - Brockham, widow [DW/PA/7/8 f.375; DW/PA/5/1612/86]
  Giles of Betchworth - Brockham [DW/PA/7/8 f.366; DW/PA/5/1612/87]
  James of Swk St Saviour - Paris Garden, waterman [DW/PA/7/9 f.46; DW/PA/5/1614/69]
  Richard of Lambeth, brewer [PRO; PCC Will 1625]
  Richard of Newington, baker [LPL; 96/1555; Will 1636]
  Thomas of Lambeth [PRO; PCC Will 1522]
  William of Newington [LPL; 96/1553; Will 1630]
KIRKHAM
  George of Richmond, gent. [PRO; PCC Will 1613]
  John of Egham, yeoman [DW/PA/7/13 f.352; 1644]
  Thomas of Egham [PRO; PCC 1642]
  William of Swk St Olave, waterman [DW/PA/7/11 f.224; DW/PA/5/1625/140]
KIRKPATRICK (KIRKPARTERICKE)
  George of Croydon [LPL; 98/1 f.72v (ren.); 1636]
KIRKTON (KYRKETON)
  John of Surrey [PRO; PCC Will 1529]
KIRRELL (KEREL,KERELL,KERRELL,KERRILL,KERYALL,KIRRELL)
  Alexander of Reigate, husbandman [DW/PA/5/1555/16]
  Elizabeth of Mortlake, widow [PRO; PCC 1643]
  Harry of Leigh [DW/PA/7/5 f.78; 1539]
  John of Horley [DW/PA/5/1591/46]
  John of Mortlake, gent. [PRO; PCC 1631]
  John of Shere [DW/PA/7/1 f.61; 1487] <Abs 205>
  Joseph of Horley [DW/PA/7/8 f.41; DW/PA/5/1607/58]
  Richard of Buckland [PRO; PCC Admon 1647]
  William of Banstead, husbandman [DW/PA/7/12 f.103; DW/PA/5/1632/59]
  William of Chipstead [DW/PA/7/7 f.448; DW/PA/5/1603/93] <Abs 849>
KIRTLAND
  Francis of Swk St Olave [DW/PA/7/13 f.268; DW/PA/5/1643/55]
KIRTON
  Margaret of Barnes, widow of Stephen, alderman [PRO; PCC Will 1573]
  William of Battersea [PRO; PCC Will 1598]
KITCHEN (KICCHIN,KICHEN)
  Ann of Egham, widow [PRO; PCC 1640]
  Gilbert of Egham, gent. [PRO; PCC 1631]
  John of Wonersh [PRO; PCC Admon 1630]
  Richard of Albury, gent. [PRO; PCC Will 1595]
  Richard of Beddington [DW/PA/5/1562/61]
  Richard of Swk St Saviour [DW/PA/7/8 f.364; DW/PA/5/1612/88]
  William of Egham [PRO; PCC Admon 1639]
  William of Richmond [PRO; PCC Admon 1637]

KITCHINER
  William of Effingham; Byfleet, yeoman [HRO; 1586 B33]
KNAP *see* KNAPP
KNAPLOCK
  William of East Clandon, esq. [PRO; PCC Will 1612]
KNAPP (KNAP,KNAPPE,KNEEP,KNEPP,KNEPPE)
  Ann of Mitcham [PRO; PCC Admon 1603]
  Ann of Mitcham [PRO; PCC Will 1604]
  Henry of Mitcham, yeoman [DW/PA/5/1581/22]
  Henry of Mitcham; Morden [DW/PA/7/7 f.472; DW/PA/5/1604/35] <Abs 891>
  John of Mitcham [DW/PA/7/4 f.4; 1532]
  John of Mitcham; Carshalton, gent. [PRO; PCC Will 1620] <Soame 107>
  Margaret, alias Margaret Shepard of Ewell [PRO; PCC Admon 1637]
  Robert of Mitcham; Carshalton; Ewell, husbandman [DW/PA/5/1602/53]
    <Abs U52>
KNARESBOROUGH (KNARISBOROUGHE,KNARISBROUGH)
  Ann of Wandsworth, widow [PRO; PCC Will 1619] <Abs SAC v.33 p.21>
  John of Mortlake, gent. [PRO; PCC Will 1599]
  Miles of Mortlake [PRO; PCC Will 1563]
  Robert of Wandsworth, yeoman [PRO; PCC Will 1612] <Abs SAC v.33 p.21>
  Thomas of Mortlake [PRO; PCC Admon 1608]
KNEEP *see* KNAPP
KNELL
  Clement of Bermondsey [PRO; PCC Admon 1620]
  Edward of Lingfield [PRO; PCC 1634]
KNEPP,KNEPPE *see* KNAPP
KNEVETT (KNIVETT,KNYVET,NEVETT)
  (Dame) Ann of Guildford [PRO; PCC Will 1582]
  John of Swk St Olave, victualler [DW/PA/7/13 f.175; DW/PA/5/1641/99]
  Richard of Swk St Mary Magdalen, luter [DW/PA/7/2 f.52; 1497]
    <Abs SAC v.1 pp.180-181>
KNIGHT (KNIGHTE,KNYGHT,KNYGHTE,KNYTT)
  Alice of Swk St Thomas [DW/PA/7/10 f.39; 1617]
  Anthony of Walton on Thames [DW/PA/7/13 f.203; DW/PA/5/1642/51]
  Christopher of Lingfield [DW/PA/5/1550/62]
  Edward, alias Edward Ellis of Ewhurst, yeoman [DW/PA/7/11 f.527;
    DW/PA/5/1630/65]
  Elizabeth of Newington, widow [LPL; 96/1561; Will 1626]
  George of Lingfield [DW/PA/7/5 f.188; 1540]
  Henry of Lambeth - Knights Hill [PRO; PCC Will 1505]
  Henry of Lambeth, yeoman [DW/PA/5/1574/24]
  Hugh of Streatham; Lambeth; Camberwell [DW/PA/5/1552/1]
  Humphrey of Surrey [PRO; PCC Will 1549]
  Joan, alias John Alyn of West Clandon [DW/PA/7/1 f.12; 1485] <Abs 41>
  John of Bermondsey, citizen and leatherseller [DW/PA/5/1576/48]
  John of Camberwell [PRO; PCC Will 1505]
  John, alias John Ellis of Ewhurst, yeoman [DW/PA/7/8 f.196;
    DW/PA/5/1610/79]
  John, alias John Ellis of Ewhurst, husbandman [DW/PA/5/1627/66]
  John of Ewhurst [HRO; 1640 AD101]
  John of Lambeth; Streatham, etc. [PRO; PCC Will 1487] <Abs. SAC v.52
    pp.32-33>
  John of Lambeth - Brockolls, yeoman [DW/PA/7/11 f.492; DW/PA/5/1628/64]
  John of Lingfield [PRO; PCC Will 1438]

KNIGHT (KNIGHTE,KNYGHT,KNYGHTE,KNYTT) [*continued*]
John of Lingfield [PRO; PCC 1647]
John of Morden, gent. [DW/PA/7/13 f.490; DW/PA/5/1648/19]
Oliver of Mitcham, yeoman [DW/PA/7/2 f.128; 1518]
Ralph, alias Ralph Ellis of Ewhurst, yeoman [DW/PA/7/12 f.395; DW/PA/5/1637/65]
Richard of Battersea [PRO; PCC 1637]
Richard of Camberwell; Lambeth [DW/PA/7/2 f.56; 1499]
Richard of Ewhurst [DW/PA/5/1580/38]
(Sir) Richard of Guildford, knight [PRO; PCC Will 1465]
Robert of Mortlake [PRO; PCC Admon 1594]
Thomas of Alfold [PRO; PCC 1642]
Thomas of Ewhurst, husbandman [DW/PA/7/11 f.23; DW/PA/5/1623/65]
Thomas of Guildford, citizen and skinner [DW/PA/7/3 f.200; 1532]
Thomas of Lingfield, yeoman [DW/PA/5/1558/172]*
Thomas of Wandsworth [PRO; PCC 1634]
Walter of Rotherhithe [DW/PA/7/12 f.257; DW/PA/5/1634/65]
William of Surrey, gent. [PRO; PCC Will 1559]
William of Camberwell - Dulwich, senior [PRO; PCC Will 1457]
William of Capel [DW/PA/5/1561/38]
William of Swk - Paris Garden, shipwright [DW/PA/5/1581/14]

KNIGHTLEY
William of Kingston, senior [PRO; PCC 1648]

KNIVETT *see* KNEVETT

KNOLLES *see* KNOWLES

KNOTT (NOTT,NOTTE)
Anthony of Thames Ditton - Ember [PRO; PCC Admon 1586]
Elizabeth of Thames Ditton, widow [PRO; PCC Will 1587]
John of Bermondsey [PRO; PCC Will 1536]
John of Croydon, yeoman [PRO; PCC Will 1625]
William of Thames Ditton; Esher; Kingston - Tolworth; Ewell, esq. [PRO; PCC Will 1576] <Abs SAC v.27 p.80 *and* v.33 p.33>
William of Swk St Saviour, servant to the bishop of Winchester [DW/PA/7/12 f.53; DW/PA/5/1631/59]

KNOWLDEN
Peter of Lingfield [DW/PA/7/11 f.113; DW/PA/5/1624/65]
Thomas of Lingfield [DW/PA/7/8 f.81; DW/PA/5/1609/49]

KNOWLES (KNOLLES)
John of Swk [DW/PA/5/1587/45]
John of Wandsworth, vicar [GL; Commissary Court of London Will 1552]
William of Croydon - Addiscombe, husbandman [PRO; PCC Will 1622]

KNOYLE
John of Lingfield, clerk and master of Lingfield College [PRO; PCC Will 1503; CCAL; 1503 f.195v]

KNYGHT,KNYGHTE *see* KNIGHT

KNYVET,KNYVETT *see* NEVETT

KOK,KOKE *see* COKE

KOOKE *see* COOKE

KRUTCHERE *see* CROUCHER

KYD
Thomas of Bermondsey [DW/PA/5/1568/86]

KYEN *see* KEEN

KYINGE *see* KING

KYLLICK,KYLLICKE,KYLLYK,KYLLYKE *see* KILLICK

KYMSOLL *see* KEMPSALL
KYNE *see* KINE
KYNG,KYNGE *see* KING
KYNGESMYLL *see* KINGSMILL
KYNGISTON,KYNGSTON *see* KINGSTON
KYNSMAN *see* KINSMAN
KYPLIN *see* KIPLING
KYPPING *see* KIPPING
KYRKEBY *see* KIRBY
KYRKETON *see* KIRKTON
KYRWYN *see* CURWEN
KYRYELL *see* KIRRELL

LABDALL
Nathaniel of Bermondsey [PRO; PCC Admon 1649]
LABORN (LALBORN)
Alice of Send, widow [DW/PA/7/2 f,8; 1491]
Thomas of Guildford, weaver [HRO; 1576 B45]
LACEY (de LACY)
James of Chessington [HRO; Reg, Wyk 2 p,231; 1387]
William of Rotherhithe, sailor [PRO; PCC Will 1618]
LACH
Thomas of Mortlake, bachelor [PRO; PCC Admon 1646]
LACKER
William of Horley, yeoman [DW/PA/7/11 f,130; DW/PA/5/1624/66]
LADD (LAD,LADDE)
Jasper of Horne; Blechingley, yeoman [DW/PA/7/7 f,117; DW/PA/5/1597/63] <Abs 217>
Jasper of Horne, yeoman [DW/PA/7/13 f,325; 1644]
Margaret of Ewell, widow [DW/PA/7/12 f,31; DW/PA/5/1631/63]
Nicholas of Horne, yeoman [DW/PA/5/1570/81]
Nicholas of Horne, yeoman [DW/PA/7/11 f,588; DW/PA/5/1630/66]
Richard of Betchworth [DW/PA/7/12 f,208; DW/PA/5/1634/67]
Richard of Buckland, bachelor [PRO; PCC Admon 1618]
Richard of Caterham, quarterman [HRO; 1609 B50]
Richard of Fetcham, yeoman [DW/PA/7/12 f,466; DW/PA/5/1638/73]
Thomas of Buckland [HRO; 1583 B50]
William of Betchworth [DW/PA/5/1580/55]
William of Buckland [DW/PA/7/12 f,135; DW/PA/5/1632/64]
LADDYN
Stephen of London, citizen and leatherseller [DW/PA/7/7 f,531; DW/PA/5/1606/52] <Abs 999>
LADE
John of Swk St Margaret, pouchmaker [DW/PA/7/4 f,51; 1533]
LAHAN
James of Newington [LPL; 98/1 f,80v; Will 1637]
LAIFORTHE
Henry, alias Henry Allen of Kingston, clerk [DW/PA/5/1579/6]*
LAINE *see* LANE
LAKE (LAKES)
Arthur of West Molesey; Harlington, Middlesex, yeoman [DW/PA/7/8 f,200; DW/PA/5/1611/70]

LAKE (LAKES) [*continued*]
Cecily of Godalming - Enton [PRO; PCC Admon 1611]
Charles of West Molesey [DW/PA/7/10 f.118; DW/PA/5/1620/73]
Francis of West Molesey [HRO; 1589 B33]
George of West Molesey [PRO; PCC Will 1557]
Richard of Haslemere [*in* DW/PA/5/1544/9]
Robert of West Molesey, husbandman [DW/PA/5/1575 B41]
see also ATLAKE
LAKER (LAYKER)
John of Alfold [PRO; PCC 1640]
John of Camberwell, husbandman [DW/PA/5/1558/174]*
John of Nutfield, yeoman [DW/PA/5/1588/17]
William of Albury; Rudgwick, Sussex; Crawley, Sussex, yeoman [DW/PA/7/10 f.271; DW/PA/5/1622/52B]
William of Horley [DW/PA/7/2 f.42; 1494]
LAKES *see* LAKE
LALBORN *see* LABORNE
LALEMORE
Elizabeth of Swk St Saviour, widow of Andrew [DW/PA/5/1578/78]
LAMB (LAMBE)
Henry of Kingston [PRO; PCC Admon 1606]
Joan of Warlingham, widow [PRO; PCC Will 1582]
John of Blechingley [DW/PA/7/2 f.131; 1519]
John of Camberwell - Peckham, gent. [PRO; PCC Wills 1602 *and* 1604] <Abs SAC v.10 pp.309-310>
John of Limpsfield, yeoman [DW/PA/5/1558/175]*
John of Lingfield, yeoman, senior [DW/PA/7/7 f.626; DW/PA/5/1608/66] <Abs 1170>
John of Rotherhithe, brewer [DW/PA/7/12 f.511; DW/PA/5/1638/79]
Juliana, alias Juliana Phillis of Wandsworth [PRO; PCC Admon 1642]
Margery, alias Margery White of Swk St George [DW/PA/5/1578/58]
Maurice of Horne [DW/PA/5/1557/71]
Richard of Blechingley, yeoman [DW/PA/7/7 f.250; DW/PA/5/1599/41] <Abs 440>
Robert of Blechingley [DW/PA/7/5 f.207; 1541]
Robert of Blechingley, shoemaker [DW/PA/7/11 f.18; DW/PA/5/1623/67]
Thomas of Blechingley [DW/PA/5/1561/7]
Thomas of Warlingham [PRO; PCC Will 1582]
William of Newington [PRO; PCC Admon 1618]
William of Newington [PRO; PCC Admon 1624]
LAMBERT (LAMBERD, LAMBURE, LUMBERT)
Andrew of Banstead, yeoman [DW/PA/7/10 f.105; DW/PA/5/1621/67]
Ann of Rotherhithe [PRO; PCC Admon 1649]
Ann of Swk St Thomas [DW/PA/7/12 f.361; DW/PA/5/1636/65]
Daniel of Woodmansterne, yeoman [DW/PA/7/10 f.265; DW/PA/5/1622/41]
Edward of Swk St George, chandler [DW/PA/7/7 f.414; DW/PA/5/1603/95] <Abs 773>
Elizabeth of Swk St Thomas, widow [HRO; 1600 B29]
Geoffrey of Banstead, yeoman [PRO; PCC Will 1567]
Geoffrey of Coulsdon, yeoman [DW/PA/7/11 f.185; DW/PA/5/1625/141]
John of Banstead; Woodmansterne; Croydon; Leatherhead; Chipstead; Ashtead; Epsom; Ewell; Cuddington; Cheam; Sutton; Carshalton; Beddington; Coulsdon; Walton on the Hill; Ewell - Kingswood; Horley; Leigh; Charlwood [DW/PA/7/4 f.45; 1533]

LAMBERT (LAMBERD,LAMBURE,LUMBERT) [*continued*]
John of Banstead, yeoman [DW/PA/7/7 f,120; DW/PA/5/1597/64] <Abs 222>
John of Banstead [PRO; PCC Admon 1618]
John of Caterham, gent, [PRO; PCC 1647]
John, alias John Gardiner of Cranleigh, ironmaker [DW/PA/5/1593/176]
John of Dorking, collier [DW/PA/7/7 f,639; DW/PA/5/1608/67] <Abs 1197>
John Lambure of Send [*This would appear to be an error in the abstract of* DW/PA/7/1 f,17 *for Barnbure,*] <Abs 58>
John of Sutton, yeoman [DW/PA/7/13 f,429; DW/PA/5/1646/34]
Luke of Swk St Olave, carman [DW/PA/7/11 f,202; DW/PA/5/1625/142]
Mark of Epsom, husbandman [DW/PA/7/7 f,367; DW/PA/5/1602/59] <Abs 673>
Martin of Bermondsey [DW/PA/7/5 f,96; 1539]
Mary of Banstead, widow [DW/PA/5/1622/53]
Matthias of Swk St Olave, joiner [DW/PA/7/13 f,144; DW/PA/5/1641/82]
Nicholas of Banstead [PRO; PCC Will 1576]
Nicholas of Banstead; Epsom; Ewell; Coulsdon; Caterham [DW/PA/7/7 f,65; 1596] <Abs 126>
Nicholas of Chipstead, gent, [DW/PA/7/9 f,87; DW/PA/5/1615/76]
Phillip of Banstead, yeoman [PRO; PCC Will 1616]
Robert of Lambeth - Lambeth Marsh [PRO; PCC Admon 1639]
Roger of Banstead [PRO; PCC Admon 1617]
Roger of Woodmansterne [PRO; PCC Admon 1649]
Samuel of Banstead [PRO; PCC Will 1594]
Sarah of Swk St Olave, widow [DW/PA/7/11 f,181; DW/PA/5/1625/143]
Walter of Carshalton [PRO; PCC Will 1545]
William of Battersea [DW/PA/7/9 f,132; DW/PA/5/1615/81]
William of Chipstead, yeoman [DW/PA/7/12 f,41; DW/PA/5/1631/66]
William of Putney [LPL; 98/1 ff,61v,71r; Wills 1634 *and* 1635]

LAMBOLD (LAMBOL,LAMBOLE,LAMBOULL)
Alice of Woking, wife of Thomas [DW/PA/5/1576/2]
Christopher of Ockham [HRO; 1561 B111-112]
John of ,,, [DW/PA/7/11 f,498; 1629]
Nicholas of Woking; Dorking, yeoman [DW/PA/5/1591/107]
Nicholas of Woking; Dorking, yeoman [DW/PA/5/1592/22]
Thomas (*and* Alice, his wife) of Woking [DW/PA/5/1576/2]
William of Bentley, Hampshire, yeoman, senior [DW/PA/7/13 f,77; DW/PA/5/1640/94]

LAME
Robert of Limpsfield [DW/PA/7/4 f,153; 1536]

LAMFORD
Richard of Battersea [DW/PA/7/9 f,184; DW/PA/5/1616/84]

LAMKYN *see* LAMPKIN

LAMMAS
Thomas of Swk St Thomas, citizen and currier [DW/PA/7/12 f,479; DW/PA/5/1638/76]

LAMOTT
Elizabeth of Mortlake, wife of John, esq, [GL; Archdeaconry Court of London Will 1644]

LAMPARD
John of Farnham [PRO; PCC 1640]
John of Leatherhead [PRO; PCC Admon 1632]
Thomas of Leatherhead [PRO; PCC 1647]

LAMPELEY *see* LAMPLEY

LAMPKIN (LAMKYN,LAMPKYN)

Richard of Sutton, husbandman [DW/PA/7/7 f.489; DW/PA/5/1604/37] <Abs 923>

Thomas of Mitcham, husbandman [DW/PA/7/4 f.61; 1533]

LAMPLEY (LAMPELEY)

Thomas of Swk St Mary Magdalen [DW/PA/7/3 f.105; 1529]

LAMPTON

Anthony of Wandsworth [PRO; PCC Admon 1593]

LAMYE (LANY)

John Lamye, alias John Lany of ,,, [*French church*] [DW/PA/5/1575/59]

LAN'

Thomas of Epsom [DW/PA/7/1 f.85; 1489] <Abs 286>

LANAWAY,LANAWBY *see* LANNAWAY

LANCASTER (LANKESTER)

Jane of Shalford, widow [DW/PA/5/1563/34]

Lawrence of Camberwell - Peckham, yeoman [DW/PA/7/7 f.146; DW/PA/5/1596/62] <Abs 270>

Thomas of Lambeth [PRO; PCC Admon 1647]

William of Swk St Olave, citizen and woodmonger [DW/PA/7/13 f.368; 1644]

LANCKFORD *see* LANGFORD

LANDER (LAUNDER)

Edward, alias Edward Estland of Godstone, yeoman [DW/PA/5/1591/10]

Erasmus, alias Erasmus Eastland of Tandridge, yeoman [DW/PA/7/8 f.320; DW/PA/5/1611/25]

Erasmus, alias Erasmus Eastland of Tandridge, yeoman [DW/PA/7/12 f.490; DW/PA/5/1638/40]

Henry, alias Henry Estlande of Tandridge; Lingfield [PRO; PCC Will 1597]

Joan, alias Joan Eastland of Tandridge, widow [PRO; PCC Will 1586]

John, alias John Eastland of Crowhurst [DW/PA/5/1592/41]

John of Godalming, yeoman [DW/PA/7/12 f.79; DW/PA/5/1633/77]

John, alias John Easteland of Tandridge, yeoman [DW/PA/7/11 f.102; DW/PA/5/1624/68]

Juliana of Godalming - Farncombe, widow [PRO; PCC 1647]

Katherine, alias Katherine Estland of Tandridge [HRO; 1597 B24]

Katherine, alias Katherine Eastlande of Tandridge; Lingfield [DW/PA/7/7 f.120; DW/PA/5/1597/33] <Abs 221>

Oliver, alias Oliver Esland of Oxted; Crowhurst, yeoman [DW/PA/7/9 f.289; 1618]

Richard, alias Richard Estlonde of Tandridge, yeoman [DW/PA/5/1570/5]

Richard of Wonersh [DW/PA/7/1 f.29; 1485] <Abs 98>

Sarah of Haslemere, spinster [PRO; PCC 1648]

Thomas, alias Thomas Estlande of Godstone [DW/PA/7/6 f.221; 1561]

LANDVEY *see* LANNAWAY

LANE (LAINE,LAYN,LEYNE)

Cicely of Egham, widow [PRO; PCC Will 1597]

Edward of Chobham [DW/PA/5/1562/53]

Edward of Egham; Thorpe [PRO; PCC Will 1596]

Elizabeth of ,,,, widow [DW/PA/5/1550/71]

George of Bermondsey; Selby, Leicestershire, citizen and leatherseller [DW/PA/5/1603/96] <Abs U76>

George of Bermondsey, citizen of London [PRO; PCC Will 1603] <Abs, SAC v.11 pp.121-122>

Gregory of Betchworth [DW/PA/7/5 f.114; 1539]

Harry of Chobham, husbandman [DW/PA/5/1562/69]

LANE (LAINE, LAYN, LEYNE) [*continued*]

Henry of Egham [PRO; PCC Will 1592]

Hugh of ... [DW/PA/5/1587/39]

Joan, alias Joan Bowyer of Bermondsey - Bermondsey Street, widow [DW/PA/7/12 f.266; DW/PA/5/1635/58]

John of Camberwell, yeoman [DW/PA/7/4 f.122; 1535]

John of Chobham, labourer [*in* DW/PA/5/1555/67]

Margery of Camberwell - Peckham [DW/PA/7/4 f.41; 1533]

Nicholas of Kingston [PRO; PCC Will 1610] <Abs, SAC v.24 pp.62-63>

Richard of Bermondsey [PRO; PCC Will 1595]

Richard of Newdigate, yeoman [PRO; PCC Will 1567]

Richard of Reigate [HRO; Reg. CCB 20 p.2; 1563]

Richard of Reigate [DW/PA/5/1563/53 *and in* DW/PA/5/1563/64]

Samuel of Morden [PRO; PCC Admon 1626]

Thomas of Chobham, yeoman, junior [HRO; 1605 B51]

Vincent of Swk St Saviour [DW/PA/7/5 f.202; 1540]

William of Chobham, husbandman, senior [DW/PA/7/1 f.53; 1487] <Abs 174>

William of Reigate [DW/PA/5/1556/5]

LANER

Thomas of Reigate, husbandman [DW/PA/7/2 f.185; 1521 *or* 1522]

LANG (LANGE)

Ann of Addington, widow [PRO; PCC 1635]

LANGBOROUGHE

William of Dunsfold; Albury; Guildford, clerk [DW/PA/5/1603/97] <Abs U77>

LANGBRIDGE

Frances, alias Frances Goodgroome of Richmond [PRO; PCC Admon 1647]

LANGDON

John of Wandsworth [PRO; PCC Will 1493]

LANGE *see* LANG

LANGFORD (LANCKFORD, LANGFORDE, LANGFORT)

Edward of Swk St Saviour, carman [DW/PA/7/7 f.97; 1596] <Abs 178>

Gregory of Elstead, husbandman [DW/PA/7/7 f.399; DW/PA/5/1602/60] <Abs 722>

John of Swk St Saviour, tanner [DW/PA/7/9 f.156; DW/PA/5/1615/77]

Luke of Bermondsey, in the Ship *Discovery* [PRO; PCC Will 1629]

Richard of Farnham [DW/PA/5/1588/54]

Thomas of Thursley [DW/PA/7/6 f.150; DW/PA/5/1559/177]

LANGHORNE

John of Camberwell [PRO; PCC Will 1405]

LANGHURST *see* LONGHURST

LANGLEY (LANGLIE)

Ann of Swk St Saviour, widow [DW/PA/7/8 f.47; DW/PA/5/1609/50]

Edward of Swk St Olave, yeoman [DW/PA/7/10 f.71; 1619]

Joan of Bermondsey, widow [DW/PA/7/11 f.109; DW/PA/5/1624/67]

John of Streatham, yeoman [DW/PA/7/13 f.246; DW/PA/5/1640/97]

Richard of Chertsey [DW/PA/5/1546/93]

Richard of Kingston - Surbiton, waterman [DW/PA/7/7 f.342; DW/PA/5/1601/58] <Abs 623>

LANGRIDGE (LANGREDGE)

James of Wandsworth, yeoman [DW/PA/7/7 f.549; DW/PA/5/1606/53] <Abs 1029>

LANGSHETTE

Thomas of Capel, citizen and cooper [GL; Commissary Court of London Will 1433]

LANGSTONE (LANGSTON)
John of Bermondsey, citizen and oil and leather dresser [DW/PA/7/11 f.534; DW/PA/5/1629/56]
William of Dorking, yeoman [DW/PA/7/10 f.64; 1618]
LANGTON
James of Kingston, gent. [PRO; PCC Will 1597]
Walter of Guildford Holy Trinity [DW/PA/7/3 f.168; 1531]
LANGWORTH
Jonathan of Rotherhithe [PRO; PCC Admon 1647]
LANIER
John of Camberwell, gent. [PRO; PCC Will 1616]
LANKESTER *see* LANCASTER
LANCKFORD *see* LANGFORD
LANNAWAY (LANAWAY,LANAWAYE,LANDVEY,LANNAWAIE,LANNAWAYE,LANWAYE,LANWEY)
George of Thursley, husbandman [DW/PA/5/1568/63]
Gillian of Pyrford [DW/PA/7/10 f.180; DW/PA/5/1620/74]
Joan of Farnham - Badshot, widow [DW/PA/7/12 f.106; DW/PA/5/1632/62]
John of Farnham - Badshot, senior [DW/PA/7/11 f.420; DW/PA/5/1626/80]
John of Godalming [DW/PA/7/5 f.40; 1538] <Abs 49>
John of Witley - Milford, husbandman [HRO; 1557 U408-409]
John of Witley [DW/PA/7/7 f.24; DW/PA/5/1595/60]
Richard of Witley, husbandman [HRO; 1557 U410-411]
Robert of Witley - Mousehill [DW/PA/7/6 f.183; DW/PA/5/1559/175]
Thomas of Godalming [DW/PA/7/2 f.35; 1493]
Thomas of Godalming [DW/PA/7/4 f.232; 1537]
Thomas of Godalming - Catteshall; Godalming - Farncombe, husbandman [DW/PA/5/1544/11]
Thomas of Godalming - Catteshall, husbandman [DW/PA/7/6 f.181; DW/PA/5/1559/176]
Thomas of Hambledon [DW/PA/7/7 f.607; DW/PA/5/1607/60] <Abs 1137>
Thomas of Witley, husbandman [DW/PA/7/12 f.136; DW/PA/5/1632/65]
LANNAY (de LANNAY)
Joan of ..., widow of Francis Queneulle [*Dutch*] [DW/PA/7/7 f.43; DW/PA/5/1595/26] <Abs 84>
LANO (de LANO)
Baldwin of Swk St Olave, skinner [DW/PA/7/1 f.46A; 1486] <Abs 151>
LANTOTTE
Edward of Camberwell, husbandman [DW/PA/7/10 f.195; DW/PA/5/1621/68]
LANWAYE,LANWEY *see* LANNAWAY
LANY
John, alias John Lamye of ... [*French church*] [DW/PA/5/1575/59]
John of Byfleet [PRO; PCC Admon 1640]
LARAMORE
Stephen of Newington [PRO; PCC Will 1593]
LARCHING
Thomas of Swk St Olave, victualler [DW/PA/7/13 f.276; DW/PA/5/1644/12]
LARDNER
Joan of Lambeth, widow [PRO; PCC Admon 1647]
LARGE (LARDGE)
Judith, alias Judith Highlord, alias Judith Parham of Camberwell [PRO; PCC Admon 1627]
Thomas of Camberwell, ironmonger, esq. [PRO; PCC 1640 *and* PCC Admon 1641]
LARMORE
Robert of Chobham, husbandman [DW/PA/5/1580/68]

LASAM *see* LASSUM
LASHFORD (LISHFORD)
Anthony of Woking, tailor, senior [DW/PA/7/13 f.500; DW/PA/5/1649/9]
William of Shere, gent. [DW/PA/7/12 f.358; DW/PA/5/1637/66]
LASSUM (LASAM)
John of Frensham, yeoman [DW/PA/7/8 f.174; DW/PA/5/1610/80]
William of Frensham [DW/PA/5/1570/44]
LASTNEY *see* LISNEY
LATCHFORD
Richard of Lambeth - Water Lambeth, baker [PRO; PCC 1630] <Scroope 290>
LATCHLEY
Richard of Kingston [PRO; PCC Admon 1597]
LATHAM
Margaret of Swk St Olave [DW/PA/7/12 f.420; DW/PA/5/1637/68]
Ralph of Pyrford [PRO; PCC Admon 1599]
Ralph of Pyrford, gent. [DW/PA/7/7 f.275; DW/PA/5/1599/42] <Abs 487>
William of Swk St Olave, butcher [DW/PA/5/1587/96]
LATHER
William of Esher, husbandman, senior [DW/PA/7/12 f.481; DW/PA/5/1638/77]
LATYMER
Henry of Weybridge, yeoman [DW/PA/5/1579/60]*
LAUNDER *see* LANDER
LAUNDIS
John of Beddington, husbandman [DW/PA/7/7 f.43; DW/PA/5/1595/61] <Abs 83>
LAURANCE,LAURENCE,LAURENS *see* LAWRENCE
LAUSIN
Henry of Swk St Olave, armourer [*Dutch*] [DW/PA/7/7 f.160;
DW/PA/5/1597/65] <Abs 297>
LAWE
Edward of Reigate [PRO; PCC 1647]
Richard of ... [DW/PA/5/1569/50]
LAWNDE
John of Swk St Saviour; Rotherhithe, vintner [DW/PA/7/8 f.29;
DW/PA/5/1608/73]
LAWNDER *see* LANDER
LAWRENCE (LAURANCE,LAURENCE,LAURENS,LORANCE)
Alice of Swk St George, widow [DW/PA/7/7 f.151; 1598] <Abs 285>
Charles of Burstow [PRO; PCC 1648]
Christopher of Ewell; Warwickshire, saddler [DW/PA/7/7 f.332;
DW/PA/5/1601/59] <Abs 599>
Edmund of St Martha's - Chilworth [DW/PA/7/6 f.202; 1560]
Edward of Blechingley, husbandman [DW/PA/7/12 f.302; DW/PA/5/1635/62]
Giles of Swk St Olave, citizen and joiner [DW/PA/7/10 f.104;
DW/PA/5/1621/69]
Harry of Swk St Mary Magdalen, tailor [DW/PA/7/2 f.72; 1500]
Jane of Lambeth - Lambeth Marsh [DW/PA/7/11 f.230; DW/PA/5/1625/144]
John of Chiddingfold, shearman, senior [DW/PA/7/7 f.169;
DW/PA/5/1597/66] <Abs 310>
John of Chiddingfold, husbandman [HRO; 1617 B35]
John of Chiddingfold, husbandman [DW/PA/7/9 f.231; DW/PA/5/1617/61]
John of Chipstead, husbandman [DW/PA/7/13 f.343; 1644]
John of Swk St George, citizen and fletcher [DW/PA/5/1569/47]
John of Walton on Thames, husbandman [DW/PA/7/7 f.335; DW/PA/5/1601/60]
<Abs 605>

LAWRENCE (LAURANCE,LAURENCE,LAURENS,LORANCE) [*continued*]
Mary of Chipstead [PRO; PCC Admon 1647]
Matthew of Cobham [HRO; Reg. Way 1 p.60; 1459]
Matthew of Swk St George, cordwainer [DW/PA/7/11 f.249; DW/PA/5/1625/145]
Richard of Coulsdon, bachelor [PRO; PCC Admon 1642]
Robert of Esher [DW/PA/5/1550/61]
Thomas of Thames Ditton, labourer [DW/PA/7/9 f.297; 1618]
Thomas of Dorking, bricklayer [DW/PA/5/1592/15]
Thomas of Swk St Olave, fisherman [DW/PA/7/4 f.70; 1534]
William of Bermondsey [PRO; PCC Will 1506]

LAWSE
Cuthbert of Rotherhithe [PRO; PCC Admon 1577]

LAWSON
Thomas of Walton on Thames, husbandman [HRO; 1602 B26]

LAYKER *see* LAKER

LAYN *see* LANE

LEA *see* LEE

LEACH (LEACHE)
Edward of Merton - Merton Abbey, mealman [DW/PA/5/1576/107]
Goodith of Swk St Saviour, widow [DW/PA/7/11 f.102; DW/PA/5/1624/70]
see also LEECH

LEACHCUM
Gabriel of ... [DW/PA/5/1561/76]

LEADFORD
John, alias John Baker of Ockley [PRO; PCC 1637]

LEAKE
Harman of Swk St Olave [DW/PA/5/1593/124]

LEAMINGTON (LYMYNGTON)
Alice of Swk St Olave, widow [DW/PA/5/1546/37]

LEANARD,LEANARDE *see* LEONARD

LEANEING (LEANNIGE)
Jane of Swk St Olave, spinster [DW/PA/7/11 f.148; DW/PA/5/1625/146]
Katherine of Swk St George, widow [DW/PA/7/11 f.478; DW/PA/5/1628/65]

LEANOLD
Edward of Egham, 'fisher' [DW/PA/7/12 f.308; DW/PA/5/1635/63]

LEASE
Richard of Egham [DW/PA/5/1569/26]

LEATHER
William of ... [DW/PA/7/8 f.337; DW/PA/5/1612/90]

LEATHERHEAD (LEDERED,LETHERED)
Henry of Esher [DW/PA/7/5 f.208; 1541]
Juliana of Leatherhead [PRO; PCC Will 1425]

LEAVER *see* LEVER

LE BLAN
John, alias John White of Swk St Olave [DW/PA/7/11 f.343; DW/PA/5/1625/147]

LECHFORD (LECHEFORD,LECHFORDE,LETCHFORD,LICCHEFORD)
(Dame) Eleanor widow of (Sir) Richard of Farnham; Leigh; Charlwood, knight [DW/PA/7/8 f.203; DW/PA/5/1612/91]
Henry of Charlwood [LPL; Reg. Abp Courtenay f.229; Will 1388]
Henry of Charlwood [PRO; PCC Will 1492]
Henry of Leigh, esq. [PRO; PCC Will 1567]
John of Horley [DW/PA/7/2 f.140; 1519]

LECHFORD (LECHEFORD,LECHFORDE,LETCHFORD,LICCHEFORD) [*continued*]
(Sir) Richard of Leigh - Shellwood; Charlwood, knight [DW/PA/7/8 f.316; DW/PA/5/1611/71]
Thomas of Horley, widower [PRO; PCC Admon 1628]
LE CLERCKE
John of Swk, combmaker [DW/PA/5/1571/7]
LE COCQ
Jehenne, alias Jehenne de Dacchin, wife of William du Pysre of Swk St Olave [DW/PA/5/1570/34]
LEDALE (LEDALL)
Ann of Swk St Margaret, widow [DW/PA/7/4 f.8; 1532]
John of Swk St Margaret, tailor [DW/PA/7/3 f.118; 1529]
LEDERED *see* LEATHERHEAD
LEDGER (LIDGER,LIGEAR,LYDGER,LYGEARD)
Alice of Burstow; Blechingley, widow [PRO; PCC Will 1578]
Andrew of Nutfield [DW/PA/5/1627/67]
Henry of West Clandon [HRO; 1596 B46]
John of Beddington [DW/PA/5/1578/49]
Nicholas of Godstone; Horne, husbandman [DW/PA/5/1604/36] <Abs U109>
Nicholas of Sutton, yeoman [DW/PA/7/11 f.93; DW/PA/5/1624/69]
Thomas of West Clandon, husbandman [DW/PA/7/6 f.282; 1560]
Thomas of West Clandon, yeoman [DW/PA/7/10 f.70; 1618]
William of Blechingley, yeoman [DW/PA/7/12 f.276; DW/PA/5/1635/60]
William of Weybridge, tailor [DW/PA/7/8 f.32; DW/PA/5/1609/51]
LEDINGTON
Timothy of Guildford [PRO; PCC Will 1596]
LEE (a LEE,ATLE,ATLEE,LE,LEA,LEGH,LEGHT,LEIGH,LEY,LEYGH,LEYS,LIGH,LIGHE, LYE,LYGHE)
Abraham of Shere [PRO; PCC 1649]
Ann of Bermondsey [DW/PA/7/12 f.512; DW/PA/5/1639/83]
Anthony of Pyrford, etc. [PRO; PCC Will 1517]
Arnold of Woking [DW/PA/7/7 f.420; DW/PA/5/1603/98] <Abs 785>
Dorothy of Woking, widow [DW/PA/7/13 f.314; DW/PA/5/1643/60]
Edmund of Frensham; Haslemere, husbandman [DW/PA/5/1593/92]
Edmund of Puttenham [DW/PA/7/6 f.249; 1560]
Edward of Chelsham - Fairchildes, gent. [PRO; PCC 1638]
Edward of Cobham, husbandman [DW/PA/7/13 f.354; 1644]
Edward of Pyrford, husbandman [DW/PA/7/13 f.403; DW/PA/5/1645/30]
Edward of Shere - Gomshall, yeoman [HRO; 1622 B27]
Elizabeth, alias Elizabeth Adlye of Ockham, widow [DW/PA/5/1571/73]
Elizabeth of Putney, widow [LPL; 96/1609; Will 1627]
Ellen of Esher, widow of John of Byfleet [DW/PA/7/12 f.340; DW/PA/5/1636/64]
Francis of Swk St George, chandler [DW/PA/7/10 f.6; DW/PA/5/1619/77]
(Sir) Francis of Addington, knight [PRO; PCC 1645] <Abs SAC v.7 pp.95-96>
Francis of Rotherhithe, gunpowder maker [PRO; PCC Will 1589]
Francis of Inner Temple; Thorpe, bachelor [PRO; PCC Admon 1638]
Henry of Carshalton [PRO; PCC Will 1486]
Henry of Chelsham [PRO; PCC Will 1561]
Henry of Chobham; Thorpe; Windlesham; Bisley, yeoman [DW/PA/7/7 f.608; DW/PA/5/1607/61] <Abs 1140>
Henry of Pirbright, senior [DW/PA/7/12 f.71; DW/PA/5/1632/60]
Henry of Woking - Sutton, husbandman [HRO; 1585 AD40]
Henry of Woking, yeoman [HRO; 1636 B19]

LEE (a LEE,ATLE,ATLEE,LE,LEA,LEGH,LEGHT,LEIGH,LEY,LEYGH,LEYS,LIGH,LIGHE, LYE,LYGHE) [*continued*]

Isabel (formerly Isabel Fitz and Isabel Hattcliff, later Isabel Fleming) of Addington [PRO; PCC Will 1544]

(Dame) Isabel of Lambeth - Stockwell [PRO; PCC Will 1527] <Abs, SAC v,51 pp,89-90>

Joan of Bermondsey, widow of Lawrence, citizen and grocer [GL; Archdeaconry Court of London Will 1639]

Joan of East Clandon, widow [DW/PA/7/7 f,367; DW/PA/5/1602/61] <Abs 672>

Joan of Horsley [DW/PA/7/8 f,88; DW/PA/5/1609/52]

Joan of Walton on Thames [PRO; PCC Will 1509]

John of Addington, senior [PRO; PCC Will 1479] <Abs SAC v,7 p,118>

John of Addington, gent, [PRO; PCC Will 1503; CCAL; 1500 f,201r] <Abs SAC v,25 pp,39-40>

John of Addington [PRO; PCC Will 1576]

John of Addington [PRO; PCC Will 1624] <Abs SAC v,7 p,89>

John of Byfleet [DW/PA/7/12 f,114; DW/PA/5/1632/63]

John of Chertsey [DW/PA/7/2 f,205; 1525]

John of Chertsey, tilemaker [HRO; 1629 B31]

John Le, alias John Atle of West Clandon, weaver [DW/PA/7/10 f,91; DW/PA/5/1615/82] <Abs U207>

John of West Clandon [PRO; PCC 1649]

John of Thames Ditton, esq, [PRO; PCC Will 1524] <Abs SAC v,8 pp,128-130>

John of Effingham [PRO; PCC Will 1507]

John of Effingham - 'Booles', yeoman [DW/PA/7/11 f,19; DW/PA/5/1623/68]

John of Ewhurst [PRO; PCC 1639]

John, alias John Spicer of Kingston [PRO; PCC Will 1502] <Abs SAC v,8 p,114>

John of Kingston [DW/PA/7/2 f,99; 1513]

(Sir) John of Lambeth - Stockwell, knight [PRO; PCC Will 1523] <Abs, SAC v,51 pp,87-88>

(Sir) John of Lambeth [PRO; PCC Will 1565] <Abs, SAC v,51 pp,90-92>

(Sir) John of Mitcham, knight [PRO; PCC Will 1624]

John of Ockham, bachelor [DW/PA/5/1562/83]

John of Shere, husbandman [DW/PA/7/13 f,219; DW/PA/5/1643/59]

John of Swk St Olave, citizen and woodmonger [DW/PA/5/1627/69]

John of Swk St Saviour - Upper Ground, waterman [DW/PA/7/13 f,37; DW/PA/5/1639/84]

John of Woking - Mayford, senior [DW/PA/7/9 f,33; DW/PA/5/1614/71]

John of Woking - Mayford, yeoman [DW/PA/7/10 f,207; DW/PA/5/1620/76]

John of Woking [DW/PA/7/11 f,563; DW/PA/5/1630/67]

John of Woking [PRO; PCC Admon 1649]

John of Wotton, husbandman [HRO; 1629 B32]

Joseph of London, citizen and leatherseller [DW/PA/7/11 f,250; DW/PA/5/1625/148]

Joyce of Woking, widow [PRO; PCC 1648]

Katherine of Swk St Saviour [BM; Add,Ms 24,925 f,11r; 1544] <Abs 20>

Michael of Battersea - Penge, gent, [PRO; PCC 1646]

Miles of Effingham, yeoman [DW/PA/7/12 f,49; DW/PA/5/1631/68 *and* DW/PA/5/1631/69]

Millicent of Horsell [? HRO; 1622]

Nathaniel of Newington, gent, [PRO; PCC 1647]

Nicholas of Addington, esq, [DW/PA/5/1581/62] <Abs SAC v,7 pp,85-86>

LEE (a LEE,ATLE,ATLEE,LE,LEA,LEGH,LEGHT,LEIGH,LEY,LEYGH,LEYS,LIGH,LIGHE, LYE,LYGHE) [*continued*]

Nicholas of Limpsfield; Titsey; Warlingham, yeoman [DW/PA/5/1600/27] <Abs U27>

Olyffe of Addington [PRO; PCC Will 1612] <Abs SAC v,7 p,92>

Phillip of Ockham, yeoman [DW/PA/5/1570/47]

Richard of Surrey, senior [PRO; PCC Will 1498]

Richard of Farnham, gent, [PRO; PCC 1646]

(Sir) Richard of Godstone, knight [PRO; PCC Will 1471]

Richard of Kingston, husbandman [DW/PA/7/8 f,136; DW/PA/5/1610/81]

Richard of Swk St Saviour, brewer [DW/PA/7/9 f,126; DW/PA/5/1615/78]

Richard of Woking - Sutton; Great Bookham; Effingham; Little Bookham; Albury; Cranleigh, yeoman [DW/PA/7/8 f,322; DW/PA/5/1611/72]

Richard of Woking - Mayford, senior [DW/PA/7/8 f,269; DW/PA/5/1613/73]

Robert of Abinger [DW/PA/7/1 f,32; 1486] <Abs 108>

Robert of Bermondsey [PRO; PCC Will 1587]

Robert of Swk St Olave, baker [DW/PA/7/7 f,509; DW/PA/5/1605/55] <Abs 955>

Robert of Walton on Thames [PRO; PCC 1648]

Roger of Surrey [PRO; PCC Will 1531]

Roger of Stoke Dabernon [DW/PA/7/13 f,72; DW/PA/5/1640/92]

Sarah of Cobham [DW/PA/7/12 f,217; DW/PA/5/1633/85]

Sarah, alias Sarah Mellersh of Effingham [PRO; PCC Admon 1635]

Simon of Woking; Worplesdon, yeoman [DW/PA/7/8 f,129; DW/PA/5/1610/82]

Stephen of Send [DW/PA/7/1 f,23; 1485] <Abs 78>

Thomas of Chelsham, senior [DW/PA/5/1581/26]

Thomas of Chelsham, yeoman [PRO; PCC Will 1604] <Abs SAC v,11 pp,299-300>

Thomas, alias Thomas Genner of Leigh [DW/PA/7/10 f,190; DW/PA/5/1621/46]

Thomas of Loughton, Essex; Swk - Horsleydown, gent, [PRO; PCC Will 1571] <Abs Emmison pp,226-227>

Thomas of Send [DW/PA/7/2 f,171; 1522]

Thomas of Swk St Saviour, sailor [DW/PA/5/1588/5]

Thomas of Walton on Thames [PRO; PCC Will 1509]

Thomas of Walton on Thames, yeoman [DW/PA/5/1624/71]

Thomas of Walton on Thames [PRO; PCC 1636]

Ursula of Guildford, widow [DW/PA/7/12 f,401; DW/PA/5/1637/67A]

William of Abinger, yeoman [DW/PA/5/1580/36]

William of Bisley [DW/PA/7/12 f,471; DW/PA/5/1638/74]

William of Bisley [DW/PA/7/13 f,494; 1638]

William of Chobham [PRO; PCC 1648]

William of Dorking [LBLAD; Surrey Deeds 1/3131; 1649]

William of Effingham, yeoman [HRO; 1640 B39]

William of Ewhurst, gent, [PRO; PCC Will 1604] <Abs, SAC v,11 p,294>

William of Guildford, bricklayer [DW/PA/7/11 f,332; DW/PA/5/1625/149]

William of Kingston - Ham, weaver [DW/PA/7/7 f,122; DW/PA/5/1597/67] <Abs 225>

William of Limpsfield [PRO; PCC 1638]

William of Morden [DW/PA/7/4 f,174; 1536]

William of Newdigate, tailor [DW/PA/7/13 f,66; DW/PA/5/1639/81]

William of Titsey, yeoman [DW/PA/7/11 f,424; DW/PA/5/1627/68]

William of Walton on Thames - Apps; West Molesey; Shepperton, Middlesex, yeoman [DW/PA/7/6 f,17; DW/PA/5/1559/16]

Wolley of Thorpe, esq, [PRO; PCC Admon 1645]

see also a LEE; ATLEE

LEECH (LEICHE)
  Francis of Swk St Olave, feltmaker [DW/PA/7/7 f.140; DW/PA/5/1597/68]
    <Abs 258>
    see also LEACH
LEEKE
  Henry of Swk, beer brewer [PRO; PCC Will 1560] <Abs SAC v.1 p.201>
  Henry of Swk St Olave, citizen and clothworker [PRO; PCC Will 1563]
    <Abs SAC v.1 pp.201-202>
  John of Carshalton, clerk [PRO; PCC Will 1526]
LEESE
  Helen, alias Helen Medcalf of Bermondsey [PRO; PCC Admon 1589]
LEESON (LESON)
  Anthony of Barnes - Barn Elms; 'Soulgrave', gent. [PRO; PCC Will 1591]
  John of Rotherhithe (died overseas) [PRO; PCC Admon 1638]
LEETE
  John of Bermondsey, esq. [PRO; PCC Will 1619]
LEG *see* LEGG
LEGATT (LEGART)
  John of Capel, weaver [PRO; PCC Will 1628]
  John of Capel, miller [PRO; PCC Will 1627]
  Richard of Puttenham [DW/PA/7/1 f.71; 1487] <Abs 235>
LEGG (LEG,LEGGE)
  John of Cobham, yeoman [DW/PA/7/13 f.403; DW/PA/5/1645/31]
  John of Richmond [DW/PA/7/4 f.217; 1537]
  Robert of Lambeth - Kennington, citizen and draper [GL; Commissary
    Court of London Will 1456]
  Thomas of Newington [LPL; 98/1 f.118v (ren.); 1640]
LEGO (LEGOO)
  Elizabeth of Swk St Olave, widow [DW/PA/7/7 f.295; DW/PA/5/1600/26]
    <Abs 529>
  Stephen of Swk St George, yeoman [DW/PA/5/1580/32]
LEGH,LEGHT *see* LEE
LEICESTER (LEYCESTRE)
  Joan of Carshalton, widow [DW/PA/7/1 f.63; 1487] <Abs 212>
  John of Carshalton, gent. [GL; Commissary Court of London Will 1455]
LEICHE *see* LEECH; LEACH
LEIGHE *see* LEE
LEIGHTON (LEYGHTON)
  Robert of Swk St Olave, currier [DW/PA/7/4 f.234; 1538]
LE JEANE
  John of Swk St George; 'Le Vonte De-la-Sen', France [DW/PA/7/11
    f.219; DW/PA/5/1625/150]
LELLE
  Richard of Swk St Olave [DW/PA/7/11 f.151; DW/PA/5/1625/151]
LEMING
  Jeremy of Swk St Saviour, citizen and ironmonger [DW/PA/7/10 f.200;
    DW/PA/5/1621/70]
le MONDE *see* TOUT le MONDE
LENAGHE
  James of Swk St Thomas Hospital [DW/PA/5/1550/77]
LENESDALL (LINESDALL,LONESDALL)
  Thomas of Stoke next Guildford, clothier [DW/PA/7/8 f.119;
    DW/PA/5/1610/83]

LENTOLL
John of Swk St Saviour, yeoman [DW/PA/7/9 f.243; DW/PA/5/1617/62]
LEONARD (LEANARD,LEANARDE,LENNARD)
Harry of Swk St Olave [DW/PA/5/1562/23]
John of Alfold, yeoman [DW/PA/7/8 f.245; DW/PA/5/1613/72]
John of Cranleigh [HRO; 1640 B40]
Margaret of Alfold, spinster [PRO; PCC Admon 1647]
Robert, alias Robert Pykkeryng of Malden, labourer [DW/PA/7/3 f.149; 1530]
Thomas of Alfold [HRO; 1617 B37]
Thomas of Alfold, yeoman [DW/PA/5/1617/68] <Abs U222>
le PEEPER
John of Camberwell - Peckham [PRO; PCC 1645]
le SAGE
Nicholas of Bermondsey [PRO; PCC Will 1590]
LESCUYER
John of ... [French church] [DW/PA/5/1592/85]
LESON *see* LEESON
LESTENEY,LESTNEY *see* LISNEY
LESTRE (De LESTRE)
Anthony De, of ... [DW/PA/5/1569/73]
LETCHFORD *see* LECHFORD
LETERFORD
Thomas of Cobham [*? Cookham, Berkshire*] [PRO; PCC Will 1448]
LETTICE (LETTES,LETTISE,LETTYS)
Ann of Farnham [*in* DW/PA/5/1558/76]*
Francis of Farnham, cooper [DW/PA/7/12 f.153; DW/PA/5/1633/79]
John of Farnham [DW/PA/7/3 f.178; 1531]
John of Farnham, weaver [DW/PA/5/1557/45]
John of Horsell, husbandman [DW/PA/7/12 f.290; 1635]
Stephen of Horsell [DW/PA/7/8 f.280; DW/PA/5/1613/74]
LETTWICK
Robert of Swk St Olave, milliner [DW/PA/5/1587/56]
LETTYS *see* LETTICE
LEVAT (LEVETT,LEVYT,LOEVET)
John of Shere [DW/PA/5/1558/177]*
Richard, alias Richard Corks of Great Bookham; Effingham, tailor [DW/PA/7/10 f.109; DW/PA/5/1619/30]
Richard of Leatherhead, clerk [DW/PA/7/13 f.483; DW/PA/5/1648/21]
Thomas of Betchworth - Brockham, esq. [PRO; PCC Will 1616]
LEVENION
Peter of St Peter le Poer, London, glassmaker [DW/PA/7/11 f.403; DW/PA/5/1627/70]
LEVER (LEAVER,LEWER)
John of Newdigate, husbandman [HRO; 1558 B386-387]
John of Streatham - Tooting Bec, yeoman [DW/PA/7/9 f.333; DW/PA/5/1620/75]
Juliana of Pirbright, widow [*in* DW/PA/5/1557/75]
Ralph of Swk St Olave; London, dyer (on voyage to the East Indies) [DW/PA/7/13 f.322; DW/PA/5/1644/13]
Valentine of Richmond [PRO; PCC 1633]
LEVERETT
William of Swk St Olave, citizen and grocer [DW/PA/7/7 f.376; DW/PA/5/1602/62] <Abs 695>

LEVERSEGGE
  Robert of Ewell, gent. [PRO; PCC Will 1435]
LEVESDALE
  Anthony, alias Anthony Lovesdale of Stoke next Guildford, yeoman [DW/PA/5/1586/29]
LEVETT,LEVYT *see* LEVAT
LEWCOKE *see* LUCOCK
LEWE
  Dorothy of Reigate, widow [DW/PA/7/12 f.2; DW/PA/5/1631/61]
LEWELLIN *see* LLEWELLIN
LEWEN,LEWENS *see* LEWIN
LEWES *see* LEWIS
LEWGER (LEWGAR)
  Elizabeth of Croydon, widow [PRO; PCC 1641]
  John of Croydon, gent. [PRO; PCC 1637]
LEWIN (LEWEN,LEWENS,LUENS)
  Garliefe of Lambeth, merchant stranger [DW/PA/7/11 f.101; DW/PA/5/1624/72]
  George of Rotherhithe [PRO; PCC 1642]
  John of Warlingham [DW/PA/7/11 f.353; DW/PA/5/1625/152]
  Joseph of Richmond; Hampton Wick, Middlesex, gent. [PRO; PCC 1643]
  Nicholas of Leigh, tanner [DW/PA/7/9 f.194; DW/PA/5/1616/88]
  Richard of Wimbledon, labourer [LPL; 96/1626A; Will 1628]
  Thomas of Sutton [DW/PA/7/4 f.18; 1532]
  Thomas of Sutton [DW/PA/5/1558/178]
  William of Croydon - Woodside [PRO; PCC Admon 1647]
  William of Newington [LPL; 98/1 f.73r; Will 1636]
LEWIS (LEWES,LEWSE,LEWYS)
  David of Swk St Saviour [DW/PA/7/11 f.370; DW/PA/5/1626/81]
  Ellen of Swk St Olave [DW/PA/7/13 f.219; DW/PA/5/1643/58]
  Harry of Frensham, bachelor [DW/PA/5/1559/12]
  Harry of Swk St Saviour, waterman [DW/PA/5/1580/15]
  Hugh of Swk St Olave, citizen and joiner [DW/PA/7/7 f.568; DW/PA/5/1606/54] <Abs 1063>
  James of Thames Ditton, mealman [DW/PA/5/1582/77]
  John of Ashtead [DW/PA/7/12 f.275; DW/PA/5/1635/59]
  John of Camberwell - Dulwich, alehousekeeper [DW/PA/7/10 f.116; DW/PA/5/1620/77]
  John of Chertsey [DW/PA/7/1 f.43; 1486] <Abs 138>
  John of Mortlake, senior, gent. [PRO; PCC Will 1585]
  John of Swk St Olave, merchant stranger [DW/PA/7/7 f.459; DW/PA/5/1603/102] <Abs 866>
  Katherine of Lambeth, widow [DW/PA/5/1579/58]*
  Lettice of Pyrford, widow [DW/PA/7/13 f.156; DW/PA/5/1641/84]
  Owen of Shere, parson [DW/PA/7/8 f.214; DW/PA/5/1612/92]
  Rees of 'Combe Park' [PRO; PCC Will 1554]
  Richard of Bermondsey [PRO; PCC Admon 1609]
  Richard of Mitcham, higler [DW/PA/7/11 f.542; DW/PA/5/1629/57]
  Richard of Reigate [DW/PA/7/8 f.1; DW/PA/5/1608/68]
  Robert of Swk St Thomas, bricklayer [DW/PA/7/7 f.222; DW/PA/5/1598/49] <Abs 392>
  Roger of Swk St Olave, feltmaker [DW/PA/7/11 f.182; DW/PA/5/1625/153]
  Thomas of Oxted, citizen and draper [PRO; PCC 1641]
  William of Lambeth [PRO; PCC Will 1547]

LEWIS (LEWES,LEWSE,LEWYS) [*continued*]
William of Swk St Saviour, blacksmith [DW/PA/5/1578/23]
William of Stoke next Guildford [PRO; PCC 1649]
LEWKENOR
Roger of Surrey, senior, esq. [PRO; PCC Will 1509]
LEWSE *see* LEWIS
LEWSTON
Humphrey of Wimbledon [PRO; PCC Will 1533]
LEWYS *see* LEWIS
LEY *see* LEE
LEYCESTRE *see* LEICESTER
LEYCROFT (LEYCROFTE)
Richard of Swk St Olave, butcher [DW/PA/5/1562/44]
Robert of Croydon, etc. [PRO; PCC Will 1486]
LEYGHTON *see* LEIGHTON
LEYNE *see* LANE
LEYS *see* LEE
LIBBE (LIBBES)
John of Clapham, esq. [PRO; PCC Admon 1615]
John of Clapham [PRO; PCC Admon 1622]
William of Swk St Olave [DW/PA/7/8 f.15; DW/PA/5/1608/69]
LIBSCOMBE *see* LIPSCOMBE
LIBSETT (LITCOTT,LYBSETT,LYPSETT)
John of East Molesey [DW/PA/5/1571/5]
(Sir) John of East Molesey, knight [PRO; PCC 1641]
Robert of Kingston, carpenter, senior [DW/PA/7/13 f.342; 1644]
Ursula of Windlesham - Bagshot [PRO; PCC Admon 1606]
William of East Molesey, yeoman [DW/PA/7/7 f.380; DW/PA/5/1602/63] <Abs 703>
LICCHEFORD *see* LECHFORD
LICHEPOLE
Thomas of Kingston [HRO; Reg. D p.57 1527]
LICKER (LYKER)
William of Leigh [DW/PA/7/1 f.21; 1485] <Abs 71>
LICKFOLD (LICKFOULD)
Alice of Seale, widow of James [DW/PA/7/8 f.281; DW/PA/5/1613/75]
Elizabeth of Seale - Tongham, widow [DW/PA/7/10 f.194; DW/PA/5/1621/73]
James of Seale - Tongham [DW/PA/7/8 f.170; DW/PA/5/1610/84]
James of Seale - Tongham, yeoman [DW/PA/7/13 f.159; DW/PA/5/1641/85]
Lawrence of Seale - Tongham [DW/PA/7/13 f.347; 1644]
LIDDLE (LYDDALL)
Robert of Kingston [PRO; PCC Will 1589]
LIDGER *see* LEDGER
LIDSEY
Richard of Thames Ditton, gent. [DW/PA/7/13 f.473; DW/PA/5/1648/20]
LIFE (LIFFE,LYFE,LYFF,LYFFE)
Edward of Reigate, barber [PRO; PCC Will 1621] [*and*] [DW/PA/5/1620/72] <Abs U244>
Elizabeth of Reigate [PRO; PCC 1634]
John of Dorking, weaver [DW/PA/7/11 f.182; DW/PA/5/1625/154]
John of Horley [DW/PA/7/4 f.55; 1533]
John of Merstham, wheelwright [LPL; 96/1636; Will 1642]
John of Reigate; Horley [DW/PA/7/11 f.416; DW/PA/5/1627/71]
Richard of Godstone, smith [DW/PA/7/9 f.196; DW/PA/5/1616/87]

LIFE (LIFFE,LYFE,LYFF,LYFFE) [*continued*]
Richard of Mitcham [DW/PA/5/1579/59]*
Richard of Reigate, blacksmith [DW/PA/7/11 f.45; DW/PA/5/1623/72]
William of Croydon [PRO; PCC 1641]
LIFELY
Thomas of Lambeth - Kennington, gardener [DW/PA/7/12 f.477; DW/PA/5/1638/75]
LIFFE *see* LIFE
LIFFORD (LYFERD,LYFFORD,LYFORD)
Henry of Mortlake [PRO; PCC Admon 1648 *and* 1649]
Thomas of Capel, victualler [DW/PA/7/10 f.293; DW/PA/5/1622/56]
William of Dorking [DW/PA/7/11 f.505; DW/PA/5/1629/58]
LIGEAR *see* LEDGER
LIGHE *see* LEE
LIGHTFOOT (LIGHEFFOTE,LYGHTFOTE)
Thomas of Witley, vicar [DW/PA/7/5 f.99; 1539]
LIGTH
George of Newington, gent. [PRO; PCC Will 1543]
LILLEY (LILLIE,LILLYE,LYLLEYE,LYLLIE,LYLLYE)
Christopher of Abinger, husbandman [HRO; 1573 B85]
John of Abinger; Ewhurst, yeoman [DW/PA/7/9 f.269; 1618]
John of Abinger, yeoman [DW/PA/7/12 f.195; DW/PA/5/1633/84]
John of Bermondsey; Swk St Olave, citizen and fletcher [DW/PA/7/7 f.404; DW/PA/5/1603/99] <Abs 749>
Nicholas of Rotherhithe [PRO; PCC Will 1622]
Richard of Abinger; Oakwood; Wotton, yeoman [DW/PA/7/9 f.263; DW/PA/5/1617/65]
Robert of Wotton, yeoman [HRO; 1560 U182-183]
LIMBDEN (LYMDEN)
William of Reigate, yeoman, senior [DW/PA/7/8 f.352; DW/PA/5/1612/93]
William of Reigate [DW/PA/5/1617/66] <Abs U220>
LIMPETT (LYMPITT)
Daniel of Swk St Saviour, falconer [DW/PA/7/7 f.462; DW/PA/5/1603/100] <Abs 873>
LINCH *see* LYNCH
LINCOLN (LINGCON,LYNCON)
Elizabeth, dowager countess of, widow of Edward Clinton, earl of, of Woking [PRO; PCC Will 1589]
Nicholas of Camberwell, husbandman, widower [DW/PA/5/1563/72 *and in* DW/PA/5/1563/65]
Richard, alias Richard Drencher of Limpsfield, husbandman [PRO; PCC Will 1618]
Thomas of Chertsey, armourer [PRO; PCC Will 1622]
William of Camberwell [HRO; Reg. CCB 20 p.10; 1563]
William, alias William Drencher of Limpsfield, yeoman [DW/PA/5/1580/57]
LINCOTT (LYMCOTTES)
Joan of Surrey; St Michael Cornhill, London, widow [GL; Commissary Court of London Will 1588]
LIND (LYNDE)
(Sir) Humphrey of Cobham, knight [PRO; PCC 1636]
William of Guildford Holy Trinity [DW/PA/7/4 f.22; 1532]
LINDER
John of ... [GMR; 97/13/1113; 1608]
LINE *see* LINES

LINEHAM
  Richard of Guildford St Nicolas; Guildford St Mary, weaver
    [DW/PA/7/10 f.267; DW/PA/5/1622/54]
LINES (LINE)
  John of Lambeth, inshore waterman [DW/PA/7/9 f.37; DW/PA/5/1614/73]
  Simon of Guildford, shearman [DW/PA/5/1578/74]
LINESDALL *see* LENESDALL
LING (LYNG,LYNGE)
  John of Lambeth [PRO; PCC Will 1551]
  John of Swk St Olave [DW/PA/7/12 f.34; DW/PA/5/1631/64]
  William of Lambeth [DW/PA/7/2 f.106; 1516]
LINGARD (LINGARDE,LYNGARDE)
  John of Croydon, gent. [PRO; PCC Will 1606] <Abs. SAC v.12 pp.197-198>
  Ralph of Farnham [DW/PA/7/3 f.193; 1531]
  William of Wimbledon [PRO; PCC Admon 1603]
LINGCON *see* LINCOLN
LINGFIELD (LINGVILE)
  Alice of Lingfield, widow [DW/PA/7/13 f.219; DW/PA/5/1642/53]
  Edward of Lingfield [PRO; PCC 1642]
LINGHAM (LYNGHAM)
  Alice of Chertsey, widow [DW/PA/7/11 f.442; DW/PA/5/1628/66]
  Thomas of Chertsey, weaver [DW/PA/7/12 f.368; DW/PA/5/1627/72]
LINGVILE *see* LINGFIELD
LINKHORN *see* FINCKHORNE
LINLEY (LYNDLEY)
  Lawrence of Kingston [PRO; PCC Admon 1612]
LINN
  John of Godstone; Lingfield; Tandridge, husbandman [DW/PA/7/10 f.83;
    DW/PA/5/1615/122]
LINNEY (LYNNYE)
  John of Christ Church Canterbury, Kent; Swk St George;
    Stoven, Suffolk; Halesworth, Suffolk, yeoman [DW/PA/7/4 f.123; 1535]
LINSELL (de LINSELL)
  Allara of London; Swk St Olave; Blandin near Tournai, France
    [French] [DW/PA/7/13 f.414; DW/PA/5/1645/32]
LINTON (de LYNTON)
  Thomas de, of Cliffe, Kent; Stoke; Wallingford, Berkshire;
    St Creed, Cornwall; Linton, Cambridgeshire, canon of St Paul's and
    canon of Windsor [LPL; Reg. Abp Courtenay f.225; Will 1387]
LINTOTT (LYNTOTT)
  Thomas of Beddington, yeoman [PRO; PCC Will 1587]
LIPPYTT
  Joan of Swk St Olave [DW/PA/5/1546/15]
LIPSCOMBE (LIBSCOMBE,LIPSCOMB,LIPPESCOMBE,LYPSCOM,LYPSCOMBE)
  Gilbert of Windlesham [PRO; PCC Will 1597]
  Hugh of Shalford, husbandman [DW/PA/7/7 f.176; DW/PA/5/1597/69] <Abs 324>
  John of Abinger, senior [HRO; 1572 B61]
  John of Cranleigh [DW/PA/5/1575/70]
  Thomas of 'Barshott' - ?Farnham - Badshot [PRO; PCC Will 1577]
  Thomas of Abinger, weaver [DW/PA/7/10 f.43; 1618]
  Thomas of Cranleigh, husbandman [HRO; 1587 B55]
LISHFORD *see* LASHFORD

LISLE (LYEL,LYELL,LYLE,LYSLE)
Edmund of Godstone, esq. [PRO; PCC Will 1622]
Katherine of Kingston, widow [DW/PA/5/1617/67] <Abs U221>
Katherine of Swk St Thomas, widow [DW/PA/7/7 f.506; DW/PA/5/1605/57] <Abs 948>
Thomas of Epsom - Horton, esq. [DW/PA/5/1550/102]
William of West Horsley, servant [PRO; PCC Will 1623]
LISNEY (LASTNEY,LESTENEY,LESTNEY,LISTNEY,LYSSNEY,LYSTNEY)
Bartholomew of Godalming; Epsom [DW/PA/7/4 f.197; 1537]
Henry of Ewell [DW/PA/7/1 f.66; 1487] <Abs 220>
John of Cobham, fuller [DW/PA/5/1593/175]
John of Croydon, yeoman [LPL; 96/1647; 98/1 f.127r; Will 1641]
John of Ewell - Loveland; Chipstead, yeoman [DW/PA/7/8 f.55; DW/PA/5/1609/53]
Juliana of Ewell; Chipstead, widow [PRO; PCC Admon 1575]
Peter of Lingfield, husbandman [DW/PA/7/12 f.181; DW/PA/5/1633/83]
Richard of Ewell; Walton on the Hill [DW/PA/7/5 f.161; 1540]
Robert of Walton on Thames - Hersham, labourer [DW/PA/5/1627/73]
Thomas of Farnham - Wrecclesham, yeoman [DW/PA/5/1592/61]
LIST
Alice, alias Alice Gunter of Newington [PRO; PCC Admon 1630]
Daniel of Lambeth [PRO; PCC Admon 1624]
LISTER (LYSTER)
Alice of Swk St Saviour, widow [DW/PA/7/6 f.251; 1560]
LISTON
Jane of Swk St George, widow [DW/PA/5/1624/73]
LITCOTT *see* LIBSETT
LITHGO (LYTHGOO)
William of Headley, parson [HRO; 1551 B85-86]
LITLE *see* LITTLE
LITLER *see* LITTLER
LITLETON *see* LITTLETON
LITTLE (LITLE)
Edward of Swk St Saviour - Bankside, waterman [DW/PA/7/10 f.117; DW/PA/5/1620/78]
Joan of Swk St Saviour, widow of Edward [DW/PA/7/11 f.48; DW/PA/5/1623/69]
LITTLEFIELD (LITTLEFEILD)
John of ... [DW/PA/7/13 f.346; 1644]
LITTLEPAGE
George of Bermondsey, yeoman [DW/PA/7/12 f.402; DW/PA/5/1637/67B]
LITTLER (LITLER)
Bridget of Putney, widow [PRO; PCC Will 1626]
LITTLETON (de LITLETON)
William de, of Guildford St Nicolas [HRO; Reg. Stra p.65; 1331]
LITTLEWELL
Thomas of Newington [LPL; 98/1 f.103r; Will 1639]
LIVERHART
John, alias John Hart of Merton [PRO; PCC Admon 1627]
William, alias William Hart of Merton [PRO; PCC Admon 1630]
LIVERSAGE
Robert of Surrey, gent. [GL; Commissary Court of London Will 1436]

LIVESEY (LYVESEY)
Amy of Streatham - Tooting Bec, widow [PRO; PCC Will 1618]
Robert of Streatham - Tooting Bec, esq. [PRO; PCC Will 1608] <Abs. SAC v.13 p.190>
LIVINGSTONE (LOVEINGSTONE,LOVINGSTONE)
Joan of Swk St Olave, widow [DW/PA/7/11 f.146; DW/PA/5/1625/156]
John of Swk St Olave [DW/PA/7/11 f.152; DW/PA/5/1625/157]
LLEWELLYN (a LLOELLEN,ap LLOELLEN,LEWELLIN)
Ann of Newington, widow [LPL; 96/1625; Will 1617]
Gawain of 'Merquiske, Flintshire'; Swk St Saviour [DW/PA/7/9 f.50; DW/PA/5/1614/99]
see also FLUELLEN
LLOYD (LLOID)
Catherine of Swk St Thomas, widow [DW/PA/7/13 f.73; DW/PA/5/1640/93]
Evan of Mitcham, chapman [DW/PA/7/12 f.319; DW/PA/5/1636/66]
Henry of Cheam [PRO; PCC Admon 1647]
LOCK (LOCKE,LOK,LOYCK)
Ann of Newington [PRO; PCC Will 1623]
Edward of Beddington [PRO; PCC 1647]
Francis of Merton; Datchet, Buckinghamshire, gent. [DW/PA/7/10 f.234; DW/PA/5/1621/71]
John of Elstead, husbandman [HRO; 1609 B45]
John of Lambeth, yeoman [DW/PA/7/7 f.13; DW/PA/5/1595/62] <Abs 28>
John of Oxted [DW/PA/7/8 f.257; DW/PA/5/1611/73]
Matthew of Merton, esq. [PRO; PCC Will 1599]
Thomas of Surrey [PRO; PCC Will 1556]
William of Chobham, innholder [DW/PA/7/13 f.30; DW/PA/5/1640/96]
(Sir) William of Merton, etc., knight [PRO; PCC Will 1550]
LOCKETT
Thomas of Newington, citizen and merchant tailor [PRO; PCC Will 1593]
LOCKIER (LOKER)
Edward of Rotherhithe, gunner [PRO; PCC 1647]
William of Chobham, gent. [PRO; PCC Will 1625] <Abs SAC v.26 p.72>
LOCKSMITH (LOCKESMYTHE,LOCKSMITHE,LOCKSMYTTHE)
Henry of Chertsey [DW/PA/5/1576/128]
Henry of Cobham, gent. [PRO; PCC 1637]
John of Bermondsey, brewer [DW/PA/7/13 f.83; DW/PA/5/1641/81]
Thomas of Chertsey [PRO; PCC Will 1594]
William of Chertsey, yeoman [DW/PA/5/1558/179]*
William of Chertsey, tanner, senior [DW/PA/7/13 f.180; DW/PA/5/1641/86]
LOCKWOOD
Hugh of Bisley [PRO; PCC Admon 1649]
Richard of Bermondsey [PRO; PCC Admon 1632]
LODGE
John of Swk St George; Burton, Yorkshire, barber surgeon [DW/PA/7/7 f.403; DW/PA/5/1603/101] <Abs 748>
LODWYN
John of Christ Church, London; Guildford, citizen and draper [GL; Commissary Court of London Will 1625]
LOEVET *see* LEVAT
LOFF *see* LUFFE
LOFFTON
Thomas of Chertsey [DW/PA/7/5 f.66; 1539] <Abs 19>
LOFLOND *see* LOVELAND

LOFTE
William of Newington [LPL; 96/1654; Will 1647]
LOFTEMAN
John of Kingston, cordwainer [DW/PA/7/6 f.66; 1559]
LOFTISMAN
George of Effingham; Little Bookham; Great Bookham, husbandman [DW/PA/7/8 f.2; DW/PA/5/1608/70]
LOGGE
John of Walton on Thames [PRO; PCC Will 1479]
LOKER *see* LOCKIER
LOMAS (LOWMASSE)
Elizabeth of Addington, widow [DW/PA/7/8 f.292; DW/PA/5/1613/78]
Henry of Addington, tailor [DW/PA/7/8 f.220; DW/PA/5/1612/94]
LOMMAN
John of Rotherhithe, sailor [PRO; PCC Will 1614]
LOND
Giles of Swk St George [DW/PA/5/1558/181]*
LONDON
John of Kingston, yeoman [PRO; PCC Will 1624]
John of Kingston [PRO; PCC 1637; PCC Admon 1637]
Thomas of Wandsworth [DW/PA/7/10 f.287; DW/PA/5/1623/70]
LONESDALL *see* LENESDALL
LONG (LONGE)
John of Croydon [PRO; PCC Will 1640]
John of Guildford St Nicolas [DW/PA/7/6 f.114; DW/PA/5/1559/119]
Robert of Surrey [PRO; PCC Will 1551]
Robert of Kingston [DW/PA/7/1 f.36; 1486] <Abs 122>
Thomas of Puttenham [DW/PA/7/4 f.103; 1535]
William of Guildford St Nicolas [DW/PA/7/1 f.45; 1486] <Abs 147>
LONGDON
John of Swk St Saviour, cooper [DW/PA/7/12 f.205; DW/PA/5/1634/66]
LONGE *see* LONG
LONGHURST (LANGHURST,LONGEHURSTE,LONGHERST,LONGHIRST,LONGHURSTE)
Edmund of Shere [DW/PA/7/13 f.119; DW/PA/5/1640/95]
George of Ockley; Ewhurst; Wotton, yeoman [DW/PA/7/9 f.319; DW/PA/5/1619/78]
James of Reigate [DW/PA/7/1 f.74; 1488] <Abs 244>
John of Ewhurst; Ockley; Billinghurst, Sussex; Pulborough, Sussex, yeoman, senior [DW/PA/5/1603/104] <Abs U79>
John of Ockley - Holbrook [DW/PA/5/1546/55]
John of Ockley [DW/PA/5/1575/20]
John of Ewhurst; Ockley; Bookham; Warnham, Sussex; Wonersh, junior [DW/PA/5/1603/103] <Abs U78>
John of Ockley, yeoman [DW/PA/7/12 f.48; DW/PA/5/1631/67]
John of Wotton [DW/PA/7/2 f.164; 1522]
Nicholas of Effingham, labourer, sen. [DW/PA/7/9 f.226; DW/PA/5/1617/63]
Robert of Great Bookham [DW/PA/7/12 f.236; DW/PA/5/1634/68]
Thomas of Ewhurst, yeoman [DW/PA/7/11 f.501; DW/PA/5/1629/59]
Thomas of Ewhurst, yeoman [DW/PA/7/13 f.319; DW/PA/5/1646/33]
Walter of Ockley, yeoman [DW/PA/7/13 f.451; DW/PA/5/1646/35]
William of Dorking [DW/PA/7/6 f.241; 1560]
William of Ewhurst; Ockley, yeoman [DW/PA/7/7 f.289; DW/PA/5/1599/95] <Abs 516>
William of Wotton - Ruckmans, yeoman [DW/PA/7/13 f.453; DW/PA/5/1647/7]

LONGTON
John of Tooting [DW/PA/7/2 f.29; 1499]
LONGTRE
William of Swk [LPL; Reg. Abp Bourgchier f.40v; Admon 1456]
LORAM
Morgan of Swk St Saviour, fruiterer [DW/PA/7/12 f.3; DW/PA/5/1631/62]
LORANCE *see* LAWRENCE
LORD (LORDE)
Alice of Sutton [PRO; PCC Will 1539] <Abs, SAC v.52 pp.47-48>
John of West Molesey, blacksmith [DW/PA/7/11 f.193; DW/PA/5/1625/155]
John of Rotherhithe, clothier [PRO; PCC Will 1603] <Abs, SAC v.11 pp.128-129>
Lawrence of Petersham [DW/PA/7/12 f.173; DW/PA/5/1633/82]
Lawrence of Petersham, tailor [DW/PA/7/12 f.249; DW/PA/5/1636/62]
Stephen, alias Stephen Lorder of Lambeth [PRO; PCC Admon 1599]
William of Swk St Olave, dyer [DW/PA/7/2 f.83; 1501]
LORDER
Stephen, alias Stephen Lord of Lambeth [PRO; PCC Admon 1599]
LORDING
Ellen of Putney, widow [LPL; 96/1659; Will 1646]
LORKIN
John of Camberwell - Great Peckham [PRO; PCC Will 1589]
LORMER
Clement of Egham, yeoman [DW/PA/7/4 f.180; 1536]
LOSELEY (LOWESLY,LOWSELEY)
Elizabeth of Swk St Mary Magdalen, widow [DW/PA/7/7 f.318; DW/PA/5/1600/30] <Abs 568>
Henry of Egham [DW/PA/5/1591/20]
LOSON
John of Swk St Mary Overy, armourer [DW/PA/7/2 f.84; 1502]
LOTT
Thomas of Newington [LPL; 96/1660; Will 1627]
LOUDER
Richard of Wonersh [DW/PA/7/1 f.85; 1486] <Abs 92>
[*see also entry for Richard Lander*]
LOUFE *see* LUFFE
LOUNDE *see* LOWNES
LOUTH (LOWETH,LOWTH)
Edmund of Swk St Olave, baker [DW/PA/7/7 f.455; DW/PA/5/1603/105] <Abs 859>
Nicholas of Swk St Olave, pinmaker [DW/PA/7/7 f.461; DW/PA/5/1603/106] <Abs 870>
LOUVER *see* LOVER
LOVE
John of Mitcham [PRO; PCC Will 1476]
(Dame) Margaret of Rotherhithe; Plymouth, Devon, wife of (Sir) Thomas, knight [DW/PA/7/11 f.296; DW/PA/5/1626/82]
Nicholas of Kingston, innholder [DW/PA/5/1575/84]
(Sir) Thomas of Rotherhithe, knight [PRO; PCC Will 1627]
LOVEDAY (LOVEDAIE)
James of Newington, carpenter [PRO; PCC Will 1625]
LOVEINGSTONE *see* LIVINGSTONE

LOVEJOY (LOVEJOYE,LOVIOY)

Phillip, alias Phillip Lovewye of Guildford St Nicolas, shoemaker [DW/PA/7/11 f.595; DW/PA/5/1629/60]

Thomas of Swk St Olave, citizen and joiner [DW/PA/7/8 f.269; DW/PA/5/1613/76]

William of Guildford St Nicolas [DW/PA/7/13 f.150; DW/PA/5/1641/83]

LOVELAND (LOFLOND,LOVELANDE,LOWELAND)

Alice of Godalming - Shackleford, widow [DW/PA/7/6 f.209; 1560]

George of Guildford St Nicolas - Loseley; Compton, husbandman [DW/PA/7/7 f.526; DW/PA/5/1607/62] <Abs 992>

George, alias George Burt of Worplesdon, husbandman [HRO; 1582 B15]

Henry of Abinger, husbandman [DW/PA/7/12 f.168; DW/PA/5/1633/81]

Henry of Pirbright, husbandman [DW/PA/7/8 f.359; DW/PA/5/1612/95]

Henry of Worplesdon [DW/PA/7/1 f.8; 1485] <Abs 28>

John of Godalming [DW/PA/7/1 f.15; 1485] <Abs 51>

John of Guildford St Nicolas, carpenter [DW/PA/5/1558/182]*

John of Horsell; Worplesdon; Ewhurst, yeoman [DW/PA/7/10 f.159; DW/PA/5/1621/72]

John of Worplesdon - Wyke [DW/PA/7/8 f.309; DW/PA/5/1613/77]

Joseph of Worplesdon [PRO; PCC Admon 1647]

Margery of Godalming [*proxy*] [DW/PA/5/1575/28]

Margery of Worplesdon, widow [*in* DW/PA/5/1558/166]

Robert of Worplesdon, carpenter [DW/PA/5/1558/184]*

Stephen of Farnham, husbandman [DW/PA/7/11 f.172; DW/PA/5/1625/158]

Thomas of Ash [DW/PA/5/1570/58]

Thomas of Dunsfold; Hascombe [DW/PA/7/6 f.263; 1560]

Thomas of Worplesdon [DW/PA/7/6 f.114; DW/PA/5/1559/76]

William of Godalming - Shackleford [DW/PA/5/1557/142]

LOVELL

Gregory of Merton, esq. [PRO; PCC Will 1597]

John of Richmond, yeoman [DW/PA/5/1550/22]

Prudence of Richmond, widow [PRO; PCC 1635]

Ralph of Richmond, waterman [DW/PA/5/1588/44]

Richard of Richmond [PRO; PCC Admon 1639]

Robert of Sutton, carpenter [DW/PA/5/1576/6]

Robert of Richmond [PRO; PCC Admon 1649]

Robert of Thorpe, carpenter [DW/PA/7/7 f.316; DW/PA/5/1600/28] <Abs 563>

Thomas of Kingston, gent. [PRO; PCC Will 1508]

Thomas of Richmond, gent., cook to the king [PRO; PCC 1632]

William of Worplesdon, blacksmith [HRO; 1633 AD56]

LOVER (LOUVER)

Stephen of Frensham, weaver [HRO; 1619 B46]

LOVERINGE

Thomas of Swk St Olave, mariner [DW/PA/7/12 f.153; DW/PA/5/1633/80]

LOVESDALE

Anthony, alias Anthony Levesdale of Stoke next Guildford, yeoman [DW/PA/5/1586/29]

LOVESTED

John of Ockham ? 'Okehampsted' [HRO; Reg. Fox 2 p.29; 1507]

LOVETT

Henry of Newington [PRO; PCC 1641]

LOVEWYE

Phillip, alias Phillip Lovejoye of Guildford St Nicolas, shoemaker [DW/PA/7/11 f.595; DW/PA/5/1629/60]

LOVEYN *see* LOVING

LOVIBONE

John of Wandsworth; Kingston [PRO; PCC Will 1532]

LOVING (LOVEYN)

(Sir) Nicholas of Poplar, Middlesex; Penshurst, Kent; Nutfield; Burstow; Cambridgeshire; Oxfordshire, knight [LPL; Reg, Abp Sudbury f,86; Will 1375]

LOVINGSTONE *see* LIVINGSTONE

LOVIJOY *see* LOVEJOY

LOWARD

Elizabeth of Swk St Saviour [DW/PA/7/11 f,471; DW/PA/5/1628/67]

LOWE

William of Newington [PRO; PCC Will 1594]

LOWELAND *see* LOVELAND

LOWLELEY

Margaret of Swk St Olave, widow [DW/PA/7/12 f,445; DW/PA/5/1639/82]

LOWER

Joan of Alfold [DW/PA/7/7 f,315; DW/PA/5/1600/29] <Abs 560>

LOWES *see* LEWIS

LOWESLY *see* LOSELEY

LOWETH *see* LOUTH

LOWICK

John of Wonersh, shearman [DW/PA/5/1587/62]

LOWKES *see* LUCAS

LOWMAN

Nicholas of Swk St Olave [DW/PA/7/5 f,70; 1539] <Abs 94>

LOWMASSE *see* LOMAS

LOWNES (LOUNDE,LOWNDE)

Gerrard of Surrey, citizen and merchant tailor [PRO; PCC Will 1572]

Katherine of Putney, widow [PRO; PCC Will 1591]

Thomas of Walton on Thames, yeoman [PRO; PCC Will 1626]

Thomas of Wandsworth, gent, [PRO; PCC 1639]

Thomasine of Wandsworth, widow [PRO; PCC 1643]

LOWSELEY *see* LOSELEY

LOWSON

John of Mitcham; All Hallows Bread Street, London [PRO; PCC 1642]

LOWSTED *see* LUSTED

LOWTH *see* LOUTH

LOYCK *see* LOCK

LOYE

Harry of Wandsworth [DW/PA/7/1 f,35; 1486] <Abs 120>

LUCAS (LOWKES,LUKAS)

Anthony of Kingston [PRO; PCC 1634]

Anthony of Swk St Saviour, servant to Mr Philpot, innholder [DW/PA/5/1568/75]

Edmund of Betchworth, yeoman [DW/PA/7/9 f,125; DW/PA/5/1615/80]

Henry of Mickleham; Leatherhead, yeoman [DW/PA/7/10 f,202; DW/PA/5/1620/79]

Joan of Epsom, widow [DW/PA/7/9 f,160; DW/PA/5/1616/85]

Joan of Godalming - Lydling, widow [DW/PA/7/13 f,463; DW/PA/5/1647/8]

John of Headley, yeoman [DW/PA/7/12 f,414; 1637]

John of Lambeth, carpenter [DW/PA/7/8 f,310; DW/PA/5/1613/79]

John of Mickleham [DW/PA/7/4 f,196; 1537]

John of Mickleham - West Humble [HRO; 1591 B49]

LUCAS (LOWKES,LUKAS) [*continued*]
Margery of Mickleham, widow [DW/PA/7/7 f.629; DW/PA/5/1608/71] <Abs 1176>
Marianne of Dorking, spinster [DW/PA/7/11 f.66; DW/PA/5/1623/71]
Mary of Swk; Bridewell, London [GL; Commissary Court of London Will 1593]
Ralph of Dorking [PRO; PCC Will 1588]
Ralph of Mickleham, husbandman, senior [DW/PA/7/7 f.238; DW/PA/5/1598/50] <Abs 419>
Richard of Betchworth [DW/PA/7/11 f.553; DW/PA/5/1629/61]
Richard of Horley, vicar [HRO; 1561 B122-123]
Thomas of Dorking [DW/PA/7/4 f.170; 1536]
Thomas of Dorking, carpenter [DW/PA/7/10 f.262; DW/PA/5/1622/55]
Thomas of Epsom, husbandman [DW/PA/7/7 f.607; DW/PA/5/1605/56] <Abs 1138>
Thomas of Headley, husbandman [DW/PA/5/1593/186]
Thomas of Malden, husbandman [DW/PA/5/1558/185]
William of Farnham [HRO; Reg. Orli 1 p.127; 1344]

LUCERE
Philpot, alias Philpot Calay of ... [French Church] [DW/PA/5/1576/103]

LUCKE
James of Swk St Saviour, butcher [DW/PA/7/8 f.27; DW/PA/5/1608/72]

LUCOCK (LEWCOKE,LUCOCKE)
Elizabeth of Capel, widow [DW/PA/7/9 f.253; DW/PA/5/1617/64]
Humphrey of Shere [DW/PA/7/4 f.30; 1533]
John of Swk St Margaret [DW/PA/7/5 f.138; 1540]

LUDGOLL (LUDGOLD,LUDGOLDE,LYDGOLD)
Catherine of Walton on Thames, widow [HRO; 1592 B34]
Margaret of Chertsey, widow [DW/PA/7/12 f.77; DW/PA/5/1632/61]
Thomas of Kingston, butcher [DW/PA/5/1580/1]

LUDLEY
Roger of Wandsworth, miller [DW/PA/7/9 f.105; DW/PA/5/1614/72]

LUDLOWE
Roger of Wandsworth, servant to Robert Miles, waterman [DW/PA/7/12 f.17; DW/PA/5/1631/60]

LUDMAN
Richard of Little Bookham [HRO; Reg. Fox 2 p.32; 1507]

LUDWELL
Thomas of Rotherhithe, citizen and merchant tailor [PRO; PCC Will 1592]
William of Carshalton, yeoman [DW/PA/7/4 f.95; 1534]

LUEN *see* LEWEN

LUFFE (LOFF,LOUFE)
Agnes of Frensham - Churt [DW/PA/5/1558/180]*
Edward of Chiddingfold [DW/PA/7/12 f.146; DW/PA/5/1633/78]
John of Frensham, junior [DW/PA/7/7 f.614; DW/PA/5/1607/63] <Abs 1148>
John of St Martha's - Chilworth; Albury, yeoman [DW/PA/7/8 f.76; DW/PA/5/1609/54]
John of Frensham, yeoman [DW/PA/7/11 f.243; DW/PA/5/1625/159]
Margaret of Frensham [DW/PA/7/11 f.144; DW/PA/5/1624/74]
Thomas of Frensham [DW/PA/5/1591/37]
Thomas of Frensham, husbandman [DW/PA/7/11 f.323; DW/PA/5/1625/160]
Thomas of Pyrford, yeoman [DW/PA/7/12 f.491; DW/PA/5/1638/78]
William of Frensham, yeoman [HRO; 1582 B61]

LUFFKYN
John of Swk St Olave [DW/PA/7/4 f.162; 1536]

LUKAS *see* LUCAS

LUKE
  Thomas, alias Thomas Awdley of Swk St Saviour; Rotherhithe - Rotherhithe Marsh, butcher [PRO; PCC Will 1610]
LULL
  Hobart of Swk, brushmaker [DW/PA/5/1563/12]
LUMBERT *see* LAMBERT
LUMLEY
  Richard of Shalford - Wintershall; Chobham, senior [DW/PA/7/10 f.58; 1618]
LUMSDEN
  James of Scotland (died in Farnham) [PRO; PCC Admon 1646]
LUNN (LUN,LUNE,LUNNE)
  Elizabeth of Farnham [? HRO; 1599 AD]
  Henry of Bentley, Hampshire, innholder [DW/PA/7/12 f.335; DW/PA/5/1636/63]
  John of Farnham, innholder [DW/PA/7/13 f.338; 1644]
  John of Swk St Thomas Hospital, carpenter [DW/PA/7/8 f.65; DW/PA/5/1609/55A]
  William of Farnham [? HRO; 1599 AD]
LUNSFORDE
  Ann of Buckland, spinster gentlewoman [PRO; PCC Will 1599] [*and*] [DW/PA/7/7 f.269; DW/PA/5/1599/43] <Abs 473>
LUNTLEY
  Rebecca of Swk St Olave, widow [DW/PA/7/13 f.362; 1644]
  Thomas of Swk St Olave [DW/PA/7/12 f.34; DW/PA/5/1631/65]
LUPI
  John of Addington [PRO; PCC Will 1604]
LUSHER (LUSHAR,LUSSHER)
  Dorothy of Haslemere, widow [PRO; PCC 1638]
  Elizabeth of Shalford, widow [DW/PA/5/1587/90]
  Jane of Puttenham - Shoelands, widow of Thomas [DW/PA/7/6 f.21; DW/PA/5/1559/20]
  Richard of Putney [PRO; PCC Admon 1616]
  Richard of Witley; Puttenham, gent. [PRO; PCC Will 1504] <Abs SAC v.31 p.124>
  Robert of Haslemere, gent. [HRO; 1637 B31]
  Thomas of Thursley, gent., junior [DW/PA/5/1587/20]
  (Lady) Thomasine of Putney, widow [PRO; PCC Admon 1642]
LUSTED (LOWSTEAD,LUSTEAD)
  Edward of Dorking, senior [DW/PA/7/11 f.472; DW/PA/5/1628/68]
  John of Dorking, bachelor [DW/PA/7/11 f.421; DW/PA/5/1626/83]
  John of Godstone [DW/PA/7/7 f.63; DW/PA/5/1596/39] <Abs 121>
  John of Tandridge, senior [DW/PA/7/2 f.45; 1495]
  Margery of Merstham, widow [PRO; PCC Will 1605] <Abs, SAC v.12 p.86>
  Robert of Godstone; Blechingley [DW/PA/7/9 f.20; DW/PA/5/1616/86]
LUTE
  John of Rotherhithe [PRO; PCC Will 1487]
LUTMAN
  Harry of Kingston [DW/PA/7/2 f.186; 1523] <Abs SAC v.1 p.187 *and* v.8 p.117>
  Thomas of Bermondsey [PRO; PCC Admon 1582]
LUTTER
  William of Guildford [PRO; PCC Admon 1603]

LUXFORD
  Robert of Wimbledon [LPL; 98/1 f.92v; Will 1638]
LYBSETT *see* LIBSETT
LYDDALL *see* LIDDLE
LYDGER *see* LEDGER
LYDGOLD *see* LIDGOLL
LYE *see* LEE
LYEL,LYELL *see* LISLE
LYFE *see* LIFE
LYFERD *see* LIFFORD
LYFF,LYFFE *see* LIFE
LYFFORD *see* LIFFORD
LYGEARD *see* LEDGER
LYGHTFOTE *see* LIGHTFOOT
LYKER [*This is a mistranscription in the calendar to* DW/PA/7/1 *for* HOKER - *see* HOOKER]
LYLE *see* LISLE
LYLLEYE,LYLLIE,LYLLYE *see* LILLEY
LYMCOTTES *see* LINCOTT
LYMDEN *see* LIMDEN
LYMPITT *see* LIMPETT
LYMYNGTON *see* LEAMINGTON
LYNACLE [*This is a mistranscription in the calendar to* DW/PA/7/1 *for* SYNACLE - *see* SINACLE]
LYNCH (LINCHE)
  George of Swk St Saviour, currier [DW/PA/7/9 f.88; DW/PA/5/1615/79]
  James of Swk St Thomas [DW/PA/5/1592/45]
LYNDE *see* LIND
LYNDLEY *see* LINLEY
LYNE,LYNES *see* LINES
LYNG *see* LING
LYNGARDE *see* LINGARD
LYNGE *see* LING
LYNGHAM *see* LINGHAM
LYNNYE *see* LINNEY
LYNTON *see* LINTON
LYNTOTT *see* LINTOTT
LYONS
  Henry of Swk St Olave, oatmealmaker [DW/PA/7/12 f.277; DW/PA/5/1635/61]
LYPSETT *see* LIBSETT
LYPSCOM,LYPSCOME *see* LIPSCOMBE
LYSLE *see* LISLE
LYSSNEY *see* LISTNEY
LYSTER *see* LISTER
LYSTNEY *see* LISTNEY
LYTHGOO *see* LITHGOO
LYVESEY *see* LIVESEY

MABANKE (MABANCKE,MABANK,MAIBANCKE,MAYBANCKE,MAYBANKE)
  Daniel of Send, senior [DW/PA/7/11 f.583; DW/PA/5/1630/68]
  Edith of Send, widow [*in* DW/PA/5/1557/75]
  Edmund of Ash, tiler [DW/PA/7/4 f.167; 1536]

MABANKE (MABANCKE,MABANK,MAIBANCKE,MAYBANCKE,MAYBANKE) [*continued*]
Edward of Effingham, brickmaker [DW/PA/7/8 f.104; DW/PA/5/1610/85]
Henry of Dunsfold, husbandman [DW/PA/7/12 f.12; DW/PA/5/1631/70]
James of Shere, weaver [DW/PA/5/1582/30]
Jeremy of Swk St Saviour [DW/PA/5/1582/59]
Joan of ...., widow [DW/PA/5/1543/12]*
Joan of Send, widow [DW/PA/7/12 f.100; DW/PA/5/1632/71]
Joan of Shere, widow [DW/PA/5/1582/47]
Joan of Woking, widow [*in* DW/PA/5/1555/1]
John of Egham, yeoman [HRO; 1576 B51]
John of Guildford St Nicolas - Artington, husbandman [DW/PA/5/1591/26]
John of Guildford St Nicolas - Artington [DW/PA/7/8 f.252; DW/PA/5/1613/80]
John of East Horsley, widower [PRO; PCC Admon 1649]
John of Send [DW/PA/5/1558/187]*
John of Shalford [DW/PA/7/12 f.152; DW/PA/5/1633/91]
John of Woking, bachelor [DW/PA/5/1576/120]
Margaret of Ripley, widow [DW/PA/5/1605/59] <Abs V155>
Nicholas of Shalford [DW/PA/7/8 f.34; DW/PA/5/1609/55B]
Ralph of Send [HRO; 1610 B50]
Reynold, alias Reynold Wheler of Send [DW/PA/7/2 f.170; 1522]
Richard of Send, yeoman [DW/PA/7/9 f.328; DW/PA/5/1619/79]
Thomas of Farnham, clothier [DW/PA/5/1580/8]
Thomas of Guildford St Nicolas - St Catherine's Hill [DW/PA/7/6 f.201; 1560]
Thomas of Pirbright [DW/PA/5/1557/91]
Walter of Hambledon, mason [HRO; 1561 B124-125]
William of Worplesdon [DW/PA/7/12 f.361; DW/PA/5/1636/68]

MABBETT
John of Bermondsey [DW/PA/7/11 f.201; DW/PA/5/1625/161]

MACE
Richard of Croydon, husbandman [LPL; 98/1 f.76v; Will 1636]
Richard of Swk St Saviour, collier [DW/PA/5/1587/6]

MACHELL
George of Lambeth [PRO; PCC Admon 1636]
John of Bermondsey, gent. [PRO; PCC Will 1575]
John of Putney, citizen and grocer [PRO; PCC Will 1570]
John of Wonersh, gent. [PRO; PCC 1647]

MACHIN (MACHON,MACHYN)
Anthony of Walton on Thames, yeoman [DW/PA/7/9 f.141; DW/PA/5/1615/91]
Anthony of Woking [DW/PA/7/12 f.242; DW/PA/5/1634/72]
Anthony of Woking, yeoman [DW/PA/7/12 f.301; DW/PA/5/1635/70]
John of Walton on Thames; Woking; Weybridge [PRO; PCC Will 1563]
Robert of Swk St Olave, fletcher [DW/PA/7/2 f.49; 1496]
Walter of Weybridge [DW/PA/7/2 f.160; 1521]
William of Walton on Thames, yeoman [DW/PA/7/10 f.274; DW/PA/5/1622/57]

MACHWYK *see* MATCHWICK

MACHYN *see* MACHIN

MACKERTH *see* MACKRETH

MACKLIN
John of Battersea, victualler [DW/PA/7/12 f.74; DW/PA/5/1632/68]

MACKRETH (MACKERTH,MAKERYTHE)
James of Kingston, yeoman [DW/PA/7/12 f.97; DW/PA/5/1633/88]
William of Camberwell; Lambeth, gent. [PRO; PCC Will 1600]

MACKWICKE *see* MATCHWICK

MACKWORTH

(Dame) Margaret widow of (Sir) Thomas of Lambeth, knight [PRO; PCC 1637]

MACOCKE *see* MAYCOCK

MACUR *see* MERCER

MACYE

Cuthbert of East Molesey [DW/PA/5/1593/101]

MADDIGALL (van MADDIGALL)

Hester of Bermondsey; Hartiegangbucke, Brabant [DW/PA/7/7 f.604; 1607] <Abs 1129>

MADDOCKS (MADDOCKE,MADDOCKES,MADDOX,MADDOXE,MADOX,MADOXE)

Alice of Swk St Olave [DW/PA/7/7 f.398; DW/PA/5/1627/74]

Alice of Swk St Thomas; Shalford, widow [DW/PA/7/8 f.334; DW/PA/5/1614/74]

John of Swk St George, baker [DW/PA/5/1592/31]

John of Swk St George, gardener [DW/PA/7/12 f.310; DW/PA/5/1635/72]

John of Swk St Thomas, porter of the Salters Company [DW/PA/7/8 f.395; DW/PA/5/1612/96]

William of Putney [PRO; PCC Will 1515]

MADDY (MADDYE)

Christopher of Rotherhithe [PRO; PCC Will 1608]

Christopher of Rotherhithe; St Michael's Island [DW/PA/7/7 f.615; DW/PA/5/1607/64] <Abs 1151>

MADELEY

Robert of Beddington - Wallington, yeoman [DW/PA/7/10 f.11; DW/PA/5/1619/80]

MADGWICK *see* MATCHWICK

MADON

Anthony of London [*Dutch Congregation*] [DW/PA/5/1561/79]

MADOX,MADOXE *see* MADDOCKS

MAECHT (de MAECHT)

Phillip of Mortlake [LPL; 98/1 f.102r; Will 1639]

MAGGOTT

Jane of Lambeth, wife of John, waterman [DW/PA/7/11 f.470; DW/PA/5/1628/69]

MAGICKE *see* MATCHWICK

MAGNUS

Henry of Rotherhithe, shipmaster [DW/PA/7/3 f.190; 1531]

MAHIEU

Daniel of Swk St Olave [DW/PA/7/11 f.257; DW/PA/5/1625/162]

MAIBANCKE *see* MABANKE

MAID (MAYD,MAYDE)

Thomas of Rotherhithe, mariner [PRO; PCC 1632]

Thomas of Rotherhithe, mariner [DW/PA/7/13 f.330; 1644]

MAIDEN (MAYDEN)

Anna of Bermondsey [PRO; PCC Admon 1647]

MAIDMAN (MAYDEMAN,MAYDMAN)

Benjamin of Windlesham, husbandman [HRO; 1630 B45]

John of Shalford; Dunsfold [DW/PA/7/5 f.119; 1539]

Richard of Bramley; Hascombe, wheelmaker [DW/PA/7/10 f.283 *and* DW/PA/7/11 f.34; DW/PA/5/1622/58]

Richard of Shalford; Dunsfold, husbandman [DW/PA/7/6 f.99; DW/PA/5/1559/77]

MAIGHTWICKE *see* MATCHWICK

MAILARDE
  Mary of Mortlake [PRO; PCC Will 1604]
MAIN *see* MAYNE
MAINFORD
  Margaret of Camberwell - Peckham, widow [PRO; PCC 1639]
MAISTER,MAISTERS *see* MASTERS
MAJOR
  Thomas of Guildford, yeoman [PRO; PCC Admon 1626]
MAKERYTHE *see* MACKRETH
MALAISE (del MALAISE)
  Jermain del, of Swk St Olave; London [DW/PA/7/11 f.412; DW/PA/5/1627/25]
MALAM (MALLAM,MALUM,MALYM)
  Christopher of Rotherhithe [PRO; PCC Admon 1645]
  John of Swk St Olave, capper [DW/PA/7/5 f.180; 1540]
  Martha of Rotherhithe [PRO; PCC Admon 1604]
  Richard of Rotherhithe [PRO; PCC Admon 1629]
  William of Rotherhithe [PRO; PCC Admon 1602]
MALBY
  Elizabeth of Streatham; Camberwell; Clapham; Battersea; Tooting, widow [DW/PA/7/4 f.93; 1534]
MALDEN
  Agnes of ... [DW/PA/7/12 f.327; 1636]
MALE (de MALE)
  Victor of Swk, dyer [HRO; Reg. Wyk 2 p.218; 1385]
MALIN
  Ferdinando of Cuddington - Nonsuch Park, gent. [PRO; PCC Will 1606] <Abs. SAC v.12 p.98>
MALLAM *see* MALAM
MALLETT
  John of Rotherhithe [PRO; PCC Will 1583]
MALLORY
  Anthony of Richmond, gent. [PRO; PCC 1641]
  William of Bermondsey - Little Barnsbye House, esq. [PRO; PCC Will 1611]
MALTBY (MALTBIE)
  Ann, alias Ann Pybus, alias Ann Crowther of Lambeth [PRO; PCC Admon 1647]
  John of Ockham, rector [HRO; Reg. Way 2 p.146; 1471]
MALTHUS (MALTHES,MAULTHOUSE)
  John of Egham, gent. [DW/PA/7/9 f.42; DW/PA/5/1614/77]
  Michael of Farnham [DW/PA/7/4 f.231; 1537]
MALUM,MALYM *see* MALAM
MAN *see* MANN
MANCHESTER (MANCHESTRE)
  John of Streatham [DW/PA/7/2 f.83; 1501]
MANDEFEILD,MANDEFELD *see* MANFIELD
MANDEKENS
  Balthasar of Swk St Olave [DW/PA/7/7 f.258; DW/PA/5/1599/44] <Abs 456>
MANDEVILL *see* MANFIELD
MANERYNG *see* MANNERING
MANETT
  James of Bermondsey [DW/PA/7/11 f.323; 1625]
MANFIELD (MANDEFEILD,MANDEFELD,MANDEVILL,MANFEILD,MAUNDEFELD,MAUNDFYLD, MAWNDEFYLD)
  Ann of Dunsfold; Godalming [DW/PA/7/4 f.57; 1533] <Abs SAC v.31 pp.76-77>
  Henry of Cranleigh, yeoman [DW/PA/7/13 f.157; DW/PA/5/1641/95]

MANFIELD (MANDEFEILD,MANDEFELD,MANDEVILL,MANFEILD,MAUNDEFELD,MAUNDFYLD, MAWNDEFYLD) [*continued*]
  Henry of Dunsfold, wheelwright, senior [DW/PA/7/7 f.297; DW/PA/5/1600/32] <Abs 533>
  Henry of Dunsfold; Shalford, yeoman, junior [DW/PA/7/7 f.298; DW/PA/5/1600/33] <Abs 534>
  Henry of Dunsfold; Shalford, yeoman [DW/PA/7/9 f.129; DW/PA/5/1615/92]
  James of Dunsfold [PRO; PCC Admon 1642]
  John of Dunsfold [DW/PA/7/1 f.1; 1484] <Abs 2>
  John of Dunsfold, husbandman [HRO; 1579 B26]
  Juliana of Godalming - Tuesley, widow [DW/PA/7/10 f.296; DW/PA/5/1622/59]
  Richard of Chiddingfold [DW/PA/7/13 f.313; DW/PA/5/1643/63]
  Richard of Dunsfold [DW/PA/7/3 f.201; 1532] <Abs SAC v.31 p.76>
  Richard of Dunsfold, husbandman [DW/PA/5/1563/36]
  Stephen of Swk St George [DW/PA/7/5 f.85; 1539]
  Stephen of Camberwell - Peckham, gent. [PRO; PCC Admon 1637]
    see also MANSFIELD
MANHAYREY
  William of Swk St George; Chester - Northgate Street, Cheshire, yeoman [DW/PA/7/10 f.45; 1618]
MANLEY
  (Sir) Richard of Lambeth - Kennington, knight [PRO; PCC Admon 1649]
  Thomas of Camberwell; Swk St George [PRO; PCC Will 1597]
MANN (MAN,MANNE)
  Ann of ...., widow [DW/PA/7/7 f.435; DW/PA/5/1603/107] <Abs 822>
  Anthony of Swk St Saviour, waterman [DW/PA/7/11 f.521; DW/PA/5/1629/62]
  Francis of Stoke Dabernon [DW/PA/7/12 f.72; DW/PA/5/1632/66]
  Henry of Sibsden, Leicestershire; Sheen [PRO; PCC Will 1566] <Abs SAC v.47 pp.27-28>
  Joan of Leatherhead, widow [DW/PA/5/1558/188]*
  John of Fetcham [DW/PA/7/4 f.91; 1534]
  John of Merrow; Send, husbandman [DW/PA/5/1593/3]
  Mary of Leatherhead, spinster [DW/PA/7/6 f.103; DW/PA/5/1559/113]
  Oliver of Kingston, gent. [PRO; PCC 1634]
  Thomas of Ashtead [DW/PA/7/5 f.139; 1540]
  Thomas of Croydon, son of Thomas citizen and haberdasher [GL; Archdeaconry Court of London Will 1638]
  Thomas of Ewell, wheelwright [DW/PA/5/1581/10]*
  Thomas of Kingston; Leatherhead, draper [PRO; PCC Will 1601] <Abs. SAC v.10 pp.302-303>
  Thomas of Send, husbandman [DW/PA/7/13 f.102; DW/PA/5/1640/105]
  Walter of Kingston, draper [PRO; PCC Will 1604] <Abs. SAC v.11 p.298>
  William of Bermondsey, citizen and sheather [GL; Archdeaconry Court of London Will 1412]
  William of Newdigate [DW/PA/7/1 f.96; 1489] <Abs 315>
  William of Titsey [DW/PA/7/12 f.99; DW/PA/5/1632/70]
MANNAM
  Richard of Farnham - Waverley [HRO; 1603 AD45]
MANNE *see* MANN
MANNERING (MANERYNG,MANWARING,MANWAYRING,MAYNWARINGE,MAYNWHYRING)
  (Sir) Arthur of Weybridge, knight [PRO; PCC 1649]
  George of Mitcham [DW/PA/7/5 f.45; 1538] <Abs 64>
  Robert of Windlesham, clerk [DW/PA/7/12 f.263; DW/PA/5/1635/77]
  Robert of Windlesham, clerk [PRO; PCC 1649]

MANNERING (MANERYNG,MANWARING,MANWAYRING,MAYNWARINGE,MAYNWHYRING)
[*continued*]
Thomas of Swk St Saviour [DW/PA/7/13 f.143; DW/PA/5/1641/88]
MANNING (MANNINGE,MANNYNG,MANYNGE)
Edward of Swk St Olave, tailor [DW/PA/7/11 f.191; DW/PA/5/1625/164]
Francis of Bermondsey [PRO; PCC Admon 1647]
Joan of Streatham - Tooting Bec, widow [DW/PA/7/13 f.367; 1644]
John of Chertsey [PRO; PCC Admon 1605]
John of Lambeth [PRO; PCC Will 1567]
Randall of Weybridge [PRO; PCC 1646]
Thomas of Limpsfield [DW/PA/5/1569/77]
MANNORY (MANNORYE,MANORY,MANORYE)
John of Farnham, tanner [DW/PA/7/13 f.350; 1644]
Richard of Puttenham [DW/PA/7/6 f.115; DW/PA/5/1559/123]
Robert of Worplesdon, yeoman [DW/PA/7/11 f.158; DW/PA/5/1624/75]
Stephen of Ash [DW/PA/5/1558/186]*
Thomas of Puttenham [DW/PA/5/1575/13]
Thomas of Puttenham, tailor [HRO; 1602 B28]
MANNSFEILD *see* MANSFIELD
MANNYNG *see* MANNING
MANSELL (MANSEWELL,MAUNCELL)
Edmund of Horley, husbandman [DW/PA/7/12 f.345; DW/PA/5/1636/67]
Geoffrey of Horsell, husbandman [DW/PA/7/12 f.376; DW/PA/5/1638/84]
Joan of Battersea [DW/PA/7/3 f.123; 1530]
Richard of Horley [DW/PA/5/1558/193]*
Thomas of Bermondsey [PRO; PCC 1649]
William of Frensham, yeoman [DW/PA/7/12 f.105; DW/PA/5/1632/73]
William of Horley, yeoman [DW/PA/7/11 f.59; DW/PA/5/1623/74]
MANSFIELD (MANNSFEILD,MANSFEILD)
Edward of Croydon [PRO; PCC Admon 1611]
Henry of Merton [DW/PA/7/9 f.243; DW/PA/5/1617/81]
Henry of Hascombe, husbandman [DW/PA/7/12 f.210; DW/PA/5/1633/96]
see also MANFIELD
MANTLE
John of Croydon, collier [LPL; 96/1686; Will 1644]
John of Merton, clerk [HRO; 1593 B48]
John of Swk St George, joiner [HRO; 1575 AD34]
MANWARING,MANWAYRING *see* MANNERING
MANYNGE *see* MANNING
MAPLESDEN
Edward of Rotherhithe, mariner [PRO; PCC 1633]
MARCE *see* MARCH
MARCELLIS
John, alias John Musselis, alias John Haunce of Rotherhithe [PRO; PCC Admon 1628]
MARCH (MARCE,MARCHE,MARRACHE)
Alice, alias Alice Jolliffe of Godalming - Tichbourne [PRO; PCC Admon 1648]
Edward of Compton [DW/PA/5/1555/11]
George of Cranleigh, yeoman [DW/PA/7/13 f.359; 1644; SRO; 212/35/43]
Joan of Dunsfold, widow [DW/PA/7/3 f.202; 1532] <Abs SAC v.31 p.75>
John of Capel, tailor [PRO; PCC Will 1616]
John of Dunsfold; Shalford; Godalming; Puttenham; Peper Harow; Compton [DW/PA/5/1552/29 *and* DW/PA/5/1552/30] <Abs SAC v.31 pp.80-81>

MARCH (MARCE,MARCHE,MARRACHE) [*continued*]

John of Dunsfold, husbandman [DW/PA/5/1558/189]*
John of Godalming, husbandman [DW/PA/7/13 f.108; DW/PA/5/1640/107]
John of Kingston [DW/PA/7/1 f.74; 1487] <Abs 243>
John of Kingston [DW/PA/7/2 f.7; 1491]
John of Shalford; Hascombe, husbandman [DW/PA/7/6 f.112; DW/PA/5/1559/80]
Nicholas of Chiddingfold, husbandman [DW/PA/7/13 f.86; DW/PA/5/1640/100]
Nicholas of Windlesham [*in* DW/PA/5/1544/6]
Richard of Dunsfold - Burningfold [PRO; PCC Admon 1583]
Richard of Dunsfold, husbandman [DW/PA/7/13 f.157; DW/PA/5/1641/94]
Robert of Hascombe [DW/PA/7/2 f.172; 1522]
Thomas of Cranleigh - Smithbrook; Hascombe; Chiddingfold, yeoman [DW/PA/7/8 f.77; DW/PA/5/1609/56]
Walter of Hascombe [DW/PA/7/6 f.104; DW/PA/5/1559/78]
William of Dunsfold [HRO; 1639 AD130]

MARCHALL,MARCHALLE *see* MARSHALL

MARCHANT (MARCHAUNTE,MERCHANT,MY'HART)

Joan, alias Joan Jenines of Frimley; Shinfield, Berkshire, widow [DW/PA/7/8 f.116; DW/PA/5/1610/86]
John of Crowhurst [PRO; PCC Admon 1599]
John of Horne, husbandman [DW/PA/7/9 f.296; 1618]
John of Swk St Olave [DW/PA/7/4 f.131; 1535]
Richard of Horne [PRO; PCC Admon 1648]
Richard of Woking [DW/PA/7/1 f.88; 1489] <Abs 296>
William of Horne, tailor [DW/PA/7/12 ff.461,505; DW/PA/5/1638/90]

MARCHE *see* MARCH

MARCHOLDE *see* MARSHALL

MARDEN (MERDEN,MERDON,MORDON,MOWDON)

Edward of Chiddingfold, carpenter [HRO; 1639 B50]
Ellen of Reigate, widow of Nicholas [DW/PA/7/5 f.41; 1538] <Abs 72>
John of Chiddingfold, carpenter, senior [DW/PA/7/9 f.143; DW/PA/5/1615/93]
John of Kingston, yeoman [DW/PA/7/13 f.58; DW/PA/5/1640/99]
John of Swk St Olave; Burstow [DW/PA/7/3 f.161; 1530]
Nicholas of Reigate, yeoman [DW/PA/7/7 f.383; DW/PA/5/1602/65] <Abs 710>
Nicholas of Wotton, husbandman [DW/PA/7/11 f.310; DW/PA/5/1626/84]
Richard of Kingston [DW/PA/7/1 f.33; 1486] <Abs 113>
Rowland of Reigate, husbandman [HRO; 1593 AD58]
Thomas of Blechingley, bachelor [PRO; PCC Admon 1648]
Thomas of Dunsfold, carpenter [*in* DW/PA/5/1557/75]
William of Farnham [DW/PA/7/4 f.67; 1534]
William of Reigate, yeoman [DW/PA/7/6 f.73; DW/PA/5/1559/105]

MARE (MAYRES,MEYRES)

Francis of Swk St Saviour [DW/PA/7/8 f.58; DW/PA/5/1609/58]
James of Rotherhithe; Alresford, Essex, mariner [DW/PA/7/10 f.192; DW/PA/5/1621/75]
John of Bermondsey [PRO; PCC Admon 1632]
John of Godstone, yeoman [DW/PA/7/11 f.106; DW/PA/5/1624/76]

MARGESSON

John of Ockley, blacksmith [DW/PA/7/10 f.342; DW/PA/5/1625/165]
Margaret of Ockley, widow [DW/PA/7/11 f.486; DW/PA/5/1628/70]

MARKBY (M'KBYE)

Thomas of Stoke Dabernon [DW/PA/7/5 f.28; 1538] <Abs 111>

MARKS
Joseph of Swk St Saviour, citizen and musician [DW/PA/7/12 f.399; DW/PA/5/1638/87]
MARKWICKE,MARKWIK *see* MATCHWICK
MARLER
Richard of Chertsey [DW/PA/7/4 f.229; 1537]
MARLIN (MARLEN,MARLINE,MARLYN,MARLYNE,MERLIN)
Amy of Worplesdon, widow [DW/PA/7/10 f.162; DW/PA/5/1621/78]
George of Puttenham, husbandman [HRO; 1573 AD20]
James of Godalming - Lydling, husbandman [DW/PA/5/1592/62]
James of Puttenham [DW/PA/7/4 f.211; 1537]
John of Godalming - Farncombe, wheelmaker, senior [DW/PA/7/12 f.465; DW/PA/5/1638/91]
Margaret of Chobham, widow of Richard [DW/PA/5/1565/11]
Margaret of Godalming - Lydling, widow [DW/PA/5/1576/7]
Richard *or* Margaret of Chobham [HRO; 1565 B58-59]
Thomas of Frensham, yeoman [DW/PA/5/1629/63]
Thomas, alias Thomas Cooper of Worplesdon - Burpham, yeoman [DW/PA/7/8 f.234; DW/PA/5/1612/97]
Thomas, alias Thomas Cooper of Worplesdon - Burpham, husbandman [DW/PA/7/12 f.284; DW/PA/5/1635/68]
MARLOWE
Miles of Egham, husbandman [DW/PA/5/1592/123]
MARMYON
Edward of Bermondsey, clerk [PRO; PCC Will 1541]
MARNER
Amy of Farnham, widow [PRO; PCC 1649]
Francis of Farnham, glover [DW/PA/7/10 f.292; DW/PA/5/1622/60]
John of Compton, labourer [DW/PA/7/7 f.600; DW/PA/5/1607/65] <Abs 1124>
John, alias John Roger of Farnham, glover [DW/PA/5/1580/7]
John of Farnham, yeoman [HRO; 1605 AD49]
John of Farnham [DW/PA/7/8 f.153; DW/PA/5/1611/74]
John of Thursley, senior [HRO; 1596 AD45]
John of Thursley, junior [HRO; 1596 AD46]
Margaret of Farnham [DW/PA/7/10 f.103; DW/PA/5/1621/76]
Margery of Farnham, widow [DW/PA/7/8 f.108; DW/PA/5/1610/87]
Richard of Farnham - Wrecclesham, husbandman [DW/PA/7/6 f.138; DW/PA/5/1559/120]
Thomas of Farnham - Wrecclesham, yeoman [HRO; 1636 B22]
MARRIOTT (MARRIAT,MARRETT,MARYOTTE)
Richard of Swk St Olave, citizen and clothworker [DW/PA/5/1568/1]
Roger of Fetcham [HRO; 1593 B49]
Thomas of Rotherhithe [PRO; PCC Admon 1603]
MARROWE
Peter of Chaldon [PRO; PCC Will 1595]
MARSH (MARSHE,MERSH,MERSHE)
Edmund of West Molesey [PRO; PCC Admon 1630]
Eleanor of Croydon, wife of Peter [PRO; PCC Admon 1576]
Francis of Beddington, gent. [PRO; PCC Will 1626; SRO; 2163/7/28]
George of Cobham, yeoman [DW/PA/7/8 f.324; DW/PA/5/1611/77]
George of Cobham [PRO; PCC 1649]
James of Cobham, husbandman [DW/PA/7/13 f.178; DW/PA/5/1641/97]
Joan of Egham [DW/PA/7/2 f.40; 1493]
Joan of Lambeth, widow [DW/PA/7/8 f.247; DW/PA/5/1613/81]

MARSH (MARSHE,MERSH,MERSHE) [*continued*]

John of Cobham, husbandman [DW/PA/7/9 f.310; DW/PA/5/1619/81]
John of Cobham, yeoman [DW/PA/7/13 f.222; DW/PA/5/1642/56]
John of Egham [PRO; PCC Will 1489]
Robert of Cobham, yeoman [DW/PA/7/7 f.217; DW/PA/5/1598/59] <Abs 385>
Robert of Cobham, yeoman [DW/PA/7/8 f.296; DW/PA/5/1613/82]
Robert of Nutfield [PRO; PCC Admon 1591]
Susan, alias Susan Gibson of Newington - Walworth [PRO; PCC Admon 1647]
Thomas of Kingston [DW/PA/7/11 f.580; DW/PA/5/1630/70]
Thomas of Walton on Thames, husbandman [DW/PA/7/12 f.91; DW/PA/5/1633/87]
William of Battersea, waterman [DW/PA/7/9 f.333; DW/PA/5/1620/80]
William of Chertsey [DW/PA/7/3 f.165; 1530]
William of Dorking, yeoman [DW/PA/5/1587/36]
William of Godalming, husbandman [DW/PA/7/12 f.355; DW/PA/5/1638/81]
William of Leigh [DW/PA/7/8 f.211; DW/PA/5/1612/106]
William of Merton, yeoman [DW/PA/7/13 f.438; DW/PA/5/1646/37]
William of Newington [PRO; PCC Admon 1632]
William of Rotherhithe [PRO; PCC Admon 1640]

MARSHALL (MARCHALL,MARCHALLE,MARCHOLDE)

Denise of Swk St Saviour, bodice maker [DW/PA/7/13 f.455;DW/PA/5/1647/9]
Edward of Thames Ditton - Marsh, husbandman [DW/PA/7/7 f.232; DW/PA/5/1598/51] <Abs 408>
Edward of Tandridge [DW/PA/5/1580/27]
Elizabeth of Putney, widow [PRO; PCC 1638]
Elizabeth of Swk St Saviour, widow [DW/PA/7/12 f.156; DW/PA/5/1633/94]
Elizabeth of Sutton, widow [DW/PA/7/13 f.241; DW/PA/5/1642/60]
(Sir) George of Putney, knight [PRO; PCC Admon 1637]
Hugh of Lambeth, waterman [DW/PA/7/12 f.371; DW/PA/5/1627/75]
Jane of Cheam, widow [PRO; PCC Will 1597]
John, alias John Allen of Blechingley, yeoman, senior [DW/PA/5/1581/8]
John of Carshalton [PRO; PCC Will 1508]
John of Compton; Wanborough, husbandman [DW/PA/7/13 f.359; 1644]
Lawrence of Ash [DW/PA/5/1563/35]
Roger of Cheam [PRO; PCC Will 1594]
Thomas of Malden; Cheam, yeoman [DW/PA/7/6 f.246; 1560]
Thomas of Seale - Tongham [DW/PA/5/1562/24]
Walter of Carshalton, yeoman [DW/PA/5/1578/55]
William of Chertsey [PRO; PCC Will 1415]
William of West Horsley, labourer [HRO; 1595 B36]
William of Lambeth, esq. [PRO; PCC Will 1579]
William of Seale, husbandman [DW/PA/5/1571/48]

MARSHAM

Elizabeth of Lambeth, widow [GL; Commissary Court of London Will 1520]
William of Lambeth, merchant haberdasher [GL; Commissary Court of London Will 1520]

MARSHAR *see* MARSHER

MARSHEPP

John of Bentley, Hampshire [DW/PA/7/5 f.52; 1538] <Abs 10>

MARSHER (MARSHAR)

Joan of Farnham, widow [DW/PA/5/1558/190]
Robert of Farnham - Wrecclesham [HRO; 1570 B280-281]

MARSON

Edward of Swk, merchant tailor [DW/PA/7/12 f.254; DW/PA/5/1635/64]
John of Guildford, saddler [DW/PA/7/12 f.528; DW/PA/5/1635/75]

MARSON [*continued*]
Robert of Guildford Holy Trinity; Guildford St Mary, saddler, senior [DW/PA/7/8 f.189; DW/PA/5/1610/88]
William of Guildford, saddler [DW/PA/7/13 f.439; DW/PA/5/1646/38]
MARSSE
William of Windlesham [DW/PA/7/3 f.103; c1529]
MARTEN *see* MARTIN
MARTER *see* MARTYR
MARTIN (MARTEN,MARTINE,MARTYN,MARTYNG,MARTYNN,MARTYNNE)
Agnes of Bermondsey [DW/PA/7/5 f.71; 1539] <Abs 91>
Alice of Blechingley, widow [DW/PA/7/8 f.396; 1613]
Ann of Egham, widow [DW/PA/7/13 f.280; DW/PA/5/1643/62]
Ann of Worplesdon, widow [HRO; 1609 B48]
Anthony of Richmond [PRO; PCC Will 1597]
Arnold of Guildford St Mary, glover [DW/PA/5/1591/82]
Denise of Cranleigh, widow [DW/PA/7/7 f.56; DW/PA/5/1596/41] <Abs 107>
Edmund of Newington [PRO; PCC Will 1596]
Edward of Bermondsey; Newington, weaver [GL; Archdeaconry Court of London Will 1646]
Eleanor of Farnham, widow [DW/PA/7/12 f.216; DW/PA/5/1633/97]
George of Chobham, husbandman [HRO; 1629 B35]
George of Swk St Olave, notary public [DW/PA/5/1593/183]
Henry of Blechingley, yeoman [DW/PA/7/7 f.507; DW/PA/5/1605/62] <Abs 950>
Henry of Farnham, glover [HRO; 1597 AD60]
Henry of Pirbright, yeoman [PRO; PCC Will 1618]
Henry of Worplesdon [HRO; 1597 B52]
Hester of Bermondsey, wife of Edward [DW/PA/7/12 f.364;DW/PA/5/1626/85]
James of Farnham - Wrecclesham, husbandman [DW/PA/5/1578/75]
James of Richmond [PRO; PCC Admon 1647]
James of Swk, smith [*Dutch*] [DW/PA/5/1558/191]*
John of Cranleigh, husbandman [DW/PA/5/1587/21]
John of Godalming [DW/PA/7/3 f.193; 1531]
John of Guildford, glover, senior [DW/PA/5/1586/28]*
John of Guildford, glover, senior [DW/PA/7/11 ff.20,37; DW/PA/5/1623/75]
John of Guildford St Mary, shearman [DW/PA/5/1580/71]
John of Merrow [DW/PA/7/11 f.504; DW/PA/5/1629/64]
John of Newington [PRO; PCC Will 1613]
John of Oxted [DW/PA/7/5 f.131; 1539]
John of Pirbright - Cowshot, husbandman [DW/PA/5/1592/63]
John of Pirbright - Cowshot [DW/PA/7/11 f.295; DW/PA/5/1626/86]
John of Rotherhithe [PRO; PCC Will 1595]
John of Shalford [DW/PA/7/6 f.99; DW/PA/5/1559/79]
John of Swk St Saviour [DW/PA/7/11 f.258; DW/PA/5/1625/167]
Katherine of Bermondsey [DW/PA/5/1586/19]
King [*King Martin, so shown in Abs 14 of* DW/PA/7/7 f.5, *is in fact Martin King*]
Lucy of Pirbright, widow [DW/PA/7/11 f.333; DW/PA/5/1625/168]
Margaret of Dorking [DW/PA/7/2 f.6; 1491]
Margery of Camberwell, widow [DW/PA/7/7 f.350; DW/PA/5/1601/61] <Abs 644>
Mary of Swk St Olave, widow of Godfrey [DW/PA/5/1587/72]
Nicholas of Shere, husbandman [DW/PA/5/1576/61]
Ralph of Battersea [DW/PA/7/5 f.86; 1539]
Richard of Guildford, clothier [DW/PA/7/13 f.457; DW/PA/5/1647/10]
Richard of Pirbright [DW/PA/7/11 f.504; DW/PA/5/1629/65]

MARTIN (MARTEN,MARTINE,MARTYN,MARTYNG,MARTYNN,MARTYNNE) [*continued*]
Richard of Swk St George [DW/PA/7/8 f.246; DW/PA/5/1613/83]
Richard of Wandsworth, cordwainer [DW/PA/7/13 f.135; DW/PA/5/1640/110]
Robert of Blechingley, husbandman [DW/PA/7/8 f.401; DW/PA/5/1612/98]
Robert of Worplesdon [PRO; PCC 1647]
Thomas of Blechingley [DW/PA/7/3 f.191; 1531]
Thomas of East Clandon, husbandman [DW/PA/7/8 f.336; DW/PA/5/1612/99]
Thomas of Compton [HRO; Ref. D3/141; 1572]
Thomas of Guildford St Mary [DW/PA/7/2 f.5; 1490]
Thomas of Lingfield, collier [DW/PA/7/8 f.47; DW/PA/5/1609/57]
Thomas of Pirbright, husbandman, senior [HRO; 1617 B42]
Thomas of Pirbright, husbandman [DW/PA/7/11 f.94; DW/PA/5/1624/77]
Thomas of Richmond [PRO; PCC Admon 1648]
Thomas of Shere - Gomshall, glover [DW/PA/7/13 f.4; DW/PA/5/1639/92]
Thomas of Woking, senior [DW/PA/7/13 f.216; DW/PA/5/1642/61]
Thomas of Worplesdon, tailor [DW/PA/7/7 f.214; DW/PA/5/1598/52] <Abs 382>
William of Bisley, yeoman [DW/PA/5/1562/39]
William of Bisley [PRO; PCC 1642]
William of Chobham [HRO; 1532 B13]
William of Thames Ditton [PRO; PCC Admon 1626]
William of Dorking, miller [PRO; PCC Will 1617]
William of Frensham, husbandman [DW/PA/5/1568/38]
William of Guildford St Nicolas [DW/PA/7/2 f.104; 1515]
William of Oxted [DW/PA/5/1576/60]
William of Swk St Saviour, falconer [DW/PA/7/7 f.409; DW/PA/5/1603/108] <Abs 756>
William of Swk, gent. [GL; Commissary Court of London Will 1455]

MARTINDALE (MARTINGDALE)
Peter of Newington [LPL; 98/1 f.83r; Will 1637]

MARTIR *see* MARTYR

MARTYMER *see* MORTIMER

MARTYN,MARTYNN,MARTYNNE *see* MARTIN

MARTYR (MARTER,MARTIR,MORTER)
Agnes of ..., spinster [DW/PA/7/9 f.205; DW/PA/5/1616/89]
Charles of Fetcham [DW/PA/7/8 f.406; DW/PA/5/1614/75]
Henry of Long Ditton, husbandman [DW/PA/5/1588/63]
John of Long Ditton - Tolworth, husbandman [DW/PA/7/8 f.239; DW/PA/5/1613/84]
John of Fetcham, yeoman [DW/PA/7/7 f.568; DW/PA/5/1606/55] <Abs 1062>
John of Fetcham - 'Hasiburne' [DW/PA/7/13 f.226; DW/PA/5/1642/57]
John of Guildford [PRO; PCC Will 1567]
John of Wonersh, yeoman [DW/PA/7/12 f.130; DW/PA/5/1632/75]
Katherine of Great Bookham [DW/PA/7/11 f.212; DW/PA/5/1625/166]
Lawrence of Effingham [DW/PA/7/13 f.433; DW/PA/5/1646/36]
Mary of Fetcham, spinster [DW/PA/7/8 f.260; DW/PA/5/1611/75]
Randolph of Croydon [LPL; 98/1 f.122r; Will 1641]
Thomas of Effingham, yeoman [DW/PA/5/1558/192]*
William of Fetcham, yeoman [DW/PA/7/13 f.10; DW/PA/5/1639/87]

MARYCHURCH
John of Rotherhithe [PRO; PCC Will 1618]

MARYOTTE *see* MARRIOTT

MASCALL
Elizabeth of Kingston - Ham, widow [PRO; PCC Will 1617]

MASHAM
Richard of Battersea, citizen and scrivenor [GL; Commissary Court of London Will 1522]

MASON (MASSON, MESONN, MESONNE)
Agnes of Oxted, widow [DW/PA/5/1580/3]
Alexander of Lambeth [PRO; PCC Will 1494]
Anthony of Battersea, yeoman [PRO; PCC Will 1609] <Abs. SAC v.23 p.146>
Edward of Swk St Saviour [DW/PA/7/10 f.51; 1618]
Elizabeth of Thames Ditton, widow [DW/PA/7/9 f.53; DW/PA/5/1614/76]
Garence of Epsom [DW/PA/5/1572/7]
Gysken of Swk St Olave, widow [DW/PA/7/5 f.138; 1540]
Joan of Dorking, weaver [DW/PA/7/13 f.153; DW/PA/5/1641/93]
Katherina of Swk St Olave [DW/PA/5/1544/10]
Peter of Swk St Olave, joiner, senior [DW/PA/7/2 f.113; 1517]
Richard of Lambeth - Stockwell, yeoman, junior [DW/PA/7/7 f.513; DW/PA/5/1605/61] <Abs 964>
Stephen of Lambeth [PRO; PCC 1636]
Thomas of Croydon, husbandman [LPL; 96/1721; 98/1 f.73v; Will 1636]
Thomas of Woking [PRO; PCC Admon 1626]
Wilsefer of Swk St Saviour [DW/PA/7/13 f.94; DW/PA/5/1640/102]

MASSAM
Mabel of Frimley [DW/PA/7/11 f.501; DW/PA/5/1629/66]

MASSEY (MASSY)
John of Wimbledon [PRO; PCC 1646]
Richard of Swk St Olave [DW/PA/7/8 f.295; DW/PA/5/1613/85]
Thomas of Swk St Margaret; West Bretton [DW/PA/7/5 f.18; 1538] <Abs 90>
William of Wimbledon [PRO; PCC 1633]

MASSINGHAM
Alice of Lambeth [PRO; PCC Will 1551]

MASSY *see* MASSEY

MASTERS (MAISTER, MAISTERS, MASTER)
Edmund of Cobham, gent. [DW/PA/7/12 f.73; DW/PA/5/1632/67]
Edward of Rotherhithe, sailor [DW/PA/5/1582/69]
Harry of Swk St Margaret, waterman [DW/PA/7/4 f.132; 1535]
John of Swk St Olave; Otham, Kent [DW/PA/5/1543/13]*
Patrick of Rotherhithe (died overseas) [PRO; PCC Admon 1641]
Peter of Swk St George, butcher [DW/PA/7/7 f.338; DW/PA/5/1601/62] <Abs 611>
William of Surrey [PRO; PCC Will 1505]
William of Limpsfield [DW/PA/5/1576/24]

MASTERTON
Matthew of Rotherhithe [PRO; PCC Admon 1648]

MATCHWICK (MACHWYK, MADGWICK, MAGICKE, MAIGHTWICKE, MARKWICKE, MARKWIK, MATCHWEEKE, MATCHWICKE, MERKWIK)
George of Elstead [DW/PA/7/11 f.203; DW/PA/5/1625/163]
John of Guildford St Nicolas [DW/PA/7/12 f.35; DW/PA/5/1631/73]
John of Witley [DW/PA/7/2 f.97; 1514]
John of Witley - Mousehill, husbandman [DW/PA/5/1570/60]
Ralph of Godalming - Tuesley, shearman [DW/PA/7/12 f.512; DW/PA/5/1638/98]
Richard of Godalming - Hurtmore, husbandman [DW/PA/7/13 f.250; DW/PA/5/1641/87]
Richard of Hambledon, husbandman [DW/PA/7/8 f.33; DW/PA/5/1609/62]
Robert of Farnham [DW/PA/7/1 f.88; 1489] <Abs 299>

MATCHWICK (MACHWYK,MADGWICK,MAGICKE,MAIGHTWICKE,MARKWICKE,MARKWIK, MATCHWEEKE,MATCHWICKE,MERKWIK) [*continued*]

Robert of Farnham [DW/PA/7/2 f.34; 1499]
Robert of Thursley [HRO; 1572 B66]
Stephen of Chiddingfold, weaver [DW/PA/7/7 f.82; 1596] <Abs 149>
Thomas of Witley - Burrow, yeoman [DW/PA/7/12 f.268; DW/PA/5/1635/66]

MATE

Joan of Dunsfold, widow [PRO; PCC 1638] [*and*] [DW/PA/7/12 f.391; DW/PA/5/1638/85]

MATHEW,MATHEWE,MATHEWES,MATHEWS; MATHEWSON *see* MATTHEWS; MATTHEWSON

MATHEY (MATHY,MATHYE)

Richard of Great Bookham, ploughwright [DW/PA/5/1582/97]
Thomas of Leigh, yeoman [DW/PA/7/13 f.444; DW/PA/5/1646/40]
William of Kingston - Hook [DW/PA/7/11 f.389; DW/PA/5/1626/87; SRO; 84/5/1]

MATKIN

Robert of Lambeth, husbandman [DW/PA/5/1588/22]

MATLOCKE

Richard of Swk St Olave, joiner [DW/PA/7/11 f.261; DW/PA/5/1625/172]

MATON

Peter of Swk St Olave [PRO; PCC Will 1517] <Abs SAC v.1 p.198>

MATTHEWS (MATHEW,MATHEWE,MATHEWES,MATHEWS,MATHOW,MATHUE,MATTHEW)

Alice of Blechingley, widow [DW/PA/7/7 f.448; DW/PA/5/1603/109] <Abs 850>
Anthony of Newdigate, husbandman [DW/PA/7/7 f.246; DW/PA/5/1599/45] <Abs 435>
Christopher of Streatham [HRO; 1594 AD43]
Edward of Woking, yeoman [HRO; 1573 B87]
Eleanor of Kingston, widow of Peter, shoemaker [DW/PA/5/1548/3]
George of Dorking, freemason [DW/PA/7/8 f.300; DW/PA/5/1613/86]
James of Carshalton [PRO; PCC Admon 1647]
James of Swk St George [DW/PA/7/11 f.231; DW/PA/5/1625/170]
Joan of Ewell, widow [DW/PA/5/1559/242]
John of Surrey [PRO; PCC Will 1498]
John of Ashtead [DW/PA/7/2 f.17; 1491]
John of Capel [DW/PA/7/2 f.79; 1517]
John of Capel [DW/PA/5/1578/95]
John of Carshalton; Chessington; Beddington, yeoman [DW/PA/7/7 f.571; DW/PA/5/1606/56] <Abs 1068>
John of Chessington, yeoman [DW/PA/7/7 f.431; DW/PA/5/1603/110] <Abs 815>
John of Kingston - Hook [DW/PA/5/1582/63]
John of Kingston [PRO; PCC 1649]
John of Leigh - Norwood, yeoman [DW/PA/7/13 f.230; DW/PA/5/1642/58]
John of Nutfield [DW/PA/7/5 f.163; 1540]
John of Reigate [DW/PA/7/12 f.254; DW/PA/5/1635/65]
Lawrence of Merton, husbandman [DW/PA/7/13 f.35; DW/PA/5/1639/89]
Margery of Albury, widow of Thomas, tailor [DW/PA/5/1587/63]
Mary of Chertsey, widow [DW/PA/7/8 f.289; DW/PA/5/1613/88]
Miles of Wandsworth [*Wrongly listed as Matthew Miles in the printed abstract of* DW/PA/7/7] [DW/PA/7/7 f.291; DW/PA/5/1600/31] <Abs 519>
Peter of ... [DW/PA/5/1546/67]
Ralph of Morden [DW/PA/7/11 f.350; DW/PA/5/1625/171]
Richard of Ashtead [DW/PA/7/4 f.173; 1536]
Richard of Beddington - Wallington, husbandman [DW/PA/7/7 f.551; DW/PA/5/1606/57] <Abs 1032>

MATTHEWS (MATHEW,MATHEWE,MATHEWES,MATHEWS,MATHOW,MATHUE,MATTHEW)
[*continued*]
Richard of Frensham, husbandman [HRO; 1618 B38]
Richard of Frensham [DW/PA/7/13 f.28; DW/PA/5/1639/88]
Richard of Hambledon, brickmaker [DW/PA/7/12 f.390; DW/PA/5/1637/73]
Richard of Horley [DW/PA/7/5 f.189; 1540]
Richard of Kingston [DW/PA/7/13 f.95; DW/PA/5/1641/92]
Richard of Lambeth [PRO; PCC Will 1593]
Richard of Leigh, husbandman [DW/PA/7/7 f.273; DW/PA/5/1599/46] <Abs 481>
Richard of Lingfield [HRO; Reg. Fox 3 p.65; 1515] [*and*] [DW/PA/7/2 f.102; 1515]
Roger of Thames Ditton - Chadsworth, collier [HRO; 1593 B51]
Stephen of ... [DW/PA/7/8 f.141; DW/PA/5/1611/76]
Thomas of Albury, tailor [DW/PA/5/1586/5]
Thomas, alias Thomas Hart of Albury, husbandman [DW/PA/7/10 f.283; DW/PA/5/1623/54]
Thomas of Carshalton, yeoman, senior [DW/PA/7/8 f.220; DW/PA/5/1612/100]
Thomas of Carshalton, yeoman [DW/PA/7/11 f.605; DW/PA/5/1630/71]
Thomas of Ewell; Epsom, husbandman [DW/PA/5/1557/72]
Thomas of Swk St Olave, waterman [DW/PA/7/9 f.5; DW/PA/5/1615/94]
Thomas of Wandsworth, yeoman [DW/PA/7/11 f.209; DW/PA/5/1625/169]
William of Albury, labourer [HRO; 1589 B38]
William of Ashtead, husbandman [DW/PA/7/10 f.186; DW/PA/5/1620/81]
William of Camberwell [PRO; PCC Admon 1630]
William of Thames Ditton [DW/PA/5/1562/1]
William of Egham, husbandman, senior [DW/PA/7/8 f.234; DW/PA/5/1612/101]
William of Frensham, yeoman [DW/PA/7/2 f.1; 1490]
William of Merstham, yeoman [LPL; 96/1727; Will 1614]
William of Morden [DW/PA/7/13 f.499; DW/PA/5/1649/10]
William of Reigate [DW/PA/7/8 f.309; DW/PA/5/1613/87]

MATTHEWSON (MATHEWSON)
Bartholomew of Lambeth [PRO; PCC Admon 1612]

MATTOCK (MATTOK)
Margaret, formerly Margaret Woderouff, of Dorking [PRO; PCC Will 1503]

MAUDSLEY (MAUDESLYE,MAWDESLIE)
John of Bramley, clerk [HRO; 1602 B29]
Thomas of Newington [LPL; 96/1732; Will 1619]
see also MOSELEY

MAUNDEFELD,MAUNDFYLD *see* MANFIELD

MAUNTE
Peter of Farnham - Runfold, weaver [HRO; 1563 B125]

MAVER
John of Cranleigh - Manning's Hill [DW/PA/7/4 f.126; 1535]

MAWBORNE
Nicholas of Dunsfold [DW/PA/5/1570/70]

MAWE
Ann of Bermondsey, widow [PRO; PCC Admon 1583]

MAWENT
William of Farnham - Badshot [*in* DW/PA/5/1544/9]

MAWER *see* MOWER

MAWHAREY *see* MANHAYREY

MAY (MAYE,MEY)
Eleanor of Abinger, widow [DW/PA/7/13 f.3; DW/PA/5/1639/86]
Elizabeth of Swk St Olave, widow [DW/PA/7/13 f.96; DW/PA/5/1640/103]

MAY (MAYE,MEY) [*continued*]
Henry of Abinger; Wotton; Ockley, yeoman [DW/PA/7/10 f.298; DW/PA/5/1622/61]
Jeremy of Egham [PRO; PCC 1647]
Joan of Farnham, widow [DW/PA/7/4 f.67; 1534]
John, alias John Reves of Bentley, Hampshire [DW/PA/7/11 f.415; DW/PA/5/1627/76]
John of Cranleigh; Ewhurst, yeoman [DW/PA/7/8 f.326; DW/PA/5/1613/89]
John, alias John Reaves of Farnham - Tilford, yeoman [DW/PA/5/1605/58] <Abs U154>
John of Merrow, husbandman [DW/PA/7/12 f.363; DW/PA/5/1638/82]
John of Swk St Saviour, minstrel [DW/PA/7/6 f.230; 1561]
Lawrence of Bermondsey [DW/PA/7/5 f.185; 1540]
Nicholas of Bramley, husbandman [DW/PA/7/13 f.148; DW/PA/5/1641/90]
Nicholas of Farnham [DW/PA/7/3 f.164; 1530]
Nicholas of Oxted, husbandman [DW/PA/7/12 f.246; DW/PA/5/1634/73]
Richard of London, citizen and skinner [DW/PA/5/1558/194]*
Richard of Bentley, Hampshire, husbandman [DW/PA/5/1558/196]
Richard of Rotherhithe, lighterman [DW/PA/7/13 f.149A; DW/PA/5/1641/91]
Robert of Swk St Olave, brewer's servant [DW/PA/7/12 f.273; DW/PA/5/1635/67]
Simon of Swk St Olave, joiner [DW/PA/7/11 f.147; DW/PA/5/1625/173]
Thomas of Rotherhithe, bachelor [PRO; PCC Admon 1639]
William of Dorking, baker [DW/PA/7/12 f.34; DW/PA/5/1631/72]
William of Swk St Saviour, citizen and vintner [DW/PA/5/1627/77]
William of Warlingham [DW/PA/7/2 f.47; 1496]

MAYCOCK (MACOCKE)
William of Swk St George, yeoman [DW/PA/7/10 f.285; DW/PA/5/1623/73]

MAYD,MAYDE *see* MAID

MAYDEN *see* MAIDEN

MAYDMAN *see* MAIDMAN

MAYE *see* MAY

MAYER (de MAYER)
Arnold of Swk St George, silk weaver [DW/PA/7/11 f.204; DW/PA/5/1625/63]
Frances of Bermondsey, wife of Robert [PRO; PCC Will 1619]
John, alias John Andrewes of Walton on Thames - Hersham; Hampton, Middlesex; Byfleet, labouringman [DW/PA/5/1604/38]
John of Swk St Thomas, weaver [DW/PA/5/1620/45] <Abs U243>

MAYHEW
Jane of Swk [DW/PA/5/1623/76]
William of Swk St Olave, yeoman [DW/PA/7/12 f.518; DW/PA/5/1639/85]

MAYLON (MAYLAN)
John of Ockley, wheelwright [HRO; 1629 B37]

MAYMAN
John of Swk St Saviour, girdler [DW/PA/7/9 f.175B; DW/PA/5/1616/90]

MAYN *see* MAYNE

MAYNARD (MAYNARDE)
Daniel of Godalming - Busbridge, yeoman [DW/PA/7/12 f.354; DW/PA/5/1638/80]
Henry of Tooting Graveney [PRO; PCC Admon 1649]
John of Swk St Thomas, draper [DW/PA/7/11 f.373; DW/PA/5/1626/88]
Thomas of Swk St Olave [DW/PA/5/1556/4]
Thomas of Tooting Graveney [PRO; PCC Admon 1649]

MAYNE (MAYN)
John of Farnham, clothier [HRO; Reg. Fox 2 p.32; 1508]
John of Beddington [PRO; PCC Will 1566]
Thomas of Swk St George, smith [DW/PA/7/6 f.203; 1560]
MAYNETTS
James of Bermondsey [DW/PA/7/11 f.201; DW/PA/5/1625/174]
MAYNWARINGE,MAYNWHYRING *see* MANNERING
MAYO
Henry of Wimbledon, husbandman [LPL; 96/1746; Will 1644]
MAYRES *see* MARE
MEACOCKE
Richard of Swk St Olave, citizen and woodmonger [DW/PA/7/13 f.370; 1644]
MEAD (MEDE,MEEDE)
Alice of Walton on Thames [PRO; PCC 1649]
Thomas of Worplesdon, tilemaker [HRO; 1568 B149-150]
MEADCALFE *see* MEDCALF
MEAKINGS (MEYKINS)
Ellen of Bermondsey, widow [DW/PA/7/11 f.399; DW/PA/5/1627/78]
MEAN
John of Guildford St Mary [DW/PA/7/2 f.197; 1524]
MEANTIS
Mary, alias Mary Dodd of Oxted, widow [PRO; PCC Admon 1648]
MEAR *see* ISAM
MEASON
John of Swk St Saviour, waterman [DW/PA/7/13 f.103; DW/PA/5/1640/106]
MEAWTYES
Henry of Farleigh [PRO; PCC Admon 1615]
MEDCALF (MEADCALFE,MEDCALFE,METCALF,METTCALF)
Anthony of Walton on Thames, yeoman, senior [DW/PA/7/7 f.488; DW/PA/5/1604/39A] <Abs 921>
Anthony of Walton on Thames - Burwood, husbandman [DW/PA/7/12 f.96; DW/PA/5/1632/69]
Christopher of Swk St Olave, citizen and currier [DW/PA/7/9 f.222; DW/PA/5/1617/82]
Helen, alias Helen Leese of Bermondsey [PRO; PCC Admon 1589]
John of Swk St Saviour, shipwright [DW/PA/5/1603/111] <Abs U80>
Peter of Rotherhithe [PRO; PCC Will 1592]
Robert of Kingston [DW/PA/7/1 f.57; 1487] <Abs 190>
Roger of Walton on Thames - Hersham, yeoman [DW/PA/7/12 f.66; DW/PA/5/1631/75]
MEDE *see* MEAD
MEDHURST (MEDEHERST)
Bennetta of Limpsfield, spinster [PRO; PCC Admon 1571]
Richard of Croydon [PRO; PCC 1632]
William of Crowhurst [DW/PA/7/4 f.88; 1534]
MEDIGALL *see* van MADDIGALL
MEDLEY Henry of Tilty, Essex; Croydon, esq. [PRO; PCC Will 1585] <Abs Emmison pp.107-109>
MEDLICOTT
Henry of Richmond, gent. [PRO; PCC 1648]
John of Bermondsey, gardener [DW/PA/7/13 f.361; 1644]
MEEDE *see* MEAD
MEEKE
Frances of Newington, spinster [LPL; 96/1752; Will 1625]

MEEKE [*continued*]
John of Lambeth [PRO; PCC Will 1519]
MEIR DE MEIER
William of Swk St Olave, merchant [DW/PA/5/1563/46]
MELBOURNE
(Sir) Thomas of Surrey, knight [PRO; PCC Will 1492]
MELERCHE,MELERSH *see* MELLERSH
MELISON
John of Bermondsey [DW/PA/5/1578/111]
MELLERSH (MELERCHE,MELERSH,MELLERCHE,MELLERSHE,MELLES,MELLEST,MELLIS, MELLISH,MELLISHE,MELLIST,MELLYSHE,MELRESH,MELYST,MILIS,MILLERSHE, MILLEST,MILLIS,MYLLERSH,MYLLEST,MYLLUST,MYLLYS)
Alice of Wonersh [PRO; PCC Will 1559]
Arnold of Hascombe [DW/PA/7/4 f.149; 1536]
Christopher of Bramley; Worplesdon, high constable, yeoman [HRO; 1582 B62]
Elizabeth of Sanderstead, gent. [PRO; PCC Will 1563]
Francis of Chobham [CCAL; 1485 f.34r]
George of Dunsfold - Graffham, yeoman [DW/PA/7/12 f.326; DW/PA/5/1637/70]
George of Godalming - Farncombe [DW/PA/7/7 f.112; 1597] <Abs 206>
George of Shalford [DW/PA/5/1562/31]
Harvey of Wonersh [PRO; PCC Will 1585]
Henry of Bramley, tailor [DW/PA/7/12 f.129; DW/PA/5/1632/74]
Henry of Godalming, clothier [PRO; PCC Will 1597]
Henry of Godalming, innholder [DW/PA/7/10 f.270; DW/PA/5/1622/62]
Henry of Horsell - Sidewood, yeoman [DW/PA/5/1576/133]
Henry of Sanderstead, merchant tailor [PRO; PCC Will 1564]
Jane of Dunsfold - Graffham; Shalford - Rushett, widow of Thomas, yeoman [DW/PA/7/8 f.369; DW/PA/5/1612/102]
John of Chertsey, yeoman [DW/PA/5/1582/85]
John of Chertsey, husbandman [DW/PA/5/1592/105]
John of Dunsfold - Graffham, yeoman [DW/PA/7/12 f.291; DW/PA/5/1635/69]
John of Godalming [DW/PA/7/2 f.209; ? c1490-1524]
John of Godalming; Wonersh; Cranleigh, yeoman [DW/PA/7/6 f.207; 1560]
John of Godalming - Farncombe [PRO; PCC Will 1567]
John of Godalming - Farncombe, yeoman [PRO; PCC Will 1623]
John of Horsell [DW/PA/7/2 f.205; 1525]
John of Horsell [DW/PA/5/1558/195]*
John of Horsell, yeoman, senior [HRO; 1610 B53]
John of Swk St Olave [DW/PA/5/1593/155]
John of Witley - Mousehill, husbandman [DW/PA/7/8 f.139; DW/PA/5/1610/89]
John of Woking [DW/PA/7/12 f.150; DW/PA/5/1633/90]
Joshua of Shalford [DW/PA/7/11 f.608; DW/PA/5/1630/72]
Katherine of Witley, widow [DW/PA/7/10 f.190; DW/PA/5/1621/77]
Lawrence of Wonersh, clothier [DW/PA/7/10 f.113; DW/PA/5/1619/82]
Matthias of Leatherhead, tanner [DW/PA/7/8 f.359; DW/PA/5/1612/103]
Oliver of Cranleigh; Hascombe, weaver [DW/PA/7/6 f.56; 1559]
Phillip of Shere [DW/PA/7/2 f.209; ? c1490-1524]
Richard of Chertsey, husbandman [HRO; 1602 B32]
Richard of Chiddingfold; Godalming; Brentford, Middlesex, yeoman, senior [DW/PA/7/10 f.18; DW/PA/5/1616/91]
Richard of Chiddingfold, yeoman [DW/PA/7/12 f.207; DW/PA/5/1634/69]
Richard of Dunsfold - High Loxley, yeoman [DW/PA/5/1579/65]*
Robert of Chertsey, yeoman [DW/PA/7/9 f.41; DW/PA/5/1614/91]

MELLERSH (MELERCHE,MELERSH,MELLERCHE,MELLERSHE,MELLES,MELLEST,MELLIS,
MELLISH,MELLISHE,MELLIST,MELLYSHE,MELRESH,MELYST,MILIS,MILLERSHE,
MILLEST,MILLIS,MYLLERSH,MYLLEST,MYLLUST,MYLLYS) [*continued*]
Robert of Chobham, husbandman [DW/PA/5/1576/91]
Robert of Guildford St Mary, shoemaker [DW/PA/5/1571/2]
Robert of Horsell [DW/PA/7/1 f.64; 1487] <Abs 215>
Robert of Horsell [DW/PA/7/4 f.109; 1535]
Robert of Sanderstead [PRO; PCC Will 1627]
Sarah, alias Sarah Lee of Effingham [PRO; PCC Admon 1635]
Solomon of Chertsey - Woodham, yeoman, junior [DW/PA/7/9 f.23;
DW/PA/5/1614/92]
Thomas of West Clandon [DW/PA/7/12 f.483; DW/PA/5/1638/93]
Thomas of Shalford; Bolney, Sussex; Woodmancote, Sussex, yeoman
[DW/PA/5/1582/56]
Thomas of Witley [DW/PA/7/8 f.379; DW/PA/5/1612/105]
Wilfred of Bramley [HRO; 1561 B142]
William of Hascombe [DW/PA/7/8 f.393; DW/PA/5/1612/104]
William of Horsell [DW/PA/7/3 f.168; 1531]
William of Horsell, yeoman [DW/PA/7/9 f.274; 1619]
William of Horsell, husbandman [DW/PA/7/12 f.495; DW/PA/5/1638/95]
William of Wonersh; Hascombe - Stovoldshill, yeoman [DW/PA/5/1570/71]
MELLSHAM *see* MELSHAM
MELLOWE
John of Swk St Saviour, chandler [DW/PA/5/1565/7]*
MELLSHAM (MELSHAM)
Edward of Stoke Dabernon [DW/PA/7/11 f.498; DW/PA/5/1629/67]
John of Cobham; Great Bookham, yeoman [DW/PA/7/10 f.144; 1621]
MELOTT
John of Cranleigh, rector [HRO; Reg. Way 2 p.151; 1472]
MELRESH *see* MELLERSH
MELSHAM *see* MELLSHAM
MELYST *see* MELLERSH
MENS
William of Swk [HRO; Reg. Fox 3 p.57; 1504]
MENTELL
John of Godstone [DW/PA/5/1561/64]
John of Horne [DW/PA/7/4 f.155; 1536]
MEPHAM
Thomas of Wandsworth [PRO; PCC Admon 1584]
MERCER (MACUR,MERSER)
Ann of Cranleigh [PRO; PCC Admon 1631]
John of Blechingley [DW/PA/7/6 f.7; 1559]
John of Cranleigh, yeoman, senior [DW/PA/5/1580/72]
Katherine of Bermondsey, widow [DW/PA/5/1592/103]
Richard of Cranleigh, yeoman [DW/PA/7/10 f.57; 1618]
Richard of Bermondsey, gent. [DW/PA/5/1592/109]
Thomas of Surrey [PRO; PCC Will 1644]
Thomas *or* Thomas Mower, of Cranleigh, yeoman [DW/PA/7/9 f.15;
DW/PA/5/1616/92] <Abs U209>
MERCHANT *see* MARCHANT
MERDEN,MERDON *see* MARDEN
MEREDITH
Evan of Ewell [PRO; PCC Will 1627]
Henry of Croydon [PRO; PCC 1640]

MERENSON
  Joys of Bermondsey [*Dutch*] [PRO; PCC Will 1593]
MEREST
  John of Guildford, citizen and haberdasher, senior [PRO; PCC Will 1570]
MERIELL *see* MERRELL
MERKWIK *see* MARKWICK
MERICKE *see* MERRICK
MERLANDE
  William of Banstead [PRO; PCC Will 1526]
MERLIN *see* MARLIN
MERRELL (MERIELL,MERYELL)
  Hamnett of Swk St Margaret, citizen and fishmonger [DW/PA/7/4 f.53; 1533]
  John of Chertsey, beer brewer [DW/PA/7/5 f.213; 1540]
  John of Swk St Thomas Hospital, clerk [DW/PA/5/1557/59]
MERRICK (MERICKE,MERRICKE)
  John of Rotherhithe (died overseas) [PRO; PCC Admon 1639]
  Margaret of Swk St Saviour, widow [DW/PA/7/9 f.216; DW/PA/5/1617/82]
MERRIDEN (MERYDEN)
  John, alias John More of Dorking [PRO; PCC Will 1489]
MERRY
  Simon of Bermondsey [PRO; PCC 1649]
MERRYFIELD (MERRYFELD)
  Edward of Swk St George, yeoman [DW/PA/7/7 f.272; DW/PA/5/1599/47] <Abs 479>
MERSHE *see* MARSH
MERSTON
  William of Kingston [HRO; Reg. Way 1 p.63; 1460]
MERYDEN *see* MERRIDEN
MERYELL *see* MERRELL
MESONN *see* MASON
MESSINGHAM (MISSINGHAM)
  Richard of Frensham [HRO; 1632 B33]
  William of Frensham - Churt, yeoman [DW/PA/7/10 f.201; DW/PA/5/1621/79]
METCALF,METTCALFE *see* MEDCALFE
METTFORD
  John of Pyrford, etc., esq. [PRO; PCC Will 1490]
METTS
  Elizabeth of Lambeth, widow [DW/PA/7/12 f.396; DW/PA/5/1638/86]
MEULEMEESTER *see* DE MEULEMEESTER
MEULEN *see* van der MEULEN
MEY *see* MAY
MEYKINS *see* MEAKINS
MEYER (de MEYER)
  John of Swk St Thomas, weaver [DW/PA/7/11 f.223; DW/PA/5/1620/45]
MEYRS *see* MARE
MEYSEY
  John of Lambeth, gent. [PRO; PCC Will 1593]
MICHAELIS,MICHAELL *see* MITCHELL
MICHEL *see* MITCHELL
MICHELBORNE *see* MITCHELBORNE
MICHELL *see* MITCHELL
MICHINALL *see* MITCHENALL
MICHENER *see* MITCHENER

MICHILD
Thomas of Shalford, carpenter [DW/PA/5/1625/175]
MIDDLEBOROW *see* MIDDLESBOROUGH
MIDDLEBROOKE
Susan of Worplesdon; Cowley, Middlesex, widow [PRO; PCC 1634]
MIDDLESBOROUGH (MIDDLEBOROW,MIDDLEBURGH,MYDDELBOROWE)
John of Thames Ditton, carpenter [HRO; 1629 B39]
Thomas of Long Ditton - Tolworth, husbandman [DW/PA/7/6 f,29; *in* DW/PA/5/1559/30]
MIDDLETON (MIDDELTON,MIDDILTON,MYDDELTON,MYDELTON)
Agnes (formerly Agnes White) of Mortlake [PRO; PCC Will 1509]
Alice of Putney, widow [PRO; PCC Will 1589]
Edward of Newington, gent, [PRO; PCC 1649]
John of Beddington [DW/PA/5/1570/61]
John of West Clandon, clerk [PRO; PCC Will 1417]
Mary of Swk St Saviour, widow [DW/PA/7/10 f,266; DW/PA/5/1622/63]
Ralph of Newington [PRO; PCC Will 1582 *and* 1583]
Richard of Egham [PRO; PCC Will 1415]
Richard of Windlesham [DW/PA/7/6 f,256; 1560]
MIGHILL
Thomas of Wonersh; Dunsfold; Shere; Cranleigh, husbandman [DW/PA/7/9 f,173; DW/PA/5/1616/93]
MILAM (MYLAM)
Clement of Kingston [PRO; PCC Will 1497] <Abs SAC v,8 pp,111-112>
MILBURY (MILBERIE)
Joan of Camberwell, widow [PRO; PCC Will 1627]
William of Camberwell, gent, [PRO; PCC Will 1622]
MILCHE
William of Croydon [PRO; PCC Will 1491]
MILDENHALL (MILDENHALE)
John of Clapham [PRO; PCC Will 1505]
Robert of Kingston [PRO; PCC Will 1476]
MILES (MYLE,MYLES,MYLIS)
Alexander of Lingfield, victualler [DW/PA/7/13 f,181; DW/PA/5/1641/98]
Alice of Blechingley, widow [DW/PA/7/12 f,310; DW/PA/5/1635/73]
Edward of Chiddingfold [DW/PA/7/11 f,506; DW/PA/5/1629/68]
Edward of Mortlake [LPL; 96/1767; Will 1618]
Edward of Mortlake, gent, [PRO; PCC Will 1618]
Elizabeth of Lambeth [PRO; PCC Will 1557]
Francis of Hambledon, husbandman [DW/PA/5/1617/80] <Abs U225>
George of Guildford St Mary, currier [DW/PA/7/7 f,306; DW/PA/5/1600/34] <Abs 549>
Henry of Nutfield, yeoman [DW/PA/7/7 f,235; DW/PA/5/1598/58] <Abs 413>
John of Blechingley, clerk [PRO; PCC Will 1601]
John of Coulsdon [DW/PA/7/3 f,163; 1530]
John of Farnham [*in* DW/PA/5/1544/9]
John of Godalming, tailor, junior [DW/PA/7/13 f,125; DW/PA/5/1640/111]
John of Lambeth [PRO; PCC Will 1555]
John, alias John Monke of Lingfield [DW/PA/7/6 f,117; DW/PA/5/1559/106]
John of Nutfield [DW/PA/7/5 f,63; 1539] <Abs 67>
John of Nutfield, labourer [DW/PA/5/1576/14]
John of Tooting [PRO; PCC Will 1469]
Nicholas of Horne [DW/PA/7/6 f,119; DW/PA/5/1559/116]

MILES (MYLE,MYLES,MYLIS) [*continued*]

Ralph of Reigate, yeoman [DW/PA/7/11 f.479; DW/PA/5/1628/71]

Richard of Chipstead, husbandman [DW/PA/5/1590/1]*

Richard of Chipstead, husbandman [DW/PA/7/7 f.73; DW/PA/5/1596/40] <Abs 137>

Richard of Croydon, mercer [PRO; PCC Will 1606] <Abs, SAC v.12 p.97>

Richard of Nutfield [DW/PA/7/3 f.133; 1530]

Richard of Nutfield [PRO; PCC Will 1587]

Richard of Reigate [DW/PA/7/11 f.347; DW/PA/5/1625/176]

Richard of Swk St Olave, victualler [DW/PA/7/10 f.56; 1618]

Robert of Guildford, shoemaker [HRO; 1632 D3/200]

Robert of Haslemere, yeoman [HRO; 1633 B42]

Thomas of Chiddingfold, woollen draper [DW/PA/5/1569/44]

Thomas of Coulsdon, yeoman [DW/PA/5/1557/60A]

Thomas of Coulsdon [PRO; PCC Will 1558]

Thomas of Nutfield [DW/PA/5/1576/50]

William of Blechingley, mercer [DW/PA/7/11 f.352; DW/PA/5/1625/177]

see also MILLS

MILIS *see* MELLERSH

MILL,MILLE *see* MILLS

MILLENS *see* MILLNES

MILLER (MYLLER)

Alice of Battersea, widow [DW/PA/5/1624/78]

Edward of Dorking [PRO; PCC Admon 1612]

Edward of Putney [LPL; 98/1 f.98v; Will 1638 [*and*] [PRO; PCC Admon 1639]

George of Rotherhithe (died overseas) [PRO; PCC Admon 1649]

Isabell of Godstone, widow [DW/PA/7/8 f.348; DW/PA/5/1612/108]

Jane of Bermondsey, widow [DW/PA/7/12 f.185; DW/PA/5/1633/95]

John of Battersea [DW/PA/7/12 f.367; DW/PA/5/1627/79]

John of Bermondsey, citizen and leatherseller [PRO; PCC Will 1621 *and* 1623]

John of Farnham, yeoman [DW/PA/7/7 f.552; DW/PA/5/1606/58] <Abs 1035>

John of Farnham [*in* DW/PA/5/1544/5]

John of Swk St George, wiredrawer [DW/PA/5/1569/22]

John of Swk St George, yeoman [DW/PA/7/7 f.410; DW/PA/5/1603/112] <Abs 758>

John of Swk St George, victualler [DW/PA/7/13 f.390; DW/PA/5/1645/34]

Margaret, alias Margaret Crooke of ...., widow [DW/PA/7/12 f.379; 1637]

Nicholas, alias Nicholas Richardson of Croydon, collier [PRO; PCC Will 1607] <Abs, SAC v.12 pp.209-210>

Richard of Richmond [PRO; PCC Will 1557]

Robert of Godstone [DW/PA/7/12 f.100; DW/PA/5/1632/72]

MILLERSHE,MILLEST *see* MELLERSH

MILLETT (MILLET,MYLLETT)

Caleb of Lambeth, bachelor, gent. [PRO; PCC Will 1627]

Henry of Staple Inn, Holborn, Middlesex; Chertsey [DW/PA/7/11 f.594; DW/PA/5/1630/73]

John of Stoke [PRO; PCC Admon 1635]

MILLING (MYLLING,MYLLYNS)

Thomas of Wimbledon, clerk [PRO; PCC Will 1540]

MILLINGTON

Jane of Newington, spinster [LPL; 96/1780; 98/1 f.70v; Will 1635]

John of Wandsworth [PRO; PCC Admon 1640]

Margaret of Wandsworth [PRO; PCC 1648]

MILLINGTON [*continued*]
Stephen of Wandsworth [PRO; PCC Admon 1647]
Thomas of Shalford, widow of Jane [PRO; PCC 1647]
MILLION (MYLYON)
John of Swk St Olave, woodmonger [DW/PA/7/3 f.196; 1532]
see also MILLMAN
MILLISON (MILLISONN)
Robert of Swk St Olave, citizen and cooper [DW/PA/7/13 f.232; DW/PA/5/1642/59]
MILLMAN (MYLMAN)
Petronell of Swk St Olave, widow [DW/PA/7/5 f.219; 1541]
see also MILLION
MILLS (MILL,MILLE,MILLES,MYLLS,MYLYS)
Arnold of Guildford St Nicolas [DW/PA/7/4 f.19; 1532]
Beatrice of Guildford St Nicolas, widow [DW/PA/7/4 f.90; 1534]
Edmund of Grays Inn, Middlesex; Petworth, Sussex; Swk [LPL; Reg. Abp Kempe f.306; Will 1452]
Edward of Frensham, yeoman [HRO; 1634 B27]
Henry of Cobham, glazier [DW/PA/7/12 f.484; DW/PA/5/1638/94]
Henry of Croydon; Carshalton; Beddington, alderman [PRO; PCC Will 1574]
James of Swk St Saviour, woolcomber [DW/PA/7/9 f.54; DW/PA/5/1614/93]
John of Surrey, esq. [PRO; PCC Will 1551]
John of Ewell [DW/PA/7/9 f.26; DW/PA/5/1614/94]
John of Guildford, clothier, senior [PRO; PCC Will 1609] <Abs. SAC v.23 pp.139-140>
John of Guildford, clothier, senior [DW/PA/7/11 f.119; DW/PA/5/1624/79]
John of Horsley [PRO; PCC Will 1503]
John of Horley [DW/PA/7/6 f.27; 1560]
John of Merstham [PRO; PCC 1639]
John of Send; Buriton, Hampshire [DW/PA/7/5 f.176; 1540]
John of Shere, husbandman [HRO; 1641 AD74]
John of Worplesdon, yeoman [DW/PA/7/7 ff.166,182; DW/PA/5/1597/70] <Abs 307>
Michael of Oxted, yeoman, junior [DW/PA/7/7 f.6;DW/PA/5/1595/63] <Abs 17>
Nicholas of Nutfield [DW/PA/7/5 f.142; 1540]
Richard of Cranleigh, yeoman [PRO; PCC 1630] <Scroope 1228>
Richard of Malden, gent. [DW/PA/5/1558/197]*
Robert of Horley, husbandman [DW/PA/7/8 f.181; DW/PA/5/1610/90]
Roger of Frensham [DW/PA/7/13 f.494; DW/PA/5/1649/11]
Sarah of Caterham, widow [DW/PA/7/13 f.415; DW/PA/5/1646/47]
Sybil of Farnham - Tilford, widow [DW/PA/7/9 f.104; DW/PA/5/1615/95]
Thomas of Chiddingfold [DW/PA/7/9 f.284; 1618]
Thomas *or* Thomas Myles of Coulsdon [PRO; PCC Will 1558]
Thomas of Frensham, yeoman [DW/PA/7/12 f.218; DW/PA/5/1633/98]
Thomas of Limpsfield [DW/PA/7/7 f.160; DW/PA/5/1597/71] <Abs 295>
Thomas of Mitcham, butcher [DW/PA/5/1576/40]
Thomas of Newington, sergeant at arms, esq. [PRO; PCC Will 1592]
Thomasine of Guildford St Mary; Guildford Holy Trinity; Guildford St Nicolas; Stoke next Guildford, widow [DW/PA/7/8 f.287; DW/PA/5/1613/90]
William of Charlwood, yeoman, senior [LPL; 96/1782; Will 1614]
William of Chertsey, gent. [PRO; PCC Admon 1641]
William of Croydon, gent. [PRO; PCC Will 1567]
William of Farnham - Runfold, yeoman [DW/PA/7/13 f.321; DW/PA/5/1644/14]

MILLS (MILL,MILLE,MILLES,MYLLS,MYLYS) [*continued*]
William of Farnham - Tilford, yeoman [DW/PA/7/7 f,325; DW/PA/5/1601/65] <Abs 583>
William of Frensham, yeoman [HRO; 1645 B12]
William of Guildford St Nicolas [DW/PA/7/4 f,34; 1533]
William of Nutfield, husbandman [DW/PA/7/9 f,131; DW/PA/5/1615/96]
William of Swk St Saviour, spurrier [DW/PA/5/1557/10]
William of Swk St Saviour - Paris Garden, waterman [DW/PA/5/1592/90]
MILLWARD (MILLWORTHE,MILWARD,MYLLWARDE,MYLWARDE,MYLWART)
Agnes of Woking, widow [DW/PA/7/5 f,7; 1538] <Abs 123>
Elizabeth of Swk St Saviour, widow [DW/PA/7/7 f,67; c1595] <Abs 128>
John of Swk St Saviour, yeoman [DW/PA/5/1563/98]
John of Woking [DW/PA/7/4 f,151; 1536]
John of Woking, husbandman [DW/PA/5/1591/28]
Richard of Pirbright [DW/PA/7/5 f,143; 1540]
Robert of Pirbright [DW/PA/7/4 f,65; 1534]
Sense, late Sense Hawkyns, of Rotherhithe [PRO; PCC Will 1549]
MILNES (MILLENS)
Roger of Ashtead, parson [HRO; 1542 B60; Reg, F p,79]
MILTON (MYLTON,MYLTONNE)
Agnes of Swk St Saviour, widow [DW/PA/7/10 f,245; DW/PA/5/1622/64]
Edward of Frimley [DW/PA/5/1555/19]
Joan of Windlesham, widow [DW/PA/5/1562/75]
John of ... [*in* DW/PA/5/1557/120]
John of Swk St Saviour, waterman [DW/PA/7/10 f,218; DW/PA/5/1621/74]
John of Windlesham [DW/PA/5/1574/45]
Richard of Chertsey, yeoman [DW/PA/7/7 f,98; DW/PA/5/1596/42] <Abs 180>
Richard of Chobham, yeoman [PRO; PCC Will 1615]
Robert of Chobham; Shere [DW/PA/7/6 f,78; DW/PA/5/1559/96]
Robert of Rotherhithe, bricklayer [DW/PA/7/12 f,258; DW/PA/5/1635/76]
Thomas of Windlesham [DW/PA/7/6 f,257; 1560]
William of Windlesham [HRO; 1594 B37]
MILWARD *see* MILLWARD
MINCHIN (MYNCHYN)
Mary of Putney [PRO; PCC Admon 1630]
William of Seale; Crondall, Hampshire [PRO; PCC 1631]
MINNE *see* MYNNE
MINORS (MYNORS)
George of Malden [DW/PA/7/13 f,397; DW/PA/5/1645/35]
Richard of Swk St Olave [BM; Add,Ms 24,925 f,13v; 1544] <Abs 26>
MINS
Richard of Swk St Thomas, citizen and girdler [DW/PA/5/1574/35]
MINSHAWE
Agnes of Swk St Olave [DW/PA/7/7 f,416; DW/PA/5/1603/113] <Abs 779>
Robert of Swk St Saviour, feltmaker [DW/PA/5/1582/48]
MINSTERLEY (MYNSTERLEY)
Andrew of Lambeth; Fulham - Padderswick, Middlesex [DW/PA/7/8 f,60; DW/PA/5/1609/60]
MINTERNE
William of Thorpe, esq. [PRO; PCC Will 1627]
MINTES
Henry of Swk St George [DW/PA/5/1582/60]

MINTON (MYNTON)
  Richard of Swk St Mary Overy, citizen and mercer [DW/PA/7/5 f,48; 1538]
    <Abs 93>
MISBOROWE
  John of Thames Ditton [? HRO; 1529]
MISBROOKE
  Elizabeth of Newdigate [DW/PA/5/1588/91]
MISKEN
  Samson of Swk St George [DW/PA/5/1606/59] <Abs U187>
MISSINGHAM *see* MESSINGHAM
MITCHELBORNE (MICHELBORNE)
  Richard of Surrey, gent, [PRO; PCC Will 1583]
MITCHELL (MICHAELIS,MICHAELL,MICHELL,MYCHAELL,MYCHELL,MYTCHELL)
  Agnes of ... [DW/PA/7/10 f,85; DW/PA/5/1615/84]
  Alice of Frensham - Shottermill, widow [HRO; 1602 B31]
  Anthony of Swk St Olave [DW/PA/7/2 f,65; 1500]
  Edward of Cranleigh [PRO; PCC 1647]
  Elias of Epsom - Horton [DW/PA/7/11 f,543; DW/PA/5/1629/69]
  Elizabeth of Epsom, widow [HRO; 1591 B55]
  Ellen of Lambeth, spinster [PRO; PCC 1647]
  Henry of Dorking, oatmealman [DW/PA/7/8 f,323; DW/PA/5/1611/78]
  Henry of Guildford, tailor, senior [DW/PA/5/1561/39]
  Isabel of Hascombe, widow [DW/PA/5/1587/68]
  Joan of Surrey; St Sepulchre, London, widow of Richard [GL; Commissary
    Court of London Will 1593]
  Joan of Chertsey, widow [HRO; 1561 B139-140]
  John of Surrey [PRO; PCC Will 1522]
  John of Chertsey [DW/PA/7/6 f,178; DW/PA/5/1559/219]
  John of Cranleigh, husbandman [HRO; 1638 B51]
  John of Epsom, limeburnmonger [DW/PA/7/10 f,95; DW/PA/5/1619/83]
  John of Lambeth [PRO; PCC Admon 1590]
  John of Lingfield [PRO; PCC Admon 1613]
  John of Mitcham [DW/PA/7/11 f,90; DW/PA/5/1624/80]
  John of Wandsworth [DW/PA/7/2 f,74; 1501]
  Margaret of Molesey [PRO; PCC Will 1455]
  Michael of West Molesey, labourer [DW/PA/7/10 f,44; 1618]
  Ninian of Lingfield, gent, [PRO; PCC Will 1558]
  Richard of Thames Ditton, faggotbinder [DW/PA/7/9 f,145;DW/PA/5/1615/83]
  Richard of Frensham - Churt [PRO; PCC Will 1601] <Abs, SAC v,10 p,146>
  Robert of Swk St Saviour, yeoman [DW/PA/7/7 f,374; DW/PA/5/1602/64]
    <Abs 691>
  Rowland of Swk St Thomas [DW/PA/5/1579/63]*
  Thomas of Surrey, gent, [PRO; PCC Will 1551]
  Thomas of Worplesdon [DW/PA/7/1 f,8; c1484] <Abs 27>
  William, alias William Burley of Bermondsey [DW/PA/7/3 f,97; 1529]
  William of Charlwood [LPL; 96/1787; Will 1616]
  William of Dunsfold, carpenter [DW/PA/7/13 f,449; DW/PA/5/1646/41]
  William of Guildford St Mary [DW/PA/7/1 f,86; 1489] <Abs 291>
  William of Kingston - Ham, yeoman [DW/PA/7/3 f,181; 1531]
  William of Kingston - Surbiton [DW/PA/5/1593/196]
  William of Kingston - 'Warnes' [HRO; 1567 B98]

MITCHENALL (MICHANELL,MICHENER,MICHENOR,MICHINALL,MICHENALL,MICHYNALE,
MICHYNALL,MITCHINALL,MITCHINER,MYCHENAL,MYCHYNALL)
Henry of Worplesdon - Wyke, fustian man [DW/PA/5/1591/80]
James of Farnham [DW/PA/7/4 f.105; 1535]
Joan of Farnham, widow [DW/PA/7/12 f.525; DW/PA/5/1635/74]
John of Ash [DW/PA/7/12 f.19; DW/PA/5/1631/71]
John of Bentley, Hampshire [DW/PA/7/5 f.146; 1540]
John of Elstead [DW/PA/7/4 f.149; 1536]
Richard of Bentley, Hampshire [DW/PA/7/5 f.146; 1540]
Richard of Seale [HRO; 1594 B45]
Robert of Elstead, yeoman [DW/PA/7/8 f.82; DW/PA/5/1609/59]
Robert of Elstead, husbandman [DW/PA/7/9 f.35; DW/PA/5/1614/90]
Robert of Wanborough - North Wanborough [DW/PA/5/1565/3]*
Stephen of Bentley, Hampshire, husbandman [DW/PA/7/8 f.345;
DW/PA/5/1612/107]
Thomas of Elstead [DW/PA/7/6 f.269; 1560]
Thomas of Seale - Tongham, yeoman [DW/PA/5/1624/81]
William of Seale, yeoman [DW/PA/7/11 f.385; DW/PA/5/1626/89]
see also MICHILD
MITTON
John *or* John Motton, of Croydon, yeoman [PRO; PCC Will 1626]
M'KBYE *see* MARKBY
MOARE *see* MOORE
MOASE *see* MOSE
MOATE (MOTE)
Henry of Swk St Saviour - Bankside, waterman [DW/PA/7/8 f.127;
DW/PA/5/1610/91]
Nicholas of Send [DW/PA/7/1 f.21; 1485] <Abs 68>
Robert of Lambeth, gent. [DW/PA/5/1576/115]
MOBERT (MOBERTE)
Christian of Swk St Thomas, widow [DW/PA/5/1581/2]
Guyllam of Swk St Thomas, currier [DW/PA/5/1576/3]
MOCKETT (MOCHETT)
John of Kingston; Walton on Thames [PRO; PCC Will 1579]
Margaret of Swk St Olave, widow [DW/PA/5/1622/65]
Robert of Swk St Olave, wheelwright [DW/PA/7/8 f.404; DW/PA/5/1614/95]
MOCKYNG (MOKKYNG)
John of Swk St Olave [HRO; Reg. Wyk 2 p.177; 1378] <Abs SAC v.1
pp.191-192>
Nicholas of Swk St Olave; master of St Lawrence Pountney, London college
[PRO; PCC Will 1424] <Abs SAC v.1 p.194>
Robert of Swk St Mary Magdalen; Swk St Olave, citizen and vintner
[PRO; PCC Will 1432] <Abs SAC v.1 pp.194-195>
Thomas of Swk, son of Thomas citizen and baker
[PRO; PCC Will 1428] <Abs SAC v.1 p.194>
MODYMAN
William of Egham [DW/PA/5/1561/59]
MOERSKYN
Henry of Swk St Olave, cooper [DW/PA/5/1558/200]*
MOGGE
Edward of Windlesham - Bagshot [DW/PA/7/9 f.331; DW/PA/5/1620/83]
MOIS
Henry of Reigate, gent. [PRO; PCC 1649]
MOLINES,MOLING,MOLLINS *see* MULLINS

MOLYNEUX (MULLENEX,MULLINEUX,MULLINEX)
Alice of Windlesham [*admon in* DW/PA/5/1558/222]*
Alice of Windlesham, widow [DW/PA/7/6 f,30; DW/PA/5/1559/32]
Edmund of Nutfield [PRO; PCC Will 1605] <Abs, SAC v,12 p,93 *and* v,31 p,92>
John, alias John Bruer of Windlesham - Bagshot [PRO; PCC Will 1548]
MOMFEILDE
John of Bermondsey, collier [DW/PA/7/8 f,62; DW/PA/5/1609/63]
MONCKE *see* MONK
MONDAY (MUNDAY)
Augustine of Swk St Saviour [DW/PA/7/8 f,293; DW/PA/5/1613/91]
Giles of Byfleet [PRO; PCC Admon 1583]
Joan of Kingston - Surbiton, widow [HRO; 1608 B52A]
Joan of Kingston - Surbiton, widow [DW/PA/7/7 f,626; DW/PA/5/1608/74] <Abs 1171>
Richard of Rotherhithe, bachelor [PRO; PCC Admon 1614]
William of Guildford St Mary [PRO; PCC 1648]
William of Kingston, carpenter [DW/PA/7/8 f,410; DW/PA/5/1614/96]
MONDEN *see* MARDEN
MONE,MONES *see* MOONE
MONEY (MONEIE,MONNEY)
Edward of Swk St Saviour, victualler [DW/PA/7/9 f,26; DW/PA/5/1614/97]
John of Bermondsey [DW/PA/5/1576/13]
Robert of Bermondsey [PRO; PCC Admon 1617]
William of Ewell [DW/PA/7/3 f,132; 1530]
MONGER (MONGAR,MONGGER,MONYAR,MOUNGER,MUNGER)
Alice of Ash [*in* DW/PA/5/1558/166]*
Benjamin of Wandsworth [PRO; PCC Will 1622]
Clement of Ash, potmaker [BM; Add,Ms 24,925 f,4r; 1544] <Abs 5>
George of Ash, woodbroker [PRO; PCC Will 1614]
Joan of Ash [DW/PA/7/7 f,232; DW/PA/5/1598/57] <Abs 409>
John of Ash [DW/PA/5/1552/21]
John of Ash [DW/PA/5/1555/12]
John of Ash, potter [DW/PA/7/7 f,496; DW/PA/5/1605/63] <Abs 931>
John of Guildford, mercer [DW/PA/5/1558/198]*
John of Guildford St Nicolas - Littleton; Godalming - Farncombe, yeoman [DW/PA/7/8 f,102; DW/PA/5/1610/92]
John of Horne; Blechingley, labourer [HRO; 1571 B124]
Nicholas of Wonersh, clothier [DW/PA/7/11 f,430; DW/PA/5/1627/82]
Robert of Ash, yeoman [DW/PA/7/12 f,317; DW/PA/5/1637/72]
Stephen of Ash [DW/PA/7/6 f,248; 1560]
William of Newdigate [DW/PA/7/5 f,82; 1539]
MONK (MONCKE,MONKE,MOUNCKE,MOUNKE,MUNCKE)
Ann of Bermondsey, spinster [DW/PA/7/11 f,107; DW/PA/5/1624/82]
John of ..., senior [DW/PA/7/9 f,35; DW/PA/5/1614/78]
John of Great Bookham [DW/PA/7/12 f,150; DW/PA/5/1633/89]
John of Camberwell - Peckham; Camberwell - Dulwich [DW/PA/7/6 f,289; 1560]
John, alias John Myles of Lingfield [DW/PA/7/6 f,117; DW/PA/5/1559/106]
Nicholas of Tatsfield [PRO; PCC Admon 1639]
Robert of Great Bookham [DW/PA/7/13 f,421; DW/PA/5/1645/33]
Thomas of Tatsfield [PRO; PCC 1638]
MONKLER (MUNCKLER)
William of Croydon - Combe, yeoman [PRO; PCC Will 1613]

MONNES *see* MOONE
MONNEY *see* MONEY
MONTAGUE (MONTAGEWE,MOUNTAGUE)
  Anthony, Viscount Mountague, of Lambeth - Stockwell [PRO; PCC Will 1592]
  Henry of Woking [DW/PA/7/13 f,378; 1644]
  John of Wandsworth [DW/PA/7/10 f,248; DW/PA/5/1622/66]
  Mary of Wandsworth, widow [DW/PA/7/11 f,131; DW/PA/5/1624/83]
  Thomas of Leatherhead [DW/PA/7/2 f,16; 1491]
  William of Woking, wheelmaker [DW/PA/7/13 f,148; DW/PA/5/1641/89]
MONTER *see* MOUNTER
MONYER *see* MONGER
MONYONS
  Alice of Swk St Saviour, widow [DW/PA/5/1592/86]
MOODY
  Thomas of Croydon, husbandman [LPL; 96/1793; 98/1 f,123r; Will 1641]
MOOELL
  Thomas of Swk St Saviour, shipwright [DW/PA/5/1550/38]
MOONE (MONE,MONES,MONNES,MOWNE)
  Edward of Farnham - Tilford [DW/PA/7/13 f,89; DW/PA/5/1640/101]
  Edward of Farnham [PRO; PCC Admon 1649]
  Eleanor of Farnham - Tilford, widow [DW/PA/7/11 f,51; DW/PA/5/1623/77]
  Eustace of Farnham ? [DW/PA/5/1587/65]
  Eustace of Farnham, gent, [DW/PA/5/1587/22]
  John of Swk St Thomas, schoolmaster [DW/PA/7/7 f,427; DW/PA/5/1603/114] <Abs 801>
  Margaret of Horne, widow [DW/PA/7/11 ff,33,77; DW/PA/5/1623/78]
  Michael of Blechingley [DW/PA/7/10 f,169; DW/PA/5/1621/80]
  Peter of Swk St Olave, joiner [DW/PA/5/1569/79]
  Richard of Great Bookham [DW/PA/7/6 f,198; 1560]
  Robert of Ash [DW/PA/5/1576/124]
  Tobias of Kingston [DW/PA/7/7 f,346; DW/PA/5/1601/63] <Abs 633>
  William *or* William Moore, of Farnham - Tilford, yeoman [HRO; 1604 B45]
  William of Seale, husbandman [DW/PA/7/13 f,346; 1644]
  William of Swk St Olave [DW/PA/5/1576/90]
MOORCOCK (MORCOCKE,MORECOCKE)
  Thomas of ... [DW/PA/5/1592/48]
  Thomas of Lingfield [PRO; PCC Will 1492]
MOORE (MOARE,MORE)
  Agnes of Lambeth, widow [DW/PA/7/7 f,350; DW/PA/5/1601/64] <Abs 646>
  Alice of Wandsworth, widow [DW/PA/7/12 f,322; DW/PA/5/1637/69]
  Ann of Battersea, widow [DW/PA/7/9 f,16; DW/PA/5/1616/94]
  Ann of Tooting - Little Tooting, widow [PRO; PCC Admon 1624]
  (Sir) Christopher of Guildford St Nicolas - Loseley, knight [PRO; PCC Will 1550]
  Edmund of Kingston [PRO; PCC Will 1536]
  Edmund of Esher; Thames Ditton, yeoman [DW/PA/7/9 f,197;DW/PA/5/1616/95]
  Edward of Croydon, blacksmith, senior [LPL; 96/1798; Will 1617]
  Edward of Dunsfold, husbandman [DW/PA/7/13 f,118; DW/PA/5/1640/98]
  Ellen of Rotherhithe, widow [DW/PA/7/13 f,217; DW/PA/5/1642/55]
  Frances of Guildford St Mary, late wife of Robert [DW/PA/7/12 f,361; DW/PA/5/1636/69]
  Frances, alias Frances Yonge of Farnham - Dippenhall, spinster [DW/PA/7/9 f,210; DW/PA/5/1616/96]

MOORE (MOARE,MORE) [*continued*]
(Sir) George of Guildford St Nicolas - Loseley Place, knight [PRO; PCC Admon 1633]
George of Lambeth, cordwainer [DW/PA/7/10 f,219; DW/PA/5/1621/82]
Henry of Esher [DW/PA/7/1 f,81; 1488] <Abs 270>
Hugh of Swk St Saviour, fishmonger [DW/PA/7/9 f,250; DW/PA/5/1617/84]
Isabella, alias Isabella Yong of Frensham [DW/PA/5/1576/34]
James of Lambeth - Water Lambeth, waterman [DW/PA/5/1588/60]
Joan of the City of Westminster, Middlesex [DW/PA/5/1606/60] <Abs U188>
John of Charlwood [PRO; PCC Will 1559]
John of Chiddingfold, yeoman [DW/PA/5/1587/64]
John of Cranleigh, yeoman [DW/PA/5/1578/66]
John of Croydon - Waddon [LPL; 96/1799; 98/1 f,129r; Will 1642]
John, alias John Meryden of Dorking [PRO; PCC Will 1489]
John of Esher [DW/PA/7/2 f,16; 1490]
John of Esher, yeoman, senior [HRO; 1532 B14]
John of Lambeth, esq. [PRO; PCC Will 1473]
John of Newington [PRO; PCC Admon 1625]
John of Newington [LPL; 98/1 f,84r; Will 1637]
John of Rotherhithe, mariner [PRO; PCC 1638]
John of Swk St Saviour, waterman [DW/PA/7/10 f,41; DW/PA/5/1617/84]
John of Chertsey - Simplemarsh [PRO; PCC Will 1597]
Mary of Esher, widow [DW/PA/7/13 f,402; DW/PA/5/1645/36]
Mary of Wandsworth, widow [DW/PA/7/12 f,154; DW/PA/5/1633/93]
Matthew of Newington [PRO; PCC Admon 1648]
Maud of Chertsey, widow [DW/PA/5/1576/101]
Nicholas of Swk St Olave, wax chandler [DW/PA/5/1576/18]
(Sir) Poynings of Guildford St Nicolas - Loseley, baronet [PRO; PCC Admon 1649]
Richard of Egham [DW/PA/7/11 f,149; DW/PA/5/1625/178]
Richard of Rotherhithe, seaman [DW/PA/7/13 f,122; DW/PA/5/1640/108]
Robert of Abinger, yeoman [DW/PA/7/12 f,363; DW/PA/5/1638/88]
Robert of Cranleigh, yeoman [DW/PA/5/1570/72]
Robert of Esher, yeoman [DW/PA/7/13 f,471; DW/PA/5/1648/23]
(Sir) Robert of Guildford St Nicolas - Loseley, knight [DW/PA/7/11 f,368; DW/PA/5/1626/90]
(Sir) Robert of Guildford St Nicolas - Loseley, knight [PRO; PCC 1647]
(Sir) Robert of Guildford St Nicolas - Loseley, knight [PRO; PCC Admon 1649]
Robert of Streatham, yeoman [DW/PA/7/12 f,412; 1637]
Rose, alias Rose Young of Farnham, widow [DW/PA/7/7 f,185; DW/PA/5/1598/93] <Abs 335>
Simon of Bermondsey [PRO; PCC Admon 1636]
Thomas of Chertsey, shoemaker [DW/PA/5/1576/96]
Thomas of Lambeth, waterman [DW/PA/7/7 f,202; DW/PA/5/1598/53] <Abs 361>
Thomas of Swk St Saviour, shipwright [DW/PA/7/8 f,10; DW/PA/5/1608/75]
William of Esher, husbandman [DW/PA/5/1556/10]
William of Esher [DW/PA/7/13 f,414; DW/PA/5/1645/38]
(Sir) William of Guildford St Nicolas - Loseley, knight [PRO; PCC Will 1600]
William of Leatherhead; Malden, gent. [PRO; PCC Will 1620] <Soame 824>
William of Morden, gent. [PRO; PCC Will 1615]
see also at MOORE
MOOREALL *see* MORRELL

MOORER (MORAR,MORER)
Francis of Buckland, husbandman [DW/PA/7/8 f,129; DW/PA/5/1610/93]
Francis of Buckland, husbandman, senior [HRO; 1610 B55]
George of Chobham [DW/PA/5/1571/63]
John of Dorking [PRO; PCC Will 1583]
John of Kingston [PRO; PCC Will 1560]
John of Kingston [PRO; PCC Admon 1569]
John of Reigate, shearman [DW/PA/5/1578/63]
John of Reigate, shoemaker [DW/PA/7/10 f,183; DW/PA/5/1620/84]
Katherine, alias Katherine Grove of Kingston [PRO; PCC Admon 1570]
Nicholas of Pyrford, husbandman [DW/PA/5/1550/93]
Richard of Ash, labourer [DW/PA/7/6 f,169; *in* DW/PA/5/1559/174]
Thomas of Abinger, husbandman [HRO; 1588 B53]
William of Kingston - Ham; Hampton Wick, Middlesex; Chessington, mercer [DW/PA/5/1550/70]
William of Send [DW/PA/7/6 f,171; *in* DW/PA/5/1559/174]
MOOREY
John of Swk St Saviour, yeoman [DW/PA/7/11 f,271; DW/PA/5/1625/179]
MOORTON *see* MORTON
MOOSE,MOOSSE *see* MOSE
MOOTHAM
John of Rotherhithe [PRO; PCC 1631]
MORANT *see* MORDAUNT
MORAR *see* MOORER
MORAUNT *see* MORDAUNT
MORCOCKE *see* MOORCOCK
MORDAUNT (MORAUNT,MORDANT,MORDIN,MORRANTT)
Edward, alias Edward Morten of Ewell, tailor [DW/PA/5/1593/152]
Joan of Lingfield, widow [DW/PA/7/2 f,38; 1494]
John of Crowhurst, bachelor [PRO; PCC Admon 1635]
William of Lingfield [PRO; PCC Will 1491]
William of Merton, senior [DW/PA/7/5 f,208; 1541]
MORDEN *see* MARDEN
MORDIN *see* MORDAUNT
MORE *see* ATMORE; MOORE
MORECOCKE *see* MOORCOCK
MORER *see* MOORER
MORES *see* MORRIS
MORESTED *see* MORSTED
MORETON *see* MORTON
MORGAN
Edmund of Lambeth - Lambeth Marsh [PRO; PCC 1649]
(Dame) Elizabeth of St Martha's - Chilworth, widow of (Sir) John, knight [PRO; PCC 1633]
Geoffrey of Chertsey, clerk [PRO; PCC Will 1508]
Hugh of Battersea, citizen and grocer, apothecary extraordinary to the king [PRO; PCC Will 1613]
Hugh of Bermondsey [PRO; PCC Will 1619]
(Sir) John of St Martha's - Chilworth, knight [PRO; PCC Will 1621]
John of Kingston [DW/PA/7/11 f,187; DW/PA/5/1625/180]
Juliana of Farnham, widow [DW/PA/7/10 f,169; DW/PA/5/1621/83]
Robert of Swk St Saviour; Llangybie, Caernarvonshire, waterman [DW/PA/7/7 f,230; DW/PA/5/1598/54] <Abs 405>
Shadrach of Bermondsey, whitster [DW/PA/7/10 f,237; DW/PA/5/1623/79]

MORGAN [*continued*]
William of St Martha's - Chilworth, esq. [PRO; PCC Admon 1603]
William of Swk St Saviour, waterman [DW/PA/7/10 f.251; DW/PA/5/1621/84]

MORINGE
John of Witley - Mousehill, husbandman [DW/PA/7/7 f.186; DW/PA/5/1598/56] <Abs 339>

MORIS,MORISE *see* MORRIS

MORLAND (MORLOND)
John of Godalming [DW/PA/7/10 f.285; DW/PA/5/1623/80]
William of Sutton, clerk [PRO; PCC Will 1492] <Abs. SAC v.52 p.45>

MORLEY (MORLAY,MORLY)
Alexander of Egham - Englefield Green [PRO; PCC Will 1594]
Elizabeth of Guildford [PRO; PCC Admon 1648]
Henry of Thursley, husbandman, junior [DW/PA/7/13 f.38; DW/PA/5/1639/90]
Henry of Thursley, yeoman [DW/PA/7/13 f.287; 1644]
John of Guildford; Ewhurst [PRO; PCC Will 1592]
Peter of Lambeth, saddler [PRO; PCC Will 1620] <Soame 227>
Ralph of Thursley, husbandman [DW/PA/5/1582/49]
Thomas of Swk St Margaret [DW/PA/7/4 f.2; 1532]

MORLOND *see* MORLAND

MORMAY
Noriah of Lambeth [PRO; PCC Admon 1648]

MORPHEW (MORPHEWE)
John of Merstham [LPL; 98/1 f.116v; Will 1640]
Thomas of Godstone, yeoman [DW/PA/7/13 f.42; DW/PA/5/1639/93]

MORRANTT *see* MORANT

MORRELL (MOOREALL)
Jane of Swk St Olave, widow [DW/PA/7/10 f.197; DW/PA/5/1621/81]
Thomas of ... [DW/PA/7/7 f.633; DW/PA/5/1608/76] <Abs 1186>
Thomas of Merton, tailor [DW/PA/5/1563/8]
Thomas of Merton, tailor [HRO; 1565 B67]

MORREY
Robert of Swk St Margaret, currier [DW/PA/7/2 f.68; 1500]

MORRIS (MORES,MORIS,MORISE,MORREYS,MORRICE,MORYS)
Christopher of Newington, citizen and founder [PRO; PCC 1645]
Edward of ... [DW/PA/7/11 f.59; DW/PA/5/1623/81]
Elizabeth of Battersea, widow [PRO; PCC 1632]
Ellis of Battersea, yeoman [DW/PA/7/8 f.233; DW/PA/5/1612/109]
Frances, alias Frances Windever of Newington [PRO; PCC Admon 1620]
Grave of Newington [PRO; PCC Admon 1633]
Henry of Wandsworth, labourer [DW/PA/7/13 f.178; DW/PA/5/1641/96]
Howell of Tooting [PRO; PCC Admon 1604]
Hugh of Swk St Mary Overy - Paris Garden, waterman [DW/PA/7/7 f.506; DW/PA/5/1605/64] <Abs 947>
John of Epsom, yeoman [DW/PA/7/13 f.474; DW/PA/5/1648/22]
John of Farnham [PRO; PCC Will 1540]
John of Guildford, musician [HRO; 1603 AD49]
John of Merrow [PRO; PCC Admon 1640]
John of Swk St George; Sevenoaks, Kent, porter [DW/PA/5/1591/85]
Lowrye of ... [DW/PA/7/9 f.227; DW/PA/5/1617/86]
Margaret of Swk St Saviour [DW/PA/7/12 f.376; 1637]
Margaret of Swk St Saviour [DW/PA/7/12 f.433; DW/PA/5/1638/83]
Mercy of Newington, widow [LPL; 96/1807; Will 1646]

MORRIS (MORES,MORIS,MORISE,MORREYS,MORRICE,MORYS) [*continued*]
  Robert of Dorking, spurrier [DW/PA/7/5 f,70; 1539] <Abs 28>
  Robert of Wandsworth [DW/PA/5/1617/87] <Abs U226>
  William of Oxted [DW/PA/7/2 f,46; 1495]
  William of Swk St Olave, cordwainer [DW/PA/7/10 f,103; DW/PA/5/1621/85]
  William of Swk St Olave [DW/PA/7/11 f,549; DW/PA/5/1629/70]
MORRISON (MORRYSON)
  Morgan of London, citizen and merchant tailor [DW/PA/7/7 f,297; DW/PA/5/1600/35] <Abs 532>
MORSE (MORS)
  John of Swk St Saviour, waterman [DW/PA/5/1575/52]
  Joyce of Guildford, widow of John [DW/PA/7/8 f,168; DW/PA/5/1610/94]
MORSEY
  Richard of Horley [PRO; PCC Admon 1636]
MORSTED (MORESTED,MORSTEDE)
  John of Betchworth [PRO; PCC Will 1421]
  Thomas of Betchworth - West Betchworth, esq. [PRO; PCC Will 1450]
MORTAIN,MORTAM *see* MORTUM
MORTEN *see* MORTON
MORTER *see* MARTER
MORTIMER (MARTYMER,MORTEMER,MORTYMER)
  Alice of Chertsey [PRO; PCC Will 1470]
  Cornelius of Newington; Swk St George [*in* DW/PA/5/1563/65]
  Cornelius of Swk St George [HRO; Reg. CCB 20 p,7; 1563]
  John of Swk St Olave, yeoman [DW/PA/7/12 f,152; DW/PA/5/1633/92]
  Mary of Swk St Olave, widow [DW/PA/7/12 f,232; DW/PA/5/1634/71]
MORTON (MOORTON,MORETON,MORTEN)
  Daniel of Bermondsey, leatherdresser [PRO; PCC Will 1622]
  Edward, alias Edward Mordin of Ewell, tailor [DW/PA/5/1593/152]
  John of Bermondsey; Swk St Olave, capper [DW/PA/7/7 f,154; DW/PA/5/1597/72] <Abs 288>
  Mary of Kingston; London, widow [PRO; PCC 1634]
  Nicholas of Frensham, yeoman [DW/PA/7/13 f,129; DW/PA/5/1640/109]
  Reginald of Swk St Olave, cooper [DW/PA/5/1576/17]
  Richard of Wimbledon [PRO; PCC Will 1489]
  (Sir) Robert of Surrey, knight [PRO; PCC Will 1514]
  (Sir) Thomas of Wimbledon, knight [PRO; PCC 1641]
  William of Croydon - Whitehorse [PRO; PCC 1630]
MORTUM
  John of Guildford St Nicolas [*in* DW/PA/5/1557/75]
MOSE (MOASE,MOOSE,MOOSSE,MOZE)
  Agnes of Cranleigh, widow [DW/PA/5/1580/44]
  Elizabeth of Shalford, spinster [DW/PA/7/13 f,150; DW/PA/5/1642/54]
  John of Alfold, husbandman [DW/PA/7/13 f,442; DW/PA/5/1646/39]
  John of Ewhurst, yeoman [HRO; 1612 B66]
  John of Wotton, husbandman [HRO; 1621 B38]
  Ralph of Mickleham, husbandman [HRO; 1585 B46]
  Richard of Dunsfold, husbandman [DW/PA/7/12 f,466; DW/PA/5/1638/92]
  Richard of Oxted [DW/PA/5/1587/86]
  Thomas of Dorking, gent. [DW/PA/7/12 f,309; DW/PA/5/1635/71]
  Thomas of Ewhurst [PRO; PCC 1640]
  William of Mickleham, yeoman [DW/PA/7/10 f,35; DW/PA/5/1617/88]
MOSELEY (MOUSLEY,MOUSLEYE,MOWSELEY,MOWESLY)
  Edward of Wandsworth, gardener [DW/PA/7/11 f,575; DW/PA/5/1630/74]

MOSELEY (MOUSLEY,MOUSLEYE,MOWSELEY,MOWESLY) [*continued*]
Henry of Battersea [DW/PA/7/9 f,260; DW/PA/5/1617/90]
Hugh of Battersea, gardener [DW/PA/7/12 f,509; DW/PA/5/1638/97]
Humphrey of Surrey, secondary of Wood Street Compter [PRO; PCC Will 1592]
Thomas of Battersea [DW/PA/7/11 f,414; DW/PA/5/1627/81]
see also MAUDSLEY
MOSSE
Gilbert of Swk St Saviour, servant to William Hodgis of Bankside, yeoman [DW/PA/5/1578/62]
MOTCHET
Peter of Kingston [PRO; PCC Admon 1614]
MOTE *see* MOATE
MOTH
John of Puttenham, tailor [DW/PA/7/12 f,374; 1637]
MOTLEY (MOTTLYE)
John of ... [DW/PA/5/1557/12]
John of Lambeth, waterman [DW/PA/5/1579/64]*
MOTT
Agnes of Rotherhithe, widow [DW/PA/5/1603/115] <Abs U81>
Arthur of Swk St Thomas, brewer [DW/PA/7/7 f,439; DW/PA/5/1603/117] <Abs 830>
John of Rotherhithe [PRO; PCC Admon 1640]
Robert of Lambeth [PRO; PCC Admon 1590]
MOTTLY *see* MOTLEY
MOTTRAM
Morgan of Merstham [GL; Archdeaconry Court of London Will 1554]
MOUDEN *see* MARDEN
MOULTON
John of Swk St Olave [DW/PA/7/11 f,132; DW/PA/5/1624/84]
John of Swk St Olave [DW/PA/7/11 f,427; DW/PA/5/1627/80]
MOULYM *see* de MOULYM
MOUNCKE *see* MONK
MOUNGER *see* MONGER
MOUNKE *see* MONK
MOUNSON
John of Kew [PRO; PCC Admon 1571]
MOUNT (MOUNTE)
John of Kingston - Coombe Nevill, yeoman [PRO; PCC Admon 1567]
Richard of Battersea [DW/PA/5/1588/1]
Thomas of Battersea, husbandman [DW/PA/7/9 f,262; DW/PA/5/1617/89]
MOUNTAGUE *see* MONTAGUE
MOUNTE *see* MOUNT
MOUNTENNEY
Leonard of Lambeth - Kennington [PRO; PCC Admon 1616
MOUNTER (MONTER)
Edmund of Betchworth - Brockham, yeoman [DW/PA/7/7 f,602; DW/PA/5/1607/66] <Abs 1126>
Joan of Leatherhead, widow [DW/PA/7/1 f,101; 1489] <Abs 329>
Richard of Leatherhead [DW/PA/7/1 f,83; 1488] <Abs 278>
Thomasine of Betchworth - Brockham [DW/PA/7/8 f,3; DW/PA/5/1608/77]
MOUNTJOY
Lord, (Sir) Walter Blount, of Surrey [PRO; PCC Will 1474]
MOUSE
Mary of Newington, widow [GL; Archdeaconry Court of London Will 1645]

MOUSLEY *see* MOSELEY

MOWCHE

John of Camberwell - Peckham, labourer [DW/PA/5/1555/80]

MOWDON *see* MARDEN

MOWER (MOWERE, MOWRE, MOWYER, MOYER)

Agnes of Cranleigh - Utworth [DW/PA/7/9 f,275; 1618]
Agnes of Shalford [DW/PA/7/11 f,439; DW/PA/5/1628/72]
Edward of Alfold, husbandman [DW/PA/7/13 f,40; DW/PA/5/1639/91]
Edward of Cranleigh, yeoman [DW/PA/7/13 f,98; DW/PA/5/1640/104]
Henry of Cranleigh - 'Pothans', yeoman [DW/PA/7/9 f,247; DW/PA/5/1617/91]
James of Walton on the Hill [DW/PA/7/10 f,53; 1619]
Joan of Cranleigh, widow [DW/PA/7/10 f,227; DW/PA/5/1621/86]
John of Cranleigh [DW/PA/7/2 f,27; 1492]
John of Cranleigh; Ewhurst; Chiddingfold; Abinger; Godalming; Hascombe [DW/PA/5/1550/44]
John of Cranleigh - Barhatch [DW/PA/5/1558/202]*
John of Cranleigh [? HRO; 1551]
John of Cranleigh - Manning's Hill; Wonersh, senior [DW/PA/7/7 f,569; DW/PA/5/1606/61] <Abs 569>
John of Cranleigh - Smithwood; Ewell, yeoman [DW/PA/7/10 f,173; DW/PA/5/1619/84]
John of Cranleigh - Smithwood; Ewell, yeoman [DW/PA/7/9 f,76; DW/PA/5/1614/79]
John of Ewhurst - Maybanks; Cranleigh; Rudgwick, Sussex, yeoman [DW/PA/7/8 f,91; DW/PA/5/1609/61]
John of Ewhurst, husbandman [DW/PA/7/12 f,36; DW/PA/5/1631/74]
John of Ewhurst, yeoman [DW/PA/7/12 f,325; DW/PA/5/1637/71]
John of Windlesham - Bagshot, yeoman, senior [DW/PA/7/11 f,105; DW/PA/5/1624/85]
Katherine of Cranleigh, widow [HRO; 1603 B38]
Oliver of Cranleigh, clothier [DW/PA/7/13 f,52; DW/PA/5/1639/94]
Peter of Kingston [PRO; PCC Will 1559]
Ralph of Cranleigh - Wyphurst, yeoman [DW/PA/7/7 f,467; DW/PA/5/1604/40A] <Abs 880>
Ralph of Cranleigh, shoemaker [DW/PA/7/12 f,374; DW/PA/5/1638/89]
Ralph of Shalford, yeoman [DW/PA/7/11 f,91; DW/PA/5/1624/87]
Richard of Alfold, shoemaker [DW/PA/5/1599/48] <Abs U25>
Richard of Alfold, yeoman [DW/PA/7/10 f,54; 1619]
Richard of Cranleigh [HRO; 1551 B105-107]
Richard of Cranleigh - Utworth, yeoman [DW/PA/5/1591/27]
Richard of Cranleigh, yeoman, senior [PRO; PCC Will 1624]
Richard of Cranleigh, husbandman [DW/PA/7/13 f,413; DW/PA/5/1645/37]
Richard of Puttenham [DW/PA/5/1561/19]
Richard of Wonersh - Whipley, yeoman [DW/PA/5/1624/86]
Robert of Cranleigh [DW/PA/5/1552/7]
Robert of Ewhurst [DW/PA/5/1575/43]
Thomas of Alfold, husbandman [HRO; 1561 B137-138]
Thomas of Cranleigh [DW/PA/5/1558/201]*
Thomas of Cranleigh, yeoman [DW/PA/7/9 f,15; DW/PA/5/1616/92]
Walter of Cranleigh, yeoman [DW/PA/5/1576/62]

MOWESLEY *see* MOSELEY

MOWLL

Richard of Swk St Margaret [DW/PA/7/4 f,59; 1533]

MOWNE *see* MOONE

MOWSELEY *see* MOSELEY
MOWSER
Robert of Tandridge [HRO; 1561 B135-136]
MOYCE *see* MOYS
MOYER *see* MOWER
MOYES *see* MOYS
MOYLE
(Sir) Thomas of Surrey, knight [PRO; PCC Will 1560]
MOYS (MOYCE,MOYES,MOYSE,MOYSES)
Edmund of Kingston, citizen and haberdasher [PRO; PCC Will 1582]
Eleanor of Banstead [DW/PA/7/11 f.598; DW/PA/5/1630/75]
John of Banstead, gent. [DW/PA/7/12 f.404; DW/PA/5/1637/74]
Josias of Limpsfield, blacksmith [DW/PA/7/12 f.228; DW/PA/5/1634/70]
Michael of Oxted, miller [DW/PA/7/12 f.504; DW/PA/5/1638/96]
Phillip of Banstead, gent. [PRO; PCC Will 1621]
Richard of Banstead [DW/PA/5/1572/16]
Thomas of Lambeth - Lambeth Marsh, yeoman [DW/PA/7/7 f.133; DW/PA/5/1597/73] <Abs 244>
Thomas of Oxted, weaver [DW/PA/7/12 f.79; DW/PA/5/1633/86]
William of Banstead, gent. [PRO; PCC Will 1613]
William of Banstead, gent. [DW/PA/7/12 f.267; DW/PA/5/1634/74]
MUCKOE
Alexander of Bermondsey, hempdresser [PRO; PCC Will 1604] <Abs. SAC v.11 p.295>
MUDDLE
William of Ewhurst, gent. [PRO; PCC 1631]
MUDGETT
Thomas of Kingston, bargeman [DW/PA/7/8 f.377; DW/PA/5/1612/110]
MUGGE
Walter of Guildford [PRO; PCC Will 1495]
MUGGERIDGE
Edward of Reigate [PRO; PCC Admon 1649]
MULFORD (MULFORDE)
Hugh of Dorking [PRO; PCC Admon 1564]
William of Rotherhithe, shipwright [DW/PA/7/7 f.205; DW/PA/5/1598/55] <Abs 365>
MULLENEX *see* MOLYNEUX
MULLENS *see* MULLINS
MULLINEUX,MULLINEX *see* MOLYNEUX
MULLINGTON (MULLYNGTON)
Agnes of Kingston [PRO; PCC Will 1507]
MULLINS (MOLINES,MOLING,MOLLINS,MULLEN,MULLENS)
Cicely of Mitcham, widow [DW/PA/7/13 f.266; DW/PA/5/1643/61]
John of Hambledon, parson [HRO; 1589 B42]
Roger of Mortlake [PRO; PCC Admon 1636]
William of Croydon, maltman, senior [LPL; 96/1820; Will 1644]
William of Croydon, maltman [LPL; 96/1821; Will 1645]
William of Dorking [PRO; PCC Will 1621] [*and*] [DW/PA/7/10 f.194; DW/PA/5/1621/87]
MULLYNGTON *see* MULLINGTON
MUMFORD
John of Guildford St Nicolas, pavior [DW/PA/7/8 f.131; DW/PA/5/1610/95]
MUNCKE *see* MONK
MUNCKLER *see* MONKLER

MUNDAY *see* MONDAY
MUNGER *see* MONGER
MUNN
  Margaret of Newington, widow [LPL; 96/1823; Will 1625]
MUNNELY
  Thomas of Bermondsey (died overseas) [PRO; PCC Admon 1641]
MUNNINGS
  Thomas of Rotherhithe, mariner [PRO; PCC 1638]
MUNROY
  John *or* John Munjoy, of Morden [DW/PA/7/11 f.1; DW/PA/5/1622/67]
MUNS
  Richard of London, citizen and basketmaker [DW/PA/7/10 f.273; DW/PA/5/1622/68]
MUNSON
  John of Kew, gent. [PRO; PCC Admon 1572]
MURGATROYD (MURGATROYDE)
  Michael of Croydon, esq. [PRO; PCC Will 1608] <Abs, SAC v.13 pp.178-179>
  Robert of Croydon, haberdasher [LPL; 96/1825; Will 1617]
MURSELE (de MURSELE)
  Hugh of Peper Harow, rector [HRO; Reg. Edn 2 p.18; 1348]
MUSCHAMP (MUSCHAMPE)
  Agmondesham of East Horsley [PRO; PCC Admon 1648]
  Agnes of Swk St Saviour, widow [DW/PA/7/8 f.408; DW/PA/5/1614/80]
  Christopher of Carshalton, Baron of the Exchequer, esq. [PRO; PCC Will 1579]
  Edmund of Swk St Olave; Shoreditch, Middlesex, gent. [DW/PA/5/1605/60] <Abs U156>
  Francis of Camberwell - Peckham, esq. [PRO; PCC Will 1617]
  Francis of Camberwell [PRO; PCC Admon 1632]
  Margery of Newington, widow [PRO; PCC Will 1624]
  Mary of East Horsley - Rowbarns [PRO; PCC Admon 1620]
  Ralph of Camberwell - Peckham, esq. [PRO; PCC Will 1559]
  Thomas of Camberwell - Peckham [PRO; PCC Will 1474]
  Thomas of Camberwell, citizen and goldsmith [PRO; PCC Will 1578]
  Thomas of Camberwell [PRO; PCC Admon 1638]
  William of Godalming, esq. [PRO; PCC Will 1606] <Abs, SAC v.12 p.197>
MUSSELIS
  John, alias John Haunce, alias John Marcellis of Rotherhithe [PRO; PCC Admon 1628]
MUSSEN
  Elizabeth of ...., widow [DW/PA/7/7 f.437; DW/PA/5/1603/118] <Abs 826>
MUSWELL (MUSSOLD)
  Thomas of Godalming, clothier [DW/PA/5/1582/17]
MYCHAELL,MYCHELL *see* MITCHELL
MYCHENALL *see* MITCHENALL
MYCHILL *see* MITCHELL
MYDDELBOROWE *see* MIDDLESBOROUGH
MYDDELTON,MYDELTON *see* MIDDLETON
MY'HART *see* MARCHANT
MYLAM *see* MILAM
MYLE,MYLES,MYLIS *see* MILES
MYLLER *see* MILLER
MYLLERSH,MYLLEST *see* MELLERSH
MYLLETT *see* MILLETT

MYLLING *see* MILLING
MYLLUST *see* MELLERSH
MYLLWARD *see* MILLWARD
MYLLYNS *see* MILLING
MYLLYS *see* MELLERSH
MYLMAN *see* MILLMAN
MYLTON *see* MILTON
MYLWARD,MYLWARDE,MYLWART *see* MILLWARD
MYLYON *see* MILLION
MYLYS *see* MILLS
MYNAR *see* MINORS
MYNCHYN *see* MINCHIN
MYNNE
  George of Epsom - Woodcote, esq. [PRO; PCC Admon 1648]
  Nicholas of Epsom [PRO; PCC Will 1528]
  (Sir) William of Epsom, knight [PRO; PCC Will 1618]
MYNORS *see* MINORS
MYNSTERLEY *see* MINSTERLEY
MYNTON *see* MINTON
MYTCHELL *see* MITCHELL

NACHTEGAL
  Josias of ... [*Dutch*] [DW/PA/7/7 f.406; DW/PA/5/1603/119] <Abs 755>
NAILE
  Alice of Farnham [DW/PA/7/7 f.53; 1596] <Abs 100>
NAILHAM
  John of Lambeth, waterman [DW/PA/7/8 f.279; DW/PA/5/1613/92]
NALDRETT (NALDRET,NALLDETT,NOLDRED)
  Henry of Guildford St Nicolas [PRO; PCC Admon 1617]
  Mary of Leatherhead [PRO; PCC Will 1599]
  Richard of Ockley [PRO; PCC Admon 1604]
  Thomas of Newdigate; Woodmansterne, yeoman [DW/PA/5/1604/39B] <Abs U111>
  William of Dorking, yeoman [DW/PA/7/11 f.437; DW/PA/5/1628/73]
  William of Horley, yeoman [DW/PA/7/7 f.135; DW/PA/5/1597/74] <Abs 249>
NALL
  Thomas of Tooting [PRO; PCC 1634]
NALLARD
  Robert of Kingston [DW/PA/5/1581/36]
NALLDETT *see* NALDRETT
NAPKIN
  Thomas of Merstham [LPL; 96/1832; Will 1648]
  William of Titsey [PRO; PCC 1649]
NAPPER
  Robert of Newington, gent. [PRO; PCC Will 1591]
NAPTON
  John of Limpsfield [DW/PA/7/2 f.96; 1514]
NARRARD *see* NORRARD
NASH (NASHE)
  Edmund of Bermondsey [PRO; PCC Will 1607]
  Edward of Putney [LPL; 98/1 f.33r; Will 1631]
  John of Beddington [PRO; PCC 1632]
  Juliana, alias Juliana Clarke of Bermondsey [PRO; PCC Admon 1649]

NASH (NASHE) [*continued*]
  Mary of Lambeth, widow [PRO; PCC Admon 1625]
  Richard of Walton on Thames, labourer [DW/PA/5/1580/28]
NAVARRE (De NAVARRE)
  Daniel of Swk St Olave [DW/PA/7/8 f.87; DW/PA/5/1609/40]
NEALE (NEALES,NEALL,NEEL,NEELES,NELE)
  Elizabeth of Beddington, widow [DW/PA/7/12 f.343; DW/PA/5/1636/70]
  John of Capel, husbandman [DW/PA/7/9 f.336; DW/PA/5/1620/86]
  John of Thames Ditton - Weston Green [DW/PA/7/11 f.536; DW/PA/5/1629/71]
  John of West Horsley [PRO; PCC Admon 1648]
  John of Leatherhead [DW/PA/7/5 f.129; 1539]
  Margery of Swk St George, widow [DW/PA/7/7 f.400; DW/PA/5/1603/120] <Abs 742>
  Richard of Leatherhead [DW/PA/5/1568/57]
  Richard of Leatherhead [DW/PA/7/7 f.329; DW/PA/5/1601/66] <Abs 589>
  Robert of Dorking, blacksmith [DW/PA/7/9 f.189; DW/PA/5/1616/98]
  Roger of Sutton, husbandman [DW/PA/5/1593/102]
  Thomas of Great Bookham; Leatherhead [DW/PA/7/4 f.167; 1536]
  Thomas of Effingham, yeoman [DW/PA/7/13 f.99; DW/PA/5/1640/113]
  Thomas of Swk St George, citizen and innholder [DW/PA/5/1563/120]
  Walter of Leatherhead, carpenter [DW/PA/7/10 f.192; DW/PA/5/1621/88]
  William of Chichester, Sussex; St Botolph Billinsgate, London; St Nicholas Olave, London; Swk [LPL; Reg. Abp Chichele i f.316; Will 1419 ?]
NEAMES (NYMYS)
  John of Guildford St Nicolas [DW/PA/7/2 f.23; 1492]
NEAVE (NEVE)
  Anthony of West Horsley, yeoman [DW/PA/7/8 f.273; DW/PA/5/1612/111]
  Anthony of West Horsley, yeoman [DW/PA/7/12 f.217; DW/PA/5/1633/99]
  Gilbert of Windlesham, husbandman [HRO; 1636 B26]
  John of Swk St Olave, citizen and haberdasher [DW/PA/7/8 f.81; DW/PA/5/1609/65]
  Richard of West Horsley, yeoman [DW/PA/7/11 f.140; DW/PA/5/1624/88]
  William of Weybridge, labourer [DW/PA/7/8 f.98; DW/PA/5/1609/64]
NEDAM *see* NEEDHAM
NEDE *see* NEED
NEDEHAM,NEDUM *see* NEEDHAM
NEED (NEDE,NEEDE,NEEDES)
  Frances of Bermondsey, wife of Robert Mayer [PRO; PCC Will 1619]
  Hugh of Swk St Olave; Much Malvern, Worcestershire, bachelor [DW/PA/7/7 f.591; DW/PA/5/1606/62] <Abs 1103>
  Richard of Rotherhithe; St Giles in the Fields, Middlesex; Malvern, Worcestershire, gunpowder maker [DW/PA/5/1603/121] <Abs U82>
  Richard of Rotherhithe [PRO; PCC Will 1603 *and* 1604] <Abs. SAC v.11 pp.117-118>
  William of Rotherhithe [PRO; PCC Admon 1600]
NEEDHAM (NEDAM,NEDENHAM,NEDOME,NEDUM)
  Alice of West Molesey, widow [DW/PA/7/9 f.177; DW/PA/5/1616/97]
  Francis of Wandsworth ['*Bandesworth*'] [PRO; PCC Admon 1626]
  Richard of Camberwell [DW/PA/7/11 f.173; DW/PA/5/1625/181]
  Thomas of Streatham [HRO; 1521 U27]
  William of Kingston [PRO; PCC Admon 1572]
NEEDLER
  Ann of Swk St Olave, widow [DW/PA/7/10 f.180; DW/PA/5/1620/85]

NEEDLER [*continued*]
  Henry of Horley, gent. [PRO; PCC Will 1613] <Abs SAC v,25 p,106>
  John of Horley, gent. [PRO; PCC Will 1623; SRO; 212/59/8] <Abs SAC v,25 p,107>
NEEL,NEELE,NEELES *see* NEALE
NEILDER (NEYLDER)
  William of Farnham [? HRO; 1545]
NELE *see* NEALE
NELOND
  John of Lingfield [PRO; PCC Will 1437]
    see also NEWLAND
NELSON (NELSONNE)
  Henry, alias Henry Elson of Swk St Olave [DW/PA/5/1582/105]
  John of Mickleham, clerk [PRO; PCC 1645]
  John of Wonersh, gent. [DW/PA/7/7 f,280; DW/PA/5/1599/49] <Abs 498>
  William of ... [DW/PA/5/1593/147]
NEPE
  Thomas of Swk St Margaret [HRO; Reg. Fox 3 p,62; 1512]
NETHERCLIFT
  Robert *or* Walter of ... [DW/PA/7/7 f,193; DW/PA/5/1598/60] <Abs 350>
NETHERCOTT
  Edward of Kingston, gent. [PRO; PCC Will 1596]
NETHERSTREET (NETHERSTRETE)
  Thomas of Rotherhithe, fishmonger [DW/PA/5/1569/16]
NETLEFOLD,NETLEFOLDE,NETLEFORD *see* NETTLEFOLD
NETLENIGHAM *see* NETLINGHAM
NETLETON *see* NETTLETON
NETLINGHAM (NETLENIGHAM,NETLINGHTON)
  Benjamin of Wandsworth [PRO; PCC 1635]
  Helen, alias Helen Barnard of Wandsworth [PRO; PCC Admon 1638]
  John of Lambeth; Camberwell, yeoman [DW/PA/7/9 f,117; DW/PA/5/1615/97]
  John *or* Robert of Lambeth [PRO; PCC Admon 1603 *or* 1605]
  Thomas of Streatham [DW/PA/5/1578/28]
  William of Camberwell [DW/PA/5/1593/78]
NETTLEFOLD (NETLEFOLD,NETLEFOLDE,NETLEFORD,NETTLEFOULD,NETYLFOLD, NETYLLFOLD,NUTLEFOLD)
  Daniel of Dorking, yeoman [DW/PA/7/8 f,340; DW/PA/5/1612/112]
  Edward of Dorking, yeoman, senior [DW/PA/7/9 f,293; 1618]
  Edward of Abinger; Headley; Ockley, yeoman [DW/PA/7/10 f,66; 1618]
  Edward of Dorking [DW/PA/5/1581/54]
  Edward of Ewhurst, yeoman [DW/PA/5/1591/34]
  John of East Clandon, husbandman [DW/PA/5/1558/204]*
  Thomas of Abinger [HRO; 1612 B67]
  William of Abinger, husbandman [HRO; 1584 B54]
  William of Dorking - Westcott, yeoman [DW/PA/5/1555/13]
  William of Dorking, husbandman [DW/PA/5/1604/41] <Abs U113>
  William of Dorking, yeoman [HRO; 1620 AD86]
NETTLETON (NETLETON)
  John of Swk - Kings Bench Prison; Hutton Cranswick, Yorkshire, gent. [DW/PA/7/7 f,142; DW/PA/5/1597/75] <Abs 259>
NEVE *see* NEAVE
NEVETT *see* KNEVETT
NEVILLE (NEVELL,NEVYLE)
  John of Charlwood [PRO; PCC Will 1551]

NEVILLE (NEVELL,NEVYLE) [*continued*]
Lawrence of Farnham, gent. [DW/PA/7/12 f.370; DW/PA/5/1627/83]
Susan of Camberwell; Newington, wife of John, esq. [GL; Archdeaconry Court of London Will 1633]
William of Kingston [DW/PA/7/2 f.47; 1496]

NEW *see* NEWE

NEWALL *see* NEWELL

NEWBOLT
John of Kingston [LPL; Reg. Abp Arundell f.174r; Admon 1400]

NEWBOROUGH (NEWBORO)
John of Guildford St Mary [DW/PA/7/4 f.201; 1537]

NEWBOWLL
William of Lambeth [HRO; Reg. CCB 20 p.15; 1563]

NEWBRIDGE (NEWBRIGGE)
Richard of Farnham, vicar [LPL; Reg. Abp Morton f.255v; Admon 1489]

NEWBURY (NEWBERY,NEWBURYE,NUBERY)
Hester, alias Hester Kente of Farnham, spinster [DW/PA/7/12 f.329; DW/PA/5/1636/61]
John of Bermondsey [PRO; PCC Admon 1627]
John of Bermondsey - Bermondsey Street, skinner [DW/PA/7/12 f.368; DW/PA/5/1627/84]
John, alias John Kent of Farnham, glover [HRO; 1600 B37]
John, alias John Kent of Farnham, fellmonger [DW/PA/7/11 f.603 *and* DW/PA/7/12 f.330; DW/PA/5/1630/63 *and* DW/PA/5/1636/60]
Margaret, alias Margaret Kent of Farnham, widow [DW/PA/7/7 f.532; DW/PA/5/1607/56] <Abs 1000>

NEWDIGATE (NEWDEGATE,NEWDYGATE,NUDIGATE)
Agnes of Newdigate, widow [HRO; 1583 B60]
Alice of Newdigate, widow of Thomas [? 1489] <Abs SAC v.6 p.261>
Alice of Newdigate, widow [DW/PA/7/4 f.75; 1534] <Abs SAC v.6 p.262>
Henry of Ashtead [PRO; PCC Admon 1635] <Abs SAC v.6 p.264>
John of Surrey [LPL; Reg. Abp Courtenay f.226; Will 1387] [*probate act only*]
John of Surrey, esq. [Register of bishop of Westminster, ff.77b and 96; 1546] <Abs SAC v.6 p.262>
Richard of Harefield, Middlesex; Newdigate; Capel, gent. [PRO; PCC Will 1545] <Abs SAC v.6 pp.262-263>
Thomas of Newdigate [? 1482] <Abs SAC v.6 p.261>
Thomas of Newdigate, gent. [DW/PA/7/2 f.110; 1517] <Abs SAC v.6 p.261>
Thomas of Newdigate, esq. [DW/PA/5/1576/42] <Abs SAC v.6 p.263-264>
Thomas of Newdigate, esq. [PRO; PCC Will 1613] <Abs SAC v.6 p.263>
Walter of Newdigate [PRO; PCC Will 1590] <Abs SAC v.6 p.264>
West of Blechingley [PRO; PCC Admon 1642]
William of Surrey [? 1377] <Abs SAC v.6 p.261>

NEWE
John of Chobham [DW/PA/7/1 f.29; 1486] <Abs 96>
Roger of Byfleet [DW/PA/5/1561/40]

NEWELL (NEWALL)
William of Croydon [LPL; 98/1 f.120r; Will 1641]

NEWENT
John of Kingston [DW/PA/7/2 f.19; 1491]

NEWINGES *see* NEWINS

NEWINGTON (NEWENTON)
Geoffrey of West Wickham, Kent; Ipswich, Suffolk; Burstow, etc. [LPL; Reg. Abp Arundel i f.179; Will 1400]
Nicholas of Merton, yeoman [DW/PA/7/13 f.250; DW/PA/5/1641/100]
Susanna of Merton, widow [DW/PA/7/13 f.211; DW/PA/5/1642/63]

NEWINS (NEWINGES,NUENS)
Richard of Swk St Saviour [DW/PA/5/1582/13]
William of Kingston, butcher [DW/PA/5/1592/120]

NEWLAND (NEWLANDS)
Alexander of Petersham [DW/PA/7/11 f.131; DW/PA/5/1624/89]
Christopher of Farnham [PRO; PCC 1645]
John of Newington [LPL; 98/1 f.64v; Will 1635]
William of Petersham, yeoman [DW/PA/7/7 f.451; DW/PA/5/1603/122] <Abs 855>

NEWMAN (NEWEMAN)
Agnes of Bermondsey [DW/PA/7/10 f.57; 1618]
Joan of Guildford, widow [PRO; PCC 1643]
John of Battersea [PRO; PCC 1646]
John of Chertsey [*in* DW/PA/5/1546/24]
John of Chiddingfold, singler [DW/PA/5/1592/87]
John of Farnham, yeoman [DW/PA/7/12 f.208; DW/PA/5/1634/75]
Nicholas of Great Bookham [DW/PA/7/1 f.75; 1488] <Abs 245>
Nicholas of Egham, gent. [PRO; PCC Will 1627]
Robert of Weybridge, yeoman [DW/PA/7/7 f.530; DW/PA/5/1607/67 *and* DW/PA/5/1607/68] <Abs 998>
Thomas of Newington [LPL; 96/1844; Will 1626]
Thomas of Newington [PRO; PCC 1642]
Thomas of Peper Harow [DW/PA/7/6 f.116; DW/PA/5/1559/124]
Walter of Egham [DW/PA/7/7 f.85; 1596] <Abs 156>
William of Chertsey, vicar [HRO; 1576 AD38]
William of Farnham, husbandman [DW/PA/7/13 f.455; DW/PA/5/1647/11]
William of Oxted [DW/PA/7/4 f.115; 1535]
William of Swk St Saviour [DW/PA/5/1593/107]
William of Thursley [HRO; 1608 B52]

NEWNHAM (NEWNAM)
John of Chobham, husbandman [DW/PA/7/7 f.112; DW/PA/5/1596/43] <Abs 204>
Thomas of Godstone [PRO; PCC 1634]
Thomas of Guildford Holy Trinity, gent. [DW/PA/7/13 f.96; DW/PA/5/1640/112]

NEWPORT
John of Newington [LPL; 98/1 f.67v; Will 1635]
Thomas of Blechingley, butcher [DW/PA/7/11 f.507; DW/PA/5/1629/72]
William of Croydon [PRO; PCC Will 1488]

NEWSAM
Margaret of Swk St Saviour, widow [DW/PA/7/11 f.358; DW/PA/5/1625/182]
Peter of Swk St Saviour, victualler [DW/PA/7/8 f.290; DW/PA/5/1613/93]
Peter of Swk St Saviour [DW/PA/7/12 f.508; DW/PA/5/1639/95]
William of Swk St Saviour [DW/PA/7/7 f.350; DW/PA/5/1601/67] <Abs 643>

NEWTON (NUTTON)
John of Croydon, yeoman [LPL; 96/1851; 98/1 f.93r; Will 1638]
John of Newington [LPL; 96/1881; 98/1 f.87r; Will 1637]
William of Newington [PRO; PCC Admon 1649]

NEYLDER *see* NEILDER

NEYLHAM *see* NAILHAM

NICHOLAS *see* NYCHOLAS
Caleb of Swk St Saviour; Lambeth, baker [DW/PA/7/10 f,214; DW/PA/5/1621/89]
Thomas of Wonersh [PRO; PCC Admon 1604]
Thrustons of Swk St Olave, hatmaker [DW/PA/5/1563/122]
Walter of Swk St Olave, papermaker [DW/PA/7/2 f,57; 1499]
NICHOLS (NICCOLLS,NICHOLES,NICHOLLES,NICHOLLS,NICKOLES,NICOLES,NICOLL, NYCOLLES)
Alice of Kingston, widow [DW/PA/7/2 f,103; 1515] <Abs SAC v,1 pp,181-183 *and* v,8 p,116>
Ann (daughter of George Ownsteed of Sanderstead) widow of Benjamin [GL; Archdeaconry Court of London Will 1626]
Christopher of Putney [LPL; 98/1 f,41v; Will 1632]
Elizabeth of Swk St Olave, widow [DW/PA/5/1563/82]
Elizabeth, alias Elizabeth Browne of Swk St Thomas Hospital, widow [DW/PA/7/13 f,229; DW/PA/5/1642/65]
George of Swk St Olave, silk weaver [DW/PA/7/7 f,574; DW/PA/5/1606/63] <Abs 1072>
Humphrey of Walton on Thames, citizen and brown baker [PRO; PCC Will 1587]
John of Frimley [PRO; PCC Admon 1632]
John of Swk St Olave, joiner [DW/PA/7/6 f,250; 1560]
Richard of Bermondsey, carman [DW/PA/7/9 f,218; DW/PA/5/1617/92]
Thomas of Bermondsey, yeoman [DW/PA/7/12 f,426; DW/PA/5/1637/75]
Walter of Ewhurst, yeoman [DW/PA/7/8 f,80; DW/PA/5/1609/66]
William of Kingston, linen draper [PRO; PCC Will 1609] <Abs, SAC v,23 p,141>
NICHOLSON (NICHOLLSON,NICOLSON,NYCOLSON)
Arnold of Swk St Thomas [DW/PA/5/1569/26]
Benjamin of Bramley, gent, [PRO; PCC Will 1600]
Paul of Swk St Thomas Hospital, purser [*Dutch*] [DW/PA/7/6 f,142; DW/PA/5/1559/137]
Thomas of Swk St Thomas [DW/PA/7/11 f,318; DW/PA/5/1626/91]
Ursula of Swk St Saviour, widow [DW/PA/7/10 f,194; DW/PA/5/1621/90]
NIEUSVEHOUSE
John of Swk St Olave [DW/PA/5/1593/69]
NIGHTINGALE (NIGHTINGALL,NYTINGALE,NYTYNGALE,NYTYNGAYLL)
John of Barnes [LPL; 98/1 f,125v (ren,); 1641]
John of Capel [DW/PA/7/4 f,117; 1535]
John of Ockley [DW/PA/7/3 f,185; 1531]
Robert of Capel, husbandman [DW/PA/7/13 f,217; DW/PA/5/1642/64]
William of Capel [DW/PA/5/1561/58]
William of Lingfield, yeoman [PRO; PCC Will 1620] <Soame 662>
William of Lingfield [PRO; PCC 1649]
NIKE *see* NYKE
NIXON (NYCKSON,NYXSON)
John of Rotherhithe (died overseas) [PRO; PCC Admon 1632]
Margaret of Walton on Thames, widow [DW/PA/5/1557/44]
Robert of Lambeth [PRO; PCC Admon 1647]
William of Lambeth [DW/PA/5/15557/112]
NOGMAN
Alice of Richmond [DW/PA/7/2 f,132; 1518]
NOKE
John of Wotton, rector [HRO; Reg, Way 1 p,6; 1449]

NOKET
  Thomas of Beddington - Wallington, citizen and draper [GL; Commissary Court of London Will 1396]
NOLDRED *see* NALDRETT
NOLLETH
  Wolfram of Rotherhithe, mariner [DW/PA/7/11 f.67; DW/PA/5/1623/82]
NONNES
  Richard of Swk St Thomas Hospital [DW/PA/5/1578/53]
NOPEN
  Nanchen of ...., widow of Gabriel Bertes [*Dutch*] [DW/PA/7/8 f.28B; DW/PA/5/1608/78]
NORBERI *see* NORBURY
NORBON (de NORBON)
  (Sir) Peter of Richmond, knight of St George, servant to the king [DW/PA/7/2 f.119; 1517]
NORBRIDGE (NORBRIGE)
  Alice of Guildford Holy Trinity; Fetcham; Wokingham, Berkshire; East Clandon; West Clandon; Compton; Haslemere; Peper Harow; St Martha's; Bramley [DW/PA/7/4 f.19; 1532]
  Henry of Guildford Holy Trinity [PRO; PCC Will 1512] <Abs SAC v.28 p.95>
  Henry of Guildford [PRO; PCC Will 1529]
NORBURY (NORBERI,NORBURYE)
  (Sir) John of Stoke Dabernon, knight [HRO; Reg. Fox 2 p.31; 1504]
  John of Stoke Dabernon, priest [HRO; 1541 U63; Reg. F pp.20,62]
  William of Richmond [DW/PA/7/2 f.10; 1491]
NORE
  Thomas of Surrey [PRO; PCC Will 1513]
NORES *see* NORRIS
NORFOLK (NORFOLKE) *for duke and duchess of, see* HOWARD
  Ann of Lambeth, widow [PRO; PCC Admon 1633]
  Ann, alias Ann Barneslay of Lambeth [PRO; PCC Admon 1649]
NORGATE
  Thomasine of Swk St Saviour [DW/PA/7/7 f.295; DW/PA/5/1600/37] <Abs 528>
  William of Newington, bachelor [PRO; PCC Admon 1629]
NORICHE *see* NORWICH
NORIS *see* NORRIS
NORMAN
  Andrew of Kingston, beer brewer [DW/PA/5/1558/205]*
  Andrew of Kingston, gent. [PRO; PCC Will 1615] [*and*] [SRO; KB35/1; 1615]
  Andrew of Kingston [PRO; PCC Admon 1649]
  Blanch of Kingston; Uxbridge, Middlesex; Hillingdon, Middlesex; Denham, Buckinghamshire, widow of James [DW/PA/7/9 f.57; DW/PA/5/1614/98]
  Bridget of Putney, widow [LPL; 96/1866; 98/1 f.66r; Will 1635]
  Jane of Putney - Roehampton; Mortlake; Chamberhowse, Berkshire, wife of Robert, gent.) [PRO; PCC 1630] <Scroope 1348>
  John of Petersham; Kingston, yeoman [DW/PA/7/1 f.63; 1487] <Abs 211>
  John of Swk, yeoman of the king's Chamber [DW/PA/7/6 f.147; DW/PA/5/1559/231]
  Nicholas of Swk St Saviour, waterman [DW/PA/7/11 f.517; DW/PA/5/1629/73]
  Peter of Swk St Olave [*French*] [DW/PA/5/1605/65] <Abs U157>
  Robert of Putney, yeoman [LPL; 96/1867; 98/1 f.68v; Will 1635]
  Robert of Swk St Olave, waterman [DW/PA/7/13 f.200; DW/PA/5/1642/62]
  William of Pyrford, yeoman [DW/PA/7/13 f.306; DW/PA/5/1644/15]

NORMANTON
Agnes of Chertsey, widow [HRO; 1522 B35]
NORRARD (NARRARD)
Elizabeth of Chobham, widow [DW/PA/7/12 f,57; DW/PA/5/1631/76]
Robert of Chobham, yeoman [DW/PA/7/7 f,306; DW/PA/5/1600/36] <Abs 548>
NORREY
Christopher Carlysle, Norroy King of Arms, of Richmond, herald [PRO; PCC Will 1511]
NORRIS (NORES,NORIS,NORRYS,NORYCE,NORYS,NORYSSE)
Alice of Kingston [DW/PA/7/4 f,139; 1536]
Henry of Lambeth [DW/PA/7/4 f,219; 1537]
John of Buckland, parson [HRO; Reg, Fox 3 p,63; 1513]
John of Rotherhithe [PRO; PCC Will 1593]
John of Swk St Saviour [DW/PA/7/8 f,400; DW/PA/5/1612/113]
John of Wandsworth, yeoman [DW/PA/7/2 f,59; 1499]
John of Wandsworth [PRO; PCC Will 1512]
Peter of Swk St Margaret [DW/PA/7/2 f,133; 1519]
Thomas of Swk St Olave, grover [DW/PA/7/5 f,230; 1541]
NORTERYCHE,NORTERYGE *see* NORTHRIDGE
NORTH (NORTHE)
John of Great Bookham [DW/PA/5/1562/3]
John of Malden [DW/PA/7/11 f,188; DW/PA/5/1625/183]
John of Sutton [DW/PA/7/1 f,55; 1487] <Abs 183>
Nathaniel of Rotherhithe, yeoman [DW/PA/7/11 f,441; DW/PA/5/1628/74]
Richard of Swk St Saviour, waterman [DW/PA/7/13 f,223; DW/PA/5/1643/65]
William of Farnham [? HRO; 1525]
NORTHALL
John of Guildford [HRO; 1570 AD42]
Thomas of Guildford, saddler [HRO; 1576 B56]
NORTHEY
Henry of Lambeth, gent, [PRO; PCC Will 1569]
NORTHRIDGE (NORTERYCHE,NORTERYGE,NORTRYG)
Gilbert of Walton on Thames [DW/PA/7/3 f,99; 1529]
Henry of Kingston [PRO; PCC Will 1543]
NORTHUPP
John of ,,, [LPL; 96/1872; Will 1622]
Watkin of Croydon, brewer [LPL; 96/1873; Will 1644]
NORTHWOOD *see* NORWOOD
NORTON (NORTONE)
Henry of Merton, gent, [PRO; PCC Will 1595]
Joan of Chertsey, widow [DW/PA/5/1562/11]
John of Frimley, esq, [PRO; PCC Will 1561]
John of Lambeth [DW/PA/5/1550/9]
Lettice of Barnes, widow [PRO; PCC 1638]
Margaret of Swk St Olave, widow [DW/PA/5/1592/70]
Nicholas of Blechingley, senior [DW/PA/7/11 f,511; DW/PA/5/1629/74]
Richard of Farnham [*in* DW/PA/5/1544/8]
Robert of Kingston, yeoman [DW/PA/7/7 f,265; DW/PA/5/1599/96] [*and*] [SRO; KB36/1; 1599] <Abs 471>
Robert of Lambeth - Stockwell, gent, [PRO; PCC Will 1627]
Roger of Leatherhead, bachelor [PRO; PCC Admon 1618]
Roger of Streatham, clerk [PRO; PCC Will 1527] <Abs, SAC v,52 pp,36-37>
Thomas of Swk St George, farrier [DW/PA/5/1627/85]
Thomas of Swk St Olave, yeoman [DW/PA/5/1592/49]

NORTON (NORTONE) [*continued*]
Walter of Godstone [DW/PA/7/2 f.92; 1510]
William of St Sepulchre, London; Godstone, citizen and grocer [GL; Commissary Court of London Will 1587]
William of Send - Newark Priory, clerk [PRO; PCC Will 1421]
William of Swk St George, miller [DW/PA/7/13 f.282; DW/PA/5/1643/64]
NORTRYG *see* NORTHRIDGE
NORWELL
Thomas of Swk St Saviour [DW/PA/5/1579/66]*
NORWICH
John of Carshalton, labourer [DW/PA/5/1587/70]
NORWOOD (NORTHWODD,NORWOD,NORWODE,NORWOODE,NURDETH)
Arthur of Chobham, yeoman [DW/PA/7/11 f.444; DW/PA/5/1628/75]
Joan of Chertsey, widow and midwife [PRO; PCC Will 1612]
John of Woking [PRO; PCC Will 1498]
John of Woking - Sutton [DW/PA/7/3 f.170; 1531]
Thomas of Bisley, husbandman [BM; Add.Ms 24,925 f.24v; 1544] <Abs 61>
Thomas of Chobham, husbandman [DW/PA/5/1558/206]*
Thomas of Horsell; Woking; Bisley [DW/PA/7/4 f.227; 1537]
Thomas of Woking [DW/PA/7/1 f.90; 1489] <Abs 306>
NORYS *see* NORRIS
NOTT,NOTTE *see* KNOTT
NOTTEMAN
William of Swk St Margaret, ? foster [DW/PA/7/2 f.62; 1500]
NOTTINGHAM
Thomas of Guildford; Crosthwaite, Westmorland clothier [DW/PA/5/1604/40B] <Abs U112>
see also HOWARD, earl of Nottingham
NOVELL (NOWELL)
John of Bentley, Hampshire, yeoman [DW/PA/7/10 f.293; DW/PA/5/1622/69]
John of Farnham - Wrecclesham, yeoman [HRO; 1609 B63]
Thomas of Farnham - Waverley, farmer [HRO; 1629 B44]
Thomas of Farnham, yeoman [DW/PA/7/13 f.243; DW/PA/5/1645/39]
NOWNES
Thomas of Carshalton [DW/PA/5/1561/4]
NOY
Robert of Newington [LPL; 98/1 87v; Will 1637]
NUBERY *see* NEWBURY
NUCE
Clement of St Giles Cripplegate - Red Cross Street, London, citizen and mercer [DW/PA/7/8 f.83; DW/PA/5/1609/67]
NUENS *see* NEWINS
NURDETH *see* NORWOOD
NUTBEAM
William of Esher [DW/PA/7/3 f.175; 1531]
NUTFIELD (NUTFILD)
John of Limpsfield, senior [PRO; PCC Will 1493]
NUTKIN (NUTTKIN)
John of Thames Ditton [DW/PA/7/12 f.345; DW/PA/5/1636/71]
Richard of Bermondsey, citizen and merchant tailor [DW/PA/7/13 f.396; DW/PA/5/1645/40]
NUTLEFOLD *see* NETTLEFOLD
NUTT
Francis of Lambeth [PRO; PCC Will 1593]

NUTTER

Daniel of Swk St Thomas Hospital [PRO; Admon in E315/483 p,56; 1649]

NUTTKIN *see* NUTKIN

NUTTON *see* NEWTON

NYCHOLAS *see* NICHOLAS

NYCKSON *see* NICKSON

NYCOLLES *see* NICHOLLS

NYCOLSON *see* NICHOLSON

NYE

John of Nutfield [PRO; PCC Admon 1647]

Oliver of Ockley, yeoman [HRO; 1612 B70]

Ralph of Shere, victualler [DW/PA/7/11 f,166; DW/PA/5/1625/184]

Richard of Blechingley [PRO; PCC 1648]

Richard of Ewhurst, yeoman [DW/PA/7/10 f,4; DW/PA/5/1619/85]

William of Abinger [DW/PA/7/5 f,66; 1539] <Abs 3>

William of Charlwood [LPL; 96/1882; Will 1615]

William of Horley, husbandman [DW/PA/7/11 f,505; DW/PA/5/1629/75]

NYKE

Thomas of Long Ditton, rector [HRO; 1542 B63; Reg, F p,75]

NYMYS *see* NEAMES

NYTINGALE,NYTYNGALE,NYTYNGAYLL *see* NIGHTINGALE

NYXSON *see* NIXON

OAKE (van OAKE)

Aganita of Swk St Olave, widow [DW/PA/7/13 f,301; DW/PA/5/1643/91]

OAKLEY (OAKLIES,OKELEY)

John of Abinger, husbandman, senior [PRO; PCC Will 1603] <Abs, SAC v,11 p,110>

Robert of Worplesdon [PRO; PCC Admon 1649]

OBBARDE (OBBERTES,OBERD)

Edward of Reigate [DW/PA/7/12 f,182; DW/PA/5/1633/100]

Joan of Limpsfield [DW/PA/5/1557/113]

Thomas of Tatsfield, yeoman [DW/PA/5/1583/2]*

Thomas of Tatsfield, yeoman [DW/PA/5/1587/51]

William of Limpsfield [DW/PA/7/5 f,91; 1539]

OCCARBE

Ralph of Farnham [DW/PA/7/6 f,110; DW/PA/5/1559/122]

OCKERSON

Henry of Kingston, tailor [DW/PA/7/8 f,299; DW/PA/5/1613/94]

OCCLE *see* OCKLEY

OCKEY

Francis of Swk St Saviour - Paris Garden, waterman [DW/PA/7/9 f,78; DW/PA/5/1614/82]

OCKLEY (OCCLE,OCKELYE,OCKLY,OKLEY)

Ann of Worplesdon; Woking, widow [DW/PA/7/8 f,333; DW/PA/5/1614/81]

Christian (later widow Ansell) of St Mary Woolchurch, London; Woodmansterne - 'Thethers', widow of George [GL; Commissary Court of London Will 1595]

Henry of Worplesdon, yeoman, senior [DW/PA/7/7 f,548; DW/PA/5/1606/64] <Abs 1028>

Jasper of Coulsdon, yeoman [PRO; PCC Will 1618]

John of Bermondsey, glover [DW/PA/7/11 f,259; DW/PA/5/1625/185]

OCKLEY (OCCLE,OCKELYE,OCKLY,OKLEY) [*continued*]
John of Guildford [DW/PA/7/2 f.135; 1519]
John of Guildford, innholder [DW/PA/5/1558/208]*
Robert of Worplesdon [DW/PA/7/5 f.14; 1538] <Abs 129>
Thomas of Worplesdon [DW/PA/7/2 f.156; 1521]
OCKLOND
Richard of Ewell [DW/PA/7/5 f.134; 1539]
OCKLY *see* OCKLEY
ODDYE
Thomas of Malden, labourer [DW/PA/7/11 f.107; DW/PA/5/1624/90]
ODE
Richard of Camberwell [PRO; PCC Will 1568]
Robert of Egham, clerk [PRO; PCC Will 1464]
ODIORNE
Robert of Rotherhithe, mariner [DW/PA/7/12 f.251; DW/PA/5/1635/78]
OFFINE
Robert of Swk St Olave, pointmaker [DW/PA/7/12 f.520; DW/PA/5/1638/100]
OFFLEY
William of Putney, widower [PRO; PCC Admon 1632]
OGDEN
Edward of Mitcham [DW/PA/7/8 f.344; DW/PA/5/1612/114]
OGLANDER
William of Shalford, gent. [PRO; PCC 1640]
OGLE
James of Wandsworth [DW/PA/7/4 f.52; 1533]
OKELEY *see* OAKLEY
OKING (OKYNG,OKYNGE)
Roger of Kingston - Ham, husbandman [DW/PA/5/1557/63]
Thomas of Kingston - Ham, husbandman [DW/PA/7/3 f.154; 1530]
William of Kingston - Ham; Petersham, husbandman [DW/PA/5/1550/84]
OKLEY *see* OCKLEY
OLIVER (OLLYVER,OLYVER)
Alice of Godalming - Eashing; Witley, widow of Stephen, husbandman [DW/PA/7/12 f.13; DW/PA/5/1631/77]
Digory of Mortlake [PRO; PCC Admon 1596]
Gervase of Swk St Margaret, tailor [DW/PA/7/5 f.121; 1539]
John *or* John Amor of Swk St Saviour [*Labelled on outside* John Amor, *possibly in error*] [DW/PA/5/1642/3] <Abs U260>
Richard of Godalming, innholder [HRO; 1565 B76-77] [*and*] [DW/PA/5/1565/4]
Stephen of Witley - Mousehill, husbandman [DW/PA/7/8 f.155; DW/PA/5/1611/79]
Thomas of Bermondsey [DW/PA/7/7 f.512; DW/PA/5/1605/66] <Abs 962>
William of Swk St Olave, beltmaker [DW/PA/7/11 f.150; DW/PA/5/1625/186]
OLMER
John of Battersea [PRO; PCC Admon 1613]
OLYFFE (OLYFF)
Henry of Camberwell - Peckham, yeoman [PRO; PCC Will 1603] <Abs. SAC v.11 p.109>
Joan of Bermondsey; Croydon; Addington, widow of John, alderman [PRO; PCC Will 1581]
John of Bermondsey [PRO; PCC Will 1479]
OMYDAY
John of Ewell, gardener [DW/PA/5/1574/18]

ONIONS (ONYONS)
Richard of Horley [DW/PA/7/8 f,48; DW/PA/5/1609/69]
ONSLOW (ONSLOWE)
(Sir) Edward of Surrey, knight [GMR; 97/13/1110; c1603 ?]
(Sir) Edward of Cranleigh - Knowle; Gloucestershire; Bramley; Wonersh; Dunsfold; ? Warlingham, knight [DW/PA/7/10 f,16; DW/PA/5/1615/98]
(Sir) Edward of Cranleigh - Knowle, knight [PRO; PCC Will 1615]
(Dame) Elizabeth of Cranleigh - Knowle, widow [DW/PA/7/11 f,559; DW/PA/5/1630/76]
Richard of Surrey, esq, [PRO; PCC Will 1571; GMR; 97/13/1108]
Rose of West Clandon [PRO; PCC Admon 1648]
Thomas of Cranleigh [PRO; PCC Admon 1617]
ORAM
William of Bermondsey, yeoman [DW/PA/7/8 f,306; DW/PA/5/1613/95]
ORCHARD (ARCHARD)
Hugh of Swk St Saviour, lighterman [DW/PA/7/7 f,527; DW/PA/5/1607/2] <Abs 993>
ORDER
Nicholas of Farnham - Wrecclesham; Hayden, Dorset; Stalbridge, Dorset; Odiham, Hampshire [DW/PA/5/1593/11]
ORGAN
Elizabeth of Swk St Saviour, widow [DW/PA/7/12 f,230; DW/PA/5/1634/76]
ORINGE
Robert of Epsom, labourer [DW/PA/7/6 f,271; 1560]
ORME
William of Kingston [DW/PA/7/1 f,37; 1486] <Abs 123>
ORMOND
James le Boteler, earl of, of Shere [LPL; Reg, Abp Courteney; Will 1386] <Abs SAC v,8 pp,223-224>
ORMESBY Arthur of North Ormsby, Lincolnshire; Swk St George; Beddington [PRO; PCC Will 1468] <Abs SAC v,43 pp,55-60>
ORMUNTON
John of Carshalton [DW/PA/7/1 f,64; 1487] <Abs 213>
ORPWOOD
Lionel of Lambeth [PRO; PCC Admon 1609]
ORROW (ORRO,ORROWE)
John of Send [DW/PA/7/4 f,81; 1534]
Robert of Ripley, yeoman [DW/PA/5/1576/131]
OSBORN (OSBORNE,OSBORNNE,OSBOURNE,OSBURNE)
Agnes of Thames Ditton - Chadsworth, widow [DW/PA/7/8 f,83; DW/PA/5/1609/68]
George of Farnham, yeoman [HRO; 1603 B42]
Joan of Rotherhithe [PRO; PCC Will 1597]
John of Chiddingfold, citizen and ironmonger [PRO; PCC Will 1581]
John of Chiddingfold [PRO; PCC Will 1595]
John of Chiddingfold, yeoman [DW/PA/7/12 f,282; DW/PA/5/1635/79]
Ralph of Thames Ditton - Ditton Marsh, yeoman [HRO; 1602 B37]
Richard of Haslemere [HRO; 1571 AD30]
Robert of Godalming [PRO; PCC Admon 1592]
Robert of Rotherhithe, mariner [DW/PA/5/1582/99]
Thomas of Thames Ditton - Chadsworth, weaver [DW/PA/7/7 f,398; DW/PA/5/1603/123] <Abs 739>
Thomas of Kingston, husbandman [DW/PA/7/10 f,289; DW/PA/5/1623/83]

OSBORN (OSBORNE,OSBORNNE,OSBOURNE,OSBURNE) [*continued*]
Thomas of Streatham [DW/PA/7/4 f,123; 1535]
William of Bermondsey, weaver [DW/PA/5/1562/17]
William of Headley, bachelor [DW/PA/7/11 f,193; DW/PA/5/1625/187]
OSCOMBE,OSCUMBE *see* ASCOMBE
OSIVER (OSSIVER)
John of Chessington; Malden [DW/PA/5/1561/30]
Richard of Epsom [DW/PA/5/1585/1]*
Richard of Reigate, blacksmith [DW/PA/7/13 f,480; DW/PA/5/1648/24]
OSSGARBY
Richard of Bermondsey, tanner [DW/PA/7/11 f,243; DW/PA/5/1625/188]
OTEWAYE *see* OTWAY
OTLEY *see* OTTELEY
OTMER
Thomas, alias Thomas Russell of Rotherhithe [PRO; PCC Admon 1589]
OTTAY *see* OTWAY
OTTELEY (OTLEY)
William of Camberwell [PRO; PCC Will 1497]
OTTER
John of Rotherhithe (died overseas) [PRO; PCC Admon 1648]
OTWAY (OTEWAYE,OTTAY,OTTWAY,OTTWAYE,OTWAYE,OTWEY)
Alice of Ashtead [DW/PA/7/10 f,36; DW/PA/5/1617/93]
Christopher of Kingston - Barwell [DW/PA/5/1593/198]
Humphrey of Ockham [DW/PA/5/1605/67] <Abs V158>
John of Ockham, husbandman [DW/PA/7/7 f,392; DW/PA/5/1603/124] <Abs 728>
John of Shere [DW/PA/7/2 f,117; c1517]
Richard of Alfold [DW/PA/5/1558/207]*
Richard of Leigh [DW/PA/7/2 f,139; 1520]
Robert of Beddington [DW/PA/7/12 f,59; DW/PA/5/1631/78]
Robert of Leatherhead [HRO; 1628 AD76]
Roger of Mitcham [DW/PA/5/1578/99]
Thomas of Ashtead [HRO; 1568 B161-162]
Thomas of Leatherhead, yeoman [DW/PA/7/12 f,348; DW/PA/5/1636/72]
Thomas of Mitcham, husbandman [DW/PA/7/5 f,163; 1540]
Thomas of Shere [*in* DW/PA/5/1557/75]
William of Albury, yeoman [DW/PA/7/7 f,358; DW/PA/5/1602/66] <Abs 656>
William of Ashtead [DW/PA/7/6 f,54; DW/PA/5/1559/97]
William of Cobham [DW/PA/7/12 f,240; DW/PA/5/1634/77]
OUESSTIN
James Wastell, alias James Ouesstin (? Weston) of ... [*French*]
[DW/PA/7/11 f,267; DW/PA/5/1625/199]
OUNSTED,OVENSTEED *see* OWNSTED
OVER
Joan of Kingston, widow [DW/PA/7/7 f,221; DW/PA/5/1598/61] <Abs 390>
John of Farnham, weaver [DW/PA/7/7 f,24; DW/PA/5/1595/64] <Abs 51>
OVERINGTON
John of Godalming; Hascombe [DW/PA/7/9 f,250; DW/PA/5/1617/94]
OVERNAM
Thomas of Oxted [PRO; PCC Admon 1641]
OVERY,OVERYE *see* AVERY
OVIATT
John of Wimbledon, gent, [PRO; PCC Admon 1649]
OWEN (OWYN)
(Sir) David of Surrey, knight [PRO; PCC Will 1542]

OWEN (OWYN) [*continued*]
  Edward of Egham, gent, [PRO; PCC Will 1612]
  Edy of ,,,, widow [LPL; 9; Will 1625]
  Evan of Esher [PRO; PCC Admon 1623]
  John of Croydon, husbandman [LPL; 98/1 f,87v; Will 1637]
  Lowry of Swk St Olave, widow [DW/PA/7/9 f,167; DW/PA/5/1616/99]
  Margaret of Swk St Olave, widow [DW/PA/7/7 f,449; DW/PA/5/1603/125] <Abs 851>
  Richard of Beddington - Wallington, yeoman [DW/PA/7/10 f,101; DW/PA/5/1621/91]
  Robert of Swk St Olave, loader [DW/PA/5/1588/86]
  Robert of Swk St Olave, shoemaker [DW/PA/7/11 f,33; DW/PA/5/1623/84]
  William of Putney [PRO; PCC Admon 1632]
  William of Rotherhithe (died overseas) [PRO; PCC Admon 1638]

OWFEILD
  (Sir) Samuel of Gatton; Hull, Yorkshire [PRO; PCC 1645]

OWLE
  Alice of Lambeth, widow [PRO; PCC 1637]
  Theodore of Lambeth [PRO; PCC 1634]
  William of Swk St Saviour, freemason [DW/PA/7/12 f,413; DW/PA/5/1638/99]

OWNSTED (OVENSTEED,OWNSTEED)
  Ann of Sanderstead, daughter of George (later Ann Nickoles) [GL; Archdeaconry Court of London Will 1626]
  George of Sanderstead, yeoman [DW/PA/7/11 f,298; DW/PA/5/1626/92]
  Henry of Croydon, yeoman [PRO; PCC Will 1615]
  Henry of Croydon [LPL; 98/1 f,91v; Will 1638]
  John of Westerham, Kent; Oxted [PRO; PCC Will 1608] <Abs, SAC v,13 pp,195-196>
  John of Sanderstead [PRO; PCC Will 1600]
  Malin of Croydon, widow [PRO; PCC 1634]
  Robert of Croydon [PRO; PCC Admon 1647]
  Robert of Farleigh; Oxted; Sanderstead - King's Wood, Selsdon; Croydon [DW/PA/7/6 f,26; DW/PA/5/1559/31]
  Robert of Sanderstead [DW/PA/7/11 f,145; DW/PA/5/1624/91]

OWSLEY
  Jane of Richmond [HRO; 1514 B11]

OWTEN
  Robert of Godalming [DW/PA/7/1 f,70; 1487] <Abs 230>

OXE
  Christopher of Streatham - Upper Tooting [PRO; PCC Will 1574]

OXELY *see* OXLEY

OXENBRIDGE (OXENBERTH,OXENBRIGGE)
  Edward of Croydon, yeoman [PRO; PCC Will 1629]
  John of Croydon [PRO; PCC Will 1575]
  Matthew of Croydon, innholder [PRO; PCC Will 1618]
  Matthew of Croydon [PRO; PCC Admon 1640]
  Robert of Surrey [PRO; PCC Will 1488]

OXLEY (OXELY)
  Thomas of Albury, bachelor [PRO; PCC Admon 1649]

OYEWELL
  John of Walton on the Hill, husbandman [DW/PA/5/1569/78]

OYNONS *see* ONIONS

PACE (PAYCE, PAYSE)
 Alice of Chipstead, widow [DW/PA/7/7 f.443; DW/PA/5/1603/130] <Abs 838>
 Andrew of Lambeth [DW/PA/7/12 f.52; DW/PA/5/1631/86]
 Christopher of Clapham [PRO; PCC 1642]
 Edmund of Lambeth - Lambeth Dean [PRO; PCC Admon 1649]
 Geoffrey of Chipstead, yeoman [PRO; PCC Will 1600]
 Harry of Cranleigh, husbandman [DW/PA/5/1558/216]*
 James of Lambeth [PRO; PCC Admon 1647]
 Joan of Wimbledon, widow of John [LPL; 96/1921; Will 1626]
 John of Betchworth - Brockham [DW/PA/7/7 f.629; DW/PA/5/1608/79] <Abs 1175>
 John of Chipstead, husbandman [DW/PA/7/4 f.108; 1535]
 John of Coulsdon, bachelor [PRO; PCC Admon 1627]
 Mary of Kingston, spinster [PRO; PCC 1643]
 Thomas of Streatham - Tooting Bec, husbandman [DW/PA/7/12 f.500; DW/PA/5/1638/110]
 William of Beddington, yeoman [DW/PA/7/8 f.326; DW/PA/5/1613/96]
PACIE
 Nicholas of Witley - Mousehill, yeoman, senior [DW/PA/7/13 f.478; DW/PA/5/1648/25]
PACKER
 Thomas of Woking, yeoman [DW/PA/7/13 f.487; DW/PA/5/1648/29]
PADDOCK (PADDICKE,PADIC,PADWICKE,PADYCKE)
 Agnes of Frensham, widow [DW/PA/7/4 f.129; 1535]
 John of Frensham [DW/PA/7/3 f.125; 1530]
 Thomas of Frensham [DW/PA/7/4 f.90; 1534]
 William of Frensham - Dockenfield [BM; Add.Ms 24,925 f.19r; 1544] <Abs 44>
 William of Puttenham, weaver [DW/PA/5/1582/79]
PADNOLL
 Margery of Putney, widow [LPL; 96/1924; 98/1 f.61r; Will 1634]
PAGE (PAGGE)
 Agnes of Horsell [DW/PA/5/1558/210]*
 Alice of Albury, spinster [DW/PA/7/12 f.366; DW/PA/5/1638/111]
 Amy *or* Amy Crabb, of Wotton, widow [DW/PA/7/6 f.285; 1560]
 Cicely of Swk St Olave [DW/PA/7/13 f.242; DW/PA/5/1643/67]
 Ellen of Walton on Thames [PRO; PCC Admon 1647]
 Helen of Walton on Thames, widow [PRO; PCC 1642]
 Henry of Rotherhithe, mariner [PRO; PCC Will 1625]
 Henry of Seale, husbandman [DW/PA/7/11 f.24; DW/PA/5/1623/85]
 James of Burstow, husbandman [LPL; 96/1927; Will 1634]
 Joan of Kingston, widow [DW/PA/7/7 f.397; DW/PA/5/1603/126] <Abs 736>
 John of Long Ditton - Tolworth, yeoman [DW/PA/7/13 f.272; DW/PA/5/1643/70]
 John of Frensham, yeoman, senior [DW/PA/7/7 f.549; DW/PA/5/1606/65] <Abs 1030>
 John of Kingston, citizen and ironmonger [GL; Commissary Court of London Will 1430]
 John of Shere [DW/PA/7/3 f.185; 1531]
 John of Wisley; Byfleet, yeoman [DW/PA/7/8 f.212; DW/PA/5/1612/116]
 Richard of Horsell, husbandman [HRO; 1589 AD44]
 Richard of Swk St Saviour, butcher [DW/PA/5/1593/139]
 Richard of Woking [DW/PA/7/1 f.7; 1485] <Abs 23>
 Robert of Chiddingfold [DW/PA/5/1557/121]

PAGE (PAGGE) [*continued*]

Robert of Elstead [DW/PA/5/1558/209]*

Thomas of Burstow [LPL; 98/1 ff.53v,65r; Wills 1633 *and* 1635]

Thomas of Farnham - Runfold, husbandman [DW/PA/7/6 f.241; 1561]

Thomas of Swk St Olave, weaver [DW/PA/7/12 f.413; DW/PA/5/1637/78]

William of Surrey [PRO; PCC Will 1500]

William of Betchworth [Essex Record Office; Court of the Archdeacon of Colchester; Will 1538]

William of Cranleigh, weaver [DW/PA/7/12 f.393; DW/PA/5/1637/77]

William of Wonersh, weaver [DW/PA/7/7 f.567; DW/PA/5/1606/66] <Abs 1061>

PAGET (PAGETT,PAGGETT)

Peter of Malden, mariner [GL; Archdeaconry Court of London Will 1609]

Richard of Newington [PRO; PCC Will 1582 *and* 1583]

PAGGE *see* PAGE

PAGGETT *see* PAGET

PAGGINGTON

John of Swk - near London Bridge [DW/PA/7/11 f.69; DW/PA/5/1623/86]

PAINE (PAIN,PAYNE)

Ambrose of Lambeth, clerk [PRO; PCC Will 1528]

Elizabeth of Frensham [DW/PA/5/1578/81]

Elizabeth of Frensham - Pitfold, widow [PRO; PCC 1645]

Elizabeth of Richmond, widow [PRO; PCC 1632]

Elizabeth of Swk St Mary Overy, widow [DW/PA/5/1558/211]*

George of Horley [HRO; 1573 B104]

Henry of Woking [DW/PA/5/1571/30]

Joan of Swk St Saviour - Bankside, widow [DW/PA/7/8 f.392; DW/PA/5/1612/118] <Abs U201>

Joan of Ash - Flexford [DW/PA/7/9 f.172; DW/PA/5/1616/107]

John of Chertsey, husbandman [DW/PA/5/1624/94]

John of Chobham, husbandman, senior [HRO; 1596 B56]

John of Chobham, husbandman [DW/PA/7/8 ff.156,380; DW/PA/5/1611/85]

John of Farnham - Runfold, yeoman [DW/PA/7/13 f.22; DW/PA/5/1639/101]

John of Godalming, senior [GMR; 5/2/234; Will 1544]

John of Godalming - Milford, gent. [DW/PA/5/1555/22]

John of Godalming - Enton, gent. [PRO; PCC Will 1602]

John of Witley - Enton, husbandman [DW/PA/7/10 f.191; DW/PA/5/1621/94]

John of Witley, senior [GMR; 5/14/15; Will 1647]

John of Woking [DW/PA/5/1574/22]

Lawrence of Godalming, bricklayer [DW/PA/7/9 f.226; DW/PA/5/1617/97]

Richard of Godalming [DW/PA/7/1 f.2; 1484] <Abs 4>

Richard of Witley - Enton [PRO; PCC Admon 1601]

Richard of Witley - Brook [DW/PA/7/12 f.5; DW/PA/5/1631/79]

Richard of Woking [PRO; PCC Admon 1628]

Thomas of Farnham - Runfold, yeoman [DW/PA/7/12 f.487; DW/PA/5/1638/105]

Thomas of Frensham - Pitfold [PRO; PCC Admon 1627]

Thomas of Ockley [SRO; 43/57/12; 1427]

Thomas of Thursley [DW/PA/5/1558/215]*

Thomas of Witley - Brook, yeoman [DW/PA/7/10 f.166; DW/PA/5/1621/95]

Walter of Swk St George, citizen and silk weaver [DW/PA/7/9 f.125; DW/PA/5/1615/102]

PAINTER (PAYNTER)

Alexander of Richmond, barber chirurgeon [DW/PA/7/13 f.287; DW/PA/5/1643/72]

John of Kingston, tailor [DW/PA/7/5 f.130; 1539]

PAINTER (PAYNTER) [*continued*]
John of Swk St Olave, currier [DW/PA/7/5 f.181; 1540]
PAKENHAM
John of Wimbledon; Streatham, gent. [PRO; PCC Will 1602] <Abs, SAC v.10 p.313>
Robert of Streatham - Tooting Bec [PRO; PCC Will 1552]
Robert of Streatham - Tooting Bec, esq. [PRO; PCC Will 1595]
PALFRAYE
John of Swk St Olave, baker [DW/PA/7/8 f.71; DW/PA/5/1609/70]
PALLAMIDES
... of Swk St Olave, sojourner [DW/PA/7/3 f.162; 1530]
PALLEY
Thomas *or* Thomas Pawley, of Surrey, senior [PRO; PCC Will 1558]
PALLING
Robert of Battersea [HRO; Reg. Fox 3 p.58; 1511]
PALMER (PALLMER,PALMERE,PAMER,PAWLMER,PAWMER)
Agnes of Clapham [DW/PA/7/11 f.547; DW/PA/5/1629/76]
Alexander of Swk St George [DW/PA/7/12 f.255; DW/PA/5/1634/80]
Denise of Headley [DW/PA/7/7 f.321; DW/PA/5/1600/38] <Abs 574>
Edmund of Lambeth [PRO; PCC Will 1620] [*and*] [DW/PA/7/9 f.340; DW/PA/5/1620/92] <Soame 841>
Edward of Clapham [DW/PA/7/8 f.306; DW/PA/5/1613/97]
Edward of Swk St Olave [DW/PA/7/13 f.486; DW/PA/5/1648/28]
Elizabeth of Capel, widow [DW/PA/7/11 f.423; DW/PA/5/1627/86]
Elizabeth of Godstone [PRO; PCC Admon 1623]
Frances of 'Pirton' [? Compton - Perton Hill], widow [PRO; PCC 1638]
George of Newington, widow [PRO; PCC Admon 1639]
Harry of Capel; Abinger; Ockley [DW/PA/5/1557/32]
Henry of Chelsham [DW/PA/7/10 f.188; DW/PA/5/1620/91]
Henry of Wotton, yeoman [DW/PA/7/8 f.149; DW/PA/5/1611/80]
Humphrey of Guildford, joiner [HRO; 1617 B48]
Jane of Lambeth, widow [GL; Archdeaconry Court of London Will 1563]
Joan of Epsom [DW/PA/7/8 f.221; DW/PA/5/1612/119]
Joan of Wotton [DW/PA/7/6 f.239; 1560]
John of ... [DW/PA/7/8 ff.12,141; DW/PA/5/1608/80 *and* DW/PA/5/1611/81]
John of Bermondsey [DW/PA/7/11 f.152; DW/PA/5/1625/189]
John of Capel, yeoman [DW/PA/7/7 f.527; DW/PA/5/1607/69] <Abs 995>
John of Dorking, senior [DW/PA/7/4 f.10; 1532]
John of Dorking, senior [BM; Add.Ms 24,925 f.8r; 1544] <Abs 14>
John of Dorking, husbandman [DW/PA/5/1570/73]
John of Dorking, husbandman [DW/PA/7/11 f.50; DW/PA/5/1623/87]
John of Epsom [DW/PA/7/9 f.145; DW/PA/5/1615/99]
John of Epsom - Horton [DW/PA/7/12 f.118; DW/PA/5/1632/79]
John of Horley [PRO; PCC 1647]
John of Lambeth [CCAL; 1500 f.32r]
John of Ockham [DW/PA/7/1 f.18; 1485] <Abs 61>
John of Swk St Saviour, glazier [DW/PA/7/13 f.234; DW/PA/5/1642/67]
Juliana, alias Juliana Smythe, of Send, widow [DW/PA/7/1 f.100; 1489] <Abs 325>
Lawrence of Lambeth - South Lambeth [PRO; PCC Admon 1593]
Margaret of Swk St Saviour, late wife of Thomas [DW/PA/7/11 f.441; DW/PA/5/1628/76]
Margery of ...., widow [DW/PA/7/7 f.478; DW/PA/5/1604/42] <Abs 902>
(Dame) Martha of Camberwell - Peckham, widow [PRO; PCC Admon 1620]

PALMER (PALLMER,PALMERE,PAMER,PAWLMER,PAWMER) [*continued*]
Phillip of Wonersh [DW/PA/7/1 f,2; 1484] <Abs 5>
Richard of Leatherhead [PRO; PCC Will 1551]
Richard of Swk St George, yeoman [DW/PA/5/1582/5]
Richard of Wotton [DW/PA/7/8 f,377; DW/PA/5/1612/120]
Robert of Cobham, husbandman [DW/PA/7/8 f,354; DW/PA/5/1612/121]
Robert of Elstead [DW/PA/7/6 f,267; 1560]
Robert of Epsom, yeoman [DW/PA/7/8 f,4; DW/PA/5/1595/65] <Abs 11>
Robert of Farnham, yeoman, senior [DW/PA/7/11 f,70; DW/PA/5/1623/88]
Roger of Lambeth [PRO; PCC Will 1603] <Abs, SAC v,11 p,117>
Roger of Rotherhithe (died overseas) [PRO; PCC Admon 1636]
Roger of Shalford [DW/PA/7/4 f,210; 1537]
Simon of Lambeth [PRO; PCC Admon 1600]
Simon of Lambeth [PRO; PCC Admon 1622]
Thomas of Battersea, citizen and goldsmith [PRO; PCC Will 1614]
Thomas of Carshalton [DW/PA/7/2 f,124; 1518]
Thomas of Croydon, citizen and fishmonger [GL; Commissary Court of London 1404]
Thomas of Guildford St Mary, shearman [DW/PA/5/1593/21]
Thomas of Mitcham [DW/PA/5/1557/69]
Thomas of Swk St Olave [DW/PA/7/12 f,98; DW/PA/5/1632/77]
Thomas of Swk St Thomas [DW/PA/5/1578/102]
William of Great Bookham, yeoman [DW/PA/7/13 f,34; DW/PA/5/1639/97]
William of Clapham [DW/PA/7/12 f,446; DW/PA/5/1639/103]
William of Dorking [PRO; PCC Admon 1648]
William of Shalford; Bramley [DW/PA/7/1 f,89; 1488] <Abs 300>
William of Walton on the Hill, husbandman [DW/PA/7/7 f,521; DW/PA/5/1606/67] <Abs 980>
William of Wonersh [DW/PA/7/3 f,140; 1530]
William of Wotton, husbandman [DW/PA/5/1558/214]*

PALTOCKE
Agnes of Kingston, spinster [DW/PA/7/8 f,128; DW/PA/5/1610/96]
Dorothy of Kingston, widow [PRO; PCC Will 1598]
Edward of Kingston [PRO; PCC Admon 1613]
Robert of Kingston; Cobham, mercer [DW/PA/7/9 f,25A; DW/PA/5/1614/83]
Thomas of Kingston, mercer [PRO; PCC Will 1603] <Abs, SAC v,11 p,108>
Timothy of Kingston, draper [DW/PA/7/10 f,236; DW/PA/5/1621/92]
William of Kingston, mercer [PRO; PCC Will 1603] <Abs, SAC v,11 p,127>

PAMER *see* PALMER

PAMPHLYN
Thomas of Newington [LPL; Reg, Abp Abbot i f,271r; Admon 1615]

PAN (de PAN)
Marguerite, or Marguerite de Pau, of Swk St Olave, widow of Gilbert Tout le Monde [*French*] [DW/PA/5/1593/144]

PANCRAS (PANKRAS)
John of Newdigate [DW/PA/7/2 f,133; 1516]

PANEFOLD *see* PENFOLD

PANINGFORD *see* PANNINGFORD

PANKHURST (PENKERST,PENKHEATH)
Robert of Swk St Saviour, citizen and merchant tailor [DW/PA/5/1576/92]
Thomas of Shalford [DW/PA/7/1 f,6; 1485] <Abs 20>

PANKRAS *see* PANCRAS

PANKRIDGE (PANKRIDG)
Alice of Ewell [PRO; PCC Admon 1604]

PANNINGFOLD (PANINGFORD)
Joan of Dorking, widow [PRO; PCC Will 1604] <Abs, SAC v,11 p,285>
William of Dorking, yeoman [DW/PA/7/7 f,412; DW/PA/5/1603/127] <Abs 767>
PANSON
John of Swk St Margaret [DW/PA/7/5 f,86; 1539]
PANTALL
Lydia of Newington [PRO; PCC Admon 1639]
William of Bermondsey [DW/PA/7/12 f,301; DW/PA/5/1635/88]
PAPRILL
John of Rotherhithe, citizen and merchant tailor, esq, [PRO; PCC 1640]
PAR' *see* PARR
PARBEN (PARBYN)
John of Swk St Olave, yeoman [DW/PA/7/7 f,508; DW/PA/5/1605/69] <Abs 952>
Mary, alias Mary Barnaby of Swk St Olave, widow [DW/PA/7/7 f,550; DW/PA/5/1606/68] <Abs 1031>
PARCKHURSTE *see* PARKHURST
PARCYVALL *see* PERCIVALL
PARHAM
Judith, alias Judith Lardge, alias Judith Highlord of Camberwell [PRO; PCC Admon 1627]
PARIS *see* PARRIS
PARISH,PARISHE *see* PARRISH
PARKAR *see* PARKER
PARKE (PARKS)
George of Godalming [DW/PA/7/6 f,151; DW/PA/5/1559/179]
John of Swk St Olave [DW/PA/5/1591/75]
Mary of Camberwell [PRO; PCC Will 1563]
Richard of Reigate [PRO; PCC Admon 1648]
Thomas of Godalming - Catteshall, yeoman [DW/PA/7/12 f,128; DW/PA/5/1632/80]
William of Egham [DW/PA/7/3 f,191; 1531]
William of Richmond [HRO; 1600 B42]
PARKEHURST,PARKEHURSTE,PARKEHUSTE *see* PARKHURST
PARKER (PARKAR,PARKERE)
Agnes of Farnham, widow [DW/PA/5/1591/92]
Alice of Stoke Dabernon [DW/PA/7/6 f,150; DW/PA/5/1559/214]
Edward of Guildford St Mary, gent, [DW/PA/7/13 f,423; DW/PA/5/1645/44]
Elizabeth of Guildford; Tewin, Hertfordshire [PRO; PCC 1648]
Elizabeth of Sutton [DW/PA/7/13 f,347; DW/PA/5/1644/2]
George of Lambeth - Stockwell, yeoman [DW/PA/5/1587/71]
George of Streatham [PRO; PCC Admon 1621]
Gregory of Bramley, gent, [DW/PA/5/1588/18]
Henry of Cobham, gent, [PRO; PCC Will 1575]
Henry of Farnham; Odiham, Hampshire; Alton, Hampshire, yeoman [HRO; 1589 B43]
Joan of Swk St Saviour, widow [DW/PA/7/8 f,143; DW/PA/5/1611/82]
Joan of Wandsworth; Kingston; Battersea, widow of John, citizen and freemason [GL; Commissary Court of London Will 1486]
John of Lambeth - Kennington [DW/PA/5/1586/37]*
John of Morden, senior [PRO; PCC Will 1494]
Josias of Swk St Olave [DW/PA/7/11 f,391; DW/PA/5/1626/93]
Margaret of Frensham, widow of William [PRO; PCC 1647]
Matthew of Lambeth, gent, [PRO; PCC Will 1574]
Matthew of Lambeth, archbishop of Canterbury [PRO; PCC Will 1575]

PARKER (PARKAR, PARKERE) [*continued*

Nicholas of ... [DW/PA/7/8 f.143; DW/PA/5/1611/83]
Nicholas of Beddington - Wallington, husbandman [DW/PA/5/1593/165]
Nicholas of Betchworth - Brockham, husbandman [HRO; 1571 B137]
Nicholas of Carshalton, yeoman [DW/PA/7/13 f.177; DW/PA/5/1641/108]
Nicholas of Epsom, carpenter [DW/PA/7/7 f.73; DW/PA/5/1596/44] <Abs 136>
Parnell of Sutton [DW/PA/5/1558/212]
Robert of Newington [LPL; 98/1 f.76v; Will 1636]
Robert of Swk St George [HRO; Reg. Wyk 2 p.253; Will 1391]
Thomas of Ewell, husbandman [HRO; 1521 B24]
Thomas of Rotherhithe [PRO; PCC Admon 1627]
Thomas of Streatham, gent., senior [PRO; PCC Will 1608] <Abs. SAC v.12 p.103>
William of Bermondsey, brewer [DW/PA/7/9 f.232; DW/PA/5/1617/95]
William of Newington - Walworth, citizen and draper [GL; Commissary Court of London Will 1442]
William of Swk St Olave [DW/PA/5/1563/100]
William of Tatsfield, rector [DW/PA/7/13 f.466; DW/PA/5/1648/26]

PARKHURST (PARKEHURST, PARKEHURSTE, PARKEHUSTE, PARKESSE, PARKESTE)

Damaris of Shere - 'Grites', spinster [DW/PA/7/13 f.74; DW/PA/5/1641/102]
Edward of Shere, yeoman [DW/PA/7/12 f.281; DW/PA/5/1636/76]
Edward of Shere [PRO; PCC Admon 1649]
George of Guildford Holy Trinity, mercer, junior [DW/PA/7/5 f.175; 1540]
George of Shere [PRO; PCC Admon 1579]
Harry *or* Henry of Guildford Holy Trinity [DW/PA/5/1579/71]*
Henry of Woking [DW/PA/7/9 f.332; DW/PA/5/1620/88]
John of Woking [DW/PA/5/1558/213]*
John of West Clandon [DW/PA/7/2 f.194; 1524]
John of Guildford, bishop of Norwich [PRO; PCC Will 1576]
John of Guildford St Mary, servant to Richard Ford [DW/PA/5/1574/1]
John of Leatherhead [DW/PA/7/6 f.110; DW/PA/5/1559/98]
John of East Molesey, yeoman [DW/PA/7/11 f.7; DW/PA/5/1622/70]
John of Shere, clothier [DW/PA/5/1563/89]
John of Shere [PRO; PCC Will 1581]
Margaret of Godalming, widow [HRO; 1587 B60]
Margaret of Shere [DW/PA/7/9 f.166; DW/PA/5/1616/106]
Nicholas of West Clandon [DW/PA/7/7 f.21; DW/PA/5/1595/66] <Abs 44>
Richard of Godalming, shearman [DW/PA/7/7 f.55; DW/PA/5/1596/45] <Abs 105>
Robert of Godalming [DW/PA/5/1568/40]
(Sir) Robert of Pyrford, knight, alderman and citizen [PRO; PCC 1637]
Robert of Shere, yeoman [DW/PA/7/7 f.215; DW/PA/5/1598/65] <Abs 384>
Robert of Shere; East Horsley; Leatherhead, yeoman [DW/PA/7/7 f.310; DW/PA/5/1600/39] <Abs 552>
William of Ewell [DW/PA/7/11 f.137; DW/PA/5/1624/92]

PARKIN, PARKINES, PARKINS *see* PERKINS

PARKINSON (PERKINSON)

Henry of Hayes, Kent; Croydon [PRO; PCC 1630]
John of Croydon, yeoman [PRO; PCC Will 1607] <Abs. SAC v.12 pp.208-209>

PARKS *see* PARKE

PARKYNS *see* PERKINS

PARLABYE

Ralph of Swk St Olave [DW/PA/7/11 f.245; DW/PA/5/1625/190]

P'ARMARANT
  Henry of Swk St Olave, linen weaver [DW/PA/5/1563/95]
PARMITER (PERMETTER)
  George of St Ann Blackfriars, London; Egham [PRO; PCC Admon 1636]
  William of Swk St Saviour, tailor [DW/PA/5/1571/61]
PARNELL
  Bartholomew of Bermondsey [PRO; PCC Admon 1629]
  Bartholomew of Bermondsey [PRO; PCC Admon 1642]
  John of Wandsworth, yeoman [PRO; PCC Will 1612]
PARR (PAR',PARRE)
  Thomas of Bermondsey, linen weaver [DW/PA/7/12 f,26; DW/PA/5/1631/82]
  William of Deptford - Hatcham; Greenwich, Kent [BM; Add,Ms 24,925 f,11v; 1544] <Abs 21>
  William of Wandsworth, husbandman [DW/PA/7/2 f,60; 1500]
PARRAT *see* PARROTT
PARRE *see* PARR
PARRIS
  Margaret of Swk St Olave, widow [DW/PA/7/12 f,337; DW/PA/5/1636/78]
PARRISH (PARISH,PARISHE)
  Francis of Cobham, yeoman [DW/PA/7/9 f,288; 1618]
  John of Limpsfield [DW/PA/7/7 f,490; DW/PA/5/1604/43] <Abs 927>
  Ralph of Epsom, labourer [DW/PA/7/7 f,457; DW/PA/5/1603/128] <Abs 862>
  Thomas of Cobham [DW/PA/7/11 f,273; DW/PA/5/1626/94]
  Thomas of Cobham [PRO; PCC 1645]
PARROTT (PARRAT,PERROTT)
  Amy of Sutton, widow [DW/PA/7/13 f,500; DW/PA/5/1649/13]
  Richard of Richmond, fisherman [DW/PA/5/1555/37]
  Robert of Merton [DW/PA/7/2 f,118; 1517]
PARRY
  David of Richmond, bachelor [PRO; PCC Will 1613]
  Knevett of Swk St Olave, bandmaster [DW/PA/5/1603/129] <Abs U83>
  Robert of London, citizen and leatherseller [DW/PA/7/8 f,336; DW/PA/5/1612/122]
  Thomas of Kingston [PRO; PCC 1648]
PARSONS (PARSON,PARSONE,PARSONES,PARSSON,PERSON)
  Ann of Guildford, widow of Thomas [DW/PA/7/13 f,336; 1644]
  Elizabeth of Molesey [PRO; PCC 1637]
  George of Swk St Olave, yeoman [DW/PA/5/1588/89]
  Henry of Swk St Saviour - Bankside, waterman [DW/PA/7/7 f,95; 1596] <Abs 175>
  Henry of Swk St George, yeoman [DW/PA/5/1624/93]
  Joan, alias Joan Glover of Godalming [DW/PA/7/4 f,232; 1537]
  John of Swk St George [DW/PA/5/1587/41]
  John of Burstow, yeoman [LPL; 96/1965; Will 1628]
  John of East Molesey, husbandman [HRO; 1587 B61]
  Mary, alias Mary Foyce of Guildford [PRO; PCC Admon 1646]
  Richard of Albury, husbandman [DW/PA/5/1588/79]
  Robert of Cobham, yeoman, senior [PRO; PCC Will 1606] <Abs, SAC v,12 p,199>
  Robert of Godstone, yeoman [DW/PA/5/1580/12]
  Robert of Haslemere [PRO; PCC Admon 1608]
  Robert of East Molesey, husbandman [DW/PA/7/7 f,29; DW/PA/5/1595/67] <Abs 60>
  Thomas of Albury, husbandman [HRO; 1639 AD156]

PARSONS (PARSON,PARSONE,PARSONES,PARSSON,PERSON) [*continued*
Thomas of Bramley - Gosden, yeoman [DW/PA/7/9 f,88; DW/PA/5/1615/100]
Thomas of West Horsley, clerk [PRO; PCC Will 1518]
Ursula of Swk St Saviour, widow [DW/PA/7/7 f,505; DW/PA/5/1605/70] <Abs 945>
Walter of East Molesey, labourer [DW/PA/7/8 f,349; DW/PA/5/1612/123]
William of Albury [HRO; 1566 B153]
William, alias William Fyschar of Lingfield - Dormansland [DW/PA/7/3 f,199; 1532]
William of Swk St Saviour, tallow chandler [DW/PA/7/11 f,338; DW/PA/5/1625/191]

PARTIN
William of Streatham, yeoman [DW/PA/7/7 f,5; DW/PA/5/1595/68] <Abs 13>

PARTRIDGE
... [see back of will DW/PA/5/1592/19]*
Nicholas of Kingston, cordwainer [DW/PA/5/1578/2]
Thomas of Kingston, mercer [DW/PA/5/1588/46]

PARVISH (PARVISHE,PARVYS,PARVYSHE,PURVOCHE,PURWYCHE)
Agnes of Stoke next Guildford - Watford [PRO; PCC Will 1601] <Abs, SAC v,10 p,148>
Ann of Shalford, widow of Henry, brickmaker [DW/PA/7/7 f,252; DW/PA/5/1599/50] <Abs 444>
George of Stoke next Guildford - Watford, gent, [PRO; PCC Will 1587]
Harry of Guildford Holy Trinity [DW/PA/7/4 f,230; 1537]
Henry of Stoke next Guildford, citizen and haberdasher [PRO; PCC Will 1593]
Joan of Stoke next Guildford [PRO; PCC Will 1597]
John of Stoke next Guildford [DW/PA/7/5 f,58; 1539] <Abs 110>
John of Stoke next Guildford [*in* DW/PA/5/1571/22]
Juliana of Farnham [DW/PA/7/3 f,123; c1530]
Thomas of Godalming [PRO; PCC Will 1510]
Thomas of Shalford, yeoman [DW/PA/5/1581/52]
Thomas of Stoke next Guildford, esq, [PRO; PCC Will 1588]

PARYSY
John of ... [*French*] [DW/PA/5/1592/102A]

PASCE
John of Leatherhead [DW/PA/5/1582/76]

PASH
Richard of Windlesham - Bagshot [PRO; PCC Admon 1648]

PATCHING (PATCHINGE)
James of Camberwell - Peckham, gent, [PRO; PCC Will 1602] <Abs, SAC v,10 pp,307-308>
Thomas of Leigh; Horsham, Sussex, yeoman [DW/PA/7/8 f,317; DW/PA/5/1611/84]

PATE
John of Richmond; Mortlake; London, yeoman [DW/PA/7/4 f,154; 1536]
William of Swk St Olave, clerk [DW/PA/5/1550/69]

PATENSON *see* PATTINSON

PATFOLD (PATFOULD,PATTEFOLLDE)
John of Woking [HRO; 1620 AD67]
Richard of Thursley, yeoman [DW/PA/7/11 f,587; DW/PA/5/1630/77]
Thomas of Thursley, shearman [DW/PA/5/1557/31]
William of Thursley [DW/PA/7/11 f,200; DW/PA/5/1625/192]

PATINSON *see* PATTINSON

PATRICK (PATRICKE)
  Giles of Egham [PRO; PCC Will 1629]
  Giles of Egham [PRO; PCC 1631]
  Sybil of Egham [PRO; PCC Admon 1640]
  Thomas of Swk St Saviour [DW/PA/7/11 f.557; DW/PA/5/1630/78]
  William of Bermondsey, cutler [DW/PA/7/9 f.240; DW/PA/5/1617/96]
PATTEFOLLDE *see* PATFOLD
PATTEN (PATTIN,PATYN)
  Agnes of Ewell [DW/PA/7/1 ff.4,5; 1484] <Abs 13>
  Baldwin of Swk St Mary Overy [DW/PA/7/11 f.82; DW/PA/5/1623/90]
  Joan of Swk St Saviour [DW/PA/5/1581/15]
PATTESON *see* PATTINSON
PATTIN *see* PATTEN
PATTINSON (PATENSON,PATTESON,PUTENSON)
  Elizabeth of Swk St Olave, widow [DW/PA/7/9 f.139; DW/PA/5/1615/101]
  Nicholas of Swk St Olave, mariner [DW/PA/7/8 f.310; DW/PA/5/1613/98]
  Peter of Carshalton, tanner [DW/PA/7/10 f.102; DW/PA/5/1621/93]
  Thomas of ... [DW/PA/7/11 f.60; DW/PA/5/1623/89]
  Thomas of Carshalton, tanner [DW/PA/5/1592/37]
PATTY (PATY)
  Robert of Swk St Margaret, bowyer [DW/PA/7/4 f.161; 1536]
PATYN *see* PATTEN
PAU (de PAU)
  Marguerite, alias Marguerite de Pan, of Swk St Olave, widow of Gilbert
    Tout le Monde [DW/PA/5/1593/144]
PAUL (PAULE,PAWLE)
  (Sir) George of Lambeth - Water Lambeth, knight [PRO; PCC 1635]
  Joan of Godstone, widow [DW/PA/7/2 f.21; 1491]
  (Dame) Joan of Lambeth - Water Lambeth, widow of (Sir) George, knight
    [DW/PA/7/11 f.300; DW/PA/5/1626/95]
  John of Blechingley [DW/PA/7/1 f.47; 1487] <Abs 156>
  John of Lambeth, bachelor [PRO; PCC Admon 1623]
  John of Mortlake [PRO; PCC Admon 1628]
  Richard of Lambeth [PRO; PCC Admon 1625]
  Thomas of Swk St Saviour, blacksmith [DW/PA/7/12 f.193;
    DW/PA/5/1633/104]
PAUSON
  John of Swk St Margaret [DW/PA/7/5 f.86; 1539]
PAVIATT (PAVIAT)
  Thomas of Croydon [PRO; PCC Admon 1597]
  Thomas of Croydon [PRO; PCC Admon 1614]
  Ursula of Croydon [PRO; PCC Admon 1597]
PAWLE *see* PAULE
PAWLEY
  Thomas *or* Thomas Palley, of Surrey, senior [PRO; PCC Will 1558]
  Thomas of Nutfield [PRO; PCC 1646]
PAWLIN
  Richard of Swk St Saviour, husbandman [DW/PA/7/11 f.570; DW/PA/5/1630/79]
PAWLMER,PAWMER *see* PALMER
PAXMAN
  William of Kingston [PRO; PCC Will 1457]
PAYCE *see* PACE

PAYLOUR
  Agnes of Banstead [PRO; PCC Will 1489] [*This entry which appears in the PCC calendar as Agnes Taylor, widow of Peter Paylour is probably a misprint.*]
PAYNE *see* PAINE
PAYNTER *see* PAINTER
PAYSE *see* PACE
PAYTOW *see* PETO
PAYTON *see* PEYTON
PEACH (PECCHE,PECHE)
  Elizabeth of Swk St Olave, widow of Edward [DW/PA/7/12 f.298; DW/PA/5/1636/77]
  Richard of Swk St Margaret, yeoman [DW/PA/7/2 f.128; 1518]
  (Sir) William of Surrey, knight [PRO; PCC Will 1488]
PEACOCK (PEACOCKE,PEICOCKE,PEYCOKE)
  Elizabeth of Swk St Saviour, widow [DW/PA/7/8 f.389; DW/PA/5/1613/99]
  George of Swk St Olave, victualler [DW/PA/7/11 f.395; DW/PA/5/1626/96]
  Isaac of Chertsey, husbandman [DW/PA/7/10 f.162; DW/PA/5/1621/96]
  Leonard of Newington [PRO; PCC Will 1574]
  Radegund of Swk St George, widow [DW/PA/7/7 f.148; DW/PA/5/1597/76] <Abs 275>
  Richard of Long Ditton - Tolworth [DW/PA/7/12 f.295; DW/PA/5/1635/86]
  Richard of Swk St George, victualler [DW/PA/7/10 f.208; DW/PA/5/1620/89]
  Robert of Swk St George, fletcher [DW/PA/7/7 f.115; DW/PA/5/1597/78] <Abs 212>
  Thomas of East Molesey, citizen and carpenter [PRO; PCC Will 1583]
  Thomas of Newington, stuff weaver [GL; Archdeaconry Court of London Will 1617]
  William of Swk St George, falconer [DW/PA/7/11 f.62; DW/PA/5/1623/91]
  William of Swk St Saviour [DW/PA/5/1558/217]*
PEAKE
  John of Swk St Olave [DW/PA/7/13 ff.266,276; DW/PA/5/1643/68]
PEAR (PEARE)
  John of Rotherhithe (died overseas) [PRO; PCC Admon 1642]
  Richard of Camberwell - Dulwich [PRO; PCC 1648]
PEARCE (PEARSE,PEERS,PEERSE,PEIRCE,PEIRSE,PERES)
  Dorothy of Blechingley [PRO; PCC Will 1629]
  Edward of Bermondsey, merchant tailor [DW/PA/7/13 f.13; DW/PA/5/1639/99]
  Elizabeth of Cranleigh [*in* DW/PA/5/1546/75]
  Ellen of Carshalton, widow [PRO; PCC Will 1614]
  Grace of Lambeth, widow [DW/PA/7/11 f.312; DW/PA/5/1626/97]
  John of Carshalton, clerk [DW/PA/7/8 f.210; DW/PA/5/1612/125]
  John of Horley [DW/PA/7/4 f.80; 1534]
  Stephen of Richmond, etc., gent., senior [PRO; PCC 1630] <Scroope 897>
  Thomas, alias Thomas Webbe of Mitcham, husbandman [DW/PA/7/5 f.103; 1539]
  William of Dorking, yeoman [DW/PA/5/1568/27]
PEARE *see* PEAR
PEAREMAN
  Joan of Swk St George, widow [DW/PA/7/9 f.7; DW/PA/5/1615/103]
PEARSE *see* PEARCE
PEARSON (PEERSON,PEIRSON,PERESON,PYERSON)
  Alice of Swk St Olave, servant to Thomas Mawe [DW/PA/5/1575/8]
  Christopher of Peper Harow, rector [HRO; Reg. D p.247; 1530]
  John of Guildford [PRO; PCC Will 1535]

PEARSON (PEERSON,PEIRSON,PERESON,PYERSON) [*continued*
  Richard of Frensham [HRO; 1559 U239-240]
  Richard of Frensham, tailor [HRO; 1598 B31]
  Thomas of Camberwell - Peckham [PRO; PCC Will 1492]
  William of Frensham - Pitfold; Haslemere, weaver [HRO; 1613 B51]
PEART
  James of Titsey - Cheverells, gent. [PRO; PCC 1646]
PEASMAN
  Ann of Bermondsey, widow [DW/PA/7/12 f.358; DW/PA/5/1636/79]
PEATE
  Edmund of Swk St Saviour - Bankside [DW/PA/7/11 f.481; DW/PA/5/1628/77]
PECARD
  Richard of Capel [DW/PA/7/1 f.25; 1485] <Abs 84>
PECCHE,PECHE *see* PEACH
PECKE
  Arnold of Godalming, husbandman [DW/PA/5/1576/125]
  Ellen of Godalming - Farncombe, widow [DW/PA/5/1622/71]
  John of Godalming [DW/PA/7/3 f.116; 1529]
  John of Godalming, yeoman [DW/PA/5/1575/35]
  Lawrence of Godalming, shearman [DW/PA/7/10 f.115; DW/PA/5/1619/86]
  Richard of Godalming [DW/PA/5/1568/36]
  Thomas of Godalming - Farncombe, yeoman, senior [DW/PA/7/10 f.127;
    DW/PA/5/1620/90]
PECKAVER
  Michael of Charlwood, gent. [PRO; PCC Will 1613]
PECKHAM
  (Sir) Edmund of Croydon, knight [PRO; PCC Will 1564]
PECKSALL
  (Sir) Richard of Surrey, knight [PRO; PCC Will 1571]
PEEPER (Le PEEPER)
  John of Camberwell - Peckham [PRO; PCC 1645]
PEERLESS
  Henry of Lingfield [PRO; PCC Will 1642]
PEERS,PEERSE *see* PEARCE
PEERSEY *see* PERCY
PEERSON *see* PEARSON
PEETER *see* PETERS
PEICOCKE *see* PEACOCK
PEILLIT
  Edward of Lambeth, blacksmith *or* nailer [DW/PA/7/8 f.145;
    DW/PA/5/1611/86]
PEIRCE,PEIRSE *see* PEARCE
PEIRSON *see* PEARSON
PEITO,PEITOE *see* PETO
PELE
  Thomas of Swk St Margaret, tailor [DW/PA/7/4 f.2; 1532]
PELHAM
  Anthony of Surrey [PRO; PCC Will 1566]
PELL
  Giles of Rotherhithe [PRO; PCC Will 1648]
  Peter of Lambeth, clothier [DW/PA/7/11 f.81; 1623]
PEMBRIDGE (PEMBRIGGE,PENBRYGGE)
  Joan of Lambeth [PRO; PCC Will 1484]
  William of Lambeth [PRO; PCC Will 1480]

PEN *see* PENN
PENBRYGGE *see* PEMBRIDGE
PENCKNEY *see* PINKNEY
PENCOSTE
  Henry of Long Ditton, matchmaker [HRO; 1598 B33]
PENDLEBERRY (PYNDYLBERY)
  James of Swk St George [DW/PA/7/5 f.230; 1541]
  William of Swk St George [DW/PA/7/7 f.436; DW/PA/5/1603/132] <Abs 824>
PENDLETON
  Elizabeth of Swk St Olave, spinster [DW/PA/7/8 f.29; DW/PA/5/1608/81]
  Ralph of Swk St George, yeoman [DW/PA/7/7 f.410; DW/PA/5/1603/131] <Abs 759>
PENFOLD (PANEFOLD,PENFOULD,PINFOLD,PONYFOLD)
  Agnes of Charlwood, widow [LPL; 96/1997; Will 1629]
  Agnes of Chiddingfold, widow [DW/PA/7/11 f.497; DW/PA/5/1629/77]
  Christopher of Dorking, yeoman [DW/PA/5/1587/52]
  James of Charlwood, yeoman [LPL; 96/1996; Will 1614]
  John of Dorking [DW/PA/5/1556/15]
  Richard of Newington [PRO; PCC Admon 1612]
PENIALE *see* PENNYALE
PENICODE *see* PENNYCOD
PENKERST,PENKHEATH *see* PANKHURST
PENN (PEN,PENNE)
  Edmund of Walton on Thames [DW/PA/5/1550/65]
  Harry of Chobham [DW/PA/5/1563/111]
  Henry of Thorpe, yeoman [DW/PA/7/12 f.166; DW/PA/5/1633/101]
  John of Send, husbandman [DW/PA/7/13 f.494; DW/PA/5/1649/12]
  John of Woking, husbandman [HRO; 1596 B57]
  Ralph of Surrey, gent. [PRO; PCC Will 1486]
  Ralph of Swk St Saviour, apothecary [DW/PA/7/8 f.245; DW/PA/5/1613/100]
PENNARD (PENNERD)
  Richard of Putney - Roehampton [LPL; 96/2004; Will 1627]
PENNE *see* PENN
PENNER
  Jane of Kingston [DW/PA/7/13 f.196; DW/PA/5/1641/112]
PENNERD *see* PENNARD
PENNICOD,PENNICOTT *see* PENNYCOD
PENNYFATHER
  Matthew of Blechingley, minister of the Word of God [DW/PA/5/1602/68] <Abs U56>
PENNING (PYNING)
  Henry *or* Thomas of Frensham [HRO; 1604 B50]
  Richard of Frensham, yeoman [HRO; 1632 B46]
  Thomas *or* Henry of Frensham [HRO; 1604 B50]
PENNINGTON (PENNYNGTON)
  Henry of Kingston, draper [DW/PA/5/1555/38]
  James of Swk St Saviour, shoemaker [DW/PA/7/8 f.228; DW/PA/5/1612/126]
  Joan of Kingston, widow [DW/PA/5/1555/47]
PENNY (PENYE)
  Joan of Woking, widow [DW/PA/5/1545/7]
PENNYALE (PENIALE,PENNYALL)
  Humphrey of Lingfield [DW/PA/7/9 f.290; 1618]
  Richard of Lingfield, yeoman [DW/PA/7/8 f.283; DW/PA/5/1613/101]
  Thomas of Godstone, weaver [PRO; PCC Will 1569]

PENNYCOD (PENICODE,PENNICOTT,PENYCOD,PENYCODE)
Agnes of Elstead, widow [DW/PA/7/7 f.185; DW/PA/5/1598/66] <Abs 337>
John of Chiddingfold [DW/PA/7/4 f.84; 1534]
John of Haslemere; Witley; Godalming, yeoman [DW/PA/7/9 f.91; DW/PA/5/1616/129]
Stephen of Elstead [HRO; 1589 AD45]
Stephen of Haslemere [PRO; PCC Admon 1596]
Thomas of Chiddingfold; Haslemere, yeoman [DW/PA/5/1550/28]
PENNYNGTON *see* PENNINGTON
PENROSE
Walter of Rotherhithe, mariner in the ship *Dolphin* (slain in war with the Turks) [DW/PA/7/9 f.213; DW/PA/5/1617/98]
PENVYE
Thomas of Chiddingfold, miller [HRO; 1574 B127]
PENWARTHEN (PENWORTHAM)
George of Rotherhithe [PRO; PCC Admon 1618]
Henry of Lambeth; Rochester St Nicholas, Kent; Bishopsbourne, Kent; Crayford, Kent, clerk, registrar to the archbishop of Canterbury [LPL; Reg. Abp Chichele i f.472; c1441]
PENYCOD,PENYCODE *see* PENNYCOD
PENYE *see* PENNY
PEPPER (PEPER,PEPYR)
John of Swk, brewer [CCAL; 1500 f.38r]
Margaret of Rotherhithe, widow [DW/PA/7/7 f.430; DW/PA/5/1603/133] <Abs 812>
Thomas of Godstone [PRO; PCC 1634]
William of Burstow [PRO; PCC Admon 1648]
William of Rotherhithe [DW/PA/7/7 f.415; DW/PA/5/1603/134] <Abs 776>
see also PEEPER
PERCHE
Margaret of Bermondsey [HRO; Reg. Fox 3 p.66; 1515]
PERCIVALL (PARCYVALL,PERSIVALL)
Anthony of Headley, yeoman [DW/PA/7/10 f.52; 1619]
Edward of Ewhurst, clerk [DW/PA/5/1579/67]*
Elizabeth of Richmond, widow [PRO; PCC Will 1595]
John of Headley, warrener [DW/PA/7/7 f.258; DW/PA/5/1599/51] <Abs 455>
Margaret of Ewhurst, spinster [DW/PA/5/1580/33]
PERCY (PEERSEY,PERESYE,PERSYE)
Henry of Lambeth [PRO; PCC Will 1587]
Joan of Swk St Olave, widow [DW/PA/5/1579/70]*
John of Swk St Margaret [DW/PA/7/4 f.25; 1532]
Simon of Swk St Olave [DW/PA/5/1579/69]*
Thomas of Swk St Mary Overy [DW/PA/7/4 f.168A; 1536]
PERES *see* PEARCE
PERESON *see* PEARSON
PERESYE *see* PERCY
PERIAR,PERIARE *see* PERRIER
PERIN *see* PERRIN
PERIOR *see* PERRIER
PERKINS (PARKIN,PARKINES,PARKINS,PARKYNS,PERKENS,PERKYN)
Alan of Newington [PRO; PCC 1632]
Harry of Richmond; Twickenham, Middlesex; Hounslow, Middlesex, gent. [DW/PA/7/4 f.12; 1532]
Henry of Petersham [DW/PA/7/9 f.74; DW/PA/5/1614/84]

PERKINS (PARKIN,PARKINES,PARKINS,PARKYNS,PERKENS,PERKYN) [*continued*
Henry of Petersham, fisherman [DW/PA/7/13 f.62; DW/PA/5/1641/103]
Henry of Richmond [DW/PA/5/1546/29]
Henry of Swk St George, silk weaver [DW/PA/7/13 f.313; DW/PA/5/1643/73]
Joanna of Swk St Olave, widow [DW/PA/7/13 f.435; DW/PA/5/1646/43]
John of Guildford [PRO; PCC Will 1530]
John of Guildford [PRO; PCC Will 1544]
Samuel of Swk St George, citizen and weaver [DW/PA/7/13 f.353; 1644]
Thomas of Swk St George, baker [DW/PA/7/8 f.378; DW/PA/5/1612/127]
William of Ockley [PRO; PCC Admon 1579]
William of Ockley [PRO; PCC Admon 1593]
PERKINSON *see* PARKINSON
PERMETTER *see* PARMITER
PERON *see* PERRIN
PERPOINTE,PERPOUNT,PERPOYNT *see* PIERPOINT
PERRIER (PERIAR,PERIARE,PERIOR,PERRERS,PERRYOR)
Alice, alias Alice Windsor of Kingston - Upminster [PRO; PCC Will 1400]
<Abs SAC v.29 p.105>
John of Dunsfold, husbandman [DW/PA/5/1581/47]
John of Godalming, yeoman [DW/PA/7/7 f.287; DW/PA/5/1599/97] <Abs 513>
John of Godalming [PRO; PCC 1632]
Joshua of Godalming, gent., senior [PRO; PCC 1649]
Thomas of Tandridge [DW/PA/7/12 f.55; DW/PA/5/1631/87]
William of Godalming [DW/PA/7/11 f.315; DW/PA/5/1626/98]
PERRIN (PERIN,PERON,PERRYN,PERRYNE,PERYN)
Edward of Lambeth, yeoman [DW/PA/5/1580/11]
Edward of Rotherhithe [PRO; PCC Admon 1604]
John of Malden [DW/PA/7/1 f.29; 1486] <Abs 94>
Magdalen of Swk St Saviour; St Helen, London, widow [DW/PA/5/1598/67]
<Abs U18>
Robert of Mitcham [PRO; PCC Admon 1646]
Thomas, alias Thomas Burges of Chiddingfold [DW/PA/5/1586/3]*
William of London, citizen and skinner [DW/PA/7/7 f.103; 1596] <Abs 185>
PERROTT *see* PARROTT
PERRY (PERRYE,PERYE)
Ann of Thorpe, widow [PRO; PCC 1647]
Elizabeth of Swk St Margaret [DW/PA/7/4 f.209; 1537]
John of Swk St Thomas [DW/PA/7/10 f.104; DW/PA/5/1621/97]
Moulde of Farnham - Tilford, widow [DW/PA/7/12 f.333; DW/PA/5/1636/75]
Thomas, alias Thomas Curtis of Ewell [PRO; PCC Will 1595 *and* 1596]
Walter of ... [DW/PA/7/13 f.165; DW/PA/5/1641/105]
William of Stoke [DW/PA/7/2 f.44; 1494]
see also PIRREY
PERRYMAN
Walter of Egham [DW/PA/5/1588/65]
PERRYN,PERRYNE *see* PERRIN
PERRYOR *see* PERRIER
PERSE *see* PURSE
PERSELL *see* PURCELL
PERSIVALL *see* PERCIVALL
PERSON,PERSONE *see* PARSONS
PERSYE *see* PERCY
PERVES,PERVEYS *see* PURVIS
PERYE *see* PERRY

PERYN *see* PERRIN

PESTER (PYSTER)

Jacob of Croydon [PRO; PCC Will 1591]

Peter, Florence son of, of Swk St Olave [DW/PA/7/4 f.218; 1537]

Peter of Swk St Olave [BM; Harleian Ms. Annals of Bermondsey Abbey; 1096] <Abs SAC v.1 p.191>

Peter of Swk St George, rector [LPL; Reg. Abp Morton f.79v; Admon 1492]

PETER (PEETER, PETERS)

Agnes of Great Bookham [HRO; 1593 AD67]

Alice of Lambeth, spinster [DW/PA/7/10 f.1 [2 entries]; DW/PA/5/1616/4]

Daniel of Reigate, gent. [PRO; PCC 1649]

Elizabeth of Dorking - Westcott, widow [DW/PA/7/12 f.36; DW/PA/5/1631/84]

Elizabeth of Ockley, widow [DW/PA/7/12 f.239; DW/PA/5/1634/79]

Geoffrey of Dorking, yeoman [DW/PA/7/13 f.483; DW/PA/5/1648/27]

Helen of Dorking, widow [DW/PA/7/13 f.271; DW/PA/5/1643/69]

Jane of Gatton, widow [PRO; PCC Will 1606] <Abs. SAC v.12 p.104>

John of Capel [HRO; 1562 B102-103]

John of Capel, husbandman [DW/PA/7/10 f.56; 1619]

John of Dorking, husbandman [DW/PA/7/12 f.468; DW/PA/5/1638/102]

John of Godalming - Farncombe [HRO; 1587 AD58]

Margaret of Guildford, widow [DW/PA/7/11 f.8; DW/PA/5/1622/72]

Owen of Cobham, yeoman [DW/PA/7/13 f.149B; DW/PA/5/1641/104]

Peter, alias Peter Peterson of Swk St Olave, in the Prince's wardrobe [DW/PA/7/10 f.192; DW/PA/5/1621/98]

Richard of Dorking - Milton, yeoman [HRO; 1632 B41]

Robert of Gatton, yeoman [PRO; PCC Will 1598]

Robert of Ockley [DW/PA/7/7 f.127; DW/PA/5/1597/77] <Abs 234>

Robert of Send [DW/PA/7/13 f.100; DW/PA/5/1640/116]

Thomas of Dorking [DW/PA/5/1571/53]

Thomas of Fetcham, husbandman [HRO; 1593 B59]

Walter of Stoke, husbandman [DW/PA/7/8 f.276; DW/PA/5/1612/124]

William of Dorking - Westcott, ploughwright [DW/PA/5/1617/99] <Abs U227>

PETERSON (PETTRSON)

Agnes of Shere [PRO; PCC Will 1555]

Derek, alias Derek Borre, of Swk St Olave, coppersmith [DW/PA/7/4 f.51; 1533]

John of Swk St Olave [HRO; Reg. Way 1 p.98; 1468]

Nicholas of Swk St Olave, joiner [DW/PA/5/1568/82]

Peter of Swk St Olave, joiner [DW/PA/7/7 f.3; DW/PA/5/1595/69] <Abs 9>

Peter, alias Peter Peters of Swk St Olave, in the Prince's wardrobe [DW/PA/7/10 f.192; DW/PA/5/1621/98]

Robert of Shere, clerk [West Sussex Record Office; Deanery of Chichester Will; 1555] <Abs SAC v.8 pp.230-232>

Thomas of Lambeth, starchmaker [DW/PA/7/13 f.190; DW/PA/5/1641/109]

PETIGRE *see* PETTIGREW

PETLEY (PETLIE, PETLY)

Edward of Wandsworth [PRO; PCC Admon 1625]

Matthew of Wandsworth, yeoman usher of the king's Chamber [PRO; PCC Will 1616]

Matthew of Wandsworth, gent. [PRO; PCC Will 1622]

William of Beddington [PRO; PCC Will 1528]

PETO (PAYTOW, PEITO, PEITOE, PETOE, PETOW, PETOWE, PETTOE, PEYTO, PEYTOE, PEYTOWE)
Agnes of Chiddingfold - Pond, widow [DW/PA/5/1579/68]*
Alice of Stoke next Guildford, widow [DW/PA/7/7 f.475; DW/PA/5/1604/44] <Abs 898>
Caleb of Godalming [PRO; PCC 1633]
David of Chiddingfold [*in* DW/PA/5/1555/14]
Harry of Chiddingfold [BM; Add.Ms 24,925 f.8r; 1544] <Abs 15>
Henry of Chiddingfold, yeoman [DW/PA/7/9 f.55; DW/PA/5/1614/86]
Henry of Godalming [DW/PA/7/12 f.187; DW/PA/5/1633/103]
Joan of Thursley [DW/PA/7/9 f.37; DW/PA/5/1614/85]
John of Chiddingfold - Combe, yeoman [DW/PA/7/2 f.120; 1518]
John of Chiddingfold - Bridge [DW/PA/7/4 f.150; 1536]
John of Chiddingfold [DW/PA/5/1592/79]
John of Chiddingfold - Dyer's Cross, yeoman [HRO; 1608 B56; SRO; 212/26/26]
John of Chiddingfold - Pond, yeoman [DW/PA/7/9 f.17; DW/PA/5/1616/100]
John of Chiddingfold - Ramsnest, yeoman [DW/PA/7/9 f.201; DW/PA/5/1616/103]
John of Chiddingfold, yeoman [DW/PA/7/10 f.282; DW/PA/5/1622/73]
John of Chiddingfold - 'Tongs' [DW/PA/7/11 f.168; DW/PA/5/1625/193]
John of Ewhurst [PRO; PCC Admon 1615]
John of Godalming [DW/PA/5/1561/36]
John of Guildford, shoemaker [DW/PA/7/6 f.164; DW/PA/5/1559/178]
John of Thursley; Chiddingfold, yeoman [DW/PA/7/10 f.153; DW/PA/5/1621/99]
Mary of Chiddingfold, spinster [DW/PA/7/12 f.460; DW/PA/5/1638/101]
Nicholas of Godalming, clothier [DW/PA/5/1582/33]
Nicholas of Chiddingfold - 'Jursty', yeoman [DW/PA/7/13 f.424; DW/PA/5/1646/42]
Robert of Godalming [DW/PA/5/1562/32]
Shadrach of Godalming [DW/PA/7/13 f.251; DW/PA/5/1641/101]
Stephen of Chiddingfold - Tugley [DW/PA/7/11 f.551; DW/PA/5/1628/78]
Stephen of Shalford; Bramley, yeoman [HRO; 1575 B61]
Thomas of Chiddingfold - Combe [DW/PA/5/1563/37]
Thomas of Chiddingfold, yeoman, senior [HRO; 1576 AD42] [died 1550]
Thomas of Chiddingfold - Gostrode, yeoman [DW/PA/7/10 f.23; DW/PA/5/1616/105]
Thomas of Chiddingfold - Chaleshurst, yeoman [DW/PA/7/12 f.100; DW/PA/5/1632/78]
Thomas of Thursley; Chiddingfold; Woolbeding, Sussex; Headley, Hampshire, yeoman [DW/PA/7/7 f.283; DW/PA/5/1599/54] <Abs 508>
Thomas of Witley [DW/PA/5/1591/88]
William of Chiddingfold; Witley [PRO; PCC Will 1596]
William of Chiddingfold, yeoman [DW/PA/7/8 f.397; DW/PA/5/1612/128]
William of Dunsfold, widower [PRO; PCC Admon 1642]
William of Farnham; Chiddingfold, yeoman [DW/PA/7/7 f.28; DW/PA/5/1595/70] <Abs 59>
William of Newington [PRO; PCC Admon 1620]

PETSAN *see* PITSOME

PETT (PETTE)
Ann *or* Ann Pott, of Newington - Walworth, widow [PRO; PCC Will 1627]
Henry of Newington - Walworth, gent. [PRO; PCC Will 1624]
John of Weybridge, widower [PRO; PCC Admon 1638]

PETT (PETTE) [*continued*
Peter of Rotherhithe [PRO; PCC Will 1589]
PETTEWORTH *see* PETWORTH
PETTICUE *see* PETTIGREW
PETTIE *see* PETTY
PETTIGREW (PETIGRE,PETTICUE)
Patrick of Swk St Olave, tapster [DW/PA/5/1592/21]
PETTOE *see* PETO
PETTRSON *see* PETERSON
PETTWYN (PETWYN)
Margaret of Swk St Olave, widow [DW/PA/7/5 f.60; 1539] <Abs 97>
Richard of Swk [DW/PA/7/5 f.26; 1538] <Abs 109>
PETTY (PETTIE)
John of Croydon, currier [PRO; PCC Will 1571]
William of Egham, yeoman [DW/PA/7/8 ff.40,93; DW/PA/5/1609/71]
PETWORTH (PETTEWORTH)
Richard of Swk, clerk [HRO; Reg. Way 1 p.55; 1458]
PETYN
John of Chobham, carpenter [PRO; PCC Will 1604] <Abs. SAC v.11 p.294>
PEVENSELL
Richard of Swk St Saviour, shoemaker [DW/PA/5/1578/40]
PEW
John of Rotherhithe, mariner [PRO; PCC Will 1627]
see also HUGHES (APEW)
PEYCOKE *see* PEACOCK
PEYTO,PEYTOE *see* PETO
PEYTON (PAYTON)
Elizabeth of Croydon, widow [LPL; 96/1981; 98/1 f.42r; Will 1633]
PEYTOWE *see* PETO
PHIFE *see* FIFE
PHIGHWARREN *see* FITZWARREN
PHILEWOOD *see* FILEWOOD
PHILLICHURCH (FEYLYSCHKYRKE,FYLYCHURCH)
Christopher of Swk St Saviour [DW/PA/5/1575/80]
Richard of Wandsworth [DW/PA/5/1555/81]
PHILIP,PHILIPS *see* PHILLIPS
PHILIPSON
Thomas of Swk St George, brewer [DW/PA/7/2 f.137; 1519]
PHILLIPS (FELYPE,FILIPPIS,FILPE,FYLPE,PHILIP,PHILIPPS,PHILLIPP,PHILLIPPES,
PHYLLIPPS,PHYLYP)
Alan of Thorpe, bargeman [DW/PA/5/1578/41]
Ann of Lambeth [DW/PA/7/12 f.273; DW/PA/5/1635/81]
Augustine of Mortlake, gent. [PRO; PCC Will 1605] <Abs.SAC v.12 pp.87-88>
Christian of Farnham, widow of Thomas, merchant tailor [PRO; PCC 1647]
Christopher of Newington [PRO; PCC 1635]
Edward of Swk St Saviour, chaplain [DW/PA/7/7 f.348; DW/PA/5/1601/68]
<Abs 637>
Elizabeth, alias Elizabeth Raunce of Farnham, widow [PRO; PCC Admon 1614]
Elizabeth of Kingston, widow [DW/PA/7/11 f.601; DW/PA/5/1630/80]
George of Sanderstead [DW/PA/7/13 f.192; DW/PA/5/1641/111]
Henry of Chobham, yeoman [DW/PA/7/11 f.103; DW/PA/5/1624/95]
Hugh of Compton, parson [DW/PA/7/9 f.314; DW/PA/5/1619/87]
John of Kingston, tailor [DW/PA/5/1591/18]
John of Newington, gent. [PRO; PCC Will 1602] <Abs. SAC v.10 p.303>

PHILLIPS (FELYPE,FILIPPIS,FILPE,FYLPE,PHILIP,PHILIPPS,PHILLIPP,PHILLIPPES, PHYLLIPPS,PHYLYP) [*continued*

John of Swk St Olave, capper [DW/PA/7/5 f.181; 1540]

John of Swk St Olave, brewer [DW/PA/7/10 f.71; 1619]

John of Swk St Saviour, butcher [DW/PA/7/10 f.116; DW/PA/5/1620/93]

John of Swk St Thomas, cutler [DW/PA/7/8 f.157; DW/PA/5/1611/87]

John of Thursley, bachelor [DW/PA/5/1587/60]

John of Wandsworth [DW/PA/7/13 f.37; DW/PA/5/1639/104]

Martin of Walton on Thames, yeoman [PRO; PCC Will 1625]

Peter of Chertsey [DW/PA/5/1588/61]

Richard of Addington [PRO; PCC Admon 1649]

Richard of Frensham [DW/PA/7/3 f.102; 1529]

Richard of Wandsworth [*in* DW/PA/5/1574/26]

Robert of Swk St Olave, shoemaker [DW/PA/7/11 f.130; DW/PA/5/1624/96]

Roger of Kingston, tailor [DW/PA/7/8 f.277; DW/PA/5/1613/102]

Roger of Richmond [PRO; PCC Will 1603] <Abs. SAC v.11 pp.113-114,121>

Rose of Swk St Olave, widow [DW/PA/7/11 f.126; DW/PA/5/1624/97]

Thomas of Chobham, yeoman [DW/PA/7/13 f.274; DW/PA/5/1643/71]

Thomas of Frensham - Churt, yeoman [HRO; 1586 B22]

Thomas of Kingston, tailor [DW/PA/7/12 f.492; DW/PA/5/1638/108]

William of Beddington, miller [DW/PA/5/1593/164]

William of Chobham [DW/PA/5/1550/29]

William of Rotherhithe (died overseas) [PRO; PCC Admon 1648]

William of Swk, curate [LPL; Reg. Morton f.79v; Admon 1492]

William of Swk St Saviour, yeoman [DW/PA/5/1588/80]

William of Swk St Saviour, tailor [DW/PA/7/7 f.294; DW/PA/5/1600/40] <Abs 526>

William of Tandridge [DW/PA/7/8 f.161; DW/PA/5/1611/88]

William of Windlesham [HRO; 1595 B42]

PHILLIS

Juliana, alias Juliana Lambe of Wandsworth [PRO; PCC Admon 1642]

PHILPOTT (FILLPOTT,FYLLPOT,FYLPOT,PHILLPOTE,PHILPOT)

George of Wandsworth, mealman [DW/PA/7/7 f.486; DW/PA/5/1604/45] <Abs 917>

Henry of Newington [LPL; 98/1 f.126r (ren.); Will 1641]

John of Seale [DW/PA/7/1 f.75; 1488] <Abs 247>

Roger of London; Swk St Olave, tailor [DW/PA/7/8 f.58; DW/PA/5/1609/77]

Susan of Long Ditton - Tolworth, widow [DW/PA/7/13 f.33; DW/PA/5/1640/114]

Thomas of Long Ditton - Tolworth; Kingston [DW/PA/5/1557/20]

William of Long Ditton - Tolworth, brown baker [GL; Archdeaconry Court of London Will 1645]

PHIPPS (PHIPES,PHIPP,PHIPPES)

Andrew of Frimley [HRO; 1640 AD124]

Elizabeth of Limpsfield, widow [DW/PA/7/13 f.376; 1644]

John of Coulsdon, clerk [PRO; PCC 1640]

John of Limpsfield, husbandman [DW/PA/7/12 f.42; DW/PA/5/1631/85]

Robert of Wandsworth, clerk [PRO; PCC Will 1603]

Susan of Coulsdon [PRO; PCC 1641]

William of ...; Wendy, Cambridgeshire [DW/PA/7/12 f.321; DW/PA/5/1636/74]

William of Swk St George - Kent Street, victualler [DW/PA/7/13 f.446; 1646]

PHITTON *see* FITTON

PHYLLIPPS,PHYLYP *see* PHILLIPS
PICKAIES *see* PICKS
PICKARD (PYKERD)
  John of Capel [*in* DW/PA/5/1544/4]
PICKE (PYCKE)
  Soynken of Swk St Olave [DW/PA/7/10 f.48; 1618]
    see also PICKS
PICKERING (PICKERINGE,PICKRING,PUCKERINGE,PUCKRING,PYKERYNG,PYKKERYNG)
  Christopher of Newington, gent. [PRO; PCC Will 1608] <Abs, SAC v.13 p.188>
  George of Morden, yeoman [DW/PA/7/11 f.463; DW/PA/5/1628/79]
  John, alias John Byhurst of Ewell, yeoman [DW/PA/7/2 f.184; 1522]
  John of Newington [LPL; 98/1 f.77r (ren.); 1636]
  Robert of Kingston [PRO; PCC Admon 1570]
  Robert, alias Robert Leonard of Malden, labourer [DW/PA/7/3 f.149; 1530]
  Sarah of Newington [PRO; PCC Admon 1609]
  Thomas of Farnham [PRO; PCC Will 1501]
  William of Newington [PRO; PCC Admon 1616]
PICKES *see* PICKS
PICKFORD
  Edward of Mitcham [PRO; PCC 1640]
PICKINGTON
  William of Swk St Olave, carpenter [DW/PA/5/1571/75]
PICKLE (PICLE)
  William of Swk St Saviour [DW/PA/7/12 f.270; DW/PA/5/1635/80]
PICKMAN (PYKMAN)
  Alice of Swk St Olave, widow [DW/PA/7/7 f.606; DW/PA/5/1607/70]<Abs 1134>
  Richard of Addington; Croydon; Farleigh; Barking, Essex [DW/PA/7/5 f.1; 1538] <Abs 4>
PICKNUTT (PYCNETT,PYKNOT)
  John of Godstone [DW/PA/7/4 f.204; 1537]
  William of Horne [DW/PA/5/1550/53]
  William of Horne [PRO; PCC 1640]
PICKRING *see* PICKERING
PICKS (PICKAIES,PICKES)
  Ann of Guildford, widow [PRO; PCC Will 1609]
  William of Rotherhithe, shipwright [PRO; PCC Will 1620] <Soame 693>
    see also PICK
PICLE *see* PICKLE
PIDDER
  John of Bisley, yeoman [DW/PA/5/1558/218]*
PIERPOINT (PERPOINTE,PERPOUNT,PERPOYNT)
  Alexander of Wimbledon; Mortlake, citizen and draper [GL; Commissary Court of London Will 1567]
  Henry of Bermondsey, gent. [PRO; PCC Will 1545]
  Jane of Mortlake, widow [PRO; PCC Will 1597]
  Mark of Mortlake [PRO; PCC Admon 1605]
  Thomas of Mortlake [PRO; PCC Will 1544]
PIGEON (PYGHAN)
  Abraham of Newington - Kentish Street [PRO; PCC Will 1595]
  Edmund of Camberwell, gent. [PRO; PCC Will 1622]
  John of Coulsdon, yeoman [DW/PA/7/10 f.54; 1618]
  John of Lingfield, citizen and grocer [PRO; PCC Will 1594]

PIGEON (PYGHAN) [*continued*

Richard of Coulsdon [HRO; 1587 B66]

Richard of Chipstead, husbandman [DW/PA/7/1 f.41; 1486] <Abs 130>

PIGG (PIGE,PYGG)

Thomas of Chobham, shoemaker [DW/PA/7/6 f.19; DW/PA/5/1559/15]

William of Chobham, husbandman [DW/PA/5/1557/34]

PIGGOTT (PIGOTT,PYGGOTT,PYGOT,PYGOTT)

Elizabeth, alias Elizabeth Deane of Newington, widow [PRO; PCC Admon 1629]

Joan of Kingston, spinster [DW/PA/7/13 f.365; 1644]

Thomas of Chertsey, abbot [LPL; Reg. Abp Morton f.81v; Admon 1492]

Thomas of Farnham, husbandman [DW/PA/7/6 f.116; DW/PA/5/1559/125]

Thomas of Swk St Olave, citizen and fishmonger [DW/PA/7/3 f.104; 1529]

PIKE (PYKE)

Henry of Mitcham, husbandman [DW/PA/5/1558/225]*

James of Camberwell [DW/PA/7/3 f.126; 1530]

John of Mitcham - Biggin [BM; Add.Ms 23,559; Will 1576]

John of Mitcham - Biggin, yeoman [PRO; PCC Will 1576]

William of Farnham - Waverley [PRO; PCC Admon 1598]

PILFOLD (PILFIOLD,PILLFOLLDE)

Roger of Swk St Saviour, citizen and chandler [DW/PA/5/1558/219]*

PILKINGTON (PILKENTON)

Joan of Swk St Olave, widow [DW/PA/7/11 f.66; DW/PA/5/1623/93]

William of Swk St Olave, barber surgeon [DW/PA/7/11 f.88; DW/PA/5/1623/94]

PILLFOLLDE *see* PILFOLD

PILSBURIE

William of Swk St Olave [DW/PA/7/7 f.372; DW/PA/5/1602/69] <Abs 686>

PINCHESTER (PYNCHESTER,PYNCHESTRE)

Charles of Kingston, yeoman [DW/PA/7/4 f.74; 1534]

William of Coulsdon - Waddington, husbandman [DW/PA/5/1555/48]

PINCKE *see* PINK

PINDAR (PYNDER)

Alice of Swk St Olave, widow [DW/PA/5/1592/23]

Edmund of Twickenham, Middlesex; Richmond; Isleworth, Middlesex, curate of Twickenham [DW/PA/7/6 f.160; DW/PA/5/1559/144]

Robert of Kingston, husbandman [DW/PA/7/7 f.116; DW/PA/5/1597/79] <Abs 214>

PINE (PYNE)

John of Croydon [PRO; PCC Will 1531]

Martha of Swk St Saviour [DW/PA/7/13 f.464; DW/PA/5/1647/13]

PINFOLD *see* PENFOLD

PINK (PINCKE,PINKE)

William of Bermondsey [DW/PA/7/8 f.98; DW/PA/5/1609/72]

William of Swk St Saviour, butcher [DW/PA/7/10 f.235; DW/PA/5/1621/100]

PINKARD (PYNCARD)

James of Swk St Olave, hatmaker [DW/PA/7/2 f.63; 1500]

PINKNEY (PENCKNEY)

Michael of Egham - Bakeham [DW/PA/7/11 f.88; DW/PA/5/1623/92]

PINNER (PYNNER)

Henry of Chessington, husbandman [DW/PA/5/1558/220]*

Henry of Chessington [DW/PA/7/12 f.480; DW/PA/5/1638/104]

Joan of Thames Ditton; Cobham [DW/PA/7/4 f.79; 1534]

Richard of Kingston [DW/PA/7/5 f.56; 1539] <Abs 60>

PINNOCK (PYNNOCKE,PYNNOK)
  Alice of Swk St George, widow [DW/PA/7/9 f.181; DW/PA/5/1616/117]
  William of Thorpe [DW/PA/7/1 f.27; 1486] <Abs 89>
PINSON (PYNSON)
  John of Chobham, husbandman [DW/PA/7/8 f.305; DW/PA/5/1613/103]
  Thomas of Chobham, labourer [DW/PA/5/1557/145]
  William of Swk St Saviour [DW/PA/5/1558/226]*
PIPER
  Thomas of Farnham, husbandman [DW/PA/7/13 f.420; DW/PA/5/1645/43]
PIRREY (PIRRYE)
  Nicholas of Lambeth [PRO; PCC Admon 1583]
  William of Swk St Olave, brewer [DW/PA/7/9 f.190; DW/PA/5/1616/101]
    see also PERRY
PISTER *see* PESTER (PYSTER)
PITCH
  Leonard of Bermondsey [PRO; PCC Admon 1637]
PITCHER (PYCHER)
  Robert of Lambeth [PRO; PCC Will 1524]
PITHER
  Edward of Wandsworth, yeoman [DW/PA/7/12 f.515; DW/PA/5/1639/96]
PITSOME (PETSAN,PITSAME,PYTSAM,PYTSAME)
  Alice of Chertsey [DW/PA/7/6 f.108; DW/PA/5/1559/101]
  Anthony of Chertsey [DW/PA/7/6 f.147; DW/PA/5/1559/234]
  Edmund of Chertsey [DW/PA/7/6 f.76; DW/PA/5/1559/100]
  George of Chertsey, mealman [DW/PA/7/13 f.20; DW/PA/5/1639/100]
  George of Chobham [DW/PA/5/1593/96]
  John of Chertsey; Chobham [DW/PA/5/1557/46]
PITTER (PYTTER,PYTTYER)
  Henry of Banstead; Woodmansterne [DW/PA/7/11 f.464; DW/PA/5/1628/80]
  Henry of Capel; Swk; Dorking; Cuckfield, Sussex, clerk [DW/PA/5/1602/67]
    <Abs U55>
  Henry of Egham [DW/PA/7/1 f.47; 1487] <Abs 159>
  John of Chaldon, husbandman [DW/PA/7/10 f.179; DW/PA/5/1620/94]
PITTS (PYTTES)
  John of Shere, clerk [PRO; PCC Will 1540] <Abs SAC v.8 pp.229-230>
PLACE
  William of Dorking, gent. [PRO; PCC Will 1627]
PLAIE *see* PLAW
PLANNER
  John of Egham [PRO; PCC Admon 1613]
PLASTED (PLAYSTED)
  Stephen of Kingston [PRO; PCC Admon 1580]
  William of Shere; Stoke; Guildford; Pyrford; West Horsley; Albury
    Brewton, Somerset; Lichfield, Staffs [PRO; PCC 1630] <Scroope 395>
  William of Swk St Olave [DW/PA/7/12 f.91; DW/PA/5/1632/76]
PLASTOWE (PLASTOW,PLAYSTOWE)
  Alice of Kingston - Surbiton, widow [DW/PA/7/7 f.243; DW/PA/5/1599/52]
    <Abs 428>
  Joan of Godalming [DW/PA/7/1 f.16; 1485] <Abs 52>
  Richard of Ewell [PRO; PCC Will 1518]
  William of Morden; Kingston; Teddington, Middlesex [DW/PA/7/7 f.94;
    1596] <Abs 172>
PLATER (PLAYTER)
  Richard of Cheam [PRO; PCC Will 1503; CCAL; 1503 f.214v]

PLAW (PLAIE, PLAWE)
Edward of Crowhurst, yeoman [DW/PA/7/13 f.176; DW/PA/5/1642/66]
Henry of Limpsfield, husbandman [DW/PA/5/1592/18]
Jasper of Lingfield [PRO; PCC 1632]
Joan of Tandridge, widow [DW/PA/5/1562/73]
John of Godstone [DW/PA/5/1588/85]
John of Tandridge - 'Water Trugges'; Lingfield, yeoman [DW/PA/7/8 f.103; DW/PA/5/1610/97]
John of Lingfield, yeoman [PRO; PCC Will 1617]
John of Tandridge [DW/PA/7/11 f.430; DW/PA/5/1627/87]
John of Westerham, Kent; Tandridge [LPL; 65 p.m. Poli; 1559 Will]
Mary of Lingfield [PRO; PCC Will 1598]
Nicholas of Tandridge, yeoman [DW/PA/5/1561/81]
Thomas of Godstone, husbandman [DW/PA/7/8 f.206; DW/PA/5/1611/89]
Thomas of Lingfield - Dormansland; East Grinstead, Sussex, yeoman [DW/PA/7/7 f.195; DW/PA/5/1598/62] <Abs 355>
William of Lingfield - Apsley [PRO; PCC Will 1596]

PLAYER
Ralph of Camberwell, husbandman [DW/PA/7/11 f.545; DW/PA/5/1629/78]

PLAYSTED *see* PLASTED

PLAYSTOWE *see* PLASTOWE

PLAYTER *see* PLATER

PLOGG
William of Camberwell - Peckham; Kent, yeoman [HRO; 1597 B57] [*and*] [DW/PA/5/1597/81] <Abs U12>

PLOMLEY *see* PLUMLEY

PLOMMER *see* PLUMMER

PLONKER (PLONCKER, PLONKAR)
John of Puttenham [DW/PA/7/5 f.57; 1539] <Abs 68>
Robert of Godalming - Catteshall, yeoman [DW/PA/7/7 f.257; DW/PA/5/1599/53] <Abs 454>

PLONKETT *see* PLUNKETT

PLUMER *see* PLUMMER

PLUMLEY (PLOMLEY)
Ellen of Titsey; Westerham, Kent; Knockholt, Kent, widow [DW/PA/7/8 f.357; DW/PA/5/1612/129]
Richard of Rotherhithe, gentleman of the king's Chapel [DW/PA/7/8 f.145; DW/PA/5/1611/90]

PLUMMER (PLOMMER, PLUMER)
John of Wandsworth [DW/PA/7/2 f.64; 1500]
John of Wandsworth, junior [DW/PA/7/2 f.72; 1500]
Thomas of Mitcham, esq. [PRO; PCC 1639]
William, alias William Hookewey of Swk St Mary Magdalen, barber [DW/PA/7/1 f.42; 1486] <Abs 134>

PLUMPTON
Henry of ? Surrey [LPL; Reg. Abp Parker f.170; Will 1560]

PLUNKETT (PLONKETT)
Mary of Newington [LPL; 98/1 f.93v; Will 1638]

PLYMOUTH
Stephen of Swk St Olave, 'hurei' [DW/PA/7/2 f.75; 1500]

POCKNELL
William of Lingfield, hoopmaker [DW/PA/7/8 f.206; DW/PA/5/1611/91]

POETT
Michael of Swk St Olave [DW/PA/7/4 f.94; 1534]

POFFLEY (POFFLIE)
Stephen of Chiddingfold, sawyer [HRO; 1639 B54]
POINTE
Alice, alias Alice Ryder of Swk St Saviour [DW/PA/7/7 f.221; DW/PA/5/1598/73] <Abs 391>
POINTZ (POYNTES)
Elizabeth of Reigate [PRO; PCC Will 1602] <Abs, SAC v.10 p.308>
William of Reigate [PRO; PCC Admon 1601]
POLE
Reginald of Lambeth, archbishop of Canterbury [PRO; PCC Will 1558]
POLGLAS
John of Swk St Olave [DW/PA/7/2 f.42; 1494]
POLL (POLLE)
John of Godstone [DW/PA/7/3 f.182; 1531]
William of Horne [DW/PA/7/2 f.131; 1518]
POLLARD (POLLORD,POULLERD)
Henry of Battersea, husbandman [DW/PA/7/7 f.426; DW/PA/5/1603/135] <Abs 796>
Isaac of Wandsworth, labourer [DW/PA/7/11 f.525; DW/PA/5/1630/81]
Joan of Godalming - Farncombe, widow [DW/PA/7/8 f.131; DW/PA/5/1610/98]
(Sir) John of Kingston, knight [PRO; PCC Will 1557]
William of Burstow, husbandman [LPL; 96/2048; Will 1626]
POLLE *see* POLL
POLLESDEN (POULSDEN,POWLESDEN)
Gilbert of Charlwood [LPL; 98/1 f.30v; Will 1631]
John of Betchworth [DW/PA/7/11 f.222; DW/PA/5/1620/97]
Thomas of Betchworth, yeoman [DW/PA/5/1557/103]
Thomas of Newdigate, yeoman [DW/PA/7/12 f.376; DW/PA/5/1638/114]
Thomas of Newdigate, yeoman [DW/PA/7/12 f.393; 1637]
POLLEXFEN
Susan of Putney, widow [PRO; PCC Admon 1646]
POLLEYN *see* PULLEN
POLLINGTON
Ellen of Cranleigh, widow [DW/PA/7/10 f.281; DW/PA/5/1622/76]
POLLORD *see* POLLARD
POLSTED
Alice of Albury, widow of Henry, esq. [PRO; PCC Will 1589]
Francis of Albury, gent. [PRO; PCC Will 1578]
Henry of Albury, esq. [PRO; PCC Will 1556] <Abs, SAC v.51 pp.95-96>
John of Guildford Holy Trinity [HRO; Reg. Way 2 p.146; 1471]
Richard of Albury, esq. [PRO; PCC Will 1576; *also* C146 9624]
Thomas of Stoke next Guildford, senior [PRO; PCC Will 1529] <Abs, SAC v.51 pp.94-95>
POLWHELE (POLWHEILE)
Jonathan of Windlesham, bachelor [PRO; PCC Admon 1649]
POMPHERET
Samuel of Esher [PRO; PCC Will 1617]
PONCHEN
Thomas *or* Thomas Punchyn of Surrey [PRO; PCC Will 1556]
POND (PONDE)
Agnes of Croydon, widow of Ralph [DW/PA/5/1593/138]
John of Guildford [PRO; PCC Admon 1630]
Ralph of Swk, oatmealmaker [DW/PA/5/1593/126]

PONDER
John of Newington, citizen and vintner [GL; Commissary Court of London Will 1393]
PONDERSON
John of Bermondsey [PRO; PCC Admon 1626]
Thomas of Bermondsey [PRO; PCC Admon 1630]
PONDMAN
William of Elstead, husbandman [DW/PA/5/1592/2]*
PONTER *see* PUNTER
PONYFOLD *see* PENFOLD
PONYNGES,PONYNGIS *see* POYNINGS
POOKE
Susan of Ewhurst, widow [PRO; PCC Admon 1626]
POOLE (de la POOLE,POOLES)
Agnes of Seale [DW/PA/7/6 f.161; DW/PA/5/1559/238]
Denise of Swk St George, widow of Nicholas [DW/PA/5/1568/80]
Elizabeth of Mitcham, spinster [PRO; PCC Admon 1616]
Humphrey of Swk St Olave, feltmaker [DW/PA/5/1582/81]
Margaret of Bermondsey - Bermondsey Monastery [PRO; PCC Will 1473]
Phillip of Swk St Saviour [DW/PA/7/10 f.7; DW/PA/5/1619/88]
Robert of Mortlake, carpenter [LPL; 96/2058; 98/1 f.24v; Will 1631]
Robert of Swk St Saviour [DW/PA/5/1561/61]
Thomas of Lambeth; Wick, Somerset; Blackfriars, London; Salisbury, Wiltshire, gent. [DW/PA/7/8 f.31; DW/PA/5/1609/73]
William of Camberwell [PRO; PCC Admon 1630]
William of Seale [DW/PA/5/1558/221]*
POOPE *see* POPE
POORE
Anthony of West Horsley [PRO; PCC 1646]
Margaret of Swk St Olave; Bermondsey, widow [DW/PA/7/7 f.44; DW/PA/5/1595/71] <Abs 86>
Stephen of Swk St Olave, butcher [DW/PA/7/8 f.82; DW/PA/5/1609/74]
Stephen of Swk St Olave, butcher [DW/PA/7/12 f.474; DW/PA/5/1638/103]
POPE (POOPE)
Edward of Croydon [PRO; PCC 1631]
George of Chipstead, husbandman [DW/PA/7/11 f.78; DW/PA/5/1623/95]
Jane of Kingston, spinster [PRO; PCC Admon 1632]
Joan of Swk St Olave, widow [DW/PA/7/7 f.567; DW/PA/5/1606/69] <Abs 1060>
John of Newdigate [DW/PA/5/1568/41]
John of Shere, canon resident at Wells [PRO; PCC Will 1475] <Abs SAC v.8 pp.228-229>
John of Windlesham [LPL; Reg. Abp Stafford f.151v; Admon 1447]
John of Tandridge [DW/PA/5/1558/223]*
Lydia, alias Lydia Rumsey of Rotherhithe [PRO; PCC Admon 1646]
Robert of Newdigate, carpenter [DW/PA/7/11 f.336; DW/PA/5/1625/194]
Roger of Kingston, gent. [PRO; PCC Will 1621] [*and*] [SRO; KB37/1; 1621]
Thomas of Haslemere [HRO; Reg. D p.50; 1527]
Thomas of Newington, husbandman [LPL; 96/2061; 98/1 f.82r; Will 1637]
William of Worplesdon, husbandman [HRO; 1576 B68]
POPELOTTE,POPLER *see* PUPLETT
POPPKIN (UPOPKIN)
Robert of Swk [DW/PA/5/1587/76]
POPSEYNT
William of Merton [HRO; Reg. Way 1 p.85; 1464]

PORT (PORTE)
Ann of Chobham, widow [DW/PA/7/12 f.197; DW/PA/5/1633/105]
Anthony of Chertsey, yeoman [HRO; 1573 B112]
Nicholas of Woking; Send, yeoman [DW/PA/7/7 f.476; DW/PA/5/1604/46] <Abs 901>
Nicholas of Woking [DW/PA/7/11 f.443; DW/PA/5/1628/81]
Oliver of Byfleet [DW/PA/5/1555/30]
Roger of Chertsey [PRO; PCC Admon 1647]
Thomas of Woking [DW/PA/7/10 f.49; 1618]

PORTER
Alice *or* Alice Potter, of Byfleet, widow [DW/PA/7/5 f.108; 1539]
Alice of Worplesdon, widow [DW/PA/7/10 f.217; DW/PA/5/1621/101]
Ann of Byfleet, widow [DW/PA/7/9 f.262; DW/PA/5/1617/100]
Augustine of Egham [PRO; PCC Admon 1599]
Benjamin of Hambledon, husbandman [DW/PA/7/13 f.45; DW/PA/5/1639/105]
Christopher of Swk [DW/PA/7/6 f.175; DW/PA/5/1559/153]
Francis of Ewell [DW/PA/7/11 f.401; DW/PA/5/1627/88]
Henry of Chipstead, clerk [PRO; PCC Will 1540]
Joan of Swk St Saviour, widow [DW/PA/5/1581/32]
John *or* John Potter of Byfleet [DW/PA/7/5 f.108; 1539]
John of Byfleet, yeoman [DW/PA/7/9 f.194; DW/PA/5/1616/92]
John of Camberwell [DW/PA/7/7 f.264; DW/PA/5/1599/55] <Abs 470>
John of Woking [DW/PA/7/7 f.282; DW/PA/5/1599/56] <Abs 503>
Margaret of Shalford - Tilsey, widow of Robert [DW/PA/7/12 f.288; DW/PA/5/1635/85]
Rachel, alias Rachel Wadeson, of Putney [PRO; PCC Admon 1649]
Richard of Byfleet, yeoman [DW/PA/7/7 f.340; DW/PA/5/1601/69] <Abs 616>
Richard of Byfleet, yeoman [DW/PA/7/9 f.34; DW/PA/5/1614/87]
Robert of Kingston [PRO; PCC Admon 1647]
Robert of Shalford - Tilsey, husbandman [DW/PA/7/12 f.274; DW/PA/5/1635/84]
Robert of Wandsworth, mealman [DW/PA/7/7 f.210; DW/PA/5/1598/63] <Abs 376>
Robert of Worplesdon [DW/PA/5/1571/31]
Robert of Worplesdon, weaver [DW/PA/7/8 f.185; DW/PA/5/1610/99]
Thomas of ... [DW/PA/7/7 f.605; DW/PA/5/1607/71] <Abs 1131>
William of Byfleet [HRO; 1639 B55]
William of Morden [PRO; PCC Will 1522]
William of Swk St Saviour, grocer [DW/PA/5/1574/9]
William of Worplesdon, husbandman [DW/PA/7/7 f.22; DW/PA/5/1595/72] <Abs 46>

PORTISSE (PORTTIS)
Paul of Swk St George [DW/PA/7/10 f.280; DW/PA/5/1622/77]
Thomas of Swk, clothworker [DW/PA/5/1561/3]

POSE
Thomas of Merton [DW/PA/5/1617/101] <Abs U228>

POSELEY (POSLY)
John of Farnham - Wrecclesham, weaver [DW/PA/7/6 f.208; 1560]
John of Farnham - Wrecclesham, yeoman [DW/PA/7/12 f.491; DW/PA/5/1638/107]

POSYER
John of Blechingley [DW/PA/7/2 f.100; 1515]

POTFLOWDE
John of Banstead [DW/PA/7/4 f.157; 1536]

POTIER

Peter of Swk St Olave; Normandy, France [DW/PA/7/5 f.68; 1539] <Abs 95>

POTT

Ann *or* Ann Pett of Newington - Walworth, widow [PRO; PCC Will 1627]

POTTER

... of Horsell; Chobham; Chertsey, senior [DW/PA/5/1550/33]

Alice *or* Alice Porter of Byfleet, widow [DW/PA/7/5 f.108; 1539]

Ann of Thorpe, widow [PRO; PCC Admon 1649]

Bridget of Swk St Saviour, spinster [DW/PA/7/8 f.2; DW/PA/5/1608/83]

Edward of Dorking, tanner [DW/PA/7/9 f.123; DW/PA/5/1615/104]

Edward of Dorking [DW/PA/7/9 f.147 (renunciation); 1616]

Edward of Lingfield [PRO; PCC 1649]

Edward of Tatsfield, clerk [DW/PA/7/8 f.362; DW/PA/5/1612/130]

Henry of Mitcham [DW/PA/5/1606/70] <Abs U189>

Joan of Horsell, widow [DW/PA/7/13 f.124; DW/PA/5/1640/118]

John *or* John Potter of Byfleet [DW/PA/7/5 f.108; 1539]

John of Surrey [PRO; PCC Will 1530]

John of Horsell, yeoman [DW/PA/7/12 f.372; DW/PA/5/1638/113]

John of London, citizen and blacksmith [DW/PA/7/10 f.204; DW/PA/5/1620/96]

John of Thorpe [DW/PA/7/12 f.431; DW/PA/5/1637/79] <Abs SAC v.23 p.80>

Margaret of Horsell, widow [*in* DW/PA/5/1555/1]

Richard of Ewhurst, yeoman [DW/PA/7/7 f.304; DW/PA/5/1600/41] <Abs 544>

Roger, alias Roger Rodnall of Swk St George, rector [HRO; Reg. Way 2 p.144; 1470]

Thomas of Surrey [PRO; PCC Will 1589]

Thomas, alias Thomas Roke of Chertsey, husbandman and tailor [DW/PA/7/5 f.199; 1540]

Thomas of Mitcham, labourer [DW/PA/5/1592/12]*

Walter of Tandridge, husbandman [DW/PA/7/11 f.588; DW/PA/5/1630/82]

William of Horsell, yeoman [HRO; 1590 B49]

William of Swk St Saviour, citizen and ironmonger [DW/PA/7/9 f.329; DW/PA/5/1620/95]

POTTERTON

Eleanor of Albury, spinster [PRO; PCC Admon 1649]

George of Albury [PRO; PCC 1649]

John of Woodmansterne, yeoman [DW/PA/7/12 f.432; DW/PA/5/1637/80]

POTTRELL

Thomas of Swk St Olave [DW/PA/5/1582/12]

POULLERD *see* POLLARD

POULSDEN *see* POLLESDEN

POULTER (POWLTER,PULTER)

Elizabeth of Dunsfold, widow [DW/PA/7/6 f.152; DW/PA/5/1559/180] <Abs SAC v.31 pp.82-83>

Elizabeth of Dunsfold, widow [DW/PA/7/10 f.85; DW/PA/5/1615/85]

Harry of Dunsfold- High Billinghurst, tailor [DW/PA/5/1568/65]

Joan of Wonersh - 'Harrolds Cornsfold' [DW/PA/7/11 f.208; DW/PA/5/1625/195]

John of Dunsfold, husbandman [DW/PA/5/1563/112]

John of Dunsfold, yeoman [DW/PA/7/12 f.447; DW/PA/5/1639/98]

Juliana of Dunsfold; Fletching, Sussex; Maresfield, Sussex, widow [DW/PA/7/6 f.141; DW/PA/5/1559/181] <Abs SAC v.31 pp.81-82>

Thomas of Dunsfold [PRO; PCC Will 1557]

POULTER (POWLTER,PULTER) [*continued*

Thomas of Swk St Saviour [DW/PA/5/1576/113]

Thomas of Wonersh, husbandman [DW/PA/7/7 f.393; DW/PA/5/1603/136] <Abs 730>

Walter of Dunsfold, husbandman [DW/PA/7/6 f.153; DW/PA/5/1559/182]

William of Chiddingfold; Dunsfold [DW/PA/7/7 f.65; DW/PA/5/1596/46] <Abs 124>

William of Dunsfold - Pond, yeoman, senior [DW/PA/7/12 f.496; DW/PA/5/1638/109]

POUNSETT

Humphrey of Chaldon, rector [DW/PA/7/13 f.288; DW/PA/5/1644/16]

POUNTER,POUTER *see* PUNTER

POWELL

Charles of Bermondsey, turner [DW/PA/7/11 f.66; DW/PA/5/1623/96]

Edward of Swk St Thomas [DW/PA/7/10 f.220; DW/PA/5/1621/102]

Eleanor of Weybridge, widow [DW/PA/7/13 f.464; DW/PA/5/1647/12]

Elizabeth of Merton, widow [DW/PA/5/1593/36]

Ellis of Swk St Olave [DW/PA/7/7 f.523; DW/PA/5/1606/71] <Abs 985>

George of Streatham - Tooting Bec, gent. [PRO; PCC Will 1627]

Isabel of Rotherhithe, widow [DW/PA/5/1588/5]

James of Guildford, yeoman [DW/PA/7/11 f.429; DW/PA/5/1627/89]

Joan of Wonersh, widow of Thomas [DW/PA/5/1576/63]

John of Blechingley [DW/PA/7/1 f.47; 1487] <Abs 156>

John of Wandsworth, gent. [PRO; PCC Will 1611] <Abs. SAC v.33 p.20 *and* v.35 p.41>

Lucy, alias Lucy Coventry, of Tooting, spinster [DW/PA/7/13 f.162; 1641]

Katherine of Swk St Olave, widow of Ellis [DW/PA/7/7 f.522; DW/PA/5/1606/72] <Abs 981>

Margery of Swk St George [DW/PA/5/1579/72]*

Margery of Streatham, spinster [DW/PA/7/13 f.247; DW/PA/5/1640/119]

Richard of Battersea, barber surgeon [PRO; PCC 1647]

Richard of Merton; Morden; Mitcham; Wimbledon, blacksmith [DW/PA/5/1593/37]

Roger of ... [DW/PA/7/8 f.54; DW/PA/5/1609/75]

Samuel of Wimbledon, yeoman [LPL; 96/2067; Will 1627]

Stephen of Wandsworth [PRO; PCC Admon 1630]

Susanna of Wandsworth, widow [PRO; PCC 1631]

Thomas of Long Ditton - Tolworth, gent. [PRO; PCC Will 1579]

Thomas of Ewell, gent. [PRO; PCC Will 1524]

Thomas of Rotherhithe, rector [PRO; PCC Admon 1607]

Thomas of Swk St Olave [DW/PA/5/1562/50]

Thomas of Wonersh, husbandman [DW/PA/5/1575/5]

William of Kingston, physician [PRO; PCC 1642]

William of Kingston, physician [PRO; PCC 1648]

see also a POWELL

POWER

John of Swk St Olave, gent. [DW/PA/7/11 f.151; DW/PA/5/1625/196]

POWLESDEN,POWLSDON *see* POLLESDON

POWLTER *see* POULTER

POWNALL

Thomas of Woodmansterne, rector [HRO; Reg. Fox 3 p.67; 1515]

POYNER

Geoffrey of Swk St Olave, feltmaker [DW/PA/7/13 f.77; DW/PA/5/1640/115]

Robert of Rotherhithe [PRO; PCC Admon 1585]

POYNINGS (de PONYNGES,PONYNGIS)
(Dame) Elizabeth (later Elizabeth Brown) of Dorking [PRO; PCC Will 1488]
Henry of Cheam [PRO; PCC 1645]
Richard, lord of Poynings, Sussex; Surrey; Kent [LPL; Reg. Abp Courteney f.223; Will 1387]
POYNTES *see* POINTZ
PRATT (PRATE,PRATTE,PRATYE)
Bartholomew of Swk St Saviour, labourer [DW/PA/7/7 f.553; DW/PA/5/1606/73] <Abs 1036>
Christopher of Bermondsey, citizen and leatherseller [PRO; PCC Will 1588 *and* 1589]
Elizabeth of Reigate, widow [DW/PA/5/1593/120]
Henry of Kingston [PRO; PCC Will 1577]
James of Bermondsey [BM; Add.Ms 24,925 f.20v; 1544] <Abs 47>
Joel of Rotherhithe, sailor [DW/PA/7/8 f.246; DW/PA/5/1613/104]
John of Epsom [DW/PA/7/5 f.141; 1540]
John of Farnham - Wrecclesham [HRO; D3/158; 1590]
John of Lambeth - Kennington [DW/PA/7/7 f.145; DW/PA/5/1597/80] <Abs 267>
John of Newington [LPL; 98/1 f.12r (ren.); Will 1630]
John of Reigate, rippier [DW/PA/5/1593/119]
John of Swk St Margaret, skinner [DW/PA/7/3 f.162; 1530]
Ralph of Bermondsey, citizen and leatherseller [PRO; PCC Will 1612]
Richard of Battersea, gent. [PRO; PCC Will 1596]
Richard of Egham - Trottsworth [DW/PA/7/12 f.488; DW/PA/5/1638/106]
Susan of Barnes, widow [PRO; PCC 1638]
Thomas of Bermondsey [PRO; PCC Admon 1608]
Thomas of Farnham - Wrecclesham, carpenter [HRO; 1614 B59]
Thomas of Newington [LPL; 98/1 f.114v; Will 1640]
PRATTER
George of Swk St George [DW/PA/7/12 f.16; DW/PA/5/1631/80]
PREIN
John of Shere [DW/PA/7/1 f.85; 1488] <Abs 285>
PREIST *see* PRIEST
PRENDERGAST
Thomas of Swk St Olave, shipowner of ship *the Peter* of Wexford, Ireland [DW/PA/5/1575/30]
PRENTICE (PRENTISE,PRENTYS,PRENTYSE)
John of Hayling Northwood, Hampshire [DW/PA/5/1616/108]
Richard of Swk St George [*This is a typescript with a note that a full transcript was made in 1938 by S.W.Prentis who also noted that it was missing in 1960; the typescript has been allocated the number the original would have had.*] [DW/PA/5/1558/224]*
Richard of Swk St Olave [DW/PA/5/1580/24]
Stephen of Farnham [? HRO; 1529]
PRENTOFT
Margaret of Swk St Olave [DW/PA/7/4 f.40; 1533]
Simon of Walton on Thames; Molesey, etc. [PRO; PCC Will 1433]
PRENTOUT
John of Chertsey [PRO; PCC Will 1423]
PRESSER
Richard of Lambeth - Water Lambeth, husbandman [DW/PA/7/12 f.29; DW/PA/5/1631/83]

PRESTON (PRESSON)

- Alice of Clapham, spinster [PRO; PCC Admon 1638]
- John of Farnham [DW/PA/7/4 f.143; 1536]
- Richard of Mortlake [PRO; PCC Admon 1625]
- Thomas of Effingham, husbandman, senior [DW/PA/7/12 f.367; DW/PA/5/1638/112]
- Thomas of Guildford Holy Trinity, weaver [DW/PA/7/12 f.220; DW/PA/5/1634/78]
- William of Seale - Tongham [DW/PA/7/8 f.28A; DW/PA/5/1608/82]

PRESTWICH

- Thomas of Lambeth [PRO; PCC Admon 1634]

PRETTIMAN

- William of Bermondsey, tailor [DW/PA/7/11 f.155; DW/PA/5/1625/197]

PRETTY (PRETTIE)

- Henry, alias Henry Albrooke of Walton on Thames, weaver [DW/PA/7/7 f.26; DW/PA/5/1595/1] <Abs 55>

PRICE (PRYCE)

- David of Newington [PRO; PCC 1641]
- Evan of Kingston, yeoman [DW/PA/7/12 f.265; DW/PA/5/1635/83]
- Henry of Dunsfold, husbandman [DW/PA/7/7 f.300; DW/PA/5/1600/42] <Abs 536>
- Jacob of St Peter le Poer, London; Kingston, citizen and skinner [PRO; PCC 1643]
- Jenkin of Kingston [DW/PA/7/11 f.295; DW/PA/5/1626/99]
- Joan of Croydon, widow of John, gent. [PRO; PCC 1635]
- John of Ashtead, clerk [PRO; PCC Will 1626]
- John of Bermondsey [DW/PA/5/1593/88]
- John of Croydon [PRO; PCC 1635]
- John of Thames Ditton [PRO; PCC Admon 1624]
- John of Kingston, gent., senior [PRO; PCC Will 1628] [*and*] [SRO; KB38/1; 1628]
- John of Lambeth - Stockwell [PRO; PCC Admon 1614]
- John of London, feltmaker [DW/PA/5/1582/66]
- John of Swk St Olave, tailor [DW/PA/7/13 f.165; DW/PA/5/1641/106]
- Matthew of Kingston [PRO; PCC Will 1549]
- Morgan of Bermondsey [PRO; PCC 1632]
- Morgan of Swk St Olave, feltmaker [DW/PA/5/1593/46]*
- Peter of Camberwell - Dulwich [PRO; PCC Admon 1606]
- Richard of Swk St Saviour, waterman [DW/PA/7/9 f.86; DW/PA/5/1615/105]
- Richard of Swk St Saviour, waterman [DW/PA/7/11 f.195; DW/PA/5/1625/198]
- Robert of Bermondsey, fellmonger, citizen and leatherdresser [PRO; PCC Will 1610] <Abs, SAC v.24 p.59>
- Roger of Croydon - Waddon, miller [PRO; PCC Will 1598]
- Thomas of Bermondsey [PRO; PCC Admon 1618]
- Thomas of Richmond [PRO; PCC 1635]
- Thomas of Swk St George, feltmaker [DW/PA/7/11 f.98; DW/PA/5/1624/98]
- William of Swk St George, victualler [DW/PA/7/12 f.349; DW/PA/5/1636/73]
- William of Swk St Olave, hatmaker [DW/PA/5/1570/25]
- William of Swk St Olave, waterman [DW/PA/7/13 f.347; 1644]

PRICHARD (ap PRICHARD)

- Ann of Bermondsey, widow [PRO; PCC Will 1621]

PRIDHAM

- John of Hambledon [HRO; 1600 B51]

PRIDY
James of Newington - Walworth [PRO; PCC Admon 1591]
PRIEST (PREIST)
William of Kingston, chirurgeon [DW/PA/7/12 f.262; DW/PA/5/1635/82]
PRIESTMAN (PRISTMAN)
John of Rotherhithe (died overseas) [PRO; PCC Admon 1646]
PRINCE (PRYNCE)
James of Rotherhithe, mariner [PRO; PCC 1635]
John of Egham, husbandman [DW/PA/5/1546/49]
PRINGLE (PRINGELL)
James of Farnham; St Martin in the Fields, Middlesex [PRO; PCC 1630]
PRIOR (PRIOUR,PRYOR)
Henry of Egham [PRO; PCC Admon 1631]
John of Chertsey [DW/PA/5/1557/53]
John of Mitcham, senior [HRO; Reg. Way 2 p.160; 1473]
Richard of Swk St Saviour, butcher [DW/PA/7/12 f.182; DW/PA/5/1633/102]
Thomas of Swk St Saviour - 'Mountaye Close' [DW/PA/7/13 f.23; DW/PA/5/1639/102]
PRISTMAN *see* PRIESTMAN
PRITCHARD
Nicholas of Esher [PRO; PCC Admon 1649]
Sarah of Esher, spinster [PRO; PCC Admon 1649]
Thomas of Esher, bachelor [PRO; PCC Admon 1649]
William of Battersea, clerk [PRO; PCC Admon 1634]
PROBY
Mary of Putney, spinster [PRO; PCC Admon 1647]
PROCTOR (PROCKER,PROCKTER,PROCTER,PROKA')
Joan of Swk St Saviour - Liberty of the Clink, widow [DW/PA/7/11 f.83; DW/PA/5/1623/97]
John of Farnham [*in* DW/PA/5/1559/25]
John of Swk St George, clothworker [DW/PA/5/1587/53]
Richard of Guildford, cardmaker [HRO; 1585 AD36]
Richard of Lambeth, yeoman [DW/PA/7/8 f.180; DW/PA/5/1610/100]
Richard of Swk St Saviour, victualler [DW/PA/7/13 f.123; DW/PA/5/1640/117]
Stephen of Rotherhithe, wherryman [DW/PA/5/1574/43]
William of Newington [PRO; PCC Admon 1636]
PROOST
William of Swk St Olave; St Peter le Poer, London, joiner [GL; Commissary Court of London Will 1619]
PROSSER
Joan of Chertsey, widow [DW/PA/5/1591/111]
William of Chertsey, gent. [PRO; PCC Will 1589]
PROWE
Elizabeth of Cheam, widow [PRO; PCC Admon 1636]
PROWSE
George of Croydon; Old Cleeve, Somerset [PRO; PCC 1646]
PROWTING
John of Lambeth, silk weaver [DW/PA/7/11 f.411; DW/PA/5/1627/90]
PRUNE (PRUYNE)
William of Surrey [PRO; PCC Will 1496]
PRYCE *see* PRICE
PRYOR *see* PRIOR

PUBNEY
  Thomas of Rotherhithe, sailor [DW/PA/5/1593/188]
PUCKERINGE,PUCKRING *see* PICKERING
PUCKRIDGE
  Nicholas of Windlesham - Bagshot [PRO; PCC Admon 1649]
PUDDIFANT (PULLYFANT)
  Thomas of Chertsey [DW/PA/7/6 f.177; DW/PA/5/1559/225]
PUDSEY
  Ralph of Richmond [PRO; PCC Will 1508]
PUE *see* HUGHES (ap PUE)
PUKE
  Thomas of Leatherhead [DW/PA/7/1 f.21; 1485] <Abs 69>
PULLER
  William of Barnes, widower [LPL; 98/1 f.85r; Will 1637]
  William of Godstone [DW/PA/7/2 f.95; 1513]
PULLEN (POLEYN,POLLEYN,PULLIN)
  Aaron of Swk St George, white baker [DW/PA/7/12 f.17; DW/PA/5/1631/81]
  John of Wandsworth, junior [DW/PA/7/2 f.89; 1503]
  John of Wandsworth, etc. [PRO; PCC Will 1506]
  Thomas of Pirbright, yeoman [HRO; 1609 B69]
  William of Wandsworth [PRO; PCC Will 1464]
PULLINGER
  Agnes of Blechingley, widow [PRO; PCC Will 1624]
  John of Blechingley, yeoman [HRO; 1609 B70]
PULLMAN
  Henry of Woking, keeper of the Queen's Park [DW/PA/7/6 f.107; DW/PA/5/1559/99]
  William of Rotherhithe, ropemaker [DW/PA/7/13 f.356; 1644] [*and*] [PRO; PCC 1644]
PULLYFANT *see* PUDDIFANT
PULTER *see* POULTER
PUMFREY
  Richard of Rotherhithe [PRO; PCC 1638]
PUNCHYN
  Thomas *or* Thomas Ponchen of Surrey [PRO; PCC Will 1556]
PUNTER (PONTER,POONTER,POUNTER,POUTER,PUNTTER)
  Elizabeth of Hambledon, widow [PRO; PCC 1632]
  Harry of Wonersh [DW/PA/7/5 f.211; 1541]
  Harry of Shalford [DW/PA/5/1558/222]*
  Henry of Bramley, husbandman [DW/PA/7/7 f.172; DW/PA/5/1597/82] <Abs 316>
  Henry of Send [HRO; 1573 B116]
  Joan of Wonersh, widow [BM; Add.Ms 24,925 f.8v; 1544] <Abs 16>
  Joan of Dunsfold - 'Harrolds in Connsfold'; Wonersh, widow [DW/PA/7/9 f.268; 1618]
  John of Bramley - Thorncombe Street, weaver [HRO; 1632 B45]
  John of Shalford - Thorncombe Street; Dunsfold, weaver, senior [DW/PA/7/9 f.233; DW/PA/5/1617/102]
  Richard of Bramley, yeoman [DW/PA/7/13 f.463; DW/PA/5/1647/14]
  Richard of Egham [PRO; PCC 1649]
  Richard of Shalford, husbandman [HRO; 1571 B157]
  Richard of Shalford; Bramley, yeoman [DW/PA/7/9 f.283; 1618]
  Robert of Godalming [DW/PA/7/4 f.128; 1535]
  Thomas of Shalford - Thorncombe Street, husbandman [DW/PA/7/13 f.390; DW/PA/5/1645/41]

PUPLETT (POPELOTTE,POPLER,PUPLET)
Avery of Banstead [DW/PA/5/1622/78]
George of Banstead, yeoman [DW/PA/7/11 f.14; DW/PA/5/1623/98]
George of Banstead [HRO; 1640 AD132]
John of Banstead [DW/PA/7/2 f.19; 1491]
John of Banstead - South Tadworth, yeoman [DW/PA/5/1545/13]
John of Banstead, husbandman [DW/PA/7/8 f.31; DW/PA/5/1609/76]
PURCAS *see* PURCHASE
PURCELL (PERSELL)
Simon of Swk St Mary Overy [DW/PA/7/4 f.88; 1534]
PURCHASE (PURCAS,PURCHAS)
Elizabeth of Lambeth, widow [DW/PA/5/1605/68] <Abs U159>
Henry of Godalming [DW/PA/7/13 f.69; DW/PA/5/1639/106]
John of Godalming, dyer, senior [PRO; PCC Will 1616]
William of Godalming, clerk [PRO; PCC 1638]
PURDAM *see* PURDHAM
PURDEY *see* PURDY
PURDHAM (PURDAM,PURDOME)
Alice of Woking, widow [DW/PA/5/1550/95]
Gilbert of Cobham [PRO; PCC Will 1576]
Joan of Woking, widow [DW/PA/7/5 f.44; 1538] <Abs 125>
Joan of Woking, widow [DW/PA/7/6 f.288; 1560]
John of Chertsey [PRO; PCC Will 1596]
Richard of Woking [PRO; PCC Admon 1622]
Robert of Horsell, yeoman [DW/PA/5/1558/227]*
PURDY (PURDEY,PURDYE)
Ann of Haslemere, widow [PRO; PCC 1648]
James of Haslemere, yeoman [DW/PA/7/13 f.416; DW/PA/5/1645/42]
John of Addington, yeoman [PRO; PCC Will 1617]
Thomas of Croydon [PRO; PCC 1647]
William of Swk St Olave [DW/PA/7/12 f.379; DW/PA/5/1637/76]
PURSE (PERSE,PURSSE)
Harry of Ash [PRO; PCC Will 1605] <Abs. SAC v.12 p.84>
John of Egham [DW/PA/7/9 f.310; DW/PA/5/1619/89]
Robert of Ash, husbandman, senior [DW/PA/7/7 f.292; DW/PA/5/1600/43] <Abs 522>
Robert, alias Robert Webbe, of Kingston; Mitcham, yeoman [DW/PA/7/6 f.233; 1561]
Robert of Worplesdon, yeoman [PRO; PCC Will 1616]
Walter of Ash, yeoman [DW/PA/7/13 f.166; DW/PA/5/1641/107]
William of Cranleigh [*in* DW/PA/5/1555/67]
PURVIS (PERVES,PERVEYS,PURVIER)
Jane of Cobham, widow [DW/PA/7/13 f.228; DW/PA/5/1643/66]
John of Cobham, tailor [DW/PA/7/12 f.300; DW/PA/5/1635/87]
John of Croydon - Bensham [PRO; PCC Will 1436]
Thomas of Croydon, gent. [PRO; PCC Will 1510]
PURVOCHE,PURWYCHE *see* PARVISHE
PURY
Nicholas of Middle Temple, Middlesex; Sanderstead, barrister [PRO; PCC Will 1587] <Abs SAC v.32 p.84>
PUTENSON *see* PATENSON
PUTT
John of Swk St Saviour, yeoman [DW/PA/7/8 f.278; DW/PA/5/1613/105]

PUTTENHAM
  William of Tandridge, etc., esq. [PRO; PCC Will 1492]
PUTTOCK (PUTTOCKE,PUTTOK)
  John of Alfold, tailor [DW/PA/7/7 f.25; DW/PA/5/1595/73] <Abs 53>
  John of Dunsfold [DW/PA/7/2 f.22; 1492]
  John of Dunsfold, yeoman [DW/PA/7/8 f.348; DW/PA/5/1612/131]
  John of Dunsfold [DW/PA/7/9 f.80; DW/PA/5/1614/88]
  Richard of Dunsfold [DW/PA/7/7 f.236; DW/PA/5/1598/64] <Abs 416>
  Richard of Dunsfold, yeoman [PRO; PCC Will 1613]
  William of Guildford, gent. [HRO; 1621 B40]
PUTTYER *see* PITTER
PYBUS
  Ann, alias Ann Crowther, alias Ann Maltbie of Lambeth [PRO; PCC Admon 1647]
PYCHER *see* PITCHER
PYCKE *see* PICKE
PYCNETT *see* PICKNETT
PYE
  Gamaliel of Bermondsey, citizen and butcher [PRO; PCC Will 1596]
PYERSON *see* PEARSON
PYGE,PYGG *see* PIGGE
PYGGOTT *see* PIGGOTT
PYGHAN *see* PIGEON
PYGOT,PYGOTT *see* PIGGOTT
PYKE *see* PIKE
PYKERD *see* PICKARD
PYKERYNG,PYKKERYNG *see* PICKERING
PYKMAN *see* PICKMAN
PYKNOT *see* PICKNUTT
PYNCARD *see* PINKARD
PYNCHESTER,PYNCHESTRE *see* PINCHESTER
PYNDER *see* PINDER
PYNE *see* PINE
PYNING *see* PENNING
PYNNER *see* PINNER
PYNNOCKE,PYNNOK *see* PINNOCK
PYNNYALL *see* PENNYALL
PYNSON *see* PINSON
PYSTER *see* PESTER
PYTSAM,PYTSAME,PYTSANNE *see* PITSOME
PYTTER *see* PITTER
PYTTES *see* PITTS

QUAIT (QUAYTE)
  George of Farnham, yeoman [DW/PA/7/13 f.182; DW/PA/5/1641/113]
QUARRELL
  Edward of Bermondsey - Bermondsey Street, glover [DW/PA/5/1604/47] <Abs U114>
QUARTERMAINE
  Roger of Swk St Thomas [PRO; E315/483 p.24; 1649]
QUAYT *see* QUAIT

QUELLER
Harry of Stoke next Guildford [DW/PA/7/2 f.178; 1522]
see also WELLER
QUENNELL (QUENELL,QUEYNELL)
Elizabeth of Dunsfold, widow [DW/PA/7/13 f.123; DW/PA/5/1640/120]
John of Haslemere, bachelor [DW/PA/7/9 f.277; 1618]
Peter of Chiddingfold; Haslemere, husbandman [DW/PA/7/6 f.167; DW/PA/5/1559/183]
Peter of Chiddingfold, yeoman [DW/PA/5/1591/94]
Peter of Haslemere, yeoman [DW/PA/5/1558/229]*
Robert of Chiddingfold - Lythe Hill; Haslemere; Compton, gent., senior [DW/PA/7/8 f.346; DW/PA/5/1612/132]
Robert of Ashtead, rector [DW/PA/7/13 f.286; DW/PA/5/1643/74]
Robert of Dunsfold, yeoman [DW/PA/7/12 f.430; DW/PA/5/1638/115]
Thomas of Alfold [PRO; PCC 1635]
Thomas of Chiddingfold [DW/PA/5/1571/40]
William of Haslemere, yeoman [DW/PA/5/1557/35]
QUENEVLLE (de QUENEVLLE)
Joan, alias Joan de Lannay, of ...., widow of Francis [*French*] [DW/PA/7/7 f.43; DW/PA/5/1595/26] <Abs 84>
QUENT
Arnold of Godalming [DW/PA/5/1568/66]
QUICK (QUICKE)
Ann of Kingston, widow [DW/PA/5/1558/228]*
Richard of Croydon, maltman [PRO; PCC Will 1617]
Roger of Swk St Thomas, joiner [DW/PA/7/11 f.442; DW/PA/5/1628/82]
William of Kingston [PRO; PCC Will 1546]
QUIDDINGTON (QUITTINGTON,QUODHEMPTON)
Anthony of Blechingley [DW/PA/7/9 f.337; DW/PA/5/1620/98]
Richard of Newdigate [PRO; PCC 1637]
see also CUDDINGTON
QUILTER (QUYLTER)
John of Guildford [PRO; PCC Will 1518]
QUINBY (QUINBYE,QUYNBY,QUYNY)
Henry of Farnham, citizen and grocer [PRO; PCC Will 1596]
John of Farnham [PRO; PCC Will 1557 (2)]
John of Swk St Margaret [DW/PA/7/5 f.124; 1539]
QUIXLEY
John of Ewell [PRO; PCC Will 1477]
QUYLTER *see* QUILTER
QUYNBY *see* QUINBY
QUYNY *see* QUINBY

RABBETT
Michael of Streatham, clerk [PRO; PCC 1631]
RACHEFORDE
Roger of Ashtead [DW/PA/7/2 f.131; 1518]
RADCLIFFE (RATCLIFFE,RATCLYFF)
Mary of Dorking, widow [DW/PA/7/12 f.279; 1635]
Richard of Battersea, gent. [PRO; PCC Will 1587]
Robert, earl of Sussex [SRO; 65/2/28; 1625]
Thomas of Surrey, earl of Sussex [PRO; PCC Will 1584 *and* 1585]
William of Dorking, gent. [PRO; PCC Will 1614]

RADFEARNE *see* REDFERN

RADFORD
- George, alias George Haynes of Newington [PRO; PCC Admon 1633]
- Mary, alias Mary Blincoe of Newington, widow [PRO; PCC Will 1627]

RADSTON
- William of Swk St Olave [HRO; Reg, Way 1 p,26; 1453]

RAFTER
- Robert of Swk St Saviour [DW/PA/5/1547/22]

RAFULLS
- John of Swk St George [DW/PA/7/5 f,183; 1540]

RAGGE (RAGG)
- Bowett of Swk St Saviour [DW/PA/7/7 f,519; DW/PA/5/1606/74] <Abs 975>
- Robert of Beddington [PRO; PCC 1638]
- Thomas of Swk St Saviour, ironmonger [DW/PA/7/8 f,131; DW/PA/5/1610/101]

RAGLES
- Thomas of Guildford, yeoman [DW/PA/7/9 f,127; DW/PA/5/1615/106]

RAINS (RAINES,RAYNES,REYNES)
- Edward of Worplesdon [DW/PA/7/11 f,495; DW/PA/5/1629/79]
- James of Barnes, gardener [LPL; 96/2147; Will 1618]
- John of Streatham, gardener [DW/PA/7/12 f,165; DW/PA/5/1633/107]
- Thomas of Surrey [PRO; PCC Will 1557]

RAINSFORD (RAYNSFORD)
- Richard of Newdigate, yeoman [DW/PA/7/13 f,450; DW/PA/5/1646/48]

RAKINS
- Nicholas of Mortlake, vintner [LPL; 96/2100; Will 1646]

RALEIGHE
- Walter of Mitcham [PRO; PCC Admon 1619]

RALINS
- Michael of Carshalton [PRO; PCC 1647]

RALPH
- Alice, alias Alice Rolph of Godalming - Eashing, widow [DW/PA/7/11 f,529; DW/PA/5/1630/83]

RAME
- Joan of Egham, widow [PRO; PCC Will 1627]

RAMPSTON
- Margaret of Chingford, Essex; Swk St Olave, widow [PRO; PCC Will 1590] <Abs Emmison pp,242-243>

RAMSDEN
- Thomas of Newington, yeoman [PRO; PCC Will 1579]
- Thomas of Swk St Olave, cordwainer [DW/PA/7/7 f,239; 1593] <Abs 421>

RAMSEY
- (Lady) Bridget of Kingston - Ham [PRO; PCC Admon 1622]
- Robert of Swk St George, yeoman [DW/PA/5/1578/104]
- (Sir) Thomas of Surrey, knight and alderman [PRO; PCC Will 1590]

RAMSOULDE
- William of Crowhurst, yeoman [PRO; PCC Will 1582]

RANALDS *see* REYNOLDS

RANCE *see* RAUNCE

RAND (RANDS)
- Joan of Oxted, wife of Ralph, clerk [PRO; PCC 1641]
- John of Clapham [PRO; PCC Will 1620]
- Mary of Oxted, widow of Ralph, clerk [PRO; PCC 1639]
- Ralph of Oxted, clerk [DW/PA/7/13 f,477; DW/PA/5/1648/32]

RANDALL
  Martha of Putney, spinster [PRO; PCC Admon 1642]
  William of Walton [PRO; PCC Admon 1641]
RANDOLPH (RANDOLF,RANDOLPHE)
  Hugh of Swk St Olave [DW/PA/5/1592/102B]
  John of Chertsey, esq. [PRO; PCC Will 1512]
RANDS *see* RAND
RANGER *see* RAUNGER
RANOLLS *see* REYNOLDS
RANS *see* RAUNCE
RAPKIN (RAPKYNE,ROPKYNE,ROPKYNS)
  Humphrey of Croydon, esq. [PRO; PCC Will 1543]
  John of Caterham, yeoman [DW/PA/5/1579/76]*
  John of Croydon [LPL; 96/2112; Will 1649]
  Thomas of Caterham [DW/PA/7/2 f.4; 1490]
RAPLEY (RAPLIE,RAPPLE,ROPLEY)
  Henry of Chiddingfold, servant [HRO; 1595 B45]
  Joan of Chiddingfold [DW/PA/7/2 f.13; 1489]
  John of Chiddingfold [DW/PA/7/1 ff.96,99; 1489] (Abs 317)
  John of Chiddingfold, fuller [DW/PA/7/4 f.210; 1537]
  John of Chiddingfold [PRO; PCC Admon 1586]
  John, by West of Chiddingfold, yeoman, senior [HRO; 1589 B45A]
  Margaret of Godalming, widow [DW/PA/5/1591/39]
  Robert of Chiddingfold [HRO; 1602 AD34]
  Robert of Wotton [PRO; PCC Admon 1648]
  Stephen of Witley; Chiddingfold, husbandman [DW/PA/7/7 f.580; DW/PA/5/1606/75] (Abs 1082)
  Stephen of Chiddingfold, yeoman [DW/PA/7/8 f.38; DW/PA/5/1609/97]
  Thomas of Chiddingfold, yeoman [DW/PA/7/11 f.75; DW/PA/5/1623/99]
  Thomas of Chiddingfold, senior [PRO; PCC Will 1624]
  Thomas of Witley [DW/PA/7/8 f.138; DW/PA/5/1610/102]
RASHALL *see* RUSSELL
RASTONE
  William of Compton, gent. [DW/PA/5/1562/37]
RATCLIFFE,RATCLYFF *see* RADCLIFFE
RATHWOOD *see* ROTHEWOODE
RAUFFE *see* ROLFE
RAUNCE (RANCE,RANS,RAWNCE,RAWNS,RAWNSE)
  Ann of Worplesdon - Wyke, widow of William, yeoman) [DW/PA/5/1557/89]
  Crecence of Thames Ditton, widow [PRO; PCC Act Book 1545-46 p.242]
  Elizabeth, alias Elizabeth Phillipps of Farnham, widow [PRO; PCC Admon 1614]
  John of Chertsey [PRO; PCC Will 1489]
  John of Farnham, mercer [DW/PA/5/1558/230]*
  John of Farnham [DW/PA/5/1563/124]
  John of Woking [DW/PA/7/6 f.239; 1560]
  Lawrence of Cranleigh, yeoman [DW/PA/5/1576/64]
  Lawrence of Chobham [DW/PA/7/8 f.362; DW/PA/5/1612/134]
  Richard of Farnham; Ash, mercer [DW/PA/5/1557/36]
  Robert of Farnham [DW/PA/7/4 f.76; 1534]
  Thomas of Farnham, yeoman [DW/PA/5/1592/67]
  William of Long Ditton, husbandman [DW/PA/7/13 f.47; DW/PA/5/1639/115]

RAUNGER
James of Frensham [HRO; 1603 AD55]
RAVELL
John of Guildford, clothier [DW/PA/5/1571/49]
RAVEN
John of Swk St Olave [DW/PA/7/4 f.153; 1536]
RAVES *see* REEVES
RAWLEY (REWELEYE)
George of Send [DW/PA/7/5 f.83; 1539]
RAWLINGSON *see* RAWLINSON
RAWLINS (RAWLYNS,RAWLYNSE)
Joan of Lambeth - Water Lambeth, widow [DW/PA/7/5 f.216; 1541]
Richard of Lambeth, waterman [PRO; PCC Will 1614]
Robert of Camberwell - Peckham Rye, husbandman [DW/PA/7/12 f.335; DW/PA/5/1636/81]
Thomas of Godalming; Chichester, Sussex; New College, Oxford; St Peter in the East, Oxford; Suffolk; Slimbridge, Gloucestershire; Magdalen College, Oxford; Swk [DW/PA/5/1605/71] <Abs U160>
Thomas of Kingston, labourer [*in* DW/PA/5/1546/11]
William of Richmond [PRO; PCC 1632]
RAWLINSON (RAWLINGSON,ROWLLYNGSON)
Alice of Swk St Olave, widow [DW/PA/7/11 f.344; DW/PA/5/1625/200]
Gilbert of Woking [DW/PA/5/1545/11]
John of Swk St George, carpenter [DW/PA/7/11 f.102; DW/PA/5/1624/99]
Margaret of Guildford, widow [PRO; PCC Will 1573]
RAWNS,RAWNSE *see* RAUNCE
RAWSON
Joseph of East Molesey [DW/PA/7/12 f.431; DW/PA/5/1637/82]
RAWSTERNE
Lawrence of Swk St Saviour, porter [DW/PA/5/1592/28]
RAWSTRICK
John of Kingston, saddler [HRO; 1567 B129-130]
RAWTHMELL
Arthur of Camberwell - Dulwich, gent. [PRO; PCC 1645]
RAYGNARD
John of Swk St George, armourer [DW/PA/5/1593/77]
RAYNER
John of Cobham, sawyer [DW/PA/7/8 f.174; DW/PA/5/1610/103]
RAYNES *see* RAINS
RAYNOLD *see* REYNOLDS
RAYNSFORD *see* RAINSFORD
READE (REDDE,REDE,REED,REEDE)
(Sir) Bartholomew of Surrey, knight [PRO; PCC Will 1505]
Charles of Lambeth, joiner [DW/PA/7/7 f.440; DW/PA/5/1603/137] <Abs 831>
Cornelius of Swk St Margaret [HRO; Reg. Fox 3 p.62; 1513]
Edward of Swk St Saviour [DW/PA/5/1593/80]
Harry of Haslemere [DW/PA/5/1563/11]
Isabel of Croydon, spinster [PRO; PCC 1648]
James of Swk St Olave, waterman [DW/PA/7/13 f.61; DW/PA/5/1640/123]
Jane of Thursley, spinster [DW/PA/7/9 f.252; DW/PA/5/1617/103]
John of Farnham [DW/PA/7/6 f.158; DW/PA/5/1559/149]
John of Stoke, brickmaker [DW/PA/7/11 f.501; DW/PA/5/1629/81]
John of Stoke next Guildford, brickmaker [HRO; 1612 B75]
John of Weybridge [PRO; PCC Will 1506]

READE (REDDE,REDE,REED,REEDE) [*continued*
Katherine of Stoke next Guildford [PRO; PCC Admon 1649]
Lettice of Kingston, widow of Thomas, citizen and dyer [GL; Commissary Court of London 1496]
Ralph of Egham [PRO; PCC Admon 1640]
Richard of Farnham, fuller [DW/PA/7/4 f.152; 1536]
(Sir) Robert of Surrey, knight [PRO; PCC Will 1518]
Robert of Godstone [DW/PA/5/1578/42]
Robert of Stoke next Guildford [DW/PA/7/11 f.475; DW/PA/5/1628/83]
Thomas of Swk St Saviour, plumber [DW/PA/5/1580/16]
Thomas of Weybridge [PRO; PCC Will 1515]
William of Wandsworth [PRO; PCC Will 1592 *and* 1593]
William of Weybridge, esq. [PRO; PCC Will 1534]

READING (REDDINGE,REDDYN,REDING,REDINGE,REDYNG)
Christopher of Kingston [PRO; PCC Admon 1649]
John of Lambeth - Lambeth Dean [PRO; PCC 1645]
John of Walton on Thames [*in* DW/PA/5/1555/68]
Margaret of Swk St Olave, widow [DW/PA/7/2 f.90; 1505]
Richard of Walton on Thames, fisherman [DW/PA/7/12 f.122; DW/PA/5/1632/83]
Robert of Walton on Thames, fisherman, senior [DW/PA/7/13 f.251; DW/PA/5/1640/127]
Thomas of ... [DW/PA/5/1587/118]
William of Molesey [PRO; PCC Will 1596]

REAMES
Robert of Newington [LPL; 96/2137; 98/1 f.14v; Will 1630]

REAVES *see* REEVES

RECORDE
John of Swk St George - Blackman Street, freemason and marbler, senior [DW/PA/5/1593/55]

RECULVER (RECULLVER)
John of Chaldon, yeoman [DW/PA/7/10 f.32; DW/PA/5/1616/122]
John of Swk St Mary Overy, prior [LPL; Reg.Abp Morton f.79v; Admon 1492]
Thomas of Lambeth, yeoman [DW/PA/7/10 f.208; DW/PA/5/1620/99]
William of Swk St Mary Magdalen [DW/PA/7/2 f.59; 1498]

REDCAN
Gosson of Swk St Saviour [DW/PA/7/7 f.372; DW/PA/5/1602/70] <Abs 684>

REDDE *see* READE

REDDINGE,REDDYN *see* READING

REDE *see* READE

REDENESSE *see* REDNESS

REDESTON
Thomas, alias Thomas Reygate of Horley [PRO; PCC Will 1472]

REDFERN (RADFEARNE)
Ellis of Godalming [DW/PA/7/10 f.191; DW/PA/5/1621/103]

REDFORD (REDEFORD,REDFORDE,RIDFORD,RIDFORDE)
Christopher of West Horsley, yeoman [DW/PA/7/13 f.461; DW/PA/5/1647/16; GMR; 54/1/65]
Frances of West Horsley, widow [DW/PA/7/10 f.295; DW/PA/5/1622/79]
George of Ewhurst, tailor [DW/PA/5/1593/22]
Joan of Wotton, spinster, daughter of George, yeoman [DW/PA/5/1593/159]
John of Albury - Farley Green, yeoman [DW/PA/7/12 f.486; DW/PA/5/1638/118]

REDFORD (REDEFORD,REDFORDE,RIDFORD,RIDFORDE) [*continued*
John of West Horsley; Shere; Ewell - Kingswood; East Horsley, yeoman [DW/PA/7/5 f.79; 1539]
John of West Horsley, yeoman [DW/PA/7/8 f.186; DW/PA/5/1610/104]
John of West Horsley, yeoman [DW/PA/7/12 f.253; DW/PA/5/1635/93]
John of Shere [DW/PA/7/2 f.106; 1516]
John of Shere [HRO; 1521 B28]
John of Wotton, yeoman [HRO; 1593 B63]
Margaret of Ockham, widow [PRO; PCC Will 1619]
Richard of Shere - Hoe [DW/PA/7/8 f.254; DW/PA/5/1611/96]
Robert of Abinger, husbandman [DW/PA/7/13 f.503; DW/PA/5/1649/17]
Robert of Wotton [DW/PA/7/3 f.203; 1531]
Thomas of West Horsley, yeoman [DW/PA/7/9 f.151; DW/PA/5/1615/107]
William of West Horsley; Shere; Abinger; Ockham, yeoman [DW/PA/7/4 f.199; 1537]
William of Ockham; West Horsley; Effingham, yeoman [DW/PA/7/8 f.328; DW/PA/5/1613/109]

REDHEAD (REDHEADE)
Bartholomew of Egham, yeoman [DW/PA/5/1576/38]
William of Horne, yeoman [DW/PA/7/11 f.522; DW/PA/5/1629/82]

REDING *see* READING

REDMAN
Elizabeth of Godalming, widow of Richard [DW/PA/7/5 f.200; 1540]
John of Lambeth, labourer [DW/PA/7/7 f.73; DW/PA/5/1596/48] <Abs 135>
Richard of Godalming [DW/PA/7/4 f.127; 1535]
see also REMNANT

REDNESS (REDENESSE)
William of Ash, rector [HRO; Reg. Wyk 2 p.135; 1375]

REDWOOD
Robert of Streatham - Tooting Bec [PRO; PCC 1631]

REDYNG *see* READING

REED,REEDE *see* READE

REELIE *see* RILEY

REEVES (RAVES,REAVES,REEVE,REVE,REVES,RYVE)
Agnes of Frensham, widow [HRO; 1573 B120]
Christiana of Farnham - Tilford, widow [DW/PA/7/11 f.141; DW/PA/5/1624/100]
Edward of Swk St George, innholder [DW/PA/7/13 f.470; DW/PA/5/1648/31]
Elizabeth of Bentley, Hampshire, widow [DW/PA/7/11 f.575; DW/PA/5/1630/84]
(Sir) Henry of Barnes, knight [PRO; PCC 1642]
John, alias John May of Bentley, Hampshire [DW/PA/7/11 f.415; DW/PA/5/1627/76]
John of Great Bookham, vicar [PRO; PCC Will 1620] <Soame 843,1344>
John, alias John May of Farnham - Tilford, yeoman [DW/PA/5/1605/58] <Abs U154>
John of Putney - Roehampton [PRO; PCC Will 1555]
Ralph of Swk St Saviour [DW/PA/5/1576/137]
Roger of Egham; Horton [? in Epsom], smith [*in* DW/PA/5/1557/75]
Roger of Egham, blacksmith [PRO; PCC Will 1566]
Thomas of Farnham, yeoman [DW/PA/7/13 f.395; DW/PA/5/1645/45]
Thomas of London; Whilton, Northamptonshire, wireworker [DW/PA/7/8 f.315; DW/PA/5/1613/106]

REEVES (RAVES,REAVES,REEVE,REVE,REVES,RYVE) [*continued*
William of Swk St Olave, citizen and carpenter [DW/PA/7/11 f.244; DW/PA/5/1625/201]
REFFOLD (REFFEW,REFFOULD)
Henry of Worplesdon, yeoman [DW/PA/7/7 f.302; DW/PA/5/1600/45] <Abs 541>
Henry of Worplesdon, yeoman [DW/PA/7/12 f.207; DW/PA/5/1634/81]
Jane of Guildford St Nicolas - Littleton [DW/PA/7/11 f.525; DW/PA/5/1630/85]
REGNARDE
John of Swk St George, armourer [DW/PA/5/1593/123]
REHAM *see* REMNANT
REIGATE (REYGATE,RYGATE)
Robert of Send [DW/PA/5/1558/240]*
Thomas, alias Thomas Redeston of Horley [PRO; PCC Will 1472]
Thomas of Wandsworth [PRO; PCC Will 1404]
REMINGTON (REMYNGTON)
William of Newington [PRO; PCC Will 1511]
REMNANT (REHAM,REMNAM,REMNAUNTE,REMPMANT,REMPNAM,REMPNANT)
... [a man] of Pirbright [DW/PA/7/2 f.122; 1518]
Anthony of Pirbright, shoemaker [DW/PA/7/10 f.110; DW/PA/5/1619/90]
Edward of Pirbright - Cowshot, yeoman [DW/PA/7/10 f.294; DW/PA/5/1622/80]
Elizabeth of Chobham, widow [DW/PA/7/10 f.39; DW/PA/5/1617/104]
George of Byfleet, yeoman [PRO; PCC Will 1626]
Henry of Pirbright, husbandman [DW/PA/7/7 f.539; DW/PA/5/1607/72] <Abs 1012>
James of Pirbright [DW/PA/5/1587/23]
John of Pirbright [DW/PA/7/1 f.34; 1486] <Abs 114>
John of Pirbright - Cowshot [DW/PA/7/4 f.184; 1536]
John of Pirbright, weaver, junior [HRO; 1579 B35]
John of Pirbright - Cowshot, senior [DW/PA/5/1580/40]
John of Pirbright, yeoman [DW/PA/5/1593/23]
John of Pirbright - Cowshot, yeoman [DW/PA/7/13 f.209; DW/PA/5/1642/68]
John of Worplesdon, yeoman [DW/PA/7/13 f.165; DW/PA/5/1641/118]
Margaret of Limpsfield [PRO; PCC Will 1573]
Matthew of Limpsfield, bricklayer [DW/PA/5/1580/53]
Richard of Guildford, mercer [PRO; PCC 1620] <*see Soane 388*>
Stephen of Godalming - Binscombe [DW/PA/7/13 f.38; DW/PA/5/1639/113]
Thomas of Compton [DW/PA/7/12 f.14; DW/PA/5/1631/88]
Thomas of Godalming [DW/PA/7/7 f.576; DW/PA/5/1606/76] <Abs 1077>
William of Chertsey [DW/PA/5/1561/27]
see also REDMAN
REMYNGTON *see* REMINGTON
RENDELL (RENDALLE)
John of Lambeth [DW/PA/7/4 f.58; 1533]
John of Frensham - Hillside [DW/PA/5/1552/20]
RENOLDES *see* REYNOLDS
RESTRYCKE
Christian of Frensham [DW/PA/7/3 f.109; 1529]
REVE *see* REEVES
REVELL
James of Streatham [PRO; PCC Will 1552] <Abs, SAC v.52 p.41>
Thomas of Swk St Saviour, dyer [DW/PA/7/9 f.287; 1618]
REVERS *see* RIVERS

REVES *see* REEVESREVELEYE *see* RAWLEY
REWMORGONY
Robert of Horsell, clerk [DW/PA/7/1 f.63; 1487] <Abs 210>
REYGATE *see* REIGATE
REYNES *see* RAINS
REYNOLDS (RANALDS,RANOOLD,RAYNOLD,RAYNOLDE,RAYNOLDES,RAYNOLDS,RENOLD, RENOLDES,REYNOLD,REYNOLDE,REYNOLDES)
Agnes of Shalford, widow [BM; Add.Ms 24,925 f.5r; 1544] <Abs 8>
Agnes of Swk St Saviour, widow [DW/PA/7/9 f.80; DW/PA/5/1614/99]
Ann of Rotherhithe, (daughter of late Richard, citizen of London [DW/PA/7/11 f.210; DW/PA/5/1625/202]
John of Bramley, husbandman [DW/PA/7/7 f.187; DW/PA/5/1598/69] <Abs 340>
John of Egham - Stroud [DW/PA/7/6 f.195; 1560]
John of East Molesey [PRO; PCC Will 1488]
John of East Molesey [PRO; PCC Will 1507]
John of Newington [LPL; 98/1 ff.59r-v; Will 1634]
John of Shalford [DW/PA/7/5 f.57; 1539] <Abs 79>
John of Swk St George [DW/PA/5/1575/18]
John of Titsey [DW/PA/5/1552/31; *cover only* DW/PA/5/1557/107]
Lambert of Kingston, cooper [DW/PA/5/1580/39]
Margaret of Kingston, widow [DW/PA/7/1 f.99; 1489] <Abs 324>
Maria of Lambeth, widow [DW/PA/7/12 f.255; DW/PA/5/1635/89]
Nicholas of Rotherhithe, goldsmith [GL; Archdeaconry Court of London Will 1602]
Phillip of Titsey [DW/PA/5/1557/106]
Richard of Lingfield; Nutfield; Titsey [PRO; PCC Will 1601]
Richard of Swk St George [DW/PA/5/1593/54]
Thomas of Egham - Stroud, husbandman [HRO; 1573 B121]
William of Ditton; Kingston [HRO; Reg. Way 1 p.86; 1465]
William of Egham [DW/PA/7/1 f.59; 1487] <Abs 196>
William of Molesey [PRO; PCC Will 1509]
William of Newington, citizen and fletcher [PRO; PCC Will 1598]
RHODES (ROADES,RODES)
Dinah of Merton, widow [DW/PA/7/11 f.430; DW/PA/5/1627/92]
Margaret of Wandsworth, widow [PRO; PCC 1643]
Richard of Reigate [PRO; PCC Will 1618]
Roger of Swk St Saviour, goldsmith [DW/PA/7/7 f.135; DW/PA/5/1597/84] <Abs 248>
Rowland of Wandsworth, waterman [DW/PA/7/13 f.105; DW/PA/5/1640/122]
William of Swk St Saviour, porter [DW/PA/7/12 f.305; DW/PA/5/1635/98]
RHYME *see* RYME
RICARD,RICARDES,RICCAS *see* RICHARDS
RICE (RYSE)
James of Seale - Hampton [HRO; 1597 B64]
Margaret of Swk St Olave; Bermondsey, widow [DW/PA/7/9 f.139; DW/PA/5/1615/108]
Tyse of Swk St Olave [DW/PA/5/1571/19]
RICH (RICHE)
Thomas of Putney [PRO; PCC Will 1513]
RICHARDS (ap PRICHARD,ap RICHERD,RICARD,RICARDES,RICCAS,RICHARDES,RICKERS)
Ann of Bermondsey, widow [PRO; PCC Will 1621]
Henry of Tooting, yeoman [DW/PA/7/7 f.85; 1596] <Abs 155>
James of Swk St Olave [DW/PA/7/6 f.176; DW/PA/5/1559/160]
John of Swk St Olave [HRO; 1527 B20]

RICHARDS (ap PRICHARD, ap RICHERD, RICARD, RICARDES, RICCAS, RICHARDES, RICKERS)
[*continued*

John of Swk St Olave [DW/PA/7/5 f.58; 1539] <Abs 100>

John of Walton on Thames, husbandman [DW/PA/7/10 f.273; DW/PA/5/1622/85]

Margery of Horley [GL; Archdeaconry Court of London Will 1382]

Thomas of Surrey [PRO; PCC Will 1488]

RICHARDSON (RICHARDESON, RYCHARDSON)

Agnes of Reigate, servant to Edmund Page [DW/PA/5/1579/74]*

Alexander of Swk St Olave, brewer's servant [DW/PA/7/11 f.269; DW/PA/5/1625/203]

Ann, alias Ann Green, of Barnes, widow [LPL; 98/1 f.81r; Will 1637]

Anthony of Blechingley, glover [DW/PA/5/1580/20]*

Bridget of Battersea, widow [DW/PA/5/1591/101]

Francis of Reigate, mercer [DW/PA/5/1592/72]

Francis of Reigate, mercer [DW/PA/7/10 f.245; DW/PA/5/1622/81]

Geoffrey of Swk St Olave, citizen and cook [DW/PA/5/1563/121]

Geoffrey of Banstead - Tadworth [PRO; PCC Will 1567]

George of Bermondsey [PRO; PCC Admon 1604]

Gregory of Battersea [PRO; PCC Will 1557]

Henry of Ockley [? HRO; 1558]

Joan of Swk St Olave; St Katherine by the Tower, widow [DW/PA/7/7 f.399; DW/PA/5/1603/138] <Abs 741>

John of Burstow [LPL; 98/1 f.86v; Will 1637]

John of Gatton; Blechingley; Merstham; Reigate, yeoman [DW/PA/7/7 f.626; DW/PA/5/1608/85] <Abs 1169>

John of Kingston [DW/PA/7/2 f.15; 1491]

John of Leatherhead [? HRO; 1529]

John of Reigate, yeoman [DW/PA/5/1591/10]

John of Reigate [DW/PA/7/11 f.404; DW/PA/5/1627/91]

John of Reigate, senior [PRO; PCC Will 1629]

John of Swk St Margaret [DW/PA/7/5 f.26; 1538] <Abs 89>

John of Swk St Mary Magdalen, brewer [Westminster Abbey; *see 4th Report of the Historical Manuscripts Commission App.I,p.197*; 1516]

John of Swk St Olave [DW/PA/7/7 f.205; 1598] <Abs 363>

John of Swk St Saviour, waterman [DW/PA/7/8 f.356; DW/PA/5/1612/136]

Katherine of Chaldon; Merstham, widow [DW/PA/7/9 f.202; DW/PA/5/1616/118]

Katherine of Reigate, widow [DW/PA/7/7 f.342; DW/PA/5/1601/70] <Abs 620>

Malachi of Blechingley [PRO; PCC Admon 1647]

Nicholas of Chaldon; St Michael Bassishaw, London; Merstham, yeoman [DW/PA/7/9 f.80; DW/PA/5/1615/109]

Nicholas, alias Nicholas Miller, of Croydon, collier [PRO; PCC Will 1607] <Abs, SAC v.12 pp.209-210>

Oliver of Leatherhead [PRO; PCC Will 1546]

Peter of Guildford [PRO; PCC Will 1559]

Peter of Swk St Saviour, freeholder [*in* DW/PA/5/1563/120]

Robert of Swk St Margaret [DW/PA/5/1538/1]

Robert of Frensham, yeoman [DW/PA/7/9 f.300; DW/PA/5/1619/91]

Sarah of Reigate, spinster [PRO; PCC Admon 1637]

Thomas of Blechingley, yeoman, senior [DW/PA/7/13 f.227; DW/PA/5/1642/70]

Thomas of Blechingley [PRO; PCC 1647]

Thomas of Farnham [DW/PA/5/1558/238]*

William of Byfleet, yeoman, senior [HRO; 1603 B48]

William of Byfleet, yeoman [DW/PA/7/13 f.153; DW/PA/5/1641/117]

RICHARDSON (RICHARDESON,RYCHARDSON) [*continued*
  William of Reigate, senior [DW/PA/7/6 f.87; DW/PA/5/1559/109]
  William of Streatham, miller [DW/PA/7/13 f.98; DW/PA/5/1640/125]
RICHBELL (RICHBEALE,RICHEBELL,RITCHBELL,RYCHBELL,RYCHEBELL)
  Avery of Epsom, yeoman [DW/PA/7/7 f.629; DW/PA/5/1608/84] <Abs 1177>
  Denise of Banstead, widow [DW/PA/7/6 f.233; 1561]
  Elizabeth of Send, wife of Thomas, yeoman) [PRO; PCC Will 1616]
  Geoffrey of Abinger, yeoman [DW/PA/7/12 f.228; DW/PA/5/1634/82]
  Geoffrey of West Horsley, yeoman [DW/PA/7/8 f.161; DW/PA/5/1611/97]
  Henry of Shere [DW/PA/7/6 f.278; 1560]
  Jane of Headley, widow [PRO; PCC 1649]
  John of Carshalton, junior [DW/PA/7/3 f.176; 1531]
  John of Carshalton, yeoman [DW/PA/7/5 f.166; 1540]
  John of Epsom, tailor [DW/PA/5/1592/100]
  John of Walton on the Hill [DW/PA/7/6 f.57; DW/PA/5/1559/108]
  Joyce, alias Joyce Frith, of Reigate, widow [PRO; PCC Admon 1619]
  Leonard of Woking [DW/PA/7/8 f.399; DW/PA/5/1612/135]
  Mary of Woking, widow [DW/PA/7/13 f.146; DW/PA/5/1641/115]
  Richard of Effingham [DW/PA/7/7 f.58; DW/PA/5/1596/49] <Abs 111>
  Susanna of Woking, spinster [DW/PA/7/13 f.456; DW/PA/5/1647/15]
  Thomas of Ashtead, husbandman [HRO; 1587 B71]
  Thomas of Great Bookham [DW/PA/7/8 f.249; DW/PA/5/1613/107]
  Thomas of Send, yeoman [DW/PA/7/11 f.556; DW/PA/5/1630/86]
  William of Banstead [DW/PA/5/1558/239]*
  William of Banstead, husbandman [DW/PA/5/1562/2]
  William of Beddington [PRO; PCC Admon 1614]
  William of Carshalton [PRO; PCC Will 1557]
  William of Epsom; Ewell, yeoman [DW/PA/5/1593/5]
RICHE *see* RICH
RICHEBELL *see* RICHBELL
RICKARDS (RICKARDES)
  John of ... [*proved at* Kingston] [DW/PA/7/8 f.402; DW/PA/5/1612/137]
  John of Ewell, carpenter [DW/PA/7/9 f.232; DW/PA/5/1617/105]
RICKEMAN *see* RICKMAN
RICKERS *see* RICHARDS
RICKFORTH (RYKFORTH)
  Robert of Swk St Saviour [DW/PA/5/1546/30]
RICKLES (RIKILS)
  Agnes of Wandsworth [PRO; PCC Will 1502]
RICKMAN (RICHMAN,RICKEMAN,RYCKMAN)
  Christopher of Newdigate [DW/PA/7/13 f.7; DW/PA/5/1640/121]
  Edward of Newdigate, husbandman [DW/PA/7/10 f.183; DW/PA/5/1620/100]
  John of Frensham - Churt [BM; Add.Ms 24,925 f.18r; 1544] <Abs 41>
  John *or* Thomas of Charlwood [LPL; 96/2162; Will 1638]
  Nicholas of Newdigate [DW/PA/5/1593/64]
  Nicholas of Newdigate; Charlwood [PRO; PCC 1639]
  Stephen of Dorking, clerk [PRO; PCC Admon 1611]
  Thomas *or* John of Charlwood [LPL; 96/2162; Will 1638]
RICKSON (RYCKSON)
  William of Swk [DW/PA/7/6 f.197; 1560]
RIDD *see* ATTRYDE; RYDE
RIDDELL
  George of Send, yeoman [HRO; 1624 AD104]
RIDE *see* RYDE

RIDEN (RIDON,RYDON)
Elizabeth of Battersea; Kingston - Kingston Hill; Clapham - Lady Acre, widow [DW/PA/5/1593/83]
Elizabeth of Pyrford [PRO; PCC Will 1612]
Henry of Battersea [PRO; PCC Will 1531]
Henry of Battersea, gent. [PRO; PCC Will 1568]
John of Battersea, yeoman [PRO; PCC Will 1500; CCAL; 1500 f.28r]
Robert of Battersea, gent. [PRO; PCC Will 1538]
see also ROYDON

RIDER (RIDAR,RYDER)
Alice, alias Alice Pointe, of Swk St Saviour [DW/PA/7/7 f.221; DW/PA/5/1598/73] <Abs 391>
Christopher of Swk St Olave, joiner [DW/PA/5/1582/104]
Jane of Swk St Saviour, widow [DW/PA/7/13 f.449; DW/PA/5/1646/45]
John of Chaldon [DW/PA/7/4 f.72; 1534]
Juliana of Kingston, widow [DW/PA/7/4 f.138; 1536]

RIDFORD, RIDFORDE *see* REDFORD

RIDGE
Benjamin of Dorking, yeoman [DW/PA/7/13 f.179; DW/PA/5/1641/119]
Jeremiah of Burstow, yeoman [PRO; PCC Will 1621]

RIDGER *see* RIGENE (RIGERE)

RIDGEWAY (RIDGEWAYE,RIDGWAY)
Margaret, alias Margaret Vergis, of West Horsley [PRO; PCC Admon 1640]
Robert of Lambeth [PRO; PCC Will 1603] <Abs. SAC v.11 p.129>

RIDING
John of Thorpe [DW/PA/7/1 f.8; 1484] <Abs 26>

RIDLEY (RIDLIE,RYDLEY,RYDLY)
Ann, alias Ann Townsend of Newington, wife of William Townsend [LPL; 98/1 f.65v; Will 1635]
Clemence of Lingfield, widow [DW/PA/5/1593/201]
Francis of Egham, gent. [PRO; PCC 1640]
George of Lingfield [PRO; PCC Will 1565]
Henry of Newdigate, husbandman [DW/PA/7/12 f.501; 1638]
Hugh of ... [*Incomplete and crossed through*] [DW/PA/7/2 f.6; c.1490]
John of Thames Ditton [DW/PA/7/8 f.84; DW/PA/5/1609/98]
John of Oxted, yeoman [DW/PA/7/13 f.419; DW/PA/5/1645/46]
Nicholas of Tooting, yeoman [DW/PA/5/1555/45]
Richard of Newington, silk weaver and victualler [LPL; 96/2164; 98/1 ff.12r,63v; Wills 1630,1634]
Robert of Lingfield - 'Ware' [DW/PA/7/5 f.188; 1540]
William of Lingfield, yeoman [DW/PA/5/1592/119]
William of Nutfield, yeoman [DW/PA/7/10 f.132; DW/PA/5/1620/101]

RIDON *see* RIDEN

RIGDON (RIGGDEN,RYGDAYN)
Henry of Frensham [DW/PA/7/5 f.7; 1538] <Abs 44>
John of Peper Harow, tailor [DW/PA/7/8 f.179; DW/PA/5/1610/105]
John of Peper Harow [DW/PA/7/9 f.238; DW/PA/5/1617/106]
Richard of Chertsey, husbandman [DW/PA/7/9 f.197; DW/PA/5/1616/119]

RIGENE (RIGERE)
William of Swk St George - Kent Street [DW/PA/7/7 f.432; DW/PA/5/1603/139] <Abs 817>

RIGGDEN *see* RIGDON

RIGGS
Randall of Bermondsey, fellmonger [PRO; PCC Will 1593]

RIGHT *see* WRIGHT
RIKILS *see* RICKLES
RILEY (REELIE,RILLEY,RILYE,RYLYE)
Adam of Woking [DW/PA/7/1 f.47; 1487] <Abs 158>
Hugh of Swk St Saviour, ale brewer [DW/PA/7/6 f.15; DW/PA/5/1559/17]
John of Lambeth [DW/PA/7/12 f.411; DW/PA/5/1637/81]
Robert of Swk, yeoman [DW/PA/5/1587/109]
Thomas of Mickleham [PRO; PCC 1649]
William of Bermondsey, tanner [DW/PA/7/11 f.372; DW/PA/5/1626/100]
RIME *see* RYME
RIMPINGDEN (RYMPYNGDEN,RYMPYNGDENE)
John of Leatherhead [PRO; PCC Will 1476]
John of Leatherhead [DW/PA/7/2 f.199; 1524]
RINGSTEAD
David of Swk St Saviour - Clink Liberty, prisoner and yeoman [DW/PA/7/9 f.315; DW/PA/5/1619/92]
RIPHAM
Robert of Richmond [PRO; PCC Admon 1570]
RIPLEY (RYPLEY,RYPPLEY)
Agnes, alias Agnes At Fylde, of Worplesdon - Burpham, widow [DW/PA/5/1574/3]
Henry, alias Henry Atfeild, of Stoke [DW/PA/7/13 f.364; 1644]
Henry, alias Henry Atfeilde, of Worplesdon - Burpham, yeoman [DW/PA/5/1578/87]
Henry, alias Henry Atfeild, of Worplesdon, senior [HRO; 1588 B1]
Henry, alias Henry Attfield, of Worplesdon - Burpham [DW/PA/7/11 f.535; DW/PA/5/1629/3]
Henry, alias Henry Atfeild, of Worplesdon - Burpham [DW/PA/7/13 f.351; 1644]
Henry, alias Henry Arfeild, of Worplesdon; Stoke; Merrow, yeoman [DW/PA/7/9 f.67; DW/PA/5/1614/100]
John, alias John Attfeild, of Worplesdon, yeoman [DW/PA/7/9 f.140; DW/PA/5/1615/3]
Juliana, alias Juliana Attfielde, of Woking - Sutton, widow [DW/PA/5/1587/3]
Thomas, alias Thomas Fyld', of Send [DW/PA/5/1558/104]*
Thomas, alias Thomas Atfeilde, of Worplesdon - Burpham, senior [DW/PA/7/11 f.380; DW/PA/5/1626/8]
Thomas, alias Thomas Attfeild, of Worplesdon, yeoman [DW/PA/7/12 f.33; DW/PA/5/1631/5]
RIPON (RYPON)
John of Stoke next Guildford [PRO; PCC Will 1464] <Abs, SAC v.51 p.93>
RISBRIDGER(ROSOBRYGER,RYSBRIGER,RYSBRIGGER,RYSBRYDGER,RYSBYGER,RYSEBRYGGER)
Alice of Albury, widow [DW/PA/7/3 ff.144,152; 1530]
Henry of Albury, yeoman [DW/PA/7/9 f.136; DW/PA/5/1615/110]
Jane of Albury, widow [DW/PA/5/1569/83]
John of Albury [DW/PA/7/2 f.113; 1517]
John of Shere [PRO; PCC Will 1564] <Abs SAC v.8 pp.232-233>
John of Shere, yeoman [DW/PA/7/12 f.38; DW/PA/5/1631/90]
Katherine of Shere, widow [DW/PA/7/7 f.122; DW/PA/5/1597/83] <Abs 227>
Richard of Witley, fuller [DW/PA/7/6 f.98; DW/PA/5/1559/104]
William of Shere [PRO; PCC 1645]
RISBROOKE
Jane, alias Jane Swarland, of Richmond [PRO; PCC Admon 1633]

RISHTON
Thomas of Surrey, sergeant at law [PRO; PCC Will 1543]
RISLEY (RYSLEY)
John of Swk St Saviour [DW/PA/5/1581/40]
RISOME (RYSOME)
William of Swk St Saviour [DW/PA/5/1579/73]*
RISSELL *see* RUSSELL
RISWICK (van RISWYK)
Bronn of Croydon [PRO; PCC Will 1502]
RITCHBELL *see* RICHBELL
RITHER
Judith of Bermondsey [DW/PA/7/11 f.28; DW/PA/5/1623/100]
Richard of Bermondsey [DW/PA/5/1592/89]
Richard of Bermondsey [PRO; PCC Will 1592]
RIVERS (REVERS,RYVER)
John of ... [DW/PA/7/5 f.60; 1539] <Abs 106>
John of Kingston, gent. [PRO; PCC Will 1506] <Abs SAC v.8 p.115>
Richard of Haslemere [DW/PA/7/12 f.241; DW/PA/5/1634/84]
RIX
Christopher of Richmond (died overseas) [PRO; PCC Admon 1642]
ROADES *see* RHODES
ROAKE (at ROKE,ROIKE,ROKE,ROOKE,ROYKE) [*Including one* ROOKE *entry which appears clearly to be a* Roake.]
Anthony of Cheam, yeoman [LPL; 96/2211; Will 1627]
Damaris of Horsell, widow [DW/PA/7/13 f.225; DW/PA/5/1642/69]
Edmund of Horsell, husbandman [DW/PA/5/1555/70]
Henry of Horsell, yeoman [DW/PA/7/13 f.493; DW/PA/5/1649/15]
Henry of Woking - Sutton, chaplain to (Sir) Richard Weston, knight [HRO; 1535 B31]
John of Horsell [DW/PA/7/4 f.163; 1536]
John of Horsell, yeoman, senior [DW/PA/7/9 f.146; DW/PA/5/1615/111]
John of Horsell, yeoman [HRO; 1636 B36]
John of Horsell, yeoman [DW/PA/7/13 f.25; DW/PA/5/1639/111]
Margaret of Horsell, widow [DW/PA/7/13 f.487; DW/PA/5/1648/35]
Robert of Horsell [DW/PA/7/8 f.158; DW/PA/5/1611/93]
Robert of Steep, Hampshire; East Molesey [DW/PA/5/1565/1]
Thomas of Horsell [DW/PA/7/1 f.14; 1485] <Abs 47>
Thomas, alias Thomas Potter of Chertsey, husbandman and tailor [DW/PA/7/5 f.199; 1540]
William of Woking - Sutton [DW/PA/7/8 f.392; DW/PA/5/1612/139]
see also ROOKES
ROBENSON *see* ROBINSON
ROBERTS (ROBARDES,ROBART',ROBARTES,ROBARTTS,ROBERTES)
Edward of Swk St Saviour, one of the king's watermen [DW/PA/5/1603/140] <Abs U84>
Ellis of [Woking ?] - Kingfield, servingman [DW/PA/7/10 f.221; DW/PA/5/1621/104]
Henry of Newington, porter [PRO; PCC Will 1625]
Hugh of Weybridge [PRO; PCC Admon 1627]
John of Swk St Olave, citizen and haberdasher [DW/PA/5/1570/94]
John of Swk St Olave, feltmaker [DW/PA/5/1603/141] <Abs U85>
Katherine of Bermondsey, widow [DW/PA/5/1580/18]
Richard of Swk St Olave, citizen and plumber [DW/PA/5/1557/56]
Thomas of ... [DW/PA/7/7 f.635; DW/PA/5/1608/86] <Abs 1189>

ROBERTS (ROBARDES,ROBART',ROBARTES,ROBARTTS,ROBERTES) [*continued*
Thomas of Malden, vicar [DW/PA/7/11 f.194; DW/PA/5/1625/204]
Thomas of Swk St Olave, glazier [DW/PA/7/12 f.35; DW/PA/5/1631/89]
William of Swk St George, writer of the court letter of London [DW/PA/7/8 f.155; DW/PA/5/1611/92]

ROBINS (ROBYN,ROBYNS)
Edward of Swk St Olave [DW/PA/7/7 f.520; DW/PA/5/1606/77] <Abs 976>
Henry of Compton, yeoman [DW/PA/5/1591/4]
John of Swk St Olave, joiner [DW/PA/7/11 f.346; DW/PA/5/1625/205]
Walter of Nutfield, rector [HRO; Reg. Way 1 p.80; 1463]

ROBINSON (ROBENSON,ROBYNSON,ROBYNSONN)
Adam of Bermondsey, leatherseller [PRO; PCC Will 1563]
Alice of Woking, widow [DW/PA/7/4 f.232; 1537]
Ambrose of Lambeth, citizen and haberdasher [PRO; PCC Will 1575]
Bridget of Swk St Olave, widow [*Dutch*] [DW/PA/5/1596/50] <Abs U9>
Christopher, alias Cadwalleder ap Robert ap Robin, of Bermondsey, citizen and leatherseller [PRO; PCC Will 1609]
Edmund of Woking [DW/PA/7/7 f.38; DW/PA/5/1595/75] <Abs 75>
Eleanor of Swk St Olave, spinster [DW/PA/7/8 f.309; DW/PA/5/1613/110]
Francis of Swk St George, yeoman [DW/PA/5/1593/136]
Francis of Swk St Olave, tanner [DW/PA/5/1575/60]
George of Godalming - Shackleford, carpenter [DW/PA/7/10 f.196; DW/PA/5/1621/105]
Henry of Clapham, parson [DW/PA/5/1550/3]
Henry of ... [DW/PA/7/13 f.276; 1643] [? *same as Richard of* St Saviour Southwark DW/PA/5/1644/17]
Hugh of Rotherhithe [PRO; PCC Will 1608] <Abs. SAC v.13 p.187>
Hugh of Rotherhithe [PRO; PCC Admon 1608]
Hugh of Rotherhithe, mariner [PRO; PCC Will 1621]
John of ... [*Flemish church*] [DW/PA/5/1580/4]
John of Battersea [PRO; PCC Will 1511]
John of Capel - Peter's, husbandman [DW/PA/7/7 f.631; DW/PA/5/1608/87] <Abs 1179>
John of Kingston, yeoman [DW/PA/7/4 f.137; 1536]
John of Rotherhithe; and ship *White Bear of London* [DW/PA/7/11 f.105; DW/PA/5/1624/101]
John of Swk St Saviour, yeoman [DW/PA/7/12 f.47; DW/PA/5/1631/92A]
John of Wotton [DW/PA/5/1558/232]*
Margery of Swk St Saviour, widow [DW/PA/7/12 f.462; DW/PA/5/1638/116]
Marie of Swk St Saviour; Greenwich, Kent, widow [DW/PA/7/7 f.313; DW/PA/5/1600/46] <Abs 557>
Marion of Swk St Thomas, widow [DW/PA/5/1579/78]*
Richard of Lambeth, citizen and basketmaker [GL; Archdeaconry Court of London Will 1603]
Richard of Lambeth [PRO; PCC Admon 1636]
Richard of Swk St Saviour [HRO; 1588 B56]
Richard of Wandsworth [PRO; PCC Admon 1591]
Samuel of Kingston - Surbiton, gent. [PRO; PCC Will 1625]
Thomas of Kingston - Norbiton; Thames Ditton, yeoman [DW/PA/5/1547/3]
Thomas of Swk St Saviour, tailor [DW/PA/7/13 f.9; DW/PA/5/1639/108]
Thomas of Swk St Thomas [DW/PA/5/1576/12]
Thomas of Walton on Thames, tailor [DW/PA/5/1585/2]*
William, alias William Robson of Crowhurst [DW/PA/7/3 f.177; 1531]
William of Kingston, fletcher [DW/PA/5/1557/135]

ROBINSON (ROBENSON,ROBYNSON,ROBYNSONN) [*continued*
William of Ockley [DW/PA/5/1591/71]
William of Swk, butcher [DW/PA/5/1588/92]
William of Swk St Olave, citizen and woodmonger [DW/PA/7/13 f.467; DW/PA/5/1648/30]

ROBSON
John of Lingfield, master of Lingfield College [HRO; 1524 B74-76]
William, alias William Robinson of Crowhurst [DW/PA/7/3 f.177; 1531]
William of Lambeth [PRO; PCC Admon 1625]

ROBYNS *see* ROBINS

ROBYNSON,ROBYNSONNE *see* ROBINSON

ROCHE (ROCHES)
Luke, alias Luke de Rupribus, of Epsom, rector and archdeacon of Surrey 1230-1239 [PRO; *in* E210 11304]
William of Swk St Olave [DW/PA/7/4 f.99; 1534]

ROCHESTER
(Sir) Robert of Richmond, knight of the garter, comptroller of the household [PRO; PCC Will 1558]

ROCKCLEY
James of Egham, gent. [DW/PA/5/1557/122]

ROCKETT
Elizabeth of Swk St Saviour; Molesey; Warwickshire; Buckinghamshire, widow [DW/PA/5/1602/46] <Abs U51>

ROCKLIFE (ROLYFF)
John of Chertsey [DW/PA/7/2 f.91; 1505]
John of Thames Ditton, gent. [DW/PA/7/9 f.240; DW/PA/5/1617/107]

ROCKWELL
Lucy of Lambeth - Stockwell, widow [PRO; PCC 1633]
Reginald of Lambeth - Stockwell, gent. [PRO; PCC Will 1616]

RODAMS
Thomas of Newdigate [PRO; PCC Admon 1636]

RODERYE
Harry of Bermondsey, miller [DW/PA/5/1563/117]

RODES *see* RHODES

RODGERS *see* ROGERS

RODNALL
Roger, alias Roger Potter of Swk St George, rector [HRO; Reg. Way 2 p.144; 1470]

ROEMAN
Robert of St Sepulchre; Swk St Mary Magdalen, mariner in Ship *Rose* [GL; Commissary Court of London Will 1620]

ROFFE (ROFE)
Geoffrey of Thursley, thatcher [DW/PA/7/7 f.537; DW/PA/5/1606/78] <Abs 1009>
Henry of Ashtead [DW/PA/7/2 f.17; 1491]
Isaac of Swk St Saviour, victualler [DW/PA/7/12 f.108; DW/PA/5/1632/82]
Richard of Egham, husbandman [DW/PA/7/8 f.164; DW/PA/5/1611/98]

ROFFEY (ROFFIE,ROFFY,ROFIE)
Edmund of Burstow [LPL; 98/1 ff.50v,65v; Wills 1633 *and* 1635]
George of Banstead, blacksmith [DW/PA/7/12 f.262; DW/PA/5/1634/85]
Hop of Reigate, tailor [DW/PA/7/7 f.538; DW/PA/5/1606/79] <Abs 1011>
Joan of Burstow, widow [LPL; 96/2188; 98/1 f.65v; Will 1635]
John of Chipstead, carpenter [PRO; PCC Will 1612]
John of Chipstead, yeoman [DW/PA/7/13 f.475; DW/PA/5/1648/33]

ROFFEY (ROFFIE,ROFFY,ROFIE) [*continued*

Katherine of Tandridge; Godstone; Oxted; Limpsfield; Chelsham, widow [DW/PA/7/10 f,204; DW/PA/5/1620/102]

Nicholas of Horne, yeoman [DW/PA/5/1579/77]*

Nicholas of Reigate [DW/PA/7/12 f,304; DW/PA/5/1635/97]

William of Horley - Norwood, yeoman [DW/PA/7/7 f,249; DW/PA/5/1599/57] <Abs 439>

William of Horley - Norwood, yeoman [PRO; PCC Will 1616]

ROGERS (RODGERS,ROGER,ROGGERES)

Alice of Cuddington [DW/PA/7/2 f,25; 1492]

Alice of Swk St Saviour, widow [DW/PA/7/7 f,614; DW/PA/5/1607/74] <Abs 1147>

Ann of Beddington - Wallington; Carshalton, widow [DW/PA/7/8 f,282; DW/PA/5/1613/111]

Edmund of Mickleham, carpenter [DW/PA/7/9 f,324; DW/PA/5/1619/93]

Edmund of West Molesey, labourer [DW/PA/7/9 f,134; DW/PA/5/1615/86]

Edward of Little Bookham [DW/PA/7/7 f,576; DW/PA/5/1606/80] <Abs 1076>

Edward of Carshalton, husbandman [DW/PA/5/1569/85]

Edward of Chertsey, gent, [PRO; PCC 1637 *and* 1638]

Edward of Cobham, yeoman [DW/PA/7/10 f,221; DW/PA/5/1621/106]

Edward of Thames Ditton, husbandman [DW/PA/7/13 f,1; DW/PA/5/1639/107]

Edward of Wotton [DW/PA/7/4 f,185; 1536]

Ellen of Kingston, widow [DW/PA/7/11 f,18; DW/PA/5/1623/102]

Friswith of Rotherhithe, widow [DW/PA/7/8 f,137; DW/PA/5/1610/106]

George of Chessington, labourer [DW/PA/7/9 f,88; DW/PA/5/1615/87]

George of Chessington, labourer [DW/PA/7/11 f,4; DW/PA/5/1622/82]

George of Godstone, yeoman [PRO; PCC Will 1618]

George of Wisley; Byfleet, yeoman [DW/PA/7/7 f,63; DW/PA/5/1596/51] <Abs 120>

Gillian of Effingham, widow [DW/PA/7/7 f,173; DW/PA/5/1597/85] <Abs 318>

Harry of Chobham - Stanners, yeoman [DW/PA/5/1580/23]

Helen of Godalming - Farncombe, widow [DW/PA/7/13 f,13; DW/PA/5/1639/110]

Hugh of Guildford Holy Trinity [DW/PA/7/1 f,89; 1489] <Abs 301>

Humphrey of Beddington - Wallington [PRO; PCC Will 1592]

Humphrey of Putney - Roehampton, gent, [PRO; PCC Will 1613]

Humphrey of Stoke Dabernon - Oxshott, labourer [DW/PA/7/9 f,95; DW/PA/5/1616/120]

James of Cobham, husbandman [DW/PA/5/1592/35]

Joan of Epsom, widow [DW/PA/7/12 f,47; DW/PA/5/1631/93]

Joan of Ockham, widow of Thomas [DW/PA/7/12 f,238; DW/PA/5/1634/83]

John of Bermondsey [PRO; PCC Admon 1637]

John of Great Bookham; Leatherhead; Fetcham [DW/PA/7/4 f,59; 1533]

John of Great Bookham [DW/PA/7/6 f,71; DW/PA/5/1559/102]

John of Great Bookham [DW/PA/7/7 f,81; 1596] <Abs 146>

John of Great Bookham [PRO; PCC Will 1597]

John of Great Bookham [DW/PA/7/8 f,85; DW/PA/5/1609/99]

John of Great Bookham, yeoman [DW/PA/7/11 f,20; DW/PA/5/1623/101]

John of Byfleet, bachelor [DW/PA/5/1581/65]

John of Long Ditton - Tolworth [DW/PA/7/6 f,48; DW/PA/5/1559/41]

John of Thames Ditton [DW/PA/7/7 f,471; DW/PA/5/1604/49] <Abs 888>

John of Effingham, oatmealman, junior [DW/PA/7/8 f,295; DW/PA/5/1613/112]

John, alias John Marner of Farnham, glover [DW/PA/5/1580/7]

John of Fetcham [HRO; 1596 B60]

ROGERS (RODGERS,ROGER,ROGGERES) [*continued*
John of Godstone, gent, [PRO; PCC Will 1626]
John of Malden [DW/PA/5/1561/72]
John of Ockham, yeoman [DW/PA/7/7 f.469; DW/PA/5/1604/48] <Abs 885>
John of Shere [DW/PA/7/1 f.49; 1487] <Abs 161>
John of Shere [DW/PA/7/1 f.50; 1487] <Abs 166>
John of Shere, husbandman [DW/PA/7/12 f.300; DW/PA/5/1635/96]
John of Sutton [PRO; PCC 1649]
Joseph of Swk St George, citizen and cutler [DW/PA/7/13 f.199; DW/PA/5/1640/126]
Lawrence of Frensham [DW/PA/5/1552/14]
Margaret of Godalming - Binscombe, widow [DW/PA/5/1571/54]
Margaret of Kingston - Surbiton, widow [DW/PA/5/1574/13]
Margaret of Leatherhead, widow [DW/PA/5/1624/102]
Margaret of Rotherhithe, widow [DW/PA/5/1627/93]
Mary of Leigh; Godstone; Horley [PRO; PCC 1620] <Soame 1269>
Nicholas of Kingston, yeoman [PRO; PCC Will 1615]
Rachel of Ashtead, widow [DW/PA/7/11 f.312; DW/PA/5/1626/101]
Richard of Beddington - Wallington; Carshalton, yeoman [DW/PA/7/8 f.215; DW/PA/5/1612/133]
Richard of Great Bookham [DW/PA/7/2 f.19; 1491]
Richard of East Clandon, blacksmith [DW/PA/7/13 f.10; DW/PA/5/1639/109; SRO; 169/1/20,23]
Richard of East Clandon, blacksmith, senior [DW/PA/7/13 f.408; DW/PA/5/1646/46]
Richard of Epsom, carpenter [DW/PA/5/1579/75]*
Richard of Ewell, senior [DW/PA/7/4 f.136; 1536]
Richard of Godalming - Farncombe, husbandman [DW/PA/7/13 f.32; DW/PA/5/1639/112]
Richard of Leatherhead, yeoman, senior [DW/PA/7/8 f.84; DW/PA/5/1609/100]
Richard of Ockham, yeoman [DW/PA/7/11 f.317; DW/PA/5/1626/102]
Richard of Sutton, yeoman [DW/PA/5/1602/72] <Abs U57>
Robert of Beddington - Wallington, husbandman [DW/PA/7/13 f.189; DW/PA/5/1641/121]
Robert of Great Bookham [DW/PA/7/2 f.186; 1523]
Robert of Great Bookham - 'Northend', yeoman [DW/PA/7/11 f.474; DW/PA/5/1628/86]
Robert of Epsom - Horton [PRO; PCC 1641]
Robert of Ewell; Cuddington; Epsom; Effingham, yeoman [DW/PA/7/4 f.42; 1533]
Robert of Guildford St Nicolas [DW/PA/7/12 f.298; DW/PA/5/1635/95]
Robert of Kingston - Surbiton [DW/PA/5/1568/9]
Robert of Kingston, widower [PRO; PCC Admon 1640]
Robert of Leatherhead, yeoman [DW/PA/5/1593/189]
Robert of Leatherhead [PRO; PCC 1631]
Robert of Malden; Chessington [DW/PA/7/4 f.226; 1537]
Robert of Stoke Dabernon [DW/PA/7/12 f.47; DW/PA/5/1631/92B] [*and*] [PRO; PCC 1631]
Stephen of Wotton [DW/PA/7/2 f.20; 1491]
Thomas of Great Bookham [DW/PA/5/1557/42]*
Thomas of Great Bookham, yeoman [DW/PA/7/7 f.79; 1596] <Abs 145>
Thomas of Great Bookham [PRO; PCC Will 1596]
Thomas of East Clandon, shearman [DW/PA/7/6 f.284; 1560]

ROGERS (RODGERS,ROGER,ROGGERES) [*continued*
Thomas of East Clandon, yeoman [DW/PA/5/1571/8]
Thomas of Cobham, husbandman [DW/PA/5/1570/57]
Thomas of Long Ditton - Tolworth, husbandman [DW/PA/5/1558/233]*
Thomas of Ewell [PRO; PCC Will 1611; SRO; 361/70/1] <Abs, SAC v,35 p,43>
Thomas of Ewell [PRO; PCC Will 1625]
Thomas of Kingston, husbandman [HRO; 1617 B55]
Thomas of Leatherhead, yeoman [DW/PA/5/1624/103]
Thomas of Newington - Blackman Street [PRO; PCC Will 1563]
Thomas of Ockham [DW/PA/7/11 f,498; DW/PA/5/1629/83]
Thomas of Swk St Saviour, waterman [DW/PA/7/7 f,276; DW/PA/5/1599/58] <Abs 489>
Thomas of Swk St Saviour, cook [DW/PA/7/9 f,301; DW/PA/5/1619/94]
Thomas of Sutton, yeoman [HRO; 1612 B80]
Thomas of Sutton [DW/PA/7/11 f,466; DW/PA/5/1628/84]
Thomas of Sutton, yeoman [PRO; PCC Will 1628]
Thomas of Streatham - Tooting Bec; Fulham, Middlesex [GL; Commissary Court of London Will 1587]
Thomas of Weybridge, yeoman [DW/PA/7/10 f,238; DW/PA/5/1621/107]
Thomas of Wisley; Byfleet; Chertsey, yeoman, senior [DW/PA/7/7 f,12; DW/PA/5/1595/74] <Abs 27>
Thomas of Wotton [DW/PA/7/3 f,206; 1532]
William of Barnes, clerk [LPL; 96/2191; Will 1617]
William of Carshalton, labourer [DW/PA/7/8 f,235; DW/PA/5/1612/138]
William of Chertsey; Stoke Dabernon - Oxshott, husbandman [DW/PA/7/7 f,443; DW/PA/5/1603/142] <Abs 836>
William of Cobham [DW/PA/7/5 f,37; 1538] <Abs 22>
William of Cuddington [DW/PA/7/2 f,24; 1492]
William of Dorking, yeoman [DW/PA/7/13 f,490; DW/PA/5/1648/34] <Abs U267>
William of Epsom, carpenter [DW/PA/7/9 f,329; DW/PA/5/1620/103]
William of Fetcham [HRO; 1561 B166-167]
William of Horsell, husbandman [DW/PA/7/13 f,492; DW/PA/5/1649/14]
William of East Horsley, husbandman [LPL; 96/2192; Will 1618]
William of Leatherhead; Fetcham; Stoke Dabernon, yeoman [DW/PA/7/7 f,202; DW/PA/5/1598/70] <Abs 362>
William of Wonersh, clothier [PRO; PCC Will 1617]
see also du ROGER

ROGERSON
Henry of Esher [DW/PA/7/3 f,120; 1529]
Henry of Walton on Thames - Hersham, husbandman [DW/PA/7/12 f,102; DW/PA/5/1632/81]

ROGGERES *see* ROGERS

ROIKE *see* ROAKE

ROKAR *see* ROKER

ROKE *see* ROAKE

ROKENHAM
Richard of Coulsdon [BM; Addtl Ms 23,731; 1479]

ROKER (ROKAR)
Edward of Witley [HRO; Reg, CCB20 p,11; 1563]
Edward of Witley [DW/PA/5/1563/74 *and, in* DW/PA/5/1563/65]
John of Chiddingfold, husbandman [DW/PA/5/1605/72] <Abs U161>
John of Witley - Milford [*in* DW/PA/5/1550/76]
Walter of Witley - Milford [*in* DW/PA/5/1550/76]

ROLANDE
John of Beddington [DW/PA/5/1558/231]
ROLES (ROLLES,ROULES)
Giles of Effingham [DW/PA/7/12 f.147; DW/PA/5/1633/106]
John of London [DW/PA/5/1552/11]
Margaret of Effingham, widow [DW/PA/7/12 f.274; DW/PA/5/1635/94]
ROLFE (RAUFFE,ROLPH)
Agnes of Swk St Saviour, widow [DW/PA/7/7 f.463; DW/PA/5/1603/143] <Abs 875>
Alice, alias Alice Ralph of Godalming - Eashing, widow [DW/PA/7/11 f.529; DW/PA/5/1630/83]
Elizabeth of Dorking [DW/PA/7/11 f.216; DW/PA/5/1625/206]
John of Kingston [PRO; PCC Admon 1570]
Richard of Godalming - Eashing, husbandman [HRO; 1626 B104]
William of Lingfield, hempdresser [DW/PA/7/13 f.502; DW/PA/5/1649/16]
William of Mickleham [DW/PA/7/1 f.67; 1487] <Abs 222>
ROLLES *see* ROLES
ROLYFF *see* ROCKLIFE
ROMAYN
Thomas of Lambeth; St Mary Aldermary, London; Clapham; Edmonton, Middlesex [LPL; Reg. Abp Reynolds f.260; 1312 - *this is probably an enrolment, not a probate, see also the Court of Hustings.*]
ROMBEM
Thomas of Wotton [PRO; PCC Will 1424]
ROMING *see* ROOMINGE
ROMNEY *see* RUMNEY
RONNELLS *see* RUNDELL
ROODES
William of Putney [LPL; 98/1 f.129r; Will 1642]
ROOFE
Ann, alias Ann Ruffe of Epsom [PRO; PCC Admon 1635]
ROOKE (ROOKES,ROUKE)
Audrey of Swk St Thomas [DW/PA/7/11 f.227; 1625]
Christopher of Bermondsey, citizen and weaver [DW/PA/7/12 f.520; DW/PA/5/1638/119]
John of Mitcham, citizen and mercer [PRO; PCC Will 1]
John of Swk St Thomas [DW/PA/7/11 f.227; DW/PA/5/1625/207]
Thomas of Mickleham, clerk [PRO; PCC Will 1492]
Thomas of Bermondsey [DW/PA/7/7 f.423; DW/PA/5/1603/144 *and* DW/PA/5/1603/145] <Abs 792>
William of West Ham - Upton, Essex; Swk, gent. [Essex Record Office; Archdeaconry of Essex; 1597] <Abs Emmison pp.63-64>
[*see also* ROAKE, *for a* ROOKE *entry which probably mistranscription for ROAKE.*]
ROOKER
Richard of Chiddingfold, husbandman [DW/PA/7/12 f.481; DW/PA/5/1638/117]
ROOKES *see* ROOKE
ROOMINGE (ROMING,ROWMING,RUMINGE,RUMMYNG,RUMYNG)
Edward of Leatherhead [DW/PA/5/1558/236]*
John of Ewhurst [PRO; PCC Admon 1642]
John of Leatherhead [DW/PA/7/5 f.192; 1540]
Thomas of Mickleham [DW/PA/7/8 f.111; DW/PA/5/1610/107]
Walter of Leatherhead [DW/PA/7/2 f.8; 1490]
ROMSEY *see* RUMSEY

ROOS *see* ROUSE
ROOTE
  Joan of Kingston [PRO; PCC 1649]
  John of Kingston [DW/PA/7/13 f.251; DW/PA/5/1641/114]
  Richard of Lambeth, bachelor [PRO; PCC Admon 1642]
ROPER
  (Lady) Alice of Cheam [PRO; PCC Admon 1647]
ROPKINS,ROPKYNE,ROPKYNS *see* RAPKIN
ROPLEY *see* RAPLEY
ROSE
  Hugh of ... [DW/PA/7/8 f.18; DW/PA/5/1608/88]
  John of Bermondsey; Ratten Manor, Wiltshire [DW/PA/7/8 f.12; DW/PA/5/1608/89]
  John of Swk St Olave - Horsleydown [DW/PA/7/13 f.295; DW/PA/5/1643/77]
ROSKE
  Thomas of Newington [LPL; 98/1 f.106r; (ren.) 1630]
ROSOBRYGER *see* RISBRIDGER
ROSSE
  John of Abinger - Oakwood, stipendiary priest [HRO; 1557 U578]
ROSYER (ROSYERE)
  George of Farnham, shoemaker [DW/PA/7/7 f.335; DW/PA/5/1601/71] <Abs 606>
  John of Windlesham - Bagshot, innholder [DW/PA/7/2 f.105; 1516]
ROTE
  Hugh of Croydon - Woodside [PRO; PCC Will 1558 *and* 1573]
ROTER *see* RUTTER
ROTH *see* WROTH
ROTHBORNE
  John of Rotherhithe [PRO; PCC Admon 1647]
ROTHELAY
  William of Streatham, rector [HRO; Reg. Wyk 2 p.135; 1375]
ROTHER
  Edward of Chobham [HRO; 1532 B18-19]
ROTHWOODE (RATHWOOD)
  Isabel of Kingston [PRO; PCC Will 1528] <Abs SAC v.8 pp.117-118>
  Thomas of Kingston [PRO; PCC Will 1526]
ROTOR *see* RUTTER
ROUGHT *see* WROTH
ROUKE *see* ROOKE
ROULES *see* ROLES
ROUND (ROUNDE,ROWNDE,ROWNE)
  Ann of Horley, widow [DW/PA/7/9 f.74; DW/PA/5/1614/101]
  Edward of Ewhurst [PRO; PCC 1635]
  Elizabeth of Charlwood, widow [LPL; 96/2219; 98/1 f.72r; Will 1636]
  John of Charlwood, yeoman [PRO; PCC Will 1629]
  John of Horley [DW/PA/7/2 f.172; 1521]
  John of Leigh [DW/PA/7/5 f.228; 1541]
  Richard of Charlwood [PRO; PCC 1644]
  Richard of Horley [PRO; PCC Will 1602] <Abs. SAC v.10 p.314>
  Richard of Leigh [PRO; PCC Will 1563]
  Thomas of Wimbledon [LPL; 98/1 f.77r; Will 1636]
  William of Horley, husbandman [HRO; 1556 U117-120]
ROUSE (ROOS,ROUS,ROWSE,ROWSSE)
  (Lady) Ann of Waverley [PRO; PCC Will 1526]

ROUSE (ROOS,ROUS,ROWSE,ROWSSE) [*continued*
Anthony of Fetcham [PRO; PCC 1632]
Hilary of Mitcham [HRO; Reg, Stra p,6; 1324]
James of Reigate, baker [DW/PA/5/1575/76]
John of Croydon, citizen and glazier [GL; Archdeaconry Court of London Will 1647]
John of Ewhurst, yeoman [DW/PA/7/11 f,383; DW/PA/5/1626/103]
Richard of Wandsworth [DW/PA/5/1576/65]
Thomas of Richmond, yeoman of the Queen's Chamber [DW/PA/5/1575/39]

ROUTER *see* ROTTER

ROWDEN
Thomas of Chertsey, yeoman of the guard [PRO; PCC Will 1597]

ROWE
Christian of Swk St Saviour, spinster [DW/PA/7/11 f,66; DW/PA/5/1623/103]
John of Barnes, husbandman [LPL; 96/2221; 98/1 f,37v; Will 1632]
William of Swk St Olave, mariner [DW/PA/7/10 f,156; DW/PA/5/1621/108]

ROWED (ROWHEAD,ROWHED)
Arnold of Coulsdon, yeoman [DW/PA/5/1593/166]
John of Croydon [LPL; 98/1 ff,39r,40r; Will 1632]
John of Croydon [PRO; PCC Admon 1649]
John of Godstone, innholder [DW/PA/5/1591/6]
Lawrence of Caterham, yeoman [DW/PA/7/10 f,32; DW/PA/5/1616/121]
Nicholas of Hascombe, husbandman [HRO; 1625 B56]
Peter of Coulsdon, yeoman [DW/PA/7/13 f,146; DW/PA/5/1641/116]
Thomas of Coulsdon - Waddington, weaver [PRO; PCC Will 1598]
Thomas of Warlingham [DW/PA/7/11 f,432; DW/PA/5/1627/94]

ROWELL *see* ROWLES

ROWHEAD,ROWHED *see* ROWED

ROWHOLT
George of Lambeth [PRO; PCC Will 1517]

ROWLAND
Thomas of Barnes, esq, [PRO; PCC Will 1625]

ROWLANDSON
Walter of Swk St Olave [DW/PA/5/1576/145]

ROWLES (ROWELL,ROWLE)
Alice of Horley; Charlwood, widow [DW/PA/7/6 f,126; DW/PA/5/1559/198]
Alice, alias Alice Staunton of Kingston, widow [PRO; PCC Will 1607] <Abs, SAC v,12 p,97>
Joan of Bermondsey [PRO; PCC Will 1597]
Joan of Swk St Olave; Cobham; Byfleet, widow [DW/PA/7/4 f,14; 1532]
John alias John Staunton of Kingston, brewer, senior [PRO; PCC Will 1603] [*and*] [SRO; KB39/1-2; 1603] <Abs, SAC v,11 pp,123-124>
Thomas of Barnes, husbandman [LPL; 96/2223; 98/1 f,88v; Will 1638]
William of Horley [DW/PA/7/6 f,22; DW/PA/5/1559/21]

ROWLEY (ROWLEYE,ROWLY)
Elizabeth of Walton on the Hill, widow [DW/PA/7/12 f,45; DW/PA/5/1631/91]
Joan of ..., widow of Richard, smith [DW/PA/7/6 f,179; DW/PA/5/1559/217]
John of Rotherhithe, citizen and ironmonger [DW/PA/7/5 f,148; 1539]
Nicholas of Horley, tailor [HRO; 1621 B43]
Richard of Buckland; Horley; Betchworth, senior [DW/PA/7/7 f,318; DW/PA/5/1600/47] <Abs 566>
Richard of Buckland, rector [PRO; PCC Will 1626]
Thomas of Betchworth, husbandman [DW/PA/7/11 f,568; DW/PA/5/1630/87]

ROWLLYNGSON *see* RAWLINSON

ROWLUFF
  John of Swk St Olave, goldbeater [DW/PA/7/6 f.227; 1561]
ROWMING *see* ROOMING
ROWND,ROWNE *see* ROUND
ROWSE,ROWSSE *see* ROUSE
ROYDON (ROYDEN)
  Elizabeth, alias Elizabeth Rydon of Pyrford, widow [PRO; PCC Will 1612]
  Humphrey of Swk St Olave; Swk St Saviour, clerk,
    minister of God's Word [DW/PA/7/7 f.525; DW/PA/5/1606/81] <Abs 989>
  Jane of Battersea, widow [DW/PA/7/11 f.327; DW/PA/5/1625/208]
  Joan of Chertsey, spinster [PRO; PCC 1635]
  John of Battersea, yeoman [DW/PA/7/8 f.335; DW/PA/5/1614/89]
  Robert of Pyrford, gent. [DW/PA/7/13 f.46; 1639]
  William of Battersea [DW/PA/7/3 f.106; 1529]
  William of Pyrford; Woking; Chertsey; Byfleet, gent. [DW/PA/7/9
    f.166; DW/PA/5/1616/124]
    see also RIDEN
ROYKE *see* ROAKE
ROYMAN
  Judith of Swk St Saviour, widow [DW/PA/7/11 f.533; DW/PA/5/1629/80]
RUCKLEY (RUCKLIE)
  Edward of Newington [PRO; PCC Admon 1625]
RUDGE
  William of Dorking [PRO; PCC 1648]
RUDSTON
  Isaac of Lingfield [PRO; PCC Admon 1607]
RUFFE
  Ann, alias Ann Roofe of Epsom [PRO; PCC Admon 1635]
RUGLESS *see* RAGLES
RUMFORDE
  Cuthbert of ... [DW/PA/5/1593/109]
RUMINGE,RUMMYNG *see* ROOMINGE
RUMNEY (RUMNEYE)
  George of Godstone [PRO; PCC Admon 1648]
  George of Woking - Sutton, servant to the countess of Arundel [PRO; PCC
    Will 1613]
RUMSEY (RUMSAY)
  James of Rotherhithe (died overseas) [PRO; PCC Admon 1636]
  John of Epsom, smith [DW/PA/5/1592/113]
  Lydia, alias Lydia Pope of Rotherhithe [PRO; PCC Admon 1646]
  Margaret of Chertsey, widow [DW/PA/7/7 f.210; DW/PA/5/1598/71] <Abs 374>
  William of Chertsey, bargeman [DW/PA/5/1593/24]
RUMYNG *see* ROOMINGE
RUNDELL (RONNELLS)
  Joan of Streatham [DW/PA/5/1547/24]
  John of Shalford [DW/PA/7/13 f.428; DW/PA/5/1646/44]
  John of Streatham, tilemaker [DW/PA/7/13 f.462; DW/PA/5/1647/17]
  Robert of Lambeth - Stockwell, yeoman [HRO; 1581 B96]
  Stephen of Camberwell - Peckham [PRO; PCC Admon 1609]
RUPRIBUS (de RUPRIBUS)
  Luke of Epsom, rector, archdeacon of Surrey 1230-1239 [PRO; *in* E210
    11304]
RUSLEY (RUSSELEY)
  John of Bermondsey; North Mimms, Hertfordshire [DW/PA/7/5 f.204; 1540]

RUSLEY (RUSSELEY) [*continued*
John of Horne, husbandman [DW/PA/7/12 f.250; DW/PA/5/1635/91]
RUSSELL (RASHALL)
Agnes of Woking, widow [DW/PA/5/1575/4]
Alice of Ash, widow [DW/PA/7/8 f.125; DW/PA/5/1610/108]
Ann of Swk St Saviour, widow [DW/PA/5/1619/95] <Abs U239>
Bernard of Ash, husbandman [DW/PA/7/6 f.208; 1560]
Edward of Mitcham, gent. [PRO; PCC Will 1597]
Elizabeth of Wimbledon [LPL; 98/1 f.98r; Will 1638]
Frances of Leatherhead, widow [DW/PA/7/8 f.15; DW/PA/5/1608/90]
George of Guildford, mercer [DW/PA/5/1555/15]
Giles of Wimbledon, husbandman [LPL; 96/2232; 98/1 f.81r; Will 1637]
Isabel of Worplesdon, widow [DW/PA/7/2 f.179; 1522]
James of Horsell, yeoman, senior [DW/PA/7/11 f.216; DW/PA/5/1625/209]
Joan of Stoke, widow [DW/PA/7/13 f.48; DW/PA/5/1639/116]
John of ...., gunner of the Ship *Hector* [PRO; PCC Will 1613] [*and*]
[DW/PA/7/8 f.300; DW/PA/5/1613/113]
John of Ash, yeoman [DW/PA/5/1569/80]
John of Chertsey [PRO; PCC Will 1596]
John of Dunsfold [DW/PA/7/8 f.86; DW/PA/5/1609/101]
John of Kingston [DW/PA/7/13 f.129; DW/PA/5/1640/124]
John of Leatherhead [DW/PA/5/1588/48]
John of Pirbright [HRO; 1587 B74]
John of Worplesdon, rector [HRO; Reg. Way 1 p.74; 1462]
John of Worplesdon, yeoman, senior [HRO; 1582 B76]
John of Worplesdon, yeoman, senior [PRO; PCC Will 1611] <Abs. SAC v.35 p.35>
John of Worplesdon, yeoman [DW/PA/7/13 f.295; 1644]
John of Worplesdon, yeoman [DW/PA/7/13 f.376; 1644]
Michael of Ash [DW/PA/7/10 f.230; DW/PA/5/1621/109]
Moses of Chertsey, husbandman [DW/PA/7/13 f.48; DW/PA/5/1639/117]
Nicholas, alias Nicholas Frye of Albury [DW/PA/5/1550/30]
Richard of Ash, yeoman [DW/PA/7/13 f.280; DW/PA/5/1643/75]
Richard of Lambeth [PRO; PCC Will 1603]
Richard of Woking, carpenter, senior [DW/PA/7/9 f.196;
DW/PA/5/1616/126]
Richard of Woking [DW/PA/7/11 f.505; DW/PA/5/1629/84]
Robert of Ash [DW/PA/5/1558/237]
Robert of Leatherhead, vicar [HRO; 1557 U581-582]
Robert of Pirbright; Woking [DW/PA/7/8 f.18; DW/PA/5/1608/91]
Thomas of Ash, weaver [DW/PA/7/4 f.228; 1537]
Thomas of Chertsey, husbandman [DW/PA/7/9 f.251; DW/PA/5/1617/108]
Thomas of Effingham [DW/PA/7/7 f.69; DW/PA/5/1596/47] <Abs 130>
Thomas of Lambeth, esq. [PRO; PCC 1635]
Thomas, alias Thomas Otmer of Rotherhithe [PRO; PCC Admon 1589]
Thomas of Worplesdon, yeoman [DW/PA/7/7 f.228; DW/PA/5/1598/72] <Abs 402>
Thomas of Worplesdon - Hurst, yeoman, senior [DW/PA/7/7 f.303;
DW/PA/5/1600/48] <Abs 543>
Thomas of Worplesdon, yeoman [DW/PA/7/9 f.82; DW/PA/5/1615/112]
Thomas of Worplesdon - Hurst, yeoman [HRO; 1619 B61]
Thomas of Worplesdon - Burpham [DW/PA/7/11 f.167; DW/PA/5/1625/210]
William of Bisley [DW/PA/5/1591/89]
William of Egham, gent. [PRO; PCC Will 1591]

RUSSELL (RASHALL) [*continued*
William of Egham, gent. [DW/PA/5/1591/65]
William of Egham [DW/PA/7/11 f.439; DW/PA/5/1628/85]
William of Guildford Holy Trinity; Worplesdon [DW/PA/5/1544/13]
William of Newington [LPL; 98/1 f.118r; Will 1640]
RUST
Joan of Shere [DW/PA/7/11 f.5; DW/PA/5/1622/83]
RUTHORNE
Richard of Bermondsey, citizen and leatherseller [DW/PA/7/8 f.254; DW/PA/5/1611/99]
RUTLADGE *see* RUTLEDGE
RUTLAND (RUTLANDE,RUTLOND)
Francis of Merton, miller [PRO; PCC Will 1592]
Nicholas of Mitcham, esq. [PRO; PCC Will 1586]
Richard of Swk St Margaret, fletcher [DW/PA/7/3 f.203; 1532]
Robert of Swk St Saviour; Swk St Olave; Swk St George, citizen and merchant tailor [DW/PA/7/7 f.582; DW/PA/5/1606/82] <Abs 1084>
RUTLEDGE (RUTLADGE,RUTLISH,RUTLISHE)
Andrew of Swk St George, yeoman [DW/PA/7/13 f.176; DW/PA/5/1625/211]
Elizabeth of Merton, widow [DW/PA/7/11 f.1; DW/PA/5/1622/84]
Elizabeth of Carshalton, spinster [DW/PA/7/13 f.286; DW/PA/5/1643/76]
Fergus of Merton, tailor [DW/PA/7/9 f.228; DW/PA/5/1617/109]
John of Carshalton, innholder [DW/PA/7/12 f.260; DW/PA/5/1635/90]
Mary of Carshalton, widow [DW/PA/7/13 f.185; DW/PA/5/1641/120]
RUTLOND *see* RUTLAND
RUTMAN
John of Coulsdon [DW/PA/7/4 f.225; 1537]
Richard of Coulsdon [DW/PA/7/4 f.78; 1534]
RUTTER (ROTER,ROTOR,ROUTER,ROTTERS)
Agnes of Bisley; Sutton [DW/PA/7/6 f.20; DW/PA/5/1559/19]
Harman of ... [DW/PA/5/1570/76]
Harman of Swk St Olave, carver [DW/PA/7/8 f.151; DW/PA/5/1611/94]
John of Bermondsey [PRO; PCC Admon 1645]
John of Bisley [DW/PA/5/1558/234]*
John of Newington [LPL; 98/1 f.126r; (ren.) 1641]
John of Windlesham [DW/PA/7/4 f.30; 1533]
Mary of Swk St Olave, widow [DW/PA/7/8 f.275; DW/PA/5/1612/140]
Oliver of Swk St Olave, joiner [DW/PA/5/1578/60]
Peter of Bermondsey; Sandwich, Kent [*Dutch*], merchant [DW/PA/7/9 f.90; 1616]
Richard of Richmond [DW/PA/7/6 f.6; DW/PA/5/1559/8]
Robert of Bisley [DW/PA/5/1563/83]
Thomas of Ash [PRO; PCC Admon 1632]
Thomas of Bisley, weaver and husbandman [DW/PA/7/4 f.29; 1533]
RYALL
William of Windlesham, rector [DW/PA/7/2 f.18; 1491]
RYCHARDSON *see* RICHARDSON
RYCHBELL,RYCHEBELL *see* RICHBELL
RYCKFORTH *see* RICKFORTH
RYCKMAN *see* RICKMAN
RYCKSON *see* RICKSON
RYCROFTE
Samuel of Richmond, widower [PRO; PCC Admon 1648]

RYDE (RIDE)
Edward of Ewhurst, yeoman [DW/PA/7/12 f.60; DW/PA/5/1631/94]
Edward of Swk St Saviour [DW/PA/7/12 f.370; DW/PA/5/1627/95]
Gillian of Send, widow [DW/PA/7/7 f.592; DW/PA/5/1607/73] <Abs 1106>
Henry of East Clandon [PRO; PCC Admon 1649]
Henry, alias Henry Attryde of Send; West Clandon; Merrow, yeoman [DW/PA/7/7 f.299; DW/PA/5/1600/44] <Abs 535>
Henry of Send, yeoman [DW/PA/7/12 f.253; DW/PA/5/1635/92]
John, alias John At Ryde of Ewhurst, yeoman [DW/PA/5/1569/40]
John of Horsell, yeoman [DW/PA/5/1562/30]
Mary of Ewhurst, widow [DW/PA/7/10 f.101; DW/PA/5/1621/110]
Thomas, alias Thomas At Ride of Ewhurst, senior [DW/PA/7/8 f.250; DW/PA/5/1613/108]
Thomas of Ewhurst, senior [PRO; PCC 1631]
Thomas, alias Thomas Atride of Send - Dedswell [PRO; PCC Admon 1613]
Thomas of Stoke next Guildford [DW/PA/5/1557/143]
see also ATTRIDE

RYDER *see* RIDER

RYDLEY *see* RIDLEY

RYDON *see* RIDEN

RYE
Richard of Camberwell, husbandman [DW/PA/7/12 f.334; DW/PA/5/1636/80]

RYGATE *see* REIGATE

RYGDAYN *see* RIGDON

RYKFORTH *see* RICKFORTH

RYLEY *see* RILEY

RYME
Abraham, alias Abraham White of Swk St Saviour [GL; Commissary Court of London Admon 1608]

RYMPYNGDEN *see* RIMPINGDEN

RYPLEY *see* RIPLEY

RYPON *see* RIPON

RYSBRIGER,RYSBRIGGER,RYSBRYDGER,RYSBYGER,RYSEBRYGGER *see* RISBRIDGER

RYSE *see* RICE

RYSLEY *see* RISLEY

RYSOME *see* RISOM

RYVE *see* REEVES

RYVER,RYVERS *see* RIVERS

SABYN
William of Swk St Saviour - liberty of Old Paris Garden, waterman [DW/PA/7/10 f.116; DW/PA/5/1620/104]

SACKVILLE (SACKFELD,SACKVILE)
Edward of Cobham, gent. [DW/PA/5/1574/36]
John of Guildford [PRO; PCC Admon 1593]

SADLER (le SADELERE)
John of Swk [HRO; Reg. Edn 2 p.42; 1360]

SAER *see* SAYERS

SAGE (le SAGE)
Nicholas of Bermondsey [PRO; PCC Will 1590]
Nicholas of Swk St Olave [DW/PA/5/1579/85]*

ST.JOHN
Alice of Lambeth, wife of Oliver [PRO; PCC Will 1566] <Abs SAC v.63 p.151>
Jane of Battersea, Viscountess Grandison [PRO; PCC Will 1631] 9*and*] [DW/PA/7/11 f.601; DW/PA/5/1630/46]
Joan of Lambeth, wife of Oliver [PRO; PCC Will 1562] <Abs SAC v.63 p.151>
(Sir) John of Battersea, baronet [PRO; PCC 1648]
John of Ewell, esq. [HRO; Reg. Fox 3 pp.62-63; 1512]
(Lady) Margaret of Battersea [PRO; PCC Admon 1637]
Oliver of Battersea, Viscount Grandison [PRO; PCC Will 1631]
Oliver of Lambeth, esq. [PRO; PCC Will 1571] <Abs SAC v.63 pp.151-152>
ST.MICHAEL (de SANCTO MICHAELE)
Lawrence of Surrey [PRO; *in* E315/46 78; Will 1282]
ST.NEOTO (de ST.NEOTO)
John of Shere, rector [HRO; Reg. Wyk 2 pp.113,116; 1374]
SAINTON *see* SAYNTON
SAKEN
William of Lambeth, gent. [PRO; PCC Will 1627]
SAKER
Alice of Betchworth - Brockham, widow [DW/PA/7/7 f.608; DW/PA/5/1607/75] <Abs 1139>
Edmund of Betchworth, husbandman [DW/PA/5/1561/15]
John of Betchworth [DW/PA/7/1 f.92; 1489] <Abs 310>
John of Betchworth - Brockham [DW/PA/5/1546/69]
John of Betchworth, yeoman [HRO; 1561 B176-177]
John of Betchworth - Brockham, yeoman, senior [DW/PA/7/9 f.338; DW/PA/5/1620/105]
Richard of Betchworth - Brockham, yeoman [DW/PA/7/9 f.228; DW/PA/5/1617/110]
Richard of Betchworth, husbandman [DW/PA/7/11 f.330; DW/PA/5/1625/212]
Robert of Betchworth, yeoman [DW/PA/7/12 f.498; DW/PA/5/1638/135]
Robert of Dorking, innholder [DW/PA/7/11 f.45; DW/PA/5/1623/104]
SALFORD
Anne, later Anne Gawsem, of Barnes [PRO; PCC Will 1509]
SALING
Thomas of Merton, etc. [PRO; PCC Will 1517]
SALLOWES (SALLO,SALLOE,SALLOWE,SALLOWS,SALLOWSE)
Francis of Rotherhithe, mariner [DW/PA/7/11 f.345; DW/PA/5/1625/213]
Humphrey, alias Humphrey Allen of Rotherhithe, mariner [PRO; PCC Will 1626]
John, alias John Allin, of Rotherhithe [DW/PA/7/7 f.631; DW/PA/5/1608/2] <Abs 1180>
John, alias John Allen of Rotherhithe; and the Ship *Darling* [PRO; PCC Will 1609]
William of Swk St Saviour [DW/PA/5/1569/64]
William, alias William Allen of Rotherhithe, mariner [PRO; PCC Will 1600]
William of Swk St Saviour, senior [DW/PA/5/1576/10]
SALMAN *see* SOLOMONS
SALONBENDE (SOLENBENE)
Lawrence of Swk St Olave, brassmaker [DW/PA/5/1555/29]
SALUSBURY
Roger of Esher; Marchwiel, Denbighshire, curate [DW/PA/5/1550/5]

SALVIN

John of Swk St Saviour, tailor [DW/PA/7/7 f.616; DW/PA/5/1607/76] <Abs 1153>

SAMBYE

Francis of Tooting; Streatham [DW/PA/7/11 f.544; DW/PA/5/1629/85]

SAMFORTH

Christian of Kingston [PRO; PCC Will 1501; CCAL; 1500 f.50B]

SAMMES

Thomas of Totham Hall, Essex; Stoke next Guildford - Stoughton Place [PRO; PCC Admon 1651 (*but in 1631-1649 volume*)]

SAMPSON

John of Kingston; Swk St George, wine porter [PRO; PCC Will 1572]

Katherine of Swk St Olave; Shirt, Derry, Donegal, Ireland, wife of Richard [DW/PA/7/13 f.164; DW/PA/5/1642/75]

Richard of Bermondsey [PRO; PCC Admon 1642]

William, alias William Eden of Newington, mariner [PRO; PCC Will 1625]

SAMPTON

Richard of Reigate [DW/PA/7/2 f.202; 1524]

SANABY

Isabel of Swk St Margaret [HRO; Reg. Way 1 p.55; 1458]

SANCKYE *see* SANKEY

SANCTO MICHAELE (de SANCTO MICHAELE)

Lawrence of Surrey [PRO; *in* E315/46 78; Will 1282]

SANDBACHE

Francis of Surrey, esq. [PRO; PCC Will 1581]

SANDDES *see* SANDS

SANDEN (SANDON)

Richard of Stoke, scrivener [DW/PA/7/11 f.609; DW/PA/5/1630/88]

Roger of Bermondsey; Ewell [PRO; PCC Will 1476]

SANDERS (SANDER,SAUNDER,SAUNDERS,SAWNDERS)

Adam of Egham - Pooley Green [DW/PA/7/9 f.335; DW/PA/5/1620/106]

Andrew of Charlwood - Rowley [PRO; PCC Will 1595]

Arnold of Swk St Saviour - Bankside, schoolmaster [DW/PA/7/7 f.160; DW/PA/5/1597/86] <Abs 296>

Edmund of East Clandon, husbandman [DW/PA/7/12 f.297; DW/PA/5/1635/107]

Edward of Bermondsey [PRO; PCC 1646]

Edward of Newington [PRO; PCC Will 1548]

Elizabeth of Malden, widow [DW/PA/7/12 f.34; DW/PA/5/1631/104]

Emma of Charlwood, widow [LPL; 96/2253; 98/1 f.61r; Will 1634]

Francis of Surrey, gent. [PRO; PCC Will 1585]

Francis of Ewell, gent. [PRO; PCC Will 1613]

George of Charlwood, yeoman [LPL; 96/2252; 98/1 f.55r; Will 1634]

Henry, alias Henry Goodwin of Egham [DW/PA/7/7 f.389; DW/PA/5/1603/58] <Abs 721>

Henry of Caterham, husbandman [DW/PA/7/9 f.122; DW/PA/5/1615/113]

Henry, alias Henry Goodwin of Egham [DW/PA/7/12 f.489; DW/PA/5/1638/56]

Henry of Epsom, gent. [PRO; PCC 1632]

Henry of Ewell, gent. [PRO; PCC Will 1518]

Jane of Ashtead [DW/PA/7/10 f.82; DW/PA/5/1619/96]

Jane of Ewell; Savoy Hospital; Swk St Mary Overy; London; Charlwood, widow [DW/PA/7/2 f.133; 1519]

Joan of Ewell, widow of William, esq. [PRO; PCC Will 1581]

Joan of Horley, widow [DW/PA/7/13 f.256; DW/PA/5/1643/78]

John of Battersea [DW/PA/5/1624/104]

SANDERS (SANDER,SAUNDER,SAUNDERS,SAWNDERS) [*continued*]

John of Battersea [PRO; PCC Admon 1635]
John, alias John Goodwyn of Egham - Egham Hythe [DW/PA/7/4 f,186; 1536]
John, alias John Goodwyn of Egham - Egham Hythe, yeoman [DW/PA/5/1579/39]*
John of Guildford St Mary [PRO; PCC Admon 1602]
John of Horley [DW/PA/7/13 f,23; DW/PA/5/1639/125]
John of Swk St George [DW/PA/5/1592/76]
Katherine of Charlwood, spinster [LPL; 96/2251; 98/1 f,37v; Will 1632]
Margaret of Bermondsey, widow [DW/PA/7/3 f,141; 1530]
Nicholas of Ewell, esq, [PRO; PCC Will 1587]
(Sir) Nicholas of Ewell, knight [PRO; PCC Admon 1649]
Richard of Ashtead [PRO; PCC Admon 1603]
Richard of Newington [LPL; 98/1 f,21v; Will 1631]
Robert, alias Robert Goodwyn of Egham - Egham Hythe [PRO; PCC 1647]
Robert of Mitcham, mealman [DW/PA/7/9 f,154; DW/PA/5/1615/114]
Robert, alias Robert Virgillo of Ockham; Send, yeoman [DW/PA/7/8 f,321; DW/PA/5/1611/116]
Thomas of Battersea, gardener [DW/PA/7/13 f,386; DW/PA/5/1645/48]
(Sir) Thomas of Charlwood, knight [PRO; PCC Will 1566 *and* PCC 1630]
Thomas of Charlwood [LPL; 96/2249; Will 1616]
Thomas of Charlwood [PRO; PCC Admon 1639]
Thomas of Charlwood - Brickhouse [PRO; PCC 1644]
Thomas of Cheam, yeoman [PRO; PCC Will 1575]
Thomas of Egham - Egham Hythe [PRO; PCC Will 1597]
Thomas of Guildford St Mary [DW/PA/7/4 f,100; 1534]
Thomas of Putney, labourer [LPL; 96/2248; Will 1614]
Thomas of Richmond [PRO; PCC Admon 1638]
Thomas of Rotherhithe [PRO; PCC Admon 1625]
Walsingham of Surrey [PRO; PCC Will 1587]
William of Barnes [LPL; 96/2250; Will 1618]
William of East Clandon, carpenter [DW/PA/5/1591/90]
William of Egham, yeoman [DW/PA/5/1558/242]*
William of Ewell, esq, [PRO; PCC Will 1571]
William of Malden [DW/PA/7/12 f,408; DW/PA/5/1638/127]

SANDERSON (SAUNDERSON)

John of Streatham [PRO; PCC Will 1490] <Abs, SAC v,52 p,34>
John of Swk St George, citizen and haberdasher [DW/PA/7/13 f,303; DW/PA/5/1642/80]
Nicholas of Swk St Saviour, carpenter [DW/PA/7/7 f,387; DW/PA/5/1602/73] <Abs 718>
William of Lambeth - 'Framyngar' [DW/PA/5/1550/66]

SANDES *see* SANDS

SANDFORD (SONDEFORD)

John of Croydon - Bensham [PRO; PCC Will 1420]

SANDON *see* SANDEN

SANDS (SANDDES,SANDES)

Ann of Fetcham; Leatherhead, gentlewoman [DW/PA/7/7 f,340; DW/PA/5/1601/72] <Abs 618>
Elizabeth of Reigate, widow [DW/PA/7/6 f,90; DW/PA/5/1559/126]
James of Reigate, weaver [DW/PA/5/1576/66]
Joan of Shere, widow [DW/PA/7/2 f,188; 1523]
John of Betchworth, gent, [PRO; PCC Will 1543]
John of Betchworth, gent, [PRO; PCC Will 1547]

SANDS (SANDDES,SANDES) [*continued*]
John of Leatherhead, gent. [DW/PA/7/12 f.225; DW/PA/5/1634/93]
Katherine of Leatherhead, wife of Thomas, formerly widow of Lawrence Pearse [PRO; PCC 1641]
Robert of Fetcham; Leatherhead, gent. [DW/PA/7/7 f.213; DW/PA/5/1598/74] <Abs 380>
(Sir) Thomas of Lingfield, knight [PRO; PCC Will 1592]
Thomas of Reigate [HRO; 1604 AD50]

SANFORD
John of Wonersh, vicar [DW/PA/7/9 f.96; DW/PA/5/1614/102]

SANKEY (SANCKYE)
Lucy, alias Lucy Skarteclyffe of Kingston [BM; Add.Ms 24,925 f.16v; 1543] <Abs 34>

SARE
Edward of Windlesham, miller [HRO; 1607 B81]
Richard of Rotherhithe, mariner [PRO; PCC Will 1620] <Soame 804>

SARGENT (SARGANT,SERGEANT,SERJEANT)
Jarman of Deptford - Hatcham [PRO; PCC 1631]
Joan of Wimbledon [PRO; PCC 1647 *and* 1648]
Joseph of Lambeth [PRO; PCC Admon 1623]
Thomas of Camberwell, gent. [DW/PA/5/1587/57]
Thomas of Lambeth, carpenter [DW/PA/7/11 f.143; DW/PA/5/1624/106]
William of Swk St Olave [DW/PA/7/3 f.158; 1530]

SARGIER
Robert of East Molesey [PRO; PCC Will 1547]
Robert of Molesey [PRO; PCC Admon 1574]

SARGRAVE
John of Swk, esq. [LPL; Reg. Abp Bourgchier f.44r; Admon 1457]

SAUNDERS *see* SANDERS

SAUNDERSON *see* SANDERSON

SAUNTON
William of Dorking [HRO; 1593 B70]

SAVAGE (SAVADGE,SAVEDGE)
Christopher of ... [DW/PA/7/9 f.179; DW/PA/5/1616/111]
Isabella of Camberwell - Peckham, widow [HRO; 1597 B65]
John of Mortlake, yeoman [LPL; 96/2268; 98/1 ff.90v,95v; Will 1638]
John of Newington, citizen and brewer [LPL; 96/2267; Will 1625]
Mary of Guildford, spinster [DW/PA/7/12 f.71; DW/PA/5/1632/84]
Mary of Guildford, spinster [DW/PA/7/12 f.91; DW/PA/5/1632/90]
Richard of Reigate [PRO; PCC Admon 1628]
Richard of Reigate; Dorking, yeoman [DW/PA/7/12 f.379; DW/PA/5/1637/83]
Roger of Camberwell [DW/PA/5/1592/97]
Seth of Kingston, yeoman [DW/PA/7/12 f.173; DW/PA/5/1633/113]
Thomas of Swk St Thomas, citizen and white baker [DW/PA/7/12 f.409; DW/PA/5/1637/88]
William of Streatham [DW/PA/7/3 f.194; 1531]
William of Wandsworth [DW/PA/5/1546/14]

SAVAKER
Judith of Swk St Olave, widow [DW/PA/7/13 f.483; DW/PA/5/1648/40]

SAWCOTT
Joan of Lambeth, widow [DW/PA/5/1592/51]*

SAWYER (SAWER,SAWYAR,SAYWYERE)
Alice of Ewhurst, widow of Nicholas [DW/PA/7/2 f.169; 1522]
Avis of Abinger, widow [PRO; PCC 1641]

SAWYER (SAWER,SAWYAR,SAYWYERE) [*continued*]
John of Shere, weaver [DW/PA/5/1561/71]
Katherine of Bermondsey, widow [PRO; PCC Will 1626]
Nicholas of Ewhurst [DW/PA/7/2 f,168; 1522]
Nicholas of Ewhurst, bachelor [DW/PA/7/3 f,139; 1530]
Richard of Abinger, yeoman, senior [PRO; PCC Will 1598]
Richard of Abinger - Parkhurst, yeoman [PRO; PCC Will 1604] <Abs, SAC v,11 p,299>
Richard of Ewhurst - Coverwood, yeoman [DW/PA/5/1581/48]
Robert of Dunsfold [DW/PA/7/4 f,85; 1534]
Thomas, alias Thomas Sayer of Abinger [PRO; PCC Admon 1639]
Thomas of Ewhurst [PRO; PCC 1631]
Thomas of Ewhurst; Abinger, yeoman [DW/PA/7/4 ff,111,153; 1535 *and* 1536]
Thomas of Walton on Thames [DW/PA/7/5 f,197; 1540]
William of Effingham [DW/PA/5/1545/16]

SAX (SAXKS)
William of Swk St Margaret [DW/PA/7/4 f,218; 1537]

SAXBY (SAXBEE,SAXBYE,SAXPES)
Katherine, alias Katherine Cooke of Lingfield, widow [DW/PA/7/10 f,84; DW/PA/5/1615/88]
Thomas of Lingfield; Hartfield, Sussex [DW/PA/5/1550/81]
Thomas of Tandridge [PRO; PCC Admon 1573]
William of Lingfield [DW/PA/7/11 f,493; DW/PA/5/1628/87]

SAY (de SAY,SEY)
Maud of Bermondsey, wife of Geoffrey, friar preacher [LPL; Reg, Abp Whittleseye f,106; Will 1369]
Robert of Weybridge [PRO; PCC 1636]
William of Carshalton [DW/PA/7/1 f,39; 1486] <Abs 126>

SAYERS (SAYER,SAYERE,SAYRE,SAYRES)
Alice of Cranleigh [PRO; PCC Admon 1616]
Edward of Tooting, yeoman [DW/PA/7/7 ff,378,386; DW/PA/5/1602/74] <Abs 702,716>
Henry of Battersea [PRO; PCC Admon 1619]
Joan of Ockham, widow [DW/PA/5/1558/241]*
Joan of Tooting Graveney, widow [DW/PA/7/9 f,199; 1617]
John of Battersea [PRO; PCC Admon 1629]
John of Shere [DW/PA/7/1 f,28; 1486] <Abs 93>
Nicholas of Tooting Graveney, yeoman [DW/PA/7/12 f,18; DW/PA/5/1631/99]
Oliver of Ockham; Effingham, yeoman [DW/PA/7/7 f,256; DW/PA/5/1599/59] <Abs 451>
Richard of Abinger, yeoman [DW/PA/7/12 f,120; DW/PA/5/1632/96]
Thomas, alias Thomas Sawyer of Abinger [PRO; PCC Admon 1639]
Thomas of Cranleigh - 'Tilchurst', yeoman [HRO; 1585 B58]
Thomas of Ewhurst, yeoman [DW/PA/7/11 f,331; DW/PA/5/1625/214]
William of East Clandon [DW/PA/5/1586/33]
William, alias William Albery of Ockham [DW/PA/5/1557/22]
see also SARE

SAYNTON
John of Egham [DW/PA/5/1546/46]

SAYWARD
Henry of Battersea, yeoman [DW/PA/7/12 f,95; DW/PA/5/1632/91]

SAYWELL (SEYWELL)
George of Swk St Olave, citizen and draper [DW/PA/5/1563/115]
Thomas of Rotherhithe, gardener [PRO; PCC 1630] <Scroope 1236>
SAYWYERE *see* SAWYER
SCALDWELL
Henry of Lambeth, widower [PRO; PCC 1635]
Jonas of Lambeth - Stockwell [DW/PA/7/13 f,131; DW/PA/5/1640/149]
SCALES
John of Swk St Saviour; Town Malling, Kent, carver [DW/PA/5/1593/114]
Thomas of Mortlake, citizen and merchant tailor [PRO; PCC 1640]
SCALHORNE
William of Newington, citizen and leatherseller [PRO; PCC Will 1591]
SCARCLYFF
Robert of Shere, Swanage, Dorset; Scarcliffe, Derbyshire [LPL; Reg, Abp Arundel ii f,158; Will 1412] <Abs SAC v,8 pp,226-228>
SCARISBRIGE
Thomas of Lambeth [DW/PA/7/4 f,87; 1534]
SCARLETT
Alexander of Swk St Olave, cooper [DW/PA/7/11 f,427; DW/PA/5/1627/96]
SCARR
Ann of Swk St Olave, spinster [DW/PA/7/8 f,8; DW/PA/5/1608/92]
SCASEBROOKE
Robert of Windlesham - Bagshot [PRO; PCC Admon 1579]
SCATLIFFE (SCATCLIFE,SKARTCLYFFE)
Henry of Kingston [PRO; PCC 1635]
John of Kingston, smith [DW/PA/7/5 f,102; 1539]
Lucy, alias Lucy Sanckye of Kingston [BM; Add,Ms 24,925 f,16v; 1543] <Abs 34>
Margaret of Kingston, widow [DW/PA/7/7 f,481; DW/PA/5/1604/52] <Abs 906>
SCATERGOOD
(Sir) Wilfred of Swk St George, knight [HRO; Reg, Fox 3 p,64; 1513]
SCHARPE *see* SHARP
SCHEPARD,SCHEPHARD *see* SHEPHERD
SCHERERS
Nicholas of Swk St Olave [DW/PA/5/1563/20]
SCHERPE *see* SHARPE
SCHESMON *see* CHEESEMAN
SCHEVENTON *see* SHEVENTON
SCHODD
Richard of Thursley [DW/PA/7/6 f,66; DW/PA/5/1559/47]
SCOCROFT
Stephen of Tooting Graveney [PRO; PCC Admon 1626]
SCOFFYNE (SCORFFYNE)
Eden of Lingfield [DW/PA/7/4 f,218; 1537]
SCOPE
William of Lingfield, yeoman [DW/PA/7/12 f,265; DW/PA/5/1635/101]
SCORFFYNE *see* SCOFFYNE
SCOT *see* SCOTT
SCOTCHER (SCOTCHIER,SCOTTYER,SCOTYER,SKOCHER)
Constancia of Guildford St Mary, widow [HRO; 1625 B62]
James of Guildford St Mary [DW/PA/5/1592/94]
James of Horsell; Chobham [HRO; 1611 B57]
John of Wonersh, husbandman [DW/PA/7/9 f,177; DW/PA/5/1616/125]
Mary of Wonersh, widow [DW/PA/7/12 f,240; DW/PA/5/1634/98]

SCOTCHER (SCOTCHIER,SCOTTYER,SCOTYER,SKOCHER) [*continued*]
William of Guildford St Mary, shearman [DW/PA/7/8 f,286; DW/PA/5/1613/114]
William of Horsell; Stoke next Guildford, ashburner, senior [DW/PA/7/7 f,483; DW/PA/5/1604/51] <Abs 909>
William of Horsell, yeoman [HRO; 1636 B40]
SCOTE *see* SCOTT
SCOTFIELD *see* SKOTFELDE
SCOTISFORD
Samuel of Newington [LPL; 98/1 f,51r; Will 1633]
SCOTT (SCOT,SCOTE,SCOTTE,SKOTT)
Agnes of Kingston, widow [DW/PA/5/1548/2]
Alice of Swk St Olave, widow [DW/PA/7/12 f,301; DW/PA/5/1636/83]
Bartholomew of Camberwell; Carshalton, esq, [PRO; PCC Will 1600]
(Sir) Edmund of Lambeth, knight [PRO; PCC Admon 1640]
Edward of Bermondsey [PRO; PCC Admon 1625]
(Lady) Elizabeth of Camberwell, widow [PRO; PCC Admon 1629]
George of Richmond, esq, of the court [PRO; PCC Will 1586]
Helen of Swk St Saviour, widow [DW/PA/7/8 f,263; DW/PA/5/1611/100]
James of Farnham [DW/PA/7/4 f,7; 1532]
James of Petersham, yeoman, senior [DW/PA/7/7 f,625; DW/PA/5/1607/77] <Abs 1166>
James of Petersham; Kingston - Ham, tailor [DW/PA/7/9 f,172; DW/PA/5/1616/123]
Joan of Rotherhithe, widow [HRO; 1595 B51] [*and*] [DW/PA/7/7 f,10; DW/PA/5/1595/76] <Abs 22>
John of Bermondsey [PRO; PCC Admon 1645]
John of Camberwell; Woodmansterne; Chipstead; Carshalton; Horley; Nutfield; Banstead; Leatherhead; Horne; Headley; Fetcham; Morden; Beddington - Wallington; Burstow; Bermondsey; Swk; Greenwich, Kent [DW/PA/7/4 f,15; 1532]
John of Camberwell, esq, [PRO; PCC Will 1558]
John of Kingston, yeoman, knight [DW/PA/7/11 f,487; DW/PA/5/1628/88]
John of Lambeth, gardener [DW/PA/7/9 f,235; DW/PA/5/1617/111]
John of Reigate [PRO; PCC 1635]
John of Swk St George [DW/PA/7/3 f,175; 1531]
(Sir) Peter of Camberwell, knight [PRO; PCC Will 1622]
Richard of Camberwell, esq, [PRO; PCC Will 1560]
Richard of Swk St Saviour [DW/PA/5/1605/79] <Abs U168>
Robert of Lambeth [PRO; PCC Admon 1631]
Thomas of Morden, labourer [DW/PA/7/12 f,321; DW/PA/5/1636/87]
Thomas of Swk St Saviour - Bankside; Walthamstow, Essex, yeoman [GL; Commissary Court of London Will 1593]
Thomas of Wandsworth [PRO; PCC 1635]
William of Camberwell - Peckham, esq, [DW/PA/5/1588/57]
William of Farnham [DW/PA/7/2 f,134; 1519]
SCOTTEN
Peter of Swk St Olave, feltmaker [DW/PA/7/7 f,193; DW/PA/5/1598/75] <Abs 351>
SCOTTYER,SCOTYER *see* SCOTCHER
SCRAFTON (SCROFTON,STRAFTON)
Edward of Godstone, weaver [HRO; 1584 B72]
John, alias John Bryan of Lingfield [PRO; PCC Will 1602] <Abs, SAC v,10 pp,305-306>

SCRAFTON (SCROFTON,STRAFTON) [*continued*]
John, alias John Bryan of Lingfield [PRO; PCC 1649]
Richard, alias Richard Bryan of Lingfield, weaver, senior [DW/PA/7/13 f,88; DW/PA/5/1640/15]
William, alias William Bryan of Lingfield, weaver [DW/PA/7/13 f,91; DW/PA/5/1640/16]
SCRAGGE
Simon of Swk St George, glover [DW/PA/7/7 f,632; DW/PA/5/1608/93] <Abs 1182>
SCREUBHAM *see* SCRUBBAM
SCREWTON
Robert of Swk St Olave, yeoman [DW/PA/7/10 f,252; DW/PA/5/1622/87]
SCRIVEN
Alice of Leigh [DW/PA/7/11 f,376; DW/PA/5/1626/104]
SCRIVENOR (SCRIVNOR)
John of Camberwell - Dulwich [DW/PA/7/13 f,73; DW/PA/5/1640/133]
William of Lambeth - Lambeth Marsh [PRO; PCC 1640]
SCROFTON *see* SCRAFTON
SCRUBBAM (SCREUBHAM,SCRUBUM)
Isabella of Swk St Olave, widow [DW/PA/5/1624/107]
Michael of ...., porter to the Skinner's Company [DW/PA/7/10 f,187; DW/PA/5/1620/107]
SCUDAMORE (SCUDMORE)
Alice, alias Alice Burton of Surrey [PRO; PCC Admon 1648]
Ann of Newington, spinster [PRO; PCC Admon 1626]
John of Lambeth - Lambeth Marsh [PRO; PCC 1637]
Mary of Swk St Olave, widow of Thomas [DW/PA/7/10 f,113; DW/PA/5/1619/97]
Richard of Bermondsey [PRO; PCC Admon 1625]
Thomas of Swk St Olave, citizen and draper [DW/PA/7/10 f,108; DW/PA/5/1619/98]
SCUDDER
John of Newington, husbandman [LPL; 96/2285; Will 1625]
Margery of Newington, widow [PRO; PCC Will 1627]
SCUDMORE *see* SCUDAMORE
SCURLOK *see* SHERLOCK
SEABROOK (SEYBROOKE)
Robert of Epsom, labourer [DW/PA/7/8 f,296; DW/PA/5/1613/115]
SEAGER (SEAGAR,SEAGURA,SEGER)
Beatrice of Guildford, widow [DW/PA/7/11 f,320; 1626]
Christian of Dunsfold, widow [DW/PA/7/13 f,154; DW/PA/5/1641/125]
Henry of Stoke next Guildford - Slyfield, husbandman [DW/PA/7/11 f,15; DW/PA/5/1623/105]
Margery of Farnham [DW/PA/7/8 f,152; DW/PA/5/1611/101]
Robert of Wanborough, husbandman [HRO; 1587 B77]
(Sir) William of Richmond, knight [PRO; PCC 1634]
SEAGOOD
Richard, alias Richard Swynnerton of Egham, bargeman [DW/PA/7/13 f,126; DW/PA/5/1640/147]
Thomas of Egham, minister [DW/PA/7/12 f,316; DW/PA/5/1636/82]
SEAGRAVE (SEGRAVE)
William of Swk St Olave, citizen and draper [DW/PA/7/3 f,159; 1530]
SEAGURA *see* SEAGER

SEALE (SEELE)
Elizabeth of Reigate, spinster [PRO; PCC 1640]
Joan of Tandridge, widow [DW/PA/7/11 f,104; DW/PA/5/1624/105]
John of Tandridge; Lingfield, yeoman [DW/PA/7/9 f,336; DW/PA/5/1620/108]
SEAMAN (SEMAN,SEMON,SEYMAN)
Agnes of Thames Ditton - Arbrook, widow [DW/PA/5/1562/57]
Elizabeth of Thames Ditton, widow [DW/PA/7/4 f,119; 1535]
Henry of Thames Ditton, husbandman [DW/PA/5/1558/243]*
James of Shere; Abinger [DW/PA/7/6 f,94; DW/PA/5/1559/81]
James of Shere, yeoman [DW/PA/7/13 f,74; DW/PA/5/1641/122]
Joan of Thames Ditton - Claygate, widow [DW/PA/7/9 f,272; 1618]
John of Bentley, Hampshire [DW/PA/7/1 f,83; 1488] <Abs 275>
John of Shalford, weaver [DW/PA/5/1587/24]
John of Shere [DW/PA/7/4 f,128; 1535]
Margaret of Effingham, spinster [DW/PA/7/12 f,185; DW/PA/5/1633/114]
Robert of Thames Ditton [DW/PA/7/8 f,352; DW/PA/5/1612/141] [*see* SAC v,18 p,265>
Robert of Shere [DW/PA/5/1557/38]
Thomas of Thames Ditton - Claygate, yeoman, senior [DW/PA/7/12 f,339; DW/PA/5/1636/90]
Thomas of Shere - Hoe [DW/PA/7/8 f,370; DW/PA/5/1612/142]
Thomas of Shere [PRO; PCC 1643]
Thomas of Swk St Saviour, victualler [DW/PA/5/1624/108]
SEARCH
Margery of Mortlake, widow [PRO; PCC Will 1597]
SEARE
Thomas of Tooting Graveney, yeoman [DW/PA/7/8 f,52; DW/PA/5/1609/103]
SEARLE (SEARLES)
Henry of Bermondsey [DW/PA/7/11 f,196; DW/PA/5/1625/215]
John of ,,, [DW/PA/7/13 f,376; 1644]
Thomas of Compton, yeoman [DW/PA/7/13 f,9; DW/PA/5/1639/122]
Thomas of Newington [LPL; 98/1 f,111v; Will 1640]
Thomas of Swk St George, silk weaver [DW/PA/7/11 f,177; DW/PA/5/1625/216]
William of Merton [DW/PA/7/13 f,200; DW/PA/5/1642/71]
SEARS (SEERES)
Thomas of Chobham [PRO; PCC 1649]
SEATON
William of Swk St George [DW/PA/5/1579/89]*
SEAVENOCKE *see* SEVENOAKS
SEAWARD *see* SEWARD
SECKINGTON (SEKYNTON)
Robert of Shere, clerk [PRO; PCC Will 1390] <Abs SAC v,8 pp,224-225>
SEDDON
Joseph of Croydon [LPL; 98/1 ff,76v,86v; Wills 1636 *and* 1637]
SEDE *see* SEED
SEDERSTON
John of Swk St George [DW/PA/7/2 f,46; 1495]
SEDGWICK (SEDGEWICKE)
Agnes, alias Agnes Chiswicke of Swk St Olave, widow [DW/PA/7/7 f,245; DW/PA/5/1599/60] <Abs 432>
SEDWELL
Richard of Richmond, gent, [PRO; PCC Will 1596]

SEED (SEDE)
William of Swk St Saviour [DW/PA/7/7 f.428; DW/PA/5/1603/164] <Abs 805>
SEEK (SEKE)
John of Ewell; Epsom [DW/PA/7/1 f.5; 1484] <Abs 17>
SEELE *see* SEALE
SEELEY (CEELY,CELYE,SEELYE,SEELLYS,SEELYS,SERLY)
Edward of Kingston - Surbiton, husbandman [DW/PA/5/1561/48]
Joan of Kingston, widow [DW/PA/5/1571/38]
John of Egham, waterman [DW/PA/5/1587/119]
John of Kingston, cooper [DW/PA/5/1570/39]
John of Kingston [PRO; PCC Will 1589 *and* 1591]
John of Kingston [PRO; PCC Admon 1592]
Rachel, alias Rachel Bellingham of Kingston [PRO; PCC Admon 1598]
William of Swk St Olave, miller [DW/PA/7/7 f.312; DW/PA/5/1600/12] <Abs 555>
SEERES *see* SEARS
SEGER *see* SEAGER
SEGRAVE *see* SEAGRAVE
SEITH
Robert of Mitcham, yeoman [HRO; 1592 B51]
SEKE *see* SEEK
SEKYNTON *see* SECKINGTON
SELBY (SELBEE,SELBIE,SELBYE)
Abraham of Bermondsey [DW/PA/7/12 f.398; DW/PA/5/1638/123]
Abraham of Putney, gent. [PRO; PCC 1646]
Giles of Lambeth - South Lambeth, yeoman [PRO; PCC Will 1625]
John of Swk St Olave, citizen and woodmonger [DW/PA/7/7 f.116; DW/PA/5/1597/87] <Abs 215>
Mabel *or* Mary of Swk St Olave, widow [DW/PA/7/9 f.222; DW/PA/5/1617/112]
Richard of Bermondsey, citizen and leatherseller, junior [DW/PA/7/12 f.417; DW/PA/5/1637/90]
Richard of Wandsworth, yeoman [PRO; PCC Will 1615]
Simon of Bermondsey, citizen and leatherseller [PRO; PCC 1637]
SELDEN
Joan of Dorking, spinster [PRO; PCC Admon 1611]
SELLECK
William of Swk St Olave, feltmaker [DW/PA/5/1625/217]
SELLERS
William of Swk St Mary Overy - liberty of the Clink [DW/PA/7/7 f.429; DW/PA/5/1603/149 *and* DW/PA/5/1603/150] <Abs 807>
SELLINGE
Samuel of Swk St Olave, citizen and haberdasher [DW/PA/5/1603/146] <Abs U86>
SELLYARD (SELYARDE)
Thomas of Lingfield [PRO; PCC Will 1535]
SELWOOD (SELWODE)
Henry of Guildford Holy Trinity, painter [HRO; 1561 B180-181]
SELWYN
John of Walton on Thames, gent. [PRO; PCC Will 1588] <Abs SAC v.33 p.17>
SELYARDE *see* SELLYARD
SEMALL
Peter of Newington; Bergen in Henegowe [PRO; PCC Will 1577]
SEMAN *see* SEAMAN
SENACLE *see* SINACLE

SENDALL
Agnes of Lambeth, widow [DW/PA/5/1545/50]
Robert of Kingston, ostler at *the Crane* [DW/PA/7/7 f,317;
DW/PA/5/1600/49] <Abs 565>
SENDE
John of Guildford Holy Trinity [DW/PA/7/1 f,15; 1485]
William of Send - Send Court; St Sepulchre, London, gent,
[GL; Commissary Court of London Will 1573]
SENDEN
Thomas of Guildford [PRO; PCC Will 1520]
SENT
John of Swk St Margaret, shearman [DW/PA/7/2 f,48; 1496]
SERELL *see* SERRELL
SERGEANT,SERGEAUNT,SERJEANT *see* SARGENT
SERRELL (SERELL,SERYLL)
John of Farnham; Aldershot, Hampshire, clothier [DW/PA/5/1550/104]
Nicholas of Farnham; Aldershot, Hampshire, clothier [DW/PA/5/1550/97]
Richard of Farnham [PRO; PCC Will 1585]
SEVENOAKS (SEAVENOCKE)
Richard of Charlwood [PRO; PCC Will 1602] <Abs, SAC v,10 p,312>
SEVERDONCK (van SEVERDONCK)
Henrik of ... [*Dutch*] [DW/PA/5/1570/83]
SEVERE
Reynold of Swk St Olave [DW/PA/7/7 f,416; DW/PA/5/1603/147] <Abs 778>
SEWARD (SEAWARD)
Christopher of Reigate, blacksmith [DW/PA/7/12 f,233; DW/PA/5/1634/96]
Richard of Farnham - ? Runwick ['Anwick'], miller [DW/PA/7/8 f,120;
DW/PA/5/1610/111]
Thomas of Bermondsey, citizen and weaver [DW/PA/7/11 f,413;
DW/PA/5/1627/97]
William of Reigate, blacksmith [DW/PA/7/12 f,505; 1638]
SEWELL
George of Mortlake [LPL; 98/1 f,126 bis; Will 1641]
Henry of Dorking [DW/PA/7/4 f,163; 1536]
John of Cobham, husbandman [DW/PA/7/7 f,99; DW/PA/5/1596/52] <Abs 181>
John of Dorking [DW/PA/5/1569/10]
SEWER
Agnes, alias Agnes Hunt of Croydon - Shirley, widow [PRO; PCC 1633]
Henry of Reigate, miller [DW/PA/5/1593/35]
Ralph of Fetcham, yeoman [DW/PA/7/11 f,293; DW/PA/5/1626/105]
SEX
Francis of Swk St Olave, cooper [DW/PA/5/1593/62]
SEXTON
James of St Laurence Pountney, London; Swk St Mary Overy [GL;
Commissary Court of London Will 1596]
SEY *see* SAY
SEYBROOKE *see* SEABROOK
SEYMAN *see* SEAMAN
SEYWELL *see* SAYWELL
SHACKLEFORD (SHAKILLFORDE,SHAKYLFORD)
Richard of Elstead [DW/PA/5/1547/9]
William of Elstead [DW/PA/5/1547/27]

SHACKLETON
  Christopher of Rotherhithe [PRO; PCC Admon 1591]
  William of Lambeth [PRO; PCC Admon 1587]
SHACRAFTE
  William of Godstone [PRO; PCC Will 1603] <Abs, SAC v,11 p,115>
SHADFORD (SHADFORDE)
  Austen of Epsom, labourer [DW/PA/7/11 f,179; DW/PA/5/1625/218]
  Nicholas of Banstead [DW/PA/7/8 f,144; DW/PA/5/1611/102]
  Thomas of Cobham, husbandman [DW/PA/5/1557/117]
SHAFTSBURY (SHAFTYSBURY)
  Edward of Kingston - Surbiton; Reigate - Colley; Long Ditton, husbandman [BM; Add,Ms 24,925 f,6r; 1544] <Abs 11>
  Robert of Kingston, bargeman [DW/PA/7/7 f,251; DW/PA/5/1599/61] <Abs 442>
SHAKESHAFT
  Thomas of St Martin in the Fields, Middlesex, yeoman [DW/PA/7/10 f,244; DW/PA/5/1622/88]
SHAKILLFORDE,SHAKYLFORD *see* SHACKLEFORD
SHALCROSS (SHALCROSSE,SHALKROS,SHAWCROSSE,SHAWLCROSSE,SHOWCROSSE)
  Alice, alias Alice Humfreye of Crowhurst, widow [DW/PA/7/9 f,303; DW/PA/5/1619/54]
  Edward of Godstone, junior [DW/PA/7/9 f,121; DW/PA/5/1615/115]
  Edward of ... [proved at Kingston] [DW/PA/7/9 f,176; DW/PA/5/1616/110]
  Humphrey of Tandridge, yeoman [DW/PA/7/12 f,25; DW/PA/5/1631/101]
  John of Godstone; Blechingley, husbandman [DW/PA/7/6 f,89; DW/PA/5/1559/127]
  Robert of Godstone, yeoman [DW/PA/7/7 f,251; DW/PA/5/1599/62] <Abs 441>
  Robert of Godstone, yeoman [DW/PA/7/7 f,470; DW/PA/5/1604/50] <Abs 887>
SHALE
  Thomas of Swk St Olave, cordwainer [DW/PA/7/9 f,331; DW/PA/5/1620/109]
SHALKROS *see* SHALCROSS
SHAMLER (SHAMBLER)
  Catherine of Guildford St Nicolas, widow [DW/PA/5/1624/109]
  James of Farnham, carpenter [DW/PA/7/13 f,92; DW/PA/5/1640/140]
SHANKE
  Walter of Lambeth, servant to the dowager duchess of Norfolk [DW/PA/7/5 f,227; 1541]
SHANSBURY
  Robert of Clapham [DW/PA/7/13 f,107; DW/PA/5/1640/143]
SHANTYBY
  John of Swk St George [DW/PA/7/5 f,180; 1540]
SHARBAN *see* SHERBORNE
SHARDELOWE
  Robert of Swk Priory, chantour of Chichester [LPL; Reg, Abp Courteney f,204; Will 1383]
SHARFE
  Elizabeth of Swk St Olave, widow [DW/PA/7/6 f,134; DW/PA/5/1559/139]
SHARNFORD
  Nicholas of Carshalton [DW/PA/7/5 f,50; 1538] <Abs 17>
SHAROLOK *see* SHERLOCK
SHARP (SCHARPE,SHARPE)
  Agnes of Merstham, widow [PRO; PCC 1641]
  Alexander of Wandsworth, yeoman [DW/PA/7/4 f,55; 1533]
  Ann of Lambeth, widow [DW/PA/7/12 f,30; DW/PA/5/1631/103]

SHARP (SCHARPE,SHARPE) [*continued*]
James of Camberwell [DW/PA/7/12 f,68; DW/PA/5/1631/108]
James of Guildford, woollen draper [PRO; PCC Will 1598]
John of Richmond, yeoman porter to the king [DW/PA/7/2 ff,144,146; 1520]
John of Swk St Olave [DW/PA/5/1558/244]*
Mary of Blechingley, citizen and wax chandler, widow of Richard [PRO; PCC Will 1617]
Nicholas of Walton on Thames - Burwood, sojourner in the house of Thomas Alee [DW/PA/5/1588/20]
Ralph of Cheam [PRO; PCC Admon 1633]
Richard, alias Richard Woodroffe of Caterham, blacksmith [HRO; 1614 B64]
Richard of Merstham, yeoman [LPL; 96/2302; 98/1 f,89v; Will 1638]
Robert of Egham [PRO; PCC Admon 1603]
Robert of Weybridge, gent, [PRO; PCC Will 1615]
Roger of Camberwell, yeoman [PRO; PCC Will 1611] <Abs, SAC v,35 p,42>
Thomas of Charlwood, yeoman [LPL; 96/2301; Will 1618]
William of Bermondsey, senior [DW/PA/7/7 f,606; DW/PA/5/1607/78] <Abs 1132>
William of Guildford [PRO; PCC Admon 1649]

SHARPARROW (SHARPAROWE)
William of Wandsworth [PRO; PCC Will 1526]

SHARPE *see* SHARP

SHASTOWE
Thomas of Bramley [PRO; PCC 1634]

SHATTELYN (CHASTELEYN)
Michael of Swk [*French*] [DW/PA/5/1571/44]

SHAVE
William of Rotherhithe [PRO; PCC Admon 1631]

SHAW (SHAWE)
Alice of Guildford Holy Trinity, widow [DW/PA/7/7 f,593; DW/PA/5/1607/79] <Abs 1108>
James of Godstone [DW/PA/7/2 f,1; 1490]
James of Guildford [PRO; PCC Admon 1594]
James of Guildford; Shalford; Stoke next Guildford [PRO; PCC Wills 1594 (two)]
John of Kingston - Surbiton, citizen and draper [PRO; PCC Will 1628]
John of Swk St Saviour [DW/PA/5/1605/80] <Abs U169>
John of Woking, vicar [DW/PA/7/11 f,176; DW/PA/5/1625/219]
Miles of Guildford, woollen draper [PRO; PCC Will 1609]
Robert of Bermondsey, mariner [DW/PA/7/10 f,228; DW/PA/5/1621/111]
Thomas of Guildford; Middle Temple, London, gent, [PRO; PCC Will 1605] <Abs, SAC v,12 pp,94-95>
Thomas of Richmond, gent, [PRO; PCC Will 1622]
William of Guildford [DW/PA/7/13 f,482; DW/PA/5/1648/38]

SHAWCROSSE *see* SHALCROSS

SHAWE *see* SHAW

SHAWLCROSSE *see* SHALCROSS

SHEALE
John *or* John Shrubb of Seale [DW/PA/7/10 f,186; DW/PA/5/1620/110]

SHEARS (SHEIRES,SHIERS)
George of Great Bookham - Slyfield, esq, [PRO; PCC 1642] [*and*] [SRO; 65/1/525-533]

SHEARS (SHEIRES,SHIERS) [*continued*]
  Roger of Chertsey - New Haw; Weybridge, yeoman [DW/PA/7/7 f.634; DW/PA/5/1608/94] <Abs 1187>
SHEARWOOD (SHEEREWOODE)
  John of Swk St Olave, yeoman [DW/PA/7/7 f.570; DW/PA/5/1606/83] <Abs 1066>
SHEATHER
  George of Walton on Thames [PRO; PCC Admon 1612]
SHEEPEY
  John of Rotherhithe, bachelor [PRO; PCC Admon 1626]
SHEEREWOODE *see* SHEARWOOD
SHEFFIELD (SHEFELD,SHEFFEILD,SHEFFEILDE)
  Alice of Swk St Olave, widow [DW/PA/7/13 f.388; DW/PA/5/1645/50]
  Blanch of Dorking - Westcott, gent., wife of John [DW/PA/7/7 f.90; 1596] <Abs 166>
  Edward of Dorking [PRO; PCC Admon 1649]
  Innocent of Dorking [DW/PA/7/10 f.185; DW/PA/5/1619/99]
  John of Dorking, gent. [DW/PA/7/7 f.381; DW/PA/5/1602/76] <Abs 706>
  John of Dorking, gent. [DW/PA/5/1603/148] <Abs U87>
  Matthew of Croydon [PRO; PCC Admon 1647]
  Robert of Dorking, senior [DW/PA/5/1550/114]
  Robert of Dorking, yeoman [HRO; 1587 B78]
  Robert of Dorking, yeoman [DW/PA/5/1587/34]
  Rowland of Godstone, esq. [PRO; PCC 1648]
  William of Abinger [PRO; PCC 1640]
  William of Abinger, miller [HRO; 1608 AD53]
  William of Dorking, tallow chandler [PRO; PCC 1634]
SHEIRES *see* SHEARS
SHELBORNE (SHILBORNE)
  Richard of Bermondsey, citizen and weaver [DW/PA/7/10 f.281; DW/PA/5/1622/89]
SHELDEN,SHELDON *see* SHELTON
SHELFORD
  Jonas of Kingston, farmer [DW/PA/7/9 f.84; DW/PA/5/1615/116]
SHELL
  William of Swk St Olave, cooper [DW/PA/5/1569/21]
SHELLEY
  Robert of Kingston - Apps Court, esq. [PRO; PCC Admon 1600]
SHELLMARDEN *see* SHERMANDINE
SHELSPORTE
  Thomas of Swk St Olave, fellmonger [DW/PA/7/2 f.41; 1494]
SHELTON (SHELDEN,SHELDON)
  Eleanor of Guildford [PRO; PCC Admon 1648]
  Ralph of Tatsfield [PRO; PCC Admon 1602]
  Reginald of Newington [PRO; PCC Admon 1596]
SHEMYN
  Giles of Swk St Thomas Hospital [DW/PA/5/1604/53A] <Abs U115>
SHEOLES
  Thomas of Swk St Saviour, saddler [DW/PA/7/7 f.339; DW/PA/5/1601/73] <Abs 614>
SHEPHERD (SCHEPARD,SCHEPHARD,SHEPARD,SHEPARDE,SHEPHEARD,SHEPPARD,SHEPPARDE, SHIPPERT)
  Alexander of St Mary le Bow, London; Richmond, bachelor [PRO; PCC Admon 1641]

SHEPHERD (SCHEPARD, SCHEPHARD, SHEPARD, SHEPARDE, SHEPHEARD, SHEPPARD, SHEPPARDE, SHIPPERT) [*continued*]
Alice of Camberwell - Peckham, widow [PRO; PCC 1649]
Bridget of Battersea, widow [PRO; PCC 1634]
George of Weybridge [PRO; PCC Admon 1649]
Henry of Kingston [PRO; PCC Admon 1616]
John of Esher [HRO; Reg, Way 2 p,163; 1473]
John of Kingston [DW/PA/7/2 f,30; 1492]
John of Peper Harow [PRO; PCC 1640]
Margaret, alias Margaret Knap of Ewell [PRO; PCC Admon 1637]
Mary of Newington, widow [PRO; PCC Will 1625]
Nicholas of Weybridge [DW/PA/7/8 f,293; DW/PA/5/1613/116]
Richard of Dorking [DW/PA/7/2 f,190; 1523]
Robert of Guildford St Mary [DW/PA/7/2 f,3; 1490]
Roger of Bermondsey [DW/PA/7/11 f,260; DW/PA/5/1625/220]
Simon of Swk St Margaret [DW/PA/7/3 f,114; 1529]
Stephen of Swk, citizen and vintner [DW/PA/7/9 f,241; DW/PA/5/1617/113]
Thomas of Bermondsey, citizen and leatherseller [PRO; PCC Will 1620] <Soame 1186>
Thomas of Ewell, brewer [PRO; PCC Will 1626 *and* regrant 1637]
Thomas of Kingston, maltster [DW/PA/7/13 f,265; DW/PA/5/1643/79]
Thomas of Newington, butcher [PRO; PCC Admon 1611]
William of Battersea [PRO; PCC Admon 1634]
William of Bermondsey, citizen and leatherseller [DW/PA/7/10 f,94; DW/PA/5/1619/100]
William of Swk St George, citizen and vintner [DW/PA/5/1578/47]
SHERARDE *see* SHERRETT
SHERBORNE (SHARBAN, SHERBAN)
Elizabeth of Streatham, widow [DW/PA/7/8 f,39; DW/PA/5/1609/102]
Jacob of Elstead [DW/PA/7/12 f,200; DW/PA/5/1633/116]
Robert of Mortlake, bachelor [PRO; PCC Admon 1629]
SHERE
Arnold of Godalming - Farncombe, shearman [DW/PA/7/8 f,304; DW/PA/5/1613/117]
Jesode of Godalming [DW/PA/7/5 f,39; 1538] <Abs 48>
John of Godalming [DW/PA/7/5 f,31; 1538] <Abs 47>
Robert of Godalming [DW/PA/7/5 f,176; 1540]
SHERFIELD (SHERFELD, SHERFILL)
John of Sutton [PRO; PCC Will 1461] <Abs, SAC v,52 p,45>
William of Putney [PRO; PCC Will 1601] <Abs, SAC v,10 p,298>
SHERLEY *see* SHIRLEY
SHERLOCK (SCURLOK, SHAROLOK, SHERLOCKE, SHIRLOCKE, SHOORLOCKE, SHORLOCKE, SHURLOCK, SHURLOCKE, SHYRLOK, SHYRLOKE)
Abraham of Ockham, husbandman [DW/PA/7/12 f,298; DW/PA/5/1635/109]
Eden of Shere [DW/PA/7/2 f,201; 1524]
Edmund of Newdigate [DW/PA/5/1591/42]
Edward of Bramley, husbandman [DW/PA/5/1588/19]
Edward of Shalford [DW/PA/7/5 f,58; 1539] <Abs 80>
Elizabeth of Bramley [DW/PA/7/11 f,488; DW/PA/5/1628/89]
George of Bramley [DW/PA/7/11 f,484; DW/PA/5/1628/90]
Joan of Send, widow [HRO; 1587 B79]
John of Alfold, yeoman [DW/PA/7/11 f,279; DW/PA/5/1625/222]
John of Chertsey, husbandman [DW/PA/7/5 f,154; 1541]
John of Shalford, husbandman [DW/PA/5/1550/89]

SHERLOCK (SCURLOK,SHAROLOK,SHERLOCKE,SHIRLOCKE,SHOORLOCKE,SHORLOCKE,
SHURLOCK,SHURLOCKE,SHYRLOK,SHYRLOKE) [*continued*]

John of Shalford - Snowdenham, yeoman [DW/PA/5/1568/64]

John of Swk St George [DW/PA/7/2 f.55; 1497]

John of Walton on the Hill, carpenter [DW/PA/7/8 f.68; DW/PA/5/1609/105]

John of Wonersh [DW/PA/7/2 f.142; 1520]

Margery of Swk St Saviour, widow [DW/PA/7/11 f.468; DW/PA/5/1628/91]

Richard of Bramley, yeoman [DW/PA/7/8 f.329; DW/PA/5/1613/118]

Richard of Shalford; Wonersh [DW/PA/7/5 f.16; 1538] (Abs 77)

Robert of Addington [PRO; PCC Admon 1619]

Robert of Albury, husbandman [DW/PA/5/1585/3]*

Robert of Beddington [DW/PA/5/1578/38]

Robert of Chertsey, husbandman [DW/PA/7/12 f.313; DW/PA/5/1636/85]

Robert of Cobham, husbandman [DW/PA/7/11 f.136; DW/PA/5/1624/112]

Robert of Compton [DW/PA/7/4 f.128; 1535]

Robert of Hascombe; Alfold; Cranleigh, boardman [DW/PA/7/6 f.97; DW/PA/5/1559/82]

Robert of Shalford [DW/PA/7/4 f.97; 1534]

Thomas of Chertsey [HRO; 1641 AD94]

Thomas of Dunsfold [*in* DW/PA/5/1558/166]

Walter of Hascombe [DW/PA/5/1591/29]

William of Albury - Farley, husbandman, senior [DW/PA/7/11 f.36; DW/PA/5/1623/106]

SHERMAN

Roger of Lambeth [PRO; PCC Will 1593]

SHERMANDINE (SHELLMARDEN,SHILMARDINE)

Edward of Swk St Olave [DW/PA/7/13 f.124; DW/PA/5/1640/146]

John of Battersea, gardener [DW/PA/7/13 f.382; DW/PA/5/1645/47]

Richard of Bermondsey; Swk St Olave, cordwainer [DW/PA/7/8 f.59; DW/PA/5/1609/104]

SHERPE *see* SHARPE

SHERRATT (SHERARDE,SHERET,SHERETT)

Dorothy *or* Joanna of Woking, spinster [DW/PA/7/13 f.311; DW/PA/5/1646/52]

Joan of West Molesey, spinster [PRO; PCC 1638]

Joanna *or* Dorothy of Woking, spinster [DW/PA/7/13 f.311; DW/PA/5/1646/52]

John of Woking, junior [DW/PA/5/1571/80]

John of Woking, senior [HRO; 1582 B78]

(Sir) Phillip of Battersea, knight [PRO; PCC Admon 1624]

Ralph of Woking, yeoman [DW/PA/5/1571/20]

Walter of Swk [DW/PA/7/11 f.464; 1628]

William of Woking, senior [HRO; 1562 D3/116]

William of Woking - Crastock, yeoman, senior [DW/PA/5/1587/28]

William of Woking, yeoman, senior [DW/PA/7/7 f.588; DW/PA/5/1607/90] (Abs 1097)

William of Woking [PRO; PCC Will 1604] (Abs. SAC v.11 p.297)

William of Woking [GMR; 46/1/5; 1645]

William of Woking - Crastock, yeoman [DW/PA/7/12 f.459; DW/PA/5/1639/119]

SHERRINGTON (SHIRINGTON)

Walter of St Bartholomew Priory, London; Uxbridge, Middlesex; Romney, Kent; Tickhill, Yorkshire; Barnes, prebendary of St Paul's; prebendary of Lichfield; prebendary of Lincoln [LPL; Reg. Abp Stafford f.170; Will 1448]

SHERWIN (SHERWYN)
  John of Newdigate [DW/PA/5/1558/245]
  Magdalen of Battersea [PRO; PCC Will 1592]
  Nicholas of Battersea [PRO; PCC Will 1616]
  William of Battersea [DW/PA/7/4 f.37; 1533]
SHERWOOD
  John of Rotherhithe, sailor [PRO; PCC Will 1581]
  John of Shalford [HRO; 1576 AD48]
SHETT
  Simon of Beddington, husbandman [HRO; 1557 U620-621]
SHEVENTON (SCHEVENTON)
  Thomas of Egham [PRO; PCC Will 1496]
SHEWELL
  John of Cobham, husbandman [DW/PA/5/1587/122]
  John of Cobham, husbandman [DW/PA/7/7 f.70; 1596] <Abs 132>
  William of Wotton, husbandman [DW/PA/5/1571/55]
SHIERS *see* SHEARS
SHILBORNE *see* SHELBORNE
SHILMARDINE *see* SHERMANDINE
SHINE (SHYNE)
  Henry of Swk St Olave, waterman [DW/PA/5/1586/39]*
  William of Wandsworth [DW/PA/5/1582/8]
SHINFIELD
  Richard of Betchworth, tanner [DW/PA/7/11 f.480; DW/PA/5/1628/92]
SHIPLEY
  Margaret, alias Margaret Dickenson of Wandsworth [PRO; PCC Admon 1634]
  Susan of Wandsworth [PRO; PCC Admon 1634]
SHIPMAN
  Roger of Barnes [PRO; PCC 1638]
SHIPPERT *see* SHEPHERD
SHIRINGTON *see* SHERRINGTON
SHIRLEY (SHERLEY,SHURLEY)
  Edmund of Warlingham, haberdasher [DW/PA/7/12 f.224; DW/PA/5/1634/91]
  George of Newington [PRO; PCC 1642]
  John of Swk St Olave [DW/PA/7/11 f.176; DW/PA/5/1625/221]
  Sybil, alias Sybil Wright of Newington, widow [PRO; PCC Admon 1641]
  Thomas of Newington [PRO; PCC Admon 1644]
SHIRLOCK *see* SHERLOCK
SHOE (SHOO,SHOOE)
  John of Horley [DW/PA/5/1605/73] <Abs U162>
  John of Ockley [PRO; PCC Will 1557]
  Richard of Dorking, yeoman [DW/PA/7/12 f.304; DW/PA/5/1636/84]
  William of Abinger, yeoman [DW/PA/7/12 f.17; DW/PA/5/1631/98]
SHONKE (SHONCK)
  Arthur of Wanborough; Guildford; Shalford, yeoman [DW/PA/7/7 f.358; DW/PA/5/1602/77] <Abs 657>
  Frances of Swk St Olave, widow [DW/PA/7/7 f.617; DW/PA/5/1607/80] <Abs 1154>
  Richard of Shalford; Guildford, beer brewer [DW/PA/7/7 f.205; DW/PA/5/1598/76] <Abs 364>
SHOOTTON
  Robert of Swk St George, yeoman [DW/PA/7/3 f.166; 1531]

SHORE
Agnes of Dorking, widow [DW/PA/7/11 f.319; DW/PA/5/1626/106]
John of Little Bookham, husbandman [DW/PA/7/9 f.101; DW/PA/5/1614/103]
John of Stoke Dabernon, yeoman [DW/PA/7/7 f.573; DW/PA/5/1606/84] <Abs 1070>
Thomas of Mickleham [DW/PA/7/13 f.24; DW/PA/5/1639/126]
Thomas of Stoke Dabernon, husbandman, senior [DW/PA/5/1558/246]*
Thomas of Stoke Dabernon, husbandman [HRO; Reg. CCB20 p.5; 1563]
Thomas of Stoke Dabernon, husbandman [DW/PA/5/1563/66 *and, in* DW/PA/5/1563/64]
SHOREY (SHORIE,SHORRY)
John of Thames Ditton - Claygate, husbandman [DW/PA/7/11 f.11; DW/PA/5/1623/107
Nicholas of Croydon [LPL; 98/1 f.24r; Will 1631]
Nicholas of Wonersh; Ewhurst, husbandman [DW/PA/7/10 f.30; 1616]
Richard of Ewhurst, husbandman, senior [DW/PA/7/7 f.276; DW/PA/5/1599/63] <Abs 491>
Robert of Guildford, saddler [DW/PA/5/1588/51]
SHORLOCKE *see* SHERLOCK
SHORRY *see* SHOREY
SHORT (SHORTE)
Humphrey of Abinger, husbandman [DW/PA/7/12 f.324; DW/PA/5/1636/88]
SHORTER
Richard of Ash; Frimley [DW/PA/5/1550/45]
Richard of Puttenham [DW/PA/7/1 f.15; 1485] <Abs 48>
Thomas of Blechingley [DW/PA/7/6 f.272; 1560]
William of Swk St Saviour, horner [DW/PA/5/1572/18]
SHOTER *see* CHUTER
SHOTT (SHOT,SHOTTE)
Angelus of Swk, goldsmith [HRO; Reg. Way 2 p.151; 1472]
Anthony of Croydon [PRO; PCC Admon 1613]
Richard of Bermondsey [HRO; Reg. Way 1 p.26; 1453]
Thomas of Oxted [DW/PA/7/4 f.191; 1536]
William of Lambeth - Lambeth Dean, husbandman [DW/PA/7/13 f.204; DW/PA/5/1642/72]
SHOVE (SHOW,SHOWE)
Agnes of Horley [DW/PA/7/9 f.78; DW/PA/5/1614/104]
Henry of Horley [DW/PA/5/1574/42]
Jeremy of Horley, yeoman [DW/PA/7/13 f.411; DW/PA/5/1645/53]
SHOVINGHURST
Richard of Ockley, husbandman [DW/PA/5/1589/2]*
SHOW,SHOWE *see* SHOVE
SHOWELL
Richard of Ashtead [DW/PA/5/1558/247]*
SHOWTER *see* CHUTER
SHREFFE
John of Newington [PRO; PCC Admon 1596]
SHREWSBURY (SHROUESBURY)
John of Surrey [PRO; PCC Will 1406]
SHRIMPTON
Michael of Blechingley, gent. [PRO; PCC 1648]
SHROUESBURY *see* SHREWSBURY

SHRUB (SHRUBB,SHRUBBE,SHRUBE)
  Joan of Seale - Tongham, widow [DW/PA/7/12 f.359; DW/PA/5/1636/92]
  John of Chobham, butcher [DW/PA/7/9 f.318; DW/PA/5/1619/101]
  John of Farnham - Wrecclesham, husbandman, senior [DW/PA/7/7 f.624; DW/PA/5/1607/81] <Abs 1164>
  John of Godalming, dyer [DW/PA/7/13 f.485; DW/PA/5/1648/42]
  John *or* John Sheale of Seale [DW/PA/7/10 f.186; DW/PA/5/1620/110] <Abs U245>
  Roger of Chobham, butcher [DW/PA/5/1593/94]
  Stephen of Farnham - Wrecclesham, weaver [HRO; 1567 B148-149]
  Thomas of Chobham, yeoman [DW/PA/7/10 f.98; DW/PA/5/1619/102]
SHUDD
  Ann of Thursley, widow [PRO; PCC Will 1616]
  Jane of Thursley; Guildford, spinster [PRO; PCC Admon 1639]
  John of Shere [HRO; 1561 B189-190]
  John of Thursley, yeoman, senior [PRO; PCC Will 1617]
  Peter of Thursley, yeoman [DW/PA/7/12 f.426; DW/PA/5/1637/94]
  Richard of Thursley; Witley; Petworth, Sussex; Wisborough Green, Sussex, yeoman [DW/PA/7/9 f.58; DW/PA/5/1614/105]
  Thomas of Thursley, yeoman [PRO; PCC Admon 1649 *and* PCC 1649]
SHUDWELL
  Thomas of Lambeth [PRO; PCC Admon 1606]
SHULTE
  Henry of All Hallows Barking, London, tailor [DW/PA/7/7 f.377; DW/PA/5/1602/75] <Abs 697>
SHURLEY *see* SHIRLEY
SHURLOCK,SHURLOCKE,SHURLOK *see* SHERLOCK
SHYNE *see* SHINE
SHYNGLETON *see* SINGLETON
SHYRLOK,SHYRLOKE *see* SHERLOCK
SIDDALL
  John of Wandsworth [PRO; PCC Will 1530]
SIDNEY (SYDNEY)
  Nicholas of Surrey, esq. [PRO; PCC Will 1512]
SIGELL
  John of Swk St Olave, cutler [DW/PA/7/5 f.218; 1541]
SIGGER (SYGAR)
  Edmund of Swk St Margaret [DW/PA/7/4 f.37; 1533]
  William of Puttenham [PRO; PCC Will 1471]
  William of Worplesdon [DW/PA/7/2 f.126; 1518]
SIGGINS (SYGON)
  Henry of Lambeth [DW/PA/7/4 f.130; 1535]
  Robert of Kingston [PRO; PCC Admon 1647 (two)]
SILGRAVE
  Margery of Beddington [PRO; PCC Will 1425]
SILKER (SYLKER)
  Richard of Farnham [DW/PA/7/2 f.19; 1491]
SILL (SILLE)
  John of ... [DW/PA/7/11 f.63; DW/PA/5/1623/108]
  Margery of Swk St Olave [DW/PA/7/11 f.613; DW/PA/5/1630/89]
SILLOCK (CILLOCKE)
  John of Carshalton, miller [DW/PA/7/11 f.96; 1624]
SILSEY (SYLSEY)
  Thomas of Swk, chaplain [LPL; Reg. Abp Morton f.79v; Admon 1492]

SILVER
William, alias William Turner of Chiddingfold, husbandman [DW/PA/7/11 f,41; DW/PA/5/1623/124]
SILVESTER
Elizabeth of Newington, widow [PRO; PCC Admon 1641]
Gabriel of Croydon, clerk [PRO; PCC Will 1512]
Miles of Peper Harow, husbandman [DW/PA/5/1624/110]
Thomas of Mitcham [PRO; PCC Will 1592]
SIMCOTT (SIMCOCK,SYMCOTE)
Henry of Lingfield, glover [DW/PA/5/1561/29]
Michael of Blechingley [DW/PA/5/1587/78]
SIMMES *see* SIMS
SIMMONS (CYMONDE,SIMANS,SIMON,SIMOND,SIMONS,SYMON,SYMONDE,SYMONDES, SYMONDS,SYMONS)
Ann of Bisley, widow [DW/PA/7/10 f,64; 1618]
Edward of Chertsey, wheelwright [PRO; PCC Will 1613]
Edward of Chertsey, bargeman [PRO; PCC Will 1625]
Edward of West Clandon; Merrow, yeoman [DW/PA/7/7 f,422; DW/PA/5/1603/151] <Abs 789>
Edward of Send, yeoman [DW/PA/7/8 f,359; DW/PA/5/1612/143]
Elizabeth of Windlesham, widow [PRO; PCC 1649]
Geoffrey of West Clandon; Send, yeoman [DW/PA/7/6 f,280; 1560]
Grace of Putney, widow of Richard, merchant [PRO; PCC 1646]
Harry of Chipstead, husbandman [DW/PA/7/7 f,245; DW/PA/5/1599/64] <Abs 434>
Henry of West Clandon [DW/PA/5/1561/60]
Henry of Kingston, gardener [DW/PA/7/10 f,277; DW/PA/5/1620/118]
James of Horsell [HRO; 1641 AD99]
John of West Clandon [DW/PA/7/1 f,17; 1485] <Abs 57>
John of West Clandon; Albury, yeoman [DW/PA/7/8 f,100; DW/PA/5/1610/109]
John of Horsell [PRO; PCC Admon 1648]
John of Lambeth [PRO; PCC Will 1504]
John of Merrow [DW/PA/7/12 f,252; DW/PA/5/1635/113]
John of Pirbright [DW/PA/5/1572/6]
John of Richmond [DW/PA/5/1575/87]
John of Ripley, yeoman [DW/PA/7/12 f,382; DW/PA/5/1637/85]
John of Swk St Saviour, citizen and white baker [DW/PA/7/12 f,278; DW/PA/5/1625/223]
Margaret of Betchworth - Brockham [DW/PA/7/8 f,145; DW/PA/5/1611/111]
Margaret of Chertsey, spinster [DW/PA/7/12 f,102; DW/PA/5/1632/92]
Margery of Bermondsey, maid [DW/PA/7/13 f,431; DW/PA/5/1646/53]
Nicholas of Camberwell, husbandman [BM; Add.Ms 24,925 f,14r; 1544] <Abs 27>
Nicholas of West Clandon, yeoman [HRO; 1626 B108]
Nicholas of Godstone, husbandman [HRO; 1611 B62]
Nicholas of Send [DW/PA/7/7 f,421; DW/PA/5/1603/152] <Abs 786>
Ralph of Surrey [PRO; PCC Will 1541]
Ralph of Swk St Olave, cooper [DW/PA/5/1562/45]
Richard of Horsell - Sidewood, yeoman [DW/PA/7/12 f,163; DW/PA/5/1633/112]
Richard of Newington [LPL; 98/1 f,8v; Will 1630]
Robert of Battersea, labourer [HRO; Reg. Fox 3 p,64; 1513]
Robert of Charlwood, husbandman [LPL; 96/2521; Will 1648]

SIMMONS (CYMONDE,SIMANS,SIMON,SIMOND,SIMONS,SYMON,SYMONDE,SYMONDES,
SYMONDS,SYMONS) [*continued*]
Robert of Charlwood, husbandman [PRO; PCC Will 1]
Robert of West Clandon [PRO; PCC 1649]
Robert of Dorking, butcher [DW/PA/5/1575/82]
Robert of Horsell [DW/PA/7/7 f.87; 1596] <Abs 159>
Roger of Swk St Saviour, citizen and woodmonger [DW/PA/7/11 f.532; DW/PA/5/1629/95]
Thomas of Albury [DW/PA/5/1580/69]
Thomas of West Clandon, yeoman [DW/PA/7/12 f.75; DW/PA/5/1632/87]
Thomas of Croydon, stationer [GL; Commissary Court of London Will 1535]
Thomas of Newdigate [DW/PA/7/2 f.141; 1520]
Thomas of Pirbright [DW/PA/7/7 f.206; DW/PA/5/1598/77] <Abs 367>
Walter of Camberwell [HRO; Reg. CCB 20 p.7; 1563]
Walter of Camberwell [DW/PA/5/1563/71 *and, in* DW/PA/5/1563/65]
William of Lambeth [PRO; PCC Will 1473]
William of Mortlake, gent. [PRO; PCC Will 1623 *and* 1624]
William of Shere; Send; Clandon [DW/PA/5/1547/2]
William of Swk St Saviour - liberty of Paris Garden, shipwright [DW/PA/7/8 f.313; DW/PA/5/1613/119]

SIMMONSON (SYMONSON)
Simon of Swk St George [DW/PA/5/1558/271]*
William of Swk St Olave, senior [DW/PA/7/5 f.73; 1539]

SIMON,SIMOND,SIMONS *see* SIMMONS

SIMPSON (SIMSON,SYMPSON,SYMSON)
Augustine of Swk St Olave [DW/PA/7/8 f.218; DW/PA/5/1612/144]
Edmund of Swk St Olave, victualler [DW/PA/7/13 f.213; DW/PA/5/1643/80]
Elizabeth of Wimbledon [PRO; PCC Will 1590]
George of Swk St George, merchant tailor [DW/PA/5/1603/153] <Abs U88>
Joan of Chigwell, Essex; Swk St Olave, widow of Nicholas, esq. [PRO; PCC Will 1560] <Abs Emmison pp.130-131>
John of Surrey [PRO; PCC Will 1497]
John of Wimbledon [PRO; PCC Will 1590]
Martha of Swk St Olave, widow [DW/PA/7/12 f.69; DW/PA/5/1631/109]
Michael of Pirbright, yeoman [DW/PA/7/6 f.208; 1560]
Richard of ... [DW/PA/5/1555/71]
Robert of Bermondsey [PRO; PCC Will 1592]
Thomas of Swk St Saviour [DW/PA/5/1578/19]
William, alias William Baker of Putney [LPL; 98/1 f.119v; (ren.) 1640]

SIMS (SIMMES,SYMES,SYMMES)
Margaret of Croydon, widow [LPL; 98/1 f.96v; Will 1638]
Richard of Swk St Margaret [DW/PA/7/3 f.142; 1530]
William of Ashtead, weaver [HRO; 1618 AD74]

SIMSON *see* SIMPSON

SINACLE,SINACKLE,SINEKELL *see* SINNACLE

SINGLETON (SHYNGLETON)
Robert of West Horsley [DW/PA/7/2 f.14; 1491]
Thomas of Swk St George [DW/PA/7/8 f.152; DW/PA/5/1611/95]

SINNACLE (LYNACLE,SENACLE,SINACKLE,SINACLE,SINEKELL,SYGNAKYLL,SYNNOCKELL)
Alice [*Appears as* Alice Lynacle *in printed calendar, but this would seem to be a transcription error.*] of Woking, widow [DW/PA/7/1 f.91; 1489] <Abs 309>
Edmund of Woking, husbandman [DW/PA/7/7 f.113; DW/PA/5/1596/53] <Abs 208>

SINNACLE (LYNACLE,SENACLE,SINACKLE,SINACLE,SINEKELL,SYGNAKYLL,SYNNOCKELL)
[*continued*]
Henry of Woking - Heathside, husbandman [DW/PA/5/1579/79]*
Henry of Woking, yeoman [DW/PA/7/11 f.598; DW/PA/5/1630/101]
Jane of Woking, widow [DW/PA/5/1591/83]
John of Woking, yeoman [DW/PA/5/1555/39]
Richard of Woking [DW/PA/7/4 f.159; 1536]
Thomas of Woking [HRO; 1611 B63]
William of Horsell [DW/PA/7/4 f.109; 1535]
SISLYE *see* CICELY
SITHEREN
John of ..., mariner [DW/PA/7/11 f.7; DW/PA/5/1622/90]
SIVEYER (SYVYER)
Eleanor of Swk St Saviour, widow of Thomas, waterman [DW/PA/7/12 f.526; DW/PA/5/1635/112]
Richard of Oxted [DW/PA/7/2 f.4; 1490]
SKAFE (a SKAFE)
John of Swk St George, victualler [DW/PA/5/1568/14]
Thomas of Swk St Saviour, feltmaker [DW/PA/7/12 f.338; DW/PA/5/1636/89]
SKARNDELL
William of Kingston, yeoman [PRO; PCC Will 1608] <Abs, SAC v.13 p.179>
SKARTCLYFFE *see* SCATLIFFE
SKEAT *see* SKEET
SKEERERS
Agnes of Newington, widow [LPL; 98/1 f.24r; Will 1631]
SKEETE (SKEAT,SKEIT,SKETE,SKETT,SKEYTE,SKITE,SKITT)
Bartholomew of Egham, yeoman [DW/PA/5/1558/250]*
Clemence of Leatherhead, widow [DW/PA/7/7 f.623; DW/PA/5/1607/82] <Abs 1162>
David of Leatherhead - Pachesham; Stoke Dabernon, husbandman [DW/PA/7/9 f.316; DW/PA/5/1619/103]
Edward of Leatherhead, yeoman [DW/PA/5/1578/21]
Edward of Leatherhead; Blechingley; Nutfield, gent. [DW/PA/7/7 f.247; DW/PA/5/1599/65] <Abs 438>
Henry of West Horsley; Little Bookham [HRO; 1585 B60]
Jane of Beddington, widow [DW/PA/7/13 f.460; DW/PA/5/1647/19]
John of Chobham, husbandman [HRO; 1601 B50]
John of Long Ditton [DW/PA/7/1 f.18; 1485] <Abs 60>
John of Leatherhead [DW/PA/7/4 f.168A; 1536]
John of Reigate [GL; Commissary Court of London Will 1395]
Margaret of Chertsey; Egham, widow [DW/PA/5/1557/54]
Nicholas of Leatherhead - Pachesham, yeoman [DW/PA/7/7 f.283; DW/PA/5/1599/66] <Abs 506>
Richard of Leatherhead [PRO; PCC Will 1491]
Richard of Leatherhead - Pachesham, yeoman [DW/PA/7/12 f.282; DW/PA/5/1635/106]
Robert of East Clandon, husbandman [DW/PA/7/13 f.17; DW/PA/5/1639/124]
Roger of Bermondsey [PRO; PCC Admon 1648]
Thomas of Leatherhead, yeoman [DW/PA/5/1546/80]
Thomas of Leatherhead [DW/PA/5/1558/249]*
Walter of Mickleham, yeoman [DW/PA/7/10 f.177; DW/PA/5/1620/119]
William of Surrey [? HRO; 1533]

SKEETE (SKEAT,SKEIT,SKETE,SKETT,SKEYTE,SKITE,SKITT) [*continued*]

William of Leatherhead - Pachesham [DW/PA/7/7 f.282; DW/PA/5/1599/67] <Abs 505>

William of Leatherhead, husbandman [DW/PA/7/10 f.60; 1618]

William of Woking, yeoman [DW/PA/7/6 f.220; 1561]

SKELTON (SKELLTON,SKILTON)

Agnes of Reigate, widow [DW/PA/7/6 f.133; DW/PA/5/1559/134]

Catherine of Swk St Saviour, widow [DW/PA/7/10 f.119; DW/PA/5/1620/111]

Christopher of Swk St Saviour [DW/PA/7/11 f.411; DW/PA/5/1627/98]

Edmund of Swk St Olave - Maze, leatherdresser [DW/PA/7/7 f.623; DW/PA/5/1607/83] <Abs 1160>

Edward of Swk St Olave [DW/PA/7/11 f.115; DW/PA/5/1624/113]

Israel of Betchworth - Brockham [PRO; PCC 1647]

James of Bermondsey, citizen and wax chandler [PRO; PCC Will 1616]

John of Bermondsey, tailor [HRO; Reg. Way 2 p.146; 1471]

John of Reigate, clerk [DW/PA/5/1555/56]

Robert of Swk St Thomas; St Botolph Bishopsgate, Middlesex, minister and pastor [DW/PA/5/1603/154] <Abs U89>

Thomas of Reigate, mercer [PRO; PCC Will 1616]

SKERES

Nicholas of Chertsey, citizen and merchant tailor [PRO; PCC Will 1566]

SKERNE (SKERN)

John of Surrey [PRO; PCC Will 1594]

Swithin of Kingston, esq.[DW/PA/7/3 f.134; 1530] <Abs SAC v.8 pp.118-119>

William of Kingston [PRO; PCC Will 1464] <Abs SAC v.8 pp.109-110>

SKETE,SKETT,SKEYTE *see* SKEETE

SKILTON *see* SKELTON

SKINGLE

John of Swk St Saviour; South Ockenden, Essex, grocer [DW/PA/7/9 f.14; DW/PA/5/1616/128]

SKINNER (SKYNNER)

Alexander of Swk [DW/PA/5/1579/86]*

Alexander of Swk St George, glover [DW/PA/7/12 f.206; DW/PA/5/1634/87]

Alice of Camberwell, widow [PRO; PCC Admon 1640]

Cuthbert of Swk St Olave, bricklayer [DW/PA/5/1563/45]

Henry of Alfold [DW/PA/7/8 f.302; DW/PA/5/1613/120]

James of Reigate, esq. [PRO; PCC Will 1558]

John of Frensham [HRO; 1615 D3/184]

John of Lingfield, yeoman [DW/PA/7/12 f.68; DW/PA/5/1631/107]

John of Putney, citizen and mercer [PRO; PCC 1636]

John of Reigate, senior [DW/PA/7/2 f.109; 1515]

John of Reigate; Kent [DW/PA/5/1543/16]*

John of Reigate, esq., senior [PRO; PCC Will 1571]

John of Reigate, esq. [PRO; PCC Will 1584]

Margaret of Reigate, widow [PRO; PCC Will 1564]

Ralph of Oxted [PRO; PCC Admon 1602]

Ralph of Oxted [PRO; PCC Admon 1612]

Richard of Camberwell - Peckham [PRO; PCC Will 1492] <Abs SAC v.26 p.5>

Robert of Cranleigh, bachelor [DW/PA/5/1569/11]

Thomas of Farnham [DW/PA/7/4 f.133; 1536]

Thomas of Godstone [PRO; PCC 1639]

Thomas of Swk St Saviour, citizen and brown baker [DW/PA/5/1578/98]

Thomas of Swk - Paris Garden [DW/PA/5/1580/10]

William, alias William Godman of Egham, yeoman [DW/PA/7/6 f.272; 1560]

SKIPWITH
  Henry of Lambeth [PRO; PCC Admon 1631]
SKITE,SKITT *see* SKEETE
SKOCHER *see* SCOTCHER
SKOPHAM
  Edmund of Richmond [PRO; PCC Will 1503]
  Richard of Richmond [PRO; PCC Will 1502]
SKOTFELDE
  John of Swk St Margaret [DW/PA/5/1546/18]
SKOTT *see* SCOTT
SKYNNER *see* SKINNER
SLACKE
  William of Chertsey [DW/PA/7/10 f.49; 1618]
SLADE
  Alice of Swk St Saviour - Upper Ground, widow of Richard, waterman [DW/PA/5/1635/114] <Abs U254>
  Mabel of Swk St Saviour, widow [DW/PA/7/9 f.316; DW/PA/5/1619/104]
  Nicholas of Worplesdon, clerk [DW/PA/7/12 f.252; DW/PA/5/1635/103]
  Thomas of West Horsley, priest [PRO; PCC Will 1539]
SLANEHEAD
  William of Lambeth [DW/PA/7/12 f.412; DW/PA/5/1637/89]
SLANNE
  Margaret of Thorpe, spinster [PRO; PCC Admon 1649]
SLARKE (SLARKES)
  Anthony of Shere, yeoman [DW/PA/5/1581/29]
  Anthony of Shere, yeoman, senior [DW/PA/7/13 f.239; DW/PA/5/1642/79]
  Anthony of Shere [PRO; PCC Admon 1652, *but in 1631-1649 volume*]
  Elizabeth of Chobham [PRO; PCC Admon 1649]
  John of Shere, yeoman [HRO; 1592 AD95]
  John of Shere, yeoman [DW/PA/7/13 f.53; DW/PA/5/1640/132]
  Richard of Shere [DW/PA/7/2 f.149; 1521]
  Thomas of Chiddingfold, yeoman [DW/PA/7/11 f.564; DW/PA/5/1630/90]
    see also SLATTER
SLATER
  Elizabeth of Swk St George - King's Bench Prison, prisoner [DW/PA/7/13 f.346; 1644]
  Richard of Mitcham, vicar [DW/PA/7/12 f.440; DW/PA/5/1638/128]
  William of Swk [? HRO 1529]
SLATT
  William of Chertsey, husbandman [HRO; 1591 B71]
SLATTER
  Richard of Reigate [DW/PA/5/1576/99]
    see also SLATER
SLATTERFORD (SLAUGHTERFORD)
  John of Chiddingfold [PRO; PCC 1649]
  Thomas of Leigh; Ringrose, Sussex; West Grinstead, Sussex [DW/PA/5/1593/43]
SLAYMAKER
  John of Putney [PRO; PCC 1649]
SLAYNY
  John of Richmond [DW/PA/5/1591/12]
SLEADE
  Thomas of Kingston - Ham [PRO; PCC Admon 1649]

SLENNE
  Hamlet of Abinger - Okewood Chapel, priest incumbent [DW/PA/5/1550/6]
SLIE *see* SLY
SLIFIELD (SLIFEELD,SLIFEILD,SLIFEILDE,SLYFEILDE,SLYFELDE,SLYFFYLD)
  Edmund of Great Bookham - Slyfield, esq. [PRO; PCC Will 1590; SRO; 65/1/518-524] <Abs SAC v.25 pp.90-91>
  Elizabeth of Great Bookham - Slyfield, widow [DW/PA/7/7 f.156; DW/PA/5/1597/88] <Abs 290>
  George of Pyrford, yeoman [DW/PA/7/13 f.109; DW/PA/5/1640/144]
  Henry of Great Bookham - Slyfield, esq., senior [PRO; PCC Will 1590; SRO; 65/1/525-533; 1598]
  Henry of West Clandon, clerk [PRO; PCC Will 1545]
  Henry of Horsell, yeoman [DW/PA/7/13 f.480; DW/PA/5/1648/36]
  Henry of Pyrford, clothworker [DW/PA/7/11 f.333; DW/PA/5/1625/225]
  James of Wonersh, yeoman [DW/PA/7/7 f.277; DW/PA/5/1599/68] <Abs 493>
  John of Byfleet, yeoman, senior [DW/PA/7/7 f.93; 1596] <Abs 171>
  John of East Clandon, yeoman [DW/PA/5/1587/37]
  John of Leatherhead, junior [PRO; PCC Will 1528]
  John of Pyrford, yeoman, senior [DW/PA/7/13 f.246; DW/PA/5/1640/150]
  Susanna of Pyrford, widow [DW/PA/5/1625/226]
  Thomas of Great Bookham [PRO; PCC Admon 1605]
SLIGHTER
  Nicholas of Battersea - Penge Green, bachelor [PRO; PCC Admon 1641]
SLUCE (SLUSE)
  Gertrude of Swk St Olave, widow [DW/PA/7/10 f.36; DW/PA/5/1617/114]
  John of Swk St Olave [*Dutch*] [DW/PA/7/9 f.332; DW/PA/5/1620/112]
  John of Swk St Olave, goldsmith [DW/PA/7/9 f.121; DW/PA/5/1615/117]
SLUTTER
  Thomas of Newington [LPL; 98/1 f.62r; (ren.) 1634]
SLY (SLIE)
  William of Kingston [PRO; PCC Admon 1616]
SLYFEILDE,SLYFELDE,SLYFFYLD,SLYFIELD *see* SLIFIELD
SLYTHAM
  Henry of Swk St George, citizen and merchant tailor [DW/PA/7/11 f.211; DW/PA/5/1625/227]
SMALE *see* SMALL
SMALEMAN *see* SMALLMAN
SMALEPAGE *see* SMALLPAGE
SMALEPEICE,SMALEPIECE *see* SMALLPIECE
SMALL (SMALE)
  Gillian of Send, widow [DW/PA/5/1558/186]*
  Robert of Send [DW/PA/7/7 f.375; DW/PA/5/1602/78] <Abs 692>
  Stephen of Newington [LPL; 96/2354; 98/1 f.46r; Will 1633]
SMALLAYE *see* SMALLEY
SMALLBONE
  Adam of Wandsworth, gardener [DW/PA/7/12 f.369; DW/PA/5/1627/99]
SMALLEY (SMALLAYE)
  John of Bermondsey, citizen and leatherseller [PRO; PCC 1646]
  Thomas of Swk St Olave, carpenter [DW/PA/5/1568/8]
SMALLMAN (SMALEMAN,SMALMAN)
  Robert of Swk St Thomas, pewterer [DW/PA/7/7 f.403; DW/PA/5/1603/155] <Abs 746>
  Thomas of Kingston [PRO; PCC Will 1584]

SMALLPAGE (SMALEPAGE)
Michael of Surrey, gent. [PRO; PCC Will 1594]
SMALLPIECE (SMALEPEICE,SMALEPIECE,SMALLPEECE,SMALLPIS,SMALPECE,SMALPEECE, SMALPEICE,SMALPES)
Alice of Shalford, widow [DW/PA/7/8 f.177; DW/PA/5/1610/112]
Ann of Godalming, spinster [DW/PA/7/12 f.454; DW/PA/5/1638/129]
James of Guildford, gent. and haberdasher [HRO; 1625 B63]
John of Compton [PRO; PCC Will 1615]
John of Cranleigh, tailor [DW/PA/7/12 f.40; DW/PA/5/1631/105]
John of Ewhurst [PRO; PCC Will 1418]
John of Ewhurst; Guildford Holy Trinity; Stoke next Guildford, yeoman [DW/PA/7/7 f.129; DW/PA/5/1597/89] <Abs 237>
John of West Horsley [BM; Add.Ms 24,925 f.14r; 1544] <Abs 28>
Katherine of Charlwood; Newdigate, widow of Thomas [PRO; PCC 1632]
Lawrence of Guildford St Nicolas, clothier, senior [DW/PA/7/13 f.406; DW/PA/5/1646/50]
Margaret of Guildford Holy Trinity, widow [HRO; 1589 B48]
Nicholas of Guildford Holy Trinity, haberdasher [HRO; 1601 B51]
Richard of Shalford; Stoke next Guildford; Guildford St Mary; Guildford St Nicolas, vicar of Shalford [DW/PA/5/1604/58] <Abs U119>
Thomas of Guildford, clothier [DW/PA/5/1571/68]
Thomas of West Horsley, husbandman [DW/PA/5/1572/12]
Thomas of Newdigate, yeoman [PRO; PCC Will 1627] [*and*] [DW/PA/7/11 f.406; DW/PA/5/1627/100]
Thomas of Newdigate [PRO; PCC Admon 1639]
Thomas of Shalford - Unstead, yeoman [DW/PA/7/10 f.193; DW/PA/5/1621/112]
William of Guildford, tailor [DW/PA/7/13 f.458; DW/PA/5/1647/18]
SMALLRIDGE (SMALREDG)
William of Bermondsey, servant to Edward Myll, esq. [PRO; PCC Will 1608] <Abs SAC v.12 p.106>
SMALLWOOD (SMALWOOD)
John of Richmond [PRO; PCC Admon 1613]
SMALMAN *see* SMALLMAN
SMALPECE,SMALPEECE,SMALPEICE,SMALPES *see* SMALLPIECE
SMALREDG *see* SMALLRIDGE
SMALWOOD *see* SMALLWOOD
SMART
Thomas of Ripley, victualler [DW/PA/7/13 f.393; DW/PA/5/1645/51]
SMEREPOUNDE
Nicholas of St Martin le Grand, London, hosier [DW/PA/5/1579/83]*
SMETHER *see* SMITHER
SMETHURST *see* SMITHURST
SMETON
Thomas, alias Thomas Smythe of Kingston [DW/PA/7/4 f.206; 1537]
SMITH (SMITHE,SMYTH,SMYTHE,SMYZTH)
... of Kingston - Ham, husbandman [DW/PA/5/1557/3]
Abraham of Swk St Olave, carman; citizen and woodmonger [DW/PA/7/11 f.76; DW/PA/5/1623/109]
Agnes of Horsell; Stoke; Woking, widow [DW/PA/5/1604/53B] <Abs U116>
Agnes of Kingston - Ham, widow [DW/PA/7/4 f.177; 1536]
Agnes of Lambeth, widow of Richard [DW/PA/7/2 f.82; 1502]
Agnes of Enfield, Middlesex; Wotton, widow [GL; Commissary Court of London Will 1603]
Alan of Banstead [DW/PA/7/12 f.268; DW/PA/5/1635/104]

SMITH (SMITHE, SMYTH, SMYTHE, SMYZTH) [*continued*]

Ann of Bermondsey, widow [DW/PA/5/1568/22]

Ann of Bermondsey, widow [DW/PA/7/10 f.251; DW/PA/5/1622/91]

Ann of Egham, widow (previously widow of Thomas Clarke) [DW/PA/7/5 f.172; 1540]

Ann of Guildford, spinster [DW/PA/7/12 f.373; DW/PA/5/1638/122]

Ann of Poplar, Middlesex; Lambeth; Kingston - Hatch, widow [DW/PA/7/9 f.318; DW/PA/5/1619/105]

Anthony of Guildford, citizen and grocer [PRO; PCC Will 1609] <Abs. SAC v.23 p.144>

Anthony of Merrow, husbandman [DW/PA/7/8 f.65; DW/PA/5/1609/107]

Anthony of Rotherhithe, mariner [PRO; PCC Will 1613]

Anthony of Wandsworth - Dunsford, gent. [PRO; PCC Will 1584]

Anthony of Witley - Milford, gent., senior [DW/PA/7/12 f.417; DW/PA/5/1637/91] [*and*] [GMR; *in* 5/4/32; 1637] <Abs SAC v.18 p.35 *and* v.33 p.40>

Augustine of Rotherhithe, carpenter [DW/PA/7/11 f.395; DW/PA/5/1626/107]

Baldwin of Guildford Holy Trinity, citizen and haberdasher [PRO; PCC Will 1557] <Abs SAC v.28 p.98>

Beatrice of Ewell, servant to John Dickins [DW/PA/5/1575/9]

Christopher of Chertsey, bachelor [PRO; PCC Admon 1630]

Cleophas of Putney [PRO; PCC Admon 1632]

Edward of Lambeth [PRO; PCC Admon 1645]

Elizabeth of Burstow [LPL; 96/2355; Will 1625]

Elizabeth of Godalming - Hurtmore [HRO; 1641 B41]

Elizabeth of Lambeth, widow [PRO; PCC Admon 1645]

Elizabeth of Swk St Saviour - Bankside, widow [DW/PA/7/10 f.80; DW/PA/5/1619/107]

Elizabeth of Wandsworth, widow [DW/PA/5/1576/152]

Ellen of Swk St Olave, widow [DW/PA/5/1563/105]

Elizabeth of Sutton, spinster [DW/PA/7/10 f.6; DW/PA/5/1619/106]

Francis of ... [DW/PA/5/1582/31]

Garret of Swk St Saviour, shoemaker [DW/PA/5/1603/156] <Abs U90>

Geoffrey of Sutton; West Cheam [HRO; 1597 B66] [*and*] [DW/PA/7/7 f.139; DW/PA/5/1597/90] <Abs 257>

George of Croydon [PRO; PCC 1634]

George of Elstead, yeoman [DW/PA/7/13 f.88; DW/PA/5/1640/139]

George of Mitcham, yeoman [DW/PA/7/8 f.391; DW/PA/5/1612/145]

George of Mitcham, esq. [PRO; PCC 1638]

George of Send - Grove Heath, husbandman [HRO; 1636 B41]

George of Worplesdon, gent. [PRO; PCC 1632]

Gosson of Swk St Olave, cordwainer [DW/PA/7/10 f.266; DW/PA/5/1622/92]

Henry of Godalming - Tuesley, husbandman [DW/PA/7/10 f.120; DW/PA/5/1620/113]

Henry of Horsell; Pyrford; Woking; Bisley, yeoman [DW/PA/7/6 f.58; DW/PA/5/1559/83]

Henry of Horsell, yeoman [DW/PA/7/12 f.471; 1638]

Henry of Horsell, yeoman [DW/PA/7/13 f.67; DW/PA/5/1639/133]

Henry of Lambeth - Water Lambeth, gent. [PRO; PCC Will 1593]

Henry of Mitcham [PRO; PCC Will 1528]

Henry of Morden, yeoman [DW/PA/7/10 f.80; DW/PA/5/1619/108]

Henry of Newington [LPL; 98/1 f.77v; Will 1636]

SMITH (SMITHE,SMYTH,SMYTHE,SMYZTH) [*continued*]

Henry of Pyrford; Chobham, husbandman [DW/PA/7/7 f.503; DW/PA/5/1605/82] <Abs 942>

Henry of Rotherhithe [PRO; PCC Admon 1638]

Henry of Limehouse, Middlesex; Swk; the Ship *Salamander* [GL; Commissary Court of London Will 1601]

Henry of Swk St Olave, feltmaker [DW/PA/5/1586/32]

Isabel of Pirbright, widow [DW/PA/7/3 f.146; 1530]

James of Cobham, husbandman [DW/PA/7/8 f.28B; DW/PA/5/1608/95]

James of Swk St Saviour, shoemaker [DW/PA/5/1571/57]

James of Swk St Saviour, bodicemaker [DW/PA/7/13 f.170; DW/PA/5/1641/129]

Jane of Peper Harow, widow [DW/PA/7/12 f.275; DW/PA/5/1635/105]

Joan of Swk St Saviour, widow [DW/PA/7/11 f.115; DW/PA/5/1624/114]

Joanna of Guildford, widow [PRO; PCC Admon 1578 (two)]

(Sir) John of Surrey, baron of the exchequer [PRO; PCC Will 1547]

John of Ash [HRO; 1559 W1 WR7 p.232]

John of Banstead, yeoman [DW/PA/7/11 f.503; DW/PA/5/1629/86]

John of Beddington [PRO; PCC 1647]

John of Bermondsey [PRO; PCC Admon 1623]

John of Bermondsey [PRO; PCC Admon 1646]

John of Blechingley [DW/PA/7/1 f.95; 1489] <Abs 313>

John of Chertsey [PRO; PCC Admon 1630]

John, alias John Clark of Egham [DW/PA/7/1 f.23; 1485] <Abs 76>

John of Ewhurst; Great Bookham [BM; Add.Ms 24,925 f.18r; 1544] <Abs 40>

John of Ewhurst [DW/PA/5/1552/18]

John of Ewhurst, carpenter [DW/PA/5/1591/2]

John of Ewhurst [PRO; PCC Will 1592]

John of Farnham, blacksmith [DW/PA/7/10 f.137; DW/PA/5/1620/115]

John of Farnham [PRO; PCC Admon 1647]

John of Frensham; Bramshott, Hampshire [DW/PA/7/3 f.113; 1529]

John of Frensham, husbandman [DW/PA/7/7 f.371; DW/PA/5/1602/79] <Abs 682>

John of Godalming - Tangley, yeoman [DW/PA/7/12 f.126; DW/PA/5/1632/98]

John of Horsell; Pyrford, yeoman [DW/PA/7/7 f.476; DW/PA/5/1604/54] <Abs 899>

John of Kingston - Ham [DW/PA/5/1571/77]

John of Lambeth, fisherman [DW/PA/7/11 f.531; DW/PA/5/1629/87]

John of Merrow [DW/PA/7/10 f.123; DW/PA/5/1620/114] <Abs SAC v.18 pp.33-34>

John of Merton [DW/PA/7/1 f.73; 1487] <Abs 240>

John of Oxted [DW/PA/5/1569/52]

John of Pirbright, husbandman [DW/PA/5/1558/252]*

John of Pirbright [PRO; PCC 1647]

John of Pyrford, husbandman [DW/PA/7/12 f.27; DW/PA/5/1631/102]

John of Reigate, tanner [DW/PA/7/2 f.180; 1522]

John of Richmond, groom almoner to the king [DW/PA/7/4 f.136; 1536]

John of Swk St George, chaplain [HRO; Reg. Way 1 p.7; 1449]

John of Swk St George, servingman [DW/PA/5/1578/100]

John of Swk St George, gardener [DW/PA/7/13 f.448; DW/PA/5/1646/55]

John of Swk St Margaret [DW/PA/7/5 f.150; 1540]

John of Swk St Mary Magdalen; Clapham; Swk St Olave [DW/PA/5/1593/87]

John of Swk St Olave [DW/PA/5/1555/34]

John of Swk St Olave, stapler [DW/PA/7/12 f.400; DW/PA/5/1637/87]

SMITH (SMITHE,SMYTH,SMYTHE,SMYZTH) [*continued*]

John of Swk St Saviour, citizen and merchant tailor [DW/PA/7/11 f.374; DW/PA/5/1626/108]

John of Stoke Dabernon [DW/PA/7/4 f.78; 1534]

John of Streatham [DW/PA/7/5 f.126; 1539]

John of Sutton, yeoman [DW/PA/5/1580/48]

John of Wandsworth [PRO; PCC Will 1574]

John of Wandsworth, gent. [PRO; PCC Will 1596]

John of Woking [DW/PA/7/4 f.202; 1537]

John, alias John at Smith, alias John Smither of Wonersh [DW/PA/5/1576/83]

Joseph of Horne; Blechingley, husbandman [DW/PA/5/1605/81] <Abs U170>

Juliana, alias Juliana Pawmer of Send, widow [DW/PA/7/1 f.100; 1489] <Abs 325>

Juliana of Swk St Olave, widow [DW/PA/7/9 f.150; DW/PA/5/1615/118]

Katherine of Thames Ditton, later Katherine Wilkynnes [PRO; PCC Will 1549]

Margaret of Pirbright, widow [DW/PA/5/1558/253]*

Marie of Banstead, widow [DW/PA/7/8 f.16; DW/PA/5/1608/96]

Mary of Croydon, widow [LPL; 98/1 f.93v; Will 1638]

Mary of Lambeth, spinster [PRO; PCC Admon 1649]

Matthias of Putney [LPL; 98/1 ff.89r,96v; Will 1638]

Miles of Kingston; Westminster St Margaret, Middlesex, mason [DW/PA/5/1558/254]*

Nicholas of Guildford, shearman, senior [DW/PA/7/7 f.55; DW/PA/5/1596/54] <Abs 106>

Nicholas of Morden, yeoman [DW/PA/7/6 ff.82,85; DW/PA/5/1559/220]

Nicholas of Swk St Olave, joiner [DW/PA/5/1575/61]

Oliver of Ash, musician [DW/PA/7/12 f.261; DW/PA/5/1634/100]

Phillip of Fetcham [DW/PA/7/3 f.184; 1531]

Phillip of Newington [LPL; 98/1 f.113r; Will 1640]

Ralph of Croydon [LPL; 98/1 f.53v; Will 1633]

Ralph of Kingston, barber [DW/PA/7/1 f.69; 1487] <Abs 228>

Ralph of Wandsworth [DW/PA/7/3 f.190; 1531]

Rebecca of Swk St Olave, widow [DW/PA/5/1593/156]

Richard of Barnes [LPL; 96/2357; 98/1 f.26v; Will 1631]

Richard, alias Richard Butler of Battersea [PRO; PCC Will 1513]

Richard of Godalming, weaver [DW/PA/5/1552/10]

Richard of Kingston, weaver [HRO; 1589 B49]

Richard of Lambeth [DW/PA/7/2 f.60; 1500]

Richard of Lambeth, yeoman [PRO; PCC Will 1597]

Richard of Mitcham, husbandman [DW/PA/7/8 f.4; DW/PA/5/1608/97]

Richard of Send, yeoman [DW/PA/7/11 f.276; 1625]

Richard of Swk - liberty of the Clink [DW/PA/7/11 f.217; DW/PA/5/1625/228]

Richard of Wandsworth [HRO; 1634 AD56]

Robert of ..., citizen and grocer [DW/PA/7/8 f.290; DW/PA/5/1613/121]

Robert of Banstead, one of the cursitors of the Court of Chancery [PRO; PCC Will 1603]

Robert of Barnes [PRO; PCC Admon 1592]

Robert of Byfleet, yeoman [DW/PA/5/1591/73]

Robert of Byfleet, yeoman [DW/PA/7/8 f.107; DW/PA/5/1610/113]

Robert of Byfleet, yeoman [DW/PA/7/13 f.400; DW/PA/5/1645/52]

Robert of Chertsey [PRO; PCC Will 1609] <Abs. SAC v.23 p.134>

SMITH (SMITHE,SMYTH,SMYTHE,SMYZTH) [*continued*]
Robert of Thames Ditton - Ember Court [DW/PA/7/5 f.167; 1540]
Robert of Godalming, yeoman [DW/PA/7/4 f.229; 1537]
Robert of Kingston - Ham, husbandman [DW/PA/5/1568/83]
Robert of Lambeth, labourer [*Latin*] [DW/PA/5/1570/29]
Robert of Newington - Kent Street, yeoman [PRO; PCC Will 1618] [*and* [Southwark Local Studies Library; Southwark Deeds 1238; 1618]
Robert of Pirbright [? HRO; 1521]
Robert of Swk St Olave, leatherseller [DW/PA/5/1563/90]
Robert of Swk St Thomas, glover [DW/PA/5/1558/255]*
Robert, alias Robert Ferror of Woking [DW/PA/7/1 f.87; 1489] <Abs 295>
Roger of Kingston - Ham Hatch, yeoman [DW/PA/7/9 f.210; DW/PA/5/1616/127]
Samuel of Bermondsey; Odierna, Brittany, France [PRO; PCC Will 1611] <Abs SAC v.35 p.45>
Samuel of Esher [PRO; PCC Admon 1617]
Simon of Lambeth - Stockwell, husbandman [DW/PA/7/9 f.197; DW/PA/5/1616/130]
Stephen of Kingston, barber and chirurgeon [PRO; PCC Will 1619]
Stephen of Putney, yeoman [PRO; PCC Will 1608] <Abs, SAC v.13 pp.189-190>
Thomas of Burstow, yeoman [PRO; PCC Will 1611] <Abs, SAC v.35 p.46>
Thomas of Chertsey [PRO; PCC Admon 1629]
Thomas of Chertsey - Hardwick Court [PRO; PCC Admon 1635]
Thomas of Cobham [DW/PA/7/4 f.225; 1537]
Thomas of Cobham; Stoke Dabernon [DW/PA/5/1558/256]*
Thomas of Dorking, sieve maker [DW/PA/7/13 f.363; 1644]
Thomas of Guildford, gent., senior [HRO; 1625 B64]
Thomas of Guildford, maltster [DW/PA/7/13 f.360; 1644]
Thomas, alias Thomas Smeton of Kingston [DW/PA/7/4 f.206; 1537]
Thomas of Lambeth, husbandman [DW/PA/7/7 f.624; DW/PA/5/1607/84] <Abs 1163>
Thomas of Lambeth - Lambeth Marsh, weaver [DW/PA/7/11 f.429; DW/PA/5/1627/101]
Thomas of Mitcham, esq. [PRO; PCC Will 1576]
Thomas of Mitcham, labourer [DW/PA/7/11 f.387; DW/PA/5/1626/109]
Thomas of Mortlake [PRO; PCC Admon 1601]
Thomas of Pirbright [DW/PA/7/8 f.275; DW/PA/5/1612/146]
Thomas of Rotherhithe, mariner [PRO; PCC Will 1609] <Abs, SAC v.23 p.138>
Thomas of Rotherhithe [PRO; PCC 1647]
Thomas of Swk; Skirlaugh, Yorkshire, husbandman [DW/PA/5/1572/17]
Thomas, alias Thomas Grange of Stoke Dabernon, yeoman [DW/PA/7/9 f.204; DW/PA/5/1616/131]
Thomas of Streatham [DW/PA/7/11 f.67; DW/PA/5/1623/110]
Thurston of Lambeth, dyer [PRO; PCC Will 1618]
Timothy of Richmond [DW/PA/7/11 f.194; DW/PA/5/1625/230]
(Sir) Walter of Great Bedwyn, Wiltshire; Send - Send Court, knight [LBLAD; Surrey Deeds 1/2287; 1643]
Walter of Deptford, Kent; Kingston, yeoman of the king's slaughterhouse [DW/PA/7/9 f.76; DW/PA/5/1614/106]
Walter of Wandsworth [DW/PA/5/1587/27]
William of Ash, labourer [? HRO; 1581]

SMITH (SMITHE,SMYTH,SMYTHE,SMYZTH) [*continued*]

William of Banstead, yeoman [DW/PA/7/7 f.552; DW/PA/5/1606/85] <Abs 1034>

William of Bermondsey, wheelwright [DW/PA/5/1579/80]*

William of Bermondsey, barber surgeon [DW/PA/5/1591/70]

William of Chertsey [DW/PA/7/1 f.73; 1488] <Abs 239>

William of Chertsey, mercer [DW/PA/7/2 f.190; 1523]

William, alias William Clerke of Croydon [LPL; 98/1 f.38r; Will 1632]

William of Croydon, gent. [PRO; PCC 1641]

William, alias William Clerke of Egham [PRO; PCC Will 1490]

William of Epsom, yeoman [DW/PA/7/12 f.319; DW/PA/5/1636/86]

William of Ewell, husbandman [PRO; PCC Will 1619]

William of Kingston - Ham, husbandman [DW/PA/7/2 f.175; 1522] <Abs SAC v.1 pp.187-189>

William of Kingston [DW/PA/7/4 f.138; 1536]

William of Kingston - Ham [DW/PA/5/1579/81]*

William of Lambeth, shipwright [PRO; PCC Will 1627]

William of Mitcham, esq. [PRO; PCC 1640]

William of Newington, citizen and innholder [GL; Archdeaconry Court of London Will 1605]

William of Swk St George [DW/PA/7/9 f.239; DW/PA/5/1617/115]

William of Swk St Saviour - liberty of Paris Garden, waterman [DW/PA/7/7 f.34; DW/PA/5/1595/77] <Abs 71>

William of Sutton; Cheam, yeoman [DW/PA/7/8 f.92; DW/PA/5/1609/108]

William of Sutton, yeoman [DW/PA/7/12 f.269; DW/PA/5/1634/102]

William of Titsey [PRO; PCC Will 1552]

William of Worplesdon, porter to the king [PRO; PCC Will 1592]

see also at Smith

SMITHER (SMETHER,SMITHERS,SMYTHER)

Benjamin of Bramley [DW/PA/7/9 f.24; DW/PA/5/1614/107]

Henry of Godalming [PRO; PCC Will 1501]

Henry of Godalming - Eashing, husbandman [DW/PA/5/1576/8]

Henry of Thursley [DW/PA/7/3 f.146; 1530]

Hugh of Shalford - Smithbrook [DW/PA/5/1591/81]

Joan of Guildford [DW/PA/7/11 f.208; DW/PA/5/1625/231]

John of Albury, husbandman [DW/PA/7/13 f.268; DW/PA/5/1644/18]

John of Bramley; Wonersh, yeoman [DW/PA/7/7 f.619; DW/PA/5/1607/85] <Abs 1156>

John of Chertsey, weaver [DW/PA/7/9 f.185; DW/PA/5/1616/132] <Abs U212>

John of Chertsey, weaver and husbandman [HRO; 1642 B35]

John of Farnham; Bramley, beer brewer [DW/PA/7/6 ff.254,276; 1560]

John of Shalford, weaver [DW/PA/5/1575/71]

John, alias John at Smithe of Wonersh [DW/PA/5/1576/83]

John of Wonersh - Tilehurst, yeoman [DW/PA/5/1622/94]

John of Wonersh - Tilehurst, yeoman [DW/PA/7/13 f.48; DW/PA/5/1639/34]

Juliana of Shalford [DW/PA/7/11 f.563; DW/PA/5/1630/91]

Margaret of Abinger, widow [DW/PA/7/10 f.90; DW/PA/5/1615/119]

Margery of Stoke; Godalming - Farncombe, widow of Edward weaver [DW/PA/5/1576/67]

Mary of Wonersh [HRO; 1631 AD92]

Richard of Windlesham, husbandman [HRO; 1639 B61]

Robert of Godalming [DW/PA/7/4 f.196; 1537]

Sarah of Woking [DW/PA/7/10 f.297; DW/PA/5/1622/93]

Thomas of Hascombe, husbandman [DW/PA/5/1558/257]*

SMITHER (SMETHER,SMITHERS,SMYTHER) [*continued*]
Thomas of Shalford [DW/PA/7/6 f.91; DW/PA/5/1559/84]
Thomas of Witley, husbandman [DW/PA/5/1622/95]
Thomas of Wonersh, yeoman [DW/PA/7/9 f.7; DW/PA/5/1615/120]
Thomas of Worplesdon, yeoman, senior [DW/PA/7/11 f.123; DW/PA/5/1623/111]
SMITHGATE (SMYTHEYATE)
John of Worplesdon [PRO; PCC Will 1559]
Thomas of Chertsey, yeoman [DW/PA/5/1561/13]
SMITHURST (SMETHURST)
Bartholomew of Pirbright, yeoman [HRO; 1576 B77]
SMITHSON (SMYTHSON)
Christopher of Newington [LPL; 98/1 f.17v; Will 1630]
John of Dorking, potter [DW/PA/7/5 f.44; 1538] <Abs 29>
SMYTH,SMYTHE *see* SMITH
SMYTHEYATE *see* SMITHGATE
SMYTHER *see* SMITHER
SMYTHSON *see* SMITHSON
SMYZTH *see* SMITH
SNAPE (SNAPES)
John of Newington [LPL; 96/2399; Will 1625]
Reginald of Weybridge, bachelor [PRO; PCC Admon 1637]
Thomas of Swk St Saviour, waterman [DW/PA/7/13 f.170; DW/PA/5/1641/128]
SNELL
Anna of Lingfield [PRO; PCC Admon 1648]
SNELLING (SNELLINGE,SNELLYNG,SNELLYNGE,SNELYNG)
Dorothy of Guildford St Mary, widow [HRO; 1573 B131]
Dorothy of Newdigate [PRO; PCC Will 1569]
Elizabeth of Swk St Saviour; Hanging Haughton, Northamptonshire, widow [DW/PA/7/10 f.291; DW/PA/5/1622/86]
Elizabeth of Witley - Milford, widow [DW/PA/7/7 f.422; DW/PA/5/1603/157] <Abs 790>
George of Kingston, mercer, senior [DW/PA/5/1568/55]
George of Kingston, gent., senior [PRO; PCC Will 1612]
George of Kingston [PRO; PCC Admon 1643]
George of Lambeth - Lambeth Marsh [DW/PA/7/10 f.119; DW/PA/5/1620/116]
Henry of Compton, yeoman [DW/PA/7/12 f.304; DW/PA/5/1635/110]
Henry of Guildford, clothier [DW/PA/7/13 f.284; DW/PA/5/1643/82]
Isabel of Swk St Saviour, late wife of Richard [DW/PA/7/11 f.482; DW/PA/5/1628/93]
Jane of Tandridge, widow [DW/PA/7/13 f.13; DW/PA/5/1639/123]
John of West Clandon, husbandman [DW/PA/5/1558/258]*
John of Elstead [HRO; 1618 B51]
John of Guildford, husbandman [DW/PA/5/1587/25]
John of Guildford St Mary, shearman [DW/PA/5/1582/50]
John of Shere, yeoman [DW/PA/7/11 f.357; DW/PA/5/1625/232]
Judith of Guildford St Mary, spinster [DW/PA/7/13 f.484; DW/PA/5/1648/41]
Margaret of Godalming, widow [DW/PA/7/12 f.130; DW/PA/5/1632/100]
Margaret of Kingston, widow [PRO; PCC Admon 1650 *but in 1631-1649 volume*]
Mark of Kingston, gent. [PRO; PCC 1634]
Matthew of Windlesham [HRO; 1601 AD37]

SNELLING (SNELLINGE,SNELLYNG,SNELLYNGE,SNELYNG) [*continued*]
Peter of Blechingley; Swk White Lion, prisoner [PRO; PCC Will 1609] <Abs, SAC v,23 p,135>
Phillip of West Horsley, smith [DW/PA/5/1578/77]
Richard of Coulsdon [DW/PA/7/11 f,489; DW/PA/5/1628/94]
Richard of Send; West Clandon; Woking, yeoman [DW/PA/7/11 f,1; DW/PA/5/1624/115]
Robert of Guildford St Mary [DW/PA/7/3 f,136; 1530]
Robert of Haslemere, farrier [HRO; 1609 B79]
Robert of East Horsley [LPL; 96/2404; Will 1623]
Robert of Puttenham, smith [DW/PA/5/1572/20]
Rose of Kingston, widow [DW/PA/7/10 f,170; DW/PA/5/1621/113]
Thomas of ,,, [DW/PA/5/1603/158] <Abs U91>
Thomas of Guildford [HRO; Reg, Fox 2 p,32; 1508]
Thomas of East Horsley [PRO; PCC Will 1504] <Abs SAC v,29 p,102>
Thomas of Kingston, gent, [PRO; PCC 1637]
Thomas of Leatherhead [? HRO; 1534]
Thomas of Puttenham, tailor [DW/PA/7/7 f,288; DW/PA/5/1599/98] <Abs 514>
Thomas of Puttenham [PRO; PCC 1640]
Thomas of Witley - Milford; Godalming - Tuesley [DW/PA/5/1598/78] <Abs U19>
Thomas of Witley, blacksmith [HRO; 1637 B41]
William of Ash; Puttenham; Godalming - Farncombe; Witley, citizen and blacksmith [GL; Archdeaconry Court of London Will 1603]
William of West Clandon [DW/PA/7/7 f,421; DW/PA/5/1603/159] <Abs 787>
William of Guildford [PRO; PCC Will 1572]
William of Haslemere, blacksmith [DW/PA/7/9 f,99; DW/PA/5/1614/108]
William of Woking, blacksmith [DW/PA/7/13 f,131; DW/PA/5/1640/148]

SNIPSTON (SNYPSTON)
John, alias John Clerk of Croydon [PRO; PCC Will 1432]

SNORING (SNORYNG)
John of Chertsey [PRO; PCC Will 1490]

SNOTT
John of Tatsfield, labourer [DW/PA/7/1 f,38; 1486] <Abs 124>

SNOW (SNOWE)
Edward of Wandsworth - Allfarthing [PRO; PCC Will 1587]
Elizabeth of St Bride, London; Lambeth - Kennington [GL; Commissary Court of London Will 1587]
Elizabeth of Surrey, widow [PRO; PCC Will 1587]
John of Cobham [DW/PA/7/5 f,112; 1539]
Judith of Richmond; Barnes, widow [DW/PA/7/7 f,480; DW/PA/5/1604/55] <Abs 905>
Katherine of Richmond; Isleworth, Middlesex; Norwood, Middlesex, widow [DW/PA/7/7 f,258; DW/PA/5/1599/69] <Abs 457>
Nicholas of Richmond, gent, and keeper of the Queen's Wardrobe [DW/PA/5/1582/24] [*and*] [PRO; PCC Will 1583]

SNOWBALL
William of Lambeth, gent, [PRO; PCC Will 1584]

SNOWE *see* SNOW

SNOWSMAN
John of Chertsey, gent, [PRO; PCC 1641]

SNYPSTON *see* SNIPSTON

SOANE *see* SONE

SOARE
  Edward of Swk St Saviour, shipwright, senior [DW/PA/7/8 f.226; DW/PA/5/1612/147]
  Edward of Swk St Saviour, shipwright [DW/PA/7/11 f.61; DW/PA/5/1623/112]
SODA
  John of Newington - Walworth, citizen and grocer [GL; Archdeaconry Court of London Will 1581]
SOLE (SOLLE)
  Robert of Swk St Saviour, brewer [DW/PA/7/8 f.246; DW/PA/5/1613/122]
  Thomas of Swk St Saviour, tailor [DW/PA/5/1561/65]
SOLENBENE *see* SALONBENDE
SOLLE *see* SOLE
SOLOMONS (SALMAN)
  Simon of Swk St Olave, feltmaker [DW/PA/5/1582/90]
  Thomas of Charlwood, etc., esq. [PRO; PCC Will 1430]
SOMER *see* SUMMERS
SOMERBY
  Robert of Kingston, clerk [PRO; PCC Will 1502] <Abs SAC v.8 pp.112-114>
SOMERSETT
  Robert of ... [DW/PA/7/11 f.64; DW/PA/5/1623/113]
SOMERTON (SOWMERTON)
  George of Lingfield; Ramsden Bellhouse, Essex, bricklayer [DW/PA/7/9 f.192; DW/PA/5/1616/133]
  Richard of Thames Ditton, husbandman [DW/PA/7/6 f.131; 1559]
SOMMERS *see* SUMMERS
SONDAR
  John of Cobham [HRO; Reg. Way 1 p.36; 1454]
SONDAY
  Mericke of ... [*proved at London*] [DW/PA/5/1587/26]
SONDE (SOWNDE)
  Henry of Dorking [PRO; PCC Will 1464]
  John of Guildford Holy Trinity [DW/PA/7/1 f.15; 1485] <Abs 50>
  Thomas of Stoke next Guildford, husbandman [DW/PA/7/7 f.170; DW/PA/5/1597/92] <Abs 312>
SONDEFORD *see* SANDFORD
SONDEZ
  Thomas of Crowhurst, clerk [PRO; PCC Will 1478]
SONE (SOANE)
  Edward of Wotton, clerk [DW/PA/5/1575/54]
  George of Blechingley, husbandman [DW/PA/7/11 f.390; DW/PA/5/1626/110]
  John of Limpsfield [DW/PA/7/7 f.148; DW/PA/5/1597/91] <Abs 274>
  Nicholas of Beddington [HRO; 1630 AD69]
  Thomas of Crowhurst; Limpsfield, yeoman [DW/PA/7/7 f.572; DW/PA/5/1606/86] <Abs 1069>
SONGHURST (CONGHURST,SONGEHURST,SONGHERST)
  Agnes of Ockley, widow [HRO; 1587 B81]
  Edith of Abinger, widow [DW/PA/7/4 f.201; 1537]
  Edmund of West Horsley, husbandman [DW/PA/7/12 f.148; DW/PA/5/1633/109]
  Eleanor of Dorking, spinster [DW/PA/7/7 f.637; DW/PA/5/1608/98] <Abs 1192>
  John of Abinger, husbandman [DW/PA/7/7 f.496; DW/PA/5/1605/83] <Abs 930>
  John of Sanderstead; Croydon, yeoman, junior [DW/PA/7/4 f.4; 1532]
  Thomas of Abinger [HRO; 1585 B64]
  Thomas of West Horsley, yeoman [DW/PA/7/10 f.248; DW/PA/5/1622/96]

SONGHURST (CONGHURST, SONGEHURST, SONGHERST) [*continued*]
  Thomas of Ockley; Wotton, yeoman [HRO; 1625 B66]
  Walter of Ockley [HRO; 1586 B50]
SOUTH
  Humphrey of Swk St George [DW/PA/7/9 f.89; DW/PA/5/1615/89]
  Richard of Ash [? HRO; 1603]
  Robert of Chobham [DW/PA/7/1 f.65; 1487] <Abs 216>
SOUTHCOTT (SOUTHCOTE)
  John of Croydon, esq. [PRO; PCC Will 1426]
  John of Merstham, esq. [PRO; PCC 1638]
SOUTHERTON
  Ellis of Richmond, gent. [PRO; PCC 1649]
SOUTHWELL (SOWTHWELL)
  Francis of Surrey, esq., senior [PRO; PCC Will 1581]
  (Sir) Robert of Surrey, knight [PRO; PCC Will 1560]
  Robert of Chertsey [PRO; PCC Admon 1586]
  (Sir) Thomas of Battersea, knight [PRO; PCC Admon 1643]
SOWMERTON *see* SOMERTON
SOWNDE *see* SOUND
SOWTHWELL *see* SOUTHWELL
SPACHERSTE *see* SPATCHURST
SPACKMAN
  Joshua of Rotherhithe [PRO; PCC Will 1623]
  Norwich of Merstham, clerk [LPL; 96/2415; Will 1617]
SPAFFOLDE
  Robert of Leatherhead [DW/PA/5/1561/77]
SPAGE
  William of Kingston [DW/PA/7/1 f.1; 1484] <Abs 1>
SPARKS (SPARKE, SPARKES, SPERCKES, SPERKES)
  John of Guildford St Nicolas [DW/PA/5/1558/260]*
  John of Albury - Weston, husbandman [DW/PA/7/7 f.359; DW/PA/5/1602/80]
    <Abs 660>
  John of Swk St Olave [DW/PA/7/4 f.208; 1537]
  Richard of Horley [DW/PA/5/1583/4]*
  Richard of Merton, husbandman [DW/PA/7/12 f.483; DW/PA/5/1638/132]
  Richard of Reigate [DW/PA/5/1558/259]*
  Richard of Wonersh, husbandman [DW/PA/7/13 f.186; DW/PA/5/1646/51]
  Samuel of Barnes, clerk [PRO; PCC Will 1609] <Abs, SAC v.23 p.136>
  Thomas of Lingfield [DW/PA/5/1543/5]*
SPARROW (SPARRO, SPARROWE)
  Alice of Reigate, widow [DW/PA/5/1576/95]
  Anthony of Chessington [DW/PA/7/11 f.499; DW/PA/5/1629/88]
  Charles of Kingston, gardener [DW/PA/5/1592/44]
  John of Swk St Margaret; Swk St George; Clapham, armourer [DW/PA/7/5
    f.76; 1539]
  Michael of Lambeth [PRO; PCC Will 1587]
  Stephen of Swk St Olave, citizen and merchant tailor [DW/PA/7/11
    ff.203,323; DW/PA/5/1625/233]
SPARROWHAWKE
  William of Swk St Olave, shipwright [HRO; Reg. CCB 20 p.5; 1563] [*and*]
    [DW/PA/5/1563/68 *and, in* DW/PA/5/1563/65]
SPATCHURST (SPACHERSTE)
  John of Lingfield, carpenter [DW/PA/7/5 f.187; 1540]
  William of Lingfield [PRO; PCC Admon 1586]

SPENCE
John of Titsey [DW/PA/7/12 f.387; DW/PA/5/1638/124]
SPENCER (SPENSER)
Edward of Reigate, gent. [DW/PA/7/8 f.137; DW/PA/5/1610/114]
Harry of Pyrford, yeoman [DW/PA/7/7 f.286; DW/PA/5/1599/99] <Abs 510>
John of Battersea [PRO; PCC 1638]
John of Camberwell [PRO; PCC Admon 1637]
John of West Horsley, yeoman [DW/PA/7/12 f.214; DW/PA/5/1633/117; GMR; *in* 22/3/8/1]
John of Swk St Saviour [DW/PA/7/7 f.15; DW/PA/5/1595/78] <Abs 32>
John of Streatham [HRO; 1510 B20 *and* Reg. Fox 2 p.33]
Mary of Battersea, widow [PRO; PCC Will 1621]
Richard of Surrey, gent. [PRO; PCC Will 1509]
Thomas of Kingston [PRO; PCC 1648]
William of Battersea, yeoman [DW/PA/7/11 f.528; DW/PA/5/1630/92]
William of Cobham, merchant tailor [GL; Archdeaconry Court of London Will 1632]
William of Lambeth [PRO; PCC 1649]
William of Reigate, gent. [DW/PA/7/9 f.211; DW/PA/5/1616/134]
William of Rotherhithe [DW/PA/7/3 f.175; 1531]
William of Woking, yeoman of the queen's guard [DW/PA/7/6 f.112; DW/PA/5/1559/85]
William of Woking [PRO; PCC Admon 1594]
SPERCKES *see* SPARKS
SPERRIN (SPERYN)
Thomas of Swk St Saviour, citizen and tallow chandler [DW/PA/5/1546/27]
SPIBYE
John of Swk St George [DW/PA/5/1591/108]
SPICER
John of Chertsey [DW/PA/7/2 f.198; c1524]
John, alias John Lee of Kingston [PRO; PCC Will 1502]
Phillip of Bermondsey, blacksmith [DW/PA/7/13 f.350; 1644]
SPICORNELL
John of Thorpe (died overseas) [PRO; PCC Admon 1637]
SPIGHT
Damaris of Bermondsey [PRO; PCC Admon 1649]
SPILLER
Robert of Sutton, esq. [PRO; PCC 1634]
(Sir) Robert of Woking, knight [PRO; PCC Admon 1637]
SPITTLE
Humphrey of Newington [LPL; 98/1 f.59v; (ren.) 1634]
SPONER *see* SPOONER
SPONGE
Edmund of Woking [BM; Add.Ms 24,925 f.24r; 1544] <Abs 60>
Henry of Chobham, yeoman [DW/PA/7/12 f.356; DW/PA/5/1638/121]
Henry of Chobham, yeoman, senior [DW/PA/7/13 f.31; DW/PA/5/1639/129]
Henry of Chobham [PRO; PCC Admon 1648]
Robert of Abinger, bachelor [PRO; PCC Admon 1647]
SPOONER (SPONER,SPONNER)
Anthony of West Clandon [DW/PA/7/7 f.141; DW/PA/5/1596/55] <Abs 210>
Elizabeth of Abinger, widow [DW/PA/7/12 f.232; DW/PA/5/1634/95]
Elizabeth of Cranleigh, widow [DW/PA/7/13 f.43; DW/PA/5/1640/130]
Harry of Ockley, husbandman [DW/PA/5/1558/261]*
Henry of Abinger, yeoman [HRO; 1603 B54]

SPOONER (SPONER,SPONNER) [*continued*]
Henry of Abinger; Ockley; Wotton, yeoman [DW/PA/7/9 f.46; DW/PA/5/1614/109]
Henry of Ockley, yeoman [DW/PA/7/12 f.111; DW/PA/5/1632/93]
John of Abinger, yeoman [DW/PA/7/12 f.117; DW/PA/5/1632/95]
Ralph of Cranleigh, yeoman [HRO; 1636 B43]
Robert of Cranleigh, yeoman [DW/PA/7/12 f.139; DW/PA/5/1632/102]
William of Ockley, yeoman [DW/PA/7/11 f.388; DW/PA/5/1626/111]
SPOORE
Edward of Swk St Olave [DW/PA/7/11 f.306; DW/PA/5/1626/112]
SPOTT
John of Cobham [PRO; PCC Admon 1648]
SPRING
Ann of Lambeth - Water Lambeth, spinster [PRO; PCC 1640]
SPRINGALL
Richard of Croydon - Trinity Hospital [LPL; 96/2422; Will 1643]
SPRINGBETT
Gilbert of Swk St Saviour, waterman [DW/PA/7/13 f.34; DW/PA/5/1639/130]
SPRINGEHAM
Matthias of Richmond, esq. [PRO; PCC Will 1620] <Soame 1099>
SPURGE
John of St Martha's - Chilworth [HRO; 1565 B102]
Thomas of Godalming - Catteshall [*in* DW/PA/5/1555/1]
SPURLINGE
Robert of Lambeth - Lambeth Dean; Streatham, yeoman [DW/PA/7/10 f.213; DW/PA/5/1620/120]
SPURSTONE
Randall of Godstone, gent. [PRO; PCC Will 1535]
SQUIBB
Stephen of Pirbright, gent. [PRO; PCC 1648]
SQUIRES (SQUIER,SQUIRE,SQUYRE,SQYRE)
Agnes of Lingfield, widow [DW/PA/7/12 f.77; DW/PA/5/1632/88]
Nicholas of Godstone [DW/PA/5/1570/8]
Robert of Beddington [PRO; PCC Admon 1625]
Thomas of Godstone [DW/PA/5/1546/60]
William of Surrey [PRO; PCC Will 1590]
William of Lingfield, husbandman [PRO; PCC Will 1618]
William of Oxted [PRO; PCC Admon 1647]
William of Rotherhithe [PRO; PCC Admon 1624]
STABLE (a STABLE)
James of Tooting Graveney [DW/PA/7/4 f.145; 1536]
STACE,STACEY *see* STACY
STACFORD *see* STACKFORD
STACIE *see* STACY
STACKFORD (STACFORD,STACKEFORD,STACKFORDE,STAKFORD,STAYCKFORD,STOKFORD)
Isabel of West Molesey, widow [DW/PA/7/5 f.195; 1540]
John of West Molesey [DW/PA/7/2 f.99; 1514]
John of West Molesey [DW/PA/5/1580/5]
John of West Molesey, yeoman [DW/PA/5/1582/82]
John of West Molesey, yeoman [DW/PA/7/13 f.75; DW/PA/5/1640/135]
Matthew of West Molesey [PRO; PCC Will 1593]
Robert of West Molesey [DW/PA/7/2 f.176; 1522]
Robert of West Molesey; Esher - Chadsworth, yeoman [DW/PA/7/7 f.76; 1596] <Abs 140>

STACKFORD (STACFORD,STACKEFORD,STACKFORDE,STAKFORD,STAYCKFORD,STOKFORD)
[*continued*]
Thomas of West Molesey; Walton; Ashford, Middlesex; East Molesey [DW/PA/7/5 f,168; 1540]
William of West Molesey [DW/PA/5/1545/12]
STACY (STACE,STACEY,STACIE,STACYE,STASEY,STALYE)
Alan, alias Alan Boone of Reigate, mason [DW/PA/7/7 f,447; DW/PA/5/1603/168] <Abs 847>
Edmund of Oxted, tanner [DW/PA/5/1579/82]*
Edward of Lingfield [PRO; PCC Admon 1624]
Elizabeth of Chertsey, widow [DW/PA/7/9 f,258; DW/PA/5/1617/116]
Joan of Ashtead, widow [PRO; PCC Admon 1649]
John of Leatherhead [DW/PA/7/9 f,200; DW/PA/5/1616/136]
John of Reigate, husbandman [DW/PA/7/7 f,157; DW/PA/5/1597/93] <Abs 292>
Nicholas of Oxted, yeoman [DW/PA/7/12 f,481; DW/PA/5/1638/131]
Paul of Leatherhead [PRO; PCC 1635]
Richard of Godstone, yeoman [DW/PA/7/8 f,123; DW/PA/5/1610/115]
Robert of Reigate; Battersea, yeoman [DW/PA/7/9 f,6; DW/PA/5/1615/123]
Robert, alias Robert Harries of Kingston - Surbiton, husbandman [DW/PA/5/1555/42]
Thomas of Camberwell, clerk [PRO; PCC Will 1527]
Thomas of Swk St Saviour, waterman [DW/PA/7/11 f,74; DW/PA/5/1623/114]
William of Godstone, husbandman [DW/PA/5/1578/110]
William of Lingfield, husbandman [PRO; PCC Will 1613]
STAFFE
Phillip of Rotherhithe (died overseas) [PRO; PCC Admon 1646]
STAFFERTE
Alexander of Swk St George; Waterford St Mary, Ireland [DW/PA/5/1593/85]
STAGING (STAGEYN)
John of Walton on Thames [PRO; PCC Will 1427]
STAINER (STAYNER)
William of Edmonton, Middlesex; Bermondsey; Swk St Olave, citizen and merchant tailor [GL; Commissary Court of London Will 1603]
STAINING (STAYNING,STAYNINGE)
Richard of Ewhurst, husbandman [DW/PA/5/1588/36; PRO; PCC Will 1588]
Thomas, alias Thomas Cooper of Dorking [PRO; PCC Admon 1626]
STAINSBY (STANESBY,STANSBY)
William of Lambeth [PRO; PCC 1637]
William of Reigate [DW/PA/7/11 f,512; DW/PA/5/1629/90]
STALYE *see* STACY
STAMFORD
Richard of Tandridge, bachelor [PRO; PCC 1644]
STANBEKE
John of Ash [DW/PA/5/1550/112]
STANBRIDGE (STANDBRIDGE,STANDIGE)
John of Dorking [PRO; PCC 1649]
John of Limpsfield, husbandman [DW/PA/7/12 f,4; DW/PA/5/1631/95]
Richard of Worplesdon, beer brewer [HRO; 1597 B68]
William of Swk St Olave, labouring man [DW/PA/7/7 f,461; DW/PA/5/1603/160] <Abs 871>
STANDEN *see* STANDON
STANDFORDE *see* STANFORD
STANDIGE *see* STANBRIDGE

STANDISH
  Francis of Esher, gent. [PRO; PCC Will 1627 *and* 1628]
  Henry of Esher [PRO; PCC Admon 1595]
STANDEN,STANDEYN *see* STANDON
STANDER
  John of Egham, vicar [DW/PA/7/10 f.224; DW/PA/5/1621/114]
STANDON (STANDEN,STANDEYN,STONDON)
  Edmund of East Molesey, gent. [PRO; PCC Will 1571]
  John of Kingston [DW/PA/7/1 f.81; 1488] <Abs 269>
  John of Kingston, fisher [DW/PA/7/3 f.163; 1530]
  John of Mitcham [PRO; PCC Will 1477]
  John of Richmond [DW/PA/7/11 f.545; DW/PA/5/1629/89]
  Lettice, alias Lettice Holte of Chertsey, widow [PRO; PCC 1640]
  Oliver of Swk St Olave, carpenter [DW/PA/5/1550/8]
  Thomas of Frimley, gent. [HRO; 1619 AD101]
  William of Mitcham, yeoman of the crown [DW/PA/7/3 f.128; 1530]
STANESBY *see* STAINSBY
STANFORD (STANDFORDE)
  Joan of Albury [DW/PA/5/1562/87]
  John of Godstone [PRO; PCC Will 1622]
  Robert of Godstone [PRO; PCC Will 1510]
STANHURST (STANNIERSTE)
  Edward of Swk St Olave, citizen and haberdasher [DW/PA/7/13 f.433; DW/PA/5/1646/54]
  Margery of Bermondsey, widow [*in* DW/PA/5/1574/26]
STANLAKE (STANLACKE,STANLOCK,STANLOCKE,STANLOKE)
  Beatrice of Shalford, widow [DW/PA/5/1550/113]
  George of Guildford St Nicolas - Artington, husbandman [DW/PA/7/13 f.50; DW/PA/5/1639/132]
  John of Compton, husbandman [DW/PA/7/12 f.258; DW/PA/5/1635/100]
  John of Guildford St Nicolas - Artington [DW/PA/7/3 f.144; 1530]
  John of Wonersh [DW/PA/7/6 f.113; DW/PA/5/1559/87]
  Margery of Chertsey, spinster [PRO; PCC Will 1617]
  Robert of Shalford, husbandman [DW/PA/7/7 f.445; DW/PA/5/1603/162] <Abs 843>
  Samuel of Godalming, yeoman [DW/PA/7/11 f.364; DW/PA/5/1626/113]
  William of Chertsey [PRO; PCC Admon 1568]
STANLEY
  Geoffrey of Kingston [PRO; PCC 1641]
  Robert of Swk St Olave; Stepney, Middlesex; Rotherhithe [DW/PA/5/1603/161] <Abs U92>
STANLOCK,STANLOCKE,STANLOKE *see* STANLAKE
STANNIERSTE *see* STANHURST
STANNINOUGH (STANNYNOUGHE)
  Lawrence of Oxted, gent. [PRO; PCC Will 1614]
STANSBY *see* STAINSBY
STANSTED
  John of Woking, yeoman [DW/PA/5/1557/144]
  John of Woking [DW/PA/5/1570/52]
  Margaret of Woking, widow [HRO; 1578 B87]
  Robert of Woking [PRO; PCC Will 1574]
STANTON (STAUNTON,STAWTON)
  Alice, alias Alice Rowle of Kingston, widow [PRO; PCC Will 1607] <Abs, SAC v.12 p.97>

STANTON (STAUNTON,STAWTON) [*continued*]
Constance of ..., widow [DW/PA/7/13 f.104; DW/PA/5/1640/142]
Edward of Bermondsey, victualler [DW/PA/7/13 f.353; 1644]
George of Ripley, innholder [DW/PA/7/8 f.90; DW/PA/5/1609/109]
Henry of Guildford St Mary [DW/PA/7/12 f.9; DW/PA/5/1631/96]
Joan of Weybridge [DW/PA/5/1571/86]
John of Buckland, senior [DW/PA/7/10 f.40; DW/PA/5/1617/117]
John of Ewell [PRO; PCC Admon 1609]
John of Ewell, yeoman [DW/PA/7/13 f.42; DW/PA/5/1639/131]
John, alias John Rowle of Kingston, brewer, senior [PRO; PCC Will 1603] [*and*] [SRO; KB39/1-2; 1603] <Abs. SAC v.11 p.123>
John of Mortlake; Lambeth [PRO; PCC Will 1523]
John of Newdigate, husbandman [DW/PA/5/1562/40]
John of Send [HRO; 1600 AD56]
Matthew of Capel [DW/PA/7/12 f.407; DW/PA/5/1638/126]
Richard of Buckland [DW/PA/7/4 f.116; 1535]
Richard of Byfleet, husbandman [DW/PA/5/1562/70]
Richard of Lingfield, victualler [DW/PA/7/13 f.160; DW/PA/5/1641/127]
Theophilus of Kingston, plumber [DW/PA/7/12 f.455; DW/PA/5/1638/130]
Thomas of Ripley, husbandman, senior [DW/PA/7/11 f.38; DW/PA/5/1623/115]
Thomas of Rotherhithe, mariner [DW/PA/7/12 f.515; DW/PA/5/1639/120]
William of Ripley, yeoman [DW/PA/5/1558/262]*
William of Ripley, yeoman [DW/PA/7/8 f.28A; DW/PA/5/1608/99]
STAPLAST *see* STAPLEHURST
STAPLE *see* STAPLES
STAPLEHURST (STAPELERST,STAPELLARSTE,STAPLAST,STAPYLHERST,STAPYLHYRSTE)
Elizabeth of Dorking, widow [DW/PA/5/1569/28]
Jacob of Ewhurst [DW/PA/5/1562/84]
James of Reigate, bricklayer [DW/PA/7/11 f.112; DW/PA/5/1624/116]
Joan of Horley, widow [DW/PA/5/1568/58]
John of Newdigate [DW/PA/7/9 f.150; DW/PA/5/1615/121]
John of Camberwell, husbandman [DW/PA/7/5 f.221; 1541]
John of Dorking [DW/PA/7/6 f.190; DW/PA/5/1559/199]
John of Horley [DW/PA/5/1558/263]*
John of Horne [DW/PA/7/12 f.19; DW/PA/5/1631/100]
John of Reigate, yeoman [DW/PA/5/1550/36]
Richard of Horley [DW/PA/7/2 f.2; 1490]
Richard of Reigate [DW/PA/7/6 f.225; 1561]
Thomas of Capel [DW/PA/5/1593/26]
STAPLES (STAPILL,STAPLE,STAPLESE)
Amy of Camberwell - Dulwich, widow of John [DW/PA/7/8 f.148; DW/PA/5/1611/103]
Joan of Oxted, widow [DW/PA/7/7 f.570; DW/PA/5/1606/87] <Abs 1065>
John of Beddington [PRO; PCC Will 1525]
John of Camberwell, husbandman [DW/PA/7/8 f.180; DW/PA/5/1610/110]
John of Godstone [DW/PA/7/2 f.26; 1492]
John, alias John Allyn of Leigh, husbandman [DW/PA/5/1592/10]
John of Oxted, miller [DW/PA/7/7 f.460; DW/PA/5/1603/163] <Abs 868>
Mark of Haslemere [DW/PA/7/11 f.602; DW/PA/5/1630/93]
Roger of Swk [DW/PA/7/6 f.172; DW/PA/5/1559/158]
Thomas of Mitcham, yeoman [PRO; PCC Will 1616]
William of Croydon; Chipstead, collier [DW/PA/7/7 f.333; DW/PA/5/1601/74 *and* DW/PA/5/1601/75] <Abs 600>

STAPLETON
John of Mitcham, husbandman [DW/PA/7/9 f.297; 1618]
Richard of Richmond [PRO; PCC 1638]
STAPLEY
Ann of Bermondsey, widow (previously widow of Christopher Sharnborne) [PRO; PCC Will 1617]
Frances, alias Frances Brewton of Lambeth, widow [PRO; PCC Admon 1641]
STAR *see* STARR
STARKEY (STARKIE,STARKY)
John of Putney [PRO; PCC 1634]
John of Bermondsey [DW/PA/7/3 f.97; 1529]
Nicholas of Kingston; Long Ditton [DW/PA/7/3 f.140; 1530]
Robert of Camberwell - Dulwich [DW/PA/7/12 f.230; DW/PA/5/1634/94]
STARR (STAR,STARRE)
Edmund of Cobham, clothworker [DW/PA/7/12 f.495; DW/PA/5/1638/134]
James of Ditton [DW/PA/5/1588/82]
James of Walton on Thames [DW/PA/7/13 f.218; DW/PA/5/1642/78]
John of ...., senior [DW/PA/7/10 f.179; DW/PA/5/1620/121]
John of Long Ditton - Tolworth, husbandman [DW/PA/5/1588/47]
John of Kingston, yeoman of the king's chamber [DW/PA/5/1569/51]
Margaret of Cobham, widow [DW/PA/7/8 f.86; DW/PA/5/1609/110]
Sense of Long Ditton - Tolworth [HRO; 1572 B96]
see also STURR
STARRAM
Daniel of Swk St Olave [DW/PA/7/11 f.430; DW/PA/5/1627/102]
STARRE *see* STARR
STARY
Thomas of Swk St Olave [DW/PA/7/6 f.224; 1561]
STASEY *see* STACY
STAUGHTON *see* STOUGHTON
STAUNTON *see* STANTON
STAYCKFORD *see* STACKFORD
STAYNER *see* STAINER
STAYNING,STAYNINGE,STEANINGE *see* STAINING
STEARE *see* STEER
STEBRANKE
Anthony of Swk St Saviour [DW/PA/7/12 f.116; DW/PA/5/1632/94]
STECELLS
Clara of Swk St Olave, widow [*Dutch*] [DW/PA/5/1593/79]
STEDE *see* STEED
STEDMAN (STIDMAN,STYDMAN)
Emery of Dunsfold, husbandman [DW/PA/5/1587/66]
George of Alfold [DW/PA/7/6 f.260; 1560]
George of Cranleigh, yeoman [DW/PA/7/13 f.44; DW/PA/5/1640/131]
Harry of Wonersh, husbandman [DW/PA/7/7 f.623; DW/PA/5/1607/86] <Abs 1161>
Joan of Wimbledon, widow [LPL; 96/2453; Will 1638]
John of Alfold, husbandman [DW/PA/7/10 f.59; 1618]
John of Bramley, husbandman [HRO; 1591 B73]
John of Godalming - Catteshall, yeoman [DW/PA/7/9 f.281; 1618]
John of Ockley, husbandman [HRO; 1618 AD76]
Richard of Cranleigh [DW/PA/5/1586/2]
Robert of Dunsfold, yeoman [DW/PA/5/1580/70]
Thomas of Cranleigh [DW/PA/5/1579/87]*

STEDMAN (STIDMAN,STYDMAN) [*continued*]
Thomas of Godalming, mercer [DW/PA/7/12 f.257; DW/PA/5/1635/99]
William of Cranleigh [PRO; PCC Admon 1581]
William of Wimbledon, yeoman [LPL; 96/2452; Will 1623]
STEED (STEDE,STEEDE,STEYD)
Elizabeth of Frensham - Pitfold, widow [DW/PA/5/1555/44]
Elizabeth of Haslemere, widow [DW/PA/7/8 f.99; DW/PA/5/1609/111]
John of Haslemere, yeoman, senior [DW/PA/7/12 f.425; DW/PA/5/1637/93]
John of Haslemere, yeoman [DW/PA/7/13 f.112; DW/PA/5/1640/129]
Thomas of Haslemere [DW/PA/7/5 f.31; 1538] <Abs 55>
William of Surrey [PRO; PCC Will 1506]
STEELE (STELE)
Alice of Swk St Olave, widow [DW/PA/5/1621/115] <Abs U251>
Bartholomew of Frensham, husbandman [HRO; 1561 B199-200]
Cornelius of Swk St Olave, cook [DW/PA/7/11 f.283; DW/PA/5/1625/234]
George of Swk St Olave, waterman [DW/PA/7/13 f.414; DW/PA/5/1646/49]
Richard of Burstow, tailor [LPL; 96/2455; Will 1628]
Richard of Frensham [DW/PA/7/7 f.328; DW/PA/5/1601/77] <Abs 588>
Richard of Slaugham, Sussex [DW/PA/7/8 f.281; DW/PA/5/1613/123]
Robert of Frensham, husbandman [HRO; 1603 AD62]
Thomas of Swk St Olave [DW/PA/7/11 f.218; DW/PA/5/1625/235]
STEELING (STELYNGE)
David of Croydon, threadmaker [LPL; 96/2459; Will 1647]
STEER (STEARE,STEERE,STER,STERE,STERRE)
Agnes of Capel, spinster [DW/PA/7/9 f.259; DW/PA/5/1617/118]
Agnes of Capel, widow [DW/PA/7/11 f.444; DW/PA/5/1628/95]
Agnes of Egham, widow [DW/PA/5/1593/195]
Alice of Capel, widow [DW/PA/5/1593/157]
Alice of Ockley, widow [DW/PA/7/4 f.76; 1534]
Alice of Send, widow [DW/PA/5/1546/3]
Edmund of Capel [DW/PA/5/1545/9]
James of Walton on Thames; East Molesey; Cobham, husbandman [DW/PA/7/6 f.199; 1560]
Jane of Ewhurst, widow of Reynold, blacksmith [DW/PA/7/13 f.371; 1644]
Joan of Capel, widow [DW/PA/7/7 f.314; DW/PA/5/1600/50] <Abs 558>
John of Capel [DW/PA/5/1570/92]
John of Capel [DW/PA/7/7 f.279; DW/PA/5/1599/70] <Abs 497>
John of Capel [DW/PA/7/7 f.624; DW/PA/5/1607/87] <Abs 1165>
John of Capel - Mosses, yeoman [DW/PA/7/8 f.327; DW/PA/5/1613/124]
John of Capel, husbandman [DW/PA/7/11 f.190; DW/PA/5/1624/117]
John of Dorking [DW/PA/7/4 f.142; 1536]
John of Dorking, husbandman [*in* DW/PA/5/1558/76]
John of Dorking, miller [DW/PA/7/8 f.165; DW/PA/5/1611/104]
John of Horley [PRO; PCC Admon 1647]
John of Ockley; Horley [BM; Add.Ms 24,925 f.5v; 1544] <Abs 9>
John of Ockley [PRO; PCC Admon 1611]
John of Ockley, husbandman [DW/PA/7/12 f.135; DW/PA/5/1632/101]
John of Woking - Heathside, husbandman [DW/PA/5/1559/86]
Katherine of Lingfield, widow [DW/PA/7/13 f.78; DW/PA/5/1640/137]
Nicholas of Thursley, husbandman [DW/PA/7/9 f.93; DW/PA/5/1616/135]
Nicholas of Stoke next Guildford, baker [DW/PA/7/11 f.173; DW/PA/5/1625/236]
Ralph of Capel, yeoman [DW/PA/7/11 f.491; DW/PA/5/1628/96]
Reynold of Ewhurst, blacksmith [DW/PA/7/12 f.238; DW/PA/5/1634/97]

STEER (STEARE,STEERE,STER,STERE,STERRE) [*continued*]
Robert of Capel, yeoman [DW/PA/7/10 f.205; DW/PA/5/1620/122]
Robert of Capel, husbandman [DW/PA/7/13 f.345; 1644]
Robert of Crowhurst, miller [DW/PA/7/12 f.154; DW/PA/5/1633/111]
Sarah of Ockley, spinster [DW/PA/7/11 f.335; DW/PA/5/1625/237]
Thomas of Capel [HRO; 1562 B126-127]
Thomas of Capel, yeoman [DW/PA/5/1571/76]
Thomas of Capel, husbandman [DW/PA/7/8 f.173; DW/PA/5/1610/116]
Thomas of Capel, husbandman [DW/PA/7/12 f.199; DW/PA/5/1633/115]
Thomas of Long Ditton - Tolworth, husbandman [DW/PA/5/1550/12]
Thomas of Lingfield [DW/PA/7/12 f.399; DW/PA/5/1638/125]
Thomas of Wotton [PRO; PCC 1646]
William of Ashtead, husbandman [DW/PA/7/7 f.447; DW/PA/5/1603/165] <Abs 846>
William of Ashtead [PRO; PCC 1649]
William of Bermondsey [PRO; PCC Admon 1604]
William of Capel [PRO; PCC Will 1561]
William of Capel [DW/PA/5/1581/35]*
William of Capel, husbandman [DW/PA/7/7 f.625; DW/PA/5/1607/88] <Abs 1167>
William of Capel [DW/PA/7/13 f.4; DW/PA/5/1640/128]
William of Dorking - Stubbs; Capel, husbandman, senior [DW/PA/5/1593/25]
William of Dorking [PRO; PCC 1648]
William of Ewhurst [PRO; PCC Admon 1649]
William of Kingston; Mickleham - Burford, milliner [DW/PA/7/7 ff.46,101; DW/PA/5/1595/79 *and* DW/PA/5/1596/56] <Abs 87,184>
William of Ockley, senior [DW/PA/7/4 f.28; 1533]
William of Ockley, yeoman [HRO; 1605 B71]
William of Windlesham [DW/PA/5/1545/5]

STEEVENS *see* STEPHENS

STEGEYN *see* STAGING

STELE *see* STEELE

STELLYMAN *see* STILEMAN

STELWELL *see* STILLWELL

STELYNGE *see* STEELING

STENNING (STEANINGE,STENING,STENYNGE,STEYENINGE,STEYNING,STEYNINGE)
John of Guildford St Nicolas, shearman [DW/PA/7/7 f.128; DW/PA/5/1597/94] <Abs 236>
John of Worplesdon, yeoman, senior [DW/PA/7/11 f.2; DW/PA/5/1622/97]
Richard, alias Richard Cowper of Rudgwick, Sussex; Cranleigh [DW/PA/7/9 f.99; DW/PA/5/1614/18]
Richard of Ewhurst [PRO; PCC Will 1588]
Richard, alias Richard Cooper of Haslemere; Lurgashall, Sussex, yeoman [DW/PA/7/8 f.71; DW/PA/5/1609/34]
William of Alfold, yeoman [DW/PA/7/13 f.206; DW/PA/5/1642/74]
William of Worplesdon, yeoman [DW/PA/7/7 f.57; DW/PA/5/1596/57] <Abs 108>

STENT *see* STINT

STEPHENS (STEAVEN,STEEVENS,STEPHANE,STEPHEN,STEPHYN,STEVEN,STEVENS,STEVYN, STEVYNS,STYVEN)
Agnes of Coulsdon, widow [PRO; PCC Will 1620] <Soame 763>
Alice of Ewell, widow [PRO; PCC Admon 1646]
Alice of Fetcham - Cannoncourt; Leatherhead; Cobham, widow [DW/PA/5/1604/56] <Abs U117>

STEPHENS (STEAVEN, STEEVENS, STEPHANE, STEPHEN, STEPHYN, STEVEN, STEVENS, STEVYN, STEVYNS, STYVEN) [*continued*]

Bartholomew of Guildford Holy Trinity, carpenter [DW/PA/7/11 f.65; DW/PA/5/1623/116 *and* DW/PA/5/1624/111]

Christopher of Fetcham; Leatherhead [DW/PA/7/5 f.65; 1539] <Abs 42>

Christopher of Leatherhead, yeoman [DW/PA/7/7 f.127; DW/PA/5/1597/95] <Abs 233>

Edmund of Great Bookham, yeoman [DW/PA/5/1586/41]*

Edward of Croydon [LPL; 98/1 f.97v; Will 1638]

Edward of Epsom, yeoman [DW/PA/7/3 f.125; 1530]

Edward of Leatherhead [DW/PA/5/1569/57]

Frances of Chessington, widow [DW/PA/7/7 f.19; DW/PA/5/1595/80] <Abs 41>

George of Ashtead [DW/PA/7/2 f.107; 1516]

George of Wonersh, husbandman [DW/PA/7/11 f.23; DW/PA/5/1623/117]

Henry of Ash, yeoman [DW/PA/7/7 f.391; DW/PA/5/1603/166] <Abs 726>

Isabel of Chobham [PRO; PCC Will 1490]

Jane of Shere - Gomshall [DW/PA/7/11 f.550; DW/PA/5/1629/91]

Joan of Guildford Holy Trinity, widow [DW/PA/7/12 f.73; DW/PA/5/1632/86]

Joan of Warlingham, widow of William [DW/PA/7/1 f.20; 1485] <Abs 66>

John of Great Bookham, yeoman [DW/PA/5/1592/122]

John of Bramley [DW/PA/7/7 f.370; DW/PA/5/1602/81] <Abs 680>

John of Long Ditton - Tolworth [PRO; PCC Will 1602] <Abs, SAC v.10 p.311>

John of Fetcham - Cannoncourt, yeoman [HRO; 1596 B65]

John of Fetcham - Cannoncourt [DW/PA/7/8 ff.103,108 *and* DW/PA/7/9 f.182; DW/PA/5/1610/117 *and* DW/PA/5/1616/112]

John of Godalming [DW/PA/5/1568/46]

John of Limpsfield [PRO; PCC Admon 1635]

John of Rotherhithe (died in Ireland) [PRO; PCC Admon 1646]

John of Shere, yeoman [DW/PA/7/13 f.481; DW/PA/5/1648/37]

John of Swk St Saviour, cooper [DW/PA/7/12 f.516; DW/PA/5/1639/121]

John of Stoke next Guildford, shearman [DW/PA/5/1571/46]

Lucy of Swk, widow [DW/PA/5/1571/37]

Mary of Abinger, widow [HRO; 1629 AD67]

Nicholas of Ash, yeoman [DW/PA/7/11 f.134; DW/PA/5/1624/119]

Nicholas of Ash [PRO; PCC 1646]

Phillip of Fetcham [DW/PA/7/2 f.204; 1524]

Ralph of Great Bookham, yeoman [DW/PA/5/1588/88]

Richard of Ashtead, husbandman [DW/PA/5/1547/10]

Richard of Blechingley [HRO; Reg. D p.47; 1527]

Richard of Coulsdon [DW/PA/7/7 f.630; DW/PA/5/1608/100] <Abs 1178>

Richard of Fetcham [DW/PA/7/12 f.205; DW/PA/5/1634/86]

Richard of West Horsley, husbandman [DW/PA/7/12 f.298; DW/PA/5/1635/108]

Richard of Send [DW/PA/7/12 f.11; DW/PA/5/1631/97]

Richard of Swk St George [DW/PA/7/12 f.208; DW/PA/5/1634/89]

Robert of Bookham [DW/PA/7/6 f.288; 1560]

Robert of Rotherhithe; Bermondsey, mariner [DW/PA/7/10 f.74; 1618]

Robert of Send [DW/PA/7/12 f.306; DW/PA/5/1635/111]

Thomas of Abinger, husbandman [HRO; 1617 B60]

Thomas of Ash [PRO; PCC 1641]

Thomas of Bermondsey, mariner [PRO; PCC Will 1604] <Abs, SAC v.11 p.295>

Thomas of Camberwell [PRO; PCC Admon 1649]

Thomas of Fetcham [DW/PA/7/11 f.106; DW/PA/5/1624/120]

Thomas of Leatherhead, husbandman [DW/PA/5/1592/33]

STEPHENS (STEAVEN, STEEVENS, STEPHANE, STEPHEN, STEPHYN, STEVEN, STEVENS, STEVYN, STEVYNS, STYVEN) [*continued*]
Thomas of Morden, husbandman [DW/PA/7/7 f,378; DW/PA/5/1602/82] <Abs 701>
Thomas of St Martha's - Tyting [DW/PA/5/1550/60]
Thomas of Send, yeoman [DW/PA/7/7 f,274; DW/PA/5/1599/71] <Abs 485>
Thomas of Send, yeoman [DW/PA/7/11 f,513; DW/PA/5/1629/92]
Thomas of Shere, yeoman [HRO; 1609 AD77]
Thomas of Swk St Saviour, yeoman [DW/PA/7/10 f,80; DW/PA/5/1619/109]
Walter of Leatherhead, labourer, senior [HRO; 1592 B54]
William of Bermondsey, weaver [PRO; PCC Will 1626]
William of Chessington, tailor [DW/PA/5/1591/115]
William of Kingston [PRO; PCC Will 1569]
William of Leatherhead [DW/PA/7/2 f,187; 1523]
William of Ockham, yeoman [DW/PA/7/10 f,130; DW/PA/5/1620/123]
William of Rotherhithe, citizen and weaver [PRO; PCC 1635]
William of Send [DW/PA/7/3 f,161; 1530]
William of Stoke Dabernon, husbandman [DW/PA/7/13 f,140; DW/PA/5/1639/134]
William of Warlingham [DW/PA/7/1 f,20; 1485] <Abs 65>
William of Wonersh, husbandman [DW/PA/7/7 f,78; 1596] <Abs 142>

STEPHENSON (STEVENSON, STEVINSON, STEVYNSON)
Andrew of Swk St Olave [DW/PA/7/13 f,216; DW/PA/5/1642/76]
George of Thorpe [DW/PA/7/4 f,195; 1537]
John of Epsom [DW/PA/7/1 f,31; 1486] <Abs 103>
Matthew of Camberwell, husbandman [DW/PA/7/4 f,192; 1536]
Nicholas, alias Nicholas Stimpson of Chertsey - 'Wheelers Green', carpenter [HRO; 1608 B70]
Richard of Chertsey, carpenter [DW/PA/7/13 f,85; DW/PA/5/1640/138]
Robert of Swk St Olave, victualler [DW/PA/7/11 f,558; DW/PA/5/1630/94]
Thomas of Bermondsey, cobbler [DW/PA/5/1581/61]
William of Egham [PRO; PCC Admon 1609]
William of Newington [LPL; 98/1 f,31v; Will 1631]

STEPHYN *see* STEPHENS
STER, STERE *see* STEER
STERKEY *see* STARKEY
STERRE *see* STEER
STERT *see* STURT

STERRY
Anthony of Swk St Olave, cooper [DW/PA/7/12 f,93; DW/PA/5/1633/108]

STERTEVANT
Sybil of Wandsworth, widow of Anthony, citizen and clothworker [PRO; PCC 1635]

STEVENS *see* STEPHENS
STEVENSON *see* STEPHENSON
STEVYNS *see* STEPHENS
STEVYNSON *see* STEPHENSON

STEWARD (STEWARDE, STUARD, STUART, STUWERDE, STYWARD)
Alice of Sutton, widow [DW/PA/7/1 f,68; 1484] <Abs 223>
Alice of Sutton, widow [DW/PA/7/1 f,32; 1486] <Abs 109>
Henry of Banstead [DW/PA/7/7 f,311; DW/PA/5/1600/51] <Abs 553>
James of Swk St Olave, sailor and mariner [DW/PA/5/1579/84]*
John of Banstead; Walton on the Hill; Sutton, husbandman [DW/PA/5/1550/50]
John of Mitcham [DW/PA/5/1558/266]

STEWARD (STEWARDE,STUARD,STUART,STUWERDE,STYWARD) [*continued*]
John of Mitcham [HRO; Reg, CCB 20 p,15; 1563]
John of Newington, citizen of London [PRO; PCC Will 1607]
John of Walton on the Hill, yeoman [DW/PA/5/1592/106]
Lewis of Mortlake [PRO; PCC Will 1593]
Richard of Mitcham [DW/PA/7/5 f,113; 1539]
Robert of Rayleigh, Essex, citizen and girdler [DW/PA/5/1578/9]
Robert of Swk St George, collier [DW/PA/7/7 f,405; DW/PA/5/1603/167] <Abs 751>
William of Bermondsey [PRO; PCC Will 1458]
William of Morden [DW/PA/7/4 f,173; 1536]
STEYD *see* STEED
STEYNING,STEYNINGE,STEYNYNGE *see* STENNING
STICHBURN
Stephen of Walton on Thames, bargeman [HRO; Reg, Fox 3 p,59; 1511]
STIDALL
Thomas, alias Thomas Stynte of Stoke Dabernon, yeoman [DW/PA/5/1571/65] [*and* [PRO; PCC Admon 1572]
STIDDOLPH (STIDDOLFE,STIDDOLPHE,STYDOLFE,STYDOLFF,STYDOLPHE)
Agnes of Chertsey - Ham Court, widow [DW/PA/5/1546/45]
Elizabeth of Mickleham, widow [DW/PA/7/8 f,47; DW/PA/5/1609/114]
George of Chertsey [PRO; PCC Will *and* Admon 1591]
John of Mickleham, esq, [DW/PA/5/1576/75]
Ralph of Limpsfield [PRO; PCC 1636]
Thomas of Mickleham [PRO; C142 72/89; 1545]
Thomas of Mickleham, bachelor [PRO; PCC Admon 1611]
William of Surrey, esq, [PRO; PCC Will 1601]
STIDMAN *see* STEDMAN
STIDWELL
William of Cobham,victualler [DW/PA/7/7 f,369; DW/PA/5/1602/83] <Abs 676>
STIFF (STIFFE)
John of Richmond [PRO; PCC Admon 1642]
STILE *see* STILES
STILEMAN (STELLYMAN,STILLEMAN,STYLEMAN,STYLMANE)
George of Surrey [PRO; PCC Will 1602]
George of Horsell, yeoman [DW/PA/7/13 f,184; DW/PA/5/1641/131A]
Giles of Swk St George, gardener [DW/PA/7/7 f,616; DW/PA/5/1607/89] <Abs 1152>
John of Horsell, yeoman [DW/PA/7/9 f,142; DW/PA/5/1615/124]
Richard of Horsell, yeoman [DW/PA/7/7 f,37; DW/PA/5/1595/81] <Abs 74>
Richard of Horsell, bachelor [DW/PA/7/8 f,122; DW/PA/5/1610/118]
Walter of Ash, husbandman [DW/PA/7/7 f,145; DW/PA/5/1597/96] <Abs 265>
Walter of Horsell, husbandman [DW/PA/5/1604/57] <Abs U118>
STILES (STILE,STYELL,STYLE,STYLES,STYLL)
(Dame) Elizabeth of Surrey, formerly Elizabeth Yarford [PRO; PCC Will 1548]
Francis of Ashtead, yeoman [DW/PA/7/11 f,583; DW/PA/5/1630/95]
Henry of Send, shearman [DW/PA/7/8 f,230; DW/PA/5/1612/151]
Joan of Swk St Saviour - liberty of the Clink, widow [DW/PA/7/8 f,346; DW/PA/5/1612/148]
John of Ashtead, yeoman [DW/PA/7/12 f,53; DW/PA/5/1631/106]
John of Betchworth [DW/PA/5/1576/76]
John of Kingston [DW/PA/5/1605/77] <Abs U166>
Margaret of Merton, spinster [DW/PA/7/13 f,486; DW/PA/5/1648/43]

STILES (STILE,STYELL,STYLE,STYLES,STYLL) [*continued*]
Richard of Frensham [DW/PA/7/4 f.84; 1534]
Thomas of Great Bookham [DW/PA/7/2 f.112; 1517]
Urian of Guildford Holy Trinity [DW/PA/7/5 f.17; 1538] <Abs 50>
Urian of Send, husbandman [DW/PA/5/1605/74] <Abs U163>
William of Swk [DW/PA/5/1581/53]
William of Chertsey, husbandman [DW/PA/7/12 f.447; DW/PA/5/1639/118]
William of Kingston, gent. [PRO; PCC Will 1601] <Abs. SAC v.10 p.149>
William of Swk St Olave [DW/PA/7/4 f.233; 1537]
STILLWELL (STELWELL,STILEWELL,STILWELL,STYLLWELL,STYLWELL)
Alice of Albury, widow [HRO; 1621 B51]
Edward of Dorking - Redlands, yeoman [DW/PA/7/12 f.123; DW/PA/5/1632/97]
Geoffrey of Dorking [DW/PA/5/1558/267]*
Geoffrey of Dorking - Westcott, yeoman [DW/PA/7/8 f.13;DW/PA/5/1608/101]
George of Elstead, yeoman [HRO; 1612 B91]
Henry of Charlwood [LPL; 98/1 ff.101r,107v; Will 1639]
Jane of Puttenham, widow [DW/PA/7/8 f.173; DW/PA/5/1610/119]
John of Betchworth, yeoman, senior [DW/PA/7/10 f.177; DW/PA/5/1620/124]
John of Dorking, senior [DW/PA/5/1558/268]*
John of Dorking - Westcott, yeoman [DW/PA/7/8 f.93; DW/PA/5/1609/112]
John of Dorking, husbandman, junior [DW/PA/7/13 f.26; DW/PA/5/1639/127]
John of Thursley, yeoman [PRO; PCC Will 1612]
John of Woking [DW/PA/5/1558/269]*
Miles of Dorking, husbandman [DW/PA/5/1576/127]
Richard of Godalming - Eashing, husbandman [HRO; 1597 B69]
Robert of Witley - Birtley, husbandman [DW/PA/7/10 f.14; DW/PA/5/1616/137]
Thomas of Witley, yeoman [HRO; 1598 B44]
Thomas of Witley - Birtley, yeoman, senior [HRO; 1624 B64]
STIMP (STYMPE)
Thomas of Thursley, husbandman [DW/PA/7/7 f.551; DW/PA/5/1606/91] <Abs 1033>
STIMPSON
Nicholas, alias Nicholas Stevinson of Chertsey - 'Wheelers Green', carpenter [HRO; 1608 B70]
Robert of Battersea [DW/PA/7/9 f.335; DW/PA/5/1620/125]
Ursula of Battersea, widow [DW/PA/7/10 f.126; DW/PA/5/1620/127]
STINT (STENT,STINTE,STYNT,STYNTE)
Abel of West Horsley [DW/PA/7/11 f.111; DW/PA/5/1624/118]
Abel of West Horsley, yeoman [HRO; 1639 B65]
Agnes of Thursley - Emley [DW/PA/5/1576/26]
Alexander of Shalford; Hascombe, weaver [DW/PA/7/6 f.243; 1560]
Alice of West Horsley, widow [DW/PA/7/12 f.220; DW/PA/5/1634/90]
Arnold of East Clandon [DW/PA/5/1576/123]
Edward of West Horsley, husbandman [DW/PA/5/1592/64]
Edward of Shere [DW/PA/7/7 f.260; DW/PA/5/1599/72] <Abs 460>
Elizabeth of West Horsley, widow [HRO; 1595 B57]
Humphrey of West Horsley [DW/PA/7/1 f.14; 1485] <Abs 44>
Humphrey of Kingston - Hook [DW/PA/7/8 f.150; DW/PA/5/1611/105]
Joan of East Clandon, widow [HRO; 1602 B47]
Joan of Ockham, widow [DW/PA/5/1555/7]
John of Farnham - Badshot, husbandman [DW/PA/7/11 f.316; DW/PA/5/1626/115]

STINT (STENT,STINTE,STYNT,STYNTE) [*continued*]

John of Guildford St Nicolas - Guildford Park, gent., senior [DW/PA/7/12 f.263; DW/PA/5/1634/101]

John of West Horsley, husbandman [DW/PA/7/6 f.214B; 1561]

John of Send; West Horsley; East Clandon; East Horsley; St Augustine, London; Ockham, haberdasher [DW/PA/7/7 f.194; DW/PA/5/1598/79] <Abs 353>

John of Thursley - Emley [DW/PA/5/1576/78]

John of Witley - Milford [HRO; 1576 B84]

Margaret of Godalming; Woking; Wonersh, widow [DW/PA/7/5 f.31; 1538] <Abs 46>

Richard of Thursley [DW/PA/7/3 f.100; 1529]

Robert of Frensham, husbandman [DW/PA/7/13 f.119; DW/PA/5/1640/145]

Robert of West Horsley [DW/PA/7/5 f.186; 1540]

Robert of West Horsley, tailor [DW/PA/7/9 f.272; 1618]

Robert of Ockham - Ockham Court, yeoman [DW/PA/5/1558/270]*

Rowland of West Horsley [DW/PA/7/11 f.320; DW/PA/5/1626/114]

Thomas of Cobham - Down Place; Wotton, yeoman [DW/PA/7/7 f.385; DW/PA/5/1602/84] <Abs 713>

Thomas of Elstead; Chertsey, husbandman [DW/PA/5/1605/75] <Abs U164>

Thomas of Kingston, gent. [DW/PA/7/13 f.309; DW/PA/5/1643/83]

Thomas of Kingston - Hook [DW/PA/7/13 f.314; DW/PA/5/1643/84]

Thomas of Send, husbandman [DW/PA/7/11 f.569; DW/PA/5/1630/96]

Thomas, alias Thomas Stidall of Stoke Dabernon, yeoman [DW/PA/5/1571/65]

Thomas, alias Thomas Arnold, alias Thomas Stidall of Stoke Dabernon [PRO; PCC Admon 1572]

Thomas of Witley, yeoman [DW/PA/5/1581/37]

William of Bramley, tailor [DW/PA/7/7 f.627; DW/PA/5/1608/102] <Abs 1173>

William of Elstead [BM; Add.Ms 24,925 f.17v; 1543] <Abs 39>

William of West Horsley, major [HRO; 1582 B81]

William of Ockham, yeoman [DW/PA/7/5 f.131; 1539]

William of Send [DW/PA/5/1550/108]

STIRTE *see* STURT

STOAT (STOYTE)

John of Newington [PRO; PCC Admon 1624]

STOCK (STOCKE,STOK)

Henry of Farnham [DW/PA/5/1575/13]

John of Swk St George [DW/PA/7/11 f.213; DW/PA/5/1625/238]

John of Swk St Olave, haberdasher [DW/PA/7/10 f.285; DW/PA/5/1623/118]

Maud of Croydon, formerly Maud Somer [PRO; PCC Will 1457]

STOCKHAM

John of Egham [PRO; PCC 1647]

STOCKTON (STOCKETON)

Richard of Swk St Saviour [DW/PA/5/1570/10]

Robert of Richmond [DW/PA/5/1571/83]

STOCKWOOD

Edward of Putney, servant to Mr Crane,esq. [PRO; PCC Will *and* Admon 1582]

STODDARD (STODERD)

George of Surrey, citizen and grocer [PRO; PCC Will 1580]

Margaret of Swk St Olave, widow [DW/PA/7/4 f.93; 1534]

Watson of Horley [PRO; PCC Will 1552]

STOFFOLD,STOFFOLDE,STOFOLD *see* STOVOLD

STOGDON
Richard of Rotherhithe [PRO; PCC Admon 1641]
STOKEBYSSHOP (de STOKEBYSSHOP)
Nicholas of Egham, vicar [HRO; Reg, Edn 2 p,19; 1348]
STOKES (STOAKES,STOK,STOKYS,STOOKES,STOYKES)
Alice of Send [CCAL; 1501 f,22r]
Ann of Chertsey [PRO; PCC Will 1593]
Henry of Sheen, citizen and tailor [GL; Commissary Court of London Will 1490]
Henry of Windlesham, yeoman [DW/PA/5/1575/15]
Henry of Windlesham [PRO; PCC Will 1579]
Hugh of Kingston - Hook [DW/PA/7/13 f,205; DW/PA/5/1642/73]
James of Swk St Saviour [DW/PA/7/11 f,462; DW/PA/5/1628/97]
Joan of Rotherhithe, widow [PRO; PCC 1647]
Joan of Windlesham, widow [DW/PA/5/1581/59]
John of Surrey [PRO; PCC Will 1595]
John of Clapham, yeoman [DW/PA/5/1575/81]
John of Rotherhithe [PRO; PCC Admon 1591]
John of Rotherhithe [PRO; PCC Admon 1647 (two)]
John of Swk; Banbury, Oxfordshire, esq, [LPL; Reg, Abp Chichele i f,380; Will 1424]
Maud of Croydon, formerly Maud Somer [PRO; PCC Will 1457]
Richard of Chobham, tailor [DW/PA/5/1557/94]
Simon of Lambeth [PRO; PCC Admon 1603]
Thomas of Lambeth, esq, [PRO; PCC Admon 1639]
Thomas of Titsey, yeoman of the guard [DW/PA/7/2 f,151; 1521]
STOKFORD *see* STACKFORD
STON *see* STONE
STONAR *see* STONER
STONDON *see* STANDON
STONE (STON)
Alice of Swk St Saviour, widow [DW/PA/5/1582/19]
Ann of Swk St Olave, widow [DW/PA/7/11 f,17; DW/PA/5/1623/119]
Edward of Effingham, husbandman [DW/PA/5/1605/78] <Abs U167>
George of Abinger, husbandman [DW/PA/7/13 f,360; 1644]
Harry of Betchworth, labourer [DW/PA/5/1557/104]
Harry of Betchworth, yeoman [DW/PA/7/6 f,232; 1561]
Henry of Capel, yeoman, senior [DW/PA/7/13 f,491; DW/PA/5/1648/44]
Henry of Chertsey, citizen and stockfishmonger [GL; Commissary Court of London Will 1473]
Henry of Wotton [HRO; 1529 U37]
Joan of Cranleigh, spinster [DW/PA/7/7 f,177; DW/PA/5/1597/97] <Abs 326>
John of ... [DW/PA/7/12 f,461; 1638]
John of Surrey [PRO; PCC Will 1643]
John of Albury [HRO; 1591 B74]
John of Dorking, husbandman [DW/PA/7/10 f,90; DW/PA/5/1615/125]
John of Ockley, yeoman [DW/PA/7/11 f,128; DW/PA/5/1624/121]
John of Swk - Bankside [DW/PA/7/11 f,570; DW/PA/5/1629/93]
John of Wotton - Goster Wood [PRO; PCC 1635]
Jonathan of Bermondsey [DW/PA/7/11 f,556; DW/PA/5/1630/97]
Katherine of Ockley, widow [PRO; PCC Will 1629]
Michael of Limpsfield [PRO; PCC 1641]
Phillip of Swk St Thomas [DW/PA/5/1588/3]
Ralph of Ockley, yeoman [DW/PA/7/7 f,364; DW/PA/5/1602/85] <Abs 667>

STONE (STON) [*continued*]
Richard of Albury, yeoman [DW/PA/7/12 f.388; DW/PA/5/1637/86]
Richard, alias Richard Astone of Shere - Dilton, yeoman [DW/PA/5/1576/106]
Richard of Chertsey [PRO; PCC Will 1504]
Robert of Horley, yeoman [DW/PA/7/13 f.73; DW/PA/5/1640/134]
Robert of Wandsworth, gent. [DW/PA/7/12 f.208; DW/PA/5/1634/88]
Thomas of Bermondsey, weaver [DW/PA/7/11 f.293; DW/PA/5/1626/116]
Thomas of Farnham [DW/PA/7/5 f.132; 1539]
Thomas of Swk St Saviour - Bankside, gardener [DW/PA/5/1578/65]
William of Cranleigh, husbandman [DW/PA/7/8 f.154; DW/PA/5/1611/106]
William of Godalming, smith [BM; Add.Ms 24,925 f.23r; 1544] <Abs 56>
William of Swk St Olave; St Martin in the Fields, Middlesex, blacksmith [DW/PA/7/9 f.239; DW/PA/5/1617/119]
see also ASTON
STONEHAM (STONHAM)
Richard of Ash; Sheet near Petersfield, Hampshire, yeoman [DW/PA/5/1605/76] <Abs U165>
Richard of Ash, yeoman [DW/PA/7/10 f.140; DW/PA/5/1620/117]
STONEHILL (STONHILL)
John of Frimley, yeoman [DW/PA/7/10 f.145; DW/PA/5/1620/126]
John of Shere, senior [PRO; PCC 1646]
John of Shere [PRO; PCC 1647]
Joseph of Frimley, yeoman [DW/PA/7/13 f.482; DW/PA/5/1648/39]
STONEMAN
James of Newington [PRO; PCC Will 1618]
STONER (STONAR)
Agnes of Ash [HRO; 1601 AD39]
Alice of Carshalton [PRO; PCC Admon 1624]
Alice of Farnham - Badshot, widow [DW/PA/7/13 f.316; DW/PA/5/1643/85]
Edith of Peper Harow - Royal, widow [DW/PA/7/8 f.164; DW/PA/5/1611/107]
Elizabeth of Swk St Saviour [DW/PA/7/11 f.558; DW/PA/5/1630/98]
James of Godalming - Hurtmore, husbandman [DW/PA/7/7 f.96; 1596] <Abs 177>
John of Farnham - Badshot, yeoman, senior [DW/PA/7/13 f.99; DW/PA/5/1640/141]
Richard of Farnham - Badshot, husbandman [DW/PA/5/1562/29]
Richard of Farnham - Badshot, husbandman [HRO; Reg. CCB 20 p.11; 1563] [*and*] [DW/PA/5/1563/73 *and, in* DW/PA/5/1563/65]
Robert of Dunsfold, husbandman [DW/PA/7/13 f.218; DW/PA/5/1642/77]
Robert of Farnham, husbandman [DW/PA/5/1557/37]
Robert of Peper Harow, husbandman [HRO; 1591 B75]
Thomas of Swk St Saviour, cordwainer [DW/PA/7/11 f.168; DW/PA/5/1625/239]
Thomas of Thursley, husbandman [PRO; PCC Will 1617]
William of Chiddingfold, husbandman [HRO; 1612 AD90]
William of Godalming - Hurtmore [DW/PA/7/12 f.356; DW/PA/5/1638/120]
STONHAM *see* STONEHAM
STONYWELL
Edward of Egham, widower [PRO; PCC Admon 1648]
STOOKES *see* STOKES
STOREY (STORY,STORYE)
Robert of ... [DW/PA/5/1563/44]
William of Camberwell, labourer [DW/PA/7/7 f.166; DW/PA/5/1597/98] <Abs 306>

STORIER

John of Charlwood, husbandman [LPL; 96/2479; Will 1626]

STORY,STORYE *see* STOREY

STOUGHTON (STAUGHTON)

Anthony of Worplesdon - Wood Street, gent. [DW/PA/5/1576/143]

(Sir) George of Stoke next Guildford - Stoughton, knight [PRO; PCC Will 1624]

Gilbert of Stoke next Guildford - Stoughton [PRO; PCC Will 1516] <Abs. SAC v.51 p.96>

Henry of Stoke next Guildford; Shalford, yeoman, senior [DW/PA/7/7 f.617; DW/PA/5/1607/91] <Abs 1155>

Henry of Woking [DW/PA/7/9 f.150; DW/PA/5/1615/126]

John of Guildford, cooper [DW/PA/5/1576/4]

John of Guildford Holy Trinity, gent. [DW/PA/7/3 f.143; 1530]

John of Guildford Holy Trinity, yeoman [DW/PA/7/13 f.387; DW/PA/5/1645/49]

John of Kingston, butcher, senior [DW/PA/7/11 f.434; DW/PA/5/1627/104]

John of Kingston [PRO; PCC Admon 1638]

Lawrence of Stoke next Guildford - Stoughton, esq. [PRO; PCC Will 1572]

(Sir) Lawrence of Stoke next Guildford; Guildford Holy Trinity, knight [DW/PA/7/9 f.1; DW/PA/5/1615/127]

Lawrence of Witley, clerk [DW/PA/7/10 f.194; DW/PA/5/1621/116]

Mary of Stoke next Guildford, widow [DW/PA/7/13 f.88; DW/PA/5/1641/123]

Richard of Send; Stoke next Guildford; Guildford St Nicolas; Guildford St Mary, yeoman [DW/PA/7/9 f.311; DW/PA/5/1619/110]

Thomas of Stoke next Guildford [DW/PA/7/2 f.96; 1514]

Thomas of Stoke next Guildford, husbandman [DW/PA/7/6 f.243; 1560]

Thomas of Stoke, esq. [PRO; PCC Admon 1576]

Thomas of Stoke next Guildford - Stoughton, gent. [DW/PA/7/8 f.147; DW/PA/5/1611/108]

Thomas of Stoke next Guildford [DW/PA/7/8 f.222; DW/PA/5/1612/149]

William of Stoke next Guildford, clerk and parson [DW/PA/7/7 f.235; DW/PA/5/1598/80] <Abs 414>

William of Stoke next Guildford - Watford, gent. [PRO; PCC Will 1612]

STOVOLD (STOFFOLD,STOFFOLDE,STOFOLD,STOVALL,STOVILL,STOVOLDE,STOVOLL)

Edward of Compton, husbandman [DW/PA/7/8 f.23; DW/PA/5/1608/103]

George of Cranleigh; Albury, husbandman, senior [DW/PA/7/8 f.135; DW/PA/5/1610/120]

Henry of Farnham - Tilford; Cranleigh; Hascombe; Dunsfold [DW/PA/7/8 f.94; DW/PA/5/1609/113]

Joan of Hascombe, widow [DW/PA/5/1550/96]

John of Alfold [*in* DW/PA/5/1558/76]

John of Cranleigh, husbandman [DW/PA/7/12 f.241; DW/PA/5/1634/99]

John of Elstead [DW/PA/7/13 f.157; DW/PA/5/1641/126]

Mary of Farnham - Tilford, widow [DW/PA/7/12 f.381; DW/PA/5/1637/84]

Richard of Farnham - Tilford, yeoman [DW/PA/7/13 f.306; 1644]

Thomas of Cranleigh; Hascombe [DW/PA/7/6 f.109; DW/PA/5/1559/88]

Thomas of Cranleigh; Hascombe [DW/PA/7/6 f.292; 1561]

Thomas of Worplesdon, yeoman [DW/PA/5/1557/127]

Thomas of Worplesdon, husbandman [DW/PA/7/7 f.276; DW/PA/5/1599/74] <Abs 490>

STOWE

Thomas of Albury [DW/PA/5/1561/41]

STOWTH
John, alias John Toothe of Swk St George, haberdasher [DW/PA/5/1576/73]
STOYKES *see* STOKES
STOYTE *see* STOAT
STRADDER
Reynold of Morden [DW/PA/5/1550/31]
STRAFTON *see* SCRAFTON
STRALFORD
Simon *or* Simon Stratford of Swk St Saviour [DW/PA/7/11 f.549; DW/PA/5/1629/94]
STRAND
John of Bermondsey [DW/PA/7/5 f.201; 1540]
STRANGE
John of Swk [HRO; Reg. Wyk 2 p.12; 1368]
STRANGRIDGE (STRANGUISH,STRANGWISSH)
... of Esher [*a man*] [DW/PA/5/1562/16]
Bartholomew of Shadwell, Middlesex, mariner [DW/PA/7/13 f.348; 1644]
Robert of Esher [DW/PA/7/11 f.320; DW/PA/5/1626/117]
STRATFIELD (STRATFEILD)
John of Camberwell [DW/PA/7/13 f.219; DW/PA/5/1643/81]
STRATFORD
Simon *or* Simon Stralford of Swk St Saviour [DW/PA/7/11 f.549; DW/PA/5/1629/94]
STRAUXHILL
William of St Paul's, London; St Benet Paul's Wharf, London; All Hallows Thames Street, London; St Bride, London; Camberwell - Peckham, citizen and skinner [LPL; Reg. Abp Stafford f.182; Will 1449]
STRAWE
Robert of Swk St Saviour [DW/PA/5/1587/92]
Thomas of ... [DW/PA/7/7 f.522; DW/PA/5/1606/88] <Abs 982>
STREET (ASTREET,STREATE,STREETE,STRET,STRETE,STRETT)
Agnes of Wonersh, widow [HRO; 1591 B76]
Alice of Kingston [PRO; PCC Will 1579]
Alice of Swk St Olave, widow [DW/PA/7/10 f.196; 1622]
Elizabeth of Shalford, widow [DW/PA/7/3 f.125; 1530]
Elizabeth of Shalford, widow [DW/PA/7/13 f.147; DW/PA/5/1641/124]
Henry of Shalford [DW/PA/7/12 f.423; DW/PA/5/1637/92]
Humphrey of Lambeth [PRO; PCC Will 1558]
Joan of Wonersh, spinster [DW/PA/7/10 f.185; DW/PA/5/1620/128]
John of Guildford St Nicolas, clothworker [DW/PA/7/10 f.27; DW/PA/5/1616/138]
John of Guildford St Nicolas; Godalming, clothworker [HRO; 1618 B55]
John of Lingfield [DW/PA/5/1592/43]
John of Shalford, husbandman [DW/PA/5/1576/57]
John of Swk St Olave [DW/PA/7/3 f.201; 1532]
John of Windlesham [DW/PA/7/4 f.189; 1536]
John of Woking - Sutton [DW/PA/7/12 f.341; DW/PA/5/1636/91]
John of Woking [DW/PA/7/13 f.76; DW/PA/5/1640/136]
John of Wonersh [*in* DW/PA/5/1559/174]
John, alias John Astreete of Wonersh [DW/PA/7/7 f.328; DW/PA/5/1601/76] <Abs 587>
Lawrence of Wonersh, yeoman [DW/PA/7/10 f.30; DW/PA/5/1616/139]
Paul of Wonersh, mercer [DW/PA/7/11 f.169; DW/PA/5/1625/240]

STREET (ASTREET,STREATE,STREETE,STRET,STRETE,STRETT) [*continued*]
Phillip of Surrey [PRO; PCC Will 1644]
Richard of Guildford [PRO; PCC Admon 1597]
Roger of Kingston [PRO; PCC Will 1573]
Thomas of Albury, tailor [HRO; 1617 B61]
Thomas of Guildford, clothier [DW/PA/7/10 f,24; DW/PA/5/1615/128]
Thomas of Shalford, yeoman [DW/PA/7/10 f,257; DW/PA/5/1622/98]
Thomas of Stoke next Guildford, shearman [DW/PA/7/7 f,473; DW/PA/5/1604/59] <Abs 893>
Thomas of Walton on Thames - Oatlands, esq. [PRO; PCC Will 1561] <Abs SAC v,33 pp,32-33>
Thomas of Wonersh [DW/PA/7/1 f,85; 1488] <Abs 287>
Thomas of Wonersh [DW/PA/7/4 f,35; 1533; GMR; *in* RB1 335]
Thomas of Wonersh [HRO; 1619 AD104]
Walter of Horley, timber hewer [DW/PA/7/9 f,124; DW/PA/5/1615/129]
William of Lambeth - Water Lambeth [DW/PA/7/4 f,58; 1533]
William of Nutfield [PRO; PCC Will 1384]
William of Windlesham - Bagshot, husbandman [DW/PA/7/7 f,113; 1597] <Abs 209>
STRETTON (STRUTEN)
Margaret of Rotherhithe [DW/PA/7/12 f,90; DW/PA/5/1632/89]
Richard of Swk St Olave, joiner [DW/PA/7/7 f,571; DW/PA/5/1606/89] <Abs 1067>
Thomas of Rotherhithe (died overseas) [PRO; PCC Admon 1647]
STRIDWEEKE *see* STRUDWICK
STRYFE (STRYFF)
James of Lambeth [DW/PA/7/1 ff,43,45; 1486] <Abs 141,149>
STRIFEN (van STRIFEN, van STRIPEN)
Walter of Bermondsey, leatherdresser [PRO; PCC Will 1604] <Abs, SAC v,11 p,285>
STRINGER (STRYNGER)
Joan of Cranleigh [DW/PA/7/4 f,143; 1536]
John of Cranleigh [DW/PA/7/4 f,104; 1535]
Margaret of Walton on Thames, widow [DW/PA/7/12 f,493; DW/PA/5/1638/133]
Thomas of Chiddingfold, yeoman [PRO; PCC Will 1606] <Abs, SAC v,12 pp,105-106>
William of Swk St Margaret, brewer [DW/PA/7/4 f,130; 1535]
STRODEWYKE *see* STRUDWICK
STRONGMALT (STRONGEMALT)
Jacob of Swk St George [DW/PA/7/11 f,238; DW/PA/5/1625/241]
Peter of Bermondsey, gardener [DW/PA/7/12 f,127; DW/PA/5/1632/99]
STROUD (STROWD,STROWDE,STRUDE)
Edward of Egham, husbandman [DW/PA/5/1569/33]
John of Alfold, miller [DW/PA/5/1627/103]
Thomas of Thames Ditton - Weston, baker [DW/PA/7/11 f,438; DW/PA/5/1628/98]
William of Egham; Windlesham, yeoman [DW/PA/7/7 f,83; 1596] <Abs 152>
William of Egham, yeoman [DW/PA/7/7 f,501; DW/PA/5/1605/84] <Abs 938>
STROWDWYKE *see* STRUDWICK
STRUDE *see* STROUD
STRUDWICK (STRIDWEEKE,STRODEWYKE,STROWDWYKE,STRUDWEEK,STRUDWICKE)
..., of Alfold [DW/PA/5/1544/2]
John, alias John of Alfold [*in* DW/PA/5/1544/8]
John of Alfold, yeoman [DW/PA/7/7 f,212; DW/PA/5/1598/81] <Abs 378>

STRUDWICK (STRIDWEEKE,STRODEWYKE,STROWDWYKE,STRUDWEEK,STRUDWICKE)
[*continued*]
John of Chiddingfold [DW/PA/7/5 f.176; 1540]
John of Chiddingfold, husbandman [DW/PA/7/10 f.245; DW/PA/5/1622/99]
Thomas of Alfold, husbandman [HRO; 1589 B55]
Thomas of Chiddingfold - Mesylls, husbandman, senior [HRO; 1604 B63]
Thomas of Dunsfold, husbandman [DW/PA/7/13 f.188; DW/PA/5/1641/131B]
STRUTEN *see* STRETTON
STRUTT
Thomas of Swk St Olave, carpenter [DW/PA/7/7 f.336; DW/PA/5/1601/78]
<Abs 607>
STRUYS
Martin of Newington [PRO; PCC Will 1587]
STRYFE,STRYFF *see* STRIFE
STRYNGER *see* STRINGER
STUARC,STUART *see* STEWARD
STUBBINGTON
Richard of Farnham [PRO; PCC Will 1527]
STUBBS (STUBBIS)
Christopher of Lambeth [PRO; PCC Admon 1614 (two)]
Thomas of Chertsey; Durham St Giles [DW/PA/7/2 f.114; 1517]
STUDD
James, alias James Tysen of Camberwell (d. overseas)[PRO; PCC Admon 1638]
STUDLEY
John of Ockham, parson [DW/PA/7/7 f.521; DW/PA/5/1606/90] <Abs 979>
STUFF
Thomas, alias Thomas Wale of Lambeth [PRO; PCC Will 1492]
STULT
Peter of Swk St Mary Overy, goldsmith [DW/PA/7/2 f.88; 1503]
STULVYNTON
Richard of Farnham, clothworker [DW/PA/5/1550/32]
STURGES
George of Ash - Henley Park [PRO; PCC Admon 1620]
Richard of Chertsey, husbandman [HRO; 1641 B43]
STURMY (STURMYE)
Ellen of Kingston, widow [DW/PA/7/8 f.336; DW/PA/5/1612/150]
Richard of Kingston, tailor [DW/PA/7/10 f.138; 1621]
Robert of Kingston, baker [DW/PA/7/8 f.314; DW/PA/5/1613/125]
STURR
George of Chobham, yeoman [DW/PA/7/6 f.72; DW/PA/5/1559/55]
James of Walton on Thames, husbandman [DW/PA/5/1582/83]
see also STARR
STURT (STERT,STIRTE,STURTE,STURTT)
George of Puttenham, yeoman [DW/PA/7/13 f.179; DW/PA/5/1641/130]
Henry of Godalming - Eashing, husbandman [HRO; 1603 B56]
Joan of Godalming - Hurtmore, widow [DW/PA/7/8 f.105; DW/PA/5/1610/121]
Richard of Farnham, senior [DW/PA/5/1562/85]
Richard of Farnham, glover [DW/PA/7/7 f.207; 1598] <Abs 368>
Richard of Godalming [DW/PA/7/1 f.11; 1485] <Abs 36>
Richard of Godalming - Shackleford, husbandman [DW/PA/7/7 f.113; 1597]
<Abs 207>
Richard of Guildford St Mary, clothier [PRO; PCC Will 1599] [*and*]
[DW/PA/7/7 f.189; DW/PA/5/1599/75 *and* DW/PA/5/1599/76 *and*
DW/PA/5/1599/77] <Abs 345>

STURT (STERT,STIRTE,STURTE,STURTT) [*continued*]
  Richard of Guildford St Mary, clothier [DW/PA/7/7 f,389; 1600] <Abs 725>
  Richard of Witley [DW/PA/7/8 f,236; DW/PA/5/1613/126]
  Robert of Farnham, turner [HRO; 1638 B79]
  Shadrach of Shalford, miller [DW/PA/7/12 f,248; DW/PA/5/1635/102]
  Thomas of Swk St Olave, carpenter [DW/PA/5/1605/85] <Abs U171>
  William of Farnham [DW/PA/5/1569/84]
  William of Farnham [DW/PA/5/1575/34]
  William of Farnham, turner [DW/PA/7/9 f,286; 1618]
  William of Godalming [DW/PA/7/3 f,165; 1530]
STUWERDE *see* STEWARD
STYDMAN *see* STEDMAN
STYDOLFE,STYDOLFF,STYDOLPHE *see* STIDDOLPH
STYELL,STYLE *see* STILES
STYLEMAN *see* STILLMAN
STYLES,STYLL *see* STILES
STYLLWELL *see* STILLWELL
STYMPE *see* STIMP
STYLWELL *see* STILLWELL
STYNT,STYNTE *see* STINT
STYVEN *see* STEPHENS
STYWARD *see* STEWARD
SUDBURY
  John of Surrey, clerk [PRO; PCC Will 1444]
SUDLOWE
  Thomas of Camberwell [PRO; PCC Admon 1603]
SUFFOLK
  Charles Brandon, duke of Suffolk, of Surrey [PRO; PCC Will 1547]
SUFFORDE
  Alice of Chobham, widow [DW/PA/5/1548/1]
SUGDEN (SUGDON)
  John of Newington [PRO; PCC Admon 1593]
SUMMERS (SOMER,SOMMERS)
  Henry of Cambridge St John the Evangelist; Edmonton, Middlesex;
    Hertfordshire; St Dunstan in the East, London; Bermondsey,
    Chancellor of the Exchequer [LPL; Reg, Abp Stafford f,183; Will 1450]
  John of Frensham, cordwainer, junior [DW/PA/7/1 f,76; 1487] <Abs 250>
  John of Farnham [PRO; PCC Will 1613]
  John of Kingston [PRO; PCC Admon 1603]
  Maud of Croydon, later Maud Stok [PRO; PCC Will 1457]
  Robert of Farnham [HRO; Reg, Fox 3 p,65; 1515]
  Robert of Merrow [PRO; PCC Admon 1615]
  Thomas of Lambeth [PRO; PCC Will 1509]
  William of Guildford [PRO; PCC Will 1493]
SUNNINGS (SUNNINGES,SUNNYNGES)
  Robert of Newington [PRO; PCC Will 1608] <Abs, SAC v,13 p,182>
  Rose of Swk St George, widow [DW/PA/7/8 f,148; DW/PA/5/1611/109]
SURMAN
  Joan of Croydon [LPL; 96/2509; 98/1 f,60r; Will 1634]
  Nicholas of Morden, yeoman [DW/PA/7/11 f,390; DW/PA/5/1626/118]
  Richard of Croydon - Waddon [PRO; PCC 1633]
SUSSEX
  Robert Radcliffe, earl of Sussex [SRO; 65/2/28; 1625]
  Thomas Radcliffe, earl of Sussex, of Surrey [PRO; PCC Will 1585]

SUTHES

William of Lambeth, citizen and goldsmith [PRO; PCC Will 1625]

SUTTON

Ann, alias Ann Harwood of 'Kegworth' [PRO; PCC Admon 1649]
Christopher of Cobham, vicar [DW/PA/7/2 f.46; 1495]
Edmund of Cobham, gent. [DW/PA/7/11 f.548; 1629]
Edward of Cobham, yeoman [DW/PA/7/10 f.254; DW/PA/5/1622/100]
George of Cobham, husbandman [DW/PA/7/11 f.482; DW/PA/5/1628/99]
James of Cobham, gent. [DW/PA/7/3 f.155; 1530]
James of Cobham - Downside, yeoman [HRO; 1608 B72]
James of Cobham, gent. [DW/PA/5/1617/120] <Abs U229>
Joan of Cobham, widow [DW/PA/7/11 f.559; DW/PA/5/1630/99]
John of Horsell, gent. [PRO; PCC Will 1604] <Abs. SAC v.11 p.133 *and* v.29 p.88>
Nicholas of Epsom [DW/PA/7/2 f.14; 1491]
Richard of Cobham, yeoman [DW/PA/7/5 f.127; 1539]
Robert of Kingston - Ham [DW/PA/7/2 f.183; 1522] <Abs SAC v.1 pp.185-186>
Thomas of Cobham, yeoman, senior [DW/PA/5/1563/49]
Thomas of Cobham, husbandman [DW/PA/5/1586/45]*
Thomas of Byfleet; Cobham; Thames Ditton - Chadsworth, yeoman [DW/PA/7/10 f.20; DW/PA/5/1615/132]
Thomas of Ewell [DW/PA/7/11 f.527; DW/PA/5/1630/100]
Thomas of Horsell, gent. [PRO; PCC Will 1604] <Abs. SAC v.11 p.138 *and* v.29 p.92>
William of Hambledon [? HRO; 1639 AD]

SWAINE (SWAYNE)

Henry of Swk St Saviour, chandler [DW/PA/7/11 f.153; DW/PA/5/1625/242]
Katherine of Swk St Saviour [DW/PA/7/11 f.378; DW/PA/5/1626/119]
Richard of Swk St George; Bradford - Horton, Yorkshire, yeoman [DW/PA/7/7 f.454; DW/PA/5/1603/168] <Abs 858>
Robert of Capel, yeoman [DW/PA/7/11 f.67; DW/PA/5/1623/120]
Robert of Rotherhithe (died overseas) [PRO; PCC Admon 1637]
Thomas of Compton - Loseley, yeoman [DW/PA/7/12 f.148; DW/PA/5/1633/110]
William of Horsell; Binfield, Berks., yeoman [PRO; PCC 1630] <Scroope 90>
William, alias William Jones of Swk St George, glover [DW/PA/5/1579/88]*
see also SWAN (for SWANE)

SWAISLAND (SWAISLANDE, SWAYLAND)

Adry of Lambeth [PRO; PCC Will 1603]
Elizabeth of Horley [PRO; PCC Admon 1628]

SWALE

John of Newington, yeoman [LPL; 96/2512; 98/1 f.108v; Will 1639]
(Sir) Richard of Rotherhithe, auditor in the Court of Audience of Canterbury, knight [PRO; PCC Will 1608] <Abs. SAC v.13 pp.183-184>

SWAN (SWANE, SWANN, SWANNE, SWHANE)

... of Tatsfield [DW/PA/7/2 f.12; 1491]
Joan of Reigate, widow [DW/PA/5/1591/113]
John of Capel [HRO; 1605 B73]
John of Capel [DW/PA/7/9 f.151; DW/PA/5/1615/130]
John of Lambeth - Water Lambeth, brewer [DW/PA/7/2 f.64; 1500]
Margaret of Bermondsey [PRO; PCC Admon 1602]
Richard of Cranleigh [DW/PA/5/1569/55]
Richard of Cranleigh [PRO; PCC Will 1574]
Richard of Cranleigh [PRO; PCC Will 1584]
Richard of Cranleigh [PRO; PCC Admon 1598]

SWAN (SWANE,SWANN,SWANNE,SWHANE) [*continued*]
  Richard of Capel, husbandman [DW/PA/7/8 f.318; DW/PA/5/1610/122]
  Richard of Reigate; Capel [DW/PA/7/5 f.113; 1539]
  Robert of Bermondsey, citizen and leatherseller [PRO; PCC Will 1593]
  Robert of Capel, yeoman, senior [DW/PA/7/8 f.199; DW/PA/5/1611/110]
  Robert of Capel [PRO; PCC Admon 1642]
  Thomas of Reigate [DW/PA/5/1568/31]
  William of Blechingley, esq., senior [PRO; PCC Will 1534]
  William of Capel, husbandman [DW/PA/7/13 f.27; DW/PA/5/1639/128]
    see also SWAINE
SWANTON
  William of Chertsey, yeoman [DW/PA/7/12 f.72; DW/PA/5/1632/85]
SWARLAND
  Jane, alias Jane Risbrooke of Richmond [PRO; PCC Admon 1633]
SWAYLAND *see* SWAISLAND
SWAYNE *see* SWAINE,SWAN (for SWANE)
SWEETING (SWEETINGE)
  John of Bermondsey, lastmaker [DW/PA/7/10 f.4; DW/PA/5/1616/140]
  William of Swk St Olave; Royston, Essex, tapster [DW/PA/5/1593/70]
SWIFT (SWIFTE,SWYFT)
  Michael of Newington [LPL; 96/2515; Will 1644]
  Richard of Bermondsey [PRO; PCC Admon 1599]
  Richard of Newington [LPL; 98/1 f.21v; Will 1631]
  Thomas of Lambeth - Stockwell [PRO; PCC Will 1413] <Abs, SAC
    v.51 pp.84-85>
  Thomas of Tooting Graveney, yeoman [DW/PA/7/7 f.192; DW/PA/5/1598/82]
    <Abs 349>
SWILLINGHURST
  William of Mitcham, victualler [DW/PA/7/9 f.156; DW/PA/5/1615/131]
SWILNERS
  Alice of Mitcham, widow [DW/PA/7/12 f.225; DW/PA/5/1634/92]
SWINBURN (SWYNBURNE)
  Agnes of Swk St Margaret [DW/PA/7/3 f.193; 1531]
SWINEHERD (de SWYNESHERED)
  John of Lyminge, Kent; Swk St Thomas, canon of Exeter; canon of Lincoln
    [LPL; Reg. Abp Whittleseye f.125; Will 1372]
SWINGFIELD (SWINGFEILD)
  John of Camberwell - Peckham [PRO; PCC Admon 1646]
  Stephen of Camberwell, citizen of London [PRO; PCC Will 1604]
  Stephen of Camberwell - Peckham [PRO; PCC Admon 1632]
  Thomas of Camberwell - Peckham, gent. [DW/PA/7/13 f.350; 1644]
  Thomas of Camberwell - Peckham, gent. [PRO; PCC 1645]
SWINGLEHURST (SWYNGLEHURST)
  Richard of Newington [LPL; 98/1 f.125v; Will 1641]
SWINNERTON (SWYNNERTON)
  Richard, alias Richard Seagood of Egham, bargeman [DW/PA/7/13 f.126;
    DW/PA/5/1640/147]
  William of Bermondsey [DW/PA/5/1576/154]
SWYFT *see* SWIFT
SWYNBURNE *see* SWINBURN
SWYNGLEHURST *see* SWINGLESHURST
SWYNESHERED *see* SWINEHERD
SWYNNERTON *see* SWINNERTON

SY
  Fremyn of ... [*French*] [DW/PA/5/1575/85]
SYDNEY *see* SIDNEY
SYGAR *see* SIGGER
SYGNAKYLL *see* SINNACLE
SYGON *see* SIGGINS
SYLSEY *see* SILSEY
SYLVER *see* SILVER
SYMCOTE *see* SIMCOTT
SYMES,SYMMES *see* SIMS
SYMON,SYMONDES,SYMONDS,SYMONS *see* SIMMONS
SYMPSON *see* SIMPSON
SYNNOCKELL *see* SINNACLE
SYSEYE,SYSLY *see* CICELY
SYVYER *see* SIVEYER

TABE
  Henry of London, citizen and stationer [DW/PA/5/1549/3]
TACKE
  Felix of Charlwood [LPL; Reg. Abp Abbot i f.277b; Admon 1615]
TACQUET
  Jacques of Swk; Marly near Valenciennes, France [DW/PA/5/1578/15]
TAGBORN
  William, alias William Bourne of Croydon [LPL; 96/2531; Will 1617]
TAILER,TAILEUR,TAILOR *see* TAYLOR
TALBOT (TALBOTT,TALPOTT)
  Arthur of Kingston, bricklayer [HRO; 1603 B57]
  Margaret of Kingston, widow [PRO; PCC Admon 1637]
  Richard of Worplesdon [PRO; PCC Admon 1580]
TALEUR *see* TAYLOR
TALLVAN
  Thomas of Witley - Mousehill [DW/PA/7/7 f.84; 1596] <Abs 154>
TALLYE
  Simon of Guildford, vintner [HRO; 1588 B65]
TALLYGE
  Robert of Swk St Olave, curate [DW/PA/5/1563/79]
TALPOTT *see* TALBOT
TALWORTH *see* TOLWORTH
TAMNER *see* TANNER
TAMWORTH
  Thomas of Surrey [PRO; PCC Will 1532]
TANER *see* TANNER
TANFIELD (TANFELD)
  Katherine of Swk St Mary Magdalen, servant to William May, lastmaker [DW/PA/5/1588/41]
TANNER (TANER,TANNAR,TANNOR)
  Ann of Swk St Olave [DW/PA/7/11 f.337; DW/PA/5/1625/243B]
  David of Godalming - Shackleford, husbandman [DW/PA/7/9 f.72; DW/PA/5/1614/110]
  Francis of Godalming - Lydling [DW/PA/7/12 f.76; DW/PA/5/1632/105]
  Harry, alias Harry Schesmon [*Cheeseman*] of Tandridge [DW/PA/7/4 f.224; 1537]

TANNER (TANER,TANNAR,TANNOR) [*continued*]

Henry of Compton - Hurtmore, yeoman [DW/PA/7/7 f,208; DW/PA/5/1598/83] <Abs 371>

Henry of Godalming - Shackleford, husbandman [HRO; 1625 B67]

John of Elstead [HRO; 1612 AD91]

John of Godalming [DW/PA/7/2 f,9; 1489]

John, alias John Bell of Godalming, tailor [DW/PA/7/10 f,67; 1618]

John of Godalming - Lydling [DW/PA/7/13 f,193; DW/PA/5/1641/134]

John of Horley [DW/PA/7/1 f,33; 1486] <Abs 110>

John of Horley [DW/PA/7/4 f,55; 1533]

John of Peper Harow; Elstead, yeoman [DW/PA/5/1605/86] <Abs U172>

John of Walton on the Hill; Leatherhead; Charlwood; Newdigate; Reigate, yeoman [DW/PA/5/1605/87] <Abs U173>

John of Walton on the Hill [PRO; PCC Admon 1648]

John of Witley, husbandman [DW/PA/5/1570/59]

John of Wonersh [DW/PA/5/1552/2]

Parat, alias Parat Bell of Godalming, widow [DW/PA/5/1587/120]

Richard of Godalming - Shackleford [DW/PA/5/1592/65]

Robert of Elstead [DW/PA/7/9 f,74; DW/PA/5/1614/111]

Robert of Wonersh - Whipley, yeoman [DW/PA/5/1622/101]

Thomas, alias Thomas Fissher of Thames Ditton [DW/PA/5/1581/38]

Thomas of Egham [? HRO; 1529]

Thomas of Ewell [DW/PA/7/7 f,592; DW/PA/5/1607/92] <Abs 1105>

Thomas, alias Thomas Bell of Godalming, tailor [DW/PA/7/7 f,105; 1596] <Abs 188>

Thomas of Guildford St Mary [DW/PA/7/2 f,108; 1516]

Thomas of Shere, farmer [DW/PA/5/1579/94]*

Thomas of Witley, husbandman [DW/PA/5/1582/57]

Walter of Swk St Olave, haberdasher [DW/PA/7/1i f,343; DW/PA/5/1625/244]

William of Chipstead [DW/PA/7/2 f,31; 1492]

William of Leatherhead [PRO; PCC Admon 1579]

William of Walton on the Hill, yeoman [DW/PA/5/1587/80]

William of Walton on the Hill, husbandman [DW/PA/7/7 f,644; DW/PA/5/1608/104] <Abs 1210>

TANNILL *see* TUNNELL

TANWORTH (TANWORTHE)

Henry of Wonersh [DW/PA/7/12 f,233; DW/PA/5/1634/104]

John of Cranleigh, yeoman [DW/PA/5/1571/34]

John of Cranleigh, husbandman [DW/PA/5/1575/22]

John of Cranleigh, husbandman [DW/PA/7/9 f,287; 1618]

John of Wonersh [DW/PA/7/11 f,107; DW/PA/5/1624/122]

Margery of Cranleigh, widow [DW/PA/5/1572/27]

TAPLIN (TEPELENE)

Richard, alias Richard Fowlemer of Lambeth; Kingston [PRO; PCC Will 1429]

TAPSELL

John of Burstow, yeoman [LPL; 96/2536; Will 1625]

see also TOPSELL

TAPSFEILD

Edith of Kingston [DW/PA/7/10 f,114; DW/PA/5/1619/111]

TARBOKE

Robert of Swk St Mary Overy [DW/PA/7/4 f,217; 1537]

TARDAUGH

Mary of Swk St Olave, widow [DW/PA/7/13 f,78; DW/PA/5/1641/131C]

TARGET
Reuben of Betchworth, glover [DW/PA/7/12 f.248; DW/PA/5/1635/116]
TARR (TARRE)
John of Ockley [DW/PA/7/1 f.10; 1485] <Abs 34>
William of Swk St Thomas, feltmaker [DW/PA/7/10 f.139; DW/PA/5/1620/131]
TARRANT (TERRENT)
Andrew of Lambeth - Lambeth Marsh, clerk and widower [PRO; PCC 1646]
TASINE
Stephen of Swk St Olave [DW/PA/7/11 f.150; DW/PA/5/1625/243A]
TASKER
Richard of Burstow, sheather [LPL; Reg. Abp Abbot i f.275; Will 1615]
TASTARD
Juliana of Kingston, widow [DW/PA/7/2 f.12; 1490]
TATERSALE *see* TATTERSALL
TATNALL
William of Merstham, yeoman [PRO; PCC Will 1626]
TATTE
William of ...., smith [DW/PA/7/8 f.80; DW/PA/5/1609/115]
TATTERSALL (TATERSALE,TETERSALL)
John of Caterham, clerk [DW/PA/5/1627/105]
Richard of Rotherhithe, citizen and draper [LPL; Reg. Abp Stafford f.178; Will 1449]
William of Epsom, vicar [? HRO; 1561]
TAUNTON
Thomas of Chobham, clerk [PRO; PCC 1649]
TAVERNER (TAVERNAR)
Henry of Battersea, yeoman [PRO; PCC Will 1623]
John of Swk St Mary Magdalen, tallow chandler [DW/PA/7/3 f.106; 1529]
John of Swk St Olave [DW/PA/7/4 f.71; 1534]
TAWLWORTH *see* TOLWORTH
TAYLOR (TAILER,TAILEUR,TAILOR,TALEUR,TAYLLER,TAYLOUR,TAYLOURE,TEYLER)
Agnes of Banstead, widow of Peter [PRO; PCC Will 1489]
Alan of Ewell, yeoman [DW/PA/7/8 f.218; DW/PA/5/1612/152]
Alan of Woodmansterne [PRO; PCC 1639]
Alexander of Great Bookham [DW/PA/5/1581/49]
Ann of Esher [DW/PA/7/12 f.360; DW/PA/5/1636/99]
Anthony of Kingston, blacksmith [DW/PA/7/13 f.278; DW/PA/5/1643/86]
Caleb of Godalming, vicar [DW/PA/7/12 f.72; DW/PA/5/1632/104]
Dorothy of Swk St Olave [DW/PA/7/11 f.232; DW/PA/5/1625/245]
Edmund of Newington [LPL; 98/1 f.50v; (ren.) 1633]
Edmund of Great Bookham [DW/PA/7/11 f.183; DW/PA/5/1625/246]
Edmund of Rotherhithe (died overseas) [PRO; PCC Admon 1638]
Elizabeth of Battersea, widow [DW/PA/7/9 f.39; DW/PA/5/1614/112]
Francis of Godalming; Lambeth, clerk [DW/PA/7/9 f.313; DW/PA/5/1619/112]
Francis of Thorpe [PRO; PCC Admon 1567]
George of Dorking [DW/PA/7/6 f.174; DW/PA/5/1559/152]
George of Esher; Thames Ditton; Long Ditton; Streatham; Chessington; Kingston - Surbiton, yeoman [PRO; PCC Will 1620]
George of Lingfield [PRO; PCC Will 1543]
George of Walton on Thames [DW/PA/7/11 f.442; DW/PA/5/1628/100]
Henry of Chobham, clothworker, senior [HRO; 1639 B66]
Henry of Lingfield, gent. [PRO; PCC Will 1595]
Henry of Walton on Thames; Cobham [DW/PA/7/5 f.15; 1538] <Abs 118>

TAYLOR (TAILER,TAILEUR,TAILOR,TALEUR,TAYLLER,TAYLOUR,TAYLOURE,TEYLER) [*continued*]

Hugh of Lambeth, citizen and vintner, bachelor [PRO; PCC 1640]
James of Great Bookham, husbandman [DW/PA/7/10 f,246; DW/PA/5/1622/102]
Joan of Dorking, widow [DW/PA/5/1588/52]
Joan, alias Joan Tylor of Esher, widow [DW/PA/7/11 f,11; DW/PA/5/1623/124]
John of Ash - Wyke [HRO; 1521 B38]
John of Betchworth - Brockham, tanner [DW/PA/5/1582/96]
John of Chobham [DW/PA/7/6 f,130; DW/PA/5/1559/194]
John of Chobham, yeoman [DW/PA/7/13 f,418; DW/PA/5/1645/56]
John of Cobham, husbandman [DW/PA/5/1617/138] <Abs U230>
John of Dorking [DW/PA/5/1575/14]
John of Ewhurst [*in* DW/PA/5/1546/38]
John of Ash - Frimley [DW/PA/5/1593/207]
John, alias John Bocher of Haslemere; Peper Harow [DW/PA/7/1 f,77; 1488] <Abs 254>
John of Kew, gent,, junior [PRO; PCC Will 1607] <Abs, SAC v,12 p,96>
John of Nutfield, yeoman [DW/PA/7/9 f,54; DW/PA/5/1614/113]
John of Ockham, butcher [HRO; 1605 B74]
John of Ockham, husbandman [DW/PA/7/13 f,202; DW/PA/5/1642/83]
John of Swk St Olave [DW/PA/7/4 f,79; 1534]
John of Swk St Saviour; Newington, gent, [DW/PA/7/7 f,209; DW/PA/5/1598/84] <Abs 373>
John of Stoke Dabernon, husbandman [DW/PA/5/1546/34]
John of Walton on Thames, carpenter [DW/PA/5/1575/42]
Joseph of Lambeth, bachelor [PRO; PCC Admon 1631]
Katherine of Swk St Saviour, widow [DW/PA/7/7 f,14; DW/PA/5/1595/82] <Abs 30>
Lancelot of Swk St Saviour, sailor [DW/PA/7/7 f,412; DW/PA/5/1603/169] <Abs 764>
Lawrence of Ockham, parish clerk [DW/PA/7/6 f,247; 1560]
Mary of Crowhurst, spinster [DW/PA/7/12 f,247; DW/PA/5/1635/115]
Mary of Woodmansterne, widow [PRO; PCC Admon 1649]
Maud of Cobham, widow [DW/PA/7/2 f,33; 1492]
Nicholas of Banstead [DW/PA/7/1 f,95; 1489] <Abs 314>
Peter of Newington - Walworth, yeoman [PRO; PCC Will 1628]
Phillip of Send [DW/PA/7/4 f,62; 1533]
Phillip of Swk St Olave, joiner [DW/PA/7/11 f,324; DW/PA/5/1625/247]
Richard of ,,, [DW/PA/7/8 f,5; DW/PA/5/1608/105]
Richard of Battersea, yeoman [DW/PA/7/6 f,23; DW/PA/5/1559/26]
Richard of Cobham, yeoman *or* husbandman [HRO; 1587 B84]
Richard of Merton, yeoman [DW/PA/5/1617/139] <Abs U231>
Richard of Shere [DW/PA/7/1 f,7; 1485] <Abs 21>
Richard of Walton on Thames, carpenter [PRO; PCC Will 1611] <Abs, SAC v,35 p,47>
Robert of Horsell, husbandman [HRO; 1565 B105-106]
Robert of Horsell, husbandman [DW/PA/5/1565/10]
Robert of Swk St George - Mermaid Court, millwright [DW/PA/7/10 f,146; DW/PA/5/1621/117]
Samuel of Walton on Thames [DW/PA/7/13 f,308; DW/PA/5/1643/89]
Samuel of Wotton, carpenter [DW/PA/7/12 f,71; DW/PA/5/1632/103]
Thomas of Surrey [PRO; PCC Will 1552]
Thomas of Battersea, gent, [PRO; PCC Will 1602] <Abs, SAC v,10 p,314>

TAYLOR (TAILER, TAILEUR, TAILOR, TALEUR, TAYLLER, TAYLOUR, TAYLOURE, TEYLER) [*continued*]

Thomas of Bermondsey [DW/PA/5/1557/129]

Thomas of Cobham [DW/PA/7/4 f.8; 1532]

Thomas of Chiddingfold, husbandman [DW/PA/5/1562/86]

Thomas of Chobham, tailor [DW/PA/7/4 f.159; 1536]

Thomas of Thames Ditton, husbandman [DW/PA/7/6 f.226; 1561]

Thomas of Harity [? Horley] [PRO; PCC 1649]

Thomas of Horley, yeoman [DW/PA/5/1617/140] <Abs U232>

Thomas of Kingston, husbandman [DW/PA/7/10 f.111; DW/PA/5/1619/113]

Thomas of Lambeth, yeoman [DW/PA/7/11 f.483; DW/PA/5/1628/101]

Thomas of Swk St Saviour - liberty of Old Paris Garden, waterman [DW/PA/7/9 f.277; 1618]

Thomas of Whitechapel, Middlesex; Swk St Saviour, glover [DW/PA/7/13 f.283; DW/PA/5/1643/87]

Thomas of Walton on Thames, carpenter [DW/PA/7/12 f.100; DW/PA/5/1632/106]

Thomas of Wandsworth [DW/PA/5/1571/11]

Thomas of Woking (died overseas) [PRO; PCC Admon 1637]

Thomas of Woking, husbandman [DW/PA/7/13 f.12; DW/PA/5/1639/138]

Walter of Guildford St Mary [DW/PA/5/1582/71]

William of Guildford St Nicholas - Artington [DW/PA/7/4 f.56; 1533]

William of Bermondsey; Derbyshire; Oxford University, Oxfordshire; Cambridge University, Cambridgeshire, fellmonger [DW/PA/7/6 f.266; 1560]

William of Capel [DW/PA/7/4 f.157; 1536]

William of Godstone [PRO; PCC Admon 1631]

William of Horley, husbandman, senior [DW/PA/7/12 f.37; DW/PA/5/1631/112]

William of Horley, yeoman [PRO; PCC 1645]

William of Swk St George [DW/PA/5/1547/12]

William of Swk St George, yeoman [DW/PA/7/9 f.92; DW/PA/5/1616/141]

William of Swk St Olave, yeoman [DW/PA/7/7 f.502; DW/PA/5/1605/90] <Abs 940>

William of Swk St Olave [DW/PA/7/10 f.212; DW/PA/5/1620/129]

William, alias William Danvile of Weybridge - Dorney; New Windsor, Berkshire [PRO; PCC 1640]

William of Woodmansterne, husbandman [DW/PA/5/1592/69]

TAYSON

John of Kingston, yeoman, junior [DW/PA/7/6 f.124; DW/PA/5/1559/209]

TEALE

Christopher of Newington [PRO; PCC Admon 1626]

TEAME (TEME)

John of Walton on Thames [DW/PA/7/6 f.186; DW/PA/5/1559/192]

John of Walton on Thames [DW/PA/7/11 f.528; DW/PA/5/1630/102]

John of Weybridge, yeoman [DW/PA/5/1579/91]*

Robert of Walton [*proved at* Kingston] [DW/PA/7/8 f.177; DW/PA/5/1610/123]

Robert of Walton on Thames, yeoman [DW/PA/7/10 f.248; DW/PA/5/1622/103]

TEARE (TEERE)

Richard of Wandsworth, carpenter [DW/PA/7/13 f.18; DW/PA/5/1639/139]

TEBBUTT (TIBBETTS, TYBBOTT)

Guy of Rotherhithe [DW/PA/7/11 f.310; DW/PA/5/1626/122]

William of Camberwell, shoemaker [DW/PA/7/2 f.66; 1500]

TECNER *see* TICKNER

TEDDER (TEDAR)

Humphrey of Swk St Saviour - Paris Garden, waterman [DW/PA/5/1592/46]

TEDHAM

William of Dorking, butcher [DW/PA/7/13 f.425; DW/PA/5/1646/56]

TEDMAN

Giles of Wandsworth [PRO; PCC Admon 1632]

TEERE *see* TEARE

TEGG (TEGGE)

Agnes of Epsom, widow [HRO; 1596 B67]

Bartholomew of Beddington, yeoman, senior [DW/PA/7/11 f.420; DW/PA/5/1626/120] <Abs U263>

Edward of Carshalton, yeoman [DW/PA/7/10 f.103; DW/PA/5/1621/118]

Geoffrey of Banstead - Tadworth; Walton on the Hill [DW/PA/5/1550/110]

John of Carshalton [PRO; PCC Admon 1588]

John of Ewell; Epsom [DW/PA/5/1579/93]*

John of Mitcham, yeoman [DW/PA/7/12 f.409; DW/PA/5/1638/136]

Richard of ... [DW/PA/7/8 f.381; DW/PA/5/1612/153]

Richard of Walton on the Hill; Betchworth; Epsom, yeoman [DW/PA/7/9 f.327; DW/PA/5/1619/114]

William of Ewell [DW/PA/7/7 f.272; DW/PA/5/1599/78] <Abs 480>

William of Morden [DW/PA/7/4 f.17; 1532]

TEGGON

Richard of Mitcham [PRO; PCC 1642]

TEIRELL *see* TERRELL

TELLER *see* ELLIS

TEKNER *see* TICKNER

TEME *see* TEAME

TEMPEST

John of Pirbright - Henley Park [PRO; PCC Admon 1603]

TEMPLE

Alice of Bermondsey [PRO; PCC Admon 1615]

John of Bermondsey, leatherseller [PRO; PCC Will 1590]

Thomas of Bermondsey [PRO; PCC Will 1604] <Abs, SAC v.11 pp.294-295>

TEMPLEMAN

Ambrose of Charlwood [LPL; 98/1 ff.91v,107v; Wills 1638 *and* 1639]

William of Swk St Olave, butcher [DW/PA/7/10 f.190; DW/PA/5/1621/119]

TENACRES (TENECRES)

George of Guildford; Clandon [PRO; PCC Will 1592]

TENCH

William of Swk St Saviour, gent. [DW/PA/7/12 f.202; DW/PA/5/1633/119]

TENECRES *see* TENACRES

TENNANT (TENNANTE)

Edmund of Swk St Olave [DW/PA/7/7 f.554; DW/PA/5/1606/92] <Abs 1039>

John of Swk St Saviour [DW/PA/7/7 f.471; DW/PA/5/1604/60] <Abs 889>

TEPAM

William of Capel, husbandman [DW/PA/7/2 f.23; 1492]

TEPELENE *see* TAPLIN

TERME

Robert of Swk St Olave [DW/PA/7/5 f.27; 1538] <Abs 103>

TERRELL (TEIRELL,TERYLL,TORRELL)

Francis of Croydon, citizen and grocer [PRO; PCC Will 1609]

Francis of Stoke Dabernon [DW/PA/5/1587/88 *and* DW/PA/5/1587/89]

Humphrey of Surrey, esq. [PRO; PCC Will 1544]

TERRELL (TEIRELL,TERYLL,TORRELL) [*continued*]
John of Abinger; Okewood; Plumstead Marsh, Kent [DW/PA/7/7 f,574; DW/PA/5/1606/100] <Abs 1074>
John of Stoke Dabernon [DW/PA/7/5 f,64; 1539] <Abs 113>
John of Stoke Dabernon, senior [DW/PA/5/1588/38]
Robert of Chertsey, joiner [PRO; PCC Will 1617]
Thomas of Newdigate, carpenter [DW/PA/7/7 f,62; DW/PA/5/1596/59] <Abs 118>
see also TIRRELL
TERRENT *see* TARRANT
TERRY (TERREY,TERRIE,TERRYE)
Alice of Farnham, widow [HRO; 1563 B176]
Andrew of Godalming, husbandman [DW/PA/7/11 f,412; DW/PA/5/1627/106]
Edward of Farnham [PRO; PCC 1646]
John of Farnham, tailor [DW/PA/7/8 f,337; DW/PA/5/1612/155]
John of Newington [LPL; 98/1 f,131r; (ren,) 1642]
Richard of Blechingley, yeoman [DW/PA/7/10 f,42; 1618]
Roger of Newdigate [DW/PA/7/12 f,418; DW/PA/5/1637/96]
Samuel of Croydon [LPL; 98/1 f,27v; Will 1631]
Thomas of Lambeth, waterman [DW/PA/7/9 f,27; DW/PA/5/1614/114]
William of Farnham, mercer [HRO; 1563 B177]
William of Farnham, woollen draper [DW/PA/7/12 f,388; DW/PA/5/1637/97]
TERYLL *see* TERRELL
TETERSALL *see* TATTERSALL
TETTISWORTH
Edmund of Swk, sergeant at arms [HRO; Reg, Wyk 2 p,227; 1386]
TEWE (TEW,TUE)
Hugh of Farnham, shoemaker [HRO; 1571 AD45]
John of Bermondsey, tailor [DW/PA/7/12 f,449; 1638]
John of Thames Ditton, yeoman [DW/PA/5/1592/27]
Robert of Guildford St Mary, yeoman [DW/PA/7/12 f,273; DW/PA/5/1636/93]
Thomas of Wanborough [DW/PA/5/1550/109]
William of Frensham, weaver [DW/PA/7/7 f,86; 1596] <Abs 158>
TEWESLEY,TEWYSLEY *see* TUESLEY
TEYDYE *see* TIDY
TEYLER *see* TAYLOR
THACCHER *see* THATCHER
THACKHAM
Ann of Wandsworth, widow [PRO; PCC Will 1625]
Matthew of Wandsworth, innholder [PRO; PCC Will 1625]
THAER,THAIRE *see* THAYER
THAMSETT *see* THOMSETT
THARLTON *see* THORNTON
THATCHER (THACCHER,THECHER,THEICHER,THESTHER,THETCHER,THOWCARD)
Gillian of Worplesdon, widow [DW/PA/5/1558/272]*
Joan of Chertsey, widow [DW/PA/5/1562/65]
Joan of Leigh [PRO; PCC Will 1528]
John of Chertsey, yeoman [DW/PA/7/4 f,236; 1527]
John of Chertsey [BM; Add,Ms 24,925 f,25r; 1544] <Abs 63>
John of Chertsey [PRO; PCC Will 1595]
John of Chertsey - Addlestone, husbandman [DW/PA/7/7 f,579; DW/PA/5/1606/93] <Abs 1080>
John of Reigate, yeoman [DW/PA/7/12 f,261; DW/PA/5/1634/105]
Margaret of Bisley, widow [DW/PA/5/1570/90]

THATCHER (THACCHER, THECHER, THEICHER, THESTHER, THETCHER, THOWCARD) [*continued*]
Thomas of Chertsey, husbandman, senior [DW/PA/5/1558/273]*
Thomas of Chertsey [DW/PA/7/6 f.177; DW/PA/5/1559/226]
Thomas of Chobham, yeoman, senior [DW/PA/7/11 f.590; DW/PA/5/1630/103]
William of Chertsey, yeoman, senior [HRO: 1589 AD57]
William of Chertsey, yeoman [DW/PA/7/7 f.537; DW/PA/5/1606/94] <Abs 1008>
William of Chertsey - Addlestone, yeoman [HRO: 1625 B69]
William of Horsell [PRO: PCC 1647]
William of West Horsley, yeoman [DW/PA/7/4 f.210; 1537]

THAYER (THAER, THAIRE, THAYRE, THEAYER, THEYER, THEYR)
Clement of Pirbright, husbandman [DW/PA/5/1550/34]
John of Ash [DW/PA/7/2 f.37; 1493]
John of Ash; Worplesdon, senior [DW/PA/7/4 f.83; 1534]
John of Frimley, husbandman [DW/PA/5/1562/13]
John of Hambledon, husbandman [HRO: 1630 B66]
Richard of Ash [DW/PA/5/1576/153]
Thomas of Pirbright, yeoman [PRO: PCC Will 1624]
Thomas of Woking [DW/PA/5/1587/116]

THEAKER
Diana Posthuma of Lambeth [PRO: PCC Admon 1630]

THEAYER *see* THAYER

THECHER, THEICHER *see* THATCHER

THERBORNE
John of West Clandon [DW/PA/7/6 f.188; DW/PA/5/1559/207]

THERESK *see* THIRSK

THESTHER, THETCHER *see* THATCHER

THEYER, THEYR, THEYRE *see* THAYER

THIRSK (THERESK)
Robert of Surrey, clerk [PRO: PCC Will 1419]

THIRLBY (THURLEBY)
William of Swk St Olave [DW/PA/7/10 f.195; DW/PA/5/1621/120]

THOERLYE *see* THORLEY

THOMARE
Passchier of Newington; Newkerck, Flanders [PRO: PCC Will 1616]
Passchier of Newington [PRO: PCC 1645]

THOMAS
(Sir) Anthony of Cobham, knight [PRO: PCC Admon 1648]
Henry of London; Oxford, Oxfordshire, citizen and ironmonger [DW/PA/5/1558/274]*
Henry of Lambeth, vintner [PRO: PCC Will 1611] <Abs, SAC v.35 p.46>
Hugh of Streatham [PRO: PCC Admon 1626]
Hugh of Wandsworth [DW/PA/7/11 f.558; DW/PA/5/1630/104]
Jenkin of Pyrford, yeoman [DW/PA/7/10 f.98; DW/PA/5/1619/115]
Joan, alias Joan Wallis of Battersea, widow [DW/PA/7/9 f.148; DW/PA/5/1615/133]
Joan of Cobham, widow [PRO: PCC 1641]
John of Battersea, waterman [DW/PA/7/12 f.51; DW/PA/5/1631/113]
John of Malden [DW/PA/7/7 f.151; DW/PA/5/1597/99] <Abs 284>
John of Swk St Olave [DW/PA/7/9 f.56; DW/PA/5/1614/115]
John of Wandsworth, tailor [DW/PA/5/1592/96]
(Lady) Katherine Daubeney, countess of Bridgewater of Lambeth formerly wife of (Sir) Rees ap Thomas, knight [PRO: PCC Will 1554]
Lewis of Swk [DW/PA/5/1561/75]
Robert of Croydon, gent. [PRO: PCC Will 1611]

THOMAS [*continued*]
  Robert of Rotherhithe, sailor [PRO; PCC Will 1623]
  Thomas of Wandsworth [PRO; PCC 1633]
  William of Esher, member of the bishop's household [HRO; Reg. Way 2 p.148; 1471]
  William of Kingston, baker [DW/PA/7/2 f.191; 1523]
  William of Swk St Mary Overy [DW/PA/7/5 f.75; 1539]
THOMBE
  John of Swk St Olave, feltmaker [DW/PA/5/1579/90]*
THOMLER
  Andrew of Swk St Saviour [DW/PA/7/11 f.209; DW/PA/5/1625/249]
THOMPLINSON *see* TOMLINSON
THOMPSETT *see* THOMSETT
THOMPSON (THOMSON,TOMPSON,TOMSON)
  David of Newington [LPL; 98/1 f.8r; (ren.) 1630]
  Edward of Croydon - Woodside, yeoman [PRO; PCC Will 1611] <Abs, SAC v.35 p.43>
  Frances of Croydon, spinster [DW/PA/5/1572/23]
  George of Bermondsey [PRO; PCC Will 1628]
  George of Swk St George [DW/PA/5/1563/92]
  Harry of Kingston, yeoman, junior [DW/PA/7/3 f.192; 1531]
  John of Addington [PRO; PCC 1631]
  John of Beddington, cook [DW/PA/5/1562/62]
  John of Bermondsey, mariner [DW/PA/7/12 f.462; DW/PA/5/1638/137]
  John of Lambeth, weaver [DW/PA/5/1575/41]
  John of Lambeth [DW/PA/7/7 f.411; DW/PA/5/1603/170] <Abs 762>
  John of Lambeth - Kennington [DW/PA/7/8 f.173; DW/PA/5/1610/124]
  John of Malden, yeoman [DW/PA/7/7 f.164; DW/PA/5/1597/101] <Abs 302>
  John of Mortlake [PRO; PCC Will 1528]
  John of Newington [LPL; 96/2575; Will 1622]
  John of Swk St Olave, whitster [DW/PA/7/12 f.342; DW/PA/5/1636/98]
  Ralph of Camberwell, yeoman [DW/PA/7/7 f.150; DW/PA/5/1597/100] <Abs 280>
  Ralph of Wandsworth [DW/PA/7/2 f.111; 1517]
  Richard of Lambeth [PRO; PCC Admon 1601]
  Richard of Swk [DW/PA/5/1569/30]
  Richard of Swk St Saviour, brewer [DW/PA/5/1593/182]
  Robert of Farnham, yeoman [DW/PA/7/12 f.287; DW/PA/5/1635/118]
  Robert of Farnham [PRO; PCC 1635]
  Robert of Farnham [PRO; PCC 1636]
  Robert of Morden [DW/PA/7/4 f.173; 1536]
  Robert of Reigate [DW/PA/7/4 f.64; 1534]
  Robert of Reigate, yeoman [DW/PA/7/7 f.444; DW/PA/5/1603/174] <Abs 841>
  Roger of Betchworth; Lambeth - Kennington [DW/PA/7/11 f.440; DW/PA/5/1628/103].
  Roger of Mitcham, husbandman [PRO; PCC Will 1604] <Abs, SAC v.11 p.293>
  Samuel of Streatham [PRO; PCC Will 1624]
  Thomas of Guildford, clothier [DW/PA/7/8 f.315; DW/PA/5/1613/131]
  Thomas of Swk St George, cordwainer, junior [DW/PA/7/11 f.508; DW/PA/5/1629/96]
  Thomas of Swk St George, yeoman [DW/PA/7/11 f.610; DW/PA/5/1630/105]
  Thomas of Swk St Olave [HRO; 1592 AD101]
  Thomas of Streatham, esq. and herald at arms [PRO; PCC 1641]
  William of Lambeth - Kennington [PRO; PCC Will 1512]

THOMPSON (THOMSON, TOMPSON, TOMSON) [*continued*]
  William of Reigate; Buxted, Sussex [DW/PA/7/5 f.27] <Abs 69>
  William of Swk St Olave, miller [DW/PA/5/1563/107]
THOMSETT (THAMSETT, THOMPSETT)
  Shadrach of Reigate [PRO; PCC Admon 1636]
  Shadrach of Reigate [PRO; PCC 1637 *and* 1637 sentence]
THORESBY (THORESBIE, THORISBIE)
  Eleanor of Lambeth - Lambeth Marsh [PRO; PCC Will 1593]
  Francis of Lambeth, esq. [PRO; PCC Admon 1599]
THORLEY (THOERLYE, THORLEYE)
  Lawrence of Kingston; Pyrford; Woking; Shalford; Guildford;
    Bramley; Walton on Thames; Kingston - Ham [DW/PA/5/1550/79]
  Thomas of Pyrford, husbandman [DW/PA/7/5 f.82; 1539]
THORBURY (THORNEBERYE)
  Walter of Swk St Mary Overy [DW/PA/7/4 f.101; 1535]
THORNCOMB (THORNCOME)
  Henry of Leatherhead - Pachesham, labourer [DW/PA/5/1599/80] <Abs U26>
  Thomas of Leatherhead, husbandman [HRO; 1631 B65]
THORNDELL
  John of Godalming [HRO; 1621 A093]
THORNDEN (THORNEDEN)
  John of Cranleigh, husbandman [DW/PA/7/9 f.56; DW/PA/5/1614/116]
  Richard of Cranleigh, husbandman [DW/PA/7/11 f.124; DW/PA/5/1624/123]
  Thomas of Cranleigh, butcher [DW/PA/7/9 f.248; DW/PA/5/1617/121]
  Thomas of Horley; Leigh, husbandman [DW/PA/7/9 f.147; DW/PA/5/1615/134]
  William of Cranleigh [DW/PA/7/8 f.204; DW/PA/5/1611/112]
  William of Godstone [DW/PA/7/11 f.507; DW/PA/5/1629/97]
THORNE
  Christopher of Ewell, husbandman [HRO; 1561 B206-207]
  Geoffrey of Coulsdon [DW/PA/7/4 f.147; 1536]
  John of Kingston, gent. [DW/PA/7/12 f.514; DW/PA/5/1639/135]
  John of Richmond [PRO; PCC Admon 1647]
THORNEBERYE *see* THORNBURY
THORNEBURGH
  Thomas of Camberwell [PRO; PCC Will 1405]
THORNEBUSH
  John of Rotherhithe (died overseas) [PRO; PCC Admon 1641]
THORNEDEN *see* THORNDEN
THORNEFFE
  Anthony of Bermondsey, mariner [DW/PA/7/12 f.335; DW/PA/5/1636/97]
THORNTON (THARLTON, THORNETON)
  Hannah of London, widow [DW/PA/7/13 f.326; 1644]
  John of Bermondsey [PRO; PCC Admon 1637]
  John of Lambeth [DW/PA/7/2 f.69; 1500]
  John of Swk St Saviour [DW/PA/7/7 f.427; DW/PA/5/1603/171] <Abs 799>
  Michael of Coulsdon [PRO; PCC Admon 1600]
  Richard of ... [DW/PA/7/7 f.597; DW/PA/5/1606/95] <Abs 1119>
  Richard of Lambeth [PRO; PCC Will 1489]
  Thomas of Kingston [PRO; PCC Admon 1612]
  Thomas of Reigate [PRO; PCC Will 1607] <Abs. SAC v.12 p.99>
THORPE (THORP)
  Edmund of Horne, yeoman [DW/PA/5/1587/69]
  George of Swk St Saviour, waterman [DW/PA/5/1581/43]
  Jane of Windlesham, widow [*in* DW/PA/5/1557/120]

THORPE (THORP) [*continued*]

John of Cobham [DW/PA/7/8 f.187; DW/PA/5/1610/125]

John of Lambeth, yeoman [*in* DW/PA/5/1547/4]

John of Thorpe, esq. [PRO; PCC Will 1438]

Richard of Thames Ditton [DW/PA/5/1580/26]

Thomas of Ash, yeoman [HRO; 1597 B73]

Thomas of Horne - Hedgecourt, gent. [PRO; PCC Will 1609]

THOWCARD *see* THATCHER

THRALE (THRALLE,THREELE)

Edward of Newington [PRO; PCC Admon 1635]

John of Lambeth - Stockwell, vintner [PRO; PCC Will 1589]

Mary of Newington, widow of Edward, esq. [PRO; PCC 1638]

William of Godalming - Shackleford, gent. [PRO; PCC Will 1560]

THRASHER (THRASSHER)

Thomas of Swk St Olave [DW/PA/5/1561/16]

THREDDER

Walter of Swk St George [DW/PA/7/13 f.153; DW/PA/5/1642/81]

THREELE *see* THRALE

THROCKMORTON (THROKMORTON)

Thomas of Surrey [PRO; PCC Will 1591]

THRONE

William of Newington [PRO; PCC 1646]

THUNDERMAN

Edward of Beddington [DW/PA/7/12 f.509; DW/PA/5/1639/136]

THURBAND

William of Ewell, curate [DW/PA/5/1571/96]

THURGOOD

John of Mortlake; Wimbledon, senior [PRO; PCC Will 1541]

THURLEBY *see* THIRLBY

THURTLE

John of Swk St Saviour, yeoman [DW/PA/7/9 f.339; DW/PA/5/1620/130]

THWAITES (THWATES,THWAYTE)

James of Swk St Olave [DW/PA/7/11 f.371; DW/PA/5/1626/121]

(Sir) Thomas of Barnes, knight [PRO; PCC Will 1503]

TIBBETTS *see* TEBBUTT

TIBBOLD (TYBBOLDE,TYBBOLL)

John of Swk St Saviour, dyer [DW/PA/5/1586/11]

Ralph of Swk St Saviour - Upper Ground, Liberty of Old Paris Garden, one of Queen's watermen [DW/PA/7/6 f.261; 1561]

TICE (TISE,TYCE,TYSE)

Edward of Swk St Olave, cordwainer [DW/PA/7/10 f.7; DW/PA/5/1619/119]

John of Chertsey [BM; Add.Ms 24,925 f.23v; 1544] <Abs 57>

John of Puttenham; Ripley, yeoman [DW/PA/7/7 f.82; 1596] <Abs 148>

John of Puttenham; Ripley, yeoman [DW/PA/7/7 f.277; DW/PA/5/1599/81] <Abs 492>

Joseph of Bermondsey [DW/PA/7/11 f.145; DW/PA/5/1625/250]

Joseph of Bermondsey [DW/PA/7/11 f.324; 1625]

William of West Clandon, rector [DW/PA/7/2 f.23; 1492]

TICHBOURN (TYCHEBOURNE,TYCHEBURNE)

John of Lingfield [PRO; PCC Will 1556]

John of Lingfield, gent. [PRO; PCC Will 1572]

Richard of Surrey, gent. [PRO; PCC Will 1549]

TICKLE (TYKHULL)

Ralph of Blechingley [PRO; PCC Will 1500; CCAL; 1500 f.99r]

TICKNER (TECNER, TEKNOR, TICKNOR, TICNOR, TYCKNOR, TYKENER, TYKNAR, TYKNER, TYKNOR, TYKNOUR)

Agnes of Cranleigh, widow [DW/PA/5/1617/141] <Abs U233>
Agnes of Bramley, widow of Stephen, yeoman [DW/PA/7/10 f.158; DW/PA/5/1621/121]
Agnes of Wonersh, widow of William, husbandman [DW/PA/5/1568/68]
Alexander of Ockham, wheelwright [DW/PA/7/7 f.467; DW/PA/5/1604/61] <Abs 881>
Alice of Wonersh - Franklin's, widow [DW/PA/5/1592/36]
Cicely of Albury [DW/PA/7/5 f.145; 1540]
Dorothy of Wonersh - Smithwood [DW/PA/7/11 f.298; DW/PA/5/1626/123]
Edward of Hambledon - 'Haytyngs', husbandman [DW/PA/7/4 f.125; 1535]
Henry of Wonersh - Franklin's, husbandman [DW/PA/7/7 f.389; DW/PA/5/1602/86] <Abs 724>
Joan of Wonersh - Franklin's, widow of Henry [DW/PA/7/7 f.490; DW/PA/5/1605/89] <Abs 928>
John of Albury - Woodhill, husbandman [DW/PA/7/13 f.244; DW/PA/5/1640/157]
John of Bramley, tanner [DW/PA/7/8 f.173; DW/PA/5/1610/126]
John of Cranleigh [DW/PA/5/1562/88]
John of Ewhurst [DW/PA/7/4 f.7; 1532]
John of Lambeth - South Lambeth, victualler [DW/PA/7/13 f.307; DW/PA/5/1643/88]
John of Ockham, yeoman [DW/PA/7/11 f.451; DW/PA/5/1628/102]
John of Send, labourer [DW/PA/7/7 f.111; 1597] <Abs 202>
John of Send [PRO: PCC 1646]
John of Shalford - Birtley, husbandman [DW/PA/5/1586/24]*
John of Wonersh - Haldish, yeoman [DW/PA/5/1579/92]*
John of Wonersh, tailor [DW/PA/7/7 f.487; DW/PA/5/1604/62] <Abs 920>
John of Wonersh - Gascon [DW/PA/7/7 f.554; DW/PA/5/1606/98] <Abs 1040>
John of Wonersh - Smithwood; Albury; Shere, yeoman [DW/PA/7/8 f.341; DW/PA/5/1612/156]
John of Wonersh - Smithwood, yeoman, senior [DW/PA/7/9 f.325; DW/PA/5/1619/116] [*proved* 1616]
John of Wonersh - Smithwood, yeoman [DW/PA/7/13 f.54; DW/PA/5/1640/153]
John of Wonersh - 'Churtses', husbandman [DW/PA/7/13 f.358; 1644]
John of Wonersh - 'Churtses' [PRO: PCC 1648]
Juliana of Wonersh, widow [DW/PA/5/1552/12]
Margaret of Dunsfold; Alfold, widow [DW/PA/5/1604/63] <Abs U120>
Margaret of Shalford [DW/PA/7/3 f.202; 1532]
Maud of Wonersh, widow [DW/PA/5/1571/36]
Ralph of Cranleigh - Utworth [PRO: PCC 1647]
Richard of ... [DW/PA/5/1613/128]
Richard of Cranleigh [DW/PA/7/3 f.185; 1531]
Richard of Leatherhead, shearman [DW/PA/7/8 f.318; DW/PA/5/1611/113]
Richard of Leatherhead, shoemaker [DW/PA/5/1613/128] <Abs U202>
Richard of Leatherhead [DW/PA/7/13 f.187; DW/PA/5/1641/132]
Richard of Cranleigh - Rapsley [DW/PA/5/1593/28]
Richard of Shalford - Birtley [DW/PA/5/1558/275]*
Richard of Wonersh [DW/PA/7/5 f.223; 1541]
Richard of Wonersh - Haldish, husbandman [DW/PA/5/1579/95]*
Richard of Wonersh - Northcote; Cranleigh, yeoman [HRO: 1596 B68]
Robert of Albury [DW/PA/7/4 f.119; 1535]
Robert of Ewhurst [DW/PA/7/8 f.372; DW/PA/5/1612/157]

TICKNER (TECNER, TEKNOR, TICKNOR, TICNOR, TYCKNOR, TYKENER, TYKNAR, TYKNER, TYKNOR, TYKNOUR) [*continued*]

Robert of Ockley [DW/PA/7/10 f.74; DW/PA/5/1619/117]
Robert of Wonersh [DW/PA/7/8 f.338; DW/PA/5/1612/158]
Stephen of Bramley, yeoman [DW/PA/7/11 f.349; DW/PA/5/1625/251]
Thomas of Thursley, husbandman [DW/PA/7/7 f.554; DW/PA/5/1607/93] <Abs 1038>
Thomas of Wonersh [DW/PA/7/2 f.22; 1491]
Thomas of Wonersh - Haldish, husbandman [DW/PA/5/1557/41]
Thomas of Wonersh [HRO; 1561 B210]
Thomas of Wonersh [HRO; 1568 B216]
Thomas of Wonersh - 'Stackhurst', yeoman, senior [DW/PA/7/9 f.22; DW/PA/5/1614/117]
Thomas of Wonersh [DW/PA/7/13 f.129; DW/PA/5/1640/156]
Thomas of Wonersh, yeoman [DW/PA/7/13 f.194; DW/PA/5/1641/135]
William of Albury; Wonersh; Ewhurst, yeoman [HRO; 1591 B81]
William of Cranleigh [DW/PA/5/1592/66]
William of Cranleigh - Snoxhall, yeoman [DW/PA/7/12 f.468; DW/PA/5/1638/138A]
William of Swk St Saviour, clerk and minister [DW/PA/7/8 f.248; DW/PA/5/1613/129]
William of Wonersh [DW/PA/7/2 f.12; 1491]
William of Wonersh - Haldish, husbandman [DW/PA/7/7 f.218; DW/PA/5/1598/85] <Abs. 386>

TIDY (TEYDYE, TYDE, TYDEY, TYDIE)

Aaron of Ewhurst, husbandman [DW/PA/7/7 f.322; DW/PA/5/1601/79] <Abs 577>
Anthony of Ockley, husbandman [DW/PA/7/7 f.589; DW/PA/5/1607/94] <Abs 1096>
Christian of Alfold [DW/PA/7/6 f.259; 1560]
Davy of Abinger, yeoman [DW/PA/7/11 f.44; DW/PA/5/1623/121]
Edmund of Ockham; Ewhurst; Abinger, husbandman [DW/PA/7/8 f.92; DW/PA/5/1609/117]
Harry of Abinger [DW/PA/5/1568/69]
Hugh of Ewhurst, husbandman [DW/PA/5/1575/18]
Joan, alias Joan Grenefeild of Capel, widow [PRO; PCC Admon 1635]
John of Abinger, yeoman [DW/PA/7/13 f.417; DW/PA/5/1645/55]
John of East Clandon, yeoman [DW/PA/7/12 f.222; DW/PA/5/1634/103]
John of Cranleigh, yeoman [DW/PA/7/7 f.51; DW/PA/5/1596/58] <Abs 95>
John of Ockley [DW/PA/5/1558/277]*
John of Wotton [HRO; 1612 AD94]
Richard of Abinger [PRO; PCC Admon 1599]
Richard of Cranleigh [DW/PA/7/7 f.581; DW/PA/5/1606/99] <Abs 1083>
Richard of Ewhurst [DW/PA/7/6 f.212; 1560]
Richard of Ockley [HRO; 1578 B90]
Robert of Send [DW/PA/7/6 f.281; 1560]
Thomas of Abinger, yeoman [DW/PA/5/1593/27]
Thomas of Abinger, yeoman [DW/PA/7/12 f.475; DW/PA/5/1638/139]
Thomas of Alfold, husbandman [DW/PA/7/8 f.118; DW/PA/5/1610/130]
Thomas of Dunsfold [DW/PA/7/8 f.17; DW/PA/5/1608/106]
Thomas of Godalming - Catteshall, miller [DW/PA/7/13 f.46; DW/PA/5/1639/143]
William of Abinger, husbandman [*in* DW/PA/5/1557/75]
William of Alfold [DW/PA/7/6 f.5; 1559]

TIE *see* TYE

TIERS *see* TYERS
TIFFIN (TIFFYN,TYFFYN)
John of Kingston, brewer [PRO; PCC 1640] [*and* [SRO; KB42/2; 1640]
John of Swk St George [DW/PA/7/4 f.24; 1532]
Robert of Kingston [PRO; PCC Admon 1620]
Thomas of Kingston, gent. [PRO; PCC 1638] [*and*] [SRO; KB42/1; 1638]
TILCOCK (TYLCOCKE)
Margaret of Bermondsey, widow [DW/PA/7/8 f.94; DW/PA/5/1609/118]
TILDEN
John of Lambeth - Kennington [PRO; PCC Will 1585]
TILE (TYLE)
Edward of Woking; Worplesdon; Pirbright, gent. [PRO; PCC Will 1580]
John of Ash, gent. [PRO; PCC Will 1608] <Abs. SAC v.12 pp.108-109>
TILER *see* TYLER
TILFORD (TYLFORD)
Richard of Farnham [HRO; Reg. Way 1 p.29; 1453]
TILL (TYLL)
Thomas of Swk St Olave [DW/PA/7/4 f.52; 1533]
TILLESLEY
John of Egham, husbandman [DW/PA/7/8 f.308; DW/PA/5/1613/130]
TILLEY (TILLY,TILLYE)
Hugh of Witley [PRO; PCC Admon 1639]
Jane of Ewell, widow [DW/PA/7/13 f.412; DW/PA/5/1645/54]
Robert of Godalming, glover [DW/PA/7/11 f.505; DW/PA/5/1629/98]
TILLIER
William of Lambeth [PRO; PCC Will 1626]
TILLING (TULLING)
Nicholas of Rotherhithe, sailor [PRO; PCC Will 1570]
TILLSWORTH (TILLISWORTH,TYLLISWORTH)
John of ... [DW/PA/7/1 f.94; 1489] <Abs 312>
Richard of Sutton [PRO; PCC Will 1500]
TILLY,TILLYE *see* TILLEY
TILNEY (TYLNEY)
Edmund of Leatherhead, master of the King's Office of the Revels, esq. [PRO; PCC Will 1610] <Abs. SAC v.24 pp.66-67>
TILSON
Thomas of Swk St Thomas [DW/PA/7/7 f.415; DW/PA/5/1603/173] <Abs 775>
TILTE (TILTH,TYLTES,TYLTH)
... of Capel [*in* DW/PA/5/1544/9]
John of Capel [DW/PA/7/5 f.105; 1539]
Robert of Capel, husbandman [DW/PA/7/9 f.179; DW/PA/5/1616/141]
Robert of Kingston, bricklayer [DW/PA/7/13 f.31; DW/PA/5/1639/141]
TIMBERTON (TIMERTON,TYMBERDYN,TYMBERTON)
John of Chertsey, labourer [HRO; 1597 B74]
Robert of Merton [DW/PA/7/4 f.171; 1536 *and* 1544] [*A second grant is listed in Campbell Cooke amongst unregistered wills* for 1544, but nothing now appears.*]
William of Windlesham [DW/PA/7/4 f.82; 1534]
TIMES (TYMES)
Giles of ... [DW/PA/7/10 f.34; DW/PA/5/1619/122]
TIMMINGS (TIMINGS)
William of Swk St Saviour, blacksmith [DW/PA/7/11 f.154; DW/PA/5/1625/255]

TIMPERLEY (TYMPERLEY)
Leonard of Kingston [PRO; PCC Will 1577]
TINDALL (TYNDALL)
Amy of Ewhurst [PRO; PCC Admon 1647]
George of Swk St Saviour; the Ship *Swan*, sailor [DW/PA/7/13 f.402; DW/PA/5/1645/57]
Isabel of Swk St Olave, widow [DW/PA/7/7 f.553; DW/PA/5/1606/96] <Abs 1037>
John of Mortlake, citizen and pewterer [PRO; PCC Will 1627]
Richard of Rotherhithe (died overseas) [PRO; PCC Admon 1645]
Thomas of Mortlake, cordwainer [LPL; 96/2599; 98/1 f.25v; Will 1631]
TINES (TYNES)
Arnold of Swk St Olave [DW/PA/5/1581/27]
TINGLE
Thomas of Swk St George [DW/PA/7/11 f.127; DW/PA/5/1624/124]
TINGLEDON (TYNGELDEN,TYNGYLDEN)
Harry of Reigate [DW/PA/7/2 f.158; 1521]
John of Reigate [PRO; PCC Will 1551]
TINNICQ *see* van TINNICQ
TINNY (TYNNY)
John of Windlesham - Bagshot [PRO; PCC Will 1531]
TIPPIN
William of Swk St Mary Overy, surveyor [DW/PA/5/1588/40]
TIPTON
John of West Clandon, clerk [DW/PA/7/10 f.253; DW/PA/5/1622/104]
TIRO (TYROE)
Elizabeth of Wandsworth, widow [PRO; PCC Will 1624]
John of Wandsworth, citizen and draper [PRO; PCC Will 1605]
TIRRELL (TYRELL,TYRRELL)
Charles of Kingston, esq., queen's gentleman pensioner [PRO; PCC Will 1570]
John of Burstow; Croydon [PRO; PCC Will 1580]
John of Burstow [PRO; PCC Will 1580]
John of Dorking [PRO; PCC Will 1604] <Abs. SAC v.11 p.130>
John of Stoke Dabernon, husbandman [DW/PA/7/13 f.12; DW/PA/5/1639/137]
Richard of Lambeth, yeoman [PRO; PCC Will 1608] <Abs. SAC v.13 p.178>
Richard of Stoke Dabernon, esq. [PRO; PCC Will 1431] <Abs. SAC v.51 p.92>
Thomas of Burstow [PRO; PCC 1638]
William of Croydon [PRO; PCC Will 1569]
see also TERRELL
TIRREY (TYRRY)
Richard of Long Sutton, Hampshire; Farnham, yeoman [DW/PA/5/1550/63]
Richard of Blechingley - South Park, yeoman [DW/PA/7/8 f.328; DW/PA/5/1613/127]
TISE *see* TICE
TISER *see* TYSER
TISON *see* TYSON
TISSARD
Agnes of Swk St Saviour, widow [DW/PA/7/9 f.146; DW/PA/5/1615/135]
TITLEY
Francis of Swk St George, baker [DW/PA/7/12 f.335; DW/PA/5/1636/96]

TOBYE

Silvester of Swk St Olave, citizen and haberdasher [DW/PA/7/7 f.628; DW/PA/5/1608/107] <Abs 1174>

TOCOTES

Robert of Lambeth [PRO; PCC Will 1504]

TODD

Brian of Bermondsey, citizen and draper [DW/PA/7/11 f.267; DW/PA/5/1625/252]

Camilla of Swk St Saviour, widow [DW/PA/7/10 f.53; 1618]

Richard of Horley [DW/PA/7/2 f.162; 1521]

TODDIE

John, alias John Farrell of Windlesham - Bagshot [HRO; 1593 AD88]

TODHAM

William of Blechingley; Horne [HRO; 1576 B89]

TOFT

John of St Martha's - Chilworth, gent. [PRO; PCC Will 1599]

TOGOOD *see* TOOGOOD

TOLL

John of Surrey [PRO; PCC Will 1517]

TOLLY

Elizabeth of West Horsley, widow of Robert [DW/PA/7/10 f.198; DW/PA/5/1621/122]

William of Newington [LPL; 96/2602; 98/1 f.12r; Will 1630]

TOLSON

William of ... [DW/PA/5/1561/23]

TOLWIN (TOLWYN)

John of Streatham [PRO; PCC Will 1584]

TOLWORTH (TALWORTH)

Joan of Carshalton, widow of John, citizen and woodmonger [GL; Commissary Court of London Will 1427]

William of Harrow on the Hill, Middlesex [DW/PA/7/2 f.54; 1496]

TOLYMONDE

William of Lambeth - Lambeth Marsh [LPL; Reg. Abp Stafford f.171; Will 1449]

TOMELL *see* TUMMELL

TOMKIS

Edward of Bermondsey, tanner [PRO; PCC Will 1616]

TOMLIN (TOMLINS,TOMLYN)

Emma of Swk St Mary Magdalen, widow [DW/PA/5/1588/34]

John of Swk St Olave, citizen and leatherseller [DW/PA/5/1568/18]

Richard of Richmond, esq. [PRO; PCC Admon 1651 - *but in 1631-1649 volume*]

TOMLINSON (THOMPLINSON,TOMLYNSON)

William of Kingston, yeoman [DW/PA/5/1578/22]

William of Swk St George [DW/PA/7/3 f.196; 1532]

TOMLYN *see* TOMLIN

TOMLYNSON *see* TOMLINSON

TOMPSON,TOMSON *see* THOMPSON

TONBRIDGE *see* TUNBRIDGE

TONGE

Francis of Swk St Olave, mariner [DW/PA/7/13 f.451; DW/PA/5/1646/57]

TONSTALL *see* TUNSTALL

TOOGOOD (TOGOOD)

Thomas of Swk St Mary Overy, yeoman [DW/PA/7/2 f.59; 1499]

TOOKE (TUKE)
Richard of Croydon [PRO; PCC Will 1499]
TOOKEY (TOOKIE)
Job of Mortlake, clerk [PRO; PCC 1638]
John of Newington [PRO; PCC Admon 1647]
TOOLEY
Nicholas of Surrey, yeoman [Ipswich and East Suffolk Record Office; Archdeaconry Court of Suffolk 1601 Ref.R38/429; W37/91]
TOOTH (TOOTHE)
Andrew of Reigate, yeoman [DW/PA/5/1588/84]
John of Mickleham, husbandman [HRO; 1590 B64]
John of Mickleham, gent. [PRO; PCC 1647]
John, alias John Stowth of Swk St George, haberdasher [DW/PA/5/1576/73]
Richard of Mickleham [PRO; PCC Admon 1634]
Richard of Reigate, husbandman [DW/PA/5/1578/64]
TOPPES *see* TOPPS
TOPPIN (TOPPYN)
Christopher of Swk St Saviour, waterman [DW/PA/7/9 f.31; DW/PA/5/1614/118]
Robert of Woking [DW/PA/7/10 f.15; DW/PA/5/1616/143]
TOPPS (TOPPES)
Dorothy of Putney; Wandsworth, widow [PRO; PCC Will 1580]
Thomas of Newington [PRO; PCC Admon 1615]
TOPPYN *see* TOPPIN
TOPSELL
Henry of Godstone; Lingfield, wheelwright [DW/PA/7/8 f.292; DW/PA/5/1613/132]
see also TAPSELL
TORFOTT
Lewis of Lambeth [BM; Add.Ms 24,925 f.14v; 1544] <Abs 29>
TORLESSE
Adam of Lambeth [PRO; PCC 1641]
TORLEY
William of Godstone [HRO; 1624 AD123]
TORNER,TORNOR *see* TURNER
TORRELL *see* TERRELL
TOTTELL
Robert *or* Robert Tuttell of Swk St Mary Overy [DW/PA/5/1593/59]
TOTTY
Hugh of Thorpe [PRO; PCC Admon 1611]
TOURNER *see* TURNER
TOUT le MONDE
Marguerite De Pau of Swk St Olave, widow of Gilbert [DW/PA/5/1593/144]
TOWELL (TOWELLE)
Elizabeth of Swk St Saviour [DW/PA/7/7 f.574;DW/PA/5/1606/97] <Abs 1073>
Isaac of Swk St Saviour - liberty of Old Paris Garden, one of the king's watermen [DW/PA/7/9 f.155; DW/PA/5/1615/136]
John of Nutfield [DW/PA/5/1552/4]
Margaret of Swk St Saviour - liberty of Old Paris Garden [DW/PA/7/11 f.447; DW/PA/5/1628/104]
TOWERS
John of Chobham, tailor [HRO; 1641 B45]
Phillip of Cobham, husbandman [DW/PA/7/12 f.299; DW/PA/5/1635/119]

TOWLESBURIE
  John of Swk St George, labourer [DW/PA/5/1570/2]
TOWLLER
  Denise of Tatsfield, widow [HRO; 1585 B67]
TOWNSEND (TOWNESEND,TOWNESENDE,TOWNSEN,TOWNSON)
  Ann, alias Ann Ripley of Newington, widow of William [LPL; 98/1 f.65v; Will 1635]
  Ann of Lambeth [PRO; PCC Admon 1647]
  Christopher of Kingston, clothworker [PRO; PCC Will 1575] [*and*] [DW/PA/5/1575/12]
  Joanna of Kingston, widow [PRO; PCC Admon 1580]
  (Sir) John of Lambeth, knight [PRO; PCC Admon 1632]
  Reynold of Swk St Olave, feltmaker [DW/PA/7/7 f.434; DW/PA/5/1603/175] <Abs 821>
  Richard of Swk St Olave, shoemaker [DW/PA/7/7 f.427; DW/PA/5/1603/176] <Abs 800>
  Robert of Chipping Wycombe, Buckinghamshire, milliner [DW/PA/7/10 f.69; 1618]
  William of Thorpe, yeoman [PRO; PCC Will 1578]
TRACY
  Hugh of St Mary Abchurch, London; Cheam, chaplain [LPL; Reg. Abp Courteney f.199; Will 1382]
TRADEWY
  William of Swk St Thomas Hospital [DW/PA/7/2 f.55; 1498]
TRANKMORE (TRANCKMORE)
  John of Bermondsey [PRO; PCC Admon 1640]
  Robert of Bermondsey [PRO; PCC 1640]
TRAPPS (TRAPPES,TREAPE)
  Frances of Battersea, widow [PRO; PCC Will 1617]
  Frances of Battersea, widow [DW/PA/7/9 f.214; DW/PA/5/1617/124]
  Henry of Swk St George, citizen and grocer [DW/PA/7/7 f.457; DW/PA/5/1603/177] <Abs 861>
  Jane of Bermondsey, widow [PRO; PCC 1633]
  Joan of Banstead, widow [PRO; PCC Will 1563]
  Robert of Surrey, esq. [PRO; PCC Will 1587]
  Robert of Cheam, esq. [PRO; PCC Will 1623]
  Roger of Cheam, gent. [PRO; PCC Will 1616]
  Rowland of Battersea, citizen and mercer [PRO; PCC Will 1616]
  Thomas of Bermondsey [PRO; PCC 1638]
  William of Lingfield, yeoman [DW/PA/7/13 f.35; DW/PA/5/1640/151]
TRAPPYN
  William of Merton, yeoman [DW/PA/5/1578/29]
TRAUGHTON *see* TROUGHTON
TRAVELL
  Richard of Swk St Thomas [DW/PA/7/12 f.271; DW/PA/5/1635/117]
TRAVIS (TRAVERS,TRAVES,TREAVICE)
  Ann, alias Ann Wright of Streatham - Tooting Bec [PRO; PCC Admon 1585]
  Christopher of Chaldon [PRO; PCC Will 1526]
  Edmund of Battersea [DW/PA/5/1575/89]
  John of Clapham, citizen and merchant tailor [PRO; PCC Will 1570]
  Margaret of Reigate; Chaldon, widow [DW/PA/7/5 f.56; 1539] <Abs 73>
TRAYMAINE *see* TREMAINE
TREADESKANT *see* TREDESCANT
TREAPE *see* TRAPPS

TREDCROFTE
  Robert of Guildford, woollen draper [DW/PA/5/1576/79]
  William of Guildford [PRO; PCC Will 1593 *and* 1594]
TREDESCANT (TREADESKANT)
  John of Lambeth - South Lambeth [PRO; PCC 1638]
TREENE
  Edmund of Swk St George, citizen and alebrewer [DW/PA/7/7 f.486;
    DW/PA/5/1604/64] <Abs 918>
TREHERNE
  John of Merton [PRO; PCC Admon 1583]
TREMAINE (TRAYMAINE)
  William of Cobham, yeoman [GL; Commissary Court of London Will 1558]
TREMLETT (TRUMPLET,TRUMPLUTT)
  Elizabeth of Frensham, widow [DW/PA/7/12 f.101; DW/PA/5/1632/107]
  Richard of Guildford [DW/PA/7/8 f.144; DW/PA/5/1611/115]
TRENTAM
  Richard of Swk, butcher [DW/PA/5/1580/17]
TRESSE
  (Sir) Thomas of Battersea, knight [PRO; PCC Admon 1635]
TREVER
  Edward of Bookham [PRO; PCC Admon 1649]
  Margery of Bermondsey [DW/PA/5/1571/67]
TREVET
  Thomas of Woking [DW/PA/7/1 f.11; 1485] <Abs 38>
TREVI
  William of Swk St Saviour [DW/PA/5/1593/160]
TREW
  William of Tandridge; Horley [DW/PA/7/4 f.11; 1532]
TREWYN
  Henry of Woolwich, Kent; Chipstead [LPL; Reg. Abp Chichele i f.349;
    Will 1421]
TRIBE (TRIBBE)
  John of Farnham, yeoman [DW/PA/7/12 f.27; DW/PA/5/1631/111]
  Richard of Godalming, weaver [DW/PA/7/9 f.55; DW/PA/5/1614/119]
TRIDDLE
  Mercy of Pirbright [DW/PA/7/11 f.547; DW/PA/5/1629/99]
TRIGG (TRIGGE,TRYGE,TRYGGE)
  Edward of Dorking [DW/PA/7/11 f.451; DW/PA/5/1628/105]
  Elizabeth of Woking, spinster [PRO; PCC Admon 1635]
  John of Frensham, husbandman [DW/PA/5/1605/88] <Abs U174>
  John of Godalming - Shackleford, husbandman [DW/PA/7/8 f.164;
    DW/PA/5/1611/114]
  Robert of Farnham - Wrecclesham, husbandman [DW/PA/7/8 f.350;
    DW/PA/5/1612/159]
  Thomas of Frensham, husbandman [DW/PA/5/1593/95]
  Thomas of Frensham, yeoman [DW/PA/7/8 f.363; DW/PA/5/1612/160]
  Thomas of Frensham, yeoman [DW/PA/7/12 f.303; DW/PA/5/1635/120]
  William of Woking [DW/PA/7/5 f.198; 1540]
TRIMNELL (TRYMNELL)
  Stephen of Newington [PRO; PCC Admon 1616]
TROCHES
  James of Barnes, gent. [PRO; PCC Admon 1627]

TROUGHTON (TRAUGHTON,TROWGHTON)
James of Lambeth - Lambeth Dean [DW/PA/7/7 f,441; DW/PA/5/1603/178] <Abs 834>
John of Lambeth, waterman [DW/PA/7/10 f,12; DW/PA/5/1619/120]
Thomas of Stoke Dabernon [DW/PA/7/1 f,5; 1484] <Abs 15>
TROUT (TROWTE)
Richard of Wandsworth, yeoman usher to the queen [PRO; PCC Will 1579]
TROWE
Edward of Egham [PRO; PCC Admon 1605]
TROWELL
William of Swk St Olave [DW/PA/7/4 f,209; 1537]
TROWERE (TRYWE)
Lance of Godalming [DW/PA/7/1 f,17; 1485] <Abs 55>
Richard of Peper Harow [DW/PA/7/1 f,13; 1485] <Abs 43>
TROWGHTON *see* TROUGHTON
TROWTE *see* TROUT
TRUBBE
Arnold of Swk St Olave [DW/PA/7/2 f,73; 1500]
TRULLEY
Rose of Swk St George [DW/PA/7/10 f,275; DW/PA/5/1621/123]
TRUMPLET,TRUMPLUTT *see* TREMLETT
TRUSSE
William of Merton, labourer [DW/PA/7/6 f,91; DW/PA/5/1559/112]
TRUSSELL
Edward of Bermondsey - Bermondsey Monastery [PRO; PCC Will 1507]
Robert of London, citizen and merchant tailor [DW/PA/5/1576/116]
TRY
John of St Leonard Eastcheap, London; Rotherhithe [PRO; PCC Admon 1642]
TRYGE,TRYGGE *see* TRIGG
TRYMNELL *see* TRIMNELL
TRYWE *see* TROWERE
TUBB
Anna of Croydon, widow [PRO; PCC Will 1629]
TUB'YE
John of Swk St Olave [DW/PA/5/1546/66]
TUBMAN
Edmund of Chertsey, butcher [DW/PA/7/8 f,136; DW/PA/5/1610/128]
John of Thorpe [PRO; PCC Will 1589]
John of Walton on the Hill, yeoman, senior [DW/PA/7/13 f,208; DW/PA/5/1642/84]
Thomas of Reigate [DW/PA/5/1604/65] <Abs U121>
TUCKE
Bridget of Battersea, widow [DW/PA/5/1605/92] <Abs U176>
see also TURKE
TUCKER (TUCKERD)
Agnes of ...., widow of Alexander [DW/PA/7/8 f,384; DW/PA/5/1612/161]
Agnes of Swk St Olave, widow [DW/PA/7/9 f,252; DW/PA/5/1617/125]
Alice of Wonersh, widow [DW/PA/7/7 f,286; DW/PA/5/1599/100] <Abs 511>
David of Egham, tailor [DW/PA/5/1593/49]
Dorothy of Limpsfield, widow [DW/PA/7/13 f,486; DW/PA/5/1648/45]
Henry of Lingfield, carpenter [DW/PA/7/12 f,182; DW/PA/5/1633/118]
Hugh of Swk St Saviour, waterman [DW/PA/7/7 f,339; DW/PA/5/1601/80] <Abs 613>
John of Chertsey [DW/PA/7/4 f,121; 1535]

TUCKER (TUCKERD) [*continued*]
John of Egham [DW/PA/7/12 f.20; DW/PA/5/1631/110]
John of Godalming, weaver [PRO; PCC Will 1617]
Morgan of Wandsworth [PRO; PCC Admon 1641]
Thomas of Egham, husbandman [DW/PA/5/1593/50]
Walter of ... [DW/PA/7/8 f.138; DW/PA/5/1610/127]
TUCKEY
Justinian of Swk St Olave, citizen and poulterer [DW/PA/7/11 f.120; DW/PA/5/1624/125]
TUDHAM
Richard of Dorking; Westerham, Kent, butcher [DW/PA/5/1605/91]
TUE *see* TEWE
TUESLEY (TEWESLEY, TEWSELY, TEWSLEY, TEWYSLEY, TUESLIE, TUYSLAY, TWERSLYE, TWYSLAYE)
Alice of Godalming, widow [DW/PA/7/3 f.186; 1531]
Elizabeth of Guildford, widow [DW/PA/5/1586/26]
Hugh of Worplesdon - Burpham; Stoke next Guildford; Merrow, husbandman [DW/PA/7/8 f.89; DW/PA/5/1609/116]
John of Guildford [PRO; PCC Will 1592]
John of Witley - Lea [DW/PA/7/6 f.253; 1560]
Leonard of Great Bookham, yeoman [DW/PA/7/7 f.282; DW/PA/5/1599/79] <Abs 502>
Richard of Cranleigh [DW/PA/7/1 f.10; 1485] <Abs 33>
Thomas of Guildford [PRO; PCC Will 1573]
Thomas of Guildford, gent. [DW/PA/7/13 f.41; DW/PA/5/1639/142]
Thomas of Witley, senior [DW/PA/7/7 f.590; DW/PA/5/1607/95 *and* DW/PA/5/1607/96] <Abs 1100>
William of Chiddingfold, husbandman [HRO; 1589 B57]
William of Farnham [DW/PA/7/5 f.221; 1541] [incomplete]
William of Witley [DW/PA/7/11 f.529; DW/PA/5/1630/107]
TUFNELL (TUFNAYLE)
Richard of Clapham, citizen and brewer [PRO; PCC 1640]
TUKE *see* TOOKE
TULLY (TULLEY)
Agnes of Guildford, widow [DW/PA/7/6 f.135; DW/PA/5/1559/35]
Hugh of Guildford Holy Trinity; Stoke next Guildford, glover [DW/PA/7/6 f.1; DW/PA/5/1559/146]
John of Horley, husbandman [DW/PA/7/7 f.15; DW/PA/5/1595/83] <Abs 33>
John of Horley, yeoman [DW/PA/7/13 f.372; 1644]
Margaret of Horley, widow [DW/PA/7/7 f.643; DW/PA/5/1608/108] <Abs 1208>
Nicholas of Horley, yeoman [DW/PA/7/10 f.193; DW/PA/5/1621/124]
TULLING *see* TILLING
TUMMELL (TOMELL, TUMWELL)
Edward of Newington [LPL; 96/2625; Will 1615]
Henry of Kingston [DW/PA/5/1568/32]
Joan of Kingston, widow [DW/PA/5/1571/88]
Thomas of Long Ditton, husbandman [HRO; 1610 B73]
TUNBRIDGE (TUNEBRYGGE)
Hugh of Mortlake [DW/PA/7/2 f.33; 1492]
John of Kingston, saddler [DW/PA/7/13 f.24; DW/PA/5/1639/140]
TUNNELL (TANNELL, TUNNILL)
William of Reigate [DW/PA/7/9 f.271; 1618]

TUNSTALL (TONSTALL, TOUNSTALL)
Christopher of Peper Harow, clerk [DW/PA/7/9 f.223; DW/PA/5/1617/123]
John, alias John Donnestale of Swk St Saviour, tailor [DW/PA/5/1582/92]
William of Camberwell - Dulwich; Bradfield [? county] [DW/PA/7/4 f.114; 1535]
TURGES
Jane of Lambeth [GL; Commissary Court of London Will 1472]
TURKE
Bridget of Battersea, widow [DW/PA/5/1605/93] <Abs U177>
Richard of Battersea, citizen and fishmonger [PRO; PCC Will 1570]
Robert of Betchworth - Brockham [PRO; PCC Will 1516]
see also TUCKE
TURNER (TORNER, TOURNER, TURNOR)
Andrew of Horne, carpenter [DW/PA/7/12 f.322; DW/PA/5/1637/95]
Andrew of Lambeth, notary [PRO; PCC 1635]
Cyril of Wimbledon [LPL; 98/1 f.56r; Will 1634]
Elizabeth of Betchworth, widow [DW/PA/5/1576/20]
Francis of Ockham, widower [PRO; PCC Admon 1648]
George of Lingfield, gent. [DW/PA/7/11 f.269; DW/PA/5/1625/253]
George of Lingfield, esq. [DW/PA/7/12 f.402; DW/PA/5/1638/138B]
Henry of Compton, yeoman [DW/PA/7/13 f.102; DW/PA/5/1640/152]
Henry of Compton, yeoman [DW/PA/7/13 f.244; 1640]
Henry of Farnham, fuller [DW/PA/5/1570/19]
Henry of Lambeth [DW/PA/7/4 f.193; 1537]
(Sir) Jeremy of Camberwell, knight [DW/PA/7/11 f.100; DW/PA/5/1624/126]
Joan of Godalming, widow [DW/PA/7/1 f.25; 1486] <Abs 82>
Joan of Kingston - Ham, widow [DW/PA/5/1558/276]
John of Blechingley [DW/PA/7/2 f.36; 1493]
John of Blechingley, esq. [DW/PA/7/7 f.594; DW/PA/5/1607/97] <Abs 1109>
John of Blechingley - West Blechingley [PRO; PCC Admon 1649]
John of Blechingley [PRO; PCC 1648]
John of Chertsey [DW/PA/5/1616/132]
John of Compton, husbandman [*in* DW/PA/5/1555/68]
John of Compton - Polsted [DW/PA/7/8 f.391; DW/PA/5/1612/162]
John of Compton, yeoman [HRO; 1639 B67]
John of Compton, husbandman [DW/PA/7/13 ff.106,111; DW/PA/5/1640/154]
John of Farnham, shearman [DW/PA/5/1563/4]
John of Farnham, yeoman [HRO; 1621 B58]
John of Frimley; Ash [DW/PA/7/3 f.101; 1529]
John of Kingston, yeoman [DW/PA/7/4 f.89; 1534]
John of Kingston [PRO; PCC Admon 1613]
John of Kingston - Ham House [PRO; PCC Admon 1649]
John of St Martha's - Tyting, husbandman [DW/PA/5/1576/80]
John of Seale [DW/PA/7/7 f.87; 1596] <Abs 160>
John of Seale - Tongham, husbandman [HRO; 1629 B62]
John of Swk St Saviour, shoemaker [DW/PA/7/11 f.220; DW/PA/5/1625/254]
Leonard of Guildford [PRO; PCC Admon 1562]
Margaret of Compton - Polsted, widow of John [DW/PA/7/11 f.545; DW/PA/5/1629/100]
Margaret of Swk St Saviour; Swk St Mary Overy, widow [DW/PA/7/9 f.24; DW/PA/5/1614/120]
Mercy of Lingfield, widow [PRO; PCC 1639]
Nicholas of Newington [PRO; PCC 1636]

TURNER (TORNER, TOURNER, TURNOR) [*continued*]

Ralph of Swk St Olave, beer brewer [DW/PA/7/7 f.2; DW/PA/5/1595/85] <Abs 4>

Richard of Thames Ditton [PRO; PCC 1642]

Richard of Witley [PRO; PCC Admon 1645]

Robert of Chertsey, citizen and fuller [DW/PA/7/5 f.15; 1538] <Abs 20>

Robert of Horley; Worth, Sussex [DW/PA/7/7 f.162; DW/PA/5/1597/102] <Abs 300>

Robert of Newington [PRO; PCC Admon 1611]

Roger of Kingston; Petersham; Esher, yeoman [DW/PA/7/5 f.67; 1539] <Abs 56>

Thomas of Compton [DW/PA/7/6 f.101; DW/PA/5/1559/90]

Thomas of Compton [HRO; 1575 B88]

Thomas of Farnham [PRO; PCC 1633]

Thomas of Lingfield, yeoman [DW/PA/7/8 f.126; DW/PA/5/1610/129]

Thomas of Mickleham; Dorking [DW/PA/7/7 f.329; DW/PA/5/1601/81] <Abs 590>

Thomas of Shalford [DW/PA/7/1 f.54; 1487] <Abs 179>

Thomas of Swk St George [DW/PA/7/11 f.548; DW/PA/5/1629/101]

Walter of Horsell; Bisley [DW/PA/7/8 f.312; DW/PA/5/1613/133]

William of Blechingley [DW/PA/5/1591/62]

William, alias William Silver, of Chiddingfold, husbandman [DW/PA/7/11 f.41; DW/PA/5/1623/122]

William of Compton, yeoman [DW/PA/7/13 f.202; DW/PA/5/1642/82]

William of Newington, citizen and woodmonger [LPL; 96/2629; 98/1 f.26r; Will 1626]

William of Petersham, yeoman [DW/PA/7/11 f.589; DW/PA/5/1630/108]

William of Swk St Saviour, baker [DW/PA/7/7 f.143; DW/PA/5/1597/103] <Abs 263>

TURNEY

John of Swk St Saviour, cheesemonger, senior [DW/PA/7/12 f.310; DW/PA/5/1636/95]

TURSWELL

Thomas of Lambeth, steward of the household of the archbishop of Canterbury [PRO; PCC Will 1583]

TUTT

John of Swk St Olave, feltmaker [DW/PA/7/12 f.286; DW/PA/5/1636/94]

William of Blechingley, husbandman [DW/PA/7/12 f.482; DW/PA/5/1638/142]

TWERSLYE *see* TUESLEY

TWETCHETT *see* TWITCHETT

TWICROFTE *see* TWYCROSS

TWIGDEN

John of Swk St George, miller [DW/PA/7/7 f.149; DW/PA/5/1597/104] <Abs 277>

TWIGG (TWYGGE)

Robert of Surrey [PRO; PCC Will 1491]

TWINE (TWYNE)

Alice of Stoke Dabernon [DW/PA/7/11 f.538; DW/PA/5/1629/102]

Anthony of Walton on Thames [PRO; PCC Admon 1628]

William of Stoke Dabernon - Oxshott, carpenter [DW/PA/7/8 f.95; DW/PA/5/1609/119]

TWINER (TWYNER)

Thomas of Godstone, yeoman [DW/PA/5/1576/11]

TWINNYHOO (TWYNYHOO)
  Margaret (formerly Margaret Carewe, and Margaret Carant) of Beddington [PRO; PCC Will 1501]
TWISDEN
  (Dame) Ann of Camberwell - Peckham, widow of (Sir) William, baronet [PRO; PCC 1638]
TWISSELL
  Alice of Swk St Margaret, widow of John [DW/PA/7/4 f.160; 1536]
TWITCHETT (TWETCHETT)
  Adam of Egham [DW/PA/5/1605/94] <Abs U178>
TWYCROSS (TWICRAFT,TWYCRASTE)
  Edward of Cranleigh, yeoman [DW/PA/7/7 f.468; DW/PA/5/1604/66] <Abs 882>
  John of West Horsley [PRO; PCC Will 1594]
TWYFORDE
  John of Shalford, gent. [DW/PA/5/1569/3]
TWYGGE *see* TWIGG
TWYNE *see* TWINE
TWYNER *see* TWINER
TWYNYHOO *see* TWINNYHOO
TWYSLAYE *see* TUESLEY
TYAS *see* TYERS
TYBBOLDE,TYBBOLL *see* TIBBOLD
TYBBOTT *see* TEBBUTT
TYCE *see* TICE
TYCHEBURNE *see* TICHBOURN
TYCKNAR,TYCKNOR *see* TICKNER
TYDE,TYDIE,TYDY,TYDYE *see* TIDY
TYFFYN *see* TIFFIN
TYCKNER,TYCKNOR *see* TICKNER
TYE (TIE)
  Elizabeth of Newdigate [PRO; PCC 1632 *and* 1634 Sentence]
  George of Croydon, blacksmith [PRO; PCC Will 1628]
  George of Sutton, yeoman [DW/PA/7/8 f.24; DW/PA/5/1608/109]
  Joan of Sutton, widow [DW/PA/7/11 f.41; DW/PA/5/1623/123]
  John of Godstone [PRO; PCC Admon 1629]
  John of Horley [DW/PA/7/2 f.32; 1494]
  Mary of Sutton, spinster [DW/PA/7/11 f.125; DW/PA/5/1624/127]
  Ralph of Richmond, butcher [DW/PA/7/7 f.138; DW/PA/5/1597/105] <Abs 254>
  Roger of Merton [PRO; PCC Will 1429]
  Thomas of Cheam [LPL; 96/2642; Will 1624]
  William of Banstead [DW/PA/5/1575/11]
TYERS (TIERS,TYAS)
  John of Bermondsey [DW/PA/7/11 f.536; DW/PA/5/1629/103]
  Robert of Battersea, esq. [PRO; PCC Will 1620] <Soame 559>
  Samuel of Bermondsey, leatherseller [DW/PA/7/7 f.463; DW/PA/5/1603/172] <Abs 876>
TYKENER *see* TICKNER
TYKHULL *see* TICKLE
TYKNAR,TYKNER,TYKNOR,TYKNOUR *see* TICKNER
TYLAR *see* TYLER
TYLCOCKE *see* TILCOCK
TYLE *see* TILE

TYLER (TILER,TYLAR,TYLOR)
Edward of Nutfield [PRO; PCC 1649]
Edward of Walton on the Hill, clerk [DW/PA/7/13 f.127; DW/PA/5/1640/155]
Henry of Cheam [PRO; PCC 1632]
Joan, alias Joan Taylor of Esher, widow [DW/PA/7/11 ff.11,38; DW/PA/5/1623/124]
Joan of Esher, widow [DW/PA/7/11 f.38; 1623]
John of Nutfield, husbandman [DW/PA/7/12 f.500; DW/PA/5/1638/143]
Katherine of Bermondsey, widow [DW/PA/7/10 f.111; DW/PA/5/1619/118]
Nicholas of Blechingley [DW/PA/5/1558/278]*
Nicholas of Esher [DW/PA/7/8 f.169; DW/PA/5/1610/131]
Richard of Chipstead, yeoman [DW/PA/7/10 f.151; DW/PA/5/1621/125]
Thomas of Nutfield [PRO; PCC 1649]
William of Gatton, yeoman [DW/PA/7/13 f.190; DW/PA/5/1641/133]
William of Newington, victualler [LPL; 96/2644; 98/1 f.60v; Will 1634]
William of Reigate, bachelor [PRO; PCC Admon 1649]
(Sir) William of Richmond, knight [PRO; PCC Will 1527]
TYLFORD *see* TILFORD
TYLL *see* TILL
TYLLISWORTH *see* TILLSWORTH
TYLNEY *see* TILNEY
TYLTES,TYLTH *see* TILTE
TYMBERDYN,TYMBERTON *see* TIMBERTON
TYMES *see* TIMES
TYMPERLEY *see* TIMPERLEY
TYNDALL *see* TINDALL
TYNGELDEN,TYNGYLDEN *see* TINGLEDEN
TYNNY *see* TINNY
TYPRE
Antoine of ... [*French*] [*Latin*] [DW/PA/5/1562/22]
TYRELL *see* TIRRELL
TYROE *see* TIRO
TYRRELL *see* TIRRELL
TYRRY *see* TIRREY
TYSE *see* TICE,TYERS
TYSEN *see* TYSON
TYSER (TISER)
Daniel of Shalford [DW/PA/7/11 f.597; DW/PA/5/1630/106]
TYSON (TYSEN)
James, alias James Studd of Camberwell (died overseas) [PRO; PCC Admon 1638]
John of Egham, gent. [DW/PA/7/7 f.592; DW/PA/5/1607/98] <Abs 1107>
TYTE
... of ... [*in* DW/PA/5/1592/19]*
Robert of Kingston, one of the children of the king's Privy Kitchen [DW/PA/5/1588/45]
TYTON
William of Swk St Saviour, waterman [DW/PA/7/7 f.374; DW/PA/5/1602/87] <Abs 689>

UBLEY (UBLY)
Henry of Chobham [PRO; PCC 1648]
Margaret of Chobham [PRO; PCC Admon 1640]
Thomas of Chobham, widower [PRO; PCC Admon 1648]
UDALL (UDALE)
Robert of ... [DW/PA/5/1576/97]
Robert of Witley [DW/PA/5/1558/279]*
UDE *see* EDE
UMFREY,UMPFREY *see* HUMPHREYS
UNDEREECK *see* UNDERWICK
UNDERHILL (UNDERHELD,UNDERHYLL,UNDIRHILL,UNDRELL)
Arthur of Crowhurst, yeoman [DW/PA/7/13 f.32; DW/PA/5/1639/144]
Edward of Lingfield, tanner [DW/PA/5/1558/280]*
Edward of Lingfield, tanner [DW/PA/7/12 f.346; DW/PA/5/1636/101]
Ellen of Lingfield, widow [DW/PA/5/1581/19]
Francis of Lingfield, tanner [PRO; PCC Will 1583]
Francis of Lingfield, bachelor [DW/PA/7/9 f.301; DW/PA/5/1619/121]
John of Lingfield [HRO; Reg. Fox 2 p.30; 1507]
John of Lingfield [DW/PA/7/5 f.135; 1540]
John of Lingfield, tanner [DW/PA/7/5 f.124; 1540]
John of Lingfield - Blackberry Street [PRO; PCC Will 1580]
Maud of Lambeth [PRO; PCC Will 1482]
Nicholas of Lingfield, yeoman [DW/PA/7/8 f.360; DW/PA/5/1612/163]
Thomas of Lingfield [DW/PA/7/4 f.203; 1537]
Thomas of Lingfield [DW/PA/5/1563/60]
Thomas of Lingfield, tanner [DW/PA/7/11 f.6; DW/PA/5/1622/105]
Thomas of Lingfield - Blackberry Street, yeoman [DW/PA/7/11 f.169; DW/PA/5/1625/256]
William of Lingfield [DW/PA/7/1 f.58; 1487] <Abs 194>
William of Swk St Saviour, victualler [DW/PA/7/12 f.261; DW/PA/5/1635/121]
UNDERWICK (UNDEREECK)
John of Swk St Olave; 'Eemeriick', Cleves, Netherlands [DW/PA/5/1543/4]*
UNDERWOOD (UNDERWOD,UNDERWOODDE,UNDERWOODE)
Agnes of Worplesdon, widow [HRO; 1585 B69]
John of Worplesdon [DW/PA/7/4 f.211; 1537]
John of Worplesdon, yeoman [DW/PA/7/11 f.139; DW/PA/5/1624/128]
Lawrence of Stoke next Guildford [DW/PA/7/8 f.139; DW/PA/5/1610/132]
Thomas of Bisley [HRO; 1585 B70]
Thomas of Lambeth [PRO; PCC Admon 1605]
Thomas of Pyrford, husbandman [HRO; 1632 B56]
Thomas of Worplesdon [DW/PA/7/6 f.173; DW/PA/5/1559/185]
William of Guildford St Nicolas - Artington [PRO; PCC Will 1597]
see also UNSWORTH
UNDRELL *see* UNDERHILL
UNGILL *see* ANGELL
UNMAN (VNMAN)
John of Swk St Olave, butcher [DW/PA/7/3 f.194; 1531]
UNSTEAD (UNSTEDE)
Joan of Addington, widow [DW/PA/5/1578/31]
UNSWORTH
Edward of Bisley,husbandman [DW/PA/7/7 f.595; DW/PA/5/1607/99] <Abs 1115>
see also UNDERWOOD

UPFOLD (UPFOLDE,UPFOULDE,UPPOLL)
Thomas of Cranleigh [DW/PA/7/4 f,81; 1534]
Thomas of Frensham, husbandman [DW/PA/7/7 f,158; DW/PA/5/1597/106] <Abs 293>
Thomas of Hascombe [DW/PA/7/5 f,110; 1539]
William of Cranleigh [DW/PA/7/4 f,103; DW/PA/5/1534/1]
William of Cranleigh [DW/PA/5/1576/9]
William of Frensham - Churt, husbandman [HRO; 1571 B187]
UPNEYE
Richard of Rotherhithe, shipwright [DW/PA/7/7 f,2; DW/PA/5/1595/84] <Abs 5>
UPOPKIN
Robert, *or* Robert Popkin, of Swk [DW/PA/5/1587/76]
UPPOLL *see* UPFOLD
UPTON
Thomas of Haslemere [PRO; PCC 1645]
URIS (VRYESE)
John of Swk St Olave [DW/PA/7/3 f,115; 1529]
URLWIN (URLWYN)
Walter of Chertsey, yeoman [PRO; PCC Will 1604] <Abs, SAC v,11 p,293>
UTTEWORTH
William of St Martha's; Shalford, gent, [DW/PA/7/1 f,40; 1487] <Abs 129>
UVEDALE (de UVEDALE)
Elizabeth of Titsey; Cranleigh; Swk St Mary Overy; Swk St Thomas [PRO; PCC Will 1488] <Abs SAC v,3 pp,163-170>
(Sir) Thomas of Titsey; Swk, knight [LPL; Reg, Abp Langham f,114; Will 1367] <Abs SAC v,3 p,150>
(Sir) Thomas of Titsey, knight [PRO; PCC Will; 1474] <Abs SAC v,3 pp,158-162
(Sir) William of Wickham, Kent; Titsey, knight, senior [PRO; PCC Will 1616] <Abs SAC v,3 pp,178-179>
(Sir) William of Titsey; Chelsham; Tatsfield; Camberwell, knight [PRO; PCC Will 1528] <Abs SAC v,3 pp,171-173>
William of Wickham, Hampshire; Tatsfield, esq, [PRO; PCC Will 1569] <Abs SAC v,3 pp,174-177>
William of Swk St Mary Overy; Nursted, Kent; Oxford All Souls College, Oxfordshire; Addington [LPL; Reg, Abp Stafford f,176; Will 1449] <Abs SAC v,3 pp,153-158>

VADEN
Eda of Swk St Olave [DW/PA/7/12 f,191; DW/PA/5/1633/121]
VAGHAM,VAGHAN *see* VAUGHAN
VALE (VAYLE)
Joan of Swk St Saviour, widow [DW/PA/7/7 f,413; DW/PA/5/1603/179] <Abs 770>
Thomas of Lingfield [PRO; PCC Will 1418]
VALENCE (VALENS)
Thomas of Wandsworth, citizen and fishmonger [GL; Archdeaconry Court of London Will 1407]
VALENTINE (FOLENTYNE,VALENTYNE)
Henry of Titsey, yeoman [DW/PA/7/6 f,290; 1560]
Humphrey of Titsey, yeoman [DW/PA/7/7 f,263; DW/PA/5/1599/82] <Abs 468>

VALENTINE (FOLENTYNE,VALENTYNE) [*continued*]
  Rose of Dunsfold [DW/PA/7/7 f,90; 1596] <Abs 167>
  William of Titsey [DW/PA/5/1558/1]*
  William of Tatsfield [PRO; PCC 1620] <Soame 448>
VALLE
  John of Swk St Saviour, waterman [DW/PA/7/7 f,1; DW/PA/5/1595/97]
    <Abs 2>
VALLER (VALLOR)
  Alice of Wonersh, widow [PRO; PCC 1640]
  Constance of Frensham - Dockenfield, spinster [HRO; 1620 B44]
  Lawrence of Wonersh [PRO; PCC 1639]
  William of Frensham, yeoman [HRO; 1600 B64]
van BURIN
  William of Swk [DW/PA/5/1579/16]*
van COLLEN
  William of ,,, [DW/PA/7/4 f,131; 1535]
VANDELDEN
  Ann, alias Ann de Caron of Lambeth - South Lambeth [PRO; PCC Admon 1635]
VANDENBRONKE *see* VANDERBROOKE
VANDENDENDEN
  Alexander of Swk St George; merchant stranger of London [DW/PA/7/13
    f,273; DW/PA/5/1644/19]
vanden DICKE
  Hans of ,,, [DW/PA/5/1570/32]
VANDERBROOKE (VANDENBRONKE)
  Abraham of Swk St George, gardener [DW/PA/7/11 f,322; DW/PA/5/1625/257]
  Abraham of Swk St George, gardener [DW/PA/7/11 f,309; DW/PA/5/1626/124]
van der MEULEN
  Anthony of Swk St Olave [*Dutch*] [DW/PA/5/1593/204]
van DIEPENRIECK
  Giles of Swk St Olave [*Dutch*] [DW/PA/7/9 f,310; DW/PA/5/1619/122]
van DROYE
  John of Swk St Olave, joiner [DW/PA/5/1563/9]
van DYMEN
  John of Swk St Olave; Utrecht, Netherlands, 'kerner' [DW/PA/7/4 f,124;
    1535]
VANHAME
  Henry of Swk St Margaret, cobbler [DW/PA/7/2 f,56; 1500]
VANHILL
  Anthony of Swk St Olave, widower [DW/PA/7/7 f,348; DW/PA/5/1601/82]
    <Abs 636>
van MADDIGALL (MEDIGALLS)
  Hester of Bermondsey; Hartiegangbuske, Brabant, Belgium, widow
    [DW/PA/7/7 f,604; DW/PA/5/1607/100] <Abs 1129>
VANNER *see* VENNER
VANOAKE
  Aganita of Swk St Olave, widow [DW/PA/7/13 f,301; DW/PA/5/1643/91]
van RISWYK
  Bronn of Croydon [PRO; PCC Will 1502]
van SEVERDONCK
  Henrik of ,,, [*Dutch*] [DW/PA/5/1570/83]
van STRIFEN (van STRIPEN)
  Walter of Bermondsey, leatherdresser [PRO; PCC Will 1604] <Abs, SAC
    v,11 p,285>

van TINNICQ
  Adam of Swk St Thomas, husband to Gertrude le Petit [DW/PA/5/1593/110]
van WINTERBEKE
  John of ... [*Dutch*] [DW/PA/5/1592/84]
VANZE
  Valentine of Swk, miller [DW/PA/5/1569/69]
VARDON *see* FINDEN
VARGIS *see* VERGIS
VARNAM
  George of Lambeth [PRO; PCC 1637]
VARNDELL
  John, alias John Ferrenden of Haslemere [PRO; PCC 1632]
VASON
  Isott of ... [DW/PA/7/10 f.285; DW/PA/5/1623/126]
VASSEUR
  Susan of Battersea [PRO; PCC 1648]
VASTON (VASTONE)
  Eleanor of Swk St Olave, widow [DW/PA/7/13 f.39; DW/PA/5/1639/145]
  Richard of Swk St Olave, blacksmith [DW/PA/7/11 f.566; DW/PA/5/1630/109]
VAUGHAN (VAGHAM, VAGHAN)
  Elizabeth of Swk St Saviour, widow [DW/PA/7/11 f.372; DW/PA/5/1626/125]
  Francis of Swk St Saviour, waterman [DW/PA/7/11 f.215; DW/PA/5/1625/258]
  Griffin of Ashtead, parson [PRO; PCC Will 1613]
  Hugh of Swk St Margaret [HRO; Reg. Fox 3 p.67; 1517]
  Thomas of ... [DW/PA/7/10 f.286; DW/PA/5/1623/125]
  William of Lambeth, gent. [PRO; PCC Will 1625]
VAUSE
  Francis of Richmond [PRO; PCC Admon 1645]
  John, alias John Frost of Swk St Saviour, butcher [DW/PA/7/12 f.156; DW/PA/5/1633/120]
VAUX
  Anthony of Lambeth [PRO; PCC Admon 1603]
  Anthony of Lambeth, vintner [PRO; PCC Will 1603] <Abs. SAC v.11 p.129>
  Anthony of Lambeth, citizen and vintner [PRO; PCC Will 1607] <Abs. SAC v.12 p.205>
  John of Lambeth, citizen and fishmonger [PRO; PCC Will 1587]
  (Lady) Mary of Petersham - Ham [PRO; PCC Admon 1618]
VAVASOR
  Thomas of Petersham - Ham, bachelor, junior [PRO; PCC Admon 1618]
VAWDY
  Robert of Wandsworth [PRO; PCC Admon 1577]
VAYLE *see* VALE
VAYRAY
  Henry of Compton; Godalming - Binscombe, yeoman [DW/PA/5/1603/180] <Abs U93>
VEER *see* VERE
VENABLES
  John of Lambeth - Lambeth Marsh, yeoman [DW/PA/7/8 f.25; DW/PA/5/1608/110]
  John of Merton [DW/PA/7/13 f.216; DW/PA/5/1642/85]
VENAR *see* VENNER
VENDYLIPP
  William of Swk St Olave, locksmith [DW/PA/7/6 f.193; 1560]

VENGHAM
Nicholas of Newington [LPL; 96/2661; 98/1 f,58v; Will 1634]
VENN *see* FENN
VENNER (VANNER,VENAR)
Andrew of Horley [DW/PA/5/1576/15]
Gabriel of Dunsfold, husbandman [DW/PA/7/10 f,2; DW/PA/5/1616/144]
Oliver of Frensham, tilemaker [HRO; 1561 B211-212]
Oliver of Frensham; Farnham [DW/PA/7/8 f,361; DW/PA/5/1612/164]
Richard of Horne [DW/PA/5/1557/125]
VENTRIS
Thomas of Lambeth - Water Lambeth, yeoman [DW/PA/7/11 f,577; DW/PA/5/1630/110]
VERBOUTS
Janneke of Swk St Olave [*Dutch*], widow [DW/PA/5/1593/71]
VERDE
John of Cheam [PRO; PCC Will 1450] <Abs SAC v,26 pp,56-57>
VERDEN
William of Rotherhithe [PRO; PCC Admon 1597]
VERE (VEER)
(Lady) Anne of Lingfield [PRO; PCC Will 1472]
John of Addington [PRO; PCC Admon 1586]
VERGIS (VARGIS,VERGYSSE)
John of West Horsley, clerk [HRO; 1636 B47]
John of Send; West Horsley, yeoman [DW/PA/7/7 f,22; DW/PA/5/1595/96] <Abs 47>
Margaret, alias Margaret Ridgway of West Horsley [PRO; PCC Admon 1640]
William of West Horsley, yeoman [DW/PA/7/5 f,134; 1539]
VERNE
Elizabeth of Swk, widow [DW/PA/7/7 f,260; DW/PA/5/1599/83] <Abs 461>
VERNEST *see* FARNHURST
VERNEY (VERNY)
John of Mortlake [PRO; PCC Will 1547]
VERNON
(Sir) Robert of Mitcham, knight [PRO; PCC Will 1617]
Thomas of Mitcham [PRO; PCC 1637]
VERNY *see* VERNEY
VERON
William of Swk St Olave, leatherdresser [DW/PA/7/7 f,241; DW/PA/5/1598/86] <Abs 423>
VERSTRATE
Phillip of ... [*Dutch*] [DW/PA/5/1593/125]
VERTEWE *see* VIRTUE
VERVORDE
Henry of Swk St Olave, gunner [DW/PA/5/1562/55]
VERYGO *see* VIRGO
VICARY *see* VICKERY
VICKERS (a VICARS,a VYCARS,VICARS,VICKARS,VYKERS)
Agnes of Swk St Saviour, spinster [DW/PA/7/11 f,152; DW/PA/5/1625/259]
John of Barnes [DW/PA/5/1561/20]
John of Guildford Holy Trinity [DW/PA/7/2 f,195; 1524]
Thomas of Guildford [DW/PA/7/5 f,157; 1540]
Thomas of Guildford [PRO; Will *in* E40 13316; 1538]
Thomas of Guildford Holy Trinity [DW/PA/7/5 f,123; 1539]

VICKERY (VICARY)
Robert of Farnham - Runfold [DW/PA/7/7 f,594; DW/PA/5/1607/101]
<Abs 1112>
VIDGEDOWNE
Richard of Richmond [PRO; PCC Admon 1635]
VIE *see* VYE
VIGNION *see* FINDEN
VINCENT (VOYSENE,VYNCENT)
David of Surrey, esq. [PRO; PCC Will 1566]
Edward of Richmond, gent. [PRO; PCC 1647]
Elizabeth of Fetcham, widow of Henry, esq. [DW/PA/7/12 f,415; DW/PA/5/1637/98]
(Sir) Francis of Stoke Dabernon, knight [PRO; PCC 1640]
Harry of Kingston [DW/PA/7/4 f,44; 1533]
Henry of Fetcham, esq. [PRO; PCC 1631]
Jane of Swk St Olave [DW/PA/7/7 f,15; DW/PA/5/1595/95] <Abs 31>
John of Egham [PRO; PCC Admon 1620]
John of Pyrford; Shepperton, Middlesex; Wisley, yeoman [DW/PA/5/1593/60]
(Sir) Thomas of Stoke Dabernon, knight [PRO; PCC Will 1614]
William of Cobham [DW/PA/5/1558/281]*
William of Pyrford, yeoman [DW/PA/5/1593/29]
William of Swk St George, citizen and wine cooper [DW/PA/7/12 f,314; DW/PA/5/1636/100]
VINDON *see* FINDEN
VINE (VYNE)
Dulcibel, alias Dulcibel Covert of Shalford [PRO; PCC Admon 1599]
Ellen, alias Ellen Babington of Chertsey [PRO; PCC Admon 1630]
Henry of Ash, esq. [DW/PA/5/1558/282]*
Henry of Ash, gent. [PRO; PCC Will 1572]
Jane of Weybridge, gentlewoman [DW/PA/7/7 f,333; DW/PA/5/1601/83]
<Abs 602>
Katherine of Godalming - Shackleford, widow and gentlewoman [HRO; 1597 B78]
Ralph of Farnham; Ash; Oxford, Oxfordshire; Berkshire, gent. [DW/PA/7/5 f,4; 1538] <Abs 40>
VINER (VYNER,VYNOR)
John of Wonersh [PRO; PCC Will 1489]
Thomas of Wonersh [DW/PA/7/1 f,50; 1487] <Abs 164>
VINTNER
John of Lambeth, yeoman [DW/PA/7/13 f,279; DW/PA/5/1643/90]
VIRGILO (VIRGILLO)
Edward of Reigate [DW/PA/7/12 f,303; DW/PA/5/1635/122]
Robert, alias Robert Sander of Ockham; Send, yeoman [DW/PA/7/8 f,321; DW/PA/5/1611/116]
VIRGO (VERYGO)
Henry of Thames Ditton; Kingston, husbandman [DW/PA/5/1555/74]
William of Kingston [DW/PA/7/2 f,114; 1517]
VIRTUE (VERTEWE)
William of Kingston, esq. [PRO; PCC Will 1526]
VIVIAN (FEVIAN)
Bartholomew, alias Bartholomew Cheseman of Leigh [DW/PA/5/1576/30]
Robert, alias Robert Cheissman of Buckland, priest and curate [DW/PA/5/1558/55]*

VLEESCHAUWERS
Elizabeth of ...., widow of Giles Bongons [DW/PA/5/1576/140]
VOECHT (de VOECHT)
Dierick of Swk, surgeon [DW/PA/5/1578/26]
VOET
John of Swk St Olave, silk weaver [DW/PA/7/8 f.159; DW/PA/5/1611/117]
VOLVAN,VOULPHAN *see* FULLFINE
VOYSENE *see* VINCENT
VRYESE *see* URIS
VULVAN *see* FULLFINE
VYE
Amy of Swk St George, widow [DW/PA/7/13 f.177; DW/PA/5/1641/136]
Ann of Swk St George, widow [DW/PA/7/13 f.180; DW/PA/5/1641/137]
Thomas of Swk St George, matmaker [DW/PA/7/12 f.428; DW/PA/5/1638/144]
VYNE *see* VINE
VYNER,VYNOR *see* VINER

WACE (WASE)
Leonard of Egham, gent. [PRO; PCC Will 1620] <Soame 1355>
WACKFORD *see* WAKEFORD
WADBROOK (WADBROKE,WADBROOKE)
George of Thames Ditton [PRO; PCC Admon 1621]
John of Thames Ditton - Weston, yeoman [DW/PA/5/1583/72]
Peter *or* Robert of Thames Ditton, gent. [PRO; PCC 1638]
WADDAM
William of Swk St George, drayman [DW/PA/7/9 f.330; DW/PA/5/1620/132]
WADDINGTON
Constance of Swk St George, yeoman [DW/PA/7/10 f.15; DW/PA/5/1616/145]
Ralph of Christ Church, London; Battersea; Chepstow, Monmouthshire, schoolmaster [GL; Commissary Court of London Will 1614]
WADE (WAIDE)
John of Rotherhithe [DW/PA/7/2 f.101; 1515]
Robert of Egham [PRO; PCC Will 1529]
WADELSHURST (de WADELSHURST)
Adam of Long Ditton [HRO; Reg. Wyk 2 p.102; 1372]
WADESON
Rachel, alias Rachel Porter of Putney [PRO; PCC Admon 1649]
WADHAM *see* WADDAM
WADSWORTH
Thomas of Swk St Saviour [DW/PA/7/9 f.48; DW/PA/5/1614/121]
WAFORD
Richard of Swk St Saviour [DW/PA/5/1581/4]
WAGGATT (WAGGOT)
Michael of Farnham, mercer [DW/PA/5/1588/14]
Phillip of Farnham, blacksmith [HRO; 1626 B117]
Richard of Woking, servant of Mr West, vicar [DW/PA/5/1572/22]
WAIDE *see* WADE
WAIGHTE *see* WAITE
WAIN (WAYNE,WEYN)
Ralph of Richmond [PRO; PCC Admon 1646]
Richard of Oxted [DW/PA/7/3 f.188; 1531]

WAINMAN (WENEMAN)
Peter of Lambeth [DW/PA/7/6 f.275; 1561]
WAINWRIGHT (WEYNWRYGHT,WRENWRIGHT)
Nicholas of Godstone [DW/PA/7/7 f.595; DW/PA/5/1607/109] <Abs 1113>
Thomas of Shalford [DW/PA/7/5 f.212; 1541]
WAITE (WAIGHTE,WAYTE,WEYTE)
Anthony of Clapham [PRO; PCC Will 1559]
Edward of Swk St Olave [DW/PA/7/11 f.435; DW/PA/5/1628/106]
John of Swk St George, brewer [HRO; Reg. Fox 3 p.64; 1515]
Lettice of Clapham, widow [PRO; PCC Will 1584]
Simon of Bermondsey, esq. [HRO; 1518 B39]
Thomas of Swk St Saviour, gardener [DW/PA/7/11 f.518; DW/PA/5/1629/107]
WAKAR *see* WAKER
WAKEFIELD (WAKEFEELD)
Peter of Swk St Saviour, white baker [DW/PA/5/1601/86] <Abs U40>
Peter of Swk St Saviour, tailor [DW/PA/5/1578/1]
WAKEFORD (WACKFORD,WAKEFORDE)
George of Ash, husbandman [DW/PA/7/9 f.8; DW/PA/5/1615/137]
George of Puttenham [DW/PA/5/1569/12]
Henry of Witley [DW/PA/7/1 f.46B; 1487] <Abs 154>
Robert of Pirbright, husbandman [DW/PA/7/9 f.73; DW/PA/5/1614/122]
Thomas of Lambeth [PRO; PCC Will 1548]
WAKER (WAKAR)
John of Beddington, yeoman [DW/PA/7/2 f.136; 1519]
John of Beddington, husbandman [DW/PA/7/5 f.94; 1539]
John of Carshalton; Sutton, yeoman [DW/PA/7/7 f.273; DW/PA/5/1599/84] <Abs 482>
John of Carshalton, yeoman [DW/PA/5/1606/107] <Abs U190>
Robert of Beddington - Wallington, yeoman [DW/PA/7/2 f.197; 1524]
Thomas of Beddington, yeoman [DW/PA/7/13 f.374; 1644]
Thomas of Carshalton [PRO; PCC Will 1566]
Thomas of Carshalton, husbandman [DW/PA/7/8 f.51; DW/PA/5/1609/121]
WAKERELL
Agnes of Mitcham [DW/PA/7/5 f.74; 1539]
Richard of Croydon, yeoman [LPL; 96/2672; Will 1617]
Richard of Croydon, yeoman [LPL; 96/2673; Will 1643]
WALBORNE *see* WALLBORNE
WALDEN (WALDON,WALLDEN,WALLDYN)
Agnes of Worplesdon [DW/PA/5/1636/113] <Abs U255>
Beatrice of Woking, widow [DW/PA/7/9 f.261; DW/PA/5/1617/126]
Harry of ... [DW/PA/5/1557/79]
Joan of Horsell; Chertsey, wife of Robert, junior [DW/PA/7/4 f.183; 1536]
Joan of Chobham, widow [DW/PA/5/1545/18]
John of Chertsey; Thorpe; Egham, husbandman [DW/PA/7/7 f.176; DW/PA/5/1597/107] <Abs 325>
John of Horsell, senior [*in* DW/PA/5/1544/5]
John of Horsell, junior [HRO; 1586 AD57]
John of Horsell, yeoman [DW/PA/7/8 f.46; DW/PA/5/1609/122]
Robert of Horsell, junior [DW/PA/7/4 f.183; 1536]
WALDRON (WALDRONE)
Walter of Swk St Margaret [DW/PA/7/4 f.108; 1535]
WALE
Thomas, alias Thomas Stuff of Lambeth [PRO; PCC Will 1492]
WALES *see* WALLES

WALEYS *see* WALLIS
WALKER
Alexander of Bermondsey, citizen and leatherseller [PRO; PCC Will 1628]
Anthony of Bermondsey; Battersea, gent, [PRO; PCC Will 1590]
Edward of Streatham [PRO; PCC Will 1602]
Gawen of Bermondsey [PRO; PCC Admon 1649]
John of Swk St George [DW/PA/7/7 f,344; DW/PA/5/1601/84] <Abs 627>
John of Swk St Saviour [DW/PA/5/1578/56]
Margery of Farnham, widow [DW/PA/7/12 f,42; DW/PA/5/1630/111]
Margery of Farnham [DW/PA/7/11 f,614; DW/PA/5/1629/112]
Matthew of Bermondsey [PRO; PCC 1637]
Nicholas of Bermondsey [PRO; PCC Will 1625]
Nicholas of Kingston, smith [HRO; 1565 B112-114]
Reginald of Swk St Olave; St Martin Vintry, London, freemason
[DW/PA/7/8 f,24; DW/PA/5/1608/112]
Thomas of Farnham [PRO; PCC Will 1587]
William of Battersea [PRO; PCC Admon 1604]
William of Swk St George, butcher [DW/PA/7/7 f,428; DW/PA/5/1603/181]
<Abs 802>
William of Worplesdon [PRO; PCC 1647]
WALL
John of Lambeth [DW/PA/7/9 f,164; DW/PA/5/1616/146]
Moses of Mickleham, minister and clerk [DW/PA/7/12 f,332;
DW/PA/5/1636/108]
Percival of Godstone, collier [DW/PA/7/8 f,185 *and* DW/PA/7/9 f,106;
DW/PA/5/1610/33 *and* DW/PA/5/1615/90]
Ralph of Swk St Saviour [DW/PA/7/12 f,501; DW/PA/5/1638/156]
Ralph of ... [DW/PA/7/12 f,504; 1638]
Richard of Farnham, clerk [PRO; PCC Will 1494]
Thomas of Lambeth, baker [PRO; PCC Admon 1584]
WALLACE *see* WALLIS
WALLBORNE
Alice of Swk St Saviour, widow [DW/PA/7/10 f,117; DW/PA/5/1620/133]
Thomas of Swk St Saviour, waterman [DW/PA/7/10 f,118; DW/PA/5/1620/134]
WALLDEN,WALLDYN *see* WALDEN
WALLER (WALLAR)
James of Alfold, husbandman [DW/PA/7/9 f,198; DW/PA/5/1616/147]
John of Alfold, husbandman [DW/PA/7/6 f,214A; 1560]
John of Newdigate [DW/PA/7/2 f,161; 1521]
Rose of Newington - Walworth, widow [PRO; PCC Admon 1622]
Thomas of Swk St Olave, rector [LPL; Reg, Abp Stafford f,165v;
Admon 1448]
William of Horley, clerk [PRO; PCC Admon 1647]
William of Rotherhithe [PRO; PCC Admon 1649]
William of Swk St George, labourer [DW/PA/7/8 f,213; DW/PA/5/1612/165]
WALLES,WALLEYS *see* WALLIS
WALLIN
Thomas of Swk St Saviour, chandler [DW/PA/7/12 f,295; DW/PA/5/1635/123]
WALLINGTON (WALYNGTON)
John of Kingston, innholder [DW/PA/7/1 f,66; 1487] <Abs 221>
WALLIS (WALEYS,WALLES,WALLEYS,WELLIS)
Agnes of Ockley; Abinger, widow [DW/PA/5/1558/286]*
Agnes, alias Agnes Frisby of Croydon [LPL; 98/1 f,53v; Will 1634]
Edmund of Ockley; Abinger [DW/PA/5/1558/284]*

WALLIS (WALEYS,WALLES,WALLEYS,WELLIS) [*continued*]
  Elizabeth of Bermondsey [DW/PA/5/1557/126]
  Henry of Epsom, vicar [HRO; Reg. Wyk 2 p.261; 1393]
  Joan, alias Joan Thomas of Battersea, widow [DW/PA/7/9 f.148; DW/PA/5/1615/133]
  John of Croydon [PRO; PCC 1633]
  John of Esher [DW/PA/7/2 f.39; 1494]
  John of Kingston [PRO; PCC Will 1499]
  John of Newdigate, yeoman, senior [DW/PA/7/9 f.321; DW/PA/5/1619/123]
  John of Swk St Olave, wax chandler [DW/PA/5/1563/101]
  John of Worplesdon, yeoman, senior [DW/PA/7/7 f.534; DW/PA/5/1607/102] <Abs 1004>
  Michael of Kingston - Ham, yeoman [DW/PA/5/1550/100]
  Nicholas of Kingston, mercer [DW/PA/7/7 f.42 *and* DW/PA/7/9 f.216; DW/PA/5/1595/94 *and* DW/PA/5/1617/127] <Abs 82>
  Nicholas of Peper Harow, clerk and parson [PRO; PCC Will 1606] <Abs. SAC v.12 p.102>
  Richard of Banstead [PRO; PCC Will 1535]
  William of Ockley [DW/PA/5/1561/21]

WALLOP
  William of Horne, gent. [PRO; PCC Will 1627]

WALLPOOLE *see* WALPOLE

WALLTER *see* WALTERS

WALPOLE (WALLPOOLE)
  Nicholas of Swk St Olave [DW/PA/7/13 f.251; DW/PA/5/1641/139]

WALSH (WALSHE)
  Thomas of Croydon, gent. [PRO; PCC Will 1600]
  William of Streatham, gent. [PRO; PCC Will 1576]

WALSHMAN
  John of Banstead, labouring man [DW/PA/7/8 f.21; DW/PA/5/1608/111]

WALSINGHAM
  (Sir) Edmund of Surrey, knight [PRO; PCC Will 1550]
  (Dame) Ursula of Barnes - Barn Elms, widow of (Sir) Francis, knight [PRO; PCC Will 1602]

WALTEN *see* WALTON

Walter, alias Walter de Clerkenwell of Ewell, rector [HRO; Reg. Stra p.25; 1326]

WALTERS (WALLTER,WALTER)
  Angel of Reigate, widow [DW/PA/7/12 f.196; DW/PA/5/1633/123]
  Edward of Swk St George [DW/PA/5/1588/87]
  George of Reigate, yeoman, senior [DW/PA/7/12 f.16; DW/PA/5/1631/116]
  Harry of Guildford St Nicolas - Loseley [DW/PA/5/1574/39 *and, in* DW/PA/5/1574/26]
  John of Thames Ditton - Arbrook; Stoke Dabernon; Cobham; Esher; Long Ditton; Kingston, yeoman, senior [DW/PA/7/9 f.160; DW/PA/5/1616/153]
  John of Thames Ditton [DW/PA/7/10 f.255; DW/PA/5/1622/106]
  John of Kingston, shearman [DW/PA/7/2 f.92; 1510]
  John of Rotherhithe [PRO; PCC Admon 1623]
  John of Shere, clerk [PRO; PCC Will 1407] <Abs SAC v.8 pp.225-226>
  Katherine of Wimbledon [PRO; PCC Will 1587]
  Katherine of Wimbledon, daughter of (Sir) William, knight [PRO; PCC 1633]
  Nicholas of Newington [LPL; 98/1 f.17r; Will 1630]
  Richard of Lingfield, yeoman [PRO; PCC Will 1619]

WALTERS (WALLTER,WALTER) [*continued*]
Robert of Lingfield [PRO; PCC 1648]
Robert of Putney - Mortlake Park [PRO; PCC Will 1595]
Thomas of Kingston [DW/PA/7/1 f.40; 1486] <Abs 128>
William of Long Ditton - Sunt, yeoman [DW/PA/7/13 f.420; DW/PA/5/1645/65]
William of Long Ditton, husbandman [DW/PA/7/2 f.97; 1514]
William of Guildford, servingman [DW/PA/5/1563/39]
William of Mitcham; Tonbridge, Kent, yeoman [HRO; 1585 B72]
William of Wimbledon, senior [PRO; PCC Will 1587]
William of Wimbledon, esq. [PRO; PCC Will 1606] <Abs. SAC v.12 p.104>
(Sir) William of Wimbledon, knight [PRO; PCC 1633]
see also ATWATER; WATERS
WALTERER *see* WATERER
WALTERI
Wallis of Swk St Olave [HRO; Reg. Fox 3 p.67; 1517]
WALTON (WALTEN,WALTHAM,WALTOM,WALTONNE)
Hugh of Croydon, innholder [LPL; 96/2690; 98/1 f.52v; Will 1633]
Jane of Shalford, widow [DW/PA/7/7 ff.27,396; DW/PA/5/1595/93 *and* DW/PA/5/1603/191] <Abs 57,734>
John of Shalford, clothier [DW/PA/5/1575/66]
Thomas of Newington [LPL; 98/1 f.68r; (ren.) 1635]
WALWORTH (de WALWORTH)
Francis of Newington [PRO; PCC Will 1576]
(Sir) William of Newington - Walworth, Lord Mayor of London [PRO; PCC Will 1385]
WALWYN
Richard of Lingfield, parish clerk [DW/PA/7/4 f.194; 1537]
WALYNGTON *see* WALLINGTON
WANKLIN (WANCKLIN)
Paul of Lambeth, yeoman [DW/PA/7/12 f.89; DW/PA/5/1633/125]
WANLINGE
John of Carshalton [DW/PA/5/1559/202]
WANNHAM *see* WONHAM
WANSLAYNE *see* WASLIN
WAPPALL
Cicely of Bermondsey [PRO; PCC 1648]
WAPSHOTT (WAPSHOTE,WAYPPESHOTTE)
Edward of Chertsey [DW/PA/7/6 f.6; DW/PA/5/1559/9]
Edward of Pirbright, husbandman [DW/PA/7/8 f.346; DW/PA/5/1612/166]
Joan of West Horsley, widow [DW/PA/5/1588/64]
John of Chertsey [DW/PA/7/1 f.72; 1487] <Abs 236>
John of Chertsey, husbandman [DW/PA/7/13 f.104; DW/PA/5/1641/138]
John of Chobham, yeoman [DW/PA/5/1579/98]*
John of Horsell, yeoman, senior [DW/PA/7/7 f.395; DW/PA/5/1603/182] <Abs 733>
Robert of Chertsey, yeoman [DW/PA/7/12 f.328; DW/PA/5/1636/106]
Robert of Chobham, bachelor [DW/PA/7/6 f.52; DW/PA/5/1559/95]
Robert of Chobham, husbandman [DW/PA/5/1591/86]
Thomas of Chertsey [DW/PA/5/1562/64]
William of Chertsey [HRO; 1578 B96]
William of Egham, yeoman [DW/PA/7/11 f.503; DW/PA/5/1629/104]
WARBLETON (WARBELTON)
William of Tandridge, esq. [PRO; PCC Will 1469]

WARD (WARDE)
Andrew of Tandridge, senior [DW/PA/7/12 f.301; DW/PA/5/1635/131]
Clement of Oxted, widow [PRO; PCC Admon 1649]
Cuthbert of Swk St Olave, yeoman [DW/PA/7/10 f.260; DW/PA/5/1622/107]
Edward of Richmond - Sheen, gent. [PRO; PCC Will 1531]
Elizabeth of Swk St Olave, widow of Edward, gardener [DW/PA/7/13 f.461; DW/PA/5/1647/20]
Ellen of Swk St Olave, spinster, senior [DW/PA/7/11 f.170; DW/PA/5/1625/260]
Frances of Swk St Olave, widow [DW/PA/5/1622/108]
Geoffrey of Swk St Saviour - Paris Garden, waterman [HRO; 1585 B73]
Henry of Battersea [DW/PA/7/11 f.110; DW/PA/5/1624/129]
Henry of Putney, citizen and merchant tailor [PRO; PCC Will 1588]
Joan of Swk [BM; Add.Ms 6,290; 1544]
John of Chertsey [DW/PA/7/3 f.110; 1529]
John of Chertsey, tilemaker [DW/PA/7/11 f.544; DW/PA/5/1629/105]
Juliana of Barnes, widow [LPL; 96/2691; Will 1614]
Michael of Ockley, clerk [PRO; PCC Admon 1587]
Richard of Oxted [PRO; PCC 1649]
Robert of Lambeth [DW/PA/5/1561/10]
Robert of Swk St Thomas [DW/PA/7/8 f.332; 1614]
Thomas of Swk St Mary Overy [DW/PA/7/4 f.172; 1536]
Thomas of Thorpe, minister [DW/PA/7/11 f.554; DW/PA/5/1629/106]
William of Kingston; island in Thames near 'Stoke Elmes', fisherman [DW/PA/7/9 f.103; DW/PA/5/1614/123]
William of Kingston, waterman, junior [DW/PA/7/13 f.133; DW/PA/5/1640/170]
William of Newington [PRO; PCC Admon 1636]
William of Richmond [PRO; PCC Admon 1641]
WARDELL *see* WARDLE
WARDEN
Anthony of Carshalton, yeoman [DW/PA/7/11 f.363; DW/PA/5/1626/126]
Christopher of Chertsey [PRO; PCC 1648]
Elizabeth of Ewell; Carshalton [DW/PA/7/11 f.368; DW/PA/5/1626/127]
Maria of Swk St Olave [DW/PA/7/11 f.415; DW/PA/5/1627/108]
Thomas of Haslemere, brickmaker [HRO; 1629 AD73]
William of Carshalton, yeoman [DW/PA/7/11 f.164; DW/PA/5/1625/261]
WARDLE (WARDELL,WARDOLL)
John of Stoke Dabernon - Oxshott [DW/PA/5/1550/64]
Robert of Lambeth - Lambeth Dean, blacksmith [HRO; 1595 AD60]
WARDNER *see* WARNER
WARDOLL *see* WARDLE
WARDROPPE
Ellen of Richmond [PRO; PCC Will 1555]
WARE
Agnes of Reigate, widow [DW/PA/7/13 f.143; DW/PA/5/1641/140]
John of Horne, husbandman [DW/PA/7/7 f.512; DW/PA/5/1605/97] <Abs 960>
Richard of Reigate, weaver [DW/PA/7/11 f.195; DW/PA/5/1624/130]
see also WARRE
WAREHAM (WARHAM)
Thomas of Croydon [PRO; PCC Will 1481; BM; Harl.Ms 112 E 35; 1481]
WARMAN
John of Swk St Saviour; Ombersley, Worcestershire, shoemaker [DW/PA/7/8 f.331; DW/PA/5/1614/124]

WARNER (WARDNER,WARNA)
Cecilia of Bermondsey [PRO; PCC Admon 1599]
Davy of Wonersh, yeoman [DW/PA/7/7 f,303; DW/PA/5/1600/53] <Abs 542>
Elizabeth of Chertsey, widow [DW/PA/7/13 f,15; DW/PA/5/1639/150]
George of Ash, gent, [PRO; PCC Will 1550]
Godlee of Godalming, widow of John, yeoman [DW/PA/7/7 f,24; DW/PA/5/1595/92] <Abs 50>
Harry of Chertsey [DW/PA/7/3 f,166; 1530]
Henry of Wotton [DW/PA/7/2 f,20; 1491]
Joan of Farnham [DW/PA/7/5 f,41; 1538] <Abs 41>
John of Chertsey [DW/PA/5/1562/63]
John of Chertsey - Woodham, yeoman [DW/PA/5/1588/67]
John of Ewhurst, etc, [PRO; PCC Will 1496]
John of Farnham - Wrecclesham [BM; Add,Ms 24,925 f,24r; 1544] <Abs 59>
John of Farnham, tailor [DW/PA/7/13 f,315; 1644]
John of Frensham [DW/PA/5/1570/6]
John of Godalming [*in* DW/PA/5/1544/6]
John of Guildford St Nicolas [DW/PA/5/1592/68]
John of Witley [DW/PA/5/1593/184]
Mary of Puttenham, widow [DW/PA/7/7 f,186; DW/PA/5/1598/87] <Abs 338>
Nicholas of Farnham, shearman [DW/PA/7/10 f,153; DW/PA/5/1620/135]
Richard of Chertsey, husbandman [DW/PA/5/1580/34]
Richard of Chertsey - Woodham [DW/PA/7/13 f,30; DW/PA/5/1640/160]
Richard of Frensham; Haslemere; Thursley, yeoman [DW/PA/7/7 f,484; DW/PA/5/1604/67] <Abs 911>
Robert of Chertsey - Woodham, yeoman [HRO; 1602 B53]
Robert of Godalming, clothier [DW/PA/5/1563/38]
Robert of Puttenham, husbandman [DW/PA/7/7 f,172; DW/PA/5/1597/108] <Abs 317>
Thomas of Dorking, blacksmith [DW/PA/7/12 f,323; DW/PA/5/1636/104]
Thomas of Farnham, wool clothing trader [HRO; 1571 B196]
Thomas of Farnham [DW/PA/7/8 f,137; DW/PA/5/1610/134]
Thomas of Farnham, cordwainer [DW/PA/7/13 f,211; DW/PA/5/1642/89]
Thomas of Weybridge, etc, [PRO; PCC Will 1478]
Thomas of Wonersh, yeoman [HRO; 1573 B139]
Walter of Horsell, tailor [HRO; 1610 B79]
William of Chertsey; Shere [DW/PA/7/6 f,56; DW/PA/5/1559/91]
William of Chobham, husbandman [DW/PA/7/6 f,277; 1560]
William of Ewhurst; Cranleigh; Alfold, citizen and merchant tailor [GL; Commissary Court of London Will 1521]
William of Lambeth, labourer [DW/PA/7/8 f,187; DW/PA/5/1610/135]

WARRE
John of Leatherhead [DW/PA/7/2 f,16; 1491]
John of Swk St Mary Overy, haberdasher [LPL; Reg, Abp Stafford f,188; Will 1450]
see also WARE

WARREN
Christopher of Swk St George [DW/PA/7/11 f,321; DW/PA/5/1626/128]
Giles of Newington - Walworth, gent, [PRO; PCC Will 1617]
Giles of Newington - Walworth [PRO; PCC Will 1620] <Soame 835>
John of Tooting Graveney, gent, [PRO; PCC Admon 1627]
John of Kingston, husbandman [HRO; 1557 U735-736]
Michael of Swk St Olave, widow [DW/PA/7/7 f,347; DW/PA/5/1601/85]
William of Ockley, labourer [DW/PA/7/8 f,138; DW/PA/5/1610/136]

WARREN [*continued*]
  William of Petersham [PRO; PCC Admon 1612]
WARWELL
  John of Newington [LPL; 96/2720; Will 1617]
WARWICK (WARWICKE)
  John of Guildford St Nicolas - Artington, carpenter [DW/PA/7/8 f.193; DW/PA/5/1610/137]
  Margaret of Camberwell - Peckham, widow [DW/PA/7/12 f.101; DW/PA/5/1632/111]
  Samuel of Croydon - Addiscombe, weaver [PRO; PCC Will 1626]
WASE *see* WACE
WASHFIELD (WASHEFEILD)
  Robert of Swk St Saviour - liberty of Old Paris Garden, waterman [DW/PA/7/8 f.165; DW/PA/5/1611/118]
WASHFORD (WASTHEFORD)
  John of Waiton on the Hill, tailor [DW/PA/7/11 f.299; DW/PA/5/1626/129]
  Thomas of Shalford [DW/PA/7/1 f.100; 1489] <Abs 326>
WASHINGTON
  Thomas of Haslemere [PRO; PCC Admon 1607]
WASLIN (WASLYN,WANSLAYNE,WASLAINE,WASTLAN,WASTLAYN,WASTLYN)
  George of Merstham [DW/PA/7/6 f.164; DW/PA/5/1559/154]
  John of Nutfield, yeoman [HRO; 1613 B75]
  Richard of Nutfield [PRO; PCC Will 1558]
  Richard of Nutfield [PRO; PCC Will 1559]
WASSELL
  John of Swk St Thomas - St Thomas Hospital [DW/PA/7/6 f.299; 1560]
  Ralph of Swk [DW/PA/7/8 f.115; DW/PA/5/1610/138]
WASTELL
  James, alias James Westin, alias James Ouesstin of ... [*French*] [DW/PA/7/11 f.267; DW/PA/5/1625/199]
WASTHEFORD *see* WASHFORD
WASTLAN,WASTLAYN,WASTLYN *see* WASLIN
WATER *see* ATWATER; WATERS
WATERARE *see* WATERER
WATERCOMBE
  Brice of Newington [LPL; 98/1 ff.78v,85v; Wills 1636 *and* 1637]
WATERER (WALTERER,WATERARE)
  Christopher of Woking, yeoman [DW/PA/7/13 f.294; DW/PA/5/1643/96]
  Denise of Woking - Mayford, widow [DW/PA/7/3 f.179; 1531]
  George of Woking, sawyer [DW/PA/7/12 f.401; DW/PA/5/1638/145]
  Henry of Woking [HRO; 1596 B69]
  John of Ewell, beer brewer [DW/PA/5/1591/9]
  John of Shalford, tailor [HRO; 1575 B91]
  John of Woking, yeoman [DW/PA/5/1558/285]*
  John of Wonersh, labourer [DW/PA/5/1582/80]
  Nicholas of Ewell [PRO; PCC Admon 1581]
  Nicholas of Ewell, yeoman [DW/PA/7/7 f.515; DW/PA/5/1605/98] <Abs 967>
  Richard of Woking - Heathside [DW/PA/7/8 f.298; DW/PA/5/1613/134]
  Robert of Woking [DW/PA/7/3 f.179; 1531]
  Robert of Woking [DW/PA/7/7 f.281; DW/PA/5/1599/85] <Abs 500>
  Thomas of Pyrford, labourer [DW/PA/5/1558/287]*
  Thomas of Reigate; Nutfield; Merstham; Buckland [DW/PA/7/5 f.153; 1540]
  Thomas of Woking - Egley, yeoman [DW/PA/7/7 f.488; DW/PA/5/1604/68] <Abs 922>

WATERER (WALTERER,WATERARE) [*continued*]
Thomas of Woking - Crastock [DW/PA/7/11 f,574; DW/PA/5/1630/112]
Thomas of Woking, yeoman [DW/PA/7/13 f,47; DW/PA/5/1639/156]
William of Woking - Mayford, yeoman [HRO; 1624 B71]
see also ATWATERER
WATERHOUSE
Henry of Tooting [PRO; PCC Admon 1642]
WATERMAN (WATTERMAN)
Alice of Horley, widow of John [HRO; 1533 B38]
John of Horley [HRO; 1533 B38]
John of Stoke [DW/PA/7/11 f,567; DW/PA/5/1630/113]
William of Walton on Thames [DW/PA/7/2 f,141; 1520]
William of Charlwood, husbandman [LPL; 96/2723; Will 1628]
WATERS (WATER)
Agnes of Shere, widow [HRO; 1601 B61]
David of Bermondsey [PRO; PCC Will 1604] <Abs, SAC v,11 p,294>
Henry of Swk St Olave [DW/PA/7/10 f,198; DW/PA/5/1621/126]
John of Guildford, joiner [PRO; PCC Will 1614]
John of Kingston, yeoman and servant to the king [DW/PA/7/10 f,209; DW/PA/5/1620/136]
John of Rotherhithe, shipwright [HRO; 1573 B140]
see also ATWATER; WALTERS
WATERSFIELD (WATERSFEILDE)
John of Surrey [PRO; PCC Will 1595]
WATFORD (de WATFORD,WATTFORDE)
John of Albury [DW/PA/7/5 f,107; 1539]
John of Guildford [HRO; Reg, Wyk 2 p,123; 1374]
Margaret of Albury, daughter of Edward, yeoman, senior [DW/PA/7/13 f,431; DW/PA/5/1646/58]
Richard of Camberwell, tilemaker [DW/PA/7/7 f,589; DW/PA/5/1607/103] <Abs 1099>
Thomas of Albury [PRO; PCC 1649]
WATKINS (WATTKINS)
Elizabeth of Barnes - Barn Elms [PRO; PCC Admon 1646]
Ellen of Swk - liberty of the Clink, widow [DW/PA/7/13 f,277; DW/PA/5/1644/21]
Robert of Bermondsey [PRO; PCC Admon 1592]
William of Swk St Saviour - liberty of the Clink, victualler [DW/PA/7/13 f,107; DW/PA/5/1640/164]
WATLINGTON (WATLYNGTON)
Christopher of Farnham [DW/PA/7/4 f,75; 1534]
Jane of Guildford St Mary [DW/PA/7/9 f,321; DW/PA/5/1619/124]
Richard of Guildford St Mary [DW/PA/7/8 f,215; DW/PA/5/1612/167]
Richard of Richmond; Warfield, Berkshire [DW/PA/5/1600/54] <Abs U28>
WATSON (WATSONN,WATSONNE,WATSYN)
Davy of Swk St Saviour, tailor [DW/PA/5/1592/73]
Gilbert of Chertsey [DW/PA/7/3 f,172; 1531]
Henry of Bermondsey, tailor [DW/PA/7/11 f,53; DW/PA/5/1623/127]
Jane of Wandsworth, spinster [PRO; PCC Admon 1628]
Joan of Horley [PRO; PCC Will 1552]
John of Egham [DW/PA/5/1592/39]
John of Swk St Thomas [DW/PA/5/1569/20]
John of Cobham [PRO; PCC Will 1545]
John of Horley [PRO; PCC Will 1545]

WATSON (WATSONN,WATSONNE,WATSYN) [*continued*]
John of Horsell, husbandman [DW/PA/7/6 f,162; DW/PA/5/1559/92]
John of Send - Ripley [DW/PA/7/8 f,248; DW/PA/5/1613/135]
John of Wandsworth [DW/PA/7/5 f,181; 1540]
Margaret of Kingston, widow [PRO; PCC Admon 1638]
Margaret of Kingston; Heston, Middlesex, widow [PRO; PCC 1638]
Robert of Kingston, gent, [PRO; PCC 1649]
Roger of Kingston [PRO; PCC Admon 1604]
Shadrach of Kingston, draper [PRO; PCC Will 1622]
Thomasine of Bermondsey, widow [DW/PA/7/11 f,370; DW/PA/5/1626/130]
William of Swk St George [DW/PA/7/1 ff,41,42; 1486] <Abs 131,135>
William of Wandsworth, gent, [PRO; PCC Will 1616]

WATTELL *see* WATTLE

WATTERMAN *see* WATERMAN

WATTES *see* WATTS

WATTFORDE *see* WATFORD

WATTKINS *see* WATKINS

WATTLE (WATTELL)
George of Reigate, yeoman [DW/PA/7/12 f,55; DW/PA/5/1631/119]
Henry of Ewell [PRO; PCC Will 1588 *and* 1589]

WATTS (WATTES,WATTYS)
Dorothy of Lambeth [PRO; PCC Admon 1626]
Edward of Frimley [PRO; PCC Admon 1649]
Edward of Swk St Olave [DW/PA/7/13 f,212; DW/PA/5/1642/90]
George of Ash, potter [DW/PA/7/13 f,246; DW/PA/5/1640/172]
George of Farnham [PRO; PCC Will 1589]
George of Farnham, yeoman [DW/PA/7/7 f,501; DW/PA/5/1605/99] <Abs 937>
George of Frimley [PRO; PCC 1637]
Henry of Haslemere, shoemaker [DW/PA/7/13 f,132; DW/PA/5/1640/168]
John of London, citizen and woodmonger [DW/PA/7/7 f,321; DW/PA/5/1601/87] <Abs 575>
John of Chertsey, blacksmith [DW/PA/7/7 f,175; DW/PA/5/1597/109] <Abs 322>
John of Farnham, yeoman [GL; Archdeaconry Court of London Will 1632]
John of Frimley, yeoman [DW/PA/7/12 f,292; DW/PA/5/1635/130]
John of Swk St Olave; Farnborough, Hampshire, yeoman [DW/PA/7/13 f,222; DW/PA/5/1643/98]
John of Worplesdon, senior [DW/PA/7/9 f,45; DW/PA/5/1614/125]
Nicholas of Farnham, yeoman [DW/PA/7/9 f,314; DW/PA/5/1619/125]
Thomas of Wandsworth [PRO; PCC Will 1498]
William of Dorking, collarmaker [DW/PA/7/9 f,147; DW/PA/5/1615/138]
William of Swk St Saviour, citizen and cook [DW/PA/7/12 f,520; DW/PA/5/1638/160]

WAVEN
John of Lambeth [DW/PA/7/2 f,75; 1501]

WAWE
Thomas of Cobham [PRO; PCC Will 1498]

WAXHAM
Hugh of Putney - Roehampton, husbandman and churchwarden of Putney [LPL; 96/2737; 98/1 f,41r; Will 1632]
John of Putney - Roehampton [LPL; 98/1 ff,59r,72v; Wills 1634 *and* 1636]

WAYES
Lambert of Swk St Olave [DW/PA/5/1582/108]

WAYLAND
Edmund of Chertsey, gent. [PRO; PCC Will 1611]
Ralph of Leatherhead [DW/PA/7/5 f.209; 1541]
WAYMAN
Richard of Swk St Olave [DW/PA/5/1563/96]
WAYNE *see* WAIN
WAYPPESHOTTE *see* WAPSHOTT
WAYTE *see* WAITE
WEADLEY
Hastings of Lambeth, spinster [PRO; PCC Admon 1631]
WEALCH *see* WELCH
WEALE (WEELL)
Edward of Holgate - Coates Manor, Shropshire,
yeoman of the queen's chamber [DW/PA/7/6 f.30; DW/PA/5/1559/36]
John *or* John Weate of Worplesdon, yeoman [DW/PA/7/12 f.349;
DW/PA/5/1636/103]
Margaret of Swk St Olave, widow [DW/PA/7/11 f.321; DW/PA/5/1626/131]
WEASTE *see* WEST
WEATE *see* WHEAT
WEATHERBY (WETHERBY,WHETHERBY)
George of Mickleham, husbandman [DW/PA/7/12 f.258; DW/PA/5/1634/114]
Julian of Nutfield [DW/PA/7/11 f.561; DW/PA/5/1630/117]
WEAVER (WEVAR,WEVER)
Anthony of Oxted; Limpsfield; Crowhurst, yeoman [DW/PA/5/1557/8]
Joan of Oxted, widow [DW/PA/5/1587/5]
Richard, alias Richard Weyn of Oxted [DW/PA/7/3 f.188; 1531]
Richard of Lingfield - Haxted, yeoman [DW/PA/7/7 f.154;
DW/PA/5/1597/110] <Abs 289>
Richard of Lingfield - Haxted [PRO; PCC Will 1597]
Richard of Lingfield - Haxted; Edenbridge, Kent; Oxted; Limpsfield,
yeoman [DW/PA/7/7 f.264; DW/PA/5/1599/86] <Abs 469>
Richard of Lingfield - Haxted, yeoman [PRO; PCC Will 1599]
William of Swk St Saviour, bone lace seller [DW/PA/7/12 f.508;
DW/PA/5/1638/158]
WEBB (WEB,WEBBE)
Anthony of Guildford St Nicolas, shearman [DW/PA/7/6 f.128;
DW/PA/5/1559/186]
Bridget of Croydon, widow [PRO; PCC 1645]
Edward of Lingfield, sheather [PRO; PCC Will 1622]
Edward of Lingfield, sheather [DW/PA/7/11 ff.12,212; DW/PA/5/1623/128]
Elizabeth of Bermondsey, spinster [DW/PA/5/1568/88]
Henry of ... [DW/PA/7/12 f.489; DW/PA/5/1638/154]
Hersey of Swk St Olave, joiner [DW/PA/5/1576/98]
James of Lambeth [PRO; PCC Admon 1603]
Joel of Oxted [DW/PA/7/10 f.40; DW/PA/5/1617/128]
John of Croydon, schoolmaster [PRO; PCC 1648]
John of Egham [DW/PA/5/1605/100] <Abs U180>
John of Farnham [DW/PA/7/11 f.396; DW/PA/5/1627/109]
John of Godalming, weaver [DW/PA/7/7 f.485; DW/PA/5/1604/69] <Abs 913>
John of Guildford St Mary, clothier [DW/PA/7/13 f.290; DW/PA/5/1643/95]
John of Lingfield, yeoman [DW/PA/7/13 f.215; DW/PA/5/1642/91]
John of Swk St Margaret [DW/PA/7/5 f.136; 1540]
Martin of Rotherhithe [PRO; PCC Admon 1622]
Nicholas of Witley - Milford, husbandman [DW/PA/5/1561/42]

WEBB (WEB,WEBBE) [*continued*]

Richard of Lambeth, yeoman [DW/PA/7/7 f,224; DW/PA/5/1598/88] <Abs 396>

Richard of Mitcham [PRO; PCC Will 1545]

Richard of Swk St Saviour, tallow chandler [DW/PA/5/1558/288]*

Robert, alias Robert Perse of Kingston; Mitcham, yeoman [DW/PA/7/6 f,233; 1561]

Robert of Windlesham [PRO; PCC 1648]

Samuel of Ockham, husbandman [DW/PA/7/13 f,34; DW/PA/5/1639/153]

Samuel of Swk St Olave - Walnut Tree Alley, yeoman [DW/PA/7/9 f,56; DW/PA/5/1614/126]

Thomas of Beddington - Wallington, yeoman [PRO; PCC Will 1616]

Thomas of Farnham [HRO; 1567 D3/127]

Thomas, alias Thomas Peerse of Mitcham, husbandman [DW/PA/7/5 f,103; 1539]

Thomas of Bermondsey [DW/PA/7/6 f,159; DW/PA/5/1559/148]

Thomas of Sutton, yeoman [DW/PA/5/1587/125]

William of London, citizen and haberdasher [DW/PA/5/1582/9]

William, alias William Whealer of Elstead [DW/PA/7/6 f,85; DW/PA/5/1559/129]

William of Swk St Olave, feltmaker [DW/PA/7/7 f,476; DW/PA/5/1604/70] <Abs 900>

WEBHAM

Nathaniel of Godalming [PRO; PCC Admon 1648]

WEBSTER (WEBSTAR)

Arthur of Swk St Thomas, citizen and armourer [DW/PA/7/9 f,259; DW/PA/5/1617/129]

John of Limpsfield, clothworker [PRO; PCC Will 1625]

John of Swk St Margaret [PRO; PCC Will 1503] <Abs SAC v,1 p,198>

John of Stoke Dabernon - Oxshott, junior [DW/PA/7/13 f,392; DW/PA/5/1645/59]

Richard of Swk St Mary Overy [DW/PA/7/2 f,63; 1500]

WECCHE *see* WEEKS

WECKES *see* WICKS

WEDGBOROWE *see* WEDGEBOROUGH

WEDGE

Richard of Swk St Saviour, yeoman [DW/PA/7/11 f,351; DW/PA/5/1625/262]

WEDGEBOROUGH (WEDGBOROWE)

William of Egham, yeoman [PRO; PCC Will 1629]

WEDNESTER

Charles of Lambeth [PRO; PCC Admon 1596]

WEDNOM

Alice of Farnham, widow [DW/PA/5/1588/70]*

WEECKE *see* WEEKES

WEEDON (WEEDEN)

Elizabeth of Lambeth, widow [PRO; PCC Will 1599]

John of Lambeth - Stockwell, husbandman [PRO; PCC 1630] [*and*] [DW/PA/7/11 f,525; DW/PA/5/1630/114] <Scroope 1244>

Richard of Croydon [LPL; 98/1 f,123v; Will 1641]

WEEKS (at WEKE,WECCHE,WEECKE,WEEKES,WEKE)

Ann of Wotton, widow [DW/PA/7/8 f,374; DW/PA/5/1612/168]

George of Wotton [PRO; PCC 1648]

John of Ockley [BM; Add,Ms 24,925 f,5v; 1545] <Abs 10>

John of Swk [HRO; Reg, Wyk 2 p,234; 1387]

John of Swk St Thomas, sawyer [DW/PA/7/11 f,478; DW/PA/5/1628/107]

WEEKS (at WEKE,WECCHE,WEECKE,WEEKES,WEKE) [*continued*]
Richard of Egham [PRO; PCC Will 1516]
Richard, alias Richard Atweecke of Thorpe; Egham - Stroud [PRO; PCC Will 1592]
see also ATWICK; WICKES
WEELL *see* WEALE
WEKE *see* WEEKS
WELBECK (WELBECKE,WELBEK,WELBEKE,YLBCKE)
Alice of Putney [PRO; PCC Will 1558]
Jane of Putney [PRO; PCC Will 1419]
John of Putney, gent. [PRO; PCC Will 1558]
Leonard of Swk St Thomas [DW/PA/5/1578/89]
Richard of Sutton [PRO; PCC Will 1515] <Abs. SAC v.52 p.47>
Richard of Putney, gent. [PRO; PCC Will 1489]
William of Putney [PRO; PCC Will 1510]
WELBELOVED (WELBELOVID,WELBELOVYD)
Edward of Kingston, bachelor [DW/PA/5/1557/98]
Thomas of Thorpe [DW/PA/7/4 f.181; 1536]
WELBURY (WELBURYE)
Robert of Swk St Saviour, shipwright [DW/PA/5/1555/31]
WELCH (WEALCH,WELCHE,WELSH,WELTCH)
Benjamin of Thursley [DW/PA/7/9 f.306; DW/PA/5/1619/126]
Edward of Elstead, clerk [DW/PA/5/1607/104]
Eustace of Farnham, yeoman [DW/PA/7/8 f.175; DW/PA/5/1610/139]
Joan of Swk St George, widow [DW/PA/5/1563/18]
John of Swk St Margaret [DW/PA/7/4 f.171; 1536]
Robert of Swk St Olave, blacksmith [DW/PA/7/10 f.223; DW/PA/5/1621/127]
William of Farnham, mercer [DW/PA/7/7 f.534; DW/PA/5/1606/101] <Abs 1005>
William of Swk St George [DW/PA/5/1562/8]
WELDE
William of Great Bookham [SRO; 65/5/29; 1638]
WELFORD (WELFARE,WELFORDE)
Nicholas of Lingfield [PRO; PCC 1634]
William of Lingfield, mason [DW/PA/5/1588/37]
see also WILFORD
WELL *see* ATWELL; WELLS
WELLAND (WELLENS)
Peter and Mary his wife (daughter of Matthew Buckers) of Swk St Thomas [DW/PA/5/1578/105] [*Joint will, proved by Mary, widow.*]
Thomas of Haslemere, senior [PRO; PCC 1649]
see also WELLINS
WELLER (WELLAR,WHELLER) [*In some early records there is confusion with Wheeler, q.v.*]
Alice of Elstead, widow [DW/PA/7/1 f.43; 1486] <Abs 137>
Ann of Woking, widow [DW/PA/7/13 f.320; 1644]
Blanch of Dorking, widow [DW/PA/7/12 f.2; DW/PA/5/1631/115]
Henry of Ewell, yeoman [DW/PA/7/13 f.196; DW/PA/5/1642/87]
Henry of Woking - Sutton [DW/PA/7/12 f.366; DW/PA/5/1638/147]
John of Byfleet, husbandman [DW/PA/7/8 f.260; DW/PA/5/1611/119]
John of Dorking, senior [DW/PA/5/1557/114]
John, alias John Atwell of Headley, husbandman [DW/PA/5/1574/44]
John of Headley [DW/PA/7/8 f.293; DW/PA/5/1613/136]
Richard, *or* Richard Wheeler of Worplesdon, husbandman [DW/PA/7/13 f.415; DW/PA/5/1645/63]

WELLER (WELLAR,WHELLER) [*continued*]
  Robert of Aldershot, Hampshire, husbandman [DW/PA/5/1563/77]
  Roger of Wandsworth [DW/PA/7/11 f.556; DW/PA/5/1630/115]
  Samuel of Croydon - Waddon, gent. [PRO; PCC Will 1604] <Abs. SAC v.11 p.288>
  Thomas of Capel, husbandman [PRO; PCC Will 1616]
  Thomas of Dorking [DW/PA/7/12 f.73; DW/PA/5/1632/108]
  Thomas of Leatherhead, husbandman [DW/PA/7/11 f.142; DW/PA/5/1624/131]
  William of Chaldon, husbandman [DW/PA/7/10 f.152; DW/PA/5/1619/128]
  William of Dorking, yeoman [DW/PA/7/10 f.107; DW/PA/5/1619/127]
  William of Farnham [DW/PA/7/12 f.206; DW/PA/5/1634/107]

WELLINS (WELLYNS)
  William of East Horsley, gardener, senior [PRO; PCC Will 1617]
  William of Wonersh, yeoman [DW/PA/7/12 f.386; DW/PA/5/1637/102]
    see also WELLAND; WELLENS

WELLIS *see* WALLIS

WELLS (WELL,WELLES)
  Edmund of Oxted, cooper [DW/PA/7/11 f.461; DW/PA/5/1628/108]
  Elizabeth of West Horsley [DW/PA/7/11 f.359; DW/PA/5/1625/263]
  Elizabeth of West Horsley, widow [PRO; PCC Will 1625]
  Harry, alias Harry at Wels of Headley [DW/PA/5/1562/4]
  James of Charlwood [LPL; 98/1 f.108r; Will 1639]
  John, alias John Awell of West Clandon [DW/PA/5/1582/21]
  John of Clapham, husbandman, senior [DW/PA/7/10 f.49; 1618]
  John of Clapham [DW/PA/7/13 f.22; DW/PA/5/1640/159]
  John of Kingston - Hatch Court, husbandman [BM; Add.Ms 24,925 f.22r; 1544] <Abs 52>
  John of Lingfield [PRO; PCC Admon 1612]
  John of Lingfield, cooper [DW/PA/7/13 f.177; DW/PA/5/1641/144]
  John of Woodmansterne [DW/PA/5/1563/40]
  Richard of Capel, yeoman [HRO; 1633 B57]
  Richard of Woodmansterne [DW/PA/7/7 f.151; DW/PA/5/1597/115] <Abs 282>
  Robert of Hambledon; Compton, weaver [DW/PA/7/3 f.206; 1532]
  Thomas of ... [DW/PA/5/1563/41]
  William of Lingfield, cooper [DW/PA/7/12 f.98; DW/PA/5/1632/110]
  William of Swk St George, gardener [DW/PA/7/12 f.342; DW/PA/5/1636/111]
  William of Woodmansterne, husbandman [DW/PA/7/4 f.222; 1537]
    see also ATWELL; HATHWELL

WELLSON *see* WILSON

WELLYNS *see* WELLINS

WELSHMAN
  Robert of Banstead, shepherd [DW/PA/7/12 f.256; DW/PA/5/1634/110]

WELSON *see* WILSON

WELY
  Richard of Bentley, Hampshire, senior [DW/PA/7/1 f.14; 1485] <Abs 45>

WENEMAN *see* WAINMAN

WEPHAM
  Nathaniel, alias Nathaniel Wexham of Godalming [DW/PA/7/13 f.489; DW/PA/5/1648/46]

WESBROOKE *see* WESTBROOK

WESKOTT *see* WESTCOTT

WEST (WEASTE,WESTE,WHEST)
  Agnes of Epsom, widow [*in* DW/PA/5/1546/11]
  Alice of Croydon [PRO; PCC Will 1594]

WEST (WEASTE,WESTE,WHEST) [*continued*]

Alice of Frensham, widow [DW/PA/5/1571/93]
Alice of Swk St Saviour, widow [DW/PA/7/9 f.288; 1619]
Ambrose of Egham, husbandman [DW/PA/5/1581/25]
Bridget of East Clandon; Litton, Dorset; Kingston, widow [DW/PA/5/1593/41]
Edmund of Abinger [PRO; PCC Admon 1589]
Edmund of Abinger [HRO; 1618 AD90]
Edmund of Horsell, husbandman [DW/PA/7/6 f.24; DW/PA/5/1559/22]
Edward of Godalming, dyer [HRO; 1573 B59]
Eleanor of Compton; Guildford, widow [DW/PA/5/1593/30]
Frances of Haslemere [HRO; 1571 AD47]
Harvey of Godalming - Farncombe, clothier [DW/PA/5/1550/46]
Henry of Godalming, yeoman [DW/PA/7/12 f.248; DW/PA/5/1636/109]
Henry of Mortlake, gent. [PRO; PCC 1637]
Henry of Swk St Olave, shipwright [DW/PA/7/11 f.218; DW/PA/5/1625/264]
Henry of Thursley, husbandman [DW/PA/7/11 f.51; DW/PA/5/1623/129]
John of Farnham [DW/PA/7/2 f.4; 1485]
John of Guildford St Mary [DW/PA/7/1 f.62; 1487] <Abs 208>
John of Hambledon; Wonersh, yeoman [DW/PA/7/9 f.258; DW/PA/5/1614/127]
John of West Horsley [DW/PA/7/10 f.284; DW/PA/5/1623/130]
John of Ockley [DW/PA/7/4 f.158; 1536]
John of Thursley [HRO; 1612 AD106]
John of Wonersh, cooper [DW/PA/7/8 f.105; DW/PA/5/1610/140]
John of Wonersh [PRO; PCC Admon 1648]
Josephus of Swk St Thomas [DW/PA/7/11 f.389; DW/PA/5/1625/265]
Mary of Thursley, widow of Robert [DW/PA/7/9 f.234; DW/PA/5/1617/130]
Nicholas of Farnham [DW/PA/7/1 f.56; 1487] <Abs 187>
Nicholas of Putney, bishop of Ely [PRO; PCC Will 1534]
Phillip of Godalming - Farncombe, clothier [DW/PA/5/1576/27]
Phillip of Godalming, gent. [PRO; PCC 1647]
Richard of Surrey [PRO; PCC Will 1591]
Richard of Bermondsey [PRO; PCC Admon 1625]
Richard of Haslemere, junior [PRO; PCC 1642]
Richard of Rotherhithe, mariner [PRO; PCC 1634]
Richard of Wonersh, cooper [DW/PA/7/13 f.1; DW/PA/5/1639/146]
Robert of Egham [? HRO; 1529]
Robert of Stoke Dabernon [DW/PA/7/5 f.49; 1538] <Abs 112>
Roger of Swk St Olave; North Somercoates, Lincolnshire [DW/PA/7/7 f.426; DW/PA/5/1603/183] <Abs 797>
Samuel of ... [DW/PA/7/9 f.189; DW/PA/5/1616/113]
Thomas of Ash, yeoman [DW/PA/7/11 f.74; DW/PA/5/1623/131]
Thomas of Lambeth, bricklayer [DW/PA/5/1578/112]
Thomas of Swk St George, yeoman [DW/PA/7/11 f.604; DW/PA/5/1630/116]
Thomas of Swk St Margaret - Bankside [DW/PA/7/5 f.49; 1538] <Abs 88>
Thomas of Swk St Saviour; Writtle, Essex; Chelmsford, Essex; carpenter [BM; Add.Ms 24,925 f.9r; 1544] <Abs 17>
Thomas of Stoke next Guildford, gent. [PRO; PCC 1644]
Thomas of Wonersh, husbandman [DW/PA/7/9 f.70; DW/PA/5/1614/128]
William of Epsom, yeoman [DW/PA/7/7 f.72; 1596] <Abs 133>
William of Swk St Saviour, chandler [DW/PA/7/7 f.266; DW/PA/5/1602/89] <Abs 670>
William of Thursley, husbandman [DW/PA/7/7 f.11; 1595] <Abs 25>
William of Croydon [PRO; PCC Admon 1635]

WESTBROOK (WESBROOKE,WESTBROCKE,WESTBROKE,WESTBROOKE,WESTBRUCKE)
Alice of Compton, widow [DW/PA/5/1558/289]*
Caleb of Godalming [PRO; PCC Admon 1635]
Christian of Godalming, widow [DW/PA/7/3 f.177; 1531]
George of Woking, butcher [DW/PA/7/7 f.312; 1600] <Abs 554>
Henry of Reigate, baker [DW/PA/7/11 f.532; DW/PA/5/1629/108]
James of Compton [HRO; 1570 B473-474]
James of Compton [HRO; 1574 B180]
John of Godalming [PRO; PCC Admon 1565]
John of Godalming, yeoman [DW/PA/7/10 f.241; DW/PA/5/1621/128]
John of Guildford, senior [GMR; *in* 85/13/160; 1543]
John of Kingston, yeoman, senior [DW/PA/7/9 f.55; DW/PA/5/1614/129]
Margaret of Godalming [PRO; PCC Will 1549]
Mungrum *or* Mungum of Farnham - Tilford, husbandman [DW/PA/7/8 f.17; DW/PA/5/1608/113]
Nicholas of Reigate [PRO; PCC Admon 1599]
Richard of Godalming - Hurtmore [DW/PA/7/3 f.169; 1531]
Richard of Godalming - Farncombe, labourer [DW/PA/7/8 f.133; DW/PA/5/1610/141]
Roger of Betchworth, husbandman [DW/PA/7/6 f.70; DW/PA/5/1559/111]
Thomas of Guildford St Nicolas, husbandman [DW/PA/5/1591/79]
Thomas of Kingston, yeoman [DW/PA/7/10 f.182; DW/PA/5/1620/137]
Thomas of Pirbright [DW/PA/7/4 f.82; 1534]
Thomas of Pirbright, husbandman [HRO; 1603 B59]
William of Farnham - Tilford, husbandman [DW/PA/5/1550/56]
William of Godalming, gent. *dated* 12 June 1537 [*Such a will is listed by Campbell Cooke, but appears now to be missing; however, it is not listed by Rodman either, so may be a mistaken entry.*]
William of Godalming, gent. [PRO; PCC Will 1550]
WESTBY
John of Lambeth [PRO; PCC Will 1516]
John of Leatherhead, vicar [DW/PA/7/2 f.16; 1491] [Sequestration]
WESTCOTT (WESKOTT,WESTCOLTE)
Robert of Malden, yeoman [PRO; PCC Will 1610] <Abs. SAC v.24 p.68>
William of Thorpe [DW/PA/5/1576/45]
WESTERBY (WESTERBEY)
William of Swk St Olave, mariner [DW/PA/7/13 f.362; 1644]
WESTERDALE (WESTURDALE)
Thomas of Battersea [DW/PA/7/2 f.86; 1503]
WESTON (WESTIN,WHISSON,WHISTON)
(Dame) Ann of Guildford [PRO; PCC Will 1548]
(Dame) Elizabeth of Sutton, widow of (Sir) Henry, knight [PRO; PCC Will 1616]
Henry of Ockham; Shere; Abinger; Ockley; Wotton; Cranleigh; Albury; Thursley; Send - Papercourt; Godstone; Horne; West Horsley; Alfold; Dunsfold; Hascombe; Shalford; Woking; Warnham, Sussex; Itchingfield, Sussex; All Hallows Barking, London; East Smithfield, London; St Botolph Aldgate, London; Fobbing, Essex; Horsham, Sussex; Slinfold, Sussex, gent., senior [DW/PA/7/9 f.107; DW/PA/5/1615/139]
Henry of Ockham, esq. [PRO; PCC Admon 1640]
(Sir) Henry of Woking - Sutton, knight [PRO; PCC Will 1592]
James, alias James Wastell, alias James Ouesstin of ... [*French*] [DW/PA/7/11 f.267; DW/PA/5/1625/199]

WESTON (WESTIN,WHISSON,WHISTON) [*continued*]
Joan of Newington, widow [PRO; PCC Will 1611] <Abs. SAC v.35 p.48>
Joan of Send, widow [DW/PA/5/1592/58]
John of Cobham; Effingham [PRO; PCC 1630] <Scroope 242>
John of Ockham, gent., senior [DW/PA/5/1592/107]
John of Croydon [LPL; 98/1 f.118v; Will 1640]
John of Ockham [PRO; PCC Will 1427]
John of Ockham, gent. [PRO; PCC Will 1548]
John of Ockham, gent. [PRO; PCC Will 1608] <Abs. SAC v.12 pp.104-105>
John of Warnham, Sussex; Ockham, gent. [PRO; PCC 1642]
Michael of Wimbledon [PRO; PCC Admon 1636]
(Sir) Richard of Woking - Sutton, knight [PRO; PCC Will 1542] <Abs. SAC v.52 p.44>
Robert of Capel [PRO; PCC Will 1622]
Robert of Frensham - Dockenfield, yeoman [HRO; 1642 AD51]
Thomas of Swk St Saviour, gardener [DW/PA/7/12 f.251; DW/PA/5/1636/112]

WESTURDALE *see* WESTERDALE

WESTWOOD (WESTWOODE)
James of Ashtead [DW/PA/7/7 f.88; 1596] <Abs 161>

WESTWRAY
Thomas of Swk St Olave; Blechingley [PRO; PCC Will 1593]

WETHERBY *see* WEATHERBY

WETHERED (WETHEREDD,WETHERYS)
George of Swk St George [DW/PA/7/5 f.182; 1540]
John of Lambeth - Water Lambeth, shipwright [DW/PA/7/6 f.198; DW/PA/5/1559/244]

WETHYMER
John of Long Ditton - Tolworth [DW/PA/7/2 f.53; 1492]

WEVAR,WEVER *see* WEAVER

WEXHAM
Nathaniel, alias Nathaniel Wepham of Godalming [DW/PA/7/13 f.489; DW/PA/5/1648/46]
Nicholas of Wimbledon [PRO; PCC Admon 1587]

WEY *see* WYE

WEYN *see* WAIN

WEYNWRYGHT *see* WAINWRIGHT

WEYTE *see* WAITE

WHARTON
Henry of Godalming [PRO; PCC Admon 1630]

WHATELEY *see* WHEATLEY

WHATMAN
John of Beddington [DW/PA/7/4 f.105; 1535]

WHEALER *see* WHEELER

WHEAT (WEATE)
Edward of Stoke next Guildford, yeoman [DW/PA/7/9 f.73; DW/PA/5/1614/130]
Elizabeth of Stoke next Guildford, widow [PRO; PCC Will 1615]
John *or* John Weale of Worplesdon, yeoman [DW/PA/7/12 f.349; DW/PA/5/1636/103]

WHEATLEY (WHEATELEI,WHEATELEY,WHEATLIE,WHEATLY,WHEATLYE,WHETLEY,WHITLEY)
Agnes of Horsell, widow [DW/PA/7/13 f.351; 1647]
Agnes of Walton on Thames, widow [DW/PA/7/7 f.598; DW/PA/5/1607/105] <Abs 1120>

WHEATLEY (WHEATELEI, WHEATELEY, WHEATLIE, WHEATLY, WHEATLYE, WHETLEY, WHITLEY) [*continued*]
Andrew of Barnes; St Gregory, London, citizen and barber surgeon [PRO; PCC 1640]
Arnold of Guildford, glover [DW/PA/7/10 f.73; 1618]
Francis of Worplesdon, yeoman [DW/PA/5/1570/62]
James of Swk St Olave, locksmith [DW/PA/5/1603/187] <Abs U95>
Joan of Farnham, widow [DW/PA/5/1582/86]
John of Chertsey [DW/PA/7/4 f.228; 1537]
John of Chertsey - Woodham [DW/PA/7/11 f.301; DW/PA/5/1626/132]
John of Chertsey - Woodham, yeoman, senior [HRO; 1637 B48]
Ralph of Worplesdon, husbandman [DW/PA/5/1557/90]
Richard of Bermondsey, esq. [PRO; PCC Will 1558]
Richard of Chertsey, yeoman, senior [DW/PA/7/7 f.330; DW/PA/5/1601/88 *and* DW/PA/5/1601/89] <Abs 594>
Richard of Walton on Thames, senior [DW/PA/5/1558/290]*
Thomas of Buckland [DW/PA/7/7 f.644; DW/PA/5/1608/114] <Abs 1211>
William of Walton on Thames, husbandman [DW/PA/7/9 f.257; DW/PA/5/1617/131]

WHEEDON (WHEDON)
John of Lambeth - Lambeth Marsh [PRO; PCC Admon 1591]

WHEELER (WHEALER, WHELAR, WHELER, WHELERE, WHILLER) [*In early records there is some confusion with Weller, q.v.*]
Agnes of Reigate, spinster [DW/PA/7/11 f.464; DW/PA/5/1628/109]
Christopher of Leigh, senior [PRO; PCC 1645]
Edward of Elstead; Godalming - Shackleford [DW/PA/7/8 f.95; DW/PA/5/1609/123]
Elizabeth of Esher, widow [PRO; PCC Will 1623]
Frusanna of Newdigate, widow [PRO; PCC Admon 1649]
Gerard of Swk St Olave, beer brewer [DW/PA/5/1562/15]
George of Haslemere [DW/PA/5/1557/39]
Henry of Elstead, yeoman [DW/PA/5/1591/95]
Henry of Elstead, husbandman [HRO; 1600 B70]
Henry of Guildford St Nicolas - Artington, yeoman, senior [DW/PA/7/13 f.165; DW/PA/5/1641/143]
Henry of Haslemere - Sturt; Thursley; Binstead, Hampshire, yeoman [DW/PA/7/8 f.271; DW/PA/5/1613/137]
Henry of Lambeth - Kennington, yeoman [PRO; PCC Admon 1658 *but in the 1631-1649 volume.*]
Henry of Leigh, yeoman, senior [DW/PA/7/13 f.198; DW/PA/5/1641/148]
Henry of Reigate, coachman [GL; Archdeaconry Court of London Will 1643]
Joan of Dorking, widow [DW/PA/7/5 f.229; 1541]
Joan of Guildford Holy Trinity, widow [DW/PA/7/1 f.56; 1487] <Abs 185>
John of Ash; Aldershot, Hampshire; Worplesdon, husbandman [DW/PA/5/1593/31]
John of Chobham [DW/PA/5/1586/27]*
John of Elstead - Westbrook, yeoman [DW/PA/7/7 f.254; DW/PA/5/1599/87] <Abs 447>
John of Elstead, bachelor [DW/PA/7/8 f.302; DW/PA/5/1613/138]
John of Guildford Holy Trinity [DW/PA/7/1 f.19; 1485] <Abs 63>
John of Guildford St Mary [DW/PA/5/1546/1]
John of Lambeth, citizen and currier [PRO; PCC 1635]
John of Leigh, yeoman [DW/PA/7/9 f.176; DW/PA/5/1616/152]

WHEELER (WHEALER,WHELAR,WHELER,WHELERE,WHILLER) [*continued*]
John of Stoke next Guildford [PRO; PCC Will 1503; CCAL; 1503 f.188v] <Abs, SAC v.51 p.94>
John of Stoke next Guildford, gent. [PRO; PCC Will 1547]
Juliana of Elstead, widow [DW/PA/7/9 f.6; DW/PA/5/1615/140]
Reynold, alias Reynold Maybank of Send [DW/PA/7/2 f.170; 1522]
Richard of Thames Ditton; Lincolns Inn, Middlesex, esq. [PRO; PCC Will 1614]
Richard of Elstead [DW/PA/5/1550/105]
Richard of Haslemere - Sturt, yeoman [DW/PA/7/12 f.327; DW/PA/5/1636/105]
Richard of Puttenham [DW/PA/7/6 f.231; 1561]
Richard of Worplesdon, husbandman [DW/PA/7/13 f.415; DW/PA/5/1645/63]
Robert of Haslemere [PRO; PCC Will 1584]
Roger of Dorking; Norfolk [DW/PA/5/1605/95 *and* DW/PA/5/1605/96] <Abs U179>
Rose of Farnham, widow [PRO; PCC 1641]
Simon of Guildford [PRO; PCC Admon 1649]
Thomas of Betchworth; Walton on the Hill; Buckland [DW/PA/5/1550/57]
Thomas of Thames Ditton [DW/PA/7/6 f.268; 1560]
William of Byfleet [DW/PA/5/1546/58]
William, alias William Webb of Elstead [DW/PA/7/6 f.85;DW/PA/5/1559/129]
William of Elstead [DW/PA/7/6 f.117; DW/PA/5/1559/128]
William of Elstead [DW/PA/5/1561/43]
William of Godalming - Enton, husbandman, senior [DW/PA/5/1579/102]*
William of Thursley, yeoman [DW/PA/7/8 f.123; DW/PA/5/1610/142]
WHELLER *see* QUELLER; WELLER
WHEST *see* WEST
WHETHERBY *see* WEATHERBY
WHETLEY *see* WHEATLEY
WHETSTONE
James of Lambeth, citizen and cutler [PRO; PCC Will 1619]
WHINYARD *see* WINEYARD
WHIP (WHYPPE)
George of Camberwell [DW/PA/5/1572/21]
WHISSON,WHISTON *see* WESTON
WHITBE *see* WHITBY
WHITBROOKE
Thomas of Putney [PRO; PCC Admon 1587]
WHITBY (WHITBE)
William of Ditton [DW/PA/7/9 f.160; DW/PA/5/1616/150]
WHITCOMBE (WYTCOMBE)
Joan of Swk St Olave, widow [DW/PA/7/8 f.11; DW/PA/5/1608/119]
WHITE (WHIT,WHITT,WHITTE,WHYTE,WHYTT,WHYTTE,WIGHT,WIGHTE,WYGHT,WYGHTE)
Abraham, alias Abraham Ryme of Swk St Saviour [GL; Commissary Court of London Admon 1608]
Agnes, alias Agnes Middelton of Mortlake [PRO; PCC Will 1509]
Alexander of Putney, baker [PRO; PCC Will 1610] <Abs, SAC v.24 p.57>
Alice of Betchworth - Brockham [HRO; 1572 B113]
Ann of Shere - Gomshall, widow [DW/PA/7/13 f.20; DW/PA/5/1639/151B]
Barbara of Swk St Thomas, widow of William, hospitaller [Essex Record Office; Archdeaconry Court of Essex Will 1569] <Abs Emmison p.294>
Daniel of Chessington [DW/PA/7/12 f.204; DW/PA/5/1634/115]
Edward of Egham, yeoman [DW/PA/7/7 f.602; DW/PA/5/1607/106] <Abs 1127>
Edward of Rotherhithe [PRO; PCC Admon 1628]

WHITE (WHIT,WHITT,WHITTE,WHYTE,WHYTT,WHYTTE,WIGHT,WIGHTE,WYGHT,WYGHTE) [*continued*]

Elizabeth of Guildford St Nicolas [DW/PA/7/11 f.385; DW/PA/5/1626/135]
Elizabeth of Leigh [DW/PA/7/8 f.334; DW/PA/5/1614/131]
Elizabeth of Swk St Margaret, widow [DW/PA/7/4 f.74; 1534]
Frances, alias Frances Gallawaye of Swk St Saviour, widow [DW/PA/5/1572/10]
Gabriel of Betchworth - Brockham, esq. [PRO: PCC Will 1622]
George of ... [DW/PA/7/8 f.350; DW/PA/5/1612/169]
Henry of Burstow [PRO: PCC Admon 1635]
Henry of Egham; Windsor, Berkshire [PRO: PCC 1647]
Henry of Leatherhead, labourer [DW/PA/7/12 f.408; DW/PA/5/1637/103]
Henry of Shere [DW/PA/7/8 f.117; DW/PA/5/1610/143]
James of Long Ditton, labourer [HRO: 1590 B67]
Joan of Bermondsey - Bermondsey Street [HRO: Act Book CCB 20 p.3; 1563]
Joan of Swk, widow [DW/PA/5/1563/62]
Joan of Swk St Saviour, widow [DW/PA/7/8 f.249; DW/PA/5/1613/139]
John of Abinger [DW/PA/7/12 f.258; DW/PA/5/1634/113]
John of Caterham, husbandman [DW/PA/7/12 f.315; DW/PA/5/1636/102]
John of Egham [DW/PA/7/8 f.201; DW/PA/5/1611/120]
John of Clapham [PRO: PCC Will 1592]
(Sir) John of Farnham, knight, alderman of London [PRO: PCC Will 1573]
John of Kingston [PRO: PCC Will 1574]
John of Leigh [DW/PA/7/2 f.131; 1519]
John of Merton, labourer [DW/PA/7/7 f.157; DW/PA/5/1597/111] <Abs 291>
John of Merton, husbandman [DW/PA/7/13 f.443; DW/PA/5/1646/60]
John of Morden, yeoman [DW/PA/7/9 f.102; DW/PA/5/1614/132]
John of Mortlake [PRO: PCC Will 1573]
John of Shere [DW/PA/7/4 f.233; 1537]
John of Shere - Hoe, husbandman [DW/PA/7/12 f.331; DW/PA/5/1636/107]
John of Shere - Gomshall, husbandman [DW/PA/7/12 f.482; DW/PA/5/1638/150]
John of Shere [PRO: PCC 1642]
John of Swk St Mary Overy, chaplain [LPL: Reg. Abp Morton f.79v; Admon 1492]
John of Swk St Olave, mariner [DW/PA/5/1587/74]
John of Swk St Saviour, oarmaker [DW/PA/5/1602/90] <Abs U58>
John of Wonersh, clothmaker [DW/PA/7/8 f.307; DW/PA/5/1613/140]
Joseph of Wimbledon, gent. [PRO: PCC Will 1614]
Joshua of London, citizen and girdler [DW/PA/5/1576/138]
Margaret of Dorking, widow [DW/PA/7/9 f.51; DW/PA/5/1614/133]
Margery, alias Margery Lambe of Swk St George [DW/PA/5/1578/58]
Margery of Swk St Olave; Bermondsey,spinster [DW/PA/5/1604/71] <Abs U122>
Mary of Thames Ditton, spinster [PRO: PCC Admon 1608]
Peter of Rotherhithe; Portsmouth, Hampshire, mariner [DW/PA/5/1598/89] Abs U20>
Rees of Guildford St Nicolas - Artington [PRO: PCC Will 1602] <Abs. SAC v.10 pp.314-315>
Richard of ..., haberdasher [DW/PA/7/13 f.267; DW/PA/5/1643/92]
Richard of Long Ditton [BM: Add.Ms 24,925 f.21r; 1544] <Abs 48>
Richard of Long Ditton; Thames Ditton, yeoman [DW/PA/7/7 f.96; 1596] <Abs 176>
Richard of Egham, yeoman [DW/PA/7/4 f.181; 1536]
Richard of Egham, husbandman [HRO: 1629 B65]
Richard of Newington [LPL: 96/2781; Will 1623]

WHITE (WHIT,WHITT,WHITTE,WHYTE,WHYTT,WHYTTE,WIGHT,WIGHTE,WYGHT,WYGHTE) [*continued*]
Richard of Pirbright [DW/PA/5/1581/34]
Richard of Pirbright [DW/PA/5/1581/45]*
Richard of Swk St Olave, fisherman [DW/PA/7/12 f.424; DW/PA/5/1637/105]
Robert of Farnham [HRO; Reg. Way 1 p.90; 1467]
Robert of Farnham [PRO; PCC Will 1467]
Robert of Farnham [PRO; PCC Will 1518]
Robert of Farnham [PRO; PCC Will 1533]
Robert of Malden; Chessington [DW/PA/7/4 f.226; 1537]
Robert of Swk St Olave [DW/PA/7/10 f.115; DW/PA/5/1619/129]
Roger of Carshalton, yeoman [DW/PA/7/2 f.6; 1491]
Stephen of Long Ditton [DW/PA/7/1 ff.4,5; 1484] <Abs 14>
Susan of Lambeth [DW/PA/5/1591/14]
Thomas of Chaldon, husbandman [DW/PA/7/13 f.121; DW/PA/5/1640/165]
Thomas of Farnham, keeper of Farnham Park [DW/PA/5/1558/291]
(Sir) Thomas of Farnham, knight [PRO; PCC 1641]
Thomas of Kingston; Twickenham, Middlesex, waterman [DW/PA/7/7 f.72; DW/PA/5/1596/60] <Abs 134>
Thomas of Shere [HRO; 1561 B223-224]
Thomas of Swk St Saviour [DW/PA/5/1568/10]
Thomas of Stoke Dabernon, husbandman [DW/PA/7/10 f.35; DW/PA/5/1617/132]
Thomas of Stoke Dabernon - Oxshott, yeoman [DW/PA/7/9 f.302; DW/PA/5/1619/130]
Thomas of Wonersh, clothier [PRO; PCC Will 1618]
Walter of Abinger [DW/PA/7/6 f.282; 1560]
William of Caterham, husbandman [DW/PA/7/9 f.193; 1616]
William of Cheam, etc. [PRO; PCC Will 1392]
William of Dorking [HRO; 1561 B225-226]
William of Leigh, yeoman [HRO; 1585 B77]
William of Malden, yeoman [DW/PA/5/1571/84]
William of Malden [DW/PA/5/1571/85]
William of Malden [PRO; PCC Admon 1649]
William of Putney [LPL; 98/1 f.117r; Will 1640]
William of Reigate, yeoman [DW/PA/7/9 f.270; 1618]
William of Shere, husbandman [DW/PA/7/12 f.277; DW/PA/5/1635/129]
William of Swk St Saviour, turner [DW/PA/5/1569/18]
WHITEGUIFTE *see* WHITGIFT
WHITEHEAD (WHITEHEADE,WHITHED,WHITHEDD,WHYTEHED)
Alexander of Esher, gent. [PRO; PCC Will 1590]
Edward of Egham, gardener [DW/PA/7/10 f.200; DW/PA/5/1621/129]
John of Guildford, gent. [DW/PA/7/13 f.373; 1644]
Oliver of Walton on Thames [PRO; PCC Will 1551]
Thomas of Streatham - Tooting Bec, labourer [DW/PA/5/1579/103]*
Thomas of Wandsworth, husbandman [DW/PA/7/4 f.63; 1534]
WHITEMORE *see* WHITMORE
WHITEWELL *see* WHITWELL
WHITFIELD (WHITEFEILD,WHITFIELDE)
William of Kingston, yeoman [HRO; 1587 B90]
WHITGIFT (WHITEGUIFTE)
John of Croydon, archbishop of Canterbury [PRO; PCC Will 1604]
Richard of Lambeth; Croydon - Waddon [PRO; PCC Will 1597]
WHITHED,WHITHEDD *see* WHITEHEAD

WHITHORNE
  Richard of Horley *or* Thursley ['Thorley'] [HRO; Reg. K p.290; 1559]
WHITING (WHITINGE)
  James of Horley; Charlwood [DW/PA/7/6 f.269; 1560]
  John of Long Ditton; Newdigate - Baldock; Morden, husbandman
    [DW/PA/7/10 f.44; 1618]
  John of Oxted [PRO; PCC Admon 1630]
WHITLEY *see* WHEATLEY
WHITMORE (WHITEMORE,WHITMOURE,WHITMOWER,WHITTMOORE)
  Ann of Lambeth, widow [PRO; PCC Will 1624]
  George of Albury [DW/PA/5/1571/23]
  George of West Horsley, yeoman [DW/PA/7/12 f.252; DW/PA/5/1635/124]
  John of Shalford; Wonersh [DW/PA/7/7 f.174; DW/PA/5/1597/112] <Abs 321>
  Paul of Compton, blacksmith [DW/PA/7/7 f.590; DW/PA/5/1607/107]
    <Abs 1101>
  Richard of Albury [PRO; PCC 1648]
  Richard of Guildford, shearman [DW/PA/5/1582/51]
  Richard of Reigate, husbandman [DW/PA/5/1575/40]
  Robert of West Horsley, yeoman [DW/PA/7/12 f.269; DW/PA/5/1634/112]
  Thomas of Albury, husbandman [DW/PA/7/11 f.54; DW/PA/5/1623/132]
  Thomas of Wonersh, husbandman [DW/PA/7/8 f.72; DW/PA/5/1609/124]
  Thomas of Wonersh, yeoman [DW/PA/7/11 f.584; DW/PA/5/1630/118]
  William of Godalming [DW/PA/7/11 f.90; DW/PA/5/1624/132]
WHITNEY (WHYTNEY,WYTNEY)
  Edward of Woking, husbandman [HRO; 1636 B50]
  Phillip of Swk St Mary Overy [DW/PA/7/4 ff.220-221; 1537]
  William of Rotherhithe [PRO; PCC Admon 1609]
  William of Rotherhithe [PRO; PCC Will 1611]
WHITROWE
  Henry of Cobham [PRO; PCC Admon 1640]
WHITT *see* WHITE
WHITTAKER (WHYTEAKERS)
  Alice of Swk St Saviour, widow [DW/PA/5/1568/19]
WHITTE *see* WHITE
WHITTINGHAM (WHYTTYNGAM)
  Edward of Croydon, citizen and merchant tailor [PRO; PCC Will 1592]
  George of Farnham, innkeeper [HRO; 1603 AD76]
  John of Battersea, citizen and grocer [PRO; PCC Will 1619]
  Robert of Swk St Olave [DW/PA/7/5 f.62; 1539] <Abs 96>
WHITTON (WITTON)
  Phillip of Bermondsey, weaver [DW/PA/7/10 f.178; DW/PA/5/1620/138]
WHITWELL (WHITEWELL,WITHWELL,WYTHEWELL,WYTHWELL,WYTTWELL)
  Joan of Worplesdon, widow [DW/PA/7/4 f.209; 1537]
  John of Lambeth, rector [PRO; PCC Will 1561]
  John of Pyrford, yeoman [DW/PA/5/1571/71]
  John of Swk St Olave, beltmaker [DW/PA/7/11 f.166; DW/PA/5/1625/266]
  Leonard of Swk St Olave, tailor [DW/PA/7/7 f.399; DW/PA/5/1603/184]
    <Abs 740>
  Richard, *or* Richard Wickwell of Horsell [DW/PA/5/1623/133]
  Richard of Pyrford [DW/PA/5/1550/90]
  Roger of Guildford Holy Trinity [DW/PA/7/2 f.42; 1494]
  Thomas of Puttenham [DW/PA/5/1575/69]
  William of Pyrford, yeoman [DW/PA/7/10 f.65; 1618]
    see also WITHLOT

WHONE *see* HONE
WHORWOD *see* HORWOOD; WIRWOOD
WHYPPE *see* WHIP
WHYTE *see* WHITE
WHYTEAKER *see* WHITTAKER
WHYTEHED *see* WHITEHEAD
WHYTT,WHYTTE *see* WHITE
WHYTTYNGAM *see* WHITTINGHAM
WIBRAND *see* WYBRAND
WICHE
John of Lingfield, master of the College [LPL; Reg. Abp Stafford f.128; Will 1445]
WICHERLEY (WITCHERLEY)
Richard of Swk, pewterer [DW/PA/7/11 f.246; DW/PA/5/1625/270]
Roger of Swk St Saviour, dyer [DW/PA/7/8 f.54; DW/PA/5/1609/127]
WICKENDON (WICKENDEANE,WYKENDEN)
John of Tandridge, yeoman, senior [DW/PA/7/12 f.385; DW/PA/5/1637/101]
Richard of Godstone [PRO; PCC Will 1524]
WICKER (WYCKER,WYKER)
Joan of Cobham, spinster [DW/PA/7/13 f.253; DW/PA/5/1643/93]
Joan of Cobham, spinster [PRO; PCC Admon 1646]
John of Esher, yeoman [HRO; 1557 U775-776]
John of Thames Ditton, husbandman [DW/PA/7/8 f.403; 1615]
Katherine of Croydon [LPL; 96/2797; Will 1629]
Richard of West *or* East Molesey, yeoman [HRO; 1588 B74]
Robert of Epsom - Horton [PRO; PCC Admon 1613]
Robert of Esher [DW/PA/5/1549/1]
Robert of West Molesey [HRO; 1576 B98]
Thomas of Molesey, husbandman [DW/PA/7/7 f.76; DW/PA/5/1596/61] <Abs 139>
William of Woking, innholder [DW/PA/7/7 f.370; DW/PA/5/1602/91] <Abs 681>
WICKERSHAM
Joan of Lambeth, gent. [DW/PA/7/12 f.256; DW/PA/5/1634/109]
WICKERSON (WYKERSON)
Dederic of Swk St Olave, barber [DW/PA/7/2 f.58; 1499]
WICKES *see* WICKS
WICKHALF (WYCHEHALFE)
Otis of Swk St Olave, citizen and bookseller [DW/PA/7/5 f.226; 1541]
WICKHAM (de WYCHAM)
Richard of Woodmansterne, rector [HRO; Reg. Stra p.10; 1324]
WICKING (WYKYNG)
William of Rotherhithe [PRO; PCC Will 1481]
WICKS (WECKES,WICKES,WIKE,WYKE,WYKES,WYKYS)
Alice of Thorpe [DW/PA/7/2 f.43; 1494]
George of Shere - Hoe, yeoman [DW/PA/5/1605/105] <Abs U85>
Harry of Chertsey; Egham; Thorpe; Chobham [DW/PA/7/5 f.169; 1540]
John of Petersham [DW/PA/7/4 f.17; 1552]
John of Shere, yeoman [DW/PA/7/12 f.275; DW/PA/5/1635/127]
John of Wonersh, yeoman [DW/PA/7/13 f.503; DW/PA/5/1649/19]
Josias of Lambeth, brewer [PRO; PCC Will 1621]
Oliver of Ockley [DW/PA/5/1579/100]*
Poole of Lambeth [PRO; PCC 1632]
William of Egham [DW/PA/7/13 f.255; DW/PA/5/1643/94]
William of Swk [PRO; PCC Will 1466] <Abs SAC v.1 p.195>
see also ATWICK; WEEKS

WICKLIFFE *see* WYCLIFFE
WICKS *see* WICKES
WICKWELL
Richard, *or* Richard Withwell of Horsell [DW/PA/7/11 f.12; DW/PA/5/1623/133]
WIDEN (WYDEN)
Robert of Farnham [DW/PA/7/1 ff.81,83; 1487] <Abs 268,276>
WIDMORE
John of Newington [LPL; 98/1 f.74r; (ren.) 1636]
WIDNELL
William of Tandridge, gent., senior [PRO; PCC Will 1602] <Abs. SAC v.10 pp.304-305>
WIGGINS
Michael of Newington [LPL; 98/1 f.128r; Will 1642]
WIGGS (WYGGS)
Francis of Lingfield, clerk of Lingfield College [DW/PA/7/5 f.186; 1540]
WIGHT,WIGHTE *see* WHITE
WIGHTMAN (WYGHTMAN)
Thomas of Lambeth - Water Lambeth, carpenter [DW/PA/7/9 f.51; DW/PA/5/1614/134]
WIGNALL
(Sir) Edward of Tandridge, clerk [PRO; PCC 1647]
Mary of Tandridge; Lingfield; Godstone, widow of William, esq. [DW/PA/7/8 f.310; DW/PA/5/1613/141]
William of Tandridge - Shawlands, esq. [PRO; PCC 1632]
WIKE *see* WICKS
WILCOX (WILCOCKES,WILCOCKS,WILCOK,WYLCOCKES)
James of Swk St Saviour, fisherman [DW/PA/5/1570/74]
John of Mitcham [PRO; PCC Will 1540]
Robert of Kingston, gent. [PRO; PCC 1639]
Robert of Swk, yeoman [DW/PA/5/1579/97]*
WILD *see* WILDE
WILDBOAR (WYLDBORE)
Joan of Farnham, spinster [DW/PA/5/1588/21]
WILDE (WILD,WYLD,WYLDE)
Henry of Byfleet [DW/PA/7/13 f.395; DW/PA/5/1645/60]
Henry of Lambeth - Camberwell Street; Camberwell [DW/PA/7/5 f.202; 1540]
Henry of Rotherhithe [PRO; PCC Admon 1586]
John of Byfleet [DW/PA/7/5 f.106; 1539]
John of Camberwell [PRO; PCC Will 1502]
John of Dorking, cook [DW/PA/7/12 f.465; DW/PA/5/1638/149]
Samuel of Reigate [DW/PA/7/11 f.380; DW/PA/5/1626/133]
Thomas, alias Thomas Edwardes of Farnham [DW/PA/7/6 f.189; DW/PA/5/1559/204]
Thomas of Farnham [PRO; PCC Admon 1648]
William of Bermondsey [PRO; PCC Admon 1612]
WILDEN
Francis of Swk St Saviour, victualler [DW/PA/7/8 f.61; DW/PA/5/1609/125]
WILDGOOSE
Richard of Lambeth [PRO; PCC Will 1628]
Richard of Lambeth [PRO; PCC Admon 1625]
Thomas of Mortlake [PRO; PCC Admon 1622]
William of Lambeth, yeoman [PRO; PCC Will 1624]
William of Lambeth [Oxfordshire Record Office; *account in* 300/6/2; 1623]

WILDSMYTH
  Thomas of Bermondsey, citizen and white baker [DW/PA/7/8 f,74; DW/PA/5/1609/126]
WILFORD (WILFORDE,WYLFFORD,WYLFORD) (*see also* WELFORD)
  Christopher of Epsom [PRO; PCC Will 1580]
  Elizabeth of Wandsworth, widow [PRO; PCC Will 1617]
  Francis of Swk St Saviour [DW/PA/7/11 f,110; DW/PA/5/1624/133]
  James of Wandsworth, esq, [PRO; PCC 1638]
  John of Buckland, parson [HRO; 1534 U45]
  John of Mitcham, senior [PRO; PCC Will 1550]
  Nicholas of Surrey [PRO; PCC Will 1551]
  Robert of Mitcham [PRO; PCC Will 1545]
  Thomas of Surrey [PRO; PCC Will 1406]
WILKES (WILKS)
  Elizabeth of Putney, widow [LPL; 96/2806; Will 1645]
  Henry of Putney - Roehampton [PRO; PCC Admon 1646]
  John of Chertsey, husbandman [DW/PA/7/10 f,114; DW/PA/5/1619/131]
  John of Epsom [PRO; PCC Admon 1631]
  Margaret of Bermondsey, widow [DW/PA/7/11 f,392; DW/PA/5/1626/134]
  Mary of Chertsey [DW/PA/7/11 f,516; DW/PA/5/1629/109]
WILKESON *see* WILKINSON
WILKINS (WILKYN,WILKYNS,WYLKYN,WYLKYNS)
  Alexander of Rotherhithe [PRO; PCC Admon 1648]
  Edmund of Bookham [PRO; PCC Admon 1625]
  Edward of Ewell, tailor [DW/PA/7/13 f,178; DW/PA/5/1641/145]
  Eleanor of Great Bookham, widow [DW/PA/7/7 f,126; DW/PA/5/1597/113] <Abs 232>
  Emery of Charlwood, carpenter [LPL; 96/2811; Will 1644]
  Harry of Great Bookham - Eastwick, husbandman [HRO; 1576 B101]
  John of Great Bookham, yeoman [DW/PA/5/1591/99]
  John of Epsom [DW/PA/7/5 f,131; 1539]
  Reynold of Ewell; Epsom, yeoman [DW/PA/5/1555/57]
  Richard of Great Bookham [DW/PA/5/1558/299]*
  Richard of Ewell, yeoman [DW/PA/5/1576/44]
  Richard of Oxted [DW/PA/7/2 f,48; 1497]
  William of Banstead [DW/PA/7/11 f,545; DW/PA/5/1629/110]
  William of Ewell [HRO; 1621 B64]
WILKINSON (WILKESON,WYLKYNSON)
  Alice of Lambeth [DW/PA/7/13 f,216; DW/PA/5/1642/92]
  Edward of Swk St Thomas - St Thomas Hospital, citizen and carpenter [DW/PA/5/1578/93]
  Gregory of Sanderstead, clerk [PRO; PCC 1630] <Scroope 1299>
  Henry of Reigate, gent, [PRO; PCC Will 1601] <Abs, SAC v,10 p,145>
  Miles of Newington [PRO; PCC Will 1595]
  Richard of Bermondsey [PRO; PCC Admon 1641]
  Thomas of Thorpe; Egham, husbandman [DW/PA/7/8 f,171; DW/PA/5/1610/144]
  William of Thorpe [DW/PA/7/5 f,115; 1539]
WILKS *see* WILKES
WILLARD (WILLARDE)
  Ann of Swk St Thomas - St Thomas Hospital, widow [DW/PA/5/1593/67]
WILLAWAYE (WILLOWAY)
  Richard of Ash - Wyke [DW/PA/5/1591/33]
  Robert of Farnham - Runwick, husbandman [DW/PA/7/7 f,485; DW/PA/5/1604/72] <Abs 915>

WILLEM (de WILLEMS)

Adltgen of Swk St Olave, widow of Christopher Williams [DW/PA/7/12 f.497; DW/PA/5/1638/155]

WILLETT (WILLATE,WILLET,WILLOTT,WYLLET,WYLLETT)

Agnes of Shere, widow of Edward [DW/PA/7/6 f.115; DW/PA/5/1559/130]

Ann of Mickleham [DW/PA/7/11 f.121; DW/PA/5/1624/134]

Edward of Shere, yeoman [DW/PA/5/1558/292]*

Edward of Wotton, husbandman [DW/PA/7/12 f.526; DW/PA/5/1635/135]

Henry of Newdigate [DW/PA/7/9 ff.195,228; DW/PA/5/1616/115 *and* DW/PA/5/1617/133]

John of Capel - Pleystowe, yeoman [DW/PA/5/1586/14]

John of Cobham [DW/PA/5/1563/48]*

John of Horne, senior [DW/PA/5/1557/67]

John of Horne [PRO; PCC Will 1558]

John of Putney, gent. [PRO; PCC 1649]

Margaret of Cuddington - Nonsuch [PRO; PCC Will 1579]

Nicholas of Newdigate [PRO; PCC 1639]

Richard of Ockley [DW/PA/5/1569/61]

Richard of Ockley, yeoman [DW/PA/7/9 f.279; 1618]

Robert of Horne, yeoman [DW/PA/7/7 f.142; DW/PA/5/1597/114] <Abs 260>

Robert of Horne, yeoman [PRO; PCC Will 1598]

WILLIAMS (GWILLIAMS,WILLIAM,WILLIAMES,WILLYAMS,WYLLMES)

Alice of Swk St Thomas; St Katherine by the Tower, London, widow [DW/PA/5/1586/20]

Ann of Swk St Olave, widow [DW/PA/7/8 f.222; DW/PA/5/1612/170]

Anthony of Mortlake, gent. [PRO; PCC Will 1557]

Cecily of Lambeth, widow [PRO; PCC Admon 1631]

Charity of Swk St Olave [DW/PA/7/11 f.137; DW/PA/5/1624/135]

Eleanor of Swk St George, spinster [DW/PA/7/13 f.83; DW/PA/5/1640/163]

Elizabeth of Swk, widow [DW/PA/5/1569/15]

Ellen of Swk St Saviour; Swk St Mary Overy, widow [DW/PA/5/1586/36]*

Evan of Swk St Olave [DW/PA/7/8 f.179; DW/PA/5/1610/146]

Griffin of Waltham Holy Cross, Essex; West Molesey, groom of the queen's cellar [GL; Commissary Court of London Will 1589]

Griffith of Swk St Olave, citizen and clothworker [DW/PA/7/8 f.355; DW/PA/5/1612/171]

Hugh of Swk St Olave, waterman [DW/PA/7/8 f.183; DW/PA/5/1610/147]

Humphrey of Swk St George, broomman [DW/PA/7/12 f.289; DW/PA/5/1636/110]

John, alias John Grigg of Surrey, gent. [PRO; PCC Will 1561]

John of Blechingley [DW/PA/7/2 f.28; 1492]

John of Lambeth [PRO; PCC Will 1522]

John of Leatherhead, yeoman [PRO; PCC Will 1615]

John of Swk, yeoman [DW/PA/7/8 f.136; DW/PA/5/1610/148]

John of Swk St Olave [DW/PA/7/3 f.127; 1530]

Mabel of Swk St Saviour, widow [DW/PA/7/12 f.394; DW/PA/5/1638/146]

Matthew of Bermondsey, citizen and leatherseller [DW/PA/7/12 f.486; DW/PA/5/1638/153]

Peter of Swk St Olave [DW/PA/5/1563/93]

Ralph of Kingston, yeoman [DW/PA/7/13 f.1; DW/PA/5/1639/149]

Rees of Newington [LPL; 98/1 f.123v; Will 1641]

Richard of Richmond, yeoman [DW/PA/7/7 f.365; DW/PA/5/1602/92]

Richard of Swk St Olave, tailor [DW/PA/7/12 f.202; DW/PA/5/1633/124]

Richard of Swk St Olave, wire drawer [DW/PA/7/12 f.277; DW/PA/5/1635/128]

WILLIAMS (GWILLIAMS,WILLIAM,WILLIAMES,WILLYAMS,WYLLMES) [*continued*]
Richard of Streatham [PRO; PCC Admon 1605]
Robert of Lambeth, collier [PRO; PCC Will 1626]
Robert of Swk St Saviour [DW/PA/7/8 f.11; DW/PA/5/1608/115]
Roger of Horley, yeoman [DW/PA/7/13 f.201; DW/PA/5/1642/88]
Thomas of ..., citizen and leatherseller [DW/PA/7/13 f.437; DW/PA/5/1646/59]
Thomas of Kingston [PRO; PCC Will 1557]
Thomas of Newington [LPL; 96/2820; Will 1627]
Thomas of Swk St Olave, silk weaver [DW/PA/7/11 f.345; DW/PA/5/1625/267]
Thomas of Walton on Thames, gent. [PRO; PCC Will 1624]
Thomas of Wandsworth, gent. [PRO; PCC 1639]
Walter of Swk St Saviour, shoemaker [DW/PA/5/1568/47]
William of Alfold, rector [DW/PA/7/12 f.306; DW/PA/5/1635/133]
William of Fetcham, clerk [DW/PA/7/7 f.95; 1596] <Abs 174>
see also WILLEMS (de WILLEMS)

WILLIAMSON (WILLIAMSONE,WYLHAMSON)
Bartholomew of East Clandon, yeoman [HRO; 1602 B57]
Henry of Streatham - Tooting Bec, gent. [PRO; PCC Will 1628]
John of Camberwell - Peckham [PRO; PCC Admon 1638]
John of Elstead, wareburner [HRO; 1594 B67]
Katherine of Streatham - Tooting Bec, widow [PRO; PCC 1632]
Richard of Swk St Olave [DW/PA/7/4 f.60; 1533]
Roger of Swk St Olave, haberdasher [LPL; Reg. Abp Stafford f.176; Will 1449]
Thomas of Swk St Olave, joiner [DW/PA/7/12 f.191; DW/PA/5/1633/122]

WILLICON (WYLLYCON)
Agnes of Thorpe, widow [*in* DW/PA/5/1544/6]

WILLINGTON (WYLLYNGTON)
Thomas of Wandsworth, baker [DW/PA/5/1587/47]

WILLINSON
William of Swk St Olave; Bermondsey; Deane, Cumberland, yeoman [DW/PA/5/1603/188] <Abs U96>

WILLIS
Gregory of Swk St Olave, blacksmith [DW/PA/5/1593/142]
Richard of Newington [LPL; 96/2832; Will 1615]
Robert of Battersea [DW/PA/7/9 f.43; DW/PA/5/1614/135]
Thomas of Swk St Saviour, yeoman [DW/PA/5/1602/54] <Abs U53>

WILLMORE *see* WILMORE

WILLMOTT (WILMOTH,WILMOTT)
Francis of Lambeth, yeoman of the queen's chamber [DW/PA/5/1591/15]
Richard of Newington [PRO; PCC Admon 1624]
William of Horley, husbandman [DW/PA/7/12 f.161; DW/PA/5/1634/106]

WILLOTT *see* WILLETT

WILLOUGHBY (WILLOUGHBYE)
Christopher of Swk St George, gent. [DW/PA/5/1586/35]*
Joan of Rotherhithe, widow [PRO; PCC Will 1622]
Thomas of Rotherhithe [PRO; PCC Admon 1613]

WILLOWAY *see* WILLAWAYE

WILLS
Henry of Lambeth [PRO; PCC Admon 1645]
Henry of Lambeth [PRO; PCC 1645]

WILLSON *see* WILSON

WILLYAMS *see* WILLIAMS

WILLYCON *see* WILLICON

WILMORE (WILLMORE,WILMER)

Francis of Bermondsey [PRO; PCC Will 1590]

George of West Ham, Essex; Swk, esq. [PRO; PCC Will 1594] <Abs Emmison pp.142-145>

WILMOTH,WILMOTT *see* WILLMOTT

WILSMORE

Medcalfe of St Giles Cripplegate, London [DW/PA/7/11 f.526; DW/PA/5/1630/119]

WILSON (WELLSON,WELSON,WILLSON,WILSONE,WYLSON)

Adam of Nutfield, doctor of Divinity [PRO; PCC Admon 1634]

Arthur of Bermondsey [DW/PA/5/1557/51]

Christopher of Newington [PRO; PCC Admon 1631]

Edward of Camberwell, clerk [PRO; PCC Will 1619]

Edward of Lambeth, baker [PRO; PCC Will 1616]

Edward of Swk St Thomas - St Thomas Hospital, currier [DW/PA/5/1561/1]

Elizabeth of Newington, wife of Thomas [PRO; PCC 1637]

Henry of Bermondsey; Swk St George; Swk St Olave; New Brentford, Middlesex, tanner [PRO; PCC 1630] <Scroope 934>

Henry of Headley; Betchworth [DW/PA/5/1570/45]

Humphrey of Chertsey, maltman [DW/PA/5/1617/142] <Abs U234>

James of Kingston [DW/PA/7/13 f.333; 1644]

James of Richmond [PRO; PCC Admon 1584]

Joan of Swk St George; Newington, widow [DW/PA/7/9 f.282; 1618]

John of Thames Ditton, husbandman [DW/PA/7/6 f.73; DW/PA/5/1559/136]

John, alias John Brounrick of Godalming, tailor [DW/PA/5/1582/52]

John of Reigate, rootman [DW/PA/7/7 f.444; DW/PA/5/1603/185] <Abs 839>

John of Swk St George, porter [DW/PA/7/9 f.260; DW/PA/5/1617/134]

John of Swk St Saviour, citizen and barber surgeon [DW/PA/7/8 f.259; DW/PA/5/1611/121]

Leonard of Camberwell [HRO; Reg. CCB 20 p.5; 1563] [*and*] [DW/PA/5/1563/67 *and, in* DW/PA/5/1563/64]

Leonard of Elstead [HRO; 1608 AD66]

Malin of Bermondsey, widow [DW/PA/5/1603/186] <Abs U94>

Nicholas of Godalming [PRO; PCC Admon 1585]

Nicholas of Newington [PRO; PCC 1635]

Nicholas of Walton on Thames [DW/PA/7/6 f.192; DW/PA/5/1559/187]

Richard of Kingston [PRO; PCC 1639]

Robert of Bermondsey [PRO; PCC Will 1576]

Robert of Swk St Margaret [DW/PA/7/4 f.94; 1534]

Robert of Swk St Saviour, innholder [DW/PA/7/5 f.227; 1541]

Roger of Chiddingstone, Kent; Farleigh, chapman [LPL; 96/6828; Will 1627]

Roland of Putney [PRO; PCC Will 1563]

Thomas of Leigh, yeoman [DW/PA/7/13 f.82; DW/PA/5/1640/162]

William of Dorking, yeoman [DW/PA/7/8 f.179; DW/PA/5/1610/149]

William of Kingston [DW/PA/5/1570/14]

William of Richmond ?, priest [DW/PA/5/1546/35]

William of Swk St Olave, citizen and goldsmith [DW/PA/5/1574/37]

William of Swk St Olave - Horsleydown; St Katherine by the Tower, London, waterman [DW/PA/7/9 f.85; DW/PA/5/1615/141]

WILTSHIRE (WYLTESCHIR)

Richard of Chertsey [GL; Commissary Court of London Will 1381]

WIMBLEDON

(Sir) Edward Cecil, Viscount, of Putney [PRO; PCC 1638]

WIMONDSELL (WYMONDESOLD)
  Elkin of Putney [LPL; 96/2916; 98/1 f,94r; Will 1638]
WINALL
  John of Swk St George, gardener [DW/PA/5/1588/31]
WINCHESTER (WYNCHESTER)
  John of Dorking, joiner [DW/PA/5/1624/136]
  John of Horley, husbandman [DW/PA/7/12 f,309; DW/PA/5/1635/134]
  John of Wonersh [DW/PA/7/5 f,81; 1539]
  Reynold of Horley; Worth, Sussex [DW/PA/5/1545/3]
  Richard of Horley, yeoman [DW/PA/7/8 f,350; DW/PA/5/1612/154]
WINCOTT (WYNCOTT)
  Margaret of Mortlake, formerly Margaret Grove [PRO; PCC Will 1513]
WIND
  John of Swk St Saviour [DW/PA/5/1558/293]*
WINDAM
  Alexander of ? Battersea [DW/PA/7/8 f,186; DW/PA/5/1610/150]
  Stephen of Swk St Olave, sailor [DW/PA/7/7 f,536; DW/PA/5/1606/102]
    <Abs 1007>
WINDEVER (WYNDOWER)
  Frances, alias Frances Morris of Newington [PRO; PCC Admon 1620]
  Robert of Kingston [DW/PA/7/2 f,47; 1496]
WINDSOR (WINSER,WYNDESORE)
  Alice, alias Alice Perrers of Upminster, Essex; Kingston [PRO; PCC Will
    1400] <Abs SAC v,29 p,105>
  Andrew, Lord Windsor, of Surrey [PRO; PCC Will 1543]
  Francis of Thames Ditton, gent, [PRO; PCC Will 1622]
  Mary of Long Ditton, widow [PRO; PCC Admon 1631]
  Thomas of Long Ditton, esq, [PRO; PCC Admon 1632]
WINEYARD (WHINYARD)
  John of Cobham [DW/PA/7/11 f,474; DW/PA/5/1628/110]
WINFIELD (WINFEILD)
  Leonard of Bermondsey, citizen and girdler [DW/PA/7/12 f,502; 1638]
WING
  Michael of Stoke Dabernon [HRO; 1595 AD64]
WINGRAVE
  William of Camberwell - Peckham [PRO; PCC 1648]
WINKFIELD (WINKEFEILD)
  William of Swk St Saviour, silkman [DW/PA/7/11 f,238; DW/PA/5/1625/268]
WINNE *see* WYNN
WINNEY (WYNNEY)
  Joan of Swk St Thomas, widow [DW/PA/7/13 f,17; DW/PA/5/1639/151A]
  William of Swk St Thomas, citizen and brewer [DW/PA/7/12 f,58;
    DW/PA/5/1631/120]
WINON (WYNON)
  Jacob of Swk St Olave, cooper [DW/PA/7/13 f,151; DW/PA/5/1641/141]
WINSLOW (WINSLOE)
  Roger of Lambeth - Water Lambeth, waterman [PRO; PCC Will 1604]
WINSPEAR (WYNSPER)
  William of Walton on Thames [DW/PA/5/1563/42]
WINSTON (WYNSTON)
  George of Weybridge, yeoman [DW/PA/5/1575/55]
  Jane of Guildford St Mary, widow [PRO; PCC Will 1618]
  Thomas of Wanborough, yeoman [DW/PA/7/7 f,51; DW/PA/5/1596/62] <Abs 97>

WINTER (WYNTER)
Elizabeth of Swk St Saviour, widow [DW/PA/7/9 f.78; DW/PA/5/1614/136]
John of Lambeth, esq. [PRO; PCC Will 1445]
Rowland of London, citizen and cordwainer [DW/PA/7/7 f.540; DW/PA/5/1606/103] <Abs 1014>
Thomas of Ash [DW/PA/7/7 f.53; DW/PA/5/1596/63] <Abs 101>
William of Bermondsey, citizen and leatherseller [DW/PA/7/11 f.217; DW/PA/5/1625/269]
William, alias William Duke alias Fuller of Chertsey [PRO; PCC Will 1414]
William of Farnham (died overseas) [PRO; PCC Admon 1647]
WINTERBEKE (van WINTERBEKE)
John of ..., [*Dutch*] [DW/PA/5/1592/84]
WINTERSHULL (WYNTERSSELL,WYNTERESHULL,WYNTRESHULL)
Henry of Guildford Holy Trinity [DW/PA/7/2 f.38; c1493]
Jane of Shalford - Wintershall [PRO; PCC Will 1596]
John of Shalford [PRO; PCC Admon 1566]
Robert of Guildford [PRO; PCC Will 1487]
Thomas of Guildford [PRO; PCC Will 1421]
WINTON (WYNTON)
Joan of Coulsdon, widow [DW/PA/5/1576/129]
WINWOOD
Margery of Swk St Saviour - liberty of Paris Garden, widow [DW/PA/7/8 f.225; DW/PA/5/1612/172]
WISDOM (WISDAM,WISDOME,WYSDOME,WYSEDOME)
Edward of Farnham, brickmaker [DW/PA/7/11 f.101; DW/PA/5/1624/137]
John of Albury, yeoman [DW/PA/5/1557/73]
Juliana *see* William
Richard of Windlesham, husbandman [DW/PA/5/1550/52]
Richard of Woking [DW/PA/7/5 f.64; 1539] <Abs 126>
Robert of Capel, bachelor [HRO; 1571 B212]
Simon of Woking [DW/PA/7/10 f.40; DW/PA/5/1617/135]
William *and* Juliana of Godalming [HRO; Reg. Wyk 2 p.150; 1377]
William of Egham - Leatherlake [PRO; PCC Will 1587]
WISE (WYSE)
John of Windlesham [DW/PA/5/1561/44]
John of Windlesham; Winkfield, Berkshire, yeoman [DW/PA/7/7 f.578; DW/PA/5/1607/108] <Abs 1079>
Martin of ...., servant to Edward, Lord Wimbledon [LPL; 96/2857; Will 1628]
WISEHEAD (WISEHEDE)
Richard of Swk St Olave, tailor [DW/PA/7/1 f.45; 1486] <Abs 150>
WISEMAN
John of Felstead, Essex; Bermondsey, esq. [PRO; PCC Will 1559] <Abs Emmison pp.145-146>
Thomas of Lambeth; Great Waltham, Essex, gent. [PRO; PCC Will 1580] <Abs Emmison pp.264-266>
WISEWALL (WYSEWALL)
Urian of Woking, clerk and vicar [DW/PA/7/5 f.19; 1538] <Abs 124>
WITCH (WYCHE)
Richard of Mitcham [PRO; PCC Admon 1625]
WITCHER (WYCHER)
Richard of West Molesey [PRO; PCC Will 1550]
William of Bermondsey, blacksmith [DW/PA/7/7 f.414; DW/PA/5/1603/189] <Abs 772>

WITCHERLEY *see* WICHERLEY
WITHALL
  Richard of Putney *or* Puttenham [DW/PA/7/8 f.400; DW/PA/5/1612/173]
  Robert of Guildford St Nicolas - Artington [DW/PA/7/13 f.41; DW/PA/5/1639/155]
WITHAM
  Christopher of Newington - Kent Street [PRO; PCC 1630]
  Dorothy of Newington, widow [PRO; PCC 1630]
WITHE
  John of Chertsey [PRO; PCC Admon 1588]
WITHERS (WYTHERS)
  David of Woking - Egley; Grays, Essex [DW/PA/5/1593/32]
  Elizabeth of Lambeth - Stockwell, widow [DW/PA/5/1592/118]
  John of Guildford, citizen and merchant tailor [PRO; PCC Will 1589]
  John of Mitcham [PRO; PCC Will 1553]
WITHLOT (WYTH'LIOT')
  Robert of Reigate; Horley [DW/PA/7/1 f.22; 1485] <Abs 73>
WITHWELL *see* WHITWELL
WITLEY
  Harman, alias Harman Awykelder [*Enticknap*] of Stoke next Guildford, beer brewer [*in* DW/PA/5/1555/1]
WITTENSTALL
  Hugh of Swk St Saviour, victualler [DW/PA/7/12 f.18; DW/PA/5/1631/117]
WITTON *see* WHITTON
WIVELL
  Marmaduke of Croydon, esq. [PRO; PCC Will 1623]
WOAN *see* HONE
WODATCHE *see* WOODHATCH
WODD,WODDE *see* WOOD
WODDEN *see* WOODEN
WODDEY *see* WOODY
WODDING *see* WOODEN
WODDYER *see* WOODYER
WODE *see* WOOD
WODECOK,WODECOKE *see* WOODCOCK
WODEHOUS *see* WOODHOUSE
WODELOND *see* WOODLAND
WODEMAN *see* WOODMAN
WODEMOSE *see* WOODMOSE
WODEN,WODENE *see* WOODEN
WODEROVE *see* WOODROOF
WODHATCHE *see* WOODHATCH
WODMAN *see* WOODMAN
WODS *see* WOODS
WODSDALE *see* WOODSDALE
WODSTOCKE,WODSTOK *see* WOODSTOCK
WODYER *see* WOODYER
WOLCRETH *see* WOOLCRETH
WOLF (WOLFE,WOLFFE,WOLLF,WULFF)
  John of Bermondsey [DW/PA/7/5 f.183; 1540]
  John of Walton on Thames [DW/PA/5/1547/29]
  John of Walton on Thames - Hersham, yeoman, senior [DW/PA/7/8 ff.349,390; DW/PA/5/1612/174]
  Richard of Chertsey; Walton on Thames, yeoman [DW/PA/7/5 f.116; 1539]

WOLF (WOLFE, WOLFFE, WOLLF, WULFF) [*continued*]
Richard of Oxted [DW/PA/5/1558/294]*
Richard of Oxted [PRO; PCC 1646]
Robert of Esher [DW/PA/7/3 f.115; 1529]
Thomas of Esher [BM; Add.Ms 24,925 f.16v; 1544] <Abs 35>
Thomasine of Lambeth - Stockwell, widow [DW/PA/5/1557/108]
WOLFORD *see* WOOLFORD
WOLLEBERGH *see* WOOLBOROUGH
WOLLETT *see* WOOLLETT
WOLLEY *see* WOOLLEY
WOLLF *see* WOLF
WOLLMAN *see* WOOLMAN
WOLLRIDGE *see* WOOLRIDGE
WOLLWARD, WOLLWOARD *see* WOOLWARD
WOLMAN *see* WOOLMAN
WOLREDGE, WOLRIDGE *see* WOOLRIDGE
WOLSROPPE *see* WOOLSROPPE
WOLWORD *see* WOOLWARD
WONHAM (WANNHAM, WONAM, WOONHAM, WORNAM, WORNEHAM, WORNHAM)
Eleanor of Kingston, spinster [DW/PA/7/13 f.308; DW/PA/5/1643/97]
Jane of Kingston, widow [DW/PA/7/10 f.273; DW/PA/5/1622/110]
Joan of Dorking, widow [DW/PA/7/12 f.458; DW/PA/5/1638/141]
John of Betchworth [DW/PA/5/1569/35]
John of Beddington [DW/PA/5/1562/59]
John of Long Ditton, yeoman [DW/PA/7/12 f.460; DW/PA/5/1638/157]
John of Long Ditton - Tolworth [PRO; PCC Admon 1639]
John of Esher, husbandman [DW/PA/7/13 f.161; DW/PA/5/1641/142]
John of Kingston, cordwainer [DW/PA/7/13 f.366; 1644]
John of Newdigate, senior [DW/PA/7/12 f.506; 1638]
John of Reigate, tanner [DW/PA/7/9 f.104; DW/PA/5/1614/137]
Miles of Dorking [DW/PA/7/11 f.560; DW/PA/5/1630/120]
Miles of Dorking, yeoman [DW/PA/7/12 f.268; DW/PA/5/1635/125]
Patience of Kingston, widow [DW/PA/7/11 f.97; DW/PA/5/1624/145]
Richard of Betchworth, yeoman [DW/PA/7/7 f.132; DW/PA/5/1597/119] <Abs 243>
Richard of Carshalton, miller [DW/PA/7/7 f.147; DW/PA/5/1597/118] <Abs 273>
Richard of Long Ditton, yeoman, senior [DW/PA/7/7 f.314; DW/PA/5/1600/56] <Abs 559>
Richard of Kingston, yeoman [DW/PA/7/12 f.519; DW/PA/5/1638/140]
Richard of Mitcham, mealman [DW/PA/7/11 f.428; DW/PA/5/1627/107]
Richard of Shalford, husbandman [DW/PA/7/9 f.331; DW/PA/5/1620/139]
Robert of Mitcham [DW/PA/7/2 f.28; 1492]
Thomas of Betchworth; Newdigate, yeoman [DW/PA/7/9 f.123; DW/PA/5/1615/142]
Thomas of Thames Ditton, yeoman [DW/PA/7/8 f.369; DW/PA/5/1612/178]
Thomas of Dorking [DW/PA/7/13 f.38; DW/PA/5/1640/158]
Thomas of Esher [DW/PA/7/9 f.233; DW/PA/5/1617/136]
Thomas of Newdigate [DW/PA/7/12 f.123; DW/PA/5/1632/112]
Thomas of Reigate [DW/PA/7/8 f.91; DW/PA/5/1609/129]
William of Betchworth [HRO; 1557 U791-792]
William of Betchworth, yeoman [DW/PA/7/10 f.257B; DW/PA/5/1622/111]
William of Newdigate [PRO; PCC 1649]

WOOD (WODD,WODDE,WODE,WOODD,WOODDE,WOODE,WOODES,WOODS,WOULD,WOULDE)

Anthony of Carshalton, yeoman [DW/PA/5/1581/11]
Anthony of Rotherhithe, mariner [PRO; PCC Will 1626]
Arnold of Swk St Olave; Bermondsey [PRO; PCC Will 1593]
Beatrice of Swk, widow [DW/PA/7/7 f.329; DW/PA/5/1601/91] <Abs 591>
Christian of ... [*in* DW/PA/5/1571/22] [*Note of admon*]
Christopher of Coulsdon, husbandman [DW/PA/5/1569/66]
David of Croydon [LPL; 98/1 f.43v; Will 1633]
Dorothy of Cobham, widow [DW/PA/5/1605/102] <Abs U182>
Dorothy of Dorking, widow [DW/PA/7/12 f.259; DW/PA/5/1634/111]
Edmund of Kingston, yeoman [DW/PA/5/1578/25]
Edward of Great Bookham, husbandman [DW/PA/7/12 f.229; DW/PA/5/1634/108]
Edward of Chelsham, husbandman [DW/PA/7/7 f.89; 1596] <Abs 163>
Edward of Richmond [PRO; PCC Will 1509]
Elizabeth of ... [DW/PA/7/8 f.264; DW/PA/5/1611/122]
Elizabeth of Chobham, widow of William, husbandman [DW/PA/7/7 f.53; DW/PA/5/1595/89] <Abs 102>
Elizabeth of Croydon, spinster [LPL; 98/1 f.103r; Will 1639]
Elizabeth of Lambeth [DW/PA/7/13 f.76; DW/PA/5/1640/161]
Elizabeth of Wandsworth, widow [DW/PA/5/1587/48]
Epaphroditus of Carshalton [PRO; PCC Will 1592]
Eusebius of Swk St Olave, citizen and clothworker [DW/PA/5/1587/103]
George of Fetcham, blacksmith [DW/PA/7/13 f.151; DW/PA/5/1642/86]
George of Godstone, clerk [PRO; PCC 1649]
Harry of Battersea [DW/PA/5/1563/86]
Henry of Chobham, husbandman [HRO; 1603 B60]
Henry of Clapham [DW/PA/7/4 f.122; 1535]
Henry of Cranleigh, yeoman [PRO; PCC Will 1627]
Henry of Croydon - Waddon [PRO; PCC Will 1539]
Henry of Godstone, clerk [DW/PA/7/9 f.310; DW/PA/5/1619/132]
Henry of Newington [LPL; 98/1 ff.75v (ren.),78r; Will 1636]
Henry of Richmond, yeoman of the kings kitchen [PRO; PCC Will 1604]
Henry of Swk St Saviour, citizen and skinner [DW/PA/7/7 f.44; DW/PA/5/1595/90] <Abs 85>
Humphrey of Oxted, husbandman [DW/PA/7/10 f.62; 1618]
Humphrey of Rotherhithe [PRO; PCC Admon 1633]
Isabel of Croydon, widow [LPL; 96/2861; 98/1 f.28r; Will 1631]
James of Merstham; Earlswood, Reigate; Chipstead, yeoman [PRO; PCC Will 1620] <Soame 1349>
James of Walton on Thames, yeoman [DW/PA/7/7 f.329; DW/PA/5/1601/90] <Abs 615>
Joan of Reigate, widow of Robert [DW/PA/5/1578/96]
John of Chaldon, bachelor [DW/PA/7/8 f.97; DW/PA/5/1609/130]
John of Chobham, tanner [DW/PA/7/13 f.320; DW/PA/5/1645/58]
John of Croydon, yeoman [PRO; PCC Will 1610]
John of Dorking, yeoman, senior [DW/PA/7/8 f.229; DW/PA/5/1612/175]
John of Dorking - Logmore, yeoman, senior [DW/PA/7/10 f.198; DW/PA/5/1621/130]
John of Dunsfold [DW/PA/7/9 f.101; DW/PA/5/1614/139]
John of Dunsfold - Howicks, yeoman [DW/PA/7/9 f.285; 1618]
John of Godalming, clothier [DW/PA/7/7 f.290; DW/PA/5/1599/101] <Abs 518>
John of Godstone - 'Senickes Barne', husbandman [DW/PA/5/1587/108]
John of Godstone [DW/PA/7/7 f.117; DW/PA/5/1597/116] <Abs 216>
John of Merstham, yeoman [LPL; 96/2862; 98/1 f.84r; Will 1637]

WOOD (WODD,WODDE,WODE,WOODD,WOODDE,WOODE,WOODES,WOODS,WOULD,WOULDE)
[*continued*]

John of Sanderstead [PRO; PCC Will 1525]
John of Swk St Saviour, merchant tailor [DW/PA/5/1593/2]
John of Tandridge [DW/PA/7/11 f.567; DW/PA/5/1630/121]
John of Weybridge, gent. [PRO; PCC Will 1598]
John of Weybridge, yeoman [PRO; PCC Will 1601] <Abs. SAC v.10 p.300>
John of Wotton [DW/PA/7/7 f.10; DW/PA/5/1595/86] <Abs 23>
Judith of Swk St Saviour, spinster [DW/PA/7/7 f.424; DW/PA/5/1603/190] <Abs 793>
Margaret of Dorking, widow [DW/PA/7/11 f.160; DW/PA/5/1624/138]
Margaret of Swk St Olave, widow [DW/PA/5/1557/15]*
Mary of Kingston, spinster [PRO; PCC Admon 1638]
Michael of Byfleet, yeoman [DW/PA/7/12 f.311; DW/PA/5/1637/99]
Michael of Chaldon [PRO; PCC 1648]
Michael of Coulsdon; Carshalton; Chipstead, yeoman [DW/PA/7/7 f.535; DW/PA/5/1606/104] <Abs 1006>
Michael of Coulsdon [PRO; PCC 1649]
Nicholas of Battersea [PRO; PCC 1648]
Nicholas of Chobham [PRO; PCC Will 1560]
Nicholas of Pirbright [DW/PA/7/7 f.519; DW/PA/5/1606/106] <Abs 973>
Peter of Battersea, yeoman [DW/PA/7/11 f.198; DW/PA/5/1624/139]
Peter of Betchworth - Brockham [DW/PA/7/12 f.412; DW/PA/5/1637/104]
Peter of Dunsfold [PRO; PCC 1641]
Richard of Carshalton [PRO; PCC Admon 1613]
Richard of Chelsham; Tatsfield; Sanderstead, yeoman [DW/PA/5/1605/103] <Abs U183>
Richard of Chelsham [PRO; PCC Admon 1635]
Richard of Coulsdon, yeoman [DW/PA/5/1570/77]
Richard of Ditton, haberdasher [PRO; PCC Will 1589]
Richard of Dorking [DW/PA/7/2 f.2; 1490]
Richard of Godstone [DW/PA/7/6 f.193; 1560]
Richard of Pirbright [DW/PA/7/12 f.76; DW/PA/5/1632/109]
Richard of Richmond [PRO; PCC Will 1521]
Richard of Swk St George, cooper [DW/PA/5/1579/99]*
Richard of Streatham - Tooting Bec, husbandman [DW/PA/7/12 f.372; DW/PA/5/1627/110]
Richard of Warlingham, yeoman [DW/PA/7/11 f.110; DW/PA/5/1624/140]
Robert of Battersea, husbandman [DW/PA/5/1604/73] <Abs U123>
Robert, alias Robert Delewood of Carshalton, weaver [DW/PA/7/7 f.52; DW/PA/5/1596/18] <Abs 93>
Robert of Chobham; Hambledon, tailor [DW/PA/7/7 f.101; DW/PA/5/1596/65] <Abs 183>
Robert of Long Ditton, husbandman [DW/PA/7/11 f.99; DW/PA/5/1624/141]
Robert of Reigate, tanner [DW/PA/5/1571/9]
Robert of Rotherhithe, bachelor [PRO; PCC Admon 1635]
Robert of Shalford, tailor [DW/PA/7/13 f.291; DW/PA/5/1644/20]
Robert of Titsey, husbandman [DW/PA/7/9 f.324; DW/PA/5/1619/133]
Thomas of Banstead; Woodmansterne; Walton on the Hill [DW/PA/5/1604/75] <Abs U124>
Thomas of Chobham, husbandman *or* labourer [HRO; 1614 B87]
Thomas of Chobham, husbandman [DW/PA/7/12 f.513; DW/PA/5/1638/159]
Thomas of Coulsdon - Waddington, yeoman [DW/PA/7/9 f.209; DW/PA/5/1616/149] [*and*] [SRO; 212/3412; 1616]

WOOD (WODD,WODDE,WODE,WOODD,WOODDE,WOODE,WOODES,WOODS,WOULD,WOULDE)
[*continued*]
Thomas of Croydon, gent., senior [PRO; PCC Will 1624]
Thomas of Dorking, yeoman [DW/PA/5/1571/18]
Thomas of Dunsfold, yeoman, senior [DW/PA/5/1605/104]
Thomas of Godalming, cordwainer [DW/PA/7/12 f.20; DW/PA/5/1631/118]
Thomas of Godstone [DW/PA/7/3 f.141; 1530]
Thomas of Lambeth [PRO; PCC Will 1594]
Thomas of Leatherhead, tanner [DW/PA/5/1593/208]
Thomas of Merton, gent. [PRO; PCC Will 1594]
Thomas of Morden, labourer [DW/PA/5/1588/26]*
Thomas of Rotherhithe [PRO; PCC 1631]
Thomas of St Michael Cornhill, London; St Benet Fink, London; Swk, pewterer [GL; Commissary Court of London Will 1571]
Thomas of Swk, skinner [DW/PA/7/7 f.142; DW/PA/5/1597/117] <Abs 261>
Thomas of Swk St Olave, glover [DW/PA/7/8 f.270; DW/PA/5/1613/142]
Valentine of Coulsdon [PRO; PCC Admon 1595]
Walter of Swk St Olave [DW/PA/5/1563/99]
William of Battersea, yeoman [DW/PA/7/11 f.603; DW/PA/5/1630/122]
William of Battersea [PRO; PCC 1647]
William of Bermondsey, baker [DW/PA/7/10 f.120; DW/PA/5/1620/140]
William of Capel [DW/PA/7/8 f.98; DW/PA/5/1609/131]
William of Chobham, yeoman [DW/PA/7/7 f.3; DW/PA/5/1595/87] <Abs 8>
William of Coulsdon, yeoman, senior [DW/PA/7/12 f.357; DW/PA/5/1637/100]
William of Effingham, husbandman [DW/PA/5/1568/61]
William of Ewhurst, ashburner [DW/PA/7/6 f.216; 1561]
William of Godstone - 'Whiteley House', yeoman [DW/PA/7/10 f.225; DW/PA/5/1621/131]
William of Mickleham, husbandman [DW/PA/5/1580/45]
William of Pirbright, husbandman [DW/PA/7/10 f.271; DW/PA/5/1622/109]
William of Swk St Olave [DW/PA/5/1558/295]*
William of Woking, husbandman [DW/PA/7/10 f.215; DW/PA/5/1621/132]
see also ATWOOD; BITHEWOOD

WOODACH *see* WOODHATCH

WOODCLERK (WOODCLERKE)
Edmund of Stoke Dabernon [DW/PA/5/1579/101]*
John of Walton on Thames - Hersham, yeoman [HRO; 1590 B68]
Richard of Walton on Thames - Hersham [DW/PA/7/5 f.169; 1540]

WOODCOCK (WODECOK,WODECOKE,WOODCOCKE)
Ann of Clapham [PRO; PCC Admon 1634]
George of Lambeth, gent. [PRO; PCC Will 1522]
Henry of Lambeth [PRO; PCC Will 1515]
James of Rotherhithe [PRO; PCC Will 1572]
James of Rotherhithe [PRO; PCC Will 1604] <Abs, SAC v.11 p.299>
James of Rotherhithe [PRO; PCC Admon 1604]
James of Rotherhithe, gent. [PRO; PCC Will 1610] <Abs, SAC v.24 p.62>
John of Surrey [PRO; PCC Will 1408]
John of 'Stanrigge, Surrey' [? Tandridge] [PRO; PCC Will 1428]
Samuel of Rotherhithe [PRO; PCC Will 1601] <Abs, SAC v.10 p.299>
William of Bermondsey, tailor [DW/PA/7/11 f.177; DW/PA/5/1625/272]
William of Rotherhithe, gent. [DW/PA/7/8 f.12; DW/PA/5/1608/116]
William of Wimbledon, clerk [PRO; PCC Will 1487]

WOODCROFT
John of Banstead, clerk [PRO; PCC Will 1465]

WOODD,WOODDE *see* WOOD
WOODDEN *see* WOODEN
WOODDY *see* WOODY
WOODE *see* WOOD
WOODEN (WODDEN,WODDING,WODEN,WODENE,WOODDEN,WOODINES)
  Elizabeth of Nutfield, widow [DW/PA/7/13 f.36; DW/PA/5/1639/154]
  John of Lingfield [? HRO; 1521]
  John of Godstone; Horne, yeoman [DW/PA/7/7 f.110; 1597] (Abs 199)
  John of Horne, husbandman [DW/PA/7/10 f.78; DW/PA/5/1619/134]
  John of Titsey, yeoman [DW/PA/7/11 f.611; DW/PA/5/1630/123]
  John of Warlingham [HRO; 1614 AD102]
  Katherine of Sanderstead, widow [DW/PA/7/13 f.122; DW/PA/5/1640/166]
  Richard of Warlingham, yeoman [DW/PA/7/8 f.143; DW/PA/5/1611/123]
  Robert of Warlingham [PRO; PCC Admon 1647]
  Thomas of Chelsham [DW/PA/7/4 f.154; 1536]
  Thomas of Nutfield [PRO; PCC Admon 1616]
  William of Warlingham [DW/PA/7/2 f.105; 1515]
  William of Warlingham [DW/PA/5/1562/21]
WOODES *see* WOOD
WOODGATE
  Henry of Croydon [LPL; 98/1 f.24v; Will 1631]
WOODGER *see* WOODYER
WOODHATCH (WODATCHE,WODHATCHE,WOODACH,WOODHACH,WOODHATCHE)
  Alice of Frensham [DW/PA/7/3 f.110; 1529]
  Robert of Shere [DW/PA/5/1587/29]
  Roger of Great Bookham, shoemaker [DW/PA/7/9 f.134; DW/PA/5/1615/143]
  Thomas of Seale - Tongham [HRO; 1608 B83]
  William of Chiddingfold [DW/PA/7/13 f.27; DW/PA/5/1639/152]
  William of Elstead; Thursley, yeoman [DW/PA/7/7 f.270;
    DW/PA/5/1599/88] (Abs 475)
  William of Thursley [DW/PA/7/9 f.297; 1618]
  William of Wanborough [DW/PA/5/1571/32]
WOODHOUSE (WODEHOUS)
  John of Camberwell - Peckham [PRO; PCC Will 1413]
WOODIER *see* WOODYER
WOODINES *see* WOODDEN
WOODLAND (de WODELOND,WODELOND,WOODLANDE)
  Elizabeth of Wandsworth [DW/PA/5/1561/63]
  Richard of Lambeth, rector
  Richard of Lambeth; Arundel, Sussex, rector of Lambeth [HRO;
    Reg. Wyk 2 p.141; 1376] [*and*] [LPL; Reg. Abp Sudbury f.82; Will 1376]
WOODMAN (WODEMAN,WOODMANE)
  Alan of Reigate, yeoman, senior [DW/PA/7/8 f.205; DW/PA/5/1611/124]
  Alice of Reigate, widow [DW/PA/5/1555/10]
  Benjamin of Reigate [DW/PA/7/11 f.481; DW/PA/5/1628/111]
  Christopher of Ewell, husbandman [DW/PA/5/1570/7]
  Elizabeth *see* Elizabeth Dubber
  Elizabeth of Epsom, widow of James [DW/PA/7/7 f.210; DW/PA/5/1598/90]
    (Abs 375)
  Henry of Reigate, yeoman [DW/PA/5/1549/2]
  John of Great Bookham; Leigh, yeoman [DW/PA/7/8 f.403;DW/PA/5/1614/138]
  John of Buckland - 'Colye' [DW/PA/7/4 f.106; 1535]
  John of Buckland - 'Colley'; Betchworth; Horley; Ashington, Sussex
    [DW/PA/7/6 f.80; DW/PA/5/1559/135]

WOODMAN (WODEMAN,WOODMANE) [*continued*]

John of Buckland - Dowdes; Reigate; Leigh; Great Bookham, yeoman [DW/PA/7/7 f,291; DW/PA/5/1600/55] <Abs 521>

John of Chessington [DW/PA/7/8 f,152; DW/PA/5/1611/125]

John of Chessington, husbandman [DW/PA/7/12 f,59; DW/PA/5/1631/121]

John of Fetcham, clothier, senior [HRO; 1637 B51]

John of Merstham [LPL; 98/1 f,70v; Will 1635]

John of Reigate [DW/PA/7/4 f,135; 1536]

Mary of Reigate [DW/PA/7/11 f,262; DW/PA/5/1625/273]

Richard of Betchworth; Headley; Penhowe, Monmouthshire, gent, [DW/PA/7/9 f,202; 1617]

Richard of Epsom, husbandman [HRO; 1608 B84]

Richard of Ewell, husbandman [DW/PA/7/11 f,95; DW/PA/5/1624/142]

Richard of Horley; Buckland, yeoman [DW/PA/7/8 f,112; DW/PA/5/1610/145]

Robert of Fetcham, husbandman [DW/PA/7/7 f,490; DW/PA/5/1604/74] <Abs 925>

Robert of Horne, husbandman [DW/PA/7/12 f,448; DW/PA/5/1638/152]

Thomas of Banstead [DW/PA/7/4 f,156; 1536]

Thomas of Carshalton [PRO; PCC Will 1472]

Thomas of Fetcham, yeoman [DW/PA/7/7 f,363; DW/PA/5/1602/94] <Abs 666>

Thomas of Epsom, yeoman [DW/PA/7/8 f,283; DW/PA/5/1613/143]

Thomas of Horley [DW/PA/7/12 f,455; DW/PA/5/1638/148]

Walter of Betchworth [PRO; PCC Will 1627]

William of Betchworth, gent, [DW/PA/7/11 f,289; DW/PA/5/1625/274]

William of Buckland, senior [DW/PA/7/2 f,10; 1491]

William of Buckland; Great Bookham, yeoman [DW/PA/7/7 f,533; DW/PA/5/1606/105] <Abs 1003>

William of Morden, husbandman [DW/PA/7/5 f,55; 1539] <Abs 66>

William of Walton on Thames, yeoman [DW/PA/7/7 f,231 *and* DW/PA/7/9 f,133; DW/PA/5/1598/91 *and* DW/PA/5/1615/144] <Abs 407>

WOODMOSE (WODEMOSE)

Thomas of Bermondsey [HRO; Reg, Way 1 p,97; 1468]

WOODROFF (WODEROVE,WOODROFFE,WOODROOF,WOODROOFE,WOODROOFFE,WOODRUFF)

(Sir) David of Seale - Poyle, knight [PRO; PCC Will 1604] <Abs, SAC v,11 pp,130-131 *and* v,32 p,32>

(Dame) Griselda of Seale, widow of (Sir) Nicholas, knight [PRO; PCC Will 1607] <Abs, SAC v,12 pp,100-101 *and* v,32 p,88>

John of Bisley, yeoman [DW/PA/5/1574/23]

John of Kingston [HRO; Reg, Way 1 p,44; 1457]

Margaret of Dorking, later Margaret Mattok [PRO; PCC Will 1503]

(Sir) Nicholas of Seale - Poyle, knight [PRO; PCC Will 1598] <Abs SAC v,32 p,87>

Robert of Seale - Poyle, esq, [DW/PA/7/13 f,2; DW/PA/5/1639/148]

WOODROSE

Edmund of Swk St Saviour - liberty of the Clink, waterman [DW/PA/7/11 f,103; DW/PA/5/1624/143]

WOODRUFF *see* WOODROFF

WOODS *see* WOOD

WOODSDALE (WODSDALE)

Nicholas of Chobham, husbandman [DW/PA/7/7 f,320; DW/PA/5/1600/52] <Abs 572>

WOODSTOCK (WODSTOCK,WODSTOCKE,WODSTOK,WOODSTOCKE)

Agnes of Sanderstead, widow [DW/PA/5/1591/17]

Henry of Farleigh, husbandman [PRO; PCC Will 1604] <Abs, SAC v,11 p,131>

WOODSTOCK (WODSTOCK,WODSTOCKE,WODSTOK,WOODSTOCKE) [*continued*]
John of Betchworth, yeoman [DW/PA/5/1558/296]*
John of Mitcham; Croydon - Waddon; Merton; Headley, yeoman [DW/PA/7/9 f.192; DW/PA/5/1616/151]
John of Oxted, yeoman [DW/PA/7/11 f.518; DW/PA/5/1629/111]
John of Sanderstead [DW/PA/7/1 f.22; 1485] <Abs 72>
John of Sanderstead, yeoman [HRO; Reg. CCB 20 p.17; 1563] [*and*] [DW/PA/5/1563/84]
Katherine of Mickleham, widow [DW/PA/7/10 f.64; 1618]
Peter of Reigate, innkeeper, senior [DW/PA/7/11 f.30; DW/PA/5/1623/134]
Richard of Mickleham; Sanderstead, husbandman [DW/PA/7/7 f.342; DW/PA/5/1601/92] <Abs 621>
Robert of Godstone, yeoman [DW/PA/7/8 ff.209,399; DW/PA/5/1612/177]
William of Sanderstead [DW/PA/7/1 f.98; 1490] <Abs 322>
WOODWARD (WOODEWARD,WOODWARDE)
Christopher of Lambeth, esq. [PRO; PCC Will 1627]
John of Caterham, yeoman [DW/PA/5/1579/96]*
John of Oxted [DW/PA/7/4 f.113; 1535]
Katherine of Lambeth - Lambeth Marsh, widow [PRO; PCC 1638]
Robert of Swk [HRO; 1573 AD36]
Thomas of Long Ditton [DW/PA/7/11 f.437; DW/PA/5/1628/112]
Thomas of Newington [LPL; 96/2896; Will 1625]
Thomas of Putney, gent. [PRO; PCC 1633]
William of Chertsey, yeoman [DW/PA/7/4 f.202; 1537]
WOODY (WOODDY)
John of Lingfield, yeoman [DW/PA/7/8 f.96; DW/PA/5/1609/128]
Richard of Lingfield, yeoman [PRO; PCC Will 1583]
Thomas of Lingfield, yeoman [PRO; PCC Will 1605] <Abs. SAC v.12 p.89>
WOODYER (WODDYER,WODYER,WOODGER,WOODIER,WOODYERE)
Bartholomew of Guildford St Nicolas, shearman [DW/PA/7/10 f.288; DW/PA/5/1623/135]
Joan of Chiddingfold [DW/PA/7/4 f.205; 1537]
John of Compton [DW/PA/7/6 f.94; DW/PA/5/1559/93]
Robert of Wonersh, husbandman [HRO; 1639 B75]
Thomas of Chiddingfold [DW/PA/7/4 f.189; 1536]
Thomas of Dunsfold, labourer [HRO; 1596 B76]
Thomas of Dunsfold; Cranleigh, labourer [DW/PA/7/7 f.64; DW/PA/5/1596/64] <Abs 123>
Thomas of Hascombe [DW/PA/7/8 f.221; DW/PA/5/1612/176]
Thomas of Witley, husbandman [HRO; 1603 B61]
William of Farnham - Wrecclesham, husbandman [DW/PA/7/11 f.327; DW/PA/5/1624/144]
William of Godalming - Eashing, yeoman [DW/PA/7/13 f.416; DW/PA/5/1645/64]
WOOLCRETH (WOLCRETH)
Katherine of Swk St Margaret [DW/PA/7/2 f.90; 1505]
WOOLLETT
Edward of Rotherhithe [PRO; PCC Admon 1596]
WOOLLEY (WOLLEY)
(Sir) Francis of Pyrford, knight [PRO; PCC Will 1609] <Abs. SAC v.23 p.147>
(Sir) John of Pyrford, knight [PRO; PCC Will 1596]
John of Swk St Olave, weaver [DW/PA/7/11 f.181; DW/PA/5/1625/271]
John of Swk St Thomas, weaver [DW/PA/7/9 f.94; DW/PA/5/1616/114]

WOOLBOROUGH (WOLLEBERGH)
  Nicholas of Nutfield [PRO; PCC Will 1407]
WOOLFALL
  Henry of Swk St Saviour, yeoman [DW/PA/7/6 f.132; 1559]
WOOLFE *see* WOLF
WOOLFORD (WOLFORD)
  Henry of Dorking [PRO; PCC Will 1435]
WOOLFRIDGE (WULFRIGGE,WULRYCHE)
  Henry of Farnham [DW/PA/7/1 f.60; 1487] <Abs 200>
  William of Farnham [DW/PA/7/1 f.60; 1487] <Abs 198>
WOOLHOUSE
  Millicent of Mitcham, widow [PRO; PCC Will 1606] <Abs. SAC v.12 p.103>
WOOLMAN (WOLLMAN,WOLMAN)
  Charles of Bermondsey [DW/PA/5/1587/82]
  Eleanor of Swk St Mary Magdalen, widow [DW/PA/5/1588/90]
  Thomas of Wimbledon [PRO; PCC Will 1629]
  Thomas of Wimbledon [PRO; PCC 1630]
WOOLMER
  Hugh of Mortlake, blacksmith [LPL; 96/2898; Will 1629]
WOOLRIDGE (WOLLRIDGE,WOLREDGE,WOLRIDGE)
  Adam of Farnham [HRO; Reg. CCB 20 p.11; 1563]
  Julian, alias Julian Hove of Lingfield [PRO; PCC Admon 1649]
  Stephen of Ewell [DW/PA/5/1593/153]
WOOLSROPPE (WOLSROPPE)
  Welfurd [? Wilfred] of Swk St Olave, hatmaker [DW/PA/7/2 f.58; 1499]
WOOLWARD (WOLLWARD,WOLWOARD,WOLWORD,WOOLLWARD)
  Elizabeth of Godalming - Farncombe, widow [DW/PA/7/13 f.136; DW/PA/5/1640/171]
  Shadrach of Godalming - Farncombe, husbandman, senior [DW/PA/7/13 f.128; DW/PA/5/1640/167]
WOONHAM *see* WONHAM
WOORLINGTON *see* WORLINGTON
WOOTTON (WOTTON)
  Christopher of Newington [LPL; 96/2900; Will 1625]
  Edmund of Chelsham [PRO; PCC Will 1524]
  Edmund of Sanderstead, priest [PRO; PCC Will 1545]
  John of Charlwood; Buxted, Sussex; Staplehurst, Kent; Maidstone, Kent, master of Maidstone College [LPL; Reg. Abp Chichele i f.309; Will 1417]
WORDSWORTH (WORSWORTH)
  Robert of Morden, vicar [DW/PA/7/2 f.29; 1492]
  William of Betchworth, vicar [HRO; 1533 B43]
WORGAN (WORGIN)
  Mary of Newington, spinster [PRO; PCC Admon 1617]
  Phillip of Rotherhithe, shipwright [PRO; PCC Will 1624]
WORLEY (WORLEIGHE,WURLEY)
  Agnes of Chertsey, widow [DW/PA/7/6 f.55; DW/PA/5/1559/94]
  John of Newington - Walworth [PRO; PCC Admon 1596]
  Mary of Reigate [DW/PA/7/11 f.490; DW/PA/5/1628/113]
  Thomas of Rotherhithe [PRO; PCC Admon 1616]
WORLINGTON (WOORLINGTON)
  James of Swk St Saviour - liberty of the Clink, waterman [DW/PA/7/7 f.275; DW/PA/5/1599/89] <Abs 488>
WORMALL
  Christopher of Lambeth - Water Lambeth, gent. [PRO; PCC 1639]

WORMALL [*continued*]
  Millicent of Lambeth [PRO; PCC 1645]
  Richard of Lambeth, bachelor [PRO; PCC Admon 1639]
WORNAM,WORNEHAM,WORNHAM *see* WONHAM
WORSFOLD (WORSFELDE,WORSFOLDE,WORSFORD,WORSHFOLDE)
  David of Cranleigh, yeoman [DW/PA/7/10 f.184; DW/PA/5/1619/135]
  Edward of Ockley [PRO; PCC 1633]
  Henry of Capel [PRO; PCC Will 1598]
  John of Abinger [PRO; PCC Will 1593]
  Richard of Ockley [PRO; PCC Admon 1599]
  Robert of Abinger [PRO; PCC Will 1522]
  Robert of Abinger, yeoman [DW/PA/5/1579/104]*
  Robert of Abinger, yeoman [DW/PA/7/12 f.506; DW/PA/5/1639/147]
  William of Wotton, yeoman [HRO; 1585 B79]
WORSHAM
  John, alias John Wyrsham of Farnham - Badshot, yeoman [DW/PA/5/1576/122]
  William of Ash, husbandman [DW/PA/7/12 f.486; DW/PA/5/1638/151]
WORSHFOLDE *see* WORSFOLD
WORSLEY (WORSLIE)
  James of Stoke next Guildford, carpenter [DW/PA/7/12 f.302; DW/PA/5/1635/132]
  John of Mitcham, gent. [PRO; PCC 1630] <Scroope 1124>
WORSOPP
  John of Clapham [PRO; PCC Will 1538]
  John of Clapham, gent. [PRO; PCC Will 1595]
  Sarah of Barnes, widow [PRO; PCC 1647]
WORSWORTH *see* WORDSWORTH
WORT
  Robert of Bermondsey, feltmaker [PRO; PCC Will 1626]
WORTH (de WORTH)
  (Sir) John of Meysey Hampton, Gloucestershire; Eton Meysy, Wiltshire; Swk, knight [LPL; Reg. Abp Courteney f.238; Will 1391]
WORTHINGTON (WORTHINTON,WORTINGTON)
  Anthony of Horsell, husbandman [HRO; 1565 B125-127] [*and*] [DW/PA/5/1565/6]
  John of Thorpe, husbandman [DW/PA/7/10 f.94; DW/PA/5/1619/136]
  Urian of Horsell; New Windsor, Berkshire; Pyrford, yeoman [DW/PA/7/9 f.265; 1618]
WORWOOD *see* HORWOOD
WOTTON *see* WOOTTON
WOULD,WOULDE *see* WOOD
WRANGHAM (WRAUGHAN)
  John of Bramley [GL; Commissary Court of London Will 1497]
WRAY (WRAYE)
  Michael of Lambeth [PRO; PCC Admon 1597]
WREN (WRENE,WRENN,WRENNE)
  Alice of Cobham [DW/PA/7/5 f.130; 1539]
  John of Epsom [DW/PA/5/1556/14]
  John of Guildford St Mary [DW/PA/7/5 f.174; 1540]
  John of Lingfield, shoemaker [DW/PA/7/13 f.132; DW/PA/5/1640/169]
  Robert of Cobham [DW/PA/7/1 f.97; 1489] <Abs 318>
  Robert of Thames Ditton [DW/PA/5/1624/146]
  Thomas of Thames Ditton [DW/PA/7/5 f.129; 1539]
  William of Thames Ditton - Claygate, husbandman [DW/PA/5/1562/58]

WRENCH (WRENTCH,WRINCH)
Richard of Swk St Saviour, gardener [DW/PA/7/11 f.332; DW/PA/5/1625/275]
Thomas of ... [DW/PA/7/9 f.79; DW/PA/5/1614/140]
William of Epsom, yeoman, senior [DW/PA/7/11 f.21; DW/PA/5/1623/136]
William of Epsom, yeoman [DW/PA/7/13 f.401; DW/PA/5/1645/61]
WRENE,WRENNE *see* WREN
WRENTCH *see* WRENCH
WRENWRIGHT *see* WAINWRIGHT
WRETILL
John of Camberwell - Peckham [PRO; PCC Will 1417]
WRIGHT (RIGHT,WRIGHTE,WRYEGHT,WRYGHT,WRYGHTE)
Agnes of Swk St Olave, widow [HRO; Reg. Fox 2 p.28; 1507]
Alice of Betchworth [PRO; PCC Will 1551]
Alice of Chertsey, widow [PRO; PCC 1647]
Ann, alias Ann Travers of Streatham - Tooting Bec [PRO; PCC Admon 1585]
Anthony of Swk St Saviour, shipwright [DW/PA/5/1579/107]*
Cicely of Swk St Olave [DW/PA/7/11 f.326; DW/PA/5/1625/276]
Edmund of Newdigate [DW/PA/5/1574/5]
Elizabeth of Richmond, spinster, daughter of (Sir) George, knight [PRO; PCC 1634]
George of Chertsey [DW/PA/5/1587/100]
(Sir) George of Richmond, knight [PRO; PCC Will 1624]
(Sir) George of Richmond, knight [PRO; PCC 1631]
George of Swk St Saviour, waterman [DW/PA/7/7 f.236; DW/PA/5/1598/92] <Abs 415>
Jane of Fetcham, spinster [DW/PA/7/13 f.187; DW/PA/5/1641/147]
John of Charlwood [PRO; PCC Admon 1618]
John of Newdigate [DW/PA/5/1555/58]
John of Newington [PRO; PCC Admon 1594]
John of Ockley, yeoman [DW/PA/7/7 f.368; DW/PA/5/1602/93] <Abs 675>
John of Oxted, husbandman [DW/PA/5/1579/105]*
John of Swk St George [DW/PA/7/11 f.608; DW/PA/5/1630/124]
John of Swk St Olave; Chatham, Kent, shipwright [DW/PA/5/1593/42]
Joseph of Bermondsey [PRO; PCC 1647]
Juliana of Rotherhithe, widow [PRO; PCC Will 1566]
Katherine of Carshalton, widow [PRO; PCC Will 1575]
Lawrence of Swk St Olave, citizen and joiner [DW/PA/5/1596/66] <Abs U10>
Mercy of Bermondsey, widow [DW/PA/7/9 f.42; DW/PA/5/1614/141]
Morgan of Reigate; Blechingley, tanner [DW/PA/7/9 f.252; DW/PA/5/1617/137]
Nicholas of Alfold, miller [DW/PA/7/13 f.413; DW/PA/5/1645/62]
Nicholas of Rusper, Sussex; Charlwood; Horley [DW/PA/7/8 f.14; DW/PA/5/1608/117]
Nicholas of Newdigate [DW/PA/5/1574/106]*
Peter of Kingston [DW/PA/7/9 f.118; DW/PA/5/1615/145]
Ralph of Egham, yeoman [DW/PA/5/1569/67]
Randolph of Beddington, clerk and parson [DW/PA/5/1578/85]
Richard of Beddington; Carshalton, husbandman [DW/PA/7/4 f.100; 1534]
Richard of Camberwell, carpenter [DW/PA/5/1574/15 *and, in* DW/PA/5/1575/26]
Richard of Clapham [PRO; PCC 1641]
Richard of Clapham [PRO; PCC Admon 1642]
Richard of Guildford, clothworker [DW/PA/7/13 f.179; DW/PA/5/1641/146]

WRIGHT (RIGHT,WRIGHTE,WRYEGHT,WRYGHT,WRYGHTE) [*continued*]
Richard of Guildford St Mary, shearman [DW/PA/7/7 f.171; DW/PA/5/1597/120] <Abs 314>
Richard of Newdigate [DW/PA/7/7 f.17; DW/PA/5/1595/18] <Abs 37>
Richard of Newdigate; Ifield, Sussex, yeoman [DW/PA/7/9 f.269; 1618]
Richard of Swk St Saviour, clothworker [DW/PA/7/9 f.80; DW/PA/5/1614/142]
Robert of Blechingley [DW/PA/5/1569/39]
Robert of Horley [PRO; PCC 1634]
Robert of Ockley, yeoman [DW/PA/7/10 f.93; DW/PA/5/1616/116] <Abs U211>
(Sir) Robert of Richmond, knight [PRO; PCC Will 1610] <Abs, SAC v.24 p.60>
Robert of Swk St Olave, shipwright [DW/PA/5/1591/63]
Robert of Swk St Saviour [DW/PA/5/1578/81]
Solomon of Charlwood [PRO; PCC Will *and* Admon 1594]
Stephen of Farnham [HRO; 1633 B59]
Sybil, alias Sybil Sherley of Newington, widow [PRO; PCC Admon 1641]
Thomas of Ashtead, husbandman [DW/PA/5/1546/17]
Thomas of Kingston - Ham Hatch, carpenter, senior [DW/PA/7/8 f.40; DW/PA/5/1607/110]
Thomas of Kingston, widower [PRO; PCC Admon 1638]
Thomas of Newdigate [DW/PA/7/2 f.176; 1522]
Thomas of Newdigate [DW/PA/7/10 f.165; DW/PA/5/1621/133]
Valentine of Newdigate [DW/PA/7/4 f.118; 1535]
William of Bermondsey, citizen and leatherseller [PRO; PCC Will 1602]
William of Kingston [DW/PA/7/11 f.221; DW/PA/5/1625/277]
William of Newdigate - Lyne [PRO; PCC Will 1607] <Abs, SAC v.12 p.204>
William of Swk St Saviour, waterman [DW/PA/7/5 f.217; 1541]
William of Swk St Saviour [DW/PA/7/8 f.8; DW/PA/5/1608/118]
William of Wandsworth, clerk [PRO; PCC Will 1528]

WRIGHTSON (WRYTHSON)
John of Swk St George [DW/PA/7/3 f.114; 1529]

WRINCH *see* WRENCH

WRINTON (WRYNTON)
Richard of Woking [DW/PA/7/5 f.143; 1540]

WROTH (ROUGHT,WROTE,WROUGHT)
Francis of Kingston; St Giles Cripplegate, London, esq. [PRO; PCC 1638]
George of Farnham [PRO; PCC 1644]
John of Farnham, bachelor [PRO; PCC Admon 1649]
Robert of Farnham, shoemaker [DW/PA/5/1571/33]

WROTTESLY
(Sir) George of Guildford, knight [PRO; PCC Admon 1637]

WROUGHT *see* WROTH

WRYEGHT,WRYGHT,WRYGHTE *see* WRIGHT

WRYNTON *see* WRINTON

WRYTHSON *see* WRIGHTSON

WULFF *see* WOLFE

WULFRIGGE,WULRYCHE *see* WOOLFRIDGE

WURLEY *see* WORLEY

WYATT (WYAT,WYOTT)
Francis of Puttenham; Compton; Isleworth, Middlesex, gent. [PRO; PCC 1635] <Abs SAC v.3 pp.304-309>
Henry of Godalming - Shackleford; Queenhithe, London [PRO; PCC Will 1645] <Abs SAC v.3 pp.304-309>

WYATT (WYAT,WYOTT) [*continued*]
Jane of Godalming, spinster [PRO; PCC Admon 1635]
Margaret of Isleworth, Middlesex; Godalming - Shackleford, widow of Richard, citizen and carpenter [PRO; PCC 1633] <Abs SAC v.3 pp.299-304>
Richard of St Peter Paul's Wharf, London; Dunsfold; Godalming - Shackleford; Puttenham; Hambledon; Compton; Chiddingfold, citizen and carpenter [PRO; PCC Will 1619] <Abs SAC v.3 pp.292-296>
Roger of Witley, gent. [DW/PA/7/11 f.400; DW/PA/5/1627/111]
Timothy of Puttenham, widow [PRO; PCC 1637]
William of Godalming - Shackleford [PRO; PCC Admon 1634]
William of Richmond, gent. [DW/PA/7/8 f.305; DW/PA/5/1613/144]
WYBRAND
Edward of Swk St Olave, dyer [DW/PA/7/11 f.248; DW/PA/5/1625/278]
WYCHAM *see* WICKHAM
WYCHE *see* WITCH
WYCHEHALFE *see* WICKHALF
WYCHER *see* WITCHER
WYCKER *see* WICKER
WYCLIFFE (WICKLIFFE,WYCLIFF)
Peter of Swk St Saviour, victualler [DW/PA/5/1570/103]
Richard of Carshalton, citizen and goldsmith [PRO; PCC Will 1577]
WYDEN *see* WIDEN
WYE (WEY)
Edward of Egham, yeoman [DW/PA/7/12 f.272; DW/PA/5/1635/126]
Henry of Cobham; Heckfield, Hampshire [DW/PA/7/4 f.151; 1536]
John of Chobham [DW/PA/5/1550/48]
John of Chobham, yeoman [DW/PA/7/13 f.491; DW/PA/5/1648/18] <Abs U268>
Richard of Chobham, husbandman [DW/PA/5/1550/47]
Richard of Wonersh [DW/PA/7/13 f.1; 1639]
Thomas of Chobham, husbandman, senior [HRO; 1601 AD49]
WYFOULD
William of Horsell, husbandman [DW/PA/5/1563/43]
WYGGS *see* WIGGS
WYGHT,WYGHTE *see* WHITE
WYGHTMAN *see* WIGHTMAN
WYKE *see* ATWICK; WICKS
WYKENDEN *see* WICKENDON
WYKER *see* WICKER
WYKERSON *see* WICKERSON
WYKYNG *see* WICKING
WYKYS *see* ATWICK; WICKS
WYLCOCKES *see* WILCOX
WYLDBORE *see* WILDBOAR
WYLD,WYLDE *see* WILDE
WYLHAMSON *see* WILLIAMSON
WYLLD *see* WILDE
WYLLFORD,WYLFORD *see* WILFORD
WYLKYN,WYLKYNS *see* WILKINS
WYLKYNSON,WILKYSON *see* WILKINSON
WYLLET *see* WILLET
WYLLIAMS,WYLLMES *see* WILLIAMS
WYLLYNGTON *see* WILLINGTON
WYLSON *see* WILSON
WYLTESCHIR *see* WILTSHIRE

WYMONDESOLD *see* WIMONDSELL
WYNCHESTER *see* WINCHESTER
WYNCOT *see* WINCOTT
WYNDESORE *see* WINDSOR
WYNDHAM *see* WINDAM
WYNDOWER *see* WINDEVER
WYNN (WINNE,WYNNE)
  Agnes of Swk St Olave, spinster [DW/PA/7/11 f.40; DW/PA/5/1623/137]
  Edward of Croydon, fellmonger [LPL; 96/2854; 98/1 f.89r; Will 1638]
  George of Swk St Olave [DW/PA/5/1558/298]*
  John of Farnham - Wrecclesham, labourer [HRO; 1570 B485-486]
  Robert of Farnham, yeoman [DW/PA/7/7 f.54; DW/PA/5/1596/67] <Abs 103>
WYNNEY *see* WINNEY
WYNON *see* WINON
WYNSPER *see* WINSPEAR
WYNSTON *see* WINSTON
WYNTER *see* WINTER
WYNTERSSELL *see* WINTERSHULL
WYNTON *see* WINTON
WYNTRESHULL *see* WINTERSHULL
WYOTT *see* WYATT
WYRSHAM
  John, alias John Worsham of Farnham - Badshot, yeoman [DW/PA/5/1576/122]
WYSDOME *see* WISDOM
WYSE *see* WISE
WYSEDOME *see* WISDOM
WYSEWALL *see* WISEWALL
WYSIM
  Phillip of Swk St Olave [DW/PA/7/3 f.151; 1530]
WYTCOMBE *see* WHITCOMBE
WYTHE
  John of Leigh, yeoman [DW/PA/5/1558/297]*
WYTHERS *see* WITHERS
WYTHEWELL,WYTHWELL *see* WHITWELL
WYTNEY *see* WHITNEY
WYTTWELL *see* WHITWELL

YALDEN (YALDENE)
  Robert of Frensham [DW/PA/7/10 f.197; DW/PA/5/1621/134]
YARDLEY (YARDELEY)
  Jasper of Guildford, master of Guildford Hospital [PRO; PCC 1639]
  John of Swk St Olave [DW/PA/7/11 f.129; DW/PA/5/1624/147]
  Robert of Swk St Olave [DW/PA/7/11 f.202; DW/PA/5/1625/279]
YARFORD
  (Dame) Elizabeth of Surrey, formerly Elizabeth Style [PRO; PCC Will 1548]
YARNER (YEARNER,YERNAR)
  Frances of Swk St Saviour, widow [DW/PA/7/10 f.117; DW/PA/5/1620/141]
  Robert of Swk St Saviour, waterman [DW/PA/7/10 f.121; DW/PA/5/1620/142]
  Robert of Swk St Saviour [DW/PA/7/11 f.229; DW/PA/5/1625/281]
YARWOOD
  Thomas of ..., servant to Richard Yarwood of London, citizen and grocer [DW/PA/7/10 f.191; DW/PA/5/1621/135]

YARWORTH
  William of Kingston; Bramcote, Nottinghamshire, gent. [PRO; PCC 1637]
YATES (YATE,YEATES)
  Avelin of Kingston, widow [DW/PA/7/12 f.1; DW/PA/5/1631/122]
  Bartholomew of Streatham [PRO; PCC Admon 1608]
  John of Swk St Olave [DW/PA/7/11 f.194; DW/PA/5/1625/280]
  Richard of Bermondsey, tanner [DW/PA/7/11 f.226; DW/PA/5/1625/282]
  William of Walton on Thames, gent. [DW/PA/7/11 f.448; DW/PA/5/1628/114]
YEARLEY (YEARLY)
  George of Swk St George - Marshalsea Prison, prisoner [DW/PA/7/11 f.572; DW/PA/5/1630/125]
  Richard of Malden, yeoman [DW/PA/5/1571/81]
YEARNER *see* YARNER
YEAST
  Gilbert, alias Gilbert East of Swk St Saviour, cordwainer [DW/PA/7/11 f.1; DW/PA/5/1622/112]
YEATES *see* YATES
YELDALE (YELDALL)
  John of Guildford St Mary, cooper [DW/PA/7/10 f.159; DW/PA/5/1621/136]
  William of Merstham [LPL; 98/1 f.20v; Will 1631]
YEOMAN (YEOMANS,YOMANS)
  Christopher of Richmond [PRO; PCC Admon 1636]
  Francis of Swk St Saviour [DW/PA/7/7 f.149; DW/PA/5/1597/122] <Abs 278>
  John of Richmond [PRO; PCC Admon 1649]
  Richard of Croydon [PRO; PCC Will 1589]
  Thomas of Croydon, yeoman [PRO; PCC Will 1602] <Abs, SAC v.10 p.307>
YERD
  John of Cheam; Kent, esq. [LPL; Reg. Abp Stafford f.188; Will c1450]
YERNAR *see* YARNER
YESTED *see* EASTED
YLBCKE *see* WELBECK
YNFELD *see* INFIELD
YNGLAR *see* INGLER
YNODE,YNWOOD *see* INWOOD
YOMANS *see* YEOMAN
YONG,YONGE *see* YOUNG
YORK (YORKE)
  Henry of Bermondsey, goldsmith [HRO; Reg. Fox 3 p.61; 1511]
  Hugh of Lambeth [PRO; PCC Will 1597]
  Joan of Richmond, widow [PRO; PCC Will 1609] <Abs, SAC v.23 p.143>
  John of Lambeth, farmer [PRO; PCC Will 1622]
YOUNG (YONG,YONGE,YOUNGE,YOYWNG,ZOYWNG)
  Anthony of Capel, weaver [DW/PA/7/11 f.379; DW/PA/5/1626/137]
  Edmund of Swk St George [DW/PA/7/11 f.365; DW/PA/5/1626/136]
  Francis, alias Francis Moore of Farnham - Dippenhall, spinster [DW/PA/7/9 f.210; DW/PA/5/1616/96]
  George of Richmond, servant and baker with ... Harford [DW/PA/5/1545/21]
  Henry of Capel, yeoman [DW/PA/5/1591/57]
  Henry of Swk St Saviour, barber surgeon [DW/PA/5/1555/85]
  Isabella, alias Isabella Moore of Farnham [DW/PA/5/1576/34]
  James of Swk St Olave, cutler [DW/PA/7/6 f.273; 1560]
  Joan of Frimley, widow [DW/PA/5/1581/55]
  Joan of Send, widow [PRO; PCC Admon 1648]

YOUNG (YONG, YONGE, YOUNGE, YOYWNG, ZOYWNG) [*continued*]
John of Beddington, husbandman [DW/PA/7/5 f.49; 1538] <Abs 7>
John of Capel [DW/PA/5/1547/11]
John of Pirbright [PRO; PCC Admon 1631]
John of Swk St Olave [DW/PA/5/1582/18]
Nicholas of Capel [DW/PA/7/5 f.33; 1538] <Abs 16>
Richard of Capel [DW/PA/7/5 f.215; 1541]
Richard of Guildford Holy Trinity, yeoman [DW/PA/7/12 f.331; DW/PA/5/1636/114]
Richard of Walton on Thames, yeoman [DW/PA/7/13 f.72; DW/PA/5/1640/173]
Robert of Capel [DW/PA/5/1547/13]
Robert of Fetcham, woodbroker [*Long list of debtors*] [DW/PA/5/1582/53]
Robert of Frimley [DW/PA/7/6 f.8; DW/PA/5/1559/14]
Robert of Limpsfield, yeoman [*in* DW/PA/5/1574/26]
Roger of Headley, husbandman [DW/PA/5/1574/19]
Roger of Walton on Thames, yeoman [DW/PA/5/1586/38]*
Rose, alias Rose Moore of Farnham, widow [DW/PA/7/7 f.185; DW/PA/5/1598/93] <Abs 335>
Solomon of Swk St George [DW/PA/5/1582/32]
Stephen of Swk St Saviour, carman [DW/PA/7/8 f.149; DW/PA/5/1611/126]
Thomas of Beddington - Wallington; Mickleham [DW/PA/7/2 f.46; 1495]
Thomas of Thorpe [DW/PA/7/11 f.451; DW/PA/5/1628/115]
Thomas of Thorpe [DW/PA/7/11 f.572; DW/PA/5/1630/126]
Thomas of Walton on Thames [PRO; PCC 1649]
William of Betchworth, yeoman [DW/PA/5/1605/101] <Abs U181>
William of Egham [PRO; PCC 1642]
William of Guildford, basketmaker [DW/PA/7/13 f.205; DW/PA/5/1642/94]
William of Guildford Holy Trinity, yeoman, senior [DW/PA/7/13 f.181; DW/PA/5/1642/93]
William of Kingston - Hatch [DW/PA/7/7 f.131; DW/PA/5/1597/121] <Abs 241>
William of Kingston, gent. [PRO; PCC Will 1614]

YSTED *see* EASTED

YVANS *see* EVANS

ZINNICQ *see* van ZINNICQ

ZINZAN
(Sir) Robert, alias (Sir) Robert Alexander of Walton on Thames, knight [PRO; PCC Will 1608] <Abs, SAC v.12 p.105>

ZOUCH
(Sir) Edward of Woking, knight [PRO; PCC 1634] <Abs SAC v.33 p.44>
James of Surrey [PRO; PCC 1643]
James of Woking, esq. [PRO; PCC 1645]

ZOYWNG *see* YOUNG

[*no name*] of Kingston [DW/PA/7/2 f.208; 1524]
[*no name*] of Thorpe (widow, Maud) [DW/PA/7/4 f.171; 1536]
[*no name*] of Cobham (widow, Ellen) [DW/PA/7/5 f.161; 1540]
[*no name*] of ... (witness; Edward Nube, curate) [DW/PA/7/5 f.223; 1541]
[*no name*] of Cobham (wife, Elizabeth, son George, brothers Edmund and James) [DW/PA/5/1544/1]
[*no name*] of ... (Richard Amies, overseer) [DW/PA/5/1550/1]
[*no name*] of Horsell (wife, Elizabeth, sons Richard, John, senior, Edmund and John, junior) [DW/PA/5/1550/13]
[*no name*] of Horley (wife, Elizabeth, sons William, Richard, Harry, Peter, Robert, John and James) [DW/PA/5/1555/52]
[*no name*] of Lingfield ? (wife, Isabel) [DW/PA/5/1557/1]
[*no name*] of Farnham (widow, Jane) [DW/PA/5/1558/2]*
[*no name*] of ... (widow, Agnes) [DW/PA/5/1558/3]*

Appendix I

[As explained more fully in the introduction, there have been produced in the past lists of Surrey wills proved in Hampshire courts. The main such list, a copy of which is in the Surrey Record Office, were compiled many years ago from calendars which include wills no longer, apparently, extant, and, which do not distinguish by county. Many wills of testators from parishes where there are Surrey and Hampshire parishes with identical or very similar names were included in this list, which are now believed to be of Hampshire testators. The list below is of the wills on the list which fall into the latter class. They have not all been examined individually, and it is possible that a very few may indeed refer to Surrey testators, but in most cases this is very unlikely.]

ALEXANDER George of Bramley (probably Bramley, Hampshire) 1617
ASTLET Thomas of Headley (probably Headley, Hampshire) 1543
ATMORE Thomas of Headley (probably Headley, Hampshire) 1547
  William of Headley (probably Headley, Hampshire) 1544
ATWELL John of Headley (probably Headley, Hampshire) 1545
AWMELL John of Headley (probably Headley, Hampshire) 1545
  William of Headley (probably Headley, Hampshire) 1542
AYLIFFE Joan of Bramley (probably Bramley, Hampshire) 1589
  Richard of Ewhurst (probably Ewhurst, Hampshire) 1597
  Robert of Bramley (probably Bramley, Hampshire) 1615

BALAM John of Kingston (probably Kingston, Hampshire) 1587
BENSTEDE John of Banstead (probably Binstead, Hampshire) 1559
BLAKE Matilda of Banstead (probably Binstead, Hampshire) 1529
BOTHE John of Banstead (probably Binstead, Hampshire) 1581
BOWKEHURSTE William of Banstead (probably Binstead, Hampshire) 1550
BRIAN John of Farleigh (probably one of two in Hampshire) 1529
BUDD Richard of Sutton (probably Bishops Sutton, Hampshire) 1547

CHAMBERS John of Bramley (probably Bramley, Hampshire) 1593
CHRISTMAS (CHRISMES) Edward of Banstead (probably Binstead, Hampshire) 1544
COLE Agnes of Sutton (probably Bishops Sutton, Hampshire) 1540
  Robert of Sutton (probably Bishops Sutton, Hampshire) 1540
  Thomasine of Sutton (probably Bishops Sutton, Hampshire) 1564
COLLEN John of Sutton (probably Bishops Sutton, Hampshire) 1542
COOPER (COPER) John of Farleigh (probably one of two in Hampshire) 1626
  Thomas of Sutton (probably Bishops Sutton, Hampshire) 1530
  Thomas of Sutton (probably Bishops Sutton, Hampshire) 1544
  William of Sutton (probably Bishops Sutton, Hampshire) 1526
COWICK Elizabeth of Ewhurst, widow (probably Ewhurst, Hampshire) 1585
COX Agnes of Kingston (probably Kingston, Hampshire) 1567

DUMPER Thomas of Sutton (probably Bishops Sutton, Hampshire) 1526

FOSTER Eleanora of Farleigh (probably one of two in Hampshire) 1552
FREMANTELL Thomas of Farleigh (probably one of two in Hampshire) 1558
FRIER William of Wotton, rector (probably Wootton, Hampshire) 1554

GEORGE William of Farleigh (probably one of two in Hampshire) 1539
GOOLD Thomas of Kingston (probably Kingston, Hampshire) 1621
GREENE Henry of Banstead (probably Binstead, Hampshire) 1543

HANNINGTON William of Combe (probably Combe, Hampshire) 1647
HASKER William of Bramley (probably Bramley, Hampshire) 1609
HEATH (HETH) Robert of Sutton (probably Bishops Sutton, Hampshire) 1546
HENTON Henry of Kingston (probably Kingston, Hampshire) 1614
HETH *see* HEATH
HOLLAND Richard of Bramley (probably Bramley, Hampshire) 1625
HOWCHIN Christiana of Chilworth (probably Chilworth, Hampshire) 1539
Robert of Chilworth (probably Chilworth, Hampshire) 1539
HUNTE Thomas of Wotton (probably Wootton, Hampshire) 1528

JERMAYNE Joan of Sutton (probably Bishops Sutton, Hampshire) 1546

KEMP (KEMPE) Robert of Combe (probably Combe, Hampshire) 1619
William of Combe (probably Combe, Hampshire) 1616
KNIGHT Nicholas of Bramley (probably Bramley, Hampshire) 1630

LETSOME Edith of Combe, widow (probably Combe, Hampshire) 1619
LISLE (LYSLE) John of Wotton (probably Wootton, Hampshire) 1591
LITTLEWORKE John of Bramley (probably Bramley, Hampshire) 1620
LONGLAND Thomas of Farleigh (probably one of two in Hampshire) 1571
LYSLE *see* LISLE

MARRYNER Margaret of Bramley (probably Bramley, Hampshire) 1581
MATHEW William of Banstead (probably Binstead, Hampshire) 1547
MEUX (Sir) John of Kingston (probably Kingston, Hampshire) 1629
(Sir) William of Kingston (probably Kingston, Hampshire) 1638
MILLS Thomas of Bramley (probably Bramley, Hampshire) 1544

OKELY Thomas of Sutton (probably Bishops Sutton, Hampshire) 1530

PALMER Alice of Farleigh (probably one of two in Hampshire) 1597
PAYCE Bernard of Bramley (probably Bramley, Hampshire) 1567
John of Bramley (probably Bramley, Hampshire) 1614
PEARCE Jane, alias Jane Tasker of Combe (probably Combe, Hampshire) 1632
Robert of Combe (probably Combe, Hampshire) 1619
PORTER Thomas of Sutton (probably Bishops Sutton, Hampshire) 1534
Thomas of Sutton (probably Bishops Sutton, Hampshire) 1566
PRINCE Robert of Bramley (probably Bramley, Hampshire) 1570
PRIOR John of Bramley, senior (probably Bramley, Hampshire) 1624

REVE Thomas of Farleigh (probably one of two in Hampshire) 1535
RIDINGEST Henry of Banstead (probably Binstead, Hampshire) 1544

SAMBOROW John of Farleigh (probably one of two in Hampshire) 1540
SEXTON Christopher of Bramley, vicar (probably Bramley, Hampshire) 1605
SHERLOCK Christiana of Farleigh (probably one of two in Hampshire) 1535
Thomas of Farleigh (probably one of two in Hampshire) 1568
SIMS Thomas of Farleigh (probably one of two in Hampshire) 1558
SPENCER Richard of Sutton (probably Bishops Sutton, Hampshire) 1514
STILEMAN Thomas of Sutton (probably Bishops Sutton, Hampshire) 1569
STONEWODE John of Wotton (probably Wootton, Hampshire) 1550

TASKER Jane, alias Jane Tasker of Combe (probably Combe, Hampshire) 1632
TERRIE George of Bramley (probably Bramley, Hampshire) 1616
THAWBUTT Richard of Banstead (probably Binstead, Hampshire) 1544

VASY Edward of Sutton (probably Bishops Sutton, Hampshire) 1558

W... John of Wotton (probably Wootton, Hampshire) 1528
WALL William of Wotton (probably Wootton, Hampshire) 1552
WAREHAM Richard of Wotton (probably Wootton, Hampshire) 1600
WATSON Thomas of Bramley (probably Bramley, Hampshire) 1558
WATTS Richard of Sutton (probably Bishops Sutton, Hampshire) 1566
WELLS Agnes of Bramley (probably Bramley, Hampshire) 1506
John of Bramley (probably Bramley, Hampshire) 1506
WHITE William of Bramley (probably Bramley, Hampshire) 1588
WILD Ambrose of Bramley (probably Bramley, Hampshire) 1628
WINSLADE John of Chilworth (probably Chilworth, Hampshire) 1549
WINTER Pexall of Bramley (probably Bramley, Hampshire) 1639
WYTCH Thomas of Farleigh (probably one of two in Hampshire) 1517

YETMANDE William of Farleigh (probably one of two in Hampshire) 1539

Appendix 2

Index of Unusual Christian Names

For some reason notes of unusual christian names have become unusual in indexes of this kind. Inevitably, editors compiling them lay themselves open to charges of subjectivity; however, many relationships are first suggested because of the use of an unusual name, and there is, therefore some utility in showing examples. Furthermore, students of christian names themselves are otherwise largely excluded from use of the index.

The index which follows has been keyed to the surname with which the christian name is linked; thus helping demonstrating some of the linkages mentioned above. To the charge that any notion of 'unusual' is subjective, the best answer is a list of those christian names the editor has omitted from this appendix, as too common.

(a) Christian names omitted from this appendix;

Abraham; Adrian; Agnes; Alan; Alexander; Alice; Ambrose; Amy; Andrew; Ann (Anna, Anne); Anthony; Arnold; Arthur; Audrey; Augustine
Barbara; Bartholomew; Beatrice; Benjamin; Bennett (Benet); Bernard; Brian; Bridget
Caleb; Catherine; Charles; Christian; Christiana; Christina; Christopher; Cicely (Cecilia, Cecily); Clement (Clemence); Cornelius
Daniel; David (Davy); Denise; Dorothy
Edmund; Edward; Eleanor; Elizabeth; Ellen; Emma; Ephraim; Eustace; Êvan (Evans); Ewan
Faith; Frances; Francis; Frederick; Frusan (Frusanna); Fulk
Gabriel; Gawain (Gawaine, Gawen); Geoffrey; George; Gerard; Gilbert; Giles; Gillian; Godfrey; Grace; Gregory; Griffin
Hannah; Harry; Helen; Henry; Hester; Hugh; Humphrey
Isaac; Isabel (Isabella)
Jacob; James; Jan; Jane; Jasper; Jenkin; Joan (Joanna); John; Jonas; Joseph; Joshua; Joyce; Judith; Juliana
Katherine
Lawrence; Leonard; Lettice; Lewis; Lionel; Lucy; Luke
Mabel; Magdalen; Margaret; Margery; Maria (Marie); Marian (Marianne, Marion, Marione); Mark; Martha; Martin; Mary; Matilda; Matthew; Matthias; Maud; Maurice; Mercy; Michael; Miles; Millicent; Morgan; Morris
Nathaniel; Nicholas
Oliver; Owen
Paul; Peter; Phillip; Phillipa; Phillis
Rachel; Ralph; Rebecca; Reginald; Reynold; Richard; Robert; Roger; Rose; Rowland
Samuel; Sarah; Simon; Stephen; Susan (Susanna); Sybil
Thomas; Thomasine; Timothy; Tobias
Ursula
Valentine; Vincent
Walter; William

(b) Unusual christian names, with the surname(s) with which they occur

Aaron Best/Pullen/Tidy; Abel Stint; Adam Burrows/Edwards/Halliday/Riley/ Robinson/Sanders/ Smallbone/ Torlesse/ Twitchett/ van Tinnicq/ Wadelshurst/ Wilson/Woolridge; Adltgen (de) Willem; Adry Swaisland; Aganita van Oake; Agmondesham Muschamp; Albert Atkinson; Allara (Allard) (de) Linsell; Alvin Child; Andrea Bassano; Angel Apple/Walters; Angelus Shott; Arlington Kelley; Artemisia Eves; Austen Shadford; Avelin Yates; Avery Butcher/Puplett/Richbell; Avis Butcher/Jones/Sawyer

Baldwin Lano/Patten; Balthasar (Balthazer) Hatrom/Mandekens; Barbaby Bainbridge; Benn Goodwin; Bennetta Medhurst; Blanch Dare/Norman/Sheffield/ Weller; Boniface Forrest; Bostock Fuller; Bowett Ragge; Boye Cochean; Brice Watercombe; Bridges Alwyn; Bronn Riswick

Calix (Celix) de Hone; Camilla Todd; Clara Stecells; Cleophas Smith; Constance Fryer/Valler/Waddington; Constancia Scotcher; Crecence Raunce; Cresset Jackson; Crispin Cotterell; Cuthbert Blackden/Buckle/Burrel/Gibson/ Hutchins/Lawse/Macye/Rumforde/Skinner/Ward; Cyril Turner

Damaris Parkhurst/Roake/Spight; Derek (Dierick) Borre/Harmanson/Janson/ Peterson/(De) Voecht; Diana Posthuma Theaker; Dierick Voecht; Digory Oliver; Dinah Husband/Rhodes; Dionis Clay/Cooper/Hunt; Dionisia Brown/ Cooper; Dismas Cordwell; Dixy Hickman; Dorcas Joiner; Dulcibel (Dulcibella) Covert/Vine

Eda Vaden; Ede Hawkins; Eden Field/Scoffyne/Sherlock; Edith Brown/Capon/ Cooper/Croyser/Mabanke/Stoner/Tapsfield; Edy Owen; Elias Allen/Davy; Ellis Bodge/Morris/Powell/Redfern/Roberts/Southerton;Emery Dawton/Gilkin/Stedman/ Wilkins; Emlin Brigham; Emming Bennett; Epaphroditus Wood; Erasmus Eastland/Ford/Gainsford/Lander; Esabe Hole; Eufhonsa Abercromby; Eugenius Alland; Eusebius Arberry/Crop/Wood; Evershed Diddlesfold

Favor Fox; Felix Tacke; Ferdinand (Ferdinando) Blake/Malin; Fergus Rutledge; Florence King; Fremyn Sy; Friswith (Frideswith) Billinge/Cross/ Rogers; Fyrmundus Deremounde

Gamaliel Pye; Garret Brian/Hone/Smith; Geanes Agalliaway; Gertrude Awcocke/ Couche/Harrison/Sluce/Tub'ye; Gervase Oliver; Gill Gwilliams; Glymet Frenchwoman; Godlee Warner; Golawayes Evans; Goodith Leach; Goraths Dodyn; Gosson Redcan/Smith; Griff ap David ap Eign; Griselda Woodstock; Guy Harman/Tebbutt; Guillam (Guyllam) Boone/Mobert; Gysken Mason

Hamlet Slenne; Hamnett Merrell; Hans Williamson Backhouse/van den Dicke; Harman Browncarde/Buckquay/Enticknap/Leake/Rutter/Witley; Harvey Blake/ Martin/West; Hastings Weadley; Haward Bickerstaff; Henrik Severdonck; Hercules Bradshaw; Hersey Webb; Hilary Rouse; Hilliard Brewer; Hobart Lull; Hop Roffey; Howell Morris; Hubert Elinck; Hugo Bush

Idonya Greenacre/Hart; Innocent Sheffield; Isebrand Court; Isott Vason; Israel Skelton

Jacques Tacquet; Jannecke Verbouts; Jaquamine Buckberry; Jarman Sargent; Jarram Hollis; Jarvis Hockett; Jehenna Cocq; Jenkin Thomas; Jeremiah Ridge;

Jeremy Bishop/Crew/Evans/Mabanke/May/Shove; Jermain del Malaise; Jesode Shere; Joachim Dennis; Job Tookey; Joel Pratt; Josephus West; Josias Moys/Nachtegal/Parker/Wicks; Josina Cantes; Joys (Joyse) Chandler/Merenson; Justinian Tuckey

Knevett Parry

Lambert Dodson/Harman/Reynolds/Wayes; Lance Trowere; Lancelot Baxter/Brewes/Burton/Johnson/Taylor; Lemuel Archer; Lowrye Morris; Lucretia Cadman/Gadbury; Lydia Pantall/Pope/Rumsey; Lyon Aleword

Malachi Chipping/Richardson; Malin (Malyn) Christmas/Wilson; Marguerite Pan; Market Bowyer; Marlyan Baldwin; Marmaduke Wivell; Medcalfe Wilsmore; Melcah Hare; Meredith Evans; Mericke Sonday; Meshach Fowle; Mome Farding de Grace; Moses Russell/Wall; Moulde Perry; Mungum (Mungrum) Westbrook

Nanchen Nopen; Neelken Coopah; Niman Bowyer; Ninian Ansty/Mitchell; Noah Beldam/Bromham; Norwich Spackman

Olberton Hancey; Oliphe Edlin; Otis Wickhalf; Otto Jameson

Parat Bell/Tanner; Parnell Burnham/Crofton/Humphreys/Parker; Passchier Thomare; Patience Wonham; Patrick Kennedy; Percival Hardy/Wall; Petronell Byworth/Millman; Phide Bolt; Philomusis Adeane; Philpot Calay/Lucere; Piers Caverley/Curtis; Pleasant Goodchild; Poole Wicks; Posthuma Theaker; Poynings Heron/Moore; Prudence Jagoe/Lovell

Quivier Clifton

Radegund Peacock; Randall Brooke/Dodd/Manning/Riggs/Spurstone; Randolph Brown/Elverston/Hellowell/Martyr/Wright; Raphael Kettell; Read Cordrey; Rees Lewis/White/Williams; Reuben Target; Rieynerus Cuypers; Roland Wilson; Rosse Avery

Samson Misken; Sancta Byrne; Sander Bray; Sebastian Hilary; Sense Broom/Hawkins/Millward/Starr; Seth (Seath) Benwell/Buckberry/Goldstone/Savage; Shadrach Peto/Sturt/Thomsett/Watson/Woolward; Sidney Atkins; Signarano Daquia; Silvester Farley/Fisher/Tobye; Solomon Martin/Young; Soynken Picke; Swithin Fox/Skerne

Thaddeus Farrell; Theophilus Brereton/Stanton; Thrustons Nicholas; Thurston Smith; Titus Alsop; Tristram Blabye/Blagden/Henson; Tyse Rice

Urian Stiles/Wise; Urithe Gage

Vaughan Cripps; Velze Anvyk; Victor de Male

Walsingham Colbrand/Hooker/Sanders; Watkin Northupp; Watson Stoddard; West Newdigate; Wilfred (Welfurd) Martin/Scatergood/Woolsroppe; Wilsefer Mason; Winifred Bexley/Burton; Wolfram Nolleth; Wolley Lee

Zachariah Elliott; Zachary Dixon/Hilder

INDEX OF BUILDINGS AND SHIPS

INDEX OF PLACES

Places Outside Surrey

INDEX OF PLACES

INDEX OF PLACES

INDEX OF PLACES